November 3–8, 2013
Barcelona, Spain

Association for
Computing Machinery

Advancing Computing as a Science & Profession

MSWiM'13

Proceedings of the 16th ACM International Conference on

Modeling, Analysis and Simulation of Wireless and Mobile Systems

Sponsored by:

ACM SIGSIM

Association for
Computing Machinery

Advancing Computing as a Science & Profession

The Association for Computing Machinery
2 Penn Plaza, Suite 701
New York, New York 10121-0701

ISBN: 978-1-4503-2353-6

Additional copies may be ordered prepaid from:

ACM Order Department
PO Box 30777
New York, NY 10087-0777, USA

Phone: 1-800-342-6626 (USA and Canada)
+1-212-626-0500 (Global)
Fax: +1-212-944-1318
E-mail: acmhelp@acm.org
Hours of Operation: 8:30 am – 4:30 pm ET

Printed in the USA

MSWIM 2013 General Chairs' Welcome

Welcome to the 16th ACM International Conference on Modelling, Analysis and Simulation of Wireless and Mobile Systems (MSWiM), and to unique Barcelona, Spain. Over the years, MSWiM has established itself as a major research venue where numerous key results in the area of performance evaluation of wireless and mobile systems have appeared; we are delighted that this year's event maintains the tradition of high quality contributions.

It is a complex procedure to put together a high quality conference and MSWIM is therefore truly a team effort. We here take the opportunity to thank this year's TPC chairs, Ravi Prakash and Cheng Li who have managed the entire technical program process, from the initial Call For Papers through the review process to the finalisation of the technical program. Of course, we also acknowledge and thank the TPC members and external reviewers whose expertise and hard work are the decisive factors for judging the quality of the contributions and facilitating the final paper selection. MSWIM also includes a poster session that has been managed by Mirela A. M. Notare and Jalel Ben-Othman. Furthermore, this year we are very happy to include a strong demonstration session, which was made possible by the hard work of Demo Chair, Laura-Marie Feeney. Finally, MSWiM 2013 also includes two distinguished keynote addresses by outstanding experts, Professors Arturo Azcorra (Universidad Carlos III de Madrid, Spain) and Robert Schober (University of British Columbia, Canada).

Along with the main conference program, four symposia and three workshops will be held, covering several specializations within mobile and wireless systems. The four symposia are: MobiWAC, PE-WASUN, DIVANet and Q2SWinet and the three workshops: WMuNeP, PM2HW2N and HP-MOSys. Over the years, these seven events have become successful and quite competitive in their own right.

We also thank the people who have managed the practical details of the event, Pan Li for advertising the conference, Robson De Grande for managing the registration process and David Rebollo-Monedero for overseeing the local arrangements. Finally, we also thank the Steering committee for their guidance behind the scenes, Azzedine Boukerche, Sajal K. Das, Lorenzo Donatiello, Jason Yi-Bing Lin, William C.Y. Lee and Simon Taylor.

Last, but not least, we wish to thank our main sponsor the ACM SIGSIM. We are very pleased to welcome you to MSWiM 2013 in Barcelona and we are confident you will find this year's event full of stimulating ideas and discussions.

Bjorn Landfeldt
MSWIM'13 General Chair
Lund University, Sweden

Mónica Aguilar Igartua
MSWIM'13 Vice General Chair
Universitat Politècnica de Catalunya, Spain

Technical Program Chairs' Welcome

The technical program of the 16th ACM International Conference on Modeling, Analysis and Simulation of Wireless and Mobile Systems (MSWiM), held in 2013 in Barcelona, Spain, continues to build upon the high standards set by previous editions of the conference.

In 2013, the call for papers attracted 184 registered papers in all areas of mobile and wireless systems of which 160 were accepted into the review process. The submitted papers came from 39 countries, and the accepted papers from 32 countries, reflecting the truly international profile of MSWiM. Members of the Technical Program Committee were drawn from 17 countries spread over five continents. The five most commonly listed topics for submissions to MSWiM'13 were:

- Performance evaluation and modeling
- Wireless network algorithms and protocols
- Wireless mesh networks, mobile ad hoc networks, VANET
- Sensor and actuator networks
- Analytical models

The submissions included a large number of papers of very high quality making the selection process difficult and competitive. In the end, we selected 42 regular papers, which is an acceptance rate of 26%. An additional 17 short papers were recommended for the program owing to their high quality and contribution.

Among the 42 regular papers, the three shortlisted as candidates for the best paper award are:

- "RECAST: Telling Apart Social and Random Relationships in Dynamic Networks," Pedro O.S. Vaz de Melo, Aline Carneiro Viana, Marco Fiore, Katia Jaffrès-Runser, Frederic Le Mouel, Antonio A.F. Loureiro.
- "Understanding the Benefits of Open Access in Femtocell Networks: Stochastic Geometric Analysis in the Uplink," Wei Bao, Ben Liang.
- "A Novel Scheduling Algorithm for Densely-Deployed Wireless Stations in Urban Areas," Hirozumi Yamaguchi, Akihito Hiromori, Teruo Higashino, Shigeki Umehara, Hirofumi Urayama, Masaya Yamada, Taka Maeno, Shigeru Kaneda, Mineo Takai.

The winner among these three papers will be announced at the conference banquet, and will be reported in the proceedings of MSWiM 2013. At this point, we take the opportunity to congratulate the winners of the best paper award for MSWiM 2012:

- "Influence of Spatial Statistics of Spectrum Use on the Performance of Cognitive Wireless Networks", J. Riihijärvi, J. Nasreddine, P. Mähönen.

Our thanks go to Professor Azzedine Boukerche and the Advisory Board for their vision in guiding MSWiM from workshop to symposium and finally to conference status over the past 15 years. A special thank you goes to the Technical Program Committee as well as the reviewers for their hard work and contributions in reviewing and judging all the submitted papers. Finally, we would like to take this opportunity to welcome you to the conference. We hope you find the technical sessions to be intellectually stimulating and rewarding.

Ravi Prakash
MSWiM'13 TPC Co-Chair
University of Texas at Dallas, USA

Cheng Li
MSWiM'13 TPC Co-Chair
Memorial University of Newfoundland, Canada

Table of Contents

Session Order 5: Wireless Sensor Networks (I)

Session Order 6: Modeling Multiple-access Channels and Networks

Session Order 7: Data Link Layer Protocols: Multiple Access and Scheduling

Session Order 8: Wireless Sensor Networks (II)

Session Order 9: Link Quality and Coverage Estimation (I)

Session Order 10: Wireless Sensor Networks (III)

Session Order 11: LTE & Cellular Networks (I)

Session Order 12: Dynamic Network Interactions

Session Order 13: Network and Transport Layer (I)

Session Order 14: Delay Tolerant Networks and WiFi Localization and Interference Modeling

Session Order 15: Vehicular Ad Hoc Networks

Session Order 16: LTE & Cellular Networks (II) and Link Quality & Coverage Estimation (II)

2013 MSWiM Conference Organization

General Chair: Bjorn Landfeldt *(Lund University, Sweden)*

Vice General Chair: Mónica Aguilar Igartua *(Universitat Politècnica de Catalunya, Spain)*

Program Co-Chairs: Ravi Prakash *(University of Texas at Dallas, USA)*
Cheng Li *(Memorial University of Newfoundland, Canada)*

Poster Co-Chairs: Mirela A. M. Notare *(Sao Jose Municipal University, Brazil)*
Jalel Ben-Othman *(University of Paris 13, France)*

Demo/Tools Chair: Laura Marie Feeney, Swedish Institute of Computer Science, Sweden

Publicity Chair: Konstantin Beznosov *(Institute of British Columbia, Canada)*

Tutorials Chair: Min Chen *(Huazhong University of Science and Technology, China)*

Publicity Chair: Pan Li *(Mississippi State University, USA)*

Local Arrangements Chair: David Rebollo-Monedero *(Universitat Politecnica de Catalunya, Spain)*

Steering Committee Chair: Azzedine Boukerche *(University of Ottawa, Canada)*

Steering Committee: Sajal K. Das *(University of Texas at Arlington, USA)*
Lorenzo Donatiello *(Università di Bologna, Bologna, Italy)*
Jason Yi-Bing Lin *(National Chiao-Tung University, Taiwan)*
William C. Y. Lee *(AirTouch Inc.)*
Simon Taylor *(Brunel University, UK)*

Program Committee: Jalel Ben-Othman *(University of Paris 13, France)*
Brahim Bensaou *(The Hong Kong University of Science and Technology, Hong Kong)*
Roberto Beraldi *("Sapienza" Università di Roma, Italy)*
Carlos Bernardos *(Universidad Carlos III de Madrid, Spain)*
Luciano Bononi *(University of Bologna, Italy)*
Raffaele Bruno *(IIT-CNR, Italy)*
Juan-Carlos Cano *(Universidad Politecnica de Valencia, Spain)*
Chi Chung Cheung *(The Hong Kong Polytechnic University, Hong Kong)*
Angel Cuevas *(Universidad Carlos III de Madrid, Spain)*
Marco Di Felice *(University of Bologna, Italy)*
Marcelo Dias de Amorim *(UPMC Sorbonne Universités, France)*
Lorenzo Donatiello *(Università di Bologna, Italy)*
Falko Dressler *(University of Innsbruck, Austria)*
Stephan Eidenbenz *(Los Alamos National Laboratory, USA)*

Program Committee (continued):

Stephan Eidenbenz *(Los Alamos National Laboratory, USA)*
Ehab Elmallah *(University of Alberta, Canada)*
Javier Gozalvez *(Universidad Miguel Hernandez de Elche, Spain)*
James Gross *(Royal Institute of Technology (KTH), Sweden)*
Isabelle Guérin Lassous *(Université Claude Bernard Lyon 1 - LIP, France)*
Andrei Gurtov *(Aalto University, Finland)*
Zygmunt Haas *(Cornell University, USA)*
Mónica Aguilar Igartua *(Universitat Politècnica de Catalunya, Spain)*
Shengming Jiang *(Shanghai Maritime University, China)*
Guillaume Jourjon *(NICTA, Australia)*
Merkourios Karaliopoulos *(National and Kapodistrian University of Athens, Greece)*
Holger Karl *(University of Paderborn, Germany)*
Peng-Yong Kong *(Khalifa University of Science, Technology & Research, UAE)*
Jerzy Konorski *(Gdansk University of Technology, Poland)*
Lavy Libman *(University of New South Wales, Australia)*
Renato Lo Cigno *(University of Trento, Italy)*
Antonio A. F. Loureiro *(Federal University of Minas Gerais, Brazil)*
Francesco Lo Presti *(Universita' di Roma Tor Vergata, Italy)*
Vincenzo Mancuso *(Institute IMDEA Networks, Spain)*
Enzo Mingozzi *(University of Pisa, Italy)*
Sotiris Nikoletseas *(University of Patras and Computer Technology Institute, Greece)*
Andrea Passarella *(IIT-CNR, Italy)*
Marius Portmann *(University of Queensland, Australia)*
Tahiry Razafindralambo *(Inria Lille - Nord Europe, France)*
Dirk Staehle *(Docomo Euro-Labs, Germany)*
Violet Syrotiuk *(Arizona State University, USA)*
Mineo Takai *(University of California, Los Angeles, USA)*
Terence D. Todd *(McMaster University, Canada)*
Yu-Chee Tseng *(National Chiao-Tung University, Taiwan)*
Damla Turgut *(University of Central Florida, USA)*
Emmanouel Varvarigos *(University of Patras and Computer Technology Institute, Greece)*
Andreas Willig *(University of Canterbury, New Zealand)*
Hongyi Wu *(University of Louisiana at Lafayette, USA)*
Yaoqing (Lamar) Yang *(University of Nebraska-Lincoln, USA)*
Hongwei Zhang *(Wayne State University, USA)*
Jingyuan Zhang *(University of Alabama, USA)*
Jun Zhang *(Telecom ParisTech, France)*

Additional reviewers:

Hamidreza Ahmadi
Qing Ai
Nadjib Aitsaadi
Shahzad Ali
Emilio Ancillotti
Xin Ao
Arash Asadi
Nils Aschenbruck
Luis Barbosa
Jan Bauer
Luca Bedogni
Alan Albert Bertossi
Bastian Bloessl
Chiara Boldrini
Yegui Cai
Alvaro Cárdenas
Giuseppe Cardone
Xi Chen
Yu Chen
Soumaya Cherkaoui
Stefano Chessa
Daniel Corujo
Oualid Demigha
Zhonghai Deng
Nikolaos Doulamis
Juergen Eckert
Mohammed El Koutbi
Milan Erdelj
Zhong Fan
Stefano Ferretti
Bo Fu
Shashidhar Gandham
Weihua Gao
Vittorio Ghini
Vasileios Gkamas
Marco Gramaglia
Ilias Gravalos
Bingyi Guo
Mian Guo
Abdulla Hammad
Shuai Han
Hanan Hassanein
Akihito Hiromori
Peng Hu
Khalil Ibrahimi
Vana Jelicic
Bo Ji
Shihab Jimaa
Adrian Kliks
Abdellatif Kobbane
Panagiotis Kokkinos
Xiangyu Kong
Dmitry Korzun
Joakim Koskela
Kostas Koumoutsos
Parag Kulkarni
Chuan Li
Xue Jun Li
Vasia Liagkou
Li Liu
Weiyi Liu
Xiaohui Liu
Madhusanka Liyanage
Ahmed Loutfi
Leonardo Maccari
David Malone
Pietro Manzoni
Gustavo Marfia
Isabel Martín-Faus
Moreno Marzolla
Khalil Massri
Nader Mbarek
Weixiao Meng
Ahmad Mezher
Karen Miranda
Alfonso Muñoz
Margit Mutschlechner
Ghasem Naddafzadeh Shirazi
Bruno Nardelli
Nidal Nasser
Qiang Ni
Ilya Nikolaevskiy
Naby Nikookaran
Jianwei Niu
Noorsalwati Nordin
Jianping Pan
Francesco Pantisano
Laurence Pilard
Andrea Reale
David Rebollo-Monedero

Additional reviewers (continued):

Yesica Saavedra Benitez
Anirudha Sahoo
Pablo Salvador
Maria Isabel Sanchez Bueno
Nandakishore Santhi
Kamil Sarac
Matthias Schwamborn
Vincenzo Sciancalepore
Michele Segata
Mohamed Shazly
Mohammad Sheikh
Zhefu Shi
Yujae Song
Weifeng Sun
Zhi Sun
Shreyas Sundaram
Stavros Toumpis
Akira Uchiyama
Takaaki Umedu
Luis Urquiza
Lorenzo Valerio
Carlo Vallati
Ivan Vidal
Christian Vitale
Pu Wang
Qing Wang
Tianqi Wang
Yuehua Wang
Zehua Wang
Zhijun Wang
Sean Williams
Qiao Xiang
Hirozumi Yamaguchi
Fang Yang
Chao Yu
Wei Yuan
Yuguang Zeng
Baoxian Zhang
Shenqiu Zhang
Lei Zhao
Dimitrios Zorbas

Sponsor: SIGSIM

Green Wireless: Towards Minimum per-bit Linear Energy Consumption in Wireless Communications

Arturo Azcorra
Universidad Carlos III de Madrid
Madrid, Spain

ABSTRACT

Low-energy communications is becoming an increasingly relevant research area, due to both economic and environmental reasons. Low-energy is particularly relevant in wireless because of the limited energy available to terminals and the high consumption of the base stations derived from wide geographical coverage. Green wireless aims to formulate a long term research goal in the wireless environment. In the talk, the speaker will present the motivation and formulation of this research goal, with an overview of the associated research challenges. The talk will also address in more detail one specific case of energy-efficiency consisting in the cross-factor, which consists of the energy penalty derived from a packet traversing the system protocol stack.

Categories and Subject Descriptors

C.2.1 [**Computer-Communication Networks**]: Network Architecture and Design—*Network communications*

Keywords

Low-energy communications, green wireless, cross-factor energy efficiency

Short Bio

Arturo Azcorra received his M.Sc. degree in Telecommunications Engineering from the Universidad Politecnica de Madrid (UPM) in 1986 and his PhD from the same university in 1989. In 1993, he obtained an MBA with honors from Instituto de Empresa.

Arturo Azcorra is an IEEE Senior Member and an ACM SIGCOMM Member. He has participated in and directed 49 research and technological development projects, including European ESPRIT, RACE, ACTS and IST programs. Azcorra has coordinated the CONTENT and E-NEXT European Networks of Excellence, and the CARMEN EU project. He has served as a Program Committee Member in many international conferences, including several editions of IEEE PROMS, IDMS, QofIS, CoNEXT and IEEE INFOCOM. He was the founder and first general chair of the CoNEXT conference series. He has published over 100 scientific papers in books, international magazines and conferences. In addition to his scientific achievements, Dr. Azcorra has a relevant track record of research management. He was deputy Vicerrector of Academic Infrastructures at U. Carlos III from 2000 to 2007. He served as Director General for Technology Transfer and Corporate Development at the Spanish Ministry of Science and Innovation from 2009 to 2010, and then appointed Director General of CDTI (Spanish agency for industrial research from 2010 to 2012. He is the founder of the international research center IMDEA Networks, and currently is its Director, with a double affiliation as Full Professor at University Carlos III of Madrid (UC3M).

MSWiM'13, November 3–8, 2013, Barcelona, Spain.
ACM 978-1-4503-2353-6/13/11.

How Much Can We Gain by Exploiting Buffers in Wireless Relay Networks?

Robert Schober
University of British Columbia
Vancouver, Canada
rschober@ece.ubc.ca

ABSTRACT

Wireless relays will play an important role in future wireless communication networks. This talk will focus on the new concept of buffer-aided relaying. In conventional relay protocols, the schedule of when the different nodes in the network transmit is pre-fixed and non-adaptive. In contrast, buffer-aided relaying protocols exploit the additional degrees of freedom introduced by relays with buffers and employ an adaptive transmission schedule which takes into account the quality of the different links in the network. We will show that this new approach leads to substantial performance improvements in relay networks with fading links. In particular, buffer-aided relays enable significant gains in throughput as well as outage and error probability at the expense of an increased delay. These gains are introduced by adaptive link selection and/or adaptive transmission mode selection. We will first introduce the basic concept of buffer-aided relaying using the example of a simple three node one-way relay network before considering more complex networks such as relay-selection networks, multi-antenna relay networks, and two-way relay networks.

We show that in some cases buffer-aided relaying protocols can double both the diversity gain and the throughput compared to conventional relaying protocols. Furthermore, in multi-antenna networks, buffer-aided relaying can also help to overcome the performance loss that half-duplex relays typically suffer compared to full-duplex relays.

Categories and Subject Descriptors

C.2.0 [**Computer-Communication Networks**]: General – *Data communications*

Keywords

Wireless communication networks, buffer-aided relaying, multi-antenna networks.

MSWiM'13, November 3–8, 2013, Barcelona, Spain.
Copyright 2013 ACM 978-1-4503-2353-6/13/11 ...$15.00.

Short Bio

Robert Schober received the Diplom (Univ.) and the Ph.D. degrees in electrical engineering from the University of ErlangenNuermberg in 1997 and 2000, respectively. From May 2001 to April 2002 he was a Postdoctoral Fellow at the University of Toronto, Canada, sponsored by the German Academic Exchange Service (DAAD). Since May 2002 he has been with the University of British Columbia (UBC), Vancouver, Canada, where he is now a Full Professor. Since January 2012 he is an Alexander von Humboldt Professor and the Chair for Digital Communication at the Friedrich Alexander University (FAU), Erlangen, Germany. His research interests fall into the broad areas of Communication Theory, Wireless Communications, and Statistical Signal Processing.

Dr. Schober received several awards for his work including the 2002 Heinz Maier Leibnitz Award of the German Science Foundation (DFG), the 2004 Innovations Award of the Vodafone Foundation for Research in Mobile Communications, the 2006 UBC Killam Research Prize, the 2007 Wilhelm Friedrich Bessel Research Award of the Alexander von Humboldt Foundation, the 2008 Charles McDowell Award for Excellence in Research from UBC, a 2011 Alexander von Humboldt Professorship, and a 2012 NSERC E.W.R. Steacie Fellowship. In addition, he received best paper awards from the German Information Technology Society (ITG), the European Association for Signal, Speech and Image Processing (EURASIP), IEEE WCNC 2012, IEEE Globecom 2011, IEEE ICUWB 2006, the International Zurich Seminar on Broadband Communications, and European Wireless 2000. Dr. Schober is a Fellow of the Canadian Academy of Engineering, a Fellow of the Engineering Institute of Canada, and a Fellow of the IEEE. He is currently the Editor-in-Chief of the IEEE Transactions on Communications.

Exploiting Graph Partitioning for Hierarchical Replica Placement in WMNs

Zakwan Al-Arnaout, Qiang Fu, Marcus Frean
School of Engineering and Computer Science
Victoria University of Wellington
Wellington, New Zealand
{zakwan.arnaout, qiang.fu, marcus.frean}@ecs.vuw.ac.nz

ABSTRACT

Content replication has gained much popularity in recent years both in the wired and wireless infrastructures. A key challenge faced by Wireless Mesh Networks (WMNs) is to determine the number and locations of content replicas (e.g. video clip) such that the mesh clients access cost is minimized. Furthermore, the dynamic nature of the wireless environment favors a distributed and adaptive solution to this problem. In this paper, we present an efficient, lightweight and scalable object replication and placement scheme for WMNs. Since the placement problem is NP-Complete, the scheme decomposes the problem into smaller sub-problems to facilitate the distributed approach in a P2P fashion. Moreover, it exploits the long-term link-quality routing metrics to augment the replica placement decision and the instantaneous link-quality metrics for replica server selection. The effectiveness of our scheme is evaluated through extensive simulation studies.

Categories and Subject Descriptors

C.2.1 [**Network Architecture and Design**]: Wireless communication; G.1.2 [**Approximation**]: Minimax approximation and algorithms

General Terms

Algorithms, Performance, Design

Keywords

Replica Placement; Distributed Algorithm; Wireless Mesh Network; Peer-to-peer Networking

1. INTRODUCTION

Wireless Mesh Networks (WMNs) are a promising solution to extend Internet access to wider areas with high bandwidth [1]. They are generally composed of three types of nodes: Mesh Clients (MCs), Mesh Routers (MRs), and Gateways (GWs). WMNs are deployed in areas where the wired infrastructure is not available or feasible such as rural areas, enterprise and university campuses. MRs compose the backbone layer through multi-hop wireless communications. A MC connects to other MCs or the Internet through its access MR. With their extended coverage and low cost, WMNs have attracted the attention of both the research community and the industry. However, similar to other wireless networks, WMNs also face challenges arising from the resource constraints and the resource demanding multimedia content retrieval [2], such as: (*i*) scalability of cache schemes with content size, network size and user population; (*ii*) poor wireless bandwidth; (*iii*) mobility of MCs; (*iv*) limited battery power of mobile clients; (*v*) poor channel quality; and (*vi*) the bottleneck effect around the GWs.

One of the key challenges for WMNs development is improving the data access efficiency and Quality of Experience (QoE), which determines the satisfaction degree of service users. Furthermore, as the Internet traffic flows through a limited number of GWs, heavy congestion around these GWs presents a serious problem. WMNs have the potential to increase network capacity by adding resource-sharing services such as content caching and replication. It has been observed [3] that for a given client population, a significant workload *locality* exists in WMNs content retrieval. Locality means that multiple users request the same content over time (and possibly at the same time). Web content caching and replication are two techniques that exploit locality to reduce the Internet traffic and access latency.

The problem we aim to address in this paper can be described as follows. We consider an infrastructure WMN where nodes (MRs) are deployed in static locations. In such networks, nodes do not join/leave the network dynamically. However, the wireless channel state between two neighbors may oscillate frequently due to various reasons. Since object replica placement is a costly operation, a replica must remain for a reasonable period of time. Most of the works in the wired/wireless literature consider minimizing the number of hops or the Euclidean distance in the placement decision. However, we argue that this approach might not yield to efficient placement since a shortest distance can lead to lossy/congested links. Other link-quality routing metrics prove to be more efficient than the simple Hop-Count such as Expected Transmission Count (ETX) [4], Expected Transmission Time (ETT) [5] and Minimum Loss (ML) [6]. In a prior work [7], we proposed a replication scheme for WMNs that builds an overlay P2P network formed by MRs. The scheme dynamically adapts the number of object replicas

MSWiM'13, November 3–8, 2013, Barcelona, Spain.

http://dx.doi.org/10.1145/2507924.2507928.

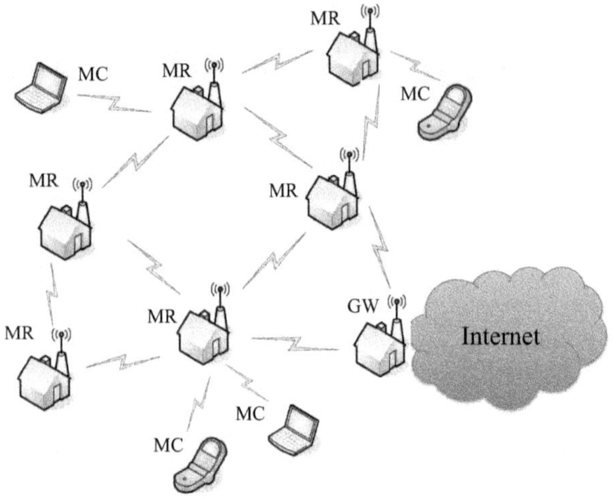

Figure 1: Network model considered in our proposed scheme.

over time based on popularity in a distributed and scalable fashion that exploits workload locality in WMNs by finding the number of replicas needed per object (e.g. video file for a Video-on-Demand service) in a time window.

We motivate our work by showing the performance gain when the replica placement considers the long-term link cost that represents its throughput or channel capacity. The short-term link cost may fluctuate frequently, whereas its long-term cost varies much slowly. In WMNs, the contention between neighboring mesh nodes for the wireless channel, together with the interference from the adjacent wireless links, results in a significant reduction in throughput over a long lossy path. Therefore, MRs that are far from the GWs suffer from long access latency and low throughput. We consider minimizing the demand-weighted distance between the requesting node and the replica server. Our contribution can be summarized as follows: (*i*) using advanced link-quality metrics to accurately gauge the client's object access cost using the long-term link-quality values for the replica placement decision, which is performed periodically. Furthermore, for replica server selection, we use the instantaneous link-quality values to satisfy a client's request; (*ii*) providing a fully-fledged replication and placement strategy for WMNs that optimally utilizes the storage capacity of MRs—by distinguishing variable sizes of objects—and avoids the creation of hotspot zones; and (*iii*) implement relevant schemes and conduct extensive simulation tests to compare the performance of our scheme with the most relevant ones. The simulation results show that our scheme *SP-DNA* (Single Partition per Delegate Node Assignment) can significantly improve the system performance.

The rest of the paper is organized as follows. Section 2 presents the network model and the proposed object replication and placement scheme is described in Section 3. In Section 4, we describe the evaluation methodology, while Section 5 discusses the results. Section 6 reviews the related work and finally, Section 7 concludes the paper.

2. NETWORK MODEL

In this section, we describe the network model of our object replica placement scheme over infrastructure WMNs. The system employs Mesh Routers (MRs) to act as content replica servers in a peer-to-peer fashion. We assume that MRs use IEEE 802.11 radios to build the wireless mesh backhaul infrastructure. MRs have replica server capabilities such as processing and storage, in other words, a MR acts as a relaying node and as a server. Fig. 1 illustrates the model considered in the paper scope. It consists of mesh access points/MRs and Mesh Clients (MCs). The MRs are interconnected by wireless links to form a multi-hop backhaul infrastructure. One or more MRs are connected to the wired Internet and are referred to as gateways (GWs). MRs are used to access and relay packets, therefore, MRs support two types of interfaces for the wireless medium. The access interface offers network access for MCs, while the relay interface is used to relay client's traffic to its destination. Typically, the two interfaces work on non-overlapping channels to prevent interference with each other.

A mesh client (e.g. laptop or smart phone) is associated with a nearby MR to access the mesh network, but it does not participate in packet relaying. To fetch an object (e.g. video file for a video on demand service), one of the structured P2P network directory services is employed (e.g. Chord [8]). A requested object is fetched first from within the mesh network. Upon a fail, the request will be forwarded to the mesh backhaul to one of the GWs and on to the origin server. We also assume that the MRs are aware of the network topology and employ one of the widely deployed routing protocols such as OLSR [9]. OLSR is defined by the IEEE 802.11s standard as the basis for future routing protocol implementations [10]. It also scales well for few hundreds of nodes. We assume that the MRs use TCP at the transport layer since it is broadly deployed for Internet access and we assume that the exchanged messages between nodes are delivered in a reliable fashion and follow their transmission order. Our scheme is implemented over the underlying TCP protocol by a user space *ReplicaDaemon*.

3. THE PROPOSED SCHEME

In this section, we present our proposed scheme. In a wireless environment, having a centralized entity to perform the placement is not suitable as it presents a bottleneck at the central entity increasing computation and communication cost resulting from acquiring popularity information about the objects. This is challenging and costly for limited resource networks such as WMNs.

Our approach is focused on decomposing the replica placement problem by using *graph partitioning* techniques. The main goal of graph partitioning is to divide a graph into a set of sub-graphs such that each sub-graph has roughly the same number of nodes and the sum of all edges that connect different sub-graphs is minimized. Therefore, graph partitioning is useful to distribute the problem into a set of partially independent sub-problems especially when dealing with large problems. The search space is split according to the computed number of replicas per object. In each partition, a predetermined *Delegate Node* (DN) solves part of the complete search space. To this end, the replica placement problem is divided into a set of smaller loosely connected ones. Thus, we can take advantage of graph partitioning techniques to solve the problem considered in a divide-and-conquer approach.

The replica placement problem can be formulated as a *p-median* [11] problem which is simply stated as: Given a graph $\mathcal{G} = (\mathcal{V}, \mathcal{E})$, find $\mathcal{V}_p \subseteq \mathcal{V}$ such that $|\mathcal{V}_p| = p$, where p may

Table 1: Notation used in the proposed scheme.

Symbol	Meaning
$\mathcal{N}$	set of demand nodes indexed by i, and potential replica servers indexed by j.
$\mathcal{N}'$	set of demand nodes within a partition indexed by i', and the set of potential replica servers indexed by j'.
$\mathcal{M}$	number of distinct objects within the WMN indexed by m.
$\mathcal{K}$	total number of the generated graph partitions indexed by k.
$\mathcal{DN}_k$	delegate node of partition k.
$\mathcal{O}_m$	identifier of object m.
$\lvert\mathcal{O}_m\rvert$	size of object m in bytes.
$\overline{X}_t$	trimmed mean of the link-quality metric (e.g. ETX, ETT and ML).
$\Gamma(\overline{X}_t)_{i'}^{j'}$	distance between demand node i' and potential replica server j' within $\mathcal{N}'$ as a function of $\overline{X}_t$.
τ	time interval window during which object requests are observed.
$\lambda_{mi}(\tau)$	number of requests for $\mathcal{O}_m$ from node i during τ.
$\lambda_m(\tau)$	total requests for $\mathcal{O}_m$ from all nodes during τ.
$\mathcal{P}r_m(\tau)$	global popularity of $\mathcal{O}_m$ during τ.
$\mathcal{P}r_{mk}(\tau)$	popularity of $\mathcal{O}_m$ during τ within partition k.
$\mathcal{P}r_{mi}(\tau)$	popularity of $\mathcal{O}_m$ at node i during τ.
$p_m(\tau+1)$	no. of replicas of $\mathcal{O}_m$ needed for $\tau+1$.
$\mathcal{SC}$	storage capacity of a node.

either be variable or fixed, and that the sum of the shortest distances from the vertices in $\{\mathcal{V}\backslash\mathcal{V}_p\}$ to their nearest vertex in $\mathcal{V}_p$ is minimized. This problem is NP-Complete for variable values of p. To distribute the replica placement problem, we simplify the *p-median* problem by partitioning the network graph into p sub-graphs, where p represents a potential number of replicas. Then we select for each partition a DN, which will be responsible for placing an object replica within its partition. The partitioning algorithm we use is proposed in [12]. In our scheme, we recursively bipartite the graph until the partition size ≤ 2. Since the total number of partitions $= \mathcal{N}-1$, each DN will be assigned at most a single partition, hence, we call it *SP-DNA*. Our scheme involves two phases, the *Network Setup Phase* and the *Content Replication and Placement Phase*. We use the notation in Table 1 to describe our scheme.

3.1 Network Setup Phase

In this phase, the aim is to build a hierarchy of partitions and assign a DN for each partition to lookup for the placement within the partition member nodes. We assume that all nodes[1] are bootstrapped with Alg. 1. To trigger the network setup phase, an application-level process called the *Content Manager* (CM)—which is a component of the *ReplicaDaemon*—starts this phase. To reduce the message overhead, the CM can be hosted by a centroid node. The CM plays a role in collecting statistical information about different objects' requests, computing the number of replicas per object for the next τ period, and assigning the placement job to the corresponding DNs. The CM selects itself to act

Algorithm 1: This function builds the DBT during the network setup phase.

1 Function BTree(*Graph g*, *String s*)
2 Graph $g_{\text{Left}}, g_{\text{Right}}$
3 Node $dn_{\text{Left}}, dn_{\text{Right}}$
4 String $s_{\text{Left}}, s_{\text{Right}}$
5 $s_{\text{Left}} \leftarrow s_{\text{Right}} \leftarrow s$
6 **if** $|g| = 2$ **then**
7 $\quad dn_{\text{Left}} \leftarrow this$
8 $\quad dn_{\text{Right}} \leftarrow \{g\} \setminus dn_{\text{Left}}$
9 $\quad$ **return** $dn_{\text{Left}} \mid\mid \{g\}$
10 **else if** $|g| = 3$ **then**
11 $\quad dn_{\text{Left}} \leftarrow rand(g) \notin s$
12 $\quad g_{\text{Right}} \leftarrow \{g\} \setminus dn_{\text{Left}}$
13 $\quad dn_{\text{Right}} \leftarrow rand(g_{\text{Right}}) \notin s$
14 $\quad$ forward $(g_{\text{Right}}, s) \rightarrow dn_{\text{Right}}$
15 $\quad$ wait (dn_{Right})
16 $\quad$ **return** $dn_{\text{Left}} \mid\mid dn_{\text{Right}}$
17 **else**
18 $\quad$ Bipartite $(g, g_{\text{Left}}, g_{\text{Right}})$
19 $\quad dn_{\text{Left}} \leftarrow rand(g_{\text{Left}}) \notin s_{\text{Left}}$
20 $\quad dn_{\text{Right}} \leftarrow rand(g_{\text{Right}}) \notin s_{\text{Right}}$
21 $\quad s_{\text{Left}} \leftarrow s_{\text{Left}} \mid\mid dn_{\text{Left}}$
22 $\quad s_{\text{Right}} \leftarrow s_{\text{Right}} \mid\mid dn_{\text{Right}}$
23 $\quad$ forward $(g_{\text{Left}}, s_{\text{Left}}) \rightarrow dn_{\text{Left}}$
24 $\quad$ forward $(g_{\text{Left}}, s_{\text{Right}}) \rightarrow dn_{\text{Right}}$
25 $\quad$ wait$(dn_{\text{Left}}, dn_{\text{Right}})$
26 $\quad$ **return** $this \mid\mid dn_{\text{Left}} \mid\mid dn_{\text{Right}}$

as a DN for the network graph $\mathcal{G}$ and runs Alg. 1 to bipartite $\mathcal{G}$, select a DN for each partition, and then forward each partition (sub-graph) to its corresponding DN. The process is recursively repeated until the partitions are fine-grained. When the base case is reached (line 6), the node running the algorithm will select itself as the DN (the term *this* refers to the node itself (line 7)). Then, the DNs in the lowest level partitions reply to their callers (parent node) with a list representing the DN and its partition members. When the caller receives the lists from its child DNs, it merges the received lists, appends its node ID and forwards the resulting list to its caller. Eventually, the CM (root node) will receive a list of DNs in the form of a balanced binary tree that we call the *Delegates Binary Tree* (DBT) as depicted in Fig. 2. Notice (Fig. 2b) that a node appears twice. Once as a parent node (i.e. partition-hosting) responsible for the descendant members (and itself) and another as a leaf node (i.e. self-hosting). We underline that this phase needs to be performed once. However, if the topology changes permanently (e.g. relocation of MRs), then we need to perform this phase again. We do not consider a temporary topology change due to temporary link variations as content replication is required for long periods.

Following the DBT creation, the CM maps the possible numbers of replicas to their DNs in the DBT, creating a MapList by running Alg. 2. It recursively divides the possible number of replicas (p) by 2 starting from the CM (root node).

[1]In order to avoid confusion throughout this paper, the terms MRs, nodes and $\mathcal{N}$ refer to the same meaning since our system is implemented by MRs decoupling it from MCs.

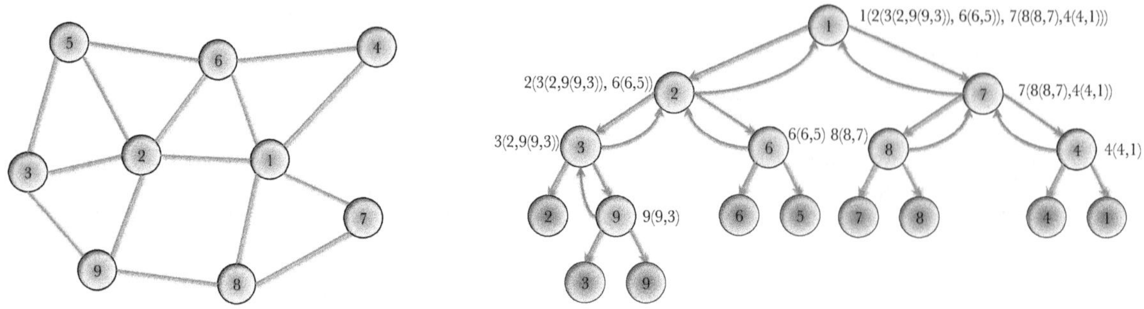

(a) Graph $\mathcal{G}$ representing mesh nodes. (b) The generated Delegates Binary Tree.

Figure 2: This figure illustrates the conversion of the network graph $\mathcal{G}$ (a) into a balanced binary tree DBT (b), where each node represents a DN for the underlying partition.

Algorithm 2: Function to map the possible number of replicas (p) to their DNs.

Function Map($Node\ n,\ int\ p$)
if $p = 1$ **then**
  if $n\ is\ leaf$ **then**
    return $n||S_{host}$
  else
    return $n||P_{host}$
else
  return $map(n.left, \lfloor \frac{p}{2} \rfloor)$ + $map(n.right, \lceil \frac{p}{2} \rceil)$

When the base case is reached (i.e. $p = 1$), it checks whether the node n is a leaf node in the DBT or not. If it is a leaf node, then it means that node n has to *self-host* the object for p replicas and returns the node ID concatenated with a flag (S_{host}) to indicate *self-hosting*. Otherwise, it returns the node ID along with a flag (P_{host}) to indicate *partition-hosting* (i.e. the DN will need to find the optimal location for the object within its partition). For every possible p, the CM creates an entry in the form of $\langle p$, set of DNs$\rangle$ and inserts it in the Map-List structure. Upon completion, the CM broadcasts the Map-List to all the nodes. This will facilitate for both the CM and the DNs to know *a priori* that for a specific p, which DNs the CM shall communicate with to assign the placement job and the DN knows from the Map-List its role whether self-hosting or partition-hosting.

3.2 Content Replication and Placement Phase

This phase consists of three steps to be performed aiming to collect statistical information about the objects, compute the number of replicas for each object and then find the placement for the replicas. These steps are described as follows:

3.2.1 During the τ period

Every node maintains a list containing an entry in the form $\langle \mathcal{N}_i, \mathcal{O}_m, \lambda_{mi}(\tau)\rangle$ that represents the request count λ_{mi} for every object $\mathcal{O}_m$ during τ at node i. An object request is counted when a MC initiates one to its access MR regardless of being served by the access MR, any other MR or even the origin server. Moreover, it will also observe the link-quality (e.g. ETX, ETT and ML) values with its neighboring nodes by logging the values of the used metric.

3.2.2 At the end of the τ period

In this step, every node finds the *trimmed mean* value of the link-quality metric with the neighboring nodes by excluding *outlier* values. Since the replica placement is intended for long periods, using the current value of the link-quality metric will not reflect the actual distance cost. Therefore, we believe that using the trimmed mean can give a precise estimation of fluctuating wireless links that captures the long-term link cost instead of using the mean or instantaneous link cost. Anomalous outlier values can completely change the mean, thus putting the link cost at big risk of errors. Therefore, it is important to identify and eliminate them as follows: We let x_1, x_2, ..., x_s be a sample of size s on measurement of a particular link-quality metric. Then the $100\alpha\%$ trimmed mean is defined as: $\overline{X}_t = \frac{\sum_{i=t+1}^{s-t} x_i}{(s(1-2\alpha))}$, where $\alpha \in (0, 1)$; $t = [s\alpha + .4]$. To simplify, we take t to be the floor of $(s\alpha + .4)$ as an approximation [13]. Every node computes $\overline{X}_t$ with its neighboring nodes to represent the range of sample points unaffected by outliers. We simply ignore t of the lowest and t of the highest sample points. Then the following sub-steps are performed:

(a) The partition members of the lowest level DNs forward their object frequency list and the computed link-quality truncated mean with the member's neighbors to the parent DN. Each DN aggregates the received lists from its children along with its own list, stores the resulting list and then forwards it to its parent node. The process of aggregate, store and forward is repeated until the CM (root node) receives the full list from all the nodes. The usefulness of this hierarchical approach is: (*i*) reducing communication overhead; and (*ii*) fusing popularity information at different levels of the DBT helps distributing this information instead of collecting it by a central node.

(b) For every $\mathcal{O}_m$, the CM computes the global popularity $\mathcal{P}r_m(\tau)$ and the number of replicas per object $p_m(\tau+1)$ according to Eq (1) and Eq (2) respectively.

$$\mathcal{P}r_m(\tau) = \frac{\sum_{i=1}^{N} \lambda_{mi(\tau)}}{\sum_{i=1}^{N}\sum_{m=1}^{M} \lambda_{mi(\tau)}} \quad (1)$$

$$p_m(\tau+1) = \frac{SC \times N \times \mathcal{P}r_m(\tau)}{|\mathcal{O}_m|} \quad (2)$$

(c) The CM creates a *Replica-List* (RL) in the form of a 4-tuple $\langle p_m(\tau+1), \mathcal{O}_m, |\mathcal{O}_m|, \lambda_m(\tau)\rangle$ grouped by $p_m(\tau+1)$ in a decreasing order to prioritize the most popular objects.

Within each group, the objects are sorted by the objects size $|\mathcal{O}_m|$ in a decreasing order. The reason behind this way of sorting is that for a group of objects of semi-equal popularity, prioritizing large objects would minimize the cost weighted by the object size given the storage constraint. However, our scheme is fair with small objects in terms of the computed number of replicas, since it divides the popularity of an object by its size (see Eq (2)).

Algorithm 3: The Distributed Replica Placement Heuristic *SP-DNA*.

```
1  foreach group ∈ RL do
2      multicast a message containing the group of object
       replicas to the corresponding list of DNs in Map-List
3  receiving DN_k performs the following:
4  lookup the Map-List for the given p_m(τ+1)
5  forall the O_m in the received group do
6      if ε_mk > η_m then
7          forward ⟨p_m(τ+1), O_m, |O_m|,
           λ_m(τ)⟩ → parent(DN_k)
8      else
9          if DN_k is flagged S_host then
10             Fetch(O_m)
11         else
12             pick a node that minimizes the cost:
                   Min Σ_{1≤i'≤N', 1≤j'≤N'} Pr_mi'(τ)Γ(X_t)_{i'}^{j'} s.t∃SC
13             assign O_m to the selected node
14             Fetch(O_m)
```

3.2.3 Replica placement

In this step, the *SP-DNA* heuristic (Alg. 3) is executed. The CM multicasts a message that contains the 4-tuple $\langle p_m(\tau+1), \mathcal{O}_m, |\mathcal{O}_m|, \lambda_m(\tau)\rangle$ to the corresponding DNs obtained from the function in Alg. 2. When each DN receives the message, a decision has to be made (line 6) to find out whether it is feasible to place $\mathcal{O}_m$ in $\mathcal{DN}_k$ partition or forward it to the parent of $\mathcal{DN}_k$ in the DBT. The corresponding $\mathcal{DN}_k$ compares the ϵ_{mk} value from Eq (3) with a threshold value η_m from Eq (4). ϵ_{mk} acts as a *feasibility index* to decide upon the feasibility of placing $\mathcal{O}_m$ within the DN's partition or forwarding it to the parent DN. η_m is inversely proportional to the number of replicas $p_m(\tau+1)$, serving as an error margin. This means that, for a given network size, a smaller $p_m(\tau+1)$ or in other words larger partitions yields a larger error margin (η_m). A larger η_m means reduced computation cost at the expense of placement accuracy. Note that, for large partitions, the computation cost is high. This is a tradeoff between computation cost and placement accuracy. The threshold η_m can be tuned using the coefficient θ, to trade off between placement accuracy and computation cost for a given partition size. If ϵ_{mk} exceeds η_m, then $\mathcal{DN}_k$ will handoff $\mathcal{O}_m$ to its parent DN, which is responsible for a larger partition where a better placement can take place. The parent DN on its turn will take the decision of placement or handoff.

$$\epsilon_{mk} = \frac{1}{p_m(\tau+1) \times \mathcal{P}r_{mk}(\tau)} - 1 \tag{3}$$

Table 2: Numerical example showing how a DN decides to *place* an object in its partition or *forward* it to its parent DN given $p_m(\tau+1) = 3$, $\theta = 1$ and $\eta_m = 0.33$.

$\mathcal{DN}_k$	$\mathcal{P}r_{mk}(\tau)$	ϵ_{mk}	Decision
3	5%	5.67	Handoff
6	30%	0.11	Place
7	40%	-0.17	Place

$$\eta_m = \frac{1}{p_m(\tau+1) \times \theta} \tag{4}$$

$$\mathcal{P}r_{mk}(\tau) = \frac{\sum_{i'=1}^{N'} \lambda_{mi'}(\tau)}{\lambda_m(\tau)} \tag{5}$$

If ϵ_{mk} is not larger than η_m (line 8), it looks up the Map-List for its role. If it has to *self-host* the replica $\mathcal{O}_m$, then it only needs to fetch it. Otherwise (i.e. *partition-host*), it computes $\mathcal{P}r_{mk}(\tau)$ using Eq (5), which represents the popularity percentage of $\mathcal{O}_m$ within partition k with respect to the whole network. $\mathcal{DN}_k$ will compute the demand-weighted total cost for every partition member and assigns $\mathcal{O}_m$ to the node that minimizes the total cost.

The distance $\Gamma(\overline{X}_t)_{i'}^{j'}$ represents the sum of the computed long-term link-quality between i' and j'. Note that if there is no sufficient space to accommodate $\mathcal{O}_m$, $\mathcal{DN}_k$ selects the second best node and so forth, even if all partition members' storage is full, the object will be forwarded to the parent DN. We note here that a parent DN waits for an acknowledgement from its child DNs when they complete the placement of the *feasible* objects so that it can start placing the forwarded objects or forward up the hierarchy. Simultaneously, it can undertake the placement of its own *feasible* objects. This rule is to make sure that when it has to place a forwarded object, the placement should consider other replicas (if any) in the underlying partitions. We give a numerical example (see Table 2) to describe how the placement decision is made using Fig. 2. Suppose an object requires 3 replicas ($p_m(\tau+1) = 3$). For instance, the DN set will be nodes 3, 6 and 7. Each DN decides based on the local popularity $\mathcal{P}r_{mk}(\tau)$ within its partition. Therefore, node 3 will forward the placement job to node 2, while both nodes 6 and 7 will find the optimal placement in each partition.

Algorithm 4: Function to fetch an object performed by the replica server node.

```
1  Function Fetch(O_m)
2  if O_m is in the node's storage then
3      goto line 10
4  else if lookup(O_m) → the Directory Service then
5      receive the list of nodes hosting O_m
6      select the nearest hosting node for O_m
7      fetch O_m from the selected replica node
8  else
9      fetch O_m from the origin server
10 update O_m(τ+1)
11 update the Directory Service with O_m(τ+1)
```

Upon successful assignment, the selected node fetches the object replica using Alg. 4 by trying to find it locally (line 2).

Upon a miss, it consults the Directory Service (e.g. Chord [8]) by sending the object's key to obtain the list of nodes hosting it. If the object is found, the replica server requests it from the closest node. Upon a miss, it requests $\mathcal{O}_m$ from the origin server. We note here that lines 10 and 11 refer to two separate updates. The first (line 10) is for the replica server to differentiate objects of the next period $(\tau + 1)$ from objects of the current period (τ). The second (line 11) is used to update the Directory Service with the node ID hosting $\mathcal{O}_m$ for the next period $(\tau + 1)$. After fetching $\mathcal{O}_m$, the node evicts an object(s) from previous τ and inserts $\mathcal{O}_m$ for $(\tau + 1)$. It can be observed that the *SP-DNA* heuristic is not fully distributed as it depends slightly on the CM that acts as a Super-Peer [14]. However, the major burden is on the replica placement which is performed by the DNs. This avoids the fully distributed approach that incurs excessive message overhead resulting from the exchange of popularity statistics between all the participating nodes.

Table 3: Default simulation parameters

Parameter	Default Value
Simulation area	3000m x 1000m
Number of MRs ($\mathcal{N}$)	150
Number of MCs	900
Radio interface	IEEE 802.11g
Link rate	54 Mbps
Transmission range	200m
Zipf-like parameter α	0.95
Threshold coefficient θ	1
Carrier frequency	2.4 GHz
Max. Tx power	2.0 mW
Noise level	-110 dBm
Channel model	Rayleigh
Percent of trimmed values t	10%
$\mathcal{M}$	3000
$\|\mathcal{O}_m\|$ range	1 -> 4 MB
τ	90 minutes
$\mathcal{SC}$	256 MB

4. EVALUATION METHODOLOGY

To evaluate our scheme, we used OMNeT++ simulator [15] with Inetmanet [16] and OverSim [17] implementations. Inetmanet provides an implementation for different MANET routing protocols with the support for multiple link-quality metrics including hop-count, ETX, ETT and ML. OverSim is a flexible overlay network simulation framework based on OMNeT++. It includes several structured and unstructured peer-to-peer protocols. In our implementation, we use Chord [8], which is a well-known distributed, scalable and DHT based content lookup protocol that is designed for structured P2P networks. We simulated a stationary WMN for different scenarios in different mesh topologies. Objects are looked-up using Chord. We used the common OLSR routing protocol augmented with one of the link-quality metrics (i.e. hop, ETX, ETT and ML). Although the schemes we are comparing with aim to minimize the Hop-Count distance, we find it unfair to compare our scheme using the other advanced metrics and use the simple Hop-Count for the other schemes. Therefore, we use the same metric for all the schemes in every simulation run. The request pattern follows a *Zipf-like* distribution.

The browsing behavior of the clients is simulated using a random think time period that represents the time elapsed between successive web page downloads by a MC. This period ranges between 5 and 10 minutes on average since the requested object represents a multimedia Web content and not the ordinary Web page browsing. The simulation results were averaged over multiple random scenarios. The application traffic is created using FTP traffic generator. In each simulation test, the baseline *Random* heuristic was run first, followed by one of the other heuristics or *SP-DNA*. For all the heuristics, requests are served from the closest replica server depending on the instantaneous value of the link-quality metric used. The simulation tests are carried out in online fashion such that object replica placement is performed whilst clients' requests are generated. Table 3 summarizes the default parameters' values used. Now, we give a brief description of the heuristics we are comparing with:

1. ***Random*** [18]: Objects are assigned to nodes randomly subject to the storage constraints. Both objects and replica servers are selected in a uniform probability until each node's storage is full. If the replica server already stores the object, a new object and a new server are selected.
2. ***Lat-CDN*** [19]: Initially, objects are stored at the origin servers and all the replica servers are empty. The heuristic selects the *object-server* pair that produces the largest network latency, and thus assign the object to the server. The cost matrix is updated following the new placement. This process is iterated until all the servers become full.
3. ***Greedy-Global*** [18]: For every node, the heuristic finds the object that yields the highest demand-weighted cost. It then picks the *object-server* pair that has the highest cost and stores the object in that node. This results in a new placement. Then it re-calculates the costs and picks the *object-server* pair that yields the highest cost. The process is repeated until all nodes' storage is full.

5. RESULTS AND DISCUSSIONS

In this section, we present the simulation results and discuss them according to the performance metrics described in each sub-section.

5.1 Mean end-to-end delay

In this subsection, the comparison is with respect to the mean end-to-end delay observed by mesh clients. This refers to the system-wide mean time taken since the initiation of a request until the completion of object's transmission. We ran multiple simulation tests for each scenario for different topologies. Fig. 3a depicts a comparison for each scenario. It can be noticed that the worst performance is obtained using the simple Hop-Count, which does not reflect the channel quality leading to lossy/congested links and as a result, yields to packet delay, loss, and retransmission due to channel congestion and degradation in signal quality. On the other extreme, it clearly shows that all the heuristics perform best using the ETT metric, which employs the link-rate information and the packet delivery ratio to represent the wireless link-quality more precisely than both ETX and ML. We can note that *SP-DNA* outperforms the other heuristics.

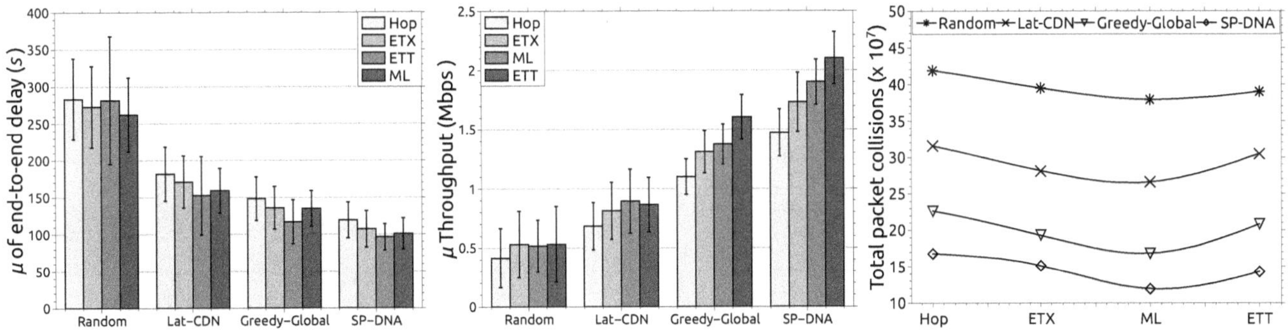

(a) Mean end-to-end delay (b) Mean throughput (c) Packet collisions

Figure 3: Performance comparison between different schemes using different link-quality metrics.

The performance gain is caused by: (*a*) given the same popularity, our scheme favors large objects over small ones when a DN makes the placement decision and as a result, the number of bytes traversing is reduced; (*b*) the shorter convergence time (as we show in subsection 5.5.2) for *SP-DNA* compared to *Lat-CDN* and *Greedy-Global* that require longer time to converge. Recall that the heuristics are evaluated in online fashion, clients' requests cannot be satisfied from nearest replica servers until the replica placement is complete; and (*c*) *SP-DNA* gives a more accurate placement than *Greedy-Global* since it considers the local popularity within the partition. We can notice that using the ETT metric yields the lowest end-to-end delay. This is because ETT improves the performance of ETX by probing the link bandwidth using fixed-size data packets periodically using two packets, a small one followed by a large one. The bandwidth is the size of the large packet divided by the minimum delay received for that link.

5.2 Mean throughput

In this subsection, we compare *SP-DNA* with the other heuristics with respect to the mean throughput in the network. This is the summation of all the sizes of served objects divided by the total time taken to complete the transmission of all the packets. The results in Fig. 3b represent the mean throughput obtained using different heuristics. It can be observed that *Lat-CDN* has a better throughput than the *Random* heuristic since servers cooperate to place objects with the high latency. However, it does not perform better than *Greedy-Global* and *SP-DNA* because it leads to improper replica placement as it considers latency cost without distinguishing the variable demand (popularity) among replica servers. We can notice that *SP-DNA* outperforms the *Greedy-Global*. This is because *Greedy-Global* does not distinguish different sizes of objects as it may not be an issue for high-performance CDN servers. However, *SP-DNA* considers this crucial factor in finding the density share for each object, which yields to a significant performance improvement. To compare with *Lat-CDN*, it clearly shows that *SP-DNA* has a significant performance gain over *Lat-CDN*. This gain is due to the same reason as in *Greedy-Global* (i.e. does not consider different sizes of object). Furthermore, it assumes similar popularity for an object among replica servers.

Although the *Greedy-Global* might lead to a better placement than *SP-DNA* in extreme situations such as when the popularity is concentrated in one partition and comparatively low in the neighboring partitions. In such a situation, *Greedy-Global* might place multiple replicas in one partition; while *SP-DNA* places a replica in each partition. However, the traffic in such situation will be concentrated in that partition; therefore, two problems will arise. The first problem is the immense traffic within that partition, which will lead to problems like the contention to access the wireless medium, packet loss, congestion and degrading the link-quality. The second problem is the load imbalance between replica servers. The servers in the hotspot partition will be overloaded and the servers in the neighboring partitions are less loaded. Our scheme can achieve a better load balance than *Greedy-Global*, since requests can be forwarded to replica servers in the neighboring partitions to avoid the aforementioned problems. For *Greedy-Global*, this might not be a problem as long as there is sufficient bandwidth and high capacity CDN servers, but in the wireless environment these resources are scarce. We can also infer that *SP-DNA* performs best using the ETT metric, which selects paths with high link rates.

5.3 Total number of packet collisions

In this subsection, the comparison is conducted with respect to the number of packet collisions. This refers to the total number of colliding packets resulting from the contention to access the wireless medium during a simulation run. Since MRs are typically stationary, link failure due to mobility is rare. However, transmission fails due to packet collisions, interference, or inadequate link rate selection. We can notice from Fig. 3c that the packet collision increases drastically for the baseline *Random* heuristic as a result of the long distance traveled by the packets, which degrades the network capacity. It can be noticed that *SP-DNA* can significantly reduce the number of packet collisions compared to the other heuristics. This performance gain is because *Greedy-Global* might lead to the creation of hotspot zones, where replicas of an object are concentrated yielding to problems such as contention and congestion in these hotspot zones that increases packet collision. The increased packet loss in *Lat-CDN* comes as a result from the assumption of similar object popularity among replica servers. This assumption is not practical in WMNs that do not have sufficient bandwidth as in CDN servers yielding improper and inefficient placement of unpopular objects in nodes that can benefit from hosting popular objects with respect to their MCs demands. As a result, the distance traveled is increased and a node's $\mathcal{SC}$ is inefficiently utilized. However, in our scheme, the traffic is distributed among the partitions to avoid the aforementioned problems. We note that in terms of packet collision, ML performs best since it is based on using the path that introduces the minimum loss rate by multiplying the success probability of each link along the path. This avoids lossy links and therefore, it reduces packet collisions.

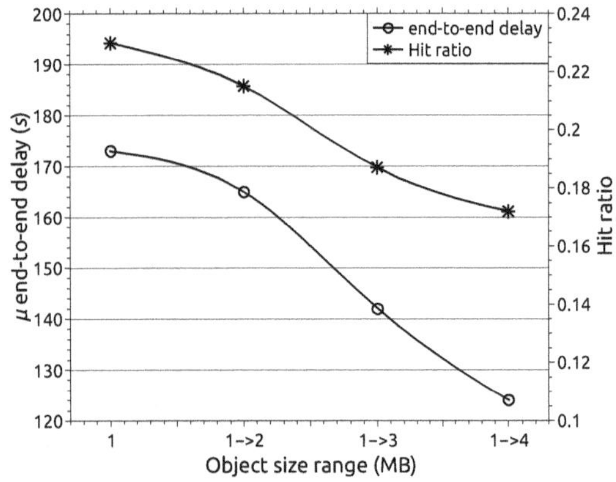

(a) Decreasing order

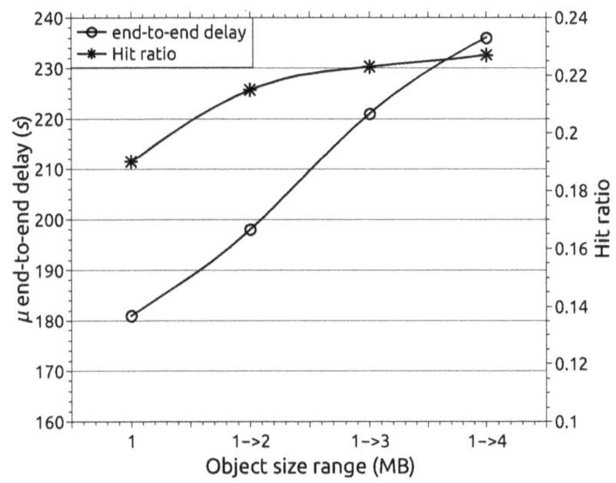

(b) Increasing order

Figure 4: The tradeoff between the mean end-to-end delay and the hit ratio vs. variable ranges of object size.

5.4 Mean end-to-end delay vs. hit ratio

In these simulation tests, we investigate the effectiveness of sorting objects of semi-equal popularity based on objects' size both in decreasing and increasing orders. This is a tradeoff between latency and hit ratio as can be noticed in both Figs. 4a and 4b. Prioritizing large objects (see Fig. 4a) shows that as the range increases, the latency improves as the placement optimality of large objects converges, which reduces the amount of packets traversing. However, the hit ratio drops slightly as the range increases. On the contrary, Fig. 4b shows a latency increment as the size gap increases and an improvement in the hit ratio since replicating smaller objects usually results in higher hit ratios [20]. However, beyond a limit (1->3) this improvement becomes slight, hence, we favor the decremental sort as the benefit in access cost is more than the benefit in the hit ratio.

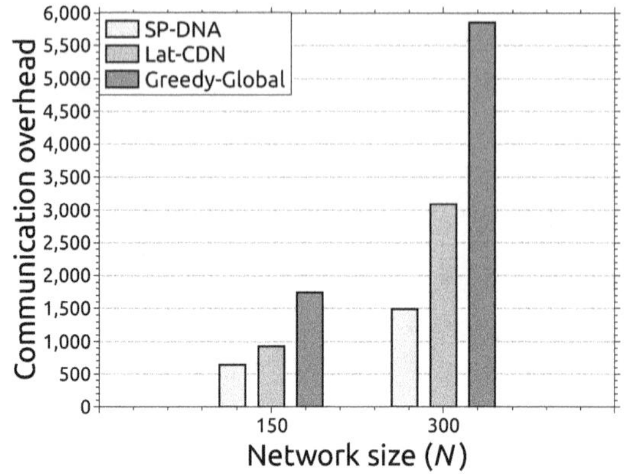

(a)

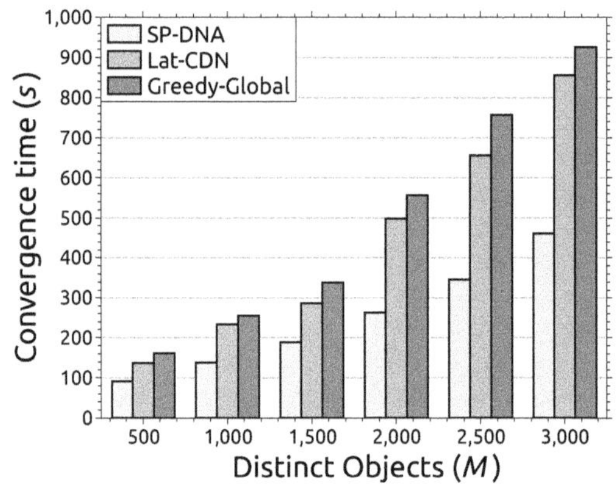

(b)

Figure 5: Comparison between different heuristics in terms of communication overhead (a) and convergence time (b).

5.5 Communication / convergence overhead

5.5.1 Communication overhead

This is the total number of control messages (wireless transmissions) generated from collecting popularity information and disseminating the placement decision on each node. Two network sizes ($\mathcal{N}$ = 150 and 300) were considered to quantify the scalability of each scheme. In the simulation runs, we considered placing the replica placement entity for both *Greedy-Global* and *Lat-CDN* in a centroid node to reduce the wireless transmissions. The results in Fig. 5a reveal that *Greedy-Global* incurs the highest overhead. This is caused by the hop-by-hop forwarding of popularity messages to the central entity, which finds the set of object replicas for each node and then forwards to each node its own replica set. *Lat-CDN* works similar to *Greedy-Global* except that it does not require the collection of popularity statistics, therefore, the overhead is reduced by approximately half. The agglomeration approach used by *SP-DNA* significantly reduces the message overhead since the partition members are in the proximity of their DN, the wireless transmissions traverse a short distance. As we go up the hierarchy, the agglomerated message might travel a longer distance, however, it combines multiple popularity messages from its descendants. On the other direction, when the CM assigns the placement job, it batches multiple object IDs in a multicast message (Alg. 3) that is forwarded to the corresponding DNs. Reducing communication overhead is a very important aspect in a wireless environment.

5.5.2 Convergence Time

This is the total time taken to decide on allocating and fetching all the object replicas on all participating nodes for the next τ period measured in seconds. We compare the heuristics for $\mathcal{N} = 300$ and for variable $\mathcal{M}$. Fig. 5b clearly shows that *Greedy-Global* and *Lat-CDN* demonstrate long time requirements to converge. This is because both of them are centralized and require heavy sorting operations since both use a two dimensional cost matrix composed of $\mathcal{N}$ and $\mathcal{M}$. Therefore, both of them require recalculating the cost function for every *Object-Server* assignment after every replica placement. As $\mathcal{N}$ increases, the growth of the convergence time for both increases dramatically. This indicates that both do not scale well with respect to $\mathcal{N}$. The performance gain for *Lat-CDN* over *Greedy-Global* is because the latter requires collecting popularity statistics about objects, which is not required by the former algorithm. In contrast, *SP-DNA* is distributed and therefore, the burden of the placement decision is performed in parallel by the DNs and runs in groups of objects. As the number of replicas $p_m(\tau+1)$ increases, the partition size ($\mathcal{N}'$) decreases yielding a decrement in convergence time. Therefore, *SP-DNA* depends on $p_m(\tau+1)$ rather than $\mathcal{N}$. However, the other heuristics depend on $\mathcal{N}$, $\mathcal{M}$, $\mathcal{SC}$ and the granularity of object size $|\mathcal{O}_m|$. Overall, the long convergence time for all heuristics is because it includes both the placement decision and the time to fetch the objects' replicas.

6. RELATED WORK

Many caching and replication algorithms have been proposed for the Internet and ad hoc networks, but there has been much less effort devoted to schemes tailored for WMNs. On one hand, many replica placement algorithms designed for the Internet are centralized and incur a high computational cost. On the other hand, caching and replication schemes in ad hoc networks focus on issues such as low bandwidth and energy constraints. In [21], the goal is to find a placement strategy that minimizes the distance that needs to be searched to find an arbitrarily chosen piece of content. However, it does not consider content popularity at different nodes since they formulate the problem as the *k-center* problem. The work in [22] proposes a strategy to determine the optimal number of replicas to minimize object access cost (defined as the Euclidean distance from the requester to the nearest replica) in WMNs when the prior knowledge on the global popularity of objects is available. *P2PMesh* was proposed in [23] for P2P file sharing system over WMNs. It aims to reduce both the number of failed lookups and the file lookup latency. However, replica placement was not considered. The authors in [24] propose *H2-VIP* to compute the optimal number of replicas of video blocks so that the overall system failure rate can be minimized. However, we consider the content placement in mesh routers storage instead of home devices. Hence, the reliability is high.

To the best of our knowledge, the closest works are given in [18, 19]. In [18] the authors proposed four heuristics: *Random*, *Popularity*, *Greedy-Single* and *Greedy-Global*. They found that *Greedy-Global* outperforms the other three heuristics. In [19] *Lat-CDN* was proposed that aims to allocate objects to replica servers with respect to the total network's latency. However, both [18, 19] are centralized and do not take into account the special features of wireless networks.

7. CONCLUSIONS

In this paper, we have proposed an efficient and scalable object replication and placement scheme for WMNs. To make our scheme distributed and hierarchical, we firstly build a balanced binary tree of multi-level partitions of the network. This is then used to facilitate replica placement and reduce communication and computation cost. The scheme makes the placement decision in a hierarchical way. A delegate node decides to place a replica in its partition when it finds that it is feasible. If not, it forwards the placement job to a larger partition up the hierarchy. As a result, the scheme is capable of making accurate placement without incurring high overhead cost. The scheme takes into account the factors of long-term link cost, object popularity and size to compute the number of replicas per object. To improve latency, the scheme favors large objects over small ones for the similar popularity. Our simulation results show that the proposed scheme can significantly improve network performance with respect to latency, throughput, packet collision and communication/computation cost.

8. REFERENCES

[1] I. F. Akyildiz, X. Wang, and W. Wang, "Wireless mesh networks: a survey," *Comput. Netw.*, vol. 47, pp. 445–487, March 2005.

[2] H. Chen and Y. Xiao, "Cache access and replacement for future wireless internet," *Comm. Mag.*, vol. 44, pp. 113–123, May 2006.

[3] S. M. Das, H. Pucha, and Y. C. Hu, "Mitigating the gateway bottleneck via transparent cooperative caching in wireless mesh networks," *Ad Hoc Netw.*, vol. 5, pp. 680–703, August 2007.

[4] D. S. J. De Couto, D. Aguayo, J. Bicket, and R. Morris, "A high-throughput path metric for multi-hop wireless routing," *Wirel. Netw.*, vol. 11, pp. 419–434, July 2005.

[5] R. Draves, J. Padhye, and B. Zill, "Routing in multi-radio, multi-hop wireless mesh networks," in *Proceedings of the 10th annual international conference on Mobile computing and networking*, MobiCom '04, (New York, NY, USA), pp. 114–128, ACM, 2004.

[6] D. Passos, C. de Albuquerque, M. Campista, L. Costa, and O. Duarte, "Minimum loss multiplicative routing metrics for wireless mesh networks," *Journal of Internet Services and Applications*, vol. 1, pp. 201–214, 2011. 10.1007/s13174-010-0015-6.

[7] Z. Al-Arnaout, Q. Fu, and M. Frean, "A content replication scheme for wireless mesh networks," in *Proceedings of the 22nd international workshop on Network and operating systems support for digital audio and video*, NOSSDAV '12, 2012.

[8] I. Stoica, R. Morris, D. Liben-Nowell, D. R. Karger, M. F. Kaashoek, F. Dabek, and H. Balakrishnan, "Chord: a scalable peer-to-peer lookup protocol for internet applications," *IEEE/ACM Trans. Netw.*, vol. 11, pp. 17–32, Feb. 2003.

[9] T. Clausen, P. Jacquet, C. Adjih, A. Laouiti, P. Minet, P. Muhlethaler, A. Qayyum, and L. Viennot,

"Optimized Link State Routing Protocol (OLSR)," 2003. Network Working Group Network Working Group.

[10] M. Campista, P. Esposito, I. Moraes, L. Costa, O. Duarte, D. Passos, C. de Albuquerque, D. Saade, and M. Rubinstein, "Routing metrics and protocols for wireless mesh networks," *Network, IEEE*, vol. 22, pp. 6 –12, jan.-feb. 2008.

[11] J. Current, M. Daskin, and D. Schilling, "Discrete network location models," *Industrial Engineering*, pp. 81–118, 2002.

[12] B. W. Kernighan and S. Lin, "An efficient heuristic procedure for partitioning graphs," *Bell System Technical Journal*, vol. 49, no. 2, pp. 291–307, 1970.

[13] A. Welsh, "The trimmed mean in the linear model," *The Annals of Statistics*, vol. 15, no. 1, pp. 20–36, 1987.

[14] B. Yang and H. Garcia-Molina, "Designing a super-peer network," *Data Engineering, International Conference on*, vol. 0, p. 49, 2003.

[15] A. Varga and R. Hornig, "An overview of the omnet++ simulation environment," in *Simutools '08: Proceedings of the 1st international conference on Simulation tools and techniques for communications, networks and systems & workshops*, (ICST, Brussels, Belgium, Belgium), pp. 1–10, ICST (Institute for Computer Sciences, Social-Informatics and Telecommunications Engineering), 2008.

[16] A. A. Quintana, E. Casilari, and A. Triviño, "Implementation of manet routing protocols on omnet++," 2008.

[17] I. Baumgart, B. Heep, and S. Krause, "Oversim: A flexible overlay network simulation framework," in *IEEE Global Internet Symposium, 2007*, pp. 79–84, 2007.

[18] J. Kangasharju, J. Roberts, and K. W. Ross, "Object replication strategies in content distribution networks," *Computer Communications*, vol. 25, no. 4, pp. 376 – 383, 2002.

[19] G. Pallis, A. Vakali, K. Stamos, A. Sidiropoulos, D. Katsaros, and Y. Manolopoulos, "A latency-based object placement approach in content distribution networks," in *Proceedings of the Third Latin American Web Congress*, (Washington, DC, USA), pp. 140–, IEEE Computer Society, 2005.

[20] C. Cunha, A. Bestavros, and M. Crovella, "Characteristics of www client-based traces," tech. rep., Boston, MA, USA, 1995.

[21] B.-J. Ko and D. Rubenstein, "Distributed self-stabilizing placement of replicated resources in emerging networks," *IEEE/ACM Trans. Netw.*, vol. 13, pp. 476–487, June 2005.

[22] S. Jin and L. Wang, "Content and service replication strategies in multi-hop wireless mesh networks," in *Proceedings of the 8th ACM international symposium on Modeling, analysis and simulation of wireless and mobile systems*, MSWiM '05, (New York, NY, USA), pp. 79–86, ACM, 2005.

[23] A. Al Asaad, S. Gopalakrishnan, and V. Leung, "Peer-to-peer file sharing over wireless mesh networks," in *Communications, Computers and Signal Processing, 2009. PacRim 2009. IEEE Pacific Rim Conference on*, pp. 697 –702, aug. 2009.

[24] J.-W. Ding, W.-T. Wang, and C.-F. Wang, "An efficient data replication scheme for peer-to-peer video streaming over wireless-mesh community networks," in *Intelligent Information Hiding and Multimedia Signal Processing, 2008. IIHMSP '08 International Conference on*, pp. 767 –770, aug. 2008.

Improving Minimum Flow Rate in Wireless Mesh Networks by Effective Placement of Directional Antennas

Yuan Li†, Michał Pióro‡†, Björn Landfeldt†
†Department of Electrical and Information Technology, Lund University, Lund, Sweden
‡Institute of Telecommunications, Warsaw University of Technology, Warsaw, Poland
{yuan.li, michal.pioro, bjorn.landfeldt}@eit.lth.se

ABSTRACT

For some time, directional antennas have been considered to solve connectivity and interference issues in wireless networks. Several scenarios have been presented and often the conclusions drawn are positive, showing increase in capacity. However, to date there has been no effort to assess a holistic picture of the benefit/cost tradeoff and previous work mainly concerns either link scheduling or antenna placement but not the two combined. Such consideration will become increasingly important in the near future with the advent of heterogeneous networks and other possible combinations of mesh and public access networks.

In order to better understand the full implications and potential of using directional antennas in such systems, we present a model for determining the maximized benefit/cost tradeoff using a combination of directional and omnidirectional antennas in wireless multihop backbones. We study the problem of maximizing the minimal flow rate from gateways to mesh routers in the mesh network. A mixed integer programming model is formulated for joint optimization of antenna placement and link transmission scheduling under an antenna-aware SINR interference constraint and a budget constraint. An accurate antenna model is used and variable modulation and coding schemes are used. The model is decomposed to a master problem and a pricing problem, and solved by a branch-and-price algorithm. Additionally, two effective heuristics are proposed as supplement methods.

Applying the introduced model makes it possible to deploy directional antennas at appropriate nodes and find a corresponding link transmission scheduling (with data rate adaptation). The numerical results show that introducing directional antennas can indeed substantially improve the considered traffic objective. Interestingly, the results also show that it is not always optimal to install directional antennas at all possible nodes because of increased interference observed at non-receiving nodes within the beam width. Finally, comparisons are made to show the effectiveness of the proposed solution methods.

MSWiM'13, November 3–8, 2013, Barcelona, Spain.

ACM 978-1-4503-2353-6/13/11 ...$15.00.
http://dx.doi.org/10.1145/2507924.2507933.

Categories and Subject Descriptors

C.2.1 [**Computer-Communication Network**]: [Network Architecture and design]; G.1.6 [**Optimization**]: [Integer programming]

Keywords

antenna-aware SINR interference; mixed-integer programming; antenna placement; link transmission scheduling

1. INTRODUCTION

Wireless Mesh Networks (WMN) have found widespread applications from public access to sensor networks. In many deployment scenarios these networks will operate in highly dense network topologies where interference from the WMN nodes themselves as well as external nodes may cause degradation of network performance. To overcome or minimize the negative effects of this interference, the use of directional antennas has been proposed [1], by focusing transmission energy between communicating pairs of nodes, resulting in increased spatial reuse and transmission range compared with omnidirectional (omni) antennas.

Directional and steerable antennas are now mature technologies and there has been a large body of work investigating their application in wireless networks. For example, [2] presented a medium access control and routing strategy based on directional antennas for wireless networks. [3] showed how directional antennas can improve the performance of ad hoc networks. In the WMN context, [4] proposed a WMN architecture utilizing low-cost directional antennas and multiple channels to exploit spatial and frequency separation which can improve the throughput greatly; [5] pointed out that directional antennas with optimized beam width can improve the performance of opportunistic routing due to the characteristics of concentrated energy.

Much related research exists on either antenna placement or link scheduling. [6] analyzes theoretical capacity bounds considering both omni and directional antennas based on the conflicted graph, i.e., a node cannot be active if it is within the interference range of any active non-intended transmitter. This is not realistic since in practice, a node can be active if the signal-to-interference-plus-noise-ratio (SINR) condition is satisfied, i.e. the ratio of the signal power received from an intended transmitter to the sum of the noise plus the signal power from other transmitters is greater than or equal to a given threshold. [7] presents a mixed integer programming (MIP) model to optimize antenna deployment to improve the throughput of wireless networks. The authors found that random antenna placement is far from optimal. However, the work is based on the conflicted graph. [8] aims to minimize the number of directional antennas on base stations needed to meet the bandwidth requirements of wireless devices; again, interference is not taken into account. In terms of transmission scheduling, many different algorithms have been proposed based on omnidirectional antennas, see [9] and included references. In the case of directional antennas, [10, 11] jointly optimize routing with link scheduling for WMN. However, they also restrict themselves to use the conflicted graph. When the SINR constraint is taken into account, a MIP model can be easily set up, see [12]. However, the model is intractable due to an excessive number of binary variables. The joint optimization of antenna placement and link scheduling has thus far received little attention. So far, the only related work [13] studied joint optimization of link scheduling and antenna beam steering to maximize spatial reuse for users sharing spectrum. The problem was formulated as non-linear mixed integer programming and was solved by a column generation combined with subgredient method. The benefit/cost tradeoff was not considered and therefore the effects of using directional antennas were not fully analyzed.

We study the problem of maximizing the minimal (max-min) flow rate between gateways and routers when omni and directional antennas are used concurrently. The routing path is fixed for each router and the links in the routing paths form the WMN topology. The max-min flow optimization not only helps to improve the fairness and throughput but also offers a non-conventional way for resources management when traffic loads and patterns are unknown [14]. In previous work [15] we compared the impact of three different strategies of placing directional antennas on the cost/benefit tradeoff for max-min flow rate optimality: deployed on leaf nodes, deployed on gateways and deployed on all nodes. However, the optimal solution for deploying directional antennas was not determined in this work.

In this paper, we present a solution for optimizing the max-min flow rate based on both placement of directional antennas and link scheduling in a WMN. We design a link scheduling algorithm based on a Time Division Multiple Access (TDMA) variant, i.e., the total time is divided to several time slots, where a group of active links satisfying the SINR constraint is selected for each time slot. Note that the SINR depends on the type of antenna installed on the nodes and we therefore derive an antenna-aware SINR constraint for transmission scheduling. The data rate of the active link is controlled by selecting different modulation and coding schemes (MCSs). Synthesizing all these components, we set up a MIP model to jointly optimize the antenna deployment and link scheduling limited by a budget constraint. By solving the model, we are able to determine the number of directional antennas needed to achieve desired performance and also where these directional antennas should be deployed.

This centralized solution yields the theoretical performance bound and therefore represents a very useful component for comparing against future work which take dynamic behavior into account and solutions which aim at achieving the same optimization goal in a distributed manner. To the best of our knowledge, this paper is the first work to jointly optimize link scheduling with antenna deployment for max-min flow optimization. The main novelties are as follows:

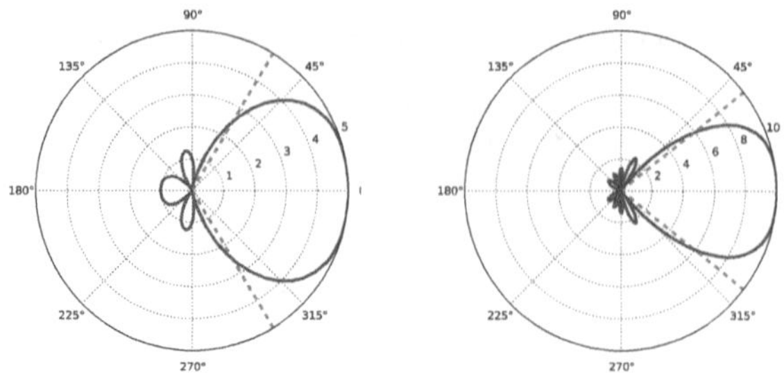

(a) N=5 (b) N=10

Figure 1: antenna radiation pattern

- We set up a general non-compact MIP model to maximize the minimal flow rate by optimizing antenna assignment and link scheduling. A branch-and-price (B&P) method is designed to solve it.
- We use a realistic antenna pattern and design a link scheduling scheme based on an antenna-aware interference model.
- We propose two effective heuristics and made several comparisons in a numerical study.

2. PROBLEM DESCRIPTION

2.1 Antenna model

An antenna's radiation pattern reflects the *antenna gain* which measures the relative power in any direction compared to an isotropic (omni) antenna. We use the terms *peak gain* referring to the maximum gain over all directions and *beam width*, denoting the angle between the two points on each side of the peak gain where the gain is 3 dB lower than the peak value.

The directional antennas can be classified into two categories: switched antennas and adaptive antennas. The switched antennas are cheap and have simple functionality at the cost of worse performance (compared with the adaptive antennas) due to their reciprocal and passive nature which preserves the system dynamic range. The adaptive antennas consist of an array of antennas and a signal processing component which can change the direction easily and fast, using a process known as beamforming. They can improve the quality of the radio signal and increase the overall system reliability [16]. The Adaptive Antenna System (AAS) has been adopted as an optional feature in IEEE 802.16. Example experimental and practical systems are detailed in [17]. In this paper, we consider adaptive antennas for all nodes.

There are different models for generating radiation patterns of directional antennas. Much previous research considered the idealized antenna models which assume the gain is 0 or a non-zero constant value outside the main beam, e.g. [12, 18]. We employ a typical realistic directional antenna pattern which has high gain in the main beam and low gain in the slide lobes and back lobes. We adopt the sinc-function antenna model [19] to generate our desired antenna patterns.

$$G(\theta) = \frac{\sin(\frac{N}{2}(kd\cos\theta + \varphi))}{\sin(\frac{1}{2}(kd\cos\theta + \varphi)} \tag{1}$$

with directional antennas. If nodes 0 and 1 used directional antennas instead of omni antennas, the max-min flow would be decreased to 5.85 because nodes 0 and 1 would then generate more interference for nodes 3 and 6, respectively.

To analyze the benefit/cost tradeoff of using directional antennas, we draw Figure 5 which illustrates the increase ratio of the max-min flow for varying budget. The increase ratio is calculated as $\frac{MMFP-MMFO}{MMFO}$ where $MMFP$ and $MMFO$ are the max-min flows when both kinds of antennas can be used and when all nodes use omni antennas, respectively. The normalized budget is the ratio of the available budget to the maximum budget $C(1) \times |V|$. We study four groups of networks and show the average results for five instances of each group. We observe that the max-min flow is a non-decreasing function of the increasing budget, and the maximum of the increase of the max-min flow is more than a half of MMFO (the starting point). What is more, the max-min flow reaches its maximum before the whole budget is used up which means not all nodes have to be equipped with directional antennas, and adding directional antennas to the network does not necessarily increase the max-min flow. A further observation is that the max-min flow gain is decaying, i.e., a small number of directional antennas deployed at critical nodes can have large effect.

The beam width of the directional antenna is also a factor affecting the increase ratio, as illustrated in Figure 6. We generate four different antenna patterns by setting the number of antenna elements N to different values according to the antenna model (1). The tested antenna patterns are: $N = 5, \theta_h = 120°$; $N = 7, \theta_h = 96°$; $N = 10, \theta_h = 80°$; $N = 15, \theta_h = 64°$. For each group of networks, we test five network instances, and plot the average and the variance. The available budget is set to $W = 2|\mathcal{V}|$ which is sufficient for all nodes to use directional antennas. We find that for the four groups of networks, the smaller the beam width, the larger the increase ratio, i.e., the directional antennas with smaller beam width offer the larger benefits. For all beam width, the increase ratio for networks with 25 nodes is the largest while that for networks with 10 nodes is the smallest. This indicates that the increase of the max-min flow due to the use of directional antennas for dense networks is bigger than that for sparse networks. However, this indication is not evident for networks with 15 nodes and 20 nodes since their differences in the number of nodes is not significant.

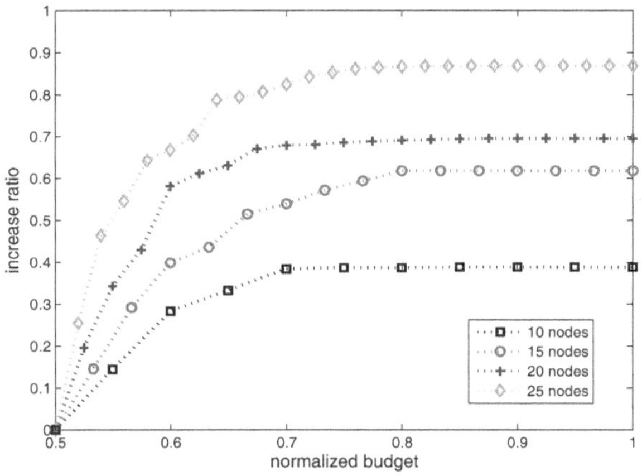

Figure 5: the benefit/cost tradeoff

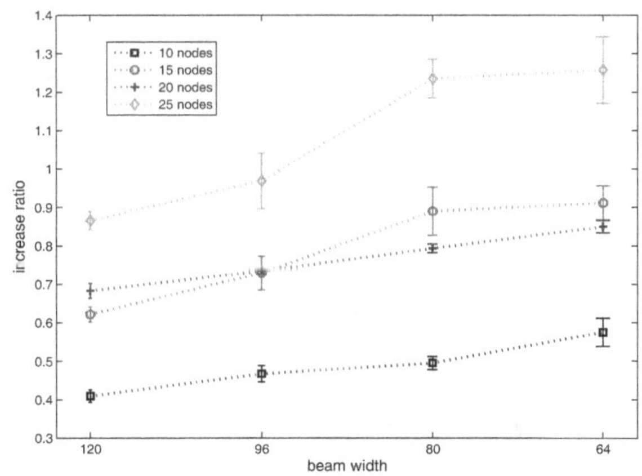

Figure 6: the impact of beam width on increase ratio

4.3 Comparisons for solution approaches

Table 3 lists the optimality gaps and running times for H1 and H2, and for B&P. The optimality gap is calculated as (objective of B&P - objective of H1 or H2) / (objective of B&P), where "objective" stands for the value of the objective function. If B&P cannot be solved in 3 hours (marked with $*$ in the table), we replace the optimal objective of B&P by the upper bound which is the solution of the root B&P node (the full linear relaxation of model (5)). Seven groups of networks with five instances each are tested and the average value for each group is shown in the table. The available budget is set to $W = 1.3|\mathcal{V}|$ and the beam width of directional antennas is 120°. The Gurobi solver is used to solve the mixed integer programming models. All the computations are executed on a computer with Inter 3.4GHz CPU, 16G RAM and 64-bit windows server 2008.

We can see that the optimality gaps are very good for H1 and acceptable for H2, even for large networks where B&P is not able to find any optimal solution in 3 hours. H1 delivers much smaller gaps than H2 while H2 needs much less time. In practice, we could use either of these methods according to the requirements.

Table 3: Comparisons for H1, H2 and B&P

Networks		H1		H2		B&P
$\|\mathcal{V}\|$	$\|\mathcal{E}\|$	gap(%)	time(s)	gap(%)	time(s)	time(s)
10	8	0.43	5	12.19	1	9
15	13	0.86	40	22.10	3	129
20	17	1.42	257	28.25	13	1879
25	22	5.61	683	29.07	29	2908
30	26	6.47	1929	31.27	60	6745
35	31	8.81	3929	33.39	67	*
40	36	11.20	8879	37.41	100	*

5. CONCLUSION

This paper presents a general model for optimizing antenna placement and link scheduling to maximize the minimal flow rate in wireless mesh networks. The problem is decomposed to a master problem with a pricing problem under the antenna-aware physical interference model. Different factors are taken into account, including the total budget, different modulation and coding schemes and the antenna pattern. The decomposition decreases the complexity of the problem and makes it more tractable. Based on the decomposition, a branch-and-price method and two heuristics are proposed. The numerical study gives a comparison for different solution strategies and shows that deploying directional antennas on all nodes does not always result in the best max-min flow rate. The tradeoff of the benefit/cost is also analyzed.

The model in this paper characterizes the optimal way to combine the use of omni and directional antennas and the amount of improvements directional antennas can bring. We notice that the pricing problem is still quite complicated and effective heuristic solutions need to be developed. Furthermore, the routing strategy and the power control mechanism could be optimized combined with antenna placement and link scheduling. Taking these into account, we conclude that there are still many unanswered questions in fully understanding the impacts directional antennas have on wireless network constructs and there are many open problems to investigate before a holistic understanding is reached.

6. ACKNOWLEDGMENT

This work was supported by the EC Marie Curie Actions project MESH-WISE (FP7-PEOPLE-2012-IAPP-324515) and ELLIIT - Excellence Center at Linköping-Lund in Information Technology. The research of Michał Pióro was also supported by National Science Centre (Poland) under grant 2011/ 01/B/ST7/02967. Yuan Li was also supported by China Scholarship Council.

7. REFERENCES

[1] G. Li, L.L. Yang, W.S. Conner, and B. Sadeghi. Opportunities and challenges for mesh networks using directional antennas. In *WiMesh workshop*, Santa Clara, USA, Sept. 2005.

[2] R.R. Choudhury, X. Yang, R. Ramanathan, and N.H. Vaidya. On designing MAC protocols for wireless networks using directional antennas. *IEEE Transactions on Mobile Computing*, 5(5):477–491, 2006.

[3] S. Yi, Y. Pei, S. Kalyanaraman, and B. Azimi-Sadjadi. How is the capacity of ad hoc networks improved with directional antennas? *Wireless Networks*, 13(5):635–648, 2007.

[4] S.M. Das, H. Pucha, D. Koutsonikolas, Y.C. Hu, and D. Peroulis. DMesh: incorporating practical directional antennas in multichannel wireless mesh networks. *IEEE Journal on Selected Areas in Communications*, 24(11):2028–2039, 2006.

[5] C. Luk, W. Lau, and O. Yue. Opportunistic routing with directional antennas in wireless mesh networks. In *IEEE INFOCOM*, pages 2886–2890, Rio de Janeiro, Brazil, Apr. 2009.

[6] Z. Jun and J. Xiaohua. Capacity analysis of wireless mesh networks with omni or directional antennas. In *IEEE INFOCOM*, pages 2881–2885, Rio de Janeiro, Brazil, Apr. 2009.

[7] O. Bazan and M. Jaseemuddin. Optimal antenna placement in multi-hop wireless networks with heterogeneous antennas. In *International Wireless Communications and Mobile Computing Conference (IWCMC)*, pages 1051–1056, Istanbul, Turkey, Aug. 2011.

[8] F. Pan and S. Kasiviswanathan. Efficient placement of directional antennas in infrastructure-based wireless networks. In *IEEE MILCOM*, pages 1796–1801, Baltimore, MD, USA, Nov. 2011.

[9] A.D. Gore and A. Karandikar. Link scheduling algorithms for wireless mesh networks. *IEEE Communications Surveys Tutorials*, 13(2):258–273, 2011.

[10] H. Su and X. Zhang. Joint link scheduling and routing for directional-antenna based 60 ghz wireless mesh networks. In *IEEE GLOBECOM*, pages 6192–6197, Hawaii, USA, 2009.

[11] P. Dutta, V. Mhatre, D. Panigrahi, and R. Rastogi. Joint routing and scheduling in multi-hop wireless networks with directional antennas. In *IEEE INFOCOM*, pages 1–5, San Diego, CA, USA, Mar. 2010.

[12] V. Ramamurthi, A. Reaz, S. Dixit, and B. Mukherjee. Link scheduling and power control in wireless mesh networks with directional antennas. In *IEEE INFOCOM*, pages 4835–4839, Phoenix, AZ, USA, Apr. 2008.

[13] E. Anderson, C. Phillips, D. Sicker, and D. Grunwald. Signal quality pricing: decomposition for spectrum scheduling and system configuration. In *IEEE Symposium on New Frontiers in Dynamic Spectrum Access Networks (DySPAN)*, pages 408–419, Aachen, Germany, May 2011.

[14] M. Pióro, M. Żotkiewicz, B. Staehle, D. Staehle, and D.Yuan. On max-min fair flow optimization in wireless mesh networks. *Ad Hoc Networks*, 2011.

[15] M. Żotkiewicz and M. Pióro. Reliability of wireless mesh networks with directional antennas. In *International Congress on Ultra Modern Telecommunications and Control Systems and Workshops (ICUMT)*, pages 1–7, Budapest, Hungary, Oct. 2011.

[16] F. E. Fakoukakis, S. G. Diamantis, A. P. Orfanides, and G. A. Kyriacou. Development of an adaptive and a switched beam smart antenna system for wireless communications. *Journal of Electromagnetic Waves and Applications*, 20(3):399–408, 2006.

[17] E. Anderson, C. Phillips, D. Sicker, and D. Grunwald. Modeling environmental effects on directionality in wireless networks. *Mathematical and Computer Modelling*, 53(11-12):2078–2092, 2011.

[18] A. Capone, I. Filippini, and F. Martignon. Joint routing and scheduling optimization in wireless mesh networks with directional antennas. In *IEEE INFOCOM*, pages 2951–2957, Phoenix, AZ, USA, Apr. 2008.

[19] C.A.Balanis. *Antenna Theory: Analysis and Design.* Wiley-Interscience, 2005.

[20] A. Goldsmith. *Wireless Communicaitons.* Cambridge University Press, 2005.

[21] M. Pióro and D. Medhi. *Routing, Flow, and Capacity Design in Communication and Computer Networks.* Morgan Kaufman, 2004.

Experimental Evaluation of a Wireless Community Mesh Network

Llorenç Cerdà-Alabern, Axel Neumann
Universitat Politècnica de Catalunya
Dept. D'Arquitectura de Computadors
Jordi Girona 1-3, E-08034 Barcelona, Spain
llorenc@ac.upc.edu, neumann@cgws.de

Pau Escrich
Guifi.net Foundation, Research group
pau.escrich@Guifi.net

ABSTRACT

Nowadays there are inexpensive WiFi devices that have fostered the deployment of wireless communities. Well known routing protocols used in the Internet do not fit well to time varying characteristic of wireless networks. This has motivated an intensive research on routing protocols for wireless mesh networks. At this time there are a number of mature and stable implementations that are being deployed in production networks. In this paper we focus on the experimental evaluation of a production Wireless Mesh network being deployed in a testbed at *Universitat Politècnica de Catalunya* (UPC) and a quarter of the city of Barcelona, Spain. To our best knowledge, this is the first paper where a production community wireless network using 802.11an is analyzed.

Categories and Subject Descriptors

C.2.1 [**Computer Communication Networks**]: Network Architecture and Design—*Wireless communication*

Keywords

Wireless Mesh Networks; Wireless Community Networks; Experimental Evaluation; 802.11an

1. INTRODUCTION

Community networks are deployed and maintained by their own users. Unlike the model used by the traditional telecommunication companies (which are business-focused), each user is owner of a part of the total infrastructure which builds the mesh network. Using an organization system (i.e. web site) they are able to understand each other and connect with neighbors, neighbors of neighbors and so on. These networks are normally open and free. Most of them use WiFi technology because it is the easiest and cheapest way to deploy an outdoor network.

A relevant example is Guifi.net [4, 29, 22, 35], the largest currently existing community network, having around 20.000 operative nodes. Guifi.net has been deployed in urban and rural areas of Spain (mostly Catalonia). Probably one of the main reasons of Guifi.net's success is the fact that it operates as an umbrella for many other small communities. Each community uses its own kind of hardware, software and organization methods (meetings, mailing lists, etc.). But all of them share probably the most important part of the Guifi.net community, the web page. It is used mainly to distribute the IPs and confederate the small networks using a common system.

Guifi.net has become a rather complex and heterogeneous network, merging wired and wireless links. Most of Guifi.net's infrastructure is wireless and the OSPF and BGP routing protocols predominate in the network.

Inside the *Quick Mesh Project* (QMP) [7] an OpenWRT [5] distribution is being developed using BMX6 as routing protocol [28]. This distribution has been adopted by one of the network communities which operate under the Guifi.net umbrella in the quarter of Sants in Barcelona, Spain. For the sake of brevity we shall refer to the quarter of Sants simply as Sants in the rest of the paper. Additionally, the EU CONFINE project [1] is deploying a research testbed at *Universitat Politècnica de Catalunya* (UPC) using QMP. CONFINE testbed has been linked to Sants, creating a network referred to as *QMPSU* (from Quick Mesh Project at Sants UPC)[1]. The QMPSU network model is expanding among other districts of Barcelona. It grows very fast and other Guifi.net groups in the city have become interested, and started the migration.

In this paper we present an experimental evaluation of QMPSU. To do so, live measurements have been taken hourly over the last 5 months. We use this data to analyze main aspects of QMPSU. These include topology, usage and network performance and characterization. To our best knowledge, this is the first academic work where a production community wireless network using 802.11an is analyzed.

The rest of the paper is organized as follows: Related work is discussed in section 2. Then, some more details about QMP project and QMPSU are given in sections 3 and 4. The measurements methodology is explained in section 5, followed by the analysis of the topology, Internet access and Usage in sections 6, 7 and 8. Then, wireless links are characterized in section 9, and some concluding remarks are given in section 10.

[1]QMPSU web site: `http://Guifisants.net`.

2. RELATED WORK

A lot of research has been done in recent years about wireless mesh networks, including design aspects (routing, scalability, security [28, 33, 25, 38, 13, 8, 27, 32, 31, 34, 9]), deployment (urban, rural, centrally-, individually-, or un-planned [14, 18, 23, 15]), measurements and analysis (topologies, performance, usage patterns, evolution, mobility [22, 35, 36, 26, 15, 11, 10, 16, 30, 12, 14, 17, 18, 23]), as well as surveys of prior work and related aspects [37, 19, 24, 29, 20].

The work presented by Brik [15] about the MadMesh network and Afansasyev [10] about the Google network in Mountain View, California present urban deployments and performance properties of large scale (several hundreds of nodes) mesh networks based on proprietary and centrally managed node systems. In contrast, the system we present is fully open source (GPL licensed) and can be deployed, managed, and maintained completely decentralized. The networks studied by both works are up to 10 times larger than the network studied in this work. While the topology in their networks is organized in a tree-like structure where each mesh node is bound to a parent node upstream to the few GW nodes where all out and incoming traffic aggregates, the topology of our network is managed in a flat (full mesh) structure where each node may become a GW node and/or a relay towards any other node. While the main focus of [10] is about usage patterns, both works present interesting and comparable performance characteristics about the links and end-to-end routes for their backbone networks.

Recent studies of Guifi net include various aspects of network and link characteristics [35, 22, 36], power laws [22], usage patterns, social participation, and evolution over the last 10 years [36]. Like in our work, links are planned individually (decentralized) but the average link length in Guifi.net is (due to its deployment also in rural environments) typically more than 10 times longer than in the QMPSU cloud. Unlike in our system, nodes in Guifi.net are clustered into zones and in fact the network presented in this work is one of these clouds. The studies distinguish between the Guifi core network (or backbone network) which includes only non-leaf nodes and the base network (which including all nodes).

In [26], LaCurts present measurement and analysis of 110 real-world 802.11 mesh networks with an average size of 13 nodes (total of 1407 APs). The focus of this paper is on link-level measurements, investigating SNR versus bit-rate correlation, benefits of opportunistic routing, and the impact of hidden stations. In contrast to our network, only 2.4GHz 802.11bgn standard has been used (QMPUS also uses 5GHz 11an) for mostly indoor deployments and few measurements are given about end-to-end performance in the studied networks.

Pioneering work on the Roofnet testbed by Bicket and Aguayo [12, 14] and on the TFA-Mesh in Houston TX by Camp [18, 17] are analyzing the multi-hop performance of purely 802.11b based mesh networks. While the size of these networks are in the same order as the QMPSU network (37 and 18 nodes respectively and up to 69 nodes in QMPSU), the density of Roofnet with 344 edges and a median of 18 links per node is outstanding and a consequence of the unplanned deployment with only omni-directional antennas.

3. QUICK MESH PROJECT

QMP [7] is an operating system for embedded network devices based on OpenWRT/Linux. It was started by some Guifi.net activists in 2011 with the objective to provide a fully open-source solution to easily and quickly deploy a mesh network and share Internet uplinks between it's users.

As main routing protocol QMP uses BMX6 [28], a destination-sequenced distance-vector protocol using UDP messages to discover other nodes and disseminate node and routing information. Some extra features have been specially developed for QMP, such as a smart gateway selection using IPIP tunnels or a short message plugin which permits to send arbitrary information to other nodes, piggybacked by the protocol packages. BMX6 obtained the best results over other mesh routing protocols tested in the Wireless Battle Mesh v6 celebrated in Aalborg (Denmark). Other important characteristics of QMP are the native IPv6 and full auto-configuration support. Each node auto-configures its own IPv6 address based on a ULA[2] prefix. IPv4 connections are enabled via tunnels over the ULA-based IPv6 network.

4. QMPSU ARCHITECTURE

QMPSU is a wireless, 802.11-based, mulit-hop, semi-static, and productively used mesh network where (topologically) all nodes provide the same routing functionality for relaying other node's traffic. Most of the network users only have the mesh network for reaching the Internet, so they depend on the community. In consequence, stability and good performance of the network are mandatory points. QMPSU is not a pure MANET network, it is being deployed following a model named by the participants: *SmartMesh*. The concept tries to explain a model placed between the complete unmanaged model used in many of the known Mesh/MANET networks and the complete organized model used in the AP/Infrastructure networks. The main points which define the *SmartMesh* deployment idea are:

- Use patch antennas with $< 90°$ as main equipment in AD-HOC mode.
- Use parabolic antennas ($< 6°$) for long shots (point-to-point links).
- Use two or more devices for some strategic locations (super-nodes).
- Use different channels to multiplex the spectrum (super-nodes make the interconnection).
- Use only 802.11an to reduce the noise and interferences (spectrum space is bigger than 802.11bgn).
- Use only stable links and devices placed in the outdoor (roof or balcony).

These requirements imply the inconvenience of planning in advance the deployments and links and requires to manually orientate antennas during the installation. But it has the advantage of reduced interference (one of the biggest problems in ISM-spectrum based networks) and fewer neighboring nodes but with better links. Following this model,

[2]RFC4193 Unique Local Address

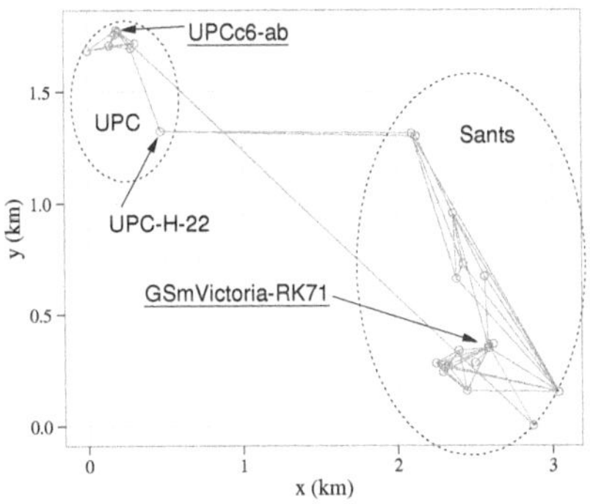

Figure 1: QMPSU network. Two main gateways are underlined.

Figure 2: Supernode.

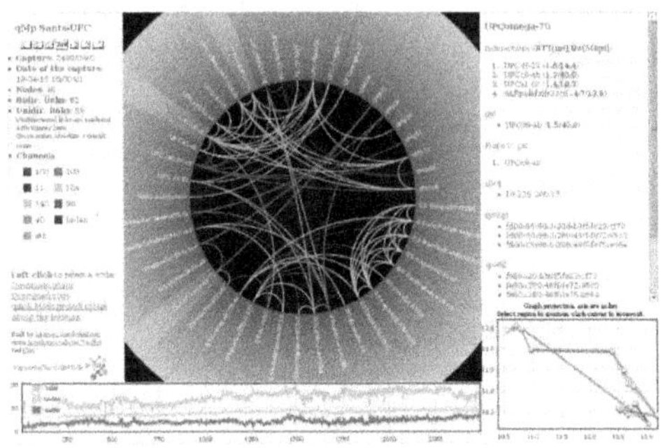

Figure 3: QMPSU network web page.

reasonable end-to-end performance could be achieved even over 7 ore more hops.

The most common hardware used in QMPSU is NanoStation M5[3], which has the following characteristics: Antenna 5GHz 16dBi, Processor Atheros MIPS 400MHz, Flash Memory 8MB, SDRAM Memory 32MB, two ethernet ports 10/100, Radio Atheros 9k 802.11AN MiMo 2T2R. For point-to-point long shots the typically used hardware is NanoBridge M5[4], a variant of the NanoStation with parabolic antenna. Finally for super-nodes, the most common equipment is a couple of Rocket M5[5] with 120° sector antennas (see figure 2).

5. METHODOLOGY

Measurements were obtained using ssh to connect to each QMPSU node and gathering information with basic system commands available in the QMP distribution. This method has the advantage that no changes or additional software had to be installed in the nodes. This is an important point, since being a community network, the users are the owner of their nodes, and so, a minimum intrusion was desirable. The data collection was done hourly from December the 29th 2012 to June the 13th 2013. A simple monitoring web page was developed, which is publicly available at [6] (see figure 3). The web page allows navigating through the graphs obtained in the captures.

QMPSU is rather dynamic. Several reasons contribute to this fact: Being a community network the growth is essentially unplanned. In Sants, nodes are added by community members using their home roofs, which are often at non optimal locations. This fact produce a high diversity on the quality of the links, making some of them to flip-flop time to time, and even some nodes to be sporadically unreachable. Other reasons of unreachability have been electricity cuts, nodes that have been upgraded, reconfigured, hanged, etc. Additionally, community members some times have re-tuned the radios of their devices, trying to achieve better performance (transmission power, channel and other parameters), thus, changing the characteristics of the links. Furthermore, during the measuring period not only new nodes have been added, but other were removed or changed their position. E.g. testing nodes only used temporarily at UPC, or users that changed residence in Sants.

Characterizing such a dynamic network is challenging. That is why in the following sections we have chosen different statistical representations depending on the parameter under study. For instance, in order to reflect the dispersion of the measured parameters, in some cases we have used standard boxplots (showing the range, median and quartiles).

6. QMPSU TOPOLOGY

Figure 4 shows the number of nodes and bidirectional and unidirectional links found in each capture. Regarding the links, we have considered those reported by BMX6 (with the command `bmx6 -c show=links`). For bidirectional links, in figure 4 we count both links in opposite direction as a single link. Figure 5 shows the nodes and links presence. We define presence as the percentage of times a given node or link is observed over the captures.

Figure 4 shows that QMPSU is growing. The solid line in the figure shows a linear regression fit, which increases from around 33 to 48 nodes. On the average 40.6 nodes have been found, 21.4 in Sants and 19.2 in UPC. Even if UPC and Sants have a similar number of nodes, at UPC the nodes are distributed in the Campus, which covers a rather smaller area than Sants (see figure 1). Overall, 69 different nodes where detected. From those, figure 5 shows that only 42 had a presence larger than 50%. Indeed, figure 5 shows that only 27 nodes were alive almost all measuring period, having a presence higher than 80%.

Figure 6 shows the link length Complementary Empirical Cumulative Distribution Function (CECDF). We have found that the link length distribution can be fitted by a mixture of 2 exponentials (solid line in figure 6). The distribution is fitted with correlation coefficient of $\rho = 0.996$. This is in line with the results reported for Guifi.net in [21, 35]. Let L be the complementary CDF of the link length, X, then: $L(x|\mu_1, \mu_2, \theta) = P(X > x) = \theta\, \mathrm{e}^{-x/\mu_1} + (1-\theta)\, \mathrm{e}^{-x/\mu_2}$ This result shows that links can be grouped in two sets: 42% of shorter links with mean $\mu_1 = 196$ m and 58% of longer distance links with mean $\mu_2 = 581$ m. Thus, an overall mean link length of 419.3 m.

Figure 7 shows the out degree distribution. To derive this figure we have proceeded as follows: We have first built the graph of each capture and its out degree ECDF. Note that the graphs may change in every capture for the reasons

[3] http://www.ubnt.com/downloads/datasheets/nanostationm/nsm_ds_web.pdf

[4] http://www.ubnt.com/downloads/datasheets/nanobridgem/nbm_ds_web.pdf

[5] http://www.ubnt.com/downloads/datasheets/rocketmgps/Rocket_M_GPS_Datasheet.pdf

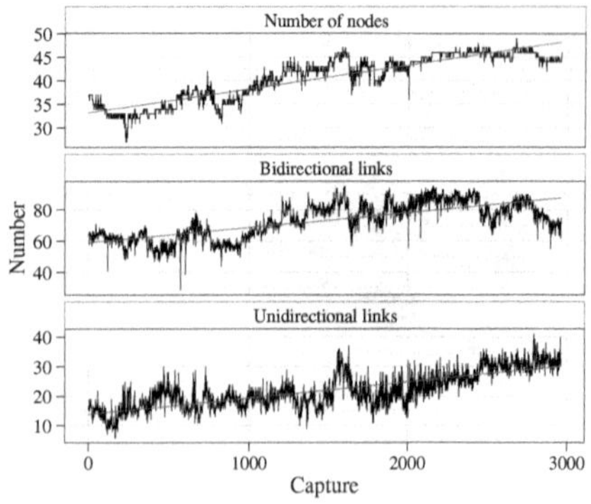

Figure 4: Number of nodes, bidirectional and unidirectional links in each capture.

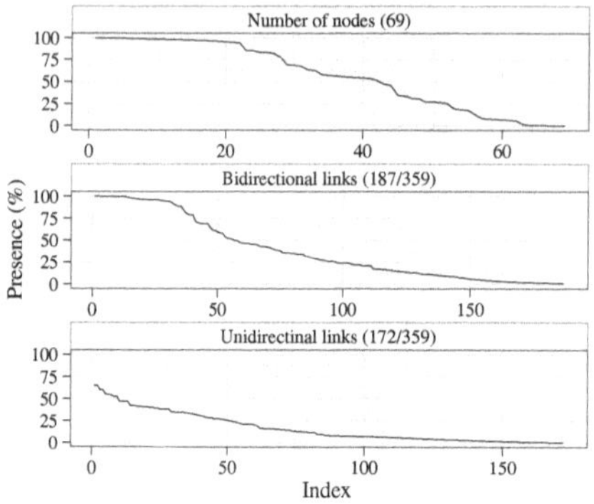

Figure 5: Nodes and links presence.

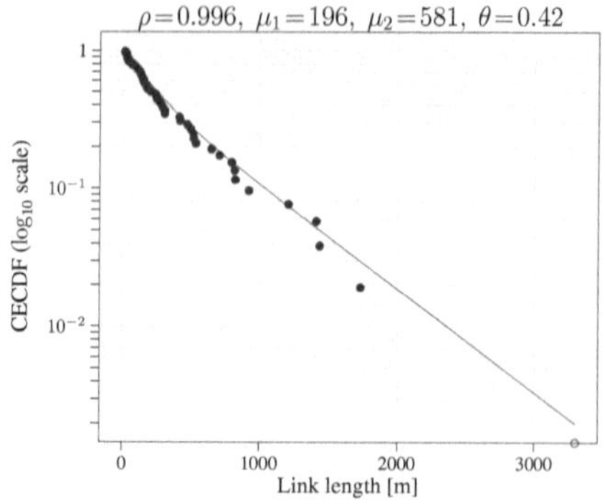

Figure 6: Link length distribution.

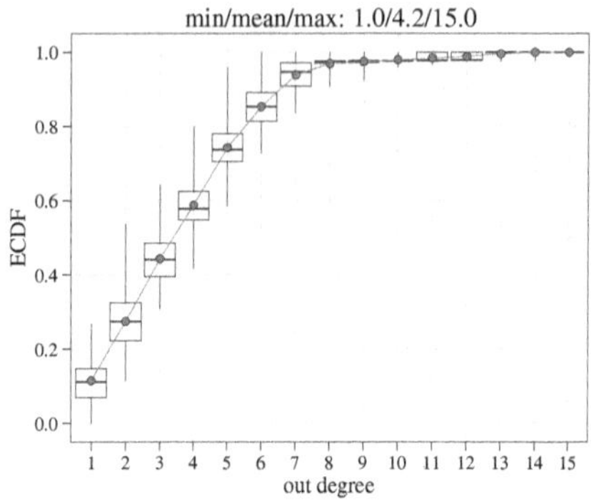

Figure 7: Average out degree ECDF.

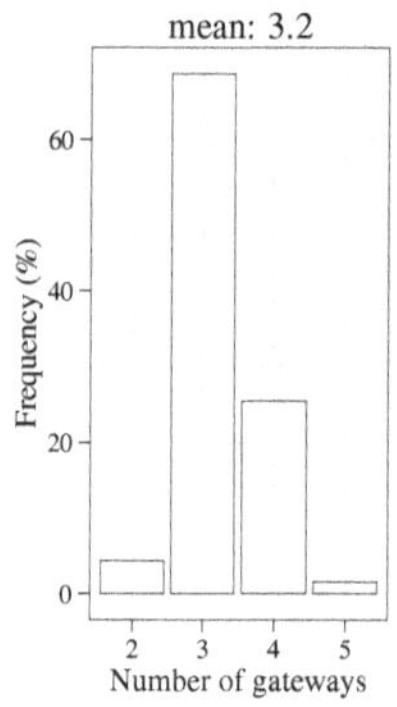

Figure 8: Number of gateways.

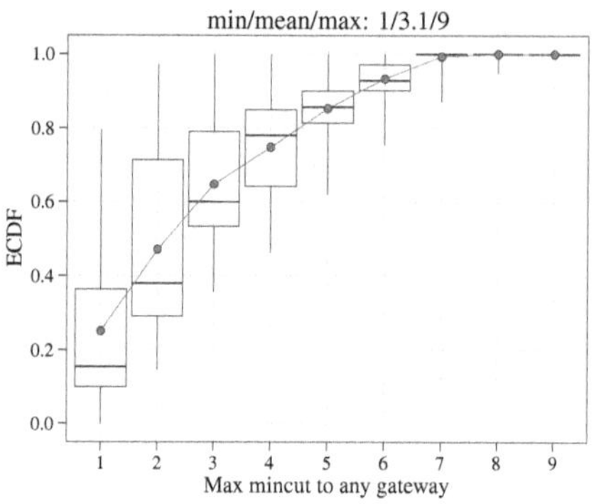

Figure 9: Average ECDF of the max-min-cut from a node to any of its gateways.

formerly described. Then, for each out degree we have taken the average of its ECDF value obtained over all captures. In order to show the variability of the out degree, in figure 7 we have added a boxplot of the out degree ECDF values obtained over the captures.

Figure 7 shows that, on the average, around 90% of the nodes have more than 1 link, and around 40% of the nodes have at least 4 links, with an overall average degree of 4.2. This is in contrast with Guifi.net[35], were the average is around 2, and only 20% of the nodes have degree higher than 3. This fact can be explained by the higher number of links that are automatically discovered and established by the nodes in the ad-hoc configuration used in QMPSU, than the static links manually configured in Guifi.net. We note that no standard distribution (including a power law) has been found to fit the average out degree. Therefore, it cannot be stated that the scale-free pattern found in the Internet applies to QMPSU. Nevertheless, the size of QMPSU (around 45 nodes) is too small to do an accurate topology fitting.

7. INTERNET ACCESS

Internet access is provided by some nodes of QMPSU having links with other nodes of Guifi.net. These nodes disseminate a default route, and we shall refer to them as *gateways*. The number of gateways has been variable during the measuring period: there were found between 2 and 5 gateways, 3.3 on the average. Figure 8 shows the frequency plot of the number of gateways. BMX6 estimates a metric to each gateway, and chooses the best one. Note that when a gateway becomes unreachable by a node, it will stop receiving its default route announcements, and BMX6 will switch to another one. Thus, in order for a node to be disconnected from the Internet, is necessary a failure in all links that allows the node to reach any of the gateways. Therefore, as an estimation of robustness of the Internet availability we define the *max-min-cut to any gateway* as the maximum min-cut between a node and any gateway of the network. Recall that the min-cut between two nodes s and t is the minimum number of edges such that, after removal, there is not directed path from s to t.[6] Figure 9 shows the average ECDF of the max-min-cuts obtained in each capture. The distribution has been obtained following the same procedure as in figure 7, i.e. taking the average of the max-min-cut ECDF obtained for each graph, and adding a boxplot in order to show the dispersion of each value. Figure 9 shows that around 75% of the nodes have a max-min-cut of at least 2 links to a gateway. We note that no standard distribution have been found to fit the average max-min-cut. Figure 8 shows that the dispersion of the max-min-cut equal to 2 is rather high: the interquartile of the ECDF values for this point is around 0.42. This is motivated by the fact that one of the nodes at UPC (called UPC-H-22, see figure 1) had a wireless link not very stable with the Sants. The failure of this link decreases the max-min-cut of many nodes.

[6] There are efficient algorithms to compute the s-t min-cut available in common numerical tools.

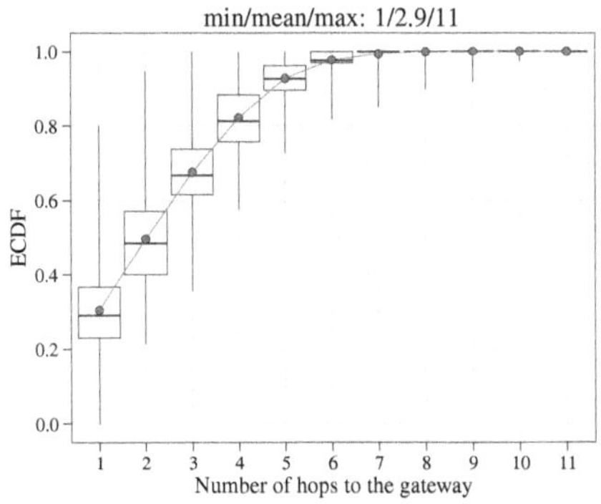

Figure 10: Average ECDF of the number of hops to the gateway.

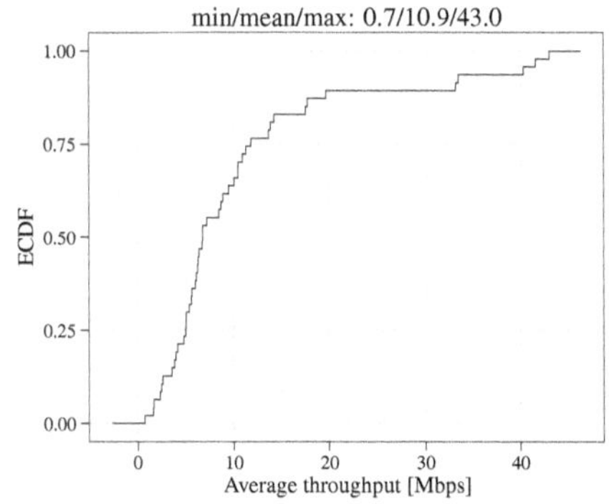

Figure 11: ECDF of the average throughput to the gateway.

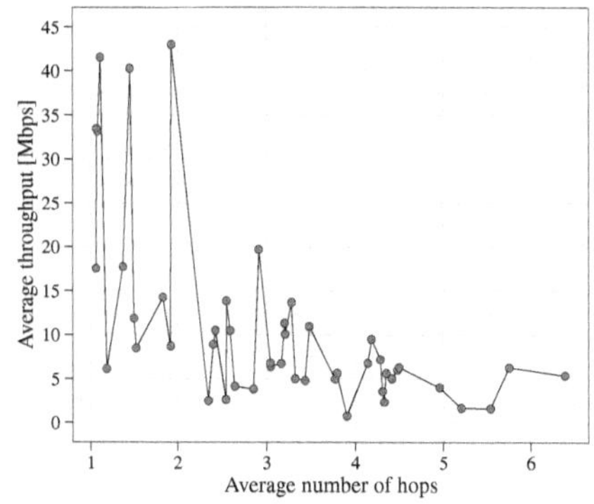

Figure 12: Average throughput vs. average number of hops to the gateway.

```
# iw dev wlan0 station dump
Station dc:9f:db:26:6a:40
 inactive time: 10 ms
 rx bytes:     3568971019
 rx packets: 135222757
 tx bytes:     3147225400
 tx packets: 167098650
 tx retries: 457952780
 tx failed:    104548
 signal:         -72 dBm
 signal avg: -73 dBm
 tx bitrate: 162.0 Mbps MCS 12 40Mhz
 rx bitrate: 120.0 Mpbs MCS 11 40Mhz
Station dc:9f:db:08:8d:a9
 ...
```

Figure 13: Output of the command iw dump.

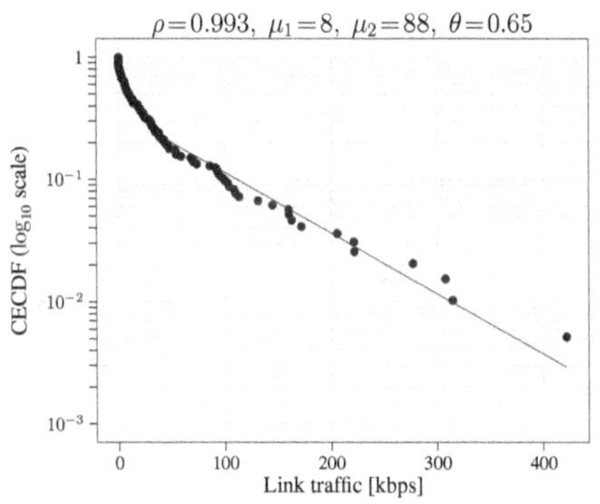

Figure 14: Link traffic CECDF.

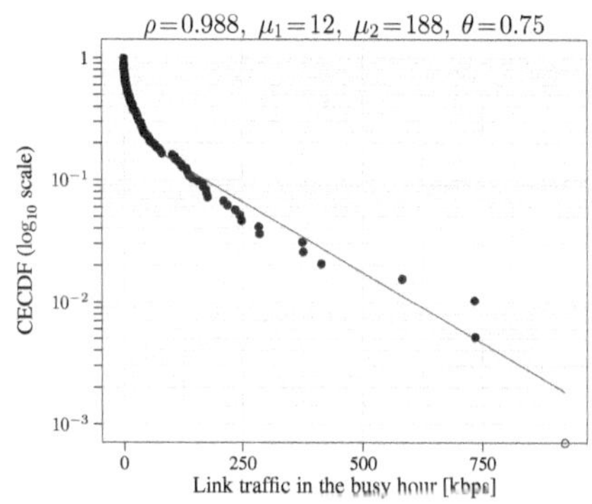

Figure 15: Link traffic in the busy hour CECDF.

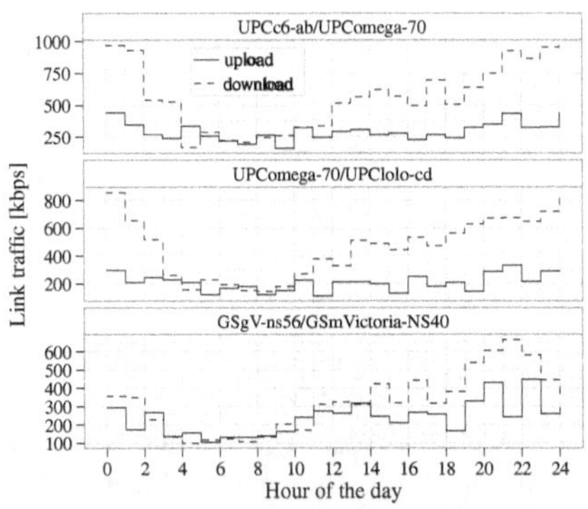

Figure 16: Traffic in the 3 busiest links.

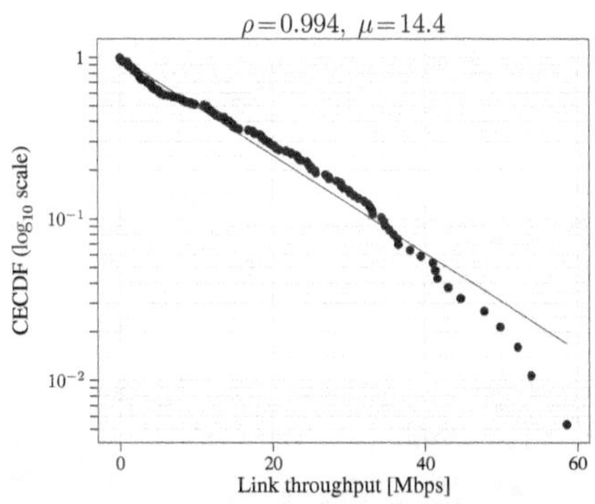

Figure 17: Throughput CECDF.

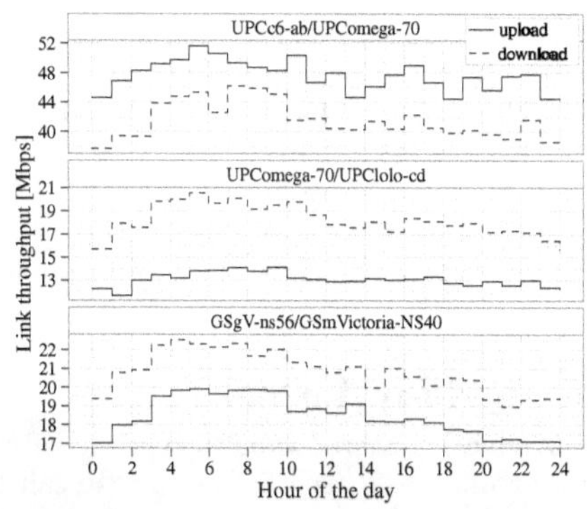

Figure 18: Throughput in the 3 busiest links.

Figure 10 depicts the average ECDF of the number of hops to the gateway of each node. This has been derived from the routing tables, which were also recorded in every capture. The plot has been obtained similarly to figures 7 and 9, i.e. taking the average of the ECDF obtained for each capture, and adding a boxplot in order to show the dispersion. Figure 10 shows that around 67% of the nodes have 3 or less hops to the gateway, with an average of 2.9 hops. We can see from the boxplots of the figure that the ECDF measured over the captures does not show strong deviations.

We have estimated links throughput using the TCP_STREAM test of netperf [3]. As before, measurements were taken hourly. The command was run from every node to its gateway. In order to limit the disturbance to the users we tried to reduce the test to the minimum time. After some trials, we observed that running netperf tests of only 3 seconds yield a good estimation. The throughput of every wireless link was also computed (link throughputs are discussed in section 9). For the link measurements IPv6 link local addresses were used, thus, assuring that no other links would be used. To avoid interferences, throughputs tests were done in serial (only one test at a time). Figure 11 depicts the ECDF of the average throughput of the nodes to their gateway measured over all captures. The figure shows that the throughputs

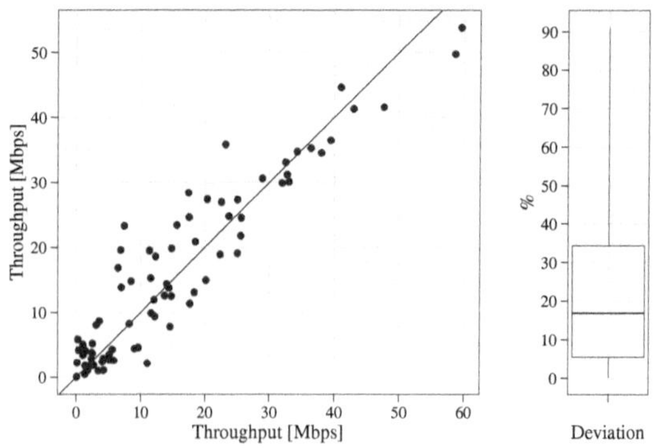

Figure 19: Throughput asymmetry.

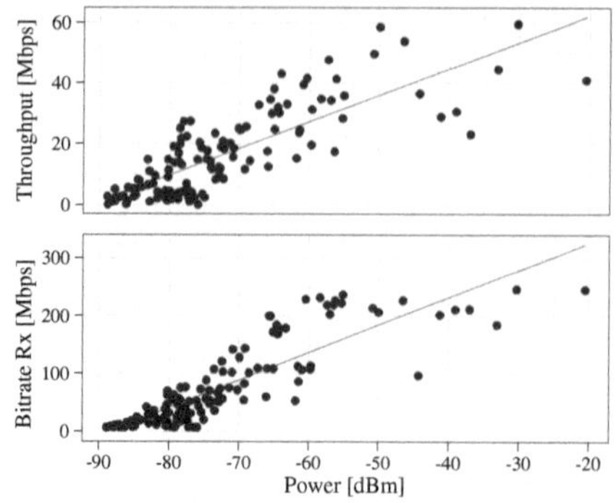

Figure 20: Throughput (top) and average bitrate of received packets (bottom) vs signal power.

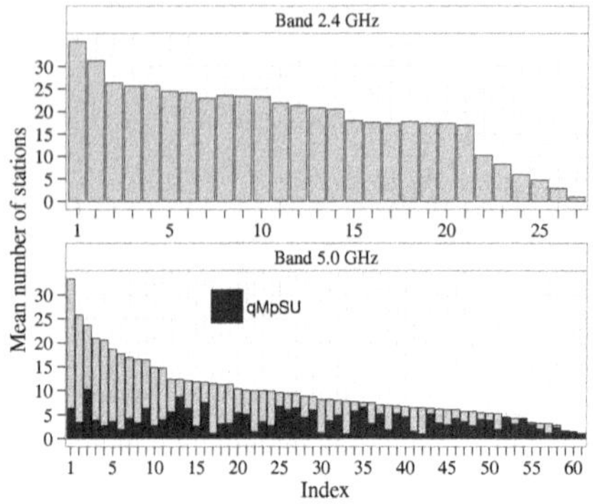

Figure 21: Number of stations per scan.

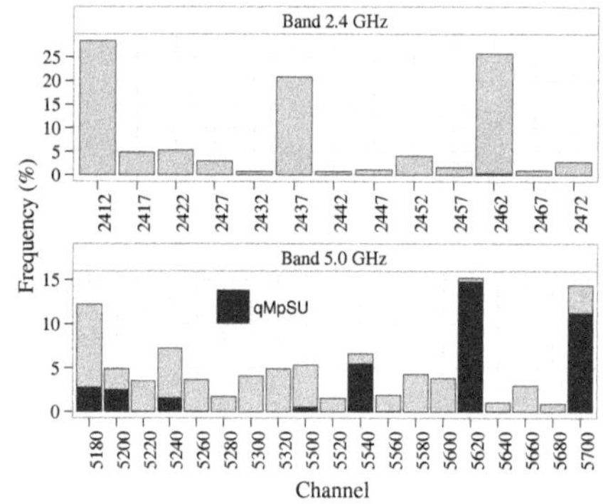

Figure 22: Channel occupancy.

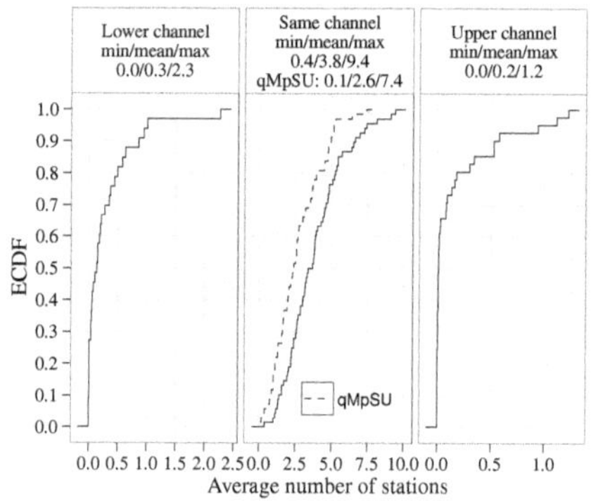

Figure 23: ECDF of the number of interfering stations.

are rather high, with an average of 10.9 Mbps. This is due to the high performance that can be achieved with MIMO 802.11an cards of most equipment. Finally, figure 12 shows the average throughput vs. average number of hops to the gateway. As expected, throughput tend to reduce as the number of hops increases. However, the line is rather irregular, due to the diversity of the links.

8. QMPSU USAGE

We have gathered the usage of the network using the linux `iw` command [2] (see figure 13). Recall that captures were done hourly. Thus, taking the difference between the transmitted bytes counter (**`tx bytes`** in figure 13) of two consecutive runs of `iw`, it is possible to estimate the average traffic sent each hour in every link.

Measurements where done using directional links, i.e. traffic sent in opposite directions between the same nodes is counted as two different links. Only wireless links, and having a presence higher than 25% (in order to avoid outliers) where considered in the statistics: 196 links in total.

Figure 14 shows the CECDF of the average traffic sent in each of these links. Interestingly, it was found that the traffic is well fitted by a mixture of 2 exponentials (solid line in figure 14): 65% with mean $\mu_1 = 8$ kbps and 35% with mean $\mu_2 = 88$ kbps (overall mean of 36 kbps). An explanation of this result is the presence of two groups of links: Those where most of the traffic belongs to a single user, and *backbone links* carrying the aggregate traffic from a number of users.

We found that the hour having the highest average traffic (*busy hour*) was between 22h and 23h. Figure 15 shows the CECDF of the average traffic sent in the busy hour. The figure shows that a mixture of 2 exponentials still gives a good fit. The overall average is now 56 kbps, almost 55% higher than before. Figure 16 shows the average traffic in both directions of the three busiest links over each hour of the day.

9. QMPSU WIRELESS LINKS

In this section we try to characterize the wireless links of the network. We start by studying their throughput, measured using netperf as described in section 7. In order to avoid outliers, only those of section 8 are considered. From the 196 links, the throughput was able to be measured in 169 (86%). Failures were due to unidirectional links (were netperf cannot run the test), or too weak links for netperf to succeed. Figure 17 shows the CECDF of the throughput of the links were netperf succeeded. The figure shows that the link throughput can be fitted with an exponential distribution with mean 14.4 Mbps. In order to see the variability of the throughput, figure 18 shows the throughput averages in both directions of the three busiest links (same links as in figure 16) over each hour of the day. Comparing figures 18 and 16 we observe that the throughput is only slightly affected by the traffic in the links. Additionally, measurements on each direction of the links are identified with the same solid or dashed lines in figures 15 and 16. Comparing the figures it is apparent that the asymmetry of the throughputs measured in both directions it is not due to the asymmetry of the users' traffic. For instance, around 5am, when the user traffic is the lowest and equal in both directions, the asymmetry of the links throughputs observed in figure 15 remains the same. We thus conclude that this asymmetry must be links characteristics, as level of interferences present at each end, or different transmission powers.

In order to measure the links' asymmetry, figure 19 depicts the throughput measured in each direction. A boxplot of the absolute value of the deviation over the mean is also depicted on the right. The figure shows that around 25% of the links have a deviation higher than 30%. Thus, we can conclude that the symmetry of the links, an assumption often used in the literature of in wireless mesh networks, is not very realistic.

Figure 20 shows the average throughput of each link (top of the figure) versus the average signal power of the received packets (measured with iw dump). The figure also show the average bitrate reported by iw dump for unicast received packets (bottom of the figure). We have assumed that unicast transmissions correspond to packets with bitrates higher than the lowest basic rate (6 Mbps in the 5 GHz band). As expected, the figure shows the clear dependency of both measures with respect of the signal power.

Finally, we have estimated the interference level by doing a scan in every node at each hourly capture. All nodes were configured in ad-hoc mode in the 5GHz band. However, some radios were dual band, and reported scans in both 2.4 and 5 GHz. We discriminated QMPSU stations because they share the same BSSID address, which is reported in the scans. Figure 21 shows the average number of stations detected in every scan of the nodes, in decreasing order. The figure shows the stations detected in both bands. The average of QMPSU stations is shown in darker color. Figure 21 shows that the 2.4 GHz band is much more crowded: only 3 non-overlapping channels of 20 MHz are available, while a much higher number of stations are detected. Figure 22 shows the number of stations detected on every channel. As expected, it can be observed as most of the stations detected in the 2.4 GHz band use the recommended 3 non-overlapping channels. In the 5 GHz it can be observed the channel where most of the QMPSU stations are located. Note that it is not possible to have high frequency diversity in QMPSU since most of the stations have only a single radio. Even if channel assignment is a key issue, it was fixed manually by QMPSU users based on trial and error. Figure 23 shows the ECDF of the average number of stations detected in the same and adjacent channels used by QMPSU nodes (5 GHz band). ECDF of detected QMPSU nodes is also reported in dashed lines. All QMPSU nodes were configured to use channel bonding (i.e. combining two adjacent 20 MHz channels). Thus, they can potentially interfere with stations located in adjacent channels. Figure 23 confirm the low number of stations belonging to external networks interfering with QMPSU nodes: around 90% of nodes detect less than 1 station, on the average, from external networks in each of the 3 channels of interest. Looking at the stations in the same channel, around 50% detect more than 3.5, from which more than 2.5 are QMPSU.

10. CONCLUSIONS

In this work we present an experimental evaluation of QMPSU, a wireless community network deployed at *Universitat Politècnica de Catalunya* (UPC) and Sants, a quarter of Barcelona, Spain. QMPSU is rather dynamic due to many reasons, e.g.: its community nature in an urban area; it is a growing network; there is a high diversity of the quality of wireless links; the mesh nature of the network.

Characterizing such a dynamic network is challenging. To do so we have performed an extensive statistical study of the main parameters. These include topological properties, Internet access, usage of the network and characterization of the radio links.

We have found simple distributions that fit some of these parameters. For instance, the network is not scale-free, the link length and traffic is fitted by a mixture of two exponentials, and the average throughput of the links is exponentially distributed. Regarding radio links, we have observed a non negligible asymmetry.

Our results show that the network is rather well connected and adaptive. Thus, demonstrating the advantages of a wireless mesh network. Furthermore, even if the network is deployed in an urban area with an average link length of around 500 m, an average link throughput of around 14 Mbps was obtained. This high performance can be attributed to the 802.11an devices used in the network.

Acknowledgments

This work was supported by the European project CONFINE `http://confine-project.eu`, and Spanish grants TIN2010-21378-C02-01 and 2009-SGR-1167.

11. REFERENCES

[1] Community Networks Testbed for the Future Internet, CONFINE. `http://confine-project.eu/`. FP7 European Project 288535.

[2] Linux utility for wireless devices. `http://wireless.kernel.org/en/users/Documentation/iw`.

[3] Netperf benchmark. `http://www.netperf.org/netperf`.

[4] Open, Free and Neutral Network Internet for everybody. `http://guifi.net/en`.

[5] OpenWrt Linux distribution for embedded devices. `https://openwrt.org`.

[6] qMp Sants-UPC monitoring web page. `http://compnet.ac.upc.edu/~llorenc/qmpsantsupc/index.php`.

[7] Quick Mesh Project. `http://qmp.cat`.

[8] M. Abolhasan, B. Hagelstein, and J.C.-P Wang. Real-world performance of current proactive multi-hop mesh protocols. In *15th Asia-Pacific Conference on Communications (APCC)*, October 2009.

[9] Loay Abusalah, Ashfaq Khokhar, and Mohsen Guizani. A survey of secure mobile ad hoc routing protocols. In *IEEE Communications Surveys and Tutorials*, 2008.

[10] M. Afanasyev, T. Chen, G.M. Voelker, and A.C. Snoeren. Usage patterns in an urban wifi network. *IEEE/ACM Transactions on Networking*, 18(5):1359–1372, 2010.

[11] Mikhail Afanasyev, Tsuwei Chen, Geoffrey M. Voelker, and Alex C. Snoeren. Analysis of a mixed-use urban wifi network: When metropolitan becomes neapolitan. In *In ACM/USENIX IMC*, 2008.

[12] D. Aguayo, J. Bicket, S. Biswas, G. Judd, and R. Morris. Link-level measurements from an 802.11 b mesh network. *ACM SIGCOMM Computer Communication Review*, 34(4):121–132, 2004.

[13] U. Ashraf, G. Juanole, and S. Abdellatif. Evaluating routing protocols for the wireless mesh backbone. In *Wireless and Mobile Computing, Networking and Communications (WIMOB)*, October 2007.

[14] John Bicket, Daniel Aguayo, Sanjit Biswas, and Robert Morris. Architecture and evaluation of an unplanned 802.11 b mesh network. In *Proceedings of the 11th annual international conference on Mobile computing and networking, MobiCom '05*, pages 31–42, Cologne, Germany, 2005.

[15] Vladimir Brik, Shravan Rayanchu, Sharad Saha, Sayandeep Sen, Vivek Shrivastava, and Suman Banerjee. A measurement study of a commercial-grade urban wifi mesh. In *Proceedings of the 8th ACM SIGCOMM conference on Internet measurement*, pages 111–124, 2008.

[16] Vladimir Bychkovsky, Bret Hull, Allen Miu, Hari Balakrishnan, and Samuel Madden. A measurement study of vehicular internet access using in situ wi-fi networks. In *Proceedings of the 12th annual international conference on Mobile computing and networking*, pages 50–61. ACM, 2006.

[17] Joseph Camp, Vincenzo Mancuso, Omer Gurewitz, and Edward W. Knightly. A measurement study of multiplicative overhead effects in wireless networks. In *in Proceedings of IEEE INFOCOM*, Uppsala, Sweden, April 2008.

[18] Joseph Camp, Joshua Robinson, Christopher Steger, and Edward Knightly. Measurement driven deployment of a two-tier urban mesh access network. In *Proceedings of the 4th international conference on Mobile systems, applications and services*, pages 96–109. ACM, 2006.

[19] G. Camponovo and D. Cerutti. Wlan communities and internet access sharing: a regulatory overview. In *Mobile Business, 2005. ICMB 2005. International Conference on*, pages 281–287. IEEE, 2005.

[20] Y. Cao, M. Krebs, G. Toubekis, and S. Makram. Mobile community information systems on wireless mesh networks-an opportunity for developing countries and rural areas. In *Fifth International Workshop on Ubiquitous Mobile Information and Collaboration Systems (UMICS'07)*, pages 11–12. Citeseer, 2007.

[21] Llorenç Cerdà-Alabern. Analysis of guifi.net's topology, extension of results. Technical Report UPC-DAC-RR-2012-15, May 2012. `http://www.ac.upc.edu/app/research-reports/html/2012/15/guifinet-topology-extension.pdf`.

[22] Llorenç Cerdà-Alabern. On the topology characterization of guifi.net. In *2012 IEEE 8th International Conference on Wireless and Mobile Computing, Networking and Communications (WiMob'2012)*, pages 389–396, Barcelona, Spain, October 2012.

[23] Kameswari Chebrolu, Bhaskaran Raman, and Sayandeep Sen. Long-distance 802.11b links: Performance measurements and experience. In *in Proceedings of ACM Mobicom*, 2006.

[24] P.A. Frangoudis, G.C. Polyzos, and V.P. Kemerlis. Wireless community networks: an alternative approach for nomadic broadband network access. *Communications Magazine, IEEE*, 49(5):206–213, 2011.

[25] D. Johnson, N. Ntlatlapa, and C. Aichele. Simple pragmatic approach to mesh routing using batman. In *2nd IFIP International Symposium on Wireless Communications and Information Technology in Devel oping Countries, CSIR, Pretoria, South Africa*, October 2008.

[26] Katrina LaCurts and Hari Balakrishnan. Measurement and analysis of real-world 802.11 mesh networks. In *Proceedings of the 10th Annual Conference on Internet Measurement (ACM)*, pages 123–136, Melbourne, Australia, 2010.

[27] D. Murray, M.W. Dixon, and T. Koziniec. An experimental comparison of routing protocols in multi hop ad hoc networks. In *Australasian Telecommunication Networks and Applications Conference (ATNAC)*, Auckland, New Zealand, 2010.

[28] Axel Neumann, Ester López, and Leandro Navarro. An evaluation of bmx6 for community wireless networks. In *1st International Workshop on Community Networks and Bottom-up-Broadband (CNBuB'2012)*, pages 651–658, Barcelona, Spain, October 2012.

[29] M. Oliver, J. Zuidweg, and M. Batikas. Wireless commons against the digital divide. In *Technology and Society (ISTAS), IEEE International Symposium on*, pages 457–465. IEEE, 2010.

[30] Joshua Robinson, Ram Swaminathan, and Edward W. Knightly. Assessment of urban-scale wireless networks with a small number of measurements. In *The 14th ACM international conference on Mobile computing and networking*, MobiCom '08, pages 187–198. ACM, 2008.

[31] Shih-Hao Shen, Yueh-Min Huang, and Jen-Wen Ding. A cross-layer design for heterogeneous routing in wireless mesh networks. In *Int. J. Pervasive Computing and Communications*, 2008.

[32] Muhammad S. Siddiqui and Choong Seon Hong. Security issues in wireless mesh networks. In *IEEE International Conference on Multimedia and Ubiquitous Engineering (MUE'07)*, 2007.

[33] C. Szabó, Z. Horváth, and K. Farkas. Wireless community networks: motivations, design and business models. In *3rd international conference on Wireless internet*, page 23. ICST (Institute for Computer Sciences, Social-Informatics and Telecommunications Engineering), 2007.

[34] Parul Tomar, P.K. Suri, and M. K. Soni. A comparative study for secure routing in manet. In *International Journal of Computer Applications*, 2010.

[35] Davide Vega, Llorenç Cerdà-Alabern, Leandro Navarro, and Roc Meseguer. Topology patterns of a community network: Guifi.net. In *1st International Workshop on Community Networks and Bottom-up-Broadband (CNBuB'2012)*, pages 612–619, Barcelona, Spain, October 2012.

[36] Davide Vega, Roc Meseguer, Leandro Navarro, and Felix Freitag. Measurement and analysis of a large-scale wireless community network. In *Submitted for SIGCOMM 2013 Barcelona*, Barcelona, Spain, 2013.

[37] S. Vural, Dali Wei, and K. Moessner. Survey of experimental evaluation studies for wireless mesh network deployments in urban areas towards ubiquitous internet. *Communications Surveys Tutorials, IEEE*, 15(1):223–239, 2013.

[38] A. Zakrzewska, L. Koszalka, and I. Pozniak-Koszalka. Performance study of routing protocols for wireless mesh networks. In *Systems Engineering, 2008. ICSENG '08. 19th International Conference*, August 2008.

On Radio Resource Sharing in Multi-Antenna Virtualized Wireless Networks

Xin Wang
School of Information Sciences
University of Pittsburgh
Pittsburgh, PA 15260
xiw54@pitt.edu

Prashant Krishnamurthy
School of Information Sciences
University of Pittsburgh
Pittsburgh, PA 15260
prashk@pitt.edu

David Tipper
School of Information Sciences
University of Pittsburgh
Pittsburgh, PA 15260
dtipper@pitt.edu

ABSTRACT

Virtualizing wireless networks has the potential to improve resource usage efficiency (system capacity) through spectrum sharing while allowing for isolation between users and customization of applications [9]. In most work related to wireless network virtualization, the sharing of spectrum is considered at the level of chunks of frequency that do not interfere. Such spectrum sharing, where service provider SP_A can use the spectrum allocated to SP_B when SP_B does not use it, results in multiplexing gains improving the resource usage (see for example, [12]). We argue that sharing *radio resources* that are a function of geography and signal strength, rather than slices of spectrum is also possible. When we consider sharing of radio resources, the transmit power, the interference, and the usage scenario (capabilities/needs of devices) become important in determining what can be shared. In this paper, the potential gain from sharing such *radio resources* while using MIMO for combating interference and exploiting spatial degrees of freedom is investigated in a two service provider collaboration scenario. The metric used is the capacity of the system (with a large cell and a small cell) as a function of separation distance, transmit power, cell range, and various MIMO settings. We show that radio resource sharing is feasible, but it has implications on isolation between users of different SPs and MIMO settings are an important factor.

Categories and Subject Descriptors

C.2 [**Computer-communication Networks**]: Network Architecture and Design

Keywords

wireless virtualization; service provider; radio resource virtualization; MIMO

MSWiM'13, November 3–8, 2013, Barcelona, Spain.

1. INTRODUCTION

Virtualization logically sets up physical resources based on user's demand to improve resource utilization while supporting isolation across users/services and enabling customization for diverse applications. In wired networks, infrastructure providers (InPs) can partition a physical network into virtual networks that share the physical routers or switches or cross-connects, physical links, and bandwidth on each link [9]. Such virtual networks then are assigned to service providers (SPs) based on the agreements they have made with InPs. Multiple SPs may operate their virtual networks on top of the same physical substrate. Wired virtualization has been widespread due to the potential improvement in utilization of physical resources [2]. The scarcity of spectrum and the demand for high data rates communications has triggered a similar interest in virtualization in wireless networks. For instance, the infrastructure and spectrum of overlapping urban cellular networks or suburban femtocells embedded in macrocells are examples of opportunities that can be exploited to pool the physical resources owned by several InPs in the same geographic area. The functions of SPs in such a case need to be decoupled from those of InPs in a manner similar to wired virtualization to facilitate spectrum/physical resource sharing. That is, InPs are only spectrum/physical infrastructure owners while SPs are in charge of providing services to mobile users (MUs) in a fashion similar to existing MVNOs. When InPs within an area agree to share their spectrum and physical resources, SPs that have agreements with any of these InPs are able to access the entire aggregate frequency bands of the InPs instead of a (typical) limited band from a single InP. A certain number of spectrum slices are allocated to a SP on a short term basis allowing the SP to use those slices for its air-interface.

Due to the fluctuating nature of the traffic demands of users supported by a given SP, the utilization of spectrum varies. Thus it is possible to increase the overall utilization of several slices of spectrum with well-designed schedulers. In most work related to wireless network virtualization, the sharing of spectrum is considered at the level of chunks of frequency. As a simple example, let us suppose that there are two slices of spectrum S_A and S_B, and two service providers SP_A and SP_B who are allocated these slices respectively by an InP. Spectrum sharing, where user SP_A can use *both the slices* S_A and S_B when SP_B **does not need/use** the slice S_B, results in multiplexing gains improving the resource usage (see for example, [12, 5]). Also, the impact of traffic characteristics and resource allocation schemes have been studied to increase the multiplexing gain to the extent possible. However, spectrum is not like a simple resource such as time slots on a wire. The works on multiplexing gain assume there is no interference (no simultaneous usage of spectrum slices in nearby geographical areas). The reality is that we should consider *radio resources* that are a function of geography and signal strength as the shared quantity, rather than orthogonal slices of spectrum. Virtualizing radio resources (simultaneous usage in a geographical area) is more likely in diverse applications (e.g., high-speed wide coverage broadband by SP_A and local applications with small coverage by SP_B or even low-speed SCADA networks by a third SP_C). When we consider radio resources, the transmit power, the interference, and the usage scenario (capabilities/needs of devices) become important in determining how much sharing is possible. This type of potential gain in utilizing spectrum has been neglected so far in the research literature. To differentiate it from separate spectrum virtualization (SSV) that results only in multiplexing gain, we call this *radio resource virtualization* (RRV).

Towards understanding and quantifying the potential benefits of RRV, we consider a two-cell system in this paper, where the coverage of one cell is a subset of another. We consider Multiple-input Multiple-output (MIMO) systems to reduce the interference to the extent possible as explained later. The aggregate spectrum efficiency and achievable data rate for each cell are obtained under various scenarios. The contribution of our work can be concluded as follow. First, we propose the RRV scheme and a hierarchical spectrum sharing arrangement which exploits both multiplexing gain and RRV gain. Second, we analyze the RRV gain as a function of transmit power, separation distance between interfering BSs, cell radius and the degrees of freedom in a MIMO setting. For this second part, a "combined signal-to-interference plus noise ratio (SINR) matrix" is used to observe the change of capacity in MIMO channels. This approach adopts an information theoretic point of view to measure the effect of co-channel interference (CCI) in MIMO channels [1], which to the best of our knowledge, an analysis like the one in this paper, that considers two tiers of cells and the capacity of each cell has not been previously performed. Third, the effect of the "degrees of freedom" in MIMO settings is illustrated by considering different numbers of antennas in the two cells (again not considered previously). While these are preliminary results, with customized MIMO settings, SPs may be able to isolate their own networks and provide diverse services to MUs.

The rest of this paper is organized as follow. Some background is provided in Section 2. Section 3 illustrates the spectrum sharing scheme and models the RRV system simply by a two-cell architecture. Section 4 presents numerical results. Finally, limitations and extended issues are discussed and this paper is concluded in the fifth section.

2. RELATED WORK

A tiered cell structure has been well-studied in LTE/LTE-A heterogenous networks (HetNets) [4]. Small cells (Femto/Pico) are deployed to enhance the coverage of macrocells and provide "offloading gain" where users are offloaded to the small cell to reduce system-wide interference and obtain a larger bandwidth. Universal and fractional frequency reuse have been applied in HetNets and so cross-tier SINR is evaluated to ensure reliable coverage in each tier [6, 11]. These works primarily consider the power, path-loss and penetration loss to model SINR and do not consider MIMO. Indoor cells may sometimes naturally provide interference separation (due to building walls, etc.) ensuring the quality of indoor transmissions without interfering with the users in the outdoor cells. But in the case of outdoor small cells, CCI may be more severe. Hence, coordinated transmissions that regulate the transmissions between the macrocell and small cell are used in HetNets. For instance, the macrocell does not transmit (or it transmits at a much lower power level) during some subframes to avoid CCI [10]. The system architecture considered in this paper is similar to an outdoor HetNet scenario. However, unlike a HetNet's single operator system, the two cells are assumed to belong to different SPs, which requires the benefit of sharing to occur on both sides. A multiple-SP virtual network may not facilitate coordinated transmissions and requires isolation as well as support for customization. To take this into account, we suggest a hierarchical scheme which switches between RRV and SSV to enable the sharing and mitigate CCI depending on the requirements of various SPs.

Further, in this paper, we harness MIMO to mitigate interference and exploit spatial degrees of freedom, unlike HetNets which simply use coordinated transmissions and only consider signal power. Previous work in MIMO at the physical layer [1] has proposed a way to evaluate the capacity of a MIMO channel with interference using a combined SINR matrix. Multiuser detection methods for combatting inter-cell interference have been developed and evaluated [3] using this matrix. The outage capacity of MIMO channels under different types of interference has been calculated in [8]. Here, we also make use of this combined SINR matrix to evaluate the MIMO channel capacity with CCI. We consider the distribution of the singular values of the combined matrix that shows some insight into the change in channel capacity and can be used to customize virtual networks.

3. SPECTRUM SHARING MODELS

In this section, we illustrate the differences between the two types of spectrum virtualization schemes - SSV and RRV, and the corresponding multiplexing gain achieved by them respectively. A simple two-cell model is used in a virtualized network setting here.

3.1 Separate Spectrum Virtualization (SSV)

In Figure 1, the base station (BS) of a large cell (SP_A's service region) transmits signals at a power P_A that maintains coverage for the large area. A smaller cell (SP_B's service region with transmit power P_B) is located within its coverage. A traditional network would distribute distinct spectrum bands for each SP in these two cells. In contrast, a virtualized network does not separate the bandwidth. SP_A and SP_B can get varying amounts of spectrum units in every time unit based on their requirements, agreements with the InP, and the corresponding policies. In SSV, the spectrum slices allocated to the two SPs in the same time interval do not overlap (this is the case considered in the virtualization research literature). The multiplexing gain with SSV can be simply explained as follows. If x denotes the fraction of total available bandwidth B assigned to SP_A in the first time unit, then $1-x$ is assigned to SP_B. SSV in Figure 2 shows that in the second time unit, SP_A takes a proportion $a(t)$ of SP_B's bandwidth for its use as determined by the fluctuating traffic load, policies, etc. The multiplexing gain for SP_A can be defined as $B_{A'}/B_A$, where $B_{A'}$ is the available bandwidth for SP_A after multiplexing and B_A is the original bandwidth assigned to SP_A (which is xB). The gain for SP_A is $1 + \frac{a(t)(1-x)}{x}$. Similarly, SP_B, could get an extra bandwidth $1 + \frac{b(t)x}{1-x}$. Since the total available bandwidth is unchanged, $a(t)$ and $b(t)$ could be positive or negative and $a(t)(1-x) + b(t)x = 0$ in every time unit. This multiplexing gain has been considered in the literature as mentioned previously [5, 12].

3.2 Radio Resource Virtualization (RRV)

We argue that *radio resources* should be considered as a function of geography and signal strength potentially allowing some spatio-temporally overlapping allocation of spectrum slices to SPs in the same time interval (RRV in Figure 2). RRV sharing can be implemented in conjunction with SSV. The combination of RRV and SSV can improve the usage of spectrum due to an RRV gain. The RRV gain depends on the amount of overlapping spectrum slices simultaneously used by SPs. Obviously, there will be interference (which may perhaps be mitigated in a multi-antenna infrastructure of an InP) within those overlapping spectrum slices, which will impact the RRV gain. To get insight of how much RRV gain is possible, we ask the question : What would happen if there is some (or complete) overlap? Also, whether or not interference in the simultaneously used spectrum slices is tolerable depends on the requirements of both of the SPs. An example of a combined SSV & RRV scheme is introduced next to illustrate this situation.

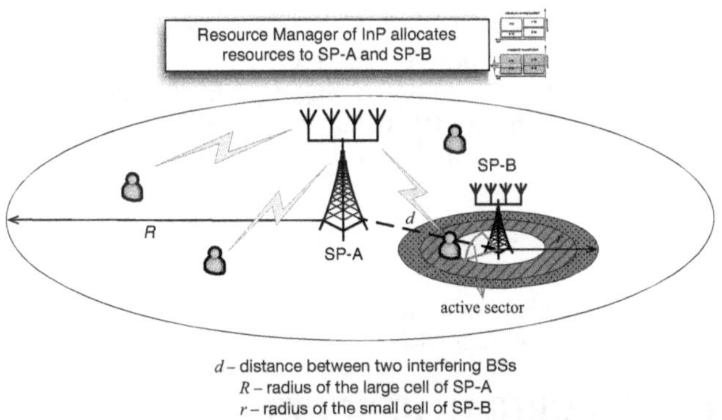

Figure 1: A two-cell system

We consider only the downlink here (and in the rest of the paper). In a wireless environment, radio propagation (that includes large-scale and small-scale fading) spatially creates "layers" of users. When SP_A and SP_B manage transmissions to certain mobile users (MUs), they may have a chance to use the same frequency bands at the same time in the same area. Suppose SP_B has three layers of MUs, indicated by three different circles in cell B in Figure 1. SP_B probably can operate its virtual network on the spectrum which has already been allocated to SP_A (and probably being used by SP_A) in the white circle. MUs in this "white layer" can possibly achieve their desired data rate because the received SINR for such users is still high enough. We call this reuse scheme as Radio Resource Virtualization (RRV). The situa-

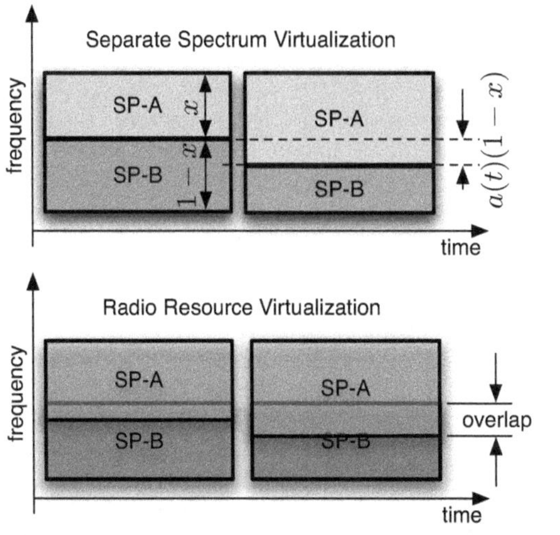

Figure 2: Separate Spectrum Virtualization Vs. Radio Resource Virtualization

tion of MUs in the "middle layer or middle ring" is not that clear. It is quite likely that some of these MUs are able to reuse the SP_A's spectrum slices, but not all of them. This implies that the SP_B can only partially share spectrum with SP_A in the middle circle, i.e., allow MUs with high SINR to utilize SP_A's spectrum and allocate separate spectrum slices to those with low SINR. As far as the "outer layer" is concerned, most MUs in this outer ring layer will face fierce interference. Hence it is better that the MUs in this layer be assigned (by a scheduler) orthogonal spectrum slices that do not overlap with those of SP_A in every time unit. When SP_A does not use a spectrum slice, SP_B can use it everywhere. In this simplified system, both SSV and RRV generate gains. Obviously, such layers exist in the larger cell as well, but we do not elaborate on it here due to space constraints. Also, we show circular coverages here, but this is not the case in reality. In this paper, we focus on the RRV gain [1] in the downlink and try to quantify its benefits in terms of answering questions such as: How large can the white circle be? What level should the transmit power be?

3.3 Mathematical Model

In the most general case, SP_A and SP_B may be using very different radio access technologies and devices. In order to get some insight into the potential of RRV gains, we resort to capacity calculations rather than specific modulation, coding, and application requirements in this paper. Our objective is to consider these specific aspects in future work to the extent possible. Here, we assume that both the downlink transmissions (by SP_A and SP_B) employ MIMO[2] for exploring spatial degrees of freedom and for combatting any interference. We assume the commonly employed frequency-flat quasi-static MIMO fading environment, where the transmission between the ith transmit antenna and the jth receiving

[1] We assume SSV is adopted in the system whether or not RRV is used and we do not consider this further here.

[2] It is possible that the applications and devices may be very different, but we assume MIMO in both cases for simplicity and to obtain insights.

antenna can be modeled by

$$y = \sqrt{D^{-\alpha}10^{\zeta/10}}h_{ij} \times x + N \quad (1)$$

where x, y are transmit and receive signals respectively, D is the distance from a transmitter to a receiver (the transmitters are the two BSs in Figure 1, but their transmissions may end up at receivers that do not belong to them as interference), α is the path loss exponent, $\zeta = N(0, \sigma)$ is the shadow fading component, h_{ij} is the Rayleigh fading channel gain of the channel between the ith transmit antenna and the jth receiving antenna, and N is the thermal noise with variance $N_0/2$. This model applies to both SPs. We change the behavior of α later in Section 4.

The area spectral efficiency of a cellular system is defined as the achievable data rate per unit area for the bandwidth available. The measure of area spectral efficiency of the combined large and small cells is in terms of bit/s/Hz/(large area) [6, 11]. Note that this is essentially a single-cell scenario, so the large cell's coverage is assumed to be the unit of area of interest. Suppose that w_m Hz of spectrum is allocated to the large cell and w_s Hz to the small cell. The total amount of available spectrum w_{tot} is $w_{tot} = w_m + w_s$. Under spectrum sharing assumptions, the MUs supported by either the large cell (SP_A) or by the small cell (SP_B) may get the permission to access the entire w_{tot} Hz spectrum in a time unit[3]. Thus the aggregate spectral efficiency is

$$\eta = \frac{C_m + C_s}{w_{tot}} \quad (2)$$

where C_m and C_s are the achievable data rates of the large cell and the small cell, respectively. They are the sum of the achievable data rate of *all the MUs* within the coverage, $C_m = \sum_{i=1}^{nu_A} C_i$ and $C_s = \sum_{j=1}^{nu_B} C_j$, where nu_A and nu_B are the number of users in the large and small cell respectively. Assume that the transmission operates in a $n_T \times n_R$ downlink MIMO channel. The achievable data rate of a single user can be estimated by the (Shannon) capacity formula [1, 3],

$$C = w \log_2 \det[(\mathbf{I}_{n_R} + (\mathbf{R}^{-1/2}\mathbf{H})P_T(\mathbf{R}^{-1/2}\mathbf{H})^H] \quad (3)$$

where w is the available bandwidth for one particular MU, and n_R is the number of receiving antennas at the MU. The transmit power is P_T. $\mathbf{H}$ is the complex channel gain matrix, consisting of $\sqrt{D^{-\alpha}10^{\zeta/10}}h_{ij}$. $\mathbf{R}$ is the interference and thermal noise combined matrix, which is given as:

$$\mathbf{R} = \mathbf{H}_I\mathbf{H}_I^H P_I + (N_0/2)\mathbf{I}_{n_R} \quad (4)$$

where $\mathbf{H}_I$ is the interfering channel matrix, P_I is the interferer's transmit power and $\mathbf{I}_{n_R}$ is an identity matrix. From an information theoretic point of view, the capacity in Eq. 3 is equivalent to the capacity of the combined channel $\mathbf{R}^{-1/2}\mathbf{H}$ under Gaussian white noise. With this interpretation, the capacity can be calculated as a Gaussian white noise channel [7]. Furthermore, we see a strong proportional relationship between capacity and the combined SINR matrix $\mathbf{R}^{-1/2}\mathbf{H}$ in Eq. 3. The effects of the separation distance d, total transmit power, cell radii r_A and r_B, and available degrees of freedom in MIMO channel are reflected in the factor $\mathbf{R}^{-1/2}\mathbf{H}$, which are investigated further in section 4.

We assume that the orthogonal sub-channels created through MIMO are dedicated to the same user, and so, the achievable data rate is

$$C = \sum_{i=1}^{min(n_T,n_R)} w \log_2(1 + \lambda_i P_i) \quad (5)$$

where P_i is power allocated in ith orthogonal sub-channel, $\sum P_i = P_T$ (P_T is the total transmit power.) and λ_i is the ith orthogonal sub-channel gain, which is obtained through a singular value decomposition (SVD) process as follows.

$$\mathbf{H}^H\mathbf{R}^{-1}\mathbf{H} = \mathbf{U}\Lambda\mathbf{U}^H \quad (6)$$

Here, $\Lambda = diag(\lambda_1, ...\lambda_{n_R})$ are the singular values of $\mathbf{H}^H\mathbf{R}^{-1}\mathbf{H}$ and $\mathbf{U}$ is a unitary matrix consisting of the eigenvectors of $\mathbf{H}^H\mathbf{R}^{-1}\mathbf{H}$. Note that, when we compute the singular values, large-scale fading (distance, path-loss, ζ) scales them in *both the interfering MIMO channel matrix and the MIMO channel matrix for a given SP's receiver.*

The transmit power allocation can be done in different fashions. If the channel condition (the matrix) is known at both the transmitter and the receiver, the classic water-filling algorithm maximizes the capacity [1, 3]. The channel capacity becomes

$$C = \sum_{i=1}^{min(n_T,n_R)} w \log_2(1 + p_i\lambda_i) \quad (7)$$

where p_i is the power allocated to the i-th orthogonal sub-channel and $\sum p_i = P_T$. [4]. However, in general, the channel condition is known only by the receiver. In this case, the transmitter allocates power equally over all the antennas to maximize the capacity (this allocation is sub-optimal). The channel capacity in this case would be

$$C = \sum_{i=1}^{min(n_T,n_R)} w \log_2(1 + \frac{P_T\lambda_i}{n_T}) \quad (8)$$

In either case, the singular values λ_i's impact the achievable data rates and change with variety of factors.

4. NUMERICAL RESULTS

In this section, first, we evaluate the RRV gain in terms of capacity for multiple scenarios. Second, the cumulative distribution functions (cdf) of the singular values of the combined SINR matrix $\mathbf{R}^{-1/2}\mathbf{H}$ are presented as a function of the separation distance between the BSs of the small and large cell, the small cell radius, and the available degrees of freedom in the MIMO channel. The aforementioned proportional relationship between the combined channel matrix and capacity can be observed by comparing the trends in the cdf as the various parameters change. The combined SINR matrix is a candidate that measures interference level or capacity. The layer (circular rings of Figure 1) of a particular

[3]We assume for simplicity that each SP manages frequency bands in frequency division multiplexing fashion for its MUs. Thus, the available bandwidth for each of SP_A's MU is $w_{tot}/(nu_A)$, while the available bandwidth for each of SP B's MU is $w_{tot}/(nu_B)$ where nu_A and nu_B are the number of users in the large and small cell respectively. In reality, the bandwidth allocation to individual users will be more complex (e.g., physical resource blocks in LTE-like systems).

[4]The optimal transmit signal covariance matrix is $\Sigma_s = (N_0/2)\mathbf{U}diag(p_1, ..., p_{n_R})\mathbf{U}^H$ where $p_i = (\mu - \frac{1}{\lambda_i})^+$ and μ is chosen such that $\sum_{i=1}^{min(n_T,n_R)} p_i = P_T$. The function $(.)^+$ compares the value with 0 and picks whichever is larger.

MU and the sharing scheme to be applied may be determined based on these numbers. Finally, the potential of MIMO enabled RRV for customization across different virtual networks is investigated. We run simulations based on a two-cell RRV system, as shown in Figure 1. r_A and r_B are the radii of the large cell and small cell (used for placing MUs) and d is the separation distance between the two BSs. A MU's coordinate can be expressed as (l, ϕ) where $l \in (0, r_B \text{ or } r_A)$ and $\phi \in (0, 2\pi)$ and we distribute MUs uniformly over the radius and the angle. Results shown are averages of 10,000 simulation runs that vary locations, ζ, and h_{ij}. Suppose a MU belonging to SP_A is at (l_i, ϕ_i), the distance between this MU and the BS of SP_B can be calculated as $L_i = \sqrt{{l_i}^2 + d^2 - 2l_i d cos(\phi_i)}$. The combined channel matrix (that includes transmissions from SP_A and interference from SP_B) can then be generated using Eq. 1. We assume that the large cell and the small cell have separate 10 MHz and 5 MHz frequency bandwidth allocation respectively and the total bandwidth is 15 MHz for the RRV system. Unless specified, at each base station (BS), $n_T = 4$ antennas are adopted while $n_R = 2$ antennas are used at each MU. The transmit power P_A is 40 dBm, P_B is the transmit power of the small BS, and $N_0/2 = -90$ dBm. α takes the value of 4 (except for the conditional $\alpha = 2$ cases – see below) and $\zeta = N(0, \sigma)$ where $\sigma = 8$.

4.1 RRV and Capacity

We calculate the aggregate spectral efficiency in Eq. 2 while varying the power ratio (P_A/P_B) for the seven different RRV scenarios described in Table 1 to obtain insights on how this changes with various parameters. Error bars correspond to one standard deviation of the mean aggregate spectral efficiency over 10,000 runs. Table 1 lists the number of MUs in the large cell and in the small cell respectively.

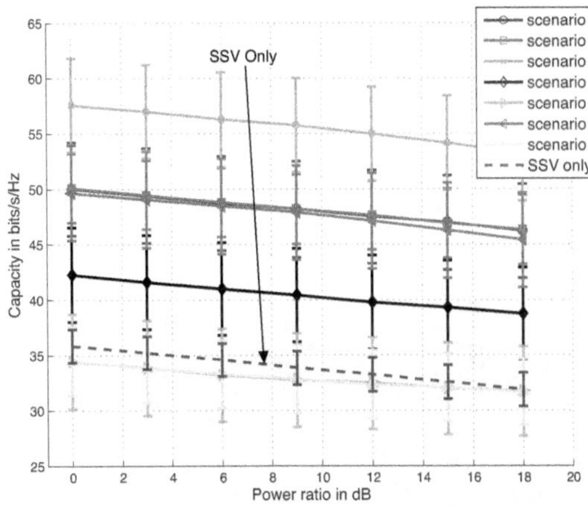

Figure 3: Aggregate achievable data rate of two cells with water-filling

4.1.1 *Aggregate Spectral Efficiency*

The aggregate spectral efficiency for the water-filling algorithm and equal power allocation is shown in Figures 3 and 4 respectively. The variation in capacity results primarily due to the location of MUs (but also due to the random fading). We omit error bars in some figures for clarity. Several preliminary conclusions can be perceived here. First, in either the water-filling or equal power allocation case, the spectral efficiency for the SSV only scheme (in Table 1) is mostly below that for all the RRV scenarios with the same parameter settings, which shows there is some gain that exclusively comes from RRV. Second, water-filling outperforms (as expected) equal power allocation approximately by 3 or 4 bits/s/Hz. Third, larger numbers of MUs in the small cell do not significantly affect the aggregate capacity because SPs are assumed to orthogonally and equally share the spectrum amongst their own MU groups. Fourth, the aggregate spectral efficiency increases as the separation distance between two BSs becomes larger but reduces when the small cell's radius increases. This implies that if the two BSs are too close (e.g., closer than 300 meters), they will not be able to adopt RRV (alternatively, the small cell should shrink further to enable RRV). Lastly, increasing the power ratio (P_A/P_B) from 0 to 18 dB changes the efficiency only a little (e.g. 3 bits/s/Hz in scenario 2). That is, the distances from SP_B's BS to SP_A's MUs are such that they make this power ratio as not a very significant factor. On the contrary, the large-scale fading for interference, which depends on the separation distance d and cell radius r_B is influential. Therefore, the separation distance and the cell radius appear to be the two major factors which have influence over the aggregate efficiency.

Table 1: Parameter Settings for Various Scenarios

ID.	r_A	r_B	nu_A	nu_B	d
1	1000	50	100	10	500
2	1000	50	100	20	500
3	1000	50	100	10	800
4	1000	50	100	10	300
5	1000	100	100	10	300
6	1000	100	100	10	800
7	1000	100	100	20	300
SSV only	1000	50	100	10	-

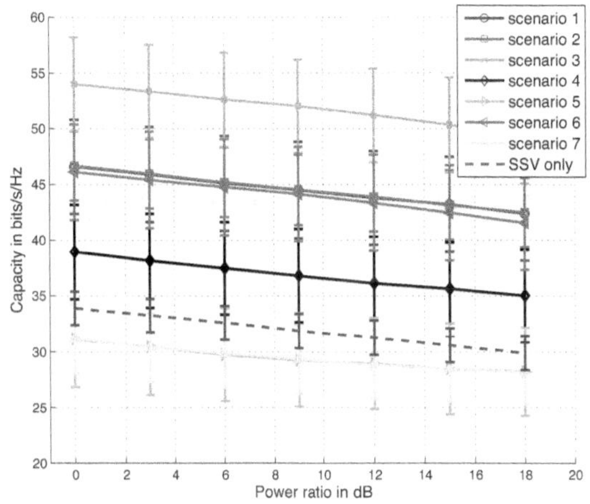

Figure 4: Aggregate achievable data rate of two cells with equal power allocation

To have a better view of how these factors affect the aggregate spectral efficiency, we evaluate them using scenario 1 as a baseline. In the cases shown here we keep r_A, nu_A and nu_B fixed and vary two factors at a time from the normalized radius r_B/r_A, the normalized distance d/r_A or the power ratio P_A/P_B. We use different values of α here ($\alpha = 4$

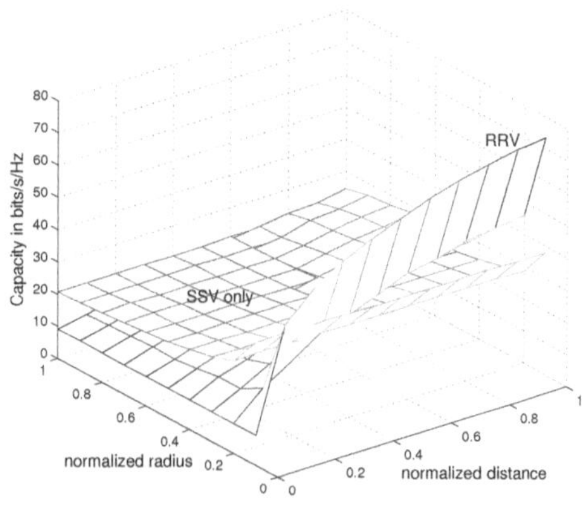

Figure 5: Aggregate Performance (Capacity) Vs. Distance & Radius ($\alpha = 4$)

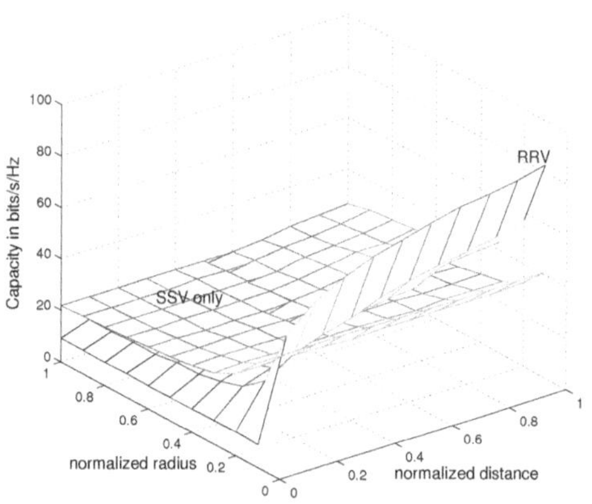

Figure 6: Aggregate Performance (Capacity) Vs. Distance & Radius (conditional $\alpha = 2$)

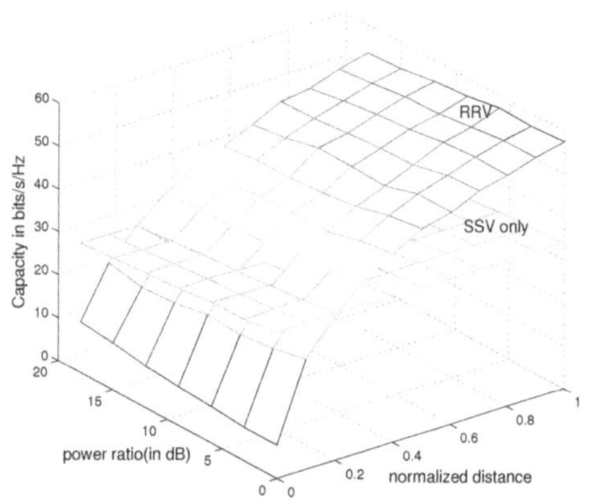

Figure 7: Aggregate Performance (Capacity) Vs. Distance & Power ($\alpha = 4$)

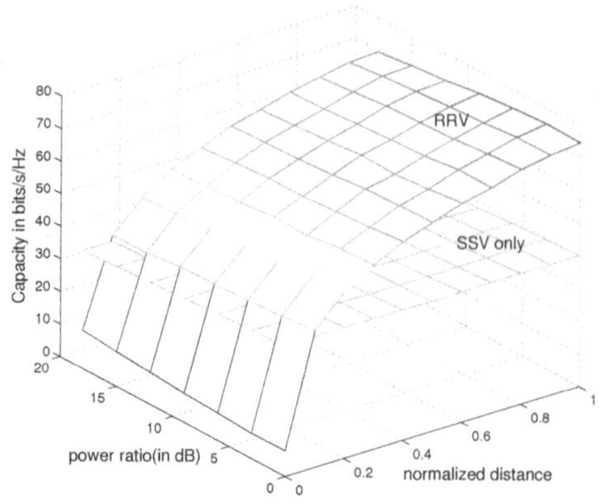

Figure 8: Aggregate Performance (Capacity) Vs. Distance & Power (conditional $\alpha = 2$)

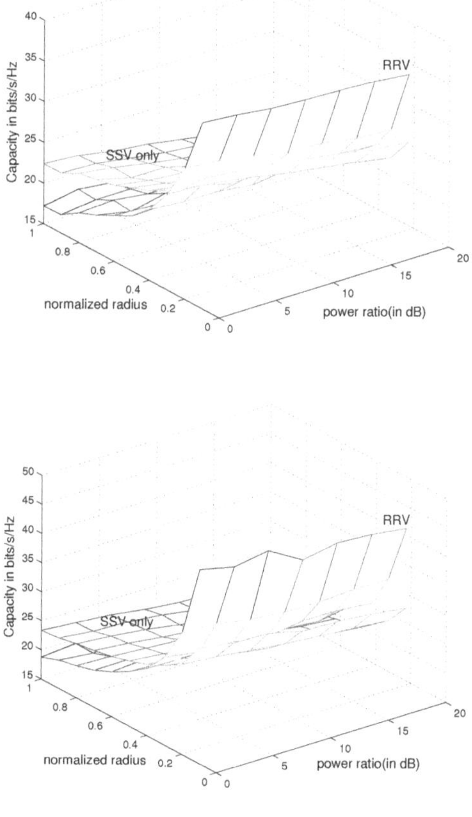

Figure 9: Aggregate Performance (Capacity) Vs. Power & Radius – top ($\alpha = 4$) and bottom (conditional $\alpha = 2$)

everywhere and $\alpha = 2$ when the distance from the transmitter is smaller than 50m - called conditional $\alpha = 2$, otherwise $\alpha = 4$). The average results are shown in Figures 5, 6, 7, 8, and 9. In Figures 5 and 6 the power ratio is fixed

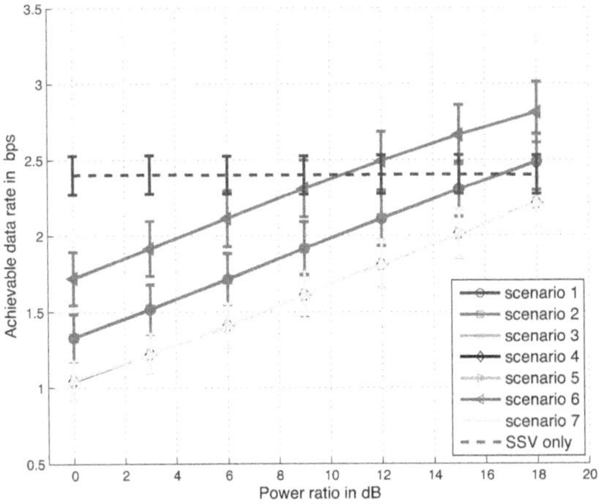

Figure 10: Achievable data rate at large cell (per MU)

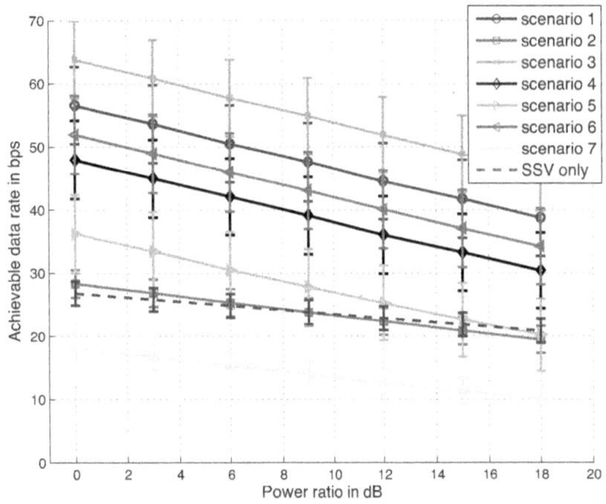

Figure 11: Achievable data rate at small cell (per MU)

at $P_A/P_B = 10$ dB and we vary the normalized radius and distance. Notice that the RRV gain is dependent on the normalized radius being small for the normalized distance to have an impact. Figures 7 and 8 show the effects of varying the power ratio and normalized distance with fixed $r_B = 50$. One can see that the power ratio has little effect compared to the normalized distance. In Figure 9, the results of varying the normalized radius and power ratio while maintaining the distance fixed at $d = 500$ are shown. Observe that the power ratio has little influence on the capacity and the normalized radius should be relatively small for the RRV gain to be large. From Figures 5 to 9, the RRV gain is greater when $\alpha = 2$ conditionally than when $\alpha = 4$ universally since the small cell benefits by a smaller α. The service providers can use these results to decide when to switch to partial spectrum sharing or only SSV instead of RRV when it fails to achieve a desired data rate.

4.1.2 Individual Cells

The average achievable data rate **per MU** of the large cell and small cell are evaluated in Figures 10 and 11 for all the scenarios using the equal power allocation scheme and $\alpha = 4$. Error bars correspond to one standard deviation of the average achievable data rate per MU over 10,000 runs. Note that MUs of each SP share the available bandwidth orthogonally. MUs in the large cell do not see a large increase in achievable data rate across the scenarios. The available bandwidth for SP_A's MUs does not increase much in the large cell which has 100 MUs in all scenarios. In the small cell however, the average data rate per user falls severely from scenario 1 (blue) to scenario 2 (red) because the number of MUs doubles in the small cell. Further, in most scenarios the achievable data rate is higher than the SSV only scheme for the small cell. It appears that most benefits, when they occur, are for MUs in the small cell.

We hypothesize that MUs of the large cell that are further away from the BS face excessive interference from the SP_B BS and this impacts their average data rates. To test this, we use a sectored scenario. We assume that the cell of SP_B is divided into three sectors (each 120°, shown in Figure 1) and RRV is used only in the one that faces the BS of SP_A (where SP_A's MUs have better channels). The achievable data rate per MU is still calculated over the seven scenarios in Table 1

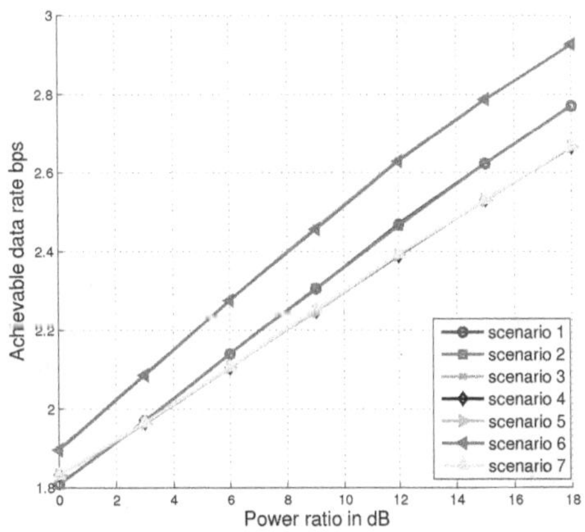

Figure 12: Average achievable data rate (per MU) at large cell with RRV employed in only one sector

with unchanged parameters. In the small cell, the achievable data rate (average) for MUs of SP_B does not change. However, for the data rate of MUs of the SP_A large cell improves as shown in Figure 12 compared with Figure 10. The achievable data rate curves with the same separation distance d still group up together and are indistinguishable. However, after the small cell moves closer toward the large cell's BS (i.e., d is 300m in scenarios 4,5, & 7), the achievable data rate per MU is improved compared to the omnidirectional case implying that MUs at the edge of the large cell suffer the most under RRV.

An interesting observation can be made from Figures 10 and 11. A minor change of data rate with the power ratio implies that even if SP_A accidentally or intentionally increases its transmit power in the RRV system, it will not cause a serious damage to MUs of SP_B. On the other hand, if SP_B intentionally transmits at a high power level, what SP_A needs to do is to adjust its own power carefully to keep the desired data rate for its MUs. This aspect, while not fully explored here, becomes important when virtualization of the wireless network considers the ***isolation*** between various services under intentional or accidental misbehavior.

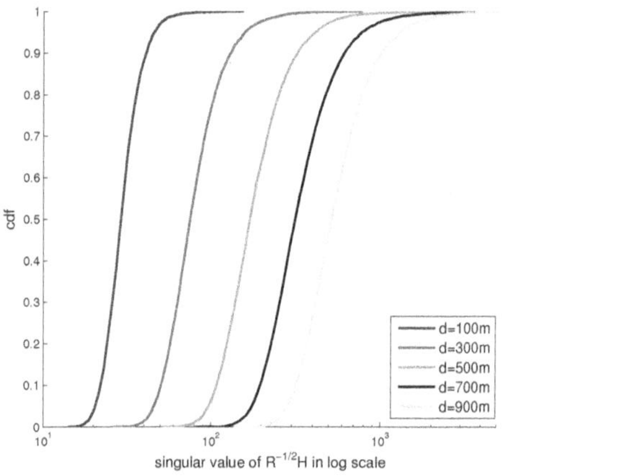

Figure 13: CDF of singular values at different separation distance (for MUs in the large cell)

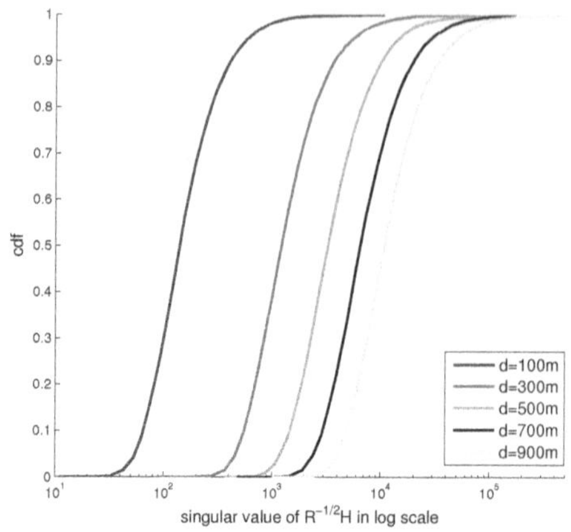

Figure 14: CDF of singular values at different separation distance (for MUs in the small cell)

4.2 Analyzing the Combined SINR Matrix

In an RRV system, estimating the channel condition is important as it helps to decide when RRV should be invoked. We consider the combined channel matrix $\mathbf{R}^{-1/2}\mathbf{H}$ here due to its relationship with capacity. From Eq. 4, $\mathbf{R}^{-1/2}\mathbf{H}$ is also a function of the separation distance d, transmit powers P_A and P_B, cell radii r_A and r_B, and available degrees of freedom (minimum number of antennas at BS or MU) in the MIMO channel. The singular values of combined channel matrix are essentially the orthogonal sub-channel gains in a MIMO channel (λ_i in Eq. 7 and Eq. 8) which represent the sub-channel quality. However, they do not include any information on the available bandwidth. Taking the amount of bandwidth into consideration provides the capacity for a given MU. Therefore, the rank of this combined channel matrix is also crucial, as it is the number of sub-channels possible (available degrees of freedom in MIMO channels). We sum all the singular values to reveal the "volume" of the MIMO channel and average it by the number of MUs in each cell while observing the singular value distributions, but how the available degrees of freedom in the MIMO channel affects the combined channel matrix is considered next. The impact of separation distance d and small cell radius r_B are examined as these two factors have a larger influence on capacity. For a fair comparison, the distribution of MUs in the area is kept fixed for both cases. For the singular value vs separation distance d case, $r_A = 1000$m, $r_B = 50$m, and P_B is 10 dB less than $P_A = 1$W. For the singular value vs radius of small cell r_B case, $r_A = 1000$m, $d = 500$m, and P_B is the same as in the previous case. All the other parameters in the simulation remain. Hence, $d = 500m$ in Figure 13 and $r_B = 50m$ in Figure 15 have the same distribution and both of them stand for scenario 1 in Table 1.

The distribution of singular values of the combined matrix $\mathbf{R}^{-1/2}\mathbf{H}$ shifts towards the right as the separation distance d becomes larger (as shown in Figure 13 and 14) both for MUs in the large cell and in the small cell (for the same locations of MUs for each d). This means, increasing the separation distance improves both the combined matrix and the resulting capacity (shown in Figure 10 and Figure 11). Figures 15 and 16 show that expanding the small cell only degrades the capacity of itself not of the large cell, which

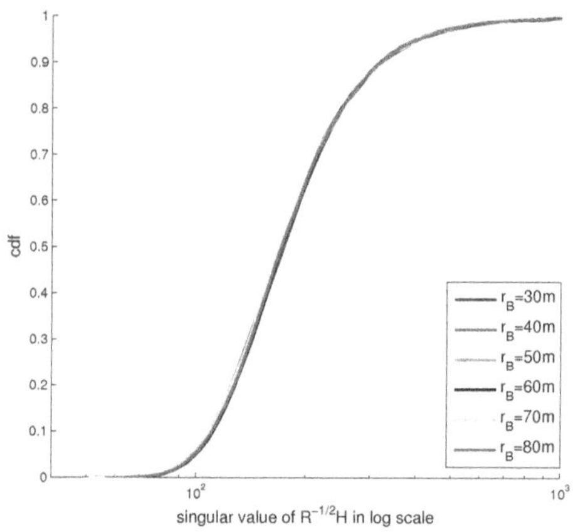

Figure 15: CDF of singular values at different radii of small cell (for MUs in the large cell)

matches what is shown in Figure 10 - the capacity curves cluster with the same d value no matter what the value of r_B is. As for the small cell, for the same number of MUs, the more compact the distribution of MUs, the higher the capacity those MUs can achieve. This conclusion can also be obtained from Figure 11 as well and is intuitive.

4.3 Customization in RRV

The essence of a virtualized network includes enabling SPs to customize their own networks based on the requirements of their MUs. Customization in this paper assumes that the devices in each SP's network can be different [5]. Here, we evaluate the relationship between the available degrees of freedom in the MIMO channel and the combined channel matrix. As shown in Eq. 7 and Eq. 8, the rank of the MIMO channel limits the system capacity in terms of the number of orthogonal sub-channels. Meanwhile, the singular values affect the capacity through the SINR in the sub-channel. Thus, the combined channel matrix not only facilitates esti-

[5]In general, customization also includes the ability of a virtual network to adjust itself to meet the need for multi-class traffic as well as adaptation to a variant environment with multiple SPs.

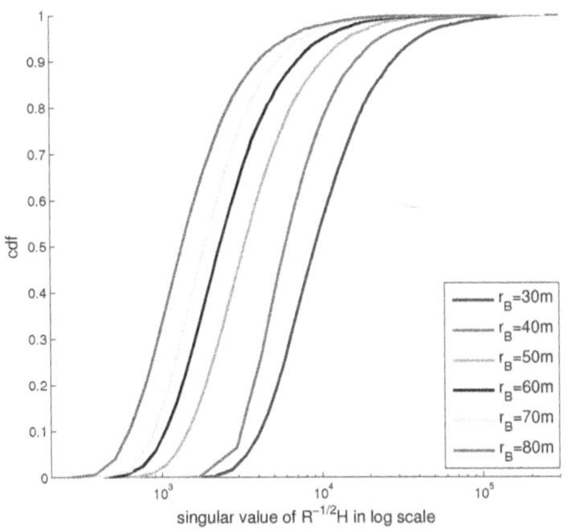

Figure 16: CDF of singular values at different radii of small cell (for MUs in the small cell)

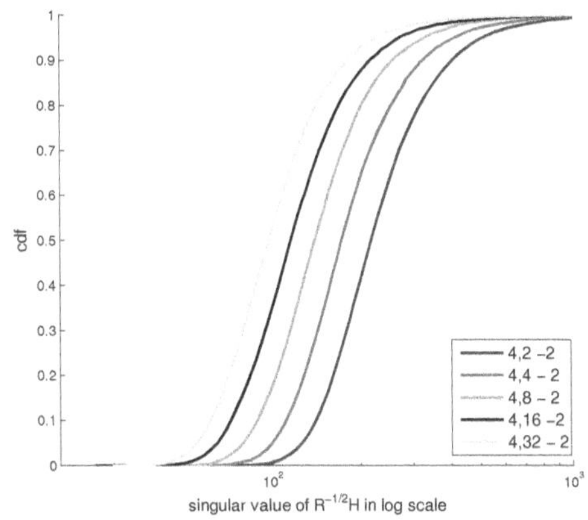

Figure 17: CDF of singular values (as seen by MUs in the large cell) with 2 MU antennas in the small cell, but varying numbers of BS antennas in the small cell

mation of capacity but also offers an opportunity for SPs to combat interference in an RRV system.

The combined SINR matrix $\mathbf{R}^{-1/2}\mathbf{H}$ is a function of separation distance, cell radii, and available degrees of freedom in the MIMO channel. The proportional relationships between this matrix and the separation distance d and the cell radii r_B are shown in Figures 13,14, 15, and16. Since large-scale fading (path loss) dominates the signal (in the received signal strength as well as the received interference), a change in capacity with either the separation distance or the radius of the small cell is clear. The small-scale fading in the MIMO channel does not impact the average received power (the small-scale fading is averaged out over the transmit signal block) but it impacts the singular values λ_i. The capacity will be significantly improved only if more antennas are adopted at the BSs and MUs of both SPs. Furthermore, if only the number of transmit antennas increases, it still improves the targeted sub-channel gain but it also causes an increased interference to the second SP's network which simultaneously operates in the same spectrum bands. Therefore, the relationship between the number of antennas at the large BS, the small BS or MUs is not straightforward. This is the focus of the investigation in this section. We set the number of antennas at the three points as (x, y-z), where x, y and z stand for the number of antennas at the large cell's BS, the small cell's BS, and MUs in the small cell respectively). MUs in the large cell still use 2 antennas.

In Figures 17 and 18, the large cell BS has 4 antennas and its MUs have 2 antennas. The small cell's MUs all have only 2 antennas, but the small cell's BS has varying numbers of antennas. The best singular value distributions for the large cell and the small cell lie at the (4, 2-2) and the (4, 32-2) values, respectively. That is, the large cell benefits from fewer BS antennas in the small cell, but the small cell suffers if it reduces the number of BS antennas! The opposite effect may be expected if we change the number of BS antennas in the large cell. On the positive side, even when the small cell uses more antennas to transmit, the large SP is not significantly impacted on average as illustrated in Table 2.

Next, we assume MUs in the small cell are able to install up to 8 antennas. The capacity in the large cell remains stable as long as the ratio x/y is unchanged (Figure 19 -

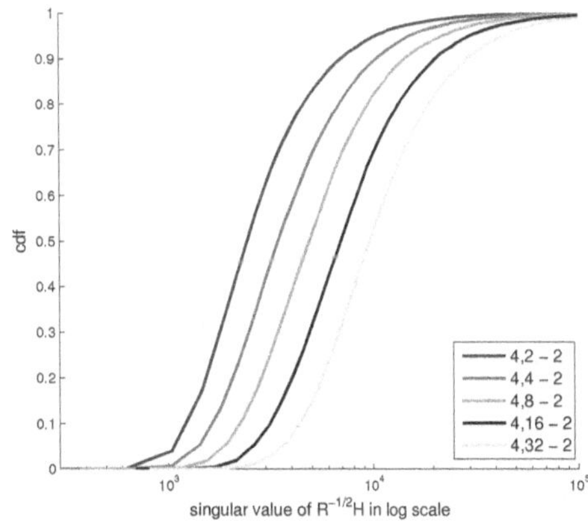

Figure 18: CDF of singular values (as seen by MUs in the small cell) with 2 MU antennas in the small cell, but varying numbers of BS antennas in the small cell

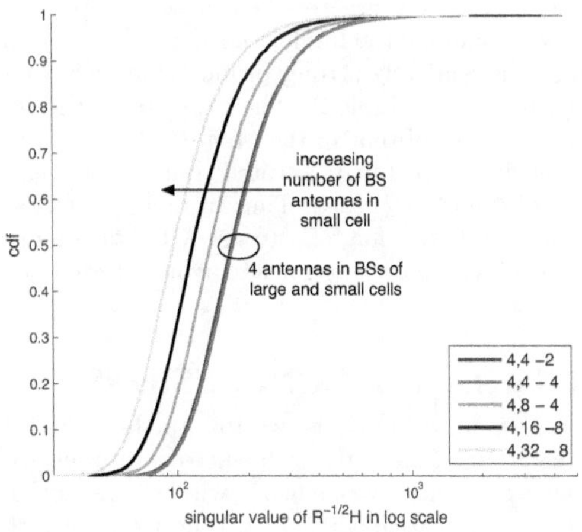

Figure 19: CDF of singular values (as seen by MUs in the large cell) with varying numbers of MU and BS antennas in small cell

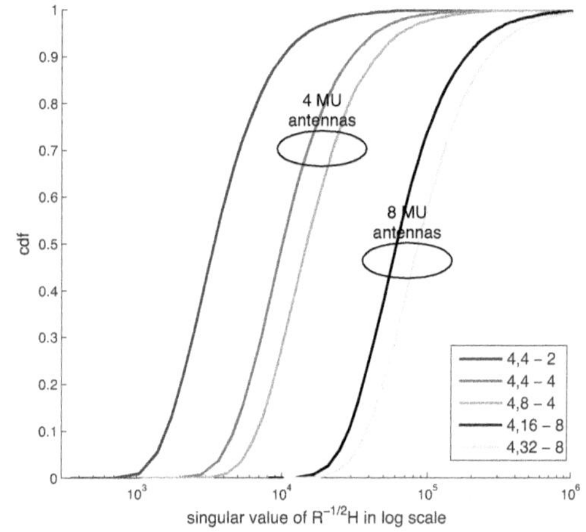

Figure 20: CDF of singular values (as seen by MUs in the small cell) with varying numbers of MU and BS antennas in small cell

Table 2: Achievable data rate (in bps) per MU

MIMO channel	large cell	small cell
(4, 2-2)	1.7325	47.1777
(4, 4-2)	1.7316	47.2488
(4, 8-2)	1.6691	48.5423
(4, 16-2)	1.6621	48.3901
(4, 32-2)	1.6414	48.6210
(4, 4-4)	1.7300	93.6539
(4, 8-4)	1.6831	98.4671
(4, 16-8)	1.6638	221.6121
(4, 32-8)	1.6538	224.3495

cases 4,4-2 and 4,4-4). The rest of the singular value distributions for the large cell remain the same as the ones shown in Figure 17 as expected since the change in number of MU antennas in the small cell does not impact the interference faced by the MUs in the large cell. The distribution of singular values in Figure 20 cluster with the available degrees of freedom in MIMO channel ($min(n_T, n_R)$) for the small cell (singular values of 4 MU antennas are together, 8 MU antennas are together). The greater the available degrees of freedom in MIMO channel, the higher the aggregate system capacity. This is a relatively strong proportional relationship which can be seen in Table 2. The capacity in the (4, 4-4) case is almost twice of that in the (4, 4-2) MIMO channel, and the capacity in the (4, 16-8) case is much more than four times that of the (4, 4-2) case. Thus from a customization point, it may be better for SP_B to use MUs with more antennas than a BS with more antennas to avoid interference to the large cell.

5. DISCUSSION AND CONCLUSIONS

In this paper, we show that it is possible to share "radio resources" rather than simply spectrum slices across service providers when we consider virtualizing wireless networks. We evaluate the downlink capacity of two service providers occupying the same geographical area, but perhaps offering different services. One service provider is assumed to have a much larger coverage and transmit power. The amount of spectrum that can be shared through simultaneous use depends on the geography and transmit powers (at a minimum). It is certainly possible to have radio resource sharing gains in a variety of circumstances. It appears that the primary factor that may impact such sharing is the interference from the smaller service provider to the mobile users of the larger service provider (affecting isolation in a virtualized network). This may be mitigated by using directional transmissions (or using disjoint spectrum slices in specific directions). There are also opportunities for customization of services at the device level. Using different MIMO settings may provide different tradeoffs between capacities across service providers. We have not considered the uplink in this work, nor have we considered interference that may be caused in a multi-cell scenario. The channel matrix assumes that the fading is independent and identically distributed while there are possible correlations in real channels. Investigation of these aspects are planned as part of our ongoing work.

6. REFERENCES

[1] R. S. Blum, J. Winters, and N. R. Sollenberger. On the capacity of cellular systems with MIMO. *IEEE Vehicular Technology Conference (Fall)*, 2001.

[2] N. M. Chowdhury and R. Boutaba. A survey of network virtualization. *Computer Networks*, 54(5):862– 876, 2010.

[3] H. Dai, A. F. Molisch, and H. V. Poor. Downlink capacity of interference-limited mimo systems with joint detection. *IEEE Transactions on Wireless Communications*, 3(2):442–453, 2004.

[4] A. Damnjanovic, J. Montojo, Y. Wei, T. Ji, T. Luo, M. Vajapeyam, and D. Malladi. A survey on 3GPP heterogeneous networks. *IEEE Wireless Communications*, 18(3):10–21, 2011.

[5] M. L. Y. Z. A. T.-G. L., Zhao and G. C. LTE virtualization: from theoretical gain to practical solution. *23rd International Teletraffic Congress (ITC)*, 2011.

[6] R. Madan, J. Borran, A. Sampath, N. Bhushan, A. Khandekar, and T. Ji. Cell association and interference coordination in heterogeneous LTE-A cellular networks. *IEEE Journal Selected Areas in Communications*, 28(9):1479–1489, 2010.

[7] D. S. Shiu. *Wireless Communication Using Dual Antenna Arrays*. Kluwer Academic Publishers, 2000.

[8] Y. Song and S. D. Blostein. MIMO channel capacity in co-channel interference. *21st Biennial Symposium on Communications.*, volume 2, 2002.

[9] X. Wang, P. Krishnamurthy, and D. Tipper. Wireless network virtualization. *International Conference on Computing, Networking and Communications (ICNC)*, 2013.

[10] Y. Wang and K. I. Pedersen. Performance analysis of enhanced inter-cell interference coordination in lte-advanced heterogeneous networks. *the 75th IEEE Vehicular Technology Conference (VTC Spring)*, 2012.

[11] B. Yong, J. Zhou, , and L. Chen. Hybrid spectrum usage for overlaying LTE macrocell and femtocell. In *IEEE Global Telecommunications Conference (GLOBECOM)*, pages 1–6, 2009.

[12] Y. Zaki, L. Zhao, C. Goerg, and A. Timm-Giel. LTE mobile network virtualization. *Mobile Networks and Applications*, 16(4):424–432, 2011.

Assessing the Appropriateness of using Markov Decision Processes for RF Spectrum Management

John Meier, Benjamin Karaus, Sreeharsha Sistla, Terry Tidwell,
Roger D. Chamberlain, and Christopher Gill
Dept. of Computer Science and Engineering
Washington University in St. Louis
{jmeier,bvkaraus,ssistla,terrytidwell,roger,cdgill}@wustl.edu

ABSTRACT

The stochastic nature of wireless communication suggests a Markov Decision Process (MDP) as a formalism for identifying and evaluating spectrum control policies. However, in practice numerous factors influence the success or failure of a transmission, so that the applicability of particular MDP models to real spectrum management problems must itself be examined. This paper presents a series of model validation studies in which correspondence between an MDP model and a discrete-event simulation (DES) model is evaluated. We test several hypotheses that together provide a foundation and an exemplar for the idea of using MDPs to guide management of shared spectrum. We conclude that there is sufficient similarity between the performance predictions made by the MDP model and the DES model that MDPs can be used effectively to determine spectrum control policies.

Categories and Subject Descriptors

C.2.1 [Computer-Communication Networks]: Network Architecture and Design—*Wireless c ommunication*; G.3 [Probability and Statistics]: Markov processes; I.6.4 [Simulation and Modeling]: Model Validation and Analysis

General Terms

Design, Performance, Verification.

Keywords

Markov decision process (MDP); discrete-event simulation (DES); spectrum allocation

1. INTRODUCTION

The advent of software defined radio [1] and techniques for cognitive radio [9] have together opened the door to dramatic improvements in the utilization of scarce RF spectrum [19][23]. Rather than ranges of spectrum being rigidly allocated to specific functions or users, it is now technically feasible for different users (e.g., transmitters) to share available spectrum efficiently, dynamically choosing not only the range of frequencies utilized, but also the modulation method, transmitter power, etc. However, while the technical capability exists to share spectrum effectively, approaches to managing and evaluating dynamic spectrum sharing are still in their infancy.

Anchora et al. [3] have extended the popular ns-3 simulator to enable the assessment of shared spectrum on the part of network operators using game theoretic techniques. At the same time, Feeney [8] cautions that there are concerns about the reliability of simulation results on the part of the wireless community. Proactively assessing the quality of performance predictions is important if the conclusions made on the basis of these predictions are to be trusted. This paper makes an initial effort in that regard for Markov decision processes applied to managing spectrum.

Markov decision processes (MDPs) [16] have been used extensively to optimize control of systems [1][18], particularly those that include stochastic elements [4]. Here, we investigate the viability of using an MDP to optimize decisions in the context of managing RF spectrum. These decisions might be admission decisions, channel allocation decisions, modulation decisions, transmitter power level decisions, or any number of other choices that are germane to managing the shared use of the spectrum.

Critical to the viability of MDP approaches is the question of whether or not the assumptions inherent in the MDP model overly simplify the underlying reality and, as a result, even an optimal choice in the space of the MDP model might or might not be even a good choice in the real world. This paper seeks to assess that question via a series of validation experiments, comparing performance predictions of a basic MDP model to those of a pre-existing discrete-event simulation (DES) model [15]. Note that the MDP will be used to choose a value-optimal policy for spectrum use. However, the DES does not make policy decisions; it only makes performance predictions for a given policy. Our purpose here is to assess the degree to which the MDP model's performance predictions agree with (or differ from) the DES model's performance predictions when they both are following the *same* policy, whether or not that policy is the value-optimal policy chosen by the MDP.

We start by presenting an MDP that models a straightforward admission control problem, one for which we presume to already know the correct allocation decisions. We next demonstrate that this MDP does, in fact, guide us to a correct policy. This is followed by testing a set of hypotheses that examine several

MSWiM'13, November 3–8, 2013, Barcelona, Spain.

http://dx.doi.org/10.1145/2507924.2507942

aspects of the assumptions made in the MDP modeling process. For each of these hypotheses, a specific experiment is designed and executed, and the validity of the hypothesis is assessed.

The three hypotheses are: (1) performance can be reasonably characterized by the mean of message durations and is relatively insensitive to their distribution; (2) even though imperfect channel allocations will occur in any real system, they are infrequent enough that ignoring them does not have a significant impact on an MDP model's ability to predict throughput accurately; and (3) value-optimal policy decisions made by the MDP are at least locally optimal as determined by the DES model.

The first two hypotheses are assessed by experiments utilizing the discrete-event simulator. The third hypothesis is assessed by comparing the performance predictions of the MDP model to those of the DES model. In all three cases, we find strong evidence to support the hypotheses, providing an indication that Markov decision processes offer a suitable mechanism for modeling and generating policies to manage the shared use of RF spectrum.

The paper is organized as follows. Section 2 describes related work in model validation and Markovian modeling of RF spectrum. Section 3 introduces the RF spectrum system model that we utilize, the MDP model, and their relationship to one another. Section 4 presents the evaluation approach, including a description of the discrete-event simulator we use for validation purposes. Section 5 presents our experimental results, and Section 6 offers conclusions and directions for future work.

2. RELATED WORK

The primary purpose of this paper is to assess the applicability of Markovian models to managing wireless radio spectrum. Perhaps the most relevant results in model applicability come from the domain of finite-element modeling [20], where explicit error estimation is used to select between p-methods and h-methods for analysis. In that work, a quantitative estimate of model error is used to assess whether or not a model is appropriate for a given task.

More commonly, assessment is an empirical exercise, in which the model in question (or more precisely, a set of predictions made by the model) is compared either with measurements of the physical system being modeled (e.g., see [4]) or with a (presumably) more robust model. For example, a frequent practice is to utilize simulation models to assess analytic models [14], as we do in this work. Such an approach makes the most sense when: (1) the simulation model explicitly incorporates aspects of the physical system being modeled that are either simplified or completely ignored in the analytic model, and (2) when the simulation model (or other reference model) has been independently evaluated. To assess the applicability of Markovian models to the problem of managing RF spectrum, we compare model predictions to a discrete-event simulation model we developed previously [15].

We are not the first to suggest using MDPs to guide decision-making in RF systems. Zhao et al. [24] propose the use of MDPs for guiding what they call *opportunistic s pectrum acces s* (the ability of secondary users to identify and exploit instantaneous spectrum opportunities that arise because of the bursty traffic patterns of primary users). Tradeoffs between optimality and complexity in such cases are examined by Djonin et al. [7]. Akbar and Tranter [2] use hidden Markov models (HMMs) to model and predict the spectrum occupancy of licensed radio bands for this same purpose.

Markovian models have been used to characterize other properties of RF systems as well. Wang et al. [22] use a Markov transition system to characterize different handoff delays associated with connections in cognitive radio networks. Geirhofer et al. [10] propose a continuous-time semi-Markov model of a WLAN's behavior, towards a better understanding of primary users' activities.

3. USING MARKOV DECISION PROCESSES FOR RF SPECTRUM MANAGEMENT

The management of RF spectrum requires a number of allocation decisions (e.g., admission, placement, overlap, and modulation) to be made. If a Markov Decision Process (MDP) model can faithfully represent the system being modeled, one then can represent these decisions as actions within the MDP and generate a value-optimal policy, with a prescribed action corresponding to each reachable state of the system. In this work, we concentrate on admission, placement, and overlap decisions, i.e., whether or not a message should be allowed to use spectrum resources and if so which channel. As future work, we also anticipate that other decisions (e.g., modulation choices) could be modeled effectively in a similar manner.

We start by describing the system model that we use to represent the RF spectrum being managed. This is followed by a brief introduction to MDP models, and then a description of the specific MDP we use for admission control.

3.1 RF Spectrum System Model

In our system model, which follows the one we developed previously [15], the system has a block of radio spectrum, divided into some number of channels, and a central controller that makes decisions about the allocation of those channels. Messages arrive via a Poisson process, and are allocated to a channel if admitted, and depart the system if not admitted. For the purposes of this evaluation, we limit the decision-making to admission and placement (including whether or not messages are allowed to overlap). The mean message arrival rate is denoted by λ, and message sizes (i.e., durations) are assumed to be uniformly distributed with mean $1/\mu$ (following the convention in queuing theory that μ is a service *rate*). The total rate of departure at any specific time, therefore, is proportional to the number of messages in the system. Multiple messages can be allocated into one channel (i.e., they can *overlap*); in that case, the success of a message delivery is a function of the RF channel model, which we describe next.

The RF channel model characterizes the success (or failure) of message delivery in terms of environmental factors and conflicts due to common channel occupancy [12]. The environmental factors (e.g., background noise, reflections, etc.) are aggregated into a single term, denoted P_{env}, representing the probability of a message delivery failure due to these factors. Message conflict is similarly characterized by a single term, denoted P_{conf}, which parameterizes a Bernoulli model of message failure. The probability that an individual message is successfully delivered, denoted P_{succ}, is therefore

$$P_{succ} = (1 - P_{env})(1 - P_{conf})^{N_m - 1}$$

where N_m is the number of messages sharing the channel.

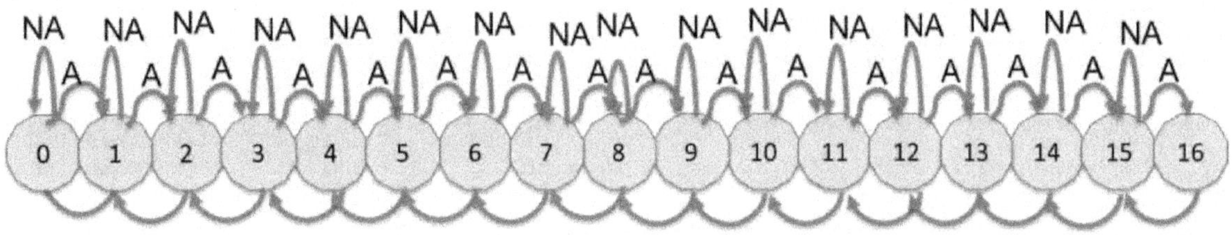

Figure 1. 4 channel, up to 16 message, Markov decision process state transition diagram.

3.2 Background on the MDP Formalism

The following description is derived from Tidwell et al. [21], which applies an MDP model to processor allocation problems[1]. An MDP is a five-tuple (X, A, P, R, γ) with *states* X and *actions* A, a *transition system* P with probabilities $P(y|x,a)$ of transitioning from state x to y on action a, and a *reward func tion* R that specifies the immediate value of each action in each state of the system. The *discount factor* $\gamma \in [0,1)$ defines how potential future rewards are weighed against immediate rewards when evaluating the impact of taking action a in a given state. A policy π for an MDP maps states in X to actions in A. At each discrete decision epoch k the agent observes the state of the MDP x_k, then selects an action $a_k = \pi(x_k)$. The MDP then transitions to state x_{k+1} with probability $P(x_{k+1}|x_k,a_k)$ and the controller receives reward $r_k = R(x_k,a_k,x_{k+1})$. Given the discount factor γ, the value of a policy, denoted V^π, is the expected sum of long-term, discounted rewards obtained while following that policy:

$$V^\pi(x) = E\left\{\sum_{k=0}^{\infty} \gamma^k r_k \,\middle|\, x_0 = x, a_k = \pi(x_k)\right\}.$$

$$R^\pi(x) = \sum_{y \in X} P(y|x,\pi(x))V^\pi(y)$$

denotes the expected reward obtained when executing action $a = \pi(x)$ in state x. Then we may equivalently define V^π as the solution to the linear system

$$V^\pi(x) = R^\pi(x) + \gamma \sum_{y \in X} P(y|x,\pi(x))V^\pi(y)$$

for each state x. When $|R^\pi(x)|$ is bounded for all states, the discount factor γ prevents V^π from diverging for any choice of policy, and can be interpreted as the prior probability that the system persists from one decision epoch to the next [13]. In practice this value is almost always set very close to 1 and in this work we set γ to 0.99.

There are several techniques for computing the value-optimal policy for an MDP with finite state and action spaces [16]. These techniques calculate the optimal action, $\pi^*(x)$, for every state $x \in X$:

$$\pi^*(x) = \underset{a \in A}{\operatorname{argmax}}\left\{R(x,a) + \gamma \sum_{y \in X} P(y|x,a)V^*(y)\right\}$$

where the optimal value, $V^*(x)$, is given by:

$$V^*(x) = \max_{a \in A}\left\{R(x,a) + \gamma \sum_{y \in X} P(y|x,a)V^*(y)\right\}.$$

The value-optimal policy is the policy that optimizes long term value, in contrast to immediate reward.

3.3 MDP Use for Admission Control

Figure 1 shows the structure of the continuous-time MDP we propose to use for admission control. Each state $x = i$ encodes the number of messages occupying a channel (i.e., currently being transmitted). Our MDP model assumes a perfect allocation of messages to channels, so if there are C channels and $x \le C$, each message is assumed to be allocated to a distinct channel. If $x > C$, we assume the number of potential conflicts (i.e., messages transmitting on a common channel) is the minimum possible.

For admission control, the two possible actions are to *allocate* or *not allocate*. One of these actions is taken whenever a message arrives in the system. In Figure 1, actions to allocate are indicated by edges labeled A in the transition from a state i to the neighboring state $i+1$. Similarly, actions to not allocate are indicated by edges labeled NA and are self-loops (i.e., transition back into the same state rather than to a new state).

Since the Poisson arrival process has mean rate λ, the transition rates for the edges labeled A and NA are both λ. The MDP treats the set of messages as a traditional birth-death process, so the departure rate is determined by the mean service rate to be $x\mu$.

The above described (continuous-time) model is converted into a discrete-time MDP by adding self-loops and converting the transition rates to transition probabilities using the uniformization technique described by Grassman [11] with uniform rate parameter δ, which is set to be greater than the largest rate in the continuous-time model[2]. As a result, the probability of an arrival is λ/δ (for an action to accept) and the probability of a departure is $x\mu/\delta$. The probability of a self-loop is $1-(\lambda + x\mu)/\delta$ (for an action to accept) and $1 - x\mu/\delta$ (for an action to not accept).

Value (from the reward function) is accrued on departure transitions, in an amount equal to the expected duration of the message time (equal to its size) multiplied by the probability of a successful transmission, P_{succ}.

Informally, we expect value-optimal admission decisions made under these conditions to result in an admission policy of accepting incoming messages up to some system occupancy and

[1] Despite the differing resources (spectrum vs. processor cycles) and semantic models (Bernoulli vs. time-utility scheduling) involved, our formulation of the MDP in this work is similarly motivated by the challenge of optimal resource use considered in that work.

[2] In the literature the uniform rate parameter is frequently represented by γ, but that symbol is already in use as part of the MDP definition.

then not accepting new messages at any higher occupancy, with the acceptance threshold being influenced in part by the value of P_{conf}, which parameterizes the penalty of sharing individual channels. This policy is known to be optimal for real-world spectrum allocation circumstances, e.g., when using FM modulation.

This intuition is confirmed by setting the value of P_{conf} to 0.97 in a 4-channel system and solving for the value-optimal policy using the MDP. At this high value of P_{conf} (i.e., high probability of message delivery failure due to conflict), sharing of channels is unlikely to benefit throughput, and the policy that is chosen via the MDP is to allocate up to 4 messages, but no more.

We expand this investigation to $P_{conf} = 0.7$ (i.e., conflicts have a lower probability of causing message delivery failure) in the same 4-channel system and again solve for the value-optimal policy. In this case, the resulting policy is to allocate up to 8 messages, but no more. This time each channel is potentially shared by up to 2 messages.

The intuition associated with these experimental results is that as P_{conf} gets smaller, the likelihood of overlapping messages being successfully delivered increases (i.e., P_{succ} goes up). Therefore, a policy with greater allowed message overlap is value-optimal.

With confirmation that our MDP is making reasonable admission decisions, we next proceed to assess the appropriateness of some of the modeling assumptions made during the development of the MDP model.

4. EVALUATION

In this section we evaluate the use of a Markov decision processes for RF spectrum allocation by empirically comparing decisions and performance predictions made by our MDP model with performance predictions made by a pre-existing discrete-event simulation (DES) model [15].

4.1 Approach

A key premise of this paper is that there is inherent value in using MDP models to manage and control RF spectrum resources. Our approach to evaluate that premise is to compare our MDP model with a different (i.e., DES) model. To appreciate both the benefits and limitations of this approach, it is important to distinguish what this empirical comparison does and does not validate. Specifically, any modeling assumption that is made in common by both the MDP model and the DES model will not be tested by this approach. We first articulate some such assumptions:

1. The arrival process of messages is assumed to be Poisson with a given mean arrival rate.
2. Messages each consume one channel of RF spectrum (i.e., the spectrum is decomposed into discrete, equal-sized channels) and collectively have a given mean duration.
3. The underlying channel model that predicts the success or failure of an individual message delivery, based on environmental factors and/or conflict with other messages, is common across the MDP and DES models.
4. Messages that fail depart the system. We do not model retries.

Although one certainly may question these assumptions, it is impractical to test them given the available experimental infrastructure, since the DES model (which also makes those same assumptions) is our comparison vehicle. As we describe in Section 3, these assumptions also come directly from the RF spectrum system model we consider.

While the above list describes what we will not test, the purpose of our evaluation is to assess the three primary hypotheses (stated in Section 1), which we *can* test:

1. the independence of message throughput on the distribution of message durations,
2. the insignificance of imperfect allocations, and
3. that value-optimal policies chosen by the MDP are at least locally optimal according to the DES model.

4.2 Discrete-Event Simulation Model

The discrete-event simulator maintains an explicit representation of the set of channels within the RF spectrum range being modeled, including occupancy of each channel over time by specifically which set of messages. Many features of the discrete event simulator are unnecessary for this evaluation (e.g., it supports a binary buddy algorithm for spectrum allocation) but since the present investigation is constrained relative to the simulator's capabilities (e.g., our comparison is limited to messages that occupy only a single channel, therefore allowing for a simple greedy allocation algorithm) we will only describe features that are directly relevant to our evaluations.

The DES uses traditional event-driven simulation techniques, in which state changes to the modeled system are represented by time-stamped events that are maintained in a time-ordered priority queue. The event with the smallest time-stamp is removed from the queue, the state change represented by that event is executed, and any subsequent future state changes implied by the event's execution are scheduled in the priority queue.

The events supported by the simulator include *message arrival* and *message departure*. As part of the execution of a message arrival event, the simulator performs a greedy allocation algorithm (i.e., it allocates the newly arrived message to a channel with the fewest conflicts with other, pre-existing messages currently using the spectrum). During the execution of a message departure event, the Bernoulli model of Section 3.1 is used to determine whether or not the message was successfully delivered.

In [15], performance predictions made by the simulator are compared with an *M/U/c/c* queueing model (i.e., *M*arkovian arrival process, *U*niformly distributed service process, *c* servers, and *c* total jobs allowed in the system). To support the evaluations we wish to perform in this work, the simulator was extended it two specific ways. First, the uniform distribution assumption for message duration was expanded to also include the option for an exponential distribution. Second, the effectiveness of the greedy allocation algorithm was measured by counting the number of messages that were delivered under imperfect allocation decisions (i.e., the message was delivered using a shared channel when a free channel was available but, at the time, unknown to the simulator).

4.3 Experimental Predictions

We now describe experimental predictions related to each hypothesis. Each experiment is designed to assess the distinctions between the MDP model and the DES model. The first two hypotheses are assessed by experiments utilizing the discrete-event simulator. The third hypothesis is assessed initially by comparing the throughput performance predictions of the MDP model to those of the DES model, followed by using the simulator to examine local optimality of the decisions made by the MDP.

The first experiment evaluates the impact of the distribution of message durations on the predicted throughput of the system. The MDP model makes the standard memory-less assumption, modeling message durations via an exponential distribution. The DES model follows a common convention in RF systems and models message durations via a uniform distribution. To test our first hypothesis we modify the simulator to support an exponential distribution for message durations, and compare the throughput predictions for uniformly distributed message durations with that for exponentially distributed message durations. We intentionally perform this experiment exclusively in the simulation model. Our experimental prediction is that there will not be a significant difference between the throughputs for the two (different) distributions of message duration. In effect, we are testing whether or not the *insensitivity property* that is well established for Erlang-loss systems [17] holds here.

The second experiment evaluates the impact of imperfect allocations on the throughput of the system. The MDP model implicitly assumes that allocation decisions are perfect (i.e., if a free channel exists in the spectrum, some other channel isn't shared). The DES model makes no such assumption, but rather implements the specific actions of a greedy allocator. By measuring the frequency of imperfect allocations (which do not meet the ideal assumptions made by the MDP model) in the simulation, we can assess the impact of this assumption on the performance predictions made by the MDP model. We predict that the frequency of these imperfect allocations is sufficiently small that its effect on throughput is within the statistical variation of the throughput predictions made by the simulator. As in the previous experiment, we use the discrete-event simulator to assess the validity of the perfect channel allocation assumption.

The third experiment is designed to assess the appropriateness of the MDP's value-optimal policy decisions. We predict that a reasonable correspondence (based on local optimality) exists between the performance predictions of the proposed MDP model and the DES model, such that value-optimal policy decisions made by the MDP correspond to optimal throughput predictions by the DES model. As true optimality is computationally impractical to test, we explicitly check for local optimality (i.e., the policy chosen by the MDP is at least a locally optimal choice as predicted by the DES model). Starting from the value-optimal policy chosen by the MDP, we ask the DES to predict performance given that policy and several "nearest neighbor" policies, with the neighborhood chosen to represent what we mean by locality.

5. EXPERIMENTAL RESULTS

In this section we describe the experiments we conducted to evaluate the hypotheses discussed above. Section 5.1 describes design details and infrastructure used to conduct our experiments, and Section 5.2 presents and discusses their results.

5.1 Experimental Setup

The MDP and DES models are configured to evaluate the models' behaviors with either a single channel or four channels of spectrum available for allocation. Each of these channels can have up to four levels of redundant use (or reuse). We describe the set up for each of these experiments, and how the evaluations take place. The MDP model is configured using a Bernoulli reward function (described in Section 3.1)[3]. All throughput predictions are made over a range of input rates that provide normalized offered load, ρ, between 0.5 and 2.5 (i.e., $0.5 \le \rho = \lambda/\mu \le 2.5$), P_{conf} ranging from 0.1 to 0.9, and $P_{env} = 0$ (the latter since P_{env} was shown in [15] to have a simple linear impact on throughput). All DES model throughput results are analyzed using the method of batch means, with 100 independent runs decomposed into 10 batches of size 10.

5.1.1 DES experiments to assess significance of message duration distribution

Our MDP model assumes exponentially distributed message durations. The DES model assumes uniformly distributed message durations. We configure the DES to test both uniform and exponential message durations and evaluate the impact. We plot the predicted throughput for both uniform and exponential message durations (using single standard deviation whiskers) for a variety of channel counts and system utilization. We call this experiment *distribution assessment*.

5.1.2 DES experiments to count and assess significance of imperfect allocations

The DES also was modified to count imperfect allocations. These were compared to the normal allocations, constructing a ratio for comparison. We modified the simulator to record the number of imperfect spectrum allocations by counting whether or not a free channel is available each time a message completes using a shared channel.

The throughput ratio (R_T) provides a normalized measure of variability in throughput that can be used to judge the impact of imperfect allocations. Defined as twice the coefficient of variation, its intent is to provide a comparison point for imperfect allocations (i.e., if the ratio of imperfect allocations to total allocations is lower than R_T, they can be considered to be infrequent enough to be within the normal stochastic variation inherent in the simulation model).

$$R_T = \frac{2 \times \textit{throughput std. dev.}}{\textit{mean throughput}}$$

The ratio of total messages transmitted relative to the number of imperfect allocations provides a measure of their significance.

$$R_I = \frac{\textit{imperfect allocations}}{\textit{total allocations}}$$

We contrast the two ratios (R_T and R_I) to evaluate the effects of imperfect allocations on the two models' throughput predictions. We call this experiment *imperfect allocations*.

5.1.3 Comparison of MDP to DES

We plot throughput predictions made by the MDP and DES models for different experimental configurations and compare trends between the two models' results. We then configure the MDP to generate a value-optimal policy for spectrum allocation. We test the local optimality of the allocations dictated by that policy by evaluating DES predicted throughput in configurations in the neighborhood of those that use the value-optimal policy. In

[3] We also considered a simple reward function based on the number of messages allocated, without considering message loss. Since the Bernoulli reward function more accurately describes semantics of FM modulation, for brevity we omit discussion of other reward functions in the rest of this paper.

these experiments, the neighborhood is defined by varying the allowed message overlap. We call these experiments *throughput evaluation*.

5.2 Experimental Results

Here, we are interested in exploring the quantitative results of the set of experiments described above. We organize the results according to the three hypotheses that we wish to evaluate:

5.2.1 Distribution Assessment Experiment

The intent of the distribution assessment experiment is to determine whether or not the mean of the message size distribution is sufficient to characterize the achievable throughput (i.e., how important is the shape of the distribution).

Figure 2 plots message throughput predicted by the DES model as a function of offered load for a pair of different circumstances:

1. $P_{conf} = 0.1$, single channel ($C = 1$), no overlap of messages ($L = 1$), and offered load ranging from 0.5 to 2.5.
2. $P_{conf} = 0.1$, four channels ($C = 4$), overlap of up to 4 messages ($L = 4$), and offered load ranging from 0.5 to 2.5.

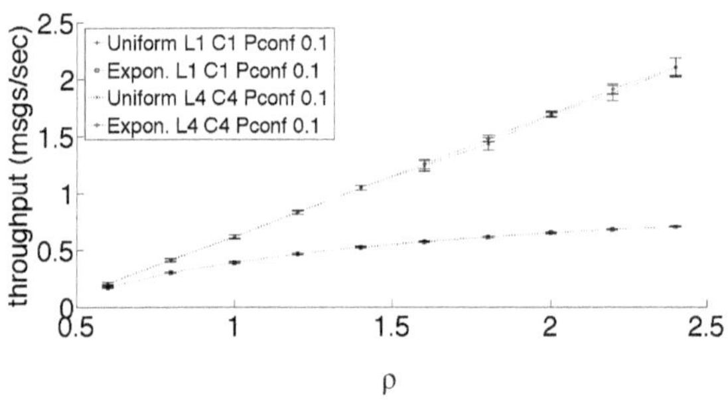

Figure 2. Throughput vs. offered load for both uniform and exponential distribution of message durations, ρ is offered load (λ/μ). Whiskers represent standard deviation.

For each of these circumstances, the simulator is configured to use both the original DES model assumption (uniformly distributed message duration) and the MDP model assumption (exponentially distributed message duration). Points represent the mean over 100 simulation executions and the whiskers represent standard deviation of 10 batches (each of size 10).

First, we observe that the throughput predictions are reasonable, with greater throughput achievable with greater capacity. As is readily apparent in the plots, the distinction in throughput between these two distribution assumptions is quite small and is well within the expected deviations due to statistical variation. This evidence thus strongly supports hypothesis 1, that "performance can be reasonably characterized by the mean of message durations and is relatively insensitive to their distribution."

To be clear, we have only truly verified the correspondence between the uniform distribution (commonly used in the RF literature and the original model assumption present in the discrete-event simulation model) and the exponential distribution (used in the Markov decision process model). Where this hypothesis might yet not be true is for extreme values of the true distribution's variance. E.g., deterministic (fixed duration) messages with zero variance or more heavy-tailed distributions with large variance. We leave this investigation for future work.

5.2.2 Imperfect Allocations Experiment

Hypothesis 2 posits insignificant performance variation due to imperfect allocations that are abstracted away in the MDP model. The imperfect allocations are recorded using the simulator to assess the significance of ignoring these occurrences. We record the occurrences when a channel is empty but allocations are yet made on already allocated channels. We examine:

1. The four channel system ($C = 4$), overlap of up to 4 messages, and offered load ranging from 0.5 to 2.5, with
2. $P_{conf} = 0.1$, 0.5, and 0.9.

We constrain the experiment to the four channel system with overlap since the other configurations cannot exhibit imperfect allocations. The 1000 independent DES simulations executed for each value of P_{conf} constitute over 500,000 allocations. The results are presented in Table 1. Recall that R_I is the ratio of imperfect allocations to total allocations and that R_T is twice the coefficient of variability in the resultant throughput predicted by the simulator.

Table 1. Frequency of imperfect allocations.

P_{conf}	R_I	R_T
0.1	0.0160	0.0156
0.5	0.0165	0.0156
0.9	0.0162	0.0156

These results indicate that only a limited number of allocations are affected by the imperfect allocations not accounted for with the MDP model (approximately equal to 2 standard deviations of the simulation output's statistical variability). As a result, the maximum impact on throughput is well within the statistical variation illustrated in Figure 2, and this evidence supports hypothesis 2. Also, the low impact of imperfect allocations implies that the greedy allocation algorithm is working quite well, i.e., essentially indistinguishable from a perfect allocator.

5.2.3 Throughput Evaluation Experiments

Hypothesis 3 examines the use of the MDP model for evaluating optimal throughput characterizations. We assess this hypothesis by examining two things: (1) throughput predictions made by both the DES and MDP models; and (2) the local optimality (as confirmed by the DES model) of value-optimal policies chosen by the MDP. The throughput predictions are from the following set of experiments:

1. $P_{conf} = 0.9$, using a single channel ($C = 1$), no overlap of messages ($L = 1$), and offered load ranging from 0.5 to 2.5 (Figure 3).
2. $P_{conf} = 0.5$, using four channels ($C = 4$), no overlap of messages ($L = 1$), and offered load ranging from 0.5 to 2.5 (Figure 4).
3. $P_{conf} = 0.1$, using four channels ($C = 4$), overlap of up to 4 messages ($L = 4$), and offered load ranging from 0.5 to 2.5 (Figure 5).

The first experiment is limited to no overlap of messages primarily because with such a large value of P_{conf}, overlapping messages do not effectively improve throughput in any event.

With only a single channel and no message overlap allowed, we expect a maximum throughput bounded above by an individual channel's capacity. The latter two experiments explore the use of additional channels and message overlap for two different values of P_{conf}. Here, we would expect to see some variation in achievable throughput between the two experiments. In each of the above experiments, we are comparing the throughput predictions of the MDP to that of the DES. To accomplish this while manually controlling the MDP policy (i.e., number of overlap levels allowed), we disable the value-optimal policy evaluation within the MDP and manually set the policy we wish to explore. This manual policy setting action transforms the Markov decision process into a traditional Markov process, for which we can determine the throughput by solving for the steady-state occupancy probabilities for each state x in the original MDP.

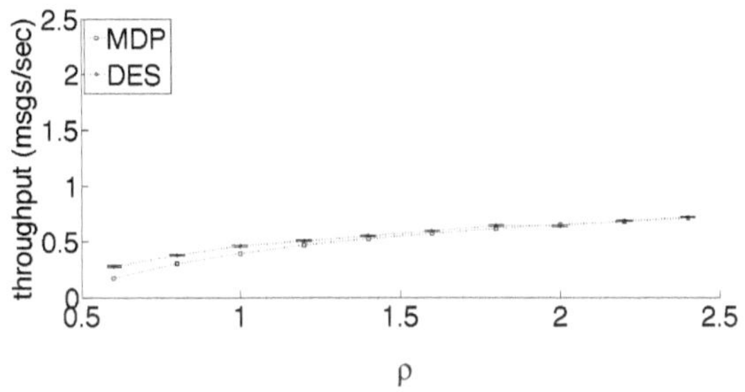

Figure 3. MDP vs. DES model throughput predictions for $P_{conf} = 0.9, C = 1, L = 1$.

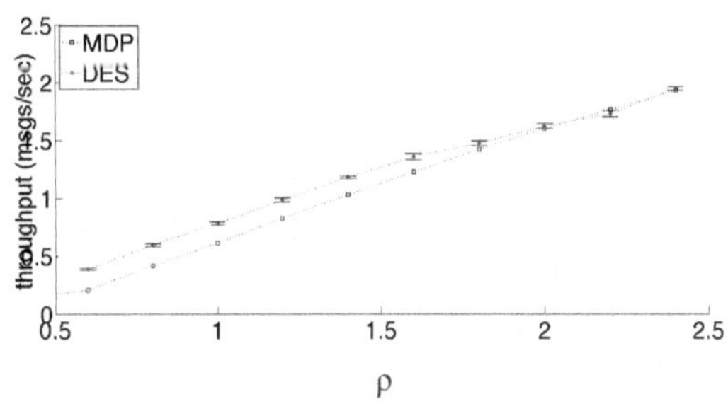

Figure 4. MDP vs. DES model throughput predictions for $P_{conf} = 0.5, C = 4, L = 1$.

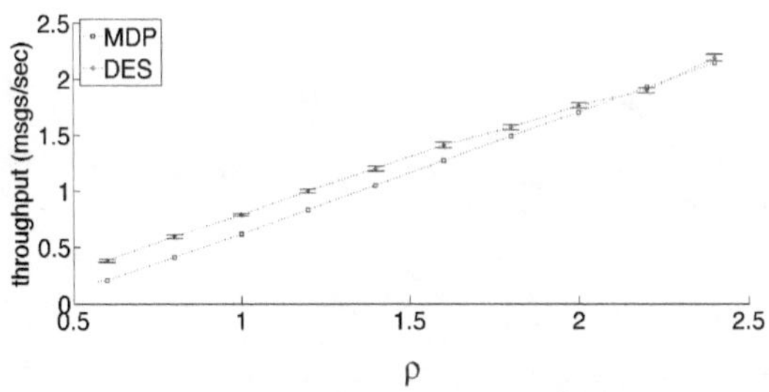

Figure 5. MDP vs. DES model throughput predictions for $P_{conf} = 0.1, C = 4, L = 4$.

As was expected, the maximum throughput achievable with only a single channel is quite limited. Achievable throughputs, however, increase as additional resources are made available.

All three plots show reasonable agreement between the throughput predictions made by the MDP model and the DES model. While the MDP model's throughput predictions are not always within one standard deviation of the DES model's mean throughput, even when they separate it is not by far. Additionally, as the offered load increases, the separation between the two models actually diminishes. Given that imperfect information is less important to an admission algorithm at low load, we are much more interested in the correspondence between the two models under high-load conditions.

After concluding that we are able to model the throughput using the MDP model, we re-enable the ability of the MDP to choose a value-optimal policy. This allows us to test the (local) optimality of the policy chosen by the MDP by using the simulator. We confirm local optimality by doing a local neighborhood search with the discrete-event simulator and assessing whether or not the policy chosen by the MDP corresponds to the local throughput maximum.

The experiment is run with $P_{conf} = 0.7$, which gives a value-optimal admission policy (provided by the MDP) of using up to 2 levels of overlap (i.e., up to 2 messages per channel, but no more). Using the simulator, we assess the throughput predictions for $L = 1$ (no overlap), $L = 2$ (value-optimal according to the MDP), and $L = 3$. The mean throughput predictions from the DES model are shown in Table 2.

Table 2. Local Optimality.

L	1	2	3
throughput	1.93	2.11	2.07

Although the separation between these throughput predictions is not very large, the throughput for $L = 2$ is clearly above that of $L = 1$ and $L = 3$. The value-optimal policy chosen by the MDP is confirmed to be locally optimal as assessed by the DES model. This provides evidence for confirming hypothesis 3.

6. CONCLUSIONS AND FUTURE WORK

This paper has assessed the use of MDP models for making management decisions for RF spectrum. We have formulated 3 distinct hypotheses, developed and conducted experiments to assess each of these hypotheses, and the empirical results all support the confirmation of the hypotheses. We therefore conclude that the use of MDPs for RF spectrum management is a reasonable (and potentially fruitful) path to explore.

The example MDP we present in this paper is suitable for admission decisions, and we have provided evidence that (for this simple case) a greedy placement algorithm is effective. In the future, we plan to expand the MDP model to incorporate additional allocation issues (e.g., explicitly including choice of modulation) and more robust channel models (e.g., to include modulation impact and/or distance measures).

7. ACKNOWLEDGMENTS

This work was supported in part by the National Science Foundation under grants CCF-0448562 and CNS-0931693, and by Object Computing, Inc.

8. REFERENCES

[1] Abundo, M., Cardellini, V., and Presti, F. L. 2011. An MDP-based Admission Control for a QoS-aware Service-oriented System. In *Proc. of IEEE 19th Int'l Workshop on Quality of Service.* (June 2011), 1-3.

[2] Akbar, I. A. and Tranter, W. H. 2007. Dynamic Spectrum Allocation in Cognitive Radio using Hidden Markov Models:

Poisson Distributed Case. In *Proc. of IEEE SoutheastCon.* (March 2007), 196-201.

[3] Anchora, L., Mezzavilla, M., Badia, L., and Zorzi. M. 2011. Simulation models for the performance evaluation of spectrum sharing techniques in OFDMA networks. In *Proc. of 14th ACM Int'l Conf. on Modeling, Analysis and Simulation of Wireless and Mobile Systems.* (2011), 249-256.

[4] Beard, J. C. and Chamberlain, R. D. 2013. Use of Simple Analytic Performance Models for Streaming Data Applications Deployed on Diverse Architectures. In *Proc. of IEEE Int'l Symp. on Performance Analysis of Systems and Software.* (April 2013), 138-139.

[5] Bethke, B., Bertuccelli, L. F., How, J. P. 2008. Experimental Demonstration of Adaptive MDP-Based Planning with Model Uncertainty. In *Proc. AIAA Guidance, Navigation and Control Conf.* (Aug. 2008).

[6] Dillinger, M., Madani, K., and Alonistioti, N. 2003. *Software Defined Radio: Architectures, Systems, and Functions.* Wiley.

[7] Djonin, D. V., Zhao, Q., and V. Krishnamurthy. 2007. Optimality and Complexity of Opportunistic Spectrum Access: A Truncated Markov Decision Process Formulation. In *Proc. of IEEE Int'l Conf. on Communications.* (June 2007), 5787-5792.

[8] Feeney, L. M. 2012. Towards trustworthy simulation of wireless MAC/PHY layers: a comparison framework. In *Proc. of 15th ACM Int'l Conf. on Modeling, Analysis and Simulation of Wireless and Mobile Systems.* (2012), 295-304.

[9] Fette, B. 2006. *Cognitive Radio Technology.* Elsevier Science & Technology Books.

[10] Geirhofer, S., Tong, L., and Sadler, B. M. 2006. A Measurement-Based Model for Dynamic Spectrum Access in WLAN Channels. In *Proc. of IEEE Military Communications Conf.* (Oct. 2006), 1-7.

[11] Grassman, W. K. 1977. Transient Solutions in Markovian Queueing Systems. *Computers & Operations Research.* 4(1):47-53 (1977).

[12] Hou, I.-H., Borkar, V., and Kumar, P.R. 2009. A Theory of QoS for Wireless. In *Proc. of IEEE Int'l Conf. on Computer Communications.* (April 2009), 486-494.

[13] Kaelbling, L. P., Littman, M., and Moore, A. 1996. Reinforcement Learning: A Survey. *Journal of Artificial Intelligence Research.* 4:237-285 (1996).

[14] Lee, B. C. and Brooks, D. 2008. Roughness of Microarchitectural Design Topologies and Its Implications for Optimization. In *Proc. of IEEE Int'l Symp. on High Performance Computer Architecture.* (2008), 240-251.

[15] Meier, J., Gill, C., and Chamberlain, R. D. 2011. Towards More Effective Spectrum Use Based on Memory Allocation Models. In *Proc. of 35th IEEE Computer Software and Applications Conf.* (July 2011), 426-435.

[16] Puterman, M. L. 1994. *Markov Decision Processes.* Wiley.

[17] Sevastyanov, B. A. 1957. An Ergodic Theorem for Markov Processes and Its Application to Telephone Systems with Refusals. *Theor. Probability Appl.* 2:104-112 (1957).

[18] Shani, G., Brafman, R. I., and Heckerman, D. 2002. An MDP-based Recommender System. In *Proc. of Conf. on Uncertainty in Artificial Intelligence.* (2002), 453-460.

[19] Staple, G. and Werbach, K. 2004. The End of Spectrum Scarcity. *IEEE Spectrum.* 41(3):48-52 (Mar. 2004).

[20] Szabó, B. and Babuška, I. 1991. *Finite Element Analysis.* Wiley.

[21] Tidwell, T., Glaubius, R., Gill, C, and Smart, W. 2010. Optimizing Expected Time Utility in Cyber-Physical Systems Schedulers. In *Proc. of 31st Real-Time Systems Symposium.* (Nov. 2010).

[22] Wang, C.-W., Wang, L. C., and Adachi, F. 2010. Modeling and Analysis for Reactive-Decision Spectrum Handoff in Cognitive Radio Networks. In *Proc. of Global Telecommunications Conf.* (Dec. 2010), 1-6.

[23] Zhao, Q. and Sadler, B. M. 2007. A Survey of Dynamic Spectrum Access. *IEEE Signal Processing Magazine.* 24(3):79-89 (May 2007).

[24] Zhao, Q., Tong, L., Swami, A., and Chen, Y. 2007. Decentralized Cognitive MAC for Opportunistic Spectrum Access in Ad Hoc Networks: A POMDP Framework. *IEEE J. on Selected Areas in Communications.* 25(3):589-600 (April 2007).

Algorithms for Channel Assignment in Mobile Wireless Networks using Temporal Coloring*

Feng Yu
City University of New York
Graduate Center
New York, NY, 10016, USA
fyu@gc.cuny.edu

Amotz Bar-Noy
City University of New York
Graduate Center
New York, NY, 10016, USA
amotz@sci.brooklyn.cuny.edu

Prithwish Basu
Raytheon BBN Technologies
Cambridge, MA, 02138, USA
pbasu@bbn.com

Ram Ramanathan
Raytheon BBN Technologies
Cambridge, MA, 02138, USA
ramanath@bbn.com

ABSTRACT

We model the problem of channel assignment in mobile networks as one of *temporal coloring* (T-coloring), that is, coloring a time-varying graph. In order to capture the impact of channel re-assignments due to mobility, we model the cost of coloring as $C + \alpha A$, where C is the total number of colors used and A is the total number of color changes, and α is a user-selectable parameter reflecting the relative penalty of channel usage and re-assignments.

Using these models, we present several novel algorithms for temporal coloring. We begin by analyzing two simple algorithms called SNAP and SMASH that take diametrically opposite positions on colors vs re-assignments, and provide theoretical results on the ranges of α in which one outperforms the other, both for arbitrary and random time-varying graphs. We then present six more algorithms that build upon each of SNAP and SMASH in different ways. Simulations on random geometric graphs with random waypoint mobility show that the relative cost of the algorithms depends upon the value of α and the transmission range, and we identify precise values at which the crossovers happen.

Categories and Subject Descriptors

C.2.1 [**Network Architecture and Design**]: Wireless Communication; G.2.2 [**Graph Theory**]: Graph algorithms

*Research was sponsored by the Army Research Laboratory and was accomplished under Cooperative Agreement Number W911NF-09-2-0053. The views and conclusions contained in this document are those of the authors and should not be interpreted as representing the official policies, either expressed or implied, of the Army Research Laboratory or the U.S. Government. The U.S. Government is authorized to reproduce and distribute reprints for Government purposes notwithstanding any copyright notation here on.

MSWiM'13, November 3–8, 2013, Barcelona, Spain.
Copyright 2013 ACM 978-1-4503-2353-6/13/11 ...$15.00.
http://dx.doi.org/10.1145/2507924.2507965.

Keywords

Channel Assignment; Mobile Wireless Networks; Graph Coloring; Random Graph; Time Varying Graph

1. INTRODUCTION

The assignment of *channels* to communicating nodes is a key part of contention-free medium access in a wireless network. Depending upon the access method, the "channel" could be time slot [19], code [11] or frequency [9]. The problem also arises in multi-channel multi-radio cognitive networks where nodes opportunistically use a subset of a large number of unused frequencies [21].

Graph coloring is a natural model for channel assignment [10,15, 19]. It can capture several access methods such as TDMA, FDMA and CDMA in a unified way [18]. In this formulation, the vertices in the graph represent nodes in a multi-hop network, edges represent links, and colors represent channels assigned to nodes. The coloring of the graph is typically done using constraints that reflect the application context. For example, for conflict-free slot assignment in TDMA one seeks to color the graphs using a minimum number of colors such that vertices within two hops (i.e., *distance-2*) of each other receive different colors, which in turn ensures that transmissions in two slots never collide.

Most of the work thus far on graph coloring has been on *static* graphs. This does not capture networks where due to mobility or other link fluctuations, the network topology is varying over time. Applying static graph coloring to successive graph "snapshots" does not capture properties that are valid *over time*, for instance, a coloring that is conflict-free for t seconds in future. Further, the mismatch between the model (static graph) and the reality (mobile networks) is far from ideal.

In this paper, we use a model that inherently captures dynamism, and hence mobility. Specifically, we model a network as a *time-varying graph* or *temporal graph* (*T-graph*). A T-graph is more than just a sequence of snapshots – it is a structure in and of itself that is manipulable *as a whole*, and for which properties can be defined *across time*. For example, a "valid coloring" property can now be attributed to (an entire) temporal graph, e.g., a contiguous sub-sequence T-graph. One can also aggregate snapshots between arbitrary points in time to get new T-graphs, as detailed later. Figure 1 illustrates a time-varying graph with a conflict-free *distance-1* time-varying color assignment.

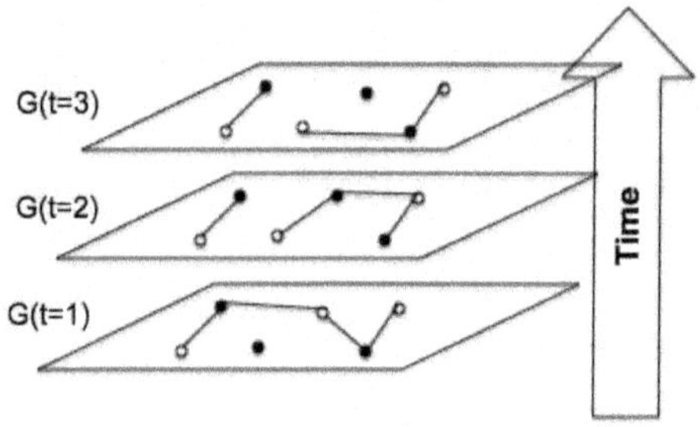

Figure 1: Temporal Graphlets for t = 1,2,3, and a conflict-free temporal coloring.

In static networks (graphs), the minimization criterion is typically just the number of channels (colors) used. In a mobile network (temporal graph), however, there are two parameters of interest: the total number of colors used, and the number of times a node has to be *re-assigned* a color due to conflicts caused by mobility. In most real-life networks, a re-assignment of time slot or frequency requires the exchange of control packets which reduces data capacity. More crucially, it may cause packet drops since the distributed algorithms that implement a re-assignment of the channel take time to converge. Note that even the addition of a single edge can cause a network-wide ripple effect of re-coloring.

In general, the relative "cost" of total colors used and the effect of re-coloring depends on the network system and its protocols. Accordingly, we use a generalized cost model where the cost of a dynamic coloring of a temporal graph is given by $C + \alpha.A$ where C is the total number of colors used, A is the number of re-assignments over a period of time T and α is a user-defined parameter that "weights" the penalty of re-assignment relative to that of the total number of colors. For example, in a cognitive radio network where spectrum holes are plentiful, α would be smaller than in a TDMA network where slots are precious. In Figure 1, for example, $C = 2, A = 2$.

We present several novel algorithms for coloring T-graphs (we call this T-coloring). We begin by taking two simple baseline algorithms that take extreme positions on the optimization function: SNAP, which colors each snapshot independently, and thus does not care about re-assignments at all; and SMASH, which takes the entire T-graph, "smashes" it into a single graph by taking the union of all edges, colors this graph, and uses the colors for the entire duration $[1, T]$. Thus, SMASH never re-assigns but makes little attempt to minimize total colors used. We then present six more sophisticated algorithms that enhance each of SNAP and SMASH in various ways, for example, by incrementally coloring or partially smashing. We evaluate the performance of several T-coloring algorithms using random geometric graph (RGG) and random waypoint mobility (RWP) models.

Our main contributions are as follows:

Temporal coloring and cost model. We present a new coloring framework that captures mobility inherently. Our cost model $C + \alpha A$ captures the relative impact of channel re-assignments and channels used in a user-selectable manner. Together, our framework better reflects real-world considerations.

Temporal coloring algorithms and analysis. We present a total of eight algorithms that cover a spectrum of strategies, including a hybrid one. We prove a number of properties on the relative performance of SNAP and SMASH. For example, we show that if $\alpha > 1$ SMASH is always better than SNAP, and if $\alpha = 0$ SNAP is never worse than SMASH, and for random graphs SNAP outperforms SMASH w.h.p. if $\alpha \leq \frac{1}{\log \frac{1}{1-p} n}$ for distance-1 coloring (we also give an analogous result for distance-2 coloring). We also derive a network dynamics based threshold for a hybrid algorithm, based on the RGG-RWP model, that we then use for switching between two algorithms.

Insights from experiments. We present several experiments comparing the algorithms and identify "pivot" points where pairs or triplets of algorithms reverse their relative performance. While no single algorithm is superior over the entire range of α, our work provides insights to practitioners to choose the best algorithm for a given scenario.

Four of our eight algorithms require the entire T-graph in advance and four do not. The former captures mobility or dynamism that are pre-defined (e.g. networks of aircraft or underwater nodes with pre-defined trajectories, scheduled sleep/wake sensor networks) or can be reasonably predicted somewhat into the future [24]. It is also applicable to dynamic job scheduling modeled as a coloring problem [1]. However, for simplicity and clarity, we assume in the description and in the experimental evaluation that all algorithms have the same input, namely the entire T-graph.

This paper follows the so-called "protocol model" for interference vice the SINR-based "physical model" [8]. While we recognize that the physical model is a better reflection of radio characteristics, our focus is on temporal aspects and a novel cost model. These are first better investigated in the simpler protocol model, with physical model extensions a topic for future work. Further, recent work [23] has shown that one can narrow the gap between the two models by appropriately setting the interference range.

Finally, while we present our algorithms as using the entire graph information (i.e., as a centralized algorithm), four of our algorithms work in a way that only uses local information at each step, and can be implemented as a distributed algorithm along the lines of [14, 27]. That is, the same techniques can be applied per (smashed) snapshot to make a distributed version of the proposed algorithms.

The rest of the paper is organized as follows. After discussing relevant background work in the next section, we provide in section 3 definitions of temporal graph and coloring. In section 4 we provide theoretical results for SNAP and SMASH. Section 5 describes six more algorithms, and section 6 compares the performance of algorithms using simulation experiments.

2. RELATED WORK

Prior work related to this paper can be broadly classified along two lines: channel assignment using a static coloring model, and recent work on time-varying graphs.

Channel assignment in multi hop wireless networks using coloring has been studied in various contexts such as FDMA [9], TDMA [5, 19] and CDMA [11]. A framework that unifies the above coloring problems is presented in [18] along with an algorithm. Most variants are NP-complete, and complexity issues have been discussed in [2]. Distributed coloring algorithms are the subject of [17, 20], while an incremental coloring algorithm is given in [15].

Graph-theoretic models of mobile or dynamic networks have been considered in [7, 12, 22, 25]. Each uses a different way of representing the time domain – labels are attached to edges in [7], while temporal reachability graphs (TVGs) are proposed in [25]. The evolution of random graphs [4] has been studied in [6].

Our work is unique in that it is the first that considers the coloring problem in a temporal graph setting with a cost model that incorporates re-assignments of colors. In achieving our advances, we have leveraged considerably from previous work, in particular, that on greedy coloring and incremental coloring.

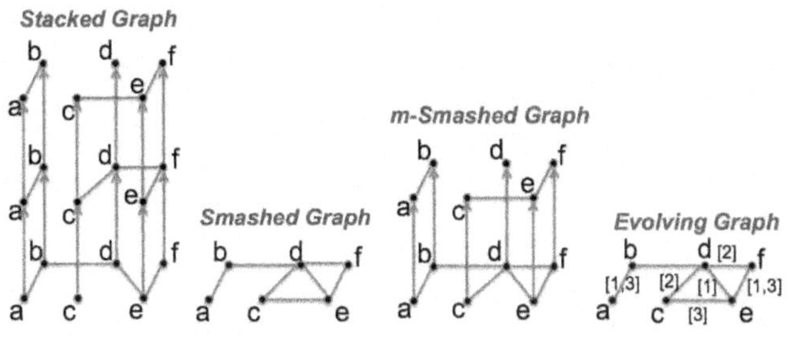

Figure 2: Various representations of temporal graphlets for the TGS in Fig. 1. A stacked graph is constructed by drawing directed edges in the direction of time between successive temporal graphlets in a TGS; a smashed graph is a "collapsed" version of the stacked graph. Alternatively, it is union of the graphlets. Both smashed and m-smashed graphs are "lossy" representations.

3. PRELIMINARIES

3.1 Temporal Graph

Assume slotted time starting at time 0. Slot $t > 0$ starts just after time $t-1$ and ends at time t. For $0 \leq T_1 \leq T_2$, a *Temporal Graphlet Sequence* (TGS) is defined as

$$TGS(T_1, T_2) = \{G(t) = (V(t), E(t))\}, T_1 \leq t \leq T_2$$

This model attempts to capture its space-time trajectory (see Figure 1). Each $G(t)$ is referred to as a *temporal graphlet*, a *graphlet*, or a *snapshot*. Alternate notations that we use, depending on the emphasis, include $G(T_1, T_2)$, $G[1, T]$ (shifting the frame of reference maintains properties), $G[T]$ (reference shifting is implied).

A *temporal graph*, called T-graph, is a single-graph representation of the TGS. Such representations include the *stacked graph (StG)*, the *smashed graph (SmG)* and its generalization the *m-smashed graph (m-SmG)*, and the *evolving graph* as shown in Figure 2. Formally,

DEFINITION 1. *Given a TGS $G[1, T]$, the* stacked graph (StG) *of $G[1, T]$ is $StG = (V_S, E_S)$, where $V_S = \cup_t V(t)$, $E_S = \cup_t E(t) \cup E_C$ where $E_C = \cup_{t,i}(u_i(t), u_i(t+1))$.*

DEFINITION 2. *Given a TGS $G[1, T]$, the* smashed graph (SmG) *of $G[1, T]$ is $SmG = (V_M, E_M)$, where each sequence of $u(t), u(t+1), \ldots$ is replaced by a single vertex $u \in V_M$, and $E_M = \cup_t E(t)$ with endpoints of edges mapped to the replaced vertices in V_M.*

DEFINITION 3. *Given a TGS $G[1, T]$, the* m-smashed graph (m-SmG) *of $G[1, T]$ is m-$SmG = (V_M, E_M)$, where the smashing operation is not performed on the entire $G[1, T]$ but on each of $G[1, m], G[m+1, 2m], G[2m+1, 3m], \ldots$ instead.*

We note that the "evolving graph" representation proposed in [7] which labels edges with the times at which they are active is equivalent to the stacked graph[1] but an evolving graph is not a traditional graph. Hence reducing to an evolving graph does not allow us to easily leverage existing algorithms or code.

3.2 Temporal Coloring

Temporal coloring (T-coloring) is the process/task of coloring a given temporal graph in a conflict free manner. Specifically, it is a vertex coloring problem with constraint *distance-1* and *distance-2* on a time varying graph such that these constraints are satisfied for every snapshot in the T-graph. The *distance-1* constraint means that every pair of adjacent nodes must receive different colors; the *distance-2* constraint means that every pair of nodes with shortest distance less than or equal to 2 must receive different colors.

[1]And deleting the labels yields a smashed graph.

DEFINITION 4. *Given a coloring constraint, a T-Coloring is a labeling function $C : [1, T] \times V \rightarrow N$ of the vertices of a temporal graph $G[1, T]$ such that $C(t, v)$ satisfies the coloring constraint for each $t \in [1, T]$ and[2] $v \in V$.*

For example, a T-Coloring with the *dist-2* constraint is a labeling function $C : T \times V \rightarrow N$ such that for any $t \in [1, T]$ and $u, v \in V$, if $dist(u, v) \leq 2$, then $C(t, u) \neq C(t, v)$.

In T-Coloring, we count the total number of colors used (denoted by C) and the total number of times any vertex changes its color between graphlets (denoted by A). The total number of colors C is the maximum label used if the positive integers $1, 2, \ldots$ are the labels. Formally,

DEFINITION 5. *Given a T-graph $G[T_1, T_2]$, and a coloring algorithm, graphlet G_i has its color set $C(G_i) = \{c_i(v_j) | v_j \in V(G)\}$, $c_i \in \mathbb{Z}^+$. Then the total number of color used is $C = max(c_i(v_j))$, and the total number of times a color is changed is*

$$A = \sum_{i=T_1}^{T_2-1} \sum_{v_j \in V(G)} c_i(v_j) \neq c_{i+1}(v_j) \,.$$

As mentioned in section 1, practical applications require minimizing both the number of colors and the number of color reassignments. Accordingly, we define a simple and natural cost function to evaluate the quality of a T-coloring.

DEFINITION 6. *The* cost *of a T-coloring X is given by $COST(X) = C(X) + \alpha \cdot A(X)$ where $\alpha \geq 0$ is a user defined parameter, and C and A are, respectively, the total number of colors used and the total number of re-assignments as defined above.*

3.3 Greedy Static Coloring

Our temporal coloring algorithms use as a key component a coloring of a graphlet. Coloring a graph is NP-hard to even approximate within a constant factor for both distance-1 and distance-2 constraints [13, 26]. While our temporal coloring algorithms are agnostic to the particular choice of static coloring method, including exponential-time optimal, we use a greedy heuristic from [18] called UxDMA with Progressive Minimum Neighbor First (we call it simply PMNF) ordering. Our implementation of PMNF has a running time of $O(|V||E|)$. However, one may replace PMNF with any other algorithm without impact on fundamental contributions, and therefore we shall refer to the procedure *static-coloring*.

4. BASELINE ALGORITHMS: SNAP AND SMASH

The set of possible T-coloring algorithms for the cost function $COST = C + \alpha A$ can be thought of as lying along a spectrum that balances the number of colors and number of re-assignments in different ways. We begin by describing and theoretically analyzing two simple and naive algorithms at the two ends of that spectrum. These algorithms are oblivious to the value of α.

[2]We note that color conflicts can occur across the directed "time" edges. T-coloring is not the same as (traditional) coloring of a T-graph.

Algorithm SNAP colors every snapshot $G[T_i]$ in the stacked graph independently and afresh using a static coloring algorithm (e.g. PMNF discussed in section 3.3). In this section, SNAP "ignores" the coloring of $G[T_{i-1}]$ when it colors $G[T_i]$. In later sections, we show that a greedy version of SNAP could do better if, for example, it considers the vertices in the same order for all the T graphlets.

Algorithm 1 SNAP for T-Coloring

```
Input: T-Graph G[1,T], constraint ∈ {dist-1,dist-2}
Output: Color assignment of each graphlet: Color[1,T]
for i from 1 to T do
    Color(i)=static-color(G_i, constraint)
end for
return Color[1,T]
```

Algorithm SMASH colors the smashed graph (refer definition in section 3.1) and the colors stay the same for all T graphlets. In other words, we simply run the static coloring algorithm on $SmG(G)$ with, say, C colors. We observe that $A = 0$ and $Cost = C$. The main drawback of SMASH is that it smashes all the T graphs, thus creating a graph whose chromatic number is too high. In later sections, we show that partial smashing could help reduce the chromatic numbers at the cost of having some color changes.

Algorithm 2 SMASH for T-Coloring

```
Input: T-Graph G[1,T], constraint ∈ {dist-1,dist-2}
Output: Color assignment: Color (same for all graphlets)
G = SmG(G[1,t]))
Color=static-color(G, constraint)
return Color
```

For the simple implementation of PMNF that was sufficient for our experiments, the worst-case running time of SNAP is $O(|V|^3T)$ and that of SMASH is $O(|V|^3+|V|^2T)$. Thus, SMASH is superior in running time.

We now consider the relative theoretical performance of SMASH and SNAP with respect to α, first with a worst-case viewpoint, then for Erdos-Renyi random graphs. First, we introduce some additional notation for *dist-2* coloring. Let G^2 denote the *dist-2* graphlet that results from adding an edge between any two nodes in G that are within two hops away from each other. Also, let $SmG(G^2)$ denote the smashed *dist-2* T-Graph $= SMASH(G_1^2, \ldots, G_T^2)$ and $SmG^2(G)$ denote the *dist-2* smashed T-Graph $= (SMASH(G_1, \ldots, G_T))^2$. It is easy to show that $SmG(G^2)$ is a subgraph of $SmG^2(G)$.

4.1 Properties of SNAP and SMASH

For clarity, consider an optimal static coloring usage for SMASH and SNAP. However, the following discussion is valid for any "reasonable" greedy alternatives as well.

For the rest of this section, we assume the *dist-1* constraint, unless otherwise specified. The next two propositions give thresholds for which one strategy outperforms the other for any T-graph.

PROPOSITION 1. *When $\alpha > 1$, SMASH is always better than SNAP.*

PROOF. Suppose we color the T-graph with a SNAP algorithm X, then we could define a new coloring: each time a vertex changes its color between G_i and G_{i+1}, we color this vertex with a new unique color in $G_1 \ldots G_{i+1}$. At the end of this process, the coloring is a legal T-coloring of the smashed graph that uses $C = C(X) + A(X)$ colors. Obviously, $C \geq C(SMASH)$, therefore $C(SMASH) \leq C(X) + A(X) < C(X) + \alpha A(X)$ since $\alpha > 1$. □

We remark that the above proposition is not true for dist-2 T-coloring on the original T-graph $(G_1, G_2, \ldots, G_T)$. However, it is true if both SMASH and SNAP were operating in dist-1 mode on the T-graph $(G_1^2, \ldots, G_T^2)$.

PROPOSITION 2. *When $\alpha = 0$, SNAP is at least as good as SMASH.*

PROOF. When $\alpha = 0$, there is no penalty for changing colors and so cost of SNAP is the chromatic number under the optimal static coloring assumption. The chromatic number is monotonic in the sense that its value for a graph G is at least its value for any sub-graph of G. Therefore, $C(G_i) \leq C(G)$. Thus, the cost of SNAP is no larger than the cost of SMASH. □

Given the above, a natural question is: in the intermediate values of $0 < \alpha < 1$, which one is better? In particular, as α is increased above 0, at what point does SNAP start to be worse than SMASH? We show that for an arbitrary sequence of graphlets there is no such threshold. However, for random graphlets such a threshold exists.

For the next two propositions we assume a "reasonable" implementation of SNAP that does not try hard to avoid changes but also does not try to generate too many changes.

PROPOSITION 3. *For any $\alpha < 1$, there exists a T-graph for which SNAP is better than SMASH.*

PROOF. Let $n = 3$ and call the vertices A, B, C. The edges $E = \{(A, B), (A, C)\}$ exist in G_1 while $E = \{(A, B), (B, C)\}$ for $G_2, \ldots, G_T$. The cost of SMASH is 3 since SMASH colors the smashed graph with 3 colors. A "reasonable" SNAP uses only 2 colors and changes the color of C once for a total cost less than 3. □

Note, that any greedy SNAP would use at most 2 colors and at most 3 changes. For an "adversarial" implementation of SNAP, the above proposition holds for $\alpha < 1/3$.

PROPOSITION 4. *For any $\alpha > 0$, there exists a T-graph for which SMASH is better than SNAP.*

PROOF. Let $n = 4$ and call the vertices A, B, C, D. The edges $E = \{(A, B), (C, D)\}$ exist in G_1. A greedy or an optimal SNAP will color G_1 with 2 colors. Without loss of generality, assume that A and C are colored with the color 1. Then $E = \{(A, B), (A, C), (C, D)\}$ for $G_2, \ldots, G_T$. A greedy or an optimal SNAP will color $G_2, \ldots, G_T$ with 2 colors but will have to change the color of at least 2 vertices. SMASH on the other hand will color the smashed graph with 2 colors in a way that is good for G_1 as well. Since $\alpha > 0$, the cost of SNAP is larger than the cost of SMASH for this T-graph. □

Note that in the above example SNAP is paying the cost of not taking into account the future state of graphlets that SMASH is naturally able to do. Also note that G_2 is defined based on the particular implementation of SNAP.

4.2 Analysis of T-coloring in Random T-graphs

In this section, we study properties of T-coloring in the simplest model of random T-graphs – each graphlet is an independently generated graph obeying the Erdos-Renyi random graph model $ER(n, p)$, in which, each of the possible $\binom{n}{2}$ edges exists with an independent probability p. We study the scaling of the number of colors necessary to color such graphs under both *dist-1* and *dist-2* constraints as a function of n and p.

We note that theoretical results for coloring in RGGs, the more relevant model for MANETs, have been more elusive even for static graphs, with the exception of the recent results by McDiarmid [16]. A theoretical study of T-coloring of RGGs is a topic of future work for us.

4.2.1 Erdos-Renyi graphlets: dist-1 constraints

THEOREM 5 (BOLLOBAS [3]). *Let χ_g denote the chromatic number under the greedy coloring algorithm, $G_{n,p}$ is an $ER(n,p)$ graph. Then $\chi_g(G_{n,p}) = \frac{n}{\log_{\frac{1}{1-p}} n}$, almost surely for any greedy algorithm and any vertex ordering.*

LEMMA 1. *$C_{SMASH} = \chi_g(G_{n,p'}) = T * \frac{n}{\log_{\frac{1}{1-p}} n}$, where $p' = 1 - (1-p)^T$.*

PROOF. The smashed graph is $ER(n,p')$ where $p' = 1-(1-p)^T$. Applying Bollobas's theorem, we have: $C_{SMASH} = \chi_g(G_{n,p'}) = \frac{n}{\log_{\frac{1}{1-p'}} n} = \frac{n}{\log_{\frac{1}{1-(1-(1-p)^T)}} n} = T * \frac{n}{\log_{\frac{1}{1-p}} n}$. The last equality is true since $\log_{x^T} n = (1/T)\log_x n$. □

LEMMA 2. *Let A_0 denote the expected number of color changes between two consecutive $ER(n,p)$ graphlets. Then $COST_{SNAP} = C_{SNAP} + \alpha A_{SNAP} = \frac{n}{\log_{\frac{1}{1-p}} n} + \alpha(T-1)A_0$.*

PROOF. We rely on the assumption that T is fixed while n tends to infinity, therefore, because of the concentration property in Bollabas' theorem mentioned above, $C_{SNAP} = \max\{C_1, \ldots, C_T\} = \frac{n}{\log_{\frac{1}{1-p}} n}$. □

The next corollary follows from the above two lemmas.

COROLLARY 6. *Let $C_0 = \frac{n}{\log_{\frac{1}{1-p}} n}$. Then with high probability SNAP outperforms SMASH iff $\alpha < \frac{C_0}{A_0}$.*

We do not know how to bound A_0 accurately. Obviously n is an upper bound on A_0. Moreover, our simulations show that A_0 is *almost surely* close to n. Applying this upper bound to the above corollary, we have the following theorem.

THEOREM 7. *For random Erdos-Renyi T-graphs, SNAP outperforms SMASH w.h.p. if $\alpha \le \frac{1}{\log_{\frac{1}{1-p}} n}$.*

We conjecture that A_0 is close to n and hence the above theorem could be modified to be an "iff" theorem.

4.2.2 Erdos-Renyi graphlets: dist-2 constraints

We now show how Bollobas' theorem mentioned in Section 4.2.1 could be applied under *dist-2* constraints as well. Some of the proofs have been omitted due to paucity of space. First, we give some basic results on *dist-2* coloring of single random graphlets and subsequently apply them to T-graphs.

LEMMA 3. *The expected number of two hop neighbors in an Erdos-Renyi random graph $G(n,p)$ is $\mathbb{E}[N_u^{(2)}] = (n-1)((1-p)(1-(1-p^2)^{n-2}))$.*

LEMMA 4. *The expected number of nodes inside the two hop neighborhood in an Erdos-Renyi random graph $G(n,p)$ is $(n-1)(1-(1-p)(1-p^2)^{n-2})$.*

PROOF. This follows from Lemma 3, the fact that $\mathbb{E}[N_u^{(1)}] = (n-1)p$, and linearity of expectation. □

THEOREM 8. *Let $\chi_g^{(2)}(G_{n,p})$ be the number of colors used by the greedy coloring algorithm under dist-2 constraints. Then, $\chi_g^{(2)}(G_{n,p}) \approx \chi_g(G_{n,p}) + \frac{n(n-2)}{\log_{\frac{1}{1-p^2}} n}$.*

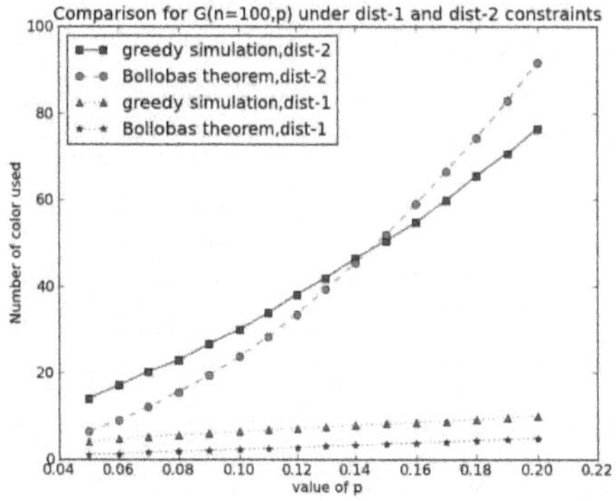

Figure 3: *dist-1* and *dist-2* coloring of Erdos-Renyi Graphs $G(n = 100, p)$. For $p \in [0.05, 0.2]$, $G(n = 100, p)$ is neither fragmented, nor is it a complete graph.

PROOF. We use Lemma 4 to create an equivalent (approximate) Erdos-Renyi graph $G(n,q)$, where $q = 1-(1-p)(1-p^2)^{n-2}$ denotes the probability of forming an edge between any node u and a node *within* the two hop neighborhood of u in $G(n,p)$. Then, we plug in this value of q into Theorem 5 to get the above estimate of $\chi_g^{(2)}(G_{n,p})$. □

Even though Bollobas' theorem is an asymptotic result, i.e., valid for large enough n for a certain fixed value of p, Figure 3 shows that the performance of a greedy T-coloring algorithm can be reasonably predicted by applying Bollobas' theorem under not only *dist-1* constraints but also *dist-2* constraints for a range of p values for which the underlying graph has a non-trivial multi-hop structure.

Assuming each graphlet in T-graph $(G_1, \ldots, G_T)$ is an Erdos-Renyi graph $G = ER(n,p)$, we have $G^2 = ER(n,q)$, where from the proof of Theorem 8 we could say approximately $q = 1-(1-p)(1-p^2)^{n-2}$.

OBSERVATION 9. *For a T-graph $G[1,T]$, $SmG(G) = ER(n, p_T)$, where $p_T = 1-(1-p)^T$; $SmG(G^2) = ER(n, q_T^1)$, where $q_T^1 = 1-(1-q)^T$; and $SmG^2(G) = ER(n, q_T^2)$, where $q_T^2 = 1-(1-p_T)(1-p_T^2)^{n-2}$.*

OBSERVATION 10. *Under* dist-2 *T-coloring, let $COST(SNAP) = C_0 + \alpha(T-1)A_0$. Then $C_0 = \chi_g(G^2) = \frac{n}{\log_{\frac{1}{1-q}} n}$ and $A_0 \le n$.*

LEMMA 5. *In dist-2 model, for any T-Graph $(G_1, \ldots, G_T)$, $\chi_g(SmG(G^2)) \le \chi_g(SmG^2(G))$.*

THEOREM 11. *In random Erdos-Renyi T-graphs, SNAP outperforms SMASH w.h.p. under dist-2 constraints if $\alpha \le \frac{1}{\log_{\frac{1}{(1-p)(1-p^2)^{n-2}}} n}$.*

PROOF. We find a lower bound for $COST(SMASH)$.

$$\begin{aligned} COST(SMASH) &= \chi_g(SmG^2(G)) \ge \chi_g(SmG(G^2)) \\ &= \frac{n}{\log_{\frac{1}{1-q_T^1}} n} = T\,\chi_g(G^2) = T\,C_0 \end{aligned}$$

Since $A_0 \le n$, so when $\alpha = \frac{1}{\log_{\frac{1}{(1-p)(1-p^2)^{n-2}}} n}$, from Obs. 10 we have $\alpha = \frac{1}{\log_{\frac{1}{1-q}} n} \le \frac{C_0}{A_0}$; $COST(SNAP) = C_0 + \alpha\,(T-1)\,A_0 \le T\,C_0 \le COST(SMASH)$. □

5. ENHANCED ALGORITHMS

In this section, we describe algorithms that seek to improve on the simple baseline algorithms from Section 4. We present two broad classes of algorithms. The first class seeks to enhance SNAP by reducing the number of re-assignments, for instance, by avoiding the independency in the coloring of successive graphlets. The second class seeks to enhance SMASH by alleviating the creation of very dense graphs that necessitates the high number of colors. In the following subsections we describe two algorithms for the first class and four for the second class.

5.1 Progressive SNAP (P-SNAP)

The main drawback of the PMNF greedy algorithm in coloring the graphlets is that the coloring might need many re-assignments even if there is little change between two consecutive graphlets. The idea behind the Progressive SNAP algorithm is to use *one* labeling (the PMNF for G_1) for all the graphlets. Then, if the graphlets evolve slowly, the coloring will remain the same for most of the vertices in the graph. Our experimental results, detailed later, bear this out.

Algorithm 3 Progressive SNAP for T-Coloring

Input: T-Graph $G[1,T]$, constraint $\in$ {dist-1,dist-2}
Output: Color assignment for each graphlet: $Color[1,T]$

label=PMNF-labeling(G_1)
for i from 1 to T **do**
  Color(i)=static-color(G_i,label,constraint)
end for
return Color$[1,T]$

5.2 Incremental (INC)

The Progressive SNAP algorithm ignores the actual changes between consecutive graphlets with the hope that a fixed global labeling would reduce the number of reassignments. The INC algorithm on the other hand adopts a very local approach. It tries to minimize the number of reassignments for each graphlet. That is, it re-colors only the vertices whose coloring from the previous graphlet is illegal. In particular, when an edge appears between two vertices and causes a color conflict, INC changes the color of each of the two vertices using the "first-fit" natural strategy. When an edge disappears, INC does not try to reduce the number of colors because it tries to avoid reassignments. This process repeats itself until all conflicts due to new edges are resolved.

The INC algorithm is roughly similar to the one in [15], with some key differences – we do not re-color on edge deletions, we don't attempt to perform "maintenance" of the coloring (both to avoid re-assignments). Also, in the [15] model, fixed position nodes appear and disappear, while in our model edges appear and disappear as a result of node mobility.

Intuitively, this strategy seems to be the best given our cost function. However, as is the case with the greedy approach, there are cases in which both baseline algorithms SNAP and SMASH outperform INC. An example is illustrated in Figure 4.

5.3 m-SMASH

Unlike the previous two strategies which were based on SNAP, the m-SMASH strategy is based on SMASH. The main drawback of SMASH is that the smashed graph might require too many colors and having no reassignments would not help reducing the COST. m-SMASH proposes a simple solution – it smashes intervals of m consecutive graphlets and generates a dynamic graph with about T/m graphlets. These graphlets are then colored using a SNAP strategy.

Algorithm 4 INC for T-Coloring

Input: T-Graph $G[1,T]$, constraint $\in$ {dist-2,dist-2}
Output: Color assignment of each graphlet: $Color[1,T]$

Color(1)=static-color($G_1, constraint$)
for i from 2 to T **do**
  $G_{i-1} = (V, E), G_i = (V', E')$
  temporal $G = G_{i-1}, Color(G) = Color(i-1)$
  while $\exists e \in E \backslash E'$ or$\exists e \in E' \backslash E$ **do**
    if $e \notin E, e \in E'$ **then**
      add edge e into G
      if coloring collision happened on G **then**
        let $e = e(u, v)$, change color of u, v in G with the first feasible color satisfying constraint.
      end if
    else delete e from G
    end if
  end while
  $Color(i) \leftarrow Color(G)$
end for
return Color$[1,T]$

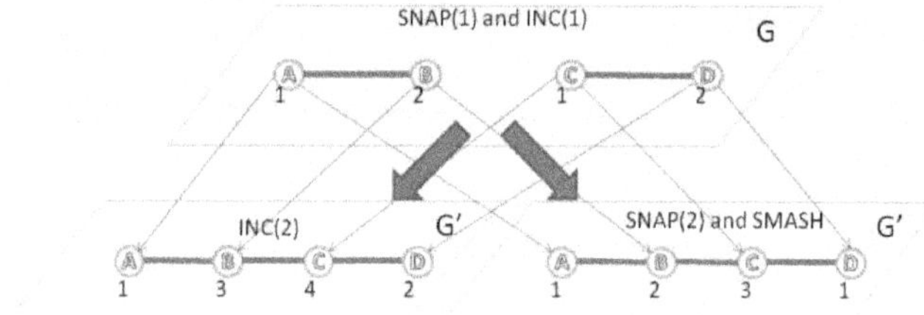

Figure 4: An example of when INC does worse than SNAP & SMASH: SNAP and INC will both color the first graphlet($2K_2$) in color sequence $(1,2,1,2)$. While INC will color the second graphlet (L_4) in color sequence $(1,3,4,2)$, SNAP will color this graphlet in color sequence $(1,2,3,1)$. SMASH will color the smashed graph of these two graphlet in color sequence $(1,2,3,1)$ too. Thus, in this case, INC uses 4 colors and number of color changes is 2; SNAP uses 3 colors and number of color changes is 1; SMASH only uses 3 colors. Therefore, for any $\alpha \geq 0$, the cost of INC is strictly greater than both INC and SMASH.

Algorithm 5 m-SMASH

Input: T-Graph $G[1,T]$, integer $m(< T)$, constraint $\in$ {dist-1,dist-2}
Output: color assignment of each graphlet: $Color[1,T]$

for i from 1 to T **do**
  if $m \backslash i$ or $i = T$ **then**
    Coloring each graphlet in $G[i - \lfloor \frac{i}{m} \rfloor + 1, i]$ with static-color($SmG(G[i - \lfloor \frac{i}{m} \rfloor + 1, i])$, constraint)
  end if
end for
return Color[1,T]

OBSERVATION 12. *For T-coloring a T-graph$G[1,T]$, m-SMASH is equivalent to SNAP when $m = 1$ and to SMASH when $m = T$.*

Recall that for small $\alpha \to 0$, SNAP outperforms SMASH almost everywhere; and for $\alpha \to 1$, SMASH outperforms SNAP almost surely. For a given α, a natural problem is to find the best value for m such that m-SMASH would outperform both SNAP and SMASH. Denote such a value by $m(\alpha)$.

OBSERVATION 13. *Under dist-1 constraints, $m(0) = 1$, and $m(1) = T$.*

5.4 Big-Change-SMASH (BC-SMASH)

The m-SMASHing algorithm is easy to implement. However, it ignores actual changes between consecutive graphlets. The BC-SMASH examines the T-graph snapshot by snapshot, and then determines the intervals to be smashed. Intuitively, when graphlets evolve slowly, the coloring set for each graphlets will be similar to each other, and similar to the coloring set for the smashed graph of these graphlets. Based on this intuition, BC-SMASH looks for two adjacent graphlets that are very different. The steps are shown in Algorithm 6.

Algorithm 6 Big-Change-SMASH

```
Input: T-Graph G[1,T], integer K(≤ T), constraint ∈ {dist-2, dist-2}
Output: color assignment of each graphlet: Color[1,T]
for i from 1 to T-1 do
    d_i ← the difference between G_i and G_{i+1}
end for
Sorting d_1, ···, d_{T-1}, let d_{p_1}, ···, d_{p_{K-1}} be the largest K-1 ones
    (assuming 0 = p_0 < p_1 < ... < p_{K-1} < p_K = T)
for i from 0 to K-1 do
    Color each graphlet in G[p_i + 1, p_{i+1}] with static-
    color(SmG(p_i + 1, p_{i+1}), constraint)
end for
return Color[1,T]
```

5.5 Accumulated-Error-SMASH

The main drawback of the Big-Change-SMASH algorithm is that the sum of many small numbers could be very large. In many cases, the BC-SMASH algorithm smashes large intervals in which consecutive graphlets are similar but the smashed graph representing this interval requires too many colors. The Accumulated-Error-SMASH algorithm (Algorithm 7) is a more sophisticated approach that finds K intervals each with about the same number of changes between its boundary graphlets. The total complexity of Algorithm 7 is $O(Kn^2)$.

Algorithm 7 Accumulated-Error-SMASH

```
Input: T-Graph G[1,T], integer K(≤ T), constraint ∈ {dist-1 dist-2}
Output: color assignment of each graphlet: Color[1,T]
for i from 1 to T-1 do
    d_i ← the difference between G_i and G_{i+1}
end for
By dynamic programming find partitioning points p_i, such that
    0 = p_0 < p_1 < p_2, ... < p_K = T for objective function
    min_{p_1,...,p_K}(max_i(Σ_{j=p_{i-1}+1}^{p_i} d_j))
for i from 0 to K-1 do
    Color each graphlet in G[p_i + 1, p_{i+1}] with static-
    color(SmG(G[p_i + 1, p_{i+1}]), constraint)
end for
return Color[1,T]
```

As was the case with m-SMASH, the two extreme cases for both Algorithms 6 and 7 are SNAP ($K = T - 1$) and SMASH ($K = 1$), respectively. A open question is to find the best K for a given α.

5.6 Adaptive Hybrid

SNAP, P-SNAP, and INC, although simple, do not perform well across all ranges of α or parameters of the RGG-RWP model (details in Section 6). Moreover, they do not utilize any knowledge of the parameters of the T-graph evolution (whether given or learnt). In this section, we present a hybrid approach that utilizes the available model information and switches between two algorithms, depending on the current level of network dynamics.

Our proposed hybrid algorithm (Algorithm 8) essentially sets an edge-change threshold for deciding whether to switch between T-coloring (pure) strategies P-SNAP and INC. For small values of α, the value of $COST$ is dominated by C, hence P-SNAP (which attempts to lower C) is the suitable coloring scheme; on the contrary, for higher values of α, $COST$ is dominated by A, hence INC (which attempts to avoid recoloring a vertex, unless essential) is the suitable T-coloring scheme.

Consider consecutive graphlets G and G' which are both RGGs and let $\Delta(G, G')$ be the symmetric difference between the edge sets of two graphs, i.e., $(E \setminus E') \cup (E' \setminus E)$. By means of simulation, we found that due to the spatial nature of the RGG, the r.v. $|\Delta(G, G')|$ is quite concentrated around its expected value, which can be shown to be bounded as follows (see Appx A): $E[|\Delta(G, G')|] < \frac{n(n-1)}{2} \frac{2\pi rs}{D^2} = \Delta^*$.

Rather than using a fixed threshold across all values of α, Algorithm 8 uses an adaptive threshold function, which is a decreasing function of α, and is denoted by $\theta(\Delta, T, \alpha)$. The rationale behind the choice of $\theta(\Delta, T, \alpha)$ is as follows: if the expected number of edge changes between consecutive graphlets is Δ and each edge change typically triggers no more than one recoloring, the contribution of the expected "recoloring" cost to the total $COST$ is $A(\Delta, T, \alpha) = \Delta T \alpha$. For fixed Δ, T, the multiplier term $e^{-A(\Delta,T,\alpha)}$ varies from 1 to 0 as α increases above 0. This achieves the adaptive switching behavior described earlier (see Sec. 6 for performance evaluation).

Algorithm 8 Adaptive Hybrid

```
Input: (Any two consecutive graphlets G, G' ∈ G[1,T]; valid coloring
    of graphlet G; RGG-RWP model parameters r, s, D, n, constraint ∈
    {dist-1, dist-2}
Output: color assignment of graphlet G'
Δ* = n(n-1) πrs/D^2
θ(Δ, T, α) = 2e^{-ΔTα}Δ
if |Δ(G, G')| > θ(Δ*, T, α) then
    Color(G') = Algorithm INC (G, G',constraint)
else
    Color(G') = Algorithm P-SNAP (G', PMNF - labeling(G),
    constraint)
end if
return Color(G')
```

6. EXPERIMENTAL ANALYSIS

In this section, we evaluate conflict-free channel assignment (over a period of time) in a MANET modeled as temporal graph coloring. We evaluate by simulation the performance of the various temporal coloring schemes described in sections 4 and 5 on a random MANET whose nodes follow the random waypoint mobility model (RWP). The parameters used in the simulation study are given in the table below. Note that all possible combinations of parameters in the table were not simulated.

Parameter and Description	Range
n (Number of nodes)	$50, 100$
D (Side of square area)	1000
s (Node speed)	$5, 10, 15, 20$
r (Transmission range)	$[25, 200]$
T (Time window of evaluation)	$100, 200$
α (Significance of reassignment)	$[0.0001, 1]$
K (Budget for smashing algorithms)	10,20
m (Number of graphlets compressed for m-SMASH)	$\sim \lceil \frac{T}{K} \rceil$

The specific combinations that were simulated have been reported in the following text.

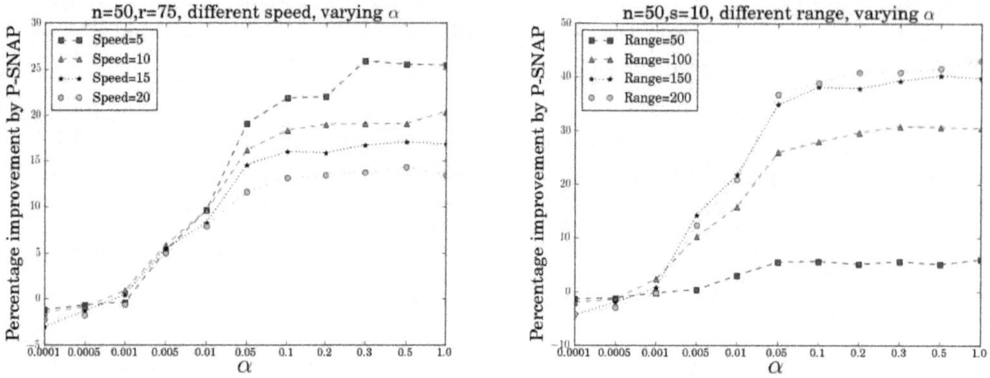

Figure 5: **For most values of α P-SNAP outperforms SNAP, especially at lower speeds and higher range.**

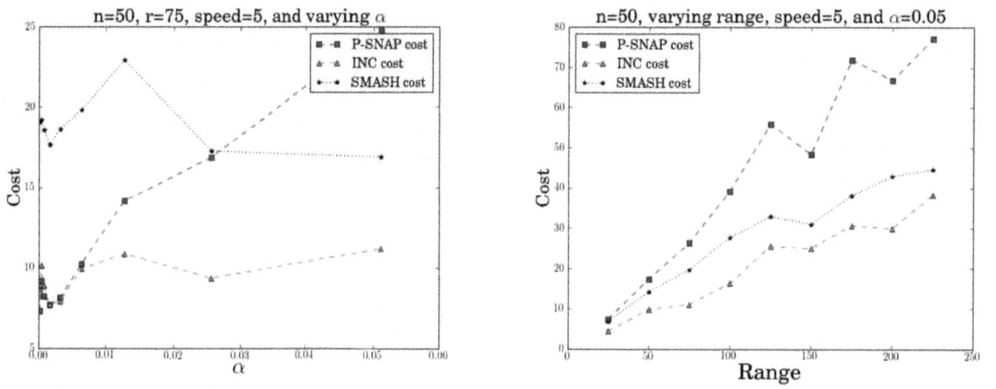

Figure 6: **INC outperforms both P-SNAP and SMASH. The relative performance of P-SNAP and SMASH depends upon the parameters.**

We focus on "pivot" or "crossover values", that is, when the relative performance (*cost*) of two or more algorithms reverse themselves. Recall that cost is $C + \alpha A$ where C is the total #colors, A total #re-assignments, and α is a user-defined parameter.

We note that SNAP, P-SNAP, INC and hybrid strictly require only one snapshot at a time whereas SMASH, m-SMASH, BC-SMASH, AE-SMASH require the entire T-graph. In order to compare all algorithms with the lowest common denominator of requirement, we assume all algorithms receive the full T-graph.

In all experiments below, we generate a T-graph based on the random geometric graph (RGG) with random waypoint mobility model (RWP). In the $RGG(n; D; r)$ model, n nodes are placed uniformly randomly in a $D \times D$ square, and two nodes have an edge between them iff they are within a transmission range r. In the $RWP(n; D; s)$ mobility model, each node picks a destination uniformly randomly in the square and moves to it at a constant given speed s, then picks another destination, and so on. There is no "pause time" at the destination. A T-graph is generated as follows. At each time slot t, graphlet $G(t)$ is the RGG based on vertex positions at time t, and we store each graph let $G(t)$ as a stacked graph for T-coloring.

In the generation of RGG and RWP, we use generic "units" – one may assign any (the same) transformation from "units" to actual metrics (e.g. 1 unit could be 10 meters). All experiments below are done using an RGG with $n = 50$ and $D = 1000$. The speed, range and the cost bias α are varied differently for each of the experiments. All of the colorings done use the *dist-2* constraint which represents broadcast scheduling for TDMA and is the most applicable vertex coloring constraint in practice. Each point in the plot represents an average over 50 random T-graph samples for all algorithms except Adaptive Hybrid for which we used 20 samples to accommodate its higher running time.

We first compare SNAP and P-SNAP. For this set of experiments, the radius $r = 75$. Figure 5 shows the percentage improvement of P-SNAP over SNAP as a function of α for varying RWP speeds and ranges. We observe that for all but very small values of α P-SNAP outperforms SNAP. As discussed earlier in section 5, for dynamism at the rates studied, two consecutive graphlets are nearly the same, and using the same ordering obviously results in better performance. At very low α, the cost is essentially the number of colors used. PMNF labeling is very effective in reducing the colors used, and since SNAP always uses PMNF while P-SNAP uses it only once at the beginning, when α is very small, SNAP uses less colors than P-SNAP.

We also observe that P-SNAP outperforms SNAP to a greater extent at lower s and higher r. Lower speeds result in similar consecutive graphlets, thus increasing P-SNAP's advantage of "sticky" labeling. At higher ranges, the graphlets are more connected and have a higher chromatic number. The higher number of colors results in a larger gap between re-assignments in SNAP and P-SNAP.

Given that P-SNAP outperforms SNAP for most of the parameter space of interest, we use P-SNAP going forward, and compare it with SMASH and INC. For this set of experiments, $r = 75$ and $s = 5$. Figure 6 shows the dependence of the cost of each algo-

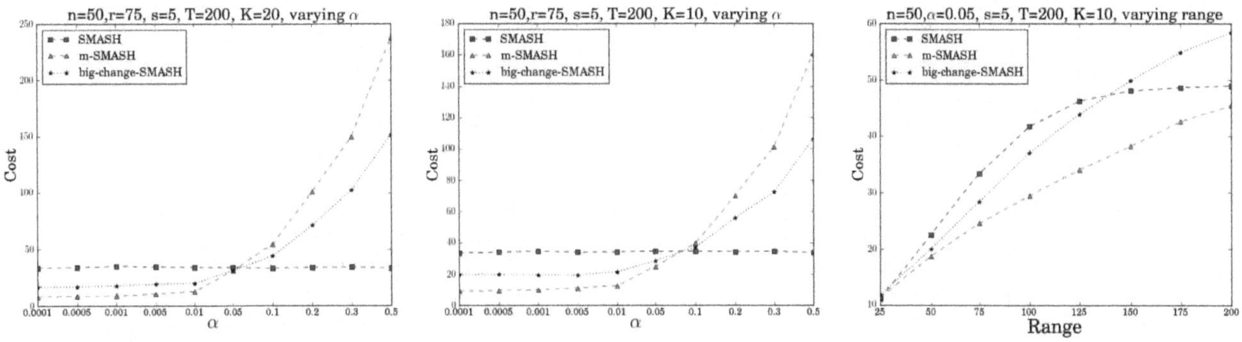

Figure 7: SMASH, m-SMASH, Big-Change-SMASH exhibit a "pivot" or "crossover" point, at approximately α=0.05

rithm as a function of α and r. INC outperforms both SMASH and P-SNAP. Thus, although we showed in section 5 that there are instances where INC incurs greater cost than both SMASH and P-SNAP, it appears that this is not evident in practice, at least in the RGG-RWP model.

However, there is no clear "winner" between SMASH and P-SNAP. There is a value of α, approximately 0.05, below which P-SNAP is better, and above which SMASH is better. At higher α, re-assignments are more costly and SMASH does not re-assign. Further, as the plot on the right in Figure 6 shows, for $\alpha = 0.05$, the gap between SMASH and P-SNAP widens with increasing range. A denser graph is more suitable for SMASH since then the difference between a single graphlet and a smashed graph narrows.

We now compare the different kinds of smashing algorithms, namely m-SMASH, Big-Change-SMASH (BC-SMASH), and regular (full) SMASH. For this set of experiments, Figures 7(a,b) show the results as a function of α for budgets $K = 10$ and $K = 20$, for different values of r. We observe an interesting phenomenon around a "pivot" value of α: when α is less than the pivot value, the cost is in the order B-C-SMASH < m-SMASH < SMASH, and when α is greater than this pivot value the cost is reversed as SMASH < m-SMASH < BC-SMASH. It is particularly interesting that the crossovers between the three algorithms occur *at the same point*, and for different combinations of range and K (we have observed this in other combinations not shown here due to lack of space). We observe that the pivot point moves to the right with decreasing K.

Figure 7(c) shows the cost versus r at $\alpha = 0.05$. A crossover can be seen between BC-SMASH and SMASH (with m-SMASH outperforming both).

Finally, we evaluate the performance of the adaptive hybrid algorithm (Algorithm 8) that switches between two online schemes P-SNAP and INC based on the current network dynamics and the value of α. Figure 8 illustrates that Algorithm 8 adaptively switches from P-SNAP (at low α) to INC (at higher α). Note that the threshold function $\theta(\cdot)$ given in Algorithm 8 is only illustrative, and other more complex functions can indeed be used instead.

Our experiments provide a way by which a user can select the right algorithm based on the kind of network, i.e,, the cost bias between colors and re-assignments, and range, among other things.

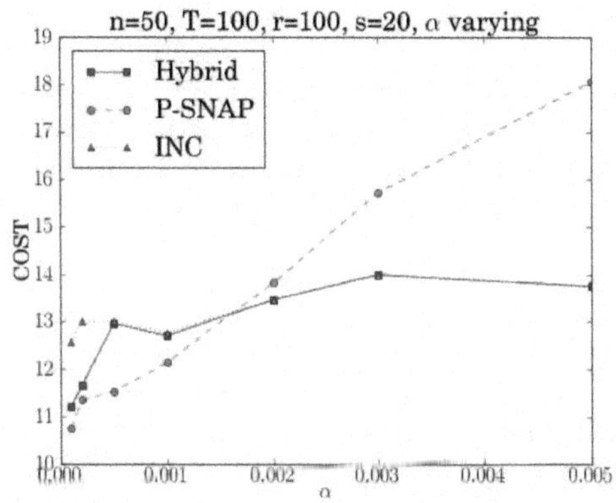

Figure 8: Hybrid online algorithm switches between P-SNAP and INC as α is varied

7. CONCLUDING REMARKS

We have considered the problem of channel assignment in mobile or otherwise dynamic networks as a graph coloring problem. We have presented a model with two novel components: a *temporal graph* and an associated *temporal coloring* model; and a cost model $C + \alpha A$ that allows a user-selectable tradeoff between number of colors (channels), and their changes over time. Using this model, we have presented a suite of algorithms ranging from simple ones such as SNAP, P-SNAP and SMASH, to more sophisticated ones such as INC, m-SMASH, Big-Change-SMASH, Accumulated-Error-SMASH, and an adaptive hybrid algorithm.

For SNAP and SMASH, we have derived bounds for when one outperforms the other, for arbitrary graphs as well as Erdos-Renyi random graphs. For all algorithms, we have presented experimental results with typically used placement and mobility models. Our study shows that there exist crossover or pivot α points between pairs or triplets of algorithms, with $\alpha = 0.05$ figuring as a kind of "magic number". Our work, with suitable adaptations, can be applied to time-, frequency- or code-based medium access in a real-life multi hop wireless network, and guide a designer to select the right algorithm for her preferred α.

Many exciting avenues for future work exist. These include further extending the theoretical bounds for distance-2 coloring and for other algorithms, especially budget-based ones, improving the performance of the online algorithms, extending to a physical propagation model and distributed implementations.

8. REFERENCES

[1] F. S. Al-Anzi, Y. N. Sotskov, A. Allahverdi, and G. V. Andreev. Using mixed graph coloring to minimize total completion time in job shop scheduling. *Applied Mathematics and Computation*, 182(2):1137 – 1148, 2006.

[2] N. Alon, A. Bar-Noy, N. Linial, and D. Peleg. On the complexity of radio communication. In *Proc. of the 21st ACM symposium on Theory of computing*, pages 274–285. ACM, 1989.

[3] B. Bollobás. The chromatic number of random graphs. *Combinatorica*, 8(1):49–55, 1988.

[4] B. Bollobás. *Random graphs*, volume 73. Cambridge university press, 2001.

[5] A. Ephremides and T. Truong. Scheduling broadcasts in multihop radio networks. *Communications, IEEE Transactions on*, 38(4):456–460, 1990.

[6] P. Erdős and A. Rényi. On the evolution of random graphs. *Magyar Tud. Akad. Mat. Kutató Int. Közl*, 5:17–61, 1960.

[7] A. Ferreira. Building a reference combinatorial model for MANETs. *Network, IEEE*, 18(5):24–29, 2004.

[8] P. Gupta and P. R. Kumar. The capacity of wireless networks. *IEEE Transactions on Information Theory*, 46:388–404, 2000.

[9] W. Hale. Frequency assignment: Theory and applications. *Proceedings of the IEEE*, 68(12):1497–1514, 1980.

[10] L. Hu. Distributed code assignments for CDMA packet radio networks. In *Proc. IEEE INFOCOM '91*, pages 1500–1509, 1991.

[11] S. Khuri, W. Moh, and F. Chung. Code assignments in CDMA networks: distributed algorithms and genetic algorithm heuristics. In *Proc. of the 6th IEEE Singapore International Conference on Networks*, volume 98, pages 91–105, 1998.

[12] V. Kostakos. Temporal graphs. *Physica A: Statistical Mechanics and its Applications*, 388(6):1007 – 1023, 2009.

[13] E. Lloyd and S. Ramanathan. On the complexity of distance-2 coloring. In *Computing and Information, 1992. Proceedings. ICCI '92., Fourth International Conference on*, pages 71 –74, may 1992.

[14] E. Lloyd and S. Ramanathan. Efficient distributed algorithms for channel assignment in multihop radio networks. *Journal of High Speed Networks*, 2(4):405–428, 1993.

[15] X. Ma and E. Lloyd. An Incremental Algorithm for Broadcast Scheduling in Packet Radio Networks. In *MILCOM*, volume 1, pages 205–210, 1998.

[16] C. McDiarmid and T. Muller. On the chromatic number of random geometric graphs. Technical report, Oxford University, 2011. http://arxiv.org/abs/1101.6065.

[17] A. Panconesi and A. Srinivasan. Improved distributed algorithms for coloring and network decomposition problems. In *Proc. of the 24th ACM symposium on Theory of computing*, pages 581–592. ACM, 1992.

[18] S. Ramanathan. A unified framework and algorithm for channel assignment in wireless networks. *Wireless Networks*, 5(2):81–94, 1999.

[19] S. Ramanathan and E. Lloyd. Scheduling algorithms for multihop radio networks. *IEEE/ACM Transactions on Networking (TON)*, 1(2):166–177, 1993.

[20] R. Ramaswami and K. Parhi. Distributed scheduling of broadcasts in a radio network. In *Proc. IEEE INFOCOM '89*, pages 497–504. IEEE, 1989.

[21] J. Redi and R. Ramanathan. The DARPA WNaN network architecture. In *MILITARY COMMUNICATIONS CONFERENCE, 2011 - MILCOM 2011*, pages 2258 –2263, Nov. 2011.

[22] S. Scellato, I. Leontiadis, C. Mascolo, P. Basu, and M. Zafer. Evaluating Temporal Robustness of Mobile Networks. *IEEE Transactions on Mobile Computing*, 12(1):105–117, 2013.

[23] Y. Shi, Y. T. Hou, J. Liu, and S. Kompella. Bridging the gap between protocol and physical models for wireless networks. *IEEE Trans. Mob. Comput.*, 12(7):1404–1416, 2013.

[24] J. Wang and B. Prabhala. Periodicity Based Next Place Prediction. *the Procedings of Mobile Data Challenge by Nokia Workshop at the Tenth International Conference on Pervasive Computing*, June 2012.

[25] J. Whitbeck, M. Dias de Amorim, V. Conan, and J.-L. Guillaume. Temporal reachability graphs. In *Proc. Mobicom '12*, pages 377–388, 2012.

[26] A. Wigderson. Improving the Performance Guarantee for Approximate Graph Coloring. *J. ACM, vol. 30, No. 4*, pages 729–735, Oct 1983.

[27] H. Wu, F. Yang, K. Tan, J. Chen, Q. Zhang, and Z. Zhang. Distributed channel assignment and routing in multiradio multichannel multihop wireless networks. *Selected Areas in Communications, IEEE Journal on*, 24(11):1972–1983, 2006.

APPENDIX

A. COMPUTING THRESHOLD Δ^* FOR HYBRID ONLINE T-COLORING

We calculate the expected number of edge-changes between two RGG-RWP graphlets G, G'. The model parameters are: area ($D \times D$), number of nodes (n), connectivity radius (r), and speed (s). We assume that G is a uniformly distributed RGG, and the future direction of each node is chosen randomly. Consider an edge (A, B) in G. Due to RWP mobility, $A \to A'$ and $B \to B'$ (change of locations in G'). Define events $Y = 1_{(A,B)\in G}$ and $Z = 1_{(A',B')\in G'}$. Then, we have, $E[\Delta(G, G')] =$

$$\tfrac{n(n-1)}{2}\{\Pr(Z|\bar{Y})\Pr(\bar{Y})+\Pr(\bar{Z}|Y)\Pr(Y)\}.$$

By assuming $D >> r$, we have $\Pr(Y) = \frac{\pi r^2}{D^2}$ and $\Pr(\bar{Y}) = 1 - \frac{\pi r^2}{D^2}$. For fixed parameters r, s, define the following function: $f(x) = \Pr(|AB| = x, |AA'| = s, |BB'| = s, |A'B'| < r)$. After geometric probability calculations (omitted due to paucity of space), it can be shown that $f(x) = \frac{1}{\pi}\int_0^{\pi}\int_0^{1} \Pr(|AB| = x, B' = B + 2ase^{i\theta}, |A'B'| < r)d\theta da$. For $x \leq r - 2s, f(x) = 1$. For $x \geq r - 2s$, let $\theta^*(x) = \arccos(\frac{(2s)^2+x^2-r^2}{2sx})$. So $1 > f(x) > 1 - \frac{1}{2}(1 - \frac{\theta^*(x)}{\pi})(1 - \frac{r-x}{2s})$. Therefore, we have:

$$\Pr(\bar{Z}|Y) = 1 - \int_0^r \frac{2x}{r^2}(1 - f(x))dx < \frac{s(3r - 2s)}{3r^2}$$

$$\Pr(Z|\bar{Y}) = 1 - \int_r^D \frac{2\pi x}{D^2 - \pi r^2}(1 - f(x))dx < \frac{\pi s(3r + 2s)}{3(D^2 - \pi r^2)}$$

Therefore, it follows that $E[\Delta(G, G')] < \frac{n(n-1)}{2}\frac{2\pi rs}{D^2}$.

OBSERVATION 14. *It is obvious that if $|AB| < r - 2s$, then $|A'B'| < r$; and if $|AB| > r + 2s$, then $|A'B'| > r$, therefore, a naive upper bound is given by*

$$\Pr((A, B)\ \textit{changing}) < \frac{\pi(r + 2s)^2 - \pi(r - 2s)^2}{D^2} = \frac{8\pi rs}{D^2}$$

Hence, our bounding technique yields a fourfold improvement over the naive upper bound.

Femtocells Sharing Management using Mobility Prediction Model

Dominique Barth, Amira Choutri,
Leïla Kloul
Université de Versailles
45, Av. des Etats-Unis
78000 Versailles, France
barth@prism.uvsq.fr,
cham@prism.uvsq.fr, kle@prism.uvsq.fr

Olivier Marcé
Alcatel-Lucent
France
Olivier.Marce@alcatel-lucent.com

ABSTRACT

Bandwidth sharing paradigm constitutes an incentive solution for the serious capacity management problem faced by operators as femtocells owners are able to offer a QoS guaranteed network access to mobile users in their femtocell coverage. In this paper, we consider a technico-economic bandwidth sharing model based on a reinforcement learning algorithm. Because such a model does not allow the convergence of the learning algorithm, due to the small size of the femtocells, the mobile users velocity and, more importantly, the randomness of their arrivals, we propose to use a mobility prediction approach based on the analysis of movements history of the mobile users. Knowing the next visited cell in advance provides more time to mobile user to negotiate with the access provider and to generate synchronized resource reservation requests that maximize the gain of the access provider.

Categories and Subject Descriptors

C.2 [**Computer Systems Organization**]: COMPUTER-COMMUNICATION NETWORKS

Keywords

Femtocell Networks ; Bandwidth Sharing Management ; Mobility Prediction ; QoS

1. INTRODUCTION

The topology and the architecture of cellular networks requires a major paradigm change from central voice, central switching and optimization of circuit, up to coverage data centralization, switching and deployment packages. Indeed with the explosion of smart-phone market and the emergence of new services (VOD, TV mobile, ...), the number of registered mobile operators has significantly increased. This has led to an unexpected increase in the mobile data requests, overloading the network infrastructure and the traffic control equipments.

Thus, today operators are faced with a capacity management problem. They must find a compromise between, in the one hand, the QoS that must be offered to the users, and on the other hand, the cost that allows providing more capacity to their final mobile customers [2, 9]. Allowing mobile users the access to 4G applications, that is, data communications with high quality of service constraints (delay, bandwidth guarantee and continuity of service) is a key issue for the operators, for which a macrocell coverage cannot meet high population density of urban areas. Moreover, in order to boost the network capacity, mobile operators have to determine the good compromise between the size of the cells and the population density in these covered area. In these urban areas, many users have contracted a wireless access point for private use, developing indoor and outdoor coverages by small cells (femtocells [2]), and consequently offering an alternative to 4G mobile deployment. [15].

In this paper, we consider a techno-economic mechanism, partially inspired from the FON system, and proposed to encourage the access point owners to share their femtocell radio resources with nomadic or mobile users [11]. This mechanism is mainly based on the use of a reinforcement learning algorithm distributed [14] among the mobile users who want to use the offered radio resources for sharing in a given cell. Our aim is to define a complete architecture for users mobility management in a femtocell coverage allowing a realistic use of the resources sharing mechanism studied in [11]. Indeed, the reinforcement learning process used in this mechanism assumes an unrealistic synchronization between competitive mobile users. This assumption is far from reality as mobile users arrive randomly to a cell. This algorithm also requires potentially long computation time and important message exchanges with the base station to converge. This cannot be compatible with the velocity of the mobile users movements in the femtocell coverage.

Thus, in order to overcome the real-time constraints faced by the bandwidth sharing model, we propose to use a mobility prediction approach which allows anticipating the next movements of the mobile users. Knowing the next visited cell in advance provides more time to mobile users to negotiate with the access provider and to generate synchronized resource reservation requests that maximize the gain of this provider. We consider the mobility prediction model developed in [6, 7] and which exploits the mobility trace of the

MSWiM'13, November 3–8, 2013, Barcelona, Spain.
Copyright 2013 ACM 978-1-4503-2353-6/13/11 ...$15.00.

mobile user to determine the next femtocell it will cross, allowing thus the network to anticipate the handover procedure.

The problem of sharing bandwidth and pricing has been already addressed, then modelled as a game. The challenging problem in this context is that bandwidth sharing requires a stable co-existence of both primary and secondary users. In game theory, this peaceful coexistence represents a stable state and is denoted by Nash Equilibrium (NE).

The property of existence of a NE in potential games, has been used for congestion game and for a real-time spectrum sharing problem with QoS provisioning [12, 1]. The approach [11] we consider in this paper is based on a decentralized learning algorithm.

Concerning prediction mobility, many studies were carried out on the mobile user behaviour. It is proved in [10] that humans follow simple reproducible patterns. The human trajectories show a high degree of temporal and spatial regularity.

In [8] and [16], the authors propose prediction models which are based on the first order of Markov chains and the second order of Markov chains, respectively. Their results show that the second order based model performs better predictions than the first order based one. In [3], Markov chains were combined with a notion of local profiles to predict the next cell of a user.

Structure of the paper: Section 2 provides a brief overview of both the resources sharing mechanism and the mobility prediction model we consider. Section 3 is dedicated to our mechanism of femtocell sharing management based on mobility prediction. Its performances are analyzed in Section 4. Section 5 concludes the paper.

2. THE MODELS

In the following, we present briefly both the bandwidth sharing model [11] and the mobility prediction model [7, 6] we consider in our solution.

2.1 The Bandwidth Sharing Model

The main actors of the techno-economic model for sharing femtocell access we consider are the service provider customers (SPC) and the service requester customers (SRC). An SPC is a femtocell owner who allows other customers of the network the access to its resources against remuneration. An SRC is a mobile user in need of a connection to the network. Note that a network customer can be both an SPC and an SRC. For the mobile users, the model consists of a learning phase and a negotiation phase. The former allows the mobile user to collect data about the SPC and the concurrent mobile users before starting the negotiations with the SPC to get the targeted amount of bandwidth.

This sharing of the femtocell access [11] is considered as a game where the players are the SRC and the shared bandwidth capacity is fixed. Using potential game characteristics, the authors have proved that a pure Nash equilibrium is reached when many service providers share the access. The choice of a strategy to apply by a player (SRC) is a probabilistic choice. The purpose of the model's learning phase is to update the probability vector of the strategies. A strategy probability increases if the gain that the SRC can obtain from the SPC, using this strategy, is maximal. The learning algorithm stops when the strategy probability is 1.

The gains of a SRC is quantified using an utility function U which is defined within the bandwidth allocation politicy of the SPC. The utility $U_i(s_i)$ of an SRC i depends on its profile and the bandwidth quantity bw_i the player obtains from the SPC.

$$U_i(s_i) = \frac{|bw_i - \mathcal{M}_i|}{M_i - m_i}$$

where $\mathcal{M}_i$ is the bandwidth quantity the player tolerates to receive. If the SRC is sensitive to the QoS then the minimum of bandwidth it tolerates to receive is the maximum of bandwidth M_i of the strategy played. If it is more sensitive to the resource price, it tolerates to receive the minimum of bandwidth m_i. For more details see [11].

The model allows us to guarantee a fair access to a femtocell between the SRC and the SPC. However, a synchronization between players must exist in the game since every player must know the available capacity. Moreover, the learning phase makes the model slow to react, and needs a lot of interactions between the service requester and the provider customers. Thus, a realistic implementation of this model becomes not easy to achieve if we consider the short time allowed to the handover procedure between femtocells and the random arrivals of the mobile requesters.

2.2 The Mobility Prediction Model

To guarantee continuous services and shorten handoff latency in wireless cellular network, mobile operators try to know the next mobile location using mobility prediction. It allows anticipating the handover process at the predicted access point.

In this paper, we consider the prediction model proposed, in the context of LTE architecture [6, 7]. This model has been proved to be efficient enough to predict the movements changes of a mobile user. The model is based on two complementary prediction algorithms. First, the Global Prediction Algorithm (GPA) allows predicting the regular movements of a mobile client. It is based on the user's mobility trace and a second order continuous-time Markov chain, whose discrete states are the cells of the network. When the GPA is unsuccessful, the approach proposes to use the Local Prediction Algorithm (LPA) which is based on the first order continuous-time Markov chain.

As at every entred cell, the algorithm computes the transition probability to every adjacent cell. Thus the prediction procedure just needs to know the adjacent cells. This information can be provided by the knowledge of the operator's network topology, or by analysing the intensity of received signals. For more details, see [6, 7].

3. FEMTOCELL SHARING MANGEMENT USING MOBILITY PREDICTION

In order to overcome the real-time constraint faced by the bandwidth sharing model in Section 2.1, we propose to use the mobility prediction model in Section 2.2. Knowing the next visited cell provides more time to mobile users to negotiate with the SPC and to generate synchronized resource reservation requests maximizing their gain.

3.1 Actors of the Model

The main actors of our model are the mobile user (SRC) and the femto base station to which the mobile is connected.

When an SRC enters a new cell a new stage t in its mobility begins.

– **Mobile Client:** it has a unique identifier id and is characterized by:

- A requested resource capacity $cap_{req}(id,t)$, at every stage t. The resource can be guaranteed or not during the client movement. We use a green color for a guaranteed resource and yellow color for non guaranteed one. For all stage t, cap_{req} is constant.
- A QoS sensitivity parameter α_{id} and a price sensitivity parameter β_{id}.
- An attachment cell $cell(id,t)$, at stage t.
- An allocated capacity $cap_{alloc}(id,t)$ such that $0 \leq cap_{alloc}(id,t) \leq cap_{req}(id,t)$.
  - **If** $\mathbf{cap_{alloc}(id,t) = cap_{req}(id,t)}$, the mobile's request is totally satisfied.
  - **If** $\mathbf{cap_{alloc}(id,t)) = 0}$ then the mobile's request is not satisfied.
- An adopted strategy $s_{id}(t)$ to formulate its request to each new reattachment cell.
- An utility $U_{id}(t)$ the SRC gets for the applying its strategy $s_{id}(t)$ and considering those adopted by its concurrent mobiles.
- A mobility trace L which contains all visited cells during T stages, $0 \leq T \leq t$.

– **Femtocell:** a femtocell $cell$ is characterized by:

- A total resource capacity $cap(cell)$ such that $cap(cell) = cap_g(cell) + cap_y(cell)$ where $cap_g(cell)$ is the guaranteed capacity and $cap_y(cell)$ is the non guaranteed one.
- A pre-emption risk P_{pre}, which is the probability that the connection is interrupted by the base station. If the connection is guaranteed then $P_{pre} = 0$, otherwise $P_{pre} > 0$.
- A maximum number of SRCs $nb_{max}(cell)$ that $cell$ can satisfy simultaneously.
- A neighborhood graph $V(cell)$, which models the network coverage. Each vertex v_i in the graph is a cell and each edge $[v_i, v_j]$ indicates that cells v_i and v_j overlap, $i,j \in [0,R]$, R being the graph size.
- A sharing resources policy that defines the way $cell$ attributes its resources to the SRCs.

We consider two resource sharing policies, a FIFO based-policy and priority-based policy. In the former, there is no distinction between mobiles who had a successful prediction at the previous stage $t-1$, and those who had a wrong one at this stage. In the latter policy, a mobile who had a successful prediction, at stage $t-1$, will have a higher priority to be satisfied, because it has prepared its resource request maximizing its gain. A wrong prediction will make a mobile joint a cell for which it did not prepare the request, unlike some of his concurrent who had success predictions. In this case, it will be assigned a low priority to be satisfied by the femtocell.

3.2 The Algorithm of the Complete Approach

At stage t, client id is attached to a femtocell $cell(id,t)$. Its terminal executes the mobility prediction algorithm in order to compute the transition probability from $cell(id,t)$ to every adjacent cell v in $V(cell)$. The procedure continues as follows:

– The mobile terminal communicates its prediction results to the base station. They consist of a probability distribution over a set of predicted cells. If more than one cell has been predicted, the base station determines the next cell of client.

– With the help of its base station, client id initiates the negotiations with the base station of the predicted cell. The negotiations make the client part of a game where mobile clients play the access to the same resources.

– Client id determines a strategy $s_{id}(t+1)$ to play during phase $t+1$ which maximizes its utility.

At stage $t+1$, mobile client id enters a new cell $cell(id,t+1)$. Two scenarios are then possible:

a) Wrong prediction: the mobile is not in the predicted cell, that is $cell(id,t+1) \neq Pred(id,t+1)$. Consequently, he is in a cell for which it did not prepare a request strategy. Thus, it can play either the strategy already prepared but for another cell, or play a strategy determined using a uniform distribution.

b) Successful prediction: the mobile is in the predicted cell, that is $cell(id,t+1) = Pred(id,t+1)$. he uses the strategy $s_{id}(t+1)$ already prepared. In this scenario, we consider two cases:

b1. One of the other players, say c, found by client id in the new cell was not supposed to be there; c made a wrong prediction. Client c may or may not play its strategy $s_c(t+1)$. Moreover, another player that is supposed to be in the cell and against who mobile client id has played has vanished because of a wrong prediction. Thus, the context of the new cell has changed for mobile client id.

b2. All players against who client id has played are in the new cell. Thus the context of this cell has not changed for client id.

For more details, we refer the readers to [5].

4. PERFORMANCE ANALYSIS

In order to assess the performances of our approach, we observe mobile clients (targeted users) requesting resources while moving in a defined environment. This one consists of a total of twelve (12) mobile users competing for a femtocell radio resource access. The data sets of the targeted users are field data collected in a major US urban area (Rice). These data sets are measured on WiFi enabled GSM cellular phones [13]. Using these data sets, a mobility trace representing all visited cells during the time period of the collection, has been extracted for each targeted user.

The performance measures we are interested in are the utility satisfaction rate and the QoS (bandwidth). Utility satisfaction rate $USR_{id}(t)$ is the ratio between the utility obtained with strategy $s_{id}(t)$ and the utility that could have been obtained with the optimal strategy. To perform these assessments we use simulation which results are obtained for a confidence level of 95%.

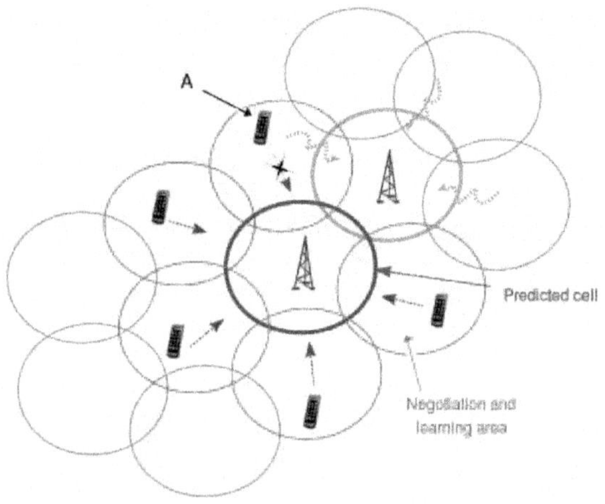

Figure 1: sharing femto access using mobile prediction.

We consider four different simulation scenarios:

- **NP** scenario: the mobility prediction is not used and users run the learning algorithm within, at most, 90 learning steps (the average number for the algorithm to converge is 115). This models the fact that without prediction, the converging time is limited since the learning algorithm can only be run when handovers occur.

- **WP** scenario: mobility prediction mechanism is used and targeted user makes a wrong prediction.

- **SP** scenario: the mobility prediction mechanism is used and all the users, including the targeted user, make a successfull prediction.

- **NSP** scenario: the prediction mechanism is used. The targeted user makes a good prediction and some other users make wrong predictions (20% prediction failure rate).

Fig. 2 shows the utility satisfaction rate obtained for user $n1$ using its mobility trace and considering different cells loads. When the cells load is low (0.5), scenario NP provides good performances since the provider has enough resources to satisfy all requesters. However, when the cells load increases, the utility decreases until reaching 0 (load equal 1.5), and the limited number of steps becomes insufficient to reach a good utility state.

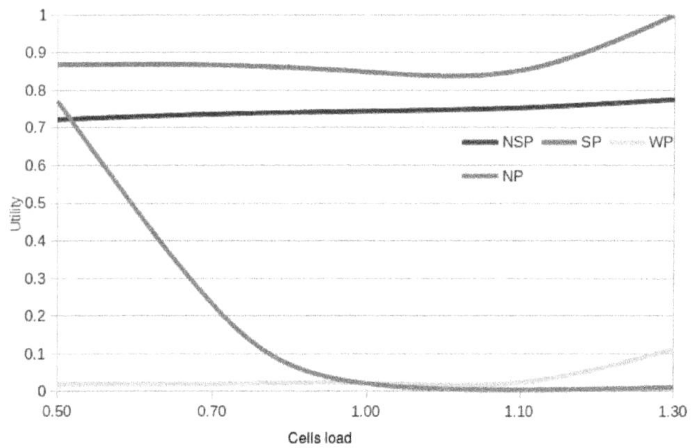

Figure 2: Utility satisfaction rate of user $n1$

The use of mobility prediction in the learning algorithm increases the obtained utility when prediction is successful (scenario SP), for different levels of cell loads. In this case, the learning algorithm has enough time to reach good utility state. Note that other simulation results show that the time to cross a cell is sufficient for the game to converge. This shows that the utility satisfaction rate and the QoS obtained can reach value 0.9 and 24, respectively, if the prediction is successful. If the targeted user makes a wrong prediction (WP curve), the obtained utility is lower than the ones obtained when good predictions are made, since the strategies have not been chosen for the corresponding crossed cells and the other mobile users having predicted these cells have priority on the resources. Indeed, the targeted user obtains a lower QoS (Figures 3, 4, 5). Moreover, even if the provider has enough resources, it will not exceed the load that it fixed beforehand. This explains why the utility in WP scenario is smaller than the one in NP scenario for low loads.

When all users make successful predictions (curve SP), the utility obtained for user $n1$ is maximal and equals to 0.9. But, if, at least one of the concurrent makes a wrong prediction, the obtained utility and the QoS decreases,. Indeed, the strategy initially chosen by the targeted user is not the optimal one anymore. Moreover, since the cells are overloaded, according to the policy of the mobile operator to satisfy the providers before the mobile users, there are users that are not served at all initially. Thus, when users do not show up in the predicted cell, there are more available resources, and the provider chooses to satisfy the minimum quantity requested by the not served mobiles. For that the provider decreases the capacity affected to the users that have already been served in the cell among which is the targeted user. That can be seen by observing the used strategies and the obtained capacities by the users in the cell.

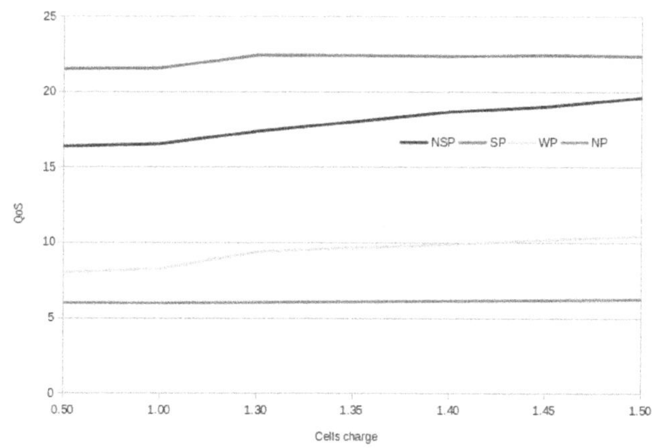

Figure 3: QoS obtained for targeted user $n1$

Targeted mobile user $n1$ has an average prediction ratio equal to 0.6 (see Fig.2, 3); it alternates between regular movements (i.e. predictable ones), for which utility success ratio is about 0.83 for 23 of QoS during 60% of the time, and irregular movements (difficult to predict), for which utility and QoS averages 0.05 and 9, respectively, in heavily loaded cells. In such cases, when WP scenario is considered the utility rate is 0.01 and the QoS is 7.

In the case of a trace (1629 cells) of irregular movements solely, like the one of user $n3$ (Fig. 5) the prediction success

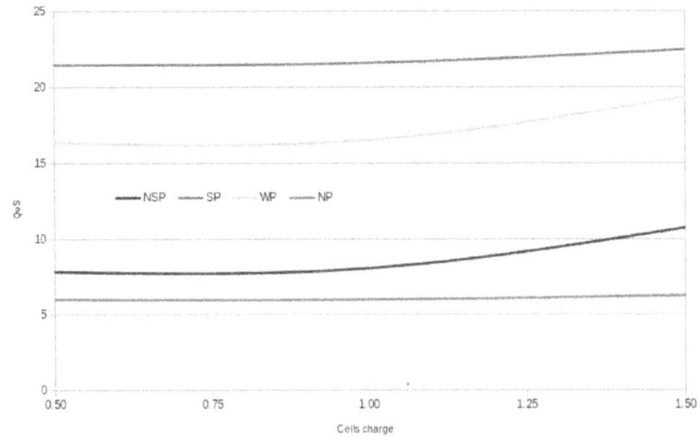

Figure 4: QoS obtained for targeted user $n2$

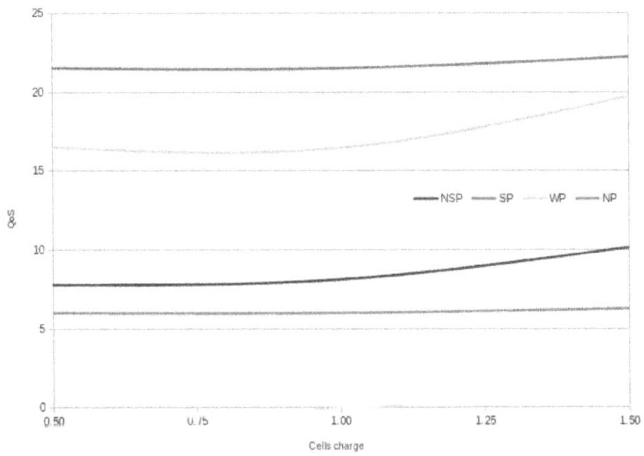

Figure 5: QoS obtained for targeted user $n3$

rate does not exceed 0.3 even if the QoS reaches 21. Thus the targeted mobile satisfayed the maximum and can express a better strategy. If the visited cells are heavily loaded, the utility rate is most of the time at 0.17, and 0.04 otherwise.

But, if the mobile user has regular movements (Fig. 4) and is able to reach a prediction success rate of 0.8 and a QoS of 24, like user $n2$ (trace of 7286 cells), most of the time, this mobile has an utility satisfaction rate and a QoS of 0.95 and 24 respectively. Its resource request is not satisfied in 20% of the crossed cells (utility rate at 0.3 and QoS at 7) which corresponds to wrong predictions.

5. CONCLUSION

The objective of this paper is to improve a techno-economic model for sharing femto access by anticipating the handover process using mobility prediction. We have assessed the performances of our approach, in terms of utility satisfaction rate and QoS. We focused on the behavior of different targeted users when they make successful/wrong predictions and the impact of the successful/failed prediction of their concurrents on their utility rate. We compared the obtained results with the ones obtained if no mobility prediction is used. These results show that we have effectively enhanced the utility obtained using the basic model for all cells loads. They also show that this enhancement depends on movements type of the users (regular, irregular, mixed).

Indeed, the mobility prediction approach we have used was penalizing for irregular movements. In the future, we plan to use a mobility prediction approach designed for such type of movements, like mobility prediction based on user profiles [3, 4]. We also plan to investigate the behavior of our algorithm in a green Femto-Macro cells network.

6. REFERENCES

[1] S. H. A. Ahmad, C. Tekin, M. Liu, R. Southwell, and J. Huang. Spectrum sharing as spatial congestion games. volume abs/1011.5384, 2010.

[2] J. G. Andrews, H. Claussen, M. Dohler, S. Rangan, and M. C. Reed. Femtocells: Past, present, and future. *IEEE Journal on Selected Areas in Communications*, 30(3):497–508, 2012.

[3] D. Barth, S. Bellahsene, and L. Kloul. Mobility prediction using mobile user profiles. In *19th IEEE MASCOTS, Singapore*, 2011.

[4] D. Barth, S. Bellahsene, and L. Kloul. Combining local and global profiles for mobility prediction in LTE femtocells. In *15th ACM MSWiM*, 2012.

[5] D. Barth, A. Choutri, L. Kloul, and O. Marcé. Femtocells Sharing Management using mobility prediction model. In *HAL-INRIA, hal-00847920, version 1*, July 2013.

[6] S. Bellahsene and L. Kloul. A new markov-based mobility prediction algorithm for mobile networks. *7th EPEW*, 2010.

[7] S. Bellahsene, L. Kloul, and D. Barth. A hierarchical prediction model for two nodes-based ip mobile networks. In *12th MSWiM*, 2009.

[8] F. Chinchilla, M. Lindsey, and M. Papadopouli. Analysis of wireless information locality and association patterns in a campus. In *IEEE* $23^{rd}INFOCOM$, 2004.

[9] M. Z. Chowdhury, Y. M. Jang, and Z. J. Haas. Network evolution and QoS provisionning for integrated femtocell/macrocell networks. *International Journal of Wireless & Mobile Networks (IJWMN)*, 2(3), 2010.

[10] M. Gonzàlez, C. Hidalgo, and A.-L. Barabàsi. Understanding individual human mobility patterns. volume abs/0806.1256, pages 779–782, 2008.

[11] M. Krichen, J. Cohen, and D. Barth. Model for sharing femto access. In *5th ICST VALUETOOLS, Paris, France*, 2011.

[12] M. Liu, S. Haji, A. Ahmad, and Y. Wu. Congestion game with resource reuse and applications in spectrum sharing. *CoRR*, abs/0910.4214, 2009.

[13] A. Rahmati and L. Zhong. Crawdad data set rice/context (v. 2007-05-23), May 2007.

[14] P. S. Sastry, V. V. Phansalkar, and M. A. L. Thathachar. Decentralized learning of nash equilibria in multi-person stochastic games with incomplete information. *IEEE Trans Systems, Man, and Cybernetics*, 24:769–777, 1994.

[15] T. Simonite. Qualcomm proposes a cell-phone network by the people, for the people, 2013.

[16] L. Song, D. Kotz, R. Jain, and X. He. Evaluating location predictors with extensive wi-fi mobility data. In *IEEE* $23^{rd}INFOCOM, HongKong, China$, 2004.

An Energy Efficient Adaptive HELLO Algorithm for Mobile Ad Hoc Networks

Danping He
Centro de Electronica Industrial
Universidad Politecnica de Madrid
danping.he@upm.es

Nathalie Mitton and David Simplot-Ryl
Inria Lille – Nord Europe
{firstname.lastname}@inria.fr

ABSTRACT

HELLO protocol or neighborhood discovery is essential in wireless ad hoc networks. It makes the rules for nodes to claim their existence/aliveness. In the presence of node mobility, no fix optimal HELLO frequency and optimal transmission range exist to maintain accurate neighborhood tables while reducing the energy consumption and bandwidth occupation. Thus a Turnover based Frequency and transmission Power Adaptation algorithm (TFPA) is presented in this paper. The method enables nodes in mobile networks to dynamically adjust both their HELLO frequency and transmission range depending on the relative speed. In TFPA, each node monitors its neighborhood table to count new neighbors and calculate the turnover ratio. The relationship between relative speed and turnover ratio is formulated and optimal transmission range is derived according to battery consumption model to minimize the overall transmission energy. By taking advantage of the theoretical analysis, the HELLO frequency is adapted dynamically in conjunction with the transmission range to maintain accurate neighborhood table and to allow important energy savings. The algorithm is simulated and compared to other state-of-the-art algorithms. The experimental results demonstrate that the TFPA algorithm obtains high neighborhood accuracy with low HELLO frequency (at least 11% average reduction) and with the lowest energy consumption. Besides, the TFPA algorithm does not require any additional GPS-like device to estimate the relative speed for each node, hence the hardware cost is reduced.

Categories and Subject Descriptors

C2.1 [**Network Architecture and Design**]: Network topology

General Terms

Algorithms

MSWiM'13, November 3–8, 2013, Barcelona, Spain.

http://dx.doi.org/10.1145/2507924.2507952.

Keywords

Adaptive Hello Algorithm; Energy Efficient; Mobile Ad Hoc Network; Neighborhood Discovery; Transmission Range; Wireless Sensor Networks

1. INTRODUCTION

Wireless Sensor Networks (WSNs) are composed of sensor nodes which have the ability to detect surrounding environments and are able to communicate with each other through specific wireless protocols. Mobility of the sensor nodes is an emerging issue and nowadays it becomes more and more under the attention of scientific community. It arises new questions such as optimization of energy consumption, connectivity of the WSN, routing in mobile networks and a lot more. Sensor nodes can be attached to animals with the purpose to track animals' habits and their natural habitat. In this case, mobility pattern is very often hard to estimate and protocols built upon this issue must take account of possible losses of connectivity or delays in the transmission of messages. Other possibility would include mobile agents (robots) which may have been given mobile pattern to follow to improve some of the parameters in the WSN [7]. In this case, overall energy efficiency of transmission can be significantly augmented using controlled mobility based smart placement of nodes related to the routing path. Due to the specific nature of mobile networks, some of the characteristic mechanisms used in static WSNs need to be redefined and adapted to the specific types of node mobility.

Neighborhood discovery is one of the most important protocols in WSN. The mechanism behind this protocol is rather simple, it includes periodically sending a specific type of message, called HELLO messages (also known as beacon messages) and gathering data from the received HELLO messages. HELLO messages contain the data of the sender id, unique identification number for the node in the WSN-usually MAC address in practical applications. Each node, usually, acquires data from all HELLO messages that it has received and organizes them into the neighborhood table which can be further used for some kind of topology control [10] or proactive routing [4].

However, finding the proper HELLO frequency is not obvious: if the HELLO frequency is too low, nodes may not be detected by their neighbors, leading to deprecated neighborhood tables, and protocol failures are likely to occur. On the contrary, if the frequency is too high, neighborhood tables are up to date, but the energy and bandwidth are wasted.

There exist many algorithms that utilize the information gathered from additional device such as GPS. The ARH algorithm presented in [6] adapts HELLO frequency when there is obvious error between the estimated speed and actual speed read from GPS. In [5], the authors deduced the relationship between the HELLO frequency and the link failure possibility for a given speed which again is obtained from GPS. The proper HELLO frequency is then calculated to guarantee that the link failure possibility is not greater than the predefined threshold. However, the speed obtained from GPS can not represent the actual changes in the surrounding environment. When a node is static or moving slowly but its neighbors are changing frequently, the HELLO frequency calculated by the previous two algorithms is lower than the required value to maintain the expected accuracy. On the contrary, when a node is moving fast with a relatively static neighborhood table, the computed HELLO frequency will be higher than the actual required value and will consume more energy.

The authors in [3] proposed a Turnover based Adaptive hello Protocol (TAP) to reduce the hardware cost and to consider the relative changes among nodes. It calculates the number of changes that appears in the neighborhood table, called *turnover*. The optimal value of *turnover* is derived and each node adapts the HELLO frequency by increasing or decreasing the value within a fixed range to keep the *turnover* as close as possible to the optimal value. In [9], the authors proposed two algorithms, one is run with GPS called *Cost*, the other called *NoTAP* relies on the TAP algorithm. Both algorithms adapt the HELLO transmission range to reduce the energy consumption. *Cost* risks sending HELLO messages with a very low power. Although the neighborhood table of *Cost* is accurate and power consumption is low, the average number of neighbors is too small to guarantee the connectivity of the network.

In this paper, a Turnover based Frequency and transmission Power Adaptation algorithm (TFPA) is presented. It is based on a previous work and allows to **dynamically adapt the HELLO frequency and its transmission power based on the estimated relative speed for each node**. The contributions of this work are:

- a theoretical analysis allowing the computing of the relative speed from the *turnover* in neighborhood,
- a theoretical analysis of the global energy optimal transmission range of HELLO message. The analysis highlights that the optimal range is independent of the speed, and hence can be applied to all nodes in the network to reduce the overall energy consumption,
- an adaptive neighborhood discovery mechanism, TFPA, that dynamically adapts jointly node transmission range and HELLO frequency, allowing accuracy and energy efficiency.

In TFPA, every node regularly checks its neighborhood and based on the observed changes and the theoretical analysis results, every node dynamically and periodically adapts both of its transmission range and HELLO frequency, allowing low energy consumption while maintaining reliable neighborhood tables. The features of TFPA are as follows:

- **Local**: in TFPA, every node only watch its neighborhood to adapt range and frequency.
- **Distributed**: every node computes the same algorithm.
- **GPS-free**: TFPA is not constraint by GPS-like devices and can be applied to general mobile ad hoc network.
- **Energy-efficient**: Results show that applying TFPA allows up to 11% energy savings.
- **Reliable**: Results show that neighborhood tables achieved through TFPA present the same error and accuracy ratios than alternative neighborhood discovery protocols.

The remainder of the paper is organized as follows: Section 2 sets the models, notations and preliminaries to this work. Section 3 provides the theoretical analysis related to this work. Section 4 presents the TFPA algorithm. Simulation results are detailed in Section 5. Section 6 gives conclusion and directions of future work.

2. MODELS AND PRELIMINARIES

2.1 Models and Notations

Wireless networks are represented by a graph $G = (V, E)$ where V is the set of nodes and $E \subseteq V^2$ is the set of edges: $(u, v) \in E$ means that u and v are neighbors (i.e., close enough to communicate). The neighborhood set $N(u)$ of a vertex u is equal to

$$v : (u, v) \in E \vee (v, u) \in E.$$

Each node is assigned a unique identifier (e.g., a MAC address). Wireless links are determined by the physical model. The most frequent one is the unit disk graph model [1]:

$$E = \{(u, v) \in V^2 | u \neq v \wedge |uv| \leq R_{max}\}$$

with $|uv|$ being the Euclidean distance between nodes u and v, and R_{max} the maximum communication range.

The basic HELLO protocol, first described in the OSPF [8], works as follows: Nodes regularly send HELLO messages to signal their presence to nodes near by, and maintain a neighborhood table. The frequency of these messages is noted f_{HELLO} and the delay between them d_{HELLO} (i.e., $d_{HELLO} = 1/f_{HELLO}$). When a node u receives such a message from a node v, u adds v to its table, or updates the time stamp of the entry if v was already there. We do not make assumptions about the content of HELLO messages, but they must contain the identifier of the sender.

The relation between HELLO frequency and relative speed is formulated (named Fopt for simplicity) in our previous work [11]. The idea of Fopt is that a node which strides a given distance in the communication area of another node has to be detected with a certain chance. If two nodes with transmission range R, move with a relative speed S, to make them discover each other with a chance of $1 - \alpha$, the optimal HELLO frequency is:

$$f_{opt} = \frac{2S}{\alpha R} \quad (1)$$

where $\alpha < 1$ predefines an expectation of accuracy of neighborhood table, e.g. the expected accuracy is 90% when $\alpha = 0.1$.

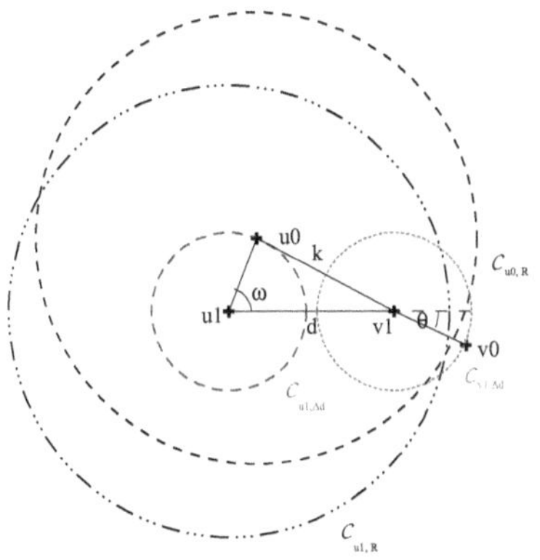

Figure 1: A new neighbor v of a node u - Global view [3].

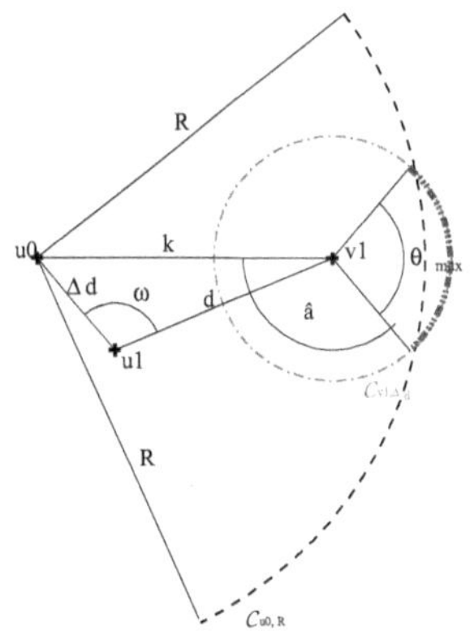

Figure 2: A new neighbor v of a node u - Zoom [3].

2.2 Turnover

The concept of *turnover* is first defined by [3], which is expressed by the ratio of new neighbors of a sensor and the number of all its neighbors between two HELLO packets. We re-establish part of the analysis provided in [3] that will be useful for the follow-up of this paper. In particular, we return the analysis of the optimal turnover ratio.

Let u_0 (resp. v_0) be the position of node u (resp. v) at time t_0 and u_1 (resp. $v1$) be its position at time t_1, the probability $P(d)$ that node v is a *new* neighbor of u is calculated through finding the probability that $|u_0v_0| > R$ knowing that $|u_1v_1| < R$. Fig. 1 illustrates the mobility model. Given the new position of a node and its traveling distance $\Delta d = S \times \Delta t$, the blue dashed circle $C_{u_1,\Delta d}$ (resp. red dotted circle $C_{v_1,\Delta d}$) represents the possible position of u_0 (resp. v_0). There exists a minimum distance $d_{min} = min(0, R-2\Delta d)$ that if $d < d_{min}$, v was an existing neighbor of u and $P(d < d_{min}) = 0$. Only the node v comes from the dotted blue angular sector of Fig. 2 can become a new neighbor of u. The $P(d)$ is expressed as:

$$P(d) = \begin{cases} \frac{1}{\pi^2}\int_{\omega_{min}}^{\pi} \theta_{max} d\omega & \text{if } d_{min} < d < R \\ 0 & otherwise \end{cases} \tag{2}$$

where $\theta_{max} = 2\arccos(\frac{R^2-\Delta d^2-k^2}{2k\Delta d})$ is the maximum angle of the dotted blue sector, $k = \sqrt{\Delta d^2 + d^2 - 2d\Delta d \cos\omega}$ and $k > R - \Delta d$ which leads to $\omega_{min} = \arccos(\frac{d^2+2R\Delta d-R^2}{2d\Delta d})$ according to the law of cosines.

In this analysis, it is assumed that nodes are randomly deployed using a Poisson Point Process (node positions are independent) with a density $\lambda > 0$, λ being the mean number of nodes per surface unit. The expected number of new neighbors that node u encounters after a time period Δt is simply equal to:

$$E[n]_{\Delta t} = \int_{d=0}^{R} 2\lambda\pi P(d) dd \tag{3}$$

By substituting (2) into (3), we have:

$$E[n]_{\Delta t} = \frac{\lambda}{\pi}\int_{d_{min}}^{R}\int_{\omega_{min}}^{\pi} d * \theta_{max} d\omega dd \tag{4}$$

In this work, $E[n]_{\Delta d}$ is used as a synonym of $E[N]_{\Delta t}$. The *turnover* of node u is expressed by the ratio of the new neighbors and number of all neighbors between two HELLO packets:

$$r = \frac{E[n]_{\Delta d}}{\lambda\pi R^2} \tag{5}$$

The above procedure shows how to deduce r from the neighborhood observation in the previous work [3]. Afterwards, we approximate the integration expression of r and the relative speed S is derived.

3. THEORETICAL ANALYSIS OF HELLO FREQUENCY AND RANGE ADAPTATION

3.1 Relationship between Turnover Ratio and Relative Speed

Fig. 3 plots the variation of $E[n]_{\Delta d}$ with different R and Δd. As can be seen, for a given Δd, $E[n]$ increases as R increases. Note that the curves vary almost linearly with R thus they can be approximated as linear variation and we have $E[n]_{\Delta d}$ expressed as:

$$E[n]_{\Delta d} = \frac{\lambda}{\pi} l(\Delta d) * R$$

where $l(\Delta d)$ is the slope of a line – a function of Δd. By checking its value for different Δd, it has $l(5) = 13\pi$, $l(10) = 26\pi$, $l(20) = 51\pi$, thus $l(\Delta d) = 2.6\pi\Delta d$ and we have $\frac{\lambda}{\pi} l(\Delta d) \approx 2.6\lambda\Delta d$. Therefore, $E[n]_{\Delta d}$ can be expressed as:

$$E[n]_{\Delta d} = 2.6\lambda\Delta d R \tag{6}$$

By substituting (6) to (5), we obtain the approximated expression for turnover ratio:

$$r = \frac{2.6\Delta d}{\pi R} \tag{7}$$

If $\Delta t = \frac{1}{f_{opt}}$, which is the optimal HELLO period (1) defined by Fopt, the $\Delta d = S \times f_{opt} = \frac{\alpha R}{2}$, then we have

$$r_{opt} = \frac{1.3\alpha}{\pi}$$

As can be noticed, r_{opt} is only a function of α and is not dependent on S, R and λ. For different α:

$$r_{opt}(0.1) \approx 0.04, \; r_{opt}(0.2) \approx 0.08, \; r_{opt}(0.3) \approx 0.12$$

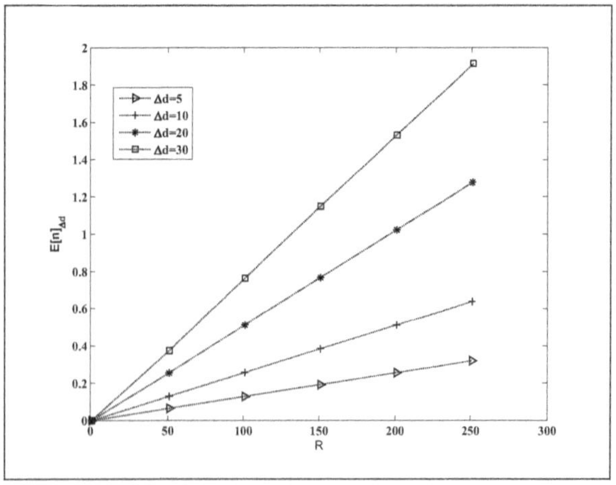

Figure 3: $E[n]_{\Delta d}$ varies with R for different Δd

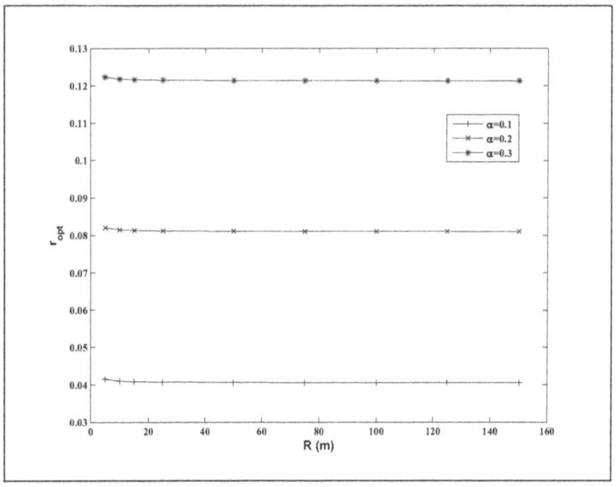

Figure 4: r_{opt} drawn by TAP [3]

When compared to the *turnover* curves drawn in TAP (see Fig. 4), the results of the simplified expression of r_{opt} correlate very well with the curves. Therefore the linear approximation of the complex integration expression in 4 is validated to be correct. The analysis will then be benefit from the linear approximated expression.

In practical application, the *turnover* r is obtained through analyzing the receiving HELLO messages for a time period Δt. Note that (7) can be represented as $r = \frac{2.6\Delta t \times S}{\pi R}$. Once r is provided, the relative speed S is calculated by

$$S = \frac{r\pi R}{2.6\Delta t} \tag{8}$$

Afterwards, the HELLO frequency f_{HELLO} and transmission range R are calculated by (1) and the adaptation solution are available to the each node.

We provide results that demonstrate the correctness of the theoretical analysis for speed estimation. In Fig. 5 the blue line represents the speed estimated through (8) by observing the *turnover* and the red line represents the speed when TAP is implemented. At the beginning of establishing the network, each sensor node is a new comer to their "neighbors", and many new neighbors are detected

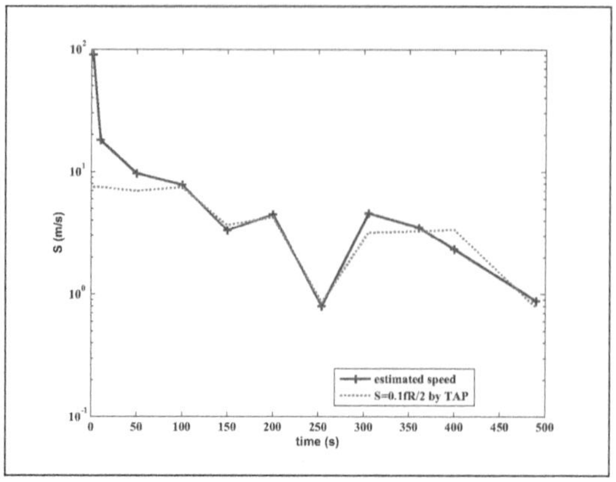

Figure 5: The comparison of speed estimated by 8 and the speed calculated by (1) in TAP

in a very short time which results in a steep rise of *turnover*, thus S is much higher than the following stable periods. The results correlate well between both methods when the network enters relative stable state. However the speed that calculated from TAP is much smaller than directly computed through (8) at the beginning, as there is a constraint to adapt the f_{HELLO} within a certain range which results TAP not as sensitive as (8) to the dynamic changes in the network.

3.2 Minimizing Energy Consumption

The energy spent in period of time Δt by a node u can be expressed as the number of sent messages sent in Δt multiplied by the energy cost of sending one message. The number of messages sent by u during Δt is equal to $\Delta t \cdot f_u(R_u, t)$ where $f_u(R_u, t)$ is the HELLO frequency of node u and R_u is the communication range of node u at time t. Energy consumption varies with both HELLO frequency and transmission range of sensor nodes. In this work, the energy consumption model of sending a HELLO message employs the one given by [2]:

$$E(R) = R(t)^A + C$$

where $A(>1)$ represents the signal attenuation coefficient along the distance, C is the overhead due to signal processing. A and C are constant as long as the deployed environment is homogeneous and the lengths of HELLO messages are identical. Based on the model, the energy spent by a sensor node on sending HELLO message during Δt is:

$$cost_{\Delta t}(R) = (R^A + C)f\Delta t \tag{9}$$

by substituting (1) into (9), we have:

$$cost_{\Delta t}(R) = (R^A + C)\frac{2S}{\alpha R}\Delta t \tag{10}$$

The objective becomes finding R_{opt} for different S that gives the minimum value of $cost_{\Delta t}$, the solution is obtained by solving the partial derivative of (10) when it equals 0:

$$\frac{\partial cost_{\Delta t}(R)}{\partial R} = [(A-1)R^{A-2} - \frac{C}{R^2}]\frac{2S}{\alpha}\Delta t = 0 \tag{11}$$

therefore we have:

$$R_{opt} = \sqrt[A]{\frac{C}{A-1}} \tag{12}$$

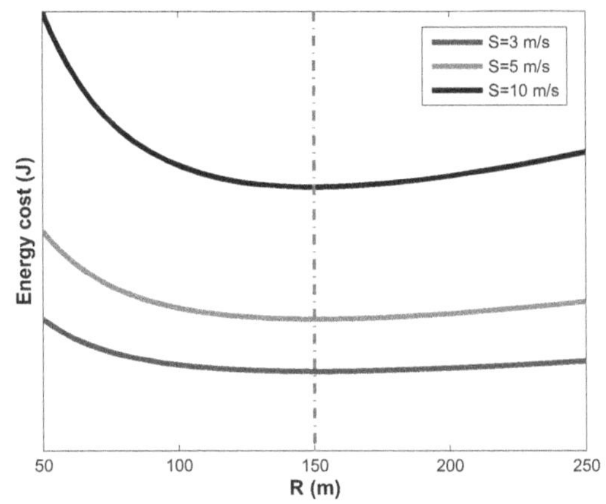

Figure 6: Curves of $cost(R)$ for different speeds

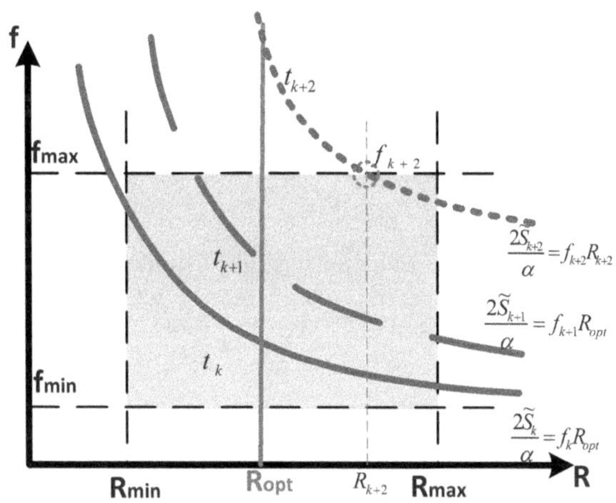

Figure 7: The example of valid region and curves of 1 for different S

Because the second derivative of $cost_{\Delta t}$ is

$$\frac{\partial^2 cost_{\Delta t}(R)}{\partial R^2} = [(A-1)(A-2)R^{A-3} + \frac{2C}{R^3}]\frac{2S}{\alpha}\Delta t \qquad (13)$$

When $A \geq 0$, the value of $\frac{\partial^2 cost_{\Delta t}(R)}{\partial R^2}|_{R=R_{opt}} > 0$. Since A is always larger than 1, it is guaranteed that $cost_{\Delta t}(R)$ reaches the global minimum value at R_{opt}. Fig. 6 shows the variations of energy consumption with R under three different speed levels. With $C = 2.25 \times 10^4$ and $A = 2$, the R_{opt} is equal to $150\ m$, and as expected, the minimum energy cost of each speed level is obtained when $R = R_{opt}$.

We notice from 12 that R_{opt} only varies with C and A, and it is independent of S, which concludes that theoretically all the sensor nodes in the same network should keep transmission range as close as possible to R_{opt} in order to minimize the energy cost and maintain high accuracy of neighborhood table simultaneously.

4. THE TFPA ALGORITHM

As discussed in the previous section, all the sensor nodes are supposed to transmit the HELLO messages with communication range close to R_{opt} in order to minimize the energy cost. However, due to the constraint on hardware device, there exists a maximum transmission range (R_{max}), and for the sake of reliable communication there is a minimum transmission range (R_{min}). Therefore, before implementing the algorithm, the value of R_{opt} should be checked. If $R_{opt} \in [R_{min}, R_{max}]$ the TFPA algorithm can be implemented directly, otherwise, if $R_{opt} \notin [R_{min}, R_{max}]$ the global minimum *cost* is not achievable. When $R_{opt} < R_{min}$, the local minimum *cost* is obtained at R_{min}, we set $R_{opt} = R_{min}$. If $R_{opt} > R_{max}$, the local minimum *cost* is obtained at R_{max}, thus $R_{opt} = R_{max}$. After truncating R_{opt} to the valid region, the TFPA algorithm can be implemented.

It should be noticed that, the change of R can be realized by modifying transmission power of antenna. There are several models for wireless communications such as free-space model, log-normal model, indoor multi-wall model and so on. Through computing the minimum transmit power to reach the computed R, the adaptation of TFPA is easily obtained. Besides, the f_{HELLO} also has an adaptation range: $[f_{min}, f_{max}]$. Fig. 7 demonstrates the valid region (gray rectangle) in which the f_{HELLO} and R can be adjusted. The curves of (1) for different S are shown in the figure as well, and the adaptations from time t_k to t_{k+2} will be explained later.

In the previous section we indeed showed that the *turnover* may be very small (e.g., $r = 0.04$ when $\alpha = 0.1$), while it is nearly impossible for a node to practically observe such a small *turnover* between two successive HELLO messages. A solution to this problem is to let nodes archive more than one table into a history of size X: if X is sufficiently large, then a correct value may be expected. The turnover will then be computed by counting neighbors present in the most recent table that are not present in the older ones and by using the current HELLO delay as:

$$r = \frac{\text{nb of new neighbor}}{\text{total nb of neighbors}} \cdot \frac{d_{HELLO}}{\Delta t} \qquad (14)$$

The implementation of TFPA algorithm is consist of two steps: *Training step* and *Adaptation step*.

In the training step, the procedure is run for $X = 10$ periods at each node to build up the historic data about neighbors which is similar as the TAP and NoTAP algorithms. It also converges the frequency and communication range to a certain level and then serves better for the adaptation step.

The adjustment of f_{HELLO} is calculated through the period between two HELLO messages d_{HELLO}, where $f_{HELLO} = \frac{1}{d_{HELLO}}$:

$$d_{HELLO} = \begin{cases} d_{HELLO} + \frac{d_{HELLO}}{factor} \cdot g(r) & \text{if } r < r_{opt} \\ d_{HELLO} - \frac{d_{HELLO}}{factor} \cdot g(r) & otherwise \end{cases} \qquad (15)$$

Function $g(r)$ is retrieved using turnover to reflect the distance between r and r_{opt}:

$$g(r) = \begin{cases} (\frac{r - r_{opt}}{r_{opt}})^2 & \text{if } r < 2 \cdot r_{opt} \\ 1 & otherwise \end{cases} \qquad (16)$$

Hence, the maximum change of d_{HELLO} at each adjustment is limited by the value of $\frac{d_{HELLO}}{factor}$, $factor > 0$. The pseudo code of *training step* is shown as follow:

TFPA: Training step

```
while X < 10 do
    Calculate r
    if r < r_opt
        Decrease f_HELLO by (15)
    else if r > r_opt then
        Augment f_HELLO by (15)
    end if
    X++
end while
```

The *Adaptation step* is run after finishing the *training step*. At each adaptation interval, each node computes the relative speed S from current turnover ratio r by using (8). The f_{HELLO} and R are then adjusted directly by (1) within the valid region. An example is shown in Fig. 7, at time t_{k+1}, the estimated speed $\widetilde{S}_{k+1}$ is higher than $\widetilde{S_k}$, the curve intersects with $R_{opt} = 150\ m$ in the valid region, thus R_{k+1} is unchanged and equals R_{opt}; while at t_{k+2}, the $\widetilde{S}_{k+2}$ is too high that the intersection with $R_{opt} = 150\ m$ is outside the valid region. However there is still a small part of the curve in the valid region, and the minimum cost will be obtained at R_{k+2} according to the theoretical analysis, therefore f_{k+2} is assigned with the maximum value f_{max}. The pseudo code of *Adaptation step* is shown below:

TFPA: Adaptation step

```
if time to send HELLO packet do
    Calculate r
    Calculate S by (8)
    if H~_optmin <= H~ = 2S/α <= H~_optmax do
        R = R_opt
        f_HELLO = H~/R
    else if H~ > H~_optmax do
        f_HELLO = f_max
        R = min(H~/f_HELLO, R_max)
    else if H~ < H~_optmax do
        f_HELLO = f_min
        R = max(H~/f_HELLO, R_min)
    end if
end if
```

Note that $\widetilde{H}_{optmax} = f_{max} R_{opt}$ and $\widetilde{H}_{optmin} = f_{min} R_{opt}$.

5. PERFORMANCE EVALUATION

In this section, the proposed TFPA algorithm is evaluated through simulation by using the WSNET[1] simulator. Because the purpose of having a HELLO algorithm is for neighborhood discovery, the algorithm must be able to keep the consistency of neighborhood tables among nodes with minimum cost. Thus in addition to HELLO frequency and power consumption, we use two evaluation metrics:

[1]http://wsnet.gforge.inria.fr/

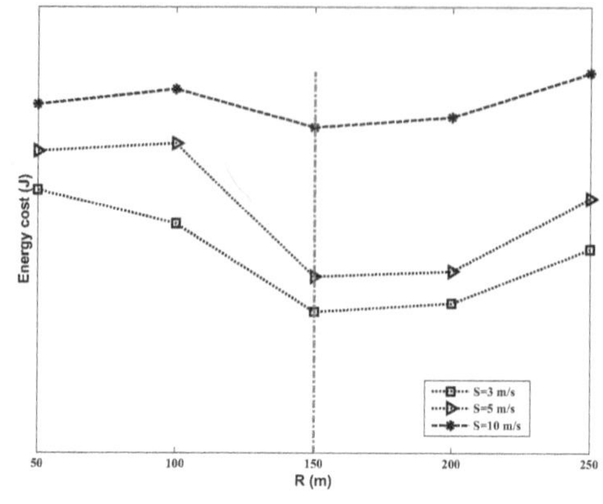

Figure 8: Validate the minimum cost curve

neighborhood accuracy and *neighborhood error*. Assuming that $N(u)$ is the set of actual neighbors of a node u, and $N'(u)$ the set of neighbors known to u (i.e. whose identifier is present in its neighborhood table), these two metrics are defined below. Notice that $acc(u) + err(u)$ is not necessarily equal to 1.

Definition 1. Neighborhood accuracy $acc(u)$ is the proportion of actual neighbors of node u that have been indeed detected by u.

$$acc(u) = \frac{|N(u) \bigcap N'(u)|}{|N'(U)|} \times 100.$$

Definition 2. Neighborhood error $err(u)$ measures both how many neighbors of node u have not been detected, and how many "false neighbors" remain in its neighborhood table (i.e. old neighbors that have not been removed).

$$err(u) = \frac{|N(u) \setminus N'(u)| + |N'(u) \setminus N(u)|}{|N(u)|} \times 100.$$

First of all, the minimum cost model stated in Sec.3.2 is validated. In the simulation, 100 nodes were randomly distributed in a square area of size 1000 $m \times$ 1000 m and the maximum speed of nodes is varied with 3 levels: $0 \sim 3\ m/s$, $0 \sim 5\ m/s\ and\ 0 \sim 10\ m/s$. The propagation employs the free-space model, and $A = 2$, $C = 2.25 \times 10^4$, therefore $R_{opt} = 150\ m$ by substituting A and C in (12) and $\lambda = \frac{100}{1000 \times 1000}$. Fig. 8 shows the energy consumption by the TFPA protocol. For each level, different $R'_{opt} \in [50\ m, 250\ m]$ are tested. Simulation lasts 100 s for each R'_{opt}. As can be seen, the energy cost at $R_{opt} = 150\ m$ is the minimum for all the mobility level and the curve varies similarly as Fig. 6, therefore the theoretical analysis on the R_{opt} is proved.

To evaluate the performance of the TFPA algorithm, we chose to compare it to four other comparable schemes: TAP algorithm[3], NoTAP algorithm[9], Fopt algorithm[11] and ARH algorithm [6]. The TFPA, TAP and NoTAP do not require nodes equipped with GPS. While Fopt sets f_{HELLO} based on the current speed and the ARH sends HELLO message when the error between the prediction of location and the real location is greater than a threshold, thus GPS

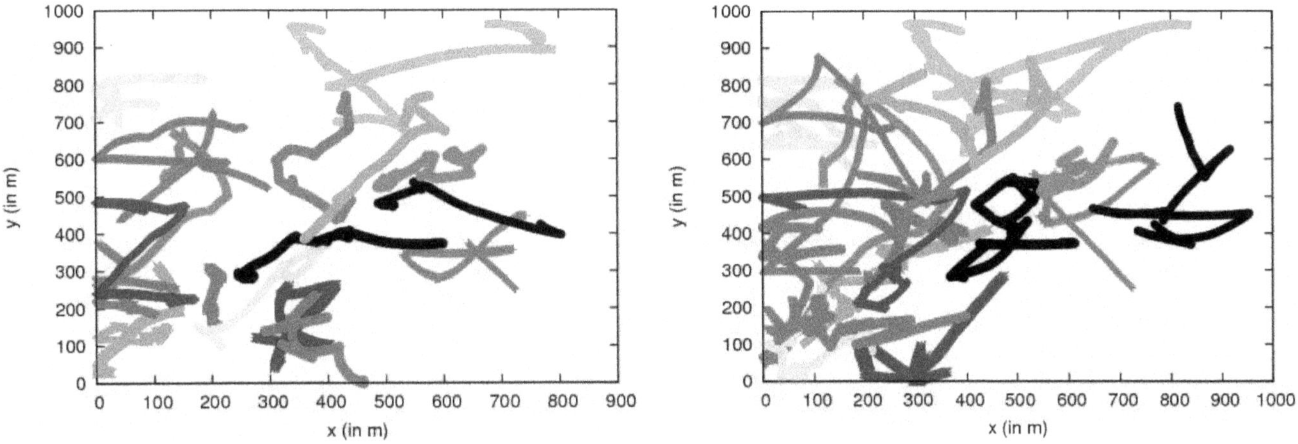

Figure 9: Real mobility trace from pedestrian runners (two examples)

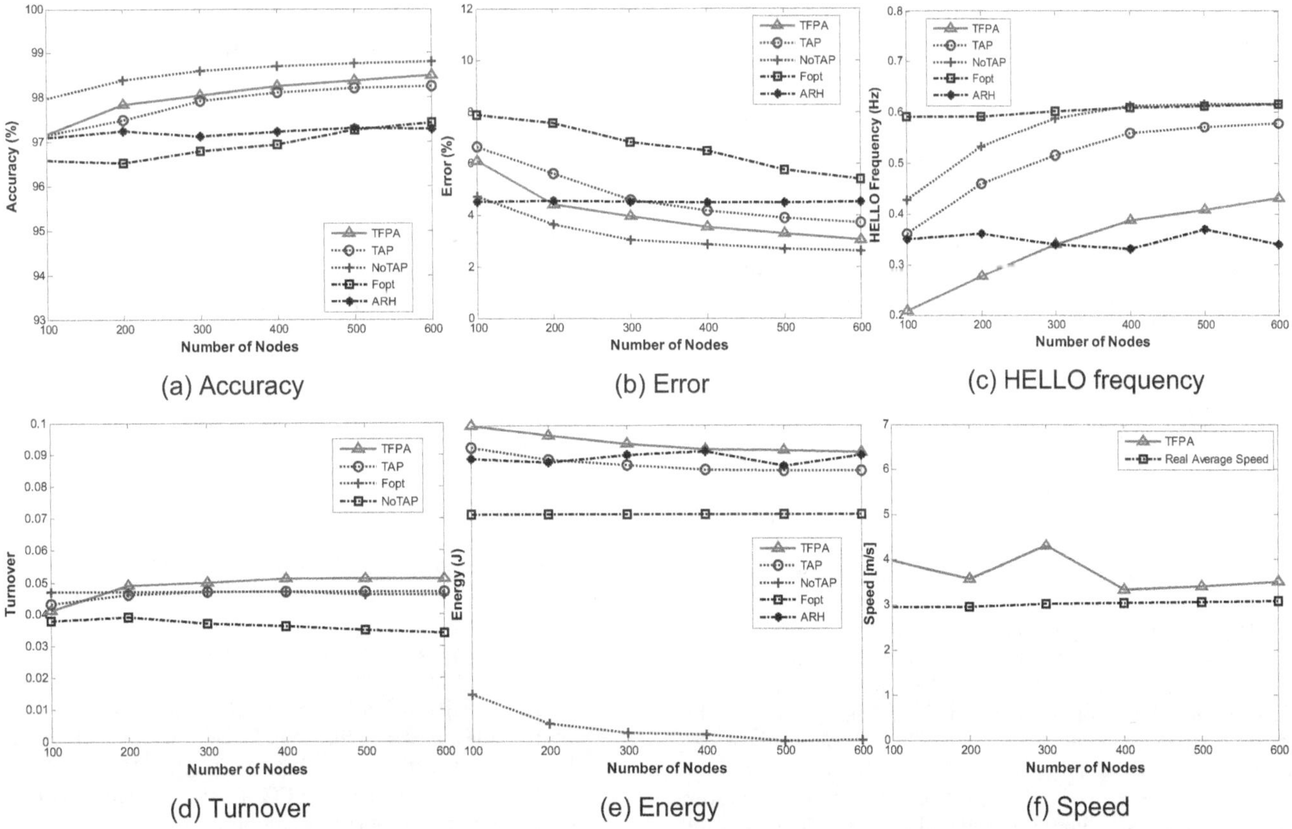

Figure 10: Different metrics of the WSN vary with number of nodes

or a localization module is needed for both Fopt and ARH algorithms.

The nodal mobility trace are generated based on log files obtained from real experiments on pedestrian runners[2]. The moving speed of each node was spread around a mean value of 3 m/s. Two examples of the mobility trace are shown in Fig. 9, where one curve stands for one runner. A varying number of nodes (from 100 to 600) were deployed in a $1000\ m \times 1000\ m$ square region. These nodes have the same optimal transmission range $R_{opt} = 100\ m$ and $R_{min} = 50\ m$, $R_{max} = 150\ m$. For each network size, we conducted 100 simulation runs and obtain the average results with 95% confidence intervals.

Fig. 10(a) and Fig. 10(b) show the accuracy and error of the neighborhood table respectively. The TFPA algorithm

[2]http://researchers.lille.inria.fr/~mitton/mobilitylog.html

performs slightly better than the TAP, Fopt and ARH, but slightly worse than NoTAP.

However, if take a look at Fig. 10(c) which compares the value of f_{HELLO} with regards to different number of nodes, we observe that the HELLO messages sent by TFPA and ARH algorithms are much less than the others. The TFPA performs better than ARH when node density is lower, while ARH performs slightly better as the number of node increases. However, in average, the f_{HELLO} of ARH is about 11% higher than TFPA. The f_{HELLO} of Fopt is 90% higher than that of TFPA, the NoTAP and the TAP are 80% and 60% higher than the f_{HELLO} of TFPA respectively. Bost of the Fopt and ARH algorithms perform consistently, but with different explanations: For Fopt algorithm, the average speed of each node is almost constant thus the average f_{HELLO} is almost constant; for ARH, the HELLO frequency depends on the error that a node detects between its position estimate and its real position, which are both independent from the number of neighbors and the total number of nodes. The curves of TFPA, TAP and NoTAP algorithms have similar variation trend and they climb slightly as the node density increases, which indicates that the dynamic of surrounded neighbors of each sensor node increases.

Fig. 10(d) demonstrates the *turnover* for all the methods except the ARH (which can not explain the *turnover*). As expected, all the turnover ratios are close to 0.04 which is in coincident with the theoretical analysis. The Fopt algorithm provides highest f_{HELLO}, thus the turnover is the lowest. The TFPA gives the lowest f_{HELLO}, thus the turnover is the highest. However, the turnover ratio of Fopt decreases as it only focuses on the absolute speed of each node and ignores the relative change on the neighbors. On the contrary, the turnovers of the TFPA, TAP and NoTAP are relatively stable because again they take into account the mobilities of the neighbors.

The remaining energy is shown in Fig. 10(e). Although the f_{HELLO} of NoTAP algorithm is less than that of Fopt, its energy consumption is the highest. Since Fopt sends HELLO messages always with R_{opt} and NoTAP intends to adapt R to achieve high accuracy, the reduction on the f_{HELLO} can not compensate the consumption on modifying the transmission range, hence the overall energy cost is at the end the highest compared to others. Meanwhile, we observe that the TFPA costs least energy among the algorithms. This can be explained by the factor that in addition to the lowest f_{HELLO}, the TFPA only adapts R when the computed f_{HELLO} reaches the boundary of valid region, while the NoTAP algorithm adapts R whenever f_{HELLO} changes. Therefore, with the lowest f_{HELLO} and quasi global optimum R, the TFPA algorithm is able to save more energy than the others.

The average speed of the WSN is also obtained, Fig. 10(f) shows that the estimated result is slightly higher than the real average speed with a mean error of 0.67 m/s. Therefore, without any GPS-like devices, the TFPA algorithm estimates properly the dynamic of the WSN which can be employed on other implementations that also require speed information.

6. CONCLUSION AND FUTURE WORKS

In this paper, a TFPA HELLO algorithm is proposed for mobile ad hoc networks. The algorithm relies on appropriate theoretical analysis in which the expression of turnover ratio r is approximated properly. By taking account of the relative change of neighborhoods, the relationship between r and relative speed S is derived which enables the sensor nodes be aware of the dynamic of their environment without using GPS-like devices and hardware cost is saved. Moreover, the optimal transmission range is deduced from the battery consumption model which makes the adaptation procedure energy efficient. The simulation results demonstrate that the algorithm is able to maintain the neighborhood table accurate with low HELLO frequency (comparable with and even lower than GPS-needed algorithm) and lowest energy consumption.

There are some open issues, such as the battery consumption modeling, as different models result in different R_{opt} with similar deduce method; the propagation model could be more practical to adapt the transmission power. We would like to further study the consequences of these more realistic assumptions and adapt TFPA protocol consequently.

7. ACKNOWLEDGMENTS

This work is partially supported by CPER Nord-Pas-de-Calais/FEDER Campus Intelligence Ambiante, ANR ECOTECH BinThatThinks and WSN DPCM project.

8. REFERENCES

[1] B. Clark, C. Colbourn, and D. Johnson. Unit disk graphs. *Discrete Mathematics*, 86(1-3):165–177, 1990.

[2] E. Fleury and D. Simplot-Ryl. *Réseaux de capteurs.* Hermes Science - Lavoisier, 2009.

[3] F. Ingelrest, N. Mitton, and D. Simplot-Ryl. A turnover based adaptive hello protocol for mobile ad hoc and sensor networks. In *MASCOTS*, pages 9–14, 2007.

[4] P. Jacquet, P. Mühlethaler, T. Clausen, A. Laouiti, A. Qayyum, and L. Viennot. Optimized link state routing protocol for ad hoc networks, 2001.

[5] N. Li, J. C. Hou, and L. Sha. Design and analysis of an mst-based topology control algorithm. *IEEE Transactions on Wireless Communications*, 4(3):1195–1206, 2005.

[6] X. Li, N. Mitton, and D. Simplot-Ryl. Mobility prediction based neighborhood discovery in mobile ad hoc networks. In *Networking (1)*, pages 241–253, 2011.

[7] V. Loscrì, E. Natalizio, and C. Costanzo. Simulations of the impact of controlled mobility for routing protocols. *EURASIP J. Wireless Comm. and Networking*, 2010, 2010.

[8] J. Moy. *OSPF - Open Shortest Path First.* RFC 1583, March 1994.

[9] J. Radak and N. Mitton. Transmission range adaptation based energy efficient neighborhood discovery. In *MSWiM12*, 2012.

[10] J. Radak, N. Mitton, and D. Simplot-Ryl. Using battery level as metric for graph planarization. In *ADHOC-NOW*, pages 58–71, 2011.

[11] A. Troël. *Prise en compte de la mobilité dans les interactions de proximité entre terminaux à profils hétérogènes.* PhD thesis, Universite de Rennes, 2004.

APDV: Making Distance Vector Routing Scale Using Adaptive Publish-Subscribe Mechanisms

Qian Li*
*Computer Engineering Department
University of California, Santa Cruz
Santa Cruz, CA 95064
liqian@soe.ucsc.edu

J.J. Garcia-Luna-Aceves*†
†Palo Alto Research Center
Palo Alto, CA 94304
jj@soe.ucsc.edu

ABSTRACT

The Adaptive Publish-subscribe Distance Vector (APDV) protocol is introduced as an example of a new approach to allowing distance-vector routing to scale by integrating it with adaptive publish-subscribe mechanisms. APDV combines establishing routes to well-known controllers using distance-vector signaling with publish-subscribe mechanisms. The latter allow destinations to publish their presence with subsets of controllers, and sources to obtain routes to intended destinations from those same controllers. Controllers are selected dynamically using a fault-tolerant distributed election algorithm to ensure that each non-controller node is covered by at least a given number of controllers within a few hops. Extensive simulation experiments are used to compare APDV with AODV and OLSR, which are representative protocols for on-demand and proactive routing. The results show that APDV achieves significantly better data delivery, attains comparable delays for delivered packets, and incurs orders of magnitude less control overhead than AODV and OLSR, even under heavy data loads.

Categories and Subject Descriptors

C.2.1 [**Computer-Communication Networks**]: Network Architecture and Design—*Wireless communication*; C.2.2 [**Computer-Communication Networks**]: Network Protocols—*Routing protocols*

Keywords

Publish-subscribe; routing; service discovery; distance vectors; hash table; distributed algorithm; MANET.

1. INTRODUCTION

Traditional routing protocols for wireless ad hoc networks rely on the network-wide dissemination of signaling packets stating either proactive updates to the state of links or distances to destinations, or on-demand requests for routes to destinations. However, as the number of network nodes, connectivity changes, and new traffic flows increase, both approaches tend to incur excessive signaling overhead, and the problem is even worse for the case of mobile ad hoc networks (MANET). Section 2 summarizes the prior work aimed at making routing more scalable in ad hoc networks. This review indicates that routing protocols for ad hoc networks are such that the signaling needed to maintain destination-based routing tables up to date works independently of the functionality needed to map the names of destinations to either their locations or routes to them.

Although considerable work has been reported on service discovery in ad hoc networks, the solutions to date either operate on top of a routing infrastructure, or augment one of the existing routing protocols to support service discovery. Interestingly, none of the prior solutions to make routing more scalable integrate destination-based routing with adaptive publish-subscribe mechanisms in a way that reduces the signaling required for both routing and service discovery.

The main contribution of this paper is presented in Section 3 and consists of introducing a new approach to routing in wireless ad hoc networks based on publish-subscribe mechanisms that is far more scalable than traditional on-demand or proactive routing. The *Adaptive Publish-subscribe Distance Vector* (APDV) protocol is presented as an example of this approach.

APDV integrates three components: (a) electing a subset of nodes to serve as controllers that maintain routes to nearby destinations, (b) maintaining routes to all known controllers using distance vectors, and (c) using publish-subscribe mechanisms with which destinations inform controllers of routes to them and sources obtain routes to destinations.

Section 4 describes the results of several simulation experiments used to compare the performance of APDV to that of AODV [16] and OLSR [9], which are representatives of traditional on-demand and proactive routing, respectively. The three protocols are compared using static and dynamic topologies. The impact that network size, traffic load, multiple access interference, and mobility have on performance are examined using packet-delivery ratio, average end-to-end delay, and signaling overhead as the performance metrics. The results from these experiments show that APDV incurs orders of magnitude less signaling overhead than AODV and OLSR while attaining similar or better packet delivery ratios and average delays.

MSWiM'13, November 3–8, 2013, Barcelona, Spain.

http://dx.doi.org/10.1145/2507924.2507925.

2. RELATED WORK

Prior routing approaches assume that the mapping of destination names to addresses or routes is done independently of routing, and includes using hierarchies, limiting the dissemination of control messages, distributed hash tables (DHT), Bloom filters, virtual or geographical coordinates, or sets of dominating nodes to reduce the size of routing tables or the amount of route signaling.

Hierarchical routing schemes organize nodes into clusters (e.g., [2], [12], [15], [20]) and some reduce signaling of clustering schemes by limiting propagation of control messages based on their distance from an originating point (e.g., HSLS [17]). The limitations of these approaches are that the affiliation of nodes to clusters is easily broken when nodes move, and re-establishing such affiliations incurs considerable overhead, and incorrect routes can result in schemes in which signaling decays based on the distance to the links.

DHT-based schemes (e.g., [14], [18], [23]) are attractive because a DHT grows only logarithmically with the number of intended destinations. However, typical DHT schemes define a virtual topology, and substantial signaling overhead can be incurred to maintain the links of virtual topologies defined in large MANETs. AIR [5] avoids the use of virtual topologies, but requires the use of variable-length prefix labels instead of addresses. Another approach consists of hashing node identifiers of destinations into Bloom filters, which are then used in routing updates [1]; however, such schemes suffer from the existence of false positives, in which case nodes incur considerable overhead.

Routing protocols that use geographical coordinates for routing (e.g., GPSR [11]) are limited by the requirement to have GPS services and still incur signaling overhead discovering the geo-locations of destinations. A number of schemes use virtual coordinates consisting of the distances of nodes to a few reference nodes (e.g., [4], [24]). The main limitation of this type of virtual coordinates is that multiple nodes may be assigned the same virtual coordinates, and there is no inherent uniqueness to a specific vector of distances to beacons. This results in either incorrect routing or the use of additional signaling (typically flooding) aimed at resolving false positives.

There are many proposals attempting to reduce the number of relays that need to forward signaling messages for a given number of destinations. The best known example of this approach is the use of multipoint relays in OLSR [9]. The main limitation of these proposals is that they call for the establishment and maintenance of connected dominating sets, i.e., the nodes selected to forward signaling messages must form a connected subgraph. This tends to require a large subset of nodes, especially in dynamic topologies.

There is a large body of work on resource and service discovery in ad hoc networks [21]. What is striking about this prior work is that all proposals either assume that names are mapped to addresses and routing to those addresses is then done independently (e.g., ADNS [8]), or augment existing routing protocols with service discovery functionality (e.g., LSD [13], AODV-SD [6], L+ [3]). The use of a common hash function to select controllers in APDV is similar to the approaches used in ADNS and L+. However, ADNS and L+ operates on top of the routing protocol assuming that directory sites or landmarks have been selected, while APDV integrates routing with the selection of controllers and the mapping of names to routes.

3. ADAPTIVE PUBLISH-SUBSCRIBE DISTANCE VECTOR (APDV)

3.1 Overview

APDV assumes that each network node is assigned a network-wide unique node identifier, and takes advantage of the broadcast nature of radio links. First, a subset of nodes are selected dynamically to serve as *controllers*. A controller acts as a directory server by maintaining the routes to destinations nearby, with destinations being denoted by their node identifiers. The distributed algorithm used to select controllers ensures that each non-controller node is within a maximum distance r from a minimum number k of *local controllers* for the node, and as a side effect informs each node about the routes to its one- and two-hop neighbors.

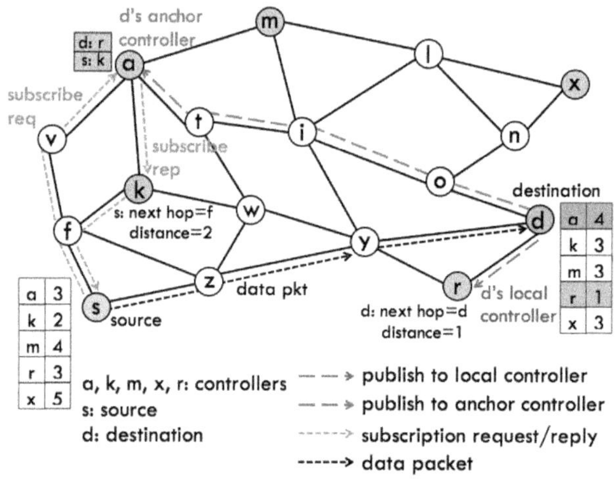

Figure 1: Example of APDV operation

Fig. 1 illustrates the basic operation of APDV assuming that each node has at least one local controller within two hops. In the example of Fig. 1, nodes a, k, m, x and r are the elected controllers of the network.

All network nodes maintain routes to all controllers using a loop-free distance-vector routing algorithm. For simplicity, we assume in this paper that a node maintains a single route to each controller, but APDV can be extended to provide multiple loop-free paths. Each node contacts each of its local controllers to publish its presence. To do this, node d sends a publish message to each of its local controllers with the mapping (d, $\{l_d^1, ..., l_d^k\}$), where l_d^i $(1 \leq i \leq k)$ is a local controller for node d. Each local controller l_d^i of node d and each relay between d and the controller receiving the publish request from d stores a tuple stating d, the next hop to d, and $\{l_d^1, ..., l_d^k\}$. In addition, node d uses a common hash function to select an *anchor controller* a_d that should store the mapping (d, $\{l_d^1, ..., l_d^k\}$), and sends such a mapping to controller a_d. The relay nodes between d and a_d can cache the mapping information. In the example of Fig. 1, node d has published its presence with its local controller (node r) and its anchor controller (node a); note that controller r has a route to node d while controller a has a route to controller r and the mapping (d, r).

A source requiring a route to destination d uses the same common hash function on the identifier of node d to find the anchor controller for d, a_d, and sends a subscription request to controller a_d stating d and $(s, \{l_s^1, ..., l_s^k\})$, where l_s^i $(1 \leq i \leq k)$ is a local controller for node s. In turn, controller a_d responds with the mapping $(d, \{l_d^1, ..., l_d^k\})$ and sends that response towards the nearest local controller for source s selected from the set $\{l_s^1, ..., l_s^k\}$. The answer is redirected to source s by either the selected controller l_s^j or the first relay node along the route from a_d to controller k with a route to s. Node s can then send data packets to destination d by sending them towards the nearest controller in the set $\{l_d^1, ..., l_d^k\}$. Those packets will be redirected to d after either reaching the selected controller in $\{l_d^1, ..., l_d^k\}$ or a node along the route from s to the selected controller with an active route to d. In the example of Fig. 1, node s subscribes to node d by contacting anchor a, which maintains the mapping (d, r) and returns it to node s by sending its response towards node k, which is the local controller of node s. Node a also caches the mapping (s, k). Node s sends data packets to d by sending them towards controller r; however, node y is in the route from s to r and also has a route to d, and forwards the data packets directly to d.

The rest of this section presents important details regarding the information and mechanisms used in APDV for selecting controllers, maintaining routes to controllers, and publishing and subscribing to destinations using controllers.

3.2 Information Stored and Exchanged

The information maintained at each node allows the node to select and route to controllers, route to local destinations, and learn the local controllers associated with distant destinations on demand. Node i maintains a *controller table* (CT^i) stating information about all controllers elected in the network; a *neighbor controller table* (NCT^i) stating information reported by each neighbor of node i regarding all controllers elected in the network; a *neighbor table* (NT^i) stating information about all one- and two-hop neighbors of node i; a *neighbor local routing table* $(NLRT^i)$ stating routing information reported by each neighbor regarding *all* destinations within two hops and *some* destinations within r hops; a *local routing table* (LRT^i) stating routing information about *all* destinations within two hops and *some* destinations within r hops; a *neighbor routing table* (NRT^i) stating information reported by each neighbor regarding distant destinations; and a *routing table* (RT^i) stating information about distant destinations.

APDV employs soft-state to operate efficiently in dynamic networks, and a node transmits its HELLOs periodically every 3 seconds and the HELLO includes some or all the updates made to node's tables. A node stores all the information from the HELLOs it receives from its neighbors, and also caches information it receives in subscription or publication requests from neighbors. Entries in RT^i and NRT^i are populated by the publish-subscribe signaling described subsequently. NT^i, CT^i, NCT^i, LCL^i, and $NLRT^i$, LRT^i, are updated by the exchange of HELLOs among one-hop neighbors.

For each controller c selected in the network, CT^i specifies: the identifier of node c (nid_c^i); the distance from i to c (d_c^i); the successors (next hops) from i to c (s_c^i); and a sequence number (sn_c^i) used to avoid routing loops. NCT^i stores the controller tables reported by each neighbor of node i. The entry for controller c reported by neighbor j and stored in NCT^i is denoted by $\{nid_{cj}^i, d_{cj}^i, sn_{cj}^i\}$.

For each neighbor j of node i, NT^i specifies: the identifier of the node (nid_j^i); a sequence number (sn_j^i) created by j and used to determine that the entry is the most recent from node j; a *controller status flag* (cs_j^i) stating whether or not node j is a controller; the *controller counter* (k_j^i) stating the number of controllers within r hops of node j; and the *local controller list* (LCL_j^i) consisting of the identifiers of all controllers within r hops of node j. An entry for neighbor v in NT^j sent in a HELLO to node i is denoted by $\{nid_v^j, sn_v^j, cs_v^j, k_v^j, LCL_v^j\}$, and the same entry stored in NT^i is denoted $\{nid_{vj}^i, sn_{vj}^i, cs_{vj}^i, k_{vj}^i, LCL_{vj}^i\}$.

An entry for destination j listed in LRT^i specifies: the identifier of the node (nid_j^i); a sequence number (sn_j^i) created by j used to avoid routing loops; the distance from i to j (d_j^i); the successor in the route to j (s_j^i); and the local controller list of node j (LCL_j^i), which may be a link to NT^i if the node is within two hops. An update made by neighbor j to LRT^j communicated in a HELLO is denoted by $\{nid_v^j$, sn_v^j, d_v^j, $LCL_v^j\}$, and the corresponding entry stored at node i in $NLRT^i$ is denoted by $\{nid_{vj}^i$, sn_{vj}^i, d_{vj}^i, $LCL_{vj}^i\}$. An entry for destination v listed in RT^i simply specifies the identifier of the node (nid_v^i) and the list of local controllers for node v (LCL_v^i), because node i maintains the routes to all controllers in CT^i.

Node i includes its own information in NT^i, i.e., it stores an entry corresponding to nid_i^i, and uses the information in its HELLOs. A HELLO from node i contains: nid_i^i, sn_i^i, cs_i^i, k_i^i, and updates to NT^i, CT^i, and LRT^i. An update to NT^i regarding neighbor j consists of the tuple $\{nid_j^i$, sn_j^i, cs_j^i, k_j^i, $LCL_j^i\}$. An update to CT^i regarding controller c consists of the tuple $\{nid_c^i$, d_c^i, $sn_c^i\}$. An update to LRT^i regarding destination v consists of the tuple $\{nid_v^i$, sn_v^i, d_v^i, $LCL_v^i\}$.

3.3 Selecting and Routing to Controllers

The distributed selection of controllers in APDV amounts to selecting a dominating set C of nodes in the network that serve as controllers, such that every node $u \notin C$ (called *simple node*) is at a distance smaller than or equal to r hops from at least k nodes in C (called *controllers*). A node u is said to be (k, r) dominated (or *covered*) if there are at least k nodes in C within r hops from u. There is a large body of work on dominating sets in graphs [7], and many distributed algorithms exist to approximate minimum connected dominating sets (MCDS) with constraints (e.g., [10]). However, the controller selection scheme in APDV is simply aimed at obtaining a set of controllers that cover all nodes but need not be a MCDS, and maintaining routes to all selected controllers. It is based on HELLO messages exchanged among one-hop neighbors. To keep the selection algorithm and signaling simple, only distances to controllers and node identifiers are used as the basis for the selection of controllers.

3.3.1 *Selecting Controllers*

The only way to add or delete controllers in the network is for nodes to self-select themselves to become controllers or stop being controllers. A given node i determines to add or delete its own entry in CT^i, respectively, according to the Controller Addition Rule (CAR) and Controller Deletion Rule (CDR) defined below.

Node i is initialized with $CT^i = \phi$ and $NT^i = \phi$, and waits for a few seconds to start receiving HELLOs from nearby nodes. Hence, according to CAR, node i will select itself as a controller when it is first initialized, unless it has received HELLOs from neighbors that prompt it not to include itself as a controller based on CDR. Node i updates an entry for $j \neq i \in CT^i$ according to the rules described in the next subsection, which ensure that no loops are formed for routes to controllers. Once node i has updated NT^i and CT^i by processing the HELLOs it receives from neighbors, it computes its local controller list (LCL^i) from CT^i, such that $v \in LCL^i$ if $d_v^i \leq r$, and sets $k_i^i = |LCL^i|$.

CAR (Controller Addition Rule):
Node i adds itself to CT^i if
$(k_i^i < k) \wedge [\ i = Min\{nid_j^i\ \forall j \in NT^i \mid (j \notin CT^i) \wedge (k_j^i < k)\}\ ]$

CDR (Controller Deletion Rule):
Node i deletes itself from CT^i if
$(k_i^i > k) \wedge [\ \forall j \in NT^i\ [\ (\ |LCL_j^i - \{i\}| \geq k\ \forall j \notin LCL_i^i\ ) \wedge$
$(nid_j^i < nid_i^i\ \forall j \in LCL_i^i)\ ]\ ]$

Fig. 2 shows an example of controller selection in APDV in a network of six nodes, assuming that each node must be covered by one controller ($k = 1$) within two hops ($r = 2$). For simplicity, the example assumes that HELLO transmissions are synchronized. The figure shows the local controller list (LCL) at each node, and each new state per node in the figure is determined by the reception of HELLOs from all neighbors, followed by the addition or deletion of controllers in the LCL resulting from applying CAR and CDR, deleting controllers that are farther than 2 hops away, or deleting a controller after the successor to that controller sends an update with a deletion of the controller (see RCR and UCR below).

As Fig. 2(a) shows, in this example each node selects itself as a controller after initialization following CAR and sends a HELLO, because nodes do not wait for HELLOs to arrive before using CAR. Fig. 2(b) shows that, after receiving a HELLO from each neighbor, a node may add new controllers reported in the HELLOs, but may delete itself from being a controller based on CDR, which is the case for nodes 30, 50 and 90. Figs. 2(c) to 2(f) illustrate the deletion of a controller entry from LCL at a given node when the successor towards the controller sends a HELLO that deletes the controller, which is the case of node 20 deleting controller 90 and node 18 deleting controllers 30 and 50 in Fig. 2(d), or nodes 30 and 18 deleting controller 20 in Fig. 2(f), for example. Fig. 2(g) illustrates the fact that nodes include in their LCLs only those controllers within $r = 2$ hops, which is the case of node 90 not including controller 10 in its LCL. Fig. 2(g) shows the final state of the LCLs for the example network.

3.3.2 *Routing to Controllers*

For simplicity of presentation, in this paper we assume that each node maintains a single route to each controller selected in the network using the updates to controller tables included in HELLOs.

APDV uses a distance-vector routing approach to maintain routes to controllers. To guarantee loop-free routes, APDV uses sequence numbers that restrict the selection of next hops towards a given controller by any node, such that only those neighbors with shorter distances to the controller or with a more recent sequence number reported by the controller can be considered as successors. An important aspect of APDV is that entries for controllers can be deleted on purpose as a result of CDR, rather than only as rare occurrences due to failures or network partitions. Together with the transmission of periodic HELLOs, the Reset Controller Rule (RCR) and the Update Controller Rule (UCR) discussed below address this functionality.

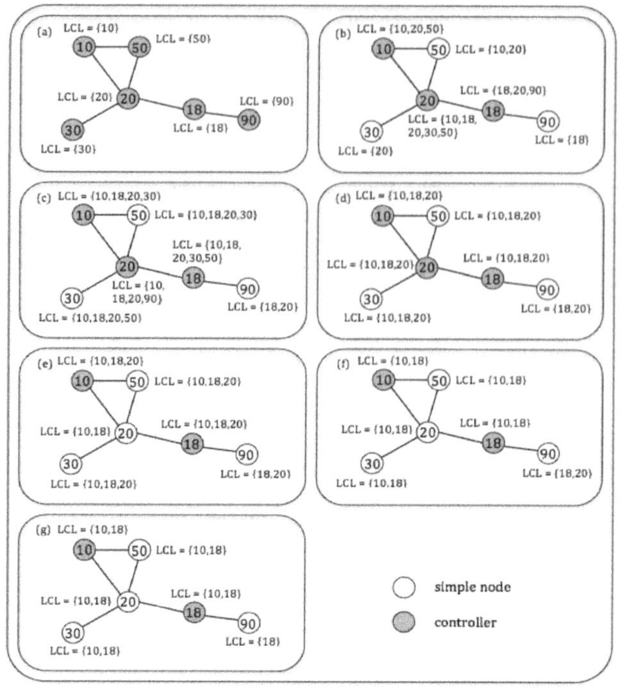

Figure 2: Example of controller selection in six-node network with $k = 1$ and $r = 2$.

Let N^i be the set of one-hop neighbors of node i. Node i updates CT_j^i as a result of HELLOs from neighbor $j \in N^i$ or the loss of connectivity to neighbor j. If node i loses connectivity to node j, the entries in CT_j^i are deleted. Once node i is selected as a controller, it is the only node that can change the sequence number for its own entry in controller-table updates sent in HELLOs.

When a given node i decides to delete itself as a controller based on CDR, its entry must be deleted in the rest of the network. To accomplish this, node i uses RCR to set its self-entry with an infinite distance and an up-to-date sequence number for a finite period of time T, before deleting its self-entry from CT^i to ensure that the rest of the nodes delete the entry for i in their controller tables. If node i receives a HELLO from j or experiences a link failure that makes it update CT_j^i for entry $c \neq i : \{nid_{cj}^i,\ d_{cj}^i,\ sn_{cj}^i\}$, node i updates its entry for c in CT^i according to UCR, which forces node i to propagate a reset update or to select a successor to controller c that is either closer to c or has reported a more recent sequence number from c.

RCR (Reset Controller Rule):
If node i must delete itself from CT^i using CDR then
set $d_i^i = \infty$; $sn_i^i = sn_i^i + 1$; $reset\text{-}timer^i = T$

UCR (Update Controller Rule):

If ($\exists q \in NT^i \mid sn^i_{cq} > sn^i_c$)
  then begin
    if ($(v = s^i_c) \wedge (sn^i_{cv} > sn^i_c) \wedge (d^i_{cv} = \infty)$)
      then set $sn^i_c = sn^i_{cv}$; $d^i_c = \infty$
      else begin
        set $d^i_c = Min\{d^i_{cf} + 1 \mid (f \in NT^i) \wedge (sn^i_{cf} = Max\{sn^i_{cv} \mid v \in NT^i)\}\}$
        set $s^i_c = j \mid (j \in NT^i) \wedge (d^i_{cj} = d^i_c - 1)$
        set $sn^i_c = Max\{sn^i_{cv} \mid v \in NT^i\}$;
  else begin
    set $d^i_c = Min\{d^i_{cf} + 1 \mid (f \in NT^i) \wedge (sn^i_{cf} = sn^i_c) \wedge (d^i_{cf} < d^i_c)\}$;
    set $s^i_c = j \mid (j \in NT^i) \wedge (d^i_{cj} = d^i_c - 1)$

3.4 Publish-Subscribe Mechanisms for Name-to-Route Resolution

Nodes learn about routes to controllers and to one- and two-hop neighbors, but have no routes to destinations many hops away as a result of the exchange of HELLOs.

To allow sources to obtain routes to arbitrary destinations without incurring network-wide dissemination of signaling messages, APDV uses a publish-subscribe mechanism for name-to-route resolution. The use of consistent hashing in APDV is similar to recent proposals for distributed name resolution in MANETs (e.g., ADNS [8]) that use consistent hashing to map the names of destinations to one of several predefined directory sites storing the name-to-address mapping for destinations. The key differences between APDV and this prior work are that: (a) the directories (i.e., controllers) are selected dynamically; (b) a node publishes its presence with multiple controllers; and (c) name resolution is integrated with the selection of and routing to controllers, rather than running on top of routing. Hence, in APDV, controllers maintain name-to-route mappings, rather than storing name-to-address mappings and then using an underlying routing protocol to obtain the routes for known addresses.

For simplicity, we describe the publish-subscribe mechanisms in APDV assuming that node identifiers constitute the names for which routes must be found. However, it should be noted that the same publish-subscribe mechanisms in APDV are applicable to support information-centric networking, such that nodes publish and subscribe to names of destinations, content or services, rather than just node identifiers.

3.4.1 Publishing Destinations

Publishing in APDV consists of having a local controller know the route to a given destination or having an anchor controller know the mapping from a node identifier to a list of local controllers. Subscribing in APDV consists of a node requesting a way to reach a named destination through an anchor controller.

In APDV, node i publishes itself with the k controllers listed in LCL^i, and with one or more anchor controllers. The local controllers in LCL^i are within r hops of node i and serve as the "landmarks" for other nodes to submit data to node i, given that nodes far away from node i do not have routes to node i. Accordingly, a local controller for node i must maintain a route to node i, and it also maintains the mapping (i, LCL^i), so that it can find alternate ways to reach node i if its route to i fails. The anchor controllers are needed for nodes far away from destinations to obtain the mappings between the identifiers of those destinations and their local controllers. For simplicity, in this paper we assume that a single anchor controller is used for any one node.

The anchor controller for node i (denoted by a_i) is obtained by using a network-wide consistent hash function that maps the identifier of node i into the identifier of one of the controllers selected in the network. Controller a_i must store the mapping (i, LCL^i), so that it can provide any node v far away from node i the list LCL^i, with which node v can send data packets towards the local controller in LCL^i that is nearest to node v according to its controller table CT^v.

The forwarding of a publication request from a node to its local controllers is done by the exchange of HELLOs. Given that nodes maintain loop-free routes to all controllers, publication requests directed to local controllers of nodes are forwarded over the reverse loop-free routes already established from local controllers to nodes. The routes maintained by local controllers to nearby nodes are refreshed periodically; each node creates a new publication request by increasing the sequence number included in the LRT self-entry of its own HELLO. If node i receives a HELLO from neighbor j with a publication request originated by node v, which consists of update to LRT^j for destination v ($\{nid^j_v, sn^j_v, d^j_v, LCL^j_v\}$), then node i forwards the request (i.e., it includes the LRT^i entry $\{nid^i_v, sn^i_v, d^i_v, LCL^i_v\}$ in its own HELLO) if it is the successor for node j to any of the controllers listed in LCL^j_v. Once a local controller c receives an entry for destination v and $c \in LCL^v$, then c publishes (i.e., stores) the entry $\{nid^c_v, sn^c_v, d^c_v, s^c_v, LCL^c_v\}$, where s^c_v is the neighbor from which it received the publication request. Controller c may also forward it if it is the successor to another controller in LCL^v for the neighbor from which it received the publication request.

The submission of a publication request from node i to its anchor controller a_i is done by node i using the network-wide consistent hash function on the set of identifiers in CT^i to obtain $hash(i) = a_i$, where $a_i \in CT^i$. After that, node i sends a publication request to its successor towards its anchor controller a_i with the tuple $\{nid^i_i, sn^i_i, d^i_i, LCL^i_i\}$. Each node v in the route from node i to controller a_i forwards the publication request towards a_i and caches the tuple $\{nid^v_i, sn^v_i, d^v_i, s^v_i, LCL^v_i\}$. Once controller a_i receives the request, it stores the tuple $\{nid^{a_i}_i, sn^{a_i}_i, d^{a_i}_i, s^{a_i}_i, LCL^{a_i}_i\}$. Hence, each node processing a publication request learns the route to the node issuing the request, and the anchor controller is able to obtain the mapping needed to redirect nodes sending subscription requests to the local controllers of node i.

3.4.2 Subscribing and Routing to Destinations

The forwarding of subscription requests is handled in much the same way described above for the case of publication requests. When node o has data for destination $j \notin CT^o$, it computes $hash(j) = a_j$, where $a_j \in CT^o$ and sends its subscription request towards a_j. The subscription request from node o regarding destination j states the identifier of node j, its anchor controller a_j, and LCL^o. When a_j receives o's request, it responds with the tuple $\{nid^{a_j}_j, sn^{a_j}_j, LCL^{a_j}_j\}$ and sends the response to the nearest controller it finds in LCL^o. Node o stores the tuple $\{nid^o_j, sn^o_j, LCL^o_j\}$ in RT^o upon receiving the reply to its subscription. Data packets from o are then sent towards the controllers in LCL^o_j

that are the closest to node o. A data packet must specify the sender, the destination, and the selected local controller of the destination. This can be done by encapsulating the header of the packet stating the origin and the destination with a header stating the origin and the selected local controller of the destination. Once the packet reaches a relay node y with an active route for the destination, the packet is forwarded directly to the destination itself, as long as the distance from node y to the destination is at most r hops.

4. PERFORMANCE COMPARISON

We used QualNet [19] (version 5.0) as the discrete event simulator to compare the performance of APDV with the performance of AODV and OLSR, which are representative protocols for the traditional on-demand and proactive routing schemes used in ad hoc networks. We use packet delivery ratio, end-to-end delay, control overhead as our performance metrics. The control overhead is the average number of control packets generated by the routing protocols. We evaluated the three protocols in static and mobile networks. In a static network, nodes are uniformly distributed in the network to avoid disconnected nodes. The random waypoint model was chosen as the mobility model for mobile networks. The routing protocols are tested using the IEEE 802.11 DCF as the underlying MAC protocol, and all signaling packets are sent in broadcast mode. Data sources produced a constant bit rate (CBR) traffic at a rate of 10 packets per second. The three protocols use the same time period to refresh their routing structures. For APDV we used $k = 2$ and $r = 3$ to select controllers. Each simulation ran for 10 different seed values. Unless otherwise stated, the simulation environment details are listed in Table 1.

Table 1: Simulation Environment

MAC Protocol	802.11	Simulation time	300s
Data source	CBR	Data rate	10 packets/s
Pkts. per flow	500	Flow duration	50s
Static Network:			
Total nodes	100-400	Node placement	Uniform
Mobile Network:			
Total nodes	100	Network size	1800 x 1800 m^2
Mobility model	Random waypoint	Pause time	10s
Min.-Max. Vel.	1-10m/s		

4.1 Results for Static Networks

4.1.1 Impact of Increasing Network Size

To evaluate the impact of network size on the performance of the protocols we used static topologies and an ideal physical layer with low data rates per sources in order to limit the impact of Multiple Access Interference (MAI) on the observed performance [22]. The number of nodes is increased from 100 to 400. To avoid having denser networks as the number of nodes is increased, the simulation area is increased proportionally to the number of nodes, so that node density is similar in all cases. The end result is that the 802.11 MAC protocol experiences perfect capture; hence, when multiple packets are received concurrently at a receiver, the receiver decodes one of them successfully. Because traffic load is kept small, MAI due to data traffic is minimum, but the effect of MAI becomes a factor when signaling traffic increases. To exercise the signaling of all protocols, each data flow lasts 50 seconds, and the total number of concurrent data flows is the same in the network at any time. CBR flows are established among randomly selected nodes, and each CBR source generates a total of 500 data packets of 256 B at a rate of 10 packets per second. To avoid bias of traffic load when the network size is changed, we used 5% and 10% of the total number of nodes for the sources with concurrent data flows. The results show that APDV scales much better than AODV and OLSR in every aspect.

The results for 5% of concurrent data flows are shown in Fig. 3(a)-(c). Fig. 3(a) shows that all protocols attain high delivery ratios when the network size is increased subject; however, APDV attains the highest delivery ratios. Fig. 3(b) shows the average control overhead induced by the protocols. APDV incurs the smallest and contrasts with the overhead induced by OLSR, which experiences a steep increase for 400 nodes. APDV incurs limited and fairly constant control overhead because only unicast publish-subscribe requests to anchor controllers are sent other than HELLOs. OLSR erroneously interprets the loss of control packets due to collisions as topology changes, triggering new topology control messages that are diffused in the network and generate more congestion. Fig. 3(c) shows that APDV attains similar end-to-end delays of delivered packets when the protocols have the same delivery ratios. APDV shows slightly higher delays than AODV for 400 nodes, which is mostly due to the fact that APDV delivers more packets than AODV, but in some cases packets may take routes slightly longer than with AODV. OLSR's longer delays are due to the queueing of packets waiting for signaling packets to be sent.

Fig. 4(a)-(c) show the results for 10% traffic load. All three protocols perform similarly up to 200 nodes. Fig. 4(a) shows that APDV scales much better than AODV and OLSR. For 400 nodes, APDV is capable of delivering close to 40% more packets than AODV and 25% more packets than OLSR. The reason behind this behavior can be observed in Fig. 4(b), which presents the average control overhead induced by the protocols. The figure shows that the control overhead incurred by APDV remains constant as the number of nodes increases, while AODV and OLSR incur more overhead as the number of nodes increases. The control overhead in OLSR is a function of the number of nodes in the network. By contrast, Figs. 3(b) and 4(b) show that the control overhead in AODV depends on the traffic load, the heavy traffic load and continuous arrival of new flows forces AODV to constantly flood the network with route requests. Under high congestion, many control packets are lost due to collisions, which is interpreted by AODV as broken links that need to be repaired, and hence nodes react to these packet losses by generating even more route requests, which congest the network even more. Fig. 4(c) shows the end-to-end delays attained by delivered data packets. We observe that APDV performs similar to or better than the other two protocols for all network sizes.

4.1.2 Impact of Increasing Number of Flows

In this scenario we increase the number of concurrent CBR sources from 10% to 40% of the 100 nodes in the static network using a real physical layer. Nodes are uniformly distributed in a simulation area of 1800×1800 m^2. The same CBR flow scheme described in Section 4.1.1 is used. The results are shown in Fig. 5(a)-(c). Fig. 5(a) shows that APDV and AODV attain similar packet delivery for 10 and

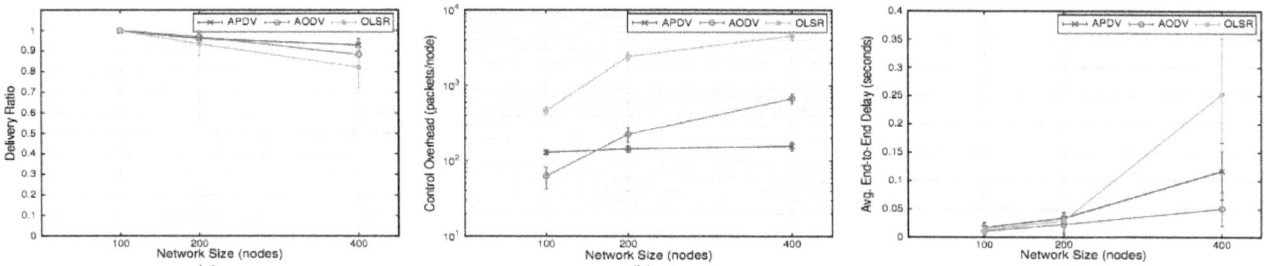

(a) (b) (c)

Figure 3: Static network with increasing network size, ideal PHY, and 5% data load: (a) Delivery ratio, (b) average number of control packets sent per node, (c) end-to-end delay of delivered data packets.

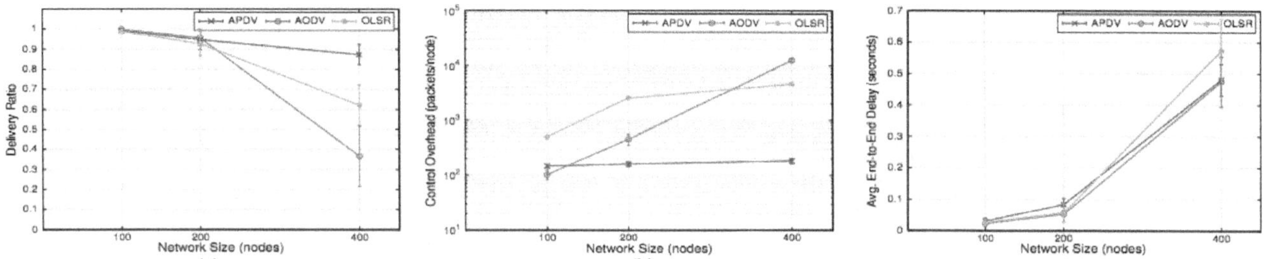

(a) (b) (c)

Figure 4: Static network with increasing network size, ideal PHY, and 10% data load: (a) Delivery ratio, (b) average number of control packets sent per node, (c) end-to-end delay of delivered data packets.

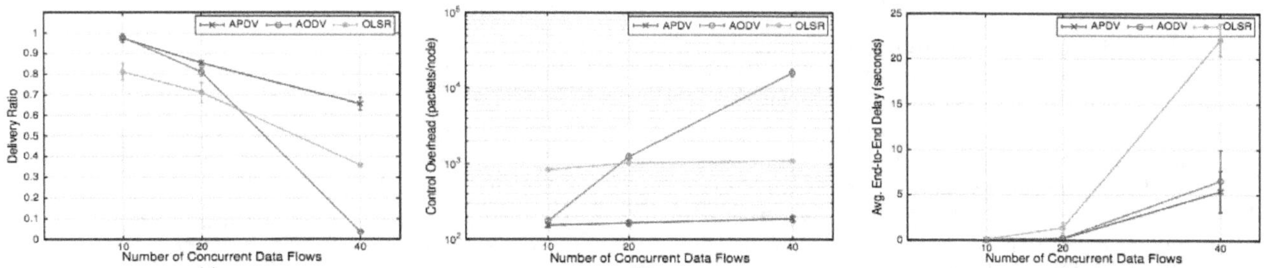

(a) (b) (c)

Figure 5: Static 100-node network with increasing number of CBR flows, and a real PHY: (a) Delivery ratio, (b) average number of control packets sent per node, (c) end-to-end delay of delivered data packets.

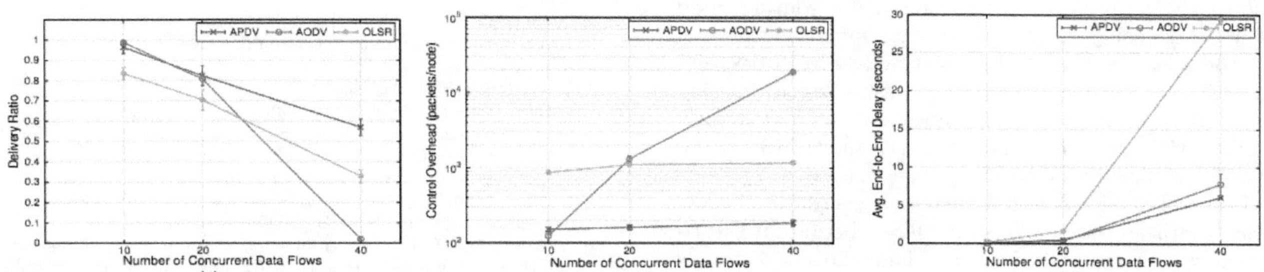

(a) (b) (c)

Figure 6: Mobile network with increasing number of CBR flows and real PHY: (a) Delivery ratio, (b) average number of control packets sent per node, (c) end-to-end delay of delivered data packets.

20 concurrent flows, and that APDV is consistently better than OLSR. APDV attains far better packet delivery than AODV and OLSR for 40 flows; APDV delivers close to 30% more packets than OLSR for 40 flows, and AODV can deliver less than 5% of the packets! Fig. 5(b) shows the control overhead induced by the protocols. APDV incurs very limited and fairly constant control overhead, which contrasts with the overhead incurred by AODV for 40 flows. Even though OLSR is able to keep the control overhead almost constant, it is still much higher than in APDV–almost an order of magnitude–even for a small number of data flows. Fig. 5(c) shows that APDV attains the smallest average end-to-end delays of delivered packets for all traffic loads, and that delays in OLSR increase dramatically for 40 data flows, which is a consequence of data packets being queued waiting for signaling packets to be sent. The delays in AODV for 40 flows appear to be better than for OLSR, but these delays are only for 5% of the packets transmitted, compared to more than 60% of the packets in APDV and more than 30% of the packets in OLSR.

4.2 Results for Mobile Networks

In this scenario we evaluate the performance of the protocols in mobile 100-node networks using a real physical layer, with the number of concurrent CBR sources increasing from 10% to 40% of the number of nodes. The simulation environment is described in Table 1. Fig. 6(a)-(c) show the results of these experiments. Fig. 6(a) shows that APDV consistently outperforms AODV and OLSR. Under heavy traffic load, APDV scales better than AODV and OLSR and is capable of delivering close to 30% more packets than OLSR for 40 flows, while AODV is ineffective and delivers less than 3% of the packets. Fig. 6(b) shows that APDV incurs limited and fairly constant signaling overhead in mobile networks, which helps to illustrate the fact that its use of controllers and adaptive publish-subscribe mechanisms is very well suited for MANETs. By contrast, AODV's overhead explodes for 40 flows, which is the reason why data packets cannot be delivered to destinations. Fig. 6(c) shows that APDV attains the smallest end-to-end delays of delivered data packets, which is a consequence of incurring limited signaling overhead that lets data packets flow faster to their intended destinations. By contrast, delays in OLSR explode for 40 flows, because data packets must wait in queues while signaling packets are transmitted.

5. CONCLUSION

We introduced the *Adaptive Publish-subscribe Distance Vector* (APDV) protocol to provide scalable routing in ad hoc networks using distance vectors by integrating routing with the selection of controllers serving as directories, and name-to-route resolution based on publish-subscribe mechanisms. We used simulation experiments to compare its performance with the performance of AODV and OLSR. APDV achieves significantly better data delivery, attains comparable delays for delivered packets, and incurs substantially less control overhead than AODV and OLSR, because it substitutes network-wide dissemination of link states or distances to destinations with publish-subscribe signaling with controllers.

More work is needed to fully exploit the approach advocated in APDV. One important aspect is the use of a hierarchy of controllers to allow destinations to be known locally, regionally or globally. The performance impact of different values of k and r, and the use of multi-path routing and load balancing among multiple loop-free paths should also be explored.

6. ACKNOWLEDGMENTS

This work was supported in part by the Baskin Chair of Computer Engineering at UCSC, and by the US Army Research Office under Grant SUB0700155/SC20070363.

7. REFERENCES

[1] P. S. Almeida, C. Baquero, N. M. Preguiça, and D. Hutchison. Scalable bloom filters. *Inf. Process. Lett.*, 101(6):255–261, 2007.

[2] J. Behrens and J. J. Garcia-Luna-Aceves. Hierarchical routing using link vectors. In *INFOCOM*, 1998.

[3] B. Chen and R. Morris. Scalable landmark routing and address lookup for multi-hop wireless networks, 2002.

[4] R. Fonseca, S. Ratnasamy, J. Zhao, C. T. Ee, D. E. Culler, S. Shenker, and I. Stoica. Beacon vector routing: Scalable point-to-point routing in wireless sensornets. In *NSDI*, 2005.

[5] J. J. Garcia-Luna-Aceves and D. Sampath. Scalable integrated routing using prefix labels and distributed hash tables for manets. In *IEEE MASS 2009*, 2009.

[6] J. A. García-Macías and D. A. Torres. Service discovery in mobile ad hoc networks: Better at the network layer? In *ICPP Workshops*, pages 452–457, 2005.

[7] T. Haynes, S. Hedetniemi, and P. Slater. *Fundamentals of Domination in Graphs*. Marcel Dekker, 1998.

[8] X. Hong, J. Liu, R. Smith, and Y.-Z. Lee. Distributed Naming System for Mobile Ad Hoc Network. In *ICWN*, pages 509–515, 2005.

[9] P. Jacquet, P. Muhlethaler, T. Clausen, A. Laouiti, A. Qayyum, and L. Viennot. Optimized Link State Routing Protocol for Ad Hoc Networks. In *IEEE INMIC 2001.*, pages 62–68, 2001.

[10] D. S. Joshi, S. Radhakrishnan, and C. Narayanan. A fast algorithm for generalized network location problems. In *ACM SIGAPP*, 1993.

[11] B. Karp and H. T. Kung. GPSR: Greedy Perimeter Stateless Routing for Wireless Networks. In *ACM MobiCom*, pages 243–254, 2000.

[12] L. Kleinrock and F. Kamoun. Hierarchical Routing for Large Networks; Performance Evaluation and Optimization. *Computer Networks*, 1:155–174, 1977.

[13] L. Li and L. Lamont. A lightweight service discovery mechanism for mobile ad hoc pervasive environment using cross-layer design. In *IEEE PerCom Workshops*, 2005.

[14] Q. Li and J. J. Garcia-Luna-Aceves. Opportunistic Routing Using Prefix Ordering and Self-Reported Social Groups. In *ICNC Workshop on Computing, Networking and Communication*, 2013.

[15] Y. Mao, F. Wang, L. Qiu, S. S. Lam, and J. M. Smith. S4: Small State and Small Stretch Routing Protocol for Large Wireless Sensor Networks. In *NSDI*, 2007.

[16] C. E. Perkins and E. M. Belding-Royer. Ad-hoc On-Demand Distance Vector Routing. In *WMCSA*, pages 90–100, 1999.

[17] C. A. Santiváñez, R. Ramanathan, and I. Stavrakakis. Making link-state routing scale for ad hoc networks. In *ACM MobiHoc*, 2001.

[18] A. Singla, P. B. Godfrey, K. Fall, G. Iannaccone, and S. Ratnasamy. Scalable routing on flat names. In *ACM CoNEXT*.

[19] S. N. Technologies. Qualnet. http://web.scalable-networks.com/content/qualnet.

[20] P. F. Tsuchiya. The landmark hierarchy: a new hierarchy for routing in very large networks. In *SIGCOMM*, 1988.

[21] C. N. Ververidis and G. C. Polyzos. Service discovery for mobile ad hoc networks: a survey of issues and techniques. *Commun. Surveys Tuts.*, 10(3):30–45, 2008.

[22] Y. Wang and J. J. Garcia-Luna-Aceves. Collision avoidance in multi-hop ad hoc networks. In *IEEE MASCOTS 2002*, 2002.

[23] B. Y. Zhao, J. D. Kubiatowicz, and A. D. Joseph. Tapestry: An Infrastructure for Fault-tolerant Wide-area Location and. Technical report, 2001.

[24] Y. Zhao, Y. Chen, B. Li, and Q. Zhang. Hop ID: A Virtual Coordinate-Based Routing for Sparse Mobile Ad Hoc Networks. *IEEE Transactions on Mobile Computing*, 6(9), 2007.

Performance Evaluation of the Anypath Routing and Forwarding Mechanism AP-OLSR

Andreas Lavén
Karlstad University
Department of Mathematics and Computer Science
651 88 Karlstad, Sweden
andreas@lavn.eu

Andreas J. Kassler
Karlstad University
Department of Mathematics and Computer Science
651 88 Karlstad, Sweden
kassler@ieee.org

Anna Brunstrom
Karlstad University
Department of Mathematics and Computer Science
651 88 Karlstad, Sweden
anna.brunstrom@kau.se

ABSTRACT

Wireless mesh networks (WMNs) consist of several small routers relaying packets wirelessly toward the destination or the Internet. A dense deployment enables the rapid creation of wireless access networks at a reasonable cost. The capacity of a wireless mesh network can be increased by using a diverse set of channels to allow simultaneous transmissions without causing interference. An interesting approach is to use one fixed wireless network interface for receiving and at least one switchable interface for sending. However, such a channel assignment suffers from switching overhead.

In order to minimize the channel switching latency, we have developed a novel packet routing and forwarding strategy, AP-OLSR, which uses multiple next hop candidates tuned to different channels. When forwarding a packet, nodes pick the neighbor which is on a channel that gives a good balance between local switching overhead and global path quality.

In this paper, we present a thorough evaluation of AP-OLSR with scenarios involving both single and multiple gateways, as well as single and competing flows.The evaluation shows that AP-OLSR can improve performance in both latency and throughput.

Categories and Subject Descriptors

C.2.1 [**Network Architecture and Design**]: Wireless communication; C.2.2 [**Network Protocols**]: Routing protocols

Keywords

Wireless Mesh Networks, Anypath Routing and Forwarding, AP-OLSR

MSWiM'13, November 3–8, 2013, Barcelona, Spain.

ACM 978-1-4503-2353-6/13/11 ...$15.00.
http://dx.doi.org/10.1145/2507924.2507934

1. INTRODUCTION

Wireless mesh networks (WMNs) are composed of radio nodes organized in a mesh topology that relay packets wirelessly towards the destination or an Internet gateway. The wireless deployment allows a dense access network to be rapidly set up at a reasonable cost. The mesh topology makes the network reliable, as the dense topology allows flows to route around failed nodes. WMNs are used by e.g. military forces, user communities and even municipalities. Due to their low cost, WMNs are considered as an interesting architectural candidate for the future wireless Internet.

By using multiple radios, the capacity of a WMN can be increased [1]. The usage of multiple radios allows simultaneous transmissions without causing interference by using a set of channels. The channel configuration of the nodes impacts both the topology and the routing of the network. Hence, an effective channel assignment is important in multi-radio mesh networks.

In static channel assignments, each network interface is assigned to a channel permanently or for a long duration of time. Dynamic channel assignments have the benefit over static channel assignments of being able to cope with external interference [2] and changes in traffic demand [3]. However, dynamic channel assignments may lead to routing problems or network disconnections. In hybrid channel assignments [4], one wireless network interface is tuned to a fixed channel and used for receiving. At least one switchable interface is used for sending. This approach has the benefit of providing a fully connected network, but may lead to high channel switching overhead.

Typical routing protocols for WMNs, such as Ad hoc On-Demand Distance Vector Routing (AODV) [5] or Optimized Link State Routing (OLSR) [6], use a single path routing algorithm. This results in one path between a sender and a receiver which is used to send packets as long as the path is available and shows a good enough quality. The routing algorithm typically calculates path costs using link state information received through control packets. Due to large differences in quality between links, the hop-count metric is not suitable in wireless mesh networks. Instead, metrics such as ETX [7] and ETT [8] are designed to cope with this problem. In multi-channel mesh networks, also channel switching overhead and channel diversity have a significant impact on route quality [4].

However, dynamically changing attributes, such as currently tuned channel, cannot be handled in single path routing mechanisms.

Anypath routing [9] gives the ability to select a path on a per packet basis instead of always using the one with the lowest average path cost. In a hybrid channel assignment a packet has to wait in a queue when the required channel is not tuned. When each node has a set of candidate forwarders for each destination, a packet may be transmitted on several channels. This increases the probability of the packet being sent immediately and reach the destination with a lower latency.

Our routing and forwarding mechanism, called AP-OLSR, follows the anypath paradigm and takes for each packet the time required to wait before transmitting on a given channel into consideration when selecting a next hop. The switching cost varies heavily during time and cannot be reflected in a routing algorithm. The key idea in our approach is to use one next hop candidate per channel and on a per packet basis select the candidate expected to make the packet reach the destination first. In this paper, we present a thorough evaluation of the AP-OLSR performance using measurements from a multi-radio mesh testbed KAUMesh [10]. The evaluation consists of scenarios with randomly selected sources and destinations involving both single and multiple gateways, as well as single and competing flows.

The key findings are that AP-OLSR decreases the latency when the network is not congested and its ability to increase throughput. The best scenario for AP-OLSR is when crossing flows exist, due to its ability to rapidly change forwarding nodes.

The remainder of the paper is structured as follows: Section 2 describes AP-OLSR, section 3 evaluates our approach and section 4 concludes the paper.

2. AP-OLSR

Wireless mesh networks using hybrid channel assignment are composed of nodes which are equipped with at least two network interfaces [4]. One interface is used for receiving data while the remaining ones are used for sending. The receiving interface is fixed to a channel known to its neighbors, and the sending interface switches its channel to match the receiving interface of the neighbor the packet should be forwarded to. Such channel assignment allows full connectivity in the network, as all nodes within reach can send data to each other. This avoids multi-channel deafness problems. In order to assign channels to the receiving interfaces several strategies exist [11].

Due to hardware limitations, switching channel on a per packet basis is too costly. Therefore, once an interface is tuned to a specific channel it will stay there for some time. All packets that are received on the receiving interface but cannot be forwarded because no sending interface is on the required channel need to be buffered. This introduces additional latency. AP-OLSR strives to decrease the time where a packet waits in queues by providing the nodes with several next hop candidates. Each candidate listens on a unique channel to increase the number of possible channels for a packet to be sent on. This increases the chance of a packet to be sent on the tuned channel instead of being placed in a queue. In wireless mesh networks there are often several paths with the same length and even a longer path has been shown to be beneficial compared to waiting in queues [12].

In the following section we will describe how Dijkstra's shortest-path algorithm [13] has been modified to find several next hop candidates for each destination. If several neighbor nodes per destination are identified which are on "good enough" paths, a forwarding algorithm is required to select for each packet the best candidate. Our forwarding algorithm will be explained after the routing algorithm.

2.1 Anypath Routing

Typically, a routing algorithm calculates the best next hop for each destination. Anypath routing needs to find multiple alternative next hop candidates. However, since we aim to reduce switching costs, the time we have to wait until a given channel is in use, we are not interested in two next hop candidates listening on the same channel. Instead, our anypath routing algorithm results only in the best next hop candidate for each destination and channel.

Given a graph $G = (V, E)$ and a source node a, the algorithm calculates the path with the lowest cost. Cost in our context is determined by the sum of the latencies of all links and the switching cost of every relay node, for every channel $f \in F$ to each destination d (see algorithm 1). Besides next hop and path cost, the algorithm also results in the number of hops for each path.

This algorithm is run independently at every node. N denotes the set of all next hop candidates, C the set of all path costs for each node and channel, H the set of all hop counts for each node and channel, and U the set of all unvisited nodes. Lines 1-9 initialize data structures N, H, C and U. Lines 10-29 visit each node, starting with the one having the smallest cost (line 11), and check all its neighbors for a better path.

The path cost is calculated by aggregating the expected transmission time $ett()$ of each link with the switching cost $sc()$ of each node. The switching cost for a given node is the average time until the required channel will be tuned, estimated by using channel usage statistics for the last second. The ETT value is given by sending a pair of packets back-to-back to the neighbor node. The neighbor node will reply with the difference in arrival time and the value is multiplied with the expected transmission count. Both the switching cost and the expected transmission time are broadcasted through the OLSR extensions. However, for the first hop (lines 13-17), we do not consider the switching cost. This is because in the routing algorithm we just have average information available, which might not reflect the actual state of the channel switch operation. Instead, the switching cost of the local node will be added in the forwarding algorithm, where the exact value for each packet is available.

If a better path is found on a channel f to a neighbor d (line 21), the next hop is stored as $N_{d,f}$ (line 22), the number of hops is stored as $H_{d,f}$ (line 23) and the *new_cost* is stored as $C_{d,f}$ (line 24). The outcome of this algorithm is then a set of next hops N, a set of required number of hops H and a set of path costs C. For each destination, each member in the next hop candidate set N is reachable via a different channel and for this given channel has the minimum cost path to destination d.

Algorithm 1 Routing(G = (V, E), a)

1: **for all** nodes $v \neq a \in V$ **do**
2:   **for all** frequencies $f \in F$ **do**
3:     $N_{v,f} \leftarrow \emptyset$
4:     $H_{v,f} \leftarrow \emptyset$
5:     $C_{v,f} \leftarrow \infty$
6:   **end for**
7: **end for**
8: $C_{a,\emptyset} \leftarrow 0$
9: $U \leftarrow V$
10: **while** $U \neq \emptyset$ **do**
11:   $u \leftarrow$extract_min(U)
12:   **for all** links $(u,d) \in E$ **do**
13:     **if** $u = a$ **then**
14:       $f \leftarrow$ get_frequency((u,d))
15:       $N_{d,f} \leftarrow u$
16:       $H_{d,f} \leftarrow 1$
17:       $C_{d,f} \leftarrow$ ett((u,d))
18:     **else**
19:       **for all** next_hops $N_{u,f} \in N$ **do**
20:         *new_cost* $\leftarrow c_{u,f}+$ sc((u,d)) + ett((u,d))
21:         **if** *new_cost* $< c_{d,f}$ **then**
22:           $N_{d,f} \leftarrow N_{u,f}$
23:           $H_{d,f} \leftarrow N_{u,f} + 1$
24:           $C_{d,f} \leftarrow$ *new_cost*
25:         **end if**
26:       **end for**
27:     **end if**
28:   **end for**
29: **end while**

2.2 Anypath Forwarding

When packets arrive at a mesh node, the forwarding mechanism looks up the next hop in the routing table. In anypath routing, the routing algorithm results in several next hop candidates for each destination. Therefore, a forwarding algorithm is required to select the best next hop candidate for each packet. The key idea is to select the next hop candidate which for each packet is expected to reach the destination fastest. This is estimated by aggregating the time until the required channel is tuned together with the expected path latency given by the routing algorithm. If several paths exist with similar path costs, latency can be reduced by avoiding time spent in queues waiting for a specific channel to be tuned. Also, a maximum number of allowed hops is used to keep the length of the path down.

Given a set of next hop candidates N, a set of required hops H and a set of path costs C, our layer 2.5 forwarding algorithm selects a next hop candidate s to the given destination d which is reached within the given remaining hops r (see algorithm 2). By considering channel scheduling information, time to wait for an interface to switch its channel can be avoided.

Algorithm 2 Forwarding(N, H, C, d, r)

1: $l \leftarrow \infty$
2: **for all** next_hops $N_{d,f} \in N$ **do**
3:   **if** $H_{d,f} \in H \leq r$ **then**
4:     $t \leftarrow$switch_delay($N_{d,f}$) + $C_{d,f} \in C$
5:     **if** $t < l$ **then**
6:       $l \leftarrow t$
7:       $s \leftarrow N_{d,f}$
8:     **end if**
9:   **end if**
10: **end for**

Line 1 initializes l, which stores the currently lowest cost to reach the destination d (line 6). Lines 2-10 loop through each next hop $N_{d,f} \in N$ and check if we can reach the destination via this neighbor and channel within r hops (line 3). If so, we calculate the total cost t (line 4), which is composed of the *actual* switching delay in the current node to tune the sending interface to the receiving channel of the given next hop candidate and the path cost $C_{d,f}$ as given by the routing algorithm. If the total cost t is lower than l (line 5), the candidate $N_{d,f}$ is stored as s (line 7). The outcome of this algorithm is then the best candidate s as perceived by the local node. The packet will then be enqueued into the channel queue which is associated with this neighbor node s.

AP-OLSR uses a variable α to balance the tradeoff between a next hop where switching delay can be avoided and keeping the length of the path down. The α variable is used to calculate the maximum number of hops allowed before the destination must be reached. A high value of α gives a packet higher probability to avoid waiting for channel switches by instead taking a longer path. This value is set by the source node and calculated by multiplying the number of hops required by the average best path, given by the routing algorithm, with the variable α, e.g. if the average best path contains 4 hops and $\alpha = 1.5$, then a packet is allowed to make 6 hops.

2.3 Implementation Details

AP-OLSR is implemented in Linux 2.6.35.7 using ath5k as wireless network driver. AP-OLSR consists of two components, a user space application responsible for routing and a kernel space module responsible for forwarding. The path information given from the routing application is sent to the kernel module using ioctl messages.

The routing application is based on [4], with a modification where AODV was replaced by OLSR [14] and an extension called Multimetric OLSR [15] which enables multiple metrics to be considered in the routing algorithm. The routing algorithm uses information generated by the ETT implementation [8].

Our kernel space module is based on Net-X [4]. It has been modified to use routing information from the user space routing application when selecting a next hop candidate. The information about the allowed number of hops is placed in each packet by overwriting the TTL value.

3. EVALUATION

This section presents the evaluation of the anypath routing and forwarding mechanism AP-OLSR.

Four different scenarios are included to analyze the performance of AP-OLSR and compare it with standard single path routing. To make the single path routing to always select the same next hop candidate for each destination, we use an average switching time also for the current node. We will evaluate the performance of single flows, multiple random flows to both one and two gateways, and also flows crossing each other.

3.1 Experimental Setup

All our experiments are run on KAUMesh [10], an experimental Wireless Broadband Mesh Network based on 802.11a/b/g WLAN devices, deployed at the Karlstad University campus. In our evaluation, we used 9 nodes placed in a topology displayed in figure 1. The notation $A : 48$ means that node A uses channel 48 at its receiving interface.

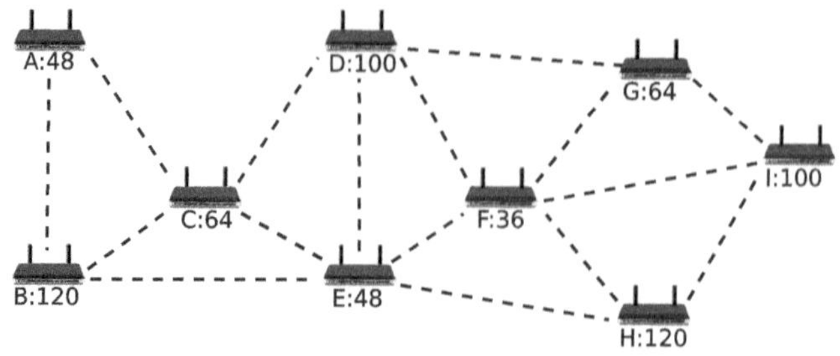

Figure 1: Topology

Each node, a Cambria GW2358-4 Network Computer, consists of an Intel IXP435 XScale CPU operating at 667 MHz, 128 MB of DDRII-400 SDRAM, and 32 MB of Flash. Each board is equipped with 3 x 802.11a/b/g Atheros miniPCI WLAN radio cards, of which two wireless network interfaces are used in our evaluation (one for receiving and one for sending). The transmission rate is fixed at 6 Mbps for each interface, using a constant sending power of 20 dBm.

In all experiments, the mgen toolset [16] is used to generate UDP packets. The packet payload size is set to 1000 bytes and generated at two different rates, 100 and 600 packets per second. The different packet rates are chosen to show the performance in both lightly and heavily loaded networks.

We use a round-robin policy for determining which channel to serve next. Once a channel is selected, the scheduler uses that channel for at least $T_{min} = 40\ ms$. After this T_{min} has expired, the scheduler picks the next channel with packets waiting to be transmitted. If there are no other channels with packets queued, then the channel switch will be postponed. To validate our results we have also run all tests with a T_{min} of 100 ms. We have also run the tests with a different receiving channel configuration on each node. The performance of each flow was slightly different, but the overall trends were the same. Due to lack of space, we present only results corresponding to our testbed setup shown in figure 1, where we use $T_{min} = 40\ ms$. The numbers indicate the receive channel config for each node. The proposed scheduling strategy for selecting the next channel is simple to implement. In a follow up version, we intend to evaluate the impact on performance using more sophisticated scheduling strategies.

3.2 Single Flow

First, we evaluate the performance of a single flow. We randomly selected Node G in our network to act as a gateway (see figure 1) and generated a packet flow from each of the 8 remaining nodes (one at the time). Each test is run 20 times and the results from this scenario are presented in figures 2, 3 and 4. The choice of 20 repetitions was made due to the low variance in the tests.

Figure 3(a) shows the average latency with a 95 % confidence interval in the lightly loaded network. The latency is the time between a packet is generated at the source node and the time it is received at the destination. The clocks of all mesh nodes are synchronized by using a wired network interface. Each bar is the average value of all flows with the given number of hops. For paths with a length of one hop, $\alpha = 2.0$ is the only configuration that is allowed to use an extra hop and the only configuration that decreases the average latency. When paths are longer, more opportunities AP-OLSR provides to make a beneficial next hop selection arise. We can see that also $\alpha = 1.5$ decreases the latency for paths longer than one hop.

Figure 3(b) shows the latency CDF over all received packets for the single flow scenario. We can see how the number of allowed extra hops decreases the latency. For example, after 40 ms about 60 % of the packets have reached the destination when using single path routing or AP-OLSR with $\alpha = 1.0$. When allowing extra hops, after the same amount of time about 75 % of the packets are delivered when $\alpha = 1.5$ and 85 % when $\alpha = 2.0$. The more extra hops we allow the more opportunities to avoid waiting for a channel switch.

Figure 2 shows the latency for 100 packets taken from the data flow between A and G (3 hops) with a packet rate of 100 packets per second. This figure shows how the latency is affected by the channel switches in the different forwarding configurations. The figure presents only 1 second, but the pattern reflects the overall latency shown in figure 3(b). We can see that the area between the line and the X axis (which is the total latency) is bigger for single path routing and for AP-OLSR where $\alpha = 1.0$, compared to AP-OLSR where $\alpha > 1.0$. The steeper curve seen for $\alpha > 1.0$ means less packets are waiting for a channel switch.

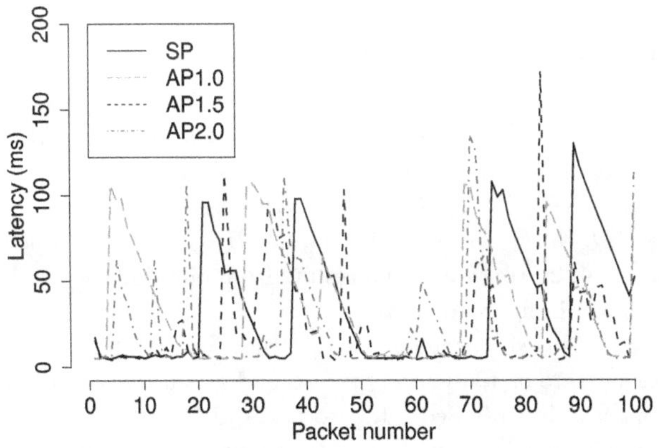

Figure 2: Latency per packet, flow A → G (100 pkts/s)

The average throughput per flow, grouped by path length, is shown in figure 3(c). The throughput is given by calculating the number of bits transferred within the data flow divided by its duration. In the lightly loaded network scenarios very few packets were lost. This leads to an equal achieved throughput for all configurations.

The results in the heavily loaded network are shown in figure 4. Figures 4(a) and 4(b) show that the latency does not always benefit from AP-OLSR in heavily loaded networks. Allowing many extra hops, $\alpha = 2.0$, results in the worst performance for short paths in the heavily loaded network. Figure 4(a) shows that the average latency of AP-OLSR ($\alpha = 2.0$) is almost 40 % higher than single path routing for all flows that traverse one hop, but lower for all 3 hop flows.

AP-OLSR splits a data flow over several paths to avoid switching costs. As all packets in a flow have the same destination all these paths need to merge (at latest at the destination node). When those subflows merge at intermediate or end nodes, at that node all packets are received by the receiving interface on the same channel (because each node listens on only one channel). This causes competition for the bandwidth which for short paths in heavily loaded networks has a negative impact greater than the gain from avoiding switching cost.

A too high value of α for short paths is not beneficial for the throughput either. As can be seen in figure 4(c), $\alpha = 2.0$ increases the throughput only for paths with 3 hops. For 1 hop paths, single path routing and AP-OLSR with $\alpha < 2.0$ all have to send directly to the destination, and therefore is the achieved throughput the same. However, for 2 hop paths the AP-OLSR with $\alpha < 2.0$ configurations are able to send regardless which channel is tuned. Hence, the achieved throughput is higher compared to single path routing.

3.3 1 Gateway, 3 Flows

In the next scenario, we randomly selected one node as a gateway to which we generated 3 flows from randomly selected source nodes. Three different sets of 1 gateway and 3 source nodes were used; (1): $G \leftarrow \{A, B, H\}$; (2): $G \leftarrow \{C, E, H\}$; (3): $G \leftarrow \{D, F, H\}$. Each test is run 20 times and the results are presented in figures 5 and 6.

Figures 5(a) and 5(b) show the latency when all flows are generated with a rate of 100 packets per second. Figure 5(a) shows the average latency for each test in our 1 gateway scenario. The only statistically significant differences in average latency between the configurations are that AP-OLSR with $\alpha = 1.5$ performs better than single path routing in the first two tests and AP-OLSR with $\alpha = 2.0$ performs better than AP-OLSR with $\alpha = 1.0$ in the third test. The reason why AP-OLSR with $\alpha = 2.0$ performs better in the third test is because all sources are close to the destination (two of them are only one hop away). In one hop paths AP-OLSR with $\alpha = 2.0$ is the only configuration that allows extra hops to avoid switching cost. In figure 5(b) we can see how AP-OLSR reduces the latency, especially when extra hops are allowed to avoid waiting for a channel switch. We can see that after 100 ms around 90 % of the packets have reached the destination when using AP-OLSR with $\alpha > 1.0$, but for single path routing it takes about 130 ms until 90 % of the packets have arrived. Again, the more opportunities

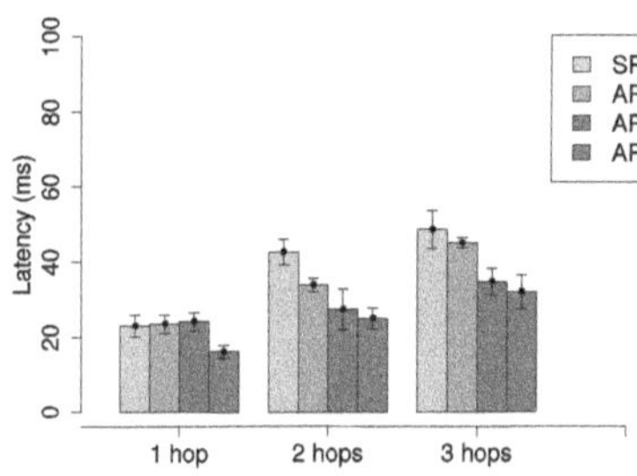

(a) Average latency

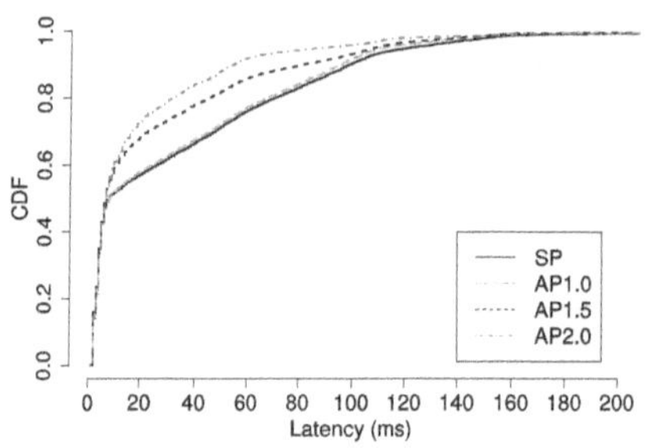

(b) Latency CDF

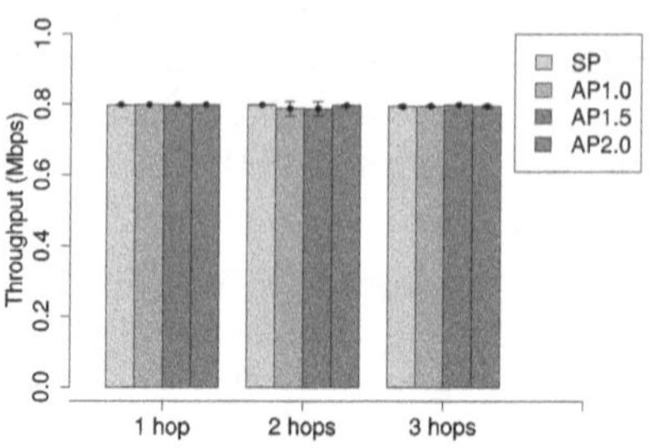

(c) Throughput

Figure 3: Single flow scenario (100 pkts/s)

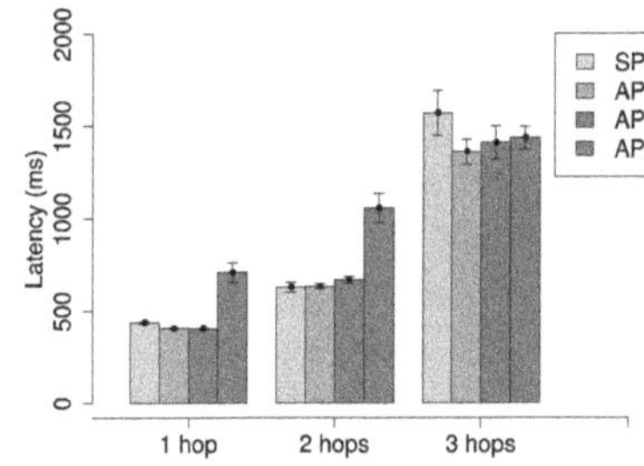

(a) Average latency

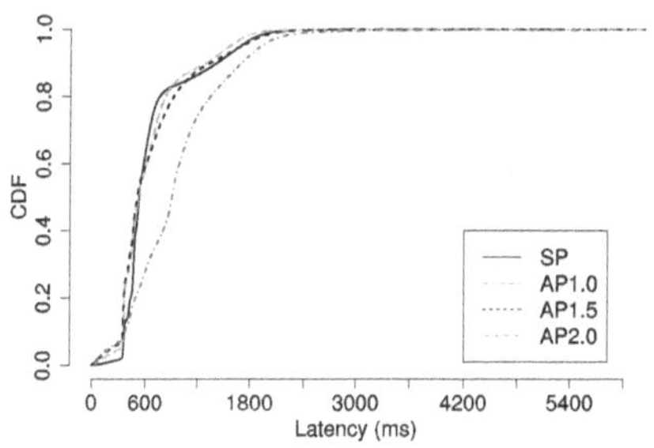

(b) Latency CDF

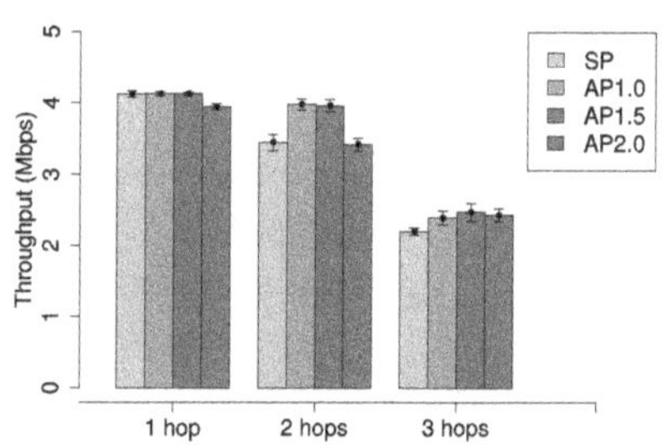

(c) Throughput

Figure 4: Single flow scenario (600 pkts/s)

to avoid a channel switch the more AP-OLSR will reduce latency.

The throughput in the lightly loaded network is shown in figure 5(c). As in the single flow scenario, in the lightly loaded network the packet loss rate is very low and therefore we cannot see any difference in throughput.

The performance in heavily loaded networks is shown in figure 6. The average latency is shown in figure 6(a). This figure shows that the average latency is similar for all configurations in test 1. In the second test, the lowest average latency is given by single path routing and AP-OLSR with $\alpha = 1.0$, while the highest is given by AP-OLSR with $\alpha = 2.0$. In the third test, all configurations of AP-OLSR have a higher average latency than single path routing. Figure 6(b) shows that AP-OLSR gets more packets delivered below 1 second than single path routing, but it also shows that the worst 50 % of the packets takes longer time when using AP-OLSR compared to single path routing. Setting $\alpha = 1.0$ performs slightly better slightly better than other configurations of AP-OLSR because it is less prone to split the data flows.

Figure 6(c) shows the average throughput in the heavily loaded network for the flows in the three different tests with one gateway. With a confidence interval of 95 %, there is no statistically significant difference in throughput for any of the configurations but AP-OLSR with $\alpha = 2.0$ in test 3 which has a lower throughput than the other. In test 3, the source nodes and destination nodes are close to each other. Therefore, all relay nodes that were selected in order to avoid a channel switch at the source node will compete with the source node to transmit data to the destination node (as discussed in the single flow scenario).

3.4 2 Gateways, 3 Flows Each

In this scenario, we randomly selected 2 nodes as gateways and 3 nodes to each gateway to generate data flows. Also, we used three different sets of gateways and source nodes; (1): $A \leftarrow \{C, D, G\}$, $B \leftarrow \{E, F, H\}$; (2): $A \leftarrow \{B, C, E\}$, $G \leftarrow \{D, E, H\}$; (3): $C \leftarrow \{B, D, E\}$, $H \leftarrow \{F, G, I\}$. Each test is run 20 times and the results from our third scenario are shown in figures 7 and 8.

Figure 7(a) shows the average latency for each test where a packet rate of 100 packets per second was used. Each bar in this graph is divided into two parts, the lower dark part is an average of all flows going to gateway 1 and the upper light part is an average of all flows going to gateway 2. The 95 % confidence intervals for the aggregated average for both gateways (this applies for all bar graphs in this scenario). The first test of this scenario differs from the remaining ones. In this test the two gateways are close to each other and they are both at the same edge of the network. This makes all the flows go in the same direction which increases the possibility that a node has to forward packets from several

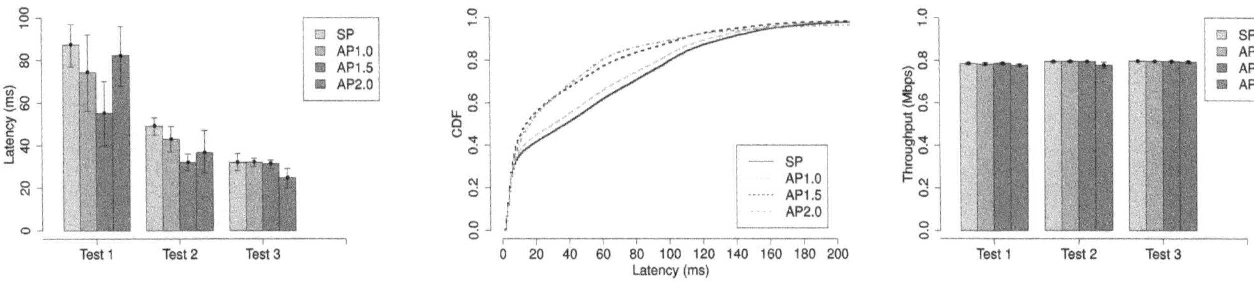

(a) Average latency (b) Latency CDF (c) Throughput

Figure 5: 1 gateway scenario (100 pkts/s)

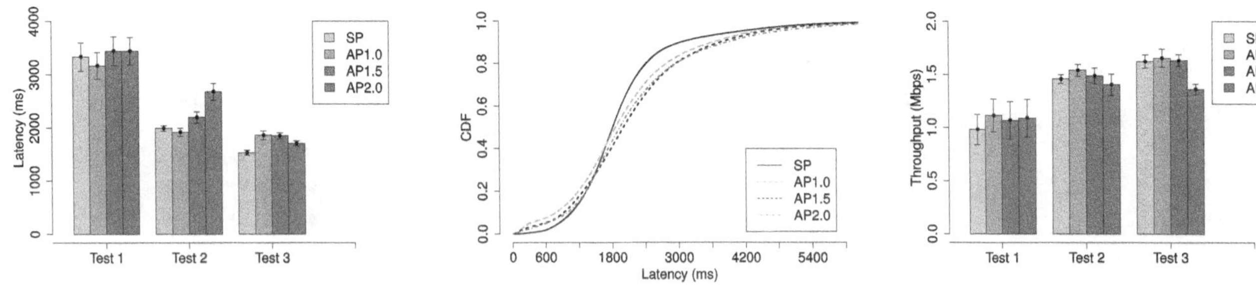

(a) Average latency (b) Latency CDF (c) Throughput

Figure 6: 1 gateway scenario (600 pkts/s)

flows, especially the nodes close to the gateways. This is even more likely for $\alpha > 1$ since packets are allowed to pass through more nodes. This is the reason why the latency is so high for AP-OLSR with $\alpha = 1.5$ and $\alpha = 2.0$. The very high latency for AP-OLSR with $\alpha > 1.0$ is naturally seen also in figure 7(b), latency CDF, where we can see that approximately one third of the packets has not reached the destination within the 200 ms shown in the graph. AP-OLSR with $\alpha = 1.0$ does not show a statistically significant difference in average latency compared to single path routing. In the second and the third test, there is no statistically significant difference between any configurations. This shows that the performance is similar as long as the network is not congested.

In figure 7(c) we can see that also the throughput is worse for AP-OLSR with $\alpha > 1.0$ in test 1. The higher the value of α the lower the throughput. Even though it is hard to see in the figure, AP-OLSR with $\alpha = 1.0$ has a higher throughput than single path routing in test 1. In the remaining two tests of this scenario, there is no difference in throughput.

Figure 8(a) shows the average latency for each test in the heavily loaded network and figure 8(b) shows the latency for each packet for all three tests. We can see that the latency is extremely high in all cases. AP-OLSR makes it even worse, especially when $\alpha = 2.0$ since packets pass through an unnecessary large number of nodes which increases the load even more. However, even though it is hard to see in the figure, all AP-OLSR configurations have more packets with a latency below 0.5 seconds compared to single path routing.

The achieved throughput in the heavily loaded network is shown in figure 8(c). Due to the high amount of flows the nodes get very loaded when $\alpha = 2.0$ which leads to higher packet loss rate. In test 1, also $\alpha = 1.5$ gives a lower throughput because of reasons mentioned above.

3.5 Crossing Traffic

In this scenario, we selected a source node, A, and a destination node, I, that is placed at a far distance from each other. We then selected two source-destination pairs where the flows cross the traffic from the first flow, $D \leftarrow B$ and $G \leftarrow E$. Each test is run 20 times and the results are shown in figures 9 and 10.

In the scenario where crossing flows exist we clearly see benefits from using AP-OLSR. The single path routing mechanism has to wait when the channel is not in use. This is always the case for one of the flows when two flows are to be forwarded on different channels. AP-OLSR, however, dynamically selects the next hop according to which channel is in use at the moment. This leads to a situation where the path may be changed on a per packet basis depending on the channel tuned.

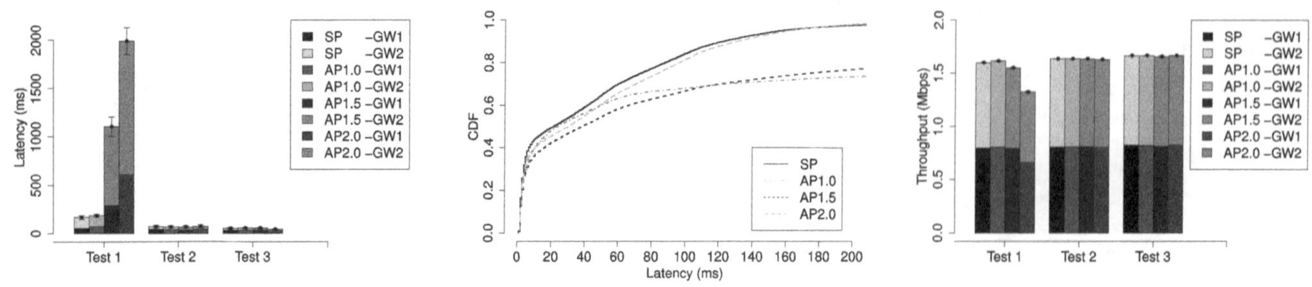

(a) Average latency (b) Latency CDF (c) Throughput

Figure 7: 2 gateways scenario (100 pkts/s)

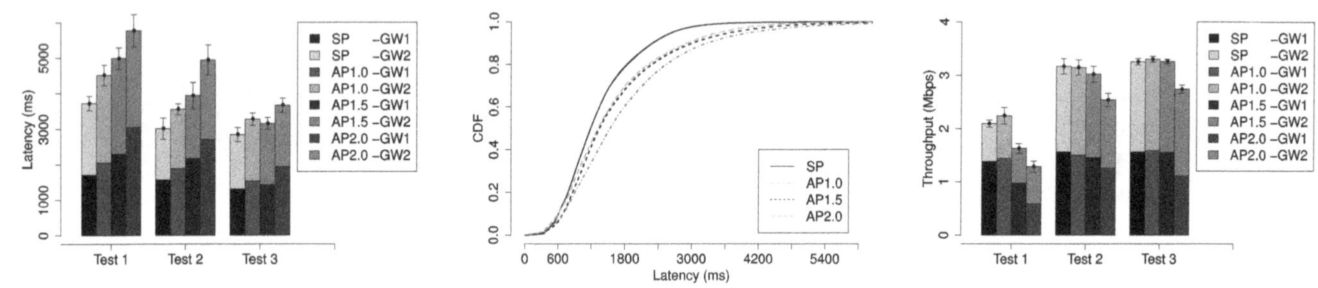

(a) Average latency (b) Latency CDF (c) Throughput

Figure 8: 2 gateways scenario (600 pkts/s)

Figure 9(a) shows the average latency in the lightly loaded network. This figure shows that $\alpha = 1.5$ has a lower average latency than single path routing. Figure 9(b) shows the latency CDF, where we can see great benefits of using AP-OLSR compared to single path. After 60 ms above 80 % of the AP-OLSR with $\alpha > 1.0$ packets have reached the destination, but under 50 % when using single path routing. Also AP-OLSR with $\alpha = 1.0$ has a lower latency compared to single path routing.

The throughput is shown in figure 9(c). Also in this scenario the packet loss rate is very low in the lightly loaded network, giving us equal throughput in all configurations.

Figures 10(a) and 10(b) show the latency when the network is heavily loaded. In figure 10(a) we can see that AP-OLSR with $\alpha = 1.0$ has a lower average latency than $\alpha > 1.0$. Allowing extra hops increases the load in the network and as in the scenarios above this has a negative impact on an already congested network. There is no statistically significant difference among the other configurations. Figure 10(b) shows that most of the packets have a lower latency when $\alpha = 1.0$. Also, we can see that all configurations of AP-OLSR have more packets received within 1 second compared to single path routing. However, the 50 worst percent of the packets have even higher latency when using AP-OLSR with $\alpha > 1.0$ compared to single path routing.

Figure 10(c) shows the throughput in the heavily loaded network. When increasing the load we see how the throughput is increased when $\alpha = 1.0$ and $\alpha = 1.5$ compared to single path routing. This is because the buffers will not fill up as quickly when more packets can be sent without waiting for a channel switch, leading to fewer packets dropped.

4. CONCLUSIONS

In this paper we have evaluated the anypath routing mechanism called AP-OLSR to see its behavior in a mesh network with different gateways and source nodes. We have seen that AP-OLSR can decrease latency and increase throughput.

The latency is decreased when the network is not congested and, typically, the latency is lower when many extra hops are allowed. However, by setting a high value of allowed number of extra hops, the load in the network increases. This may cause congestion and have a negative impact on both latency and throughput. This is especially a problem in short paths and at high network load.

AP-OLSR performs best when crossing flows exist. Thanks to its ability to rapidly change forwarding nodes on a per packet basis, AP-OLSR is very well suited for these scenarios. As future work, we plan to evaluate the proposed approach under more realistic traffic conditions and using larger network topologies.

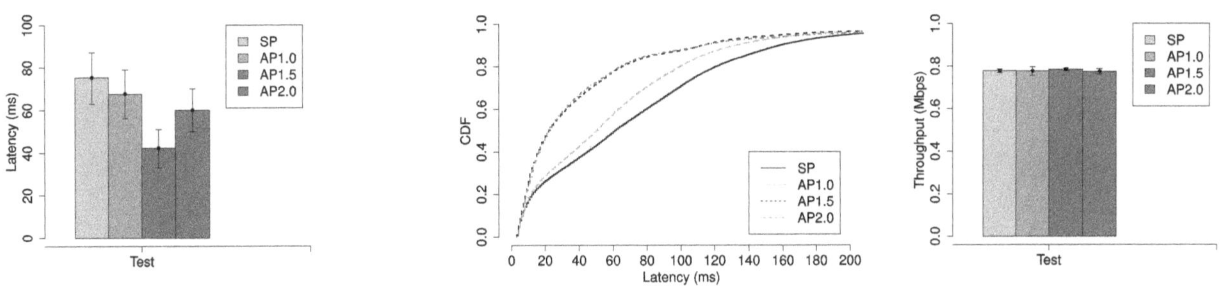

(a) Average latency (b) Latency CDF (c) Throughput

Figure 9: Crossing flows scenario (100 pkts/s)

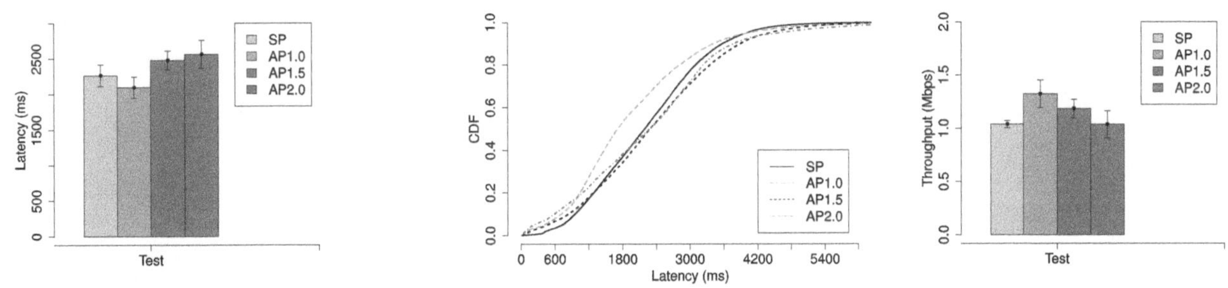

(a) Average latency (b) Latency CDF (c) Throughput

Figure 10: Crossing flows scenario (600 pkts/s)

5. REFERENCES

[1] J. Li, C. Blake, D. S. J. De Couto, H. I. Lee and R. Morris, "Capacity of ad hoc wireless networks," in *Proc. of 7th ACM MOBICOM*, 2001.

[2] K. N. Ramachandran and E. M. Belding and K. C. Almeroth and M. M. Buddhikot, "Interference-Aware Channel Assignment in Multi-Radio Wireless Mesh Networks," Proc. of INFOCOM, 2006.

[3] M. Alicherry, R. Bhatia, Li Erran Li, "Joint Channel Assignment and Routing for Throughput. Optimization in Multi-radio Wireless Mesh Networks," Proc. of ACM MOBICOM, 2005.

[4] P. Kyasanur, C. Chereddi, and N. H. Vaidya, "Net-X: System eXtensions for Supporting Multiple Channels, Multiple Interfaces, and Other Interface Capabilities," Tech. Rep., University of Illinois at Urbana-Champaign, August 2006.

[5] Ad hoc On-Demand Distance Vector (AODV) Routing, RFC: http://www.ietf.org/rfc/rfc3561.txt [Accessed December, 2012].

[6] UniK OLSR daemon software, Available: http://www.olsr.org/ [Accessed December, 2012].

[7] D.S.J. De Couto, D. Aguayo, J. Bicket, R. Morris, "A high-throughput path metric for multi-hop wireless routing," Wireless Networks, v 11, n 4, pp. 419-34, 2005.

[8] P.M. Esposito, M. Campista, I.M. Moraes, L. Costa, O. Duarte, M.G. Rubinstein, "Implementing the expected transmission time metric for OLSR wireless mesh networks," in *2008 1st IFIP Wireless Days*, pp. 5, 2008.

[9] R. Laufer, H. Dubois-Ferriere, L. Kleinrock, "Multirate anypath routing in wireless mesh networks," in *2009 Proceedings IEEE INFOCOM.*, pp. 37-45, 2009.

[10] KAUMesh http://www.kau.se/en/kaumesh/ [Accessed: December, 2012].

[11] J. C. Chuang, "Performance issues and algorithms for dynamic channel assignment," IEEE J. Select Areas Commun., vol. 11, no. 6, pp. 955-963, 1993.

[12] J. A. A. Lavén, A. J. Kassler, "Multi-Channel Anypath Routing in Wireless Mesh Networks," in *IEEE Globecom 2010 Workshop on Heterogeneous, Multi-hop Wireless and Mobile Networks*, Miami, FL, USA, 2010.

[13] Dijkstra, E. W. "A note on two problems in connexion with graphs." Numerische mathematik 1.1 (1959): 269-271.

[14] M. C. Castro, P. Dely, A. J. Kassler, F. P. D'Elia, S. Avallone, "OLSR and Net-X as a Framework for Channel Assignment Experiments," in *ACM International Workshop on Wireless Network Testbeds, Experimental Evaluation and Characterization (WiNTECH)*, co-located with *ACM MobiCom 2009*,

Beijing, China, September 21st 2009.

[15] J. A. A. Lavén, P. Hjärtquist, "Multimetric OLSR and ETT," in *5th OLSR Interop & Workshop*, October 2-4, 2009 in Vienna, Austria.

[16] Multi-Generator, Naval Research Laboratory (NRL) http://cs.itd.nrl.navy.mil/work/mgen/ [Accessed: December, 2012].

Sequence Numbers Do Not Guarantee Loop Freedom —AODV Can Yield Routing Loops—

Rob van Glabbeek
NICTA, Australia
University of New South Wales, Australia
rvg@cs.stanford.edu

Peter Höfner
NICTA, Australia
University of New South Wales, Australia
Peter.Hoefner@nicta.com.au

Wee Lum Tan
NICTA, Australia
University of Queensland, Australia
WeeLum.Tan@nicta.com.au

Marius Portmann
NICTA, Australia
University of Queensland, Australia
marius@itee.uq.edu.au

ABSTRACT

In the area of mobile ad-hoc networks and wireless mesh networks, sequence numbers are often used in routing protocols to avoid routing loops. It is commonly stated in protocol specifications that sequence numbers are sufficient to *guarantee* loop freedom if they are monotonically increased over time. A classical example for the use of sequence numbers is the popular Ad hoc On-Demand Distance Vector (AODV) routing protocol. The loop freedom of AODV is not only a common belief, it has been claimed in the abstract of its RFC and at least two proofs have been proposed. AODV-based protocols such as AODVv2 (DYMO) and HWMP also claim loop freedom due to the same use of sequence numbers.

In this paper we show that AODV is not a priori loop free; by this we counter the proposed proofs in the literature. In fact, loop freedom hinges on non-evident assumptions to be made when resolving ambiguities occurring in the RFC. Thus, monotonically increasing sequence numbers, by themselves, do *not* guarantee loop freedom.

Categories and Subject Descriptors

C.2.2 [**Network Protocols**]: Routing protocols; Protocol verification; F.3.1 [**Specifying and Verifying and Reasoning about Programs**]: Invariants

Keywords

AODV; loop freedom; process algebra; routing protocols; wireless mesh networks

MSWiM'13, November 3–8, 2013, Barcelona, Spain.
Copyright 2013 ACM 978-1-4503-2353-6/13/11 ...$15.00.
http://dx.doi.org/10.1145/2507924.2507943 .

1. INTRODUCTION

Wireless Mesh Networks (WMNs), which can be considered to include Mobile Ad-hoc Networks (MANETs), have gained considerable popularity and are increasingly deployed in a wide range of application scenarios, including emergency response communication, intelligent transportation systems, mining and video surveillance. They are self-organising wireless multi-hop networks that can provide broadband communication without relying on a wired backhaul infrastructure, a benefit for rapid and low-cost network deployment.

Highly dynamic topologies are a key feature of WMNs and MANETs, due to mobility of nodes and/or the variability of wireless links. This makes the design and implementation of robust and efficient routing protocols for these networks a challenging task, and a lot of research effort has gone into it.

Loop freedom is a critical property for any routing protocol, but it is particularly relevant and challenging for WMNs and MANETs. Descriptions as in [9] capture the common understanding of loop freedom: "*A routing-table loop is a path specified in the nodes' routing tables at a particular point in time that visits the same node more than once before reaching the intended destination.*" Packets caught in a routing loop, until they are discarded by the IP Time-To-Live (TTL) mechanism, can quickly saturate the links and have a detrimental impact on network performance. It is therefore critical to ensure that protocols prevent routing loops.

Sequence numbers, indicating the freshness of routing information, have been widely used to guarantee loop freedom, in particular for distance vector protocols such as DSDV [20], AODV [19], AODVv2 (formerly known as DYMO) [21] and HWMP [14]. These protocols claim to be loop free due to the use of monotonically increasing sequence numbers. For example, the AODV RFC states: AODV "*uses destination sequence numbers to ensure loop freedom at all times (even in the face of anomalous delivery of routing control messages), ...*" [19], and a similar claim is made in the IETF draft of AODVv2 [21]: "*AODVv2 uses sequence numbers to assure loop freedom [Perkins99].*"[1] A proof of loop freedom of AODV has been provided in [22]. Another, more recent

[1]Here, [Perkins99] is our reference [22].

proof is [26].[2] It is therefore a common belief that the use of sequence numbers in this context guarantees loop freedom.

However, while this use of sequence numbers can be an efficient approach to address the problem of routing loops, we show in this paper that sequence numbers by themselves do not guarantee loop freedom. We illustrate this using AODV as a running example.

We show that loop freedom can be guaranteed only if sequence numbers are used in a careful way, considering further rules and assumptions on the behaviour of the protocol. The problem is, as shown in the case of AODV, that these additional rules and assumptions are not explicitly stated in the RFC, and that the RFC has significant ambiguities in this regard. We demonstrate that routing loops can be created—while fully complying with the RFC, and making reasonable assumptions when the RFC allows different interpretations. As a consequence, which is a *key contribution* of this paper, we obtain that routing protocols using sequence numbers as described in [19] are not a priori loop free. We argue that the lack of precision and the corresponding ambiguity of the protocol definition in the RFC is a key problem here—and for RFCs in general. As *another contribution* we show details of several ambiguities and contradictions in the AODV RFC, and discuss which interpretations will lead to routing loops. A *third contribution* of this paper is an analysis of five key implementations of the AODV protocol, and a discussion of their corresponding loop freedom properties.

To address the problem of ambiguities and contradictions in RFCs, we argue for the benefit of more precise and formal approaches for the specification of protocols, which are sufficiently expressive to model real networks and protocols, while maintaining usability. As a *final contribution* we show how formal methods can be used to avoid ambiguities in RFCs and to guarantee properties such as loop freedom.

The remainder of the paper is organised as follows: in Section 2 we recapitulate the basic principles of the AODV protocol. We state what we mean by loop freedom and discuss the existing proofs of AODV's loop freedom. In Section 3, nearly all plausible readings of the AODV RFC, resolving its ambiguities and contradictions, are discussed. Each of the presented interpretations is analysed w.r.t. loop freedom. In Section 4 we show an example of a routing loop occurring in the AODV routing protocol, as a result of following a reasonable and plausible interpretation of the RFC. Having the various RFC interpretations and the loop example in mind, we then analyse five different key implementations of AODV w.r.t. routing loops. Finally, in Section 6, we sketch how formal methods—here in the form of process algebra—can be applied to model routing protocols and verify the presented results on routing loops. Before we conclude with a short discussion in Section 8, we present major related work in Section 7.

2. AODV

To prove that sequence numbers do not a priori guarantee loop freedom, we use AODV as an example. We expect that other routing protocols such as AODVv2 and HWMP behave similarly. AODV [19] is a popular routing protocol designed for MANETs, and is one of the four protocols currently standardised by the IETF MANET working group[3]. It also forms the basis of new WMN routing protocols, including the upcoming IEEE 802.11s wireless mesh network standard [14]. AODV is designed for wireless and mobile networks where links are particularly unreliable.

2.1 Brief Overview

AODV is a reactive protocol, which means that routes are established only on demand. If a node S wants to send a data packet to a node D, but currently does not know a route, it temporarily buffers the packet and initiates a route discovery process by broadcasting a route request (RREQ) message in the network. An intermediate node A that receives the RREQ message creates a routing table entry for a route towards node S referred to as a *reverse route*, and re-broadcasts the RREQ. This is repeated until the RREQ reaches the destination node D, or alternatively a node that knows a route to D. In both cases, the node replies by unicasting a corresponding route reply (RREP) message back to the source S, via a previously established reverse route. When forwarding RREP messages, nodes create a routing table entry for node D, called the *forward route*. When the RREP reaches the originating node S, a route from S to D is established and data packets can start to flow. Both forward and reverse routes are maintained in a routing table at every node—details are given below. In the event of link and route breaks, AODV uses route error (RERR) messages to notify the affected nodes: if a link break is detected by a node, it first invalidates all routes stored in the node's own routing table that actually use the broken link. Then it sends a RERR message containing the unreachable destinations to all (direct) neighbours using this route.

In AODV, a routing table consists of a list of entries—at most one for each destination—each containing the following information:

- the destination IP address;
- the destination sequence number;
- the sequence-number-status flag—tagging whether the recorded sequence number can be trusted;
- a flag tagging the route as being valid or invalid—this flag is set to invalid when a link break is detected;
- the hop count, a metric to indicate the distance to the destination;
- the next hop, an IP address that identifies the next (intermediate) node on the route to the destination;
- a list of precursors, a set of IP addresses of those 1-hop neighbours that use this particular route; and
- the lifetime (expiration or deletion time) of the route.

The destination sequence number constitutes a measure approximating the relative freshness of the information held—a higher number denotes newer information. The routing table is updated whenever a node receives an AODV control message (RREQ, RREP or RERR) or detects a link break.

During the life time of the network, each node not only maintains its routing table, it also stores its *own sequence number*. This number is used as a local "timer" and is incremented whenever a new route request is initiated.

Full details of the protocol are outlined in the request for comments (RFC) [19], the official specification of AODV.

[2]We discuss problems with these proofs later in this paper.
[3]`http://datatracker.ietf.org/wg/manet/charter/`

2.2 Loop Freedom

The "naive" notion of loop freedom is a term that informally means that "a packet never goes round in cycles without (at some point) being delivered". This dynamic definition is too restrictive a requirement for AODV. There are situations where packets are sent in cycles, but which should not be considered "harmful". This can happen when the network topology keeps changing. The sense of loop freedom is much better captured by a static invariant, saying that *at any given time the collective routing tables of the nodes do not admit a loop*. Such a requirement does not rule out the dynamic loop alluded to above. However, in situations where the topology remains stable sufficiently long it does guarantee that packets will not keep going around in cycles.

2.3 Proofs Based On Sequence Numbers

As mentioned before, AODV "*uses destination sequence numbers to ensure loop freedom at all times*" [19, Page 2]. Moreover, it has been "proven" at least twice that AODV is loop free [22, 26].

In both papers a main argument is that messages relating to a particular route request are handled only once at every node; moreover that every route discovery process has a unique sequence number. The latter is guaranteed since a node's own sequence number is incremented whenever a new route discovery is initiated. Each sequence number stored in any routing table for destination *dip* is ultimately derived from *dip*'s own sequence number at the time such a route was discovered.

The proof sketch given in [22] uses the fact that when a loop in a route to a destination Z is created, all nodes X_i on that loop must have route entries for destination Z with the same destination sequence number. "*Furthermore, because the destination sequence numbers are all the same, the next hop information must have been derived at every node X_i from the same RREP transmitted by the destination Z*" [22, Page 11]. The latter is not true at all: some of the information could have been derived from RREQ messages, or from a RREP message transmitted by an intermediate node that has a route to Z. More importantly, the nodes on the loop may have acquired their information on a route to Z from different RREP or RREQ messages, that all carried the same sequence number. This will be illustrated in our forthcoming loop example.

The proof of [26] was established in two steps: (i) a mathematical model of AODV was derived[4]; (ii) based on the derived model loop freedom was proven using the interactive theorem prover Isabelle [18].[5] In the model of [26] route replies generated by intermediate nodes [19, Sect. 6.6.2.] are not considered. Since this is a key feature of AODV (and, as we shall see, an essential ingredient in the creation of routing loops), the work of [26] cannot be said to pertain to the full protocol.

3. AMBIGUITIES IN THE AODV RFC

"*A Request for Comments (RFC) is a publication of the Internet Engineering Task Force (IETF) and the Internet Society [...]. A RFC is authored by engineers and computer scientists in the form of a memorandum describing methods, behaviors, research, or innovations applicable to the working of the Internet and Internet-connected systems. [...] The IETF adopts some of the proposals published as RFCs as Internet standards.*"[6] Not all RFCs are standards [13]. However, in the case of the AODV routing protocol, the RFC 3561 [19] is the de facto standard.

RFCs are typically written in English and are not equipped with a formal description language. This has the advantage that everybody can read any RFC. However, it holds the disadvantage that the RFC contains contradictions and ambiguities. Additionally, there may be unexpected situations occurring in real networks that are not described or anticipated by the RFC. In sum, this yields a variety of interpretations for every RFC; some interpretations being more plausible than others.

In this section, we discuss some of the ambiguities found in the specification of AODV. We catalogue and analyse the variants of AODV arising from interpretations consistent with the reading of the RFC and show which of them yields routing loops. Our analysis is based on a rigorous, formal, and mathematical approach [7]. A full and detailed analysis is given in [8]. Table 1 summarises the results; section numbers refer to [19].

One of the crucial aspects of AODV is the maintenance of routing tables. Hence the update of routing table entries with new information has to be performed carefully. Unfortunately, the RFC specification only gives hints how to update routing table entries; an exact and precise definition is missing.

1. Updating the Unknown (Invalid) Sequence Number in Response to a Route Reply. If a node receives a RREP message, it might have to update its routing table: "*the existing entry is updated only in the following circumstances: (i) the sequence number in the routing table is marked as invalid [...]*" [19, Sect. 6.7]. Here it is relevant that, through the sequence-number-status flag, any sequence number can be marked as unknown or invalid. In the same section it is also stated what actions occur if a route is updated. Among others it is stated that "*the destination sequence number is marked as valid, [...] and the [new] destination sequence number [in the routing table] is the Destination Sequence Number in the RREP message.*" [19, Sect. 6.7]. The interpretation that follows these lines literally is denoted 1a in Table 2. It can decrement sequence numbers, which immediately yields routing loops, as explained in [8, Sect. 8]. This update mechanism contradicts Sect. 6.1 of [19], which states that any information from an incoming AODV control message that carries a lower sequence number than the corresponding entry in the routing table MUST be discarded (Interpretation 1b). The routing loops resulting from following Sect. 6.7 strongly indicate that this contradiction in the RFC should be resolved in favour of Sect. 6.1.

2. Updating with the Unknown Sequence Number. Whenever a node receives a forwarded AODV control message from a 1-hop neighbour, it creates a new or updates an existing routing table entry to that neighbour. For example, "*[w]hen a node receives a RREQ, it first creates or updates a route to the previous hop without a valid sequence number*" [19, Sect. 6.5]. In case a new routing table entry is created, the sequence number is set to a default value (typically 0, as is done in implementations such as AODV-UU [2], AODV-UIUC [15] and AODV-UCSB [4]) and the sequence-

[4] In [26] the model is only given partially.

[5] Again only snippets of the proofs can be found in [26].

[6] `http://en.wikipedia.org/wiki/Request_for_Comments`

Table 1: Analysis of different interpretations of the RFC 3561 (AODV)

1.	**Updating the Unknown (Invalid) Sequence Number in Response to a Route Reply**	
1a.	the destination sequence number (DSN) is copied from the RREP message (Sect 6.7)	may decrement sequence numbers, which causes loops
1b.	the routing table is not updated when the information that it has is "fresher" (Sect. 6.1)	does not cause loops
2.	**Updating with the Unknown Sequence Number (Sect. 6.5)**	
2a.	no update occurs	does not cause loops, but opportunity to improve routes is missed.
2b.	overwrite any routing table entry by an update with an unknown DSN	may decrement sequence numbers, which causes loops
2c.	use the new entry with the old DSN	does not cause loops
3.	**(Dis)Allowing the Creation of Self-Entries in Response to a Route Reply**	
3a.	allow (arbitrary) self-entries	loop free only if used with Interpretations 4d or 4e below
3b.	allow optimal self-entries only; store own sequence number in optimal self-entry	does not cause loops
3c.	disallow self-entries; if self-entries would occur, ignore msg.	does not cause loops
3d.	disallow self-entries; if self-entries would occur, forward	does not cause loops
4.	**Invalidating Routing Table Entries in Response to a Route Error Message**	
4a.	always copy DSN from RERR message (Sect. 6.11)	may decrement sequence numbers, which causes loops (when allowing self-entries (Interpretation 3a))
4b.	only invalidate if the DSN in the routing table is smaller than or equal to the one from the RERR message (Sect. 6.1)	causes loops (when allowing self-entries)
4c.	take the maximum of the DSN of the routing table and the one from the RERR message	causes loops (when allowing self-entries)
4d.	take the maximum of the increased DSN of the routing table and the one from the RERR message	does not cause loops
4e.	only invalidate if the DSN in the routing table is smaller than the one from the RERR message (Sect. 6.2)	does not cause loops

number-status flag is set to `unk` to signify that the sequence number corresponding to the neighbour is unknown. But, what happens if there exists already a routing table entry? Following the quote above, the routing table has to be updated. Unfortunately, it is not stated how the update is done.[7] There are three reasonable options:

(2a) no update occurs. This interpretation is harmless with regard to routing loops, but misses an opportunity to improve some routes. It can be argued that the RFC rules out this option by including "or updates" in the quote above.

(2b) All information is taken from the incoming AODV control message; since that message formally does not contain a sequence number for the neighbour, the destination sequence number is set to value 0. Since this can decrease sequence numbers, routing loops might occur. Hence this interpretation must not be used.

(2c) The information from the routing table and from the incoming AODV control message is merged.[8] This interpretation does not give rise to loops.

3. (Dis)Allowing the Creation of Self-Entries in Response to a Route Reply. In any practical implementation, when a node sends a data packet to itself, the packet will be delivered to the corresponding application on the local node without ever involving a routing protocol and therefore without being "seen" by AODV or any other routing protocol. Because of this it seems that it does not make a difference whether any node using AODV stores routing table entries to itself.

In AODV, when a node receives a RREP message, it creates a routing table entry for the destination node if such an entry does not already exist [19, Sect. 6.7]. If the destination node happens to be the processing node itself, this leads to the creation of a self-entry. The RFC does not mention self-entries explicitly; it only refers to them at one location: "*A node may change the sequence number in the routing table entry of a destination only if: – it is itself the destination node [...]*" [19, Sect. 6.1]. This points at least to the possibility of having self-entries. We have analysed various implementations of AODV and found that the Kernel-AODV [1], AODV-UIUC [15], AODV-UCSB [4] and AODV-ns2 implementations allow the creation of self-entries.

If arbitrary self-entries are allowed (Interpretation 3a in Table 2) this can, in combination with other plausible assumptions, yield routing loops, as we will show in the next section. However, storing only optimal self-entries in routing tables (Interpretation 3b) does not cause loops. For example, Kernel-AODV maintains the nodes' own sequence numbers in this way.

On the other hand, there are two possibilities to disallow self-entries: if a node receives a route reply and would create a self-entry, it silently discards the message (Interpretation 3c). This interpretation has the disadvantage that replies are lost. The alternative is that the node forwards the message without updating its routing table (3d). Both variants by themselves do not yield routing loops.

4. Invalidating Routing Table Entries in Response to a Route Error Message. If a node receives a RERR message, it might invalidate entries of its routing table based on information from this message. When invalidating routing table entries, destination sequence numbers should be "*copied from the incoming RERR*" [19, Sect. 6.11]. This is Interpretation 4a in Table 1. In particular, this part of the RFC prescribes the replacement of an existing destination sequence number in a routing table entry with one that may be strictly smaller, which contradicts Sect. 6.1 of the RFC.

[7]Section 6.2 of [19] further explains in which circumstances an update occurs. It does not resolve this ambiguity (cf. [8]).

[8]By taking the destination sequence number from the existing routing table entry and all other information from the AODV control message.

To make invalidation consistent with Sect. 6.1 of the RFC, one could use two possible variants instead. The first (4b), strictly following Sect. 6.1, invalidates only if the destination sequence number in the routing table is smaller than or equal to the destination sequence number provided by the incoming RERR message; it aborts otherwise. The second (4c) invalidates in all circumstances, but prevents a decrease in the destination sequence number by taking the maximum of the stored and the incoming number.[9] In the next section we will show that each of these three interpretations can yield routing loops, when used in conjunction with non-optimal self-entries.

There are two reasonable solutions to avoid routing loops in these circumstances. As a modification of Interpretation 4c, one can first increment the destination sequence number of the routing table by one and then use the maximum of this updated sequence number and the one from the RERR message (Interpretation 4d). Alternatively, one could invalidate only if the destination sequence number in the routing table is (strictly) smaller than the destination sequence number provided by the incoming RERR message (4e), and abort if it is larger or equal. The latter interpretation is at least consistent with Section 6.2 of the RFC, which states that "*The route is only updated if the new sequence number is either (i) higher than the destination sequence number in the route table, or [...]*".

4. AODV YIELDS LOOPS

In the previous section, we discussed some of the ambiguities found in the specification of AODV, and catalogued the variants of AODV that arise from interpretations consistent with the RFC. In the following we describe an example of a routing loop in AODV, based on a reasonable and plausible interpretation of the RFC, following Interpretations 3a and any out of 4a, 4b and 4c of AODV, in resolving the ambiguities from Table 1.

4.1 Creating Routing Loops

The given example (shown in Figure 1) consists of four parts: (1) First, a standard RREQ-RREP cycle occurs (Figures 1(a)–(b)); (2) Then, a node stores information about *itself* in its routing table (Figures 1(c)–(e)); Such information is called a *self-entry*. (3) Another standard RREQ-RREP cycle occurs (Figure 1(f)); (4) Finally, a link break in combination with another route discovery yields the loop (Figures 1(g)–(h)).

1. Standard RREQ-RREP Cycle. In Figure 1(a), we show the initial network topology, with the nodes' sequence numbers depicted inside the circles. Figure 1(b) shows node D searching for a route to node A. We see that the sequence number for node D is increased to 2 ("*The Originator Sequence Number in the RREQ message is the node's own sequence number, which is incremented prior to insertion in a RREQ.*" [19, Sect. 6.3]). Figure 1(b) also shows the nodes' routing tables. Each routing table entry (depicted as a 5-tuple) contains information about the destination, the destination's sequence number, the validity of the routing table entry, the hop count and the next hop (cf. Section 2.1). We do not show the sequence-number-status flag, the list of precursors in the routing table entries and the lifetime of a route as they constitute auxiliary information that is not critical to the loop example here. Due to the successful exchange of RREQ-RREP messages, nodes D and A create routing table entries to each other in their routing table.

2. Self-Entries. In Figure 1(c), we see node S searching for a route to node D. In Figure 1(d), the link between nodes S and D goes up (e.g. due to node mobility) and node S then searches for a route to node X. The route request message $\mathrm{RREQ}_{S\to X}$ is forwarded by nodes D and A since they do not have any information on the destination node X. From the information contained in the $\mathrm{RREQ}_{S\to X}$ message, a routing table entry to node S is created in the routing tables of nodes D and A. "*Then the node searches for a reverse route to the Originator IP Address [...] If need be, the route is created, or updated using the Originator Sequence Number from the RREQ in its routing table.*" [19, Sect. 6.5]. Node S also receives the forwarded $\mathrm{RREQ}_{S\to X}$ message from node D, and before silently discarding the message (since it is the originator of the RREQ message), updates its routing table to create an entry to node D. "*When a node receives a RREQ, it first creates or updates a route to the previous hop without a valid sequence number.*" [19, Sect. 6.5]. We use the value 0 for an unknown/invalid sequence number created in this manner, as is also done in implementations like AODV-UU [2], AODV-UIUC [15] and AODV-UCSB [4].

At some point, $\mathrm{RREQ}_{S\to D}$ finally reaches node A (Figure 1(e)). Since node A has a valid routing table entry to node D, it generates an intermediate route reply message using the information from its routing table [19, Sect. 6.6 and 6.6.2]. The $\mathrm{RREP}_{S\to D}$ message is unicast to node D, the next hop on the path towards node S. "*Once created, the RREP is unicast to the next hop toward the originator of the RREQ, as indicated by the routing table entry for that originator.*" [19, Sect. 6.6]. Node D processes the $\mathrm{RREP}_{S\to D}$ message, updates its routing table and forwards the message to node S, which establishes a route to node D. When updating its routing table, node D creates a self-entry (following Interpretation 3a in Table 1) since the $\mathrm{RREP}_{S\to D}$ message contains information about a route to node D [19, Sect. 6.7].

3. Standard RREQ-RREP Cycle. In Figure 1(f), the link between nodes S and X goes up, while the link between nodes D and A goes down. Node D also searches for a route to node X. Due to the successful exchange of RREQ-RREP messages, the routing tables of nodes D, S, and X are updated accordingly.

4. From Self-Entries to Loops. The loop example continues with the link between nodes S and X going down (Figure 1(g)). In addition, node D detects that its link to node A is broken. Following from this, node D initiates processing for a RERR message. "*A node initiates processing for a RERR message [...] if it detects a link break for the next hop of an active [(`val`)] route in its routing table while transmitting data*" [19, Sect. 6.11]. In this process, "*the node first makes a list of unreachable destinations consisting of the unreachable neighbor and any additional destinations [...] in the local routing table that use the unreachable neighbor as the next hop.*" [19, Sect. 6.11]. In addition, the routing table for node D has to be updated for these unreachable destinations as follows: "*1. The destination sequence number of this route entry, if it exists and is valid, is incremented*

[9] Although this is not really a plausible reading of the RFC, Interpretation 4c can be seen as a compromise between Sections 6.11 and 6.1 of the RFC—it seems a natural way to avoid a decrement of destination sequence numbers and still take all information from the RERR message into account.

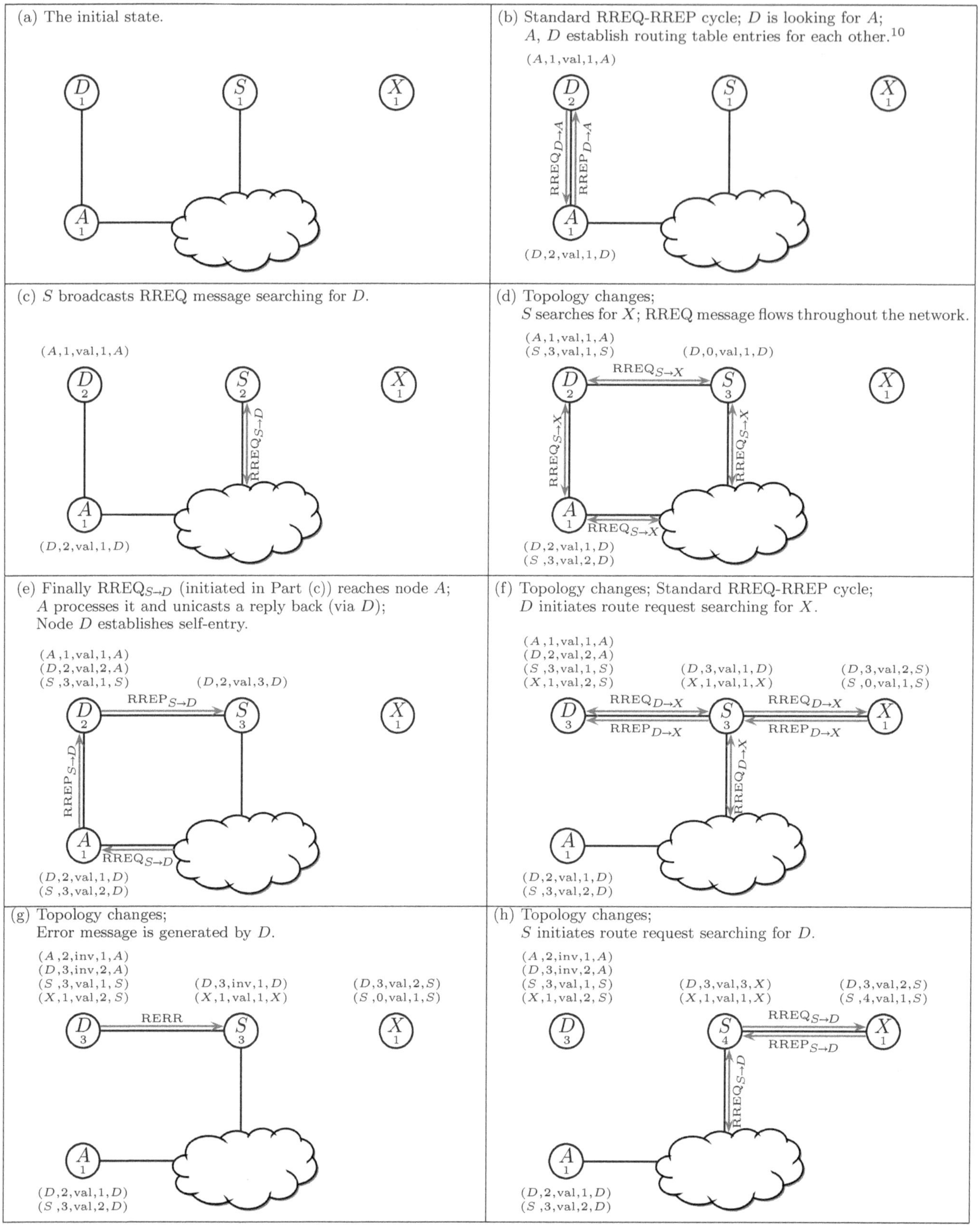

Figure 1: Creating routing loops

[10]Each routing table entry has the form (*destination*, *sequence number*, *validity*, *hop count*, *next hop*).

[...]. 2. The entry is invalidated by marking the route entry as invalid". [19, Sect. 6.11]. The result of this process is that the sequence numbers of routing table entries for the unreachable destination nodes A and D are increased, and the entries invalidated, as shown in the routing table of node D in Figure 1(g).

The RERR message generated by node D contains information about the unreachable destination nodes A and D, taken from the routing table of node D. The message is sent to node S since it is the precursor for the unreachable destination node D. Node S receives the RERR message, and updates its routing table as follows: "*1. The destination sequence number of this routing entry [...] is copied from the incoming RERR. [...] 2. The entry is invalidated by marking the route entry as invalid*". [19, Sect. 6.11]. Therefore, the entry to node D in node S's routing table is updated to $(D, 3, \mathtt{inv}, 1, D)$.[11]

In Figure 1(h), the link between nodes S and D goes down, while the link between nodes S and X goes up. Node S also searches for a route to node D. Accordingly, the destination sequence number in the $\text{RREQ}_{S\to D}$ message is set to the value 3 since "*a previously valid route to the destination [...] is marked as invalid. [...] The Destination Sequence Number field in the RREQ message is the last known destination sequence number for this destination and is copied from the Destination Sequence Number field in the routing table.*" [19, Sect. 6.3]. The RREQ message is received by node X, which generates an intermediate RREP message since "*it has an active route to the destination, the destination sequence number in the node's existing route table entry for the destination is valid and greater than or equal to the Destination Sequence Number of the RREQ*" [19, Sect. 6.6]. Due to this, node X unicasts a $\text{RREP}_{S\to D}$ message back to node S. Finally, node S receives this message and updates its routing table, as shown in Figure 1(h).

A routing loop between nodes S and X for destination node D is now established. When either of the nodes has a data packet to send to destination node D, the data packet will loop between the two nodes.

In this section, we have shown that AODV is not a priori loop free. The presented example can create loops if (i) sequence numbers are implemented in a way consistent with the RFC, (ii) self-entries are allowed, and (iii) destination sequence numbers are copied directly from RERR messages—even when this copying is only executed if it does not cause a decrement in the destination sequence number in the routing table. This shows that loop freedom hinges on non-evident assumptions to be made when interpreting the RFC and not only on monotonically increasing sequence numbers.

5. AODV IMPLEMENTATIONS

To show that our results are not only theoretically driven, but *do* occur in practice, we analyse five different open source implementations of AODV:

- *AODV-UU* [2] is an implementation of AODV, developed at Uppsala University.
`http://aodvuu.sourceforge.net/`
- *Kernel-AODV* [1] is an implementation developed at NIST.
`http://w3.antd.nist.gov/wctg/aodv_kernel/`
- *AODV-UIUC* [15] (Univ. of Illinois at Urbana-Champaign) is an implementation that is based on an early draft (version 10) of AODV.
`http://sourceforge.net/projects/aslib/`
- *AODV-UCSB* [4] (Univ. of California, Santa Barbara) is another implementation that is based on an early draft (version 6) of AODV. `http://moment.cs.ucsb.edu/AODV/aodv-ucsb-0.1b.tar.gz`
- *AODV-ns2* is an AODV implementation in the ns2 network simulator, originally developed by the CMU Monarch project and improved upon later by S. Das and E. Belding-Royer (the authors of the AODV RFC [19]). It is based on an early draft (version 8) of AODV. It is frequently used by academic and industry researchers to simulate AODV.
`http://ns2.sourcearchive.com/documentation/2.35~RC4-1/aodv_8cc-source.html`

Although these implementation behave differently, all of them *do* capture the main aspects of the AODV protocol, as specified in the RFC [19]. As we have shown in the previous sections, implementing the AODV protocol based on the RFC specification does not necessarily guarantee loop freedom: routing loops may occur when following either Interpretation 1a, Interpretation 2b or the combination of Interpretation 3a with any of 4a–c of Table 1. Therefore, we look at these five concrete AODV implementations to determine whether any of them is susceptible to routing loops. In particular, we examine the code of these implementations to see if routing loops can occur. Table 2 shows the results of this analysis: it indicates for each of the implementations which of the interpretations of Table 1 they follow and whether they can create routing loops or not.

We found that none of the five implementations makes use of the sequence-number-status flag, so a positive sequence number can never be marked as unknown. As a result, Ambiguity 1 of Table 1 does not arise.

In AODV-UU, self-entries are never created because a check is always performed on an incoming RREP message to make sure that the destination IP address is not the same as the node's own IP address. In terms of Table 1 it follows Interpretations 2c, 3c and 4a. It is shown in [8] that this interpretation of the RFC (avoiding self-entries) is loop free.

In Kernel-AODV, which follows Interpretations 2a, 3b and 4a of Table 1, an optimal self-entry (with hop count 0 and next hop being the node itself) is always maintained by every node in the network. The optimal self-entry is created during node initialisation. The node also maintains its own sequence number in this entry. Since the self-entry is already optimal, a node will never update the self-entry when processing any incoming RREP messages that contain information about itself. As such, a routing loop as described by the example in Section 4.1 will never occur.

AODV-UIUC follows the Interpretations 2b, 3a and 4a, whereas AODV-UCSB implements 2b, 3a and 4b. Due to Interpretation 3a, both implementations allow the occurrence of self-entries. These self-entries are not created during node initialisation, but generated based on information contained in received RREP messages.

The processing of RERR messages in AODV-UIUC and AODV-UCSB does not adhere to the RFC specification (or even the draft versions that these implementation are based upon). Due to this non-adherence, we are unable to recreate the routing loop example in Section 4.1. However, we note that if both AODV-UIUC and AODV-UCSB were

[11] Each of the Interpretations 4a, 4b and 4c in Table 1 will produce the same update in this scenario.

Table 2: Analysis of AODV implementations

Implementation	Interpretation	Analysis
AODV-UU [2]	2c, 3c, 4a	Loop free, since self-entries are explicitly excluded.
Kernel-AODV [1]	2a, 3b, 4a	Loop free, due to optimal self-entries.
AODV-UIUC [15]	2b, 3a, 4a	Yields loops, through decrement of sequence numbers, by use of Interpretation 2b.
AODV-UCSB [4]	2b, 3a, 4b	Yields loops, through decrement of sequence numbers, by use of Interpretation 2b.
AODV-ns2	2a, 3a, 4b	Yields routing loops in the way described in Section 4, following plausible interpretations of the RFC w.r.t. Ambiguities 3 and 4.

to strictly follow the RFC specification with respect to the RERR processing, loops would have been created.

Even though the routing loop example of Section 4.1 could not be recreated, both implementations allow a decrease of destination sequence numbers in routing table entries to occur, as a result of following Interpretation 2b. This contradicts the idea of monotonically increasing destination sequence numbers, and can give rise to routing loops in a straightforward way [8, Sect. 8.1].

In AODV-ns2, self-entries are allowed to occur in nodes and the processing of RERR messages follows the RFC specification. It follows Interpretations 2a, 3a and 4b. However in AODV-ns2, whenever a node generates a RREQ message, sequence numbers are incremented by two instead of by one as specified in the RFC. We have modified the code such that sequence numbers are incremented by one whenever a node generates a RREQ message, and are able to replicate the routing loop example of Section 4.1 in the ns2 simulator, with the results showing the existence of a routing loop between node S and node X in Figure 1(h). However, we note that even if the code remains unchanged and sequence numbers are incremented by two, AODV-ns2 can still yield loops; the example is very similar to the one presented and only varies in subtle details.

In sum, we discovered not only that three out of five AODV implementations can produce routing loops, but also that there are essential differences in various aspects of protocol behaviour. This is due to different interpretations of the RFC by the developers of the AODV implementations.

6. METHODOLOGY

In Section 3 we discussed several interpretations of the RFC. We also stated which of these interpretations are loop free and which are not. To show that there is a possible routing loop, a single example, like the one we have given in Section 4, is sufficient.

The statement that a particular interpretation is loop free is much harder to show. Looking at the specification of AODV and AODV-based protocols, loop freedom is claimed in the preamble; the justification is then given by a short informal statement. For example, AODV "*uses destination sequence numbers to ensure loop freedom at all times (even in the face of anomalous delivery of routing control messages), avoiding problems (such as "counting to infinity") associated with classical distance vector protocols.*" [19, Sect. 1]. As we have shown, these statements are not sufficient and not necessarily true. The only way to guarantee loop freedom for some interpretations and to analyse all (reasonable) interpretations in a systematic manner is by the use of formal modelling and analysis.

6.1 Formal Modelling and Analysis

Ideally, any specification is free of ambiguities and contradictions. Using English prose only, this is nearly impossible to achieve. Hence every specification should be equipped with a formal specification. The choice of an appropriate specification language is often secondary, although it has high impact on the analysis. The use of *any* formal language helps to avoid ambiguities and to precisely describe the intended behaviour. Examples for modelling languages are (i) the Alloy language, which is used to model Chord [24]; (ii) timed automata, which are the input language for the UPPAAL model checker, used by Chiyangwa, Kwiatkowska [5] and others [6] to reason about AODV; (iii) routing algebra as introduced by Griffin and Sobrinho [11] or (iv) AWN, a process algebra particularly tailored for (wireless mesh) routing protocols [7, 12].

The analysis yielding the results presented in this paper is based on a formal model using AWN. The reason why we chose this formal language is two-fold: on the one hand it is tailored for wireless protocols and therefore offers primitives such as **broadcast**; on the other hand, it defines the protocol in a pseudo-code that is easily readable by any network or software researcher/engineer. (The language itself is implementation independent). Table 3 presents the main primitives of AWN; the full specification of AODV in AWN can be found in [8].

Table 3: AWN language (main primitives)

$X(exp_1, \ldots, exp_n)$	process name with arguments
$P + Q$	choice
$[\varphi]P$	if statement: execute P if condition φ holds
$[\![\mathtt{var} := exp]\!]P$	assignment followed by P
$\mathbf{broadcast}(ms).P$	broadcast ms followed by P
$\mathbf{groupcast}(dests,ms).P$	iterative unicast to all destinations $dests$
$\mathbf{unicast}(dest,ms).P \blacktriangleright Q$	unicast ms to $dest$: if successful proceed with P; otherwise with Q
$\mathbf{deliver}(data).P$	deliver data to application layer
$\mathbf{receive}(msg).P$	receive a message
$P \| Q$	parallel composition of nodes

Based on a formal specification one can now perform a careful analysis of the model to see if the model is consistent and if it satisfies properties such as loop freedom. Our analysis uses "classical" paper-and-pen verification techniques, and, in this end, guarantees the loop freedom of some interpretations of the AODV specification.

6.2 Using Formal Methods to Augment RFCs

Though we have not shown our proofs in the present paper—the purpose was to show that sequence numbers do not a priori guarantee loop freedom and that formal methods are needed—our analysis is based on a rigorous, formal and mathematical approach. As mentioned before, each interpretation of the RFC has been formalised in an unambiguous way.

We strongly believe that a "good" specification should consist of both a formal specification such as the one given in [12, 8] *and* an English description. The English text then serves the purpose of informing the reader about the main behaviour of the protocol and explains design decisions; the formal specification gives all the details, without allowing any ambiguities.

The IETF argues for the value of formal methods for specifying, analysing and verifying protocols.

> "*Formal languages are useful tools for specifying parts of protocols. However, as of today, there exists no well-known language that is able to capture the full syntax and semantics of reasonably rich IETF protocols.*" [IETF Web page[12]]

The quote is dated 1 Oct 2001; we believe that since then formal methods have advanced to such a state that they are now able to capture the full syntax and the full semantics of protocols and should be used for protocol specification and analysis.

7. RELATED WORK

Analysing and verifying routing protocols has a long tradition. Merlin and Segall [16] were amongst the first to use sequence numbers to guarantee loop freedom of a routing protocol. As we have pointed out, at least two proofs for AODV's loop freedom have been proposed [22, 26]. These proof attempts are discussed in Section 2.3. Besides, other researchers have used formal specification and analysis techniques to investigate the correctness of AODV; we point only at some examples.

A preliminary draft of AODV has been shown to be not loop free by Bhargavan et al. in [3]. Since then, AODV has changed to such a degree that the analysis of [3] has no bearing on the current version [19]. Furthermore, their loop had to do with timing issues (as is also the case in [10, 23]), whereas ours is time-independent. In the same paper they show the use of model checking on a draft of AODV, demonstrating the feasibility and value of automated verification of routing protocols. Using the model checker SPIN they were able to find/verify the routing loop in the preliminary draft. Musuvathi et al. [17] introduced the CMC model checker primarily to search for coding errors in implementations and used AODV as an example. Chiyangwa and Kwiatkowska [5] use the timing features of the model checker UPPAAL to study the relationship between the timing parameters and the performance of route discovery. A "time-free" model of AODV is exhaustively analysed by Fehnker et al. in [6], where variants of AODV, which yield performance improvements, are proposed and analysed. The presented model is based on the process algebra AWN introduced by the same authors in [7]; the complete model of AODV can be found in [8].

Next to the analysis of AODV with various formal methods, formal languages are also used for the specification and verification of other reasonably rich protocols. In [11], Griffin and Sobrinho use path algebras and algebraic routing to define a metarouting language that allows the definition of routing protocols. Their main interest lies in the combination of different algebras with applications in interdomain routing protocols such as BGP. Zave et al. provide abstractions for implementing the SIP protocol; the major elements of the language are presented in [25].

8. DISCUSSION & CONCLUSION

We have shown that, in contrast to common belief, sequence numbers do not guarantee loop freedom, even if they are increased monotonically over time and incremented whenever a new route request is generated. This was mainly achieved by analysing the Ad hoc On-demand Distance Vector (AODV) routing protocol. We have shown that AODV can yield routing loops.

Of course, one could argue that the given loop example does not occur in practice very often, since the sequence in which different requests have to be initiated and afterwards handled by different nodes might be really rare. However, it has been claimed that routing loops are avoided in *all possible scenarios* by the use of sequence numbers—this has been proven to be incorrect. Here, it does *not* matter how often this scenario occurs in real life. The fact that the example exists and can occur, makes the protocol flawed and disproves the fact that monotonically increasing sequence numbers are sufficient to guarantee loop freedom.

Next to that we have analysed several different interpretations of the AODV RFC. It turned out that several interpretations can yield unwanted behaviour such as routing loops. We also found that implementations of AODV behave differently in crucial aspects of protocol behaviour, although they all follow the lines of the RFC. This is often caused by ambiguities, contradictions or unspecified behaviour in the RFC. Of course a specification "*needs to be reasonably implementation independent*"[12] and can leave some decisions to the software engineer; however it is our belief that any specification should be clear and unambiguous enough to guarantee the same behaviour when given to different developers. As demonstrated, this is not the case for AODV, and likely not for many other RFCs provided by the IETF.

Our work confirms that RFCs written merely in a natural language contain ambiguities and contradictions. As a consequence, the various implementations depart in various ways from the RFC. Moreover, semi-informal reasoning is inadequate to ensure critical safety-properties like loop freedom. We believe that formal specification languages and analysis techniques—offering rigorous verification and analysis techniques—are now able to capture the full syntax and semantics of reasonably rich IETF protocols. These are an indispensable augmentation to natural language, both for specifying protocols such as AODV, AODVv2 and HWMP, and for verifying their essential properties.

Acknowledgement.

NICTA is funded by the Australian Government as represented by the Department of Broadband, Communications and the Digital Economy and the Australian Research Council through the ICT Centre of Excellence program.

[12]`http://www.ietf.org/iesg/statement/pseudocode-guidelines.html`

9. REFERENCES

[1] Kernel AODV (ver. 2.2.2), NIST. `http://www.antd.nist.gov/wctg/aodv_kernel/` (accessed September 27, 2013).

[2] AODV-UU: An implementation of the AODV routing protocol (IETF RFC 3561). `http://sourceforge.net/projects/aodvuu/` (accessed September 27, 2013).

[3] K. Bhargavan, D. Obradovic, and C. Gunter. Formal verification of standards for distance vector routing protocols. *J. ACM*, 49(4):538–576, 2002.

[4] I. Chakeres and E. Belding-Royer. AODV routing protocol implementation design. In *24th International Conference on Distributed Computing Systems Workshops (WWAN'04)*, pages 698–703. IEEE Press, 2004.

[5] S. Chiyangwa and M. Kwiatkowska. A timing analysis of AODV. In *Formal Methods for Open Object-based Distributed Systems (FMOODS'05)*, volume 3535 of *LNCS*, pages 306–322. Springer, 2005.

[6] A. Fehnker, R. J. van Glabbeek, P. Höfner, A. McIver, M. Portmann, and W. L. Tan. Automated analysis of AODV using UPPAAL. In C. Flanagan and B. König, editors, *Tools and Algorithms for the Construction and Analysis of Systems (TACAS'12)*, volume 7214 of *LNCS*, pages 173–187. Springer, 2012.

[7] A. Fehnker, R. J. van Glabbeek, P. Höfner, A. McIver, M. Portmann, and W. L. Tan. A process algebra for wireless mesh networks. In H. Seidl, editor, *European Symposium on Programming (ESOP'12)*, volume 7211 of *LNCS*, pages 295–315. Springer, 2012.

[8] A. Fehnker, R. J. van Glabbeek, P. Höfner, A. McIver, M. Portmann, and W. L. Tan. A process algebra for wireless mesh networks used for modelling, verifying and analysing AODV. Technical Report 5513, NICTA, 2013. `http://www.nicta.com.au/pub?doc=5513`.

[9] J. J. Garcia-Luna-Aceves. A unified approach to loop-free routing using distance vectors or link states. In *Symposium Proceedings on Communications, Architectures & Protocols (SIGCOMM '89)*, volume 19(4) of *ACM SIGCOMM Computer Communication Review*, pages 212–223. ACM Press, 1989.

[10] J. J. Garcia-Luna-Aceves and H. Rangarajan. A new framework for loop-free on-demand routing using destination sequence numbers. In *IEEE International Conference on Mobile Ad-hoc and Sensor Systems (MASS)*, pages 426–435, 2004.

[11] T. Griffin and J. Sobrinho. Metarouting. In *Proceedings of the 2005 Conference on Applications, Technologies, Architectures, and Protocols for Computer Communications (SIGCOMM '05)*, volume 35(4) of *ACM SIGCOMM Computer Communication Review*, pages 1–12. ACM Press, 2005.

[12] P. Höfner, R. J. van Glabbeek, W. L. Tan, M. Portmann, A. McIver, and A. Fehnker. A rigorous analysis of AODV and its variants. In *Modeling, Analysis and Simulation of Wireless and Mobile Systems (MSWIM'12)*. ACM Press, 2012.

[13] C. Huitema, J. Postel, and S. Crocker. Not all RFCs are standards. RFC 1768 (Informational), 1995.

[14] IEEE P802.11s. IEEE draft standard for information technology—telecommunications and information exchange between systems—local and metropolitan area networks—specific requirements—part 11: Wireless LAN Medium Access Control (MAC) and physical layer (PHY) specifications-amendment 10: Mesh networking, July 2010.

[15] V. Kawadia, Y. Zhang, and B. Gupta. System services for ad-hoc routing: Architecture, implementation and experiences. In *Proceedings of the 1st international conference on Mobile systems, applications and services*, MobiSys '03, pages 99–112. ACM, 2003.

[16] P. M. Merlin and A. Segall. A failsafe distributed routing protocol. *IEEE Transactions on Communications*, com-27(9), 1979.

[17] M. Musuvathi, D. Y. W. Park, A. Chou, D. R. Engler, and D. L. Dill. CMC: a pragmatic approach to model checking real code. In *Operating Systems Design and Implementation (OSDI'02)*, 2002.

[18] T. Nipkow, L. C. Paulson, and M. Wenzel. *Isabelle/HOL — A Proof Assistant for Higher-Order Logic*, volume 2283 of *LNCS*. Springer, 2002.

[19] C. Perkins, E. Belding-Royer, and S. Das. Ad hoc on-demand distance vector (AODV) routing. RFC 3561 (Experimental), 2003. `http://www.ietf.org/rfc/rfc3561.txt`.

[20] C. Perkins and P. Bhagwat. Highly dynamic destination-sequenced distance-vector routing (DSDV) for mobile computers. In *Conference on Communications, Architectures, Protocols & Applications (SIGCOMM '94)*, volume 24(4) of *ACM SIGCOMM Computer Communication Review*, pages 234–244. ACM Press, 1994.

[21] C. Perkins and I. Chakeres. Dynamic MANET on-demand (AODVv2) routing. Internet Draft (Standards Track), 2013. `http://tools.ietf.org/html/draft-ietf-manet-dymo-26`.

[22] C. Perkins and E. Royer. Ad-hoc On-Demand Distance Vector Routing. In *2nd IEEE Workshop on Mobile Computing Systems and Applications*, pages 90–100, 1999.

[23] H. Rangarajan and J. J. Garcia-Luna-Aceves. Making on-demand routing protocols based on destination sequence numbers robust. In *IEEE International Conference on Communications (ICC)*, volume 5, pages 3068–3072, 2005.

[24] P. Zave. Using lightweight modeling to understand CHORD. *SIGCOMM Comput. Commun. Rev.*, 42(2):49–57, 2012.

[25] P. Zave, E. Cheung, G. W. Bond, and T. M. Smith. Abstractions for programming SIP back-to-back user agents. In *International Conference on Principles, Systems and Applications of IP Telecommunications*, IPTComm '09, pages 11:1–11:12. ACM Press, 2009.

[26] M. Zhou, H. Yang, X. Zhang, and J. Wang. The proof of AODV loop freedom. In *Wireless Communications & Signal Processing (WCSP09)*, pages 1–5. IEEE Press, 2009.

Efficient, Distributed Coordination of Multiple Mobile Chargers in Sensor Networks

Adelina Madhja
Computer Technology Institute and Press "Diophantus" (CTI) & University of Patras, Greece
madia@ceid.upatras.gr

Sotiris Nikoletseas*
Computer Technology Institute and Press "Diophantus" (CTI) & University of Patras, Greece
nikole@cti.gr

Theofanis P. Raptis†
Computer Technology Institute and Press "Diophantus" (CTI) & University of Patras, Greece
traptis@ceid.upatras.gr

ABSTRACT

We investigate the problem of efficient wireless energy recharging in Wireless Rechargeable Sensor Networks (WRSNs). In such networks special mobile entities (called the Mobile Chargers) traverse the network and wirelessly replenish the energy of sensor nodes. In contrast to most current approaches, we envision methods that are distributed and use limited network information. We propose four new protocols for efficient recharging, addressing key issues which we identify, most notably (i) what are good coordination procedures for the Mobile Chargers and (ii) what are good trajectories for the Mobile Chargers. Two of our protocols (DC, DCLK) perform distributed, limited network knowledge coordination and charging, while two others (CC, CCGK) perform centralized, global network knowledge coordination and charging. As detailed simulations demonstrate, one of our distributed protocols outperforms a known state of the art method, while its performance gets quite close to the performance of the powerful centralized global knowledge method.

Categories and Subject Descriptors

C.2.1 [**Network Architecture and Design**]: Distributed Networks; Network Communications; Wireless Communication

General Terms

Algorithms; Experimentation; Performance

*Research supported by the European Union (European Social Fund ESF) and Greek national funds through the Operational Program "Education and Lifelong Learning" of the National Strategic Reference Framework (NSRF) - Research Funding Program: Thalis-DISFER, Investing in knowledge society through the European Social Fund.

†Research supported by the EU/FIRE IoT Lab project - STREP ICT-610477.

MSWiM'13, November 3–8, 2013, Barcelona, Spain.

http://dx.doi.org/10.1145/2507924.2507938.

Keywords

Sensor Networks; Energy Efficiency; Mobility; Distributed Algorithms; Wireless Recharging

1. INTRODUCTION AND CONTRIBUTION

The technology of highly-efficient wireless energy transmission was proposed for efficient, non-radiative energy transmission over mid-range. The work in [12] has shown that through strongly coupled magnetic resonances, the efficiency of transferring 60 watts of power over a distance in excess of 2 meters is as high as 40%. Industry research also demonstrated that it is possible to improve transferring 60 watts of power over a distance of up to two to three feet with efficiency of 75% [11]. Together with the research efforts on wireless energy transmission, several international organizations, such as the *Wireless Power Consortium* (WPC, [5]) and the *Alliance for Wireless Power* (A4WP, [1]), aim at maximizing the use of these technologies. WPC, an open-membership cooperation of Asian, European, and American companies in diverse industries, including electronics manufacturers and original equipment manufacturers, is working towards the global standardization of wireless charging technology. A4WP, an independently operated organization composed of global wireless power and technology industry leaders, focuses on a new wireless power transfer technology that provides spatial freedom for charging of electrical devices in cars, on table tops and for multiple devices simultaneously. Commercial products utilizing wireless energy transmission are already available on the market such as those in [3], in [2] and in [4].

These technologies lead the way towards *a new paradigm* for wireless sensor networks; the Wireless Rechargeable Sensor Networks (WRSNs). WRSNs consist of sensor nodes that may be either stationary or mobile, as well as few mobile nodes with high energy supplies. The latter, by using wireless energy transmission technologies are capable of charging sensor nodes. This way, the highly constrained resource of energy can be managed in great detail and more efficiently. Another important aspect is the fact that energy management in WRSNs can be performed passively from the perspective of sensor nodes and without the computational and communicational overhead introduced by complex energy management algorithms. Finally, WRSNs allow energy management to be studied and designed independently of the underlying routing protocol used for data propagation.

The Problem. Let a Wireless Rechargeable Sensor Network (WRSN) comprised of *stationary* sensor nodes and *special mobile entities called the Mobile Chargers.* The Mobile Chargers have significant (yet finite) energy supplies, that are much larger than those of each sensor node, and are thus capable of charging the sensors in the network. We aim at designing and evaluating efficient protocols for the chargers' coordination and charging procedures in order to improve energy efficiency, prolong the lifetime of the network and also improve important network properties (such as the quality of network coverage and the robustness of data propagation).

In particular, we view the chargers' coordination as a distinct procedure, on top of the sensor nodes charging mechanism. Unlike other methods in the state of the art, we do not couple the chargers' coordination neither with the sensor nodes charging process nor with the underlying network energy information data propagation; actually, we wish to perform efficient coordinated wireless energy transfer in a way which is agnostic of the network energy status, via adaptive techniques that *implicitly (based on the chargers' status) adapt to the network's energy evolution.*

Remark. We note that, although the wireless recharge problem might look similar to other related research problems (such as aggressive data collection via mobile sinks), it admits special features that necessitate a direct approach, while the optimization of concrete trade-offs and the fine-tuning of design alternatives that arise in wireless recharging necessitate the distinct investigation of special protocol design parameters.

Finally, we note that Mobile Charger optimization problems are (inherently) computationally hard e.g. in [6] we have formulated the wireless recharge problem as the Charger Dispatch Decision Problem - CDDP, and showed that it is $\mathcal{NP}$-complete (via reduction from the Geometric Traveling Salesman Problem, G-TSP; see e.g. [8], p. 212).

Our Contribution. While interesting research has been lately contributed to the wireless recharge problem and particularly to the scheduling of a single mobile charger, most methods so far necessitate significant (in many cases even global) network knowledge (e.g. it is assumed that the charger knows the energy levels of all sensors in the network) and the solutions are centralized. On the contrary, our methods are *distributed, and use (at most) local network information.* Also, unlike other multiple chargers state of the art approaches that opt for integration and coupling of the coordination and charging procedures, our methods distinguish the network operations in three separate levels: *the coordination procedure*, *the charging process* and *the routing mechanism.* We identify the necessity of this demarcation as an efficient approach to the design of more detailed and better fine-tuned charger protocols.

In particular, we propose and evaluate selected *alternative strategies for efficient recharging* in stationary WRSNs via multiple Mobile Chargers. Our design provides concrete, different solutions to some *key issues (and the associated trade-offs)* of wireless recharging which we identify, most notably

i assuming a number of Mobile Chargers in the network, *in what way should they coordinate,*

ii given that the Mobile Chargers have coordinated, *what are good trajectories for the chargers to follow.*

More specifically, a) we first distinguish two fundamental network operations, *charger coordination* and *node charging* b) taking into account the capability of *both centralized and distributed processing* we design selected charger coordination alternatives that efficiently split the network area and assign subregions to the Mobile Chargers c) assuming *different levels of network knowledge* we design different charging traversal strategies employed by the chargers in their region of interest.

We provide four new coordination and charging protocols based on their network knowledge (from global to local and to absence of knowledge) and their processing ability (from distributed to centralized). The CC and DC protocols perform centralized and distributed coordination respectively with no network knowledge, the DCLK protocol performs distributed coordination with local knowledge and the CCGK protocol performs centralized coordination with global knowledge. Actually, we view the centralized coordination with global knowledge CCGK protocol as a kind of performance upper bound to which the two distributed, partial knowledge protocols are compared with.

2. RELATED WORK AND COMPARISON

Recently there has been much research effort in the field of WRSNs using *a single Mobile Charger.* In [13], the authors build a proof-of-concept prototype by using a wireless power charger installed on a robot and sensor nodes equipped with wireless power receivers and carry out experiments on the prototype to evaluate its performance in small-scale networks of up to ten nodes. In [15], the authors introduce the necessary and sufficient conditions such that the wireless charging problem can be studied as an optimization problem, with the objective of maximizing the ratio of the Mobile Charger's vacation time over the network traveling time. In [6], the authors study the impact of the charging process to the network lifetime for selected routing protocols by proposing a protocol that locally adapts the circular trajectory of the Mobile Charger to the energy dissipation rate of each sub-region of the network. In [18], the authors co-locate the mobile base station on the Mobile Charger and minimize the energy consumption of the entire system while ensuring none of the sensor nodes runs out of energy. All above works are advancing the topic, but do not address the capability of a network to support more than one Mobile Chargers. Such a capability could be vital for the lifetime prolongation of large networks that consist of several thousand nodes (and thus their maintenance is not feasible using one single charger).

On the other hand, in the field of WRSNs using *multiple Mobile Chargers* there has been limited research effort. In [19] the authors introduce collaborative mobile charging, where Mobile Chargers are allowed to charge each other (in our case, the model is different since we do not address chargers charging each other). They investigate the problem of scheduling multiple Mobile Chargers which collaboratively charge nodes over one dimensional WSNs, to maximize the ratio of the amount of payload energy to overhead energy, such that no sensor runs out of energy but in contrast to our work, they restrict their algorithms only in line-graphs. In [17] the authors nicely leverage concepts and mechanisms from NDN (Named Data Networking) to design energy monitoring protocols that deliver energy status information to Mobile Chargers in an efficient manner. They interestingly study how to minimize the total traveling cost of multiple chargers while ensuring no node failure and derive theoretical results on the minimum number of mobile vehicles required for perpetual network operations. They present a sophisticated heuristic algorithm and conduct simulations to demonstrate the effectiveness and efficiency of the proposed design but in contrast to our approach, they propose only one charging scheme of simple charger coordination and node selection procedures i.e., they do not really elaborate on the coordination aspect. Also, unlike our work, in both above approaches, the chargers' coordination is performed centrally and not distributively. That may not be considered realistic in large scale networks as it introduces high communication overhead (i.e. every charger has to propagate its status over large distances) and does not scale well with network size. We have chosen to compare with the protocol presented in [17], for comparison fairness in terms of similar model assumptions.

3. THE MODEL

Our model features three types of devices: stationary sensors, Mobile Chargers and one stationary Sink. We assume that there are N sensors of wireless communication range r uniformly distributed at random in a circular area $\mathcal{A}$ of radius R and K Mobile Chargers initially deployed at coordinates $(x,y) = (\frac{R}{2}\cos(\frac{\pi}{K}(2j-1)), \frac{R}{2}\sin(\frac{\pi}{K}(2j-1)))$ of the circular area, where $j = 1, 2, ..., K$. The Sink lies at the center of the circular area. In our model we assume that the Mobile Chargers do not perform any data gathering process.

We denote by E_{total} the total available energy in the network. Initially,

$$E_{total} = E_{sensors} + E_{MC}(t_{init})$$

where $E_{sensors}$ is the amount of energy shared among the sensor nodes and $E_{MC}(t_{init})$ is the total amount of energy that the Mobile Chargers have and may deliver to the network by charging sensor nodes. The maximum amount of energy that a single node and a single charger may store is E^{max}_{sensor} and E^{max}_{MC} respectively. Energy is split among the sensor nodes and the chargers as follows:

$$E^{max}_{sensor} = \frac{E_{sensors}}{N} \text{ and } E^{max}_{MC} = \frac{E_{MC}(t_{init})}{K}.$$

In our model the charging is performed point-to-point, i.e. only one sensor may be charged at a time from a Mobile Charger by approaching it at a very close distance so that the charging process has maximum efficiency. The time that elapses while the Mobile Charger moves from one sensor to another is considered to be very small when compared to the charging time; still the trajectory followed (and particularly its length) is of interest to us, since it may capture diverse cost aspects, like gas or electric power needed for charger movement. We assume that the charging time is equal for every sensor and independent of its battery status.

We assume a quite heterogeneous data generation model. Each sensor node chooses independently a relative data generation rate $\lambda_i \in [a, b]$ (where a, b constant values) according to the uniform distribution $\mathcal{U}[a, b]$. Values of λ_i close to a imply low data generation rate and values close to b imply high data generation rate. The routing protocol operates at the network layer, so we are assuming appropriate underlying data-link, MAC and physical layers. We refer to [9, 7] for greedy, single path, underlying routing protocol.

To transmit a k-bit message, the radio expends $E_T(k) = \epsilon_{trans} \cdot k$ and to receive a k-bit message, the radio expends $E_R(k) = \epsilon_{recv} \cdot k$ where ϵ_{trans} and ϵ_{recv} are constants.As usual, the power needed to transmit a message at distance d is roughly d^α where $2 \leq \alpha \leq 6$ a constant; for simplicity we take $\alpha = 2$.

4. DEMARCATED PROTOCOL PHASES

In contrast to other known works, we split the charging process in two phases, the *coordination phase* and the *charging phase*. The demarcation of the chargers' operations in phases allows us to focus on each aspect separately and fine-tune the protocols more precisely.

Coordination Phase. A Mobile Charger's energy is consumed as it replenishes the energy of the sensor nodes. The energy dissipation rate among Mobile Chargers may not be the same, since the non-uniform generation rate of events can eventually lead to stressed network regions and burden some chargers more than others. For this reason, the Mobile Chargers periodically communicate with each other and deal out their charging regions fairly (for example, a weaker Mobile Charger in terms of energy should be assigned to a smaller network region). This coordination process can be achieved either in a *centralized* or a *distributed* manner.

In the centralized case the coordination is performed using information from all K chargers. We assume that the calculations for this type of coordination are performed by a computationally powerful network entity, e.g. the Sink. Centralized coordination is generally more powerful than distributed coordination, thus centralized protocols' performance serves as an upper bound on performance which the distributed methods are compared to. In the distributed case, a charger is informed about the status of its neighboring chargers resulting in a more secluded coordination between close chargers.

Charging Phase. Charging traversal alternatives have been widely studied in the case of a single Mobile Charger. In our approach, where the charger's operation is dual, we give emphasis to the *amount of knowledge* possessed by protocols in terms of locality. In order to appropriately design the charging phase of a protocol we distinguish the protocol's knowledge amount among *global knowledge, local knowledge, no knowledge* and *reactive knowledge.*

In the case of global knowledge, we suppose that a Mobile Charger can use information from all over the network (sensor nodes and other chargers). Such an amount of knowledge makes the Mobile Charger powerful but it may be unrealistic in large networks and do not scale well with network size. On the contrary, in the more realistic case of local knowledge, a Mobile Charger is allowed to use limited information derived from its neighborhood. We consider a charger to be "blind" when it has no knowledge on the network and thus cannot use a sophisticated charging method. The reactive knowledge is a special case of real time acquisition of global knowledge, by spending some energy for information messages exchanging among nodes and chargers. Note that the amount of knowledge can also be diversified in the coordination phase, among the Mobile Chargers.

5. THE PROTOCOLS

We present four new Mobile Chargers protocols and another, state the art protocol ([17]) that we compare with.

5.1 Centralized Coordination protocol CC

The CC protocol performs centralized coordination among the chargers and assumes no knowledge on the network. In particular, the coordination process is able to use information from all Mobile Chargers (energy status, position etc), but is agnostic of the underlying network and sensor nodes attributes (energy status, position etc.). This approach virtually partitions the network elements in two completely separate levels, the Mobile Chargers level and the sensor nodes level.

Coordination phase. Each Mobile Charger is assigned to a network region. Since the initial charger deployment coordinates are $(x, y) = (\frac{R}{2}\cos(\frac{\pi}{K}(2j-1)), \frac{R}{2}\sin(\frac{\pi}{K}(2j-1)))$, where $j = 1, 2, ..., K$, we can split the network area in Slices, with one charger assigned to each Slice. When the coordination process is initialized, the region of each charger is computed. Each charger should be assigned to a region of size analogous to its current energy level, so that the energy dissipation among the chargers is balanced. In order to compute the size of the region of charger j, it suffices to compute the central angle ϕ_j corresponding to the charger's Slice. In particular

$$\phi_j = 2\pi \cdot \frac{E_j}{\sum_{j=1}^{K} E_j}, \text{ where } \sum_{j=1}^{K} \phi_j = 2\pi.$$

Charging phase. During this phase, charger j traverses the network region it is assigned to (Slice defined by angle ϕ_j) and charges the corresponding sensor nodes. The CC protocol assumes no knowledge on the network. For this reason the path followed by the Mobile Charger is restricted to several naive alternatives (some presented in [6]). In our approach we use a "blind" scanning of the region where the Mobile Charger starts form the Sink and traverses an exhaustive path until it reaches the boundaries of the network area. The advantage of this movement is that due to its space filling attributes, the Mobile Charger covers the whole Slice and almost every node is charged, until the energy of the Mobile Charger is totally depleted. On the other hand, due to lack of knowledge, this movement is not adaptive, i.e. it does not take into account differences of the energy depletion rates of the network area caused by the underlying message propagation.

5.2 Distributed Coordination protocol DC

Coordination phase. The DC protocol performs distributed coordination among chargers and assumes no network knowledge. We split the network area in Slices and assign one Slice per charger. Angle ϕ_j corresponds to the central angle of jth charger's Slice. The chargers distributively define their Slice limits (i.e. the two radii that define the Slice), according to the size of the region each one can handle, w.r.t. their energy status. Each charger can shift their right and left Slice limits resulting in either a widening or a shrinkage of the region of interest. This task is performed distributively and each region limit movement is determined through a cooperation of the two adjacent Mobile Chargers. A limit movement of j's region is expressed as a change of ϕ_j. The coordination process uses two critical charger parameters for definition the region of interest, the charger's current energy level E_j and the charger's energy consumption rate since the last coordination ρ_j. The change $\Delta\phi_j^l$ of ϕ_j for the left Slice limit is defined by the following computation:

if $\min\{E_j, E_{j-1}\} = E_j$ **then**
  $\Delta\phi_j^l = -\phi_j \cdot \frac{|\rho_{j-1}-\rho_j|}{\max\{\rho_{j-1},\rho_j\}}$
else
  $\Delta\phi_j^l = \phi_{j-1} \cdot \frac{|\rho_{j-1}-\rho_j|}{\max\{\rho_{j-1},\rho_j\}}$
end if

Similarly, for the change $\Delta\phi_j^r$ of ϕ_j for the right Slice limit:

if $\min\{E_j, E_{j+1}\} = E_j$ **then**
  $\Delta\phi_j^r = -\phi_j \cdot \frac{|\rho_j-\rho_{j+1}|}{\max\{\rho_j,\rho_{j+1}\}}$
else
  $\Delta\phi_j^r = \phi_{j+1} \cdot \frac{|\rho_j-\rho_{j+1}|}{\max\{\rho_j,\rho_{j+1}\}}$
end if

The new angle (denoted by ϕ_j') is computed as $\phi_j' = \phi_j + \Delta\phi_j^l + \Delta\phi_j^r$. Note that, between two adjacent chargers j_1 and j_2, the change of their common slice limit is $\Delta\phi_{j_1}^r = -\Delta\phi_{j_2}^l$ so that the charger with the lower energy level provides its neighbor with a portion of its region of interest. Also, it is their energy level that determines which charger should reduce its region of interest and the energy consumption rate that determines the size of the reduced area. The size of the angle change is not computed by considering the energy levels of the two chargers because energy consumption rate shows how quickly will this energy level be reduced. For example, if ρ_j is high then j's Slice is critical, causing a rapid reduction of E_j, independently of its current level.

Charging phase. Since this protocol operates under the no knowledge assumption, the charging phase follows the same pattern with the CC protocol (Slice scanning).

5.3 Centralized Coordination Global Knowledge protocol CCGK

The CCGK protocol, similarly to the CC protocol, performs centralized coordination. However, the assumption of global knowledge on the network further extends the Mobile Chargers' abilities. For this reason, it is expected to outperform all other strategies that use only local information, thus somehow representing a performance bound. The global knowledge assumption would be unrealistic for real large-scale networks, as it introduces large communication overhead (i.e. nodes and chargers have to propagate their status over large distances).

Coordination phase. Instead of using the same coordination process with the CC protocol, we integrate the global knowledge assumption in the coordination phase. As a result, the network is not partitioned in two separate levels (Mobile Chargers, sensor nodes) and the Mobile Chargers are allowed to use network information during this phase. Each Mobile Charger is assigned to a network region. The region of interest of charger j is a cluster of nodes. Node i belongs to the cluster of charger

$$j' = \arg\min_j \left\{ \left(1 + \frac{dist_{ij}}{2R}\right) \cdot \left(2 - \frac{E_j}{E_{MC}^{max}}\right) \right\}$$

where $dist_{ij}$ is the distance between node i and charger j and E_j the residual energy of charger j ($E_j > 0$). In other words, a node selects a charger which is close and with high amount of energy. Note that the centralized computation of the charger region in the CCGK protocol is more powerful compared to other methods, since it uses information about the distance among every charger with every node.

Charging phase. The global knowledge charging phase we suggest uses energy and distance in a ranking function. In each round the charger moves to the sensor in the corresponding cluster, that minimizes the product of each node's energy times its distance from the current position of the Mobile Charger. More specifically, in each moving step the charger j charges node

$$i' = \arg\min_{i \in C_j} \left\{ \left(1 + \frac{dist_{ij}}{2R}\right) \cdot \left(1 + \frac{E_i}{E^{max}_{sensor}}\right) \right\}$$

where E_i is the residual energy of sensor node i. In other words, this protocol prioritizes nodes with low energy and small distance to the Mobile Charger.

5.4 Distributed Coordination Local Knowledge protocol DCLK

Coordination phase. The coordination phase follows the same pattern with the coordination phase of DC protocol (distributed ϕ_j angle computation).

Charging phase. The DCLK protocol operates with local knowledge assumption. The Slice corresponding to charger j is divided into k Sectors S_{jk} of the same width. Charger j prioritizes its Sectors w.r.t. high number of sensor nodes with low level of residual energy.

DEFINITION 1. *E^{min}_{jk} is the lowest nodal residual energy level in the Sector S_{jk}.*

DEFINITION 2. *$E^{min+\Delta}_{jk}$ is an energy level close to E^{min}_{jk}:*

$$E^{min+\Delta}_{jk} = E^{min}_{jk} + \delta \cdot \frac{E^{max}_{sensor}}{E^{min}_{jk}}, \delta \in (0, 1).$$

DEFINITION 3. *$N(S_{jk})$ is the number of nodes in Sector S_{jk} with residual energy between E^{min}_{jk} and $E^{jk}_{min+\Delta}$:*

$$N(S_{jk}) = \sum_{e=E^{min}_{jk}}^{E^{min+\Delta}_{jk}} N(e)$$

where $N(e)$ is the number of nodes with energy level e.

Charger j charges Sector S_{jk} which maximizes the product

$$\max_{S_{jk}} \{N(S_{jk}) \cdot (E^{max}_{sensor} - E^{min}_{jk})\}.$$

The intuition behind this charging process is the grouping of nodes in each Slice and the selection of a critical group. A critical group is a Sector containing a large number of sensor nodes that require more energy than other nodes throughout the network.

5.5 Centralized Coordination Reactive Knowledge protocol CCRK ([17])

The CCRK protocol acquires global knowledge in exchange for some in-network message aggregation. The Mobile Chargers obtain the most up-to-date energy information from sensor nodes and make decisions in real time. The energy information is aggregated by several special nodes in the network that act as representatives of partitioned network regions.

Coordination phase. Mobile Chargers communicate with each other to know their positions. To avoid conflicts where multiple Mobile Chargers choose the same node for recharge, the Sink stores and updates the availability of each node. The procedure is similar to that for shared memory access in operating systems, e.g. see [16], p. 125. The Sink maintains a $0-1$ valued node list. Once a sensor is chosen, its value is set to 1 (locked). Otherwise, it is 0. The value should be changed back from 1 to 0 when a Mobile Charger finishes charging that node. A Mobile Charger can simply communicate with the Sink, exclude nodes already selected by other Mobile Chargers, and notify the Sink of the status of nodes it chooses.

Charging phase. Two important metrics impact the charging order between node i and node i': the traveling time between node i to node i', and their residual lifetime L_i and $L_{i'}$. If node i' has a small $L_{i'}$ such that it would be dead if a Mobile Charger charges node i first, node i' should be visited first. In this protocol we use a weighted sum of traveling time from current node i to next node i' and the residual lifetime of node i',

$$w_{ii'} = \alpha t_{ii'} + (1 - \alpha) L_{i'}.$$

$w_{ii'}$ is used to decide which node i' to charge next. A sensor node with a smaller weighted value should be visited at a higher priority. When $\alpha = 1$, the algorithm reduces to nearest node selection that the Mobile Chargers always charge the closest node first regardless of battery deadlines; when $\alpha = 0$, it picks the node with the earliest battery deadline first regardless of the traveling distance.

6. EXPERIMENTAL EVALUATION

The simulation environment for conducting the experiments is Matlab 7.11. The Sink is placed at the center $(x, y) = (0, 0)$ of the circular deployment area. The number of sensors is set to 2000 and the number of chargers to 6. We simulate experiments of 4000 generated events. For statistical smoothness, we apply several times the deployment of nodes in the network and repeat each experiment 100 times. For each experiment we simulate large numbers of data propagations and the average value is taken. The statistical analysis of the findings (the median, lower and upper quartiles, outliers of the samples) demonstrate very high concentration around the mean, so in the following figures we only depict average values.

Since the N sensors are uniformly distributed in the circular area $\mathcal{A}$ of radius R, we apply a well known connectivity threshold, in order to maximize the probability that the produced random instances are connected. More strictly, since $\mathcal{A} \subset \mathbb{R}^2$, an instance of the *random geometric graphs model* $\mathcal{G}(\mathcal{X}_N; r)$ is constructed as follows: select N points $\mathcal{X}_N$ uniformly at random in $\mathcal{A}$. The set $V = \mathcal{X}_N$ is the set of vertices of the graph and we connect two vertices if their euclidean distance is at most r. In [10, 14] it is shown that the connectivity threshold for $\mathcal{G}(\mathcal{X}_N; r)$ is $r_c = \sqrt{\frac{\ln N}{\pi N}}$. In this paper we consider random instances of $\mathcal{G}(\mathcal{X}_N; r)$ of varying density, by selecting $r = \sqrt{\frac{c \ln N}{\pi N}}$, for different values of $c > 1$, which guarantees that the produced random instance is connected with high probability.

We focus on the following performance metrics: a) **alive nodes over time**, that is the number of nodes with enough residual energy to operate, during the progress of the experiment, b) **connected components over time** which indicates the number of strongly connected components of the network graph throughout the experiment c) **routing robustness** and **average routing robustness**, in terms of the nodes' average alive neighbours during the progress of the experiment, d) **coverage ageing**, that is the average coverage number (number of sensors having the point in their range) of 1000 randomly selected points in the network over time.

6.1 Protocols' impact on network properties

i) The application of charging protocols results in a great reduction in the overall death rate of the network (in terms of *alive nodes* over time), as shown in Fig. 1a. The CCGK as expected outperforms all other protocols and rather serves as an upper bound of their performance. The power of CCGK comes from the great amount of knowledge it assumes and from the robust centralized coordination of the Mobile chargers. The DCLK protocol, with limited network knowledge is an efficient distributed alternative, since it manages to achieve a performance close to the upper bound and outperform the reactive CCRK protocol. CC and DC protocols which assume no network knowledge are ourperformed by other protocols. Note that the upward curve of the DC protocol after 1500 generated events indicates a temporary starvation, after which the chargers revive some of the dead nodes when passing by areas with high amounts of dead nodes.

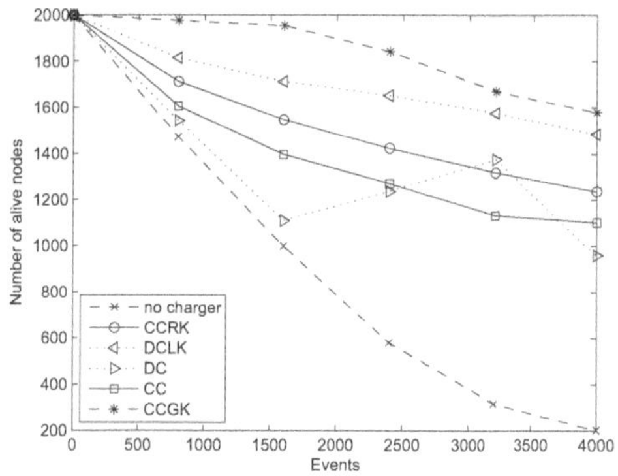

(a) Alive nodes over time.

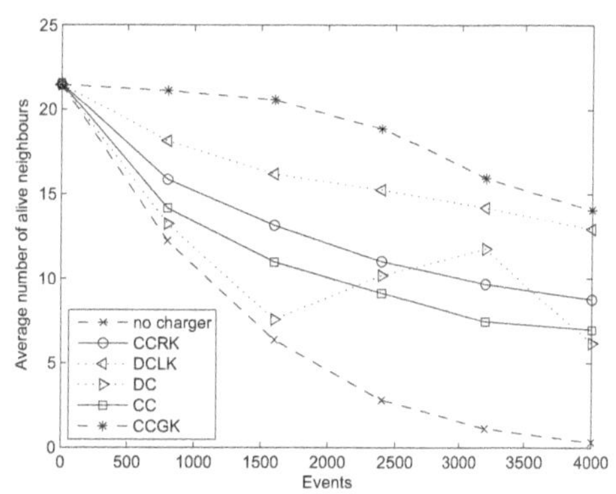

(b) Average routing robustness.

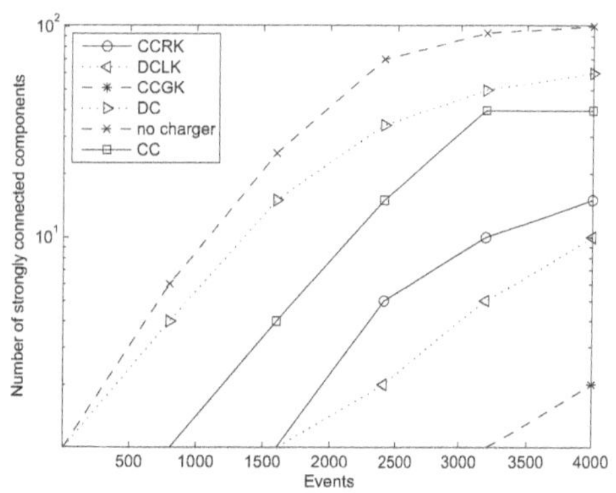

(c) Graph connected components over time.

Figure 1: Various metrics.

ii) *Routing robustness* is critical for wireless sensor networks, as all data collected have to be sent to the Sink. Path breakage occurs frequently due to node failure, mobility, or channel impairments, so the maintenance of a path from each node to a control center is a challenging task. A way of addressing the routing robustness of a wireless sensor network is by counting the number of its alive neighbors over time for each node. This can be seen as an implicit measure of network connectivity. For our protocols, the average number of alive neighbors is depicted in Fig. 1b. A more detailed evolution of the network's routing robustness is depicted in Fig. 2. The average routing robustness follows the same pattern as the death rate of nodes in the network. This is natural, since more dead nodes in the network result in loss of neighbors for each node. In Fig. 2 we can see that in the no charger case the white bar (representing number of neighbors < 7) is increasing, whereas the black bar (number of alive neighbors > 16) is rapidly decrasing. On the other hand, CCGK, CCRK and DCLK protocols achieve reliable routing robustness.

iii) Similarly to the routing robustness, the number of *strongly connected graph components* is an overall measure of connectivity quality in a wireless sensor network. Disconnected components are unable to communicate with each other and support efficient data propagation, resulting in high data delivery failures. A strategy of improving data delivery latency is the maintenance of a small number of connected components in the network. High numbers of components may lead to isolation of critical nodes, thus loss of important information. Fig. 1c depicts the evolution of the number of network components throughout the experiments. As we noted earlier, DC and CC protocols lead to a higher node death rate in comparison to CCRK and DCLK protocols, a fact that results in early disconnections and sharp increase of connected components. The powerful CCGK maintains a single strongly connected component for much longer.

iv) *Point coverage* problem regards the assurance that some selected points in the network are covered by an adequate number of sensors and is an important aspect in numerous wireless sensor networks functionalities (e.g. localization, tracking etc.). A point that is covered by k sensors is called k-covered. In Fig. 3 we can see the coverage ageing of 1000 randomly selected points scattered throughout the network. We examine how many points are $< 2, 2, 3, > 3$ covered for 4000 generated events. Each bar in the plot represents a number of the covered points. In the no charger case, the number of $<$ 2-covered points is increasing in contrast to the the number of > 3-covered points that is decreasing. CCGK, DCLK and CCRK protocols improve the network coverage by reducing the rate that the coverage of > 3-covered points is decreasing. The absolute difference of the number of < 2 and > 3-covered points, between different time instances, is not increasing quickly, compared to the no charger case.

6.2 The impact of knowledge

An important fact that comes up from the observation of the aforementioned metrics is that the CC and DC protocols are outperformed by their improved alternatives, CCGK and DCLK. The CC protocol, which uses a strong, centralized computation in order to calculate the regions of interest for the chargers, is outperformed even by the DCLK protocol that employs distributed computation (but assumes more knowledge on the network). This leads to the conclusion that the nature of the coordination procedure is less significant than the design of the charging traversal, when the latter relies on a greater amount of knowledge. Of course, when assuming the same amount of knowledge, the coordination procedure is still important (e.g. CC vs DC).

Also, the comparison between CCGK and CCRK protocols enlighten us about the size of the impact for acquiring knowledge on the network w.r.t. energy cost. The CCRK protocol is provided with global knowledge on the network but (in contrast to CCGK) the information maintenance relies on an underlying message propagation mechanism which is dissipating node and charger energy. As shown by the experimental evaluation, the degradation from global knowledge to local knowledge assumption (DCLK) is more efficient than a costly acquisition of global knowledge.

6.3 Traveling distance

Traveling distance of the Mobile Chargers indirectly reflects the efficiency of the coordination procedure and the charging process. Although the investigation of traveled distance does not display the impact on crucial network parameters, it can lead to useful conclusions about the balance of the chargers activity. Also, traveling distance can be associated with relevant cost for movement.

Fig. 4 depicts the total distance traveled by all (six) Mobile Chargers in the network. It is clear that CCGK, CCRK and DCLK protocols achieve the required charging process by traveling less distance than DC and CC protocols. Fig. 5 is comprised of five piecharts, one per protocol. A piechart consists of slices, the size of which is proportional to the distance traveled by the corresponding charger. We observe that in contrast to DC and CC protocols, CCGK, CCRK and DCLK protocols achieve balanced distribution of traveled distance among the chargers.

7. CONCLUSIONS AND FUTURE WORK

In this work we have studied the problem of efficient wireless energy recharging in Wireless Rechargeable Sensor Networks (WRSNs), in which Mobile Chargers traverse the network and wirelessly replenish the energy of sensor nodes. We

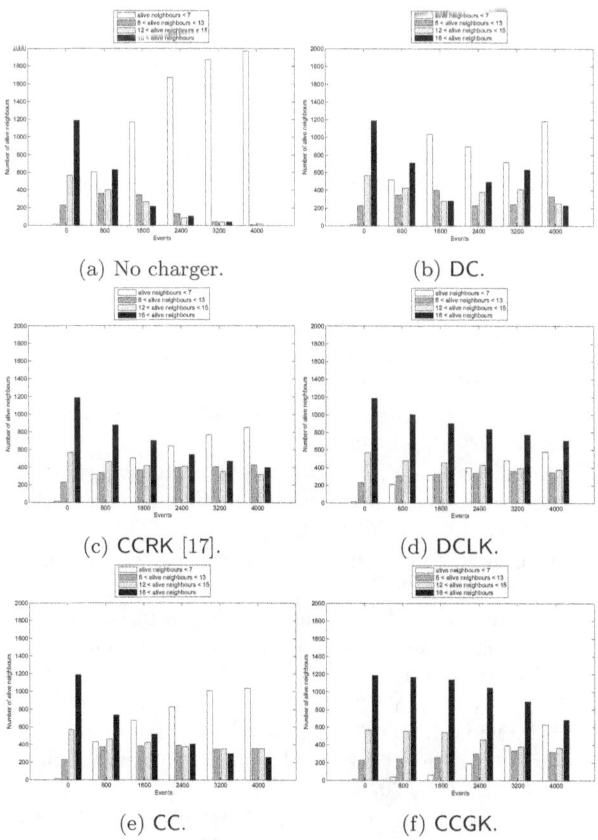

(a) No charger. (b) DC. (c) CCRK [17]. (d) DCLK. (e) CC. (f) CCGK.

Figure 2: Routing robustness.

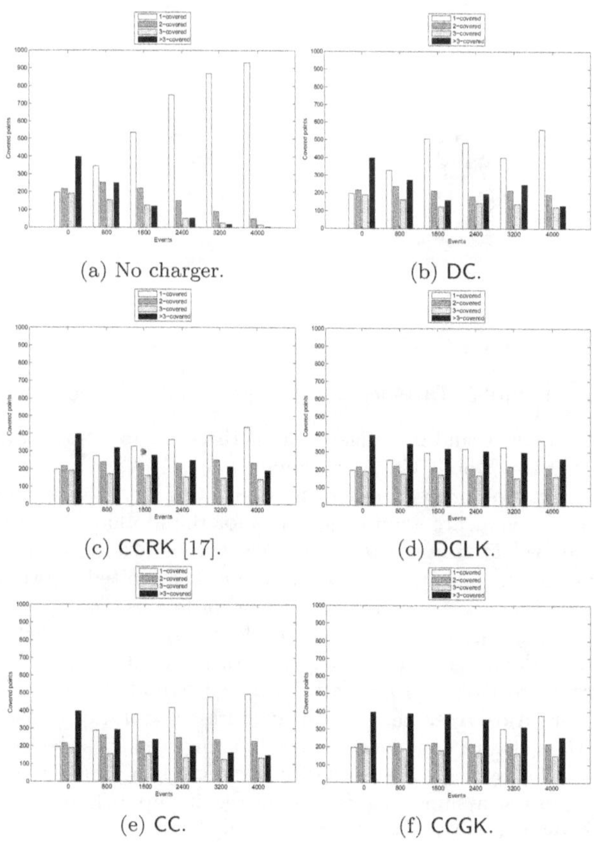

(a) No charger. (b) DC. (c) CCRK [17]. (d) DCLK. (e) CC. (f) CCGK.

Figure 3: Coverage ageing.

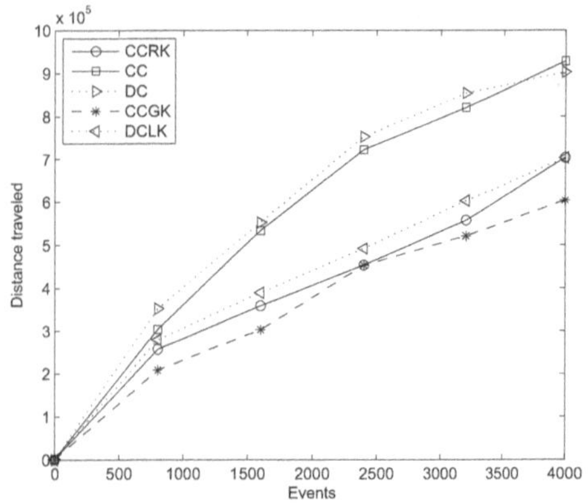

Figure 4: Distance traveled by Mobile Chargers.

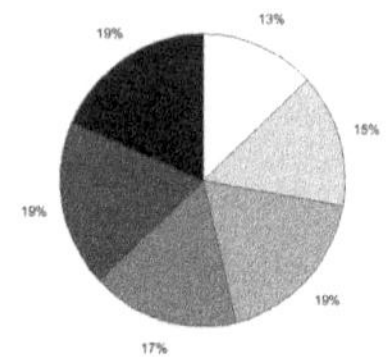

(a) CCGK.

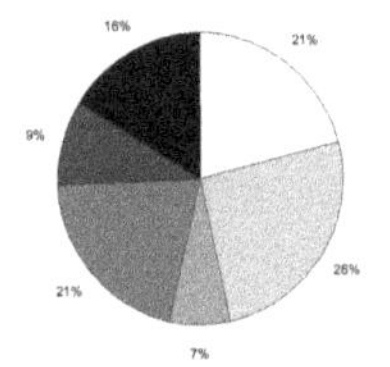

(b) DC.

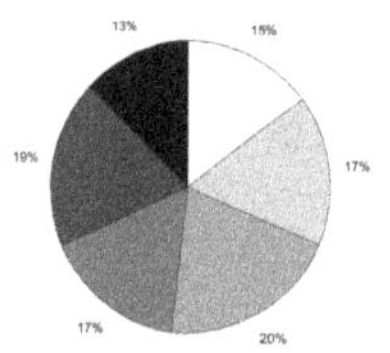

(c) CCRK [17].

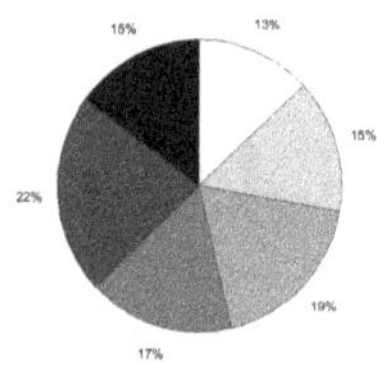

(d) DCLK.

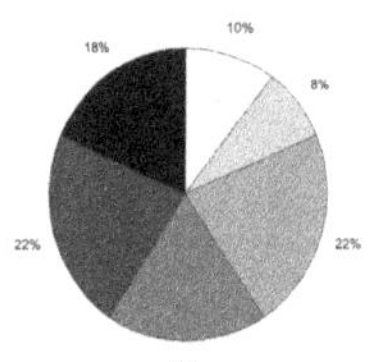

(e) CC.

Figure 5: Distance traveled per Mobile Charger.

first identify and investigate some critical issues and trade-offs of the Mobile Chargers configuration (i) what are good coordination procedures for the Mobile Chargers to perform and (ii) what are good trajectories for the Mobile Chargers to follow. In contrast to most current approaches, we envision methods that are distributed and use limited network information. We propose four new protocols for efficient recharging assuming different levels of network knowledge (from global to local and no network knowledge), and different processing (from centralized to distributed).

For future research, we plan to address non-uniform cases of the network deployment, since in many scenarios the network deployments are limited by the underlying terrain and we can not assume that the target region supports uniform deployments. We also plan to investigate the impact of different execution periods of the coordination phases. Another future research direction is the case of collaborative charging (as nicely addressed in [19]), where Mobile Chargers are allowed to charge each other. This model variant may lead to new protocols for charger configuration. Also, recent advances in magnetic resonant coupling shows that multiple nodes can be charged at the same time. This enables us to to consider new design alternatives for the charging problem. Finally, we plan to implement selected protocols in small/medium scale real experiments (e.g. with robotic elements and wireless recharge technology).

8. REFERENCES

[1] Alliance for wireless power. `http://www.a4wp.org/`.

[2] Murata manufacturing. `http://www.murata.com/`.

[3] Powercast. `http://www.powercastco.com/`.

[4] Texas instruments. `http://www.ti.com/`.

[5] The wireless power consortium. `http://www.wirelesspowerconsortium.com/`.

[6] C. M. Angelopoulos, S. Nikoletseas, T. P. Raptis, C. Raptopoulos, and F. Vasilakis. Efficient energy management in wireless rechargeable sensor networks. In *MSWiM*, 2012.

[7] D. Efstathiou, A. Koutsopoulos, and S. Nikoletseas. Analysis and simulation for parameterizing the energy-latency trade-off for routing in sensor networks. In *MSWiM*, 2010.

[8] M. R. Garey and D. S. Johnson. *Computers and intractability.* W. H. Freeman and Company, 1979.

[9] O. Gnawali, R. Fonseca, K. Jamieson, D. Moss, and P. Levis. Collection tree protocol. In *SenSys*, 2009.

[10] P. Gupta and P. Kumar. Critical power for asymptotic connectivity in wireless networks. *Stochastic Analysis, Control, Optimization and Applications*, 1998.

[11] Intel. Wireless resonant energy link (wrel) demo. `http://software.intel.com/en-us/videos/wireless-resonant-energy-link-wrel-demo/`.

[12] A. Kurs, A. Karalis, R. Moffatt, J. D. Joannopoulos, P. Fisher, and M. Soljacic. Wireless power transfer via strongly coupled magnetic resonances. *Science*, 317:83, 2007.

[13] Y. Peng, Z. Li, W. Zhang, and D. Qiao. Prolonging sensor network lifetime through wireless charging. In *RTSS*, 2010.

[14] M. Penrose. *Random Geometric Graphs.* Oxford University Press, 2003.

[15] Y. Shi, L. Xie, Y. T. Hou, and H. D. Sherali. On renewable sensor networks with wireless energy transfer. In *INFOCOM*, 2011.

[16] A. Tanenbaum. *Modern Operating Systems, 3rd Ed.* Prentice Hall, 2007.

[17] C. Wang, J. Li, F. Ye, and Y. Yang. Multi-vehicle coordination for wireless energy replenishment in sensor networks. In *IPDPS*, 2013.

[18] L. Xie, Y. Shi, Y. T. Hou, W. Lou, H. D. Sherali, and S. F. Midkiff. Bundling mobile base station and wireless energy transfer: Modeling and optimization. In *INFOCOM*, 2013.

[19] S. Zhang, J. Wu, and S. Lu. Collaborative mobile charging for sensor networks. In *MASS*, 2012.

Performance Evaluation of Wireless Sensor Networks in Realistic Wildfire Simulation Scenarios

Sinan Isik *
NETLAB †
Bogazici University, Turkey
isiks@boun.edu.tr

M. Yunus Donmez ‡
NETLAB
Bogazici University, Turkey
donmezme@boun.edu.tr

Can Tunca
NETLAB
Bogazici University, Turkey
can.tunca@boun.edu.tr

Cem Ersoy
NETLAB
Bogazici University, Turkey
ersoy@boun.edu.tr

ABSTRACT

Forest fires lead to high amount of environmental and economic loss all over the world. Prevention and early detection efforts aim to eliminate or minimize the damage that will be caused by a fire incident. Current surveillance systems for forest fires do not provide dense real-time monitoring and hence they lack prevention or early detection of a fire threat. Wireless sensor networks (WSNs), on the other hand, can collect real-time information such as temperature and humidity from almost all points of a forest and can provide fresh and accurate data for the fire-fighting management center quickly. In this work, we aim to evaluate the reporting performance of a WSN under realistic workload. Since fires are destructive and burning a deployed WSN is not feasible, simulation is the appropriate way to assess the reporting capability of a WSN during a forest fire. We integrate WSN simulator with a realistic fire propagation simulator which is modified to provide time based temperature field information while the fire propagates through the deployment area. Temperature information is used for the generation of realistic workloads and the determination of sensor destruction times that affects the routing decisions in WSN simulations. We present the effects of WSN related factors; such as reporting rate, number of the sinks, and the sink locations together with the effects of environmental factors such as the wind speed and the number of ignition points in terms of temperature reporting performance and freshness of temperature map.

*Dr. Isik is also with the Department of Mathematics, Bogazici University.

†NETLAB, Computer Networks Research Laboratory, Department of Computer Engineering, Bogazici University, Bebek, Istanbul 34342, Turkey.

‡Dr. Donmez is also with R&D, Information Technologies, NETAŞ, Istanbul, Turkey.

MSWiM'13, November 3–8, 2013, Barcelona, Spain.

http://dx.doi.org/10.1145/2507924.2507941.

Categories and Subject Descriptors

C.2 [**Computer-Communication Networks**]; C.2.2 [**Network Protocols**]; C.2.3 [**Network Operations**]

Keywords

Wildfire; fire propagation estimation; wireless sensor networks; simulation; performance evaluation

1. INTRODUCTION

Together with fire prevention precautions, early warning and fire spread monitoring systems for fires are very valuable for improving the efficiency of fire fighting activities. Although there are satellite remote sensing [1] and camera based early warning systems available [2, 3], these systems cannot function efficiently during all types of weather conditions. Their success depends on the time of the day, the existence of line of sight and other visibility constraints. Hence, if these systems can be supported by a wireless network of sensors such as temperature, humidity, smoke sensors, the resulting multimodal fire surveillance system can be more successful.

The most important goals in fire surveillance are quick and reliable detection and accurate localization of the fire. While the dimensions of the fire are still small, and the location of the fire is known, it will be much easier to suppress the fire without allowing much time for spreading. In this respect, besides timely detection of the fire, wireless sensor networks [4] can help in providing information about the location of the fire, about the extent of spread of the fire, and about temperature or smoke conditions at various locations which are highly valuable for firefighting management. With that information at hand, firefighting staff can be guided towards the target to block the fire or to suppress it quickly by utilizing the required firefighting instruments and vehicles.

During the last few years, significant advances in embedded hardware and software technologies are driving down the cost of wireless sensors. There is a variety of wireless sensor nodes that have become commercially available [5, 6, 7]. Although their prices are not yet very suitable to be

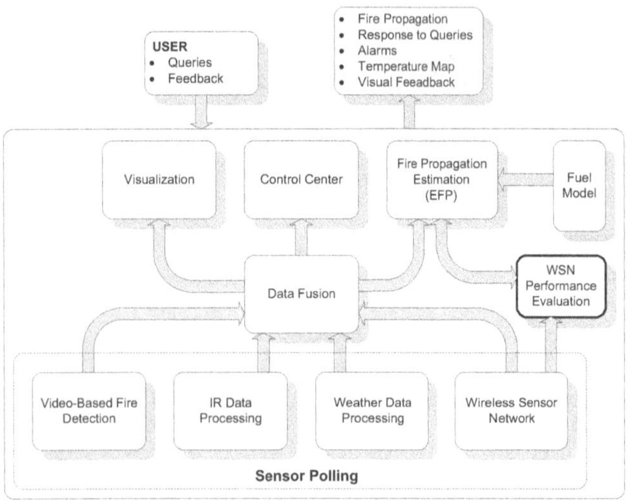

Figure 1: FIRESENSE system architecture

deployed in thousands to very large areas, several hundred sensors can be deployed around critical or important areas and used for improving the efficiency of the fire monitoring systems.

The work in this paper is contained as a sub-block in the block structure of a fire monitoring and detection system (Figure 1) named FIRESENSE [8] which is a Specific Targeted Research Project (STReP) of the European Union's 7th Framework Programme Environment. FIRESENSE aims to develop an automatic early warning system to remotely monitor areas of archaeological and cultural interest from the risk of fire and extreme weather conditions. The system is based on an integrated approach that uses innovative systems for early warning. It takes the advantage of recent advances in multisensor surveillance technologies. The key idea is to place a Wireless Sensor Network (WSN), capable of monitoring temperature, and optical and infrared cameras on the deployment site. The signals collected from these sensors are transmitted to a monitoring center, which employs intelligent computer vision and pattern recognition algorithms as well as data fusion techniques to automatically analyze sensor information. The system is capable of generating automatic warning signals for local authorities whenever a dangerous situation arises. FIRESENSE provide real-time information about the evolution of fire using wireless sensor network data. Furthermore, it estimates the propagation of the fire based on the fuel model of the area and other important parameters such as wind speed, slope and aspect of the ground surface. A 3-D Geographic Information Sytem (GIS) environment provides visualization of the predicted propagation.

Since fires are destructive and burning a deployed wireless sensor network is not feasible, simulation is the appropriate way for evaluating the fire detection performance of a WSN during a forest fire. Here, we need an integrated simulation framework which contains both a realistic fire propagation simulation component and a realistic WSN simulation component. In this framework, the fire propagation simulation component should include a temperature field model such that it can evaluate and report the temperature values at specific geographic coordinates as an incident of a wildfire propagates in an environment with given ignition locations and environmental conditions. On the other hand, the WSN simulation component should include a sensor destruction model where the sensors deployed into an environment are destructible due to high temperatures caused by a propagating fire incident. Moreover, the WSN simulation component should include a distributed routing model which can maintain its functionality with fast route restoration and minimal overhead under such dynamic network topologies. In the integrated simulation framework, the temperature map evolution output of the fire propagation component is fed into the WSN simulation component as an input for the performance evaluation of WSNs in realistic forest fire simulation scenarios.

For the WSN simulation component, we used OPNET modeler [9] and for the fire propagation simulation component we used EFP [10]. OPNET is a commercial network design, analysis and research tool and it can be used both prior to or after the deployment for assessing the reporting performance of a WSN in a forest fire scenario. EFP is developed in the FIRESENSE project and it aims to predict the propagation of a real fire incident by considering the environmental models such as ground and fuel models and current weather conditions as input. In the project various temperature field modeling algorithms are developed and embedded into EFP which allows modeling of the temperature variation at specific pre-defined sensor node locations, as a wildfire spreads starting from specific locations and under specific environmental conditions. The temperature map evolution is then used in OPNET for the sensor data generation and for the determination of sensor destructions. As the routing algorithm, we used a recent multisink routing algorithm, MLBRF [11], which is suitable for wildfire applications, where sensors are dynamically destroyed and sensor topology changes as the fire propagates in the environment.

In this paper, we aim evaluate the reporting performance of WSNs under realistic fire scenarios by enabling temperature based workload generation with dynamic topology changes due to sensor destructions caused by very high temperatures. We present the effects of WSN related factors; such as the reporting rate, the number of sinks, and the sink locations together with the effects of environmental factors such as the wind speed and the number of ignition points in temperature reporting performance and freshness of the temperature map.

The rest of the paper is organized as follows: An overview of the related works on WSNs for forest fire detection is presented in Section 2. A summary of MLBRF routing algorithm and its route restoration mechanism is given in Section 3. The simulation model and the performance evaluation of WSN in various scenarios are presented in Section 4. Section 5 concludes the paper.

2. FIRE DETECTION USING WSN

There has been a considerable amount of work carried out for fire detection application of wireless sensor networks. In [12] real experiments through controlled fires are done with a system of ten sensor nodes with GPS capability. The sensor nodes are deployed with ranges up to one kilometer and they sense and forward temperature, humidity and barometric pressure values to a base station. The system was implemented and real-world observations were gathered from the field. However, because of the long distances between sensor nodes, the data arriving to the sink is not valuable enough to detect a fire quickly and forecast the spread direction of the fire. Also, with the growth of fire and burning out some of the sensor nodes, the sensor network could fail in delivering the data from all sensor nodes to the base station.

A wireless local area network (WLAN) together with sensor-node technology for fire detection is used in [13]. The proposed system mixes multi-sensor nodes with IP-based cameras in a wireless mesh network setting in order to detect and verify a fire. When a fire is detected by a wireless multi-sensor node, the alarm generated by the node is propagated through the wireless network to a central server on which a software application runs for selecting the closest wireless camera(s). Then, real time images from the zone are streamed to the sink. Combining sensory data with images is the most important contribution of this study.

A multi-tiered portable wireless system for monitoring environmental conditions, especially for forest fires is developed and presented in [14]. Integrating web-enabled surveillance cameras with wireless sensor nodes, the system can provide real-time weather data from a forest. Three different sensor networks are deployed to different parts of a forest and the communication between the networks is enabled by powerful wireless devices that can send data up to ten kilometers range. The objective of the study is to determine the behavior of forest fires rather than their detection. With a wireless sensor network around an active fire, they measure the weather conditions around the fire. Webcams are also used to get visual data of the fire zone. Data gathered from the sensor nodes and the webcams are aggregated at a base station which has the capability of providing long distance communication using satellites. Periodically, the sensor nodes measure the temperature, relative humidity, wind speed and direction, and web-cams provide continuous visual data to the base station.

A forest fire surveillance system in South Korea is proposed by [15] in which a dynamic minimum cost path forwarding protocol is applied. After gathering data, a sink node makes several calculations regarding the relative humidity, precipitation and solar radiation, and produces a forest fire risk level. Additionally, [15] applies a minimum cost path forwarding method that causes some sensor nodes (especially the ones that are closer to the sink) to consume their energy much faster than the others.

A method is presented in [16] which applies neural network techniques for in-network data processing in environmental sensing applications of wireless sensor networks. Several data fusion algorithms are presented in this study. Maximum, minimum and average values of temperature and humidity data are calculated by the cluster-heads. Data are propagated to the sink only if a certain threshold is exceeded.

A general reliability-centric framework for event reporting in wireless sensor networks which can also be used in forest fire detection systems is provided in [17]. They consider the accuracy, importance and freshness of the reported data in environmental event detection systems. They present a data aggregation algorithm for filtering important data and a delay-aware data transmission protocol for rapidly carrying the data to the sink node.

A proactive routing method for wireless sensor networks is proposed in [18] to be used in disaster detection. The protocol is developed to be aware of a node's destruction threat and it can adapt the routes in case of a sensor node's death. The method can also adapt the routing state based on a possible failure threat indicated by a sensed phenomenon.

A wireless sensor network for forest fire detection is developed in [19] based on Fire Weather Index (FWI) system which is one of the most comprehensive forest fire danger rating systems in USA. The system determines the spread risk of a fire according to several index parameters. It collects weather data via the sensor nodes, and the data collected is analyzed at a center according to FWI. A distributed algorithm is used to minimize the error estimation for spread direction of a forest fire.

A simulation environment is presented in [20] that can create a model for a fire by analyzing the data reported by sensor nodes and by using some geographical information about the area. The use of topography of the environment distinguishes the study from some other solutions. The estimation of the spread of a fire is sent to hand-held devices of fire fighters to help them in fighting against the fire in field.

A framework for the use of wireless sensor networks for forest fire detection and monitoring is proposed in [21]. Framework includes proposals for the wireless sensor network architecture, sensor deployment scheme, and clustering and communication protocols. The aim of the framework is to detect a fire threat as early as possible and yet consider the energy consumption of the sensor nodes and the environmental conditions that may affect the required activity level of the network. Proposed framework is validated and evaluated via simulations to show that the framework can provide fast reaction to forest fires while also consuming energy efficiently.

3. SUITABILITY OF MLBRF FOR WILDFIRE APPLICATIONS

3.1 An overview of MLBRF

Deployment of multiple sinks is a candidate solution for the congestion problem in WSNs which also provides extra benefits in terms of energy-efficiency and reliability. Extra sinks in the environment relieves the burden around any sink. In addition, the average path length, consequently, the number of hops that a frame has to travel between a sensor and a sink decreases due to shorter geographic distances. Traveling shorter hops results with less energy consumption on the whole network due to the degradation in the number of sensors employed as a relay node. Moreover, usage of extra sinks relieves the unbalanced energy consumption among the sensors and improves the lifetime of a deployed sensor network. A multi-sink sensor network also becomes more robust against the inaccessibility of a sink node due to single point of failures such as node failures (energy exhaustion), node destructions (wildfire) or communication destructions (jamming).

In order to gain the maximum benefit from the deployment of multiple sinks, it is essential to distribute the load among the sinks evenly. MLBRF (Multi-Sink Load Balanced Reliable Forwarding) [11] is a cross layer geographic forwarding scheme which aims to provide reliable and energy efficient data delivery in a multi-sinked WSN for target tracking by maintaining load balancing among the deployed sinks.

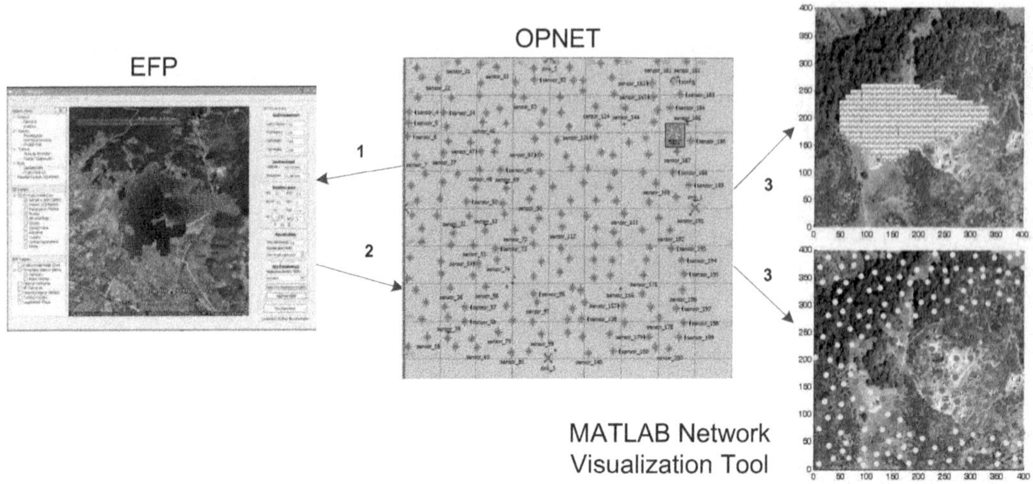

Figure 2: Block Diagram of OPNET and EFP

MLBRF uses a sink selection mechanism based on fuzzy logic. In order to evaluate the traffic density in the direction of a sink, it uses a fuzzy inference system to combine two dynamic criteria which are the number of contenders and the buffer occupancy levels in the neighborhood with a static criterion which is the distance of the candidate relay sensor to the sink. The result of the fuzzy engine is the current membership value of the sensor for a sink. Subsequent to the evaluation of the current membership values of the sensor for each sink, the destination sink for a frame is determined as the one with the greatest membership value.

3.2 Route restoration mechanism of MLBRF

MLBRF uses a special solution to route the packets around dead-ends. For this purpose, it introduces routing-classes in order to discriminate the forwarding capabilities of the sensors.

The own routing-class of a sensor is determined according to the gathered routing-class information of the neighbors which are acquired by extracting the piggy-backed information from each received MAC layer packet and stored in neighbor information table. In case of any change in the routing-class information from a neighbor, a sensor checks and updates its own routing-class accordingly. In that way, these changes iteratively diffuse in the network over time and the routing-classes in the network reach to a steady state.

The routing-class of a node is updated either in the initialization phase or in case of a topological change in the network such as energy depletion, sensor destruction or a long-term communication disruption. If for a sufficiently long time no packet is received from a neighbor, than the routing-class of that sensor is set to be unreachable and are not involved in any forwarding decision. A sensor determines its neighbors that belong to this class at the time of each frame delivery by controlling the last packet reception times in neighbor information table and re-evaluates its own routing-class. If any subsequent packet is received from an unreachable neighbor, the routing-class of the neighbor and the node itself is updated accordingly.

4. PERFORMANCE EVALUATION OF A WSN FOR FIRE DETECTION

The structure of the integrated WSN performance evaluation system is presented in Figure 2. In the integrated system, initially, the WSN topology (area dimensions, sensor locations, grid size, and ignition point(s)) that will be used in OPNET simulations is generated and fed to the EFP module (1). Various additional parameters are then specified by the user or are automatically obtained based on various information sources, e.g.: slope/aspect (estimated from 100m STRM files for the area of interest), fuel maps (converted from CORINE maps corresponding to the area of interest),weather parameters such as temperature, humidity, precipitation, wind speed and wind direction (current or forecasted, obtained by FIRESENSE weather stations or supported external (Internet) weather services). EFP estimates and outputs the temperature variation with respect to time for each sensor location for the given topology. Each cell of the grid may either be ignited or not, as the fire is propagated, and the temperature at each predefined sensor location can be modeled based on the locations and fire-related parameters (e.g. flame length) of the ignited cells closest to the sensor. The temperature variation for each sensor is estimated for the whole time-span of the WSN simulation and used by OPNET to determine the temperature reporting rate and the time instant of sensor destructions. The overall network and fire propagation behaviour is observed using the Network Visualization Tool implemented in MATLAB (3).

In our simulation model temperature sensors are randomly deployed into the forest. Initially, all the sensors are alive and start sensing and communication as a regular WSN. Sensors generate periodic data packets that contain the temperature values reported by the EFP software and deliver them in a multi-hop manner to the sinks using a routing protocol. These report packets are used to create a temperature map of the environment. The sensor data generation model supports two modes of operation, which are normal and alarm modes. In these operation modes, the sensors report temperature readings with different periods where the

(a) (b)

Figure 3: WSN topology change due to sensor destructions

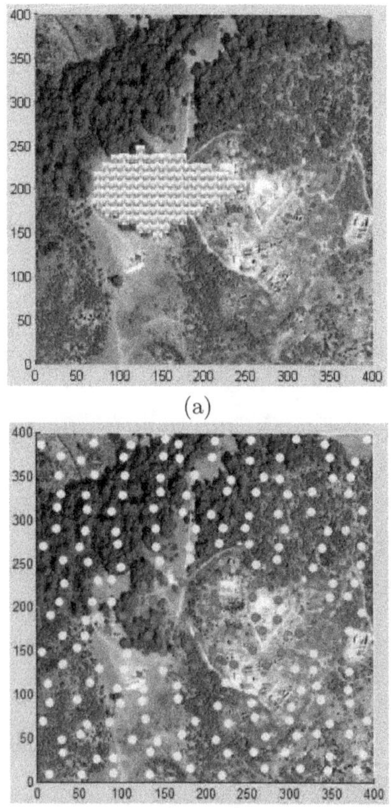

(a) (b)

Figure 4: Simulated fire scenario and the WSN

period is longer in the normal mode and shorter in the alarm mode. Related with the operation modes of the sensors, there are two temperature thresholds defined in the model. The first temperature threshold value is the one that determines the sensors to switch from the normal operation mode to alarm operation mode. The second temperature threshold value is the one that defines the temperature value over which the sensors are destructed. The destructed sensors will cease both sensing and relaying activities, and alternative routes to sinks are considered (Figure 3).

We designed experiments to to explore the effects of WSN related factors; such as reporting rate, number and location of the sinks together with the effects of environmental factors such as the wind speed and the number of ignition points in terms of temperature reporting performance and freshness of temperature map.

4.1 Simulation Setup and Parameters

In the default simulation scenarios, 200 sensors are deployed into an environment of 400m x 400m. The environment is assumed to be in the ancient city of Rhodiapolis in the Antalya region in Turkey which is one of the FIRE-SENSE pilot sites [22] and the environmental parameters such as fuel maps and slope/aspect are configured accordingly. The location of the sinks are varied in order to evaluate the effect of sink locations on the reporting performance of the WSN. In Figure 4, the simulated fire scenario and the simulated WSN are presented. The alert mode temperature threshold of the sensors are set to 60 °C which is 20 °C above the ambient temperature assumed to be 40 °C in a summer day which is of a high risk season. The destruction temperature threshold of the sensors are set to 120 °C where the sensors are assumed to be in a protective casing. The routing protocol used is MLBRF [11] which is modified to deal with sensor destructions for finding alternative routes. In the MAC layer, we used the SMAC [23] protocol with 1 duty cycle. Table 1 presents other simulation parameters.

Table 1: Simulation parameters

Normal Period	10 minutes
Alarm Period	0.25, 0.5,1,2,4 minutes
Alarm & Destruction Thresh.	60 °C & 120 °C
Data Packet & Buffer Size	100 bits & 10 packets
Channel Rate	250 Kbps
MAC Layer	SMAC
Duty Cycle	1%
Transmission Range	60 m
Initial Energy	200 J
TX Power	81 mW
RX Power	30 mW
IDLE Power	30 mW
SLEEP Power	0.003 mW

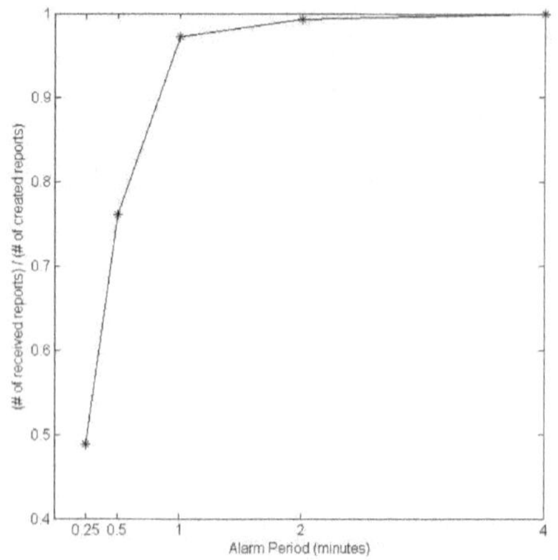

(a)

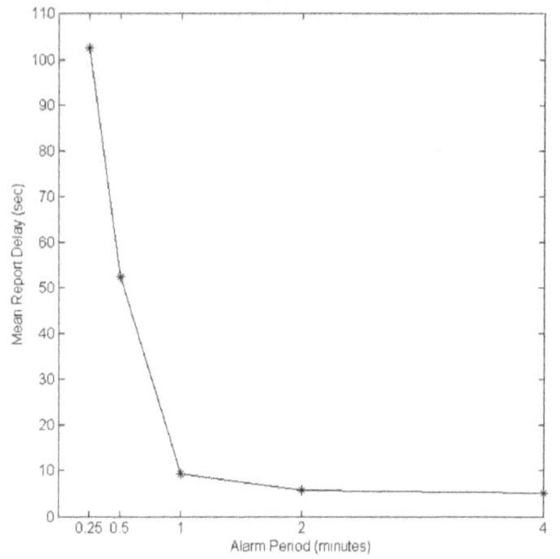

(b)

Figure 5: Report delivery ratio and report delay

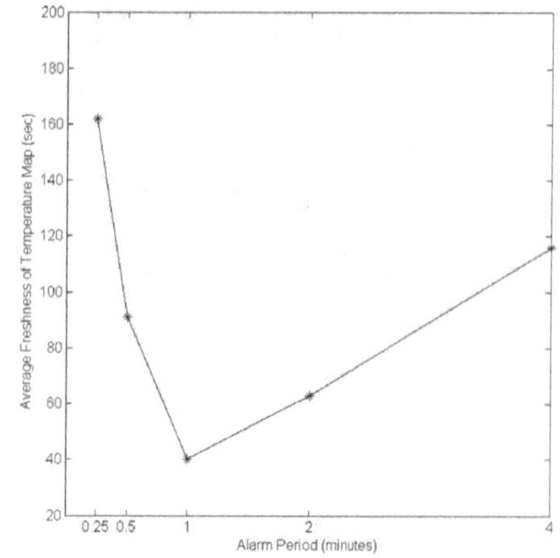

(a)

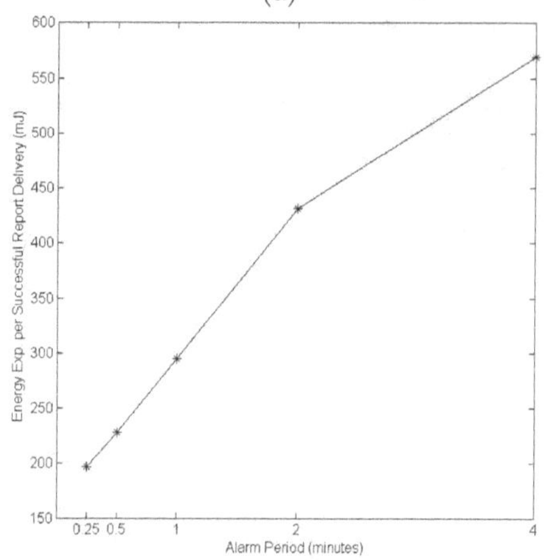

(b)

Figure 6: Report freshness and energy expenditure per report

The radio power consumption parameters are set as in [24], which are typical values for Mica2 Mote sensors.

4.2 Single Sink Scenarios

In the first set of experiments, the sink is located at the center of the right edge and the wind speed is set as 3 mph in EFP. During fire propagation, 33 sensors are destructed which are shown in red (dark colors) in Figure 4.b. In these experiments, we varied the alarm period of the sensors and observed the delivery performance of the WSN in terms of the report delivery ratio (Figure 5.a), the reporting delay (Figure 5.b), the freshness of the temperature map (Figure 6.a) and the energy expenditure per successful report delivery (Figure 6.b). Freshness of temperature reports from a sensor is measured in seconds and it corresponds to the average inter-arrival time among the report packets. Likewise, freshness of the temperature map provided by a WSN is the average freshness of all sensors in the network.

When the alarm period is at the lowest value, we observe that the report delivery ratio is low and the mean report delay is very high due to high level of congestion created by the excessive number of report packets. For the alarm period value of 0.5 minutes, the congestion level is still quite high which results with a delivery ratio below 0.8 and mean delay above 50 seconds. When the alarm period is 1 minute and above, the congestion is relieved and the WSN performance is acceptable in terms of both metrics,i.e., the delivery ratio is above 0.9 and the mean delay is below 10 seconds.

On the other hand, the average freshness of the temperature map results in Figure 6.a suggest that the alarm period should be set as 1 minute where we get the best value among the measured ones. Freshness is worse for the lower alarm period values due to high level of congestion. As we increase the alarm period beyond 1 minute, although the congestion level decreases, average freshness increases due to the larger inter-arrival times of the report packets. For the choice of 1 minute alarm period, delivery ratio and report delay figures also provide quite acceptable results.

Figure 6.b presents the effectiveness of the WSN in terms of energy expenditure per successful report delivery. As the alarm period increases, the number of report packets created by the network decreases but the energy expenditure of the WSN per report increases. This result is due to the MAC protocol which operates with a static duty cycle and suggests a MAC protocol that has a dynamic duty cycle management.

In the second set of experiments, the alarm period is set as 1 minute and the location of the sinks are varied to be

Table 2: Performance results for different sink locations

	R	L	T	B
Delivery Ratio	0.97	0.95	0.91	0.9
Delay (sec)	9.26	20.23	11.71	21.58
Av. Temp. Map Freshness (sec)	40	56	52	65

Table 3: Performance results for two sinks case

	L	L-R	T-B
Delivery Ratio	0.72	0.77	0.78
Delay (sec)	66.81	44.54	46.16
Av. Temp. Map Freshness (sec)	111	85	86

in the centers of Top (T), Bottom (B) and Left (L) edges of the environment. Table 2 presents the performance results for each sink location including Right (R) edge. From the results, it can be observed that when the sink is located in the right edge, which is the fire propagation direction, we get better results in each performance metric.

4.3 Multiple Sinks Scenarios

In the first set of experiments, the number of sinks in the environment is increased to two. The alarm period is also set as 0.5 minute to increase the load of the network for this and the other set of experiments. The locations of the sinks in one setup are the centers of the left and the right edges of the environment. In the other setup, the locations are the centers of the top and the bottom edges. The two setup results are compared to the case where there is a single sink in the environment located in the center of the left edge. Table 3 presents the performance results. The performance of the WSN for both setup with two sinks are similar. Introduction of a second sink reduces the congestion in the network especially around the sinks compared to the single sink case and improves the performance of the WSN in terms of each metric.

In two other set of experiments, we increased the number of sinks in the environment to three and four sinks, the results of which are presented in Table 4 and Table 5 respectively. From each set of experiments, we observe that as the number of sinks in the environment increases, the degree of congestion decreases and the performance of the WSN improves in terms of each metric. In addition, the results show that the location of the sinks is an important factor that provides a significant differentiation in the performance of the WSN. The location of ignition and the direction of fire propagation make the location of the sinks an influential parameter.

Table 4: Performance results for three sinks case

	L-R-T	L-R-B	L-T-B	R-T-B
Delivery Ratio	0.87	0.84	0.84	0.87
Delay (sec)	28.62	34.99	34.09	24.59
Av. Temp. Map Freshness (sec)	55	68	63	51

Table 5: Performance results for four sinks case

	Edge Centers	Corners
Delivery Ratio	0.92	0.95
Delay (sec)	19.24	17.94
Av. Temp. Map Freshness (sec)	42	38

Table 6: Performance results for different wind speed for four sinks case

Wind speed	1 mph	2 mph	3 mph	4 mph
Delivery Ratio	1	0.99	0.95	0.96
Delay (sec)	2.36	4.29	17.94	16.09
Av. Temp. Map Freshness (sec)	24	21	38	34
Destructed	2	6	33	70

4.4 Effect of the Wind Speed

In this set of experiments, we look at the effect of wind speed in the delivery performance of the WSN. For this purpose, keeping the ignition point as it is in the previous experiments and the number of sinks as four located in the corners, we varied the wind speed. As can be seen in Table 6, as the wind speed increases, the number of destructed sensors increases up to 70. The increase in the destructed sensors affects the operation of the routing algorithm by creating routing holes and topology changes. However, we observe that the routing algorithm finds alternative routes and achieves fairly good results in each performance metric despite the increased number of sensor destructions. We observe that the report delivery ratio increases and the report delay decreases as the wind speed changes from 3 mph to 4 mph, which is also related with the increased number of sensor destructions that leads to decreased level of the created load in the network and hence the decreased level of congestion.

4.5 Effect of the Number of Ignition Points

In the first set of experiments, we set the alarm period as 0.5 minutes and the wind speed as 3 mph. In Figure 7, the simulated fire scenario and the simulated WSN are presented. During the fire propagation, 86 sensors are destructed (Figure 7.b) which are shown in red (dark colors). We varied the number of sinks in the environment. Table 7 presents the performance results. We repeated the same set of experiments for the case where the wind speed is set as 4 mph. In Figure 8, the simulated fire scenario and the

Table 7: Performance results for two ignition points (Wind speed=3 mph)

	T	T-B	L-T-B	L-R-T-B
Delivery Ratio	0.58	0.83	0.91	0.95
Delay (sec)	49.79	47.15	28.96	24.97
Av. Temp. Map Freshness (sec)	130	83	62	50

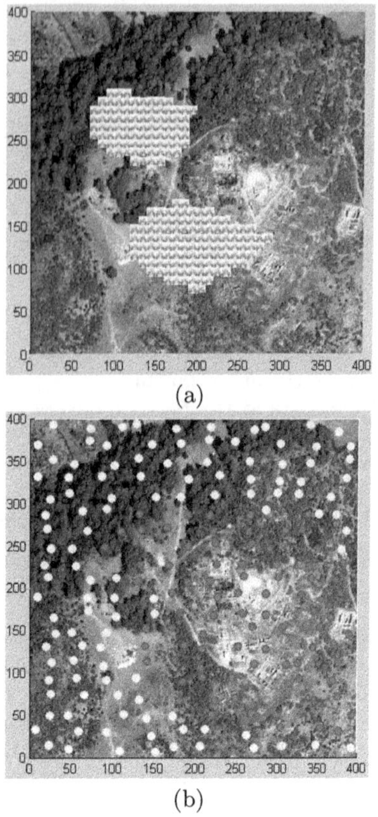

(a) (b)

Figure 7: Two ignition points fire scenario and the resulting WSN simulation (Wind speed = 3mph)

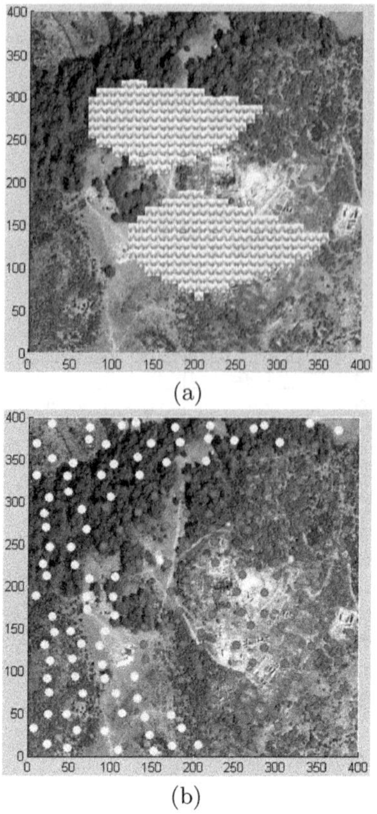

(a) (b)

Figure 8: Two ignition points fire scenario and the resulting WSN simulation (Wind speed = 4mph)

simulated WSN are presented. During the fire propagation, 119 sensors are destructed (Figure 8.b). The performance results for this case are presented in Table 8.

As expected, the increase in the number of ignition points in the environment increases the number of destructed sensors which causes to frequent topology changes. The results show that with multiple sinks in the environment the routing algorithm successfully deals with the frequent topology changes and finds alternative routes for delivering the temperature reports to the sink nodes, where the delivery ratio increases up to 95%.

5. CONCLUSION

In this work, we evaluated the performance of a WSN under realistic fire scenarios using the OPNET modeler, which is integrated with a realistic fire propagation simulator that provides time based temperature information from the deployment area. We presented the performance of WSN under various load conditions determined by the reporting rate in terms of the report delivery ratio, the reporting delay, the freshness of temperature map and the energy expenditure. The results show that, for the cases studied, 1 report per minute gives the best result in terms of freshness and quite acceptable results in terms of the delivery ratio and the delay. In addition, energy expenditure results suggest a MAC protocol that adjusts its duty cycle dynamically according to the level of the load in the network for the effective use of scarce energy. The results also show that the location of the sinks is an important factor that affects the performance of the WSN. Hence they have to be arranged according to the main wind directions in the monitored area. We also evaluated the reporting performance of WSNs in scenarios with multiple sinks where we observed that the increase in the number of the sinks provides a significant gain in terms of each performance metric. The increase in the the wind speed and the number of ignition points in the environment causes higher number of sensors to be destructed which leads to dynamic and frequent topology changes. The results show that the routing algorithm is successful in coping with the frequent topology changes and finding alternative routes for delivering the temperature reports to the sink nodes.

Table 8: Performance results for two ignition points (Wind speed=4 mph)

	T	T-B	L-T-B	L-R-T-B
Delivery Ratio	0.58	0.85	0.94	0.96
Delay (sec)	51.98	36.73	19.21	11.06
Av. Temp. Map Freshness (sec)	115	64	48	34

As the next step, we want to design and implement a load aware MAC protocol that is tailored for the needs of WSNs for forest fire monitoring. Then, we can compare the performance of WSN using the novel MAC with the results obtained in this work. We also want to design additional experiments to further investigate the effects of the environmental parameters such as vegetation and aspect/slope characteristics of an environment on the detection and delivery performance of WSNs. In addition, we want to improve the prediction capability of the fire propagation estimation software in a real fire scenario by enabling the temperature map information to flow from the WSN to the fire propagation software. In that case, we can compare the accuracy of the WSN-integrated fire propagation estimation with the original EFP software.

6. ACKNOWLEDGMENTS

This work is supported by the European Community's Seventh Framework Programme (FP7-ENV-2009-1) under the grant agreement FP7-ENV-244088 FIRESENSE.

7. REFERENCES

[1] The Advanced Very High Resolution Radiometer (AVHRR) Web Page. http://noaasis.noaa.gov/NOAASIS/ml/avhrr.html/, 2013.

[2] Aerovision Web Page. http://www.aerovision-uav.com/, 2013.

[3] B.C. Fire Lookout Towers Web Page. http://www.firelookout.com/bc.html/, 2013.

[4] . ick, B. Mukherjee, and D. Ghosal. Wireless sensor network survey. *Computer Networks*, 52(12):2292–2330, 2008.

[5] Libelium. Wireless Sensor Networks - igBee - Mesh Networks. http://www.libelium.com/, 2013.

[6] Shimmer. Wireless Sensor Platform for Wearable Applications. http://www.shimmer-research.com/, 2013.

[7] ARDUINO. http://www.arduino.cc/, 2013.

[8] FIRESENSE Project. http://www.firesense.eu/, 2013.

[9] OPNET Modeler. http://www.opnet.com/products/modeler/home.html, 2013.

[10] Fire Propagation Estimation Software. FIRESENSE, http://www.firesense.eu/, 2013.

[11] D. M. Doolin and N. Sitar. Wireless sensor nodes for wildfire monitoring. In *Proceedings of SPIE Symposium on Smart Structures and Materials*, San Diego, pp. 477–484, 2006.

[12] S. Isik, M. . Donmez, and C. Ersoy. Multi-sink load balanced forwarding with a multi-criteria fuzzy sink selection for video sensor networks. *Computer Networks*. 56(2):615–627, 2012.

[13] . Lloret, M. Garcia, D. Bri, and S. Sendra. A wireless sensor network deployment for rural and forest fire detection and verification. *Sensor Nodes*, 9(11):8722–8747, 2009.

[14] C. Hartung and R. Han. FireWxNet: A multi-tiered portable wireless system for monitoring weather conditions in wildland fire environments. In *Proceedings of International Conference on Mobile Systems*, Applications and Services, pages 28–41, 2006.

[15] B. Son. A design and implementation of forest-fires surveillance system based on wireless sensor networks for South Korea mountains. *International Journal of Computer Science and Network Security*, 6(9B), 124–130, 2006.

[16] L. u, N. Wang, and X. Meng. Real-time forest fire detection with wireless sensor networks. In *Proceedings of International Conference on Wireless Communications, Networking and Mobile Computing (WiMob)*, pages 1214–1217, 2005.

[17] E. Ngai, . hou, M. Lyu, and . Liu. A delay-aware reliable event reporting framework for wireless sensor-actuator networks. *Ad Hoc Networks*, 8(7):694–707, 2010.

[18] B. Wenning, D. Pesch, A. Giel, and C. Gorg. Environmental monitoring aware routing: Making environmental sensor networks more robust. *Springer Science Business Media Telecommunication Systems*, 43(1–2):3–11, 2009.

[19] M. Hefeeda and M. Bagheri. Forest fire modeling and early detection using wireless sensor networks. *Ad Hoc Sensor Wireless Networks*, 7:169–224, 2009.

[20] E. M. Garcia, and M. A. Serna. Simulating a WSN-based wildfire fighting support system. In *Proceedings of IEEE International Workshop on Modeling, Analysis and Simulation of Sensor Networks (MASSN)*, pages 896–902, 2008.

[21] . E. Aslan, I. Korpeoglu, and O. Ulusoy. A framework for use of wireless sensor networks in forest fire detection and monitoring. *Computers, Environment and Urban Systems*, 36:614–625, 2012.

[22] FIRESENSE Pilot Sites. http://www.firesense.eu/index.php?option=com_content&view=article&id=55&Itemid=103&lang=en, 2013.

[23] W. e, . Heidemann, and D. Estrin. Medium access control with coordinated adaptive sleeping for wireless sensor networks, *IEEE/ACM Transactions on Networking*. 12(3):493–506, 2004.

[24] M. . Miller and N. H. Vaidya. A MAC protocol to reduce sensor network energy consumption using a wakeup radio. *IEEE Transactions on Mobile Computing*, 4(3):228–242, 2005.

Efficient Data Aggregation Scheduling in Wireless Sensor Networks with Multi-Channel Links

Miloud Bagaa
Dep. of Theo and,
Comp Eng, CERIST,
Algiers, Algeria
bagaa@mail.cerist.dz

Mohamed Younis
Dep. of Comp Sc.
& Elect Eng, Univ. of
Maryland Baltimore County
younis@cs.umbc.edu

Nadjib Badache
CERIST, Algiers, Algeria
badache@mail.cerist.dz

ABSTRACT

In-network data aggregation is often pursued to remove redundancy and correlate the data en-route to the base-station in order to save energy in wireless sensor networks (WSNs). In this paper, we present a novel cross-layer approach for reducing the latency in disseminating aggregated data to the base-station over multi-frequency radio links. Our approach forms the aggregation tree with the objective of increasing the simultaneity of transmissions and reducing buffering delay. Aggregation nodes are picked and time-slots are allocated to the individual sensors so that the most number of ready nodes can transmit their data without delay. Colliding transmissions are avoided by the use of different radio channels. Our approach is validated through simulation and is shown to outperform previously published schemes.

Categories and Subject Descriptors

C.2.1 [**Computer Communication Networks**]: Network Architecture and Design— *Wireless communication, Network topology*; F.2.2 [**Analysis of Algorithms and Problem Complexity**]: Nonnumerical Algorithms and Problems— *Sequencing and scheduling*

Keywords

wireless sensor network, data aggregation, multi-channels, media access scheduling

1. INTRODUCTION

Wireless sensor networks (WSNs) are composed of a large number of miniaturized and low-cost wireless sensor nodes, that can gather data about some phenomena in the environment. Each sensor node can collaborate with other sensors to route the sensed data to a processing center, which is also called the base-station or sink node. However, the sensor nodes have limited resources in term of battery power, computational capacity, and communication bandwidth. To save these resources, aggregation of the data collected by the individual sensors en-route to the base-station is one of the popular optimization strategies. Data aggregation opts to eliminate redundant packet transmissions by filtering repeated and unnecessary data readings and thus cut on the energy used in communication.

WSNs have numerous applications such as, early detection of forest fire [4] and security surveillance [3]. In these applications, it is very critical to deliver alarms about serious events in a timely manner so that an appropriate action can be taken in response. Therefore, the network design should strive to minimize the delay in disseminating the data to the base-station. One of the most effective schemes is to limit medium access latency by adopting reservation based protocols such as *TDMA* (Time Division Multiple Access). In-network data aggregation helps in limiting medium access contention and reduces the number of transmitted packets, and thus can help in finding low-latency medium access schedule.

Recently cross-layer methodologies have been deemed advantageous and a number of techniques have emerged to combine the formation of the aggregation tree with medium access scheduling [2] and [5]. These solutions assume that the network nodes use only one channel to communicate. However, the use of multi-channel radio transceivers in *WSN* has recently become popular. Exploiting the availability of multiple channels would allow increased simultaneous transmissions, i.e., time slots reuse, and would thus reduce the data latency. In this paper, we pursue a novel cross-layer approach for establishing data aggregation over multi-channel links (*DAS-MC*) that minimizes data delivery latency. *DAS-MC* considers setups in which each node can transmit and receive on multiple radio frequencies. Unlike published solutions, *DAS-MC* intertwines the tree construction and transmission scheduling. *DAS-MC* does not purse breadth-first ordering. When a node that is L-hop away from the sink (i.e., in level L) becomes ready to schedule, it selects its parent from nodes in level $L-1$, L, or $L+1$ and its time slot as the earliest one in all the channels. This relaxed approach, which has not been proposed before, lowers the latency and increases the network throughput.

The rest of this paper is organized as follows. Related work is summarized in section 2. The problem formulation and the basic idea of our approach are presented in section 3. The approach details are presented in section 4. The simulation results are discussed in section 5. Finally, the paper is concluded in section 6.

2. RELATED WORK

The existing solutions aim to maximize the network throughput by gathering the data from all network nodes in the

MSWiM'13, November 3–8, 2013, Barcelona, Spain.
Copyright 2013 ACM 978-1-4503-2353-6/13/11 ...$15.00.
http://dx.doi.org/10.1145/2507924.2507995.

least time. To observe data freshness requirements, the slot allocated to a parent would be greater than all the ones of its children. Chen et al. [2] have proved that the minimum delay data aggregation scheduling problem is *NP-hard*, and proposed an iterative scheduling procedure applied on the formed tree. Huang et al. [5] proposed a centralized solution, called *NCA*. *NCA* uses the Connected Dominating Set (*CDS*) as an aggregation tree. Malhotra et al. [8] observed that the data path from the nodes to the sink in the *CDS* based aggregation tree is not necessarily optimal and proposed an algorithm, which uses a *Balanced Shortest Path Tree* instead of a *CDS* as a data aggregation structure. Bagaa et al. proposed a centralized algorithm in [1] in which no information about candidate parents or children are provided to the scheduling algorithm. The tree construction and the scheduling are performed concurrently.

However, the proposed solutions in [2, 5, 8, 1] do not support multi-channel links when scheduling network nodes. For this reason the solutions [6], [7], [9] and [10] have been proposed to exploit the capabilities of the new transceiver. The network nodes in [10] are organized into clusters. The cluster head aggregates the data and routes the cell report to the base-station over an inter-cluster-head tree. To increase the network throughput, each branch of the tree is assigned a different channel. Receiver-Based Channel Assignment (*RBCA*) has been proposed in [6]. In *RBCA*, the children of the same parent use the same channel (i.e., the parent's channel) to transmit their data. A Tree-Based Multichannel Protocol (*TMCP*) has been proposed in [9]. The aggregation tree in *TMCP* is divided into a set of subtrees, such that the root of each of them is a neighbor of the sink. In order to minimize the interference in the subtrees, *TMCP* assigns a different channel for each subtree. Meanwhile, a Joint Frequency Time Slot Scheduling (*JFTSS*) has been proposed in [7]. The links of the tree are sorted in *JFTSS*, such that the link which conflicts with most number of other links has high priority for channel reassignment. However, these solutions de-couple the tree construction from the nodes scheduling. Moreover, in the approaches of [9], [7] and [6], the parent's transmission slot can be earlier than the child' one, which leads to aggregating the data of different periods together. Thus, the data freshness is not ensured.

3. PROBLEM DEFINITION AND SOLUTION STRATEGY

Devising a non-conflicting medium access schedule that achieves minimum delivery latency subject to flow constraints is a known NP-hard problem [2]. Therefore, heuristics are usually pursued. *DAS-MC* opts to reduce time latency by increasing the time slot reuse and by selecting for each node the smallest time slot in all the channels which ensures the aggregation freshness. *DAS-MC* intertwines the tree construction and nodes scheduling. Therefore, at each moment in *DAS-MC* execution, each node in the network can have two kinds of neighbors: (*i*) a set of nodes which has already designated its parent and set its time slot (i.e., scheduled node); (*ii*) set of nodes which are not yet scheduled. For each channel i the neighbors $\gamma(u)$ of a node u can be grouped into three disjoint subsets according to a time slot τ. The subset $\delta_i^\tau(u)$ includes nodes that, (*a*) are not selected as parent at time slot τ on channel i, and (*b*) cannot hear at this time slot using channel i due to collision. Each node v in $\delta_i^\tau(u)$ has at least one node in $\gamma(v)$ which has already designated its parent and set its time slot to τ and its channel to i (i.e., scheduled node); The subset $\varrho_i^\tau(u)$ has nodes which are selected as parents by other scheduled nodes at time slot τ and channel i. The neighbors of nodes in this subset are prevented from using τ on channel i due to collision. The subset $\varphi_i^\tau(u)$ has the nodes which can be parents of node u at time slot τ on channel i and can be formally defined as:

$$\varphi_i^\tau(u) = \gamma(u) - (\delta_i^\tau(u) \cup \xi^\tau(u) \bigcup_{j=1}^{k} \varrho_j^\tau(u)) \qquad (1)$$

such that $\xi^\tau(u)$ is the set of u's neighbors which are (*i*) scheduled and (*ii*) their time slot lower or equal to τ. We remove $\xi^\tau(u)$ from $\varphi_i^\tau(u)$ to ensure data freshness and prevent the creation of cycles. If $\varrho_i^\tau(u) \neq \emptyset$ or $\varphi_i^\tau(u) = \emptyset$, node u should select a time slot that is higher than τ in order to avoid introducing collision.

Each node u in *DAS-MC* should use only one channel CH_u and one time slot TS_u to transmit its data to the parent node $\rho(u)$. CH_u and TS_u should be selected such that the time latency is reduced. Therefore, TS_u should be selected as the smallest time slot in all the channels, whereas CH_u should the channel which does not cause the collisions and also allows more time slot reuse. *DAS-MC* aims to capture this trade-off by assigning for each node u the time slot TS_u and channel CH_u which reduce the time latency and increase the potential of the time slot reuse.

While all nodes in $\gamma(u)$ cannot receive another packet when u transmits at time slot TS_u on channel CH_u, a node $v \in (\gamma(u) - \{\rho(u)\})$ can transmit to a node $w \in \gamma(v)$ at TS_u on channel CH_u as long as $w \notin \gamma(u)$ and $\rho(u) \notin \gamma(v)$. Moreover, if v uses a channel different than CH_u, it can transmit to any node in $w \in \gamma(v) - \{\rho(u)\}$ at TS_u. *DAS-MC* leverages this observation to boost the simultaneity of transmissions, and consequently minimize the data delivery latency, by increasing the chance to find a u's parent $\rho(u)$ in which u can use a smallest time slot. To select the smallest time slot for a node u, we should increase the size of $\varphi_i^\tau(u)$ for each channel i as much as possible. To achieve this objective, *DAS-MC* intertwines the tree construction and data aggregation scheduling. In addition, *DAS-MC* allows a node u in level L, where L is the shortest distance between u and the sink, to select its parent from its neighbors in (1) level $L-1$ (upper-level), (2) level L (same-level), and (3) level $L+1$ (lower-level) providing that does not create cycle. Favoring parents that have the fewest number of neighbors in and not yet scheduled enables increased time slots reuse.

4. MULTI-CHANNEL DATA AGGREGATION SCHEDULING

To reduce the time latency three fundamental issues are to be addressed; (1) what the transmission order constraints among nodes are, (2) how channels are assigned to links, and (3) how parents and children are associated on the aggregation tree so that time slot reuse is maximized. The balance of this section opts to explain the operation of *DAS-MC* and how it tackles these issues. In addition to CH_u, TS_u, $\rho(u)$, $\gamma(u)$, δ_i^τ, ϱ_i^τ, φ_i^τ defined earlier, the following notation will be used in the discussion:

- (u, v): Link between the nodes u and v.
- SC_u: Set of nodes in $\gamma(u)$ which are scheduled, i.e., the nodes which already select their parents and set their time slot.

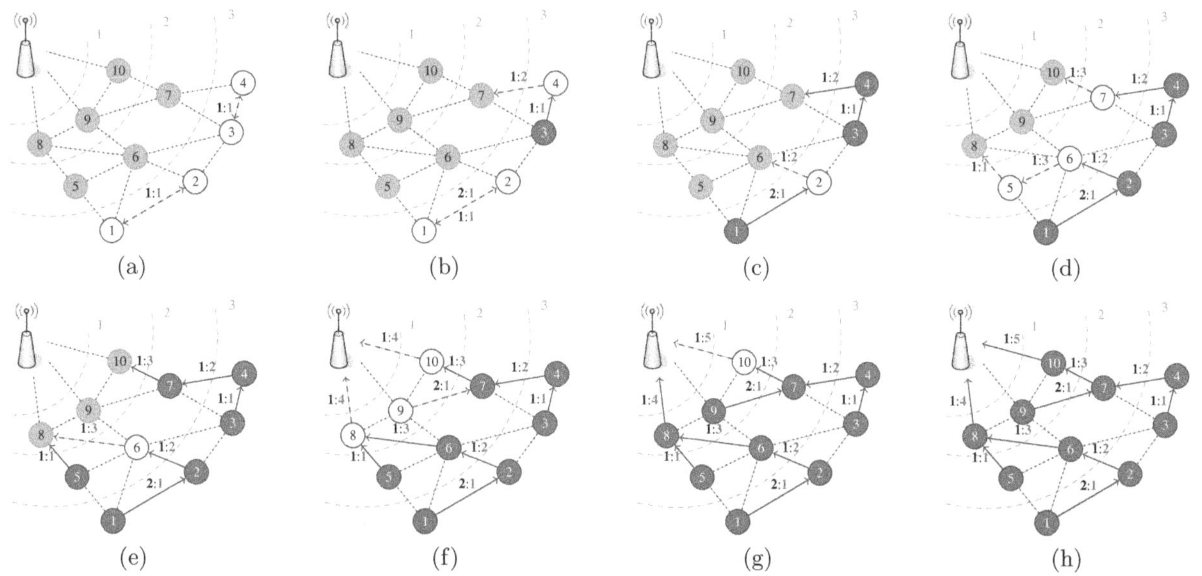

Figure 1: Detailed illustrative example to show how DAS-MC is applied

- $\overline{SC_u}$: Set of nodes in $\gamma(u)$ which are unscheduled i.e., the nodes in $\gamma(u)$ which have not yet selected their parents. Formally, $\overline{SC_u} = \gamma(u) - SC_u$.
- T_i^j: The use of time slot j on channel i.
- η_i: Node whose identifier is i. η_0 is the base station.
- $\psi_i(u)$: The parent of node u on channel i.
- $TC(u)$: The maximum time slot of u's children, initially is set to zero.

In order to facilitate the presentation of *DAS-MC*, Figure 1 will be referenced throughout the discussion. Figure 1 shows an example of *DAS-MC* execution. In this example, we consider that there is only two channels and the depth of the breadth-first tree is three (i.e., 3 levels). In the figure, the gray, white and black circles represent the unready, ready and scheduled nodes, respectively. A dashed arrow between two nodes a and b indicates that a has chosen b as its best parent when the arrow becomes solid it indicates that the link (a, b) is scheduled. The dotted lines represent the graph connectivity. The gray number besides the dashed and solid arrow (a, b) represents a's transmission slot. The black number besides the dashed and solid arrow (a, b) represents a's transmission channel.

4.1 Temporal ordering of transmissions

The nodes in *DAS-MC* are scheduled bottom-up, level by level in a breadth-first order. Each node in level L will not get scheduled until all its $L+1$ neighbors are assigned transmission slots. For example in Figure 1(a) η_1, η_2, and η_3, which are in level L, should be scheduled before η_5, which is in level $L-1$. The scheduling of nodes in a breadth-first order does not mean that the aggregated data is also routed on a breadth-first tree. In *DAS-MC* when a node in level L gets scheduled, it selects its parent from $L-1$, L or $L+1$ levels. For example in Figure 1(c) η_2, which is in level L, selects its parent η_6 from level $L-1$, whereas in Figure 1(f) η_9, which is in level L, selects its parent η_7 from level $L+1$.

4.2 Assigning parents and time slots

Let T_i^τ be the earliest time slot on channel i which ensures the data freshness and prevents message collision. Formally T_i^τ is defined as the earliest time slot (i) which is higher than all u's children and (ii) which fulfills that $\varrho_i^\tau(u) = \emptyset$ and $\varphi_i^\tau(u) \neq \emptyset$. In *DAS-MC* $\psi_i(u)$ is selected from $\varphi_i^\tau(u)$ as the node which has the fewest number of neighbors and not yet scheduled to encourage time slots reuse. That is if a node u selects $\psi_i(u)$ which has many unscheduled neighbors, the set ϱ_i^τ at many nodes will not be empty and then many nodes will be prevented from reusing T_i^τ.

A node in *DAS-MC* should use only one channel CH_u and one time slot TS_u to send the aggregated data to its parent $\rho(u)$. CH_u, TS_u and $\rho(u)$ should be selected such that (1) the messages collision is prevented, (2) data freshness is ensured, and (3) the time latency is reduced. To reduce the time latency, CH_u is set to be the channel i which offers the earliest time slot T_i^τ. If there is many channels which qualify, CH_u is picked to enable the selection of the parent with the fewest number of neighbors and not yet scheduled. If there is more than one channel which fulfill the above conditions, the channel with the smallest *ID* will be selected. Meanwhile, $\rho(u)$ and TS_u will be selected according to CH_u value. $\rho(u)$ and TS_u are set to $\psi_{CH_u}(u)$ and $T_{CH_u}^\tau$ values, respectively. In the selection of CH_u, *DAS-MC* gives the first priority to the smallest TS_u then the parent $\rho(u)$ with smallest number of unscheduled neighbors. If we give priority to the parent which has the fewest unscheduled neighbors many time slots never be used creating gaps, and thus the time slot reuse will diminish.

In the previous solutions, when a node u gets scheduled, it should select its parent from $\overline{SC_u}$ to prevent creation of cycles. Therefore, the gaps slot is never used and thus the time slot reuse will be significantly decreased. Unlike the published solutions, *DAS-MC* explores the gaps slots by allowing each node u to select its parent from scheduled nodes, i.e., $\{\rho(u)\} \cap SC(u) \neq \emptyset$. From equation 1 a node u in *DAS-MC* selects its parent w from $\varphi_i^\tau \cap SC_u$ if and only if $TS_u < TS_w$, thus the data freshness is ensured and creation of cycles are prevented. Finally, it is important to note that the parent selection criteria of *DAS-MC* allows the parent of a node in level L to be picked from level L, $L-1$ or $L+1$, and thus the aggregation is not restricted to a breath-first tree as on previously published work.

To illustrate, let us use node η_1 in the example in Figure 1(a). $\varrho_1^{\#1}(1) = \emptyset$, and $\varphi_1^{\#1}(1) = \{\eta_2, \eta_5, \eta_6\}$. The earliest available time slot for channel 1 that can be assigned to η_1 is #1. The number of nodes in $\overline{SC}$ of η_2, η_5 and η_6 are 3, 3 and 6, respectively. It is obvious that the choice which maximizes the time slot reuse is $\psi_1(1) = \eta_2$ or $\psi_1(1) = \eta_5$. As η_2 has lowest ID, $\psi_1(3) = \eta_2$. For the same reason in channel 2 the earliest available time slot that can be assigned to η_1 is #1 and its parent $\psi_2(1) = \eta_2$. As the two channels offer the same time slot and whose parents have the same number of unscheduled neighbors, η_1 selects the channel which has the smallest ID, which is 1. Thus, CH_1, TS_1 and $\rho(1)$ will be set to 1, #1 and η_2, respectively. In this case, η_1 which is in level L selects its parent $\rho(1)$ from the same level. Figure 1(f) shows an example to illustrate the selection of a parent of η_9 from scheduled nodes and level $L+1$. In the Figure $\varrho_1^{\#1}(9) = \{\eta_8\}$, which means that the time slot #1 with channel 1 is reserved by the children of η_8, and if η_9 uses this time slot on channel 1 a collision will occur at η_8. If node η_9 uses channel 1 with time slot 2 (resp., 3) a collision will occur at node η_6 (resp., η_8). $\varrho_1^{\#4}(9) = \emptyset$ and $\varphi_1^{\#4}(9) = \{\eta_0, \eta_8, \eta_10\}$, the earliest time slot that can be assigned to η_9 on channel 1 is #4 and its parent $\psi_1(9) = \eta_8$. In the same Figure, $\varrho_2^{\#1}(9) = \emptyset$, $\xi^{\#1}(9) = \emptyset$, $\delta_2^{\#1}(9) = \{\eta_6\}$ and $\varphi_2^{\#1}(9) = \gamma(9) - (\delta_2^{\#1}(9) \cup \xi^{\#1}(9) \bigcup_{j=1}^{2} \varrho_j^{\#1}(9)) = \{\eta_0, \eta_7, \eta_{10}\}$. As η_7 has the smallest number of unscheduled neighbors, the earliest time slot that can be assigned to η_9 on channel 2 is #1 and its parent $\psi_2(3) = \eta_7$. As channel 2 offers the earliest time slot, CH_9, TS_9 and $\rho(9)$ will be set to 2, #1 and η_7, respectively.

4.3 Scheduling the transmitting nodes

The parent selection step discussed above is node-centric in the sense that it is limited to node u when picking a parent, and assigning a time slot and channel. However, conflicts may exist among the individual nodes which are not neighbors on the same level L. To illustrate, consider the example in Figure 1(a). Based on the parent selection criteria discussed above, nodes η_1 and η_2 each one select the other as its parent at $T_1^{\#1}$. Nodes η_3 and η_4 are also each one select the other as its parent at $T_1^{\#1}$. If η_1, η_2, η_3 and η_4 are scheduled at $T_1^{\#1}$ a collision will be occurred. *DAS-MC* resolves such a conflict by considering every pair for ready nodes u and v in the level that is being scheduled. A conflict exists between nodes u and v if one of the following conditions is hold:

1. A collision: If $TS_u = TS_v$ and
   (a) $\rho(u) = \rho(v)$ or
   (b) $CH_u = CH_v$ and ($\rho(u) \in \gamma(v)$ or $\rho(v) \in \gamma(u)$).
2. Violation of data freshness or creation of cycle: If a ready node selects another one as its parent i.e., $\rho(u) = v$ or $\rho(v) = u$.

To resolve a collision, *DAS-MC* picks the one among the two nodes u and v whose parent collectively has the least number of unscheduled interfering nodes (i.e., smallest size of $\overline{SC}$) and reschedule its transmission in order to enable the most reuse. In case of a tie, the node, either u and v, that has the least number of unscheduled interfering nodes will keep the earliest slot in order to allow as many nodes as possible to be parent in this slot with channel CH_u, i.e., reduce the size of $\delta_{CH_u}^{TS_u}$. In the case both u and v, fulfill the above conditions, the node with the smallest ID will be scheduled. Meanwhile, the violation of data freshness or creation of cycles are resolved as follows: If $\rho(u) = v$ or $\rho(v) = u$ then the node which has the earliest time slot, say u, should be scheduled first. That is if node v sets u as its parent and v is scheduled first, node u should change its time slot to be later than TS_v to ensure the data freshness. If $TS_u = TS_v$, the conflict will be resolved using the same approach.

Coming back to the example in Figure 1(a), let us consider the four nodes η_1, η_2n η_3 and η_4. For η_1 and η_2, if η_1 is scheduled first, the set $\varrho_1^{\#1}$ of the two unscheduled interfering nodes of η_1's parent (i.e., $\overline{SC}_2 - \{\eta_1\}$), will not be empty and will be prevented from transmitting at $T_1^{\#1}$. Meanwhile, assigning slot #1 to η_2 makes η_1 locked and will affect also 2 unscheduled interfering nodes (i.e., $\overline{SC}_1 - \{\eta_2\}$). Moreover both nodes prevent the same number of nodes from serving as parents at time slot TS_u on channel CH_u (i.e., they make $\delta_i^T(u)$ of the same number of nodes not empty), so the node which has the smallest ID would be scheduled first. Thus, node η_1 should be scheduled before node η_2. As there is a conflict between nodes η_1, η_3 and η_4, one of them should be scheduled first. Node 4 prevents three nodes to use time slot #1 (i.e., $\overline{SC}_3 - \{\eta_4\}$), whereas assigning slot #1 to η_3 makes η_4 locked and will affect only one node. Therefore, nodes η_3 is to be allocated $T_1^{\#1}$ before η_2, η_4 and η_1 as depicted in Figure 1(b). Such a decision leads to higher time slot utilization, and hence minimum latency is likely to be achieved.

5. SIMULATION RESULTS

In this section, we discuss the performance of our solution and compare to that of *JFTSS* [7], *TMCP* [9] and *RBCA* [6]. The algorithms are evaluated in terms of the following metrics:

- *Time latency (last time slot):* is defined as the time required for the base station B to receive the aggregated data from all the sensor nodes;
- *Channel utilization variance* σ^2*:* This metric shows the capability of compared solutions in exploring the available channels. If the channels are evenly utilized over the network, the time slot reuse would be maximized and consequently the time latency will be significantly decreased. σ^2 is defined as the variance of random variable χ_i, such that χ_i represents the percentage of nodes which use channel i;

In the simulation experiments, N nodes are randomly deployed according to a uniform random distribution. The algorithms evaluation is performed by varying the number of nodes N and number of channels K. We conduct two types of experiments:

- Vary N and fix ψ to 50;
- Vary K while fixing N and ψ to 300 and 50 respectively;

K takes one of the following values 1, 2, 4 and 8 when varying the number of nodes.

As *JFTSS*, *TMCP* and *RBCA* do not meet the data freshness requirement and in order to fairly compare *DAS-MC*

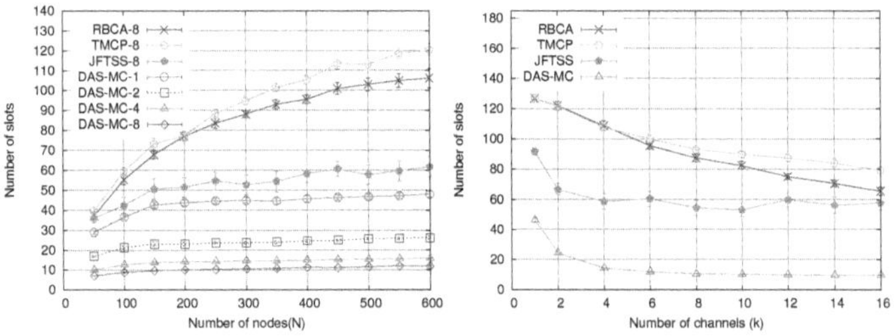

(a) (b)

Figure 2: Comparison of the data delivery latency of *DAS-MC* and the baseline approaches

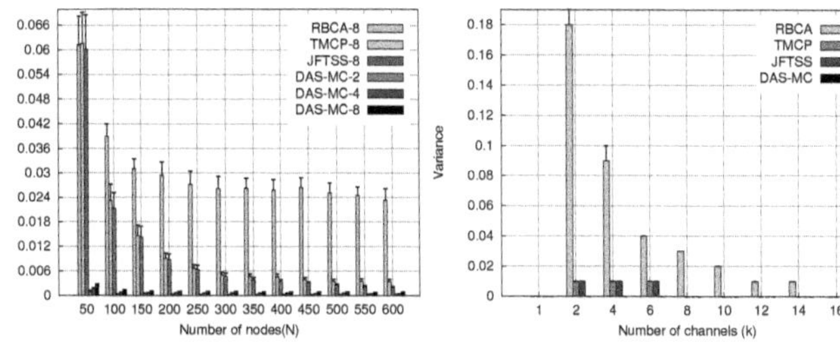

(a) (b)

Figure 3: Comparing the variability in channel utilization among the compared approaches and under varying network parameters

with them, we have slightly modified their implementations so that the data freshness would be ensured. Basically, when the parent node is ready to be scheduled, it is assigned a time slot later than all its children. In our simulation results, each plotted point represents the average of 35 executions. We plot the 95% confidence interval on the graphs.

5.1 Time latency

Figure 2 shows time latency as a function of N and K. Figure 2(a) shows that when 8 channels are used and the number of nodes is 600, the time latency of *TMCP*, *RBCA* and *JFTSS* is more than 120, 105 and 62 slots, respectively, whereas *DAS-MC* does not exceed 12 slots if 8 channels are used. Figure 2(c) shows that our solution *DAS-MC* outperforms the other solution whatever the number of channels K. *DAS-MC* outperforms all baseline approaches in term of data latency due to the use of (i) intertwining the tree formation and node scheduling, and (ii) the selection criteria for choosing parent nodes. It is worth noting that *DAS-MC* achieves a lower latency even when only one channel is available, which demonstrates the effectiveness avoiding gaps and increased time slot reuse.

5.2 Channel utilization variance σ^2

Balanced use of the available channels enables better utilization of the available transceiver's capacity and decreases the time latency. Figure 3 shows the variance of channels distribution among network nodes as a function of N and K. Figures 3(a) and 3(c) show that for all values of N and K, *DAS-MC* equitably distributes the channels over the network nodes (i.e., σ^2 is not more than 0.0018) whereas σ^2 in *RBCA*, *TMCP* and *JFTSS*, in some cases, is more than 0.07, 0.05 and 0.05, respectively. Given the significantly low variance for our approach, it is not visible in Figure 3(a).

6. CONCLUSION

In time-sensitive applications minimal delay should be experienced in delivering data to the base-station. To achieve this objective, time-based medium access arbitration is often pursued and the transmission of the individual sensor nodes are scheduled in a breadth first order according to the aggregation tree. Each node gets scheduled (i.e., assigned a time slot and a channel) only after all its children. However, such an approach, which is pursued in previously published solutions, significantly constrains the optimization of the time latency. To deal with this issue, we have proposed *DAS-MC* which provides two main features: (i) it intertwines the tree construction and nodes scheduling so that an optimal time-slot and channel assignment can be achieved, and (ii) it associates parents to nodes on the aggregation tree in a way that maximizes the choices of parents for each node and maximizes time slot reuse. The simulations results have shown that *DAS-MC* scales very well with respect to number of nodes and number of channels, and outperforms the contemporary solutions in terms of time latency.

7. REFERENCES

[1] M. Bagaa, A. Derhab, N. Lasla, A. Ouadjaout, and N. Badache. Semi-structured and unstructured data aggregation scheduling in wireless sensor networks. In *Proc. of IEEE INFOCOM*, March 2012.

[2] X. Chen, X. Hu, and J. Zhu. Minimum data aggregation time problem in wireless sensor networks. volume 3794 of *Lecture Notes in Computer Science*, pages 133–142. Springer, 2005.

[3] D. Dudek, C. Haas, A. Kuntz, M. Zitterbart, D. KrÃijger, P. Rothenpieler, D. Pfisterer, and S. Fischer. A wireless sensor network for border surveillance. In *Proc. of the 7th ACM Conference on Embedded Networked Sensor Systems*, Berkeley, 2009.

[4] M. Hefeeda and M. Bagheri. Forest fire modeling and early detection using wireless sensor networks. *Ad Hoc & Sensor Wireless Networks*, 7(3-4):169–224, 2009.

[5] S. C.-H. Huang, P.-J. Wan, C. T. Vu, Y. Li, and F. F. Yao. Nearly constant approximation for data aggregation scheduling in wireless sensor networks. In *Proc. of IEEE INFOCOM*, Anchorage , AK, May 2007.

[6] Ö. D. Incel, A. Ghosh, B. Krishnamachari, and K. Chintalapudi. Fast data collection in tree-based wireless sensor networks. *IEEE Trans. Mob. Comput.*, 11(1):86–99, 2012.

[7] X. Lin and S. Rasool. A distributed joint channel-assignment, scheduling and routing algorithm for multi-channel ad-hoc wireless networks. In *Proc. of IEEE INFOCOM*, Anchorage, Alaska, May 2007.

[8] B. Malhotra, I. Nikolaidis, and M. Nascimento. Aggregation convergecast scheduling in wireless sensor networks. *Wireless Networks*, 17(2):3319–335, 2011.

[9] Y. Wu, J. A. Stankovic, T. He, and S. Lin. Realistic and efficient multi-channel communications in wireless sensor networks. In *Proc. of IEEE INFOCOM*, Phoenix, AZ, 2008.

[10] M. Younis and S. Bushra. Efficient distributed medium access arbitration for multi-channel wireless sensor networks. In *Proc. of IEEE ICC*, Glasgow, Scotland, 2007.

Optimal Radius for Connectivity in Duty-Cycled Wireless Sensor Networks *

Amitabha Bagchi
Dept. of Comp. Sci. and Engg.
IIT Delhi, India
bagchi@cse.iitd.ernet.in

Cristina M. Pinotti
Dept. of Comp. Sci. and Math.
University of Perugia, Italy
cristina.pinotti@unipg.it

Sainyam Galhotra
Dept. of Comp. Sci. and Engg.
IIT Delhi, India
cs1100246@cse.iitd.ernet.in

Tarun Mangla
Dept. of Comp. Sci. and Engg.
IIT Delhi, India
cs1100260@cse.iitd.ernet.in

ABSTRACT

We investigate the condition on transmission radius needed to achieve connectivity in duty-cycled wireless sensor networks (briefly, DC-WSN). First, we settle a conjecture of Das et. al. (2012) and prove that the connectivity condition on Random Geometric Graphs (RGG), given by Gupta and Kumar (1989), can be used to derive a weak sufficient condition to achieve connectivity in DC-WSN. We also present a stronger result which gives a necessary and sufficient condition for connectivity and is hence *optimal*. The optimality of such a radius is also tested via simulation for two specific duty-cycle schemes, called the *contiguous* and the *random selection* duty-cycle scheme.

Categories and Subject Descriptors

C.2.1 [**Network Architecture and Design**]: Wireless Communication

Keywords

duty-cycled wireless sensor networks; connectivity radius

1. INTRODUCTION

Careful control of transmission power is required in wireless sensor networks to ensure that data can be sent while wasting minimum energy in interference and collision. This tradeoff translates into the question: what is the optimal radius for the connectivity of the WSN graph? This has been studied using the Random Geometric Graph (RGG) model by Gupta and Kumar [3] among others.

*This work has been partially supported by the Research Grant 2010N5K7EB from MIUR and Project Sapienza 2011 "Green and Secure Wireless Networking".

MSWiM'13, November 3–8, 2013, Barcelona, Spain.

http://dx.doi.org/10.1145/2507924.2507985.

To save energy even during sensing and processing activities, often sensors are organized in Duty-Cycled Wireless Sensor Networks (briefly, DC-WSNs). In such networks, sensors alternate between the *awake* and the *sleep* mode. During the sleep mode, the sensors recharge or conserve their batteries; during the active mode, the sensors sense, process and communicate. However, for the duty-cycled network to function as it should, we need two properties: (a) *Time coverage,* i.e. data generated at any time must be sensed and relayed by the network, and (b) *connectivity,* i.e. every node should be connected to every other node. The study of the conditions that guarantee these properties is the focus of this paper. This problem was initially investigated in [2], where it was conjectured that the DC-WSN is connected if in every time slot the nodes awake form a RGG connected in that time slot. We have settled this conjecture although we do not have space to present the proof here [1]. We have also established that the radius of connectivity that this conjecture implies is not optimal, i.e. a lower connection radius is sufficient. This lower connection radius, we call it the *strong radius* as opposed to the *weak radius* conjectured in [2], is also to be optimal in the sense that it provides a necessary condition for connectivity. We present two natural duty-cycling schemes, called the *contiguous* scheme and the *random selection* scheme that both satisfy the time coverage property. Apart from being useful duty-cycling schemes for real applications, these schemes also highlight the contribution of this paper since they have the same weak radius of connectivity but very different strong radii.

Related work and Motivation.

Power conservation mechanisms for WSNs may be classified into two main categories: active and passive [4]. Active mechanisms achieve energy conservation by smartly defining energy-efficient network protocols. Since they do not turn off the sensors, the connectivity property of the wireless sensor networks is preserved. Passive mechanisms save power by turning off the radio/sensing sensor module. As surveyed in [4], passive mechanisms can apply turn-off techniques at the physical layer for reducing the CPU energy in idle system states, or at the MAC layer by leading such a layer to decide when there is a frame destinated to it and then turn-off the radio interface for the remaining time of the frame, or utilizing higher layer application informations to decide when turn-off the radio. Since turning off the sensors makes the topology of the wireless sensor networks dynamic, the connectivity of such networks needs to be investigated.

2. THE DUTY-CYCLE MODEL

We first define our notation and the model following [2]. A *random geometric graph* $\mathrm{RGG}(n, r)$ is a graph with vertex set V of n points distributed uniformly at random in the unit circle centred at the origin. To this we add a point at the origin. There are edges between any two $u, v \in V$ such that $d(u, v) \leq r$ where $d(\cdot, \cdot)$ is a distance defined on $\mathbb{R}^2$.

In the duty-cycled setting all the nodes in the network are assumed to be synchronized and following a periodic pattern of sleeping and waking. Although the sleeping and waking patterns of different sensors may be different, they all share the same period, and each cycle of this periodic pattern (known as a *duty cycle*) begins and ends at the same time for all the nodes. As described in [2], the primary parameters of a duty-cycled wireless sensor network are L, *length* of the duty cycle, and d, the *number of waking slots* where $d < L$ and we use the notation $\delta = \lceil d/L \rceil$ to indicate the *duty-cycle ratio*, which is a measure of the energy spent by each sensor in each cycle. Each sensor u chooses its waking slots which we denote by the set A_u where $A_u \subseteq \{0, 1, \ldots, L-1\}$ and $|A_u| = d$. Given a scheme $\mathcal{A}$ for choosing these waking slots, we define the *duty-cycle graph* $\text{DC-WSN}_{\mathcal{A}}(n, r, \delta, L)$ as follows: it has the same vertex set as $\mathrm{RGG}(n, r)$ and its edge set is: $E = \{(u, v) : d(u, v) \leq r, A_u \cap A_v \neq \emptyset\}$. Namely, for two vertices u and v that are within transmission range of each other to be connected, they must share a slot where they are both awake. When the context requires it, we will also use the notation $\text{DC-WSN}_{\mathcal{A}}(n, r, \delta, L, \gamma)$ to denote a duty-cycle graph wherein the probability of two vertices u and v that are within transmission range of each other sharing a waking slot is γ.

A fundamental property desired of any duty-cycled sensor network is connectivity i.e. *it should be possible to send data generated at any time at any node to any other node in the network (within reasonable time).*

Whenever the awake period of each sensor is (strictly) more than half the duty cycle then each edge of the original graph $\mathrm{RGG}(n, r)$ is available for at least one time slot because any two waking periods must share a slot, i.e.

FACT 2.1. *If $\delta > 1/2$ then $DC\text{-}WSN(n, r, \delta, L)$ is connected whenever $RGG(n, r)$ is connected.*

However, for $\delta \leq 1/2$, connectivity is not a given under our current definition. Not only is it a random event whose probability needs to be determined, it may also be an event which occurs with probability 0. To ensure that the model admits connectivity with non-zero probability we will need a technical condition we call the *reachability condition.* Consider a scheme $\mathcal{A}$ for selecting the waking slots of nodes. Given the set $\mathcal{L} = \{A : A \subset \{0, 1, \ldots, L-1\}, |A| = d\}$, let us denote by $\mathcal{L}(\mathcal{A})$ all those subsets in $\mathcal{L}$ that have non-zero probability of being selected as a waking schedule for a node. Then, the reachability condition on $\mathcal{A}$ is the following:

Reachability. There is a finite $k \geq 0$ such that for any $A_1, A_2 \in \mathcal{L}(\mathcal{A})$, there are $A_1 = B_0, \ldots, B_k = A_2$ such that $B_i \in \mathcal{L}(\mathcal{A}), 0 \leq i \leq k$, and $B_i \cap B_{i+1} \neq \emptyset, 0 \leq i < k$.

We also need a notion which ensures that a duty-cycling scheme does not allow time slots where no sensor is awake. We call this notion *time coverage.*

Time coverage. For each $k \in \{0, 1, \ldots, L-1\}$, the probability that a node u is awake in slot k is $\delta_k > 0$, where δ_k may be a function of d and L but is not dependent on the number of nodes in the network.

If all the δ_k are equal then we say that there is *uniform coverage.*

3. CONNECTIVITY RESULTS

In this section we present a weak and a strong condition on transmission radius needed to achieve connectivity.

The weak result.

The weak result Theorem 3.1 is a generalization of the result first presented in Das et. al. [2].

THEOREM 3.1. *Given a duty-cycling scheme $\mathcal{A}$ with $0 < \delta \leq 1/2$ and $d = \lceil \delta L \rceil > 1$, and the marginal probability of a node being awake in slot i denoted by δ_i, the probability that $DC\text{-}WSN_{\mathcal{A}}(n, r(n), \delta, L)$ is connected tends to 1 as $n \to \infty$ if $\mathcal{A}$ satisfies the reachability condition and the coverage condition and if*

$$\pi r^2(n) \delta_{\min} = \frac{\log n + c(n)}{n}, \tag{1}$$

such that $c(n) \to \infty$ as $n \to \infty$, where $\delta_{\min} = \min_{k=0}^{L-1} \delta_k$.

We prove the theorem by considering a set of L subgraphs of $\text{DC-WSN}_{\mathcal{A}}(n, r, \delta, L)$, one for each time slot in a typical duty cycle. The proof proceeds by using Gupta and Kumar's result to show that each of these subgraphs is connected with probability that goes to 1 as $n \to \infty$ and that these subgraphs are all connected with probability tending to 1 as $n \to \infty$. We omit details of the proof due to lack of space.

In the uniform coverage situation, i.e. $\delta_0 = \ldots = \delta_{L-1} = \delta = \delta_{\min}$, Theorem 3.1 gives us the theorem of [2].

The strong result.

In this section we develop and present our strong connectivity result for duty-cycled WSNs, i.e. the most important contribution of our paper. Proving this result involves defining a new "vertex-based" random connection model. This model has four parameters. There are two finite positive real numbers λ, r. The third parameter is a random variable Z defined on some probability space $(\Omega, \mathcal{F}, \mathrm{P})$, that is a function of the form $Z : \Omega \to Q$ where Q is some domain. The fourth parameter is a function $f : Q \times Q \to \{0, 1\}$. The vertex set V is a Poisson point process in $\mathbb{R}^2$ with density λ with an additional point at the origin. With each $u \in V$ we associate a random variable Z_u which is a copy of Z. All the random variables in the collection $\{Z_u : u \in V\}$ are independent of each other. Two vertices u and v with distance r are connected by an edge if $f(Z_u, Z_v) = 1$. Clearly, for this model to be useful, there should be non-zero probability of an edge being formed between two points that are within distance r of each other.

Since the vertex-based random connection model is a new continuum percolation model, it is necessary to establish certain properties like the existence of a critical density for percolation (i.e. the formation of an infinite component), the non-triviality of the critical density, and the uniqueness of the infinite component. Since this is not directly relevant to the duty-cycled networks setting and due to the lack of space, we omit it here.

We now come to our main result dealing with the high-density situation. Define the quantity $q_k(\lambda) = P_\lambda(|W| = k), k \geq 1$ where W is the connected component containing the origin i.e. $q_k(\lambda)$ is the probability that the component containing the origin has size k for all finite values of k. Our key contribution is that we can prove that the following result proved by Penrose [5] for the high-density setting of the random connection model also holds for the vertex-based random connection model:

LEMMA 3.2.

$$\lim_{\lambda\to\infty} \frac{\sum_{k=1}^{\infty} q_k(\lambda)}{q_1(\lambda)} = 1$$

Since $\sum_{k=1}^{\infty} q_k(\lambda)$ is the probability that the origin is part of a finite sized component with at least 2 points in it, the implication of the theorem is that as $\lambda \to \infty$, the origin is either isolated or part of the infinite component with probability 1.

We are now ready to denote by VB-RGG(n, r, γ), the vertex-based random connection model graph with vertex set consisting of n points uniformly distributed in the unit circle centred at the origin, with radius bound r, and a connectivity function g that uses a function f and and random variable Z such that for any Z_1 and Z_2 that are independent copies of Z, $\gamma = P(f(Z_1, Z_2) = 1)$. Now, we are ready to state our strong connectivity result in Theorem 3.3. We omit the proof due to space constraints.

THEOREM 3.3. *P(DC-WSN$_{\mathcal{A}}(n, r, \delta, L, \gamma)$ is connected) $\to$ 1 as $n \to \infty$ if and only if*

$$\pi r(n)^2\gamma = \frac{\log n + c(n)}{n}, \tag{2}$$

where $c = \lim_{n\to\infty} c(n) = \infty$ *as* $n \to \infty$.

4. SIMULATION RESULTS

In this section, we illustrate the significance of our results for two specific duty-cycle schemes: the *contiguous* (we will denote it DC-C-WSN) and the *random selection* (we will denote it DC-R-WSN) schemes. The *contiguous* model has been studied in [2]. There A_u is chosen as follows: Each sensor u independently chooses an integer i_u from the set $\{0, 1, \ldots, L-1\}$ and is awake for the all the time slots i_u to $i_u + d - 1$, then asleep from all the time slots $i_u + d$ to $i_u + L$, repeating this cycle indefinitely. In the *random selection* model, each node chooses a set A_u of size d at random from $\{0, 1, \ldots, L-1\}$.

In the rest of this section, we first test the weak radius by measuring the percentage of sensors belonging to the largest component in DC-C-WSN and DC-R-WSN for various values of n, L and δ. Then, we repeat the experiments using the optimal radius.

Experimental setup.

In regard to the duty-cycle parameters, we select δ varying between 0.05 and 0.5 according to Fact 2.1. Then either we calculate $d = \lceil \delta L \rceil$ by fixing $L = 100$, or we derive $L = \lceil d/\delta \rceil$ by fixing $d = 5$. In addition to d, L, and $r(n)$, some informations are stored in the file for each sensor, depending on the duty-cycle scheme. For DC-C-WSN, we store for each sensor its start time, generated at random. For DC-R-WSN, we store a bitmap of length L. This bitmap will have d of its bits set to 1, which implies that the sensor is awake in that time slot, and the rest of them set to 0. To add an edge between two sensors, we check if they lie within the connectivity radius and if they share a common awake slot. To find the connected component, we make use of the Union Find algorithm. We start assigning unique flags to each point (i.e., each sensor belongs to an isolated component). Initially these flags point to themselves. As and when we get an edge between two points, we combine the connected components of both the points by pointing the head flag of one component to the head flag of the other component. When all edges have been added, the number of the distinct connected components in the graph and their sizes are traced. Each experiment is repeated at least three times and the average value is reported. The *kd*-tree spatial data structure was used to process pairs of points in $\theta(n)$ time, and the connected components were created in $\theta(n \log n)$ time. As a result testing connectivity for a random graph model with 10^6 node took approximately 20 minutes.

Weak connectivity condition.

Let the *weak radius* be the radius $r(n)$ that satisfies Theorem 3.1. Since both contiguous and random selection schemes satisfies the uniform coverage situation with $\delta = \lceil d/L \rceil$, the weak radius for both schemes yields:

$$r(n) = \sqrt{\frac{\log n + c(n)}{\pi n \delta}} \tag{3}$$

with $c(n) \to +\infty$ as $n \to +\infty$.

Under the weak radius, in all our experiments in DC-C-WSNs more than 99% sensors belong to the largest connected component, while all the sensors belong to the largest component in DC-R-WSNs. We omit these curves for lack of space.

Note that the weak radius is much larger than the transmission radius required to achieve the connectivity in RGG. In fact it is $\frac{1}{\sqrt{\delta}}$ times the RGG radius given in [3]. Such an increase in the transmission radius means on average that, since the power spent by each node in transmission is proportional to the square of the radius and since $n\delta$ sensors are awake, the overall energy spent is almost the same as in regular (i.e. all awake) WSNs, thereby negating the effect of duty-cycling.

Strong connectivity condition.

To apply the strong connectivity condition in Theorem 3.3 for the contiguous and random duty-cycle scheme, we need to compute the probability γ in the VB-RGG model.

In DC-C-WSNs, a sensor v will share at least one slot with node u if v chooses as its starting point any of $i_u - (d-1)$ mod $L, \ldots, i_u, \ldots i_u + (d-1)$ mod $L, \ldots, i_u - (d-1)$ mod L slots. Hence, two sensors have probability $\gamma = \frac{2d-1}{L}$ of sharing one slot. Now, let the *strong DC-C-WSN radius* be the radius $r(n)$ that satisfies Theorem 3.3 when $\gamma = \frac{2d-1}{L}$. We have:

COROLLARY 4.1. *When $\gamma = \frac{2d-1}{L} < 1$, P(DC-C-WSN is connected) $\to 1$ as $n \to \infty$ if and only if*

$$r(n) = \sqrt{\frac{\log n + c(n)}{(2\delta - 1/L)\pi n}}, \tag{4}$$

where $c = \lim_{n\to\infty} c(n) = \infty$.

Note that if $\gamma = \frac{2d-1}{L} > 1$, the radius in (4) goes below the lowest possible radius and it is no longer meaningful.

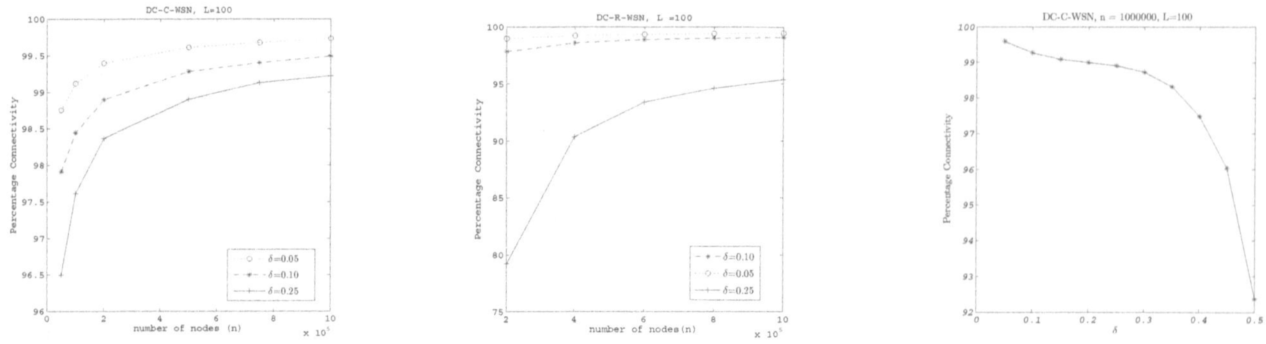

(a) (b) (c)

Figure 1: Strong radius:(a) in DC-C-WSN when n varies (b) in DC-R-WSN when n varies (c) in DC-C-WSN when δ varies

However, $\gamma = \frac{2d-1}{L} > 1$ implies $\delta > 1/2$, and by Fact 2.1 the RGG radius given in [3] guarantees connectivity.

In DC-R-WSNs, when a node u has chosen d slots, another node v has d possibilities to choose one slot in common with u and the probability of doing that is at least δ each time. Hence, the probability that two sensors share one slot is $\gamma > \left(1-(1-\delta)^d\right)$. Therefore, by Theorem 3.3, the *strong DC-R-WSN radius* must satisfy:

COROLLARY 4.2. *P(DC-R-WSN is connected)* $\to 1$ *as* $n \to \infty$ *if and only if*

$$r(n) = \sqrt{\frac{\log n + c(n)}{(1-(1-\delta)^d)\pi n}}, \tag{5}$$

where $c = \lim_{n\to\infty} c(n) = \infty$.

Under the strong radius, Figures 1a and 1b show the percentage of sensors belonging to the largest component when $L = 100$, $c(n) = \log\log n$, $10^5 \le n \le 10^6$, $\delta = 0.05, 0.15$ and 0.25. For both schemes, fixing a value of δ, the size of the largest connected component increases when n increases since (3) holds for $n \to +\infty$. On the other hand, fixing a value of n, when δ increases, the the number of nodes in the largest connected component slightly decreases according to the fact that the radius $r(n)$ decreases. Nonetheless, for all the experiments on DC-C-WSNs, more than 90% of the sensors belong to the largest component. Such a percentage is disregarded by the DC-R-WSNs only for small values of n and large values of δ, as for $n = 2\cdot 10^5$ or $n = 4\cdot 10^5$ and $\delta = 0.25$ (see Figure 1b). This shows that the reliance on the asymptotic condition for n is stronger for DC-R-WSNs than for DC-C-WSNs.

Figures 1c and 2 depict the percentage of sensors belonging to the largest component in both schemes when $n = 10^6$, $L = 100$, $c(n) = \log\log n$ and $0.1 \le \delta \le 0.5$. The results are almost as good as the ones for the weak radius, but the strong radius is much smaller than the weak one (see Table 1). Fig. 2 shows a drop off in the percentage of connectivity when $\delta = 0.20$, although the connectivity remains high at more than 90%. The gain between the strong and the weak radius in Table 1 is about a factor of $\sqrt{2}$ for the contiguous scheme, while is more important for the random scheme. In conclusion, the strong connectivity condition undoubtedly leads to a great gain in the radius length, and a great energy saving in power transmission for both schemes.

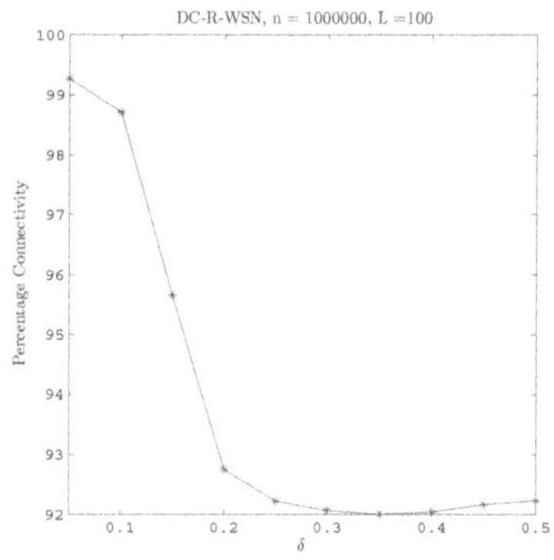

Figure 2: Strong radius in DC-R-WSN when δ varies.

	$L = 200$		$L = 100$	
δ	DC-C-WSN	DC-R-WSN	DC-C-WSN	DC-R-WSN
0.10	1.396	3.374	1.378	3.918
0.15	1.402	2.591	1.390	2.702
0.20	1.405	2.236	1.396	2.249
0.50	1.410	1.414	1.407	1.414

Table 1: The ratio of the weak to the strong radius in DC-C-WSN and DC-R-WSN for different δ and L.

5. REFERENCES

[1] A. Bagchi, S. Galhotra, T. Mangla, and C. M. Pinotti. Connectivity in duty-cycled wireless sensor networks. Technical report, Department of Computer Science and Mathematics, University of Perugia, May 2013.

[2] S. K. Das, A. Di Saverio, G. Ghidini, A. Navarra, and C. M. Pinotti. Broadcast analysis in dense duty-cycle sensor networks. In *Proc. ICUIMC '12*, 2012.

[3] P. Gupta and P. R. Kumar. Critical power for asymptotic connectivity. In *Proc. 37th IEEE Conf. on Decision and Control*, pages 1106–1110, 1998.

[4] N. A. Pantazis and D. D. Vergados. A survey on power control issues in wireless sensor networks. *IEEE Communications Surveys and Tutorials*, 9(1-4):86–107, 2007.

[5] M. D. Penrose. On a continuum percolation model. *Adv. Appl. Probab.*, 23(3):546–556, September 1991.

A Multi-metric Routing Protocol with Service Differentiation for Cognitive Radio Ad-Hoc Networks

Samar Moursi
Computer and Systems Engineering Dept.
Alexandria University
Alexandria, Egypt 21544
samar.moursi@gmail.com

Mustafa ElNainay
Computer and Systems Engineering Dept.
Alexandria University and Virginia Tech MENA
Alexandria, Egypt 21544
ymustafa@alexu.edu.eg

ABSTRACT

In Cognitive Radio Networks, secondary users are affected by the the activity of primary users on licensed channels. To solve this problem, most routing protocols select the most stable links/channels, or use the minimum delay route and switch to other channels when primary users become active. However, these approaches may lead to competition between the secondary users on the most preferred links/channels which may cause congestion and affect the quality of the transmissions. In this paper, a multi-metric routing protocol with service differentiation is proposed. The main idea is to use different routing metrics for different traffic types to select routes that satisfy the specific requirements of each traffic type and to make load balancing across the network. Simulation results show that, compared to other related approaches, our protocol provides better end-to-end delay and increases the aggregate throughput. It also achieves load balancing across the network.

Categories and Subject Descriptors

C.2.2 [**Computer-Communication Networks**]: Network Protocols—*Routing protocols*

Keywords

Cognitive Radio Networks; Multi-metric Routing

1. INTRODUCTION

In traditional wireless communications, spectrum resources are fixed and pre-allocated. This fixed spectrum assignment policy is becoming unsuitable for today's wireless communication according to the Federal Communications Commission (FCC) report [1]. It results in poor utilization and spectrum holes. In order to make good use of the unutilized bands, devices with cognitive capabilities can be networked to form Cognitive Radio Network (CRN), in which there are two types of users sharing a common spectrum portion but with different rules: Primary Users (PUs) which have the priority to use the spectrum within the band they have licensed, and Secondary Users (SUs) that must opportunistically access the spectrum without interfering with PUs.

MSWiM'13, November 3–8, 2013, Barcelona, Spain.

ACM 978-1-4503-2353-6/13/11
http://dx.doi.org/10.1145/2507924.2507992 ...$15.00.

The research in Cognitive Radio (CR) is primarily on spectrum sensing and spectrum sharing [2, 3]. In the routing layer, many challenges are added due to the dynamic behavior of PUs, and their effects on changing spectrum opportunities (SOPs) availability of SUs. To solve this problem, most routing protocols try to avoid regions of PUs and select the most stable routes, or make use of the minimum end-to-end delay routes and switch to other channels or perform re-routing upon PU appearance. However, these approaches can lead to competition/congestion among secondary users.

In this paper, a Multi-metric Routing protocol with SErvice Differentiation for CRNs (MRSED) is proposed to solve the problem of competition among CR nodes for the most preferable links and channels due to the use of a single routing metric. It switches among many routing metrics to satisfy the Quality of Service (QoS) requirements of each traffic.

The rest of the paper is organized as follows: Section 2 describes the related work in this area. The system model is presented in Section 3. Section 4 presents the details of the proposed routing protocol and the suggested metrics. In Section 5, we evaluate the proposed protocol using NS2 simulation scenarios and present the simulation results. Finally, Section 6 concludes the paper.

2. RELATED WORK

Most of the existing research work on Cognitive Radio (CR) has been mainly focused on the physical layer and the issues of the medium access control. Recently, many routing protocols are introduced for CRNs. The authors in [4] categorize routing protocols according to the metric used to assess route quality into three main categories: Delay-based solutions, link quality/stability based solutions, and throughput based solutions.

Delay-aware routing metrics are proposed in [5, 6, 7, 8, 9], which consider different delay components such as switching delay, backoff delay, queuing delay, and propagation delay. The work in [5, 6] introduces a metric for multi-hop CRN that is aware of both the switching delay and the backoff delay. This metric is generalized in [7, 8] to add the queuing delay, which occurs at intersecting relay node that serves many incoming flows. Moreover, a location-based routing protocol is introduced in [9] which considers both propagation and switching delays.

Many link stability aware metrics are proposed recently for routing in CRNs due to the dynamic nature of such networks. Gymkhana [10] is a routing scheme which routes packets across paths that avoid network zones with unstable links. In [11], spectrum tree based on demand routing protocol is introduced. It uses a routing metric that combines link quality and spectrum availability. In [12], the authors introduce a new definition of route stability based on the concept of route maintenance cost where routes with minimum maintenance cost are the candidate routes.

The above mentioned solutions for both delay-aware or link stability-aware metrics can help nodes to select the minimum end-to-end delay route or the most stable route, respectively, but by forcing all CR nodes to use the same routing metric for all traffic types. The competition among them for the most preferable routes and channels may result in high contention and collision problems and subsequently, affect link utilization and the overall network performance.

As each traffic type has its own characteristics and service requirements, using multi-metric routing can give better performance for networks that have different traffic types. Multi-metric concept is introduced in some routing protocols for traditional ad hoc networks. In [13, 14], an extension for the proactive routing protocol Optimized Link State Routing (OLSR) is proposed. Two additional metrics are added to satisfy QoS requirements; bandwidth availability and link quality. In [15], multi-metric routing framework is proposed based also on OLSR with the ability to add many metrics, but there is no switching between the metrics during runtime; the metric that will be used in the routing tables is decided in advance during compile-time.

In this paper, we propose MRSED as a multi-metric routing protocol for CRNs, the main contributions of our work presented in this paper include: (1) A Multi-metric routing protocol with service differentiation that uses different routing metrics for different traffic types to satisfy the specific QoS requirements of each traffic type. (2) A new route maintenance process that can recover routes affected by PUs appearance fast and with minimum routing overhead.

3. SYSTEM MODEL

A multihop cognitive radio ad hoc network that has m licensed channels, n mobile secondary users (SUs), and k stationary primary users (PUs) is considered. Each secondary user is equipped with two interfaces; a *control interface* which is used for exchanging control messages through a common control channel (CCC) (that is not subject to PUs interruptions). The other interface is *data interface* which is used for sending or receiving data messages. The PU activity is modeled as exponential ON-OFF process. The duration of the ON and OFF periods follows exponential distribution with parameters μ_{on} and μ_{off}, respectively. The average transmission range of the PUs is known, and SUs are not allowed to use the licensed channel when a nearby PU is operating on this channel (this also protects primary receivers).

4. MULTI-METRIC ROUTING PROTOCOL WITH SERVICE DIFFERENTIATION

As shown in Figure 1, MRSED consists of three main modules. One of them is an external module which is the Spectrum Sensing Module. It is responsible for sensing the spectrum and inform each secondary user with its available SOPs. The other two modules are the Route Discovery and Route Maintenance Modules. The function of the Route

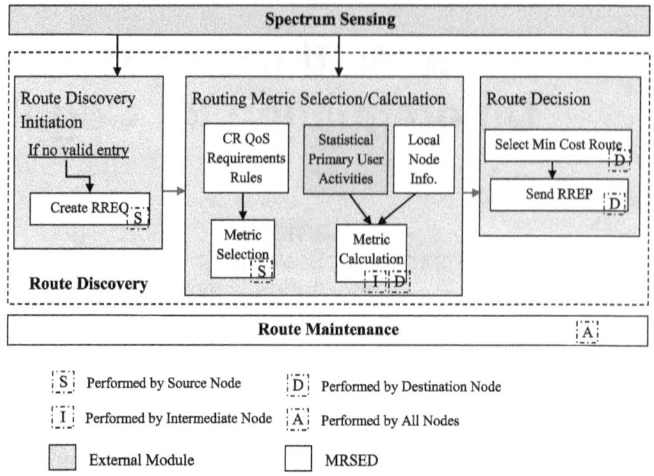

Figure 1: MRSED Architecture

Discovery Module is to discover all possible paths between a source node and a destination node by propagating RREQ through intermediate nodes, calculating the cost of each of them and select the minimum cost route. It incorporates three sub-modules: Route Discovery Initiation sub-module; Routing Metric Selection/Calculation sub-module in which the suitable metric that will be used to assess the route is selected based on predefined CR QoS requirements rules, and is calculated using statistical PU activities and local node information. Finally, in the Route Decision sub-module, the destination node examines a list of candidate routes and selects the route with the minimum cost. On the other hand, the route maintenance module is responsible for recovering route failure due to PU appearance or mobility issues. Routing metrics used in our protocol are presented in this section and then the route discovery and route maintenance processes are explained.

4.1 Routing metric selection

As previously discussed, the use of one routing metric can not lead to the optimal route selection, specially in CRNs where spectrum bandwidth is an opportunistic resource that should be allocated wisely according to CR users QoS requirements. In our proposed protocol (MRSED), three routing metrics are used: delay, link stability and load balancing metrics for three main traffic types: VoIP/UDP, FTP/TCP and CBR/UDP, respectively. VoIP traffic is used to represent unreliable and delay-sensitive applications and FTP traffic is used to represent reliable and delay-tolerant applications. Finally, CBR traffic is used to represent applications that have minimum QoS requirements and have the less priority among others. Table 1 identifies the different traffic categories, the used metric for each of them, and mapping to applications that are used in the simulation.

4.1.1 Delay metric

The delay metric as presented in [6] is composed of two components: switching delay and back-off delay. Switching delay is the delay incurred when a node switches from one frequency band to another. Backoff delay is produced by MAC layer when there is a contention on identical frequency bands. Backoff delay on band i is obtained as:

$$D_{backoff_i} = \frac{1}{(1-p_c).[1-(1-p_c)^{\frac{1}{(Num_i-1)}}]}.W_0 \quad (1)$$

where Num_i is the number of contending nodes, p_c is the probability that a contending node experiences collision, and W_0 represents the minimum contention window size.

If an end-to-end route r is composed of H hops, the accumulated delay $Delay_r$ can be calculated as:

$$Delay_r = \sum_{j=1}^{H}(\min_{i\in 0,1,..,m} D_{backoff_i}(j)) + M.D_{switch} \quad (2)$$

where M is the number of channel switches along route r.

4.1.2 Link stability metric

As in [11], we select a link-stability based metric that considers both link quality and link stability. The link stability cost S_i of link l_i is calculated as:

$$S_i = \left(O_{ca} + O_p + \frac{P_{kt}}{r_i}\right).\frac{1}{1-e_{pti}}.\frac{1}{T_{l_i}} \quad (3)$$

where O_{ca}, O_p and P_{kt} are constants for specific access technology and represent the channel overhead, protocol overhead and packet size, respectively. r_i is the link rate (in Mbps), e_{pti} is the packet error rate on the link, and T_{l_i} is the spectrum band available time for the link l_i. T_{l_i} reflects the integration of the link stability to the link quality. Its value can be easily determined from previous history of PUs activities. Hence, the stability cost $Stability_r$ of an end-to-end route r composed of H links is:

$$Stability_r = \sum_{j=1}^{H}(\min_{i\in 0,1,..,m} S_i(j)) \quad (4)$$

4.1.3 Load balancing metric

Load-balancing is a technique that is used to distribute the network load over different paths in order to decrease the congestion at intermediate nodes and improve the packet delivery ratio. In our case, traffics that have no special requirements (low priority traffics) may use different routes than traffics that need high quality routes. A new routing metric that targets load balancing is proposed in [17]. The key idea of the metric is that the load is usually maximal at the center of the network and it decreases as we go further to the network edges. Thus, selecting nodes that have minimum routing table size is an indication of nodes that do not participate much in routing. Selecting those nodes achieves load balancing. We made some modifications on this metric to fit in the CRNs context. Therefore, the load balancing metric of an end-to-end route r can be calculated as follows:

$$LoadBalancing_r = \frac{1}{n}.\sum_{k=1}^{n}(\min_{i\in 0,1,..,m} size(rtable_i(k))) \quad (5)$$

where $size(rtable_i(k))$ refers to the number of routing table entries of a node k that use the band i for transmission, the band that has the minimum routing table entries is selected, n is the number of nodes participating in the route r.

4.2 Route Discovery

As mentioned previously, MRSED is built on top of the AODV protocol. Thus, some fields are added to the AODV-style RREQ, RREP packets and routing table as shown in

Traffic Category	Routing Metric	Application
(1) Multimedia	Minimum Delay	VoIP/UDP
(2) Important data	Maximum Stability	FTP/TCP
(3) Ordinary data	Load balancing	CBR/UDP

Table 1: Traffic categories, their assigned metrics and the used application for each category in the simulation

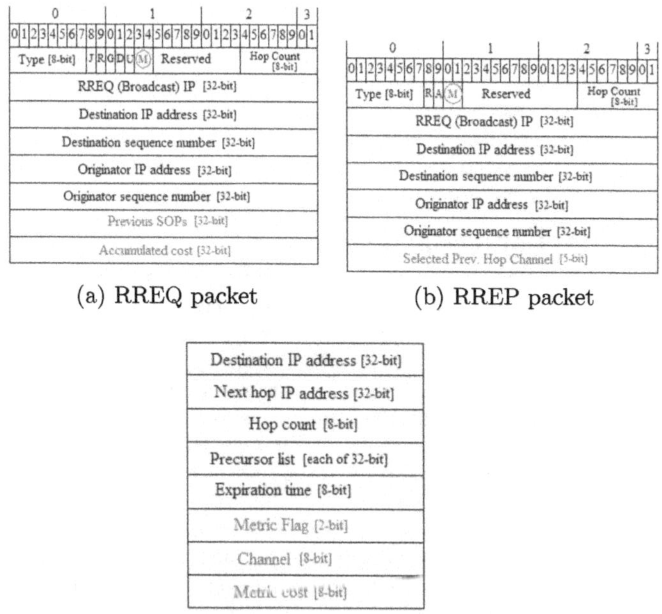

(a) RREQ packet (b) RREP packet

(c) Routing table entry

Figure 2: MRSED packet formats and routing table entry

Figure 2. For the RREQ, three fields are added which are: $PreviousSOPs$ (holds the spectrum availability of the previous hop node that forwards the RREQ), metric flag (M) (holds one of three values: [D] for selecting the delay metric, [S] for the link stability metric, and [L] for load balancing metric) and $Accumulatedcost$ (is used for calculating the total cost of the route for specific metric). Two fields are added to the RREP packet which are: metric flag (M) (is used to specify the metric that will be added to the routing table entry for the selected route), $SelectedPrevHopChannel$ (also to be added to the routing table entry).

If a source node N_s has some data to send to the destination node N_d for which it has valid routing entry that meets the traffic type requirements, the source node sends the data (packet) to the next hop immediately. Otherwise, it initiates a route discovery process. The route discovery process can be summarized in the following steps:

1. The source node N_s creates and broadcasts a RREQ packet to its neighboring nodes containing its $SOPs$ and metric flag (M) which is assigned according to the traffic type (as stated in Table 1).

2. Once a node receives a RREQ packet, it replaces its $SOPs$ information and forwards it to its neighbors if and only if there is an intersection between the $SOPs$ of this node and the previous hop node. By doing this, RREQ is forwarded towards the destination using routes that are feasible in both space and spectrum availability.

3. Each intermediate node N_k calculates the required routing metric (Delay metric, link stability metric or load balancing metric according to the metric flag field (M)) based on its local information and adds it to the *Accumulatedcost* in the RREQ before forwarding it.

4. When the destination node N_d receives a RREQ packet, it waits for certain time to collect all RREQ messages. After that it selects the route with the minimum cost specified in the RREQ and unicasts a RREP message on the reverse path of the selected route.

5. While the RREP is traversing the reverse path, routing table entries are added/updated for the specified metric, and the *SelectedPrevHopChannel* is extracted from the RREP and inserted into these entries.

6. Immediately, the source node N_s starts sending the queued data upon receiving the RREP packet.

4.3 Route Maintenance

Due to the stochastic nature of the PU activities, we introduce a new route maintenance process that can recover routes affected by PUs appearance fast and with minimum routing overhead. When a PU becomes active on an established route, each affected SU suspends any current transmissions and the following process is performed.

- Affected node(s) send(s) Channel Switch (CSWTCH) packet to previous and next hop nodes involved in the current transmission sessions.

- When a node receives CSWTCH packet, it firstly queues any current transmissions to the specified destination. Then, it calculates the best channel to be used based on the common SOPs between it and the initiator node. Previous hop just switches to the new selected channel but the next hop node must reply to the initiator node with CSWTCH-Reply packet containing the new selected channel.

- When a node receives CSWTCH-Reply, it updates its corresponding routing table entry with the new selected channel, and starts sending any queued data.

- If two adjacent nodes in the same route detect the presence of the PU and send CSWTCH packet, the node that is near to the destination will be responsible of selecting the new channel, and the other node will just ignore the received CSWTCH packet to avoid redundancy/conflict decisions.

- If the affected node does not find any channel between itself and the previous or the next hop node, it sends a Route Suspend (RSUSP) packet to the source to suspend the current session and start a new route discovery process.

5. PERFORMANCE EVALUATION

In this section, we evaluate the performance of MRSED using NS2 with multi-radio multi-channel extension [18].The three types of traffics that specified in Table 1 are generated with equal proportions. All simulation parameters are shown in Table 2. In our experiment, we compare MRSED to the Delay motivated On-demand Routing Protocol (DORP) [7] and the Spectrum-Tree based On-Demand routing protocol (STOD-RP) [11]. The impact of increasing the number of channels and PUs have been investigated. Moreover, the performance of VoIP and TCP transmissions has been measured in terms of percentage of delayed calls and loss ratio, respectively. Simulation results were computed using a 90% confidence interval.

Parameter	Value range	Nominal value(s)
Area	(1000X1000)m	(1000X1000)m
Number of SUs (n)	150	150
Number of PUs (k)	0, 4, 8, 16	4
Number of active flows	3, 6, 9, 12, 15	15
Number of licensed channels (m)	2, 3, 4, 5	3
Channel switching time	5 ms	5 ms
SU transmission range	120 m	120 m
PU transmission range	200 m	200 m
μ_{on}	$\in$[2 to 5]	$\in$[2 to 5]
μ_{off}	$\in$[10 to 20]	$\in$[10 to 20]
W_0	12	12
O_{ca}	75 μ	75 μ
O_p	110 μ	110 μ
P_{kt}	8224	8224

Table 2: NS2 Simulation Parameters

1) *Effect of increasing number of channels:* Figure 3 shows that as the number of channels increases, MRSED can achieve less end-to-end delay and significantly improve the aggregate throughput. That is because MRSED uses different metrics for different traffic types. Thus, it makes best utilization of the available channels and balances the channel load. Furthermore, STOD-RP tends to use the most stable routes, so its throughput is better than DORP, but has greater delay.

2) *Effect of increasing number of PUs:* Figure 4 shows that when there is no PUs, DORP and STOD-RP are close to each other because STOD-RP will select minimum hop routes when there is no PU, and DORP selects minimum end-to-end delay routes. However, as the number of PUs increases, the performance of all protocols is affected as the number of available routes and channels for SUs decreases. DORP has a slight performance advantage as it tries to minimize the end-to-end delay considering the backoff delay, but STOD-RP targeting most stable routes is better in terms of aggregate throughput. MRSED has the best performance among the other two protocols because in addition to make load balancing by distributing traffics among different available routes and channels, route maintenance process that is performed upon sudden appearance of PUs for already established routes makes significant advantage over other protocols which normally make re-route discovery.

3) *Performance of VoIP transmissions:* According to ITU Recommendation G.114, delay in VoIP applications should never exceed 400 ms otherwise the quality of the VoIP stream is significantly degraded. In order to measure the effectiveness of the proposed protocol for VoIP applications, we measure the percentage of delayed packets which incur delay larger than 400 ms. Figure 5 (a) shows that as the number of flows increases, the percentage of delayed calls increases significantly with STOD-RP and smoothly with DORP. However, MRSED has the minimum percentage of delayed packets even with large number of active flows.

4) *Performance of TCP transmissions:* To measure the effectiveness of MRSED for TCP transmissions, we measure the loss ratio while increasing the number of flows. Figure 5 (b) shows that as the number of flows increases, STOD-RP and DORP have almost identical performance, unless when the number of flows is 20, the performance of STOD-RP is worse than DORP because of the congestion on the most stable routes. However, MRSED with its load balancing still has a significant advantage over the other protocols.

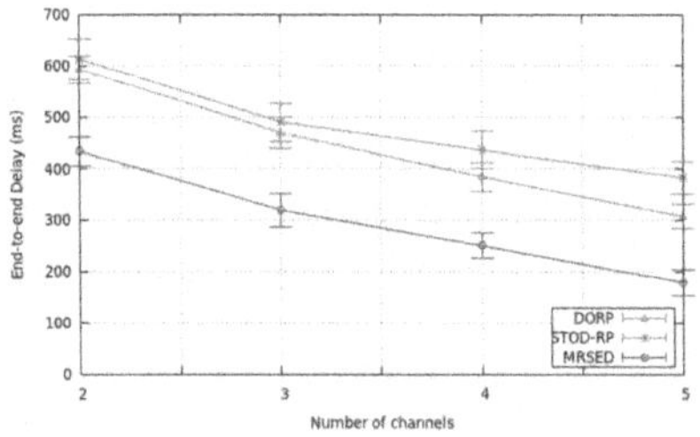

(a) End-to-end delay

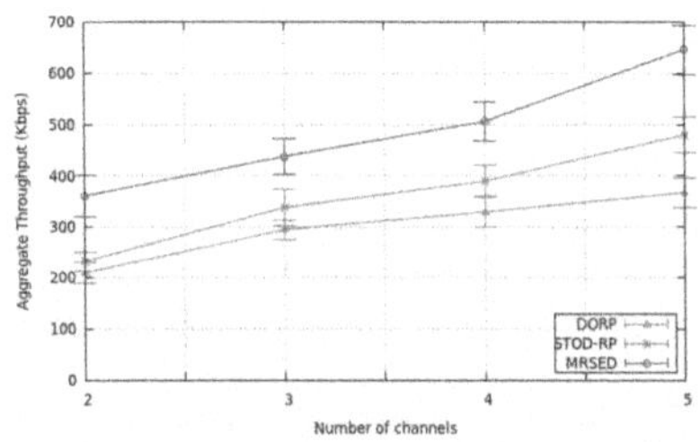

(b) Throughput

Figure 3: Impact of increasing number of channels

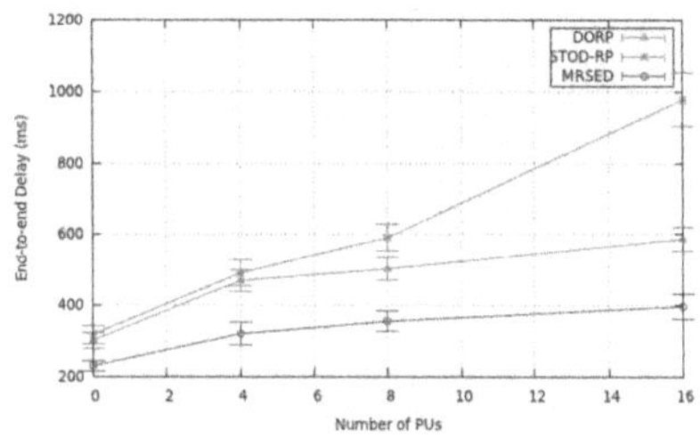

(a) End-to-end delay

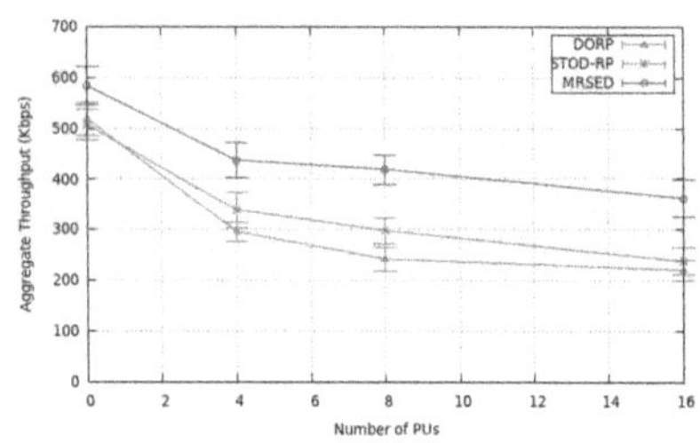

(b) Throughput

Figure 4: Impact of increasing number of PUs

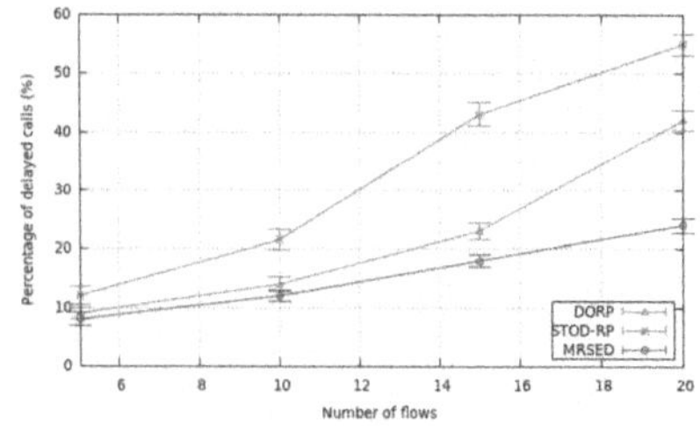

(a) Percentage of delayed VoIP packets

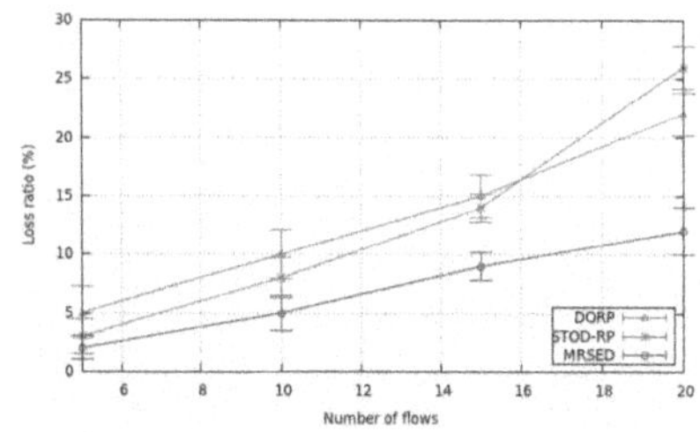

(b) Loss ratio of TCP transmissions

Figure 5: Performance evaluation of VoIP and TCP transmissions

6. CONCLUSION

In this paper, a multi-metric routing protocol with service differentiation for cognitive radio networks is proposed. The key concept in this protocol is to use different routing metrics according to the traffic type. This achieves load balancing and satisfies the QoS requirements of different traffic types. We have validated the effectiveness of the protocol by simulation and the proposed protocol was shown to outperform DORP and STOD-RP protocols.

7. REFERENCES

[1] F. C. Commission. Fcc adopted rules for unlicensed use of television white spaces. tech. rep. et docket no. 04-1862004.

[2] I. Akyildiz, W.-Y. Lee, M. Vuran, and S. Mohanty. Next generation/dynamic spectrum access/cognitive radio wireless networks: a survey. *Computer Networks*, pages 2127–2159, 2006.

[3] T. Yucek and H. Arslan. A survey of spectrum sensing algorithms for cognitive radio applications. *Communications Surveys and Tutorials, IEEE*, pages 116–130, 2009.

[4] M. Cesana, F. Cuomo, and E. Ekici. Routing in cognitive radio networks: Challenges and solutions. *Elsevier Ad Hoc Networks*, pages 228–248, 2011.

[5] X. M. H. Ma, L. Zheng and Y. luo. Spectrum aware routing for multi-hop cognitive radio networks with a single transceiver. *CrownCom 2008*, pages 1–6, 2008.

[6] G. Cheng, W. Liu, Y. Li, and W. Cheng. Spectrum aware on-demand routing in cognitive radio networks. *IEEE DySPAN*, pages 571–574, 2007.

[7] G. Cheng, W. Liu, and Y. Li. Joint on-demand routing and spectrum assignment in cognitive radio networks. *IEEE ICC*, pages 6499–6503, 2007.

[8] Z. Yang, G. Cheng, W. Liu, W. Yuan, and W. Cheng. Local coordination based routing and spectrum assignment in multi-hop cognitive radio networks. *Mobile Networks and Applications*, pages 67–81, 2008.

[9] K. Habak, M. Abdelatif, H. Hagrass, K. Rizc, and M. Youssef. A location-aided routing protocol for cognitive radio networks. *ICNC'13*, pages 729–733, 2013.

[10] A. Abbagnale and F. Cuomo. Gymkhana: a connectivity-based routing scheme for cognitive radio ad hoc networks. *IEEE INFOCOM*, pages 1–5, 2010.

[11] G. Zhu, I. Akyildiz, and G. Kuo. Stod-rp: a spectrum-tree based on demand routing protocol for multi-hop cognitive radio networks. *IEEE GLOBECOM*, pages 1–5, 2008.

[12] E. E. I. Filippini and M. Cesana. Minimum maintenance cost routing in cognitive radio networks. *6th IEEE MASS'09*, pages 284–293, 2009.

[13] J. Cao and W. Wu. A multi-metric qos routing method for ad hoc network. *International Conf. on Mobile Ad-hoc and Sensor Networks*, pages 99–102, 2008.

[14] M. B. Jaroslaw Krygier and K. Maslanka. Evaluation of the multimetric proactive routing protocol implementation for mobile ad-hoc networks. *Microwaves Radar and Wireless Communications (MIKON)*, pages 259–261, 2012.

[15] A. Laven and P. Hjartquist. Multimetric olsr and ett. *5th OLSR Interop and Workshop*, 2009.

[16] C. E. Perkins and E. M. Royer. Ad hoc on-demand distance vector routing. *IEEE WMCSA'99*, pages 90–100, 1999.

[17] M. F. Oussama Souihli and M. B. Hamouda. Load-balancing in manet shortest-path routing protocols. *Elsevier Ad Hoc Networks*, pages 431–442, 2009.

[18] Cognitive radio cognitive network simulator. *http://stuweb.ee.mtu.edu/ ljialian/*.

Performance Modeling and Analysis of IEEE 802.11 Wireless Networks with Hidden nodes

Myung Woo Lee
Department of Mathematical Sciences and Telecommunication Engineering Program
KAIST
Daejeon, Republic of Korea

Ganguk Hwang
Department of Mathematical Sciences and Telecommunication Engineering Program
KAIST
Daejeon, Republic of Korea
guhwang@kaist.edu

Sumit Roy
Department of Electrical Engineering
University of Washington
Seattle, USA
roy@ee.washington.edu

ABSTRACT

This work seeks to develop an analytical model for the per-node throughput analysis of IEEE 802.11 WLAN networks with *hidden nodes* by extending the Bianchi's model. With the analytic model we derive the per-node throughput of each node and quantify the impact of hidden nodes on per-node throughput. Through our analysis, we find that nodes having more hidden nodes are likely to have worse throughput performance than nodes having less hidden nodes, so resulting in unfairness in per-node throughput.

We next propose a new algorithm, called the fake collision algorithm, to solve the unfairness due to hidden nodes. The proposed fake collision algorithm allows nodes with poor throughput to acquire more transmission opportunities by slightly modifying the Binary Exponential Backoff algorithm of the IEEE 802.11 Distributed Coordination Function. To this end, the fake collision algorithm uses a new control parameter called the fake collision probability which can be obtained from a computation algorithm that we develop based on our analytic model. We show that the fairness in per-node throughput can be achieved with the fake collision probability for each node through simulation.

Categories and Subject Descriptors

C.2.5 [**Computer-Communication Networks**]: Local and Wide-Area Networks—*Access Schemes*

Keywords

Performance modeling, WLAN, IEEE 802.11, Hidden Node Problem

1. INTRODUCTION

Performance of Distributed Coordination Function (DCF) protocol for the IEEE 802.11 WLANs has been well analyzed, starting with the seminal work of Bianchi [1]. However, the limitations of this train of analysis is well-known, notably it's lack of inclusion of 'hidden' nodes [2]. If two (source) nodes N_1, N_2 are outside the carrier sensing range of each other, N_1 may initiate a transmission to a common receive node, while it is already receiving a packet from N_2, resulting in a packet collision[1].

The hidden node problem is commonplace in dense, infrastructure 802.11 networks [5, 6]. In addition, obstacles such as walls or partitions, lead to additional hidden nodes. Thus it is most desirable to improve analytical estimates of 802.11 network performance by incorporating hidden nodes.

We have two main objectives in this work. The first is to develop an analytic model that provides improved estimates of 802.11 network in the presence of hidden nodes. To this end we extend the Bianchi's model [1] as described next. In the Bianchi's model, the state of a node is observed at slot times, called embedded epochs from now on, where the backoff counter of the node are decremented by one. Assuming that the collision probability of a node is constant, the backoff counter and the backoff stage at each embedded epoch form a two dimensional discrete time Markov chain (DTMC). The performance of the IEEE 802.11 DCF is then analyzed by using the stationary distribution of the DTMC. It is assumed in the Bianchi's model that the network does not have any hidden nodes, so that all embedded epochs of all nodes in the network are *almost* synchronized and hence the use of a single DTMC suffices for analysis. However, in the presence of hidden nodes, the embedded epochs of nodes are not well synchronized, i.e., a node may decrease its backoff counter when a hidden node transmits or freezes its backoff counter. To capture such characteristics of the hidden node problem, we consider *different DTMCs for different nodes* and compute the collision probability of each node in a completely different way, distinct from the Bianchi's model. As a result, we compute the per-node throughput of each node separately, that in turn allows us to investigate network *unfairness*. As expected, if a node has more hidden nodes than others, the per-node throughput of the node worsens relatively. In addition, we see that 802.11 WLANs

MSWiM'13, November 3–8, 2013, Barcelona, Spain.

http://dx.doi.org/10.1145/2507924.2507947.

[1]The carrier sensing range is the range inside which the received signal power at any receive node exceeds a sensing threshold value [3]. Any nodes that lie within the same carrier sensing range of each other, cannot transmit simultaneously.

with RTS/CTS enabled performs better than WLANs with basic access mode as reported in [7, 8], so it is recommended to use the RTS/CTS mode in the presence of hidden nodes. We validate our analytic model through simulation by using different types of network topologies both in the basic access mode and in the RTS/CTS mode. The per-node throughputs from simulation and our analytic model are compared, and we see that our analytic results are well matched with the simulation results.

Our second objective is to mitigate the unfairness problem in per-node throughput due to hidden nodes. By observing the reasons underlying the unfairness, e.g., the nodes with more hidden nodes have less transmission opportunities than those with fewer hidden nodes, we propose a new algorithm, called the *fake collision algorithm*, where the nodes with more hidden nodes are allowed to acquire more transmission opportunities than in the Binary Exponential Backoff (BEB) algorithm. To this end in the fake collision algorithm, when a node transmits its packet successfully, it stochastically *increases* its backoff stage by one according to the fake collision probability, thereby falsely mimicing a packet collision. More details are given in Section 3. Obviously, the higher the fake collision probability of a node, the fewer transmission opportunities it has. The fake collision probability thus acts a control parameter. We develop a computation algorithm to obtain the fake collision probability for each node that can achieve given feasible target ratios in per-node throughput. It is anticipated that introduction of the fake collision probabilities will cause a degradation in network throughput, but we show through simulation that this degradation is negligible.

Several works have attempted to modeling the hidden node problem [9]-[13]. The performance under unsaturated traffic condition is considered in [9, 10]. In [9], all nodes are assumed to have the same number of hidden nodes, a clearly impractical scenario. Uplink and downlink throughputs are analytically derived in [10], but they do not consider the unfairness problem. In [11] the authors consider a special case where the number of nodes in the carrier sensing range is the same as the number of hidden nodes and investigate the throughput performance in the presence of hidden nodes. To solve the unsynchronization problem caused by hidden nodes (i.e., while a node transmits its packet, its hidden node still decreases its backoff counter) in the mathematical modeling, a new DTMC is proposed where embedded epochs are extended to all time points with fixed interval in [12]. [13] categorizes the collisions induced by a hidden node based on the packet transmission times of the hidden node. Most of previous studies investigate network throughput but per-node throughput is not investigated. In this paper, we propose a mathematical model to analyze the per-node throughput and this is essential to investigate fairness in per-node throughput.

Fairness issue in the hidden node problem is studied in [14]-[22]. In [14], the fairness problem when the packet length is variable is investigated in ad-hoc networks and a new algorithm is proposed to achieve fairness in the case. In [15, 16] they solve the hidden and exposed node problem by using power control algorithms. The fairness issues in the performance of the TCP protocol in ad-hoc networks with the IEEE 802.11 DCF is considered in [17]-[19], and the performance of the UDP protocol in ad-hoc networks with the IEEE 802.11 DCF is also studied in [20]. The unfairness in the three-flow problem is studied in [21] and its generalization is done in [22]. Previous studies on fairness consider ad-hoc networks, but the current use of IEEE 802.11 is mostly in infrastructure networks. Moreover the probability of the presence of hidden nodes is high in infrastructure networks because of the widespread use of smartphones, laptop computers and etc. To the best of our knowledge, our work is the first work to deal with fairness in per-node throughput in an infrastructure network and to propose an algorithm to solve the unfairness problem.

The organization of this paper is as follows. In Section 2, we develop an analytic model to analyze the per-node throughput of the IEEE 802.11 DCF infrastructure network with hidden nodes. We validate our analytic model through simulation and investigate the per-node throughput and fairness of the IEEE 802.11 WLAN in the presence of hidden nodes. In Section 3, the fake collision algorithm is proposed to mitigate unfairness due to hidden nodes. In Section 4, we give our conclusions.

2. SYSTEM MODEL

We consider an IEEE 802.11 infrastructure network with a single Access Point (AP). There are N nodes in the network including the AP. All nodes always have packets to transmit and use a single transmission rate. In the infrastructure network, we assume that all nodes except the AP always transmit their packets (such as RTS (Request-To-Send), CTS (Clear-To-Send), data packets, etc.) to the AP for communication, i.e., there are no direct communications between nodes except the AP. We do not consider the capture effect [23] in this paper, so any simultaneous transmissions by nodes always result in collision.

In this paper, we consider two transmission modes - the basic access mode and the RTS/CTS mode. While a winning node (backoff counter reaches 0) transmits its data packet in the basic access mode, a node first transmits an RTS packet in the RTS/CTS mode. To consider both modes in a single mathematical framework, we use the term *the first packet* to denote the packet to be transmitted first by a node with backoff counter 0 in both modes. We implicitly assume that there are no other sources of packet loss such as link failure except packet collisions.

2.1 Carrier Sensing Range

Suppose that node i denotes a source node, and $d(i,j)$ is the distance between nodes i and j. The received signal power at node j is then given by $\frac{P_{tx,i}\lambda_w^2}{16\pi^2 d(i,j)^n}$ [3], where $P_{tx,i}$ is the transmit power of node i, λ_w is the wavelength and n is the path loss exponent. If the received signal power at node j is greater (lower) than the carrier sensing threshold $\gamma_{cs,j}$ of node j, node j determines that the channel is busy (idle). Let $R_{cs,ij}$ denote the distance from node i at which the received signal power at node j is equal to $\gamma_{cs,j}$, i.e.

$$\gamma_{cs,j} = \frac{P_{tx,i}\lambda_w^2}{16\pi^2 R_{cs,ij}^n} \quad \text{or} \quad R_{cs,ij} = (\frac{P_{tx,i}\lambda_w^2}{16\pi^2\gamma_{cs,j}})^{1/n}.$$

If $d(i,j) < R_{cs,ij}$, then node j can sense the transmission of node i, and if $d(i,j) > R_{cs,ij}$, then node j cannot sense the transmission of node i, i.e., node i is hidden from node j.

Suppose that node i can sense all nodes in the network, then it freezes its backoff counter whenever any node in the network transmits and consequently node i minimizes the probability of collisions through channel sensing. If however node i can sense few nodes, it consequently experiences relatively high collision probability. So the carrier sensing range structure is one of key parameters in determining the per-node throughput of the WLAN.

In the following subsection, we introduce the carrier sensing (CS) matrix to represent the carrier sensing range structure of an arbitrary network. Note that the AP and any node in the network can sense each other. We assume that all nodes have the same carrier sensing threshold and use the same fixed transmit power, i.e. $P_{tx} := P_{tx,i}$, $\gamma_{cs} := \gamma_{cs,j}$ and $R_{cs} := R_{cs,ij}$.

2.2 The CS matrix

Let $M_{cs} = (m_{ij})$ be the matrix whose (i,j)-th element, m_{ij}, is 1 if the distance $d(i,j) < R_{cs}$ and equals 0 otherwise. Note that the matrix M_{cs} is symmetric by our assumption. Since we assume that the infrastructure network topology is known *a priori*, the matrix M_{cs} is also pre-determined. The topology is assumed to be static, so that M_{cs} is fixed.

From the matrix M_{cs}, we can determine, for any source node, all hidden nodes. Hence for source node i, all other nodes can be classified into two categories as follows, denoting the sensed and hidden node sets, respectively.

$$\begin{aligned} C(i) &= \{j \in \{1,2,\cdots,N\}\backslash\{i\} | d(i,j) < R_{cs}\}, \\ H(i) &= \{j \in \{1,2,\cdots,N\}\backslash\{i\} | d(i,j) > R_{cs}\}. \end{aligned}$$

2.3 Collision Probability Analysis

For node i, $1 \le i \le N$, we develop its state transition diagram as in [1], by extending the Bianchi's model to consider the interference by hidden nodes. When $i = N$, node N denotes the AP in the model. Let η be the number of slot times to transmit the first packet - a data packet in the basic access mode and an RTS packet in the RTS/CTS mode, and $p_{i,c}$ be the collision probability when node i transmits a packet. Note that the collision probabilities can be different from node to node due to different hidden nodes. Hence, each node has its own state transition diagram as follows. For node i, by taking the time epochs where the backoff counter of node i is decreased by 1 as the embedded points of node i and using the same method as in [1], we can develop the state transition diagram of $\{(BS_i(k), BC_i(k))\}$ where $BS_i(k)$ and $BC_i(k)$ are the backoff stage and the backoff counter values of node i at the k-th embedded point, respectively.

To compute the collision probability $p_{i,c}$ of node i when node i transmits its first packet at the time epoch that backoff counter is 0, recall that the first packet of node i is successfully transmitted only when it is not interfered by any other transmissions of the other nodes during its transmission.

Suppose that node i starts to transmit its first packet at time t, i.e., time t is an embedded point of node i and the backoff counter of node i is 0 at time t. Note that the embedded points of node i can be different from those of the other nodes. So if node i is not the AP, then there are two possible cases - case 1 where time t is also an embedded point of the AP and case 2 where time t is not an embedded point of the AP. If node i is the AP, i.e., $i = N$, only case 1 can occur. If time t is also an embedded point of the AP (case 1), then there are no other nodes transmitting packets at time t because the AP freezes its backoff counter whenever

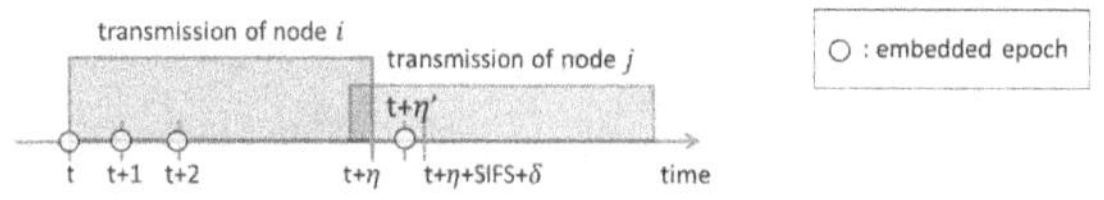

Figure 1: Vulnerable period of node i.

any node in the network transmits. On the other hand, if time t is not an embedded point of the AP (case 2), which implies that the AP freezes its backoff counter at time t, then there exists at least one node that is obviously hidden to node i and is transmitting at time t. In this case, the transmission of node i obviously fails.

Let $P_{em,i}$ denote the probability that an embedded point of node i is also an embedded point of the AP. Observe that the AP always freezes its backoff counter whenever any node transmits a packet. This implies that the set of the embedded points of the AP is a subset of the set of the embedded points of node i. So $P_{em,i}$ is computed by

$$P_{em,i} = \lim_{t\to\infty} \frac{N_N(t)/t}{N_i(t)/t} = \frac{E[T_i]}{E[T_N]}, \tag{1}$$

where $N_i(t)$ is the number of embedded points of node i during $[0,t]$ and $E[T_i]$ is the expected length of two consecutive embedded points of node i. Note here that $N_N(t)$ and $E[T_N]$ are the number of embedded points of the AP and the expected length of two consecutive embedded points of the AP, respectively. The derivation of $E[T_i], 1 \le i \le N$, will be done in the next subsection.

The collision probability $p_{i,c}$ of node i is then given as follows:

$$p_{i,c} = (1 - P_{em,i}) \times 1 + P_{em,i} \times P\{F_i|E_i\},$$

where E_i is the event that an embedded point of node i is also an embedded point of the AP and F_i is the event that the transmission of node i is interfered by other nodes.

To compute $P\{F_i|E_i\}$, suppose that node i starts to transmit its first packet at time t, which is also an embedded point of the AP. We consider two cases - one for a pair of (i,j) with $j \in H(i)$ and the other for a pair of (i,j) with $j \in C(i)$.

For $(i,j), j \in H(i)$, note that the transmission instants of nodes i and j are not mutually known. If the transmission of the first packet by node i is interfered by node j for at least one slot time or more, the transmission by node i fails. This implies that the vulnerable period of node i due to node $j \in H(i)$ is at least of length η slots. In addition, when the AP successfully receives the first packet from node i at time $t + \eta + \delta$ where δ is the propagation delay, it waits $SIFS$ and then transmits the ACK or CTS packet. So, if node j transmits within $\delta + SIFS$ after the end of the packet transmission by node i, the AP cannot transmit successfully the ACK or CTS packet. This observation suggests that the vulnerable period of node i should be $[t, t + \eta + SIFS + \delta)$, denoted by $I(t,\eta)$, as in Fig. 1. Let τ_{ij}^h denote the probability that node $j \in H(i)$ transmits its first packet during a vulnerable period $I(t,\eta)$ of node i when time t is an embedded point of the AP. Note that $\eta + SIFS + \delta$ may not be an integer, so we let η' be the largest integer which is less than $\eta + SIFS + \delta$ for the analysis. Then τ_{ij}^h is computed as follows:

$$\begin{aligned}\tau_{ij}^h &:= P\{\text{node } j \text{ transmits its first packet during } I(t,\eta) \\ &\qquad \mid \text{time } t \text{ is an embedded point of the AP}\} \\ &= \sum_{s=0}^{M} \sum_{b=0}^{min\{\eta',W_s-1\}} \pi_{j;s,b}, \end{aligned} \tag{2}$$

where M is the maximum backoff stage, W_s is the window size of backoff stage s and $\{\pi_{j;s,b}\}$ denote the steady state probabilities of $\{(BS_j(k), BC_j(k)\}$ of node j, i.e.,

$$\pi_{j;s,b} := \lim_{k\to\infty} P\{BS_j(k) = s,\ BC_j(k) = b\}.$$

Similar to the Bianchi's model, $\{\pi_{j;s,b}\}$ are given by

$$\begin{aligned}\pi_{j;s,b} &= \frac{W_s - b}{W_s}\pi_{j;s,0},\ \pi_{j;s,0} = \begin{cases} p_{j,c}^s \pi_{j;0,0} & \text{for } 0 \le s < M \\ \frac{p_{j,c}^M}{1-p_{j,c}}\pi_{j;0,0} & \text{for } s = M \end{cases} \\ \pi_{j;0,0} &= \frac{2(1-2p_{j,c})(1-p_{j,c})}{(1-2p_{j,c})(W+1) + p_{j,c}W(1-(2p_{j,c})^M)}. \end{aligned} \tag{3}$$

For the detailed derivation of (3), refer to [1].

For a pair of $(i,j), j \in C(i)$, the vulnerable period due to node j in $C(i)$ is just one slot time as in the Bianchi's model because two nodes i and j can sense each other. Let τ_{ij} be the probability that node j transmits at an arbitrary embedded point. Then τ_{ij} is given by

$$\tau_{ij} = \sum_{s=0}^{M} \pi_{j;s,0}. \tag{4}$$

Since τ_{ij}^h and τ_{ij} do not depend on i, we use $\tau_j^h := \tau_{ij}^h$ and $\tau_j := \tau_{ij}$ henceforth.

We are now ready to compute the collision probability $p_{i,c}$ of node i. By combining the above results and using the assumption that all nodes behave independently, $p_{i,c}$ is computed as follows:

$$\begin{aligned} p_{i,c} &= 1 - P_{em,i} + P_{em,i} \times P\{F_i|E_i\} \\ &= 1 - P_{em,i} + P_{em,i} \times (1 - \prod_{j\in C(i)}(1-\tau_j)\prod_{j\in H(i)}(1-\tau_j^h)) \\ &= 1 - P_{em,i} \times \prod_{j\in C(i)}(1-\tau_j)\prod_{j\in H(i)}(1-\tau_j^h). \end{aligned} \tag{5}$$

Using $p_{i,c}$ obtained above and $\{\pi_{i,s,b}\}$ given in (3), we can recursively compute the collision probabilities $p_{i,c}$ and $\{\pi_{i,s,b}\}$ for all nodes, provided that we know $E[T_i]$ for all $i, 1 \le i \le N$. The derivation of $E[T_i]$, $1 \le i \le N$, is given in the next subsection.

2.4 Throughput

In this subsection, we compute $E[T_i]$ and the per-node throughput of node i, denoted by S_i, for $1 \le i \le n$. Let L_i be the amount of a payload successfully transmitted by node i between two consecutive embedded points of node i and T_i be the length of two consecutive embedded points of node i, called a virtual slot of node i, in steady state. Then S_i is defined by

$$S_i = \frac{E[L_i]}{E[T_i]}. \tag{6}$$

We call T_i the length of a virtual slot of node i.

By some abuse of notation, we use the same terminology for both the basic access mode and the RTS/CTS mode, in the expectation that the two are distinguishable. For the basic access mode, we use

$$\begin{aligned} T_s &= H + E[P] + SIFS + \delta + ACK + DIFS + \delta, \\ T_c &= H + E[P] + DIFS + \delta, \\ T_s^h &= ACK + DIFS + \delta, \end{aligned}$$

and for the RTS/CTS mode, we use

$$\begin{aligned} T_s &= RTS + SIFS + \delta + CTS + SIFS + \delta \\ &\quad + H + E[P] + SIFS + \delta + ACK + DIFS + \delta, \\ T_c &= RTS + DIFS + \delta, \\ T_s^h &= CTS + SIFS + \delta \\ &\quad + H + E[P] + SIFS + \delta + ACK + DIFS + \delta \end{aligned}$$

where H and P are the time durations to transmit the packet header and the packet payload, respectively, and RTS, CTS and ACK are the time durations to transmit these packets.

Note here that T_s^h is the time duration of a virtual slot where node i cannot sense a transmission by its hidden node in the network but the transmission by the hidden node results in a success. This can happen if node i receives the ACK packet in the basic access mode and the CTS packet in the RTS/CTS mode from the AP. In this case, node i freezes its backoff counter only after it receives the ACK packet in the basic access mode and the CTS packet in the RTS/CTS mode from the AP. This is the explanation why T_s^h is of the form given above.

Virtual slots of node i are classified into four types.

1) The first type of a virtual slot of node i occurs when there are no transmissions by any nodes in $\tilde{C}(i) := C(i) \cup \{i\}$ and no successful transmission by any nodes in $H(i)$. During the first type of a virtual slot, node i does not freeze its backoff counter so the length of the virtual slot in this case is σ. So we have

$$\begin{aligned} &P\{T_i \text{ is of the first type}\} = (1-P_{tr,i})(1-P_{s,i}^h), \\ &E[T_i|T_i \text{ is of the first type}] = \sigma, \end{aligned}$$

where $P_{tr,i} = 1 - \prod_{j\in\tilde{C}(i)}(1-\tau_j)$ is the probability that at least one node including node i transmits and the transmission is sensed by node i, and $P_{s,i}^h = \sum_{j\in H(i)} \tau_j(1-p_{j,c})$ is the probability that one of hidden nodes to node i successfully transmits its transmission.

2) The second type of a virtual slot of node i occurs when there are no transmissions by any nodes in $\tilde{C}(i)$ but there is a successful transmission by a hidden node in $H(i)$. Note that node i cannot freeze its backoff counter during the transmission of the first packet by a hidden node in $H(i)$ but node i can freeze its backoff counter after the AP acknowledges. Let α be the probability that the first packet of the hidden node is being successfully transmitted during the second type of a virtual slot. Then we have $\alpha = (H + E[P])/T_s$ in the basic access and $\alpha = RTS/T_s$ in the RTS/CTS mode. It follows

that

$$P\{T_i \text{ is of the second type}\} = (1 - P_{tr,i})P^h_{s,i},$$
$$P\{T_i \text{ is of the second type and the first packet is being transmitted during } T_i\} = (1 - P_{tr,i})P^h_{s,i}\alpha,$$
$$P\{T_i \text{ is of the second type and a packet other than the first packet is transmitted during } T_i\} = (1 - P_{tr,i})P^h_{s,i}(1 - \alpha),$$
$$E[T_i|T_i \text{ is of the second type and the first packet is being transmitted during } T_i] = \sigma,$$
$$E[T_i|T_i \text{ is of the second type and a packet other than the first packet is transmitted during } T_i] = T^h_s.$$

In the above, the first packet means the first packet of the hidden node which successfully transmits the packet.

3) The third type of a virtual slot of node i occurs when there occurs a successful transmission by a node in $\tilde{C}(i)$. Note that node i can sense any transmission from any node in $\tilde{C}(i)$ and hence freezes its backoff counter. So we have

$$P\{T_i \text{ is of the third type}\} = P_{s,i},$$
$$E[T_i|T_i \text{ is of the third type}] = T_s,$$

where $P_{s,i} = \sum_{j\in\tilde{C}(i)} \tau_j(1 - p_{j,c})$ is the probability that a node including node i whose transmission is sensed by node i, transmits successfully.

4) The fourth type of a virtual slot of node i occurs when there is at least one transmission by one of nodes in $\tilde{C}(i)$ but it is not successful. In this case, the backoff counter of node i is freezed for a time duration of length T_c. So we have

$$P\{T_i \text{ is of the fourth type}\} = P_{tr,i} - P_{s,i},$$
$$E[T_i|T_i \text{ is of the fourth type}] = T_c.$$

By using the above results and unconditioning on the types of a virtual slot of node i, we have the following.

$$E[T_i] = (1 - P_{tr,i})[(1 - P^h_{s,i})\sigma + P^h_{s,i}(\alpha\sigma + (1 - \alpha)T^h_s)] + P_{s,i}T_s + (P_{tr,i} - P_{s,i})T_c. \quad (7)$$

In addition, since L_i is the amount of a payload successfully transmitted by node i during a virtual slot of length T_i, we have

$$E[L_i] = \tau_i(1 - p_{i,c})P. \quad (8)$$

By plugging (7) and (8) into (6), we compute the per-node throughput S_i of node i..

The network throughput S is then given by $S = \sum_{i=1}^{N} S_i$. Note that, if $C(i) \cup \{i\} = \{1, 2, \cdots, N\}$, i.e., there are no hidden nodes in the network, all values mentioned in this section become identical to those of the Bianchi's model.

2.5 Model validation

We validate our model by comparing our analytic results with simulation results conducted in MATLAB. For the physical (PH) layer, Frequency Hopping Spread Spectrum (FHSS) is assumed [24]. Transmission power P_{tx} = 15 dBm, wavelength λ_w = 12.5 cm, carrier sensing threshold is −70 dBm and the path loss exponent n = 2.9. In this case, R_{cs} = 35.49 m. The length of a payload is fixed to 4600 bits and the data rate is 1 Mbps. In this case, η' is 100 in the basic access mode and 6 in the RTS/CTS mode. Simulation time of each run is 10^8 slot times.

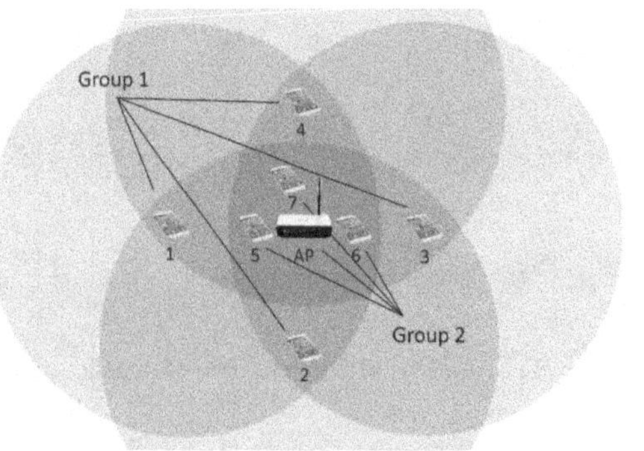

Figure 2: Network topology

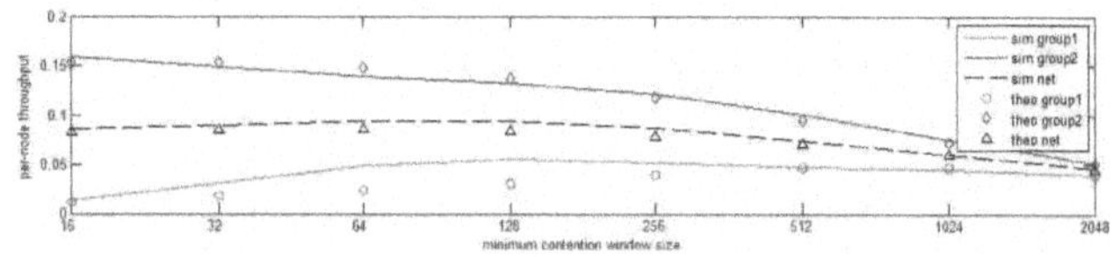

(a) Basic access

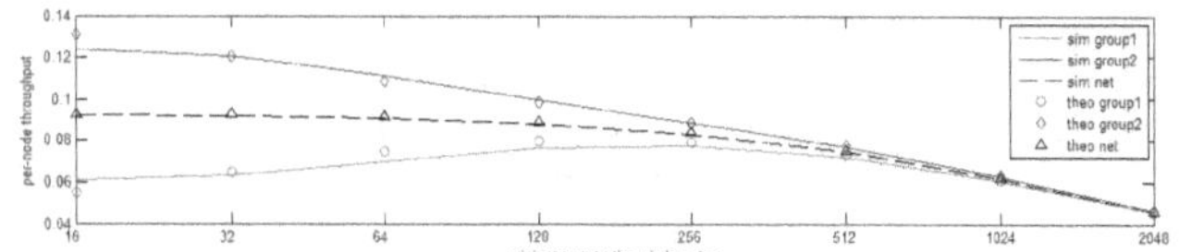

(b) RTS/CTS

Figure 3: Model validation

The network topology shown in Fig. 2 is used to validate our model. The gray areas in Fig. 2 are the carrier sensing ranges of nodes. We write the index of each node in Fig. 2 to avoid confusion. 3 nodes are near the AP and 4 other nodes are 20 m away from the AP and placed at the different vertices of a square whose center is the AP. In the network, nodes $1, 2, 3, 4$ and nodes $5, 6, 7, 8$ form groups 1 and 2, respectively. The 8th node is the AP. Nodes in group 2 can sense all nodes in the network and nodes in group 1 have one hidden node in group 1 as shown in Fig. 2. For example, node 1 and node 3 are hidden from each other and both are in the carrier sensing ranges of node 2, node 4 as well as all nodes in group 2. Fig. 3 shows the per-node throughput of each group in this case. The maximum backoff stage M is fixed to 5 in this paper. In the figure, 'net' means the network throughput divided by the number of nodes N. In addition, 'sim' means the simulation results and 'theo' means the analytic results obtained in the previous subsections. As shown in the figure, both simulation and analytic results are well matched, especially for the RTS/CTS mode. In addition, we see the unfairness between two groups, and the unfairness problem is less significant in the RTS/CTS mode.

From our analysis, we conclude that the RTS/CTS mode is recommended in the presence of hidden nodes in the IEEE 802.11 WLAN. However, RTS/CTS does not resolve the unfairness problem unless the minimum window size W is relatively large. Refer to Fig. 3. Since such a large value of W degrades network throughput as shown in Fig. 3, we

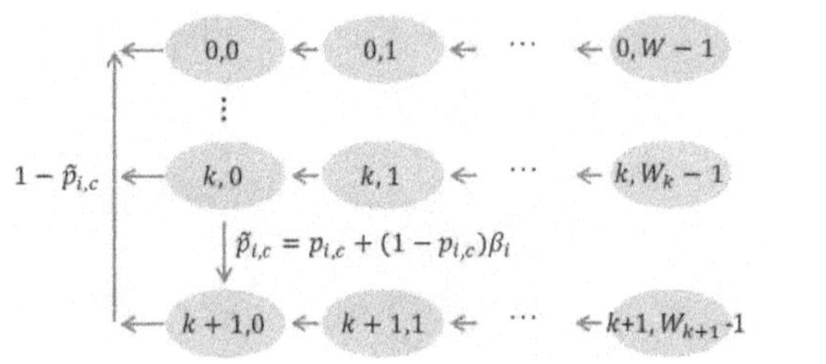

Figure 4: Transition diagram for the fake collision

propose a new solution to fix the unfairness problem while preserving network throughput in the next section.

3. FAKE COLLISION ALGORITHM

According to the Binary Exponential Backoff (BEB) algorithm of the IEEE 802.11, if a node transmits a packet successfully, its backoff stage is reset to 0. Suppose that node 1 and node 2 are hidden from each other and that node 2 has a topological benefit, e.g., node 2 has only 1 hidden node whereas node 1 has more hidden nodes. In this case, since node 2 can sense all nodes except node 1, it experiences less packet collisions. On the other hand, since node 1 has more hidden nodes than node 2, node 1 experiences more packet collisions and sees relatively higher backoff stages. Thus node 2 acquires more transmission opportunities than node 1. From our simulation study, we see that node 1 maintains its backoff stage close to the maximum, while the backoff stage of node 2 is close to 0.

The objective of the fake collision algorithm is to allow a node having more hidden nodes to acquire more transmission opportunities than in the BEB algorithm of the IEEE 802.11. Thus if node i transmits successfully, it increases its backoff stage by one with probability β_i as if the transmission failed, or it changes its backoff stage to 0 with probability $1-\beta_i$ as in the BEB algorithm. When $\beta_i = 0$, then the fake collision algorithm is the same as the BEB algorithm of the IEEE 802.11. To achieve fairness in terms of per-node throughput, a correct choice of the fake collision probability β_i of node i, is critical. Obviously, the fake collision probability β_i depends on the local topology around node i. The fake collision probability β_i is calculated based on our model developed in the previous section with appropriate modification. Since node i increases its backoff stage by one with probability β_i even when it transmits successfully, the transition diagram for the embedded Markov chain of node i is modified as given in Fig. 4. So $\pi_{i;0,0}$ in (3) is changed by replacing $p_{i,c}$ by $\tilde{p}_{i,c}$ as follows:

$$\begin{aligned}\tilde{p}_{i,c} &= p_{i,c} + (1-p_{i,c})\beta_i, \qquad (9)\\ \pi_{i;0,0} &= \frac{2(1-2\tilde{p}_{i,c})(1-\tilde{p}_{i,c})}{(1-2\tilde{p}_{i,c})(W+1)+\tilde{p}_{i,c}W(1-(2\tilde{p}_{i,c})^M)}.\end{aligned}$$

Expressions for $P_{tr,i}$, $P_{s,i}$ and $E[L_i]$ are the same as in the previous section because the expressions of τ_i and $\tau_i(1-p_{i,c})$ are not affected by the introduction of the fake collision probability β_i.

Now suppose that the target ratios $(R_1, R_2, \cdots, R_{N-1})$ are given where $R_1 = \frac{S_N}{S_1}, R_2 = \frac{S_N}{S_2}, \cdots, R_{N-1} = \frac{S_N}{S_{N-1}}$. Then, by using the expressions of the per-node throughputs S_i given in (6) and using the target ratios $(R_1, R_2, \cdots, R_{N-1})$ we can numerically solve for the fake collision probabilities $\beta_i, 1 \le i \le N$. The computation algorithm to get the solution, denoted by $(\beta_1^*, \beta_2^*, \cdots, \beta_N^*)$, is provided in the next subsection.

3.1 Computation Algorithm for finding Fake Collision Probabilities

To explain our computation algorithm, we first derive two important equations on the system behavior. From (6) and (8), we know $E[T_i] = \frac{\tau_i(1-p_{i,c})P}{S_i}$, from which we have, with the help of (1),

$$P_{em,i} = \frac{S_N}{S_i}\cdot\frac{\tau_i(1-p_{i,c})}{\tau_N(1-p_{N,c})}. \qquad (10)$$

Combining (10) with (5) yields

$$p_{i,c} = 1 - \frac{S_N}{S_i}\cdot\frac{\tau_i(1-p_{i,c})}{\tau_N(1-p_{N,c})}\prod_{j\in C(i)}(1-\tau_j)\prod_{j\in H(i)}(1-\tau_j^h).$$

Supposing that $p_{i,c} < 1$, which is obviously true in practice, the above equation is reduced to

$$1 = \frac{S_N}{S_i}\cdot\frac{\tau_i}{\tau_N(1-p_{N,c})}\prod_{j\in C(i)}(1-\tau_j)\prod_{j\in H(i)}(1-\tau_j^h). \qquad (11)$$

Furthermore, since $p_{N,c} = 1-\prod_{1\le j\le N-1}(1-\tau_j)$ from (5), (11) becomes

$$1 = \frac{S_N}{S_i}\cdot\frac{\tau_i(1-\tau_N)}{\tau_N(1-\tau_i)}\prod_{j\in H(i)}\frac{(1-\tau_j^h)}{1-\tau_j}, 1\le i\le N-1. \qquad (12)$$

Suppose that $\beta_i^*, 1\le i\le N$, form a solution for the target ratios $(R_1,\cdots,R_{N-1})$. Let $\tilde{p}_{i,c}^*, 1\le i\le N$, be the resulting values computed from (9) and $\tau_i^{h*}, \tau_i^*, 1\le i\le N$, be the probabilities corresponding to $\tilde{p}_{i,c}^*$, computed from (2) and (4). Let $p_{i,c}^*, 1\le i\le N$, be the resulting (actual) collision probabilities when we use the solution $\beta_i^*, 1\le i\le N$.

Since $\beta_i^*, 1\le i\le N-1$, are a solution, (12) yields

$$1 = R_i\cdot\frac{\tau_i^*(1-\tau_N^*)}{\tau_N^*(1-\tau_i^*)}\prod_{j\in H(i)}\frac{(1-\tau_j^{h*})}{1-\tau_j^*}, 1\le i\le N-1. \qquad (13)$$

Moreover, from (1) and (5) the collision probabilities $p_{i,c}^*, 1\le i\le N$, satisfy

$$p_{i,c}^* = 1 - \prod_{j\in C(i)}(1-\tau_j^*)\prod_{j\in H(i)}(1-\tau_j^{h*})\frac{E[T_i^*]}{E[T_N^*]} \qquad (14)$$

where $E[T_i^*]$ and $E[T_N^*]$ are the values of $E[T_i]$ and $E[T_N]$ from (7) corresponding to $p_{i,c}^*, 1\le i\le N$.

From (13) and (14) we have the following observations.

Observation 1. Suppose that β_N^* is given. $(\tau_1^*, \tau_2^*, \cdots, \tau_N^*)$ in (13) can be found as follows. First, observe that $p_{N,c}^* = 1-\prod_{1\le j\le N-1}(1-\tau_j^*)$ and β_N^* is given. So $\tilde{p}_{N,c}^*$ (and accordingly τ_N^*) can be computed from (9) if we know the point $(\tau_1^*, \tau_2^*, \cdots, \tau_{N-1}^*)$, equivalently, $(\tilde{p}_{1,c}^*, \tilde{p}_{2,c}^*, \cdots, \tilde{p}_{N-1,c}^*)$.

Let A_i be defined by

$$A_i := R_i\cdot\frac{\tau_i(1-\tau_N)}{\tau_N(1-\tau_i)}\prod_{j\in H(i)}\frac{(1-\tau_j^h)}{1-\tau_j}, 1\le i\le N-1,$$

which come from the right hand side of (13). Then A_i is a function of $(\tilde{p}_{1,c},\cdots,\tilde{p}_{N-1,c})$, i.e., $A_i = A_i(\tilde{p}_{1,c},\cdots,\tilde{p}_{N-1,c})$ because τ_i is a function of $\tilde{p}_{i,c}$ for $1\le i\le N$ and $\tilde{p}_{N,c}$ can be obtained from $(\tau_1,\cdots,\tau_{N-1},\beta_N^*)$ by using (5) and (9).

Now define by $G := (G_1, G_2, \cdots, G_{N-1})$ where

$$G_i := \min(\tilde{p}_{i,c} A_i(\tilde{p}_{1,c}, \cdots, \tilde{p}_{N-1,c}), 1), 1 \leq i \leq N-1.$$

Then G is a continuous function from $[0,1]^{N-1}$ to $[0,1]^{N-1}$. From Brouwer's fixed-point theorem [25][2], we know G has a fixed point $\tilde{p}_c^f := (\tilde{p}_{1,c}^f, \cdots, \tilde{p}_{N-1,c}^f)$, i.e., $\tilde{p}_c^f = G(\tilde{p}_c^f)$. Note that, if the fixed point $\tilde{p}_c^f$ satisfies (13), then we have $\tilde{p}_{i,c}^* = \tilde{p}_{i,c}^f, 1 \leq i \leq N-1$. Conversely, if there exists a solution $(\tilde{p}_{1,c}^*, \tilde{p}_{2,c}^*, \cdots, \tilde{p}_{N-1,c}^*)$, it is obviously a fixed point of G. From this observation, we can compute $(\tilde{p}_{1,c}^*, \tilde{p}_{2,c}^*, \cdots, \tilde{p}_{N-1,c}^*)$ and $\tilde{p}_{N,c}^*$ by examining the fixed points of the function G, provided that $\beta_N^* (= \beta_N)$ is given. Moreover, if all fixed points of G do not satisfy the condition (13), then we know the problem is infeasible for the given β_N.

Observation 2. Suppose that we obtain $(\tilde{p}_{1,c}^*, \tilde{p}_{2,c}^*, \cdots, \tilde{p}_{N,c}^*)$. We next compute $(p_{1,c}^*, p_{2,c}^*, \cdots, p_{N,c}^*)$ that satisfies (14), so that we finally compute the fake collision probabilities $(\beta_1^*, \beta_2^*, \cdots, \beta_{N-1}^*)$. As before, since

$$p_{N,c}^* = 1 - \prod_{1 \leq j \leq N-1} (1 - \tau_j^*),$$

it suffices to compute $(p_{1,c}^*, p_{2,c}^*, \cdots, p_{N-1,c}^*)$. To this end, define by $K := (K_1, \cdots, K_{N-1})$ where, for $1 \leq i \leq N-1$

$$\begin{aligned} K_i &= K_i(p_{1,c}, p_{2,c}, \cdots, p_{N-1,c}) \\ &:= 1 - \prod_{j \subset C(i)} (1 - \tau_j^*) \prod_{j \in H(i)} (1 - \tau_j^{h*}) \frac{E[T_i]}{E[T_N]}, \end{aligned}$$

which come from the right hand side of (14). Recalling from (7) that $E[T_i]$ and $E[T_N]$ are continuous functions of $p_{i,c}, 1 \leq i \leq N$, it is easy to show that K is a continuous function from $[0,1]^{N-1}$ to $[0,1]^{N-1}$. From Brouwer's fixed-point theorem [25] again, we see that K has a fixed point. Let $p_c^f := (p_{1,c}^f, p_{2,c}^f, \cdots, p_{N-1,c}^f)$ be a fixed point of K. If the fixed point p_c^f satisfies the condition that $p_{i,c}^f \leq \tilde{p}_{i,c}^*$ (this comes from (9)), then it is a solution of (14), i.e., $p_{i,c}^* = p_{i,c}^f, 1 \leq i \leq N-1$. Conversely, if there exists a solution $(p_{1,c}^*, p_{2,c}^*, \cdots, p_{N-1,c}^*)$, then it is obviously a fixed point of K. From this observation, we can compute $(p_{1,c}^*, p_{2,c}^*, \cdots, p_{N-1,c}^*)$ and $p_{N,c}^*$ by examining the fixed points of the function K. Moreover, if all fixed points of K do not satisfy the condition that $p_{i,c}^f \leq \tilde{p}_{i,c}^*$, then we know the problem is infeasible.

From the above observations, our computation algorithm has the following steps.

Step 0. Set $\beta_N = 0$ and let   be a small positive real number, called the step size.

Step 1. Find a fixed point of G. If the point $(\tau_1^*, \tau_2^*, \cdots, \tau_N^*)$ corresponding to the fixed point of G, satisfies (13), go to Step 2. If no solution of (13) is found, then we increase the value of β_N by   and go to Step 1 until $\beta_N \geq 1$.

Step 2. For $(\tau_1^*, \tau_2^*, \cdots, \tau_N^*)$ that we find in Step 1, we find a solution $(p_{1,c}^*, p_{2,c}^*, \cdots, p_{N,c}^*)$ that satisfies (14), obtain the resulting values of $(\beta_1^*, \beta_2^*, \cdots, \beta_{N-1}^*)$, and set $\beta_N^* = \beta_N$. We keep increasing the value of β_N by   and go to Step 1 until $\beta_N \geq 1$.

[2]Every continuous function from a convex compact subset of a Euclidean space to itself has a fixed point.

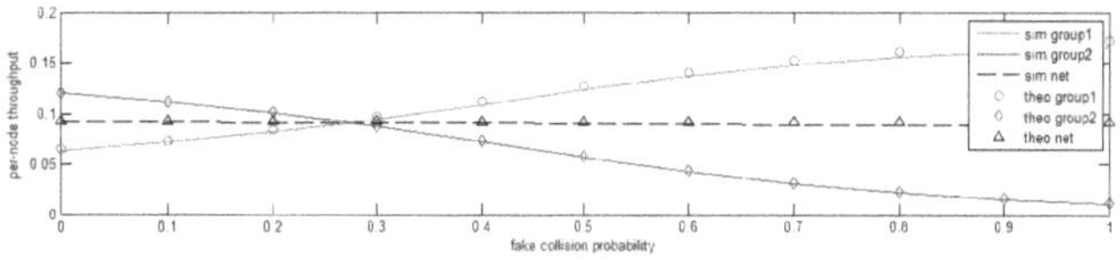

Figure 5: The results for the fake collision algorithm

Step 3. If we find no solution until $\beta_N \geq 1$, then we declare the target ratios $(R_1, R_2, \cdots, R_{N-1})$ are infeasible.

Remark For given target ratios $(R_1, R_2, \cdots, R_{N-1})$ it is obvious that there exist multiple solutions $(\beta_1^*, \beta_2^*, \cdots, \beta_N^*)$. Let V denote the set of all such solutions, called the valid solution set. It is then natural to use the solution $(\beta_1^*, \beta_2^*, \cdots, \beta_N^*)$ in V that maximizes the network throughput, i.e.,

$$argmax_{(\beta_1^*, \beta_2^*, \cdots, \beta_N^*) \in V} \sum_{i=1}^{N} S_i.$$

3.2 Validation

As an example we use $R_i = 1, 1 \leq i \leq N-1$, i.e., $S_1 = S_2 = \cdots = S_N$. To show that there exists a solution $(\beta_1^*, \beta_2^*, \cdots, \beta_N^*)$ to achieve $S_1 = S_2 = \cdots = S_N$, we consider the network in Fig. 2 and the RTS/CTS mode (which is recommended to use in the presence of hidden nodes). In Fig. 5 we plot simulation and analytic results for the per-node throughputs of group 1 and group 2 as we change the fake collision probability of group 2, β_i, $i \in \{5, \cdots, 8\}$ (all of which are the same due to the same topological structure) from 0 to 1. W is fixed to 32 and the fake collision probability of group 1, β_i, $i \in \{1, \cdots, 4\}$ is fixed at 0. We see from simulation that, when the fake collision probability of group 2 is about 0.27, all per-node throughputs are the same. Our analytic model also provides a value of 0.268 for the fake collision probability of group 2. Moreover, we see from the figure that the network throughput is not much degraded by the use of the fake collision probability, validating the usefulness of the fake collision algorithm.

4. CONCLUSIONS

In this paper, we develop an analytic model to analyze the throughput performance of the IEEE 802.11 WLAN with hidden nodes. In the analytic model, the backoff stage and counter of each node are modeled by a two dimensional discrete time Markov chain. By considering the characteristics of hidden nodes' behavior in the analytic model, we can compute the per-node throughput of each node in the network. The analytic model is validated through simulation and we investigate unfairness in per-node throughput due to hidden nodes. To solve unfairness in per-node throughput, we propose the fake collision algorithm where the fake collision probability is introduced to mitigate unfairness in per-node throughput. A computation algorithm to get the desired fake collision probabilities is provided based on our analytic model. We validate that the fake collision algorithm performs well and mitigate unfairness in per-node throughput through simulation.

Acknowledgments

This research was supported by Basic Science Research Program through the National Research Foundation of Korea

(NRF) funded by the Ministry of Education, Science and Technology (2011-0022026).

5. REFERENCES

[1] G. Bianchi, Performance analysis of the IEEE 802.11 distributed coordination function, IEEE . Select. Area Commun., vol.18, no.3, pp.535-547, Mar 2000.

[2] F. Tobagi and L. Kleinrock, Packet Switching in Radio Channels: Part II–The Hidden Terminal Problem in Carrier Sense Multiple-Access and the Busy-Tone Solution, IEEE Trans. Commun.,vol.23, no.12, pp. 1417- 1433, Dec 1975.

[3] H. Ma, R. Vijayakumar, S. Roy, and . hu, Optimizing 802.11 Wireless Mesh Networks Based on Physical Carrier Sensing, IEEE/ACM Trans. Netw., vol.17, no.5, pp.1550-1563, Oct. 2009.

[4] . Deng, B. Liang, P. K. Varshney, Tuning the carrier sensing range of IEEE 802.11 MAC, GLOBECOM '04. IEEE, vol.5, pp. 2987- 2991 Vol.5, 29 Nov.-3 Dec. 2004.

[5] . Tseng, S. Ni and E. Shih, Adaptive Approaches to Relieving Broadcast Storms in a Wireless Multihop Mobile Ad Hoc Network, IEEE Trans. Comput., vol. 52, no. 5, pp. 545-557, May 2003.

[6] L. Hwang, S. Sheu, . Shih, and . Cheng, Grouping strategy for solving hidden node problem in IEEE 802.15.4 LR-WPAN, in: Proceedings of 1st Int. Conf. on Wireless Internet, uly 2005, pp. 26-32.

[7] V. Bharghavan, A. Demers, S. Shenkar, and L. hang, MACAW: A media access protocol for wireless LANs, in Proc. SIGCOMM '94, Aug. 1994, pp. 212-225.

[8] . Weinmiller, H. Woesner, P Ebert, and A. Wolisz, Analyzing the RTS/CTS mechanism in the DFWMAC media access protocol for wireless LANs, in IFIP TC6, 1995.

[9] O. Ekici and A. ongacoglu, IEEE 802.11a Throughput Performance with Hidden Nodes, IEEE Commun. Lett., vol.12, no.6, pp.465-467, une 2008.

[10] . W. ang, . K. Kwon, H. . Hwang, and D. K. Sung, Goodput analysis of a WLAN with hidden nodes under a non-saturated condition, IEEE Trans. Wireless Commun., vol.8, no.5, pp.2259-2264, May 2009.

[11] T. Kim and . Lim, Throughput analysis considering coupling effect in ieee 802.11 networks with hidden stations, IEEE Commun. Lett., vol.13, no.3, pp.175-177, March 2009.

[12] H. Wu, F. hu, Q. hang, and . Niu, WSN02-1: Analysis of IEEE 802.11 DCF with Hidden Terminals, IEEE GLOBECOM ąr06., pp.1-5, Nov. 2006.

[13] A. Tsertou, D. I. Laurenson, and . S. Thompson, A new approach for the throughput analysis of IEEE 802.11 in networks with hidden terminals, Int. Workshop Wireless Ad-hoc Netw., London, U.K., 2005.

[14] . Wang and B. Bensaou, Achieving Fairness in IEEE 802.11 DFWMAC with Variable Packet Lengths, IEEE GLOBECOM ąr01, vol. 6, pp. 3588-3593, 2001.

[15] L.B. iang and S.C. Liew, Improving Throughput and Fairness by Reducing Exposed and Hidden Nodes in 802.11 Networks, IEEE Trans. Mobile Comput., vol. 7, no. 1, pp. 34-49, an. 2008.

[16] . hou and S. M. Nettles, Balancing the hidden and exposed node problems with power control in CSMA/CA-based wireless networks, IEEE WCNC 2005, vol.2, no., pp. 683- 688, March 2005.

[17] S. Xu and T. Saadawi, Does the IEEE 802.11 MAC protocol work well in multihop wireless ad hoc networks , IEEE Commun. Mag., vol.39, no.6, pp.130-137, un 2001.

[18] . Fu, P. erfos, H. Luo, S. Lu, L. hang, and M. Gerla, The impact of multihop wireless channel on TCP throughput and loss, INFOCOM 2003, vol.3, no., pp. 1744- 1753, March 2003.

[19] K. Tang and M. Gerla, Fair Sharing of MAC under TCP in Wireless Ad-hoc Networks, Proc. IEEE MMT ąr99, Venice, Italy, Oct. 1999.

[20] P. C. Ng and S. C. Liew, Re-routing instability in IEEE 802.11 multi-hop ad-hoc networks, the 29th Annual IEEE Int. Conf. on Local Computer Networks, pp. 602- 609, 16-18 Nov. 2004.

[21] C. Chaudet, I. G. Lassous, and B. Gaujal, Study of the impact of asymmetry and carrier sense mechanism in IEEE 802.11 multi-hop networks through a basic case, PE-WASUN ąr04, Venice, Italy, 2004.

[22] A. Margolis, R. Vijayakumar, and S. Roy, Modelling Throughput and Starvation in 802.11 Wireless Networks with Multiple Flows, IEEE GLOBECOM '07, pp. 5123-5127, Nov. 2007.

[23] K. Whitehouse, A. Woo, F. iang, . Polastre, and D. Culler, Exploiting the Capture Effect for Collision Detection and Recovery, IEEE EmNetS-II, May 2005.

[24] IEEE, IEEE Standard for Information Technology-Telecommunications and Information Exchange Between Systems-Local and Metropolitan Area Networks-Specific Requirements - Part 11: Wireless LAN Medium Access Control (MAC) and Physical Layer (PH) Specifications, IEEE Std 802.11-2007, une 2007.

[25] S. Kakutani, A generalization of Brouwer's fixed point theorem, Duke Mathematical ournal, pp. 457-459, 1941.

Hierarchical Modeling of IEEE 802.11 Multi-hop Wireless Networks

Thiago Abreu
Université Lyon 1 - LIP
France
thiago.wanderley@ens-lyon.fr

Bruno Baynat
Université Pierre et Marie Curie - LIP6
France
bruno.baynat@lip6.fr

Thomas Begin
Université Lyon 1 - LIP
France
thomas.begin@ens-lyon.fr

Isabelle Guérin-Lassous
Université Lyon 1 - LIP
France
isabelle.guerin-lassous@ens-lyon.fr

ABSTRACT

IEEE 802.11 is implemented in many wireless networks, including multi-hop networks where communications between nodes are conveyed along a chain. We present a modeling framework to evaluate the performance of flows conveyed through such a chain. Our framework is based on a hierarchical modeling composed of two levels. The lower level is dedicated to the modeling of each node, while the upper level matches the actual topology of the chain. Our approach can handle different topologies, takes into account Bit Error Rate and can be applied to multi-hop flows with rates ranging from light to heavy workloads. We assess the ability of our model to evaluate loss rate, throughput, and end-to-end delay experienced by flows on a simple scenario, where the number of nodes is limited to three. Numerical results show that our model accurately approximates the performance of flows with a relative error typically less than 10%.

Categories and Subject Descriptors

C.4 [**Performance of Systems**]: Modeling techniques

Keywords

Multi-hop wireless chains; Markov Chains; performance evaluation; IEEE 802.11 modeling

1. INTRODUCTION

IEEE 802.11, based on CSMA/CA principles, is one of the leading communication protocols for wireless networks. Its deployment has been largely supported by its distributed property as well as by the simplicity and the low cost associated with its implementation. Various underlying topologies for IEEE 802.11 exist. Clearly, the most frequent example is the infrastructure network, commonly referred to as a WiFi hotspot, where communications occur exclusively between nodes and the access point. Other examples include multi-hop wireless networks, where communications between nodes may involve relay nodes, that act like forwarding entities.

Throughout this paper we refer to the sequence of nodes involved in the communication between two nodes as being a chain. The behavior and associate performance of such a chain can not be easily derived since the latter is subject to many factors, e.g. the number and position of nodes in the chain, and it may exhibit complex phenomena like the freezing period of backoff, the hidden node problem, etc.

Despite these intrinsic complexities, analytical models can represent a convenient means to forecast and explain the performance of flows travelling along a multi-hop wireless network. However, only few models have been proposed for characterizing their behavior. Indeed, most of the analytical studies on IEEE 802.11 are devoted to either cell networks, or multi-hop networks with single-hop flow [2, 11, 5, 9]. Considering the few works dealing with multi-hop flows [1, 6], they consider simplifying assumptions (e.g. buffers with infinite length to queue extra datagrams, ideal physical layer for transmitting frames, specific scenarios where the network is overloaded or even totally saturated) that significantly deviate from some of the fundamental properties arising in IEEE 802.11 chains, and thus they may not be accurate when applied to realistic scenarios.

We present new a modeling framework to evaluate the performance of a flow conveyed through a chain. Our framework is based on a hierarchical modeling composed of two levels. The lower level is dedicated to the modeling of each node, while the upper level takes into account the actual shape (topology) of the chain. Thus, given the shape of the actual chain, the channel degradation pattern due to Bit Error Rate and the rate of the flow conveyed through the chain, the model delivers approximate values for customary performance parameters, e.g. loss rate, throughput, end-to-end delay, using a simple fixed-point iteration between the two modeling levels.

The remainder of the paper is organized as follows. Section 2 reminds the principles of IEEE 802.11 protocol and

MSWiM'13, November 3–8, 2013, Barcelona, Spain.
Copyright 2013 ACM 978-1-4503-2353-6/13/11 ...$15.00.
http://dx.doi.org/10.1145/2507924.2507949.

describes the considered scenario in this work. Section 3 presents our modeling framework. In Section 4, we compare the performance delivered by our model with the actual ones coming from a discrete-event simulator. Section 5 concludes this paper.

2. SYSTEM DESCRIPTION

2.1 IEEE 802.11

In this section, we remind the main principles of IEEE 802.11 DCF protocol [7]. Basically, the transmission of a datagram occurs as follows. First, the node continuously senses the channel until the latter is found to be idle for a time DIFS. Second, the node postpones the transmission of the frame associated to this datagram by a time whose length is randomly drawn within an interval determined by the contention window (also denoted CW hereafter). This latter delay is expressed as a number of slot times and is referred to as the *backoff*. Then, the backoff value is continually decremented (by one) whenever the channel is sensed idle during an entire slot time. If the channel is sensed as busy, the backoff value remains constant. It is said to be in *freezing* state. The backoff quits this freezing state, and hence resumes its decrement, if the channel is sensed idle during a DIFS period. As the backoff value reaches zero, the node can start its transmission. Note that a backoff period can be interrupted several times due to multiple transmissions in its neighborhood.

A node considers that its frame has been successfully transmitted to its neighbor node when it receives the acknowledgment. If the node does not receive an acknowledgment before a timeout, which includes a SIFS, it assumes the corresponding frame has been lost, and thus attempts to retransmit it up to a given limit [7]. Note that at each retransmission of a frame, the contention window size is doubled. If the transmission of a frame as well as the following retransmissions fail, the node simply discards the corresponding datagram. Finally, each successful transmission of a frame (as well as a complete discard) resets the contention window to its initial value.

IEEE 802.11 includes an optional mechanism to avoid collisions, known as RTS/CTS. When activated, prior to each frame transmission, a node sends a RTS (Request-to-Send) frame and should receive a CTS (Clear-to-Send) frame in the aim of getting exclusive use of the channel. Note that since RTS/CTS has been shown to be inefficient in the case of a chain [12], we did not consider it in our study.

2.2 Studied chain and associated scenario

We consider the case of a wireless multi-hop chain with N nodes (labeled from 1 to N). We now itemize the main assumptions regarding our system. First, each node can only communicate with its 1-hop neighbors. Second, the carrier sense range of each node covers all its 2-hop neighbor nodes. Third, we consider a non-perfect physical layer that affects the channel quality, and can cause erroneous frame transmissions. We assume that the Bit Error Rate (BER) does only depend on the distance between nodes. Here, we use the values reported in [8].

We assume that the network chain conveys a single flow, starting at one border node and traveling up to the other border node. The flow may represent the traffic generated by a single (or multiple) user or application. A flow is com-

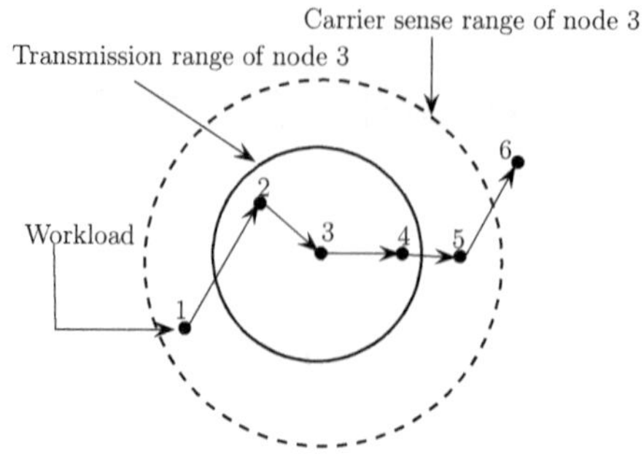

Figure 1: A multi-hop chain with a single flow and N=6 nodes.

posed of equally sized datagrams. The rate at which this flow generates datagrams determines the level of workload of the chain. Note that our system will be described as being in saturation if the flow always have datagrams to be sent across the chain. Figure 1 illustrates a possible example of our system with 6 nodes. As exhibited by this figure, nodes in the chain do not have to be aligned along a straight line, nor being equally spaced as long as they meet the assumptions mentioned above.

We now detail the scenario that will be used as case study throughout the next sections. In this scenario, we consider a multi-hop chain with N=3 nodes that conveys a single flow travelling from node 1 to node 3 through node 2. We position node 2 at different distances in between nodes 1 and 3, and we consider several levels of rates for the flow workload. Clearly, the performance of the flow will vary against the distance between the nodes since each distance leads to a different BER, and thus to a different rate of erroneous frame transmission. Although this scenario does not face the hidden node problem (since all nodes are in the detection range of each other), it has to cope with several other issues, e.g. heavy dependence between nodes, freezing periods of the backoff, recurrent starvation of the relay node.

3. HIERARCHICAL MODELING

We have developed a hierarchical modeling framework for performance evaluation of a general multi-hop wireless chain. Our model is made of two levels: 1) a global high-level queueing network model and 2) several local low-level Markov chain models. In the global model, each queue is associated with a node of the wireless chain, and the routing between queues matches the topology of the chain. In order to parameterize the global model, we use several local Markov chain models, each one being associated to a given queue of the global model, i.e., to a given node of the chain. As a first step in the development of this general framework, we describe our hierarchical model on a simple scenario in Sections 3.1 and 3.2. As detailed in these two subsections, the inputs of the global model are the outputs of the local models, and vice versa. The performance of the resulting model will thus be the solution of a fixed-point iterative algorithm described in Section 3.3.

3.1 Global model

As explained before, in this paper we restrict the description of the model to a simple scenario made of three nodes, 1, 2 and 3, although we believe it can be extended to more

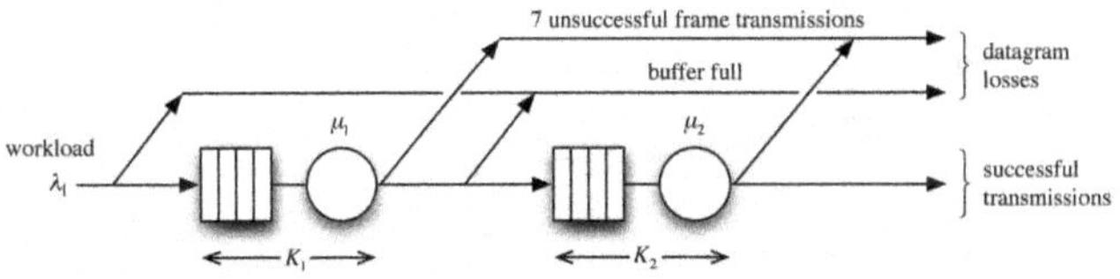

Figure 2: Global queueing model.

complex scenarios. Node 1 generates a flow of datagrams to transmit to node 3, through relay node 2, which has an intermediate position between 1 and 3. We naturally associate with this scenario the queueing network depicted in Figure 2. The customers of this queueing model are the datagrams of the wireless network and both queues have a single server modeling transmission of datagrams. Every single queue of this network corresponds to a node of the system that has to transmit datagrams, i.e., nodes 1 and 2. Indeed, in our simple scenario, node 3 is the receiver and only sends acknowledgment frames.

Each queue i of the model has a single server with rate μ_i and a finite capacity K_i that matches the buffer size of the wireless cards. These finite capacities will result in datagram losses due to buffer overflows. As illustrated in Figure 2, our model also takes into account the other potential cause of datagram losses, that again closely matches IEEE 802.11 specifications, which corresponds to excessive retransmissions. In our model, we consider that, after seven unsuccessful frame transmissions, a datagram is discarded [7]. Finally, it is important to emphasize that our model is a queueing network with a routing that matches the chain structure of our wireless system. Hence, the average number of datagrams that a relay node receives by unit of time and has to transmit over the radio channel, matches the average number of datagrams by unit of time that have been correctly transmitted without error by the preceding node in the chain. As will be seen in the Section 4, this implies that, even in a saturated case where one border node of the chain has always datagrams to transmit, nodes "in the middle" of the chain may not be saturated and can even suffer from starvation. This starvation has a significant impact on the performance of the system.

One important feature of our model lies in the definition of the service times of the different queues. For queue i ($i = 1$ or 2 in our initial simple scenario), the service time of the queue represents the time separating the instant when a datagram is ready to be sent by node i over the radio channel, from the instant where it is either acknowledged or discard because of excessive retransmissions. The service time of a customer of the model thus includes transmission times of all frames that are necessary to transmit the datagram, as well as backoff times preceding any transmission, freezing times of backoff periods due to canal occupation by other transmissions, and all required protocol delays (DIFS SIFS, timeout).

The originality of the model is to include the freezing time of a backoff in the definition of the service of a datagram. By doing so, the model works around the complexity of representing the strong synchronization between the different nodes of the system, namely the fact that, when a node transmits, it not only prevents nodes (that can sense its transmission) to transmit, but also freezes all ongoing backoffs. Instead, we opt for decoupling the two queues of the global model, by including in the definition of the service time of each queue, the average freezing time caused by transmission of the other one. We come up with a desynchronized queueing network model of a strong synchronized system. We really believe that this feature will be crucial to scale up our model to larger scenarios.

In order to solve our queueing model, we first decompose it into two isolated single queues, as illustrated in Figure 3. It is important to emphasize that this was not necessary for the scenario we consider (with only two queues), as we could, under certain assumptions, solve this open queueing network. However, we wanted our methodology to be easily generalizable to more complicated and realistic scenarios, including more than three nodes and independent flows in opposite directions. By decomposing the global model into single queues, we believe that this approach can be extended pretty easily to other scenarios.

The first assumption of this decomposition, consists in assuming that the arrival process at each queue of the network is a Poisson process, resulting in two isolated $M/G/1/K$ queues. Assuming that datagrams are generated by the source (node 1) according to a Poisson process is a classical assumption, made in many papers [2, 4]. Let λ_1 be the rate with which datagrams are injected in the network. Though, in our original queueing model, the output process of queue 1 is generally not Poisson, this assumption will not have a significant impact on the accuracy of the model and drastically simplify its solution.

The second approximation we make, always with the objective of making the model easily tractable and expandable, is to consider that the service times of the two isolated queues are exponentially distributed. The resulting model thus consists in two isolated $M/M/1/K$ queues (see Figure 3) and is therefore very easy to solve, provided that we know the values of the service rates μ_1 and μ_2, as well as those of the datagram loss probabilities p_{d1} and p_{d2} due to excessive retransmissions (outside buffer overflows that are performance parameters of the queueing model). We will derive in the next subsection the estimation of the service rates. Now, as we are only interested here in datagram loss probabilities resulting of seven consecutive unsuccessful frame transmissions, their expressions can directly be obtained from frame error probabilities p_{f_i} as:

$$p_{d_i} = p_{f_i}^{7} \tag{1}$$

A frame transmission error can be the result of the BER (Bit Error Rate) or a collision with another node transmission. In our simple scenario, we assume that the three nodes are within each other carrier sense range, and we can thus consider that no collisions take place in this system. The frame error probability p_{f_i} can then be classically estimated

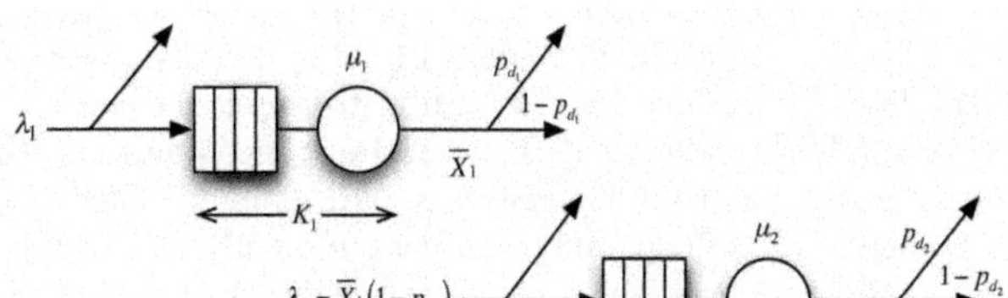

Figure 3: Decoupled queueing model.

from the BER that is function of the distance between the sender (say node i) and the receiver (node $i+1$), extracted from manufacturers card specifications [8].

All performance parameters of our global queueing model can then be obtained from the well known results of the $M/M/1/K$ queue. The output throughput of station i, corresponding to the average number of datagrams that are correctly transmitted by unit of time from node i to node $i+1$, is:

$$\overline{X}_i = \mu_i(1 - \pi_i(0)) \tag{2}$$

where $\pi_i(n)$ is the probability of having n customers in the i-th $M/M/1/K$ isolated queue.

The average number of customers in queue i, corresponding to the average number of datagrams waiting or in transmission at node i, is given by:

$$\overline{Q}_i = \sum_{n=1}^{K_i} n\pi_i(n) \tag{3}$$

From Little's law, we can derive the mean sojourn time of an admitted customer in queue i, corresponding to the average time a datagram that is not lost because of buffer overflow, stays in node i before being transmitted to node $i+1$ (or discarded because of excessive retransmissions):

$$\overline{R}_i = \frac{\overline{Q}_i}{\overline{X}_i} \tag{4}$$

The utilization of queue i, corresponding to the proportion of time node i is not empty, is:

$$\overline{U}_i = 1 - \pi_i(0) \tag{5}$$

And finally, from PASTA theorem, we can obtain the rejection probability, corresponding to the probability that a datagram is rejected because the buffer of the destination node is full at its arrival instant:

$$p_{r_i} = \pi_i(K_i) \tag{6}$$

3.2 Local models

In order to estimate the missing parameters of the global queueing network model, i.e., the rates μ_i ($i = 1, 2$) of the two $M/M/1/K$ queues, we propose to associate with each queue, a Continuous-Time Markov Chain (CTMC) describing precisely the transmission process of a node according to the IEEE 802.11 DCF protocol.

Throughout this subsection, we will then focus on the CTMC associated with each single queue i of the global decomposed model ($i = 1$ or 2). The objective of this CTMC is to provide an estimation of the mean service time S_i, inverse of the service rate μ_i, of the associated $M/M/1/K$ queue i. To do this, the CTMC has to precisely describe the succession of the different states a node has to go through in order to transmit a datagram over the wireless channel. The CTMC is depicted in Figure 4 and is globally made of seven "lines", each one corresponding to a given stage k of the backoff and modeling the backoff time preceding the k-th transmission of a given datagram (provided the $k-1$ preceding transmission of the datagram were in error). Recall that a maximum of seven unsuccessful transmissions is considered for a same frame associated to a datagram, after which the datagram is discarded. In order to simplify the drawing of this CTMC and the derivation of its performance parameters, we remove in the following, unless necessary, the index

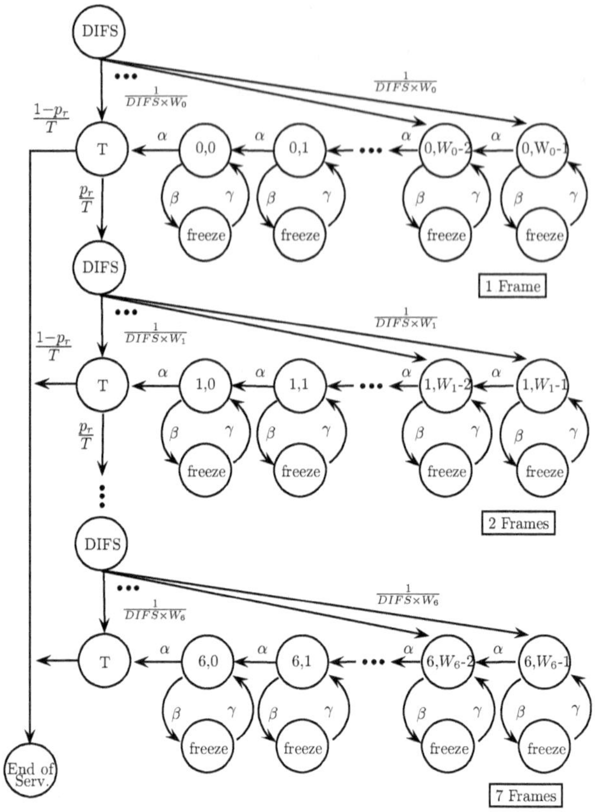

Figure 4: Local CTMC model for each node.

i from all notations (and use for example β instead of β_i). Let us however remind that there is a CTMC (with different parameters) associated with each transmitting node i.

As explained in Section 2, any transmission attempt starts with a DIFS time and then enters a backoff procedure, that can be interrupted anytime when the node senses a busy canal, and ends with a transmission time, that can be either successful leading to the "end of service" state with a rate $\frac{1-p_f}{T}$, or in error bringing the process to the next stage of the backoff with a rate $\frac{p_f}{T}$. In these rates, p_f is the frame error probability and T is the average of a time corresponding to the transmission of a frame plus the defer time SIFS plus a timeout value corresponding to the duration of an acknowledgment. A state $\{k, j\}$ corresponds to the k-th stage of the backoff (i.e., the k-th transmission attempt of the datagram) with an actual contention window equal to j ($j \in [0, W_k - 1]$). Exiting the k-th "DIFS" state, the process randomly chooses any state $\{k, j\}$ or the transmission state with a uniform probability (equal to $\frac{1}{W_k}$). From any state $\{k, j\}$, we can either reach state $\{k, j-1\}$ (or transmission state if $j = 0$) if the canal has remained idle during the current time-slot, or reach a "freeze" state if the canal has been sensed busy. The corresponding rates are denoted α and β. α is simply the inverse of a time-slot duration and is fixed by IEEE 802.11 specifications. The inverse of β corresponds to the time separating two backoff freezing, provided that the node is in backoff. The rate out of any "freeze" state is γ, whose inverse corresponds to the freezing duration, which is nothing, in our simple scenario, but the transmission time of the other node (including the return-

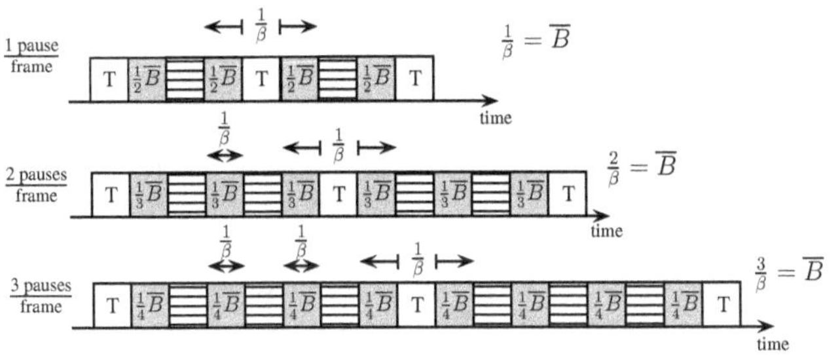

Figure 5: Illustration of the relation between β, $\overline{np}$ and $\overline{B}$.

ing time of the acknowledgment) plus a DIFS time that is always deferred before any backoff retake.

As a result, most of the parameters of this CTMC come directly from IEEE 802.11 specifications, except the frame error probability p_f and the rate β. As developped in Section 3.1, the frame error probability can be classically estimated from the BER and the distance between the consider node and the next one in the chain. Estimating the last remaining parameter β is much more difficult and we now turn our attention to it.

As explained before, it is easier to consider the inverse of parameter β which corresponds to the mean time between two successive backoff freezing (provided a node is in backoff). This quantity is related to the average number of freezing of the backoff of the considered node i, denoted as $\overline{np}$ and the mean backoff duration $\overline{B}$. This is illustrated in Figure 5, where the hashed areas correspond to freezing periods of the backoff. If we assume that a) each backoff is paused exactly one time, we can see from the figure that, in average, $1/\beta = \overline{B}$; b) each backoff is paused exactly two times, $2 \times 1/\beta = \overline{B}$; and c) each backoff is paused exactly three times, $3 \times 1/\beta = \overline{B}$. We can easily extend these results to an average number of pauses in the backoff, $\overline{np}$, and obtain the following (pretty intuitive) relation:

$$\frac{\overline{np}}{\beta} = \overline{B} \tag{7}$$

It turns out that parameter β can be directly obtained from the estimation of the average number of backoff freezing and the mean backoff duration. This last parameter can easily be estimated from the following average:

$$\overline{B} = \frac{\frac{CW_1}{2} f_1 + \frac{(CW_1+CW_2)}{2} f_2 + \cdots + \frac{(CW_1+CW_2+\cdots+CW_7)}{2} f_7}{f_1 + 2f_2 + \cdots + 7f_7} \tag{8}$$

where CW_j is the size of the contention window at the j-th frame transmission attempt by assuming an initial CW of 31 and a maximal CW of 1023, see Section 4):

$$CW_j = \max(2^{4+j} - 1, 1023) \tag{9}$$

and f_j is the probability that the transmission of a datagram requires exactly j frames, and can be derived from the frame error probability as:

$$f_j = p_f^{j-1}(1 - p_f) \text{ for } j \leq 6 \text{ and } f_7 = {p_f}^6 \tag{10}$$

Now it remains to estimate the average number of pauses in the backoff of a node. Let us remind that the backoff of a given node i is paused whenever any node j in the carrier sense range of i makes a transmission. Now going back to our simplified scenario (with 3 nodes, but where only node 1 and 2 transmit datagrams), let us consider backoff of node 1. Figure 6 illustrates the successive transmissions of node 1 in a saturated case, i.e., when node 1 has always datagrams to transmit. In this case, between two frame transmissions there is always a backoff that is paused by transmissions of node 2. The average number of pauses of each backoff is thus equal to the average number of frame transmissions of node 2 in between two conscutive frame transmissions of node 1. If we denote by $\overline{F_i}$ the average number of frames transmitted by node i by unit of time ($i = 1, 2$), we thus have: $\overline{np}_1 = \frac{\overline{F_2}}{\overline{F_1}}$. (Note that we need here to put back the indexes corresponding to nodes in the notations.) We now consider the general case where node 1 is not saturated, illustrated in Figure 7. Between two transmissions there may occur an idle time (of average duration x on the figure) before the beginning of the backoff. Some transmissions of node 2 freeze the backoff of node 1, whereas others do not (because they happen during idle periods of node 1). The average number of pauses in the backoff of node 1 has thus to be adjusted with a corrective factor δ_1 as: $\overline{np}_1 = \frac{\overline{F_2}}{\overline{F_1}} \times \delta_1$. This corrective factor corresponds to the proportion of time node 1 is idle between two successive frame transmissions: $\delta_1 = \frac{y}{x+y}$. The final question relies on estimating the frame throughput $\overline{F_i}$, as well as the corrective factors δ_i. Intuitively, the average number of frame transmissions by unit of time $\overline{F_i}$ is related to node i datagram throughput $\overline{X_i}$ and the corrective factor δ_i is related to node i utilization $\overline{U_i}$. It turns out that both quantities are performance parameters that can be derived from the global model described in the previous subsection.

First, the frame throughput $\overline{F_i}$ can easily be obtained from the datagram throughput $\overline{X_i}$ of $M/M/1/K$ queue i of the global model, by multiplying it by the average number of frame transmissions necessary to transmit a datagram:

$$\overline{F_i} = \overline{X_i}\, n_{f_i} \tag{11}$$

where n_{f_i} is expressed from the f_n probability as:

$$n_{f_i} = \sum_{n=1}^{7} n\, f_n \tag{12}$$

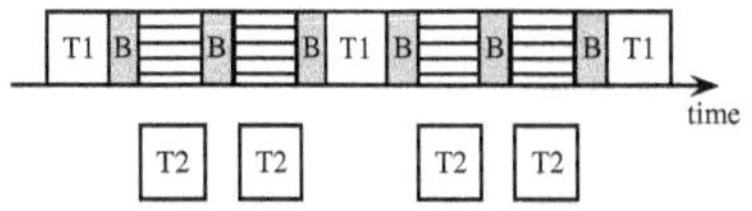

Figure 6: Relation between transmissions in neighbor nodes and backoff freezing in a saturated case.

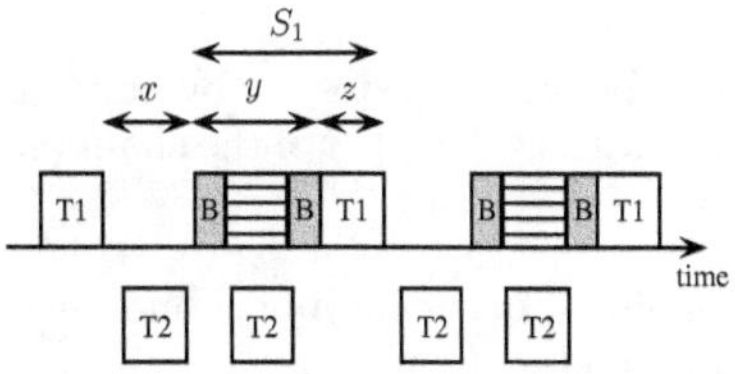

Figure 7: Relation between transmissions in neighbor nodes and backoff freezing in a non-saturated case.

Then in order to obtain the correcting factor δ_i, we first express the utilization $\overline{U}_i$ of queue i with notations of Figure 7:

$$\overline{U}_i = \frac{S_i}{S_i + x} \tag{13}$$

and use it in the expression of the corrective factor:

$$\delta_i = \frac{y}{x+y} = \frac{S_i - z}{S_i \frac{1-\overline{U}_i}{\overline{U}_i} + S_i - z} \tag{14}$$

where z is just the actual transmission time of a frame.

Finally, by using together previous equations, we get the following expression for the missing parameters β_i:

$$\beta_i = \frac{\overline{X}_j n_{f_j}}{\overline{X}_i n_{f_i}} \frac{\delta_i}{\overline{B}} \tag{15}$$

with the convention that $j = 2$ if $i = 1$, and $j = 1$ if $i = 2$.

Now that all the parameters of the CTMC have been estimated, we can use it to get a fair estimation of the service rate μ_i of the associated $M/M/1/K$ queue i. The inverse of this rate corresponds to the average time that is necessary to reach the state "end of service", starting from the first "DIFS" state of the Markov chain, and is given by:

$$\frac{1}{\mu_i} = t_0 + p_{f_i} \times (t_1 + p_{f_i} \times (t_2 + ... + p_{f_i} \times t_6)))))) \tag{16}$$

where t_k corresponds to the average time spent by the process in "line" k of the CTMC:

$$t_k = \text{DIFS} + \frac{W_k}{2} \times r + T \tag{17}$$

and r is the average time spent in any pair of loop states $(\{k, j\}, \{freeze\})$:

$$r = \frac{1}{\alpha} \times \left(1 + \frac{\beta}{\alpha}\right) \tag{18}$$

3.3 Fixed-point solution of the model

As developed in the two previous subsections, the global model takes as an input the service rates μ_i of all queues and provides the global performance parameters, among which datagram throughputs $\overline{X}_i$ (relation (2)) and node utilizations $\overline{U}_i$ (relation (5)). Conversely, the local models assume known values of datagram throughputs $\overline{X}_i$ and node utilizations $\overline{U}_i$ to parameterize the CTMCs (thanks to relations (8)-(15)) and give estimations of the service rates μ_i (relations (16)-(18)). It is then quite obvious to resort on a fixed-point iteration to obtain the values of the subsequent parameters. We detail the iterative procedure below:

0. Initialize rates β_i (with non-absurd values, e.g. by taking $np_i = 1$).

1. Calculate the service rates μ_i by solving the CTMC associated with each node i of the chain (equation (16)-(18)).

2. Solve the global queueing model and derive its performance parameters (equations (2)-(6)).

3. Update rates β_i (equations (8)-(15)).

4. Repeat algorithm until convergence.

Parameter	Value
DIFS	50μs
SIFS	10μs
Time slot	20μs
Contention window size (min,max)	31, 1023
Frame transmission limit	7

Table 1: IEEE 802.11 parameters

Once the algorithm has converged, we can obtain the performance parameters of interests from the well parameterized global model: the average throughput of datagrams that have reached the destination without error, $\overline{X}_2$, the datagram rejection probabilities at both nodes, p_{r1} and p_{r2}, and the end-to-end delay of correctly transmitted datagrams, $\overline{R}_1 + \overline{R}_2$.

4. NUMERICAL RESULTS

We simulate the scenario described in previous sections with *Network Simulator 2* (ns-2.35) [10], which is tuned to incorporate a non-perfect physical layer implementation in wireless transmissions [3]. Nodes 1 and 3 are fixed, 500m away from each other. The relay node can be positionned in several spots within the interval [110m,390m] away from node 1. The communication and carrier sense ranges cover 399m and 700m, respectively. The links capacities are configured at 11Mb/s, using a 2-ray ground propagation model.

We compare the results of our model with those delivered by simulation, for different levels of workload. In our simulations, similarly to our model, datagrams are generated by the source according to a Poisson process. Datagrams have a size of 1500 bytes while acknowledgments are limited to 14 bytes. For both queues we set the buffer size to 50 datagrams. We remind that no RTC/CTS handshake mechanism is used. All the other used values of the IEEE 802.11 parameters are given in Table 1. Note that our model can use and be adapted to any value of the IEEE 802.11 parameters.

Figure 8 compares the mean values of the service time of a datagram (as described in Section 3.1) obtained with our model with the values collected from simulation, with a workload of 6Mb/s and for different relay positions. As seen in this figure, the service time, which is a key parameter for our model, closely matches the values of the simulation, with a difference between both results smaller than 10%. Overall, the model presents good performance for most of the positions of the relay node. The existence of a high BER affects the results of our model for the extreme positions. As expected, when node 1 (source node) is distant of the relay node, we see the service time in the first queue being multiplied by a factor of 10. Nevertheless, our model satisfactorily represents this behavior.

Figure 9 shows the mean time spent in backoff freezing before transmitting a frame, another key parameter of our model. For a workload of 6Mb/s the accuracy of our model. The relative error between the results is less than 10% for the worst cases and typically less than 5%. For the relay node, the mean values of backoff freezing increase substantially when this node is distant from the destination (node 3). This is due to losses by BER, which increases with the distance. The necessary retransmissions yield greater contention windows, which increases the probability that a neighbor node transmits and freezes the backoff decrement. For the source

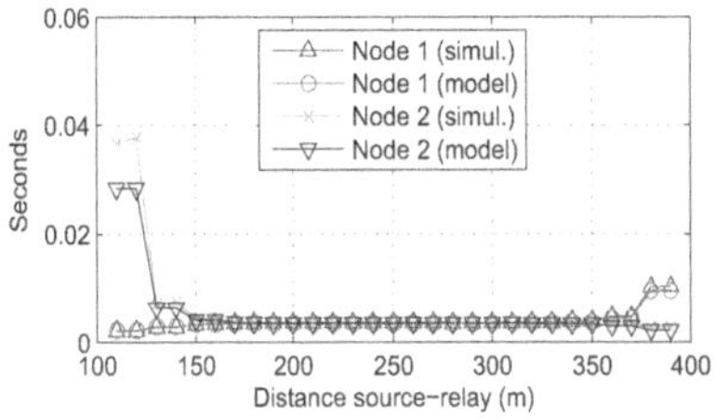

Figure 8: Mean service times of datagrams for a workload of 6Mb/s.

node, this behavior is not observed, despite the elongation of the mean backoff duration due to losses. If few datagrams are correctly transmitted from the source, clearly the relay node will very likely go to starvation. Therefore, it will not be able to freeze the backoff decrement at the source node. This behavior shows that there is no symmetry between the source and relay nodes, which may not be obviously initially.

Figure 10 shows the performance of our model, regarding the mean throughput of a node, datagram rejection probability by buffer overflows and mean end-to-end delay. These performance parameters correspond to characteristics of our model, as seen in Equations (2), (6) and (4). Figure 10(a) shows the throughputs of both nodes obtained from our model and from simulation, for a workload of 3Mb/s. Under these circumstances, depending on the actual distance between nodes 1 and 2, node 1 can be in saturation. We clearly see that the relative error between the results of our model and those from simulation is very low (around 3%). In a wide range of relay positions (between 150m and 350m), we see that the system is capable of conveying the entire workload. On the other hand, when source and relay nodes are close, the throughput of node 2 decreases due to high BER and the network can not cope with the workload. In the other extreme position (source and relay nodes are distant), due to BER, there are more retransmissions for node 1 with consequent service time elongation and buffer overflows in node 1. Figure 10(d) shows that, when the system workload is set to 6Mb/s, the best performance of the system are obtained in several points around the middle position for node 2, where the effect of BER is less significant. With this workload, the system is not capable of conveying all datagrams and is in saturation (buffer overflows).

Figure 10(b) and 10(e) compare the datagram rejection probabilities of our model with simulation, for the same levels of workload. The accuracy of our model is clearly seen, since the relative error, when comparing to the simulation results, remains low for both cases (less than 5%). The rejection probability for the relay node is significantly more important when it is close to source node. This is due to the high rate of arriving datagrams from node 1 and to the frame losses between nodes 2 and 3 due to high BER. These losses increase the frame retransmissions and the mean service time of a datagram for node 2, which leads to a higher buffer occupation. Regarding the source node, it also loses several datagrams by buffer overflow whenever the BER is important. Moreover, for the workload of 6Mb/s, the chain is not capable of conveying the entire workload, and datagrams are rejected by the source node.

Finally, Figure 10(c) and 10(f) show the mean end-to-end delay of a datagram. The relative errors between our model results and those from simulation are low, ranging from 3% (best cases) up to 10% (worst cases). As expected, these values increase significantly when the BER is more important (long distances between nodes), leading to values up to 12 times larger when compared to the best cases around the middle position. To the best of our knowledge, our model is the only one to also estimate this performance parameter.

Given the accuracy of our model, we believe it can be used as a prediction tool to forecast the flow performance for different positions of the relay node. Figure 11 shows the behavior of the system throughput for several workloads, ranging from 0.1Mb/s up to 8Mb/s, and for five different distances between source and relay nodes. We can see the impact of saturation in the overall throughput, when the relay node is 150m away from the source. This scenario presents a performance degradation when the workload exceeds a certain limit (around 3.2Mb/s). This behavior can be exacerbated for other scenarios, and a prediction tool is thus of high importance, in order to to prevent the system from such a performance degradation.

We have also developed and validated a model for the scenario where two independent flows are conveyed throughout the chain, each starting at one border node and traveling up to the other border node. However, due to space constraints, related results are not presented in this work.

5. CONCLUSION

In this paper, we present a hierarchical modeling framework to evaluate the performance of flows conveyed through a multi-hop wireless chain. This latter approach is thought to deal with different topologies of the chain, can handle various channel degradation patterns due to Bit Error Rate and can be applied to flows with rates ranging from light

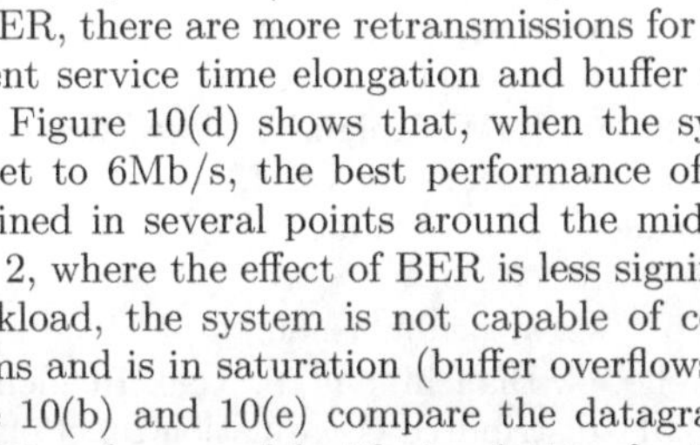

Figure 9: Mean backoff freezing duration for a workload of 6Mb/s.

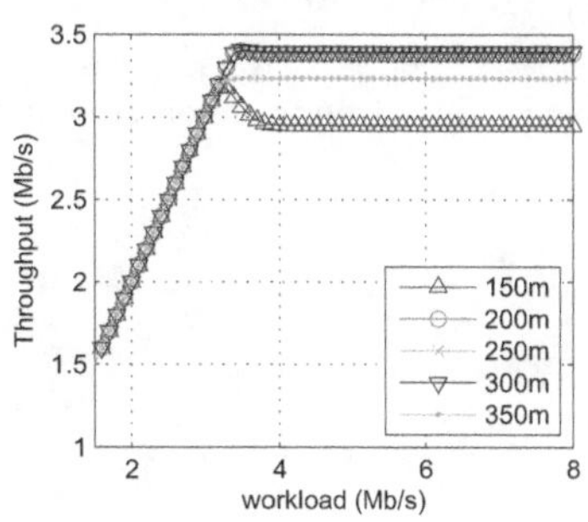

Figure 11: Evolution of the mean throughput as a function of the workload.

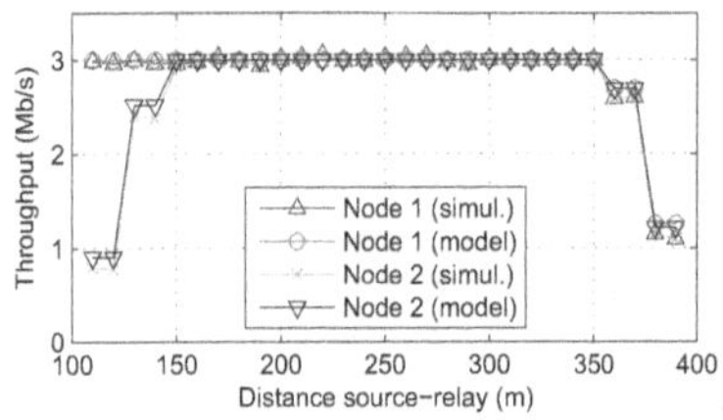

(a) workload: 3Mb/s

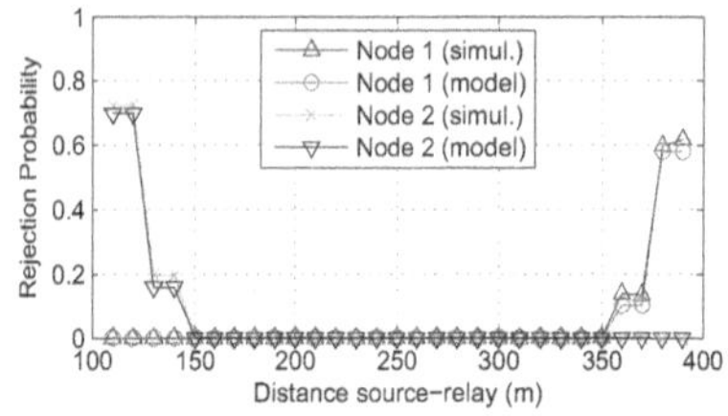

(b) workload: 3Mb/s

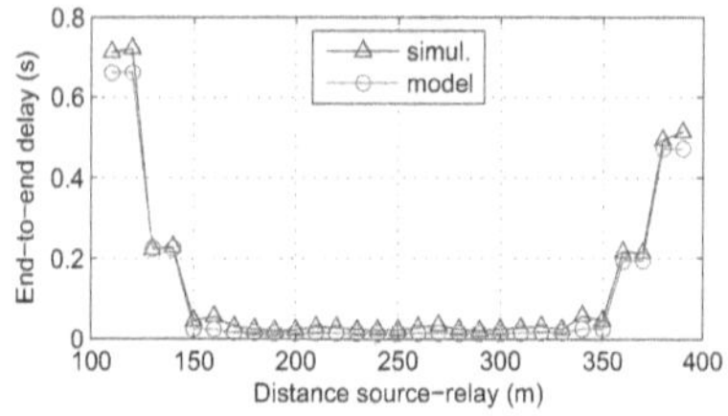

(c) workload: 3Mb/s

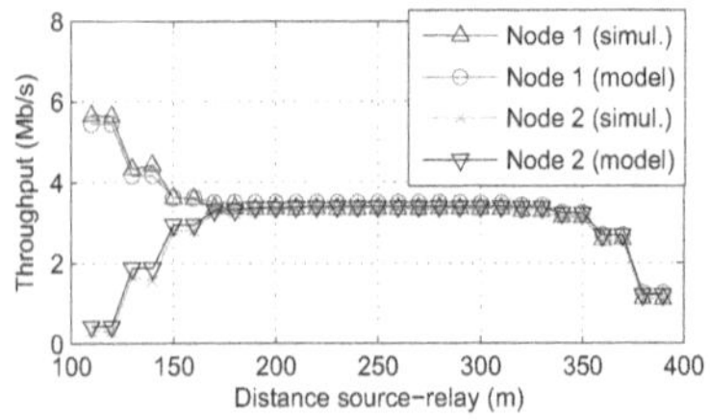

(d) workload: 6Mb/s

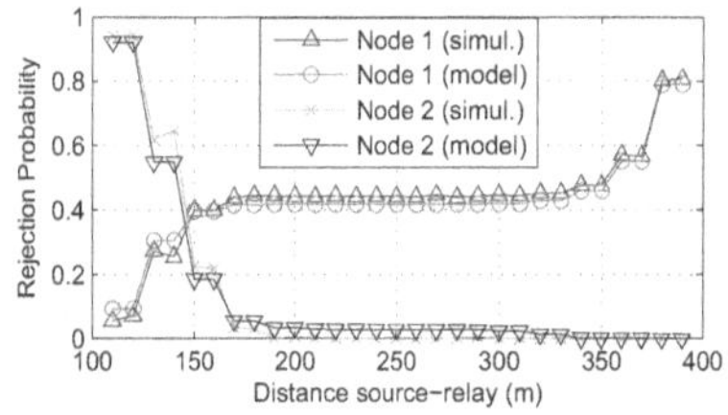

(e) workload: 6Mb/s

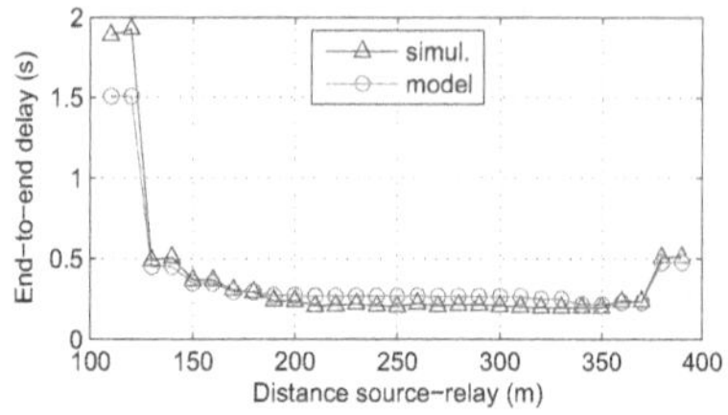

(f) workload: 6Mb/s

Figure 10: Mean throughput (a,d), rejection probability by buffer overflow (b,e) and end-to-end delay (c,f).

to heavy workloads. The resulting model is simple to implement and to parameterize. Its solution is easily obtained using a simple fixed-point iteration.

We validate our modeling framework on a simple scenario where the number of nodes in the chain is limited to three, yet the positioning of the relay node and the rate of the incoming flow may vary significantly. We compare the values provided by our modeling approach for customary performance parameters, e.g. loss rate, throughput, end-to-end delay, with simulation. Numerical results show that our model is able to accurately approximate the performance of flows. The relative difference is in general less than 10%.

Acknowledgments

This work was partially funded by the French National Research Agency (ANR) under the project ANR VERSO RESCUE (ANR-10-VERS-003). The authors wish to thank Nghi Nguyen for his valuable help with ns-2.

6. REFERENCES

[1] A. Aziz, M. Durvy, O. Dousse, and P. Thiran. Models of 802.11 multi-hop networks: Theoretical insights and experimental validation. In *IEEE COMSNETS*, 2011.

[2] G. Bianchi. Performance analysis of the IEEE 802.11 distributed coordination function. In *IEEE JSAC*, 18(3), 2000.

[3] M. Fiore. http://perso.citi.insa-lyon.fr/mfiore/research.html.

[4] M. Garetto, T. Salonidis, and E. W. Knightly. Modeling per-flow throughput and capturing starvation in CSMA multi-hop wireless networks. In *IEEE INFOCOM*, 2006.

[5] M. Garetto, J. Shi, and E. W. Knightly. Modeling media access in embedded two-flow topologies of multi-hop wireless networks. In *ACM MobiCom*, 2005.

[6] M. M. Hira, F. A. Tobagi, and K. Medepalli. Throughput analysis of a path in an IEEE 802.11 multihop wireless network. In *IEEE WCNC*, 2007.

[7] IEEE 802.11 Working Group and others. IEEE 802.11-2012 Part 11: Wireless LAN Medium Access Control (MAC) and Physical Layer (PHY) specifications. In *IEEE 802.11 Wireless LAN Standards*, 2012.

[8] H. Intersil. Direct sequence spread spectrum baseband processor, February 2002.

[9] B. Nardelli and E. W. Knightly. Closed-form throughput expressions for CSMA networks with collisions and hidden terminals. In *IEEE INFOCOM*, 2012.

[10] NS2. http://www.isi.edu/nsnam/ns/.

[11] I. Tinnirello, G. Bianchi, and Y. Xiao. Refinements on IEEE 802.11 distributed coordination function modeling approaches. In *IEEE Transactions on Vehicular Technology*, 59(3), 2010.

[12] K. Xu, M. Gerla, and S. Bae. Effectiveness of RTS/CTS handshake in IEEE 802.11 based ad hoc networks. In *Ad Hoc Networks*, 1, 2003.

Multiple-access Channel Capacity of Diffusion and Ligand-based Molecular Communication

Qiang Liu
School of Communication & Information Engineering
University of Electronic Science and Technology of China
Chengdu, China
+8613668210955
liuqiang@uestc.edu.cn

Kun Yang
Network Convergence Laboratory, School of Computer Science & Electronic Engineering
University of Essex
Colchester, UK
+4401206872770
kunyang@essex.ac.uk

ABSTRACT

Molecular communication is a novel paradigm that uses molecules as an information carrier to enable nanomachines to communicate with each other. The two major components of a diffusion-based molecular communication are diffusion in the medium and the ligand-reception. In this paper, using the principles of diffusion theories and natural ligand-receptor binding mechanisms in biology, we first develop and present model for the molecular single-access channel. Then, we derive the capacity expressions of the molecular single-access channel. Furthermore, we extend it to multiple-access channel in which multiple transmitters communicate with a single receiver. The objective of this paper is to study the capacity of multiple-access channel which is effected by the parameters of diffusion channel and ligand-receptor binding mechanisms. The numerical results show that the overall channel capacity is restricted by the physical parameters of diffusion channel and ligand-receptors and some different characteristics are presented in multiple-access channel scenario comparing with single-access channel scenario.

Categories and Subject Descriptors

H.1.1 [**Information Systems**]: Models and principles –System and Information.

Keywords

Molecular communication, diffusion process, ligand-receptor, multiple-access channel capacity, On-Off Keying

1. INTRODUCTION

Molecular communication (MC) has recently become a rapidly growing communication paradigm within communications and information theory and an interdisciplinary research area that spans nanotechnology, biotechnology, and communication technology. [1][2]. Since the speech by Nobel laureate Richard Feynman, it is widely believed that quantum and molecular approaches may replace part of the future needs of semiconductor technology. MC is inspired by biological micro-organisms which transmit information by propagating molecules which carried information from a sender to a receiver. Information can be encoded onto the molecules in different ways, such as using concentration, timing or the types of the molecules themselves. The information molecules are unloaded from the carrier molecules at the receivers. The receivers, upon receiving the information molecules, decode the information encoded onto the information molecules and react biochemically to the information molecules. It is a consensus that a bio-inspired molecular communication approach will govern the development of future nanonetwork communications [3]. MC would potentially enable some new applications in the health care areas as well as information processing and communication areas such as drug/DNA delivery system. In the future, the potential applications of MC system are unlimited prospective on biomedical, environmental, industrial and limitary aspects.

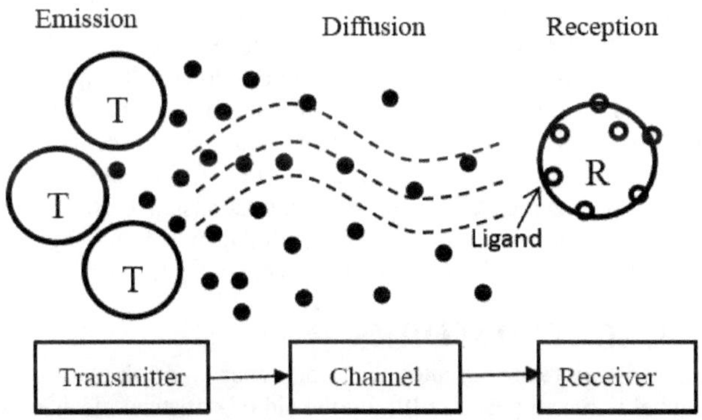

Figure 1: Model of the diffusion-based molecular communication

Unlike traditional electronic communication technology to transmit information with the electromagnetic wave, molecules are used to carry the information from transmitter nanomachine to receiver nanomachine in MC system. There are several different kinds of forms to propagate the information in MC such as molecular motors for short-range, bacteria chemotaxis for medium-range, pheromone diffusion and ion diffusion for long-range communication [4]. Arguably, the most dominating form of the communication at the micrometer scale is diffusion-based molecular communication, i.e., embedding the information in the alteration of the concentration of the molecules and relying on diffusion to transfer the information to the destination [5]. Just as the diffusion process shown in Fig. 1. The transmitters send molecules to the medium and these molecules diffuse to the

MSWiM'13, November 3–8, 2013, Barcelona, Spain.

destination by Brownian movement. Moreover, in nature, biological entities communicate with each other via the ligand-receptor binding mechanism [6]-[8]. As shown in Fig. 1, in a MC system, the receiver absorbs molecules by the ligand receptors on its surface.

We can treat the process that a molecule transmitted by a transmitter propagates to a receiver as a communication channel from the point of communication theory. For this channel, it is essential to find out molecular delivery capacity between transmitter and receiver to understand how to enable molecular communication with high molecule delivery capacity, especially for multiple access channels. The molecule delivery capacity could be affected by some parameters of the channel and physical properties of the environment such as diffusion coefficient and characteristics of ligand-based receptors. Therefore, it is imperative to find out capacity of the molecular channel and to understand how it varies with the properties of the channel and environment.

The focus of this paper is on the multiple-access channels capacity of diffusion-based and ligand-based hybrid, since they can be considered the most typical in nature. Up to date, there exist some researches to study the capacity of single-access and diffuse-based channel, but there are very limited researches has addressed the problem of the multiple-access molecular capacity of this hybrid diffusion and ligand-based MC from an information theoretical point of view. Considering multiple transmitters and single receiver, we at first established a time division discrete channel model for single-access channel scenario in this paper. Then, we deduce the express of the capacity of multiple-access channel based on single-access channel model.

The remainder of this paper is organized as follows. Section 2 introduces some related works about the capacity of single-access and multiple-access channel of MC. In section 3, a basic diffusion-based channel and system model studied in this paper is presented. Based this system model, the overall capacity of diffusion and ligand-based system with single-access and multiple-access channel are derived in section 4. Then in section 5, we give the numerical results on the relationship between the channel capacity and some parameters of diffusion and ligand-based channel. Finally, in section 6, we conclude the paper.

2. RELATED WORKS

Most of related studies focus on capacity of single-access channel in recent years. In [9], by the aid of statistical mechanics and thermodynamic entropy theory, a closed-form mathematical expression for the information capacity of diffusion-based MC is derived as function of physical parameters, such as the size of the system, the temperature and the number of molecules as well as of the bandwidth of the system and the transmitted power. The capacity and modulation schemes can also be analyzed by modeling the channel as a time slotted binary channel [10]. Taking account into the channel noise factor, a diffusion-based propagation channel can be regarded as the additive inverse Gaussian noise (AIGN) channel model [1][11], the upper and lower bounds on channel capacity can be developed, and a maximum likelihood receiver can be derived [1]. In [12], the design of a binary digital communication system is proposed based on particle diffusion. Stochastic signaling through On-Off Keying (OOK) for random particle emission and a diffusion channel with memory is considered, and the optimal decision threshold for the receiver detection is derived through mutual information maximization. In the ligand-based researching, assuming the input signal and noise are normal distribution, Atakan et al. derive a capacity expression for single molecular channel in which a single Transmitter Nanomachine communicates with a single Receiver Nanomachine by using the principles of natural ligand-receptor binding mechanisms in biology. Then, they investigate the capacity of the molecular multiple-access channel in which multiple transmitters communicate with a single receiver [13]. In the work of [14], the combination of results for these two components with single-access channel, i.e., the diffusion channel and the ligand receptor, gives a full model for diffusion-based molecular communication and cascading the two components gives an upper bound for overall information transmission rate of it.

3. BASIC SYSTEM MODELS

We consider molecular communication between several senders and a single receiver, i.e. there are multiple transmitters and only one receiver in this system. The schematic diagram of a diffusion-based channel and ligand-receptor MC system is shown in Figure.1, in which the '*T*' indicates the transmitter, the '*R*' indicates the ligand-based receiver.

The transmitter sends the molecules into the medium around in environment. Molecules are released by means of a molecule flux which is able to modulate the molecule concentration rate at transmitter location as a function of the time. The transmitter stimulates an outgoing molecule flux, thus encoding the input message into variations in the molecule concentration rate.

The channel is physically related to the diffusion process that occurs when the concentration of molecules is not homogeneous. During the diffusion process the molecules make the Brownian motion between the transmitter and the receiver following the Fick's second diffusion laws [15] [16], as shown in Eq. (1).

$$\frac{\partial c(x,t)}{\partial T} = D\nabla^2 c(x,t) + r(x,t). \tag{1}$$

Here $c(x, t)$ is the concentration of molecules at point x from the source and time t. $\nabla^2 c(x, t)$ is the sum of the n-dimension spatial second derivatives of $c(x, t)$. D is the diffusion coefficient of the medium. $r(x, t)$ is the molecule production rate at the source. The impulse response of (1) is the Green's function as follows:

$$g_d(x,t) = \frac{1}{(4\pi Dt)^{3/2}} exp(-\frac{x^2}{4Dt}). \tag{2}$$

Given a modulated number of emitted molecules $m(x,t)=r(x,t)\sigma(x)$, we will have

$$c(x,t) = g_d(x,t) * m(x,t). \tag{3}$$

The molecule movement propagates the message that was encoded in the molecule concentration rate at the transmitter location. The channel delivers the message through variations on the molecule concentration at the receiver location, as a function of the time.

The reception process at receiver side involves capture or release of molecules from/into the medium by several ligand-based receptors, as shown in Fig. 1. When the sender emits one kind of molecule instantaneously, the receiver must receive the molecule with binding the molecule to the ligand on their surface. In generally, there are sufficient chemical receptors on the surface are used to receive information coming from the diffusion process. The capture and release of molecules is modeled according to the chemical theory of the ligand-receptor binding process [17]. The binding reaction occurs with a probability k_1 when the receptor was not previously bound to a molecule. The release reaction occurs with a probability constant k_{-1} when there is a complex formed by a molecule and the chemical receptor. Finally, the receiver decodes the message from the molecule concentration rate.

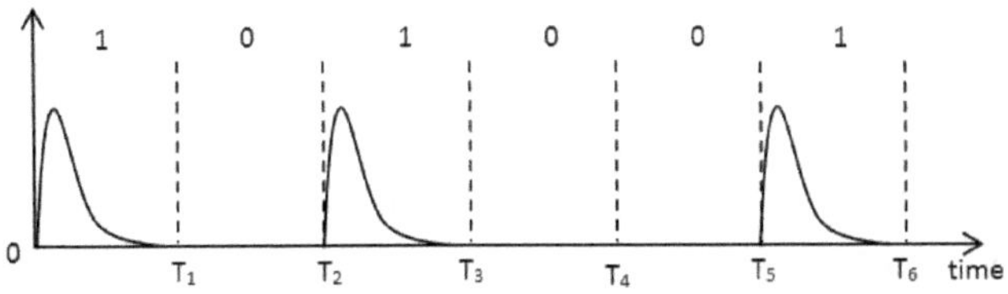

Figure 2: Binary signals transmission with OOK scheme.

In this paper, we assume the transmitter adopts On-Off Keying (OOK) to transmit 1 or 0 signal. Figure 2 shows an example of binary signals transmission produced by a transmitter. Each signal is sent in corresponding time slot. With a priori probability p, a random number of molecules are emitted in an instantaneous fashion by transmitters at the beginning of each time slot to signify 1; no molecule is emitted to signify 0. Receiver counts the number of molecules that arrive in each time slot and chemically reacts to that number of molecules to decode information of 0 or 1 at the end of each time slot.

4. CAPACITY OF SYSTEM CHANNEL

In this section, we apply an information-theoretic approach to analyse the single molecular communication channel at first and then, derive the capacity expression for the multiple-access and diffusion-based channel with ligand-receptors.

4.1 Single Molecular Communication Channel

We consider a communication between only one transmitter and one receiver. When the sender emits molecules to medium and propagation to the receiver, the concentration of molecules in random point of space follows the Fick's second law. According to Eq. (3), Molecules transmitted by transmitter arrive at receiver stochastically and they degrade over time. Considering the channel memory, the InterSymbol Interference (ISI) could exist, i.e. the overlap in molecule concentration between the signal transmitted in current time slot and the remainder signals transmitted in previous time slots. The probability that a molecule transmitted in slot $i \in \{1, 2, \cdots, n\}$ arrives in slot n can be expressed as [10]:

$$q'_v = \int_{vT}^{(v+1)T} g_d(t) \int_t^{\infty} m_n(u)\,du\,dt \tag{4}$$

here, $v=n-i$. T is the length of a time slot. $m_n(u)$ is the pdf of the molecule life expectancy (or the stability of the molecule in the environment) and is given as an exponential distribution function: $m_n(u) = \lambda e^{-\lambda u}$ with the mean of $1/\lambda$.

Assume that the distance between the transmitter and receiver is r, then the receiver binding rate is k_1 and release rate is k_{-1}, using the ligand-receptors binding model given in [11][17], then the concentration of by bound molecules of the receiver denoted by B can be given as

$$B = \frac{k_1 NA}{k_{-1}} \tag{5}$$

Where k_1 and k_{-1} are the constant binding and release rate, respectively. k_{-1} is a constant which is affected by physical properties of the receptors on receiver and it does not change as long as the physical properties of the receptors on receiver do not change. We assume that k_1 is a constant which is only affected by the several environmental factors such as molecular diffusion coefficients, temperature, and distance between transmitter and receiver. In the literature, there are several realistic models for k_1 that are experimentally tested for certain biochemical. In this paper, we use the following model [13] for k_1,

$$k_1 = \frac{4\pi D r_0 \beta}{1-(1-\beta)\frac{r_0}{r_\infty}} \tag{6}$$

where r_0 is the radius of receiver and r_∞ is the radius of the whole spherical shaped environment. β is the ratio of the radius of one molecule to the distance between transmitter and receiver, i.e. $\beta=r_0/r$. A is the concentration of the molecules sent by the transmitter. N is the concentration of the ligand-based receptors on the receiver's surface. The coefficient of the A i.e. k_1N/k_{-1} could be treated as the probability of successfully reception of the receiver. Thus, considering the condition with ligand-based receptors, the probability that a molecule transmitted in slot i arrives in slot n can be modified as

$$q_v = \frac{k_1 N}{k_{-1}} q'_v = \frac{k_1 N}{k_{-1}} \int_{vT}^{(v+1)T} g_d(t) \int_t^{\infty} m_n(u)\,du\,dt \tag{7}$$

As mentioned above in Sec. II, we consider a diffusion-based communication system for transmission of binary digital information. The transmitter adopts On-Off Keying (OOK) to transmit 1 or 0 signal. The basic binary communication model is shown in Figure 3. When transmitter send 0 or 1, respectively, the probability of the receiver detect correctly are P and Q. the signal of 1 or 0 is transmitted in different time slot. In here, we assume the transmitter and receiver has perfect synchronize in term of time.

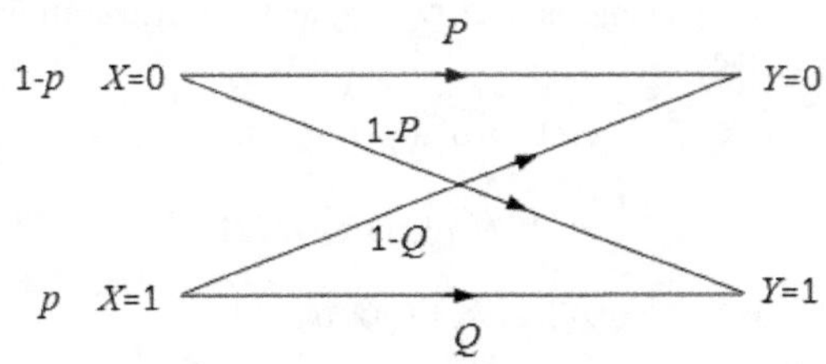

Figure 3: Representation of a diffusion channel as a binary test channel

We thus describe the probabilities of successful bit transmission as follows:

$$P[Y_n = 0 \mid X_n = 0] = P_n \tag{8}$$

$$P[Y_n = 1 \mid X_n = 1] = Q_n \tag{9}$$

Respectively, the false probability is 1-P and 1-Q.

We adopt the results derived in [10], for n=1, Q_1=q_0 and P_1=1, i.e., communicating a '0' is always successful. For $n > 2$, considering a recurrence relation for Q_n and P_n, we have

$$Q_n = 1-(1-q_0)\prod_{i=1}^{n-1}(1-pq_i), \tag{10}$$

$$P_n = \prod_{i=1}^{n-1}(1-pq_i). \tag{11}$$

The information capacity of a communication system is expressed by the general formula from Shannon [18]. For single-access channel, the general formula defines the information capacity as the maximum difference between the entropy $H(Y)$ of the signal x in input to the channel and the equivocation $H_Y(X)$:

$$C = max\{I(X;Y)\} = max\{H(Y) - H_Y(X)\}, \tag{12}$$

where $H_Y(X) = H(Y|X)$. For discrete binary system, the single-access channel capacity obtained from slot 1 to n is then expressed as

$$C_s = \frac{1}{T}\sum_{i=1}^{n}\frac{max\, I(X_i;Y_i)}{n} \quad bps \tag{13}$$

when n approaches ∞, (13) represents the channel capacity.

The critical problem is to find the $I(X;Y)$. For discrete system, Shannon has given out the entropy in the case of two possibilities with probabilities ξ and $1-\xi$, namely

$$H = -\xi log\xi - (1-\xi)log(1-\xi). \tag{14}$$

Following the (12) and (14), the mutual information in time slot n is represented as

$$\begin{aligned} I(X_n;Y_n) &= H(Y_n) - H(Y_n|X_n) \\ &= \chi((1-p)P_n + p(1-Q_n)) \\ &\quad -\{p\chi(Q_n) + (1-p)\chi(P_n)\} \end{aligned} \tag{15}$$

Where p=$P[X_n$=1] and $\chi(\xi) = -\xi log\xi - (1-\xi)log(1-\xi)$ are assumed. The proof of (15) is shown as Appendix.

For n=1, there should be that $Q_1 = q_0$ and $P_1 = 1$, substituting to (15), we have

$$\begin{aligned} I(X_1;Y_1) &= \chi((1-p)P_1 + p(1-Q_1)) \\ &\quad -\{p\chi(Q_1) + (1-p)\chi(P_1)\} \\ &= \chi(1-pq_0) - p\chi(q_0) \\ &= log_2\frac{(1-p)^{p(1-q_0)}}{p^{pq_0}(1-pq_0)^{1-pq_0}} \end{aligned} \tag{16}$$

In the same way, for $n > 2$, substituting (10), (11) to (15), we have

$$\begin{aligned} I(X_n;Y_n) &= \chi((1-p)\prod_{i=1}^{n-1}(1-pq_i) + p(1-(1-(1-q_0)\prod_{i=1}^{n-1}(1-pq_i)))) \\ &\quad -\{p\chi(1-(1-q_0)\prod_{i=1}^{n-1}(1-pq_i)) + (1-p)\chi(\prod_{i=1}^{n-1}(1-pq_i)) \end{aligned} \tag{17}$$

Substituting (7) to (17), from $\frac{dI(X_n;Y_n)}{dp}\Big|_{p=p_{max}} = 0$, we can determine the value of p_{max}. The overall channel capacity of single-access channel is finally derived as

$$C_s = \max_p \frac{1}{T}\sum_{i=1}^{n}\frac{I(X_i;Y_i)}{n} \quad bps \tag{18}$$

By applying (18), we can finally achieve the overall single-access channel capacity.

4.2 Capacity of Molecular Multiple-Access Channel

In the molecular multiple-access channel, a number of T_s ($T_1 \dots T_n$) communicate with a single R. Each Transmitter has a self-identifying label and adheres the label to the emitted molecules. This mechanism provides a simple addressing scheme to allow R to distinguish the molecules emitted by each communicating T. Here, we also assume that T_i is located to the distance d_i from R and transmits molecules A with concentration A_i using the binding and release rate k_{1i} and k_{-1}, respectively.

In [8], a model is proposed to find concentration of bound molecules (delivered molecules) for the case in which different molecules bind to a single kind of receptors with a constant concentration. Using this model introduced in [8], the concentration of molecules emitted by T_i and bind to the receptors on R, i.e., B_i, can be given as

$$B_i = \frac{k_{1i}NA_i}{k_{-1}(1+\sum_{j\neq i}^{f}\frac{E(A_j)k_{1j}}{k_{-1}})} \tag{19}$$

Where $E(A_j)$ is the expectation of A_j, N is the concentration of the receptors on R. Thus, from (7), the probability of q_v can be expressed as

$$\begin{aligned} q_v &= \frac{k_{1i}N}{k_{-1}(1+\sum_{j=i}^{n}\frac{E(m_n(u))}{k_{-1}})}q_v' \\ &= \frac{k_{1i}N}{k_{-1}(1+\sum_{j=i}^{n}\frac{1}{\lambda k_{-1}})}\int_{vT}^{(v+1)T} g_d(t)\int^{\infty} m_n(u)dudt \end{aligned} \tag{20}$$

Similar as single-access channel, substituting (20) to (17), and from $\frac{dI(X_n;Y_n)}{dp}\Big|_{p=p_{max}} = 0$, we can also determine the value of p_{max} and the overall channel capacity of single-access C_j.

For multiple-access channels, if the number of channel is f, then the total capacity of channel can be expressed as

$$\begin{aligned} C_m &= \sum_{j=1}^{f} C_j \\ &= \sum_{j=1}^{f}(\max_p \frac{1}{T}\sum_{i=1}^{n}\frac{I(X_i;Y_i)}{n}) \quad bps \end{aligned} \tag{21}$$

By applying (21), we can finally achieve the overall multiple-access channel capacity.

5. NUMERAL RESULTS

In this section we present the numerical analysis on the single-access channel and multiple-access channel capacity of hybrid of diffusion-based channel and ligand-based receptors. The aim of this analysis is to determine the molecular multiple channel characteristics in the environment with the both two components. We also aim to observe the changes in these characteristics according to the molecular communication physical parameters such as number of channel m, number of slot time n, width of the interval of slot time T, binding rate k_1, the priori probability p, interference probability q_m and the concentration of molecules N. By comparing the capacity between single and multiple-access channel, we found that there are obviously some different characteristics in multiple-access channel scenario than in single-access channel scenario. We perform the numerical analysis using Matlab.

5.1 Parameters setting

All the results are computed for a common set of parameters, whose values are assigned as follows. The diffusion coefficient D is set to 1 um^2/sec [5]. The values of k_1 are set in the interval from 0.1 to 0.4, and we consider that the value of k_{-1} depends only on the properties of receiver receptors and cannot be changed and is set to a constant with 0.08. The concentration of the receptors N which are on the surface changes from 0.01 to 1 *umol/liter* [12]. The distance d between the transmitter and receiver is set to 10 *nm*. The *pdf* of the molecule life expectancy $m_n(u)$ is assumed as an exponential distribution function: $\lambda e^{-\lambda u}$ with the mean of $1/\lambda$. The value of λ is set to 0.01-0.5. Considering the diffusion velocity and interference in molecular communication, the interval width of time slot T is set to 10-20 *s*.

5.2 The numerical results

In Figure 4, the capacity of single-access channel is shown with varying priori probability p for different k_1. The channel capacity C_s is a function of p and the curve is a convex function in which the top point is the capacity of the nth time interval. That reveals that p is a vital parameter for channel capacity. In order to achieve the biggest capacity, the transmitter should produce molecules in a way that approximately, does not make p close to either 1 or 0, in each transmission. In reality, the value of p is determined by coding scheme of the original signal source. From this figure, as the number of time slots n increases, the channel capacity C_s is decrease respectively. Because k_1 indicats the binding reaction probability, so increasing in k_1 means that the more molecules are binded by the receptors and C_s is improved. And we should also note that C_s increases no more as k_1 achieves 1, i.e. the maximum of binding probability.

Figure 5 shows the capacity of multiple-access channel with varying priori probability p for different k_1. Unlike the single-access channel, the capacity of multiple-access channel has no change k_1 as increases. In molecular multiple-access channel, due to the contention among T_s to capture the receptors on R, molecular communication capacity severely reduces with respect to single molecular communication channel on the order of 10^{-8}. Furthermore, contrary to the single molecular channel, as k_1 increases for all T_s contending on the channel, C_m cannot be improved because the excessive contention with the increasing k_1 cannot be mitigated by T_s.

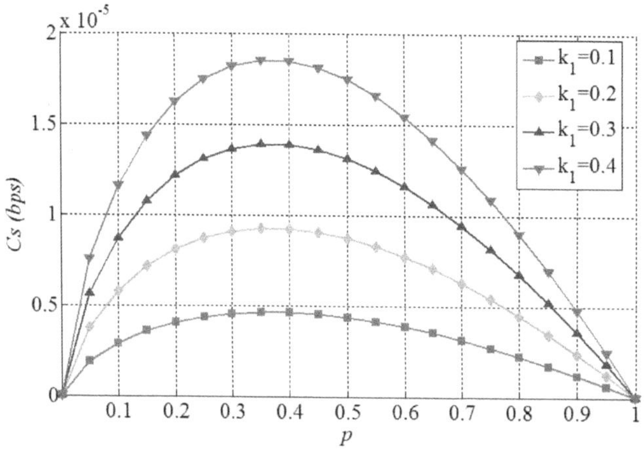

Figure 4: The capacity of single-access channel vs p for different k_1. n=1,T=20s, N=0.01, λ=0.01.

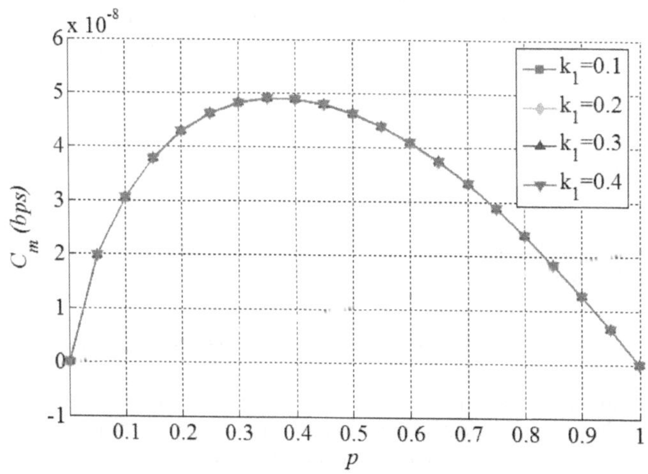

Figure 5: The capacity of multiple-access channel vs p for different k_1. n=1, m=4, T=20s, N=0.01, λ=0.01.

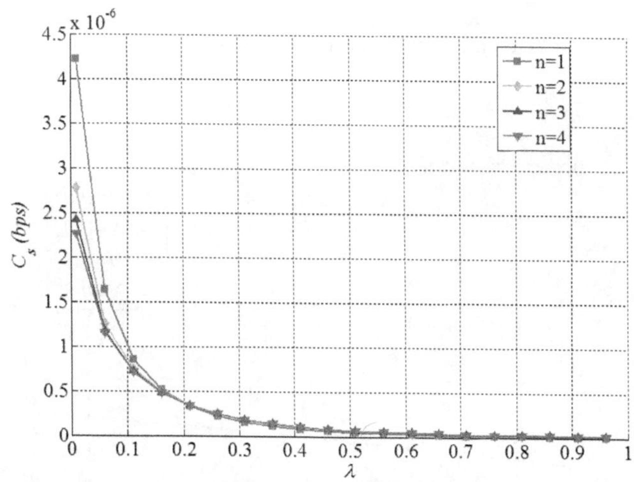

Figure 6: The capacity of single-access channel vs n for different λ. p=0.4, T=20s, N=0.01, k_1=0.1.

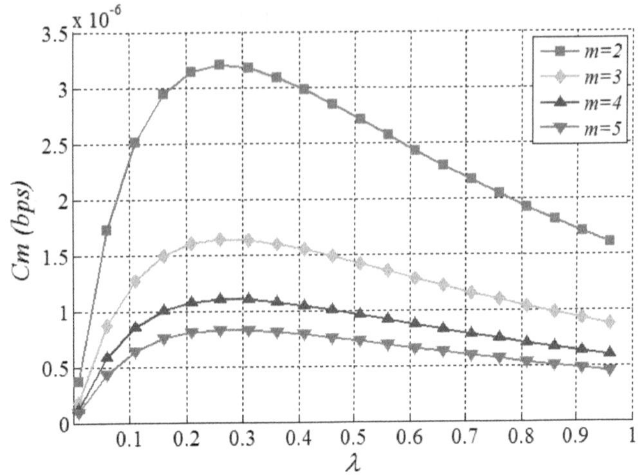

Figure 7: The capacity of multiple-access channel vs n for different λ. p=0.4, n=1, N=0.01, T=20s, k_1=0.1.

Figure 6 shows the capacity of single-access channel with varying λ for different number of time slot n. As the number of time slots n increases, the single-access channel capacity is decrease respectively. This means the interference is also increase by increasing the number of time slot. In the other words, the more transmitting signals, the more interference of previous time slots were added on current time interval. However, the farer from current time slot, the smaller interference is. So the rate of decline descends gradually. Figure 6 also shows that the channel capacity is decreases as λ increases. Because the amount of molecules sent by transmitters declines when λ increases, the capacity also declines respectively.

Figure 7 shows the capacity of single-access channel with varying λ for different number of channel m. For the same reason, the amount of channel capacity is also a bit less than single-access channel's. Furthermore, contrary to the single molecular channel, C_m first increases and then declines slowly as λ increases. When λ increases first, the concentration of molecules sent by each transmitter will be decline. There is more less contention among T_s to capture the receptors, and C_m increases respectively. However, as λ continue to increase, the amount of all molecules in channel is too little and C_m declines respectively.

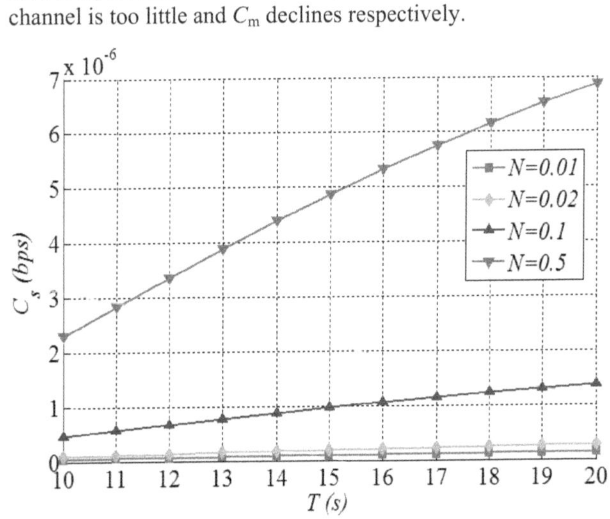

Figure 8: The capacity of single-access channel vs T for different N. p=0.4, T=20s, k_1=0.1, λ=0.01.

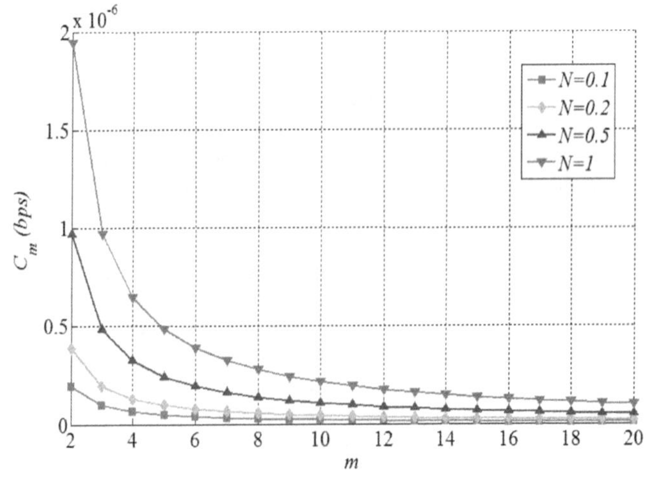

Figure 9: The capacity of mutiple-access channel vs m for different N. p=0.4, T=20s, k_1=0.1, λ=0.01.

Figure 8 shows the C_s as a function of T, i.e. interval of time slot. When T increases from 10s to 20s, C_s increases respectively. At the same time, as the concentration of the receptors N increase, C_s increase also. The figure indicates that the interval of time slot and the concentration of the receptors both are important parameters that determine the channel capacity. The concentration of the signal in a time slot attenuate as the width of this time slot increasing. As a consequence, the molecules that remain in environment and interfere with future bit transmission are also decrease and channel capacity is improved. N increase means the number of the receptors increase. Receiver has more receptors to bind the molecules and C_s increase.

Figure 9 shows C_m with varying number of channel m for different N. We can see that C_m decreases as m increases. This is also due to the contention among T_s to capture the receptors on R. The contention can get harder as m increases. So, C_m gets smaller gradually. Same as single-access channel, C_m also increases due to receiver has more receptors as N increases.

6. CONCLUSION

In this paper, considering the two components, i.e. diffusion-based channel and ligand receptors, we investigate capacity of molecular communication with single and multiple-access channel. The objective of this work is to study the characteristics of channel capacity in those scenarios. We first model the single-access channel similar to discrete binary channel with time slot. We then derive the capacity expression base on this model. Furthermore, we extend it to the multiple-access channel. The provided channel capacity expression takes into account the two main effects, namely diffusion-based channel and ligand-based reception. Numerical results reveal that the capacity of this kind of channel is relative with some physical parameters of real channel such as number of slot time n, number of channel m, width of the interval of slot time T, binding rate k_1, the priori probability p, interference probability q_v and the concentration of molecules N. Some different characteristics are presented with multiple-access channel comparing with single-access channel. It is not an available method to promote molecular communication channel capacity by adding the number of transmitters. The present results also provide a basis for further studies on channel coding, time slot design and reception scheme etc.

Future work includes developing other multiple-access models such as single transmitter to multiple receivers or multiple transmitters to multiple receivers, using multiple channels to improve the channel capacity, and studying the interference and synchronization among multiples.

7. REFERENCES

[1] K. V. Srinivas, A. W. Eckford and R. S. Adve. Molecular Communication in Fluid Media: The Additive Inverse Gaussian Noise Channel, *IEEE transactions on information theory*, 58(7): 4678-4692, 2012.

[2] Y. Moritani, S. Hiyama, and T. Suda. Molecular Communication for Health Care Applications. *The Fourth Annual IEEE International Conference on Pervasive Computing and Communications Workshops 2006*, pages 548-553. 2006.

[3] L. P. Giné, I. F. Akyildiz. Molecular communication options for long range nanonetworks. *Computer Networks*, 53: 2753–2766. 2009.

[4] I. F. Akyildiz, F. Brunetti and C. Blázquez. Nanonetworks: A new communication paradigm. *Computer Networks*, 52(12): 2260 -2279. 2008.

[5] M. Pierobon, I. F. Akyildiz. Capacity of a Diffusion-based Molecular Communicatioin System with Channel Memory and Molecular Noise. *IEEE Transactions on Information Theory*, 59(2): 942-954. 2013.

[6] J. P. Rospars, V. Krivan and P. Lansky. Perireceptor and receptor events in olfaction. Comparison of concentration and flux detectors: a modeling study. *Chemical Sense*, 25: 293–311. 2000.

[7] V. Krivan, P. Lansky and J. P. Rospars. Coding of periodic pulse stimulation in chemoreceptors. *Biosystem (Elsevier)*, 67: 121–128. 2002.

[8] R. Malaka, T. Ragg and M.Hammer. Kinetic models of odor transduction imple-mented as artificial neural networks. *Biological Cybernetics*, pages 73195–207. 1995.

[9] M. Pierobon, I. F. Akyildiz. Information Capacity of Diffusion-based Molecular Communication in Nanonetworks. In *Proc. IEEE Int. Conf. Computer Communication (INFOCOM) 2011*, pages 506 – 510. 2011.

[10] T. Nakano, Y. Okaie and J. Liu. Channel Model and Capacity Analysis of Molecular Communication with Brownian Motion. *IEEE communications letters*, 16(6): 797-800. 2012.

[11] Khormuji, M. Nasiri. On the capacity of molecular communication over the AIGN channel. In *45th Annual Conference on Information Sciences and Systems (CISS)*, pages 1-4. 2011.

[12] L. S. Meng, P. C. Yeh, K. C. Chen and I. F. Akyildiz. A Diffusion-Based Binary Digital Communication System. *IEEE International Conference Communication (ICC) 2012*, pages 4985 – 4989. 2012.

[13] B. Atakan, O. B. Akan. Single and Multiple-Access Channel Capacity in Molecular Nanonetworks. In *Proc. ICST/ACM Nano-Net 2009*, pages 1-10. 2009.

[14] A. Einolghozati, M. Sardari and F. Fekri. Capacity of Diffusion-based Molecular Communication with Ligand Receptors. *IEEE Information Theory Workshop (ITW), 2011*, pages 85-89. 2011.

[15] E. L. Cussler, Diffusion. Mass Transfer in Fluid Systems. *2nd edition, Cambridge University Press*, 1997.

[16] J. Philibert. One and a half century of diffusion: Fick, Einstein, before and beyond. *Diffusion Fundamentals*, 2: 1.1–1.10. 2005.

[17] R. Malaka, T. Ragg and M. Hammer. Kinetic models of odor transduction implemented as artificial neural networks. *Biological Cybernetics*, 73: 195–207. 1995.

[18] C. E. Shannon. A mathematical theory of communication. *The Bell System Technical Journal*, 27. 1948.

8. APPENDIX

The possible value of Y is 0 or 1. The probability of 0 is

$$P[Y=0]=(1-p)P+p(1-Q)=\xi \tag{22}$$

Respectively, the probability of 1 is

$$P[Y=1]=pQ+(1-p)(1-P)=1-\xi \tag{23}$$

Substituting (22) and (23) to (14), we have

$$\begin{aligned} H(Y) &= -\xi\log\xi-(1-\xi)\log(1-\xi) \\ &= \chi((1-p)Q+p(1-P)) \end{aligned} \tag{24}$$

Similarly,

$$\begin{aligned} H[Y|X=0] &= (1-p)[-P\log P-(1-P)\log(1-P)] \\ &= -(1-p)\chi(P) \end{aligned} \tag{25}$$

$$\begin{aligned} H[Y|X=1] &= p[-Q\log Q-(1-Q)\log(1-Q)] \\ &= -p\chi(Q) \end{aligned} \tag{26}$$

$$H(Y|X)=H(Y|X=0)+H(Y|X=1) \tag{27}$$

Substituting (24) and (27) to (12), we have

$$\begin{aligned} I(X;Y) &= H(Y)-H(Y|X) \\ &= \chi((1-p)Q+p(1-P)) \\ &\quad -\{p\chi(Q)+(1-p)\chi(P)\} \end{aligned} \tag{28}$$

Where $p=P[X=1]$ and $\chi(\xi)=-\xi\log\xi-(1-\xi)\log(1-\xi)$ are assumed.

ATR-MAC: Deadline Driven Data Collection from Smart Meters in Absence of Aggregation

Ehsan Nourbakhsh, Ravi Prakash
Department of Computer Science
The University of Texas at Dallas
{ehsaan,ravip}@utdallas.edu
http://dslab.utdallas.edu

ABSTRACT

Deployment of Smart Grid networks throughout cities introduces a realistic scenario for a large scale sensor network. Smart Meters create a wireless mesh network for receiving commands and sending metering reports back to provider company. The challenges of reliable and timely communication call for a fresh review of the well studied topic of Wireless Sensor Networks (WSN). We provide a centralized MAC solution for data collection, *ATR-MAC*, that relaxes requirements in general purpose WSNs, but emphasizes on difficulties a Smart Metering deployment will face. *ATR-MAC* considers variable reuse distances for minimizing propagation delay. It also increases efficiency of collection deadline instead of energy efficiency, a common concern of general-purpose WSN MAC protocols. We provide time and buffer size analysis of our algorithm, prove its correctness and show experimental results using implementation on a testbed.

Categories and Subject Descriptors

J.7 [**Computer Applications**]: Computers in other systems—*Smart Grid*

Keywords

smart grid; network infrastructure; evaluation

1. INTRODUCTION

It is widely assumed that smart meters will communicate their information to a data collection point through wireless connections. As the wireless communication range of the meters is limited, and there could be a variety of obstructions to signal propagation, all meters will not be able to directly communicate with the data collection point. So, we consider a model proposed in literature wherein the smart meters form a wireless mesh to relay their signal to the data collection point. Any increase in the frequency of updates from the smart meters will increase the load on the wireless mesh network.

At first glance, one may be tempted to model this problem as that of wireless sensor nodes communicating their data to a sink. However, there are some interesting differences: some favorable, and some unfavorable. Unlike several sensing scenarios, data from individual meters cannot be aggregated, nor is data loss desirable. Each meter's data must be delivered in a reliable and timely fashion to the data collection point. On the other hand, unlike sensor networks there is a certain predictability about the volume of traffic offered by each meter. So, rather than employing contention-based wireless media access, we propose that each smart meter should transmit messages as per a pre-defined schedule. The predictability of traffic pattern, coupled with relatively stable network topology, enables such transmission scheduling. Also, appropriately scheduled communication can preclude collision of wireless transmissions, increase channel throughput, and enable large scale smart meter deployment even in dense urban settings.

As Lichtensteiger *et al.* [5] discuss, it is common practice in smart grid networks to add a relaying router with higher radio range to connect a disconnected community of houses to our mesh. In a traditional tree structure for data collection such as S-MAC[18], it is implicitly assumed that the tree is more-or-less balanced. However, the relaying router in the smart metering context will have a significantly higher number of neighboring nodes, resulting in a skewed tree. This would also be the case for suburban environments in which houses are located along tertiary streets with smart meters along the street forming a long chain of wireless links. These scenarios are all similar to worst case scenarios that algorithms such as TreeMAC[15] and TRAMA[12] are designed to handle.

We propose a centralized contention-free MAC approach to determine the order in which nodes transmit their messages. As described later in Section 3, we model the problem of transmission scheduling as multiple iterations of graph coloring and graph pruning. Colors associated with edges map to time slots during which meter readings are relayed along those edges. For a smart meter with multiple neighboring meters there may be a sequence of time slots during which the meter receives data more often than it forwards data, resulting in an increase in buffer occupancy. However, such sequences are followed by periods during which the buffer is steadily emptied. Following an analysis of correctness of *ATR-MAC* in Section 4.1, we quantify maximum buffer occupancy in Section 4.2 as it will help determine the

MSWiM'13, November 3–8, 2013, Barcelona, Spain.
Copyright 2013 ACM 978-1-4503-2353-6/13/11 ...$15.00.
http://dx.doi.org/10.1145/2507924.2507963.

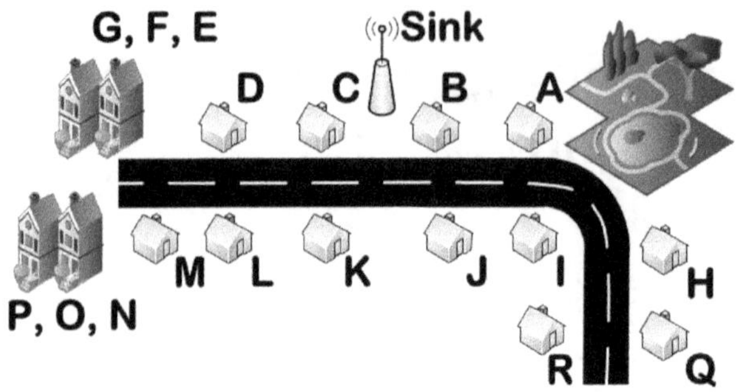

Figure 1: Map of houses in a residential area

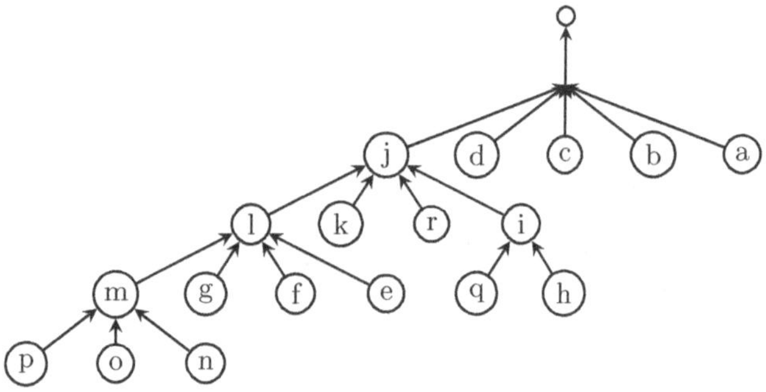

Figure 2: One possible data acquisition tree by *ATR-MAC* corresponding to map of Figure 1

maximum storage requirement of each smart meter. We also provide some discussion about time it would take for the sink to collect all reports using *ATR-MAC* in Section 4.3.

2. SYSTEM MODEL

Each smart meter i is able to communicate with some neighboring nodes, U_i. It may also sense transmissions of some other neighbors, C_i, without decoding them. If $j \in C_i$, we conclude that i is in "interference range" of j. The union of C_i and U_i a set of all its neighbors, Nbr_i. There is a network-wide requirement of sending messages with a frequency of f. So, the time corresponding to $1/f$ is the duration of one *cycle*. Nodes report their readings back to a sink node s once every cycle. Total number of nodes (smart meters) in the network is N. We denote the wireless mesh network of smart meters as a graph $G_{mesh} = (V, E_{mesh})$. V, the set of vertices, denotes the set of smart meters. For a pair of smart meters x and y such that $x \in Nbr_y$ and $y \in Nbr_x$, the edge $(x, y) \in E_{mesh}$. A schedule of transmissions for collecting data from all nodes to the sink will form a subgraph $G = (V, E)$ where $E \subseteq E_{mesh}$. E represents the set of edges that form a tree rooted at the sink. Furthermore, in the tree we consider each edge to be directed from a node to its parent, indicating the direction in which smart meter reports flow towards the sink. So, $\vec{xy}$ denotes that node x is a child of node y in the tree. The number of nodes in the subtree rooted at node i is represented by *count*(i). So, *count*(*sink*) $= N$. The tree edge directed from node i to its parent is initially assigned an integer equal to *count*(i). This value signifies the number of messages to be sent along this edge per cycle. Value of an edge originating from x is equal to $1 + \sum values\ of\ edges\ into\ x$.

In the context of a Smart Grid, we follow the model presented by Lichtensteiger *et al.* [5], based on an actual deployment of smart meters. Each smart meter is a sensor node and the sink acts as one of the regional data *collectors*. The collector can use other forms of communication, such as 3G wireless or wired network, to send the messages to the head-end system (HES).

It is required that in time less than or equal to one cycle duration, the sink must receive one consumption report generated by each smart meter. Unit of time scheduling is a *frame*, and frame length can vary over time. Multiple frames will be needed to send all reports to the sink node. This number of frames is called a *cycle*. Times at which node i transmits are $T(i)$, such that

$$T(i) = \{(t, d) | t : \text{time sent}, d : \text{immediate destination node}\}$$

$$T_d(s) = \{t : (t, d) \in T(s)\}$$

Time at which report sent by node i at round r is received by the sink is $R(i, r)$. Both of these times are relative to start of current round.

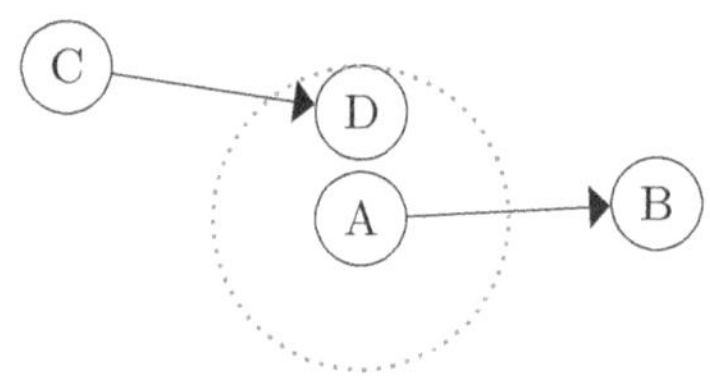

Figure 3: Two interfering edges belonging to the same network.

Consider two edges as shown in Figure 3. Simultaneous communication along the edges should not be permitted if it will cause interference at either b or d, i.e., if c is within interference range of b or a is within interference range of d. So, if both $\vec{ab}$ and $\vec{cd} \in E$ then the set of slot(s) during which node a transmits to b should be disjoint from the set of slot(s) during which c transmits to d, in other words:

$$\vec{ab} \in E \wedge \vec{cd} \in E \ \wedge \ (d \in C_a \vee b \in C_c) \Rightarrow T_b(a) \cap T_d(c) = \phi$$

Considering the above definitions in Section 2, the problem to solve is as follows. We are responsible for devising a Time Division Multiple Access (TDMA) Media Access Control (MAC) solution for Advanced Metering Infrastructure (AMI) aspect of all smart meters, routers and the sink. In this solution sink node is responsible for scheduling transmission times of the nodes.

The assumption is transmissions we schedule here are only from nodes towards the sink and have a periodic nature. The network managed by each sink can be few hundred nodes, as described by Lichtensteiger *et al.* [5]. Due to privacy concerns, reading data by each node may be encrypted and only readable by the sink node. An example of such key management, an ongoing theoretical and practical challenge, is described by Metke *et al.* [8]. This further highlights the requirement of freedom from data aggregation throughout our solution.

Each node may experience wireless interference. Nodes may be subject to interference from other devices, however our solution should avoid causing interference between nodes in the same network. It should also be able to intelligently cope with interference from neighboring Smart Grid networks whose activity has a periodic nature. In the latter case, an intelligent method to detect and include schedule of the other device is preferable.

Main objective of this solution is to minimize cycle time of network while avoiding loss of reports from nodes in its network. As mentioned earlier, our target network is a group of Smart Meters which are connected to power sources, mitigating the energy consumption concerns. These two design goals make a third goal, scalability, achievable. In other words if $R(i, r)$ represents the time at which report sent by node i at round r is received by the sink, then:

$$min(max(R(i,j))) \qquad \forall i \in V, \forall j$$
subject to
$$count(R(i,j)) = N$$
and
$$x, y \in E \wedge (x \in I(y) \vee y \in I(x)) \Rightarrow T(x) \cap T(y) = \phi$$

3. SOLUTION DESCRIPTION

In a network as described in Section 2, each smart meter is transmitting its data towards the sink. But as we get closer to the sink, each node is also responsible for forwarding data it has received from its descendants in the tree. As a result as we go higher in the tree, amount of data that each node forwards increases. In each cycle a node i should be allowed to transmit in as many slots as the cardinality of the subtree rooted at it, *i.e*, $count(i)$. This is because the cardinality of the subtree rooted at node i is the number of messages it generates or relays on behalf of its descendants, per cycle. To ensure efficiency and scalability the schedule should be as short as possible and maximize concurrency.

To solve this problem, we consider the following three collision avoidance principles. 1) Each node has to be silent if any of its neighbors are receiving. 2) Node x cannot transmit to node y if y is experiencing interference. 3) Also given our assumption of half-duplex communications, x cannot transmit if y itself is transmitting. So each node i requires to *own* at least $|Nbr_i|$ silent time slots to be able to receive data from its neighbors. It also requires one dedicated time slot to transmit to next hop towards sink in that frame. So if frame length is set to $1 + \max_{\forall i} |Nbr_i|$, each node in the network is guaranteed to have at least one time slot to transmit towards the sink. This yields **correctness**. But it is not an efficient solution, because many allocated time slots will be wasted when their owner node has no more data to transmit.

Now, to address **efficiency** we try to optimize cycle length by allowing reuse of time slots. If each node i knows and broadcasts amount of traffic it has to forward, adjacent nodes will know when it has no more packets to transmit. This allows them to reduce frame length and as a result reuse dedicated time slots to node i. As time passes, more nodes are silent and in the end only the node with highest ratio of descendants to frame length is still transmitting. We form a tree structure and use it to count descendants of each node and gather information about its neighbors.

Figure 1 shows an example, where smart meters a to r are located along a street. Smart meters e, f, g are on one building and n, o, p are on another, while the rest are meters belonging to houses in the area. A hierarchy similar to Figure 2 might result. In this case, nodes j, l, m relay data to higher layers but the rest are leaves.

Time slot assignment is done in a centralized manner because the schedule for one cycle is calculated once and repeated after that unless network changes occur. So we construct a modified graph $G' = (V', E')$ such that: $V' = \{(a,b) : a, b \in V \wedge \vec{ab} \in E\}$ and $E' = \{(a,b)(c,d) : \vec{ab} \in E \wedge \vec{cd} \in E \wedge (c \in Nbr(b) \vee a \in Nbr(d))\}$. Vertices that are neighbors in G' represent edges in the actual tree that should not be scheduled for communication during the same time slot because concurrent communication along these tree edges will result in interference.

Algorithm 1: Algorithm to assign time slots

```
slot_number ← 0;
G'' ← G';
forall the (x,y) ∈ V'' do
    begin
        find (x',y') ∈ V' corresponding to (x,y)
        (x,y).integer ← (x',y').integer
begin
    changed ← TRUE;
    while G'' ≠ NULL do
        if changed == TRUE then
            perform vertex coloring of G'' ;
            n =number of colors in vertex color of G'' ;
        ∀i : 1 ≤ i ≤ n: for all vertices (x,y) of G''
        assigned color c_i schedule transmission by meter
        x to meter y during time slot slot_number + i;
        slot_number ← slot_number + n ;
        forall the (x,y) ∈ V'' do
            (x,y).integer − −
        changed ← FALSE;
        forall the (x,y) ∈ V'' do
            if (x,y).integer == 0 then
                delete (x,y) and all edges incident on it;
                changed ← TRUE;
```

Prior to initiating the execution of the scheduling solution, as described in Algorithm 1, each vertex (a,b) in G' is assigned the same integer value as the value of the corresponding tree edge $\vec{ab}$ in G. Then the following steps are executed:

1. A vertex coloring heuristic is run on the graph G'. The colors assigned to each vertex correspond to a time slot during which one unit of information can be transmitted in a conflict-free manner from a smart meter to its parent in the tree.

2. Schedule one transmission by each smart meter to its parent in the tree, based on the color assigned to the edge between the node and its parent. The corresponding sequence of slots constitutes a frame.

3. After a run of the steps described above, one unit of data has moved from each smart meter to its parent in the tree. So, we prune graph G' in the following manner: reduce the value associated with each vertex by 1

(to denote that it has one less data value to transfer to its parent until completion of the cycle), and eliminate all vertices whose value is reduced to zero as a result, and all the edges incident on the removed vertices.

4. If the graph is pruned completely, exit.
5. If the graph topology is unchanged, go back to Step 2.
6. If the graph topology is modified, go back to Step 1.

Each vertex in $G^{'}$ gets scheduled for as many time slots at the integer value associated with it. This means that for each edge $\vec{ij}$ in the original tree, there are as many time slots as the number of nodes in the subtree rooted at i. There are as many frames in a cycle as the number of times Steps 2 and 3 of the algorithm are executed. Different frames may have different lengths, depending on the number of nodes in the graph $G^{''}$.

Like any TDMA schedule, interferences from outside of the network may result in some transmissions to fail. As a result, nodes with outstanding messages will transmit their messages to their parents based on a Carrier sense Multiple Access (CSMA) protocol after the TDMA schedule is finished. *ATR-MAC* records interference occurrences, and if interference observed by a node repeats periodically or is constantly present the schedule is updated to avoid allocating transmissions in time slots affected by it (Algorithm 2 described in Section 3).

3.1 Neighbor Discovery and Tree Formation

Prior to executing the scheduling algorithm we need to form a tree of the smart meters rooted at the sink, as described below. First, each smart meter discovers its neighbors by listening for heart beat messages broadcasted periodically. Sink will trigger formation of tree by broadcasting a JOIN message to all its neighbors. Each smart meter will absorb the JOIN message if it has not already joined the tree as the child of another smart meter or sink. On joining the tree a smart meter will also broadcast the JOIN message to its neighbors. Otherwise it will send a negative acknowledgment to the sender of the JOIN message. In this manner the JOIN message diffuses through the network of smart meters and forms a tree rooted at the sink. Starting from the leaves of the tree and moving up, meter i communicates the number of meters in the subtree rooted at it (N_i), all its children, and the set of all its neighbors (Nbr_i) to its parent. Thus, the sink ultimately gets all the information it needs to reconstruct the tree and execute Algorithm 1.

3.2 Refinement and Maintenance

Neighbor discovery and tree formation is required when the network is being set up, or a significant change to number of nodes or environment has occurred. However, an urban area deployment of nodes will be exposed to a variable radio propagation environment. To add to this factor, it is possible that installation of new meters is done in rounds. This means a sizable number of sensors (meters) are installed about the same time. But after they have initiated and formed their network, new nodes are added gradually. Proposed solution should handle these additions gracefully and without disruption. The rest of this section describes this solution.

To maintain the neighbor and conflict relationships more accurately, the sink periodically runs a scanning routine. Once the node identities are known, the sink distributes a schedule of the following format

$$S = \{(i,t) | i \in V, t = \textit{unique time slot from a reference time}\}$$

Each node is present exactly once in this schedule, and the beginning and end of the scanning routine are announced to all nodes based on the synchronized time between the nodes. The sink also announces a time length, τ.

After the reference time has passed, each node transmits a message containing its identity and pads it so the resulting message lasts τ units of time. If a node is not transmitting, it is sensing the environment. Each node in sensing mode records when it receives a message or it detects a transmission without decoding, and timestamps each observation. Each of these observations are recorded as (t, y, id) where t is the time of observation, y is type of observation, i.e., a meaningful reception of the message or simply sensing an ongoing transmission. Since transmissions by all nodes have the same length, τ, a node can distinguish between background noise. Once the scanning routine is finished, all nodes send the set of their observations to the sink.

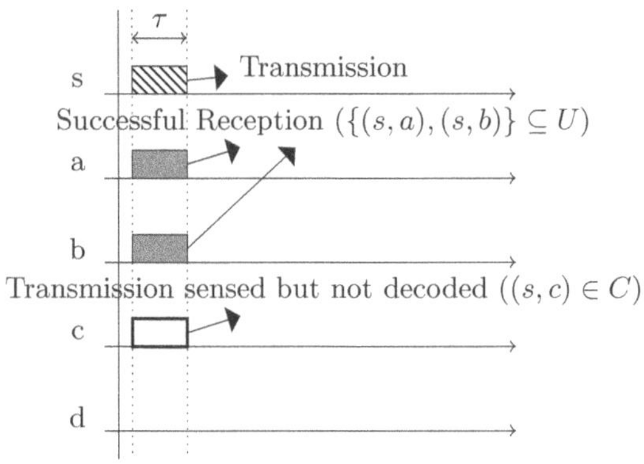

Figure 4: Overview of scanning routine based on schedule provided by sink

The sink is able to use the above data to infer which nodes are able to communicate with each other or are affected by transmission of any other node. This results in two sets of tuples, conflict $C = (i, j)$ and communication sets $U = (i, j)$. If (i, j) is present in C, it means transmissions by node i are sensed at node j and node j will experience interference if it is concurrently receiving a message from another node. However, node j is not capable of decoding the message sent by i. But if (i, j) is present in U, it means node j can successfully receive messages sent from node i. Based on this definition, $C \bigcap U = \emptyset$. Please note that the sets are not necessarily symmetrical. This means presence or absence of (i, j) in one of the sets does not necessarily impact presence or absence of (j, i) in the same set or the other. Thus the Nbr_i set defined earlier is $\{j : (i, j) \in U \vee (j, i) \in C\}$. An example of the transmission schedules and some of the resulting sets are shown in Figure 4.

We also need to maintain observed quality of time slots. If a time slot is marked as Interference more than *threshold* number of times, the node will increase number of its neighbors and asks the sink to re-assign time slots. Details are shown in Algorithm 2.

Algorithm 2: Maintaining scheduled time slots over time

```
change ← FALSE;
if RSS quality of current time slot is undesirable then
    update the history array with negative observation;
    use above array to count how many times this time
    slot has had low RSS quality;
    if count(low quality observations) ≥ threshold
    then
        mark this time slot as a conflict with itself;
        changed ← TRUE;
    if changed then
        recalculate maximum neighbor count;
        if neighbor set has changed then
            report new neighbor set to sink through
            parent;
            sink runs Algorithm 1 on new set;
        if sink responded with new time slots then
            replace current schedule;
else
    update the history array with positive observation;
```

3.3 External Algorithms: Coloring and Time Synchronizing

As any other TDMA MAC protocol, we require time synchronization between the nodes to prevent collisions. We use work by Maróti *et al.* [7] for time synchronization. We further enhance time synchronization between the nodes by piggybacking time information in the periodic heart beat messages they transmit.

For coloring, we utilize the heuristic algorithm by Welsh *et al.* [16]. It is worth mentioning that the coloring is used only when scheduling the network, and is only required when the network topology is changed. Furthermore, the G'' graph from Algorithm 1 is only re-colored when pruning has changed it.

4. ANALYSIS

4.1 Proof of Correctness

DEFINITION 4.1. *A scheduling algorithm A provides* ***weak interference avoidance*** *if no two nodes within reception range of each other use same TDMA time slot for transmission.*

DEFINITION 4.2. *A scheduling algorithm A provides* ***strong interference avoidance*** *if no two nodes a and b within interference range of each other use the same TDMA time slot for transmission. This requirement holds even if a and b are not able to communicate.*

LEMMA 4.1. ATR-MAC *can provide weak interference avoidance after the Time Assignment phase.*

Proof. **Case 1**: No link failure has occurred.

We provide proof by contradiction. Assume nodes a and b are assigned the same time slot t to transmit to their respective parents. Each of these nodes will use a time slot only if no other node has indicated they are using them. Since a and b are in reception range of each other, they will both report identity of the other in their neighbor set. Sink will assign them time slots such that each is silent when the other is active according to Algorithm 1.

Case 2: Link failure has occurred.

If the wireless link has broken between h and its parent p, they both realize this approximately at the same time since they both use same failure mechanism. Until then t is still reserved for h, and after failure detection h will disassociate itself and inform its children. So even in this case t will not be used by more than one node. □

LEMMA 4.2. ATR-MAC *can provide strong interference avoidance after limited number of runs of Maintenance procedure (Section 3.2).*

Proof. Assume the interference is happening for nodes a and b. If both nodes belong to the same network, weak interference avoidance can also indicate the strong case. If the two nodes are able to receive messages from each other, during the Time Assignment phase they marked each other's time slots as Interference. But it is possible that they are unable to communicate, for example when they are in interference range of each other but not in communication range.

For this case assume Maintenance procedure (Section 3.2) has run more than *threshold* number of times. So the counter is larger than the threshold, and that time slot will be marked as Interference. Then it will obtain an updated schedule that avoids using that time slot. It is very likely that the frame and cycle length of these networks are not the same and one, for example a, has smaller frame length. Value of *threshold* decides if this irregular interruption is sufficient to mark the time slot as Interference or it is ignored. □

4.2 Buffer size

In the first frame each node i sends its own message to its parent, and receives messages from its immediate children. For all subsequent frames it relays one message per frame from messages that are in its buffer. Number of messages buffered at i increases as long as at least two of its children are forwarding packets to it. As a result buffer length starts decreasing from its maximum length when there are no more incoming messages, i.e., its child with largest subtree has forwarded its last packet. So at frame *count(largest subtree of i)* node i has received all $count(i)$ messages in its own subtree and its queue starts shrinking. Since i was sending one message per frame to its parent, total size of buffer is upper bound by $count(i)$ – *count*(largest subtree of i).

As stated earlier, our algorithm is directly targeting situations similar to Figure 2 where the tree is highly skewed. As a result, the above value is going to be very small. The worst case scenario occurs when the largest subtree of node i has size equal to 1, i.e., is a leaf node. Hence, all other "subtree"s are also leaf nodes. In this unlikely case, the size of buffer for node a is equal to $n-1$. However, the schedule created for this node is going to be perfectly packed: first round includes all of its children sending it their messages (and a sending its own to the sink), and rounds two to $n+1$ will be node a forwarding the buffered messages to the sink. Imposing a limit on the buffer size to avoid such extreme scenarios may lengthen the active time of the network but eliminate this problem.

4.3 Cycle Length

Let us assume a minimum of k edges are removed from G'' in each run of the *while* loop in Algorithm 1. The value of k depends on how many leaves were eliminated from the tree in each frame. Since each run of this while loop corresponds to one frame of the schedule, upper bound for total number of frames will be

$$\frac{\text{total edges}}{\text{estimated number of eliminated nodes in each round}} = \lceil \frac{N}{k} \rceil$$

Number of time slots in each frame is variable and equals to number of colors used in vertex coloring of G'' in that frame. The coloring algorithm we use [16] provides an upper bound for number of colors used. This upper bound is equal to maximum degree of all nodes plus one. Since graph G'' is shrinking as *ATR-MAC* assigns time slots in Algorithm 1, it is safe to assume the maximum number of colors is also shrinking. In the worst case scenario this value will be the first number of colors used which we call c.

In short, the *while* loop runs $\lceil \frac{N}{k} \rceil$ times and each time a maximum of c time slots are scheduled. So the cycle length will be equal to $\lceil \frac{N}{k} \rceil \times c$.

One might argue that in the worst case scenario, $k = 1$ and $c = N$. But it would mean that every node is causing interference to all other nodes, and a chain is formed so each frame only eliminates one node from G''. A more realistic assumption would lead to values for k and c to be comparatively small constant values proportional to maximum direct neighbors among all nodes.This will result in a cycle size of $\lceil \frac{c}{k} \times N \rceil = O(N)$.

5. RELATED WORK

The focus of earlier sensor network MAC protocols was to address energy conservation using low-duty cycling. B-MAC [10] is one of the most well known examples which tries to reduce idle listening with adaptive sampling. S-MAC [18] is also targeting energy consumption by customized sleep cycles. Given that our sensors in this current scenario are smart meters, the higher level of focus on energy saving can be relaxed. Furthermore, the attachment of said meters to houses eliminates possibility of constant movement and makes interference and variable noise a higher concern. In other words, we are able to create more optimized solution for the specific scenario of Smart Grid networks rather than providing a general purpose solution.

Data gathering MAC (D-MAC) [6] can be viewed as an extension to S-MAC with a time adapting scheme. Active time of each node is determined based on its depth in the formed tree. To avoid interference with higher layers, a 3 time slot gap is used. However, length of this gap is based on the assumption that no higher level of internal interference beyond two hops is present. D-MAC does not use TDMA and relies on CSMA for contention avoidance in local neighborhoods.

TreeMAC [15] utilizes a tree architecture to create a localized TDMA MAC protocol that ensures conflict-free sending, receiving and snooping. Frame length in TreeMAC is three and cycle size is calculated based on size of the network. Similar to D-MAC, TreeMAC allocates transmission time within one frame based on the depth of each node in formed tree. *ATR-MAC* has a more generalized approach as we use number of children, and not only depth in tree, to allocate time slots. We also change frame length to address declining number of senders in each frame and as a result cycle time is minimized.

TRAMA [12] is also a TDMA based approach which uses flow information in assigning time slots. Nodes are required to periodically report their future traffic trend. They can also allow re-use of time slots if the actual traffic is less than the amount predicted. The obvious downside of this approach is overhead of information sharing. FLAMA [11] addresses this issue by only requesting flow information when necessary. However, accuracy of resulting schedules depends on how closely changes can be predicted. By focusing on requirements and assumptions specific to smart metering, we are able to relax these issues.

DRAND [14] is a distributed scheduling algorithm that uses graph coloring for time slot reuse. Z-MAC [13] uses DRAND for distributed TDMA time slot arrangement that extends to the two-hop neighbors. Z-MAC distinguishes two modes of operation, Low Contention Level (LCL) and High Contention Level (HCL). In LCL, any node can compete to transmit in any slot, but in HCL, only the owners of the current slot and their one-hop neighbors are allowed to compete. Underlying assumption of DRAND is all nodes are similar in internal interference and main interference is contained within two hop neighborhood. Z-MAC assign frame sizes of fixed length, given that no assumption about the application is made in its design.

Iyer *et al.* [3] provide an analysis of performance of two routing protocols on a wireless mesh network used for Advanced Metering Infrastructure (AMI). This marks an interesting path for developing customized routing protocols or adjusting existing ones for such applications.

6. EVALUATION

We used 24 MICA2 868-916MHz motes [1] for evaluating our algorithm. These experiments were conducted using our testbed, ASSERT. Complete details of *ASSERT* are provided in [9]. In our setup, each node has up to 8 neighbors which is consistent with connectivity requirements shown by Xue *et al.* [17]. Given this configuration, we expect our results to be scalable for larger networks.

Sensed values as well as quality of the links between motes were controlled to emulate changes in environment. For comparison, we ran Collection Tree Protocol (CTP) designed by Gnawali *et al.* [2] on B-MAC [10] as well as Z-MAC [13]. Duration of each experiment is 30 minutes. Sensors report their virtual reading every 2 minutes to one sink.

Parameter	value
Transmission Power	-10dBm
Slot size	20 ms
Heartbeat interval	30s

Table 1: *ATR-MAC* experiment parameters

For the initial step of constructing the neighbor and conflict graph, we set $\tau = 32.5ms$. To reduce the chance of missing detections, each node repeats transmissions 11 times. Receiving nodes report a neighbor/conflict only if they detect more than 6 such detections. There is a constant silence time following each transmission, and a larger one before the next node started its sequence. This total time for each node would be $5,500ms$. Thus, the total time for this step is $k \times 5.5s$, where k is total number of nodes controlled by same root node. This constant conflict detection time is not included in reported setup times.

We used attenuation traces obtained by Lee *et al.* [4] from real world measurements to recreate those topologies. For each experiment size, we chose three *connected* subsets of nodes and repeated our experiment on each of these three topologies. The provided results are an average over these three different topologies, unless otherwise stated. Table 1 shows some of the main parameters used in our experiments.

6.1 Results and Comparison

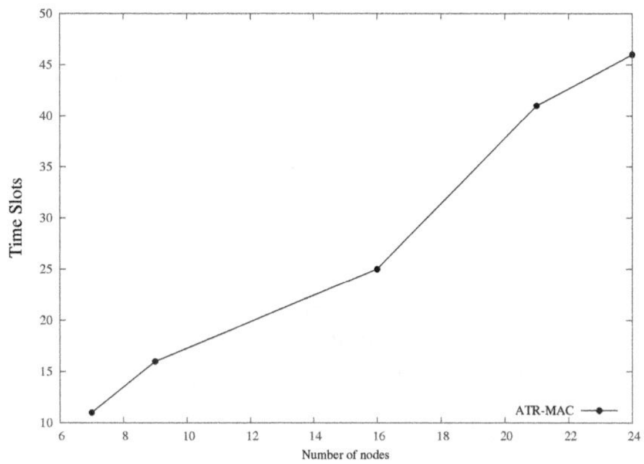

Figure 5: Average calculated cycle duration for three runs of *ATR-MAC* on multiple topologies

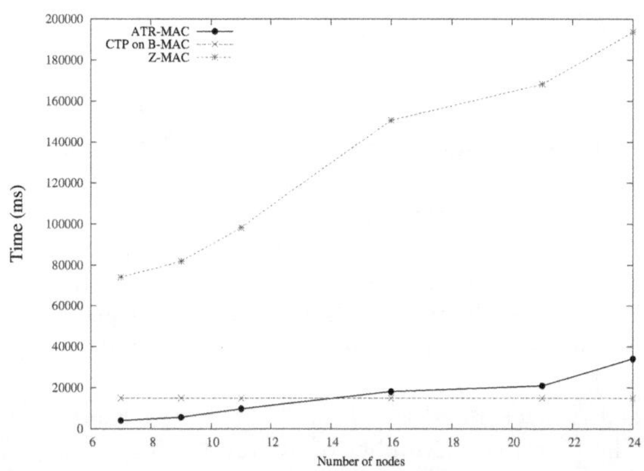

Figure 6: Average setup time versus number of sites

As shown in Figure 6, amount of time taken by *ATR-MAC* to form the trees is relatively small. Setup time for CTP is not dynamic and is adjustable. In our experiments we set this setup phase to be 15 seconds. Setup time of Z-MAC is mainly dedicated to running DRAND. We would like to acknowledge that DRAND would have a better performance in comparison with centralized algorithms when network size is large. However, in a smart metering application each sink is only responsible for a smaller number of nodes. Reaction of CTP to network changes is also only visible when new queries are submitted, and thus not comparable with our proactive approach. Cycle duration calculated by sink using *ATR-MAC* is shown in Figure 5.

To measure the reaction time of nodes, we create a random link failure. The time network takes to react to this inter-

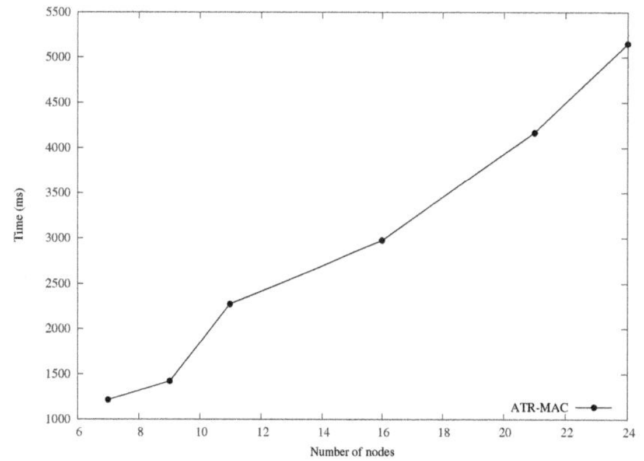

Figure 7: Average reaction time to network changes

ruption is shown in Figure 7. The small amount of time can be attributed to the fact that most of the time it is a local disruption without major message transmissions with other neighbors. However, a link failure between a node with higher number of children and its parent can result in higher reaction time. Cycle changes are sent to nodes after end of current cycle and before start of the next one. Similar reaction in Z-MAC would require running DRAND locally on affected nodes. But a common approach is to schedule DRAND to run periodically to address network changes. In our experiments DRAND was scheduled to run every 10 minutes.

Time at which sink receives last pending message for current cycle is considered propagation time. This propagation time is shown in Figure 9. As it can be observed, performance of *ATR-MAC* is close to Z-MAC, and a much better improvement over performance of CTP. The values reported are average of maximum delays observed by all the nodes.

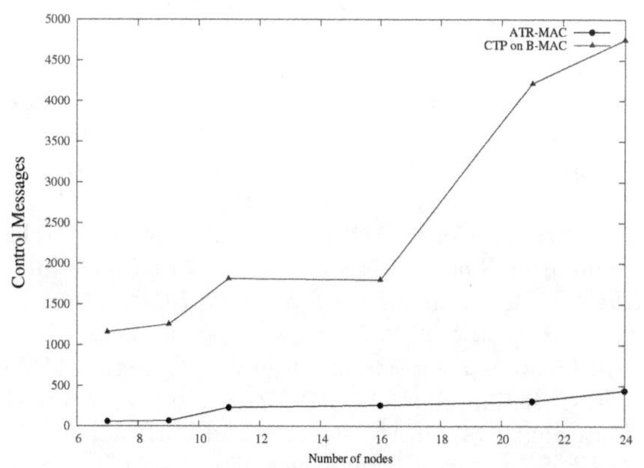

Figure 8: Average control messages overhead

In comparison to CTP, *ATR-MAC* has far less control messages (Figure 8). While B-MAC does not require control messages, CTP will require beacons and route establishment messages which are included in the figure.

7. CONCLUSION AND FUTURE WORK

We proposed *ATR-MAC*, a centralized MAC specifically designed taking into account specific requirements of smart

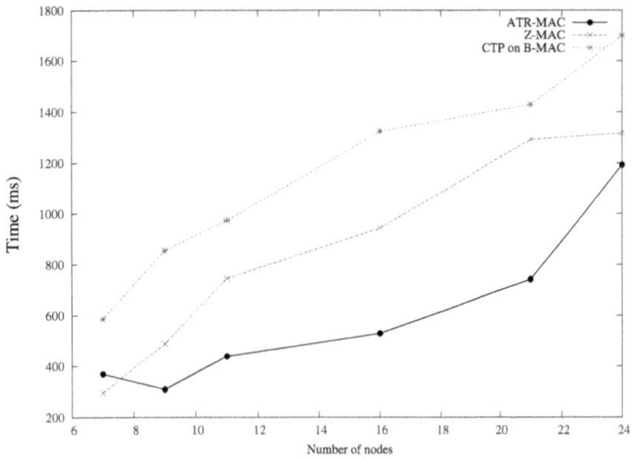

Figure 9: Average of Maximum Propagation time

metering wireless networks. We aim to enhance our work by designing a distributed version of this MAC protocol.

As demonstrated by Lemma 3.2, we can handle interferences caused by other generic devices or networks. *ATR-MAC* also provisions an intelligent way to detect and coexist with periodic interference such as other AMI networks. An extension of this work would study precise impact of presence of multiple networks in vicinity of each other. By focusing on timeliness and contention reduction, *ATR-MAC* is able to provide a scalable solution for data gathering without aggregation in Smart Grid networks. *ATR-MAC* performs efficiently where most MAC protocols perform suboptimally. This is made possible by relaxing the energy efficiency requirement, as is permitted in Smart Grid applications.

8. REFERENCES

[1] MICA2 Platform by MEMSIC, Inc.

[2] O. Gnawali, R. Fonseca, K. Jamieson, D. Moss, and P. Levis. Collection Tree Protocol. In *Proceedings of the 7th ACM Conference on Embedded Networked Sensor Systems*, SenSys '09, pages 1–14, 2009.

[3] G. Iyer, P. Agrawal, E. Monnerie, and R.S. Cardozo. Performance Analysis of Wireless Mesh Routing Protocols for Smart Utility Networks. In *IEEE SmartGridComm*, pages 114 –119, 2011.

[4] H.J. Lee, A. Cerpa, and P. Levis. Improving Wireless Simulation Through Noise Modeling. In *Proceedings of the 6th International Conference on Information Processing in Sensor Networks*, page 30, 2007.

[5] Bill Lichtensteiger, Branko Bjelajec, Christian Muller, and Christian Wietfeld. RF MeshSystems for Smart Metering: System Architecture and Performance. In *IEEE SmartGridComm*, pages 379–384, 2010.

[6] Gang Lu, Bhaskar Krishnamachari, and Cauligi S. Raghavendra. An Adaptive Energy-Efficient and Low-Latency MAC for Data Gathering in Wireless Sensor Networks. In *IEEE IPDPS*, 2004.

[7] Miklós Maróti, Branislav Kusy, Gyula Simon, and Ákos Lédeczi. The Flooding Time Synchronization Protocol. In *Proceedings of the 2nd international conference on Embedded networked sensor systems*, SenSys '04, page 39–49, 2004.

[8] A.R. Metke and R.L. Ekl. Security technology for smart grid networks. *IEEE SmartGridComm*, 1(1):99–107, 2010.

[9] Ehsan Nourbakhsh, Jeff Dix, Paul Johnson, Ryan Burchfield, S. Venkatesan, Neeraj Mittal, and Ravi Prakash. ASSERT: A Wireless Networking Testbed. In *Proceedings of TridentCom '10: LNICST 46*, pages 209–219, 2010.

[10] J. Polastre, J. Hill, and D. Culler. Versatile Low Power Media Access for Wireless Sensor Networks. In *Proceedings of the 2nd International Conference on Embedded Networked Sensor Systems*, pages 03–05, 2004.

[11] V. Rajendran, J.J. Garcia-Luna-Aveces, and K. Obraczka. Energy-efficient, application-aware medium access for sensor networks. In *IEEE International Conference on Mobile Adhoc and Sensor Systems Conference*, pages 8 pp. –630, 2005.

[12] Venkatesh Rajendran, Katia Obraczka, and J. J. Garcia-Luna-Aceves. Energy-efficient, Collision-free Medium Access Control for Wireless Sensor Networks. *Wireless Networks*, 12:63–78, 2006.

[13] I. Rhee, A. Warrier, M. Aia, J. Min, and M.L. Sichitiu. Z-MAC: A Hybrid MAC for Wireless Sensor Networks. *IEEE/ACM Transactions on Networking (TON)*, 16(3):511–524, 2008.

[14] I. Rhee, A. Warrier, J. Min, and L. Xu. DRAND: Distributed Randomized TDMA Scheduling for Wireless Ad Hoc Networks. *IEEE Transactions on Mobile Computing*, pages 1384–1396, 2009.

[15] Wen-Zhan Song, Renjie Huang, Behrooz Shirazi, and Richard LaHusen. TreeMAC: Localized TDMA MAC Protocol for Real-time High-data-rate Sensor Networks. *Pervasive and Mobile Computing*, 5(6):750–765, 2009.

[16] D.J.A. Welsh and MB Powell. An Upper Bound for The Chromatic Number of a Graph and Its Application to Timetabling Problems. *The Computer Journal*, 10(1):85, 1967.

[17] Feng Xue and P.R. Kumar. The Number of Neighbors Needed for Connectivity of Wireless Networks. *Wireless networks*, 10(2):169–181, 2004.

[18] W. Ye, J. Heidemann, and D. Estrin. An Energy-efficient MAC Protocol for Wireless Sensor Networks. In *IEEE Proceedings Twenty-First INFOCOM 2002.*, volume 3, pages 1567–1576, 2002.

An Intelligent Routing Scheme Effectively Utilizing Mass Storage Embedded on Satellites to Mitigate Network Congestions

Kazuma Kaneko, Yuichi Kawamoto, Hiroki Nishiyama, and Nei Kato
Graduate School of Information Sciences, Tohoku University
Sendai, Japan
{kaneko, youpsan,bigtree, kato}@it.ecei.tohoku.ac.jp

Shinichi Yamamoto, and Naoko Yoshimura
Wireless Network Research Institute, National Institute of Information and Communications Technology,
Tokyo, Japan
{yamamoto, naoko}@nict.go.jp

ABSTRACT

Recently, since many kinds of wireless devices have been widely used and a large amount of contents is available on the Internet, a network system that provides adequate services anytime and anywhere is required. In this research, we focus on satellite networks using mass storage devices to provide the above mentioned services. In this kind of network, multiple satellites are used to cover the whole surface of the earth, and each satellite is equipped with a mass storage device. By using mass storage devices, the satellite network can manage a high buffer capacity to handle large amounts of data. However, no routing method has been developed for such kind of satellite network that can utilize the storage devices and manage the large amount of data in the network effectively. In this paper, we propose a novel routing scheme for the efficient utilization of the mass storage on satellites to mitigate network congestion. The proposed method is analyzed mathematically. The numerical results validate the effectiveness of our proposed method.

Categories and Subject Descriptors

C.2.2 [**Computer-Communication Networks**]: Network communication

Keywords

satellite networks, storage, route control, collision congestion control

1. INTRODUCTION

In recent years, the widespread use of wireless devices such as smart-phones and tablets makes it possible to easily access to Internet anytime and anywhere. Together with the development of technologies, the demands for using high quality services have been quickly increased. For example, uploading large data such as high quality videos became more common. Using cloud computing to share and manage data has been also more popular. The total amount of data communicated in Internet may reach to several zettabytes. One more reason for the increase of network load is the development of Machine-to-Machine (M2M) that enables machines to connect and share data with others more easily. It leads to higher requirements for contemporary networks.

Terrestrial networks consist of ground-based stations. And thus, in the areas having no station such as seas or mountains, we cannot use the networks. Similarly, in the disaster areas where the stations have been broken, the networks cannot be used. For example, after the great earthquake in March 2011 in apan, many people have suffered from the lack of communications. Therefore, the next generation networks need to not only handle a large amount of data but also provide easy Internet access to users anytime and anywhere. Because of these factors, satellite networks have attracted much attention.

Particularly, we focus on the satellite networks using mass storage devices [1]. In this kind of networks, each satellite can keep big amount of data in the storage and provide high quality services to many people. Satellite networks provide worldwide communication environment since they have wide coverage and the advantages of simultaneous transmissive communication. In disaster areas, we can use them instead of the destroyed ground network systems. The satellite networks using mass storage devices are considered as a good candidate for next generation network systems to manage large amount of data. However, in the previous researches on routing method for the satellite networks using mass storage devices, there are not any methods efficiently utilizing the network and the storage devices. Therefore, in this paper, we propose a new routing method which utilize the mass storage devices on the satellites in order to manage high amount of data in the satellite networks. We also analyze the utilization of the links with mathematical expressions. Moreover, we confirm the effectiveness of our proposed routing scheme and the correctness of the analysis on the link utilization by using numerical calculations.

The remainder of this paper is organized as follows. Section 2 describes general satellite constellations and the ex-

MSWiM'13, November 3–8, 2013, Barcelona, Spain.

http://dx.doi.org/10.1145/2507924.2507951.

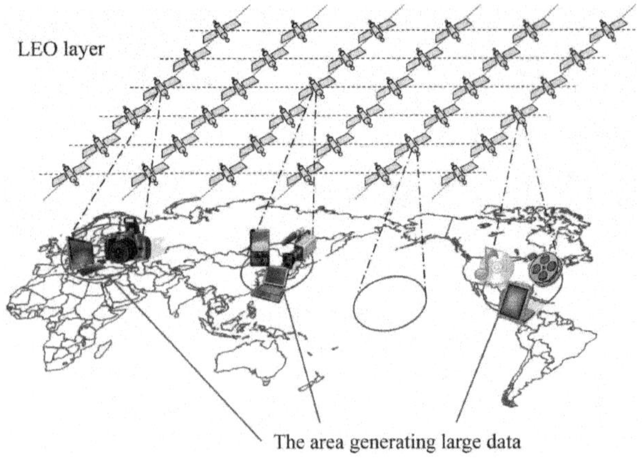

Figure 1: An example of a constellation constructed by LEO satellites using mass storage devices.

isting routing methods for satellite networks. The proposed routing method and the analyses regarding the link utilization are introduced in Section 3. The numerical results are presented in Section 4. Finally, this paper is concluded in Section 5.

2. SATELLITE CONSTELLATIONS AND EXISTING ROUTING METHODS

2.1 General satellite constellations

Satellites are generally categorized into Low Earth Orbit (LEO), Medium Earth Orbit (MEO), and Geostationary Earth Orbit (GEO) satellites according to their altitude [2] [3]. Each satellite constellation has different advantages [4] [5]. In these constellations, we take particular note of LEO satellite constellations for their lower delay and electric power saving aspects. Since they have lower altitude orbit than GEO and MEO satellites, they can communicate with small antennas on the ground. As a result, LEO satellites are suitable for mobile communications. However, in order to cover all over the world, it is necessary to build a network between LEO satellites. Iridium is a famous LEO satellite constellation which is a system to provide worldwide communication environment. It consists of 66 satellites orbiting 780km high, has a mesh type topology which constructs 6 orbits, and has 4 Inter Satellite Links (ISLs) with adjacent satellites. In this paper, we focus on networks consisting of mesh type LEO satellite constellations and each satellite has a mass storage device.

2.2 Existing routing method and its shortcomings

In satellite networks, traffic is sent from satellite earth stations to LEO satellites, and then go through other LEO satellites to go to the destination. To realize efficient traffic delivery, the route control of traffic is necessary. Most of the existing route control methods are implemented based on the Dijkstra's Shortest Path (DSP) algorithm, which selects the path whose link cost is minimal. Transmission delay or hop count is generally utilized as the link cost in DSP [6] [7]. Since DSP is known as one of the simplest routing schemes, it has been employed in various networks including satellite networks. However, traffic distribution on the earth is very inhomogeneous because users of the network tend to converge to big cities against sea or mountain areas. The distribution of the amount of generated traffic is similar to that of population. Thus, much traffic gathers to some LEO satellites covering populated areas. Traffic congestion causes the decrease in the performance of the network such as packet drop, throughput degradation, and the increase of delay. To avoid the congestion, many route control methods for satellite networks have been developed based on DSP [8] [9] [10]. As one example, Explicit Load Balancing (ELB) is proposed as a traffic control method that can handle acute changes of traffic [11]. In ELB, each satellite constantly measures its queue occupancy as an indicator of traffic loads. Each satellite also exchanges congestion information. The traffic detouring is performed depending on the condition of the traffic load. As a result, when a satellite has heavy traffic load and congestion occurs, its load is immediately decreased by traffic detouring. Even though ELB is able to mitigate the congestion at relay satellites, there has not been any method which can efficiently avoid the congestion at the destination concentrating high traffic.

In order to come up with a solution for that problem, we consider satellite networks where each satellite has a mass storage device. Satellites can save and bring the data when they orbit the earth. In other words, satellites are able to deliver a packet to destination without using the link among satellites. However, an efficient routing method is required to take such advantage of the embedded mass storage devices.

3. PROPOSED ROUTING METHOD CONSIDERING STORAGE DEVICES

We consider a simple scenario as shown in Figure 2 in order to make a clear explanation for our method. In this scenario, at first, satellite E covers the area where there is traffic concentrating. Satellite E has four links among adjacent satellites. These satellites move together in the direction of the arrow in Figure 2. After that, the hand-over from satellite E to satellite A occurs and satellite A moves to this area as shown Figure 2(b).

3.1 Deterioration of the link utilization

In this section, we propose a new routing method to improve link utilization and avoid network congestion. For satellite networks, roundabout traffic has negative effects because it wastefully use links that do not need to be used. On the other hand, since unnecessary detouring leads to delay, traffic should only use the necessary links. Thus, link utilization improves when only necessary links are used, and degrades when wasteful links are used. When much traffic concentrates on one satellite, the congestion might occur. In the case of not having storage device, satellites cannot save packets temporally, and thus adjacent satellites continue sending packets to the satellite having congestion. In our new routing method, adjacent satellites reduce the amount of traffic to the satellite having congestion by detouring or saving some traffic. Although our routing method is proposed for general cases, in order to keep the simplicity of the explanation, the proposed algorithm is explained based on the above mentioned scenario.

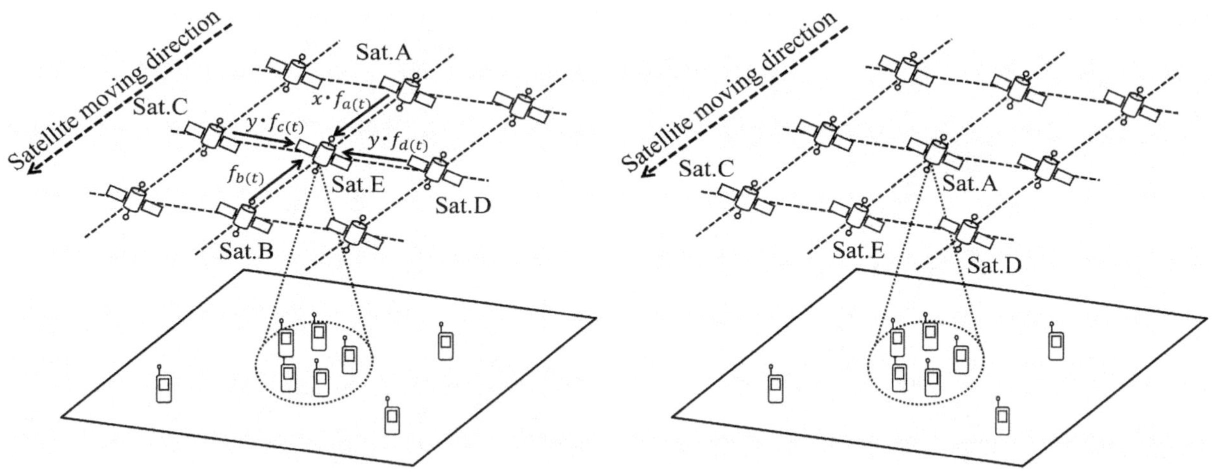

(a) Before hand-over (b) After hand-over

Figure 2: Considered model.

When our new routing method is not applied, the amount of the traffic from satellite A to E at the time of t is defined by $f_a(t)$, and those from B, C, D are defined by $f_b(t)$, $f_c(t)$, and $f_d(t)$, respectively. t_h is the time when satellite E moves out of the communication range of the destination. In this research, we only consider the traffic that is sent to destination through satellite E. The amount of all traffic to satellite E, $F(t)$ is expressed as the following equation.

$$F(t) = f_a(t) + f_b(t) + f_c(t) + f_d(t). \quad (1)$$

We assume that all satellites have the ability to send the traffic with the amount of T_{capacity} to the destination per time unit. Since satellite E covers the area where there is much traffic concentrating, it is likely that $F(t)$ becomes larger than T_{capacity}. If $F(t)$ is greater than T_{capacity}, either satellite E has to save data to storage device or adjacent satellites need to reduce the amount of traffic to satellite E.

Firstly, we consider the case where satellite E saves all the which is over T_{capacity} in storage device. When satellite E moves out of the communication range of the destination at the time t_h, satellite A covers the area that was previously covered by satellite E as shown in Figure 2(b). In this case, if satellite E saved the data in its storage device, it has to send that amount of data to satellite A using satellite-satellite links. To prevent using these links, we consider the another case where adjeacent satellites reduce the amount of traffic to satellite E by sending that traffic to satellite A beforehand. Since satellite A saved that data in its storage device, it can send that data to the destination without using any more satellite-satellite links. As a result, the link utilization will be improved. On the other hand, if the traffic from adjacent satellites to satellite E is too small, satellite-destination link cannot be used adequately and it deteriorates the utilization of satellite-destination links. Therefore, it is necessary to maximize the use of the link between satellite E and destination, and minimize the amount of data that satellite E needs to send to satellite A. It is important to note that futher describe how adjacent satellites send traffic to satellite A. Satellite A does not send traffic and save it in its storage device, but another satellites have to send traffic to satellite A using satellite-satellite links. Satellite C and satellite D have to use two satellite-satellite links and satellite B has to use four satellite-satellite links. Obviously, the amount that adjacent satellites send to satellite A should change taking into account the positions of the satellites.

When $F(t)$ reaches T_{capacity}, satellite E sends signaling packets to its adjacent satellites. Satellite A which received this signaling packets reduces the amount of traffic actually flowing to satellite E to $xf_a(t)$, where x represents the ratio of the amount of traffic when our method is applied to amount of traffic when the method is not applied. $x = 1$ means satellite A sends all traffic with the destination is satellite E, and $x = 0$ means satellite A does not send any such traffic. Similar to satellite A, after receiving signaling packets from satellite E, satellite C and D reduce the amount of traffic actually flowing to satellite E to $yf_c(t)$ and $yf_d(t)$, respectively. Note that the value of x and y imply all cases that only satellite E saves data to its storage device, or only the adjacent satellites reduce the amount of traffic to satellite E, or both. When satellite C and D reduce their traffic, based on the moving direction of the constellation as shown in Figure 2, the remaining traffic from satellite C and D should be detoured to satellite A. After that, satellite A can save those data and directly send to the destination because satellite A will cover the area instead of satellite E. The amount of traffic which satellite C and satellite D detour to satellite A are $(1-y)f_c(t)$ and $(1-y)f_d(t)$, respectively. After the adjustment, the amount of traffic which adjacent satellites actually send, $F'(t)$, becomes the following equation.

$$F'(t) = xf_a(t) + f_b(t) + y\{f_c(t) + f_d(t)\}. \quad (2)$$

If the adjacent satellites reduce the amount of traffic to satellite E, but $F'(t)$ is still greater than T_{capacity}, satellite E saves the data that cannot be sent to destination. If $F'(t)$ becomes below T_{capacity} after using storage device on satellite E, satellite E sends the data saved in its storage device to the destination.

3.2 Improvement of the link utilization

In this section, we compare the link utilization in two cases of using storage device on satellite E or on satellite A.

We assume that every adjacent satellites of satellite E generates the same amount of traffic having Gaussian distribu-

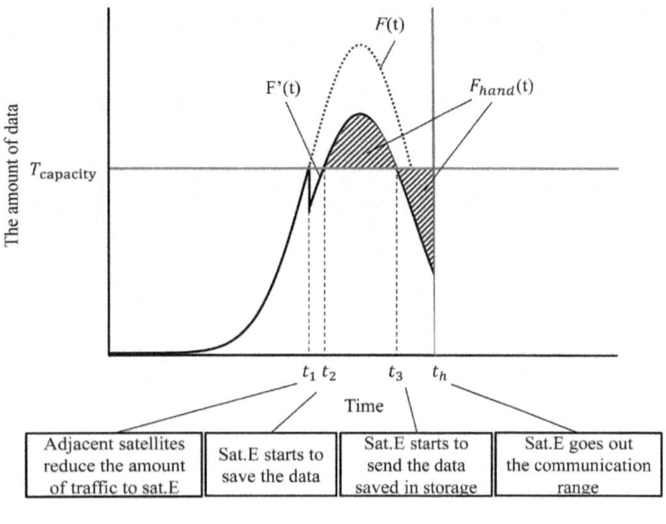

Figure 3: The relationship between $F(t), F'(t)$, and T_{capacity}.

tion in terms of time, which is expressed as Eq. 3, where σ is the standard deviations of t, and μ is the mean of t.

$$f(t) = \frac{1}{\sqrt{2\pi}\sigma} \exp\left(-\frac{(t-\mu)^2}{2\sigma^2}\right). \tag{3}$$

Gaussian distribution has the peak at μ, and traffic decreases gradually from this peak but is limited by zero. The shape of the distribution depends on the value of σ. $F(t)$ and $F'(t)$ can be calculated as follows.

$$F(t) = 4f(t). \tag{4}$$

$$F'(t) = (1 + x + 2y)f(t). \tag{5}$$

We consider the case $F(t)$ becomes larger than T_{capacity}, when satellites need to use storage device. The time when $F(t)$ becomes over T_{capacity} is defined by t_1 as shown Figure 3. This parameter is related to traffic distribution and T_{capacity}. As mentioned earlier, adjacent satellites reduce the traffic to $F'(t)$ at t_1. In the case $F'(t)$ becomes over T_{capacity} in spite of reducing traffic to satellite E, we call that time t_2. And when $F'(t)$ falls below T_{capacity}, we call that time t_3. Similar to t_1, t_2 and t_3 change with the changes of traffic distribution and T_{capacity}. In addition, t_2 and t_3 are related to the amount of traffic from adjacent satellites, which are affected by x and y. According to traffic distribution, relationship with t_3 and t_h is categorized in two types, $t_3 \leq t_h$, and $t_h < t_3$. Figure 3 indicates only one case which is $t_3 \leq t_h$.

The amount of data that satellite E has to send to satellite A after hand-over occurs, F_{hand}, is expressed as follows.

$$F_{hand} = \int_{t_2}^{t_h} \{F'(t) - T_{\text{capacity}}\} dt \tag{6}$$

In Figure 3, F_{hand} is indicated by the shaded area. When $F'(t)$ is larger than T_{capacity}, satellite E starts to save the data in its storage device. After $F'(t)$ falls below T_{capacity}, satellite E sends the data saved in its storage device. If the amount of the data that satellite E temporarily saved is larger than the amount of data that satellite E can send until the hand-over occurs, F_{hand} has a positive value. This means that satellite E has to send that data to satellite A after the hand-over. On the other hand, if the amount of the data that satellite E temporarily saves is smaller than the amount of data that satellite E can send until hand-over occurs, F_{hand} has a negative value. In this case, no traffic is sent from satellite E to satellite A after the hand-over. However, when satellite E does not use the satellite-destination links at its maximum, the link utilization between satellite and destination decreases. As a result, to maximize link utilization, satellite E should always send traffic with an amount equal to T_{capacity} to the destination, and thus, the incoming traffic to satellite E is limited such that no traffic is transmitted from satellite E to satellite A after the hand-over. This results in a value of $F_{hand} = 0$. In the next section, we analyze the existence of x and y that makes $F_{hand} = 0$.

Table 1: parameter settings

	case1	case2
σ	1.0	1.0
μ	8.0	9.0
x	0.00-1.00	0.00-1.00
y	0.00-1.00	0.00-1.00

4. NUMERICAL ANALYSIS

In this section, we aim to verify the relationship between the utilization of satellite-satellite links and that of satellite-destination links. Moreover, we declare the existence of the optimal amount which adjacent satellites send to satellite E with some numerical calculation results.

The parameter settings that characterize traffic are summarized in Table 1. In this numerical analysis, T_{capacity} is set to 0.5GB. The time period between when satellite E starts covering the destination to when the hand-over occurs is set to 10 minutes. We analyze two different cases that are described as follows. In Case 1, we set σ to 1.0 and μ to 8.0, and the percentage of traffic amount x and y varies from 0.00 to 1.00 with a step of 0.01. If there is a particular combination of x and y which makes $F_{hand} = 0$, it means that satellite E always send T_{capacity} traffic and there are no traffic needed to send from satellite E to satellite A after hand-over. In short, we find the optimal combination of x with y such that the link utilization becomes maximum. In Case 2, we set σ to 1.0 and μ to 9.0, and vary x and y in the same way as the Case 1. By indicating particular combination of x and y which makes $F_{hand} = 0$ using another parameter, it can be said that the optimal combination of x and y exists regardless of the traffic.

Figure 4 shows the relationship between the amount of traffic from adjacent satellites and the storage device utilization of satellite E. Figure 4(a) and Figure 4(b) represents Case 1 and Case 2, respectively. In Figure 4(a), F_{hand} increases with the increase of x and y. In the area with small x and y, F_{hand} keep a constant value. In this area, x and y is too small and $F'(t)$ does not reach T_{capacity}. In this case, t_2 and t_3 do not exist, so we can not calculate F_{hand}. Therefore we use the minimum value of F_{hand} for F_{hand} in the area. The plane of F_{hand} crosses zero plane at particular x and y, which means that the optimal combination exists

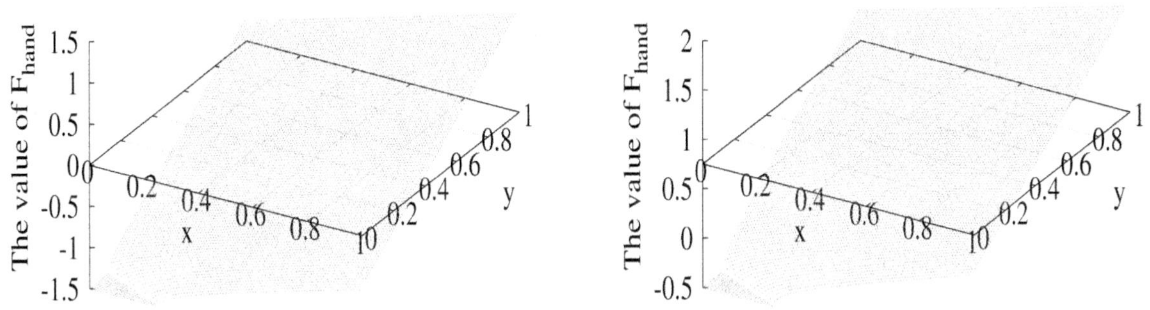

(a) Case 1

(b) Case 2

Figure 4: The relationship between the amount of traffic from adjacent satellites and the utilization of storage device on satellite E.

and that is the optimum value. Also, in Figure 4(b), the plane F_{hand} crosses zero plane at different value of x and y, so the optimal combination of x with y exists. These results show that there is a combination of x and y that makes the link utilization maximum regardless of the traffic.

5. CONCLUSION

In this paper, we proposed a new routing method for satellite networks using mass storage devices, which is a good candidate for next generation networks to manage large amount of data. By applying our new routing method, satellite networks can mitigate congestion due to the concentration of traffic. Furthermore, we analyzed the link utilization of satellite-satellite and satellite-destination links. From the analysis of over use of the satellite-satellite links and inadequate use of the satellite-destination links, the existence of the optimal amount of traffic from adjacent satellites to the satellite having congestion in terms of maximizing link utilization is indicated. Finaly, we showed that the appropriate routing method achieves to avoid congestion for satellite networks without wasteful consumption of network resource.

Part of this research belongs to Research of communication control techniques in next generation satellite-routed sensor system, supported by National institute of Information and Communications Technology (NICT).

6. REFERENCES

[1] Ministry of Internal Affairs and Communications, 2011 WHITE PAPER Information and Communications in apan, Part 1, 2011.

[2] . W. Lee, . W. Lee, T. W. Kim, and D. U. Kim, Satellite over Satellite (SOS) Network: A Novel Architecture for Satellite Network, in *Proc. IEEE INFOCOM*, pp. 315–321, Nov. 2000.

[3] S. Bayhan, G. Gur, and F. Alagoz, Performance of Delay Sensitive Traffic in Multi-layered Satellite IP Networks with On-board Processing Capability, *International Journal of Communication Systems*, vol. 20, no. 12, pp. 1367–1389, an. 2007.

[4] M. Asvial, R. Tafazolli, and B. G. Evans, Satellite constellation design and radio resource management using genetic algorithm, *Communications, IEEE Proceedings*, vol. 151, no. 3, pp. 204–209, un. 2004.

[5] . Kawamoto, H. Nishiyama, N. Kato, N. oshimura, N. Kadowaki, A delay-based traffic distribution technique for Multi-Layered Satellite Networks, *Wireless Communications and Networking Conference 2012 IEEE*, pp. 2401–2405, Apr. 2012.

[6] F. Alagoz, O. Korcak, and A. amalipour, Exploring the routing strategies in next-generation satellite networks, *Wireless Communications, IEEE*, vol. 14, no. 3, pp. 79–88, un. 2007.

[7] E. W. Dijkstra, Note on Two Problems in Connexion with Graphs, *Numerische Mathematik*, vol. 1, no. 1, pp. 269–271, Dec. 1959.

[8] . Tada, H. Nishiyama, N. oshimura, and N. Kato, An Effective Route Control Method on Multi-layered Satellite Networks, *International Astronautical Congress*, IAC-10.B2.1.5, Prague, Czech Republic, Sep. 2010.

[9] I. F. Akyildiz, E. Ekici, and M. D. Bender, MLSR: a novel routing algorithm for multilayered satellite IP networks, *IEEE/ACM Transactions on Networking*, vol. 10, no. 3, pp. 411–424, un. 2002.

[10] C. Chen and E. Ekici, Routing Protocol for Hierarchical LEO/MEO Satellite IP Networks, *Wireless Networks*, vol. 11, no. 4, pp. 507-521, ul. 2005.

[11] T. Taleb, D. Mashimo, A. amalipour, N. Kato, and . Nemoto, Explicit Load Balancing Technique for NGEO Satellite IP Networks With On-Board Processing Capabilities, *IEEE/ACM Transactions on Networking*, vol. 17, no. 1, pp. 281–293, Feb. 2009.

Wake-up Radio as an Energy-Efficient Alternative to Conventional Wireless Sensor Networks MAC Protocols

Joaquim Oller, Ilker Demirkol, Jordi Casademont, Josep Paradells
Department of Telematics Engineering
Universitat Politecnica de Catalunya
i2CAT Foundation
Barcelona, Spain
{joaquim.oller, ilker.demirkol, jordi.casademont, teljpa}@entel.upc.edu

Gerd Ulrich Gamm, Leonhard Reindl
Institut für Mikrosystemtechnik – IMTEK
Albert-Ludwigs-Universität
Freiburg
{gerd.ulrich.gamm, reindl}@imtek.uni-freiburg.de

ABSTRACT

The use of duty-cycling in Medium Access Control (MAC) protocols effectively helps improving the energy efficiency of wireless networks. However, while the benefits of these protocols are unquestionable, most of them still suffer from overhearing and idle listening, two issues that prevent duty-cycled systems from achieving optimum energy usage, which is a crucial aspect in specific types of wireless networks such as Wireless Sensor Networks (WSN). Wake-up Radio (WuR) systems have been employed recently to overcome these issues. Under this approach, the nodes' MicroController Unit (MCU) and main radio transceiver are completely switched off and only activated when a secondary, extremely low-power receiver in the node is triggered by a particular wireless transmission. Wake-up Radio systems allow for drastic energy savings since receiver nodes are only activated on-demand, maximizing their battery lifetimes. In this paper, we have modeled and simulated a real, recent and promising WuR hardware platform based on its time and energy consumption characterization. By comparing such WuR approach to B-MAC and IEEE 802.15.4, two well-known and widely employed MAC protocols, we show it effectively outperforms the conventional WSN MAC approaches in terms of energy efficiency. To the best of authors' knowledge, this is the first study to include a comparative analysis for multi-hop networks based on a real WuR platform, which shows WuR systems represent an energy-efficient solution that also provides a good tradeoff between latency, packet delivery ratio and applicability.

Categories and Subject Descriptors

C.2.0 [**Computer-communication Networks**]: General—*Data communications*; C.2.1 [**Computer-communication Networks**]: Network Architecture and Design—*Wireless communication*

MSWiM'13, November 3–8, 2013, Barcelona, Spain.

ACM 978-1-4503-2353-6/13/11 ...$15.00
http://dx.doi.org/10.1145/2507924.2507955.

General Terms

Design, Measurement, Performance.

Keywords

Wake-up radio, wake-up receiver, energy-efficient communications, MiXiM, OMNET++, WSN, duty-cycling, low-power listening, MAC.

1. INTRODUCTION

Since the wireless communication of the nodes is a dominant energy consuming operation of a network, to achieve optimum energy utilization has been a main target of the wireless networking research community. A conventional solution to reduce the energy waste caused by redundant activation of the radio has been duty-cycling, where the nodes are put to sleep state and wake up periodically to check the medium for potential incoming packets. However, duty-cycling approaches do not completely overcome the problems of idle listening, which happens when a node checks the medium but no communication is present, or overhearing, which happens when a communication is being received by a node, although it is not intended for that node. Examples of duty-cycling approaches are B-MAC [14] and X-MAC [4], which are common default MAC choices for wireless sensor nodes.

Both B-MAC and X-MAC protocols are based on Low Power Listening (LPL), in which the transmitter node generates a preamble prior sending the real data. In B-MAC, such preamble is slightly longer than the sleeping period of the nodes' duty-cycle to ensure the receiver node to hear the preamble. The preamble is detected as a medium-busy tone by the receiver, which waits until its end and then switches to *real* data reception mode, where the transceiver presents higher current consumption since now it requires demodulation and decoding capabilities. Undoubtedly, such preamble-based way of operation introduces severe medium occupancy and latency issues. These issues can be reduced by increasing the duty-cycle, i.e., by shortening the sleep period, of the MAC protocol, which in turn increases the energy consumption.

A predominant MAC protocol for Wireless Sensor Networks (WSN) is the IEEE 802.15.4, which is the basis of network layer specifications such as ZigBee and 6LoWPAN. IEEE 802.15.4 does not consider duty-cycling in its widely employed non-beacon enabled mode. Without duty-cycling, IEEE 802.15.4 achieves high throughput and low delay, since it does not incur large overhead as in LPL.

A recent and promising energy-efficient alternative to exploit the trade-off between duty-cycling approaches and non-beacon enabled IEEE 802.15.4 is Wake-up Radio (WuR), which enables wireless devices to remain in very low-power deep-sleep mode until woken up by remote triggering. In a WuR system, when a node requires to communicate it first sends a Radio Frequency (RF) signal through its wake-up transmitter (WuTx) to the ultra low-power Wake-up Receiver (WuRx) attached to the destination node, which MicroController Unit (MCU) and main radio are in deep sleep mode. Upon reception of such radio signal, so-called Wake-up Call (WuC), the WuRx raises a hardware interruption in the node's MCU, which in turn activates the main radio transceiver. From this moment on, traditional data communication may take place. Thus, compared to duty-cycled preamble-based MACs, WuR allows for significant latency improvements by optimizing the wireless medium's occupancy. On the other hand, when compared to proposals such as non-beacon enabled IEEE 802.15.4, WuR provides much better energy management by reducing the energy waste caused by idle listening and overhearing, while still promising acceptable throughput and delay performance.

Recently, a very low-power WuR system has been proposed in [6, 5] that we refer as SubCarrier Modulation Wake-up Radio (SCM-WuR), which achieves very low WuRx power consumption and long operational distances. In this paper, we target to quantify the advantages of using SCM-WuR in a multi-hop network scenario, and compare its performance to B-MAC and IEEE 802.15.4. We evaluate the network performances of all three approaches in terms of packet delivery ratio, latency, mean current consumption and energy efficiency, i.e., the energy required by nodes to successfully deliver one bit. For these evaluations, we implement a complete model for SCM-WuR in OMNET++ [3] using its MiXiM framework [2] and show its corresponding results when deployed in the same network as the other two approaches.

The rest of the paper is structured as follows. Section 2 contains a brief state of the art of the works related to wake-up radio simulations. Section 3 introduces our Wake-up Radio MiXiM model. Section 4 describes the analyzed scenario and employed parameter set, and presents the performance analysis of the different kind of nodes when operating in such scenario. Finally, Section 5 concludes the paper.

2. RELATED WORK

The literature on MAC protocols for wireless sensor networks and related performance evaluations is known to be extensive [7]. Unfortunately, comparing their performance to multi-hop networks with WuR-equipped nodes is not common, since most WuR proposals do not contemplate multi-hop capabilities. In fact, until late 2010 the current consumption of wake-up receivers was not sufficiently low and the corresponding operational ranges were not large enough for their deployment to be considered as feasible and beneficial.

There are many WuR hardware proposals in the literature [13, 12, 8] but few simulations evaluate their network performance, if any. The work in [15] provides a comparison between preamble-sampling and wake-up radio systems, but basically from the point of view of the density of nodes required to cover a geographical area under each approach. A more detailed and current overall comparison of WuR systems can be found in [10]. Unfortunately, the presented results are limited to quantify the consumption featured by receivers when activated certain number of times per hour, not including latency or other metrics, and not comparing them to duty-cycled approaches. Finally, in other works such as [11] the employed WuR system architecture is not even explicitly detailed.

In this paper, we provide an implementation of a recent, completely detailed Wake-up Radio system, and contrast the multi-hop network performance it achieves when compared to MAC protocols. In order to provide a meaningful comparison, we study not one but several metrics. To the best of our knowledge, we are the first to provide these comparative analysis results for multi-hop networks based on a real WuR system.

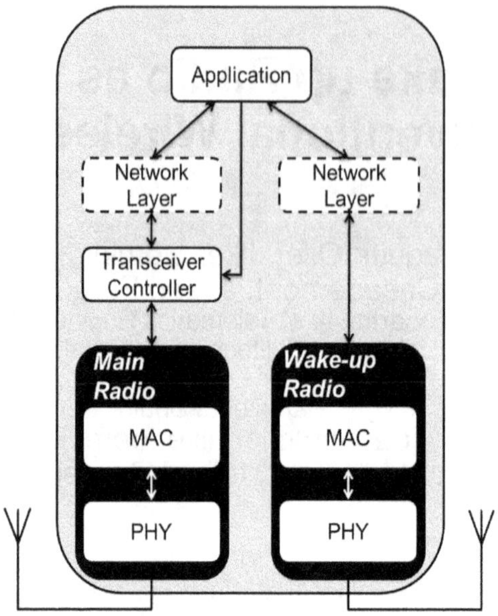

Figure 1: Developed MiXiM model for a WuR-equipped node.

3. DEVELOPED MIXIM MODELS

MiXiM (MiXed siMulator) is a software framework built on top of the well-known OMNET++ simulation engine designed for modeling communication networks. MiXiM offers detailed models of radio wave propagation, interference estimation, power consumption, timing, etc. which become extremely useful for evaluating wireless MAC protocols. Compared to OMNET++, MiXiM provides MAC protocols that are not generic yet much more focused to subjects of wireless sensor networks, body area networks and adhoc networks, among others. For example, both B-MAC and non-beacon enabled IEEE 802.15.4 approaches are included by default in MiXiM, but not in OMNET++. We develop our SCM-WuR system model on MiXiM because of its integration to OMNET++ and the models it provides for concepts related to WSN, such as the CC2420 transceiver and the B-MAC and IEEE 802.15.4 MAC protocols.

Our model is compatible with the latest software versions of OMNET++ and MiXiM 4.3 and 2.3, respectively. In order to avoid redesigning existing parts, it takes profit of several concepts already implemented such as the Clear Channel Assessment (CCA) procedure. As it can be seen in Figure 1, in our model, WuR-equipped nodes feature two radio transceivers: the *main* transceiver and the *wake-up* transceiver. This two-radio model enables the simulation of WuR systems either with two separated radio interfaces or with a shared transceiver such as in SCM-WuR. In real SCM-WuR devices, wake-up radio transmissions and data transmissions are generated by the same transceiver [6] and the input/output RF path is managed by an ADG918 antenna switch [1] by the node's MSP430 MCU.

Independently of its architecture, in any WuR system the MCU and the main data communication transceiver are initially switched off to reduce the energy consumption while the wake-up radio is left activated to monitor the channel. When a WuC is received by the WuRx, it generates an interruption to wake-up the node's MCU, which in turn switches on the main transceiver (and the input RF path, in case of a shared transceiver) so that upcoming data frames can be received in a traditional fashion through the main radio. After the MCU of the node is activated, it may perform several jobs before disabling the data transceiver and going to low-power WuR mode again, such as doing a measurement from a temperature sensor and sending back the data, or forwarding the incoming data frame. In our model, incoming and outgoing WuCs are managed in the right path of the Figure 1, while traditional communications take the left one. For the 868MHz CC1101 transceiver in the SCM-WuR's MiXiM model, appropriate current consumption values are adapted from the manufacturer's datasheet [9].

In Figure 1, the *Application* module contains the code for the user application, e.g., to initialize the node or to generate packets. The main radio is managed by a sub-module so-called *Transceiver Controller*, which allows the application to monitor and control the status of the transceiver, as done in the source code of the real SCM-WuR boards. Different routing protocols may be implemented in the *Network* layer module in Figure 1, which may also be omitted.

Currently, there exist two real hardware implementations of the SCM-WuR system. A version capable to transmit up to 40 meters is introduced in [6], where as an enhancement for a transmitter capable of achieving an operational range of up to 100 meters is proposed in [5]. In this paper, we consider a SCM-WuR model that can operate up to 100 meters. Such WuR board features as low as 3.5μA when operating in low-power wake-up mode when no WuC is detected. This value increases up to 8μA when the WuRx is decoding the address embedded in a WuC. Regarding transmitter side, the WuTx requires up to 152mA when sending a WuC to achieve the 100 meters range. WuR present lower operational ranges than traditional wireless communications due to the fact the WuRx design must be kept simplistic in order to operate in the microamper order of magnitude. Accordingly, wake-up calls in SCM-WuR require to be transmitted with noticeably more power than conventional wireless transmissions to be detected.

Real SCM-WuR nodes are powered by means of four 1.5V AA batteries providing a capacity of 1500mAh each. Correspondingly, a value of 3000mAh and 3V is contemplated for our simulations. Such battery configuration is common in wireless sensor networks' deployments.

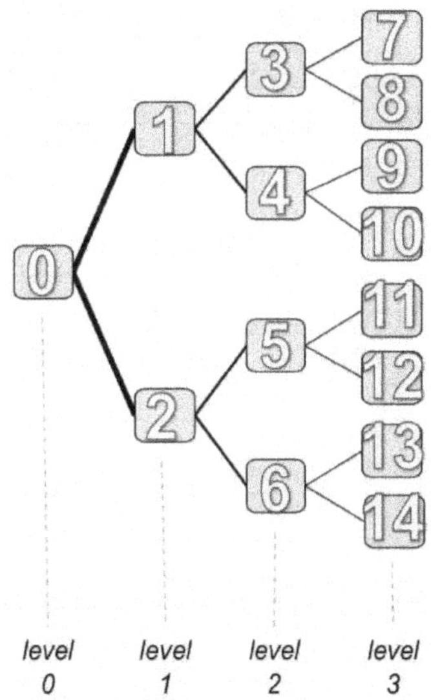

Figure 2: Simulated multi-hop network.

4. PERFORMANCE EVALUATION

In order to effectively compare the performance of the studied approaches, a realistic multi-hop scenario is considered, for which a binary tree is defined as shown in Figure 2. Packet routes are predefined and fixed to do the performance comparison independently of the employed routing protocol. Nodes in the proposed simulation topology periodically generate data packets. The period, i.e., the time between consecutive packet generations, is varied to evaluate the network performance under different traffic loads. Each node generates packets destined to Node 0, i.e., the sink of the network, and sends such packets to their parent nodes to be forwarded to the sink. This way, if the packet inter-generation time is 10 seconds, a node placed at penultimate level of the tree will have to forward 20 pkts/sec, 10 from each child, as well as to generate its own 10 packets, for a total of 30 pkts/sec. The nodes closer to Node 0 are in charge of forwarding much more packets than the nodes closer to the leaf nodes.

For each evaluated parameter set, we ran 10 repetitions with different random seeds in order to increase the representativeness of the results. We provide the 95% confidence intervals in the plots based on these repetitions. Each node randomly chooses its initial offset for packet generation. We define λ to be the packet rate, i.e., the inverse of packet inter-generation times. Hence, the considered network is tested for data loads of λ = 10, 1, 0.2, 0.1, 0.03, 0.02, 0.01, 0.006 pkts/sec, which are generated by each node of the network but the sink. We tested two implementations already present in MiXiM, non-beacon enabled IEEE 802.15.4 and B-MAC, and compare their performances to that of SCM-WuR implementation. The results are processed entirely by using specific OMNET++ packages for the R statistical software.

Approach	Parameter	Value	Unit
Common	Tree level distance	100	m
	Packet payload	100	bytes
	Queue buffer length	10	pkts
	Supply Voltage	3	V
	Battery Capacity	3000	mAh
B-MAC	Sleep Current	0.02	mA
	Rx Current	16.4	mA
	Tx Current	17	mA
	Bit-rate	15.360	kbps
	Check Interval	10	ms
	Slot Duration	1	s
IEEE 802.15.4	Rx Current	18.8	mA
	Tx Current	17.4	mA
	Bit-rate	250	kbps
	Slot Duration	100	ms
	Backoff Number	3...8	slots
SCM-WuR	Sleep Current	3.5	μA
	Rx Current main radio	18.8	mA
	Rx Current (WuRx)	8	μA
	Tx Current main radio	18.8	mA
	Tx Current (WuTx)	152	mA
	Bit-rate main radio	250	kbps
	Bit-rate (WuR)	1	kbps

Table 1: Simulation Parameter Set.

4.1 Simulation Parameter Set

The configurable parameter set is found to be extremely large in MiXiM as well as in OMNET++. Table 1 summarizes the simulation parameters that are crucial for the evaluations carried out.

In the simulations, we have not modified any parameter value or source code for MiXiM's IEEE 802.15.4 and B-MAC implementations.

4.2 Packet Delivery Ratio Analysis

We evaluate the packet delivery ratio (PDR) as the number of packets received at the sink divided by the total number of packets generated during the experiment. This metric is an important measure of the network performance for convergecast type of traffic, where packets are forwarded towards a sink that acts as a gateway to an external network. Figure 3 shows the packet delivery ratio achieved by the three approaches investigated, namely B-MAC, IEEE 802.15.4 and SCM-WuR, under different packet traffic loads. As seen in the figure, B-MAC results in a PDR close to 0 for packet rates higher than 1 pkt/sec, since the preamble duration is also 1 second, a circumstance which saturates the network. In B-MAC, wait periods due to busy medium can be significant due to the long preamble duration and, in addition, during this procedure both transmitting node and nodes that are detecting the preamble cannot receive any packets from other nodes. Moreover, surrounding nodes' energy consumption is increased, since they cannot sleep until receiving the data frame which carries the address of the destination node and comes after the preamble. Thus, in our topology, B-MAC quickly collapses for increased λ values.

In the case of IEEE 802.15.4, as it is a CSMA-based approach, a node desiring to access the channel must first assure no other transmitter is using the medium. If the node senses the medium to be busy after such CCA operation, it performs a randomized back-off and tries to transmit after the chosen back-off time. Since in CSMA no preamble or wake-up packet is needed, transmissions can be performed in much less time and more quickly than in B-MAC. This is one reason why IEEE 802.15.4 presents good PDR results. Indeed, evaluating the non-beacon IEEE 802.15.4 approach is useful to establish performance limits for PDR, since it provides the upper limit of the network's capacity due to no energy-conserving sleeping and no overhead.

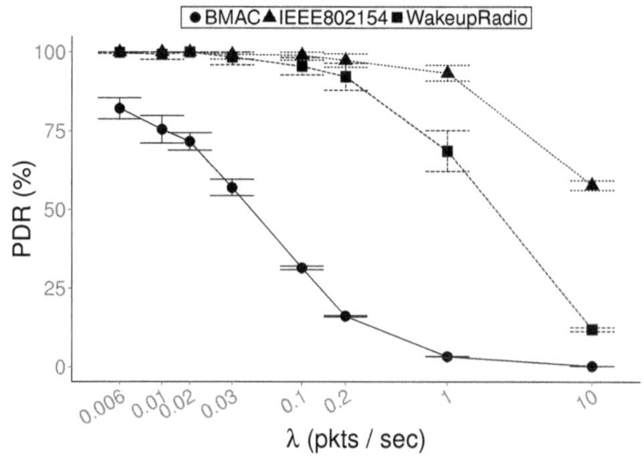

Figure 3: Packet Delivery Ratio Analysis.

Regarding our SCM-WuR model, the PDR results are found to be satisfactory up to a value of $\lambda = 0.2$ pkts/sec, i.e., up to 1 packet every 5 seconds. Yet the data rates observed in most sensor network applications are lower than this rate. For more aggressive values of λ, SCM-WuR begins to saturate. Thus, simulation results show how SCM-WuR effectively outperforms B-MAC, and present similar PDR results to non-beacon enabled IEEE 802.15.4 for $\lambda \leq 0.2$.

4.3 Latency Analysis

Latency is calculated in the MiXiM framework as the difference between a packet's reception time at the destination and the time the packet was generated. In Figure 4, the total delay for a packet to travel from the leaf Node 7 to the network's sink is shown as an illustrative example. Such measure can be seen as the total time it takes for a packet generated at the furthest tree level to go through all the levels of the proposed network topology.

For preamble-based MACs, a preamble is generated at the same time as a data packet and sent just before it. In B-MAC, data packets may suffer long wait periods due to surrounding preamble transmissions before being able to be transmitted. Such issue is repeated in all hops up to the sink and becomes more and more important as data load increases. Again, BMAC is observed to saturate as λ gets close to 0.1 pkt/sec.

Obviously, IEEE 802.15.4 obtains the best latency results due to being constantly active for monitoring the channel and for not incurring any delay overhead except the CCA prior the packet transmissions. However, this comes with a cost in consumed power.

For its part, SCM-WuR performs efficiently in terms of latency when compared to the other two approaches, with

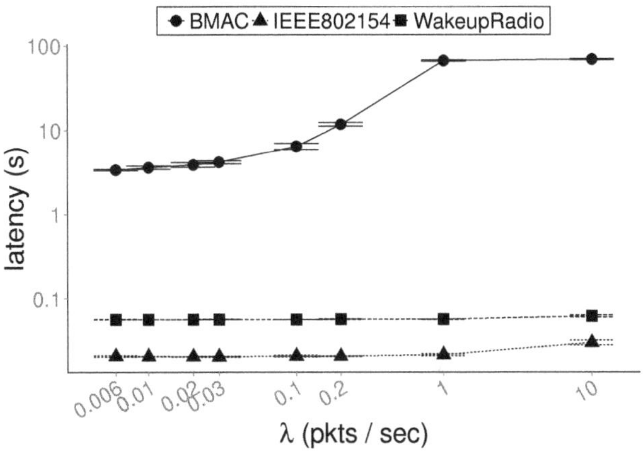

Figure 4: Latency Analysis.

values not higher than 60 milliseconds for packets to go through the entire network. This value is logical if we consider the amount of time needed for the WuC (12ms), the transition of the MCU and main network interface card from sleep to receiving state (1.79ms), the reception of the data packet ((100bytes * 8) / 250000bps = 3.2ms) and average contention and processing-related times (1.5ms) for a total of 18.5ms. Such value, multiplied by 3 hops (4 levels) from Node 7 to reach the sink, sums up to a total of approximately 60ms.

WuR systems are not limited to the obtained latency values. Other WuR systems may implement two transceivers working at different frequencies for main and wake-up radio, thus the data and WuC transmissions can be carried in a parallelized fashion, achieving better utilization of the medium and lower delay.

4.4 Lifetime Analysis

By making use of the energy framework in MiXiM, we measure the average power consumption of each node of the network. Figures 5a and 5b depict such consumption for the sink node and Node 1, one of the sink's child nodes, respectively. Node 1 is the one of the two most power consuming descendants of the sink in all tests because of being in charge of forwarding the packets from half of the nodes in the network depicted in Figure 2.

In the evaluated scenario, the sink node does not need to transmit, so its power consumption in Figure 5a is only related to reception. Note that under very high data loads, the sink node's power consumption featured by SCM-WuR is greater than that of B-MAC due to the fact it effectively receives more packets in the SCM-WuR approach. For transmitting nodes such as Nodes 1 and 7, Figures 5b and 5c show the clear benefits of SCM-WuR, respectively. On the contrary, IEEE 802.15.4 presents a constant power consumption in all the nodes due to the always-on radio. Its power consumption value corresponds to the multiplication of the voltage (3V) by the current consumption of the nodes when transmitting or receiving (17.4mA and 18.8mA, respectively). Note that IEEE 802.15.4 is continuously listening the channel, only switching when a transmission is required. Thus, the predominant power-demanding component is reception.

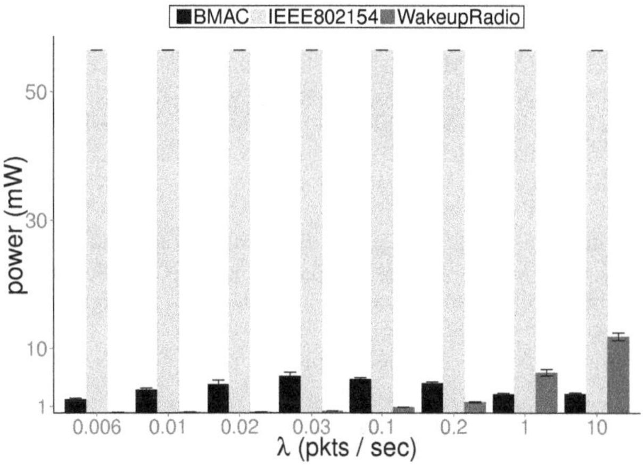

(a) Sink node

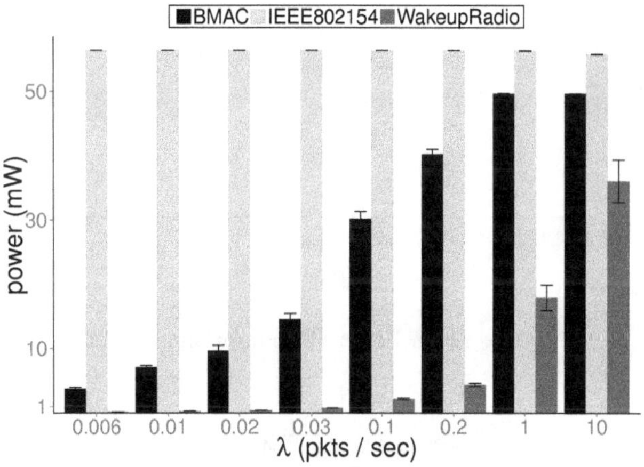

(b) Node 1

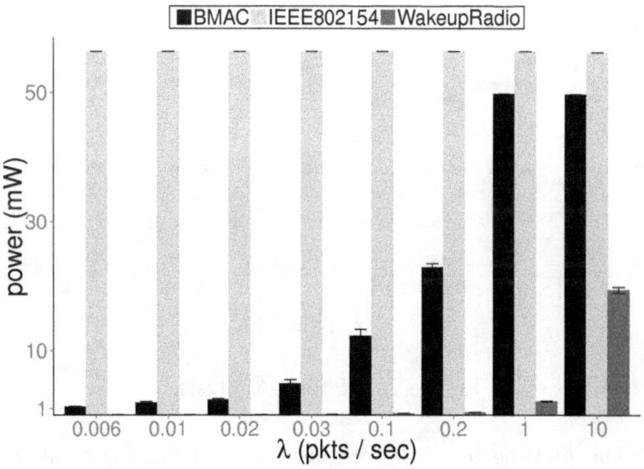

(c) Node 7

Figure 5: Mean power consumption of individual nodes.

In addition to characterizing the power profiles of individual nodes, also the whole network's average node power consumption is analyzed. Figure 6 shows such global comparison between the three approaches. As expected, non-beacon enabled IEEE 802.15.4 nodes consume the highest average power among all three approaches due to continuous listening of the channel. The purpose of duty-cycled protocols such as B-MAC is precisely to reduce such energy-demanding continuous idle listening, and B-MAC effectively accomplishes that for λ values up to 0.2 pkt/sec although resulting in low PDR, as seen in Figure 3. As a numerical example, at λ value of 0.03 pkts/sec, B-MAC and SCM-WuR provide energy savings up to 85% and 99%, respectively, when compared to IEEE 802.15.4. In fact, SCM-WuR keeps offering good power consumption values even for higher data loads.

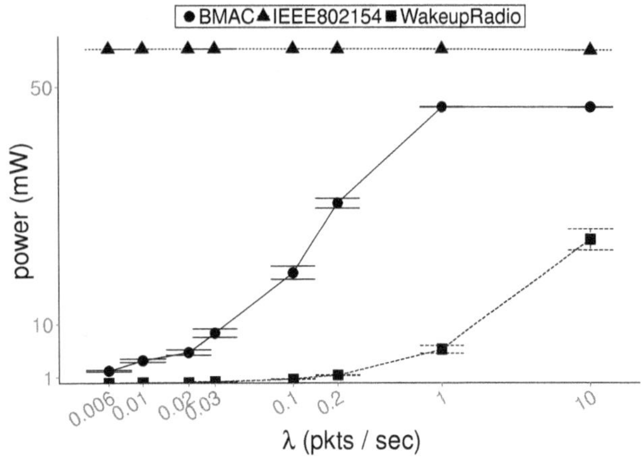

Figure 6: Mean Power Consumption Analysis.

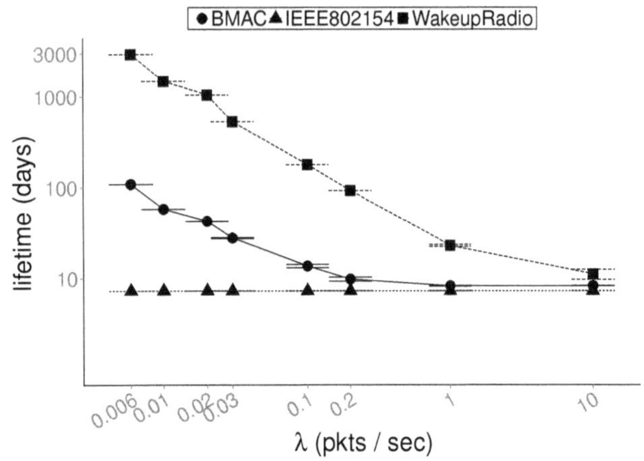

Figure 7: Lifetime Analysis.

The lifetime of a network is also a crucial performance metric. Among different alternatives, we choose and evaluate the lifetime metric that corresponds to the minimum time the network operates until the first node runs out of battery, which enables the network designer to know how long it takes for each MAC approach before battery replacement or recharging is required.

In Figure 7, we present the lifetime performances of the three approaches. Even though a WuC requires several times more current consumption than a traditional wireless data communication, it is important to note how SCM-WuR can offer lifetime values which outperform the other approaches in orders of magnitude. This confirms that most part of energy required by wireless nodes is devoted to reception, which is drastically reduced in WuR systems. Even for a quite stressing packet generation rate of 1 packet every 10 seconds ($\lambda = 0.1$), the SCM-WuR approach enables up to 100 days of network operation time, while B-MAC and IEEE 802.15.4 approaches can only provide 5 and 2 days, respectively. For lower data generation rates, the difference becomes even more noticeable, with up to 3000 days for SCM-WuR nodes in front of less than 100 days for the other approaches. The lifetime and mean power consumption of SCM-WuR can be further improved using less power for WuC transmissions if lower operational ranges than 100m are enough for the intended application. In such case, the relative gain of the SCM-WuR would be much higher since the WuC transmission is the main power-demanding procedure in SCM-WuR.

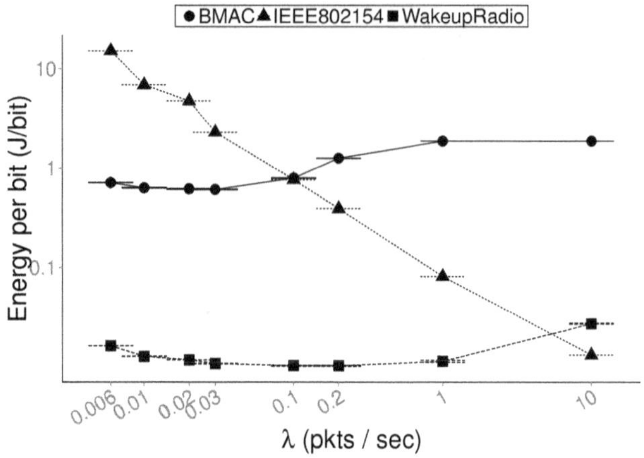

Figure 8: Energy per bit Analysis.

4.5 Energy per bit Analysis

The amount of energy per transmission of one successful bit is shown in Figure 8. This metric is calculated by dividing the total energy consumed in the network by the total number of bits received at the sink node. As seen in Figure 8, the energy per bit performance of non-beacon enabled IEEE 802.15.4 improves as the data rate gets higher. The reason is that IEEE 802.15.4 consumes energy independently of the traffic rate because of an always-on state, thus the energy efficiency increases in accordance with the data load. However, although the energy efficiency of IEEE 802.15.4 is better than that of SCM-WuR for very high data rates (e.g., at the rate of 10 pkts/sec), such data rates are not common in WSN. For its part, B-MAC requires more energy than SCM-WuR, due to the long preamble it sends for each data packet.

To quantify the components of such energy consumption at the nodes, the percentage of time employed in each state of the main transceiver is depicted for B-MAC, IEEE 802.15.4 and SCM-WuR in Figures 9a, 9b and 9c, respectively. Clearly, SCM-WuR obtains its energy advantages from the fact that the main radio interface is in the sleeping mode most of the time. This contrasts with the high ratio of time that B-MAC nodes are in transmit or reception modes. The transceiver's switching procedure is performed very fast, thus its time component is not very significant in the figures.

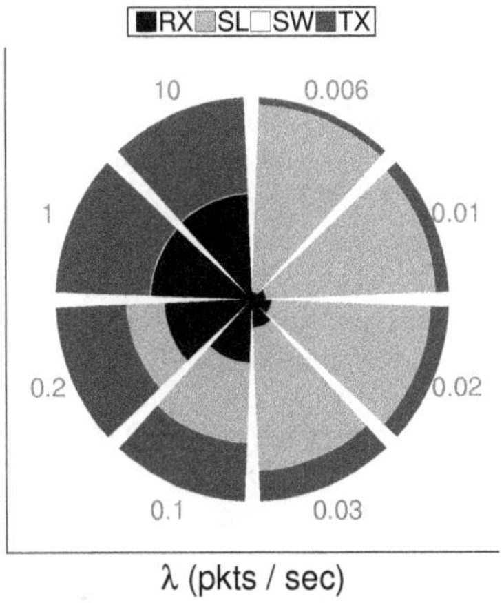

(a) B-MAC

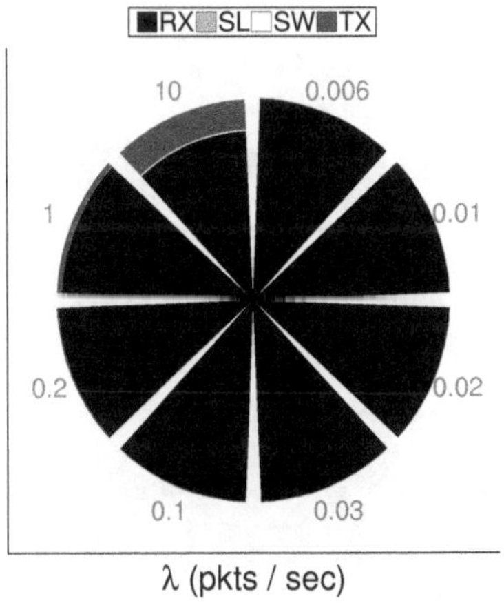

(b) Non-beacon enabled IEEE 802.15.4

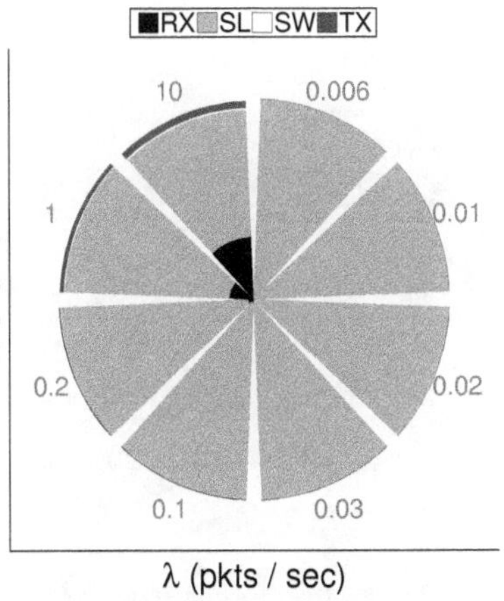

(c) SCM-WuR

Figure 9: Time percentage the main transceiver of Node 1 is in each mode. Inside out: RX (receiving), SL (sleeping), SW (transceiver switching) and TX (transmitting).

5. CONCLUSIONS AND FUTURE WORK

Energy efficiency is one of the most important concerns in nowadays wireless networks. Unfortunately, such energy efficiency presents a trade-off with latency and packet delivery ratio, or requires solutions with global time synchronization, a feature which is not trivial to achieve in wireless deployments. Wake-up radio systems present an energy-efficient solution while providing a good tradeoff between latency, packet delivery ratio and applicability. This paper describes the implementation and simulation of a novel WuR solution, namely SCM-WuR. For the simulation parameters, we use current consumption and timing values obtained by physical measurements of real SCM-WuR hardware boards. Such SCM-WuR approach is compared to two well-known WSN MAC protocols, namely B-MAC and non-beacon enabled IEEE 802.15.4, which are commonly used in WSN. Simulation results show that SCM-WuR effectively outperforms the conventional WSN MAC approaches in terms of energy efficiency for realistic traffic loads expected in WSN. Future work plans include the evaluation of other MAC protocols, as well as other topologies such as mobile networks.

6. ACKNOWLEDGMENTS

This work has been supported by the Spanish Government's Ministerio de Economía y Competitividad through project TEC2012-32531 and by MICINN through project TEC2009-11453. Joaquim Oller was supported by FEDER and by the Spanish Government through a FPI grant.

7. REFERENCES

[1] Adg918: Wideband, 43db isolation 1ghz, cmos 1.65v to 2.75v switch. `http://www.analog.com/en/rfif-components/rf-switches/adg918/products/product.html`.

[2] Mixim: mixed simulator. `http://mixim.sourceforge.net/`.

[3] Omnet++ network simulation framework. `http://www.omnetpp.org/`.

[4] M. Buettner, G. V. Yee, E. Anderson, and R. Han. X-mac: a short preamble mac protocol for duty-cycled wireless sensor networks. In *Proceedings of the 4th international conference on Embedded networked sensor systems*, SenSys '06, pages 307–320, New York, NY, USA, 2006. ACM.

[5] G. Gamm and L. Reindl. Range extension for wireless wake-up receivers. In *9th International Multi-Conference on Systems, Signals and Devices (SSD)*, pages 1–4, 2012.

[6] G. Gamm, M. Sippel, M. Kostic, and L. Reindl. Low power wake-up receiver for wireless sensor nodes. In *Sixth International Conference on Intelligent Sensors, Sensor Networks and Information Processing (ISSNIP)*, pages 121–126, 2010.

[7] P. Huang, L. Xiao, S. Soltani, M. Mutka, and N. Xi. The evolution of mac protocols in wireless sensor networks: A survey. *Communications Surveys Tutorials, IEEE*, 15(1):101–120, 2013.

[8] X. Huang, S. Rampu, X. Wang, G. Dolmans, and H. De Groot. *A 2.4 GHz/915MHz 51uW wake-up receiver with offset and noise suppression*, page 222–223. IEEE, 2010.

[9] T. Instruments. Cc1101: Low-power sub-1 ghz rf transceiver datasheet, 2012.

[10] V. Jelicic, M. Magno, D. Brunelli, V. Bilas, and L. Benini. Analytic comparison of wake-up receivers for wsns and benefits over the wake-on radio scheme. In *Proceedings of the 7th ACM workshop on Performance monitoring and measurement of heterogeneous wireless and wired networks*, PM2HW2N '12, pages 99–106, New York, NY, USA, 2012.

[11] R. Jurdak, A. Ruzzelli, and G. M. P. O'Hare. Adaptive radio modes in sensor networks: How deep to sleep? In *SECON '08. 5th Annual IEEE Communications Society Conference on Sensor, Mesh and Ad Hoc Communications and Networks*, pages 386–394, 2008.

[12] S. J. Marinkovic and E. M. Popovici. Nano-power wireless wake-up receiver with serial peripheral interface. *IEEE Journal on Selected Areas in Communications (JSAC)*, 29:1641–1647, 2011.

[13] N. M. Pletcher, S. Gambini, and J. Rabaey. A 52uw wake-up receiver with -72 dbm sensitivity using an uncertain-if architecture. *IEEE Journal of Solid-State Circuits*, 44(1):269–280, 2009.

[14] J. Polastre, J. Hill, and D. Culler. Versatile low power media access for wireless sensor networks. In *Proceedings of the 2nd international conference on Embedded networked sensor systems*, pages 95–107, New York, NY, USA, 2004. ACM.

[15] R. Su, T. Watteyne, and K. Pister. Comparison between preamble sampling and wake-up receivers in wireless sensor networks. In *Global Telecommunications Conference (GLOBECOM 2010), 2010 IEEE*, pages 1–5, 2010.

Efficient Algorithm for Serial Data Fusion in Wireless Sensor Networks*

Ahmed Mostefaoui
FEMTO-St Institute DISC dep.
University of Franche Comte
Belfort, 90000, France
ahmed.mostefaoui@univ-fcomte.fr

Mahmoud Melkemi
LMIA laboratory
University of Haute Alsace
Mulhouse 68093, France
mahmoud.melkemi@uha.fr

Azzedine Boukerche
PARADISE Research Lab,
University of Ottawa
Ottawa, Canada
boukerch@site.uottawa.ca

ABSTRACT

Although Wireless Sensor Networks (WSNs) are capable of generating a huge amount of data, the ultimate objective of the underlying applications/end-users is to derive an estimate of a parameter or function of interest through queries sent to nodes containing raw data. The way these queries are handled by the network has a deep impact on its overall performances (e.g., required communications, consumed energy, etc.). Among the numerous centralized and distributed approaches addressing this issue, serial ones have shown an interesting improvements in terms of reducing communication needed for each query and hence reducing required energy. Nevertheless, serial approaches suffer two main drawbacks: (a) they require to construct a path passing through all nodes of the network (which is known to be a NP-Complete problem) and (b) they experience poor scalability. In this paper, we investigate these issues by proposing a novel localized serial approach, called *Peeling Algorithm (PA)*. The proposed approach, because of its localized nature (i.e., no extra-information is needed rather than what it is already available at each node), has shown better support for scalability while reducing significantly needed communications to accomplish a query. The extensive simulation evaluations we made have confirmed the effectiveness of our proposed approach in comparison to other serial approaches. We also provide in this paper formal proofs of its correctness i.e., our distributed approach terminates (free of looping) and visits all connected nodes in the network.

Categories and Subject Descriptors

C.2.4 [**Computer communication networks**]: Distributed applications

Keywords

sensor networks; serial data fusion; distributed and localized algorithm

---

*This work is partially supported by NSERC, Canada Research Chairs program, and MRI/ORF Research Funds.

MSWiM'13, November 3–8, 2013, Barcelona, Spain.

http://dx.doi.org/10.1145/2507924.2507964.

1. INTRODUCTION

Recent technological advances have lead to the emergence of Wireless Sensor Networks (WSNs) as a promising technology for many applications in several domains [4] (environmental monitoring, health-care diagnostics, animals tracking, etc.). A WSN consists in a collection of nodes, each of which provided with sensing, computing and wireless communication capabilities. Nodes are then deployed in a region of interest, usually in an random fashion, for monitoring purposes. Sensors collect data that is forwarded to the base station, also called *Sink*, in order to answer the application/end-user queries. This process is referred to as *query processing*.

Because of their intrinsic constraints (energy limitation, large deployment, etc.) query processing in WSNs remains a challenging research problem. Many approaches have been proposed in the literature and could be classified into three categories: (a) Centralized approaches [3], also called *warehouse approaches*, in which raw data are first collected by sensors and sent to the sink. The latter, with the help of a database management system, could then answer the queries. In those approaches, the query processing is independent of the the data collection. Although centralized approaches are simple and efficient in terms of queries answering, they however have several drawbacks among them we note overutilization of network resources, mainly communications, and poor scalability. (b) Distributed approaches [8] have then been proposed to specifically overcome these limitations. In such approaches, as the general objective is to derive an estimate of a parameter or function of interest from raw data (e,g., average, source location [15], , ...), sensor nodes do not need to hold global knowledge about the current network topology since each node communicates only with its immediate neighbors. The unknown parameter is then successively (i.e., iteratively) carried out through local computation from the exchanged data between neighbors. The advantages of such approaches are numerous: (1) no central base station is required as every node holds the estimate of the unknown parameter; (2) multi-hop communications are avoided and consequently maintaining rooting data is not needed any more; (3) better behavior is observed in front of communication and nodes unreliability. Nevertheless, distributed approaches observe an important resources consumption, particularly communications as the number of iterations could be important. Furthermore, because of their synchronized iterations, these approaches generate an important number of packets collisions which may decrease the overall network performances (query responsiveness). (c) Serial approaches [13, 12] have then been proposed as an interesting alternatives to reduce communications, including collisions, overhead observed previously in both centralized and distributed approaches. The basic idea behind is to let one node initiating the query and the estimate is then successively (i.e., serially) updated from node to node until all nodes of the network are visited. The last node holds the correct estimate [10]. As stated in [13], serial approaches perform very efficiently in terms of reducing needed communications.

Although theoretical foundations of serial approaches have been provided into [13, 11, 10], some practical issues have not been, to the best of our knowledge, addressed yet: in fact, serial approaches make the assumption that an hamiltonian path within the network exists. However, constructing such a path is known to be a NP-Complete problem [6] which is not easy to meet, especially in sparce and large scale networks. The cost of finding such a path, in a decentralized manner to ensure scalability, could generate a prohibitive communication cost. In [12], the authors propose to use *space filling curves* to derive a path through the network. Besides of its poor scalability, this approach does not efficiently handle irregular network topologies, i.e., networks with holes. Moreover, it does not ensure all nodes visiting.

In this paper, we propose a novel serial data fusion approach that is totally *distributed and efficient.* Two important requirements have guided our work. First scalability which means that the protocol should be totally distributed to scale proportionally with the size of the network. Second, completeness which means that all nodes of the network should be visited i.e. contribute in the parameter estimate. Our approach, thanks to its localized nature i.e., no extra-information than what is usually available (1 hop-information), well fulfills the scalability and robustness requirements as the next hop decision is taken locally and independently by each node. We also provide theoretical proofs of its completeness. The simulation results show clearly the effectiveness of our approach in terms of reducing communication, energy and responsiveness time in comparison to other serial approaches.

The rest of the paper is organized as follows: in Section 2 we present our serial algorithm. Section 3 provides proofs of correctness of the proposed approach. Performance evaluation and results are presented into Section 4 while Section 5 concludes the paper.

2. PEELING ALGORITHM

In this section we present our proposed serial approach, named Peeling Algorithm (PA). We begin first by sketching the overall PA behavior through illustrative examples. Then after, we present the boundary traversal algorithm we used which of course fulfills our major requirement (e.g., of a distributed and localized nature).

We consider a geographic wireless sensor network in which nodes are static and homogeneous, with R as their communication range. We note $\mathcal{N}$ as the set of nodes and $\mathcal{E}$ as the set of links. We consider that each node is aware of its location by means of a positioning system like GPS or as a result of a localization process [2]. Furthermore, each node N_i is aware of its neighboring set $V_i = \{N_j \mid E_{(i,j)} \in \mathcal{E}\}$ and their corresponding locations.

The commonly communication model used in wireless sensor networks is of a broadcasting nature [4] i.e., when a node sends a packets, all neighbors within its transmission range will receive it. Hence, it is worthwhile to notice that the listening process does not incur any additional transmission (no explicit request is sent to the transmitter). This interesting feature of the communication model will be used later on in our approach to update, without any additional communication costs, the visited neighbors table of each node.

We refer in the rest of the paper to the node that issues the request as the *"Query Initiator Node" (QIN).* In opposition to other approaches, mainly centralized ones, the QIN in our approach could be any node in the network.

We now introduce some definitions used later to highlight our peeling approach.

Definition 1. *(Boundary Node)*
A node N is said to be a boundary node in the direction $\angle N_iNN_j$, noted BN, iff it has at least two angularly adjacent neighbors N_i, N_j such that N_i could not communicate with N_j or the angle $\angle N_iNN_j \geq \pi$

In other terms, messages issued on a boundary must remain on the same boundary. Hence, a node is facing a boundary (hole or network boundary) if any message coming from its right neighbor to its left neighbor "transits" by it. Two cases are possible: either its neighbors could not communicate with each others or the angle is greater or equal to π as illustrated into Figure 1. Each node could face at most six boundaries.

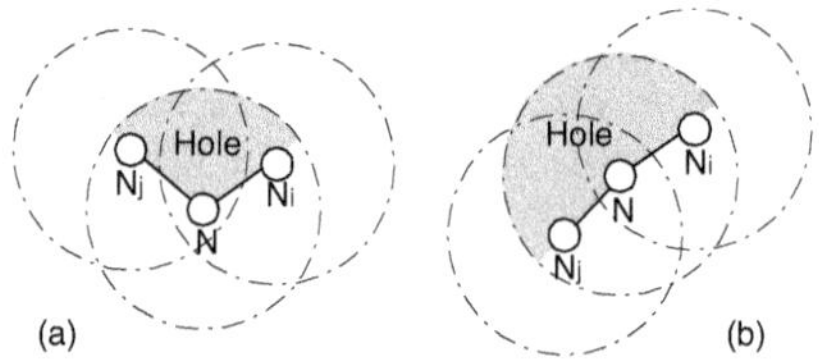

Figure 1: Boundary Node.

With the help of this definition, every node in the network could locally determine if it is located either on the boundary of a hole inside the network or on the boundary of the network. The computation can be performed with only information on 1-hop neighbors.

Definition 2. *(Hole Boundary Nodes)*
For each hole, noted H, we define the set of nodes belonging to it as a cyclic sequence of boundary nodes:
$H = \{N_j, N_{j+1}, ..., N_{j+k}, N_j\}$ *such that the closed region bounded by this non self-intersecting polygonal sequence is empty of any node.*

Definition 3. *(Network Boundary Nodes)*
We define the set of Network Boundary nodes as a cyclic sequence of boundary nodes: $NBN = \{N_i, N_{i+1}, ..., N_{i+k}, N_i\}$ such that the closed region bounded by this non self-intersecting polygonal sequence contains all nodes of the network.

As explained below, our serial query processing approach starts from a network boundary node. The identification of such node is not straightforward and could not be processed locally as it was the case for boundary nodes. To this end, we present below a distributed and localized algorithm that is able to identify a starting network boundary node.

Definition 4. *(unvisited Sub-Network)*
We define the current unvisited sub-network, noted Ω, as the set of all currently unvisited nodes.

2.1 PA Overview

The key idea behind our algorithm is to let the serial process visiting nodes, starting from one node, located on the external boundary of the network, by means of a boundary traversal process. Hence, from this node, the process starts visiting nodes based on their localization on the boundary of the unvisited region Ω. Initially, for any query we have $\Omega = \mathcal{N}$. Then, at every step of the serial process, the currently visited node is removed from Ω (marking itself as visited) and in turn it selects the next unvisited node located on the boundary of Ω. This process is repeated until all nodes are visited: the last node that has all its neighbors visited detects query termination and sends the result to the QIN by mean of any geographical routing approach [5]. The term peeling comes from the fact that all currently visited nodes belong to the boundary of Ω. Figure 2(a) illustrates the peeling process.

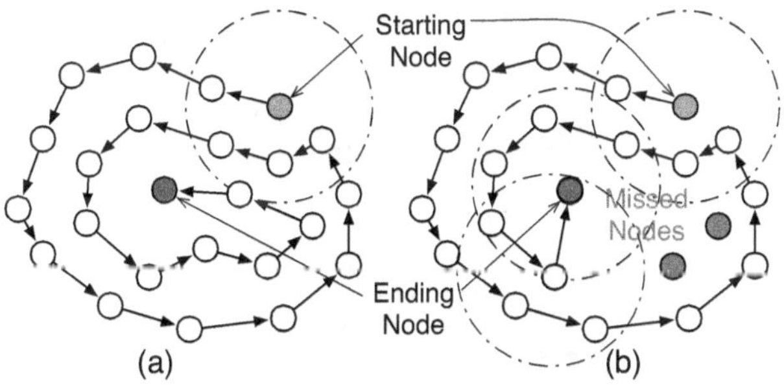

Figure 2: Peeling Serial Algorithm.

This simple process whereas it behaves very efficiently in dense and hole free topologies (it nearly derives the optimal path), it however does not ensure completeness (i.e., be able to visit all nodes) for all network topologies. A simple example is when a node is connecting two parts of the network. Once the latter is visited, the unvisited region connectivity is not ensured any more leading thus to *missed unvisited nodes* as illustrated into Figure 2(b).

To prevent this situation, certain nodes have to be maintained *"alive"* to ensure network connectivity even though they have been visited. For this reason, we have introduced the notion of **Bridge Node** as follows:

Definition 5. *(BRidge Node)*
A node is said Bridge Node, noted BRN, when it verifies the two following conditions: (a) at least two of its unvisited or BRN neighbors could not communicate and (b) none of the other unvisited or BRN neighbors are able to connect these two neighbors.

In other terms, the current node is the only node able to ensures connectivity between these two neighbors. An illustration of BRN is given into Figure 3. The left node is considered as BRN whereas the right one is not.

It has to be noted that the current node could locally decide whenever it is a BRN or not based only on neighboring information. No additional information than what is already available is required. This ensures that our approach

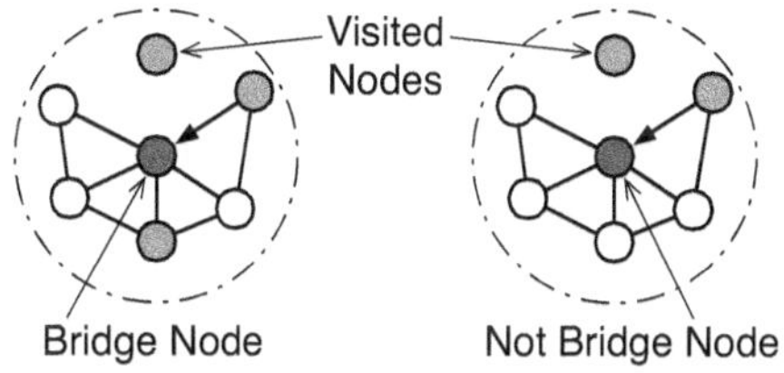

Figure 3: Bridge Node definition.

remains localized and does not generate any additional communication overhead. We also note that a node could change its "status" from BRN to visited node depending on its localization on one hand and on its currently visited neighbors on the other hand. The broadcasting/listening nature of the communication model used in wireless sensor networks ensures that neighboring status updates do not incur any additional communication overhead.

Property 1.
Bridge nodes ensure unvisited sub-network (e.g. Ω) connectivity

PROOF. We prove by contradiction. Initially Ω is connected. We assume that the current node, N_i is not a bridge node whereas at the same time it breaks Ω connectivity. From Definition 5, if N_i is not a bridge node, this means that for every pair of its neighbors, there is a link connecting them without passing by N_i. Hence, Ω is then connected which contradicts the fact that N_i breaks Ω connectivity. □

Although bridge nodes resolve the problem of unvisited sub-network connectivity, they however rise another problem when the network contains hole. In fact, according to Definition 5, all hole boundary nodes, belonging to the same hole H, will be marked as bridge nodes. The consequence, in this case, is that some nodes, with particular localization around the hole, could not be visited any more i.e., they prevent the peeling process to access those nodes leading hence to query completeness violation as illustrated into Figure 4. Moreover, as all hole nodes are "labeled" as bridge's nodes, the termination of the peeling process, as stated earlier, is not guaranteed too. It leads usually to looping situation as showed into the example of Figure 4.

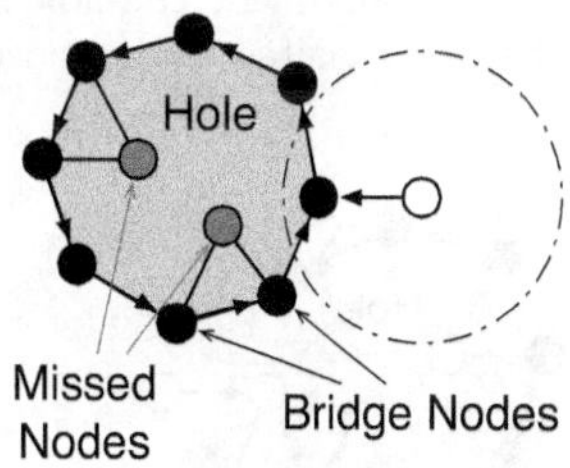

Figure 4: Example of peeling looping.

To resolve these two important issues, while continuously maintaining the connectivity of the unvisited nodes (e.g., Ω), we have associated a particular rule to special hole nodes defined as follow:

Definition 6. *(Hole Gate Node (HGN))*
For each hole H, we define its Hole Gate Node (HGN) ($HGN \in H$) as the first node that holds the peeling process.

The goal behind defining Hole Gate Nodes is to let the peeling process going inside the hole. By doing so, we avoid situations in which nodes, located *"around"* holes, could not be visited as explained in the example. The questions that follow are how a node could be labeled as HGN? and what is/are the associated rule(s)?

To answer the first question, two steps are necessary: (a) a node must first determine if it is located on the boundary of a hole or not? As explained above in Definition 1, this could be done locally by each node thanks to the neighboring available information ; (b) Secondly, when a node is aware of its localization on the boundary of a hole, it could determine if it is the HGN of this hole or not when it receives the peeling message for the first time: if the peeling comes from a node that does not belong to the hole then it deduces that it is the first visited node of the hole and consequently it is the HGN of this hole. Otherwise, the hole has already its HGN. According to that, we note that each hole has only one corresponding HGN. For these two steps, we mention that no extra-information is needed and could then be processed locally.

The second question has to be handled carefully in order to prevent looping inside the hole. We observe that each hole node has two hole neighbors. We note them the *Left Neighbor (LN)* and the *Right Neighbor (RN)* as presented into Figure 5. When a node detects itself as a HGN, it performs the following steps:

1. It contributes into the query process and marks it self as a HGN.

2. According to the peeling direction (i.e., clockwise or counterclockwise), it chooses either LN or RN as the next query holder. For sake of simplicity, we assume that it chooses LN as the next hop.

3. Node RN is then notified to update its neighbors table with "visited" label for node HGN even when the latter is considered as BRN. In other terms, we break the link between the two nodes *HGN* and *RN* (see Figure 5).

4. HGN sends the query to LN.

When LN holds the query, the process could continue normally by using the boundary traversal algorithm. Step 3 prevents the peeling to loop inside the hole since RN will at its turn consider HGN as visited node and could not select it as next hop.

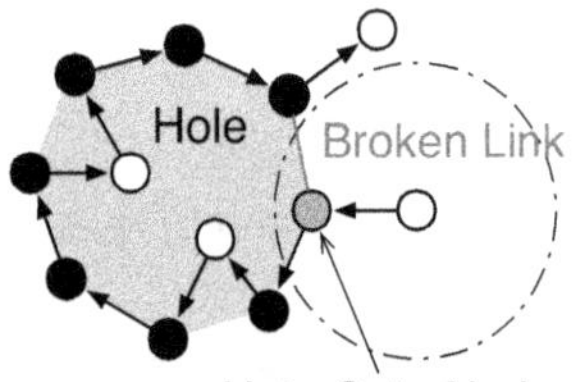

Figure 5: Hole Gate Node Rule.

These rules, applied by the HGN of each hole, were practically sufficient to ensure query completeness. In fact, among the numerous network configurations, generated randomly as explained into Section 4, none has experienced network completeness violation i.e., all alive nodes in the network have been visited by our approach. Nevertheless, from theoretical point of view, we have constructed by hand some topologies in which our approach fails to visit all nodes. An example of such a topology is presented into Figure 6(a). When node N_1 receives the query, it considers itself as the HGN of $hole_1$ and applies the corresponding rules according to previous steps. Hence, the link $E_{(1,17)}$ is broken and the query is oriented toward node N_2. Similarly, when node N_4 receives the query, it considers itself as the HGN of the hole located on its left side and decides to break the link $E_{(4,5)}$. It sends then the query to node N_{10}. By doing so, all nodes located on $hole_2$ are lost and could never be visited later on. The origin of this misbehavior comes from the fact that node N_4 could not locally know that it is located on the same hole. In other terms, node N_4 locally "views" two holes whereas it is the same hole, leading hence to a *False HGN* detection. This information is not available for N_4 at the moment of receiving the query.

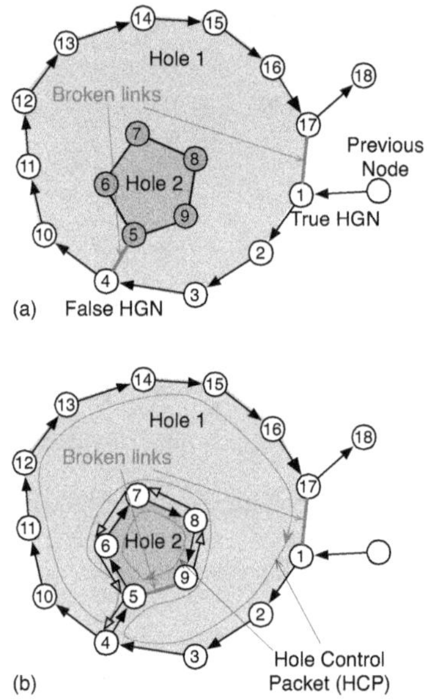

Figure 6: Peeling Misbehavior.

To alleviate this problem, we have added an additional rule to the HGN, when it detects itself as a HGN. Before selecting its next hop according to step 2, it first sends a control packet, named Hole Control Packet (HCP), toward the hole as showed in Figure 6(b). The objective of this packet is twice: first it informs all hole nodes that the hole has "got" its HGN and consequently they will not consider this hole when they receive the query. Secondly, it allows nodes to detect if their "local holes" do not belong to the same hole. For instance, node N_4 will know that its left and right holes belong to the same hole, which has already got its HGN. In this case, when it receives the query, it will not consider itself as HGN of this hole and hence lets the peeling process continuing after contributing in it. However, node N_5 could be able to detect itself as the HGN of $hole_2$ and apply consequently the corresponding rules i.e, sending a HCP and breaking the link with the right neighbor as shown into Figure 6(b).

The HGN rules could be seen somehow as a way of *linearizing* holes preventing hence looping situations and allowing inside holes exploration. On the other hand, they always preserve the unvisited region connectivity i.e, the removed links could not lead to Ω partition.

Property 2. *HGN rules do not partition the unvisited region Ω i.e., Ω connectivity remains.*

PROOF. We assume that the broken link, says $E_{(HGN,RN)}$, leads to Ω partition. This means that no path could connect nodes HGN and RN. However, we note that both sides of the broken link $E_{(HGN,RN)}$ could not by construction belong to the same hole, thanks to HCP rule lunched by the HGN of the hole. Also, by construction, each hole holds one and only one HGN. Consequently, it exists a path connecting HGN to every node in the hole without passing through link $E_{(HGN,RN)}$, in particular node RN. This contradict the initial assumption. □

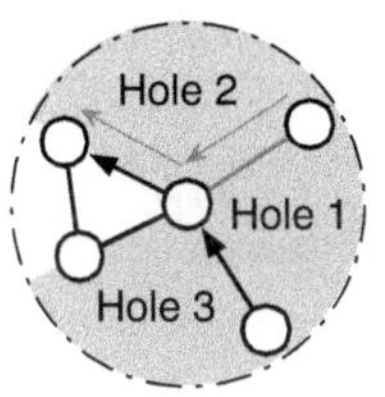

Figure 7: Node's local holes selection.

The overall serial query algorithm, executed by each node receiving the query message, is depicted into Algorihm 1. We assume that the boundary traversal algorithm is using counterclockwise direction.

Algorithm 1 Peeling Algorithm.

```
Require: Receive message M from the previous hop
if (Not visited for this query) then
    Contribute in the query.
    Mark itself as visited node for this query.
    if (current node is HGN) then
        // In case where the current node is located on more
        // than one unexplored hole (see Figure 7).
        From the incoming message, select the first counterclockwise hole among local unexplored holes.
        Send HCP toward the selected hole
        Upon receiving the HCP, mark itself as HGN
        Select the left neighbor as the next hop.
    else
        Select the next hop among unvisited and BRN neighbors.
    end if
else
    Select the next hop among unvisited and BRN neighbors
end if
Compute its status (i.e., is the current node a BRN or not?)
send the message to the next hop N_next
```

2.2 Boundary Traversal Algorithm

As seen before, the use of a boundary traversal algorithm is crucial in our peeling algorithm to ensure its completeness (i.e., visiting all nodes). Of course, the distributed and localized nature of the boundary algorithm must be maintained in order to reach good communication performances. In previous work [9], we have proposed an efficient boundary traversal algorithm, called Curved Stick (CS). In addition to deriving shorter paths, this approach has the advantage of being fully localized while at the same time formally ensures boundary traversal. It works as follows:

The process always starts from a boundary node, called Boundary Traversal Initiator (BTI). The BTI initiates a *"Curved Stick"* (CS) which has the form of an arc with radius of R (node's communication range). Initially the CS, hinged at the current node, is oriented in the direction of the hole/network boundary as shown into Figure 8. From this position, the BTI sweeps the CS counterclockwise[1] until a neighbors is hit. The latter is then selected as the next hop and will repeat the same process starting from its corresponding *"starting point"*, defined as fellow:

Definition 7. *(Starting Point)*
We define the Starting Point of node N_{i+1}, noted SP_{i+1} as the intersection point between the two circles of range R, centered at N_i and N_{i+1} and following the direction $\angle N_{i-1}N_iN_{i+1}$ where N_{i-1} is the previous hop of node N_i and N_{i+1} is the next hop of N_i.

And so on until the message gets back to the BTI which means that a cycle has been achieved (hole boundary detection for instance).

Theorem 1.
Whenever started from a boundary node, curved stick process ensures boundary traversal.

PROOF. Because of space limitation, we provide here just the idea behind our proof. Details can be found in [9]. We assume that CS does not ensure boundary traversal i.e., there is a node located in the grey area if Figure 8 which is not hit by CS and show that this leads to a contradiction. □

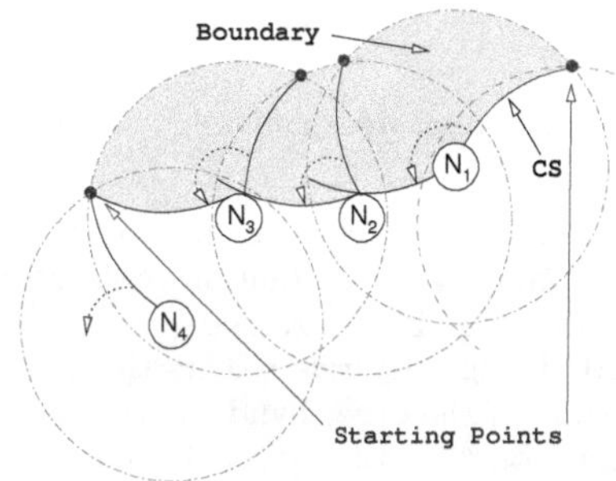

Figure 8: Curved Stick boundary traversal algorithm.

In our peeling implementation, we have made use of the curved stick approach.

2.3 Starting Node Detection

As mentioned previously, our peeling approach must start from a node located on the external boundary of the network. Furthermore, each network boundary node must update the list of its local holes in order to avoid considering the external network boundary as a hole.

[1]The sweeping direction does not impact the process i.e., the clockwise direction could also be used but the direction must remain the same during the whole process.

Several approaches could be developed to inform nodes about their localization on the external boundary of the network. One could though about a centralized approach in which every node sends its localization information to the sink and the latter, through local processing, detects those located on the external boundary of the network. After, this information is sent back to NBNs. Besides its important energy consumption, this approach presents another very limitative weakness: it is not scalable any more. Scalability remains however an important requirement to protocols in large-scale sensor networks.

To overcome these limitations, we propose a distributed and localized approach, inspired from our previous work [9], to ensure external boundary nodes detection. This approach does not require any additional knowledge than node's localization and neighbors information.

The key idea behind our approach is to use geographic greedy routing to try to reach a virtual node located outside the network area, as illustrated into Figure 9. Hence, a message is initiated from a source node, usually the sink, to reach this virtual node. The source node, knowing the location of the destination node, sends the packet to its 1-hop neighbor which is the closest node to the destination among all neighbors. Knowing the destination location from the received message, every node in the path repeats this process until the message fails into local minimum situation (i.e., the message could not be delivered to the next hop as the current node is the closest one to the destination). From this node, also called local minimum node, recovering process is lunched using Curved Stick boundary traversal approach as explained earlier. This process is repeated until the current selected node is close to the virtual node than the local minimum node. Then the greedy forwarding is used again, and so on.

Following this approach and knowing that the virtual node is unreachable by construction, the message will make a cycle and gets back to the last local minimum node, noted N_l.

Property 3.
The last local minimum node, noted N_l, belongs to the set NBN.

Proof. Initially, all nodes of the networks are connected (i.e., network connectivity assumption). Also, from the fact that CS ensures boundary traversal (c.f., Theorem 1) on one hand and that greedy rule selects the closest node to the virtual node on the other hand, it results that the last local minimum node has the lowest distance to the virtual node among all nodes of the network. Hence it is located on the network boundary. □

Once a node has been identified as belonging to the set NBN, we note Node N_l (N_{14} in the example of Figure 9), from this node and using the CS boundary traversal algorithm, all visited nodes belong to the set of network boundary nodes. Hence the latter could easily update their local holes list.

3. PROOF OF CORRECTNESS

As for any decentralized algorithm, we provide in this section correctness proofs of our peeling algorithm. More precisely, we prove that it terminates (i.e., does not fail into looping) and visits all nodes of the networks (i.e., query

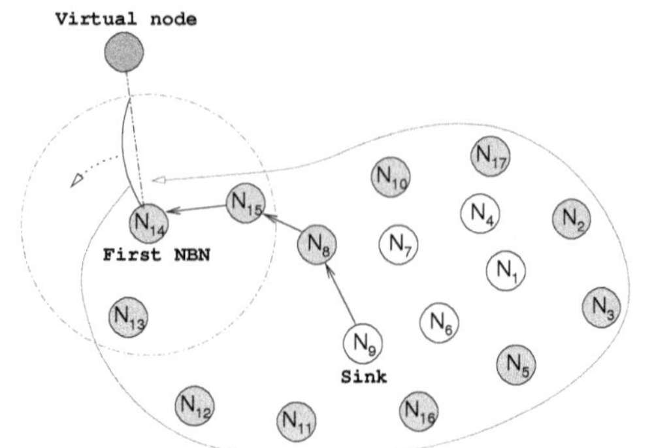

Figure 9: Network Boundary Nodes detection process.

completeness). We point out that PA is based on two main ideas. The first one is to iteratively shrink the resulting network by visiting the external boundary without loss of connectivity (Property 1), while the second one (i.e., HGN rules) allows the transformation of the input network into a connected one without holes (Property 2).

Formally, PA constructs iteratively the set Ω_i, following the recurrent relationship defined as follows:

$$\begin{cases} \Omega_0 = \mathcal{N} \\ \Omega_{i+1} = \Omega_i - \{P_i\} \end{cases}$$

Where P_i is the first visited node which is not a bridge node during the scan of Ω_i. For instance, in Figure 6(b), if we note the sub-network of nodes 1 to 18 as Ω_k, then $\Omega_{k+1} = \Omega_k - \{N_1\}$, $\Omega_{k+2} = \Omega_{k+1} - \{N_2\}$, $\Omega_{k+3} = \Omega_{k+2} - \{N_3\}$, $\Omega_{k+4} = \Omega_{k+3} - \{N_9\}$, $\Omega_{k+5} = \Omega_{k+4} - \{N_8\}$, ...

Lemma 1.
At each iteration i, PA visits a no bridge node P_i (i.e., P_i exists).

Proof. Suppose that at step i, P_i does not exist. Since CS ensures boundary traversal (cf. Theorem 1), this means that all visited nodes are bridge nodes . Consequently, the visited nodes form a hole. This contradicts the no existence of holes guaranteed by HGN rules. Therefore, we deduce that at each step i, P_i exists. □

With the help of the previous lemma, we have:

Theorem 2.
PA generates a finite sequence $\mathcal{P} = \bigcup_{i=0}^{k} P_i$ (i.e., PA terminates).

Proof. To prove that PA performs a finite number of iterations and terminates, we should show that the number of nodes in Ω_i decreases as i grows. Initially we have $\Omega_0 = \mathcal{N}$, which is a finite set of nodes. From Lemma 1, P_i exists at each iteration i. Therefore, it exists k such that $\Omega_{k+1} = \emptyset$. Hence, we prove that $\mathcal{P}$ is finite and PA terminates. □

We define the set of Ω_i boundary nodes, noted $B(\Omega_i)$, as follows:

Definition 8. *(Ω_i Boundary Nodes)*
The boundary of Ω_i is a cyclic sequence of unvisited or bridge boundary nodes such that the closed region bounded by this non self-intersecting polygonal sequence contains all the nodes of Ω_i.

Lemma 2.
At each iteration i, node $P_i \in B(\Omega_i)$ i.e., P_i is on the boundary of the current sub-network Ω_i.

PROOF. We prove by induction. Initially, PA starts at a node located on the boundary of the network Ω_0 and scans the nodes of the boundary of Ω_0 (as explained in Boundary Traversal Algorithm, see Subsection 2.2) until it hits P_0. Thus P_0 is on the boundary of Ω_0, hence the property is true for $i = 0$. Suppose that the property is true for i and we should show that it remains true for $i+1$. As the property is true for i, the current node is P_i and it is located on the boundary of Ω_i. Boundary Traversal Algorithm guarantees that next hop P of P_i is on the boundary of Ω_i. This next hop is also on the boundary of Ω_{i+1}. If P is not a bridge then $P_{i+1} = P$ otherwise starting at P, PA scans the boundary nodes of Ω_{i+1} until it hits a no bridge node P_{i+1}. Hence the property is also true for $i + 1$. □

Theorem 3.
The sequence $\mathcal{P}$ generated by PA contains all nodes of the network (i.e $\mathcal{P} = \mathcal{N}$).

PROOF. We assume that $\mathcal{P}$ is different from $\mathcal{N}$ and we seek to derive a contradiction. We note N_u as an unvisited node missed by PA algorithm, namely $N_u \neq P_i$ for all $i = 0, ..., n$. Specifically, consider the integer $0 < j < n$ such that N_u belongs to Ω_j and does not belong to Ω_{j+1} (i.e N_u is missed at iteration j). As at step j, PA hits only nodes on the boundary of Ω_j and does not miss any boundary node (cf. Lemma 2 and Theorem 1) then N_u cannot be located on the boundary of Ω_j. Thus N_u belongs to Ω_{j+1}, which contradicts the fact $N_u \notin \Omega_{j+1}$, and consequently contradicts the initial assumption. □

In fine, PA terminates and ensures query completeness.

4. PERFORMANCE EVALUATION

For comparison purposes, we have implemented, in addition to our peeling algorithm, the well known serial approach called Depth First Search (DFS) [14]. DFS constructs a rooted tree by expending, at each time, this tree towards unvisited nodes. Hence, each node, except the root, has a "father" node and each node has one or several children except the leafs. To explore a network with N connected nodes, this algorithm requires $2 * (n - 1)$ communications whereas an optimal Hamiltonian path, that does not exist in every network, requires $(n - 1)$ hops. DFS ensures completeness since it allows visiting all nodes. We have used OMNET++ simulator [1], with the Castalia Package to run our simulations.

In our comparison, we have considered three main metrics: (a) *communications efficiency* which records the number of communications needed to end a query; (b) *energy consumption* [7] of all nodes to finish a query and (c) *Time-To-End* that reflects the time taken by each query to deliver the result.

The overall simulation parameters are depicted into Table 1. For each query configuration (i.e., network deployment and query initiator), we have run the two studied approaches and recorded the obtained results. The presented results below are the mean values of 30 runs for each network configuration.

Figure 10 plots the results of required communications (e.g., number of hops). We have also plotted the theoretical

Parameter	value(s)
Network Area (m^2)	250 x 250
Transmission range (m)	50
Nodes distribution	Uniform
Number of nodes	25, ..., 300
Query initiator location	Random
Packet size	50 Bytes

Table 1: Simulations parameters

optimal path which does not necessary exist in any network configuration.

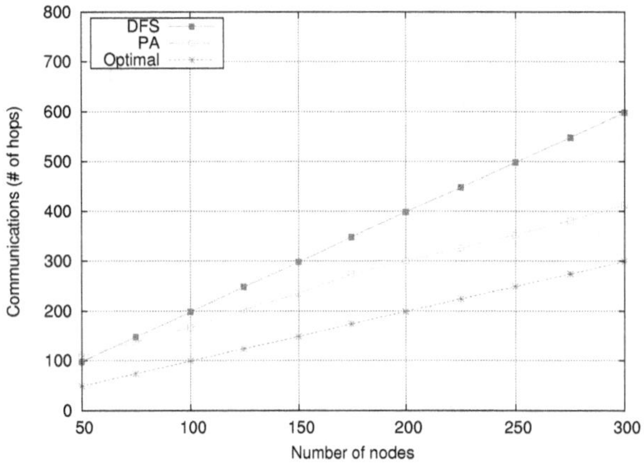

Figure 10: Communication requirement for one query.

As expected, the communication requirement increases with the increase of the number of nodes in the network for the two approaches. This increase is linear for DFS approach. In sparce networks, with low densities, DFS slightly outperforms PA. This is due to the fact that in such networks, the probability of facing linear topologies is high. We recall that linear topologies are the most disadvantageous configurations for our peeling algorithm. In fact, a deep analysis of PA behavior in such topologies reveals that the initialization phase (i.e., starting node detection) is the most communications consuming part. As an example, we have constructed a linear topology composed of 10 nodes, and chosen the worst case where the query initiator was located on the opposite side of the virtual node, as explained into Subsection 2.3. In this configuration, the initialization phase required $[9 + (2 * 9)] + (2 * 9)$ communications, representing respectively the starting node detection and the notification of external network boundary nodes, whereas the query processing required 9 communications. In comparison, DFS required $(2 * 9)$ communications. Nevertheless, it is worthwhile to notice that our approach does not require explicitly initialization phase for each query execution. In fact, once a node has detected itself as the starting node and noticed all network boundary nodes about their localization during the first query, it could avoid this operation for all the remaining queries. For instance, in our linear example, the second query, even in the worst case (i.e., initiated from a node located far away form the starting node), will require 9 communications to reach the starting node and 9 communications to execute the query. An so on. Finally, for an evaluation of k queries, in the worst cases, peeling approach requires $[9+(2*9)+(2*9)]+k(9+9)$ communications whereas DFS requires $k(2*9)$ communications. When k becomes large, the difference between peeling and DFS in terms of communication performance will not be noticeable. This analysis is valide only in the worst network configuration for our peeling approach (i.e., linear topologies). However, in randomly deployed networks, beyond a certain density, PA largely outperforms DFS as shown in the figure, even for single query as it is the case in our results. For instance, the improvement when the network is composed of 300 nodes is more than 31%.

Figures 11 and 12 present the obtained results for the total energy consumption and the query duration (i.e., time to end) respectively. Similarly, PA algorithm presents better behavior than DFS from a certain network density (e.g. 75 nodes). For energy consumption, the improvement ranges from 5% in sparce networks to 43% in dense networks whereas the query responsiveness reduction ranges from 7% to 30%. In summary, the overall results show clearly the effectiveness of our proposed peeling algorithm.

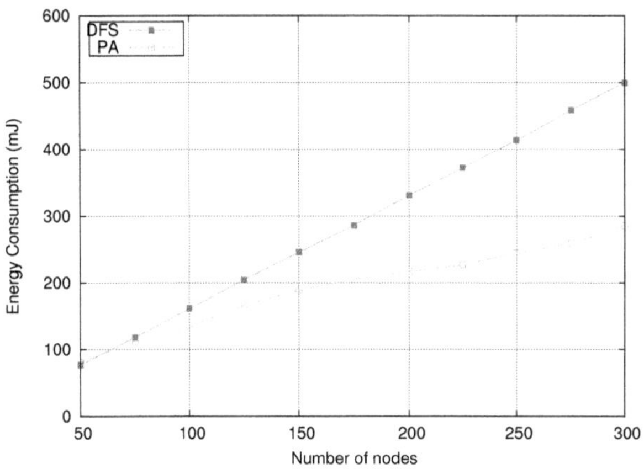

Figure 11: Total energy consumption for one query.

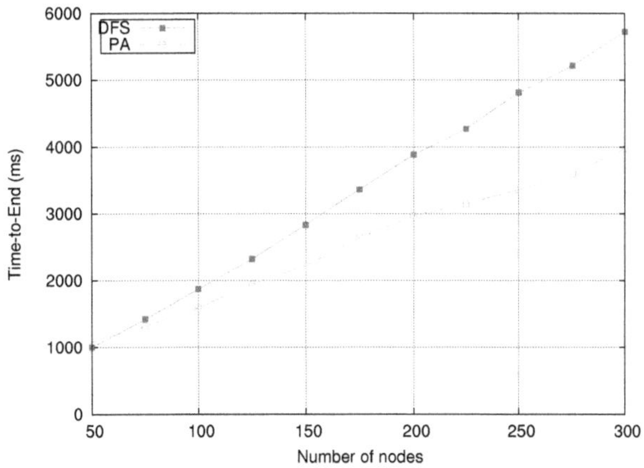

Figure 12: One query duration.

5. CONCLUSION AND FUTURE WORKS

Serial approaches for data fusion in WSNs have shown their effectiveness in terms of reducing communication overheads as well as energy consumption. Nevertheless, previous research works have not explicitly addressed the key issue of constructing the serial path. Moreover, the query completeness (in the sense of visiting all nodes) was not ensured any more. In this paper, we have tackled this important issue by proposing a *localized approach*, named peeling algorithm. The main advantage of our approach is that does not require any additional knowledge than what is traditionally available in WSNs. It is one hop approach and does not require any knowledge about the topology of the network. We have formally proven that our approach ensures query completeness and is free of looping. The obtained simulation results have highlighted its effectiveness in terms of reducing communications requirement, energy consumption and time responsiveness to accomplish one query.

In future work, we plan to consider additional network nodes distributions than the uniform one. In fact, some preliminaries results on other distributions, while they confirmed again the effectiveness of our peeling algorithm, have highlighted however other possible enhancements because we have noticed that some links and bridge nodes are solicited more frequently than the average. We believe that introducing additional rules for these specific nodes will enhance our peeling algorithm.

Another important issue, that we plan to address in future work, is robustness. in fact, serial approaches are known to be vulnerable to links and nodes failures. How to make our peeling algorithm robust will constitute our future challenge.

6. REFERENCES

[1] http://www.omnetpp.org/.

[2] J. Bahi, A. Makhoul, and A. Mostefaoui. Localization and coverage for high density sensor networks. *Computer Communications*, 31(4):770–781, 2008.

[3] P. Bonnet, J. E. Gehrke, and P. Seshadri. Towards sensor database systems. In *Second International Conference on Mobile Data Management*, pages 3–14, January 2001.

[4] A. Boukerche. *Algorithms and Protocols for Wireless Sensor Networks*. Wiley Series on Parallel and Distributed Computing, ISBN-10: 0471798134, 2008.

[5] A. Boukerche, B. Turgut, N. Aydin, M. Ahmad, L. Bölöni, and D. Turgu. Routing protocols in ad hoc networks: a survey. *Computer Networks (Elsevier)*, 55(13):3032–3080, 2011.

[6] M. R. Garey and J. D. S. *Computers and Intractability: A Guide to the Theory of NP-Completeness*. New York: W. H. Freeman, p. 199, 1983.

[7] W. B. Heinzelman, A. P. Chandrakasan, and H. Balakrishnan. An application-specific protocol architecture for wireless microsensor networks. *IEEE Transactions on Wireless Communications*, 1(4):660–670, 2002.

[8] B. Khaleghi, A. Khamis, and F. O. Karray. Multisensor data fusion: A review of the state-of-the-art. *Information Fusion*, 14(1):28–44, 2011.

[9] A. Mostefaoui, M. Melkemi, and A. Boukerche. Routing through holes in wireless sensor networks. In *15th ACM international conference on Modeling, analysis and simulation of wireless and mobile systems*, pages 395–402, 2012.

[10] A. Nedic and D. P. Bertsekas. Incremental subgradient methods for nondifferentiable optimization. *SIAM Journal on Optimization*, 12(1):109–138, 2001.

[11] R. Nowak. Distributed em algorithms for density estimation and clustering in sensor networks. *IEEE Trans. on Sig. Proc.*, 51(8):3, August 2003.

[12] S. Patil, S. Das, and A. Nasipuri. Serial data fusion using space-filling curves in wireless sensor networks. In *IEEE Conference on Sensor and Ad Hoc Communications and Networks, IEEE SECON*, pages 182–190, 2004.

[13] M. Rabbat and R. Nowak. Quantized incremental algorithms for distributed optimization. *IEEE Journal on Selected Areas in Communications*, 23(4):798–808, 2005.

[14] E. Shimon. *Graph Algorithms (2nd ed.)*. Cambridge University Press, pp 46-48, 2011.

[15] F. Zhao and L. Guibas. *Information Processing in Sensor Networks*. Springer LNCS, 2003.

Movement Assisted-Topology Control and Geographic Routing Protocol for Underwater Sensor Networks*

Rodolfo W. L. Coutinho
Dept. of Computer Science
UFMG, Brazil
rwlc@dcc.ufmg.br

Luiz F. M. Vieira
Dept. of Computer Science
UFMG, Brazil
lfvieira@dcc.ufmg.br

Antonio A. F. Loureiro
Dept. of Computer Science
UFMG, Brazil
loureiro@dcc.ufmg.br

ABSTRACT

Underwater sensor networks have recently been proposed as a way to observe and to explore the lakes, rivers, seas, and oceans. A challenging issue in these networks is the communication, mainly due to the impairments of the acoustic transmission. Thus, efficient mechanisms to improve the data delivery must be proposed. In this work we present a novel anycast greedy geographic forwarding protocol and two topology control mechanisms. The proposed geo-routing protocol considers the anycast network architecture in the data forwarding process. The proposed centralized topology control (CTC) and distributed topology control (DTC) mechanisms organize the network via depth adjustment of some nodes. The simulation results show that with these mechanisms, the data packet delivery ratio achieves more than 90% even in hard and difficult scenarios of very sparse or very dense networks, the end-to-end delay and energy consumption per delivered packet is reduced.

Categories and Subject Descriptors

C.2.2 [**Computer-Communication Networks**]: Network Protocols

Keywords

Underwater sensor networks; topology control; geographic routing; local maximum problem

1. INTRODUCTION

Recently, underwater sensor networks (UWSNs) have been suggested as a powerful technology for monitoring lakes, rivers, seas, and oceans. [1, 2]. In SEA (Sensor Equipped Aquatic) swarm architecture nodes deployed underwater, equipped with a large number of sensors and with acoustic modem, could monitor environmental variables such as water temperature, pressure, conductivity, turbidity and certain pollutants, and then report relevant collect data for any one of surface sonobuoys through acoustic multihop communication. Moreover, each node has a winch-based apparatus or floating buoy that can be inflated by a pump, and its depth can be adjusted [3]. The sonobuoys are equipped with both acoustic and radio communication, and have the function of getting the collected data from sensor nodes through acoustic communication and offload the data to a monitoring center by means of radio communication (WiFi or satellite communications).

A key issue in the underwater sensor network is the communication. A challenging task is the design of efficient mechanisms to effectively deliver data from underwater nodes to the monitoring center. In underwater communication we have a high propagation delay due to the speed of acoustic signals in water which is about 1500m/s, severely limitod available bandwidth, and high and dynamic packet loss probability, which leads to lots of retransmissions, a high energy consumption, and lower reliability [4]. Due to the above characteristics of underwater, the conventional reactive and proactive routing protocols used in terrestrial wireless sensor networks are not suitable for UWSNs. These routing protocols rely on systematic flooding for route discovery and maintenance, potentially causing excessive energy consumption and collisions [5]. In these scenarios, position-based or geographic routing is preferable as it does not require the establishment or maintenance of complete routes and there is no need to transmit routing messages to update states [6].

Geographic routing uses the position information to route packets towards the destination. Every node, aware of its geographical location, forwards packets to a locally optimal next-hop node closest to destination. This strategy makes geographic routing protocols simple and scalable. Moreover, there is not additional communication overhead since source node requires to know only 1-hop neighbors locations to select the next-hop. However, geographic routing suffers from a serious drawback called *communication void region*. The communication void region occurs whenever the sender fails to locate a next-hop node in its neighborhood, i.e., it is the closest one to the destination [7]. The node located in a *communication void region* is called *void node*. Whenever a packet gets stuck in a void node, the routing protocol should attempt to route the packet using some recovery method or discard it.

Some works in the field have invested efforts to cope with the communication void problem. Most of them use message transmission-based procedures to circumvent the void region. For instance, the VBVA [8] routing protocol, which is an extension of the VBF [9], attempts to route the data

*This work was partially supported by CNPq and CAPES.

MSWiM'13, November 3–8, 2013, Barcelona, Spain.

packet along the boundary of the communication void by shifting the forward vector of the data packet and by a back-pressure method when the vector-shift method fails (convex voids). In Hydrocast [5], when a node determines that it is located at a local maximum, it performs a search for a node whose depth is lower than its depth and explicitly maintains a path to the node. In VAPR [10], the presence of the void nodes is known by means of periodic beacons. The next-hop selection is done according to the match of the forwarding direction (upwards or downwards). The drawback of these approaches is that an explicit path must be discovered and maintained. Additionally, to circumvent the void region, data packets are routed along more hops, leading to the congestion and an increase in the energy consumption, if this route is highly used.

We advocate that instead of using message transmissions-based procedures, topology control approaches can be effective to cope with the communication void region problem. In this context, the objective of the topology control is to devise network topologies where communication void regions can be minimized or even eliminated. Particularly, the topology control through movement assisted (depth adjustment) of some nodes can organize the topology in a favorable way to use the greedy geographic routing protocol. In this approach, we have a initial energy cost dependent on the depth adjustment technology to move the nodes to new locations. This cost is diluted in the long-term of network operation, i.e., the energy per delivered packet is amortized. Furthermore, according to the application, the gain in the network performance can justify paying this cost.

Our Contributions. In this work we propose an anycast greedy geographic routing protocol and two topology control algorithms. The proposed routing protocol (Section 3) considers the *anycast* nature of the underwater sensor network SEA swarm architecture for next-hop forward selection. We use the distance from the neighbors to its closest sonobuoy and the one with the smaller distance value will be selected as the next-hop forwarder. The topology control algorithms are designed to better organize the network topology through depth adjustment of some nodes, aiming significantly to reduce the impact of the communication void problem in the network performance. We consider only the scenarios where nodes can move on the vertical axes, not x, y as occurs with current technology. We present a centralized topology control (CTC) algorithm in Section 4 that determines which nodes do not have a path to a sonobouoy (isolated nodes) and which ones are in a communication void region and, then, compute new depth to them. Moreover, we present a distributed topology control (DTC) algorithm in Section 5 where each node locally determines if it is in a communication void region and computes its new depth to overcome this problem.

The nodes moved to new locations can effectively participate in the data forwarding process to the sonobuoys. Thus, we have a significant improvement in the network performance as compared with the traditional underwater sensor networks routing protocols. With both the geographic routing protocol and topology control proposed mechanisms, the fraction of the data delivered packet was higher than 95% for CTC and 80% for DTC, which represents a gain of 25% when compared with analyzed routing protocols, even in hard and difficult scenarios of very sparse or very dense networks. Moreover the fraction of sensing coverage area and the energy consumption per delivered packet were improved.

2. PRELIMINARIES

Our network model consists of a set $\mathcal{N}$ of nodes in the network, with $|\mathcal{N}| = N$. In the set $\mathcal{N}$ there are two subsets of nodes, namely (i) the set $\mathcal{N}_n$ of sensor nodes, and (ii) the set $\mathcal{N}_s$ of sonobuoys.

The sensor nodes $\mathcal{N}_n = \{n_1, n_2, \ldots, n_{N_n}\}$, are evenly deployed in a Euclidean space $D \in \Re^3$, attached into buoys and/or anchors which allow them to remain fixed in its deployed location. Moreover, it can control its depth, moving vertically with velocity v, through winch-based apparatus (e.g., AquaNode [3]) or floating buoy that can be inflated by a pump. The function of these nodes is to monitor local underwater activities and periodically report time-critical data to any destination (sonobuoys) through multihop acoustic communication.

The sonobuoys $\mathcal{N}_s = \{s_1, s_2, \ldots, s_{N_s}\}$, are special nodes on the sea surface, with capabilities to communicate with both sensor nodes and a monitoring center. They can be deployed in a planned manner and are responsible to deliver the data packets from the sensor network to a monitoring center. These nodes are equipped with both acoustic and radio transceivers, which they use acoustic links to send commands and receive data from sensor nodes and the radio links to forward the data packets to a monitoring center.

We represent the network topology as a graph $\mathcal{G} = (\mathcal{V}, \mathcal{E})$, where $\mathcal{V} = \{\mathcal{N}_n \cup \mathcal{N}_s\}$ corresponds to nodes and $\mathcal{E}$ is the finite set of links between them. Two nodes n_u and n_v are *neighbors* and are *directly connected* via a *link*, if they can directly, mutually, and consistently communicate over an acoustic channel, that is, given the communication radius equals to r_c and its locations $(x_{n_u}, y_{n_u}, z_{n_u})$ and $(x_{n_v}, y_{n_v}, z_{n_v})$ respectively, they are neighbors (n_u can receive $n_v'{}s$ broadcast and vice versa) if the Euclidean distance between them is less than or equal to r_c ($\| n_u - n_v \| \leq r_c$). We define $N(n_u)$ as the set of nodes that are node $n_u'{}s$ neighbors with $n_u \notin N(n_u)$. The node knows its neighboring through beacons dissemination.

With respect to the geographic routing protocols, it usually consists of a *geographic forwarding strategy* and a *void node recovery* process. The first dictates how the packet will be routed in direction to the destinations, that is, how is the rule of select the next-hop forwarder between the neighbor nodes, aiming to move the packet in direction to destination. The second one deals with the void communication problem, that is, how packets from nodes located in a maximum local will be moved in direction to destination.

We use the greedy forwarding strategy to the next-hop forwarder selection. Thus, always that an intermediate node S receives a packet, it forwards the packet to a neighbor X lying closest to destination D, i.e., in every hop the packet is routed to a locally optimal next-hop node towards to destination. We use the *packet advance (ADV)* [11] which is defined as the distance between the source node S and the destination node D minus the distance between the neighbor X and D, to select the best next-hop candidate to continue the progress of the packet in direction to destination. The proposed anycast greedy geographic routing model is described in the following section.

3. GEOGRAPHIC ROUTING PROTOCOL

As in the underwater sensor SEA swarm architecture for long-time monitoring has N_s destinations (the sonobuoys), and the data packet is considered successfully received if it reaches any destination, we define the packet advance (ADV) as

$$ADV(n_j) = D(n_j, s^*_{n_j}) - D(n_i, s^*_{n_i}) \quad (1)$$

where n_i and n_j are the source and neighbor nodes, respectively. $D(n, s)$ denotes the Euclidean distance from the nodes n and the destination s. $s^*_{n_i}$ is the closest destination (sonobuoy) from n_i, given according to

$$s^*_{n_i} = \arg \min_{s \in \mathcal{N}_s} \{D(n_i, s)\}. \quad (2)$$

Let $\mathcal{F}_{n_i} = \{n_j \in N(n_i) : ADV(n_j) > 0\}$ be the set of neighbors candidate of n_i that are able to act as a next-hop forwarder. From Eq.(1) and Eq.(2), if n_i lacks of direct connectivity with a sonobuoy, it will select the next-hop forwarder as

$$n^*_j = \arg \max_{n_k \in \mathcal{F}_{n_i}} \{ADV(n_k)\}. \quad (3)$$

Whenever a packet gets stuck in a void node, the routing protocol should attempt to route the packet using some recovery method or discard it. A survey of approaches to deals with void node problem in 2D networks are presented in [6]. In contrast, Durocher et al. in [12] has been shown that there is not a k-local routing algorithm that guarantees delivery messages on 3D networks modeled as all unit ball graphs. Herein, we deal with the communication void problem by means of the topology control through depth adjustment of some nodes. Before the network operation phase, we perform a rearrangement of some nodes by means of adjusting its depth aiming to derive a new network topology such that the fraction of nodes in communication void regions is drastically reduced or even eliminated. Therefore, during the phase of network operation, the anycast greedy geographic routing protocol does not need to execute any procedure to circumvent communication void regions.

4. CENTRALIZED TOPOLOGY CONTROL (CTC) ALGORITHM

The proposed centralized topology control (CTC) algorithm runs in the monitoring center and needs the geographic location of all nodes $\mathcal{N}$. Its objectives are: to determine which nodes do not have a path to any sonobuoy (isolated nodes), which ones are in a communication void regions, and organize the network topology to cope with these drawbacks. A preliminary version of the CTC was presented in [13]. In this section, we have enhanced the protocol design and elaborated description of the proposed protocol.

We use the localization system proposed by Erol et al. [14] to get the location of the nodes. In this localization system, autonomous underwater vehicle (AUVs) dives to a fixed depth following a predefined trajectory and then broadcast a wakeup beacon to declare their presence. The sensor which has received the beacon, starts range measurement by sending a location request packet. When the AUV receives a location request message, it replies with a response packet the includes its coordinates. Thus, the estimated coordinates of the sensor nodes are obtained by the range measurements and the received AUV coordinates. This localization system does not require a priori infrastructure or synchronization between sensor nodes. At the end of AUV-aided localization operation, the monitoring center has the position information about all sensor nodes. For this, the AUVs can disseminate the nodes' location to sonobuoys along their trajectory or then send directly to a monitoring center.

Thereafter, CTC determines which nodes are isolated. From the graph $\mathcal{G}$, we run the Depth First Search (DFS) algorithm from each $s_i \in \mathcal{N}_s$ as the root and the, we get $d_{n_i}(s_i)$ the number of hops needed from n_i reaches the sonobuoy s_i. If $d_{n_i}(s_i)$ is equal to zero, the node n_i do not have a path to the sonobuoy s_i. The set Φ of isolated nodes is determined from $d_{n_i}, \forall n_i \in \mathcal{N}_i$, as

$$\Phi = \{n_i \in \mathcal{N}_n : \sum_{s_i \in \mathcal{N}_s} d_{n_i}(s_i) = 0\}. \quad (4)$$

Afterward, CTC determines which must be the new depth of these nodes such that they have a path to some sonobuoy. Let $\Upsilon = \overline{\Phi}$ be the set of nodes that has a path to a sonobuoy. For each node $n_i \in \Phi$, we determine the set $\mathcal{C}_{n_i}$ of neighbor candidates nodes in Υ such that n_i can reach all nodes in $\mathcal{C}_{n_i}$ and, consequently it reaches some sonobuoy. The set $\mathcal{C}_{n_i}$ is determined as

$$\mathcal{C}_{n_i} = \{n_j \in \Upsilon : \sqrt{(x_{n_i} - x_{n_j})^2 + (y_{n_i} - y_{n_j})^2} \le r_c\}. \quad (5)$$

Intuitively, the set of neighbor candidates for an isolated node is formed by the nodes that have a path to some sonobuoy and the Euclidean distance between themselves and the isolated node, considering only the (X,Y)-axes, is less than or equals to the communication radius. Thus, we determine in what depth $z^{n_j}_{n_i}$, that will be refereed just as z^j_i for clarity purpose, the isolated node n_i must be for that it can communicate with each n_j neighbor candidate in $\mathcal{C}_{n_i}$ by solving the quadratic equation

$$(x_{n_i} - x_{n_j})^2 + (y_{n_i} - y_{n_j})^2 + (z^j_i - z_{n_j})^2 = r^2_c. \quad (6)$$

Finally, n_i will be moved to the new depth that will lead to the smallest displacement, *i.e.*, $z^*_i = \arg\min_{\forall z^j_i}\{|z_{n_i} - z^j_i|\}$, and the set Φ is updated, $\Phi = \Phi \cup \{n_i\}$. Along this adjustment, it is possible that a node, even at the surface ocean, i.e., $z = 0$, cannot have a path to any sonobuoy. For these cases the node is left isolated.

CTC copes with the communication void region problem after the previous phase is finished. It determines which nodes are in the communication void region examining the neighborhood of each node and then, it calculates what must be the depth such that this node can participate effectively in the routing data process using anycast greedy geographic routing strategy. We have the set $\Gamma = \{n_i \in \mathcal{N}_n : D(n_i, s^*_{n_i}) \le D(n_j, s^*_{n_j}), \forall n_j \in N(n_i)\}$ of nodes in the communication void region. As in the previous phase, we determine the set of neighbors candidates $\mathcal{C}_{n_k}, \forall n_k \in \overline{\Gamma}$, and the new depths z^k_i that the void node n_i must be to that it can communicate with each $n_k \in \Gamma$. However, the depth z^k_i is only satisfactory if $D(n_k, s^*_{n_k}) < D(n_i, s^*_{n_i})$ is held. As above, the void node will be moved to the new depth that will lead to the smallest displacement.

After determining the new depths of the isolated and void nodes, we use the AUVs to inform these nodes, what is the depth that they must move to. Furthermore, the AUVs broadcast a beacon informing a delay that all nodes should wait before starting the data collection and reports. This delay corresponds to the time required to the AUVs to disseminate the information and the isolated and void nodes to reach their new depths.

5. DISTRIBUTED TOPOLOGY CONTROL (DTC) ALGORITHM

In the distributed topology control (DTC) each node locally determines if it is in a communication void region and then starts the process of depth adjustment, if necessary. Due to the distributed way, DTC uses control messages during the process of topology control. This leads to an extra energy consumption on the nodes besides of the energy cost for nodes' movement, resulting in an increase in the network operation cost. However, differently of CTC, DTC does not incurs in additional network project cost because it does not require the use of the AUV-aided localization system.

To better understand the proposed protocol, we define the following concepts used throughout this section:

- **Wait time for depth adjust decision:** is the time which the node must wait before verifing if it is in a communication void region. The need to use this time is to ensure that the depth adjustment of the void nodes occurs in a prioritized manner so that the shorter the distance to the closest sonobuoy, the shorter it is the waiting time to decide if it must move to a new depth or not. When a void node starts it depth adjustment, all void nodes with the smaller distance to its closest sonobuoy is already apt to act as a next-hop forwarder to some sonobuoy using anycast greedy geographic routing protocol. The wait time for the node n_i is $t_i^w = D(n_i, s_{n_i}^*)/v$.
- **Status of a node:** During the topology control phase, a node can have the following status:
  - WAITING: when the node is waiting the time t_i expires.
  - ADJUSTING: when the node is moving to a new depth.
  - DONE: when the node already performed the adjustment decision and is already in the new depth.
- **MSG_INFORM_ADJUST:** it is the message periodically disseminated by void nodes during the depth adjustment. This message contains the *id* of the void node and *its updated distance* to its closest sonobuoy.
- **MSG_REPLAY:** is the message sent by a node which already performed the depth adjust procedure (status equals DONE) in response to the received message MSG_INFORM_ADJUST, to inform the void node that it can stop its adjustment and it must use the node id contained into the message as next-hop forwarder. Furthermore, the MSG_REPLAY contains the distance of the sender to its closest sonobuoy.

The DTC procedure is described in the Algorithm 1. First of all, the sensors determine which will be the time that it must wait before to start the depth adjustment (lines 1-5). After that, the nodes verify if it must move to a new depth or not (lines 7-21). The node does not need to adjust its depth if *i) it has direct connectivity with any sonobuoy; or ii) it has a neighbor that can act as a next-hop forwarder using the greedy geographic forward strategy.* In the first one (lines 8-11) if the node has direct communication with its closest sonobuoy, it updates its status to DONE and broadcast a beacon with its both *id* and *distance* to its closest sonobuoy, to inform the neighbors of its condition. When a node receives a beacon and its status is *WAITING*, it updates its neighbor table. An important aspect of the DTC is that there is not a periodic beacon procedure. The neighbor table is updated from beacons sent by nodes that have either direct communication with any sonobuoy, a neighbor with status equal to DONE that can act as next-hop forwarder, or that finish the depth adjustment and now it is located in a new depth where is possible to send data using the greedy geographic routing protocol. In the second one (lines 12-15) the node examines its neighbor table and it does not adjust its depth if it has a neighbor that it can use as a next-hop forwarder. When a node is in a communication void region and it can move to a new depth in order to solve it (lines 16-20), it starts the vertical movement in direction to the new depth and, periodically with interval T, runs the procedure *depthUpdate()* (lines 23-32). In this procedure, the node gets the current depth information, and if

Algorithm 1. DTC procedure.

1: **procedure** startTopologyControl()
2:     $t_i^w \leftarrow D(n_i, s_{n_i}^*)/v$
3:     status $\leftarrow$ *WAITING*
4:     Schedule depthAdjustmentDecision (t_i).
5: **end procedure**
6:
7: **procedure** depthAdjustmentDecision()
8:     **if** $D(n_i, s_{n_i}^*) \leq r_c$ **then**
9:         status $\leftarrow$ *DONE*
10:         next_hop $\leftarrow s_{n_i}^*$
11:         broadcast Beacon
12:     **else if** $\exists n_j \in N(n_i) \mid ADV(n_j) > 0$ **then**
13:         status $\leftarrow$ *DONE*
14:         next_hop $\leftarrow n_j$
15:         broadcast Beacon
16:     **else if** $(x_{n_i} - x_{s_{n_i}^*})^2 + (y_{n_i} - y_{s_{n_i}^*})^2 \leq r_c^2$ **then**
17:         status $\leftarrow$ *ADJUSTING*
18:         $z_{n_i}^* \leftarrow \sqrt{r_c^2 - [(x_{n_i} - x_{s_{n_i}^*})^2 + (y_{n_i} - y_{s_{n_i}^*})^2]}$
19:         depthUpdate()
20:     **end if**
21: **end procedure**
22:
23: **procedure** depthUpdate()
24:     $z_{n_i} \leftarrow \pi(n_i)$
25:     **if** $z_{n_i} = z_{n_i}^*$ **then**
26:         status $\leftarrow$ *DONE*
27:         broadcast Beacon
28:     **else**
29:         broadcast MSG_INFORM_ADJUST
30:         Schedule depthAdjust (T)
31:     **end if**
32: **end procedure**

it reaches the new specified depth, it stops the depth adjustment and broadcast a beacon. Otherwise, the node sends a MSG_INFORM_ADJUST and reschedule a new call for the *depthUpdate()* procedure.

During the depth adjustment of a void node, if a node that has a status equal *DONE* receives a MSG_INFORM_ADJUST, it determines if it can act as next-hop from the void node, examining its distance to the closest sonobuoy and the distance from the void node to its closest sonobuoy contained into the MSG_INFORM_ADJUST. If it can, it sends a MSG_REPLAY to inform the void node that it can stop the depth adjustment. After that, both nodes broadcast a beacon to inform the neighboring of its condition.

6. IMPACT OF THE TOPOLOGY CONTROL

6.1 Energy Consumption

We define E_d as the energy cost by meter in order to measure the consumption of energy of the nodes due to the depth adjust task. Let $\mathcal{N}_d$ be the set of nodes which performed the depth adjustment and let $n_i \in \mathcal{N}_d$ be a node which was located initially in the depth z_{n_i} and after the topology control (CTC or DTC), in a new depth $z^*_{n_i}$. The displacement of n_i is $\delta_{n_i} = |z_{n_k} - z^*_{n_k}|$. The total displacement in the network is given by

$$\Delta^n = \sum_{n_i \in \mathcal{N}_d} \delta_{n_i}. \quad (7)$$

Thus, the energy consumption for the topology control through nodes' depth adjustment is

$$E_{tc} = \Delta^n \times E_d. \quad (8)$$

In DTC, besides the cost of nodes' movement we also have the energy spent by control messages. Therefore, the energy consumption for the topology control operation in DTC is

$$E_{tc} = \Delta^n \times E_d + E_o, \quad (9)$$

where E_o represent the energy consumption of the send and reception operations of control messages. We derive E_o using similar approach of [11] as follows. As an ADJUSTING node updates the information about its current depth and sends a MSG_INFORM_ADJUST periodically with interval T, from Eq.(7), the number of these messages disseminated in the network is $n = \Delta^n/vT$. Thus, let L_m be the size of a MSG_INFORM_ADJUST message and P_t the transmission power of the nodes, we approximate the energy consumption required to send n of these messages, through a channel with bandwidth equals to B as

$$E^s_{MIA} = P_t \times \frac{nL_m}{B}. \quad (10)$$

Let $\mathcal{N}_r(i)$ be the set of nodes which have received the ith MSG_INFORM_ADJUST message and $\mathcal{N}_p(i) \subseteq \mathcal{N}_r(i)$ the set of nodes that might act as next-hop forwarder and then responded this message with a MSG_REPLAY message, with size equals L_r, and posteriorly with a beacon of size L_b. The energy consumption to the reception of MSG_INFORM_ADJUST messages when P_r is used as the energy needed by the transceiver circuit to receive one bit, and to send MSG_REPLAY is given by Eq.(11) and Eq.(12), respectively.

$$E^r_{MIA} = P_r \times \sum_{i=1}^{n} \frac{|\mathcal{N}_r(i)|L_m}{B} \quad (11)$$

$$E^s_{MR} = P_t \times \frac{(L_r + L_b)\sum_{i=1}^{n} |\mathcal{N}_p(i)|}{B} \quad (12)$$

After, we approximate the energy consumption relative to the reception of MSG_REPLAY messages. Due to the broadcast nature of the acoustic transmissions, all nodes within the radius communication of a sender will receive the message. However, as the MSG_REPLAY messages are addressed to a specific node, all the other nodes which have received the message will discard it after examine the header and determine that it is not the destination. Thus, we compute only the energy consumption in the nodes where the MSG_REPLAY and the beacons are processed as

$$E^r_{MR} = P_r \times \frac{(L_r + L_b)\sum_{i=1}^{n} |\mathcal{N}_p(i)|}{B}. \quad (13)$$

Finally, the energy consumption of of the send and reception operations of control messages is

$$E_o = E^s_{MIA} + E^r_{MIA} + E^s_{MR} + E^r_{MR}. \quad (14)$$

6.2 Sensing Coverage Rate

In this section we model the fraction of sensing coverage area in order to evaluate the impact of the topology control proposed algorithms in this task. As in [15], we consider that the sensing range of a sensor n_u is a sphere of radius r_s, centered at ξ_u $(x_{n_u}, y_{n_u}, z_{n_u})$ and defined by the point of the set

$$\mathcal{C}^{n_u}_o(r_s) = \{\xi \in \Re^3 : \| \xi_u - \xi \| \leq r_s\} \quad (15)$$

where $\| \xi_u - \xi \|$ is the Euclidean distance between the locations ξ_u and ξ. For approximate the rate of covered area, the area of interest D is divided into $(L_x \times L_y \times L_z)/l^3$ sames cubes with side l. Thus, we define a Boolean function $f(\xi_i, u)$ to determine if a cube whose the center point is $\xi_i(x_i, y_i, z_i)$ is covered by the sensor $n_u \in \mathcal{N}_n$, as

$$f(\xi_i, n_u) = \begin{cases} 1, & \xi_i \in \mathcal{C}^{n_u}_o(r_s) \\ 0, & \text{otherwise.} \end{cases} \quad (16)$$

In determining the ratio of sensing covered area, we consider only those nodes that have a path to some sonobuoy and can delivery the collected data. For this, we define the function of reachability of node $n_u \in \mathcal{N}_n$ by

$$g(n_u, s) = \begin{cases} 1, & \exists s \in \mathcal{N}_s \mid n_u \rightsquigarrow s \\ 0, & \text{otherwise.} \end{cases} \quad (17)$$

From Eq.(16) and Eq.(17), the coverage rate is defined fraction of the cubes that are covered by at least one sensor node that has a path to some sonobuoy, as

$$C_o = \frac{\sum_{i=0}^{(L_x.L_y.L_z)/l^3} \max_{n_u \in \mathcal{N}_n} \{f(\xi_i, n_u) \times g(n_u, s)\}}{\frac{L_x.L_y.L_z}{l^3}} \tag{18}$$

7. SIMULATIONS SETUP

To evaluate the performance of the geographic routing after the proposed topology control algorithms we conduct a series of simulations on Aqua-Sim[1]. Aqua-Sim is developed on NS-2 and can effectively simulate the impairment of acoustic communication, like the acoustic signal attenuation and packet collisions in underwater sensor networks [16]. We comparatively evaluate the performance of our greedy geographic routing protocol after both the centralized topology control (CTC) and distributed topology control (DTC) proposed algorithms against the DBR [17] and VAPR [10] underwater routing protocols. In these routing protocols, the next-hop forwarder selection is based on the depth information of the neighbors. The metrics we concentrate on during simulations are the *packet delivery ratio* that is the fraction of the packets that were received by the sonobuoys; the *delay* that is the average latency for a packet to reach any of sonobuoys and the *number of redundant packets* that is the mean of redundant copies of data packets received by all sonobuoys.

We randomly deploy varying numbers of nodes ranging from 150 to 400 in 3D region of size $1500m \times 1500m \times 1500m$. The sensor nodes have a transmission range of $r_c = 250m$, data rate of $50Kbps$, and CSMA MAC protocol, as in [17, 10]. Every packet transmission is performed through MAC layer broadcasting. In CSMA, a node waits a back-off period and attempts to sense the carrier again when the channel is busy. Regarding the deposition of the sonobuoys, we divide the surface area of the region of interest into $K = 9$ sub-areas with side equals to $s = 500$, and then we evenly deposited N_s/K sonobuoys are in each sub-area such that $N_s = \{9, 45\}$ to evaluate the impact of the increase on the number of surface sonobuoys in the network performance. The packet payload size if of 100 bytes. The values of energy consumption were $P_t = 2W$, $P_r = 0.1W$, *10mW* and $E_d = 15J/m$[18] for sensors operations of transmission, reception, idle and depth adjustment, respectively. The traffic rate generated by each sensor node follows a Poisson process with the same parameter $\lambda = 0.01 pkts/min$. In our simulation each run lasts 1 day. This configuration is used throughout this work if not otherwise specified. The results correspond an average value of 50 runs with 95 percent confidence interval.

8. SIMULATION RESULTS

8.1 Network performance analysis

We first analyze the impact of the proposed topology control algorithms on the network connectivity and sensing coverage area. We analyze the impact on the network connectivity through the fraction of nodes which do not have a path to any destination (isolated nodes) and the fraction of nodes in a communication void regions.

[1]http://obinet.engr.uconn.edu/wiki/index.php/Aqua-Sim

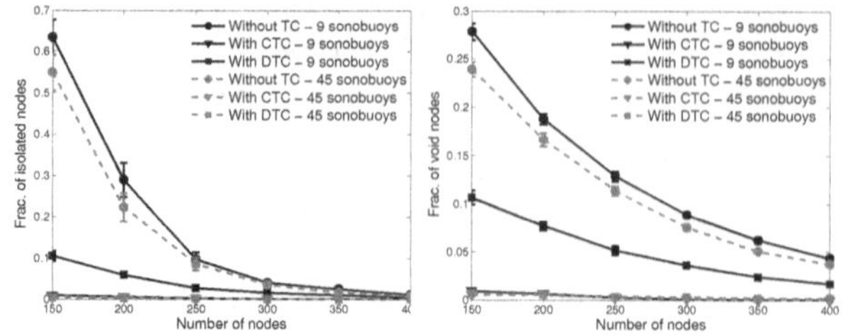

(a) Frac. of isolated nodes. (b) Frac. of void nodes.

Figure 1: Topology related experimental results.

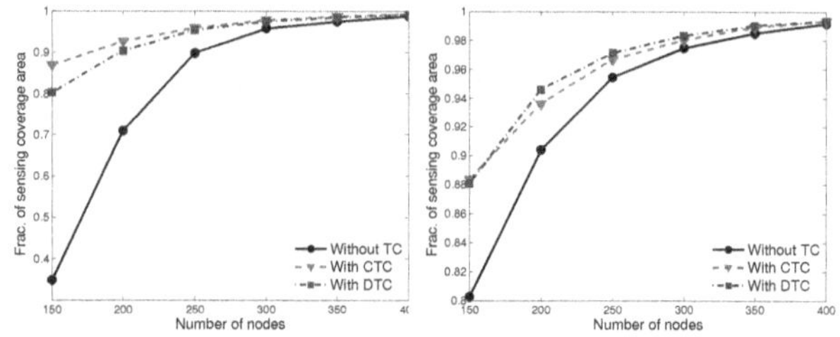

(a) 9 sonobuoys (b) 45 sonobuoys

Figure 2: Sensing coverage area with r_s=250m.

In Fig.1a, the result shows that when the network density increase, the fraction of isolated nodes decrease. We also can see that the increase in the number of sonobuoys does not significantly reduce the fraction of isolated nodes. CTC and DTC derive new topologies from the nodes' depth adjustment such that the fraction of void nodes was approximately zero when 45 sonobuoys were used. For the architecture with 9 sonobuoys, the resulting network topology after DTC algorithm still showed about 10% of isolated nodes. This happens due to the existence of nodes which even at the sea surface, do not have the possibility of direct communication with any sonobuoy. Thus, these nodes do not perform the depth adjustment. Similar behavior happens for the fraction of void nodes considering the anycast greedy geographic strategy as next-hop rule selection, as shown in Fig.1b. The results clearly show the efficiency of the topology control proposed algorithms to derive more adequate topologies.

Fig.2 shows the impact of the topology control in the sensing coverage area obtained from Eq.(18), with $l = 10m$. The overall results show that with the proposed topology control algorithms the fraction of the sensing area is increased due to the reduction of the isolated nodes which will fail to deliver the collected data, as corroborated by previous results. In Fig.2a, when we have a network architecture with an extreme case of low density, the increase of the fraction of sensing area is around 160% and 180% for DTC and CTC, respectively.

Fig.3 examines the packet delivery ratio of GR after CTC and DTC, VAPR, and DBR with 9 and 45 sonobuoys on the surface. The overall trend of the four protocols is quite consistent with the network topology results, shown in Fig.1a. The packet delivery ratio of GR with topology control (CTC and DTC) outperforms those of the rest of routing protocol for both scenarios. The VAPR and DBR have similar behavior because the way of the sonobuoys are deposed at sea surface. However, the performance of VAPR is slightly bet-

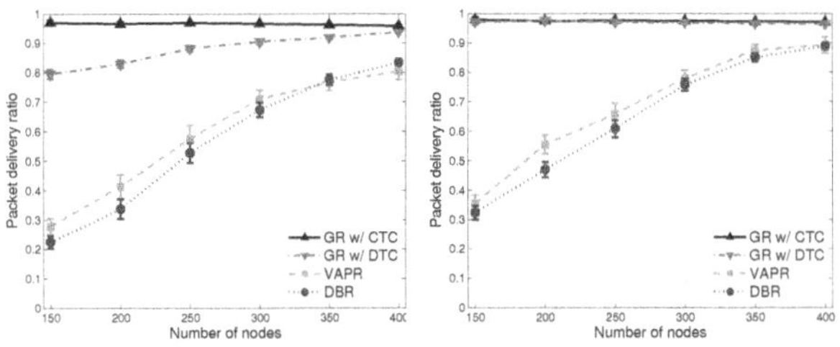

(a) 9 sonobuoys. (b) 45 sonobuoys.

Figure 3: Packet delivery ratio.

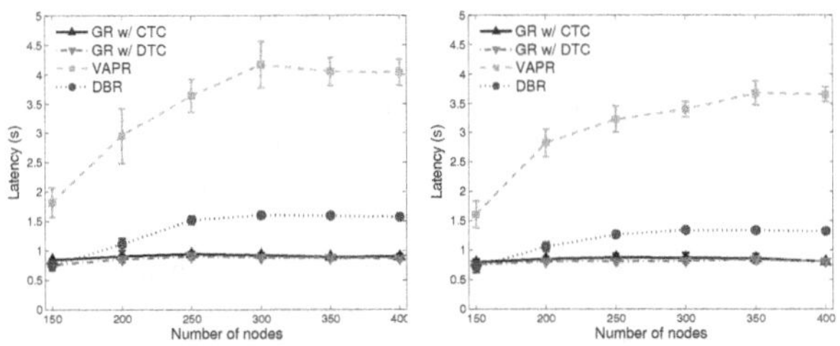

(a) 9 sonobuoys. (b) 45 sonobuoys.

Figure 4: Average end-to-end latency.

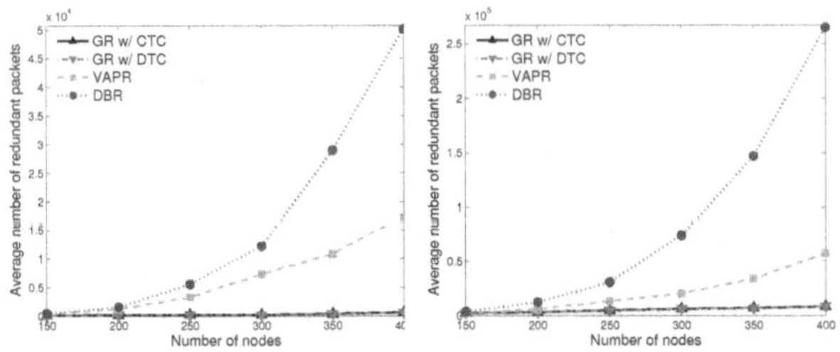

(a) 9 sonobuoys. (b) 45 sonobuoys.

Figure 5: Average number of redundant packets.

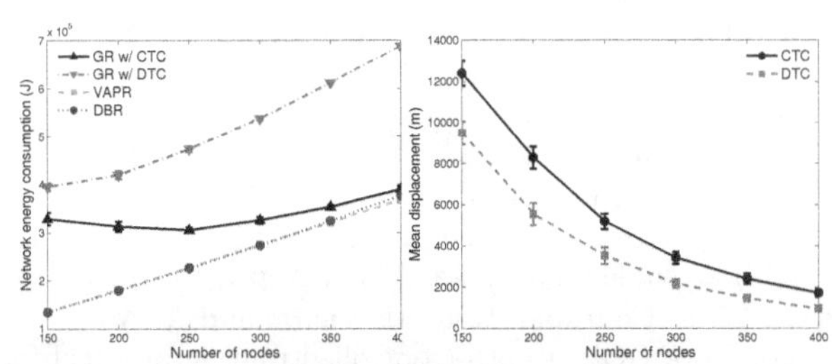

(a) Net. energy consumption. (b) Disp. of moved nodes.

Figure 6: Performance measurements.

ter than DBR because it is aware of void regions and routes the packet through directional trails in direction to some sonobuoy. For scenario with 9 sonobuoys, the performance of GR with DTC is significantly lower than GR with CTC because the fraction of void nodes is over 5% (see Fig.1b).

Fig.4 shows the average latency for all delivered packets. Here, VAPR shows the worst performance due to the mechanisms used to reliability, as opportunistic routing and ARQ at the routing layer which uses ACK packets to suppression of redundant transmission. Thus, the data packet transmissions compete with the ACK packets for the use of the shared channel which leads to an increase in the delay due to the backoff mechanism. As DBR uses a depth-based timer to schedule the forward transmissions, it has a delay upper than the GR proposed protocol where data packets are immediately forwarded. We note that the increase on the number of sonobuoys (Fig.4b) leads to a decrease in the latency for all routing protocols.

Fig.5 examines the average number of redundant copies of data packets received by the sonobuoys. The GR with CTC, GR with DTC have similar performance. For these protocols, the redundant copy results due to broadcast nature of the transmission. Thus, the nodes located next to sea surface, can be located in the communication area of the more than one sonobuoy. For these cases, the transmission of the node will be received by several sonobuoys. In VAPR, fails on the reception of ACKs due to collisions leads to a duplicated transmission. In DBR, the average number of redundant copies grows significantly with the increase in the number of nodes due to failure in the suppression of data transmission on the lower priority nodes given that the heuristic to next-hop set selection no guarantee that the nodes will hearing each one.

8.2 Energy consumption analysis

As shown in the previous section, the approach of topology control through movement assisted of some nodes leads to an increase of the network performance. In this section we investigate the trade-off between the energy cost used to organize the topology of the network and the improvement of the network performance. The question that motivates us in this investigation is *"under what conditions is profitable to pay the price for the topology control through movement assisted?"*. Herein, we analyze the experiments described in Section 7 for the scenario with 9 surface sonobuoys. The winch-based apparatus used to vertically move the sensor nodes consume a significant amount of energy. In our experiments, the energy per meter to move the node was $E_d = 15J/m$ as in [18], leading to a high overall energy consumption, as shown Fig.6a.

However, a considerable amount of this energy consumption is relative to the nodes' movement. This is corroborated by the results in Fig.6b that shows the displacement of the nodes which adjusted their depth. Fig.7 examines the overall energy consumption due to both topology control and data packet transmission operation. As expected, the trend is that the energy consumption referent to topology control decreases with an increase in the network density because there is a reduction on the number of nodes in a communication void region. Since the displacement is greatest when CTC is used than DTC (Fig.6b), the energy consumption for topology control in the CTC is greater. This because CTC derive more adequate topologies, verified mainly in Figs.1a, 1b and 3a. We also can see that with an increase in the network density, the data communication energy consumption also increases due to the large amount of data packet generated by the network.

Fig.8a shows the overall energy consumption per delivered packet per node. This is an important metric that well represents the trade-off between the cost of the topology control through nodes' movement assisted and the network performance. Despite the high energy consumption of topology control, it is diluted with the significant increment on the fraction of delivered packet, as shown in Fig.3a. Therefore, for long-term operation and for applications where large amounts of data are produced in the network which need

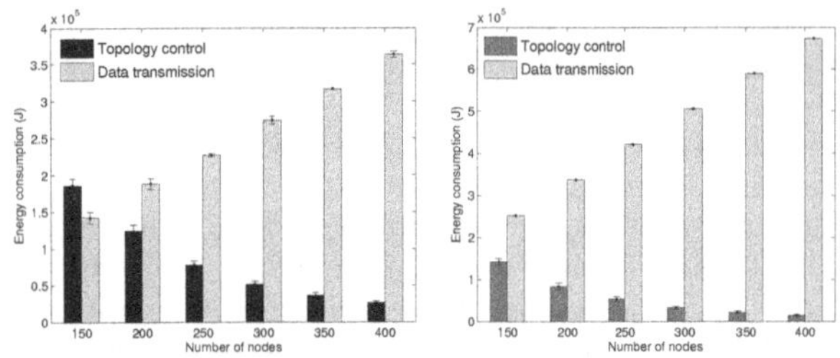

(a) With CTC. (b) With DTC.

Figure 7: Average energy consumption for network operation.

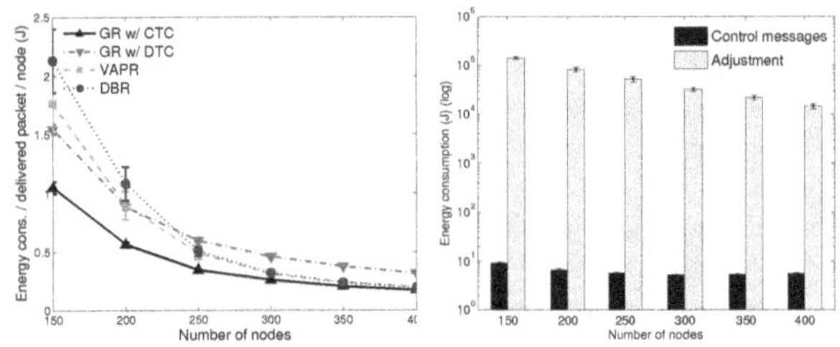

(a) Energy consumption per delivered packet per node. (b) TC task in DTC.

Figure 8: Energy consumption measurements.

to be effectively delivered with a strong restriction in the fraction of the losses that the application can support, like for marine life or oil spill plumes monitoring, this approach is thoroughly adequate. Besides, with mechanisms that efficiently can adjust the depth of the nodes with the minimal energy consumption, this topology control methodology can be applied to improve the overall network performance. This is because, as show in Fig.8b, the depth adjustment task has much more energy consumption due the message control overhead.

9. CONCLUSIONS AND FUTURE WORKS

We propose and investigate the geographic routing protocol and two topology control algorithms (CTC and DTC) for long-time monitoring underwater sensor networks. The topology control approach uses the movement assisted of the nodes by means of the depth adjustment, aiming to derive favorable topologies to use the anycast greedy geographic routing protocol. Simulation results showed that when the network density is lower and consequently, the number of isolated nodes is higher, CTC and DTC effectively derive new network topology such that the fraction of delivered packet data is upper than 90% for most cases. Moreover, we investigate the impact of the depth adjustment in the network energy consumption. The results showed that the topology control through nodes' movement leads to a higher energy cost which is diluted with the increase of the fraction of delivered packets. Besides, with energy efficient depth adjustment mechanisms this methodology is very attractive to effectively use in underwater sensor networks. As future work, we plan to investigate the topology control through movement assisted in underwater sensor network scenarios where sensor nodes can freely drift with sea current. Besides, we plan to derive an analytical model to investigate the efficiency of topology control via power adjustment and topology control via movement assisted, in underwater sensor networks.

10. REFERENCES

[1] I. Vasilescu, K. Kotay, D. Rus, M. Dunbabin, and P. Corke. Data collection, storage, and retrieval with an underwater sensor network. SenSys '05.

[2] J. Partam, J. Kurose, and Levine B. N. A Survey of Practical Issues in Underwater Networks. In *WUWNet'06*.

[3] C. Detweiler, M. Doniec, I. Vasilescu, and D Rus. Autonomous Depth Adjustment for Underwater Sensor Networks: Design and Applications. *IEEE/ASME Transactions on Mechatronics*, 2012.

[4] M. Stojanovic. On the relationship between capacity and distance in an underwater acoustic communication channel. In *WUWNet'06*.

[5] U. Lee, P. Wang, Y. Noh, L. F. M. Vieira, M. Gerla, and J.-H. Cui. Pressure routing for underwater sensor networks. In *INFOCOM'10*.

[6] D. Chen and P. K. Varshney. A survey of void handling techniques for geographic routing in wireless networks. *IEEE Comm. Surveys Tutorials*, pages 50 –67, 2007.

[7] F. Kuhn, R. Wattenhofer, and A. Zollinger. Worst-Case optimal and average-case efficient geometric ad-hoc routing. In *MobiHoc '03*.

[8] P. Xie, Z. Zhou, Z. Peng, J.-H. Cui, and Z. Shi. Void avoidance in three-dimensional mobile underwater sensor networks. In *WASA '09*.

[9] P. Xie, J.-H. Cui, and L. Lao. VBF: Vector-Based Forwarding Protocol for Underwater Sensor Networks. In *IFIP Networking'06*.

[10] Y. Noh, U. Lee, P. Wang, B. Choi, and M. Gerla. VAPR: Void aware pressure routing for underwater sensor networks. *IEEE Trans. on Mob. Comput.*, 2012.

[11] T. Melodia, D. Pompili, and I. F. Akyildiz. Optimal local topology knowledge for energy efficient geographical routing in sensor networks. In *INFOCOM '04*.

[12] S. Durocher, D. Kirkpatrick, and L. Narayanan. On routing with guaranteed delivery in three-dimensional ad hoc wireless networks. *Wirel. Netw.*, 16, 2010.

[13] R. W. L. Coutinho, L. F. M. Vieira, and A. A.F. Loureiro. DCR: Depth-Controlled routing protocol for underwater sensor networks. In *IEEE ISCC '2013*.

[14] M. Erol, L. F. M. Vieira, and M. Gerla. AUV-Aided Localization for Underwater Sensor Networks. In *WASA '07*.

[15] B. Liu, F. Ren, C. Lin, Y. Yang, R. Zeng, and H. Wen. The redeployment issue in underwater sensor networks. In *IEEE GLOBECOM 2008*.

[16] P. Xie, Z. Zhou, Z. Peng, H. Yan, T. Hu, J.-H. Cui, Z. Shi, Y. Fei, and S. Zhou. Aqua-Sim: An NS2 based simulator for underwater sensor networks. 2009.

[17] H. Yan, Z. J. Shi, and J.-H. Cui. DBR: depth-based routing for underwater sensor networks. In *NETWORKING'08*.

[18] M. O'Rourke, E. Basha, and C. Detweiler. Multi-modal communications in underwater sensor networks using depth adjustment. In *WUWNet '12*.

Cooperative Localization Revisited: Error Bound, Scaling, and Convergence

Shigeo Shioda
Graduate School of Engineering, Chiba University
1-33 Yayoi, Inage, Chiba 263-8522, Japan
shioda@faculty.chiba-u.jp

Kazuki Shimamura
Graduate School of Engineering, Chiba University
1-33 Yayoi, Inage, Chiba 263-8522, Japan
11tm0327@chiba-u.jp

ABSTRACT

Cooperative localization, where sensors exchange the information with each other to determine their locations, has received considerable attention. In this work, we study the cooperative localization in order to investigate several fundamental properties that have not been well addressed so far. We formulate the cooperative localization in a general setting, where a relative or absolute location map is obtained, depending on the number of anchors. The (relative or absolute) location map is the output of an optimization problem, where the objective function is given as a norm of a space where a vector composed of distances between sensors is defined. We show that several error bounds and the estimation bias of the cooperative localization can be obtained by simple arguments (*e.g.* by using triangle inequality) without specifying the detail of the objective function. Next, we theoretically and numerically verify that the cooperative localization has a preferable scaling property such that the estimation becomes more accurate as sensors are more densely deployed. Finally, we consider the problem that the objective functions used in the cooperative localization are usually multimodal and have a number of local optima and saddle points. We show that the gradient descent algorithm starting from a random prior (initial estimates) often fails to find the optimal solution when the distance measurements between some pair of sensors are not available. We propose a new prior, called *shortest-path-distance-based prior*, which is very powerful for obtaining accurate estimates even when the distances between some sensor pairs are not measurable.

Categories and Subject Descriptors

C.2.4 [**Distributed Systems**]: [Network operating systems]; C.4 [**PERFORMANCE OF SYSTEMS**]: [Modeling techniques]

General Terms

Theory

Keywords

localization; sensor networks; position estimation; optimization

MSWiM'13, November 3–8, 2013, Barcelona, Spain.

ACM 978-1-4503-2353-6/13/11...$15.00.
http://dx.doi.org/10.1145/2507924.2507937.

1. INTRODUCTION

Recent progress in electronics and micromechanics allows us to have small, low-cost, and low-power sensors, which have built-in battery and wireless-communication capability to transmit sensed data to a data center via a single or multi-hop wireless link. Such sensors present us with great opportunities for a wide range of applications including tracking, surveillance, or environment monitoring. Even if each sensor provides little amount of data, we can obtain respectable information on a field of watch by aggregating large amount of data sensed by densely deployed sensors.

When aggregating sensed data, knowledge of the geometrical locations of sensors is very important in order to identify at which location each piece of data is collected. Knowing sensors' locations is also valuable for geographical routing or topology control of sensor networks. A straightforward solution for knowing sensors' locations, usually referred to as *localization*, is to equip each sensor with a Global Positioning System (GPS) receiver, but it is prohibited because of the size, cost, and power consumption constraints of sensors.

One of common approaches for localization is to use a small number of sensors, called *anchors* or *reference nodes*, that know their geographical coordinates typically via GPS and that give information on locations to neighbor sensors. In conventional localization, a sensor estimates its location based on anchors' locations and its ranges (or the number of hops) to anchors. Sensors with unknown locations, however, could also help each other to determine their locations by exchanging their location estimates. The additional information exchanged between sensors with unknown locations would enhance the accuracy of localization. A considerable number of studies have been made on such a localization system, which is typically called *cooperative localization* [23, 19, 34]. Note that the cooperative localization could realize the anchor-free localization, which outputs a relative map of sensors although it does not provide absolute coordinates of sensors. A relative map is still helpful for some applications including shape recognition of a target object [5, 32, 31] or direction-based routing.

In this work, we study the cooperative localization in order to give some insights that have not been addressed well in the previous studies. To this end, we formulate the cooperative localization in a general setting, which allows us to have a relative location map or an absolute location map, depending on the number of anchors. The relative or absolute location map is obtained as the output of an optimization problem, where the objective function to be minimized is given as a norm of the space where a vector composed of distances between sensors is defined. First, we show that several fundamental properties of the location estimator, including the error bounds and the estimation bias, can be derived even without specifying the detail of the objective function. Next, we theoretically and numerically verify that the cooperative localization has a preferable scaling property such that the estimation error becomes smaller as sensors are more densely deployed.

The objective functions used in the cooperative localization are usually multimodal and have a number of local optima and saddle points. The gradient descent algorithm is often used in the cooperative localization, and thus it may fail to find the global optimal solution. Finally, we consider this issue and show that the gradient descent algorithm starting from a random prior often fails to find the optimal solution when the distance measurements between some pair of sensors are not available. We propose a new prior, called *shortest-path-distance-based (STD-based) prior*, which allows us to have almost optimal estimates even when the distances between some sensor pairs are not measurable.

This manuscript is organized as follows: in Sec. 2, we overview related work concerning the sensor localization. In Sec. 3 we explain several assumptions and notions used in this work. In Sec. 4 we formulate the cooperative localization as a non-linear optimization problem, and show several mathematical characteristics of the cooperative localization. In Sec. 5 we numerically evaluate the cooperative localization using simulation experiments. Finally, we conclude the study in Sec.6.

2. RELATED WORK

Existing studies on localization are classified as range-base and range-free. In range-based methods, sensors with unknown locations measure distances to anchors based on signal strength or time of arrival, and estimate their locations using the process of trilateration, triangulation, or Maximum Likelihood estimation. GPS uses the time of arrival from a satellite for localization [13]. Several studies [2, 36, 37] use Received Signal Strength Indicator (RSSI) for distance measurement because most sensor nodes have radio transmitters and receivers. The RSSI-based distance measurement relies on theoretical or empirical model to translate signal strength into distance estimates. The RSSI-based measurement techniques, however, have a difficulty that multi-path effect, antenna orientation, or unknown path loss factor inevitably causes measurement errors. Time of Arrival (TOA) of ultrasound was used for distance estimation in [33, 11], where a small ultrasonic transducer attached to a target object emits a pulse of ultrasound and receivers in rooms record the time of arrivals of pulses from the transducer to determine its location using the multilateration. Time difference of arrival (TDOA) between simultaneously transmitted radio and ultrasound signals was used for distance estimation in Cricket [25], AHLoS [27]. TPS [6] used the TDOA-based sensor localization without using ultrasound transducers or receivers.

Sensors with unknown locations could help each other to determine their locations by sending their location estimates. This observation yields a new paradigm of localization, called *cooperative localization*, and a number of studies have been made so far. Centralized algorithm, in which a central processor gathers the distance measurements from sensors and determine the locations of all sensors by solving some global optimization problem, is the simplest implementation of the cooperative localization [9, 20, 30, 15]. For example, Shang *et al.* proposed the centralized algorithm [30] for *connectivity-based* cooperative localization, where the distance between two connected sensors is defined to be 1, while the distance between two sensors not in range is given by the number of hops in the shortest path between them. They also proposed the extension of their work [29], where sensors respectively build local maps using information on their neighbors and merge these maps together to form a global map. Centralized algorithms are usually not scalable, so most of algorithms for cooperative localization are distributed [28, 17, 23, 7, 1] (see also [34] and references therein). If the probability distribution of the error in the distance measurements between sensors is known *a priori*, maximum likelihood estimation [8] or Bayesian estimation [14, 24] can be used for the localization.

The cooperative localization determines the locations of sensors by solving some optimization problems, which are usually multimodal and have a number of local optima and saddle points. Some studies address this problem under the multilateration setting where a node localize itself based on the distances to multiple (more than three) anchors [26, 3].

Range-free methods rely only on the information on the locations of anchor nodes without using the distance measurements. In Centroid algorithm [4], anchors are placed with overlapping regions of coverage and transmit periodic beacon signals to provide their positions to their neighbor sensors. Each sensor localizes itself to the centroid of anchor nodes, from which beacon signals are received. DV-HOP algorithm [22] assumes a network consisting of sensors and a small number of anchors. Each anchor floods packets containing its physical location throughout the network. A flooded packet maintains a running hop-count along the way; each sensor receiving the flooded packet knows how many hops are required to reach the corresponding anchor node as well as its physical location, which are in turn used to estimate the position of the sensor. Over the past few years, several articles have been devoted to the extension of DV-HOP algorithm [21].

3. PRELIMINARIES

3.1 Basic Assumptions

Consider a two-dimensional area where N sensors are deployed. Among N sensors, the first n sensors, labeled 1 through n, are so called anchors whose absolute locations are known, and the rest $N-n$ sensors, labeled $n+1$ through N, are ordinary sensors, whose locations are unknown. Each sensor is assumed to have functions for approximately estimating distances between neighbor sensors, and for sending estimation results to a central server via single long-range wireless link. The central server has the information on the distances between sensors, based on which it conducts all the computations for solving a global optimization problem mentioned later to obtain the locations of sensors. Let s_i denote the location of sensor i ($i = 1, \ldots, N$), and let d_{ij} and $d_{ij}^{(m)}$ respectively denote the real and estimated distance between sensors i and j. Note that $d_{ij}^{(m)} \neq d_{ji}^{(m)}$ in general, although $d_{ij} = d_{ji}$. We use the following variables:

$$m(i,j) \stackrel{\text{def}}{=} \begin{cases} 1 & \text{sensor } i \text{ can measure the distance to sensor } j (\neq i), \\ 0 & \text{otherwise,} \end{cases}$$

$$M(i) \stackrel{\text{def}}{=} \{j \in (1, \ldots, N) | m(i,j) = 1\},$$

$$\boldsymbol{d} \stackrel{\text{def}}{=} (\underbrace{d_{12}, d_{13}, \ldots, d_{ij}, \ldots, d_{NN-1}}_{j \in M(i)}), \quad M \stackrel{\text{def}}{=} \sum_i |M(i)|$$

$$\boldsymbol{d}^{(m)} \stackrel{\text{def}}{=} (\underbrace{d_{12}^{(m)}, d_{13}^{(m)}, \ldots, d_{ij}^{(m)}, \ldots, d_{NN-1}^{(m)}}_{j \in M(i)}),$$

$$S_1 \stackrel{\text{def}}{=} (s_1, \ldots, s_n), \quad S_2 \stackrel{\text{def}}{=} (s_{n+1}, \ldots, s_N),$$

$$S \stackrel{\text{def}}{=} (S_1, S_2) = (s_1, \ldots, s_n, s_{n+1}, \ldots, s_N).$$

Note that d ($d^{(m)}$) is a vector sorting d_{ij} ($d^{(m)}_{ij}$) in a lexicographic order, while skipping d_{ij} ($d^{(m)}_{ij}$) if $j \neq M(i)$[1].

Remark 1. *Although we mentioned that the localization is conducted at the central server, the distributed implementation is also possible. We will explain the distributed implementation in Sec. 4.3.*

Remark 2. *For simplifying the framework for localization, we assume that the probability distribution of the error in the distance measurements between sensors is not known a priori. So, the maximum likelihood estimation or Bayesian estimation is not discussed in this work.*

3.2 Relative Locations

Even if the number of anchors is less than three, the cooperative localization can estimate the relative locations of sensors although the absolute coordinates of sensors are not available. Since the locations of sensors are accurate relative to one another under the transformations of translation, rotation, and reflection, we use these three transformations (translation, rotation, and reflection) for the formal definition of the relative locations.

Definition 1. *We say that $P \stackrel{\text{def}}{=} (p_1, \ldots p_N)$ is a set of relative locations of sensors with co-ordinates S, if applying one of the three transformations (translation, rotation, and reflection) or its combination to S yields P.*

Let $P \stackrel{\mathcal{R}}{\sim} S$ denote the fact that P is a set of relative locations of S.

Note that relation $\mathcal{R}$ is an *equivalence relation* in $\mathbb{R}^{2N}$; $\mathcal{R}(S)$ defined below is its *equivalent class* with representative S:

$$\mathcal{R}(S) \stackrel{\text{def}}{=} \left\{P \in \mathbb{R}^{2N} \middle| P \stackrel{\mathcal{R}}{\sim} S\right\}.$$

An arbitrary element of $\mathcal{R}(S)$ is a set of relative locations of S. That is, there are multiple (infinite) sets of relative locations of sensors even if absolute location of each sensor is uniquely given. We introduce another equivalent relation.

Definition 2. *We say that P is equivalent to S in the sense of inter distances if*

$$\forall i \in (1, \ldots, N),\ \forall j \in M(i) \quad |p_i - p_j| = |s_i - s_j|.$$

We denote it by $P \stackrel{\mathcal{R}_d}{\sim} S$.

Relation $\mathcal{R}_d$ is also an equivalent relation in $\mathbb{R}^{2N}$; $\mathcal{R}_d(S)$ defined below is its equivalent class with representative S:

$$\mathcal{R}_d(S) \stackrel{\text{def}}{=} \left\{P \in \mathbb{R}^{2N} \middle| P \stackrel{\mathcal{R}_d}{\sim} S\right\}.$$

Definition 3. *If $\mathcal{R}_d(S) = \mathcal{R}(S)$, then we say that sensors are relatively localizable based on the inter distances.*

In this work, assuming the relative localizability of sensors, we consider the problem to determine a set of relative locations (an element of $\mathcal{R}(S)$) from $d^{(m)}$.

Remark 3. *Relative localizability (Definition 3) is equivalent to the notion of global rigidity [16, 10, 18, 12]. A graph is rigid if one cannot continuously deform the graph on the plane without changing the edge length, and a graph is globally rigid if there is a unique realization on the plane. Relative localizability is also closely related to the notion of localizability; a graph is localizable if there is a unique location of every node under the given edge length and some additional constraints [35].*

[1]Because of the limited effective range, the distance between two sensors separated far from each other cannot be measured.

4. FRAMEWORK FOR COOPERATIVE LOCALIZATION

4.1 Mathematical Formulation

We define the following mapping $d^{(e)} : \mathbb{R}^{2N} \to \mathbb{R}^M$.

$$\begin{aligned} d^{(e)}(X_1, X_2) &= d^{(e)}(x_1, \ldots, x_n, x_{n+1}, \ldots, x_N) \\ &= \underbrace{(|x_1 - x_2|, |x_1 - x_3|, \ldots, |x_i - x_j|, \ldots, |x_{N-1} - x_N|)}_{j \in M(i)}. \end{aligned}$$

Note that $d^{(e)}(X_1, X_2)$, a vector sorting $|x_i - x_j|$ in a lexicographic order, is a set of distances between sensors if x_i is co-ordinate of sensor i.

Most of previous studies use $\hat{P}_2 = (\hat{p}_{n+1}, \ldots, \hat{p}_N)$ defined below as an estimator of the location map of sensors with unknown locations.

$$\begin{aligned} \hat{P}_2 &\stackrel{\text{def}}{=} \arg\min_{X_2} \|d^{(e)}(S_1, X_2) - d^{(m)}\|, \qquad (1) \\ &(= \arg\min_{(x_{n+1}, \ldots, x_N)} \|d^{(e)}(s_1, \ldots, s_n, x_{n+1}, \ldots, x_N) - d^{(m)}\|,) \end{aligned}$$

where $\|\cdot\|$ is a norm defined in the space $\mathbb{R}^M$. The following L1 or L2 norm can be used for the computation of $\hat{P}_2$.

$$\|d^{(e)}(X_1, X_2) - d^{(m)}\|_1 = \sum_i \sum_{j \in M(i)} \left| |x_i - x_j| - d^{(m)}_{ij} \right|, \qquad (2)$$

$$\|d^{(e)}(X_1, X_2) - d^{(m)}\|_2 = \sqrt{\sum_i \sum_{j \in M(i)} (|x_i - x_j| - d^{(m)}_{ij})^2}. \qquad (3)$$

Since $\|d^{(e)}(S_1, \hat{P}_2) - d^{(m)}\|$ is the difference between the estimated and measured distances between sensors, the optimization problem in the right-hand side of (1) is equivalent to finding the solution minimizing the estimation error.

Consider a case of $n = 0$ where $(S_1, \hat{P}_2) = \hat{P}_2$. Since $\|d^{(e)}(\hat{P}_2) - d^{(m)}\|$ remains the same under the three transformations (translation, rotation, and reflection), an arbitrary element of $\mathcal{R}(\hat{P}_2)$ is to be an estimator of relative locations of sensors. That is, the optimization problem in the right-hand side of (1) has multiple (infinite number of) solutions. This comes from the nature of the problem of relative localization. The optimization problem has multiple solutions when $n \leq 2$; otherwise, it has the unique solution.

4.2 Characteristics of the Estimator

In this subsection, we derive several fundamental characteristics of the estimator, including the error bounds and the estimation bias, without specifying the detail of the objective function.

Definition 4. *We say that $d \in \mathbb{R}^M$ is feasible if there exists $X_2 \in \mathbb{R}^{2(N-n)}$ such that $d = d^{(e)}(S_1, X_2)$.*

Let $\mathcal{D}_f(S_1) \subset \mathbb{R}^M$ denote the set of feasible elements in $\mathbb{R}^M$, called *feasible space* in the following, and for $d \in \mathcal{D}_f(S_1)$ we define

$$\mathcal{P}(d, S_1) \stackrel{\text{def}}{=} \left\{X_2 | d = d^{(e)}(S_1, X_2)\right\}.$$

Observe that

$$\min_{X_2} \|d^{(e)}(S_1, X_2) - d^{(m)}\| = \min_{d \in \mathcal{D}_f(S_1)} \|d - d^{(m)}\|.$$

Thus, solving the optimization problem in the right-hand side of (1) is equivalent to finding the projection from $d^{(m)}$ to $\mathcal{D}_f(S_1)$ defined below

$$\pi_f(d^{(m)}) \stackrel{\text{def}}{=} \arg\min_{d \in \mathcal{D}_f(S_1)} \|d - d^{(m)}\|,$$

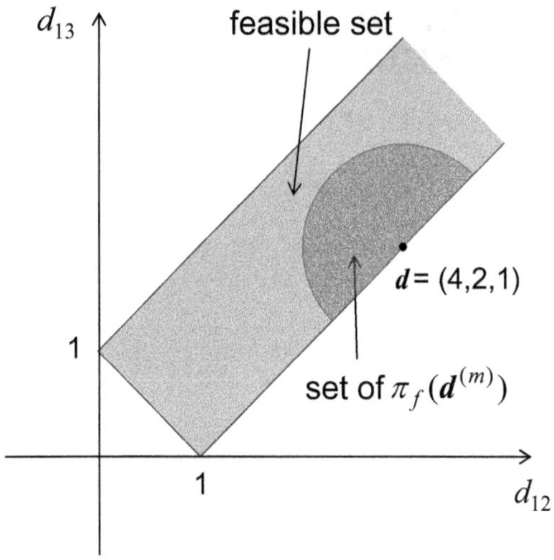

Figure 1: Example where $\hat{P}_2$ is biased.

and obtaining an element of $\mathcal{P}(\pi_f(\boldsymbol{d}^{(m)}), S_1)$. Note that $\boldsymbol{d}^{(e)}(S_1, \hat{P}_2) = \pi_f(\boldsymbol{d}^{(m)})$.

Estimator $\hat{P}_2$ depends on the measured distances between sensors $\boldsymbol{d}^{(m)}$, which is a random variable including random measurement error, and thus $\hat{P}_2$ is also a random variable. Note that when $n < 3$ the direct comparison between $\hat{P}_2$ and S_2 has no meaning because $\hat{P}_2$ is a set of *relative* coordinates while S_2 is a set of *absolute* coordinates of sensors. So, we use the following definition for the unbiasedness of $\hat{P}_2$.

Definition 5. *We say $\hat{P}_2$ is unbiased if $E[\boldsymbol{d}^{(e)}(S_1, \hat{P}_2)] = \boldsymbol{d}$.*

It follows from Definition 5 that $\hat{P}_2$ is unbiased if $E[\pi_f(\boldsymbol{d}^{(m)})] = E[\boldsymbol{d}^{(m)}] = E[\boldsymbol{d}]$. This result means that the shape of space $\mathcal{D}_f(S_1)$ and the statistical characteristics of $\boldsymbol{d}^{(m)}$ determines whether $\hat{P}_2$ is unbiased. Unfortunately, $\hat{P}_2$ is biased in general. To see this, we consider the case of $N = 3$, where $\boldsymbol{d}$ is feasible when

$$\begin{aligned} &d_{12} = d_{21}, \quad d_{23} = d_{32}, \quad d_{13} = d_{31}, \\ &d_{12} < d_{13} + d_{23}, \quad d_{13} < d_{12} + d_{23}, \quad d_{23} < d_{12} + d_{13}. \end{aligned}$$

Figure 1 illustrates the feasible space of this case on the plane of $d_{23} = 1$. Now, we assume that $\boldsymbol{d} = (d_{12}, d_{13}, d_{23}) = (4, 2, 1)$ and $\boldsymbol{d}^{(m)}$ are uniformly distributed within a disk with range of 1 centered at $\boldsymbol{d}$. Under these assumptions, the projection of $\boldsymbol{d}^{(m)}$ on $\mathcal{D}_f$, $\pi_f(\boldsymbol{d}^{(m)})$, is distributed as illustrated in Fig. 1 and its centroid is different with $\boldsymbol{d}$. That is, $\hat{P}_2$ is biased.

Although $\hat{P}_2$ is biased in general, we can obtain several upper bounds of the estimation error. The next lemma, proved by the triangle inequality, shows that the difference between estimated and real distances between sensors is less than the twice of the error in the distance measurement.

Lemma 1.

$$\|\boldsymbol{d}^{(e)}(S_1, \hat{P}_2) - \boldsymbol{d}\| \leq 2\|\boldsymbol{d} - \boldsymbol{d}^{(m)}\|.$$

Proof. It follows from the definition of $\hat{P}_2$ that

$$\|\boldsymbol{d}^{(e)}(S_1, \hat{P}_2) - \boldsymbol{d}^{(m)}\| \leq \|\boldsymbol{d} - \boldsymbol{d}^{(m)}\|.$$

Then, the proof readily follows from the observation that

$$\begin{aligned} \|\boldsymbol{d}^{(e)}(S_1, \hat{P}_2) - \boldsymbol{d}\| &= \|\boldsymbol{d}^{(e)}(S_1, \hat{P}_2) - \boldsymbol{d}^{(m)} + \boldsymbol{d}^{(m)} - \boldsymbol{d}\| \\ &\leq \|\boldsymbol{d}^{(e)}(S_1, \hat{P}_2) - \boldsymbol{d}^{(m)}\| + \|\boldsymbol{d} - \boldsymbol{d}^{(m)}\| \\ &\leq 2\|\boldsymbol{d} - \boldsymbol{d}^{(m)}\|. \end{aligned}$$

□

Tighter bounds on $\|\boldsymbol{d}^{(e)}(S_1, \hat{P}_2) - \boldsymbol{d}\|$ than Lemma 1 hold if the following L2 Euclidean norm is used in (1).

$$\begin{aligned} &\|\boldsymbol{d}^{(e)}(S_1, \hat{P}_2) - \boldsymbol{d}^{(m)}\| \\ &\stackrel{\text{def}}{=} \sqrt{(\boldsymbol{d}^{(e)}(S_1, \hat{P}_2) - \boldsymbol{d}^{(m)}) \cdot (\boldsymbol{d}^{(e)}(S_1, \hat{P}_2) - \boldsymbol{d}^{(m)})} \\ &= \sqrt{\sum_i \sum_{j \in M(i)} (d_{ij}^{(e)}(S_1, \hat{P}_2) - d_{ij}^{(m)})^2}. \end{aligned}$$

Lemma 2.

$$\|\boldsymbol{d}^{(e)}(S_1, \hat{P}_2) - \boldsymbol{d}\| \leq \sqrt{2(\boldsymbol{d}^{(e)}(S_1, \hat{P}_2) - \boldsymbol{d}) \cdot (\boldsymbol{d}^{(m)} - \boldsymbol{d})}.$$

Proof. First observe that

$$\begin{aligned} &(\boldsymbol{d}^{(e)}(S_1, \hat{P}_2) - \boldsymbol{d}^{(m)}) \cdot (\boldsymbol{d}^{(e)}(S_1, \hat{P}_2) - \boldsymbol{d}^{(m)}) \\ &= (\boldsymbol{d}^{(e)}(S_1, \hat{P}_2) - \boldsymbol{d} + \boldsymbol{d} - \boldsymbol{d}^{(m)}) \cdot (\boldsymbol{d}^{(e)}(S_1, \hat{P}_2) - \boldsymbol{d} + \boldsymbol{d} - \boldsymbol{d}^{(m)}) \\ &= \|\boldsymbol{d}^{(e)}(S_1, \hat{P}_2) - \boldsymbol{d}\|^2 + \|\boldsymbol{d} - \boldsymbol{d}^{(m)}\|^2 \\ &\quad + 2(\boldsymbol{d}^{(e)}(S_1, \hat{P}_2) - \boldsymbol{d}) \cdot (\boldsymbol{d} - \boldsymbol{d}^{(m)}). \end{aligned}$$

Combining the fact $\|\boldsymbol{d}^{(e)}(S_1, \hat{P}_2) - \boldsymbol{d}^{(m)}\| \leq \|\boldsymbol{d} - \boldsymbol{d}^{(m)}\|$ with the above yields

$$\begin{aligned} \|\boldsymbol{d} - \boldsymbol{d}^{(m)}\|^2 \geq \|\boldsymbol{d}^{(e)}(S_1, \hat{P}_2) - \boldsymbol{d}\|^2 + \|\boldsymbol{d} - \boldsymbol{d}^{(m)}\|^2 \\ + 2(\boldsymbol{d}^{(e)}(S_1, \hat{P}_2) - \boldsymbol{d}) \cdot (\boldsymbol{d} - \boldsymbol{d}^{(m)}). \end{aligned}$$

Thus, we obtain

$$2(\boldsymbol{d}^{(e)}(S_1, \hat{P}_2) - \boldsymbol{d}) \cdot (\boldsymbol{d}^{(m)} - \boldsymbol{d}) \geq \|\boldsymbol{d}^{(e)}(S_1, \hat{P}_2) - \boldsymbol{d}\|^2,$$

which completes the proof. □

Lemma 3. *If $E[\boldsymbol{d}^{(m)}] = \boldsymbol{d}$, then*

$$E[\|\boldsymbol{d}^{(e)}(S_1, \hat{P}_2) - \boldsymbol{d}\|] \leq \sqrt{2Cov[\boldsymbol{d}^{(e)}(S_1, \hat{P}_2), \boldsymbol{d}^{(m)}]},$$

where

$$\begin{aligned} &Cov[\boldsymbol{d}^{(e)}(S_1, \hat{P}_2), \boldsymbol{d}^{(m)}] \\ &\stackrel{\text{def}}{=} E[(\boldsymbol{d}^{(e)}(S_1, \hat{P}_2) - E[\boldsymbol{d}^{(e)}(S_1, \hat{P}_2)]) \cdot (\boldsymbol{d}^{(m)} - E[\boldsymbol{d}^{(m)}])]. \end{aligned}$$

Proof. It follows from Lemma 2 that

$$\begin{aligned} &E[\|\boldsymbol{d}^{(e)}(S_1, \hat{P}_2) - \boldsymbol{d}^{(m)}\|^2] \\ &\leq 2E[(\boldsymbol{d}^{(e)}(S_1, \hat{P}_2) - \boldsymbol{d}) \cdot (\boldsymbol{d}^{(m)} - \boldsymbol{d})] \\ &= 2E[(\boldsymbol{d}^{(e)}(S_1, \hat{P}_2) - E[\boldsymbol{d}^{(e)}(S_1, \hat{P}_2)]) \cdot (\boldsymbol{d}^{(m)} - \boldsymbol{d})] \\ &\quad + 2E[(E[\boldsymbol{d}^{(e)}(S_1, \hat{P}_2)] - \boldsymbol{d}) \cdot (\boldsymbol{d}^{(m)} - \boldsymbol{d})] \\ &= 2E[(\boldsymbol{d}^{(e)}(S_1, \hat{P}_2) - E[\boldsymbol{d}^{(e)}(S_1, \hat{P}_2)]) \cdot (\boldsymbol{d}^{(m)} - \boldsymbol{d})] \\ &\quad + 2(E[\boldsymbol{d}^{(e)}(S_1, \hat{P}_2)] - \boldsymbol{d}) \cdot E[\boldsymbol{d}^{(m)} - \boldsymbol{d}] \\ &= 2E[(\boldsymbol{d}^{(e)}(S_1, \hat{P}_2) - E[\boldsymbol{d}^{(e)}(S_1, \hat{P}_2)]) \cdot (\boldsymbol{d}^{(m)} - \boldsymbol{d})]. \end{aligned}$$

Thus, it follows from Jensen's inequality that

$$\begin{aligned} (E[\|\boldsymbol{d}^{(e)}(S_1, \hat{P}_2) - \boldsymbol{d}^{(m)}\|])^2 &\leq E[\|\boldsymbol{d}^{(e)}(S_1, \hat{P}_2) - \boldsymbol{d}^{(m)}\|^2] \\ &\leq 2Cov[\boldsymbol{d}^{(e)}(S_1, \hat{P}_2), \boldsymbol{d}^{(m)}], \end{aligned}$$

which completes the proof. □

LEMMA 4. *If* $E[\boldsymbol{d}^{(m)}] = \boldsymbol{d}$, *and* $\boldsymbol{d}^{(e)}(S_1, \hat{P}_2)$ *and* $\boldsymbol{d}^{(m)}$ *are statistically independent, then*

$$||\boldsymbol{d}^{(e)}(S_1, \hat{P}_2) - \boldsymbol{d}|| = 0.$$

PROOF. The proof readily follows from Lemma 3. □

Note that

$$Cov[\boldsymbol{d}^{(e)}(S_1, \hat{P}_2), \boldsymbol{d}^{(m)}] = \sum_i \sum_{j\in M(i)} Cov[d_{ij}^{(e)}(S_1, \hat{P}_2), d_{ij}^{(m)}].$$

Thus, if $E[d_{ij}^{(m)}] = d_{ij}$ for all (i, j) pairs, it follows from Lemma 4 that $\boldsymbol{d}^{(e)}(S_1, \hat{P}_2) = \boldsymbol{d}$ if $d_{ij}^{(e)}$ and $d_{ij}^{(m)}$ are statistically independent. In general, $d_{ij}^{(e)}$ and $d_{ij}^{(m)}$ are positively correlated because $d_{ij}^{(m)}$ is the first-order approximation of $d_{ij}^{(e)}$. However, we conjecture that this positive correlation may vanish as $|M(i)|$ tends to infinity because distance measurements between sensors overdetermine $d_{ij}^{(e)}$ and the measurement error in $d_{ij}^{(m)}$ seems to balance against errors in distance measurements between sensors other than the pair of (i, j). To verify the conjecture, consider a case where many sensors are densely deployed and the following normalized norm is used:

$$||\boldsymbol{d}^{(e)}(S_1, \hat{P}_2) - \boldsymbol{d}^{(m)}|| = \sqrt{\frac{1}{\sum_i |M(i)|} \sum_i \sum_{j\in M(i)} (d_{ij}^{(e)}(S_1, \hat{P}_2) - d_{ij}^{(m)})^2}.$$

THEOREM 1. *If* $|M(i)|$ *tends to infinity as* $N \to \infty$ *for all i, and*

$$\arg\min X_2 ||\boldsymbol{d}^{(e)}(S_1, X_2) - \boldsymbol{d}^{(m)}||^2 \quad (4)$$

has the unique solution, then

$$\lim_{N\to\infty} \boldsymbol{d}^{(e)}(S_1, \hat{P}_2) = \boldsymbol{d}.$$

PROOF. Define

$$\hat{P}_2^{(i,j)} \overset{\text{def}}{=} \arg\min_{X_2} g_{ij}(X_2),$$

where

$$g_{ij}(X_2) \overset{\text{def}}{=} \sqrt{\frac{1}{\sum_k |M(k)|} \sum_k \sum_{l\in M(k);(k,l)\neq(i,j)} (d_{kl}^{(e)}(S_1, X_2) - d_{kl}^{(m)})^2}.$$

Note that $\hat{P}_2^{(i,j)}$ is statistically independent with $d_{ij}^{(m)}$ because $g_{ij}(X_2)$ does not include $d_{ij}^{(m)}$, and thus $d_{ij}^{(e)}(S_1, \hat{P}_2^{(i,j)})$ and $d_{ij}^{(m)}$ are mutually independent. Observe that

$$g_{ij}(X_2)^2 = ||\boldsymbol{d}^{(e)}(S_1, X_2) - \boldsymbol{d}^{(m)}||^2 - \frac{1}{\sum_k |M(k)|}(d_{ij}^{(e)}(S_1, X_2) - d_{ij}^{(m)})^2$$
$$\longrightarrow ||\boldsymbol{d}^{(e)}(S_1, X_2) - \boldsymbol{d}^{(m)}||^2 \quad (N \to \infty),$$

because of the assumption that $|M(i)|$ tends to infinity as $N \to \infty$ for all i. Combining this fact with the uniqueness of the solution of (4) yields that $\lim_{N\to\infty} \hat{P}_2^{(i,j)} = \hat{P}_2$, and thus $d_{ij}^{(e)}(S_1, \hat{P}_2)$ and $d_{ij}^{(m)}$ are statistically independent in the limit of $N \to \infty$. Combining this fact with Lemma 4 completes the proof. □

In Section 5, we numerically show that the estimation error becomes smaller as sensors are more densely placed.

4.3 Solution of the Optimization Problem

The optimization problem is written in the following form when L1 norm (2) is used:

$$\min_{X_2} ||\boldsymbol{d}^{(e)}(S_1, X_2) - \boldsymbol{d}^{(m)}||_1$$
$$= \min \sum_i \sum_{j\in M(i)} t_{ij} \quad \text{subject to } - t_{ij} \le d_{ij}^{(e)}(S_1, X_2) - d_{ij}^{(m)} \le t_{ij}.$$

The objective function is linear, but the constraints are not linear and thus we cannot directly apply solutions for linear-programming problems. In this sense, the L1 norm might not be a good choice.

All existing studies concerning the cooperative localization choose the L2 norm and often apply gradient descent algorithm. The gradient of $(||\boldsymbol{d}^{(e)}(S_1, \hat{P}_2) - \boldsymbol{d}^{(m)}||_2)^2$ is given as below

$$\frac{\partial}{\partial \hat{\boldsymbol{p}}_i}(||\boldsymbol{d}^{(e)}(S_1, \hat{P}_2) - \boldsymbol{d}^{(m)}||_2)^2 = 2 \sum_{j=1;j\in M(i)}^{n} \left(1 - \frac{d_{ij}^{(m)}}{|\hat{\boldsymbol{p}}_i - \boldsymbol{s}_j|}\right)(\hat{\boldsymbol{p}}_i - \boldsymbol{s}_j)$$
$$+ 2 \sum_{n<j;j\in M(i)}^{N} \left(1 - \frac{d_{ij}^{(m)}}{|\hat{\boldsymbol{p}}_i - \hat{\boldsymbol{p}}_j|}\right)(\hat{\boldsymbol{p}}_i - \hat{\boldsymbol{p}}_j).$$

More sophisticated algorithm [15, 7] for solving the optimization problem can be obtained by observing

$$(||\boldsymbol{d}^{(e)}(S_1, \hat{P}_2) - \boldsymbol{d}^{(m)}||_2)^2 = g(S_1, \hat{P}_2, \hat{P}_2) \le g(S_1, \hat{P}_2, Q_2),$$

where

$$g(S_1, \hat{P}_2, Q_2)$$
$$\overset{\text{def}}{=} \sum_{i>n}^{N} \sum_{j=1;j\in M(i)}^{n} \left\{|\hat{\boldsymbol{p}}_i - \boldsymbol{s}_j|^2 + (d_{ij}^{(m)})^2 - 2(\hat{\boldsymbol{p}}_i - \boldsymbol{s}_j)(\boldsymbol{q}_i - \boldsymbol{s}_j)\frac{d_{ij}^{(m)}}{|\boldsymbol{q}_i - \boldsymbol{s}_j|}\right\}$$
$$+ 2\sum_{i>n}^{N} \sum_{j>n;j\in M(i)}^{N} \left\{|\hat{\boldsymbol{p}}_i - \hat{\boldsymbol{p}}_j|^2 + (d_{ij}^{(m)})^2 - 2(\hat{\boldsymbol{p}}_i - \hat{\boldsymbol{p}}_j)(\boldsymbol{q}_i - \boldsymbol{q}_j)\frac{d_{ij}^{(m)}}{|\boldsymbol{q}_i - \boldsymbol{q}_j|}\right\},$$

and $Q_2 \overset{\text{def}}{=} (\boldsymbol{q}_{n+1}, \ldots, \boldsymbol{q}_N)$. Assume that we have the lth location estimates $\hat{P}_2^{(l)}$. Minimizing $g(S_1, \hat{P}_2, \hat{P}_2^{(l)})$ is achieved by finding $\partial g(S_1, \hat{P}_2, \hat{P}_2^{(l)})/\partial \hat{\boldsymbol{p}}_i = 0$ where

$$\frac{\partial g(S_1, \hat{P}_2, \hat{P}_2^{(l)})}{\partial \hat{\boldsymbol{p}}_i} = 2 \sum_{j=1;j\in M(i)}^{n} \left\{(\hat{\boldsymbol{p}}_i - \boldsymbol{s}_j) - (\hat{\boldsymbol{p}}_i^{(l)} - \boldsymbol{s}_j)\frac{d_{ij}^{(m)}}{d_{ij}^{(e:l)}}\right\}$$
$$+ 2 \sum_{j>n;j\in M(i)}^{N} \left\{(\hat{\boldsymbol{p}}_i - \hat{\boldsymbol{p}}_j) - (\hat{\boldsymbol{p}}_i^{(l)} - \hat{\boldsymbol{p}}_j^{(l)})\frac{d_{ij}^{(m)}}{d_{ij}^{(e:l)}}\right\},$$

where

$$d_{ij}^{(e:l)} = \begin{cases} \hat{\boldsymbol{p}}_i^{(l)} - \boldsymbol{s}_j & \text{if } n < i \le N,\ 1 \le j \le n, \\ \boldsymbol{s}_i - \hat{\boldsymbol{p}}_j^{(l)} & \text{if } 1 \le i \le n,\ n < j \le N, \\ \hat{\boldsymbol{p}}_i^{(l)} - \hat{\boldsymbol{p}}_j^{(l)} & \text{if } n < i, j \le N. \end{cases}$$

The $(l+1)$th location estimates satisfying $\partial g(S_1, \hat{P}_2, \hat{P}_2^{(l)})/\partial \hat{\boldsymbol{p}}_i = 0$ are then given by

$$(\hat{p}_{(n+1)x}^{(l+1)}, \ldots, p_{Ny}^{(l+1)})^T = A^{-1}(\beta_{(n+1)x}^{(l)}, \ldots, \beta_{Nx}^{(l)})^T,$$
$$(\hat{p}_{(n+1)y}^{(l+1)}, \ldots, p_{Ny}^{(l+1)})^T = A^{-1}(\beta_{(n+1)y}^{(l)}, \ldots, \beta_{Ny}^{(l)})^T, \quad (5)$$

where

$$\boldsymbol{\beta}_i^{(l)} = \hat{\boldsymbol{p}}_i^{(l)} \sum_{j=1;j\in M(i)}^{N} \frac{d_{ij}^{(m)}}{d_{ij}^{(e:l)}}$$
$$+ \sum_{j=1;j\in M(i)}^{n} \boldsymbol{s}_j\left(1 - \frac{d_{ij}^{(m)}}{d_{ij}^{(e:l)}}\right) - \sum_{j>n;j\in|M(i)|}^{N} \hat{\boldsymbol{p}}_j^{(l)} \frac{d_{ij}^{(m)}}{d_{ij}^{(e:l)}},$$

$$A = \begin{pmatrix} |M(n+1)| & -m(n+1, n+2) & \ldots & -m(n+1, N) \\ -m(n+1, n+2) & |M(n+2)| & \ldots & -m(n+2, N) \\ \vdots & \vdots & \ddots & \vdots \\ -m(N, n+1) & -m(N, n+2) & \ldots & |M(N)| \end{pmatrix}.$$

Note that $\hat{p}_{ix}^{(l+1)}$ ($\hat{p}_{iy}^{(l+1)}$) is x-coordinate (y-coordinate) of $\hat{\boldsymbol{p}}_i^{(l+1)}$ and $\beta_{ix}^{(l)}$ ($\beta_{iy}^{(l)}$) is x-coordinate (y-coordinate) of $\boldsymbol{\beta}_i^{(l)}$. Repeated substitution of the location estimates via (5) constantly decreases the objective function and should reach the point minimizing the objective function.

The gradient descent algorithm requires some prior knowledge on the location map of sensors, and thus the solution by the gradient descent algorithm has dependence on the prior (initial location estimates) because the objective function would have multiple local minimum and the gradient descent algorithm may stagnate at one of these suboptimal solutions. We experimentally found that the gradient descent algorithm or the repeated substitution through (5) obtains the optimal solution almost surely despite of the prior when all pair-wise distances of sensors are measurable and any anchor is not placed (see Sec. 5.2). When the distances between all sensor pairs are measurable, the classical multidimensional scaling algorithm [30, 15] can be applied for the localization and the solution is found by eigen-decomposition. In such a case, the objective function itself seems to have a good structure, where the standard gradient descent algorithm can find the optimal solution.

By contrast, when the distances between some sensor pairs are not measurable due to the constraint of radio range, different priors generally lead to different solutions whose objective-function values are different (see Sec. 5.3). So, in order to have better results, we should carefully choose the prior (initial location estimates). In Sec. 5.3, we propose a promising choice of the prior, which enables us to have the good estimates even when the distances between some sensor pairs are not measurable.

The gradient descent algorithm or the repeated substitution through (5) can be implemented in a distributed fashion. To see this, for example, please observe that $\hat{\boldsymbol{p}}_i^{(n+1)}$ can be computed if $d_{ij}^{(m)}$, $\hat{\boldsymbol{p}}_j^{(n)}$, and $\boldsymbol{s}_j^{(n+1)}$ are known for all $j \in M(i)$. In case of distributed localization, each node periodically broadcast its location estimate to neighbor nodes. Node i can update its location estimate using the measured distances to node $j \in M(i)$ and the location estimate of node $j \in M(i)$, which is periodically broadcasted from node j.

Note that the centralized algorithm can obtain various final location estimates by starting from various initial estimates, and it can choose the best one. The distributed algorithms, however, cannot do it; in the distributed algorithms, each sensor needs to choose an initial estimate of its coordinate before starting the algorithm. This feature of the distributed algorithms would cause a serious problem because the performance of the cooperative localization largely depends on the choice of the initial estimates as mentioned in the above.

5. EVALUATION

5.1 Simulation Conditions

We evaluated the performance of the cooperative localization through a set of simulations. In a square region with side of 100 m, sensors were randomly placed. Four sensor networks with different sizes were used for the simulations: the numbers of sensors (N) in the networks were respectively 40, 100, 400, and 1000. The distance measurement error was given by

$$d_{ij}^{(m)} - d_{ij} = e d_{ij} U, \tag{6}$$

where U is a random variable following the uniform distribution between -1 and 1, and e is a parameter for varying the error size. To solve the optimization problem in (1) with L2 norm (3), we obtained 100 different solutions starting from 100 initial location map and, among those, chose the best one that minimized the objective function. Each initial location map was obtained by randomly choosing an initial estimate of location of each sensor within the region. We applied the repeated substitution by (5) to obtain the final solution of the optimization problem. Each sensor was assumed to be able to measure the distances to neighbor sensors when real distance was less than a given radio range d_{mea}; that is,

$$m(i,j) = \begin{cases} 1 & d_{ij} < d_{mea} \text{ and } i \neq j, \\ 0 & \text{otherwise.} \end{cases}$$

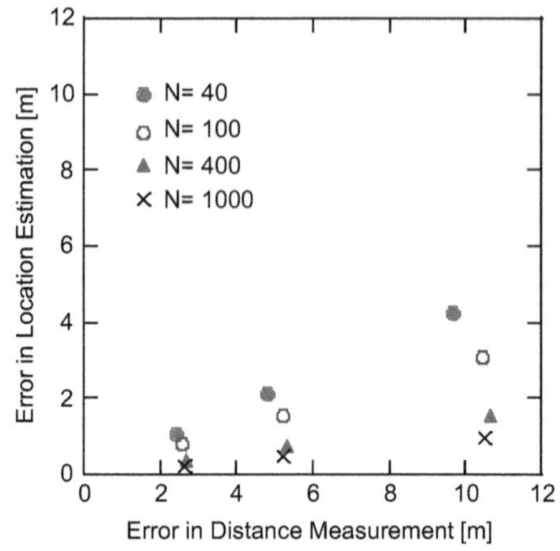

Figure 2: Relationship between location estimation error and distance measurement error: $n = 0$ **and** $d_{mea} = \infty$**.**

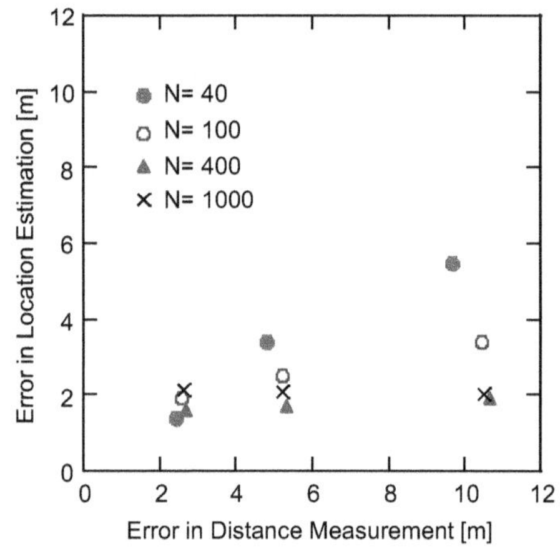

Figure 3: Relationship between location estimation error and distance measurement error: $n = 3$ **and** $d_{mea} = \infty$**.**

5.2 Simulation Results: Scenario 1

We first evaluated the performance of the cooperative localization in a scenario (Scenario 1) where all pair-wise distances of sensors are measurable; that is, $d_{mea} = \infty$.

5.2.1 Accuracy of Localization

Figure 2 shows the relationship between the location estimation error and the distance measurement error when no anchor was placed for localization. We carried out simulation experiments using ten different placement patterns of sensors, and the figures show the average for the ten placement patterns. The error in location estimation means the average distance between estimated and real absolute locations of sensors. Note that the cooperative localiza-

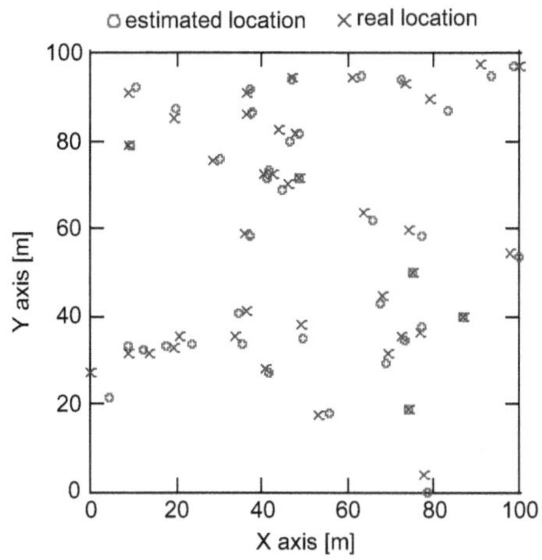

Figure 4: Estimated and real sensor locations: N = 40, n=3, $d_{mea} = \infty$, and $e = 0.2$.

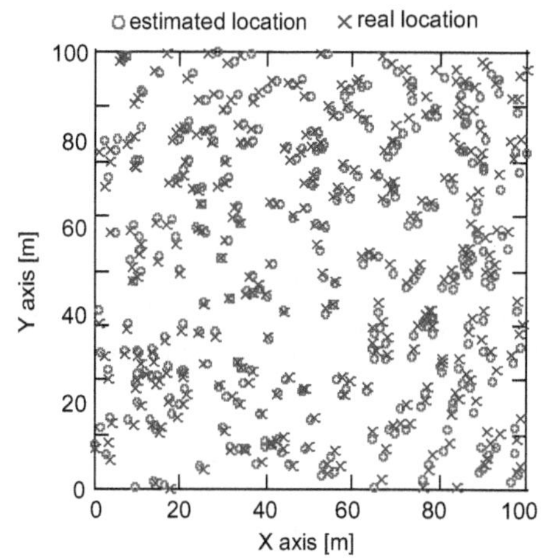

Figure 5: Estimated and real sensor locations: N = 400, n=3, $d_{mea} = \infty$, and $e = 0.2$.

tion outputs an estimated relative map of sensors, not the absolute map, when no anchor is placed. To evaluate the estimation accuracy, we transformed the estimated relative map through translation, rotation, and reflection, and obtained the absolute map, which minimizes the sum of squares of the errors between the real and estimated locations of sensors. The resultant absolute map was used for qualifying the accuracy of the localization error.

We find three features of the cooperative localization in the figure. First, the relationship between the location estimation error and the distance measurement error is almost linear. Second, the location estimation error is much smaller than the distance measurement error. For example, when N = 1000, the location estimation error was less than 1 m in average when the distance measurement error was larger than 10 m. Finally, the location estimation error decreases as the number of sensors increases. The final finding is consistent with Theorem 1 in Sec. 4.2.

Figure 3 shows the relationship between the location estimation error and the distance measurement error when three anchors were placed. Interestingly, the location estimation error with three anchors is larger than that without anchors. As shown in Sec. 5.2.2, placing just three anchors significantly changes the structure of the objective function: the objective function after placing three anchors seems to have a lot of local maxima and thus the repeated substitution via (5) seems to fail to find the optimal solution.

Figures 4 and 5 respectively compare the estimated and real absolute locations of sensors when N = 40 and 400. The distance measurement involved maximally 20% error (e = 0.2 in (6)) and three anchors were placed for localization. All figures show that the estimated locations are very consistent with real locations of sensors. Overall, the performance of estimation is very satisfactory when all pair-wise distances of sensors are measurable.

5.2.2 Dependence on the initial estimates

As explained in Sec. 5.1, solving the optimization problem by repeated substitution via (5) requires to have some prior (initial location estimates), and thus the estimation results would have dependence on the initial estimates. Figures 6(a) (without anchor) and 6(b) (with three anchors) plot the relative frequency of errors involved in the final location estimates, which were respectively obtained from 100 different initial estimates. The number of sensors (including anchors) placed was 40 and the distance measurement involved maximally 40% error (e = 0.4 in (6)). Interestingly, the distribution of the location estimation error significantly depends on the placement of anchors; when no anchor is placed, the estimates obtained by the cooperative localization have the same size of errors despite of the choice of the initial estimates. When three anchors are placed, however, the estimation errors are widely distributed; that is, the choice of the initial estimates largely affects the accuracy of the location estimation. These results demonstrate that placing just three anchors should significantly change the structure of the objective function, and that the relative localization (localization without anchor) is easier and more stable than the absolute localization (localization with anchors).

Figures 6(c) (without anchor) and 6(d) (with three anchors) shows the relative frequency of errors in the location estimates when N = 1000. We also find the same dependence of the estimation error distribution on the placement of anchors.

5.3 Simulation Results: Scenario 2

Next, we evaluated the cooperative localization in another scenario (Scenario 2) where each sensor cannot measure distances to its neighbors located outside the radio range; that is, $d_{mea} < \infty$.

5.3.1 Accuracy of Localization

Figures 7 (without anchor) and 8 (with three anchors) shows the effect of the radio range for distance measurement on the location estimation error when the distance measurement involved maximally 40% error (e = 0.4). The location estimation error tends to increase as the distance-measurement range becomes shorter. In particular, the estimation errors when d_{mea} = 30 m are very large, where the repeated substitution via (5) seems to fail to find the optimal solution.

To have better location estimates, we investigated another choice of the prior. We first estimate the location map under the *shortest-path-distance assumption*, where $d_{ij}^{(m)}$ for (i, j) pair with $m(i, j) = 0$ assumes to be equal to the length of the shortest path between (i, j) pair, which is composed of links between (distance-measurable) sensor pairs. Here, we expect that the gradient descent algorithm would obtain the optimal solution despite of the choice of the prior when all pair-wise distances of sensors are measurable as shown in Sec. 5.2. The resultant location map is in turn used as a prior for conducting the gradient descendent algorithm, where we do not use

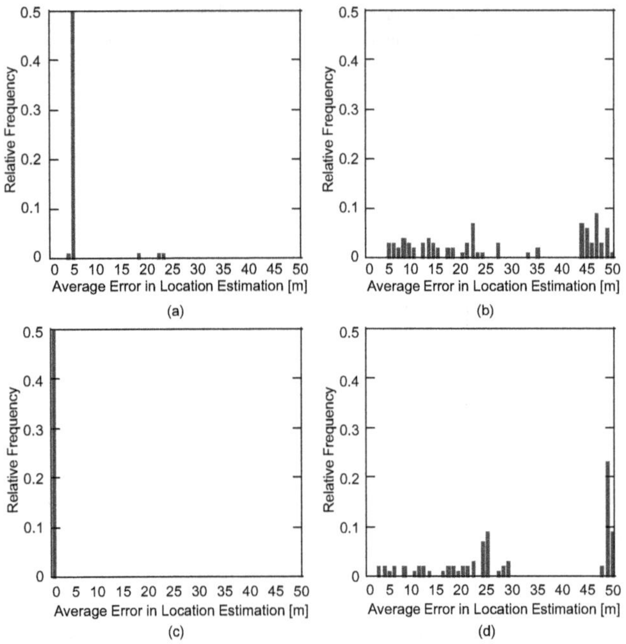

Figure 6: Distribution of the location estimation errors due to the difference of initial estimates ($d_{mea} = \infty$): (a) $N = 40$, $n = 0$, (b) $N = 40$, $n = 3$, (c) $N = 1000$, $n = 0$, (d) $N = 1000$, $n = 3$.

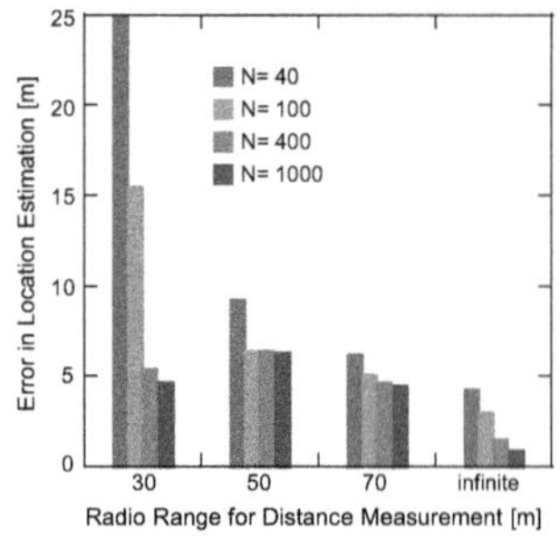

Figure 7: Effect of distance measurement range ($n = 0$): random prior.

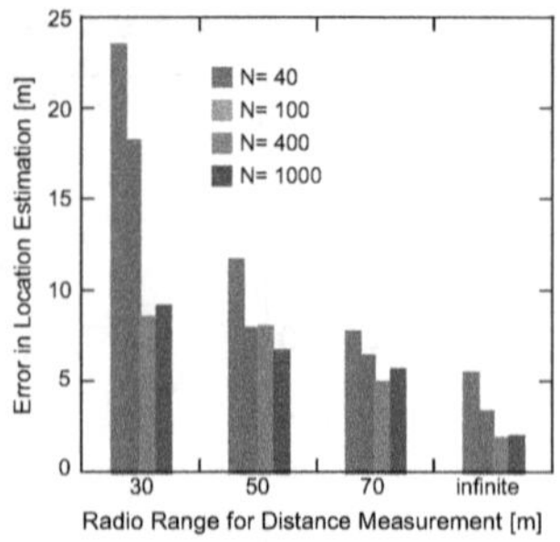

Figure 8: Effect of distance measurement range ($n = 3$): random prior.

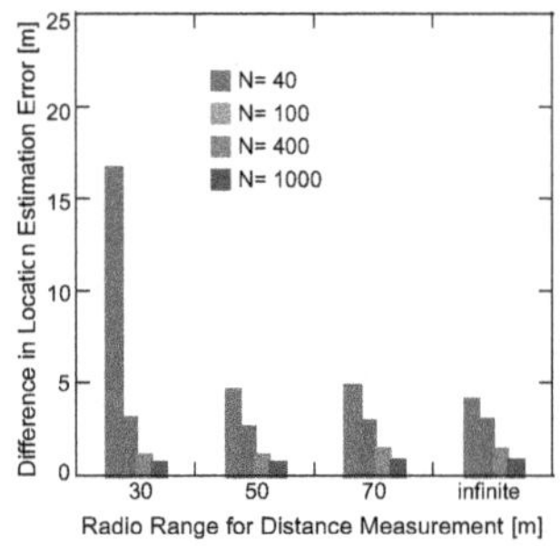

Figure 9: Effect of distance measurement range ($n = 0$): prior of shortest-path-distance assumption.

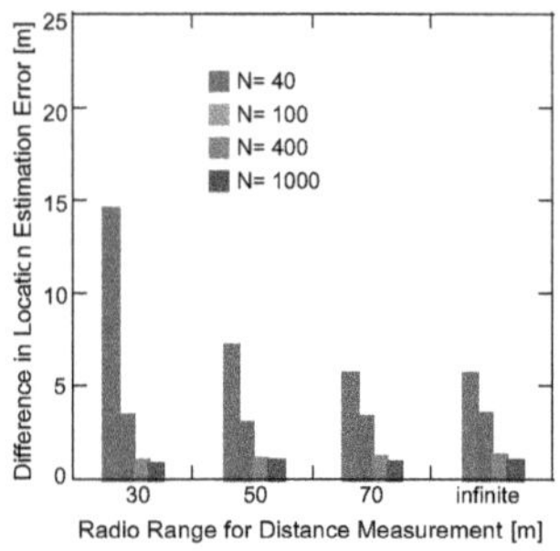

Figure 10: Effect of distance measurement range ($n = 3$): prior of shortest-path-distance assumption.

the shortest-path-distance assumption. This prior is referred to as the *shortest-path-distance-based* (SPD-based) prior in this work.

Figure 9 (without anchor) and 10 (with three anchors) show the location estimation error when the SPD-based prior was used. The distance measurement also involved maximally 40% error ($e = 0.4$). The location estimation error is much smaller than the results in Figs. 7 and 8 where random priors (100 random initial estimates) were used.

To further investigate the performance of the cooperative localization using the SPD-based prior, we obtained the location estimates using *the best prior*, where the real location map was used as a prior of the gradient descent algorithm. Figure 11 (without anchor) and 12 (with three anchors) show the location estimation error when the *best prior* was used. We do not find the significant difference between the results in Figs. 9 and 10 and the results in Figs. 11 and 12. Since location estimates with the best prior would be the optimal solution, this indicates that the SPD-based prior allows us to have almost optimal solutions even when the distances between some sensor pairs are not measurable.

Figures 13 ($N = 40$) and 14 ($N = 400$) compare the estimated and real absolute locations of sensors when $d_{mea} = 30$ m. The location estimation was conducted with the SPD-based prior. The distance measurement involved maximally 20% error ($e = 0.2$ in (6)) and three anchors were placed for localization. Only small discrepancies between estimated and real absolute locations of sensors are found in both figures. Note that the SPD-based prior is only available for the centralized algorithm. So, if the distributed implementation is used, the dependence on the initial estimates still causes a very serious problem of the cooperative localization.

Placing more than three anchors would decrease the location estimation errors of the cooperative localization. Figure 15 ($N = 100$) and Figure 16 ($N = 1000$) show the effect of anchor placement on the estimation accuracy when the SPD-based prior is used. The distance measurement involved maximally 40% error ($e = 0.4$), and the ratio of anchors was increased from 0.01 ($N = 1000$) or 0.03 ($N = 100$) to 0.1. The average error of location estimates was computed over 10 sensor deployment patterns. Both figures indicate that the improvement by placing anchors is not significant. This is because the location estimation is conducted very accurately even with only three anchors.

5.3.2 Dependence on the initial estimates

Figures 17(a) (without anchor) and 17(b) (with three anchors) plot the relative frequency of errors involved in the location estimates, which were respectively obtained from 100 different random priors, when 40 sensors were placed and $d_{min} = 30$ m. The distance measurement involved maximally 40% error ($e = 0.4$). In contrast to Scenario 1, regardless of the placement of anchors, the estimation errors are widely distributed; the choice of the initial estimates largely affects the accuracy of the location estimation. As shown in the figures, using the SPD-based prior yields much better results than using the random prior.

Figures 17(c) (without anchor) and 17(d) (with three anchors) show the relative frequency of errors in the location estimates when 1000 sensors were placed and $d_{min} = 30$ m. The estimation errors are also widely distributed, but the large probability mass is found around the optimal solution (average error is about 5 m) in Fig. 17(c) ($n = 0$). Because of this, it is rather easier to find the optimal solution when $n = 0$ even starting from a random initial location map. The SPD-based prior also yields much better results than using the random prior.

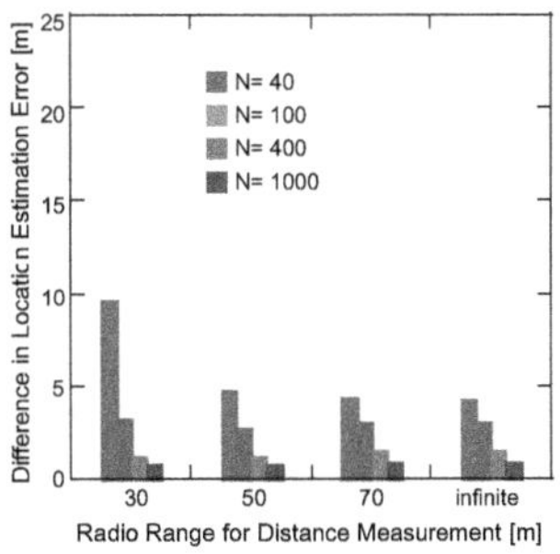

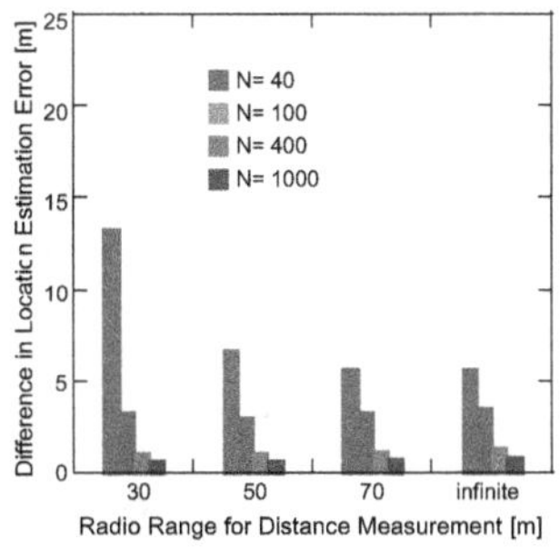

Figure 11: Effect of distance measurement range (n = 0): the best prior.

Figure 12: Effect of distance measurement range (n = 3): the best prior.

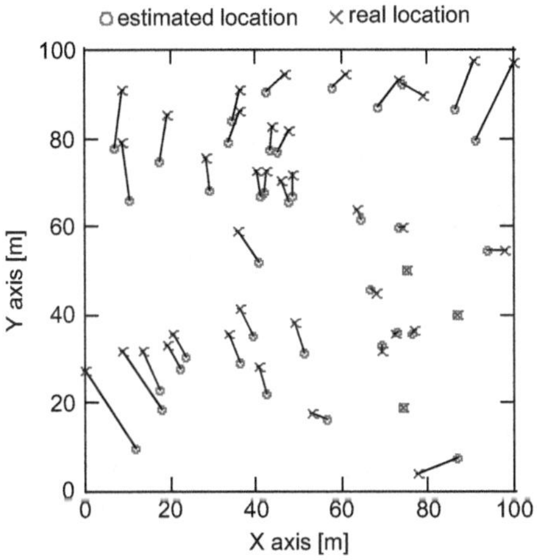

Figure 13: Estimated and real sensor locations: N = 40, n=3, d_{max} = 30 m, and e = 0.2 (with the prior of shortest-path-distance assumption).

6. CONCLUSION

In this work, we have theoretically and numerically investigate the property of the cooperative localization. In most of previous studies, the cooperative localization is performed by the gradient descent algorithm, but the use of the gradient descent algorithm inevitably causes the dependence of the localization accuracy on the prior information about the sensor locations. In this work, we found that this dependence is very large and it should lead to a serious problem especially when the distances between several sensor pairs cannot be measured due to the limitation of radio range. To mitigate the dependence, in this work, we propose the SPD-based prior, which is very powerful for obtaining accurate estimates even when the distances between some sensor pairs are not measurable. Note that the SPD-based prior is only available when the cooperative localization is implemented in a centralized fashion. The choice of priors for the distributed implementation remains as a future work.

There exist other approaches for the cooperative localization including the multi dimensional scaling (MDS) exist. We have compared the performance of our proposal with these exiting approaches, the results of which will be reported in near future.

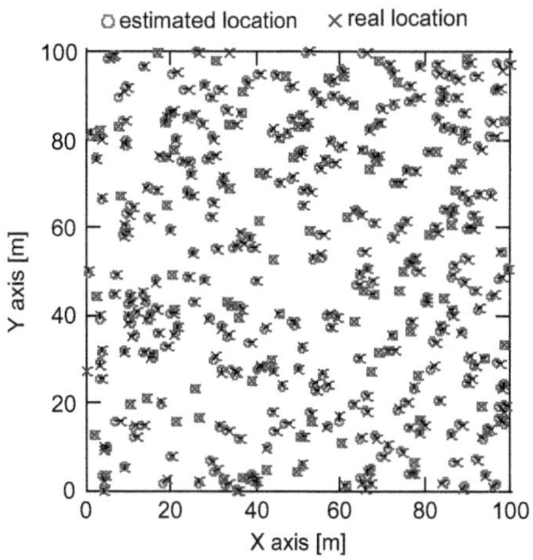

Figure 14: Estimated and real sensor locations: N = 400, n=3, d_{max} = 30 m, and e = 0.2 (with the prior of shortest-path-distance assumption).

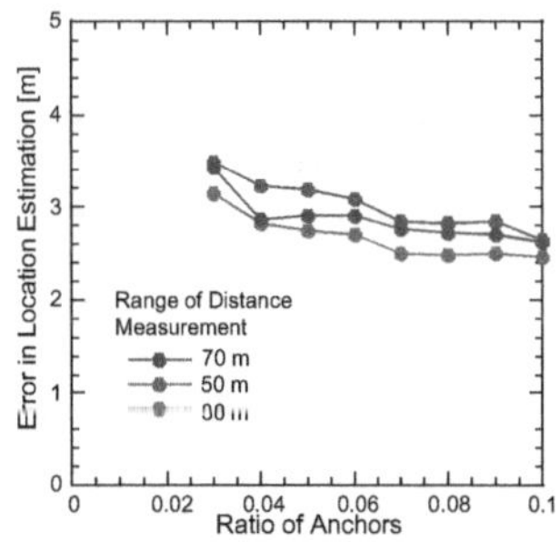

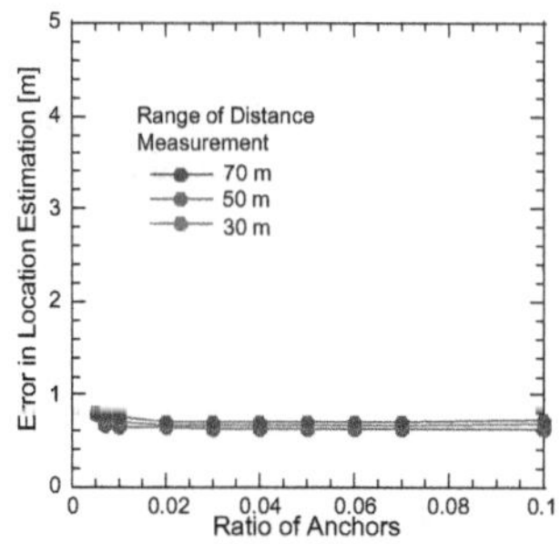

Figure 15: Localization error and anchor ratio (N = 100).

Figure 16: Localization error and anchor ratio (N = 1000).

7. ACKNOWLEDGMENTS

This work was supported by JSPS KAKENHI Grant Number 25330099.

8. REFERENCES

[1] A. Alsindi, K. Pahlavan, B. Alavi, and L. Xinrong. A novel cooperative localization algorithm for indoor sensor networks. In *IEEE PIMRC*, 2006.

[2] P. Bahl and V. Padmanabhan. RADAR: an in-building rf-based user location and tracking system. In *IEEE INFOCOM*, 2000.

[3] D. Blatt and A. Hero III. Energy-based sensor network source localization via projection onto convex sets. *IEEE Trans. Signal Processing*, 54(9):3614–3619, 2006.

[4] N. Bulusu, J. Heidemann, and D. Estrin. GPS-less low cost outdoor localization for very small devices. *IEEE Personal Communication magazine*, 7(5):28–34, 2000.

[5] C. Buragohain, S. Gandhi, J. Hershberger, and S. Suri. Contour approximation in sensor networks. In *Proc. IEEE DCOSS*, 2006.

[6] X. Cheng, A. Thaeler, G. Xue, and D. Chen. TPS: a time-based positioning scheme for outdoor wireless sensor networks. In *IEEE INFOCOM*, pages 2685–2696, 2004.

[7] J. Costa, N. Patwari, and A. Hero III. Distributed weighted-multidimensional scaling for node localization in

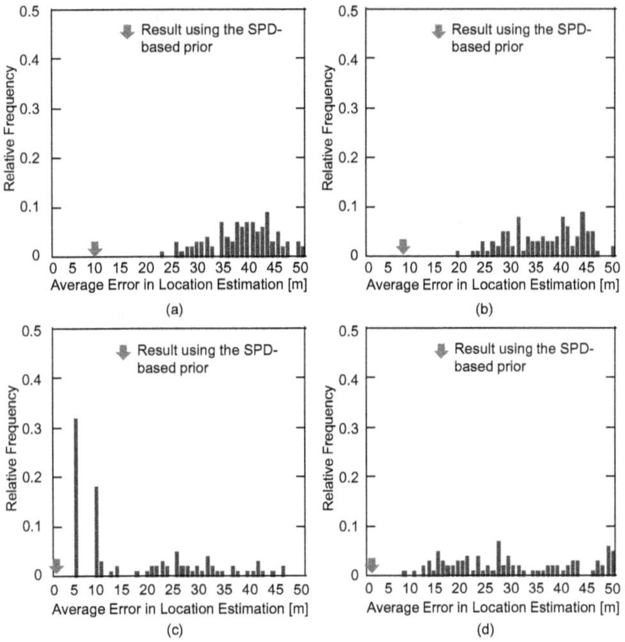

Figure 17: Distribution of the location estimation errors due to the difference of initial estimates (d_{mea} = 30 m): (a) N = 40, n = 0, **(b)** N = 40, n = 3, **(c)** N = 1000, n = 0, **(d)** N = 1000, n = 3.

sensor networks. *ACM Transactions on Sensor Networks*, 2(1):39–64, 2006.

[8] B. Denis, J.-B. Pierrot, and C. Abou-Rjeily. Joint distributed synchronization and positioning in UWB Ad Hoc networks using TOA. *IEEE Trans. Microwave Theory and Techniques*, 54(4):1896–1911, 2006.

[9] L. Doherty, K. Pister, and L. Ghaoui. Convex position estimation in wireless sensor networks. In *IEEE INFOCOM*, pages 1655–1663, 2001.

[10] T. Eren, O. Goldenberg, W. Whiteley, Y. Yang, A. Morse, B. Anderson, and P. Belhumeur. Rigidity, computation, and randomization in network localization. In *IEEE INFOCOM*, 2004.

[11] A. Harter, A. Hopper, P. Steggles, A. Ward, and P. Webster. The anatomy of a context-aware application. In *ACM MobiCom*, pages 59–68, 1999.

[12] B. Hendrickson. Conditions for unique graph realizations. *SIAM J. Comput*, 21(1):65–84, 1992.

[13] B. Hofmann-Wellenhot, H. Lichtenegger, and J. Collins. *Global Positioning System*. Springer Verlag, 1997.

[14] A. Ihler, J. Fisher, R. Moses, and A. Willsky. Nonparametric belief propagation for self-localization of sensor networks. *IEEE J. Sel. Areas Commun.*, 23(4):809–819, 2005.

[15] X. Ji and H. Zha. Sensor positioning in wireless Ad-Hoc sensor networks using multidimensional scaling. In *IEEE INFOCOM*, volume 4, pages 2652–2661, 2004.

[16] G. Laman. On graphs and rigidity of plane skeletal structures. *J. Eng. Mathematics*, 4(4):331–340, 1970.

[17] K. Langendoen and N. Reijers. Distributed localization in wireless sensor networks: a quantitative comparison. *Computer Networks*, 43(4):499–518, 2003.

[18] S. Lederer, Y. Wang, and J. Gao. Connectivity-based localization of large-scale sensor networks with complex shape. *ACM Transactions on Sensor Networks*, 5(4), 2009.

[19] G. Mao, B. Fidan, and B. Anderson. Wireless sensor network localization techniques. *Computer Networks*, 51(10):2529–2553, 2006.

[20] R. Moses, D. Krishnamurthy, and R. Patterson. An auto-calibration method for unattended ground sensors. In *IEEE ICASSP*, 2002.

[21] R. Nagpal, H. Shrobe, and J. Bachrach. Organizing a global coordinate system from local information on an Ad Hoc sesnor network. In *Proc. Second ACM/IEEE Int'l Conf. Information Processing in Sensor Networks (IPSN)*, 2003.

[22] D. Niculescu and B. Nath. DV based positioning in Ad Hoc networks. *Telecommunication Systems*, 22(1–4):267–280, 2003.

[23] N. Patwari, J. Ash, S. Kyperountas, A. Hero, R. Moses, and N. Correal. Locating the nodes: cooperative localization in wireless sensor networks. *IEEE Signal Processing Magazine*, 22(4):54–69, 2005.

[24] R. Peng and M. Sichitiu. Probabilistic localization for outdoor wireless sensor networks. *ACM SIGMOBILE Mobile Computing and Communications Review*, 11(1):53–64, 2007.

[25] N. Priyantha, A. Chakraborty, and H. Balakrishnan. The cricket location-support system. In *ACM MobiCom*, 2000.

[26] M. Rydstrom, E. Strom, and A. Svensson. Robust sensor network positioning based on projections onto circular and hyperbolic convex sets (POCS). In *IEEE SPAWC*, 2006.

[27] A. Savvides, C.-C. Han, and M. Strivastava. Dynamic fine-grained localization in ad-hoc networks of sensors. In *ACM SIGMOBILE*, volume 4, pages 2673–2684, 2001.

[28] A. Savvides, H. Park, and M. Srivastava. The bits and flops of the n-hop multilateration primitive for node localization problems. In *ACM WSNA*, 2002.

[29] Y. Shang and W. Ruml. Improved MDS-based localization. In *IEEE INFOCOM*, 2004.

[30] Y. Shang, W. Ruml, Y. Zhang, and M. Fromherz. Localization from mere connectivity. In *Proc. ACM MobiHoc*, 2003.

[31] S. Shioda and T. Hayashi. Inner-distance-based shape recognition of target object using binary sensors. In *IEEE ICPADS*, 2012.

[32] S. Srinivasan and K. Ramamritham. Contour estimation using collaborating mobile sensors. In *Proc. DIWANS '06*, 2006.

[33] A. Ward, A. Jones, and A. Hopper. A new location technique for the active office. *IEEE Personal Communications*, 4(5):42–47, 1997.

[34] H. Wymeersch, J. Lien, and M. Win. Cooperative localization in wireless networks. *Proceedings of the IEEE*, 97(2):427–450, 2009.

[35] Z. Yang and Y. Liu. Understanding node localizability of wireless Ad Hoc and sensor networks. *IEEE Trans. Mobile Computing*, 11(8):1249 – 1260, 2012.

[36] K. Yedavalli and B. Krishnamachari. Sequence-based localization in wireless sensor networks. *IEEE Trans. Mobile Computing*, 7(1):81–94, 2008.

[37] Y. Zhang, L. Zhang, and X. Shan. Ranking-based statistical localization for wireless sensor networks. In *IEEE WCNC*, 2008.

Voronoi Trees for Hierarchical In-Network Data and Space Abstractions in Wireless Sensor Networks

Mohamed M.Ali Mohamed
University of Illinois at Chicago
Chicago, IL. USA
mali25@uic.edu

Ashfaq Khokhar
University of Illinois at Chicago
Chicago, IL. USA
ashfaq@uic.edu

Goce Trajcevski
Northwestern University
Evanston, IL. USA
g-trajcevski@nothwestern.edu

ABSTRACT

We address the problem of spatial queries in Wireless Sensor Networks (WSN) via hybrid overlays, where the data values may correspond to different physical phenomena and sensors may be correlated with spatial constraints. We show how hierarchical data and space abstractions can be used to represent Voronoi Cell based partitions of the sensing field and use Voronoi Trees to efficiently map the hierarchical abstractions for energy-efficient processing. The proposed scheme is simulated on the SidNET, a JiST/SWANS based sensor network simulation platform. The performance results show significant advantages in terms of accurate field representation at different levels of the tree hierarchy with a trade-off in query processing delay.

Categories and Subject Descriptors

C.2.4 [**Distributed Systems**]: Distributed Applications; E1 [**Data Structures**]: distributed data structures, graphs and networks.

General Terms

Algorithms, Design, Experimentation.

Keywords

Wireless Sensor Networks, Computational Geometry.

1. INTRODUCTION

Wireless Sensor Networks (WSN)s have become tools for distributed data gathering and query processing [1] in a plethora of application domains. Retrieving a perfectly accurate (spatial distribution of) data is expensive in terms of energy usage and processing time, and is not always needed [1]. We investigate issues related to distributed in-network indexing and query processing, taking into consideration that due to the imperfections of sensing devices, approximate responses with bounded error may be acceptable in various contexts. Since reduction in accuracy can also decrease resources utilization, we aim at designing abstractions for answering queries pertaining to overlapping heterogeneous data and/or spatial regions, at various levels of accuracy.

MSWiM'13, November 3–8, 2013, Barcelona, Spain.

http://dx.doi.org/10.1145/2507924.2507999

Traditional indexing structures (K-D trees, R-Trees, B-Trees, or variations) used for efficient retrieval in spatial databases [3] have lead to distributed index structures for WSNs [5-9]. However, the particular challenge that we address in this work is efficient in-network processing of hybrid queries, by minimizing communication, computation, and storage overheads. These queries combine sensed values within a specific geographic region, and the spatial extent at which the sensed data falls within a specific range, like, for example:

Q1: *Retrieve all the prairie regions in DuPage county that are near river and have between 15% and 45% of salinity decline in the next 3 hours.*

Motivated by the well-studied properties of Voronoi diagrams from Computational Geometry [4] and the fact that a Voronoi cell centroid is optimal for sensor allocation in terms of sensing accuracy [12], in this paper we investigate the use of Voronoi Treemaps [2] as a hierarchical indexing structure in WSN.

Voronoi tessellations have been used for tackling various objectives in WSN research, where the data-centric nature of the underlying sensed phenomena matches some basic properties satisfied in a region bounded by a Voronoi cell [12]. Voronoi Treemaps create hierarchical spatial data structure that splits the given space in multiple granulation levels by creating contiguous non-overlapping regions, and without producing holes.

Our proposed techniques are carefully designed to accommodate different query types and provide responses within specified accuracy, incurring diminutive update costs that do not increase across the network. This enables load balancing and prolonging the overall network lifetime. We use rank order statistics, regular sampling, and bitmap representations to interleave the management of physical- as well as data space queries. The proposed techniques are implemented on SIDnet simulator [11]. Our experimental observations show the benefits and trade-offs.

2. PRELIMINARIES

We assume a dense WSN where each node s_i knows its coordinates (x_i, y_i) with respect to a reference coordinate system, and the locations of all of its 1-hop neighbors. Users may be interested in the sensed phenomena across the field or parts of it, but the location of sensed values is also important as the value itself – , e.g., fire occurrence requires specifying where this event is detected. In this work, we are focusing on two main types of queries: (1) inquiring the values of sensed phenomenon (physical-space queries), and (2) inquiring the location of sensor nodes with certain sensed values (data-space queries). Queries may be confined to a regional space of the field or a range of values – a constraint term specifying the search bound. Allowing limited (im)precision of the answer to decrease resources utilization, we focus on conjunction of query predicates, pertaining to heterogeneous types and (sensed) values.

2.1 Voronoi Diagrams and Hierarchies

One of the most studied concepts in Computational Geometry [4] is the Voronoi diagram of a collection of points, along with its geometric-dual, Delaunay triangulation. Given n distinct points $P = \{p_1, p_2, ..., p_n\}$ contained inside a convex polygon S in R^2, the bounded Voronoi tessellation $V_{\cap S}(P) = \{V(p_1)\cap S, V(p_2)\cap S, ..., V(p_n)\cap S\}$ is defined as the decomposition of the space S into n convex polygons, called Voronoi regions. Each Voronoi region $V(p_i)$ associated with the point p_i, has the property that for an arbitrary point $q(x,y)$, if $q(x,y)$ is inside $V(p_i)$, than $dist(q, p_i) > dist(q, p_j)$, for any other $p_j \in P$ $(i \neq j)$. The function *dist* represents a specified distance measure between two points, which can be as simple as Euclidean distance, or may include other functions that parameterize more context-related information. A specific example is the centroidal Voronoi tessellation (CVT) - a Voronoi tessellation with the property that the generating point for each Voronoi region is the center of mass of the region.

A bottom-up approach for constructing a hierarchy based on Voronoi cells was presented in [13], where at each level of the hierarchy, a Voronoi tessellation is calculated such that each set of Voronoi cells in a given level is contained in one Voronoi cell in the higher level. However, the boundaries of the Voronoi cells between levels are not guaranteed to fully coincide, resulting in non-containment of lower level cells in higher levels.

Tree-Maps [10] visualized hierarchical information structures by mapping the full hierarchy onto a rectangular region in a space-filling manner. Voronoi Treemaps [2] build a hierarchical spatial data structure that is based on CVTs in a top-down manner, partitioning a given convex polygon space into a set of centroidal Voronoi cells, and recursively partitioning each cell into further CVT, given the generating points.

A given space is split in multiple granulation levels by creating contiguous non-overlapping regions without producing holes.

3. ABSTRACTIONS AND MODELS

We firstly present data and physical space abstractions that will be used to represent sensor data and its location at different levels of the Voronoi Treemap (see [5] for a preliminary version), in the context of orthogonal bisection based KD-trees. We then follow with a detailed discussion on Voronoi-based partitioning.

3.1 Physical-space Abstraction

Our focus is on representing the sensed data in the field of interest at multiple scales with respect to the geographical location of the sensing nodes. Given a hierarchical spanning tree $T(V',E')$ of depth d, and *(w.l.o.g.)* a fixed fan-out f, in a graph $G(V, E)$, where each leaf node $v_{d,i}$ represents a Voronoi Cell, we want to find an abstract representation $p_{v'di}$ of the sensed values in the region associated with node $v'_{d,i}$, such that: *average error*, *communication cost*, and *computation cost* are minimized. A more formal definition can be found in [5].

Each node $v'_{d,i}$ in the spanning tree $T(V',E')$ gathers the sensed from its set of sensor nodes v_{ij} in its vicinity and stores them. Upon acquiring its population's readings, each node $v'_{d,i}$ rank-orders the sensed data and stores it in an array along with their corresponding sensor nodes' physical locations. The abstract representation $p_{v'di}$ is introduced as an array of a fixed-size (k) and its values are chosen by regularly sampling the sorted array of the population nodes with interval (D/k), including the first and last elements of the sorted array, as depicted in Figure 1.

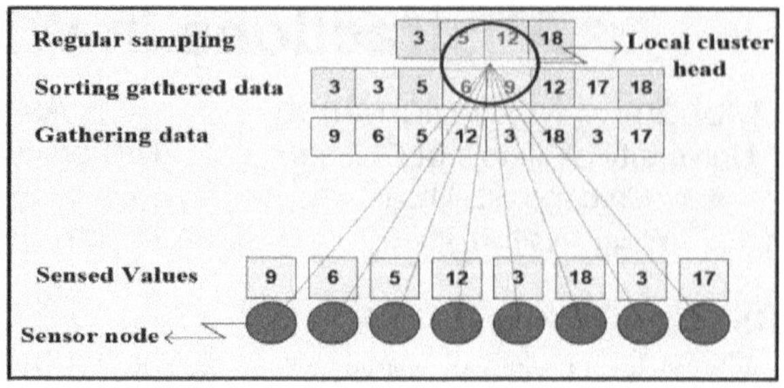

Figure 1. Leaf (cluster-head) create the representation construct by sorting and sampling sensed values.

To develop abstract representations of larger regions represented by the non-leaf nodes of the spanning tree, each leaf node $v'_{d,i}$ compresses and transmits the representation $p_{v'di}$ to its parent in the spanning tree. Each non-leaf node receives from its children a set of f arrays, representing the physical-phenomenon at spatially non-overlapping regions in the field, and merges them into a larger one representing the sensed phenomenon in the area enclosing the f regions. The new physical-space abstraction of the larger region is created by regularly sampling the merged array with a given sampling interval (f). Upon completion, the new construct is of the same size as the received (input) arrays. It provides a regular sorted sample of the larger population, but in a coarser form. The data-payload is updated throughout the participating nodes by using fixed size messages, keeping the communication workload equally distributed.

3.2 Data-space Abstraction

We assume that the possible values of the sensed phenomenon are delimited within a finite range [min, max] for the potentially queried data-space. Our objective is to provide a hierarchical multi-resolution abstraction scheme to obtain approximate answers to queries that involve localizations of the related sensor nodes. The data-space abstraction aims to find a representation construction $L_{v'di}$ of the sensor nodes location distribution *w.r.t* its sensed value for each leaf node $v'_{d,i}$, such that the *average error*, *communication cost*, and *computation cost* are decreased.

Each set of sibling leaf nodes represents a group of neighboring clusters within a region splitting the data-space into q data ranges, where $q \geq f$. The responsibility of the data-space in each region gets distributed among the managing f leaf nodes. Each cluster head node (i.e., leaf node $v'_{d,i}$) keeps the position of the sensors which report value within its data range(s) of responsibility inside its containing region. For example, for a sensed phenomenon whose possible range of values is [1-100], a split between four nodes is: {[1,25], [26,50], [51,75], [76,100]}. Thus, each leaf node reports to its f-1 siblings the positions of the nodes of its population conforming to their assigned data range.

In order to create the representation construct $L_{v'di}$ of nodes positions for each leaf node $v'_{d,i}$, a bit-map is created. A bit-map is a is a 2D array of a size that maps to the physical region it represents, where each entry represents an area that can be occupied by no more than a single sensor node. We note that the resolution of the map (i.e. cell size) is application dependent. The map entries/cells are initialized to zero. A leaf node, then, sets the cells occupied by sensor nodes that reported values within its data range. The resulting map can be viewed as a highly sparse 2D array of zeroes and ones, which is compressed using Run-length coding technique. Figure 2 depicts an example of bit-map construction for the sensed values within one region.

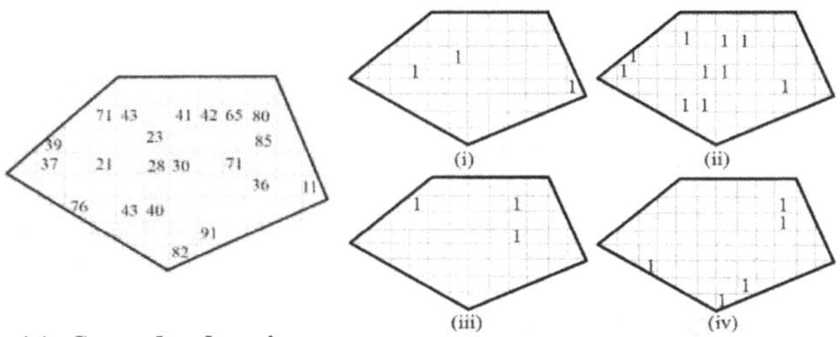

(a). Sensed values in a range [1,100] reported in a region. **(b). Corresponding four bitmaps for ranges [1,25], [26,50] [51,75] and [76, 100], respectively.**

Figure 2. Illustrative example of the bitmap creation.

For each data range, the corresponding responsible nodes (f in total) at level i send their compressed maps to the node in level j responsible for the same data range in the containing region. Upon receiving the f maps for the data range, the recipient node concatenates them according to their geographic locations, which generates one larger map for the data range of responsibility in the whole region.

In order to provide approximate representation and keep message size fixed across the indexing structure, the concatenated map needs to be zoomed out with a scale that reduces its size with a $1/f$ factor on average. In this fashion, nodes keep approximating maps of different data ranges as they elevate through the indexing structure, providing the ability to supply proper approximations for the data-space as shown in Figure 3.

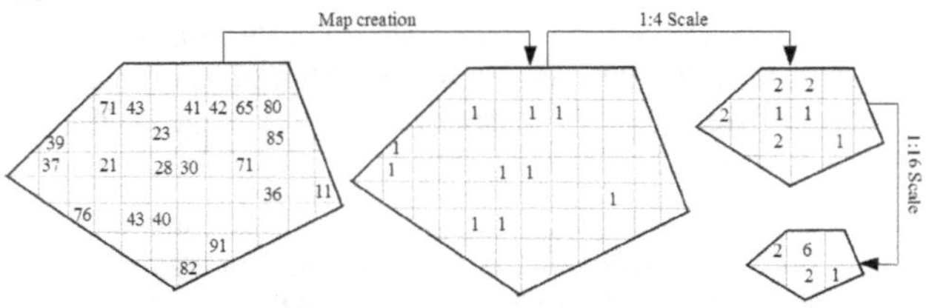

Figure 3. Map creation for data range [26-50], and zooming out twice with 1:4 factors.

3.3 Voronoi Treemaps and Queries

The Voronoi treemap (cf. Sec. 2.1.) is created using a top-down approach, in which the field is subdivided into a set of centroidal Voronoi cells, according to a given set of generating points which are selected via a given function having prior knowledge of the distribution of the sensed phenomenon. Within each cell, a node is placed at the centroid point and considered responsible of managing the data abstraction processes, and reporting them to the sink node. The same process is repeated within each centroidal Voronoi cell, to create the next level of spatial division in the field corresponding to the next level of indexing nodes in the Voronoi Treemap. This recursion stops at the last level of Voronoi cells – local clusters - surrounding the phenomenon sources. After constructing Voronoi treemap, sensor nodes are deployed in each local cluster surrounding the cell centroid point, which has the local cluster head node, and represents the source of the sensed phenomena in the cell. Figure 4 shows a color-coded description of the elected nodes at 3 inner-levels of a Voronoi Treemap. Leaf nodes create maps for the data ranges of their regions, transmit them to the upper level nodes responsible for the same data range. Upper level nodes zoom-out the maps and recursively apply the same process until the sink node is reached. Queries originate at a sink, which we assume is connected to a base station. Upon receiving a query, the root node first checks the query type to decide which representation is inquired. It then analyzes the bounding constraints –if any exists– for range queries, where through the bounding region and bounding data range constraints the node can determine which nodes need to participate in the processing. The solution path is determined step by step, where each node that receives the query checks the intersection of the query's geometric and data range bounds with the geometric area and data range(s) that it covers. The decision of being able to answer the query at each node is taken according to the accuracy requirement of the query.

Once the query reaches the node(s) capable of answering it with satisfactory accuracy, the response is backtracked through the same path it took from the root node. Each intermediate node waits to receive the response from all the nodes it forwarded the query to. Once received, it combines the query responses. The data-space query results are obtained by concatenation of the response maps, while physical-space queries merge the arrays of sensed values. In the case of extreme values (min or max) the merging trivially preserves the smallest or largest values.

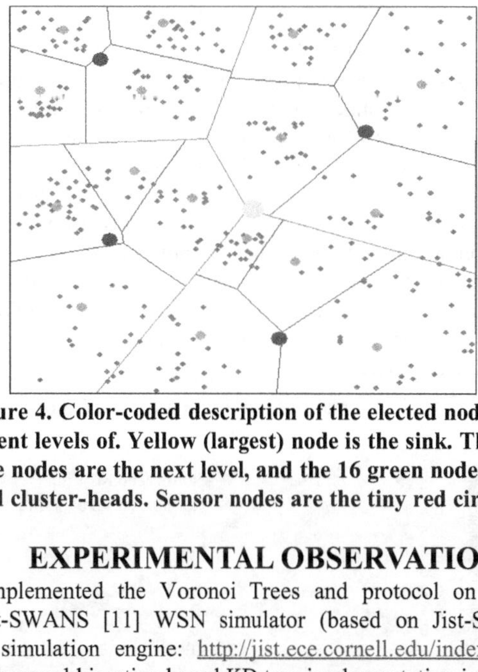

Figure 4. Color-coded description of the elected nodes at different levels of. Yellow (largest) node is the sink. The four blue nodes are the next level, and the 16 green nodes are local cluster-heads. Sensor nodes are the tiny red circles.

4. EXPERIMENTAL OBSERVATIONS

We implemented the Voronoi Trees and protocol on top of SIDnet-SWANS [11] WSN simulator (based on Jist-SWANS event simulation engine: http://jist.ece.cornell.edu/index.html). An orthogonal bisection based KD tree implementation in SIDnet (cf. [3]) was used to compare the performance of Voronoi treemaps. While there are many different binary space partitioning methods, we opted to use KD-tree because, to the best of our knowledge, there are no indexing methodologies in the literature that encompass data space abstractions. Hence, we resorted to our own implementation for this, as well as hybrid-settings. The WSN has 500 nodes deployed in a square field of 300x300 meters square, using MAC802.15.4, and Shortest Geographic Path for routing. The power consumption characteristics are based on Mica2 Motes specifications, MPR500CA.

Phenomenon Values Impact: The quality of representing the sensed values via hierarchical abstraction(s) is limited by the ability of the sensors to report values that match the distribution of the sensed phenomenon. For this, sensor nodes should be located in positions that correspond to the sensed phenomenon distribution across the field. We tested the indexing structures in terms of accurately representing data field. We simulated the data field using 2D Gaussian distributions by varying their variance. We reconstruct the field by looking at the variance at different levels of the hierarchy in these indexing structures. Figure 5 shows that the Voronoi Treemaps achieve lower error when reconstructing "sharp" Gaussian distributions (i.e., lower variance) than KD trees. This is intuitive in the sense that the Voronoi cells are created based on the properties of the physical field being sensed. Hence, closer mapping of sensor nodes to data sources yields reconstructed values that are closer to the phenomenon's spatial distribution.

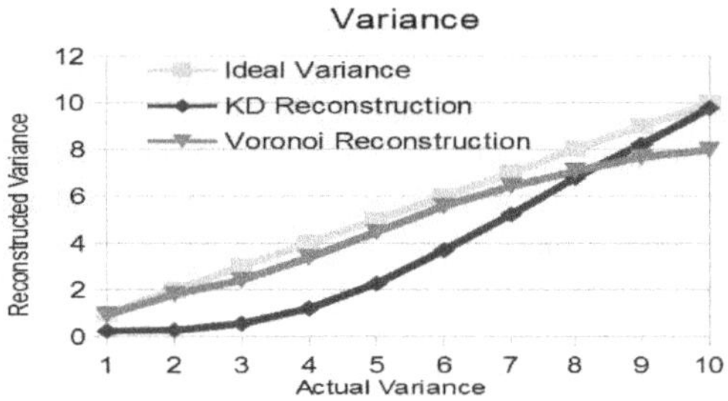

Figure 5. Reconstructed Variance

Similar observations are present in Figure 6, which shows the normalized error values. On the contrary, random deployment on which the KD tree is built is more likely to have less accuracy in the reconstructed data field. This will be particularly true for sharp Gaussian distributions. For distributions with significantly larger variances, the KD tree starts to perform better in reconstructing the field than the Voronoi treemap. The reason is that Voronoi treemap deploys nodes around the data source, whereas KD-trees, covering larger area between children and cluster head, may incorporate the readings from sensors that are away from the source.

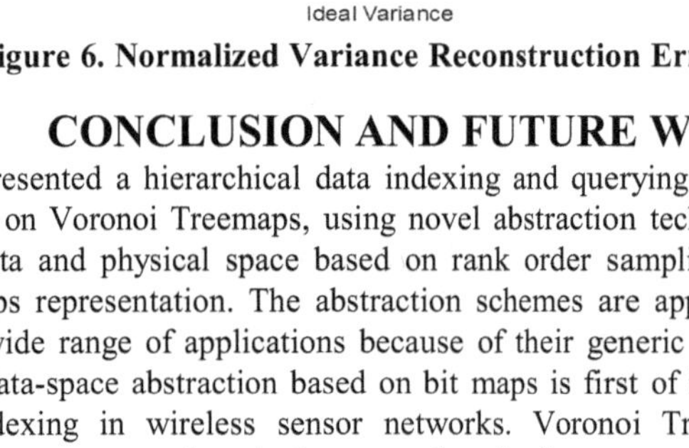

Figure 6. Normalized Variance Reconstruction Error

5. CONCLUSION AND FUTURE WORK

We presented a hierarchical data indexing and querying system based on Voronoi Treemaps, using novel abstraction techniques for data and physical space based on rank order sampling and bitmaps representation. The abstraction schemes are applicable to a wide range of applications because of their generic nature. The data-space abstraction based on bit maps is first of its kind in indexing in wireless sensor networks. Voronoi Treemaps provide sensor nodes deployment that is better capable of capturing the phenomenon distribution. The proposed system gives a generic way to answer different queries of various phenomena with high efficiency. Fixed size update messages ensure load balancing across the network, enabling longer network life time. Our ongoing efforts are focused on incorporating spatio-temporal evolution of the Voronoi treemaps for WSN with mobile sensors.

6. ACKNOWLEDGEMENTS

This research has been supported in part by the NSF grants CNS 0910988, 0910952 and III 1213038.

7. REFERENCES

[1] Zhao, F. and Guibas, L. 2004. *Wireless Sensor Networks: An Information Processing Approach*. Morgan Kaufman.

[2] Balzer, M., Deussen, O. and Lewerentz, C. 2005. Voronoi treemaps for the visualization of software metrics. *In Proc. of* ACM Symp. on Software visualization.

[3] Shekhar, S. and Chawla, S. 2003. *Spatial Databases: A Tour*. Prentice Hall.

[4] De Berg, M., Cheong, O., Van Kreveld, M. and Overmars, M. 2008. *Computational Geometry Algorithms and Applications*. Springer.

[5] Ali Mohamed, M. M., Khokhar, A., Trajcevski, G., Ansari, R. and Ouksel, A. 2012. Approximate hybrid query processing in wireless sensor networks. *In Proc. of* ACM GIS.

[6] Greenstein, B., Estrin, D., Govindan, R., Ratnasamy, S. and Shenker, S. 2003. DIFS: A Distributed Index for Features in Sensor Networks. Ad Hoc Networks, Vol. 1, pp. 333-349.

[7] Ganesan, D., Greenstein, B., Estrin, D., Heidemann, J. and Govindan, R. 2005. Multiresolution Storage and Search in Sensor Networks. ACM Transactions on Storage (TOS), Vol. 1, pp. 277-315.

[8] Ciancio, A., Pattem, S., Ortega, A. and Krishnamachari, B. 2006. Energy-Efficient Data Repres and Routing for Wireless Sensor Networks Based on a Distributed Wavelet Compression Algorithm. IPSN.

[9] Meliou, A., Guestrin, C. and Hellerstein, J. 2009. Approximating Sensor Network Queries Using In-Network Summaries. IPSN Johnson, B. and Shneiderman, B. 1891.

[10] Tree-maps: A space-filling approach to the visualization of hierarchical information structures. In Proc. IEEE Visualization Conf.

[11] Ghica, O., Trajcevski, G., Scheuermann, P., Bischoff, Z. and Valtchanov, N. 2008. Sidnet-swans: A simulator and integrated development platform for sensor networks applications. ACM SenSys.

[12] Ammari, H.M., and Sajal K.D. 2008. Promoting heterogeneity, mobility, and energy-aware voronoi diagram in wireless sensor networks. IEEE Trans. Parallel and Distributed Systems, IEEE Transactions on 18(7)

[13] Gold, C. and Angel, P. 2006. Voronoi Hierarchies. Geographic Information Science (pp. 99-111). Springer Berlin Heidelberg.

Indoor Coverage Estimation from Unreliable Measurements using Spatial Statistics

Elena Meshkova, Janne Riihijärvi, Junaid Ansari, Petri Mähönen
Institute for Networked Systems, RWTH Aachen University
Kackertstrasse 9, D-52072 Aachen, Germany
Email: {eme, jar, jan, pma}@inets.rwth-aachen.de

ABSTRACT

Estimating the coverage of a wireless network is one of the key problems in network planning and management. In outdoor environments this is usually done using modern network planning tools combined with intensive drive tests. However, in indoor environments the problem is much more difficult. Solutions based on propagation modeling require precise building information for accuracy, and even then their performance is highly varying. Refining such predictions using measurements from mobile terminals is a promising possibility, but is not straightforward due to the noisy and unreliable measurement quality. In this paper we study the performance of spatial statistics techniques for coverage prediction in indoor environments. Using data collected in an indoor testbed with 60 low cost radio receivers, we show that such techniques can yield accurate coverage predictions provided suitable preprocessing and filtering of the data is performed. Further, a simple optimization approach enables high prediction accuracy to be achieved using only a small subset of the available measurement devices. These results are also highly relevant to the minimization of drive tests (MDT) approach currently being developed in 3GPP to enable mobile terminals carry out coverage measurements for wireless networks.

Categories and Subject Descriptors

C.2 [**Computer-Communication Networks**]: Miscellaneous; G.3 [**Probability and Statistics**]: Statistical computing; I.6.4 [**Simulation and Modeling**]: Model Validation and Analysis; I.6.5 [**Simulation and Modeling**]: Model Development

Keywords

Performance evaluation; indoor coverage estimation; cognitive wireless networks; spatial statistics

MSWiM'13, November 3–8, 2013, Barcelona, Spain.

http://dx.doi.org/10.1145/2507924.2507957 ...$15.00.

1. INTRODUCTION

Coverage estimation is one of the key tasks in planning, deployment and management of wireless networks. For outdoor deployments, such as large-scale cellular networks, sophisticated planning tools are commonly used incorporating complex propagation models that take into account effects of surrounding buildings and other environmental details. After initial deployment the coverage estimates are further refined through extensive drive tests. Unfortunately this approach does not work very effectively for indoor deployments due to several reasons. First, indoor propagation is very hard to model exactly, and even sophisticated approaches such as raytracing need calibration through measurements to yield acceptable results [6, 7, 9, 18]. Second, indoor propagation environment tends to be highly dynamic, with positions of furniture, people, and even doors and windows playing a role in the shadowing and fading [1]. Third, classical drive tests are obviously infeasible indoors, and similar high quality measurements are costly to perform and repeat regularly. A promising alternative is to rely on the deployed network nodes, such as Wi-Fi access points or femtocells to carry out coverage measurements possibly together with mobile terminals. Unfortunately the quality of the measurements carried out by such devices is much lower than obtained through drive tests due to cheaper hardware used, uncertainties in antenna patterns, and the complex dynamic indoor propagation environment.

In this paper we study the use of spatial statistics techniques for automatic and dynamic coverage estimation from such unreliable measurements. These techniques have been found very effective in processing drive test types of measurements outdoors and for simulated indoor data (see, for example, [2, 4, 5, 11, 13, 16]), but only a few applications to measurement based indoor propagation estimates can be found in the literature [17]. We also propose techniques for dealing with unreliable measurement sources and outliers in the data. We discuss how preprocessing of the measurement data can be used to form coverage estimates for multiple different transmitters operating on the same frequency band, provided the dynamics of these are sufficiently different. We also show how small subset of the available terminals can be selected to carry out measurements while still achieving high prediction accuracy, reducing considerably the measurement overhead. Overall, we show that the measurement-based approach is highly promising for coverage estimation in emerging femtocell networks [15, 19], as well as large Wi-Fi deployments. Improved coverage estimates have several key applications as the networks are becoming more dense, ranging from cooperative interference management solutions to localization services.

The rest of this paper is structured as follows. In Section 2 we give an overview of the testbed used for gathering the measurement data that forms the base of our study. We then give in Section 3 a concise overview of the spatial statistics techniques for coverage estimation, and establish a baseline for their performance for indoor coverage estimation. In Section 4 we study the effects of incorporating additional knowledge on the radio environment into the predictions, as well as discuss how to deal with unreliable measurements and outliers in the data. Finally, impact filtering of the measurement data before spatial estimation is discussed in Section 5 before concluding the paper in Section 6.

2. TESTBED AND MEASUREMENTS

For studying the problem of indoor coverage estimation we use a dedicated testbed for indoor propagation studies, described earlier in [12]. This testbed is deployed in a typical office building, and in this paper we use readings from 60 TelosB wireless sensor nodes [14] spread across five rooms. All of the sensor nodes are used as low cost spectrum measurement devices, running a custom measurement software sweeping through the 2.4 GHz ISM band with resolution bandwidth of 5 MHz. The overall area covered by the testbed is approximately 20 m × 12 m, and the propagation conditions in this area are extremely variable. Some of the rooms are relatively empty, while other have computers and typical office equipment set up, resulting in a dense multipath environment traditionally challenging for coverage estimation. Walls between the rooms are also of varying thickness, ranging from soft partitions to heavy supporting concrete walls. For a more precise description of the testbed layout and the building, see [12] as well as Figure 2.

Several signal sources were used to test the proposed coverage estimation methods, ranging from continuous narrowband transmissions from sensor nodes and signal generators to highly bursty Wi-Fi traffic. The number of concurrently active sources ranged from one to three depending on the measurement run. The sensors have been placed in varying orientations to better mimic unplanned measurements where antenna orientations cannot be precisely controlled (see Figure 1 for illustration).

One of the sensor devices turned out to have faulty hardware causing more than 20 dB difference to the noise floor reported by the other devices. In some of the measurements the second node failed the same way. These faulty reports are not included in the estimation of the results shown below, as they are always automatically filtered out by the proposed outlier rejection methods. Complete list of the different measurement scenarios is given in Table 1 at the end of the paper, where summary of prediction performance of the proposed estimation techniques are also given in detail.

3. COVERAGE ESTIMATION WITH SPATIAL STATISTICS

3.1 Mathematical Foundations

The received signal strength at any given location can be considered as a stochastic process. Statistics of this process, such as the mean received signal strength, form another stochastic process, this time defined over *space* rather than

Figure 1: Part of the testbed deployment showing the sensor devices used for spectrum measurements.

time. Such spatial stochastic processes are called *random fields* [3,8], and they play a central role in the formalization of the coverage estimation problem.

Denote now the region inside which we seek to carry out coverage estimation by D. Then the coverage area related to a random field $Y(\boldsymbol{x})$ of received signal strength, with $\boldsymbol{x} \in D$, is the *excursion set* [3]

$$D_{\mathrm{CA}} \equiv \{\, \boldsymbol{x} \in D \,|\, Y(\boldsymbol{x}) \geq \theta_{\mathrm{S}} \,\}, \qquad (1)$$

where θ_{S} is a technology-specific decodability threshold. For technologies utilizing rate adaptation, such as Wi-Fi or cellular systems, we would have such a set for each coding and modulation scheme. Since the set D_{CA} is completely determined by $Y(\boldsymbol{x})$, the coverage estimation problem is reduced to estimating the value of $Y(\boldsymbol{x})$ for all $\boldsymbol{x} \in D$ based on some possibly noisy and unreliable measurements related to Y.

We shall adopt a simple additive error model in the following, dealing with more complex outliers in the data preprocessing phase as opposed to the estimation phase. Therefore we assume that a vector of measurements

$$\boldsymbol{Z} \equiv \big(Z(\boldsymbol{x}_1), \ldots, Z(\boldsymbol{x}_n)\big)' \qquad (2)$$

is used to estimate $Y(\boldsymbol{x})$, where

$$Z(\boldsymbol{x}) \equiv Y(\boldsymbol{x}) + \varepsilon(\boldsymbol{x}). \qquad (3)$$

Here $\varepsilon(\boldsymbol{x})$ is used to model both location independent as well as location dependent errors, such as receiver noise, contaminations from random antenna orientation, effects of multipath fading, and so on. The underlying random field $Y(\boldsymbol{x})$ of received signal strength is assumed to be of the form

$$Y(\boldsymbol{x}) = \boldsymbol{t}(\boldsymbol{x})'\boldsymbol{\alpha} + \nu(\boldsymbol{x}), \qquad (4)$$

where $\boldsymbol{t}$ are covariates, $\boldsymbol{\alpha}$ is a vector of coefficients to be estimated, and ν is assumed to be a process of zero mean and spatial covariance function

$$C(\boldsymbol{x}, \boldsymbol{y}) = \mathrm{Cov}\big(\nu(\boldsymbol{x}), \nu(\boldsymbol{y})\big). \qquad (5)$$

The covariates are used to incorporate information such as number of walls between the transmitter and the measurement location or the distance between them, if such side information is available. The covariance function is of course not known, and must be estimated from the data. In practice this is done by assuming weak stationarity and estimating the *semivariogram*

$$\gamma(\boldsymbol{x} - \boldsymbol{y}) = \frac{1}{2}\,\mathrm{Var}\{Z(\boldsymbol{x}) - Z(\boldsymbol{y})\} \qquad (6)$$

by the method of moments, after which a parametric semivariogram model is fitted to the estimate. After this is done, the covariance function is obtained using the identity

$$\gamma(\boldsymbol{\tau}) = C(\mathbf{0}) - C(\boldsymbol{\tau}), \tag{7}$$

where $\boldsymbol{\tau} = \boldsymbol{x} - \boldsymbol{y}$. A commonly used example for parametric correlation models is the *exponential semivariogram model*

$$\gamma(\boldsymbol{\tau}; \boldsymbol{\beta}) = \beta_0 + \beta_1 \left(1 - \exp\left(\frac{-\|\boldsymbol{\tau}\|}{\beta_2}\right)\right), \tag{8}$$

where the parameter β_0 is used to account for variance arising from measurement inaccuracies, short-range variations, or superimposed noise. The parameter β_1 controls the variance of Z, and β_2 is the *range parameter*, scaling the correlation distance of the model. These parameters can be fitted with usual regression techniques to the estimated semivariogram. This overall process might seem unduly complicated, but is in fact computationally lightweight, and results in estimates that are highly robust against outliers. Naturally it rarely suffices to use a single semivariogram model. Instead, usually we fit several, and utilize the one giving the best fit for subsequent estimation steps. See [8] for definitions of other common semivariogram models, such as the Matérn, Cauchy and spherical models. These were considered in addition to the exponential model in the following when selecting the best parametric representation for the measured correlations.

Combining these assumptions we obtain a generalized linear model of the form

$$\boldsymbol{Z} = \boldsymbol{T}\boldsymbol{\alpha} + \boldsymbol{\delta}, \tag{9}$$

where $\boldsymbol{T}$ is the matrix of known covariates at different measurement locations (if any), and $\boldsymbol{\delta} = \boldsymbol{\nu} + \boldsymbol{\epsilon}$ is a zero-mean random process. Writing $(\boldsymbol{C})_{ij} \equiv C(\boldsymbol{x}_i, \boldsymbol{x}_j)$ the covariance matrix $\boldsymbol{\Sigma}$ of $\boldsymbol{\delta}$ can be written as

$$\boldsymbol{\Sigma} = \boldsymbol{C} + \boldsymbol{V}, \tag{10}$$

where $\boldsymbol{V}$ is a diagonal matrix. The coverage estimation problem now becomes that of forming an estimate $\widehat{Y}(\boldsymbol{x}_0)$ at a location $\boldsymbol{x}_0 \in D$ for which measurements might not be available. The "best" such estimate in the sense of being both unbiased and having the minimal estimation variance is given by the conditional expectation

$$\widehat{Y}(\boldsymbol{x}_0) = \mathbb{E}\{Y(\boldsymbol{x}_0) \mid \boldsymbol{Z}\}. \tag{11}$$

In general conditional expectation is difficult to compute, but if the underlying random fields are assumed to be Gaussian the resulting predictor has simple form given by

$$\widehat{Y}(\boldsymbol{x}_0) = \boldsymbol{t}(\boldsymbol{x}_0)'\widehat{\boldsymbol{\alpha}} + \boldsymbol{c}(\boldsymbol{x}_0)'\boldsymbol{\Sigma}^{-1}(\boldsymbol{Z} - \boldsymbol{T}\widehat{\boldsymbol{\alpha}}), \tag{12}$$

where the estimate $\widehat{\boldsymbol{\alpha}}$ is of the generalized least square form given by

$$\widehat{\boldsymbol{\alpha}} = (\boldsymbol{T}'\boldsymbol{\Sigma}^{-1}\boldsymbol{T})^{-1}\boldsymbol{T}'\boldsymbol{\Sigma}^{-1}\boldsymbol{Z}, \tag{13}$$

and $\boldsymbol{c}(\boldsymbol{x}_0) \equiv \big(C(\boldsymbol{x}_0, \boldsymbol{x}_1), \ldots, C(\boldsymbol{x}_0, \boldsymbol{x}_n)\big)'$. This is the *kriging estimator* of spatial statistics, and its estimated error, usually called the *kriging standard deviation* in the literature, can also be computed analytically for the Gaussian case (see [8] for details).

Of course, one cannot expect received signal strengths to be exactly Gaussian even when measured in the logarithmic scale (i.e., in dBm or dBW). However, since it is well known that sums of log-normal distributions of received powers are relatively well approximated by individual log-normals, the

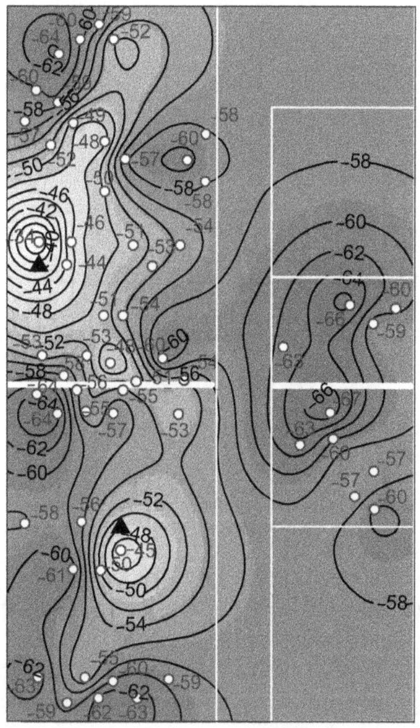

Figure 2: Kriging prediction for the received signal strength from one access point and a Wi-Fi client denoted by triangles together with the raw measurements. White lines indicate walls between the rooms in which the measurement devices were deployed in. The thick white line in the middle indicates the supporting concrete wall, other walls are plaster-based.

Gaussian approximation is quite reasonable. Further, as shown in [8], the kriging predictor is relatively robust also against deviations from Gaussianity (unlike maximum likelihood based approaches). We shall in this paper see that this robustness holds for spatial prediction of received signal strength readings as well.

3.2 Baseline Performance and Optimized Selection of Sensors

We shall now apply the kriging predictor (12) on the measurement data collected from the testbed. Figure 2 shows the layout of the sensor nodes across the different rooms, the raw measurement values for each sensor (the figures in blue), as well as a contour plot of the kriging predictor. In the shown example two Wi-Fi nodes were active, the upper one being the Access Point (AP), the other being the receiving TCP client. The locations of the nodes are shown with triangles in the figure. The obtained results are quite intuitive, as we can see the roughly uniform and isotropic decay of received power away from the transmitters.

For estimating the accuracy of the predictions, we apply *cross-validation* [8]. In cross-validation the available data set is divided into two parts. First is used to estimate the model and to perform the prediction, and the second part is used to study the accuracy of the method. A special case of cross-validation often applied for spatial data is the *leave one out* cross-validation, in which each data location is removed in turn, and predicted using the rest of the data. Applied on the data set of Figure 2 this process yields the estimated RMSE or standard deviation of 3.9 dB, which is comparable

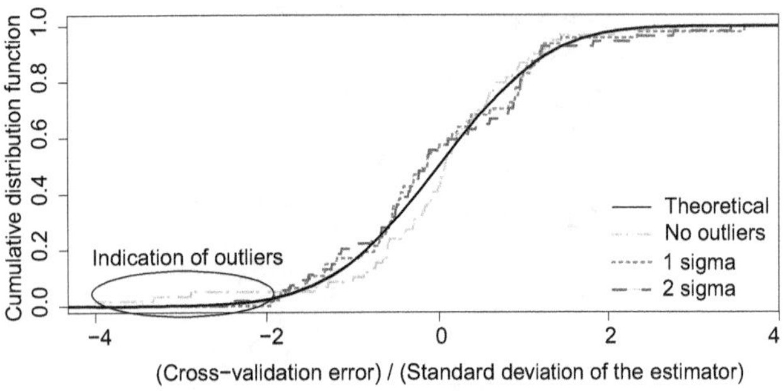

Figure 3: The cumulative distribution function of the standardized cross-validation errors with and without prefiltering for outliers.

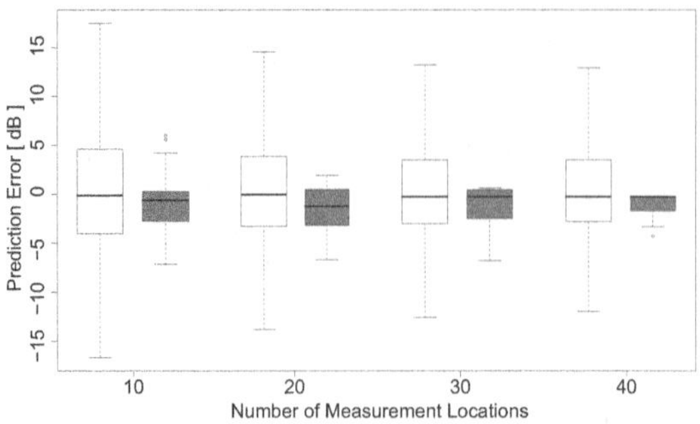

(a) Box plots of the distribution of cross-validation errors with random subsampling (white) and using the genetic algorithm approach (red shading).

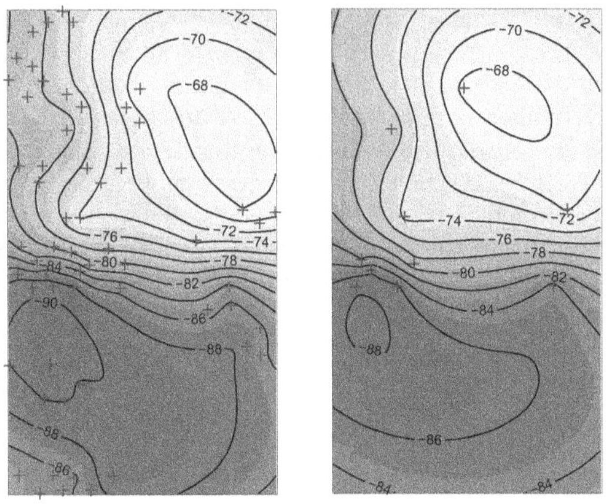

(b) Kriging predictions with all nodes (left) and subset of 10 nodes (right) obtained using the genetic algorithm.

Figure 4: Performance of genetic algorithm based measurement location selection.

to or better than what is achieved by most sophisticated raytracing models calibrated against measurements reported on in similar environments [6, 9, 18].

While this initial result is certainly encouraging, there are few serious limitations remaining on the accuracy of the kriging approach when applied indoors. First, due to multipath fading effects, there are several significant outliers in the data that can seriously limit the accuracy of the proposed predictions approach. Second, in our example relatively dense measurement network is used for obtaining the results. For practical applications this would imply several femtocells, Wi-Fi access points, or mobile terminals carrying out continuous measurements, leading into potentially excessive energy consumption and measurement overhead. We shall now discuss how these two problems can be avoided.

Local outliers due to failed measurement devices or non-representative measurements caused by deep fades can be removed by a simple spatial filtering approach. The marginal distribution of the measurements within a particular region is readily computable from (12) combined with the estimated RMSE of the kriging predictor. This marginal distribution is normal with a given standard deviation. We propose to compute these marginals in regions centered on each measurement point in turn with radius dependent on the estimated correlation range (in our case typically around 4 m), and filter out measurements from successive processing that are sufficiently far below the estimated conditional mean. Figure 3 illustrates the effect of such filtering on the prediction accuracy compared against the theoretical RMSE for the estimator. The different sigma-values in the figure correspond to the number of standard deviations a measurement should be away from the conditional mean in order to be interpreted as an outlier. We see from the figure that not only the proposed filtering clearly alleviates the impact of outliers in the tails of the error distribution, but also that the theoretical RMSE estimates fit very well with the realized ones. This is a powerful result as it indicates that the kriging based predictions are not only accurate, but also the corresponding estimates on their accuracy are of high quality as well.

For reducing the number of measurements needed, and to improve the quality of the predictions further, we propose a simple iterative approach based on metaheuristics. The iteration begins by requesting few measurements from all the available devices, followed by finding the optimal subset of measurement locations that minimizes the standard deviation of the cross-validation error. Since this optimization problem is basically equivalent to a non-linear integer programming problem, we tackle it using a standard genetic algorithm. The results shown in Figure 4a compare the performance of the proposed scheme with the genetic algorithm using a population size of 300 over 1000 iterations against selection of random subsets of 10–40 nodes from the 60 possible. The optimization based approach clearly reduces the estimation error significantly, and enables accurate coverage estimation with as few as 10 measurements within the region covered by our testbed. The results obtained with the genetic algorithm using just 10 selected nodes are similar or better in terms of standard deviation of the cross-validation error than the results obtained using all the 60 sensors. Figure 4b shows the resulting estimates before and after optimization, in the latter case with 10 nodes.

4. INCORPORATING KNOWLEDGE ON RADIO ENVIRONMENT AND FILTERING OUTLIERS

We shall now study in more detail the impact of the different modeling choices on the quality of the obtained received signal strength predictions. Without considering outliers or

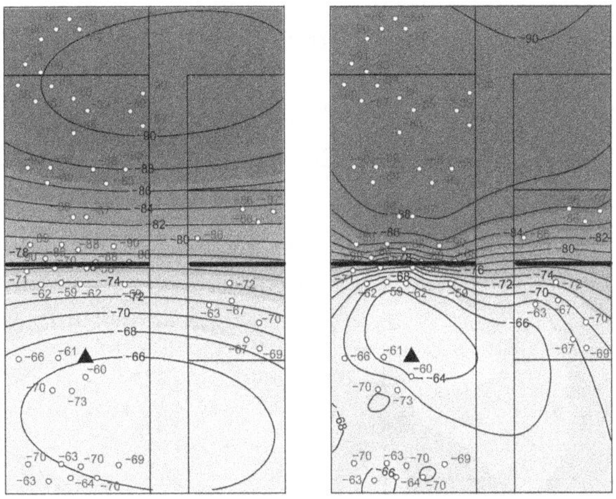

(a) Matérn (b) Exponential

Figure 5: Results for the signal generator transmitting with 20 MHz bandwidth and power of 20 dBm over using two different correlation models (Matérn and exponential) fitted over distances of 8 and 16 meters, respectively.

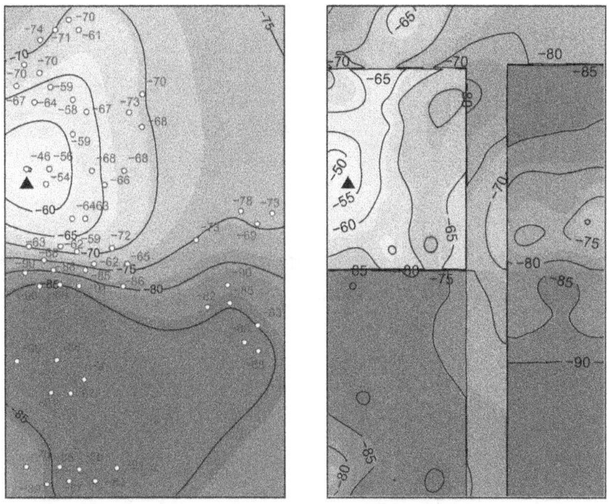

(a) Without covariates (b) With room covariates

Figure 7: Influence of incorporating room information as a covariate into the predictions for a beaconing Wi-Fi access point. Notice how the predictions change at room boundaries, following the expected physical structure of the environment much better with the covariates included.

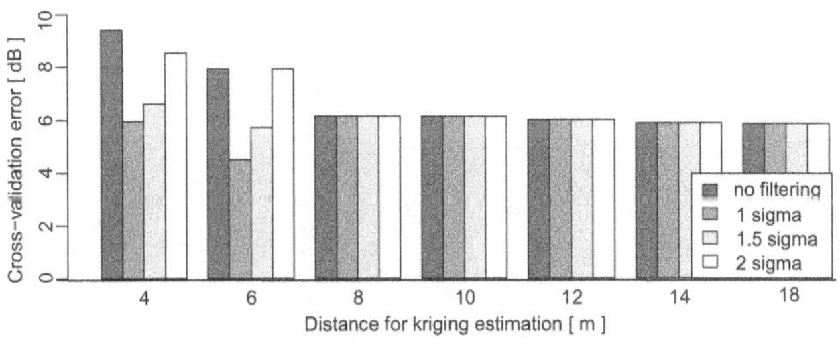

(a) Signal generator dataset with 5 MHz bandwidth and power of 20 dBm with the Cauchy model.

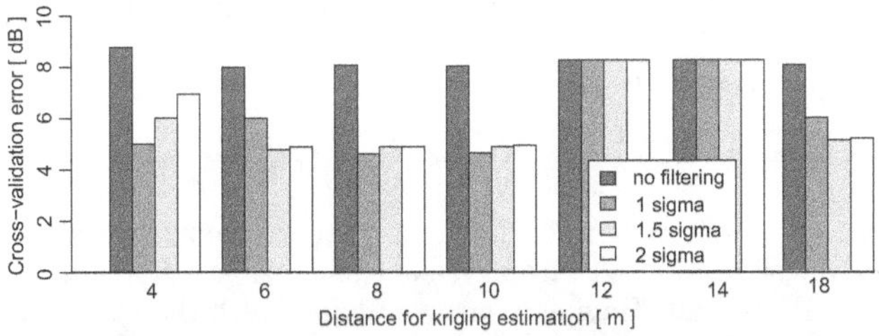

(b) TCP client and access point with the Matérn model.

Figure 6: The influence of different levels of outlier filtering on cross-validation error.

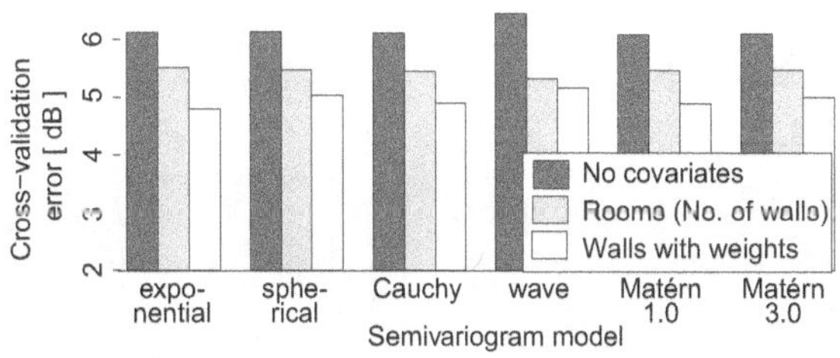

Figure 8: Influence of choice of covariates and the semivariogram model on the cross-validation error for the Wi-Fi beaconing scenario of the figure above.

possible covariates, the main modeling choice lies in the parametric model for the correlation function or semivariogram over distance. Here the key decisions are the choice of the parametric family and the range of distances over which the model is fitted to the empirical data. The former has major impact on the smoothness of the arising predictions, whereas the latter mainly influences the overall aggregate prediction accuracy. This tradeoff is illustrated in Figure 5 contrasting the predictions obtained with two different choices of the correlation models and the distance ranges used.

Figure 6 illustrates further the impact of outlier filtering as well as the correlation range considered on the prediction accuracy for two of the measurement data sets. Both of these are for narrower bandwidths, namely 5 MHz for the signal generator case, and for the TCP transmission a frequency band on the border of the transmission mask was chosen. These data sets were selected since such transmissions are more prone to experience multipath effects, and thus are more challenging for any spatial prediction scheme. We see that selecting a too short correlation range results in a significant increase in prediction errors, whereas beyond the shortest studied correlation range the results are relatively stable. For outlier filtering small values of the cutoff parameter sigma typically perform the best in overall terms, although for the TCP transmission data set all studied outlier detection schemes result in almost identical performance, in each case yielding improvements over the baseline.

Let us now study the influence of different possible covariates on the prediction accuracy. Recall from Section 3.1 that in order to incorporate additional information into our predictions, we need to specify the deterministic covariate field $\boldsymbol{t}$ in the term $\boldsymbol{t}(\boldsymbol{x})'\boldsymbol{\alpha}$. Since our prediction model is

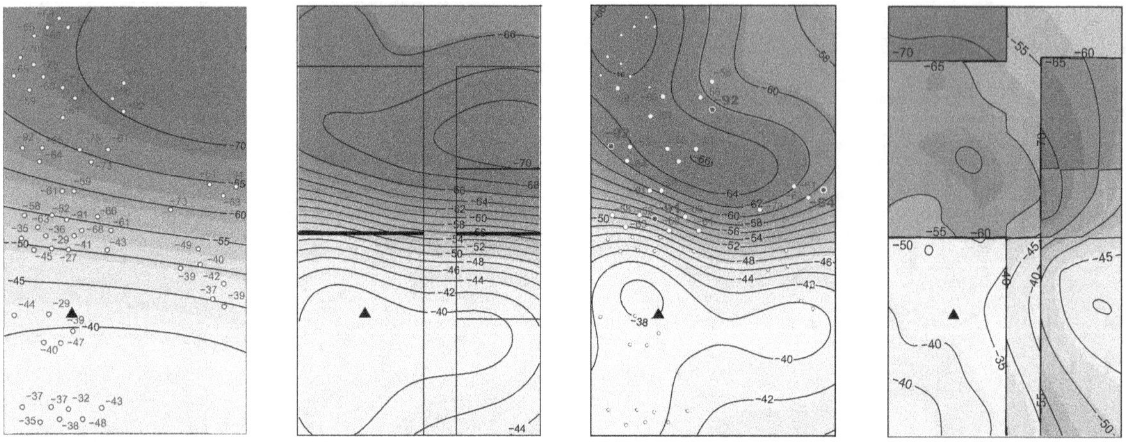

(a) Baseline (b) Maximum distance (c) Outlier filtering (d) Covariates

Figure 9: Illustrating the impact of different data processing steps on the kriging predictions with the narrowband signal generator (5 MHz / 20 dBm) data set. All results are obtained using the Cauchy semivariogram model.

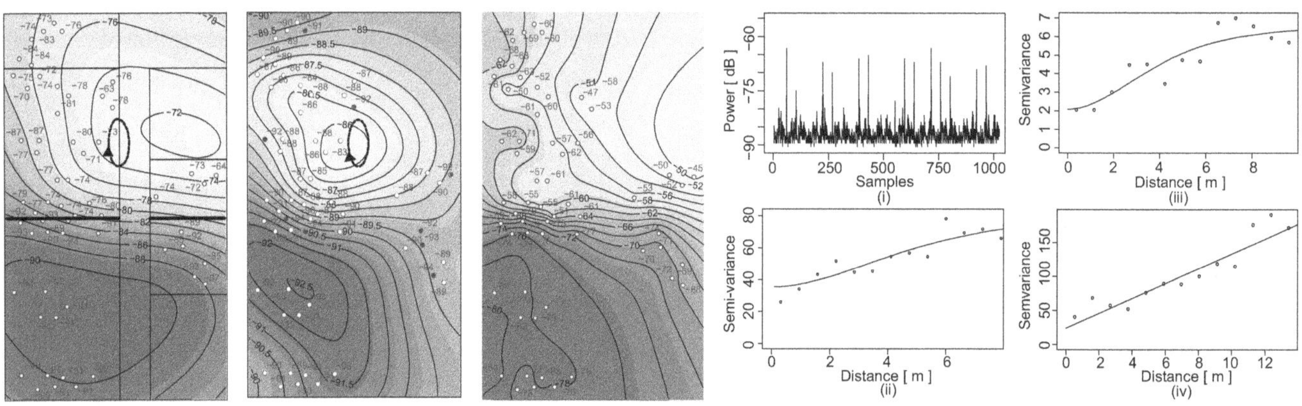

(a) No preprocessing (b) 70th percentile (c) 99.5th percentile (d) Example measurements and semivariograms

Figure 10: Using time-domain filtering to separate sources.

linear, these covariates should have roughly linear impact on the received signal strength in order to be useful for the predictions. Most obvious of these is to use information on the locations of walls, since penetration losses are additive when measured in the logarithmic scale (that is, in dBs). Another choice would be to use t to index the distance in rooms from the transmitter, resulting in a somewhat cruder measure but which is simpler to compute from building information. Figures 7 and 8 show the impact of difference choices of covariates on the prediction errors. First examples in the figure use just the raw number of walls between the transmitter and the sender as a covariate, effectively fitting a single wall-loss value for the entire scenario. Our second choice is to use a vector of covariates, corresponding binary functions encoding whether a given point is shadowed by a given wall. This choice enables individual loss values per wall to be fitted based on the measurements. We see from the results that both choices are beneficial, and that the prediction accuracy is indeed further increased as additional information is made available.

We shall conclude this section with a more complete example on how the different data processing steps influence the obtained predictions. As a data set we use measured received signal strength from a signal generator set to transmit a 5 MHz signal. Having a narrower bandwidth than the previous examples, this signal is more susceptible to multipath propagation effects, and the expected performance of plain kriging is expected to be worse. Indeed, without further processing kriging achieves standard deviation of cross validation error of only 12 dB which is relatively poor. The corresponding prediction surface is shown in Figure 9a, which clearly seems unphysical. Figures 9b and 9c show the impact of first limiting the maximum correlation range used to more reasonable 8 m, and then applying outlier filtering before the predictions. The filtered out sensor readings are shown in boldface numbers of Figure 9c, and are clearly unreasonably low due to the corresponding sensors experiencing deep fades. Finally, Figure 9d shows the impact of incorporating room information as covariates, resulting in a both most accurate and physically meaningful predictions. Altogether, the above steps reduce the standard deviation of the prediction error from 12 dB to 6.12 dB.

Table 1: Summary of the obtained results with kriging interpolation. The results give the semivariogram models yielding best predictions, the corresponding maximum range used in estimating the model parameters, as well as the level of filtering used for detecting outliers. Values in parentheses correspond to adjacent channel estimates which are more susceptible for multipath effects.

Scenario description	Transmit power [dBm]	Bandwidth [MHz]	Cross-validation error [dB] and kriging parameters: Default	Outliers	Covariates[1] (default / outliers / wall info)
Beaconing AP	20	20	6.23 spherical / 8 m	6.07 spherical / 8 m / 1σ	5.28 / 5.45 / 4.65
AP and one TCP client in two rooms	20	20	3.94 (7.92) Matérn $\kappa = 1$ / 8 m	3.86 (4.53) Matérn $\kappa = 1$ / 6 m (8 m) / 1σ	not beneficial (7.65) / 3.79 (4.53) / 3.75 (not beneficial)
AP and two UDP clients in two rooms	20	20	4.83 exponential / 10 m	not beneficial	not beneficial
Rogue AP	20	20	4.6 Matérn $\kappa = 1$ / 14 m	4.43 Matérn $\kappa = 1$ / 10 m / 1σ	4.43 / 4.35 / 3.9
Signal generator	20	20	5.84 exponential / 14 m	not beneficial	4.11 / 4.11 / 3.53
Signal generator	20	5	12.0 Cauchy / 8 m	8.03 Cauchy / 8 m / 2σ	11.65 / 6.67 / 6.12
Moving train with TelosB sensor node	0	5	4.2 exponential / 8 m	3.64 spherical / 6 m / 1σ	3.68 / 3.59 / 3.03
Stationary sensor node	0	5	3.78 (6.03) Matérn $\kappa = 3$ (exponential) / 8 m	3.69 (5.7) Matérn $\kappa = 3$ (exponential) / 8 m (6 m) / 1σ	3.72 (5.66) / 3.42 (not beneficial) / 3.22 (5.11)
Two sensor nodes in different rooms	0	5	8.26 exponential / 10 m	7.33 exponential / 10 m / 1σ	7.75 / 6.95 / 6.95
Train and rogue AP	0/20	5/20	5.61 Matérn $\kappa = 3$ / 10 m	not beneficial	4.64 / 4.64 / 4.42
Two sensor nodes with 50 and 25 DC in two rooms	0	5	6.35 exponential / 8 m	4.89 exponential / 8 m / 1.5σ	5.95 / 4.75 / 4.73

5. IMPACT OF TIME DOMAIN FILTERING

In this final section we study the problem of coverage or interference footprint estimation for multiple sources exhibiting highly different temporal dynamics. For this we use the data set illustrated in Figure 10a. The two transmitters active are a narrowband wireless sensor node mounted on a toy train, constantly traversing the ellipsoidal trajectory shown in the figure, and the rogue access point above the upper-right corner of the testbed region. Typical measurement results for this setup are shown in Figure 10d, subpanel (i), where one clearly sees the superposition of periodic high power beacons with the small scale variation from the sensor node on the train. The predictions based on raw measurements shown in Figure 10a apply thus to the aggregate mean power only, which is not very descriptive of the individual transmission patterns of these two sources.

Since the time-domain dynamics and the power values measured from these sources are highly different, simple filtering of the power measurements before spatial prediction phase suffices to obtain more information from the coverage areas of the sources. In Figures 10b and 10c predictions preceded by filtering the 70th percentile and 99.5th percentile of the power readings are shown. The first of these filters extracts typical active phase of the sensor transmissions, but is not sensitive to beacons due to their rarity, whereas filtering for the 99.5th percentile effectively finds the peaks from the data sets. The resulting received signal strength maps are much more descriptive regarding the coverage regions of the two sources. In particular, the estimate for the sensor node mounted on the train in Figure 10b has the maximum at exactly the correct region, and the attenuation follows the layout of the rooms well even without the latter information being used in the predictions directly.

6. CONCLUSIONS

In this paper we have studied the use of spatial statistics methods with different preprocessing approaches for indoor coverage estimation. Our experiments show that the proposed scheme can achieve prediction accuracy of 3.1–6.9 dB in terms of standard deviations of prediction errors with simple outlier rejection scheme to remove measurements from measurement devices experiencing deep fades or hardware faults estimation errors. With optimized selection measurement locations, only small number (≈ 10) of the devices were needed to achieve high prediction accuracy. These results are comparable to or better than what have been achieved by more complex approaches, which require more detailed prior information on the environment.

Table 1 gives a summary of all the different measurement data sets collected, and the prediction accuracies achieved. From the table it is clear that even without outlier detection or using additional covariates for improving prediction accuracy, the results are typically very good. However, for selected data sets especially involving narrow-band signals occasionally poor prediction results are obtained, mainly due

[1]The kriging parameters for the values in this column correspond to the respective values provided in the previous columns. The third values, where the covariates coefficients include the specifics of individual wall propagation, are given for the cases where the outliers have been filtered out.

to the dense multipath environment typical of indoor propagation environments. The simple outlier detection approach suggested in the paper effectively removes these problems, and use of additional information on the radio environment can bring further improvements of the overall estimation accuracy. We emphasize that all steps, including the selection of the semivariogram model, the distance ranges used for estimation, as well as the level of outlier filtering applied are all automated, and do not require manual intervention for determining the best models or their parameters. We strongly believe that such measurement-based approaches are also highly promising for processing data from future minimization of drive tests (MDT) deployments, where mobile phones are used to estimate outdoor and outdoor-to-indoor cellular network coverage [10].

Acknowledgement

We thank RWTH Aachen University and the German Research Foundation (Deutsche Forschungsgemeinschaft, DFG) for providing financial support through the UMIC research centre.

7. REFERENCES

[1] Z. Abbas, J. Nasreddine, J. Riihijärvi, and P. Mähönen. Long-term indoor propagation models for radio resource management. In *Proceedings of 2012 IEEE International Symposium on a World of Wireless, Mobile and Multimedia Networks (WoWMoM)*, pages 1–9, 2012.

[2] A. Achtzehn, J. Riihijärvi, G. Martinez, M. Petrova, and P. Mähönen. Improving coverage prediction for primary multi-transmitter networks operating in the TV whitespaces. In *Proceedings of 2012 9th Annual IEEE Communications Society Conference on Sensor, Mesh and Ad Hoc Communications and Networks (SECON)*, pages 623–631, 2012.

[3] R. Adler. *The geometry of random fields*, volume 62. SIAM, 1981.

[4] M. Akella, E. Delmelle, R. Batta, P. Rogerson, and A. Blatt. Adaptive cell tower location using geostatistics. *Geographical Analysis*, 42(3):227–244, 2010.

[5] A. Alaya-Feki, S. Ben Jemaa, B. Sayrac, P. Houze, and E. Moulines. Informed spectrum usage in cognitive radio networks: Interference cartography. In *Proceedings of IEEE PIMRC 2008*, pages 1–5, 2008.

[6] J. B. Andersen, T. S. Rappaport, and S. Yoshida. Propagation measurements and models for wireless communications channels. *IEEE Communications Magazine*, 33(1):42–49, 1995.

[7] G. E. Athanasiadou and A. R. Nix. A novel 3-D indoor ray-tracing propagation model: The path generator and evaluation of narrow-band and wide-band predictions. *IEEE Transactions on Vehicular Technology*, 49(4):1152–1168, 2000.

[8] N. Cressie. *Statistics for spatial data.* Wiley-Interscience, 1993.

[9] K. El-Kafrawy, M. Youssef, A. El-Keyi, and A. Naguib. Propagation modeling for accurate indoor wlan rss-based localization. In *Proceedings of IEEE 72nd Vehicular Technology Conference Fall (VTC 2010-Fall)*, pages 1–5, 2010.

[10] W. A. Hapsari, A. Umesh, M. Iwamura, M. Tomala, B. Gyula, and B. Sebire. Minimization of drive tests solution in 3GPP. *IEEE Communications Magazine*, 50(6):28–36, 2012.

[11] A. Konak. A kriging approach to predicting coverage in wireless networks. *International Journal of Mobile Network Design and Innovation*, 3(2):65–71, 2009.

[12] E. Meshkova, J. Ansari, D. Denkovski, J. Riihijärvi, J. Nasreddine, M. Pavloski, L. Gavrilovska, and P. Mähönen. Experimental spectrum sensor testbed for constructing indoor radio environmental maps. In *Proceedings of the 2011 IEEE Symposium on New Frontiers in Dynamic Spectrum Access Networks (DySPAN)*, pages 603–607, 2011.

[13] C. Phillips. *Geostatistical Techniques for Practical Wireless Network Coverage Mapping.* PhD thesis, University of Colorado, 2012.

[14] J. Polastre, R. Szewczyk, and D. Culler. Telos: enabling ultra-low power wireless research. In *Proceedings of the Fourth International Symposium on Information Processing in Sensor Networks (IPSN 2005)*, pages 364–369, 2005.

[15] S. Rangan and R. Madan. Belief propagation methods for intercell interference coordination in femtocell networks. *IEEE Journal on Selected Areas in Communications*, 30(3):631 -640, april 2012.

[16] J. Riihijärvi, P. Mähönen, M. Wellens, and M. Gordziel. Characterization and modelling of spectrum for dynamic spectrum access with spatial statistics and random fields. In *Proceedings of IEEE PIMRC 2008*, pages 1–6, 2008.

[17] F. Seco, C. Plagemann, A. R. Jiménez, and W. Burgard. Improving rfid-based indoor positioning accuracy using gaussian processes. In *Proceedings of the International Conference on Indoor Positioning and Indoor Navigation (IPIN)*, pages 1–8, 2010.

[18] L. Subrt and P. Pechac. Advanced 3d indoor propagation model: calibration and implementation. *EURASIP Journal on Wireless Communications and Networking*, 2011(1):1–10, 2011.

[19] R. Tandra, M. Mishra, and A. Sahai. What is a spectrum hole and what does it take to recognize one? *Proceedings of the IEEE*, 97(5):824–848, 2009.

An Empirical Study of Link Quality Estimation Techniques for Disconnection Detection in WBANs

Majid Nabi[1], Marc Geilen[1], Twan Basten[1,2]
[1]Department of Electrical Engineering, Eindhoven University of Technology, the Netherlands
[2]TNO-ESI, Embedded Systems Innovation by TNO, Eindhoven, the Netherlands
{m.nabi,m.c.w.geilen,a.a.basten}@tue.nl

ABSTRACT

Sensor nodes in many Wireless Body Area Network (WBAN) architectures are supposed to deliver sensed data to a gateway node on the body. To satisfy the data delivery requirements, the network needs to adapt itself to the changes in connection status of the body nodes to the gateway. As a prerequisite, Link Quality Estimation (LQE) needs to be done to detect the connection status of the nodes. The quality of links in WBANs is highly time-varying. The LQE technique should be agile to react fast to such link quality dynamics while avoiding frequent fluctuations to reduce the network adaptation overhead. In this paper, we present an empirical study on using different LQE methods for detecting the connection status of body nodes to the gateway in WBANs. A set of experiments using 16 wireless motes deployed on a body are performed to log the behavior of the wireless links. We explore the trade-offs made by each LQE method in terms of agility, stability, and reliability in detecting connection changes by analyzing the experimental data. Moreover, different LQE methods are used in an adaptive multi-hop WBAN mechanism, as a case study, and their impact on the Quality-of-Services (QoS) are investigated.

Categories and Subject Descriptors

C.2.1 [**Computer-Communication Networks**]: Network Architecture and Design; C.4 [**Performance of Systems**]: Modeling Techniques; Performance Attributes

Keywords

Link Quality Estimation; Wireless body area network; Disconnection detection; Quality-of-service.

1. INTRODUCTION

In a Wireless Body Area Network (WBAN), several small-scale wireless sensor devices are deployed on a human body to sense and transmit biological signals of the body. In common network architectures, one node plays the role of a gateway node to gather data from all nodes in the WBAN and transmit it to a higher level network (e.g., a central station).

MSWiM'13, November 3–8, 2013, Barcelona, Spain.
Copyright 2013 ACM 978-1-4503-2353-6/13/11
http://dx.doi.org/10.1145/2507924.2507959 ...$15.00.

Thus the body nodes are supposed to deliver their sensed data to the gateway node. There are several approaches for data delivery to the gateway nodes, from a one-hop star architecture to multi-hop data forwarding mechanisms.

Regardless of the used network protocol for data delivery to the gateway, applications have specific Quality-of-Service (QoS) requirements that should be satisfied by the networking protocol. In particular, Data Delivery Ratio (DDR) to the gateway node and energy consumption are important parameters. The network protocol is responsible for meeting the data delivery requirements of the application while minimizing the energy consumption of the nodes to prolong the life-time of the sensor nodes.

WBANs are very dynamic and the network topology and the quality of wireless links varies over time (due to posture changes and body movement). The protocol needs to adapt itself to these dynamics to continuously meet the QoS requirements. This can be done by data retransmission, data forwarding through nodes with good wireless links to the gateway as relay nodes, or transmit power adaptation, for instance. An adaptation mechanism is triggered when the connection status of some nodes to the gateway changes. A node is connected to the gateway node if it is able to properly reach the gateway directly to satisfy the data delivery requirements; otherwise, it is disconnected.

The connection status of the body nodes to the gateway is detected by monitoring the quality of wireless links to the gateway. Thus, Link Quality Estimation (LQE), aiming to quantify the quality of the wireless links, is a prerequisite for (dis)connection detection. Several LQE techniques for Wireless Sensor Networks (WSNs) exist, each with specific features [1]. Accuracy, agility to follow link quality dynamics, stability, energy efficiency, and computation overhead are characteristics that should be taken into account for selecting an LQE method for a specific network. WBANs are a special kind of networks with frequent topology changes and link quality variations. Thus an LQE method for WBANs needs to be firstly agile to react fast to such frequent link quality variations. Link quality directly affects DDR for the nodes that experience a change in their connection state. As the LQE result is going to be used for triggering the adaptation mechanism of the underlying network protocol, it should be stable enough to avoid frequent fluctuations. In addition, the method needs to be energy efficient with as little as possible required computation and hardware support to be used by ultra-low power body sensor devices.

The main contribution of this paper is to experimentally study the performance of different LQE methods presented for WSNs for (dis)connection detection in WBANs. We deployed 16 wireless nodes on a human body and performed several experiments with different network configurations (such as different transmit power levels of the nodes). The status of the links was logged during each experiment. This experimental data is then used to investigate the characteristics of various LQE methods and also to explore the trade-offs made by each method and its configurations in terms of agility, stability, and reliability. Although there are several work in the literature that investigate the performance of LQE methods for WSNs and ad hoc networks, to the best of our knowledge, this is the first effort to experimentally study these techniques in WBANs. We also present an LQE method, Smoothed Link Likelihood Factor, which is able to make a very good trade-off for various performance metrics in many WBAN scenarios. Finally, we use different LQE methods in an adaptive WBAN mechanism [2], as a case study, to investigate the impact of using each method on the WBAN performance (i.e., energy consumption and DDR).

The paper is organized as follows. The next section describes the problem of disconnection from the gateway in WBANs. Sec. 3 discusses the classification of LQE methods for WSNs from [1] and their suitability for WBANs. In Sec. 4, our experimental setup and the used metrics for investigating the characteristics of different LQE methods are described. Sec. 5 presents data analysis results for various LQE methods and different configurations, and gives an impression of the characteristics of each estimator. In Sec. 6, the use case is presented and the achieved QoS by using different LQE methods are compared. Sec. 7 concludes.

2. PROBLEM STATEMENT

We consider $S = \{s_1, s_2, ..., s_N\}$ as the set of N Body Sensor nodes (BSNs) deployed on a body, forming a WBAN. One of these nodes, say s_N, plays the role of a gateway (hub) to gather sensed data from all nodes in the WBAN. As the nature of various body signals being sensed is different, there is usually a high diversity in data sampling and also data delivery requirements for different BSNs. This implies that each sensor needs to be treated considering its own specifications.

$\mathcal{R}^t(s_i)$ is defined as the Data Delivery Ratio (DDR) of node s_i at time t that shows the percentage of the $\mathcal{H}$ last data items sampled by node s_i before time t that reached the gateway, calculated by Eqn. 1.

$$\mathcal{R}^t(s_i) = \frac{1}{\mathcal{H}} \sum_{k=1}^{\mathcal{H}} D^{t,k}(s_i) \quad (1)$$

where $D^{t,k}(s_i)$ is a 0 or 1 valued parameter that shows whether the kth data item sampled by node s_i before/at time t (starting to count backward from time t) has reached the gateway; a value of 1 indicates a successful delivery. The application may specify a constraint $\mathcal{RC}(s_i)$ for DDR of each node s_i. It means that the application expects the value of $\mathcal{R}^t(s_i)$ to remain above this threshold ($\mathcal{R}^t(s_i) \geq \mathcal{RC}(s_i)$). However, because of the stochastic nature of the network, this may not be 100% satisfiable during the network operation. Therefore, the application needs to have tolerance to a certain percentage of violations of its constraint $\mathcal{RC}(s_i)$. As an example, an application may require the DDR for a node s_i to be higher than 80% in 95% of the time.

All nodes are initially supposed to send their data directly to the gateway. This is a common communication approach (e.g., [3, 4, 5]) because of the small scale of WBANs. However, the direct link to the gateway may fail because of body influence on the wave propagation, or the very low transmission power of some nodes. Each node has a certain packet transmission period and each data packet has some retransmission budget to be delivered to the gateway. The data packet gets lost if it cannot be delivered using the available (re)transmission opportunities.

Definition: *A body sensor node s_i is said to be disconnected from the gateway iff it cannot satisfy the required data delivery ratio $\mathcal{RC}(s_i)$ by sending its packets directly to the gateway node within the available transmission budget.*

Taking this definition, disconnection of a node depends on the quality of its wireless link to the gateway, data sampling and transmission rates, and the DDR requirements for that node. This means that we may have two nodes with the same link quality, where one is considered connected and the other is considered disconnected, because of different sampling specifications and DDR requirements. When a node goes to a disconnected state, the network protocol should adapt itself to improve data delivery for the disconnected node and to bring the DDR of the node within the acceptable range. The protocol should also adapt when a node reconnects to the gateway to optimize the consumption of network resources.

Here we consider two common solutions that may be used to deal with this disconnection problem. The first one is to provide multi-hop data routing, by getting help of other BSNs that have currently good links to the gateway (e.g., [2], [6]). The second approach is to adapt the transmit power of the node (e.g., [7] and [8]), hoping to improve the link quality to the gateway and getting out of the disconnection state. This method resolves the issue as far as a higher transmit power is available for the BSN. A combination of these two approaches may also be applied.

Regardless of the method that the networking protocol uses to deal with disconnections, a mechanism for detecting connection changes should be in place to trigger the adaptation mechanism. As the data sampling and transmission period, and DDR constraints ($\mathcal{RC}(s_i)$) are known, we only need to measure the quality of the wireless link between the BSNs and the gateway to detect connection state of the nodes. The speed and accuracy of the LQE method influence the performance of the WBAN protocol. Because of very frequent topology and link quality changes in WBANs, the LQE method should react fast enough to follow the changes in the quality of links. Late disconnection detection may lead to data loss or even violation of DDR requirements for the BSNs. Late reconnection detection is also expensive, because the protocol may be performing unnecessary data forwarding or the BSN uses unnecessarily high transmit power. The method should not be very sensitive to incidental link failures or connections. It needs to be stable enough to avoid frequent fluctuations in order to to keep the overhead of the adaptation mechanism low and to make it robust.

There are several LQE methods in the literature of WSNs. In [9], the performance of prominent software-based LQE techniques are compared by applying them in simulating static WSNs. The quality of wireless links and the kind of network dynamics in WBANs substantially deviate from typical WSNs. In this paper, we investigate the performance of LQE methods for detecting connection changes in real-world WBANs. This is done by performing comprehensive experiments using wireless motes deployed on a body, logging the status of the wireless links, and applying different LQE methods on the logged data. It allows us to explore the trade-offs in terms the agility, stability, and reliability of the estimators in detecting connection changes. These performance metrics and the method for measuring them are described in Sec. 4.2.

3. LQE FOR WSNS AND WBANS

3.1 Classification of LQE Techniques

Techniques for estimating the quality of wireless links in WSNs are firstly categorized as *hardware-based* and *software-based* methods [1]. Link Quality Indicator (LQI), Received Signal Strength Indicator (RSSI), and Signal-to-Noise Ratio (SNR) are hardware-based LQE methods provided by many radio devices. The hardware-based link quality values are directly given by the radio device and no further computation is necessary in software. However, these techniques suffer from some limitations. First, the provided values are only for successfully received packets and the lost packets are not taken into consideration. This may lead to overestimating the link quality. Second, the hardware-based LQE techniques are only suitable for classifying the links as very good or very bad and are not accurate enough to provide a fine-grained estimation of the link quality [10]. Another fact that further limits the use of hardware-based techniques is that not all radio chips are equipped with a link quality estimator (e.g., Nordic nRF24L01[11]).

Software-based LQE methods are done in software base on the ability of the links to deliver the whole packets (data packets or beacons). These estimators are classified into *sender side* and *receiver side* methods. Sender side techniques compute or approximate the average number of times a data item should be (re-)transmitted until it is correctly received by the receiver. This is done by the sender of the packets and uses the acknowledgment that is sent by the receiver. Thus, asymmetric links degrade the accuracy of these methods. Required Number of Packet transmissions (RNP) [12], the Link Inefficiency metric (LI) [13], Expected Transmission Count (ETX) [14], and four-Bit [10] are examples of sender side LQE techniques.

In this work, we investigate the behavior of *receiver side LQE methods* for estimating the quality of links toward the gateway node in WBANs. Sender side methods rely on acknowledges from the receiver (gateway here), which is costly for energy constrained BSNs, and it is not done in many WBAN scenarios. Moreover, the main flow of data in typical WBANs is from BSNs to the gateway. So the gateway can use the existing data traffic for LQE without the need for beacon transmission by BSNs. In the following, the receiver side LQE techniques under investigation are described.

3.2 Receiver-side LQE Methods for WBANs

Assume that each BSN periodically transmits packets to the gateway node with round sequence numbers denoted by τ. $Link^{\tau}$ is a logical value (0 or 1), which is 1 if the packet transmitted at round number τ is directly received by the gateway; otherwise, it is 0. In fact, $Link^{\tau}$ shows the reception status of the packet at round τ. Based on this knowledge, the gateway is able to quantify the quality of its incoming links using the following estimators.

Packet Reception Ratio (PRR) at any time is the ratio of last w transmitted packets that are successfully received by the receiver, given by Eqn. 2.

$$PRR^{\tau} = \frac{1}{w}\sum_{k=0}^{w-1} Link^{\tau-k} \quad (2)$$

Actually, PRR is a moving average of link status and parameter w is the window size of the moving average. A smaller window size leads to more agile estimation at the cost of less stability (more fluctuations). Especially when the quality of the link is not on the extreme good or bad sides, a greater window size is required to accurately quantify the link quality [12]. PRR can be used as an LQE itself, but it is also the basis for some other LQE techniques. Fig. 1 depicts a block diagram of calculating the LQE techniques that are mostly based on PRR, and the involved parameters.

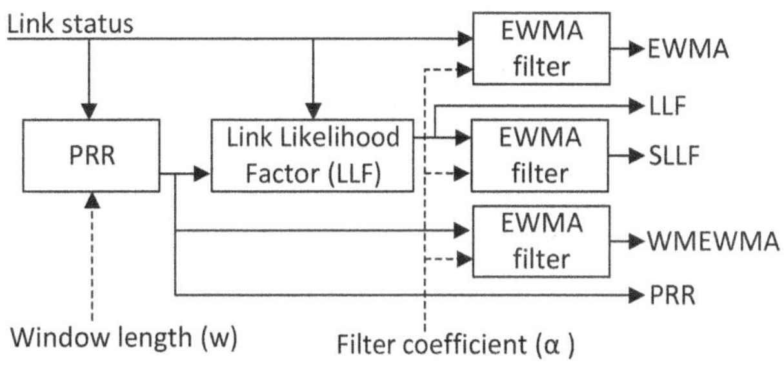

Figure 1: Block diagram of link quality estimators.

Time Weighted Moving Average (TWMA) calculates a moving average over a window of size w using a linear weighting function. It places heavier weight on more recent samples to make the quality estimation more reactive to temporal dynamics comparing to PRR. Eqn. 3 calculates this estimate.

$$TWMA^{\tau} = \frac{\sum_{k=0}^{w-1}\left((w-k)\times Link^{\tau-k}\right)}{\sum_{k=1}^{w} k} \quad (3)$$

Exponentially Weighted Moving Average (EWMA) is a type of infinite impulse response filter that applies exponentially decreasing coefficients (infinite window with exponential weights). Calculating this estimate is simple and memory efficient as a recursive calculation, given in Eqn. 4, only requires storage of the previous estimate.

$$EWMA^{\tau} = \alpha \times Link^{\tau} + (1-\alpha)\times EWMA^{\tau-1} \quad (4)$$

The coefficient $0 < \alpha \leq 1$ represents the degree of weighting decrease. A higher value of α discounts previous link states faster, which leads to a more agile LQE. In general, the technique has the property of being reactive to small dynamics of the link quality even for very intermittent link fluctuations. However, it severely suffers from frequent fluctuations, which cause an unstable estimation.

Window Mean with EWMA (WMEWMA) is proposed in [15] to smooth the PRR estimate using the EWMA filter aiming to make the estimation more stable, but still agile. It is a generalization of both PRR and EWMA. It is sometime referred to as Smoothed PRR (SPRR) [9]. The recursive calculation of the estimation is given by Eqn. 5.

$$WMEWMA^{\tau} = \alpha \times WMEWMA^{\tau-1} + (1-\alpha)\times PRR^{\tau} \quad (5)$$

WMEWMA has two control parameters, which are the window size w in calculating PRR and the history control coefficient $0 \leq \alpha \leq 1$. A higher value of coefficient α leads to a filter that passes lower frequency fluctuations on PRR, which means a more stable estimate. Setting $\alpha = 0$ converts WMEWMA to the base PRR estimate. In [15], it is claimed that this metric performs best overall because it provides the most stable estimate and is simple to calculate. However, the slow reaction of the estimator to link dynamics is a weakness of the estimator.

Link Likelihood Factor (LLF) is also a PRR-based LQE method, which is proposed in [6], specifically for estimating the quality of wireless links in WBANs. This metric tries to represent the likelihood for the link to be connected at any given time. The main point is to differentiate incidental link status from long-term behavior of the link taking the history of the link into account. Eqn. 6 gives the recursive calculation of LLF estimation. The only control parameter of the estimator is the window size w for calculating PRR on which the LLF estimate is built.

$$LLF^{\tau} = \begin{cases} LLF^{\tau-1} + (1 - LLF^{\tau-1}) \times PRR^{\tau} & Link^{\tau} = 1 \\ LLF^{\tau-1} \times PRR^{\tau} & Link^{\tau} = 0 \end{cases} \tag{6}$$

If the receiver successfully received the last transmitted packet ($Link^{\tau} = 1$), the metric is increased towards 1 with a rate determined by the history of this link (PRR) and the deviation of the previous value of the metric from its maximum value (i.e., one). Notice that if the link has shown a good connection in the recent history of length w, LLF will converge to one very fast. On the other hand, if the link has a poor PRR, the last successful reception is considered as a likely temporary connection and so LLF increases with a lower rate. In the second case, in which the last packet is lost ($Link^{\tau} = 0$), the metric is decreased, again with a rate proportional to the history of the link (PRR). If PRR is high, the last link failure is supposed to be an intermittent disconnection and the metric decreases with a low rate. The main idea behind this is that if the link has shown a good record, incidental disconnections do not decrease the metric too much and vice versa. Based on this, the LLF estimator is expected to respond fast to real dynamics of the link quality and tolerate intermittent link states. However, experiments show that for medium quality links, this estimator suffers from frequent fluctuations.

Smoothed Link Likelihood Factor (SLLF) is proposed in this paper to alleviate the stability problem of the LLF method. Experimental evaluations show that LLF is very agile in detecting connection changes in WBANs, but it suffers from frequent fluctuations. We use an EWMA filter to smooth the LLF estimate, similar to the filter which is used to smooth the PRR in the WMEWMA estimator. This filter is able to improve the stability of LLF at the cost of low degradation of the speed of detections. Eqn. 7 shows the calculation for SLLF.

$$SLLF^{\tau} = \alpha \times SLLF^{\tau-1} + (1 - \alpha) \times LLF^{\tau} \tag{7}$$

where $0 \leq \alpha \leq 1$ is the history control coefficient. Actually, this technique is expected to trade off the high agility of LLF for acquiring more stable estimations.

3.3 Disconnection Detection using LQE

To find out if node s_i is disconnected from the gateway, a threshold ℓ_i is considered for the estimated quality of the link from s_i to the gateway. This threshold is given individually for each node based on particular DDR requirements and sampling rate of that node. In [2], we presented a method for determining this threshold based on the DDR requirement $\mathcal{RC}(s_i)$, the transmission and sampling rate of node s_i

Note that for disconnection detection using any LQE method, hysteresis is introduced to prevent too frequent switches when the value of the LQE is around the threshold. A link moves from a connected to disconnected state when the LQE drops below the given threshold $\ell_i - \Delta\ell$. Accordingly, for moving to connected state from disconnected state, the quality factor should go higher than $\ell_i + \Delta\ell$.

4. EXPERIMENTS

Comparison of some LQE methods are previously presented in [15], [9], and [12]. Authors in [15] use a stochastic link data generation for static WSNs. In [9], wireless link models [16] available in the TOSSIM simulator [17] are used to generate link behavior data for static WSNs. Considering high node mobility and frequent topology changes in WBANs due to body movements and postural changes, simulation radio models fail to mimic near-realistic link behavior in these mobile networks. Although in [12] real experiments were performed to evaluate LQE techniques, it is done for static WSNs. The behavior of wireless links in WBANs substantially deviates from their behavior in static WSNs. This makes performing experiments for measuring the links in WBANs very important. Moreover, we aim to compare the described LQE techniques specifically for detecting disconnection from the gateway in WBANs.

We performed extensive experiments to record the behavior of wireless links from all nodes to the gateway node ($Link^{\tau}$) in a real WBAN. Then different LQE techniques are applied on the links' status records to check the performance of the estimators.

4.1 Setup and Performed Experiments

We deployed 16 *MyriaNed* [18] wireless nodes on various positions of a body. Fig. 2(a) depicts the node placement in the experiments. *MyriaNed* uses the *Nordic* nRF24L01 radio chip [11] as transceiver. This works in the 2.4GHz ISM band, which is one of the proposed carrier frequency bands in IEEE 802.15.6 for WBANs. The data rate is 2Mbps and packets have a fixed size of 32 bytes. Four transmit power levels (-18, -12, -6, 0dBm) are available for the radio. This allows us to test the links in various link conditions.

A TDMA-based mechanism is exploited for communication of the BSNs. Each node is given an exclusive time slot for packet transmission. Therefore, links behavior is not influenced by collisions. The TDMA frame length is set to $100ms$. Thus every node periodically transmits 10 packets per second. All body nodes including the gateway listen to all slots and record packet receptions from all other nodes at each TDMA round in their 4MByte flash memory. This way full traces of all links between all pairs of nodes are logged. All experiments were done in an indoor environment.

Body posture is a determining factor in the quality of the radio links in WBANs. We consider 6 postures in our experiments, namely *running*, *walking*, *standing*, *sitting on a chair*, *sitting on the ground*, and *lying down*. As the posture transitions are very important to evaluate the reaction of LQE methods upon link dynamics, we have all possible transitions between different postures during each experiment (Fig. 2(b)). Therefore, we performed a posture pattern of 36 postures having all possible combinations in which each posture was repeated 6 times. The duration of each posture is 2 minutes. Thus each experiment lasts 72 minutes. We performed four different experiments with four available transmit power levels. During one experiment, all nodes use a uniform transmit power level. In total, we gather link behavior of 15 BSNs to the gateway in 288 minutes of experiments with packet transmission period of $100ms$.

4.2 Metrics for LQE Characterization

To investigate the characteristics of LQE methods in detecting connection changes, we first need to have a *reference connection state* for each node. We use the future link states to calculate the packet reception rate of the link at each packet transmission round. At any round τ, we compute the packet reception ratio in a window of size $\mathcal{H} = 50$

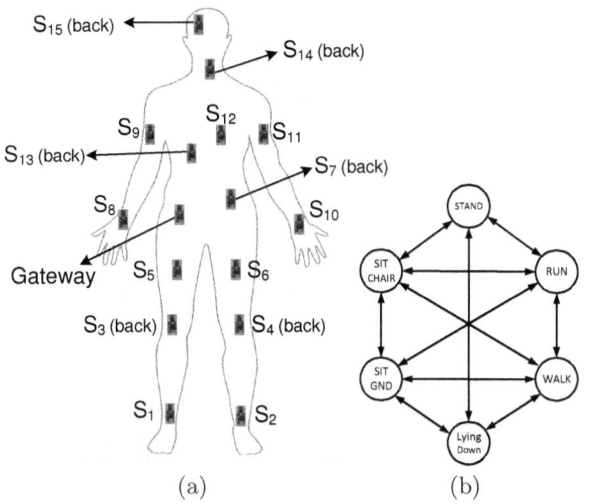

Figure 2: a) The position of 16 MyriaNed nodes on the body for the experiments. Nodes $s_{3,4,7,13,14,15}$ are deployed on the back side of the body. b) The postures of the person wearing the WBAN during the experiments. All possible posture transitions are performed in each experiment.

around τ. The calculated reception rate is then compared to a threshold ℓ to determine the reference connection state of the link at round τ. Fig. 3 illustrates the calculated PRR using future link states and the reference connection state using $\ell = 0.3$ and $\ell = 0.7$ for a time period of one of our experiments. This connection detection is then compared with the connection state produced by using the LQE techniques under investigation (described in Sec. 3). Note that the LQE methods do not have access to future information online during network operation. For each experiment, we run the analysis for 7 different values of the threshold (i.e., $\ell = 0.2$, 0.3, 0.4, 0.5, 0.6, 0.7, and 0.8), applying a margin $\Delta\ell = 0.1$ for hysteresis. High threshold values indicate that the data losses are hardly tolerable and the links are tagged as disconnected with low number of packet losses. Lower values of threshold allow higher rate of packet losses before the link is tagged as disconnected. Accordingly, the link is reconnected with showing lower rate of successful receptions. By applying various threshold values, we evaluate the LQE metrics with various application requirements. The same values of the threshold and its hysteresis margin ($\Delta\ell = 0.1$) are used in detecting connection status using each LQE method. In presenting the results, we show the average of the results over all experiments with different transmit power levels and various values of the threshold ℓ.

We investigate *agility*, *stability*, and *reliability*, as three metrics for characterizing the behavior of different LQE techniques. Agility aims to show how fast an estimator detects a connection change, once it happens. To measure it we compute the delay (in terms of rounds) from occurring a change in the reference connection status and the detection using the particular LQE method.

Stability shows the fluctuations in announcing a link as connected or disconnected. It actually aims to reveal the ability of the estimator in ignoring short-term link quality variations, which are very common in WBANs. To measure this metric, we count the average number of switches of (dis)connection detection using each LQE method. When comparing different LQE techniques, higher number of changes is a sign of less stability of the method, as all methods are applied on the same data set. This metric is in

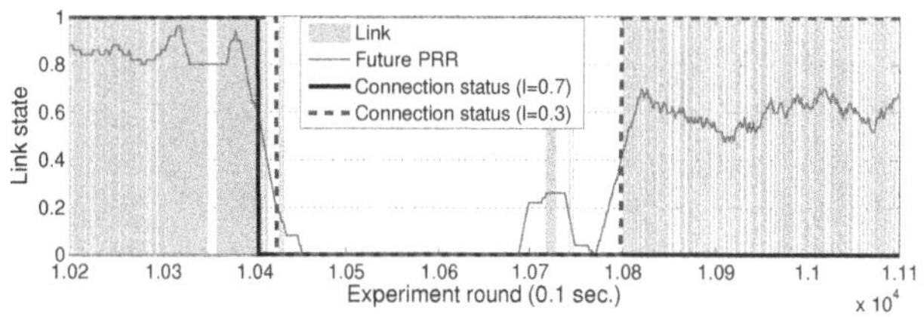

Figure 3: Reference connection status of the link from node s_1 to the gateway for a certain time period using two threshold values of $\ell = 0.3$ and $\ell = 0.7$.

conflict with the agility of the estimator and we target to explore the trade-off that each LQE method is able to make between agility and stability.

The reliability of the method measures the ratio of changes in the reference connection status that is detected by an LQE metric. If an estimation is overestimating or underestimating the quality of the links, it may fail in detecting a change in connection status. Moreover, a high delay in detection for slow estimators may lead to failure in detecting short duration disconnections or connections.

5. ANALYSIS OF LQE CHARACTERISTICS

In this section, we first investigate the impact of the configuration parameters of the estimators on their performance and go through some detailed behavior of the metrics for a certain period of time. Then we show the trade-offs made by each estimator to compare them and investigate the best fitting estimators for WBANs from various points of view.

5.1 Configuration of the LQE Methods

To show the response of the estimators to variations of the link quality, we zoom into the status of the link from node s_1 to the gateway over a short period of time (between rounds 10200 and 11100) in an experiment with the lowest transmit power level. In this time period shown in Fig. 3, there are some changes in the connection status of the link. Note that the reference connection status depends on the used threshold value (ℓ) for disconnection and reconnection detection. Using $\ell = 0.3$, for instance, the link goes from connected to disconnected state around round 10400 and vice versa at round 10800, whereas the link is not considered reconnected around round 10800 when using $\ell = 0.7$. There are also transient receptions and intermittent link failures in this time period, which are useful to observe the reaction of the estimators to these phenomena. Fig. 4 shows the link status ($Link^{\tau}$) at all rounds together with the estimated link quality. For each estimator, several settings are applied to depict its behavior with different parameter configurations.

Fig. 4(a) shows the PRR of the link for five different values of averaging window length. As expected, increasing the window length w increases the delay in detecting connection changes. TWMA (Fig. 4(b)) has smoother curves with faster reaction compared to PRR with the same window length.

EWMA (Fig. 4(c)) reacts very fast to any change in the link connection status. The estimated link quality in this figure is not properly visible because of many fluctuations. When the value of parameter α is closer to one, the estimator reacts faster, but it is more fluctuating. Note that parameter α in EWMA has an opposite effect of the same parameter in other estimators (WMEWMA and SLLF). In EWMA, α is the coefficient for the new value of $Link^{\tau}$. Therefore, increasing it puts higher weight on the state of the link in the last round and puts lower weight on the previous estimate.

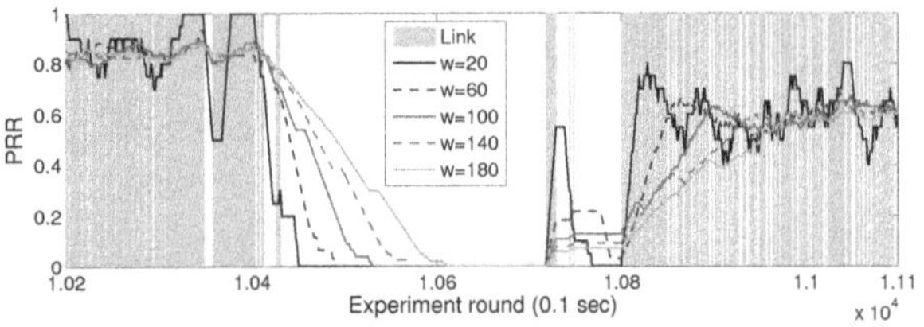

(a) PRR using different lengths of averaging window.

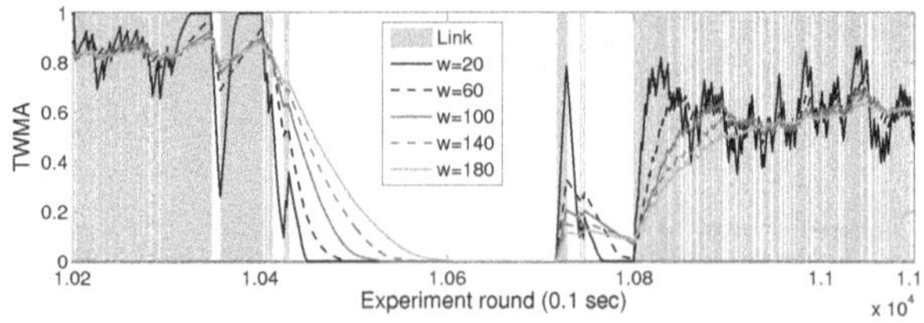

(b) TWMA using different lengths of averaging window.

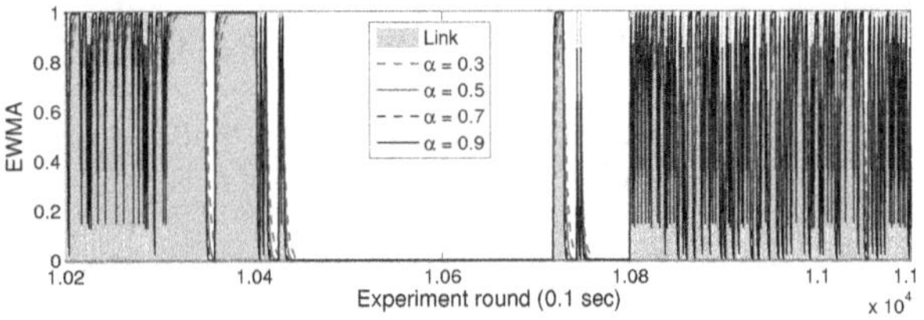

(c) EWMA using various values of last round control coefficient (α).

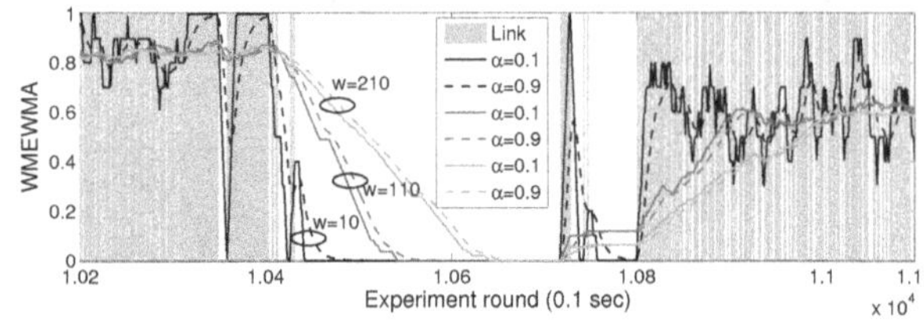

(d) WMEWMA using different values of w and history control coefficient α.

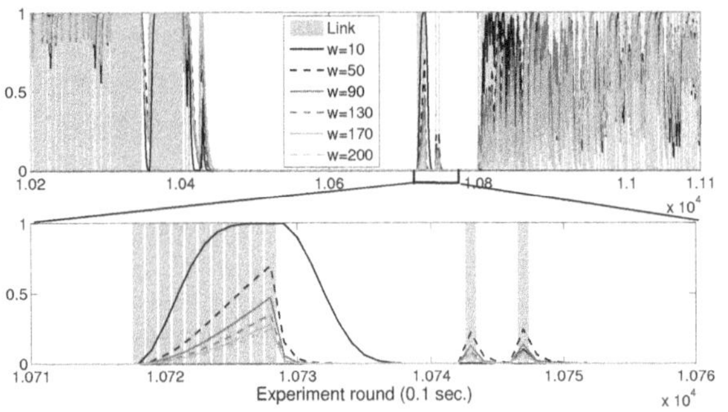

(e) LLF using different values of averaging window length (w). The lower graph zooms into a short period of time from the upper graph.

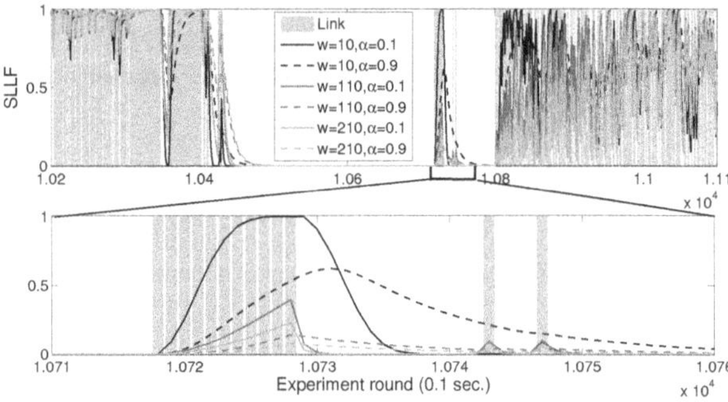

(f) SLLF using various values of w and α. The lower graph zooms into a short period of time from the upper graph.

Figure 4: The quality of the link from node s_1 to the gateway for a certain time period estimated by various settings of different LQE techniques.

Fig. 4(d) shows the value of the WMEWMA estimator using some values of window length and history control coefficient. Results of using two values of $\alpha = 0.1$ and $\alpha = 0.9$ are shown as two (near-)extreme behaviors for each window length. One observation here is that the parameter w has a major impact on the delay and stability of this estimator. For each value of w, having a bigger α smoothes the curve more, which leads to slightly more stable estimation at the cost of slower reaction. Decreasing the value of α makes the performance of the WMEWMA estimator more similar to that of PRR.

The relation between the behavior of the LLF method and the averaging window size is more complicated than that of other estimators. When w is lower, a link is considered faster as a good or bad link according to the PRR value with the given window size. The lower graph in Fig. 4(e) zooms into a time period (between rounds 10710 and 10760) with short-term receptions. Around round 10720 in this graph, some successful receptions are observed, the curve for $w = 10$ goes up earlier than others as the PRR quickly gets higher values. After this short period of successful receptions, it goes down later than others as the PRR with $w = 10$ has become one in this short period. For the LLF with $w = 90$, for instance, the link is not considered good any time during this period since the PRR value is low after this time period. Therefore, with observing the link failures starting from round 10730, the estimate goes down quickly (multiplication with a low PRR value in Eqn. 6).

SLLF in Fig. 4(f) smoothes LLF, which results in a slightly slower reactions, but less fluctuations. Transient receptions do not make a visible change on the value of SLLF, especially for higher values of α. Thus SLLF is better able to avoid transient link states than the base LLF estimator. The SLLF curve with $w = 110$ and $\alpha = 0.9$ in Fig. 4(f) makes a good balance in reasonably fast reacting to real changes in link quality and bypassing intermittent link behaviors. Such transient behavior is very common for wireless links in typical WBANs.

Fig. 5 depicts the relation between the average performance of different LQE methods in detecting link connection changes and the configuration parameters of these techniques. Lower delay and lower number of changes are considered better as they show more agile and stable estimators, respectively. Higher detection ratio is better as it reveals more reliable detection. Fig. 5(a) shows the dependencies on the value of α in the estimators that have this parameter. Among all, the performance of EWMA substantially varies with changing the value of α. Values of α close to one make the metric very unstable. Considering the high link fluctuations in WBANs, the results strongly recommend to avoid using values above $\alpha = 0.5$ for EWMA. Overall, EWMA shows the most agile estimator with the lowest sta-

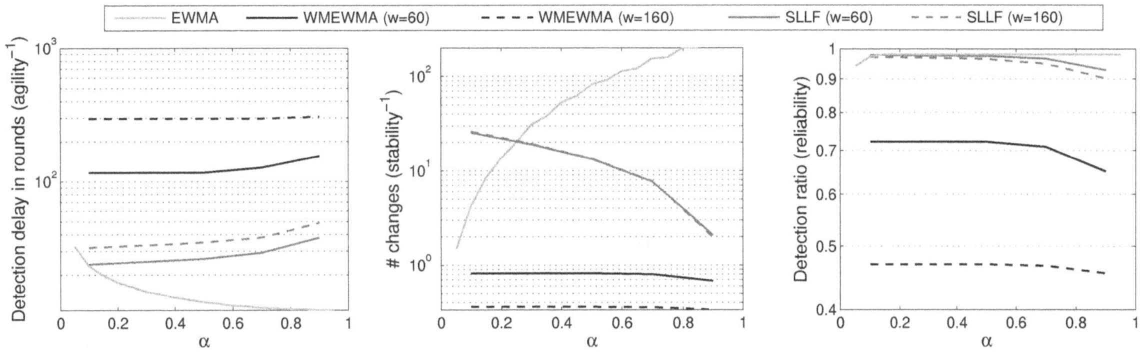

(a) The effect of the history control coefficient (α) on agility, stability, and reliability of LQE methods. *The vertical axis is logarithmic.*

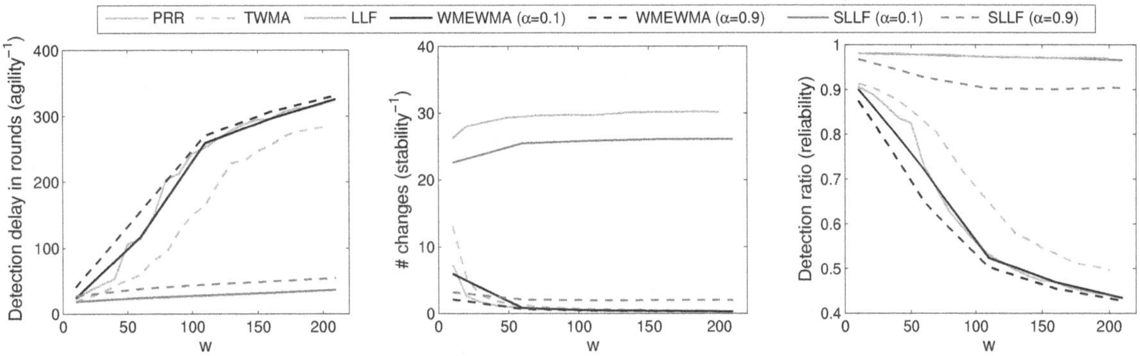

(b) The effect of averaging window length (w) on agility, stability, and reliability of LQE methods.

Figure 5: The effect of configuration parameters on the performance of different LQE techniques.

bility among all investigated metrics. Another observation is that both the WMEWMA and SLLF estimators perform better for high values of α. According to the results shown in Fig. 5(a), increasing the value of α improves the stability of the WMEWMA and SLLF estimators at the cost of a limited worsening of the delay. Thus increasing the value of α up to a value around 0.9 improves the overall performance of these metrics.

Fig. 5(b) shows the effect of the averaging window size w. For the LQE techniques having parameter w (all methods except EWMA), the agility decreases when increasing the window size. Among all, the agility of LLF-based estimators depends least on the window size. WMEWMA with $\alpha = 0.9$ shows to be overall the least agile estimator. The stability of the estimators shows in general a weaker dependency on the value of w, comparing to agility. Increasing the window size considerably decreases the detection ratio (reliability) except for the metrics that are based on LLF. The reason is the high reactivity of these techniques to link dynamics. One important observation in Fig. 5(b) is the behavior of the SLLF method with $\alpha = 0.9$. It has a good agility, high stability, and a detection ratio close to that of LLF (the most reliable one in Fig. 5(b)). In particular, setting the window size around 100 for this estimator seems to be a proper choice to balance different performance metrics.

5.2 Concluding LQE Characteristics

Fig. 6 show the achieved performance of different estimators and their configurations to show the trade-offs made by each estimator and to help in making decisions about using an LQE method. Note that almost all metrics make trade-offs in terms of different performance metrics, in particular, in terms of agility and stability. In the following, we sort the estimators according to the overall achieved results and detailed observations in our experiments for disconnection and reconnection detection in WBANs.

Agility: The EWMA method is found to be the most agile estimator that can exactly follow any link quality variation. Setting α very close to one makes the estimation equal to the link state at each round. The following ordered list presents all investigated LQE metrics from most agile to least agile, based on the results presented in Fig. 6(a). The slowest estimator in detecting connection changes is WMEWMA.

$$\textit{Agility: } \{EWMA,\ LLF,\ SLLF,\ TWMA,\ PRR,\ WMEWMA\} \quad (8)$$

Stability: Again EWMA and WMEWMA are on both extremes for stability. WMEWMA shows to be the most stable estimator. This result conforms with the conclusions made in [15] and [9], although their evaluation of stability is based on the coefficient of variations of the estimate (the ratio of the standard deviation to the mean). EWMA is overall the most fluctuating estimator. The following list shows the investigated estimators from best stable to worst stable estimator.

$$\textit{Stability: } \{WMEWMA,\ PRR,\ SLLF,\ TWMA,\ LLF,\ EWMA\} \quad (9)$$

Reliability: The reliability of the estimators in detecting the connection changes conforms to the agility of the estimator. EWMA (with $\alpha = 0.5$) can detect 98% of the connection changes. The ratio is around 97% and 95% for LLF and SLLF (with $\alpha = 0.9$), respectively. PRR, TWMA, and WMEWMA show a low detection ratio (sometimes even

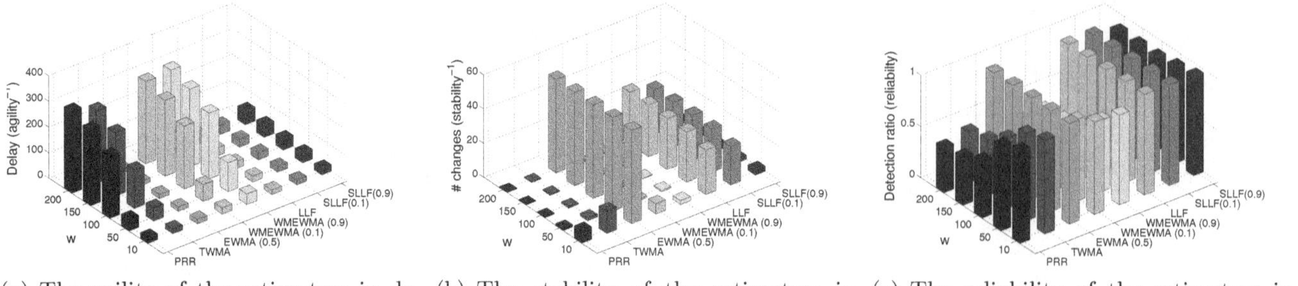

(a) The agility of the estimators in detecting connection changes. A lower delay value shows a more agile estimator.

(b) The stability of the estimators in detecting connection changes. A lower number of fluctuations is a sign of a more stable estimator.

(c) The reliability of the estimators in detecting connection changes. Higher detection ratio means more reliable detection.

Figure 6: Comparing the trade-offs made by different LQE methods for disconnection detection in the performed experiments for WBANs.

less than 50%). To have a good detection ratio using these methods, we need to decrease the window size, which leads to very slow estimation.

6. IMPACT ON WBAN PERFORMANCE

So far in this paper, we investigated the characteristics (agility and stability) of the receiver-side LQE techniques using real WBAN link traces. In this section, the relation between the characteristics of the LQE techniques and the QoS of a WBAN application is investigated. We first present a qualitative discussion of the impact of the estimators' characteristics on the performance of a WBAN such as data delivery behavior and energy consumption. Then we use various estimators in an adaptive WBAN protocol as a case study, and investigate their impact on the achieved network performance. Finally, some guidelines for decision making about the most appropriate estimator based on the requirements of a WBAN application are provided.

6.1 Qualitative Discussion

Suppose that the quality of the link from a body node, say s_i, to the gateway is very good, with sporadic intermittent failures. Due to a posture change, for instance, this link may go to a low quality state. A more agile estimator detects such a transition faster and hence, the network protocol adapts itself earlier to avoid data losses from the node s_i. Agile estimators such as EWMA, LLF, and SLLF perform the best and provide the least data losses during such transitions. It takes some time for a slow estimator like WMEWMA to detect these transitions. Also in a reverse transition (from a poor link quality to a very good state), more agile estimators cause less unnecessary usage of network resources (e.g., energy). Therefore, more agile estimators perform better for detecting the transitions between extreme link quality states from perspectives of both data delivery performance and energy consumption. Among the three aforementioned most agile estimators, LLF and SLLF are also able to ignore intermittent link behavior, while EWMA may unnecessarily react to such transient changes. Failure in ignoring intermittent link states leads to both data losses and energy wastage.

When a link is in a medium quality state, we may face frequent interchanging link successes and failures. Such link states are common in WBANs especially for the nodes that are deployed on mobile parts of the human body such as legs and hands. Empirical measurements in [5] show periodic variations of the quality of the link between a node on a hand and the gateway installed on the belly while walking. The period of such changes from good to bad quality and vice versa is measured as 1.2 second, which matches the duration of the walking steps. Depending on the frequency of such periodic quality changes and also the frequency of link measurements, we may decide to track the changes by using an agile estimator or to have a stable average estimation by using a stable LQE method. The time that a network adaptation takes to be accomplished and become effective is an important factor. The period of link quality changes should be much higher than the adaptation time; otherwise, it does not make sense to trigger an adaptation. Using a stable estimator like WMEWMA or PRR can provide an overall sense of link quality and avoids too many network adaptations, while an unstable estimator such as EWMA and LLF for the links with frequent quality changes triggers frequent network adaptations without giving the network enough time to perform adaptations. Tracking frequent quality changes using an unstable estimator also leads to data losses in many cases. When the estimator tags the link as connected with observing few link successes, the network stops supporting that node. Soon after that, because of fluctuating link quality, several failures may happen resulting in data losses.

This qualitative analysis reveals that it may be the best to use different LQE techniques for different links in the WBAN, based on the behavior of the links. To provide an overall best performance trade-off, a certain level of agility and stability is necessary for an estimator. This inspires that an estimator such as SLLF, which balances between agility and stability, makes the best compromise. This way, this estimator can make a fast detection of the transitions between extreme link quality states ignoring intermittent link behaviors, and also a stable estimation for the links with high quality fluctuations.

6.2 Case Study

In [2], we developed an adaptive on-demand listening and data forwarding (ODLF) mechanism for WBANs. All nodes use a star architecture to directly send their data packets to the gateway. At the same time, the gateway estimates the quality of all its incoming links. Using this LQE and taking the sampling specification and DDR requirements of individual nodes into account, the gateway checks if some nodes are disconnected. Then the gateway requests the body nodes to listen to the disconnected nodes and forward their data. Thus an adaptive multi-hop data forwarding is established when it is necessary. We simulate the ODLF mechanism using various receiver-side LQE methods using the link traces

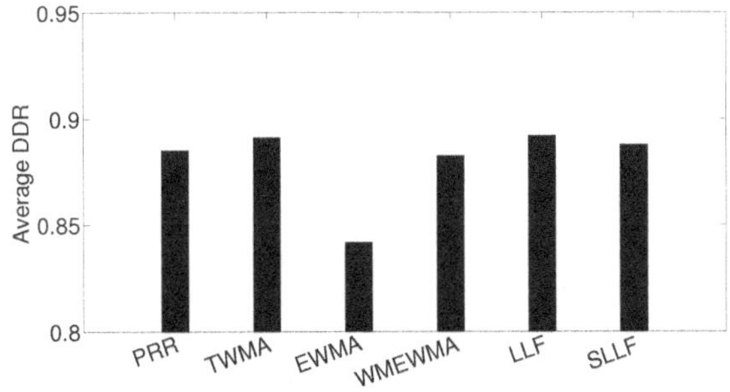

(a) Average data delivery ratio over nodes with low quality links to the gateway.

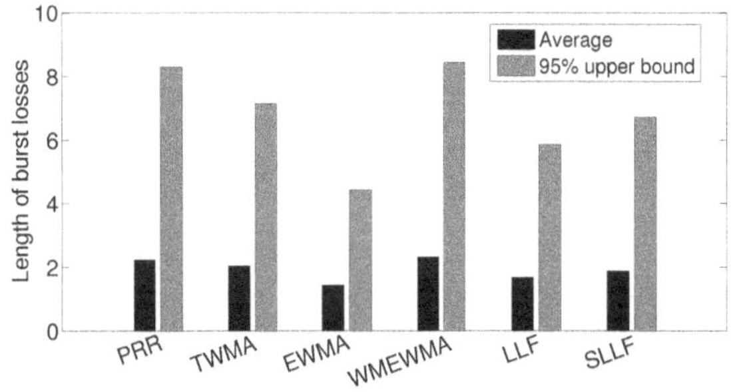

(b) Average length of burst data losses and the upper bound of the length of 95% of burst data losses.

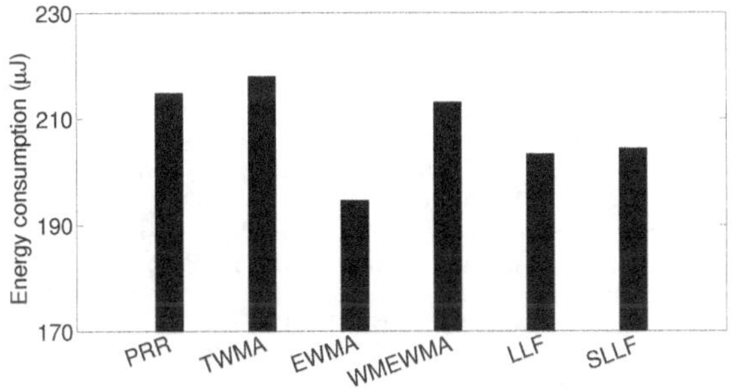

(c) Radio energy consumption of nodes per TDMA frame (100 ms).

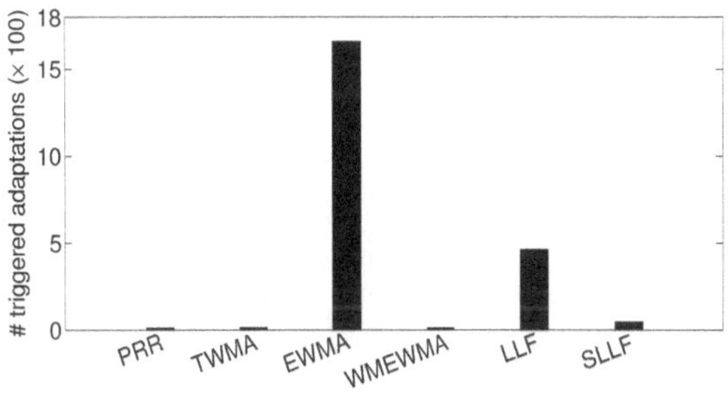

(d) Average number of triggered adaptations in the WBAN protocol using different estimators.

Figure 7: Achieved quality-of-services in the WBAN experiments that run the adaptive ODLF [2] protocol, using different LQE techniques for detecting disconnection from the gateway.

of the experimental setup of Fig. 2. Because we are using real logged link traces of the experiments, the behavior of the ODLF mechanism is the same to that of running ODLF on wireless body nodes.

Fig. 7 presents the achieved performance results of the ODLF mechanism in the WBAN experiments, when using different LQE techniques for (dis)connection detection. Fig. 7(a) shows the average DDR over nodes s_2, s_3, s_4, s_{10}, s_{11}, s_{13}, and s_{14}. These nodes have shown to have poor wireless links to the gateway in the experiments. By using different LQE techniques, the achieved DDR values vary. EWMA led to the worst DDR. As discussed in the previous subsection, this is expected because the EWMA estimation fluctuates frequently, especially when the link quality is highly dynamic. Considering overall DDR performance, LLF performed the best in this case study.

The distribution of data losses over time is also an important aspect of data delivery performance. Loss of several subsequently generated data samples may lead to a failure of the WBAN application even if the overall DDR lies in the acceptable range. To evaluate this, we calculate the length of burst data losses (the number of subsequent losses of data samples) during the experiments. Fig. 7(b) shows the average length of burst data losses, on average over the aforementioned nodes. We also show the upper bound of this length when considering 95% of the occurrences of data losses. WMEWMA shows the worst performance in this sense. Considering the low agility of this estimator, this result is expected. Because of very fast reactions, EWMA is able to avoid long burst data losses. The LLF and SLLF estimators are the next estimators in the row for providing the best performance in this aspect.

Nodes running the ODLF mechanism consume energy for listening to the disconnected nodes from the gateway. When the network connectivity is poor and more nodes are detected as disconnected, average energy consumption increases due to the need for more on-demand listening and data forwarding. Fig. 7(c) shows the average energy consumption of body nodes per TDMA frame using the ODLF mechanism, which differs when using different LQE techniques. EWMA causes less energy consumption compared to the other estimators. The reason is that with observing a very few link successes, EWMA quickly tags the link as connected and hence, other nodes stop listening to that node. However, in many cases, it leads to degradation of data delivery performance, as it is shown in Fig. 7(a) that this estimator provides the least overall DDR among the examined LQE techniques. LLF and SLLF are the next estimators that cause less energy consumption.

As the last performance observation, we count the number of triggered network adaptations in the ODLF by different LQE techniques. Each adaptation may be costly for the protocol. Behaviors of different estimators substantially differ from each other in this aspect. EWMA, the most agile estimator, triggered a very high number of adaptations. This number is also quite high for LLF compared to the other estimators. This limits the applicability of the unstable estimators for many WBAN applications and protocols, when the network adaptation is time- or energy-costly. In this case study (ODLF mechanism), the overhead of network adaptation is low. Otherwise, very fluctuating metrics such as EWMA would have been less convincing.

Considering all performance metrics, SLLF provides good DDR and energy consumption close to those of LLF, but with much fewer triggered adaptations. This is because of the balance that SLLF is able to make between agility and stability.

6.3 Guidelines for Decision Making

In Sec. 5, we observed the conflicts between different LQE techniques in terms of agility and stability. This leads to a trade-off between different network performance metrics, as some were explored in the previous subsection. Because of that, it is not straight-forward to suggest an estimator as the best choice for all WBAN applications. Network specifications and application demands should be then taken into account to select the most appropriate estimator.

In a WBAN scenario for which the stability of disconnection and reconnection detection is the only objective, WMEWMA with $\alpha \approx 0.9$ is the most appropriate LQE technique. When the protocol adaptation after a disconnection or reconnection has a very high overhead, this approach may help to have as little as possible adaptations. However, this estimator provides such stability at the cost of very slow detection with a high chance of missing the connection changes. On the other extreme, if the WBAN scenario needs to deal with every connection change very fast, the EWMA estimator with $\alpha \approx 0.4$ can be the best solution. However, the overhead of the protocol adaptation should be very low. Otherwise, a very high number of announced connection changes by this estimator causes a high overhead.

The above two scenarios are extreme cases. In other WBAN scenarios, we need to make an appropriate trade-off between different performance metrics. Thus a reasonably fast, stable, and reliable detection of the connection changes is preferred. In those scenarios, SLLF is the best fitting estimator for detecting connection changes. A configuration of SLLF with $w \approx 100 - 150$ (10-15 seconds) and $\alpha \approx 0.9$ provides the best performance. On the one hand, the agility of SLLF is very close to that of EWMA and LLF, and substantially deviates from the low detection speed of PRR and WMEWMA. On the other hand, SLLF is very stable, very close to the stability of WMEWMA. These mean that SLLF is able to make the best trade-off between the different performance metrics.

7. CONCLUSIONS

This paper investigates using Link Quality Estimation (LQE) techniques for detecting connection changes in Wireless Body Area Networks (WBANs). A node is connected to the gateway node in the WBAN, when it can properly reach the gateway to satisfy the data delivery requirements. Otherwise, the link is said to be disconnected. Detecting connection changes is of great importance to adapt the network protocol and node configurations during the network operation. The paper reviews the existing receiver-side LQE techniques and proposes a new method called Smoothed Link Likelihood Factor (SLLF). A set of experiments using 16 nodes deployed on different positions of the body are performed to log the behavior of the wireless links to the gateway node. Different estimators are applied on the logged data and their characteristics (agility, stability, and reliability) in detecting connection changes are investigated. Then the relation between different characteristics of the estimators and the WBAN performance is explored. The estimators have been used in an adaptive WBAN protocol as a case study and their impact on the performance of the network is studied.

Based on the detailed analysis of the results, the trade-off between the three mentioned criteria made by each estimator is explored and the best and worst estimators from the point of view of different characterizing metrics are discussed. No estimator is able to perform the best in terms of all performance metrics or in all WBAN applications. However, the SLLF method is able to balance different aspects and provides the best trade-off between the different performance metrics for many WBAN scenarios.

8. REFERENCES

[1] N. Baccour et al, "Radio link quality estimation in wireless sensor networks: a survey," *ACM Trans. Sen. Netw. (TOSN)*, vol. 8, no. 4, 2012.

[2] M. Nabi, M. Geilen, and T. Basten, "On-demand data forwarding for automatic adaptation of data propagation in WBANs," in *Proc. IEEE Communications Society Conf. on Sensor, Mesh and Ad Hoc Communications and Networks (SECON)*. IEEE, 2012, pp. 250–258.

[3] C. Otto et al, "System architecture of a wireless body area sensor network for ubiquitous health monitoring," in *Journal of Mobile Multimedia*, vol. 1. Rinton Press, 2006, pp. 307–326.

[4] A. Marinkovic et al, "Energy-efficient low duty cycle MAC protocol for wireless body area networks," *IEEE Transactions on Information Technology in Biomedicine (TITB)*, vol. 13, no. 6, pp. 915–925, 2009.

[5] K. Shashi Prabh and J.-H. Hauer, "Opportunistic packet scheduling in body area networks," in *Proc. of the 8th European Conf. on Wireless Sensor Networks (EWSN)*. Springer-Verlag, 2011, pp. 114–129.

[6] M. Quwaider and S. Biswas, "Probabilistic routing in on-body sensor networks with postural disconnections," in *Proc. 7th ACM MobiWAC*. ACM, 2009, pp. 149–158.

[7] M. Nabi et al, "A robust protocol stack for multi-hop wireless body area networks with transmit power adaptation," in *Proc. 5th Int'l Conf. on Body Area Networks (BodyNets)*. ICST, 2010.

[8] D. Smith, L. Hanlen, and D. Miniutti, "Transmit power control for wireless body area networks using novel channel prediction," in *Proc. Wireless Communications and Networking Conference (WCNC)*. IEEE, 2012, pp. 684–688.

[9] N. Baccour et al, "A comparative simulation study of link quality estimators in wireless sensor networks," in *Proc. IEEE Symposium on Modeling, Analysis and Simulation of Computer and Telecommunication Systems (MASCOTS)*. IEEE, 2009, pp. 1–10.

[10] R. Fonseca et al, "Four bit wireless link estimation," in *Proc. Sixth Workshop on Hot Topics in Networks (HotNets VI)*, 2007.

[11] "NORDIC Semiconductor. nRF24L01 data sheet, 2007."

[12] A. Cerpa et al, "Temporal properties of low power wireless links: modeling and implications on multi-hop routing," in *Proc. ACM symposium on Mobile ad hoc networking and computing (MobiHoc)*. ACM, 2005.

[13] D. Lal et al, "Measurement and characterization of link quality metrics in energy constrained wireless sensor networks," in *Proc. IEEE Global Telecommunications Conference (GLOBECOM)*. IEEE, 2003.

[14] D. Couto, D. Aguayo, J. Bicket, and R. Morris, "A highthroughput path metric for multi-hop wireless routing," in *Proc. 9th Int'l Conf. on Mobile computing and networking (MobiCom)*. ACM, 2003.

[15] A. Woo and D. Culler, "Evaluation of efficient link reliability estimators for low-power wireless networks," EECS Department, University of California, Berkeley, Tech. Rep. UCB/CSD-03-1270, 2003. [Online]. Available: http://www.eecs.berkeley.edu/Pubs/TechRpts/2003/6239.html

[16] H. Lee, A. Cerpa, and P. Levis, "Improving wireless simulation through noise modeling," in *Proc. Int'l Conf. on Embedded networked sensor systems (SenSys)*. ACM, 2007.

[17] P. Levis et al, "TOSSIM: accurate and scalable simulation of entire tinyos applications," in *Proc. Int'l Conf. on Embedded networked sensor systems (SenSys)*. ACM, 2003.

[18] F. van der Wateren, "The art of developing WSN applications with MyriaNed," Chess Company, the Netherlands, Tech. report, 2008.

Equilibrium Sensing Time for Distributed Opportunistic Access in Cognitive Radio Networks

Sofia Bouferda
RITM-ESTC
ENSEM-GREENTIC
Hassan II University
Casablanca, Morocco
sofiabouferda@gmail.com

Essaid Sabir
ENSEM-GREENTIC
Hassan II University
Casablanca, Morocco
e.sabir@ensem.ac.ma

Aawatif Hayar
ENSEM-GREENTIC
Hassan II University
Casablanca, Morocco
a.hayar@greentic.uh2c.ma

Mounir Rifi
RITM-ESTC-GREENTIC
Hassan II University
Casablanca, Morocco
rifi@email.com

ABSTRACT

In this paper, we consider a distributed opportunistic access (D-OSA), in which cognitive radio (CR) users attempt to access a channel licensed to a primary network. In this context, we formulate the problem of designing the equilibrium sensing time in a distributed manner, in order to maximize the throughput of CR users while guarantying a good protection to the primary users (PU). Next, we study the Nash equilibrium of the system, we also propose a combined learning algorithm for continuous actions that is fully distributed, and allows to the CR users to learn their equilibrium payoffs and their equilibrium sensing time. The simulation results show that the system can learn the sensing time and converge to a unique Nash equilibrium, which come to prove the theoretical study. A surprising feature is that there exists a correlation between the transmit probability and the sensing time. More precisely, lower transmit probability induces lower sensing times.

Categories and Subject Descriptors

C.2.1 [**Network Architecture and Design**]: Distributed networks; C.2.1 [**Network Architecture and Design**]: Wireless communication; C.2.5 [**Local and Wide-Area Networks**]: Access schemes; G.3 [**Probability and Statistics**]: Probabilistic algorithms (including Monte Carlo)

Keywords

Distributed Spectrum sensing, Nash equilibrium, combined fully distributed learning

MSWiM'13, November 3–8, 2013, Barcelona, Spain.
Copyright 2013 ACM 978-1-4503-2353-6/13/11 ...$15.00.
http://dx.doi.org/10.1145/2507924.2507944

1. INTRODUCTION

1.1 Our daily life and new trends

The great development of communication has created huge demand of radio spectrum, which has become a scarce resource. Nevertheless, it has been found that the major licensed bands are underutilized and some of the remaining bands are heavily used [7]. This is in a part due to the actual resource allocation strategies, which allocate a fixed frequency band to a single licensed system.
Cognitive radio is a promising solution to this radio spectrum wastage, it allows the simultaneous access to the same spectrum band by PU and secondary users (SU), by using spatial, temporal and frequency spectrum holes left by idles PU [12].

Spectrum sensing has been identified as a key enabling cognitive radio to not interfere with PU, by reliability detecting PU signals. It motivates the concept of opportunistic spectrum access (OSA), which allows secondary cognitive radio (CR) systems to opportunistically exploit the under-utilized spectrum. A basic component of OSA is a sensing strategy at the MAC layer for spectrum opportunity tracking. Due to hardware limitations, energy constraints, a secondary user may not be able to sense all channels in the spectrum simultaneously, and due to throughput constraints Secondary users can not sense channels for a long time, in general the longer the sensing time, the less time available for the CR user to transmit data during the rest of the time frame. In this case a sensing strategy for intelligent channel selection and sensing time optimisation is necessary.
The presence of high priority PU and the requirement that the cognitive users should not interfere with them define a medium access paradigm called cognitive medium access. Cognitive medium access control is relevant to both the cognitive radio and the coexistence community. Cognitive medium access control protocols play an important role to exploit the spectrum opportunities, manage the interference to primary users, and coordinate the spectrum access amongst secondary users [10],[13], [14].

1.2 Literature review

Cognitive medium access control game formulations have been studied in[8, 1, 11] using different approaches. Cognitive medium access control coupled with state estimation and detection for identifying and exploiting instantaneous spectrum opportunities is one of the central challenges. In addition, the opportunistic spectrum access needs to take into consideration energy constraints of sensing, exploration, exploitation and transmission. Then the question is how to develop cognitive sensing and access strategies that learn from observations and offer improved fairness and performance over time [1], [11] without central controllers or dedicated communication/control channels. In[19] the authors examined evolutionary game theoretic perspective of the classical medium access control. Cognitive considerations are not discussed.[14] proposed memory management for distributed spectrum sharing under limited spectrum sensing.

In [8] the authors examine cognitive medium access and the relation to competitive multi-armed bandit problem. The arm bandit problem is well understood for single CR, which wishes to opportunistically exploit the availability of resources in the spectrum. For multiple users however the outcomes are not clear. This difficulty is in particular due to the interactive behavior of the underlying processes of decision making in dynamic environment. The authors proposed a Bayesian approach to identify a trade-off metric between exploring the availability of other free channels/time slots and exploiting the opportunities identified. In[11], a game theoretic learning and pricing have been proposed. In the above references, stochastic formulations of the medium access problem are examined. These formulations often lead to intractable configurations. Authors in [16], proposed a new two-step game where sensing and opportunistic access are jointly considered. A full characterization of the Nash equilibria and analysis of the optimal pricing policy, from the network owner view, for both centralized setting and decentralized setting, are also provided. Next, a combined learning algorithm that is fully distributed and allows the cognitive users to learn their optimal payoffs and their optimal strategies in both symmetric and asymmetric cases is proposed.

1.3 Our contribution

In this paper, we propose to associate game theory to learning strategies in cognitive medium access, to find the equilibrium sensing time. To the best of our knowledge, this is the first paper devoted to analyze distributed sensing. Meanwhile, the related literature usually considers the sensing time from an optimization perspective ([2, 5, 9]). In contrast to the classical literature of medium access games, which does not focus on the random nature of cognitive radios, we propose a fully distributed strategic learning to learn the equilibrium payoff and the associated equilibrium strategies. Moreover, we provide many insightful results to understand the possible relationship between sensing time and transmit probability. Next, we analyze the impact of starting point and speed of learning on convergence to Nash equilibrium.

1.4 Organization of the paper

This paper will be organized as follows: In section II, the system model, the main notations and spectrum sensing preliminaries are presented. In section III, we describe the utility function of the game and equilibrium analysis, in section IV, we propose a distributed learning algorithm, Performance evaluation and results analysis are provided in section V.

2. SYSTEM MODEL AND MAIN NOTATIONS

2.1 System model

We consider a secondary network that coexists with a primary network where each PU is licensed to transmit whenever he/she wishes for most of time except for the case when the channel is occupied by another PU. The duration of a primary frame is denoted T. We consider that we have N SU trying to access the spectrum of the PU. Throughout this work the following consideration are taken into account:

- Energy-based spectrum sensing: the primary network activity is determined by measuring the signal strength traveling over the channel. If the received signal power exceeds some given threshold, the channel is declared busy, it is declared idle in the other case.
- Imperfect sensing in the sense that SUs may declare a busy channel while it is idle (false alarm).
- Random access for data transmission of CRs. Here, we consider that SUs follow a slotted aloha-like protocol to transmit data.

During primary users activities, each SU i receives some given signal. SU i samples the received signal at sampling frequency f_s without loss of generality, we assume that all SUs use the same sampling frequency. The discrete received signal at the SU i can be represented as:

$$Y_i = \begin{cases} h_i.S(t) + n(t) & : \text{Hypothesis } H_1 \text{ (Busy)} \\ n(t) & : \text{Hypothesis } H_0 \text{ (Idle)} \end{cases} \tag{1}$$

Where $S(t)$ is the transmitted signal, h_i is the channel gain experienced by SU i and n(t) is an circular symmetric complex Gaussian noise with mean 0 and variance $E[|n(t)^2|] = \sigma$. The channel state is considered as the binary hypothesis test H_0 and H_1.

2.2 Energy based spectrum sensing

Spectrum sensing is often considered as a detection problem. Many techniques were developed in order to detect the holes in the spectrum band. Focusing on each narrow band, existing spectrum sensing techniques are widely categorized into energy detection [20] and feature detection [3]. Although this is not a restriction of our work, we will use energy detection throughout the paper. τ_i being the sensing time and N the number of considered samples. Thus, we have $N = [\tau f_s]$.it follows that the average energy detected by SU i is:

$$T_i(Y) = \frac{1}{N} \sum_{1}^{N} |Y_i(t)|^2 \tag{2}$$

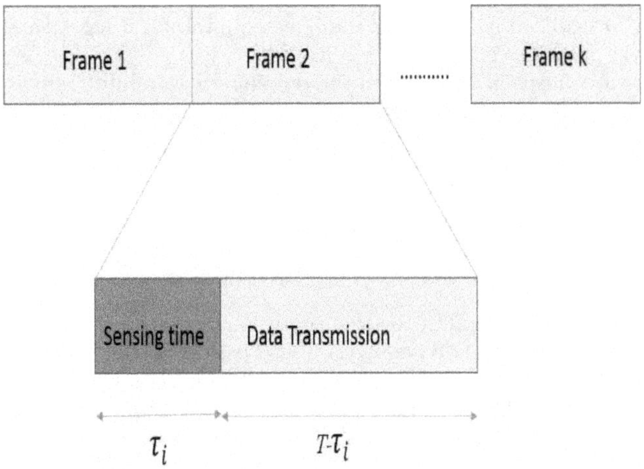

Figure 1: Frame structure of the cognitive radio network.

2.3 Imperfect sensing

We consider throughout this work a scenario where the spectrum sensor has imperfect detection performance. In other terms, each SU i has a false alarm probability P_{fi}, i.e., the probability that the channel is sensed to be busy while it is actually idle.

$$P_{fi}(\epsilon, \tau_i) = Pr(T_i(Y) > \epsilon \backslash H_0) \tag{3}$$

Where ϵ denotes the threshold which specifies the collision tolerance bound of PUs.
We assume that the primary signal is i.i.d complex Phase shift keying modulated, with zero mean. We also assume that the primary signal and noise are independent. Using energy detection, the false alarm probability $P_{fi}(\epsilon, \tau_i)$ can be estimated by the following:

$$P_{fi}(\epsilon, \tau_i) = \frac{1}{2} erfc\left(\left(\frac{\epsilon}{\sigma^2} - 1\right)\sqrt{\tau_i f_s}\right) \tag{4}$$

Where the complementary error function is given by:

$$erfc(x) = \frac{2}{\sqrt{\pi}} \int_x^{\infty} e^{\frac{-t^2}{2}} dt \tag{5}$$

Each SU i senses the channel for a duration τ_i Fig.1. This duration affects directly the false alarm probability $P_{fi}(\epsilon, \tau_i)$ that the tagged SU i will experience. This relationship could be stated as: long sensing time leads to a more accurate sensing operation (equivalently low false probability) but generates short transmission opportunity and high competition. Thus, the experienced throughput would be affected drastically by the outcome of the sensing operation. The issue is then how to find a good trade-off between sensing and received throughput.
In [9], it is shown that there exists an optimal sensing time that maximizes the throughput of CR users. Similar result can be found in [5]. In both papers, authors consider the case of centralized control, in this work unlike the papers mentioned above we consider equilibrium sensing time in a distributed framework.

3. EQUILIBRIUM ANALYSIS

In absence of primary network activity (i.e., under hypothesis H_0), the average Throughput of SU i is given by:

$$U_i(\tau_i) = \frac{T - \tau_i}{\tau_i}(1 - P_{fi}(\epsilon, \tau_i)) P_i \prod_{j \neq i}(1 - P_j(1 - P_{fj}(\epsilon, \tau_j))) \tag{6}$$

Where:
T is the time slot duration, τ_i is the sensing time for user i and P_i is the probability of access to the channel for user i.

In the proposed game G each SU chooses an appropriate sensing time to maximize its utility function, which is equivalent to its throughput. In this context, it is important to ensure the stability of the system. A concept which relates to this issue is the Nash equilibrium. As definition in [15], a pure strategy profile $\{\tau_j^*\}_{j \neq i}, j \in \{1, ..M\}$ is a Nash equilibrium of the proposed game if, for every player i (i.e. SU i):

$$U_i(\tau_i^*, \tau_{-i}^*) \geq U_i(\tau_i, \tau_{-i}^*) \forall i \in \{1, ..M\} \tag{7}$$

A Nash equilibrium can be regarded as a stable solution, at which none of the users has the incentive to change its sensing time τ_i.

3.1 Existence of Nash equilibrium

PROPOSITION 1. *Game G admits at least one Nash equilibrium.*

PROOF. The conditions for the existence of Nash equilibrium in a strategic game are given in [4]:

1. The set τ_i is a nonempty, convex, and compact subset of some Euclidean space for all i.
2. The utility function $U_i(\tau_i; \tau_- i)$ is continuous on τ and quasi-concave on τ_i.

On one hand and according to the above description of the strategy space, it is straightforward to see that it is nonempty, convex and compact. On the other hand, the utility function U_i is a continuous and quasi-concave function. Hence, game G admits at least one Nash equilibrium.

$$\begin{aligned} U_i(\tau_i, \tau_j) &= \\ &\frac{T - \tau_i}{\tau_i}(1 - P_{fi}(\epsilon, \tau_i)) P_i \prod_{j \neq i}(1 - P_j(1 - P_{fj}(\epsilon, \tau_j))) \\ &= \frac{T - \tau_i}{T}\left(1 - \frac{1}{2} erfc\left((\frac{\epsilon}{\sigma^2} - 1)\sqrt{\tau_i f_s}\right) P_i \right. \\ &\prod_{j \neq i}\left(1 - P_j\left(1 - \frac{1}{2} erfc\left((\frac{\epsilon}{\sigma^2} - 1)\sqrt{\tau_i f_s}\right)\right)\right) \end{aligned} \tag{8}$$

G being the primitive of $e^{-\frac{t^2}{2}}$,

$$erfc(x) = \frac{2}{\sqrt{\pi}}(G(+\infty) - G(x))$$

$$\Rightarrow erfc'(x) = \frac{-2}{\sqrt{\pi}} G'(x) = \frac{-2}{\sqrt{\pi}} e^{-\frac{x^2}{2}} \tag{9}$$

For simplicity of the derivation we can put:

$$A = \frac{\epsilon}{\sigma^2} - 1. \quad (10)$$

$erfc\left(\frac{\epsilon}{\sigma^2} - 1\right)$ is then written as follows:

$$erfc(A\sqrt{\tau_i f_s}) \quad (11)$$

From (9) we can deduce the first derivative of (11) :

$$erfc'(A\sqrt{\tau_i f_s}) = \frac{Af_s}{2\sqrt{\tau_i f_s}}\frac{-2}{\sqrt{\pi}}e^{\frac{-2\tau_i f_s}{2}} = -A\sqrt{\frac{f_s}{\tau_i \pi}}e^{\frac{-A^2\tau_i f_s}{2}} \quad (12)$$

$$\frac{\partial(U_i(\tau_i,\tau_j))}{\partial\tau_i} = K\left(\frac{-1}{T}\left(1 - erfc(A\sqrt{\tau_i f_s})\right) + \frac{T-\tau_i}{T}\frac{1}{2}A\sqrt{\frac{f_s}{\tau_i\pi}}e^{\frac{-A^2\tau_i f_s}{2}}\right) \quad (13)$$

Where:

$$K = P_i\prod_{j\neq i}\left(1 - P_j\left(1 - \frac{1}{2}erfc\left(\left(\frac{\epsilon}{\sigma^2} - 1\right)\sqrt{\tau_i f_s}\right)\right)\right) \quad (14)$$

To simplify the second derivative we put:

$$G(\tau) = \frac{T-\tau}{T}\frac{1}{2}A\sqrt{\frac{f_s}{\tau\pi}}e^{\frac{-A^2\tau f_s}{2}} \quad (15)$$

$$\frac{\partial G}{\partial\tau} = \frac{-A}{2T}\sqrt{\frac{f_s}{\tau\pi}}e^{\frac{-A^2\tau f_s}{2}} + A\frac{T-\tau}{2T}e^{\frac{-A^2\tau f_s}{2}}\frac{-f_s}{\pi\tau^2}\frac{1}{2\sqrt{\frac{f_s}{\tau\pi}}} + A\frac{T-\tau}{2T}\sqrt{\frac{f_s}{\tau\pi}}\frac{-A^2 f_s}{2}e^{\frac{-A^2\tau f_s}{2}}$$

$$= \frac{-A}{2T}\sqrt{\frac{f_s}{\tau\pi}}e^{\frac{-A^2\tau f_s}{2}}\left(1 + \frac{T-\tau}{2\tau} + \frac{T-\tau}{2}A^2 f_s\right) \quad (16)$$

Thus, the second derivative of U can be written as follows:

$$U''(\tau_i,\tau_j) = K\left(G'(\tau_i) - \frac{-A}{2T}\sqrt{\frac{f_s}{\tau\pi}}e^{\frac{-A^2\tau_i f_s}{2}}\right)$$

$$= \frac{-KA}{2T}\sqrt{\frac{f_s}{\tau\pi}}e^{\frac{-A^2\tau_i f_s}{2}}\left(2 + \frac{T-\tau_i}{2}\left(A^2 f_s + \frac{1}{\tau_i}\right)\right) \quad (17)$$

- It's obvious that K is a positive term.
- If $P_{fi}(\epsilon,\tau_i) = \frac{1}{2}erfc\left(A)\sqrt{\tau_i f_s}\right) \leq 0.5$.
  Then: erfc$\left(A\sqrt{\tau_i f_s}\right) \leq 1$ and A$\sqrt{\tau_i f_s} \geq 0$. Thus A is positive.
- The other terms of (17)are all positives

Thus the second derivative is negative and the function is quasi-concave. □

3.2 Uniqueness of the Nash equilibrium

We turn now to examine the uniqueness of Nash equilibrium of the sensing-time game.

PROPOSITION 2. *The sensing-time game G admits a unique Nash equilibrium.*

PROOF. The game has a unique equilibrium if it satisfies the Rosen's conditions cited in [17].
If a concave game satisfies the dominance solvability conditions [17] given by:

$$-\frac{\partial^2 U_i}{\partial^2\tau_i} - \sum_{j\neq i}\left|\frac{\partial^2 U_i}{\partial\tau_i\partial\tau_j}\right| \geq 0 \quad (18)$$

Then it also satisfies Rosen's conditions.
For simplicity of the analysis we derive the utility function for 2 users, and check the sign of (23) using Maple software and found that is a positive term, thus the utility function satisfies the Dominance Solvability conditions and admits one Nash equilibrium. Simulation results eventually comes to prove this result.

$$\frac{\partial(U_i(\tau_i,\tau_j))}{\partial\tau_i} = -\frac{\left(1 - \frac{1}{2}\,erfc\left(A\sqrt{\tau_i f_s}\right)\right)P_i\left(1 - P_j\left(1 - \frac{1}{2}\,erfc\left(A\sqrt{\tau_j f_s}\right)\right)\right)}{T} + \frac{1}{2}\frac{(T-\tau_i)\,e^{-A^2\tau_i f_s}Af_sP_i\left(1 - P_j\left(1 - \frac{1}{2}\,erfc\left(A\sqrt{\tau_j f_s}\right)\right)\right)}{\sqrt{\pi}\sqrt{\tau_i f_s}T} \quad (19)$$

$$\frac{\partial^2(U_i)}{\partial^2\tau_i} = -\frac{e^{-A^2\tau_i f_s}Af_sP_i\left(1 - P_j\left(1 - \frac{1}{2}\,erfc\left(A\sqrt{\tau_j f_s}\right)\right)\right)}{\sqrt{\pi}\sqrt{\tau_i f_s}T} - \frac{1}{2}\frac{(T-\tau_i)\,A^3{f_s}^2e^{-A^2\tau_i f_s}P_i\left(1 - P_j\left(1 - \frac{1}{2}\,erfc\left(A\sqrt{\tau_j f_s}\right)\right)\right)}{\sqrt{\pi}\sqrt{\tau_i f_s}T} - \frac{1}{4}\frac{(T-\tau_i)\,e^{-A^2\tau_i f_s}A{f_s}^2P_i\left(1 - P_j\left(1 - \frac{1}{2}\,erfc\left(A\sqrt{\tau_j f_s}\right)\right)\right)}{\sqrt{\pi}\,(\tau_i f_s)^{\frac{3}{2}}\,T} \quad (20)$$

$$\frac{\partial(U_i(\tau_i,\tau_j))}{\partial\tau_j} = -\frac{1}{2}\frac{(T-\tau_i)\left(1 - \frac{1}{2}\,erfc\left(A\sqrt{\tau_i f_s}\right)\right)P_iP_je^{-A^2\tau_j f_s}Af_s}{\sqrt{\pi}\sqrt{\tau_i f_s}T} \quad (21)$$

$$\frac{\partial^2(U_i)}{\partial\tau_i\partial\tau_j} = \frac{1}{2}\frac{\left(1 - \frac{1}{2}\,erfc\left(A\sqrt{\tau_i f_s}\right)\right)P_iP_je^{-A^2\tau_j f_s}Af_s}{\sqrt{\pi}\sqrt{\tau_j f_s}T} - \frac{1}{4}\frac{(T-\tau_i)\,e^{-A^2\tau_i f_s}A^2{f_s}^2P_iP_je^{-A^2\tau_j f_s}}{\pi\sqrt{\tau_i f_s}\sqrt{\tau_j f_s}T} \quad (22)$$

From (22) and (20) we can write:

$$
\begin{aligned}
& -\frac{\partial^2 U_i}{\partial^2 \tau_i} - \sum_{j \neq i} \left| \frac{\partial^2 U_i}{\partial \tau_i \partial \tau_j} \right| = \\
& \frac{\mathrm{e}^{-A^2 \tau_i f_s} A f_s P_i \left(1 - P_i \left(1 - \frac{1}{2}\, erfc\left(A\sqrt{\tau_j f_s}\right)\right)\right)}{\sqrt{\pi}\sqrt{\tau_i f_s} T} \\
& + \frac{1}{2} \frac{(T - \tau_i) A^3 {f_s}^2 \mathrm{e}^{-A^2 \tau_i f_s} P_i \left(1 - P_j \left(1 - \frac{1}{2}\, erfc\left(A\sqrt{\tau_j f_s}\right)\right)\right)}{\sqrt{\pi}\sqrt{\tau_i f_s} T} \\
& + \frac{1}{4} \frac{(T - \tau_i) \mathrm{e}^{-A^2 \tau_i f_s} A {f_s}^2 P_i \left(1 - P_j \left(1 - \frac{1}{2}\, erfc\left(A\sqrt{\tau_j f_s}\right)\right)\right)}{\sqrt{\pi} (\tau_i f_s)^{\frac{3}{2}} T} + \\
& \left| -\frac{1}{2} \frac{\left(1 - \frac{1}{2}\, erfc\left(A\sqrt{\tau_i f_s}\right)\right) P_i P_j \mathrm{e}^{-A^2 \tau_j f_s} A f_s}{\sqrt{\pi}\sqrt{\tau_j f_s} T} \right. \\
& \left. + \frac{1}{4} \frac{(T - \tau_i) \mathrm{e}^{-A^2 \tau_i f_s} A^2 {f_s}^2 P_i P_j \mathrm{e}^{-A^2 \tau_j f_s}}{\pi \sqrt{\tau_i f_s} \sqrt{\tau_j f_s} T} \right| \quad (23)
\end{aligned}
$$

□

4. DISTRIBUTED LEARNING ALGORITHM

In this section, we introduce an adaptive scheme to learn equilibria in the proposed Game. Learning is important in cognitive medium access control because the above payoff can be noisy due measurement, feedback errors or acknowledgment errors. Learning will help us to understand the behavior of the users during the interactions. In the proposed game the sensing time represent a continuous action, a convenient class of learning scheme of our game is the class of COmbined fully DIstributed Payoff and Strategy learning (CODIPAS) for continuous actions[18]. In the CODIPAS scheme each player seeks to learn her payoff functions as well as the associated equilibrium strategies.CODIPAS scheme, is well-adapted to cognitive radio networks for multiple reasons:

- CODIPAS is designed for random environment;
- It is only based on numerical measurements and include noisy observation, measurement error and outdated measurements. In particular, no specific knowledge of the utility function is required;
- The player does not need to know the others actions or their respective payoffs. It only need to observe the realization of its utility during previous iterations.

$\tau_{i,k}$ is the sensing time for user i at time k, $\tau^*_{i,k}$ is an intermediary variable. a_i, Ω_i and ϕ_i represent the amplitude, frequency and phase of the sinus perturbation signal respectively[6]. $\mathrm{U}_{i,k+1}$represents the reward or the utility of user i at time $k+1$.

At each time instant k, each transmitter updates its sensing time $\tau_{i,k}$, by adding the sinus perturbation to the intermediary variable $\tau^*_{i,k}$ using equation (24), and makes the transmission using τ_i, k. Then, each transmitter gets a realization of the reward $\mathrm{U}_{i,k+1}$ from its corresponding receiver at time $k+1$ which is used to compute $\tau^*_{i,k+1}$ using equation (24).

The sensing time $\tau_{i,k+1}$ is then updated using equation (25). This procedure is repeated for the whole transmission window T. The algorithm is in discrete time and is given by:

$$
\tau^*_{i,k+1} = \tau^*_{i,k} + \lambda_k l_i a_i sin(\Omega_i k^* + \phi_i) U_{i,k} \quad (24)
$$

$$
\tau_{i,k+1} = \tau^*_{i,k+1} + a_i sin(\Omega_i k^* + \phi_i) \quad (25)
$$

Where $k^* := \sum_{k'=1}^{k} \lambda_k . \forall i$ should be selected to be small.For example $\lambda_k = \frac{1}{k+1}$. $\phi_i \in [0, 2\pi] \forall i, k \in \mathbb{Z}$

Algorithm 1 CODIPAS for Continuous Sensing Time

I. Initialization :
Each secondary user i
1. initializes $\tau^*_{i,0}$
2. transmits

II. Learning pattern :
Each secondary user
1. Observes the realization $U_{i,k}$
2. Estimates $\tau^*_{i,k+1}$ according to Equation (24)
3. Updates $\tau_{i,k+1}$ using Equation (25).

5. SIMULATION RESULTS

In order to validate the theoretical ideas discussed above, simulation results are presented in this section,the primary signal is considered to be i.i.d complex shift keying modulated with bandwidth 6Mhz.

The parameters of simulations are set to be : T=100ms, $f_s = 6Mhz$, $P_{fi}(\epsilon, \tau_i) \leq 0.5$, $\Omega_i = 0.9$, $\phi_i = 0$, $a_i = 0.9$. The numerical setting could be tuned in order to make the convergence slower or faster. Each simulation setup is rum several times in order to smooth up the results and to eliminate the random behaviour effect during learning phase.

Fig.2 shows that the SUs converge to an equilibrium sensing time, the sensing time is not the same for all users because SU does not have the same probability of access to the channel. The simulations are repeated several times and the convergence is always to a unique point for a given set of parameters which assist our finding that the equilibrium is unique. A surprising feature is the observed correlation between transmit probability and sensing time. Explicitly, we notice that the lowest is the probability of access, the lowest is the sensing time. This could be explained as follows. In order to respect licensed user (primary user) in terms of false alarm and detection probability, secondary users finetune their couple (transmit probability, sensing time). As a SU transmit with low probability, then even if it senses the channel for a brief period, this would not have a penalizing impact on PU activity. However, as a tagged SU becomes more aggressive (transmit at high probability), it needs to sense the channel during a longer period, so as it can catch the right PU's activity.

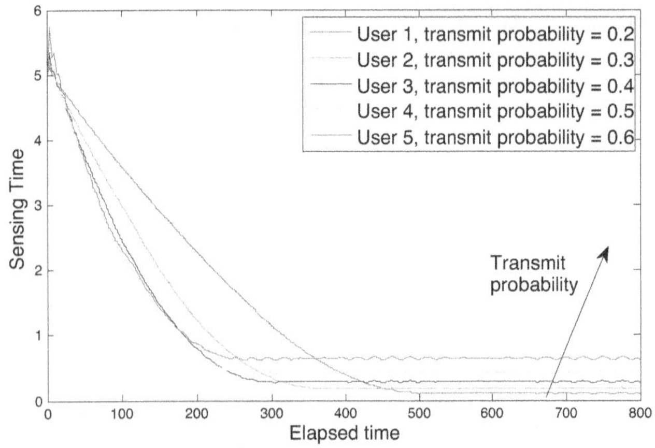

Figure 2: Convergence and sensing time evolution for 5 users under $\lambda_k = \left(\frac{1}{k+1}\right)^{0.2}$.

Fig.3 illustrates the convergence when the starting points are changed, we started here from different smaller points compared to Fig.2, we notice that the users converge quickly to their equilibrium sensing time depending on their starting points, the more the starting points are small, the more the users converge quickly to their equilibrium sensing time. The users converge to the same equilibrium in Fig.2 and Fig.3 even if the starting points are changed.

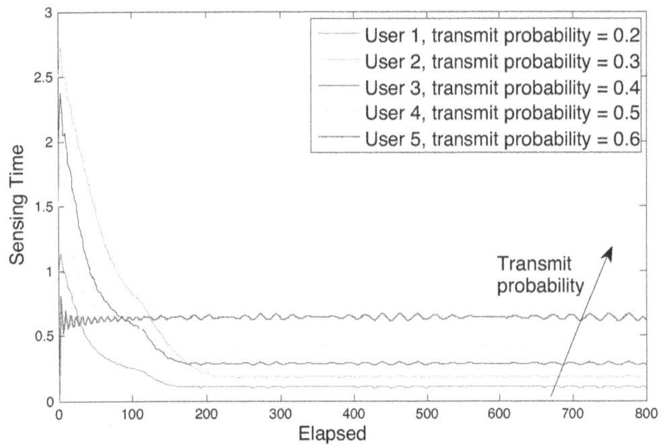

Figure 3: Impact of the starting point on the convergence speed for 5 users under $\lambda_k = \left(\frac{1}{k+1}\right)^{0.2}$.

Fig.4 is a logarithmic representation for Fig.3 to highlight the start of the convergence that we can not see clearly in Fig.3. The users are starting from different points compared to Fig.2 and they converge to the same equilibrium sensing times. The uniqueness of the equilibrium sensing time is well illustrated in the case of user 5, we have seen in Fig.2 that the user 5 converge to the higher equilibrium sensing time because of its higher probability of access, in Fig.4 we can see that even if it starts from 0 ms it converges to the higher sensing time, which comes to prove the uniqueness of the equilibrium.

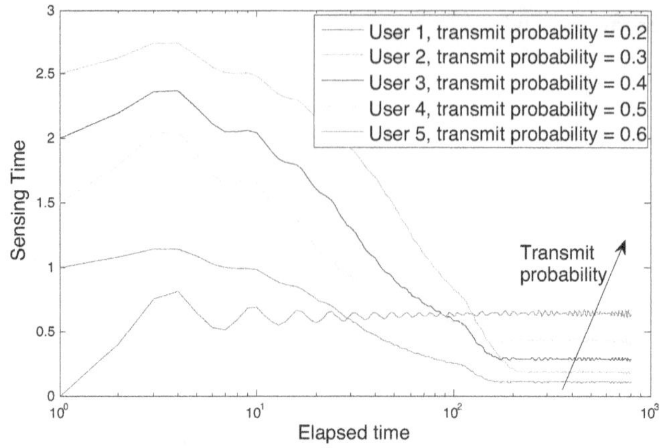

Figure 4: Convergence in a logarithmic scale for 5 users under $\lambda_k = \left(\frac{1}{k+1}\right)^{0.2}$.

Next, we depict in Fig.5 the learning evolution for a speed of convergence $\lambda\left(\frac{1}{k+1}\right)^{0.5}$. By comparing Fig.5 with Fig.2, where λ is set to a lower value $\left(\frac{1}{k+1}\right)^{0.2}$, we can see that the convergence is faster as λ increases. As expected the more the step is small, the more the convergence is slow, but the less fluctuations are strong. Thus, we need to define a trade-off between accuracy of convergence and speed of convergence.

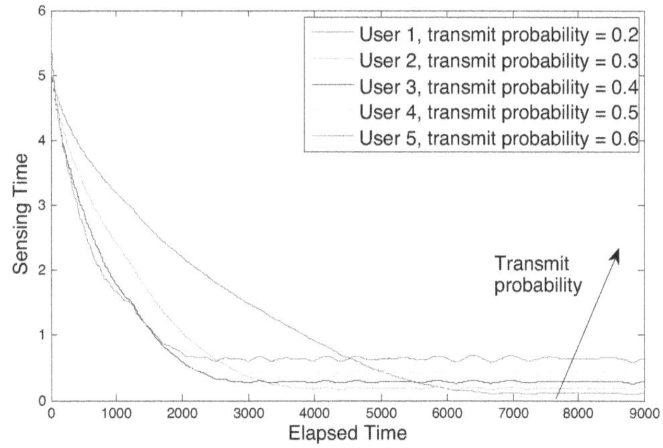

Figure 5: Convergence and sensing time evolution for 5 users under $\lambda_k = \left(\frac{1}{k+1}\right)^{0.5}$.

6. CONCLUSIONS

In this paper, we proposed a distributed method for designing the sensing time in cognitive radio networks. We analyzed the sensing interaction among secondary users as a non-cooperative game. Then, we studied the equilibrium of this sensing time game and proved that there exist a unique equilibrium for the proposed game. Furthermore, we proposed a learning algorithm that is fully distributed and allows the cognitive users to learn jointly their payoffs and sensing time without use of any centralized controller. A special feature is that lower transmit probability induces lower sensing times.

As an extension to this paper we are in process to develop a comparison in terms of sensing time and throughput between the proposed solution and a centralized one, by the mean of price of anarchy. Moreover we are working towards proving theoretically convergence of CODIPAS for Continuous Sensing Time.

7. REFERENCES

[1] ANANDKUMAR, A., MICHAEL, N., TANG, A. K., AND SWAMI, A. Distributed algorithms for learning and cognitive medium access with logarithmic regret. *IEEE JSAC on Advances in Cognitive Radio Networking and Communications 29*, 4 (April 2011), 781–745.

[2] CARDENAS-JUAREZ, M., AND GHOGHO, M. Spectrum sensing and throughput trade-off in cognitive radio under outage constraints over nakagami fading. *IEEE Communication letters, 15(10), 2011 15* (June 2011).

[3] DANDAWAT, A., AND GIANNAKIS, G. B. Statistical tests for presence of cyclostationarity. *IEEE Trans. Signal Processing 42*, 9 (1994), 2355–2369.

[4] FUDENBERG, D., AND TIROLE, J. Game theory. *Cambridge, MIT Press* (1991).

[5] GHASEMI, A., AND SOUSA, E. Optimization of spectrum sensing for opportunistic spectrum access in cognitive radio networks. In *in Proc of 4th IEEE Consumer Communications and Networking Conference (CCNC), Las Vegas, USA* (Jan 2007).

[6] HANIF, A. F., TEMBINE, H., ASSAAD, M., AND ZEGHLACHE, D. Distributed stochastic learning for continuous power control in wireless networks. *Signal Processing Advances in Wireless Communications (SPAWC), 2012 IEEE 13th International Workshop* (June 2012).

[7] HAYKIN, S. Cognitive radio: brain-empowered wireless communications. *IEEE J. Sel. Areas in Commune. 23* (Feb 2004), 201–220.

[8] LAI, L., GAMAL, H. E., JIANG, H., AND POOR, H. V. Cognitive medium access: Exploration, exploitation and competition. *IEEE Transactions on Mobile Computing 10*, 2 (Feb 2011), 239–253.

[9] LIANG, Y. C., ZENG, Y. H., PEH, E., AND HOANG, A. T. Sensing-throughput tradeoff for cognitive radio networks. *IEEE Transactions on Wireless Communications 7*, 4 (April 2008), 1326–1337.

[10] LIU, K. J. R., AND WANG, B. Cognitive radio networking and security: A game theoretical view. *Cambridge University Press* (2010).

[11] MASKERY, M., KRISHNAMURTHY, V., AND ZHAO, Q. Game theoretic learning and pricing for dynamic spectrum access in cognitive radio. *in Cognitive Wireless Comm. Networks. Springer* (2007).

[12] MITOLA, J. Cognitive radio: An integrated agent architecture for software defined radio. *Doctor of Technology, Royal Inst. Technol. (KTH), Stockholm, Sweden* (2000).

[13] NIYATO, D., HOSSAIN, E., AND HAN, Z. Dynamics of multiple-seller and multiple buyer spectrum trading in cognitive radio networks: A game theoretic modeling approach. *IEEE Transactions on Mobile Computing 8*, 8 (august 2009), 1009–1022.

[14] PARK, J., AND VAN DER SCHAAR, M. Cognitive mac protocols using memory for distributed spectrum sharing under limited spectrum sensing. *IEEE Transactions on Communications 59*, 9 (2011), 2627–2637.

[15] ROSENTHAL, R. W. A class of games possessing pure-strategy nash equilibria. *International Journal of Game Theory 2* (1973), 65–67.

[16] SABIR, E., TEMBINE, H., AND HADDAD, M. Joint strategic spectrum sensing and opportunistic access for cognitive radio networks. In *IEEE GLOBECOM* (December 2012).

[17] SHI, P. Summary of what's known about convergence in concave games.

[18] TEMBINE, H. *Distributed Strategic Learning for Wireless Engineers.* CRC Press/ Taylor Francis, ISBN: 9781439876442, May 2012.

[19] TEMBINE, H., ALTMAN, E., ELAZOUZI, R., AND HAYEL, Y. Evolutionary games in wireless networks. *IEEE Transactions on Systems, Man, and Cybernetics,Part B: Cybernetics 40*, 3 (2010), 634–646.

[20] URKOWITZ, H. Energy detection of unknown deterministic signals. In *Proceeding of the IEEE* (April 1967), vol. 54, pp. 523–531.

Understanding the Benefits of Open Access in Femtocell Networks: Stochastic Geometric Analysis in the Uplink

Wei Bao and Ben Liang
Department of Electrical and Computer Engineering, University of Toronto
Toronto, Ontario, Canada
wbao@comm.utoronto.ca, liang@comm.utoronto.ca

ABSTRACT

We introduce a comprehensive analytical framework to compare between open access and closed access in two-tier femtocell networks, with regard to uplink interference and outage. Interference at both the macrocell and femtocell levels is considered. A stochastic geometric approach is employed as the basis for our analysis. We further derive sufficient conditions for open access and closed access to outperform each other in terms of the outage probability, leading to closed-form expressions to upper and lower bound the difference in the targeted received power between the two access modes. Simulations are conducted to validate the accuracy of the analytical model and the correctness of the bounds.

Categories and Subject Descriptors

C.2.1 [**Network Architecture and Design**]: Wireless communication

Keywords

Femtocell; uplink interference; stochastic geometry; open access

1. INTRODUCTION

In deploying wireless celluar networks, some of the most important objectives are to provide higher capacity, better service quality, lower power usage, and ubiquitous coverage. To achieve these goals, one efficient approach is to install a second tier of smaller cells, which are referred to as femtocells, overlapping the original macrocell network [17]. Each femtocell is equipped with a short-range and low-cost base station (BS).

In the presence of femtocells, whenever a User Equipment (UE) is near a femtocell BS, two different access mechanisms may be applied: closed access and open access. Under closed access, a femtocell BS only provides service to its local users, without further admitting nearby macrocell users. In contrast, under open access, all nearby macrocell users are allowed to access the femtocell BS. The open access mode increases the interference level from within a femtocell, but it also allows macrocell UEs that might otherwise transmit at a high power toward their faraway macrocell BS to potentially switch to lower-power transmission toward the femtocell BS, therefore reducing the overall interference in the system. However, the relative merits between open access and closed access remain unresolved within the research community, as they may concern diverse factors in communication efficiency, control overhead, system security, and regulatory policies.

In this work, we contribute to the current debate by providing new technical insights on how the two access modes may affect both macrocell users and local femtocell users, in terms of the *uplink* interference and outage probabilities. We seek to quantify the conditions to guarantee that one access mode improves the performance of macrocell or femtocell users. It is a challenging task, as we need to account for the diverse spatial patterns of different network components. Macrocell BSs are usually deployed regularly by the network operator, while femtocell BSs are spread irregularly, sometimes in an anywhere plug-and-play manner, leading to a high level of spatial randomness. Furthermore, macrocell users are randomly distributed throughout the system, while femtocell users show strong spatial locality and correlation, since they aggregate around femtocell BSs. Whenever open access is applied, we also need to consider the effects of handoffs made by open access users, which brings even more complication to the analytical model.

We develop stochastic geometric analysis schemes to derive numerical expressions for the uplink interference and outage probabilities of open access and closed access by modeling macrocell BSs as a regular grid, macrocell UEs as a Poission point process (PPP), and femtocell UEs as a two-level clustered Poisson point process, which captures the spatial patterns of different network components. However, uplink interference analysis is notoriously complex even for traditional single-tier cellular networks. For the two-tier network under consideration, our analysis yields non-closed forms requiring numerical integrations. This motivates us to further develop closed-form sufficient conditions for open access and closed access to outperform each other, at both the macrocell and femtocell levels.

Based on the above analysis, we are able to extract a key factor that influences the performance difference between open access and closed access: the power enhancement factor ρ, which is the ratio of the targeted received power of

MSWiM'13, November 3–8, 2013, Barcelona, Spain.
Copyright 2013 ACM 978-1-4503-2353-6/13/11 ...$15.00.
http://dx.doi.org/10.1145/2507924.2507945.

an open access user to its original targeted received power in the macrocell. We investigate the threshold value ρ^* (resp. ρ^{**}) such that macrocell (resp. femtocell) users may benefit through open access if $\rho < \rho^*$ (resp. $\rho < \rho^{**}$) as we apply open access to replace closed access. Tight upper and lower bounds of ρ^* are derived in closed forms, and the bounds of ρ^{**} can be found by numerically searching through closed-form equations, providing system design guidelines with low computational complexity. To the best of our knowledge, this is the first paper to theoretically analyze the uplink performance difference between open access and closed access of femtocell networks that considers the impact of random spatial patterns of BSs and UEs.

The rest of the paper is organized as follows: In Section 2, we discuss the relation between our work and prior works. In Section 3, we present the system model. In Sections 4 and 5, we analyze the performance at the macrocell and femtocll levels, respectively. In Section 6, we validate our analysis with simulation results. Finally, concluding remarks are given in Section 7.

2. RELATED WORKS

The downlink interference and outage performance in cellular networks have been extensively studied using the stochastic geometric approach. [9, 10] analyzed the downlink performance of heterogeneous networks with multiple tiers by assuming the signal-to-interference plus noise ratio (SINR) threshold is greater than 1. [14] studied the maximum tier-1 user and tier-2 cell densities under downlink outage constraints. [11] studied the downlink interference considering load balance. [19] studied the downlink user achievable rate in a heterogeneous network considering both SINR and spatial user distributions. [13] studied open access versus closed access in femtocell networks in terms of downlink performance.

The analysis of uplink interference in multi-tier networks is more challenging compared with the downlink case. For uplink analysis, the interference generators are the set of UEs, which are more complicatedly distributed compared with the interference generators (i.e., BSs) in downlink analysis. Under closed access, without considering random spatial patterns, [15] studied the uplink performance of a single tier-1 cell and a single femtocell, while [16] extended it to the case of multiple tier-1 cells and multiple femtocells. [1] studied the co-channel uplink interference in LTE-based multi-tier cellular networks, considering a constant number of femtocells in a macrocell. However, none of [1,15,16] considered the random spatial patterns of users or femtocells.

By considering random spatial patterns, [18] analyzed uplink performance of cellular networks, but it was limited to the one-tier case. [7] evaluated the uplink performance of two-tier networks considering random spatial patterns. However, several interference components were analyzed based on approximations, such as (1) BSs see a femtocell as a point interference source and (2) Femtocell UEs transmit at the maximum power at the edge of cells. [8] studied both uplink and downlink interference of femtocell networks based on a Neyman-Scott Process. However it assumed that each UE transmits at the same power and femtocell users are uniformly distributed in an infinitesimally thin ring around the femtocell BS. With a more general system model, [5] derived the uplink interference in a two-tier network with multiple types of users and small cell BSs, but no closed-form result

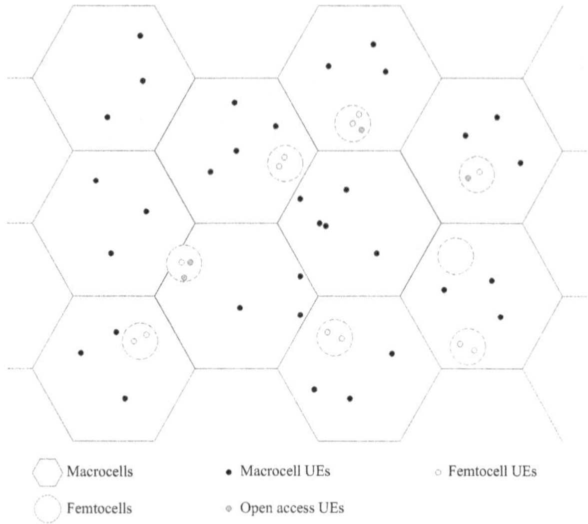

Figure 1: Two-tier network with macrocells and femtocells.

was obtained. Moreover, [5, 7, 8] considered only the closed access case.

The analysis of open access in femtocell networks is even more complicated. This is because the model for open access needs to capture the impact of the users disconnecting from the original macrocell BS and connecting to a femtocll BS. In order to satisfy mathematical tractability, the previous analysis of open access was based on simplified assumptions. [23] compared the performance of open access and closed access based on a model with one macorcell, one femtocell, and a given number of macrocell users, while [21] was based on a model with one macorcell, a constant number of macrocell users, and randomly distributed femtocells. Although [23] and [21] have provided useful insights into the performance comparison between open access and closed access, due to their limited system models, they have not addressed the challenging issues brought by the diverse spatial patterns of BSs and UEs.

Finally, several other works studied the performance of femtocells based on experiments [2, 24], which provided important practical knowledge in designing a real system. Compared with these works, our theoretical approach is an essential alternative that allows more rigorous reasoning to understand the performance benefits of open access compared with closed access, by considering more general system models and behaviors instead of specific experimental scenarios.

3. SYSTEM MODEL

3.1 Two-Tier Network

We consider a two-tier network with macrocells and femtocells as shown in Fig. 1. Following the convention in literature, we assume that the macrocells form an infinite hexagonal grid in the two-dimensional Euclidean space $\mathbb{R}^2$. Macrocell BSs are located at the centers of the hexagons $\mathbb{B} = \{(\frac{3}{2}aR_c, \frac{\sqrt{3}}{2}aR_c + \sqrt{3}bR_c)|a, b \in \mathbb{Z}\}$, where R_c is the radius of the hexagon. Macrocell UEs are randomly distributed in the system, which are modeled as a homogeneous Poisson point process (PPP) Φ with intensity λ.

Because femtocell BSs are operated in a plug-and-play fashion, inducing a high level of spatial randomness, we assume femtocell BSs form a homogeneous PPP Θ with intensity μ. Each femtocell BS is connected to the core network by high-capacity wired links that has no influence on our wireless performance analysis.

Each femtocell BS communicates with local femtocell UEs surrounding it, constituting a femtocell. We assume R as the communication radius of each femtocell BS. Given the location of a femtocell BS at $\mathbf{x}_0$, we assume that its femtocell UEs, denoted by $\Psi(\mathbf{x}_0)$, are distributed as a non-homogenous PPP in the disk centered at $\mathbf{x}_0$ with radius R. Its intensity at $\mathbf{x}$ is described by $\nu(\mathbf{x}-\mathbf{x}_0)$, a non-negative function of the *vector* $\mathbf{x}-\mathbf{x}_0$. Note that the user intensity $\nu(\mathbf{x}-\mathbf{x}_0)=0$ if $|\mathbf{x}-\mathbf{x}_0|>R$. The femtocell UEs in one femtocell are independent with femtocell UEs in other femtocells, as well as the macrocell UEs. We assume the scale of femtocells is much smaller than the scale of macrocells [17], $R \ll R_c$.

To better understand the spatial distribution of femtocell BSs and femtocell UEs, the femtocell BSs Θ can be regarded as a parent point process in $\mathbb{R}^2$, while femtocell UEs Ψ is a daughter process associated with a point in the parent point process, forming a two-level random pattern. Note that the aggregating of femtocell UEs around a femtocell BS implicitly defines the location correlation among femtocell UEs.

Let $\mathcal{H}(\mathbf{x})$ denote the hexagon region centered at $\mathbf{x}$ with radius R_c; let $\mathcal{B}(\mathbf{x},R)$ denote the disk region centered at $\mathbf{x}$ with radius R; let $\mathcal{BS}(\mathbf{x})$ denote the hexagon center nearest to $\mathbf{x}$ (i.e., $\mathcal{BS}(\mathbf{x})=\mathbf{x}_0 \Leftrightarrow \mathbf{x}\in\mathcal{H}(\mathbf{x}_0)$).

3.2 Open Access versus Closed Access

If a macrocell UE is covered by a femtocell BS (i.e., within a distance of R from a femtocell BS), under closed access, the UE still connects to the macrocell BS. Under open access, the UE is handed-off to connect to the femtocell BS and *disconnects* from the original macrocell BS; the UE is then referred to as an *open access UE*.

Given a femtocell BS located at $\mathbf{x}_0$, let $\Omega(\mathbf{x}_0)$ denote the point process corresponding to the open access UEs connecting to it. Note that because the radius of a femtocell is much smaller than that of macrocells, the probability of two femtocells overlapping is small. Thus, $\Omega(\mathbf{x}_0)$ corresponds to points of Φ inside the range of the femtocell BS at $\mathbf{x}_0$, which is a PPP with intensity λ inside $\mathcal{B}(\mathbf{x}_0,R)$.

Let $\overline{\nu}=\int_{\mathcal{B}(\mathbf{0},R)}\nu(\mathbf{x})d\mathbf{x}$ be the average number of local femtocell UEs inside a femtocell, and $\overline{\lambda}=\pi R^2\lambda$ be the average number of open access UEs inside a femtocell (in the open access case only).

3.3 Pathloss and Power Control

Let $P_t(\mathbf{x})$ denote the transmission power at $\mathbf{x}$ and $P_r(\mathbf{y})$ denote the received power at $\mathbf{y}$. We assume that $P_r(\mathbf{y})=\frac{P_t(\mathbf{x})h_{\mathbf{x},\mathbf{y}}}{A|\mathbf{x}-\mathbf{y}|^\gamma}$, where $A|\mathbf{x}-\mathbf{y}|^\gamma$ is the propagation loss function with predetermined constants A and γ (where $\gamma>2$ in practice), and $h_{\mathbf{x},\mathbf{y}}$ is the fast fading term. Corresponding to common Rayleigh fading with power normalization, $h_{\mathbf{x},\mathbf{y}}$ is independently exponentially distributed with unit mean. Let $H(\cdot)$ be the cumulative distribution function of $h_{\mathbf{x},\mathbf{y}}$.

We follow the conventional assumption that uplink power control adjusts for propagation losses [6,7,12,22]. The targeted received power level of macrocell UEs, femtocell UEs and open access UEs are P, Q, and P', respectively[1]. Given the targeted received power P_T ($P_T=P$, $P_T=Q$, or $P_T=P'$), receiver at $\mathbf{y}$, and transmitter at $\mathbf{x}$, the transmission power is $P_TA|\mathbf{x}-\mathbf{y}|^\gamma$. Then, the resultant interference at $\mathbf{y}'$ is $\frac{P_T|\mathbf{x}-\mathbf{y}|^\gamma h_{\mathbf{x},\mathbf{y}'}}{|\mathbf{x}-\mathbf{y}'|^\gamma}$.

Let $\rho=P'/P$, which is the targeted received power enhancement if a macrocell UE becomes an open access UE. In this paper, we study the performance variation when open access is applied to replace closed access. Therefore, as a parameter corresponding to open access UEs, ρ is regarded as an important designed parameter. Other parameters, such as P,Q, and γ are considered as predetermined system-level constants.

3.4 Outage Performance

In this paper, the performance of macrocell UEs and femtocell UEs (under open access or closed access) is examined through the outage probability, which is defined as the probability that the signal to interference ratio (SIR) is smaller than a given threshold value T. Because we focus on the interference analysis, the thermal noise is assumed to be negligible in this paper.

3.5 Scope of This Work

The above model assumes a single shared channel for all UEs. However, the model is applicable for the orthogonal multiplexing case (e.g., OFDMA) [10]. In that case, the spectrum is partitioned into n orthogonal resource blocks, and thus the density of UEs is equivalently reduced by a factor of n when we assume random access of each resource block.

4. OPEN ACCESS VS. CLOSED ACCESS AT THE MACROCELL LEVEL

In this section, we analyze the uplink interference and outage performance of macrocell UEs. Consider a reference macrocell UE, termed the *typical UE*, communicating with its macrocell BS, termed the *typical BS*. We aim to investigate the performance of the typical UE.

Due to stationarity of point processes corresponding to macrocell UEs, femtocell BSs, and femtocell UEs, throughout this section we will re-define the coordinates so that the typical BS is located at $\mathbf{0}$ [3]. Correspondingly, the typical UE is located at some $\mathbf{x}_U$ that is uniformly distributed in $\mathcal{H}(\mathbf{0})$, since macrocell BSs form a deterministic hexagonal grid [3].

Let Φ' be the point process of all other macrocell UEs conditioned on the typical UE, which is called the *reduced Palm point process* [3] with respect to (w.r.t.) Φ. Because the reduced Palm point process of a PPP has the same distribution as its original PPP, Φ' is still a PPP with intensity λ [3]. Therefore, for presentation convenience, we still use Φ to denote this reduced Palm point process.

[1]We assume a single fixed level of targeted received power at the macrocell or femtocell level for mathematical tractability. We show that our model is still valid when the targeted received power is randomly distributed through simulations in Section 6.

4.1 Open Access Case

4.1.1 Interference Components

The overall interference in the uplink has three parts: from macrocell UEs not inside any femtocell (denoted by I_1), from open access UEs (denoted by I_2), and from femtocell UEs (denoted by I_3).

I_1 can be computed as the sum of interference from each macrocell UE:

$$I_1 = \sum_{\mathbf{x}\in\Phi^0} \frac{P|\mathbf{x} - \mathcal{BS}(\mathbf{x})|^\gamma h_{\mathbf{x},\mathbf{o}}}{|\mathbf{x}|^\gamma}, \tag{1}$$

where Φ^0 denotes the points of Φ not inside any femtocell.

I_2 can be computed as the sum of interference from all open access UEs of all femtocells:

$$I_2 = \sum_{\mathbf{x}_0\in\Theta}\sum_{\mathbf{x}\in\Omega(\mathbf{x}_0)} \frac{P'|\mathbf{x} - \mathbf{x}_0|^\gamma h_{\mathbf{x},\mathbf{o}}}{|\mathbf{x}|^\gamma}. \tag{2}$$

I_3 can be computed as the sum of interference from all femtocell UEs of all femtocells:

$$I_3 = \sum_{\mathbf{x}_0\in\Theta}\sum_{\mathbf{x}\in\Psi(\mathbf{x}_0)} \frac{Q|\mathbf{x} - \mathbf{x}_0|^\gamma h_{\mathbf{x},\mathbf{o}}}{|\mathbf{x}|^\gamma}. \tag{3}$$

The overall interference of open access is $I = I_1 + I_2 + I_3$.

4.1.2 Laplace Transform of I

In this subsection, we study the Laplace transform of I, denoted by $\mathcal{L}_I$, which leads to the following theorem[2]:

Theorem 1.

$$\mathcal{L}_I = \mathbf{E}\Big(\prod_{\mathbf{x}\in\Phi} u(\mathbf{x})\Big) \cdot \mathbf{E}\Bigg[\prod_{\mathbf{x}_0\in\Theta} \frac{\mathbf{E}\Big(\prod_{\mathbf{x}\in\Omega(\mathbf{x}_0)} v(\mathbf{x},\mathbf{x}_0)\Big)}{\mathbf{E}\Big(\prod_{\mathbf{x}\in\Omega(\mathbf{x}_0)} u(\mathbf{x})\Big)} \mathbf{E}\Big(\prod_{\mathbf{x}\in\Psi(\mathbf{x}_0)} w(\mathbf{x},\mathbf{x}_0)\Big)\Bigg], \tag{4}$$

where $u(\mathbf{x}) = \exp\Big(-\frac{sP|\mathbf{x}-\mathcal{BS}(\mathbf{x})|^\gamma h_{\mathbf{x},\mathbf{o}}}{|\mathbf{x}|^\gamma}\Big)$, $v(\mathbf{x},\mathbf{x}_0) = \exp\Big(-\frac{s\rho P|\mathbf{x}-\mathbf{x}_0|^\gamma h_{\mathbf{x},\mathbf{o}}}{|\mathbf{x}|^\gamma}\Big)$, and $w(\mathbf{x},\mathbf{x}_0) = \exp\Big(-\frac{sQ|\mathbf{x}-\mathbf{x}_0|^\gamma h_{\mathbf{x},\mathbf{o}}}{|\mathbf{x}|^\gamma}\Big)$.

Proof: See our technical report [4].

4.1.3 Numeric Computation of $\mathcal{L}_I$

In this subsection, we present a numeric approach to compute $\mathcal{L}_I$ derived in (4), which will facilitate later comparison between open access and closed access. Let $\mathcal{L}_0 = \mathbf{E}\left(\prod_{x\in\Phi} u(\mathbf{x})\right)$, which is a generating functional corresponding to Φ [3, 20]. It can be re-written in a standard integral form as follows:

$$\begin{aligned}\mathcal{L}_0 &= \exp\Bigg(-\lambda\int_{\mathbb{R}^2}\Big(1-\int_{\mathbb{R}+} e^{-\frac{sP|\mathbf{x}-\mathcal{BS}(\mathbf{x})|^\gamma h}{|\mathbf{x}|^\gamma}} H(dh)\Big)d\mathbf{x}\Bigg)\\ &= \exp\Bigg(-\lambda\int_{\mathbb{R}^2}\frac{\frac{sP|\mathbf{x}-\mathcal{BS}(\mathbf{x})|^\gamma}{|\mathbf{x}|^\gamma}}{\frac{sP|\mathbf{x}-\mathcal{BS}(\mathbf{x})|^\gamma}{|\mathbf{x}|^\gamma}+1}\Bigg)d\mathbf{x}.\end{aligned} \tag{5}$$

Given the location of a femtocell BS at $\mathbf{x}_0$, let $\mathcal{W}(\mathbf{x}_0) = \mathbf{E}\Big(\prod_{\mathbf{x}\in\Psi(\mathbf{x}_0)} w(\mathbf{x},\mathbf{x}_0)\Big)$, which is a generating functional corresponding to $\Psi(\mathbf{x}_0)$. It can be expressed in a standard form through the Laplace functional of PPP $\Psi(\mathbf{x}_0)$,

$$\mathcal{W}(\mathbf{x}_0) = \exp\Bigg(-\int_{\mathcal{B}(\mathbf{0},R)}\frac{\frac{sQ|\mathbf{x}|^\gamma}{|\mathbf{x}+\mathbf{x}_0|^\gamma}}{\frac{sQ|\mathbf{x}|^\gamma}{|\mathbf{x}+\mathbf{x}_0|^\gamma}+1}\nu(\mathbf{x})d\mathbf{x}\Bigg). \tag{6}$$

Similarly, let $\mathcal{V}(\mathbf{x}_0) = \mathbf{E}\left(\prod_{\mathbf{x}\in\Omega(\mathbf{x}_0)} v(\mathbf{x},\mathbf{x}_0)\right)$, and $\mathcal{U}(\mathbf{x}_0) = \mathbf{E}\left(\prod_{\mathbf{x}\in\Omega(\mathbf{x}_0)} u(\mathbf{x})\right)$, we have

$$\mathcal{V}(\mathbf{x}_0) = \exp\Bigg(-\lambda\int_{\mathcal{B}(\mathbf{0},R)}\frac{\frac{s\rho P|\mathbf{x}|^\gamma}{|\mathbf{x}+\mathbf{x}_0|^\gamma}}{\frac{s\rho P|\mathbf{x}|^\gamma}{|\mathbf{x}+\mathbf{x}_0|^\gamma}+1}d\mathbf{x}\Bigg), \tag{7}$$

$$\mathcal{U}(\mathbf{x}_0) = \exp\Bigg(-\lambda\int_{\mathcal{B}(\mathbf{x}_0,R)}\frac{\frac{sP|\mathbf{x}-\mathcal{BS}(\mathbf{x})|^\gamma}{|\mathbf{x}|^\gamma}}{\frac{sP|\mathbf{x}-\mathcal{BS}(\mathbf{x})|^\gamma}{|\mathbf{x}|^\gamma}+1}d\mathbf{x}\Bigg). \tag{8}$$

Let $\mathcal{J}(\mathbf{x}_0) = \frac{\mathcal{V}(\mathbf{x}_0)}{\mathcal{U}(\mathbf{x}_0)}\mathcal{W}(\mathbf{x}_0)$, which is numerically computable through (6)-(8). Finally, we note that

$$\begin{aligned}&\mathbf{E}\Bigg[\prod_{\mathbf{x}_0\in\Theta}\frac{\mathbf{E}\Big(\prod_{\mathbf{x}\in\Omega(\mathbf{x}_0)} v(\mathbf{x},\mathbf{x}_0)\Big)}{\mathbf{E}\Big(\prod_{\mathbf{x}\in\Omega(\mathbf{x}_0)} u(\mathbf{x})\Big)}\mathbf{E}\Big(\prod_{\mathbf{x}\in\Psi(\mathbf{x}_0)} w(\mathbf{x},\mathbf{x}_0)\Big)\Bigg]\\ =&\mathbf{E}\Bigg[\prod_{\mathbf{x}_0\in\Theta}\Big(\frac{\mathcal{V}(\mathbf{x}_0)}{\mathcal{U}(\mathbf{x}_0)}\mathcal{W}(\mathbf{x}_0)\Big)\Bigg] = \mathbf{E}\Big(\prod_{\mathbf{x}_0\in\Theta}\mathcal{J}(\mathbf{x}_0)\Big)\\ =&\exp\Big(-\mu\int_{\mathbb{R}^2}(1-\mathcal{J}(\mathbf{x}_0))\,d\mathbf{x}_0\Big),\end{aligned} \tag{9}$$

where (9) is derived from the generating functional with respect to PPP Θ. Substituting (5) and (9) into (4), we can numerically compute $\mathcal{L}_I$:

$$\mathcal{L}_I = \mathcal{L}_0 \exp\Big(-\mu\int_{\mathbb{R}^2}(1-\mathcal{J}(\mathbf{x}_0))\,d\mathbf{x}_0\Big). \tag{10}$$

4.1.4 Outage Probability

Given the SIR threshold T, the outage probability of the typical UE can be computed as the probability that the signal strength $Ph_{\mathbf{x}_U,\mathbf{o}}$ over the interference I is less than T:

$$P_{out}^o = \mathbf{P}(Ph_{\mathbf{x}_U,\mathbf{o}} < TI) = 1 - \mathcal{L}_I\big|_{s=\frac{T}{P}}. \tag{11}$$

The last equality above is due to $h_{\mathbf{x}_U,\mathbf{o}}$ being exponentially distributed with unit mean. As a result, P_{out}^o can be derived directly from $\mathcal{L}_I$.

4.2 Closed Access Case

Different from the open access case, the overall interference has only two parts: from macrocell UEs (denoted by $\widehat{I}_1$) and from femtocell UEs (denoted by $\widehat{I}_3$).

$\widehat{I}_1$ can be computed as the sum of interference from each macrocell UE:

$$\widehat{I}_1 = \sum_{\mathbf{x}\in\Phi}\frac{P|\mathbf{x}-\mathcal{BS}(\mathbf{x})|^\gamma h_{\mathbf{x},\mathbf{o}}}{|\mathbf{x}|^\gamma}. \tag{12}$$

$\widehat{I}_3$ is exactly the same as I_3 in (3).

Then, the total interference can be computed as $\widehat{I} = \widehat{I}_1 + \widehat{I}_3$. Similar to Section 4.1.3, the Laplace transform of $\widehat{I}$ is

$$\mathcal{L}_{\widehat{I}} = \mathbf{E}\Big[\prod_{\mathbf{x}\in\Phi}u(\mathbf{x})\prod_{\mathbf{x}_0\in\Theta}\prod_{\mathbf{x}\in\Psi(\mathbf{x}_0)}w(\mathbf{x},\mathbf{x}_0)\Big]$$

[2]For presentation convenience, we omit the variable s in all Laplace transform expressions.

$$=\mathcal{L}_0\mathbf{E}\Bigg[\prod_{\mathbf{x}_O\in\Theta}\Big(\mathcal{W}(\mathbf{x}_O)\Big)\Bigg]=\mathcal{L}_0\exp\Big(-\mu\int_{\mathbb{R}^2}(1-\mathcal{W}(\mathbf{x}_O))d\mathbf{x}_O\Big), \tag{13}$$

where $\mathcal{L}_0$ is the same as (5), and $\mathcal{W}(\mathbf{x}_O)$ is the same as (6).

Finally, the outage probability of the typical UE can be computed as

$$P^c_{out}=\mathbf{P}(Ph_{\mathbf{x}_U,\mathbf{0}}<T\widehat{I})=1-\mathcal{L}_{\widehat{I}}|_{s=\frac{T}{P}}. \tag{14}$$

4.3 Parameter Normalization

From the above performance analysis of both open access and closed access, we see that one can can normalize the radius of macrocells R_c to 1, so that R is equivalent to the ratio of the radius of femtocells to that of macrocells ($R\ll 1$). Also, we can normalize the target received power of macrocell UEs P to 1, so that Q is equivalent to the ratio of the target received power of femtocell UEs to that of macrocell UEs, and $P'=\rho$. Therefore, in the rest of this section, without loss of generality, we set $R_c=1$ and $P=1$.

4.4 Open Access vs. Closed Access

We compare the outage performance of open access and closed access at the macrocell level. Due to the integral form of the Laplace transform, the expressions of outage probabilities for both open and closed access cases are in non-closed forms, requiring multiple levels of integration. As a consequence, we are motivated to derive closed-form bounds to compare open access and closed access.

Let $\mathbf{V}_{\max}=4\pi^2R^4(T\rho)^{\frac{2}{\gamma}}\left(\frac{1}{8}+\frac{1}{4(\gamma+2)}+\frac{1}{(\gamma+2)(\gamma-2)}\right)$, $\mathbf{V}_{\min}=2\pi^2R^4(T\rho)^{\frac{2}{\gamma}}\left(\frac{1}{8}+\frac{1}{4(\gamma+2)}+\frac{1}{(\gamma+2)(\gamma-2)}\right)$, and C_u be a system-level constant predetermined by T and γ, shown in (42) of the proof to Theorem 2. The closed-form bounds are presented in the following theorem:

Theorem 2. $-\mathbf{V}_{\max}+\pi R^2C_ue^{-\overline{\nu}}>0$ is a sufficient condition for $P^o_{out}<P^c_{out}$, and $-\pi R^2C_ue^{\overline{\lambda}}+\mathbf{V}_{\min}e^{-\overline{\lambda}-\overline{\nu}}>0$ is a sufficient condition for $P^c_{out}<P^o_{out}$.

Proof: See Appendix for the proof.

Through Theorem 2, the closed-form expressions can be used to compare the outage probabilities between open access and closed access without the computational complexity introduced by numeric integrations in (10) and (13).

In the following, we focus on the performance variation if open access is applied to replace closed access. The parameter corresponding to open access UEs, ρ, is regarded as a designed parameter. If we fix all the other network parameters, increasing ρ implies better performance for open access UEs, but it will also increase the interference from open access UEs to macrocell BSs. As a consequence, we aim to derive ρ^*, such that $P^o_{out}=P^c_{out}$. At the macrocell level, macrocell UEs experience less outage iff $\rho<\rho^*$. Thus, ρ^* is referred to as the *maximum power enhancement tolerated at the macrocell level.* Thus, in the deployment of open access femtocells, the network operator is motivated to limit ρ below ρ^* to guarantee that the performance of macrocell UEs under open access is no worse than that under closed access. One way to derive ρ^* is through numerical computation of (10) and (13) and numerical search, which introduces high computational complexity due to the multiple levels of integrations. A more efficient alternative is to find the bounds of ρ^* through Theorem 2. Simple algebra manipulation leads to

$$\rho^*_{\min}=\frac{1}{T}\left(\frac{C_ue^{-\overline{\nu}}}{4\pi R^2\left(\frac{1}{8}+\frac{1}{4(\gamma+2)}+\frac{1}{(\gamma+2)(\gamma-2)}\right)}\right)^{\frac{\gamma}{2}}, \tag{15}$$

$$\rho^*_{\max}=\frac{1}{T}\left(\frac{C_ue^{\overline{\nu}+2\overline{\lambda}}}{2\pi R^2\left(\frac{1}{8}+\frac{1}{4(\gamma+2)}+\frac{1}{(\gamma+2)(\gamma-2)}\right)}\right)^{\frac{\gamma}{2}}, \tag{16}$$

where $\rho^*_{\min}$ and $\rho^*_{\max}$ are the lower bound and upper bound of ρ^*, respectively. If the network operator limits $\rho<\rho^*_{\min}$, the performance of macrocell UEs under open access can be guaranteed no worse than their performance under closed access.

Through (15) and (16), we observe that $\rho^*_{\min}=\mathcal{O}(\frac{1}{R^\gamma})$ and $\rho^*_{\max}=\mathcal{O}(\frac{1}{R^\gamma})$, leading to the following corollary:

Corollary 1. $\rho^*=\mathcal{O}(\frac{1}{R^\gamma})$.

Intuitively, as a rough estimation, open access UEs have their distance to the BS reduced approximately by a factor of R, leading to the capability to increase their received power by the corresponding gain in the propagation loss function, as their average interference level is maintained. However, Corollary 1 cannot be trivially obtained from the above intuition. This is because the outage probability does not only depend on the average interference, but also depends on the distribution of the interference (i.e., the Laplace transform of the interference). Comparing (10) with (13), we note that if we switch from closed access to open access, the distribution of the interference will change drastically. Corollary 1 can be derived only after rigorously comparing and bounding the Laplace transforms of interference under open access and closed access.

Finally, because $\rho^*_{\min}$ and $\rho^*_{\max}$ have the same scaling behavior, Corollary 1 also demonstrates the tightness of the bounds in (15) and (16).

5. OPEN ACCESS VS. CLOSED ACCESS AT THE FEMTOCELL LEVEL

In this section, we analyze the uplink interference and outage performance of femtocell UEs. Given a reference femtocell UE, termed the *typical femtocell UE,* connecting with its femtocell BS, termed the *typical femtocell BS,* we aim to study the interference at the typical femtocell BS. We also define the femtocell corresponding to the typical femtocell BS as the *typical femtocell,* and the macrocell BS nearest to the typical femtocell BS as the *typical macrocell BS.*

Similar to Section 4, we re-define the coordinate of the typical macrocell BS as $\mathbf{0}$. Correspondingly, the typical femtocell BS is locating at some $\mathbf{x}_B$ that is uniformly distributed in $\mathcal{H}(\mathbf{0})$ [3]. Given the typical femtocell centered at $\mathbf{x}_B$, let Θ' denote the point process of other femtocell BSs conditioned on the typical femtocell BS, i.e., the reduced Palm point process w.r.t. Θ. Then, Θ' is still a PPP with intensity μ [3]. For presentation convenience, we still use Θ to denote this reduced Palm point process. Let $\widetilde{\Psi}(\mathbf{x}_B)$ denote the other femtocell UEs inside the typical femtocell conditioned on the typical femtocell UE. Similarly, $\widetilde{\Psi}(\mathbf{x}_B)$ has the same distribution as $\Psi(\mathbf{x}_B)$. Let $\widetilde{\Omega}(\mathbf{x}_B)$ denote open access UEs connecting to the typical femtocell BS.

5.1 Open Access Case

The overall interference in the uplink of the typical femtocell UE has five parts: from macrocell UEs not inside any femtocell ($I'_1(\mathbf{x}_B)$), from open access UEs outside the typical femtocell ($I'_2(\mathbf{x}_B)$), from femtocell UEs outside the typical femtocell ($I'_3(\mathbf{x}_B)$), from local femtocell UEs inside the typical femtocell ($I'_4(\mathbf{x}_B)$), and from open access UEs inside the typical femtocell ($I'_5(\mathbf{x}_B)$). We have

$$I'_1(\mathbf{x}_B) = \sum_{\mathbf{x}\in\Phi^0} \frac{P|\mathbf{x}-\mathcal{BS}(\mathbf{x})|^\gamma h_{\mathbf{x},\mathbf{x}_B}}{|\mathbf{x}-\mathbf{x}_B|^\gamma}, \tag{17}$$

$$I'_2(\mathbf{x}_B) = \sum_{\mathbf{x}_0\in\Theta}\sum_{\mathbf{x}\in\Omega(\mathbf{x}_0)} \frac{\rho P|\mathbf{x}-\mathbf{x}_0|^\gamma h_{\mathbf{x},\mathbf{x}_B}}{|\mathbf{x}-\mathbf{x}_B|^\gamma}, \tag{18}$$

$$I'_3(\mathbf{x}_B) = \sum_{\mathbf{x}_0\in\Theta}\sum_{\mathbf{x}\in\Psi(\mathbf{x}_0)} \frac{Q|\mathbf{x}-\mathbf{x}_0|^\gamma h_{\mathbf{x},\mathbf{x}_B}}{|\mathbf{x}-\mathbf{x}_B|^\gamma}, \tag{19}$$

$$I'_4(\mathbf{x}_B) = \sum_{\mathbf{x}\in\widetilde{\Psi}(\mathbf{x}_B)} Qh_{\mathbf{x},\mathbf{x}_B}, \tag{20}$$

$$I'_5(\mathbf{x}_B) = \sum_{\mathbf{x}\in\widetilde{\Omega}(\mathbf{x}_B)} \rho Ph_{\mathbf{x},\mathbf{x}_B}. \tag{21}$$

The overall interference is $I'(\mathbf{x}_B) = \sum_{i=1}^{5} I'_i(\mathbf{x}_B)$.

Similar to the derivations in Sections 4.1.2 and 4.1.3, the Laplace transform of $I'(\mathbf{x}_B)$, denoted by $\mathcal{L}_{I'}(\mathbf{x}_B)$, is derived as

$$\mathcal{L}_{I'}(\mathbf{x}_B) = \mathcal{L}'_0(\mathbf{x}_B)\exp\left(-\mu\int_{\mathbb{R}^2} 1- \frac{\mathcal{V}'(\mathbf{x}_0,\mathbf{x}_B)\mathcal{W}'(\mathbf{x}_0,\mathbf{x}_B)}{\mathcal{U}'(\mathbf{x}_0,\mathbf{x}_B)} d\mathbf{x}_0\right)\frac{\mathcal{W}''(\mathbf{x}_B)\mathcal{V}''(\mathbf{x}_B)}{\mathcal{U}''(\mathbf{x}_B)}, \tag{22}$$

where

$$\mathcal{L}'_0(\mathbf{x}_B) = \exp\left(-\lambda\int_{\mathbb{R}^2}\frac{\frac{sP|\mathbf{x}-\mathcal{BS}(\mathbf{x})|^\gamma}{|\mathbf{x}-\mathbf{x}_B|^\gamma}}{\frac{sP|\mathbf{x}-\mathcal{BS}(\mathbf{x})|^\gamma}{|\mathbf{x}-\mathbf{x}_B|^\gamma}+1}d\mathbf{x}\right), \tag{23}$$

$$\mathcal{W}'(\mathbf{x}_0,\mathbf{x}_B) = \exp\left(-\int_{\mathcal{B}(\mathbf{x}_0,R)}\frac{\frac{sQ|\mathbf{x}-\mathbf{x}_0|^\gamma}{|\mathbf{x}-\mathbf{x}_B|^\gamma}}{\frac{sQ|\mathbf{x}-\mathbf{x}_0|^\gamma}{|\mathbf{x}-\mathbf{x}_B|^\gamma}+1}\nu(\mathbf{x}-\mathbf{x}_0)d\mathbf{x}\right), \tag{24}$$

$$\mathcal{V}'(\mathbf{x}_0,\mathbf{x}_B) = \exp\left(-\lambda\int_{\mathcal{B}(\mathbf{x}_0,R)}\frac{\frac{s\rho P|\mathbf{x}-\mathbf{x}_0|^\gamma}{|\mathbf{x}-\mathbf{x}_B|^\gamma}}{\frac{s\rho P|\mathbf{x}-\mathbf{x}_0|^\gamma}{|\mathbf{x}-\mathbf{x}_B|^\gamma}+1}d\mathbf{x}\right), \tag{25}$$

$$\mathcal{U}'(\mathbf{x}_0,\mathbf{x}_B) = \exp\left(-\lambda\int_{\mathcal{B}(\mathbf{x}_0,R)}\frac{\frac{sP|\mathbf{x}-\mathcal{BS}(\mathbf{x})|^\gamma}{|\mathbf{x}-\mathbf{x}_B|^\gamma}}{\frac{sP|\mathbf{x}-\mathcal{BS}(\mathbf{x})|^\gamma}{|\mathbf{x}-\mathbf{x}_B|^\gamma}+1}d\mathbf{x}\right), \tag{26}$$

$$\mathcal{W}''(\mathbf{x}_B) = e^{-\frac{sQ\overline{\nu}}{sQ+1}}, \mathcal{V}''(\mathbf{x}_B) = e^{-\frac{s\rho P\overline{\lambda}}{s\rho P+1}}, \tag{27}$$

$$\mathcal{U}''(\mathbf{x}_B) = \exp\left(-\lambda\int_{\mathcal{B}(\mathbf{x}_B,R)}\frac{\frac{sP|\mathbf{x}-\mathcal{BS}(\mathbf{x})|^\gamma}{|\mathbf{x}-\mathbf{x}_B|^\gamma}}{\frac{sP|\mathbf{x}-\mathcal{BS}(\mathbf{x})|^\gamma}{|\mathbf{x}-\mathbf{x}_B|^\gamma}+1}d\mathbf{x}\right). \tag{28}$$

Similar to (11), the outage probability (given $\mathbf{x}_B$) is

$$\begin{aligned}\widehat{P}^o_{out}(\mathbf{x}_B) =& \mathbf{P}(Qh_{\mathbf{x}_U,\mathbf{x}_B} < TI'(\mathbf{x}_B)) \\ =& 1-\mathcal{L}_{I'}(\mathbf{x}_B)|_{s=T'},\end{aligned} \tag{29}$$

where $\mathbf{x}_U$ is the coordinate of the typical femtocell UE (irrelevant to the result), $T' = \frac{T}{Q}$, and T is the SIR threshold. Because $\mathbf{x}_B$ is uniformly distributed in $\mathcal{H}(\mathbf{0})$, the average outage probability can be computed as $\int_{\mathcal{H}(\mathbf{0})}\widehat{P}^o_{out}(\mathbf{x}_B)d\mathbf{x}_B/|\mathcal{H}(\mathbf{0})|$, where $|\mathcal{H}(\mathbf{0})| = \frac{3\sqrt{3}R_c^2}{2}$ is the area of a macrocell.

5.2 Closed Access Case

The overall interference has three parts: from macrocell UEs ($\widehat{I}_1(\mathbf{x}_B)$), from femtocell UEs outside the typical femtocell ($\widehat{I}_3(\mathbf{x}_B)$), and from femtocell UEs inside the typical femtocell ($\widehat{I}_4(\mathbf{x}_B)$). $\widehat{I}_1(\mathbf{x}_B)$ can be computed as

$$\widehat{I}_1(\mathbf{x}_B) = \sum_{\mathbf{x}\in\Phi}\frac{P|\mathbf{x}-\mathcal{BS}(\mathbf{x})|^\gamma h_{\mathbf{x},\mathbf{x}_B}}{|\mathbf{x}-\mathbf{x}_B|^\gamma}, \tag{30}$$

and $\widehat{I}_3(\mathbf{x}_B)$ and $\widehat{I}_4(\mathbf{x}_B)$ are exactly the same as $I'_3(\mathbf{x}_B)$ in (19) and $I'_4(\mathbf{x}_B)$ in (20), respectively.

Thus, the overall interference is $\widehat{I}'(\mathbf{x}_B) = \widehat{I}_1(\mathbf{x}_B)+\widehat{I}_3(\mathbf{x}_B)+\widehat{I}_4(\mathbf{x}_B)$. Then, the Laplace transform of $\widehat{I}'(\mathbf{x}_B)$ is

$$\mathcal{L}_{\widehat{I}'}(\mathbf{x}_B) = \mathcal{L}'_0(\mathbf{x}_B)\cdot\exp\left(-\mu\int_{\mathbb{R}^2}1-\mathcal{W}'(\mathbf{x}_0,\mathbf{x}_B)d\mathbf{x}_0\right)\cdot\mathcal{W}''(\mathbf{x}_B). \tag{31}$$

The outage probability (given $\mathbf{x}_B$) is

$$\widehat{P}^c_{out}(\mathbf{x}_B) = 1-\mathcal{L}_{\widehat{I}'}(\mathbf{x}_B)|_{s=T'}. \tag{32}$$

The average outage probability is $\int_{\mathcal{H}(\mathbf{0})}\widehat{P}^c_{out}(\mathbf{x}_B)d\mathbf{x}_B/|\mathcal{H}(\mathbf{0})|$. Similar to the discussion in Section 4.3, we still can normalize R_c and P. Hence, in the rest of this section, without loss of generality, we set $R_c = 1$ and $P = 1$.

5.3 Open Access vs. Closed Access

In this subsection, we compare the outage performance of open access and closed access at the femtocell level.

Let $\mathbf{V}'_{\max} = 4\pi^2R^4(T'\rho)^{\frac{2}{\gamma}}\left(\frac{1}{8}+\frac{1}{4(\gamma+2)}+\frac{1}{(\gamma+2)(\gamma-2)}\right)$, $\mathbf{V}'_{\min} = 2\pi^2R^4(T'\rho)^{\frac{2}{\gamma}}\left(\frac{1}{8}+\frac{1}{4(\gamma+2)}+\frac{1}{(\gamma+2)(\gamma-2)}\right)$; let $C'_u = \int_{\mathbb{R}^2}\left(\frac{\frac{T'|\mathbf{x}-\mathcal{BS}(\mathbf{x})|^\gamma}{|\mathbf{x}-\mathbf{x}_B|^\gamma}}{\frac{T'|\mathbf{x}-\mathcal{BS}(\mathbf{x})|^\gamma}{|\mathbf{x}-\mathbf{x}_B|^\gamma}+1}\right)d\mathbf{x}$, which is a system-level constant similar to C_u in Theorem 2; let

$$\mathcal{R}_{\min} = \begin{cases}\pi\int_0^R\frac{\frac{T'(|\mathbf{x}_B|)^\gamma}{r^\gamma}r}{\frac{T'(|\mathbf{x}_B|)^\gamma}{r^\gamma}+1}dr & \text{if } |\mathbf{x}_B|\le R,\\ \pi\int_0^R\frac{\frac{T'(|\mathbf{x}_B|-R)^\gamma}{r^\gamma}r}{\frac{T'(|\mathbf{x}_B|-R)^\gamma}{r^\gamma}+1}dr+\pi\int_0^R\frac{\frac{T'(|\mathbf{x}_B|)^\gamma}{r^\gamma}r}{\frac{T'(|\mathbf{x}_B|)^\gamma}{r^\gamma}+1}dr & \text{if } |\mathbf{x}_B|> R,\end{cases} \tag{33}$$

and

$$\mathcal{R}_{\max} = \pi\int_0^R\frac{\frac{T'(|\mathbf{x}_B|+R)^\gamma}{r^\gamma}r}{\frac{T'(|\mathbf{x}_B|+R)^\gamma}{r^\gamma}+1}dr+ \pi\int_0^R\frac{\frac{T'(\sqrt{|\mathbf{x}_B|^2+R^2})^\gamma}{r^\gamma}r}{\frac{T'(\sqrt{|\mathbf{x}_B|^2+R^2})^\gamma}{r^\gamma}+1}dr, \tag{34}$$

where $\mathcal{R}_{\min}$ and $\mathcal{R}_{\max}$ are in closed forms if γ is a rational number[3]. Then we have the following theorem:

[3]It is acceptable to assume γ as a rational number in reality, because each real number can be approximated by a rational number with arbitrary precision.

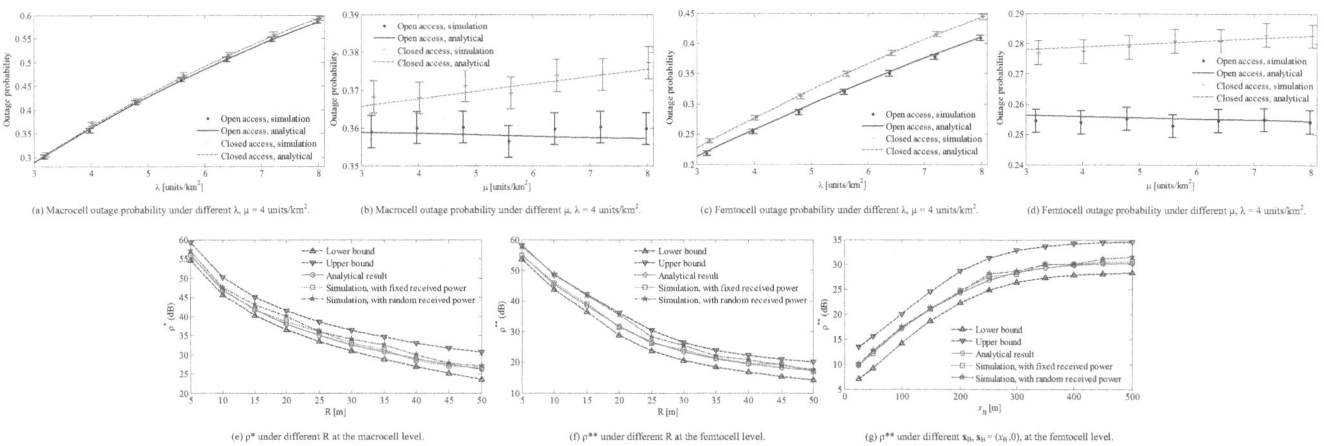

Figure 2: Numerical results.

Theorem 3. Given $\mathbf{x}_B$, $K_1 \triangleq -\mu\mathbf{V}'_{\max} + \mu\pi R^2 C'_u e^{-\overline{\nu}} - \frac{\pi R^2 T'\rho}{T'\rho+1} + \mathcal{R}_{\min} > 0$ is a sufficient condition for $\widehat{P}^o_{out}(\mathbf{x}_B) < \widehat{P}^c_{out}(\mathbf{x}_B)$, and $K_2 \triangleq -\mu\pi R^2 C'_u e^{\overline{\lambda}} + \mu\mathbf{V}'_{\min} e^{-\overline{\nu}-\overline{\lambda}} + \frac{\pi R^2 T'\rho}{T'\rho+1} - \mathcal{R}_{\max} > 0$ is a sufficient condition for $\widehat{P}^c_{out}(\mathbf{x}_B) < \widehat{P}^o_{out}(\mathbf{x}_B)$.

Proof: See our technical report [4].

Through Theorem 3, the closed-form expressions can be used to compare the outage probabilities between open access and closed access without the computational complexity introduced by numeric integrations in (29) and (32).

Similar to the discussion in Section 4.4, let ρ^{**} denote the value of ρ, such that $\widehat{P}^o_{out}(\mathbf{x}_B) = \widehat{P}^c_{out}(\mathbf{x}_B)$. At the femtocell level, given that a femtocell BS is located at $\mathbf{x}_B$ (the relative coordinate w.r.t. the nearest macrocell), its local femtocell UEs experience less outage iff $\rho < \rho^{**}$. Thus, ρ^{**} is referred to as the *maximum power enhancement tolerated by the femtocell.*

Instead of deriving ρ^{**} through (29) and (32), which introduces high computational complexity due to multiple levels of integrations, we can find the lower bound $\rho^{**}_{\min}$ and upper bound $\rho^{**}_{\max}$ of ρ^{**} through Theorem 3. Accordingly, $\rho^{**}_{\min}$ is the value satisfying $K_1 = 0$ and $\rho^{**}_{\max}$ is the value satisfying $K_2 = 0$. Thus, $\rho^{**}_{\min}$ and $\rho^{**}_{\max}$ can be found by a numerical search approach w.r.t. the closed-form expressions.

6. NUMERICAL STUDY

We present simulation and numerical studies on the outage performance in the two-tier network with femtocells. First, we study the performance of open access and closed access under different user and femtocell densities. Second, we present the numerical results of ρ^* and ρ^{**}. Unless otherwise stated, $R_c = 500$ m, $R = 50$ m, $\gamma = 3$; and fast fading is Rayleigh with unit mean. Each simulation data point is averaged over 50000 trials. The SIR threshold T is set to 0.1.

First, we study the performance under different user and femtocell densities[4]. The network parameters are as follows: $\nu(\mathbf{x}) = 80$ units/km^2 if $|\mathbf{x}| < R$, and $\nu(\mathbf{x}) = 0$ otherwise; $P = -60$ dBm, and $Q = P' = -54$ dBm ($\rho = 6$ dB).

[4]As discussed in Section 3.5, these intensities may already account for the multiplicative factor introduced by orthogonal multiplexing.

Fig. 2 (a) and (b) show the uplink outage probability of macrocell UEs under different λ and μ respectively. Fig. 2 (c) and (d) show the uplink outage probability of femtocell UEs under different λ and μ respectively. The analytical results are derived from the exact expressions in Sections 4.1, 4.2, 5.1, and 5.2, without applying any bounds. The error bars show the 95% confidence intervals for simulation results. The plot points are slightly shifted to avoid overlapping error bars for easier inspection. The figures illustrate the accuracy of our analytical results. In addition, the figures show that the macrocell UE density strongly influences the outage probability of both macrocell and femtocell UEs, while the femtocell density only has a slight influence. At the macrocell level, increasing the density of femtocell leads to more proportion of macrocell UEs becoming open access UEs, which gives higher performance gap between open access and closed access. At the femtocell level, the interference is observed at femtocell BSs, and the average number of macrocell UEs in a femtocell becomes a more important factor influencing the performance gap.

Next, we present the numerical results of ρ^* and ρ^{**}. The network parameters are as follows: $\lambda = 4$ units/km^2, $\mu = 4$ units/km^2; $\nu(\mathbf{x}) = 20$ units/km^2 if $|\mathbf{x}| < R$, and $\nu(\mathbf{x}) = 0$ otherwise; $P = -60$ dBm, and $Q = -54$ dBm.

Fig. 2 (e) presents the value of ρ^* at the macrocell level. We compute the actual value of ρ^* by numerically searching for the value such that (11) is equal to (14). Through the closed-form expressions in Theorem 2, we are able to derive the upper and lower bounds of ρ^*. Through simulation, we can also search for the value of ρ^* such that the simulated outage probability of open access is equal to that of closed access. Furthermore, we also simulate a more realistic scenario, in which each macrocell UE randomly selects a targeted received power level among $0.5P$, P, $1.5P$, and $2P$ with equal probability. If a macrocell UE is handed-off to a femtocell, then its targeted received power is multiplied by ρ no matter which power level it has selected. The figure shows that ρ^* is indeed within the upper bound and the lower bound, and the simulated ρ^* agrees with the analytical ρ^*, validating the correctness of our analysis. Furthermore, this remains the case when the targeted received power is random, indicating the usefulness of our analysis in more practical scenarios.

Figs. 2 (f) and (g) present the value of ρ^{**} at the femtocell level. Fig. 2 (f) shows ρ^{**} under different R as we fixed $\mathbf{x}_B = (0, 100\text{m})$. Fig. 2 (g) shows ρ^{**} under different $\mathbf{x}_B$ ($\mathbf{x}_B = (x_B, 0)$) as we fixed $R = 50$ m. The results show that ρ^{**} is indeed within the upper and lower bounds, and the simulated values of ρ^{**} agree with their analytical values, validating the correctness of our analysis. Furthermore, ρ^{**} decreases in R at a rate slightly faster than that of ρ^*, while it increases in x_B, until saturating when the femtocell BS is near the macrocell edge. This quantifies when femtocells are more beneficial as they decrease in size and increase in distance away from the macrocell BS.

7. CONCLUSIONS

In this work, we provide a theoretical framework to analyze the performance difference between open access and closed access in a two-tier femtocell network. Through establishing a stochastic geometric model, we capture the spatial patterns of different network components. Then, we derive the analytical outage performance of open access and closed access at the macrocell and femtocell levels. As in most uplink interference analysis, the outage probability expressions are in non-closed forms. Hence, we derive closed-form bounds to compare open access and closed access. Simulations and numerical studies are conducted, validating the correctness of the analytical model as well as the usefulness of the bounds.

8. ACKNOWLEDGEMENTS

This work has been supported in part by grants from Bell Canada and the Natural Sciences and Engineering Research Council (NSERC) of Canada.

APPENDIX

Proof of Theorem 2.

PROOF. In this proof, we use the fact that P and R_c can be normalized and set $P = R_c = 1$. Furthermore, we substitute $s = T$ into (6), (7) and (8) such that $\mathcal{W}(\mathbf{x}_0, T) = \exp\left(-\int_{\mathcal{B}(\mathbf{0},R)} \frac{\frac{TQ|\mathbf{x}|^\gamma}{|\mathbf{x}+\mathbf{x}_0|^\gamma}}{\frac{TQ|\mathbf{x}|^\gamma}{|\mathbf{x}+\mathbf{x}_0|^\gamma}+1}\nu(\mathbf{x})d\mathbf{x}\right)$, $\mathcal{V}(\mathbf{x}_0, T) = \exp\left(-\lambda \int_{\mathcal{B}(\mathbf{0},R)} \frac{\frac{T\rho|\mathbf{x}|^\gamma}{|\mathbf{x}+\mathbf{x}_0|^\gamma}}{\frac{T\rho|\mathbf{x}|^\gamma}{|\mathbf{x}+\mathbf{x}_0|^\gamma}+1}d\mathbf{x}\right)$, and $\mathcal{U}(\mathbf{x}_0, T) = \exp\left(-\lambda \int_{\mathcal{B}(\mathbf{x}_0,R)} \frac{\frac{T|\mathbf{x}-\mathcal{BS}(\mathbf{x})|^\gamma}{|\mathbf{x}|^\gamma}}{\frac{T|\mathbf{x}-\mathcal{BS}(\mathbf{x})|^\gamma}{|\mathbf{x}|^\gamma}+1} d\mathbf{x}\right)$.

(a) A sufficient condition for $P^o_{out} < P^c_{out}$
According to (10), (11), (13), and (14), $P^o_{out} < P^c_{out}$ iff

$$\frac{\exp\left(-\mu\int_{\mathbb{R}^2}\left(1-\frac{\mathcal{V}(\mathbf{x}_0,T)}{\mathcal{U}(\mathbf{x}_0,T)}\mathcal{W}(\mathbf{x}_0,T)\right)d\mathbf{x}_0\right)}{\exp\left(-\mu\int_{\mathbb{R}^2}\left(1-\mathcal{W}(\mathbf{x}_0,T)\right)d\mathbf{x}_0\right)} > 1, \tag{35}$$

which is equivalent to

$$\int_{\mathbb{R}^2}\left(\frac{\mathcal{V}(\mathbf{x}_0,T)}{\mathcal{U}(\mathbf{x}_0,T)} - 1\right)\mathcal{W}(\mathbf{x}_0,T)d\mathbf{x}_0 > 0. \tag{36}$$

Let $V(\mathbf{x}_0) = \int_{\mathcal{B}(\mathbf{x}_0,R)} \frac{\frac{T\rho|\mathbf{x}-\mathbf{x}_0|^\gamma}{|\mathbf{x}|^\gamma}}{\frac{T\rho|\mathbf{x}-\mathbf{x}_0|^\gamma}{|\mathbf{x}|^\gamma}+1}d\mathbf{x} = \int_{\mathcal{B}(\mathbf{0},R)} \frac{\frac{T\rho|\mathbf{x}|^\gamma}{|\mathbf{x}+\mathbf{x}_0|^\gamma}}{\frac{T\rho|\mathbf{x}|^\gamma}{|\mathbf{x}+\mathbf{x}_0|^\gamma}+1}d\mathbf{x}$, and $U(\mathbf{x}_0) = \int_{\mathcal{B}(\mathbf{x}_0,R)} \frac{\frac{T|\mathbf{x}-\mathcal{BS}(\mathbf{x})|^\gamma}{|\mathbf{x}|^\gamma}}{\frac{T|\mathbf{x}-\mathcal{BS}(\mathbf{x})|^\gamma}{|\mathbf{x}|^\gamma}+1}d\mathbf{x}$. Then, (36) becomes

$$\int_{\mathbb{R}^2}\left(\frac{\exp(-\lambda V(\mathbf{x}_0))}{\exp(-\lambda U(\mathbf{x}_0))} - 1\right)\mathcal{W}(\mathbf{x}_0,T)d\mathbf{x}_0 > 0. \tag{37}$$

It is easy to see that the following inequality is a sufficient condition for (37):

$$\int_{\mathbb{R}^2}\left(-\lambda V(\mathbf{x}_0) + \lambda U(\mathbf{x}_0)\right)\mathcal{W}(\mathbf{x}_0,T)d\mathbf{x}_0 > 0. \tag{38}$$

Let $W_{\min}$ and $W_{\max}$ be the lower bound and upper bound of $\mathcal{W}(\mathbf{x}_0, T)$, respectively. According to (6), $W_{\max} = 1$ and $W_{\min} = e^{-\overline{\nu}}$. Thus, the following is a sufficient condition for (38):

$$-W_{\max}\int_{\mathbb{R}^2} V(\mathbf{x}_0)d\mathbf{x}_0 + W_{\min}\int_{\mathbb{R}^2} U(\mathbf{x}_0)d\mathbf{x}_0 > 0. \tag{39}$$

Let $\mathbf{V} = \int_{\mathbb{R}^2} V(\mathbf{x}_0)d\mathbf{x}_0$, we have the following lemma corresponding to the upper and lower bounds of $\mathbf{V}$.

Lemma 1. $\mathbf{V}_{\max} = 4\pi^2R^4(T\rho)^{\frac{2}{\gamma}}\left(\frac{1}{8} + \frac{1}{4(\gamma+2)} + \frac{1}{(\gamma+2)(\gamma-2)}\right)$, $\mathbf{V}_{\min} = 2\pi^2R^4(T\rho)^{\frac{2}{\gamma}}\left(\frac{1}{8} + \frac{1}{4(\gamma+2)} + \frac{1}{(\gamma+2)(\gamma-2)}\right)$, then $\mathbf{V}_{\min} \leq \mathbf{V} \leq \mathbf{V}_{\max}$.
Proof: See the next subsection.

Hence, the following is a sufficient condition for (39):

$$-W_{\max}\mathbf{V}_{\max} + W_{\min}\int_{\mathbb{R}^2} U(\mathbf{x}_0)d\mathbf{x}_0 > 0. \tag{40}$$

In addition, we have

$$\int_{\mathbb{R}^2} U(\mathbf{x}_0)d\mathbf{x}_0 = \int_{\mathbb{R}^2}\int_{\mathcal{B}(\mathbf{x}_0,R)}\left(\frac{\frac{T|\mathbf{x}-\mathcal{BS}(\mathbf{x})|^\gamma}{|\mathbf{x}|^\gamma}}{\frac{T|\mathbf{x}-\mathcal{BS}(\mathbf{x})|^\gamma}{|\mathbf{x}|^\gamma}+1}\right)d\mathbf{x}d\mathbf{x}_0$$

$$= \pi R^2\int_{\mathbb{R}^2}\left(\frac{\frac{T|\mathbf{x}-\mathcal{BS}(\mathbf{x})|^\gamma}{|\mathbf{x}|^\gamma}}{\frac{T|\mathbf{x}-\mathcal{BS}(\mathbf{x})|^\gamma}{|\mathbf{x}|^\gamma}+1}\right)d\mathbf{x} = \pi R^2 C_u, \tag{41}$$

where

$$C_u = \int_{\mathbb{R}^2}\left(\frac{\frac{T|\mathbf{x}-\mathcal{BS}(\mathbf{x})|^\gamma}{|\mathbf{x}|^\gamma}}{\frac{T|\mathbf{x}-\mathcal{BS}(\mathbf{x})|^\gamma}{|\mathbf{x}|^\gamma}+1}\right)d\mathbf{x} \tag{42}$$

is only related to predetermined system-level constants T and γ.
As a consequence, (40) becomes

$$-W_{\max}\mathbf{V}_{\max} + W_{\min}\pi R^2 C_u > 0. \tag{43}$$

(b) A sufficient condition for $P^o_{out} > P^c_{out}$
According to (10), (11), (13), and (14), $P^o_{out} > P^c_{out}$ iff

$$\frac{\exp\left(-\mu\int_{\mathbb{R}^2}\left(1-\mathcal{W}(\mathbf{x}_0,T)\right)d\mathbf{x}_0\right)}{\exp\left(-\mu\int_{\mathbb{R}^2}\left(1-\frac{\mathcal{V}(\mathbf{x}_0,T)}{\mathcal{U}(\mathbf{x}_0,T)}\mathcal{W}(\mathbf{x}_0,T)\right)d\mathbf{x}_0\right)} > 1, \tag{44}$$

Then the following is a sufficient condition for (44):

$$\int_{\mathbb{R}^2}\left(-\lambda U(\mathbf{x}_0,T) + \lambda V(\mathbf{x}_0,T)\right)\frac{\mathcal{V}(\mathbf{x}_0,T)}{\mathcal{U}(\mathbf{x}_0,T)}\mathcal{W}(\mathbf{x}_0,T)d\mathbf{x}_0 > 0. \tag{45}$$

Let $W'_{\min}$ and $W'_{\max}$ be the lower bound and upper bound of $\frac{\mathcal{V}(\mathbf{x}_0,T)}{\mathcal{U}(\mathbf{x}_0,T)}\mathcal{W}(\mathbf{x}_0,T)$, respectively. According to (6), (7), and (8), $W'_{\max} = \exp\left(\overline{\lambda}\right)$ and $W'_{\min} = \exp\left(-\overline{\lambda}-\overline{\nu}\right)$. Finally, the following is a sufficient condition for (45):

$$-W'_{\max}\pi R^2 C_u + W'_{\min}\mathbf{V}_{\min} > 0. \quad (46)$$

□

Proof of Lemma 1.

PROOF. **Upper Bound of V**

$$\mathbf{V} = \int_{\mathbb{R}^2}\int_{\mathcal{B}(\mathbf{x}_0,R)} \frac{\frac{T\rho|\mathbf{x}-\mathbf{x}_0|^\gamma}{|\mathbf{x}|^\gamma}}{\frac{T\rho|\mathbf{x}-\mathbf{x}_0|^\gamma}{|\mathbf{x}|^\gamma}+1} d\mathbf{x}d\mathbf{x}_0 \quad (47)$$

$$= \int_{\mathbb{R}^2}\int_{\mathcal{B}(\mathbf{x},R)} \frac{\frac{T\rho|\mathbf{x}-\mathbf{x}_0|^\gamma}{|\mathbf{x}|^\gamma}}{\frac{T\rho|\mathbf{x}-\mathbf{x}_0|^\gamma}{|\mathbf{x}|^\gamma}+1} d\mathbf{x}_0 d\mathbf{x}$$

$$= \int_0^\infty 2\pi r_1 \int_0^R \frac{\frac{T\rho r_2^\gamma}{r_1^\gamma}}{\frac{T\rho r_2^\gamma}{r_1^\gamma}+1} 2\pi r_2 dr_2 dr_1 \quad (48)$$

$$\leq \int_0^\infty 2\pi r_1 \int_0^R \mathbf{1}(T\rho\frac{r_2^\gamma}{r_1^\gamma} \geq 1) 2\pi r_2 dr_2 dr_1 +$$

$$\int_0^\infty 2\pi r_1 \int_0^R \mathbf{1}(T\rho\frac{r_2^\gamma}{r_1^\gamma} < 1)\frac{T\rho r_2^\gamma}{r_1^\gamma} 2\pi r_2 dr_2 dr_1 \quad (49)$$

$$= 4\pi^2 R^4 (T\rho)^{\frac{2}{\gamma}} \left(\frac{1}{8} + \frac{1}{4(\gamma+2)} + \frac{1}{(\gamma+2)(\gamma-2)}\right). \quad (50)$$

In (48), the integrated item is in the form of $\frac{X}{X+1}$, where $X = \frac{T\rho r_2^\gamma}{r_1^\gamma} \geq 0$. The bound of the integrated item can be found as follows: if $X \geq 1$, $\frac{1}{2} \leq \frac{X}{X+1} \leq 1$; otherwise, if $X < 1$, $\frac{X}{2} \leq \frac{X}{X+1} \leq X$. Accordingly, we can separate the integration region into $\frac{T\rho r_2^\gamma}{r_1^\gamma} \geq 1$ region and $\frac{T\rho r_2^\gamma}{r_1^\gamma} < 1$ region. As a consequence, the upper bound of (48) can be derived as (49).

Lower Bound of V

Following a similar approach as above, we have

$$\mathbf{V} = \int_0^\infty 2\pi r_1 \int_0^R \frac{\frac{T\rho r_2^\gamma}{r_1^\gamma}}{\frac{T\rho r_2^\gamma}{r_1^\gamma}+1} 2\pi r_2 dr_2 dr_1 \quad (51)$$

$$\geq \int_0^\infty 2\pi r_1 \int_0^R \mathbf{1}(T\rho\frac{r_2^\gamma}{r_1^\gamma} \geq 1)\pi r_2 dr_2 dr_1 +$$

$$\int_0^\infty 2\pi r_1 \int_0^R \mathbf{1}(T\rho\frac{r_2^\gamma}{r_1^\gamma} < 1)\frac{T\rho r_2^\gamma}{r_1^\gamma} \pi r_2 dr_2 dr_1 \quad (52)$$

$$= 2\pi^2 R^4 (T\rho)^{\frac{2}{\gamma}} \left(\frac{1}{8} + \frac{1}{4(\gamma+2)} + \frac{1}{(\gamma+2)(\gamma-2)}\right). \quad (53)$$

□

9. REFERENCES

[1] X. An and F. Pianese. Understanding co-channel interference in LTE-based multi-tier cellular networks. In *Proc. of ACM PE-WASUN*, Paphos, Cyprus, Oct. 2012.

[2] M. Y. Arslan, J. Yoon, K. Sundaresan, S. V. Krishnamurthy, and S. Banerjee. FERMI: a femtocell resource management system forinterference mitigation in OFDMA networks. In *Proc. of ACM MobiCom*, Las Vegas, NV, Sept. 2011.

[3] F. Baccelli and B. Blaszczyszyn. Stochastic geometry and wireless networks, volume 1: Theory. *Foundations and Trends in Networking*, 3(3-4):249 – 449, 2009.

[4] W. Bao and B. Liang. Understanding the benefits of open access in femtocell networks: Stochastic geometric analysis in the uplink. *arXiv:1308.2454 [cs.NI]*.

[5] W. Bao and B. Liang. Uplink interference analysis for two-tier cellular networks with diverse users under random spatial patterns. In *Proc. of IEEE/CIC International Conference on Communications in China (ICCC)*, Xi'an, China, Aug. 2013.

[6] C. C. Chan and S. Hanly. Calculating the outage probability in a CDMA network with spatial Poisson traffic. *IEEE Trans. on Vehicular Technology*, 50(1):183 – 204, Jan. 2001.

[7] V. Chandrasekhar and J. Andrews. Uplink capacity and interference avoidance for two-tier femtocell networks. *IEEE Trans. on Wireless Communications*, 8(7):3498–3509, Jul. 2009.

[8] W. C. Cheung, T. Q. S. Quek, and M. Kountouris. Stochastic analysis of two-tier networks: Effect of spectrum allocation. In *Proc. of IEEE International Conference on Acoustics, Speech and Signal Processing (ICASSP)*, Prague, Czech Republic, May 2011.

[9] H. Dhillon, R. Ganti, F. Baccelli, and J. Andrews. A tractable framework for coverage and outage in heterogeneous cellular networks. In *Information Theory and Applications Workshop*, San Diego, CA, Feb. 2011.

[10] H. Dhillon, R. Ganti, F. Baccelli, and J. Andrews. Modeling and analysis of K-tier downlink heterogeneous cellular networks. *IEEE Journal on Selected Areas in Communications*, 30(3):550–560, Apr. 2012.

[11] H. S. Dhillon, R. K. Ganti, and J. G. Andrews. Load-aware heterogeneous cellular networks: Modeling and SIR distribution. In *Proc. of IEEE GLOBECOM*, Anaheim, CA, Dec. 2012.

[12] K. Gilhousen, I. Jacobs, R. Padovani, A. Viterbi, L. Weaver, and C. Wheatley. On the capacity of a cellular CDMA system. *IEEE Trans. on Vehicular Technology*, 40(2):303–312, May 1991.

[13] H.-S. Jo, P. Xia, and J. G. Andrews. Open, closed, and shared access femtocells in the downlink. *arXiv:1009.3522 [cs.NI]*, 2010.

[14] Y. Kim, S. Lee, and D. Hong. Performance analysis of two-tier femtocell networks with outage constraints. *IEEE Trans. on Wireless Communications*, 9(9):2695– 2700, Sept. 2010.

[15] S. Kishore, L. Greenstein, H. Poor, and S. Schwartz. Uplink user capacity in a CDMA macrocell with a hotspot microcell: exact and approximate analyses. *IEEE Trans. on Wireless Communications*, 2(2):364–374, Mar. 2003.

[16] S. Kishore, L. Greenstein, H. Poor, and S. Schwartz. Uplink user capacity in a multicell CDMA system with hotspot microcells. *IEEE Trans. on Wireless Communications*, 5(6):1333–1342, June 2006.

[17] D. Knisely, T. Yoshizawa, and F. Favichia. Standardization of femtocells in 3GPP. *IEEE Communications Magazine*, 47(9):68–75, Sept. 2009.

[18] T. D. Novlan, H. S. Dhillon, and J. G. Andrews. Analytical modeling of uplink cellular networks. *arXiv:1203.1304 [cs.IT]*, 2012.

[19] S. Singh, H. S. Dhillon, and J. G. Andrews. Offloading in heterogeneous networks: Modeling, analysis and design insights. *arXiv:1208.1977 [cs.IT]*, 2012.

[20] D. Stoyan, W. Kendall, and J. Mecke. *Stochastic Geometry and Its Applications*. Wiley, second edition, 1995.

[21] P. Tarasak, T. Q. S. Quek, and F. P. S. Chin. Uplink timing misalignment in open and closed access OFDMA femtocell networks. *IEEE Communications Letters*, 15(9):926–928, Sept. 2011.

[22] A. J. Viterbi, A. M. Viterbi, K. Gilhousen, and E. Zehavi. Soft handoff extends CDMA cell coverage and increases reverse link capacity. *IEEE Journal on Selected Areas in Communications*, 12(8):1281–1288, Oct. 1994.

[23] P. Xia, V. Chandrasekhar, and J. Andrews. Open vs. closed access femtocells in the uplink. *IEEE Trans. on Wireless Communications*, 9(12):3798–3809, Dec. 2010.

[24] J. Yoon, M. Y. Arslan, K. Sundaresan, S. V. Krishnamurthy, and S. Banerjee. A distributed resource management framework for interference mitigation in OFDMA femtocell networks. In *Proc. of ACM MobiHoc*, Hilton Head Island, SC, June 2012 2012.

Efficient Energy Management and Data Recovery in Sensor Networks Using Latent Variables Based Tensor Factorization

Bojan Milosevic*, Jinseok Yang†, Nakul Verma†, Sameer S. Tilak†, Piero Zappi‡
Elisabetta Farella*, Luca Benini*, Tajana S. Rosing†

*University of Bologna, Via Risorgimento 2, Bologna, Italy
†UCSD, 9500 Gilman Dr., La Jolla, USA
‡Qualcomm Inc., 5775 Morehouse Dr., San Diego, USA

ABSTRACT

A key factor in a successful sensor network deployment is finding a good balance between maximizing the number of measurements taken (to maintain a good sampling rate) and minimizing the overall energy consumption (to extend the network lifetime). In this work, we present a data-driven statistical model to optimize this tradeoff. Our approach takes advantage of the multivariate nature of the data collected by a heterogeneous sensor network to learn spatio-temporal patterns. These patterns enable us to employ an aggressive duty cycling policy on the individual sensor nodes, thereby reducing the overall energy consumption. Our experiments with the OMNeT++ network simulator using realistic wireless channel conditions, on data collected from two real-world sensor networks, show that we can sample just 20% of the data and can reconstruct the remaining 80% of the data with less than 9% mean error, outperforming similar techniques such is distributed compressive sampling. In addition, energy savings ranging up to 76%, depending on the sampling rate and the hardware configuration of the node.

Categories and Subject Descriptors

G.3 [**Probability and Statistics**]: Multivariate statistics; I.5.1 [**Pattern Recognition**]: Statistical models

Keywords

Statistical Modeling; Data Recovery; Energy Management; Wireless Sensor Networks; Latent Variables; Tensor Factorization

*{*firstname.lastname*}@unibo.it
†{*jiy011, naverma, sameer, tajana*}@ucsd.edu
‡pzappi@qti.qualcomm.com

MSWiM'13, November 3–8, 2013, Barcelona, Spain.

http://dx.doi.org/10.1145/2507924.2507953.

1. INTRODUCTION

Modern applications of WSNs typically require measuring several variables (such as temperature, humidity, etc.) for extended periods of time over a large area. To meet the application requirements, the design and deployment of a WSN has to carefully balance between two competing goals: (1) high spatio-temporal resolution to ensure the accuracy of the collected data, and (2) minimal energy consumption to maximize the network lifetime and limit node maintenance. The amount of data that a node collects and processes directly affects both its power consumption and the accuracy of the information obtained [8, 22].

Extending the uptime of a sensor node - especially when the nodes are deployed in difficult to access remote locations - is an active topic of research in WSNs. Common approaches try to enhance the battery life *directly* by harvesting energy from the environment and employing low-power hardware architectures [4, 5], or using improved wireless protocols and distributed computation for data processing [27]. More recently, researchers are optimizing the battery life *indirectly* by reducing the overall amount of sensed data [24]. Here, the data is selectively sampled according to a predetermined protocol, reducing the total amount of samples collected by the individual sensor nodes, thus minimizing the energy consumption [11]. To maintain an acceptable amount of total measurements, the missing data is inferred according to statistical models that capture how the data evolves. In addition to enhancing the battery life, these approaches are also able to estimate any lost or corrupted data, making them a popular choice.

In this paper we propose an energy efficient, data driven technique to estimate missing data within a heterogeneous sensor network. Our approach extends the standard latent variable factorization model - which typically considers only dyadic interactions in data - to multivariate spatio-temporal data, by applying tensor decomposition techniques [15]. The key advantage of using a latent variable model is that it provides a compact representation of the gathered data that can be used to recover the missing samples. In order to perform well under extreme sampling conditions, we extend the standard technique to explicitly incorporate the spatial, temporal, and inter-sensor correlations.

This study focuses on the trade-off between the accuracy in recovering the missing data and the energy consumption when sensor nodes duty cycle to save energy. The proposed technique drastically reduces the amount of sampled data at each node, thus allowing the nodes to spend more time in a low-power sleep mode and save energy. The lower amount of sampled data implies a lower amount of data to transmit from the node to a central gathering station, reducing also the power consumptions associated with the radio communications. To test our approach, in a realistic setting (e.g., realistic channel conditions) we simulated our sensor network deployments using the OMNeT++ [21] network simulator. We used two different deployments: one is an environmental monitoring WSN with weather stations displaced across the state of California [9], and the another is a smaller scale WSN used for a structural health monitoring application [1]. Our results show that we can effectively reconstruct the un-sampled data with under 9% error even when we are sampling only about 20% of the CIMIS dataset. The 3ENCULT dataset achieve a mean reconstruction error of 6.3% when using 4-hop networks. We compared our technique with a state-of-the-art approach based on Distributed Compressive Sensing (DCS) [13], which has a comparable approach and reconstructs individual signals from sub-sampled versions. The result show how our approach is better in the case of higher percentage of missing samples, and with signals that show lower temporal correlations. We observed up to 50% of energy saving across the network of sensors, depending on the sampling frequency. Lower energy savings when using a longer sampling period are expected because the sensor nodes spend most of the time in a low power sleep state. Thus, the energy consumption within the sleep state dominates the overall savings.

2. RELATED WORK

Selectively sampling the data in order to improve the overall energy consumption is an active area of research. Various compression [6, 3], subsampling [11, 18] and data recovery techniques [16] have been proposed in the literature, based on application characteristics.

Compressed Sensing (CS) has emerged as a powerful framework to summarize (compress) and recover missing values when the data is sparse. It has recently been applied in WSNs to reduce transmission bandwidth and improve the energy consumption [6, 3, 13]. In [6], for instance, a random basis is used to compress data gathered from temperature sensors. A feedback mechanism allows the network nodes to adapt their sampling rate dynamically while minimizing the data acquisition and transmission costs. The distributed compressed sensing (DCS) framework [13] exploits both intra-signal and inter-signal correlations through the concept of joint sparsity. The work in [3], presents a distributed algorithm, robust to increases in the number of network, that optimizes the transmission bandwidth via DCS. Research has also optimized the energy consumption by minimizing data acquisition and various subsampling schemes have been proposed [11, 18, 16]. The work in [11] treats sensor networks as a database, adopting an interactive sensor querying approach enriched with statistical modeling techniques. They demonstrate that such models, coupled with the appropriate selection of sensors, can help provide answers that are both more meaningful, and, by introducing approximations with probabilistic confidences, significantly more efficient for computing. In [18] similar types of nodes are clustered and data is sampled from one node in each cluster at a time. The missing values are predicted using a linear combination of the sampled entries. A Bayesian approach to find patterns in data is used in [16]. The missing data is reconstructed by using these patterns. They use simple spatial and temporal correlations (last values and one-hop neighbors) to improve the final prediction.

Latent variable and decomposition techniques have also been proposed in literature, for various applications. Matrix factorization learning of latent variables has been used for recovering missing data in sensor networks in [25]. Tensor decomposition techniques have been applied on WSNs only in [21], where the learned models are used to find the damages in a structural health monitoring application. Other applications of tensor decomposition techniques include data classification and recovery in multichannel electroencephalograms [10] or network analysis [2].

The previously presented algorithms only consider homogeneous sensor streams, dealing with one sensor at a time, and do not consider varying sampling costs across sensor types. In our work we correlate data from different types of sensors across different node locations over time. Our approach focuses on the multivariate nature of the collected data. It expands the tensor factorization techniques by employing spatio-temporal and intra-sensor correlations for more robust and better results than the existing methods. The DCS has a similar approach when considering the network nodes, but adopts different reconstruction techniques. We included a comparison with our work to highlight the benefits of a correlation-based approach, that has better reconstruction capabilities with lower percentages of sampled data.

3. LATENT VARIABLES AND TENSOR FACTORIZATION

Latent variable based factorization is a simple yet powerful framework for modeling data, and has been successfully applied in several application domains [17]. The main idea behind this framework is to model the large number of observed variables (the *observed data*) in terms of a much smaller number of unobserved variables (the *latent variables*). The latent variables are learned from the observed data and are used to estimate the missing samples, modeling complex interactions between the observed variables through simple interactions between the latent variables.

More specifically, given some multivariate data that is collected by a heterogeneous WSN in a large field over time, we can naturally organize it in a three dimensional data array (or a *3-tensor*). Each of the three dimensions corresponds to a different variate of a particular measurement (e.g. the time, the location and the sensor type associated with each reading). Once the data is organized in this way, we can then associate a low-dimensional *latent* variable with each unique location, time slice and sensor type. We can thus model a particular observation (at a given location, time and type) as a noisy combination of the associated latent variables. In many scenarios, a multiplicative combination of these latent variables is able to capture intricate dependencies in the data [15, 2]. The goal then is to learn a good set of latent variables (that is, find a factorization) that can efficiently represent our observed data.

3.1 Modeling Details

We now define formally our model. For each unique time instance t, sensor type s, and node location n, we associate a unique K-dimensional vector a_t, b_s and c_n respectively. These unobserved vectors are called the latent factors or variables, and are assumed to control the location-, time-

and sensor-specific interactions present in the observed data. Then, given a $[T \times S \times N]$ tensor $\mathcal{X}$ of sensor readings from S different sensor types collected at N different nodes and T different time instances, with possible missing entries, we model $\mathcal{X}$ as follows. We assume that each reading x_{tsn} (reading at time t, for sensor type s, at node location n) is a noisy realization of the underlying true reading that is obtained by the interaction of the time specific latent variable a_t, with the sensor specific latent variable b_s and with the location specific variable c_n. That is,

$$x_{tsn} = \sum_{k=1}^{K} a_{tk} b_{sk} c_{nk} + \varepsilon, \qquad (1)$$

where ε is modeled as independent zero-mean Gaussian noise ($\varepsilon \sim \mathcal{N}(0, \sigma^2)$). Observe that under this model once all the latent variables are known, one can recover the true readings of all sensors at all locations and times. Thus the goal is to find the most predictive set of vectors a_t, b_s and c_n for all $t = 1, \ldots, T$, $s = 1, \ldots, S$, $n = 1, \ldots, N$. Such a representation models the entire data of size $[T \cdot N \cdot S]$ by just $[K \cdot (T + N + S)]$ modeling parameters. The choice of the free parameter K provides a key trade-off: a large K increases the number of modeling parameters and thus can help model the observed data exactly. But this lacks the capability on predicting unobserved/missing data due to overfitting. A small K, on the other hand, escapes the overfitting problem, but the corresponding model lacks sufficient richness to capture salient data trends. The exact choice of a good K is typically application dependent and is derived empirically.

3.1.1 *Learning the latent variables*

Finding the optimal set of K-dimensional latent variables given the observations is equivalent of factorizing the given tensor into three matrices each of rank at most K [15]. Thus, assuming that all the data is known (that is, every entry in the tensor is observed), we can find the latent factors by employing the CanDecomp/ParaFac (CP) tensor factorization [15]. This is simply a higher-order generalization of the matrix singular value decomposition (SVD), and decomposes a generic third order tensor in three matrix factors A, B, and C. By restricting the ranks of each of the matrix factors to at most K, yields the best rank K approximation. Algorithmically, the matrix factors are found by an alternating least squares approach (ALS) [2], which starts from a random initialization and iteratively optimizes one matrix factor at a time, while keeping the other two fixed.

This technique can be generalized to work with tensors that have missing entries. Since sensor nodes can periodically go offline due to duty-cycling or run out of energy (preventing all sensors on a node from collecting any data for an extended period of time), we need to extend our basic model to deal with data missing from multiple sensors or nodes, resulting in entries and rows of missing data in the collected tensor. In order to do well in this regime we extend the basic tensor factorization model to explicitly incorporate spatial, temporal and sensor specific information from neighboring observations by explicitly learning and enforcing the corresponding correlations.

3.2 Incorporating correlations

To successfully interpolate the sensor interactions to contiguously missing blocks of data, we need to explicitly model spatial, temporal and sensor-specific trends within each of our latent variables a_t, b_s and c_n. Such trends ensure that the latent variables a_t and $a_{t'}$ (respectively b_s and $b_{s'}$, and c_n and $c_{n'}$) take similar values when times t and t' are "similar" (respectively sensors types s and s', and locations n and n'). Note that similarity can mean anything based on the context. For locations, it can mean that variables associated two locations that are close in distance should have similar characteristics, while for time, it can mean that variables associated with times that are same hour of the day or same day of the week should have similar characteristics. Here we take a data driven approach to infer the best notion of similarity using correlations directly computed from the data. We use a limited sample of data collected from the network to learn the correlations, which are then applied to the subsequent slot of data to reconstruct the unsampled values.

The similarity constraints are modeled in the same way for all the three sets of latent variables, and here we illustrate the case for the a_t's. Since each a_t is a K-dimensional variable, let a_{tk} denote its kth coordinate. We model a_{tk} (independently for each coordinate k) as

$$\begin{aligned} a_{:k} &= \mu_{ak} + \alpha_{:k} \\ \alpha_{:k} &\sim \mathcal{N}(0, \Sigma_a). \end{aligned} \qquad (2)$$

Here $a_{:k}$ represents the collection of all a_t's (across $t = 1, \ldots, T$) in the kth coordinate and μ_a represents their mean value. The distributional constraint over $\alpha_{:k}$ (as $\mathcal{N}(0, \Sigma_a)$) enforces the similarity constraints via the $T \times T$ covariance matrix Σ_a. By changing the t, t' entry of Σ_a we can encourage/discourage the corresponding a_t and $a_{t'}$ to take similar values – a high positive value at $\Sigma_a(t, t')$ encourages a positive correlation, a high negative value encourages negative correlation, while a value close to zero does not encourage any correlation. We enforce similar constraints on b_s and c_n variables as well.

To get the right similarity constraints Σ_a, Σ_b and Σ_c (for latent variables a_t, b_t and c_n), we compute them from the data we are considering. For spatial similarity constrains, we computed the averaged pairwise Pearson correlation coefficients between data from different pairs of locations, and averaged over different time and sensors. We do the same to approximate inter-sensor and temporal similarities. We can have only one global correlation constraint along each of the dimensions.

3.3 Parameter learning

We can learn the underlying latent variables in a probabilistic framework using a *maximum a posteriori* (MAP) estimate. In particular, let θ denote all the model parameters (i.e. $\theta = \{\{a_t\}, \{b_s\}, \{c_n\}, \sigma\}$), then the optimum choice of parameters θ_{MAP} given the data $\mathcal{X}$ is obtained by:

$$\theta_{MAP}(\mathcal{X}) := \underset{\theta}{\operatorname{argmax}} \underbrace{p(\mathcal{X} \mid \theta)}_{\text{likelihood}} \underbrace{p(\theta)}_{\text{prior}}$$

$$= \underset{\theta}{\operatorname{argmax}} \sum_{t,s,n \in \text{observed}} \log p(x_{tsn} \mid a_t, b_s, c_n, \sigma) +$$

$$\sum_{k=1}^{K} \log p(a_{:k}) + \sum_{k=1}^{K} \log p(b_{:k}) + \sum_{k=1}^{K} \log p(c_{:k}).$$

The first term (the likelihood) takes the form of Eq. (1), and the other terms represent the priors for each latent variable and each one of them takes the form of Eq. (2). We take a

	Nodes	Sensors per node	Variables Reported	T_S [min]
	128	7	10	60
ULT	23	3	3	10

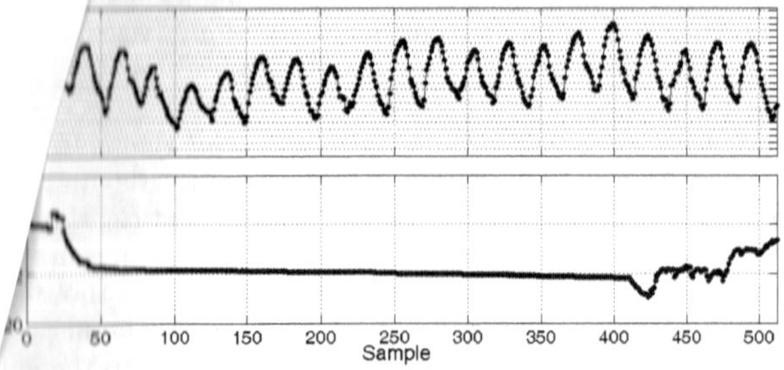

'igure 1: **Comparison of the temperature signal col-ected from the CIMIS network (above) and the 3ENCULT network (below).**

uniform prior over σ, the standard deviation of the residuals in Eq. (1) so it doesn't explicitly show in the equation.
This optimization does not have a closed form solution. Standard gradient based techniques can be used to get a locally optimal solution. Here we can do an alternating hill-climb approach by optimizing the value of one variable while keeping all others fixed to get a good solution. As for the standard factorization technique, this iterative approach uses a random initialization of the latent variables.

4. HARDWARE, NETWORK AND POWER MODELS

To evaluate the proposed technique we use real-world data from two sensor networks, with different hardware configurations and spatio-temporal resolutions. The composition of the two networks is summarized in Table 1.
Our first data set comes from an environmental monitoring WSN from the California Irrigation Management Information System (CIMIS) [9]. It is a program that manages a network of 232 automated weather stations (128 functioning at the moment), displaced across the state of California. Each station provides hourly readings of 12 different measurements from its embedded sensors. The second data set comes from a case study of the 3ENCULT European project [1], deployed by our research group. This is a structural health monitoring application where a network of 23 low-power sensor nodes is deployed across the three floors of a historic building at the University of Bologna.
The two data sets have different sampling periods (one hour for CIMIS and ten minutes for 3ENCULT) and different spatial coverage and distribution (state-wide coverage for CIMIS and indoor coverage of a 3-store building for 3ENCULT). Table 2 summarizes the variables reported by each station for the two datasets. Even if some variables are shared among the two datasets, the network characteristics, the nature of the captured signals and the resulting correlations are different because of the differences in the sensed environment. As an example, we can observe the Figure 1 where a block of 512 samples of temperature readings from the two data sets is reported.

4.1 Hardware

We used the hardware configuration of the nodes in the two data sets to estimate each node's power consumption. For the environmental monitoring stations in the CIMIS dataset we used the Vaisala WHT250 sensor station [23] which

Variables	CIMIS	3ENCULT
Solar Radiation $[W/m^2]$	X	X
Net Radiation $[W/m^2]$	X	
Soil Temperature $[°C]$	X	
Air Temperature $[°C]$	X	X
Pressure $[kPa]$	X	
Wind Speed $[m/s]$	X	
Wind Direction $[0 - 360°]$	X	
Precipitation $[mm]$	X	
Ref. ETo $[mm]$	X	
Rel. Humidity $[\%]$	X	X

Table 2: Sensor list for the different datasets.

has detailed power consumption information available. This type of station is used at several locations in the CIMIS network. Since the WHT250 does not embed any radio, we assume that the radio communication is performed through a commercially available Zigbee wireless transceiver (XBee PRO [12]).
The node employed in the 3ENCULT network is a custom wireless node (W25TH) that is based on an NXP system on chip module with an 32-bit RISC processir and a $24GHz$ IEEE802.15.4-compliant transceiver. Sensors include a Sensirion SHT21 for temperature and humidity, and a BH1715 for Light. Timing reference and power information is obtained either using the values reported in the datasheet (CIMIS) or direct measurements using a GPIO trigger connected to an oscilloscope (3ENCULT). Data on power consumption of the various subsystems is not reported due to lack of space, but the reader can refer to Tables 3 and 4 for key power parameters, including the measured currents in the case of the 3ENCULT nodes.

4.2 Network model

In a sensor network we can consider that each node samples the signals for a period of time T, called acquisition period, ideally gathering $N = T * f_s$ number of samples at a f_s sampling frequency, before sending the data to the collection point. If each node adopts a sub-sampling policy with an under-sampling ratio α then the number of samples actually gathered by the node is $M = \alpha N$.
The under-sampling pattern is locally generated by each node using its own ID and the timestamp as seed for the randomization of the sampling pattern, which has inter-measurement intervals that are always multiple of the sampling period $T_k = T/N$.
We used the OMNET++ network simulator to simulate the packet loss characteristics of a realistic wireless channel [20]. We leveraged the commonly used log-normal path loss model, which is defined as:

$$P_r(d)[dBm] = P_t[dBm] - PL(d_0) - 10nlog(d/d0) - X_\sigma \quad (3)$$

where $P_r(d)$ is the received signal strength (in dBm), P_t is transmitted power, $PL(d_0)$ is the measured path loss at the reference distance d_0, n is the path loss exponent, and X_σ is a normal random variable with a zero mean and variance σ (in dB).
The path loss exponent measures the rate at which the received signal strength decreases with distance [19], while the term X_σ models the shadowing effect, which introduces signal variations because of various types of artifacts in the environment [7]. In ideal channel conditions, with line of sight path and no shadowing effects, the loss model has n=2

and σ=0. In this case, the collection center can successfully receive all the sensor measurements without any loss. In order to mimic harsher channel conditions such as an urban scenario, we use the results of [14] which investigate the path loss characteristic of nine urban streets in Cambridge. From their observations, one of nine street has a path loss exponent (n) equal to 2.6, so we used this value as parameter. In addition, the placement of the transmitter determines the fraction of rays, which might vary from 2 to 5 dB [14]. Thus, we set σ is 3 in our simulation. Each sensor node has maximum 80m transmission distance with maximum 2mW transmit power. The maximum distance is evaluated by free space model [20].

4.3 Sensor node power models

We introduce an architecture level power model to evaluate the energy consumption of the node when the subsampling parameters are changed. Using this power model with data from real hardware and measurements, we can easily evaluate how changing the parameters influences the energy consumption and the lifetime of the network.
Starting from the assumption reported in the previous section, the average energy consumption in each period of duration T_k, for a sub-sampling factor ρ, is:

$$E_k = \rho\,(E_{\text{setup}} + E_{\text{sample}} + E_{\text{store}}) + E_{\text{sleep}} + N^{-1}\,(E_{\text{nv}} + E_{\text{send}}) \tag{4}$$

where E_{sleep} is the energy spent in sleep mode, E_{setup} is the energy used for waking up and setting up the device, E_{sample} is the energy for sampling each sensors, E_{send} is the energy used to send the acquired data, E_{store} is the energy to store the acquired sample in non volatile memory and E_{nv} is the energy spent during the recovery of the data from non volatile memory. We used the hardware configuration of the nodes in the two data sets to estimate each node's power consumption.
The energy consumption of the environmental monitoring sensor stations is summarized in Table 3. This data is obtained from the components' data sheets, considering the average consumption for each operation, and using the World Meteorological Organization (WMO) specifications for environmental data gathering [26]. The wind measurements (speed and direction) need to be reported in 1 minute increments, thus costing a lot of energy. Pressure, temperature and humidity sensors have the same power consumption ($9.6mW$) as they are part of the same module, but each sensor has to be read individually. With an 1 hour sampling period, the energy consumed at each interval is $5.62J$, 75% of which is spent in the sleep mode. Of the active energy, 96% is consumed for the sampling of the sensors, 3.5% for data transmission and 0.5% by the CPU. Our model considers all the contributions even if the sampling energy is the dominating component in this scenario.

The energy consumption of the nodes of the 3ENCULT network is summarized in Table 4. In this case the radio transmission represents the main source of energy consumption. There is $24.1mJ$ of energy per each 10 minutes sampling period, of which almost 82% is for the sleep mode. Of the active power, 86% is consumed by the radio transmission of the acquired packets, 13% by the CPU and 1% by the sensors.
In both cases the influence of the energy spent in the sleep mode increases with an increase of the sampling period, since

Sensor or State	Power [mW]	Time [s]	Energy [mJ]
Sleep (all node)	1.2	-	-
CPU Active	42.9	-	-
Wind speed & direction	20	60	1200
Pressure	9.6	5	48
Temperature	9.6	5	48
Humidity	9.6	5	48
Rain	0.84	10	8.4
Data transmission	158.4	0.05	8

Table 3: Power consumption of the different components of an environmental station used by CIMIS. The energy consumption refers to a single sampling event or a single packet transmission.

Sensor or State	Current [mA]	Power [mW]	Time [ms]	Energy [mJ]
Sleep (all node)	0.01	0.578	-	-
CPU Active	8.08	24.7	-	-
Temperature	0.3	0.495	0.002	0.001
Humidity	0.3	0.495	0.002	0.001
Light	0.3	0.495	0.002	0.001
Data transmission	18	102.3	0.05	5.115

Table 4: Power consumption of the different components of the sensor node used in 3ENCULT.

the node spends more time waiting for the next interval. With longer periods, even aggressive duty cycling policies will have a smaller benefit in terms of energy saving, since they reduce only the active energy spent for sampling and data transmission.

5. EXPERIMENTAL RESULTS

5.1 Data preprocessing

Our statistical model treats data from each heterogeneous sensor equally. Since raw data from different sensor types are at widely different scales (e.g. the temperature ranges from about 10 to $40°C$, while relative humidity measurements range from 0 to 100%), we preprocess all the variables to ensure they have zero mean and unit variance. This normalization brings all measurements to the same scale and allows us to apply our multivariate tensor factorization technique. The normalized prediction can easily be translated back into the original scale by rescaling and adding back the mean value. The reconstruction error is evaluated in the original scale for each variable, adopting the Normalized Root Mean Squared Error ($NRMSE$) defined as: $NRMSE = \sqrt{E[(\hat{\boldsymbol{x}} - \boldsymbol{x})^2]}/(x_{max} - x_{min})$, where $\boldsymbol{x}$ and $\hat{\boldsymbol{x}}$ are respectively the actual and predicted data for each variable, x_{max} and x_{min} are the maximum and minimum values for the same variable.

5.2 Tensor factorization

Here we evaluate the effectiveness of our tensor-based latent variable factorization technique to model our datasets. In our approach, the data collected from the sensor network is organized in a $[T \times S \times N]$ tensor $\mathcal{X}$ and is factored in three matrix factors A, B and C of size $[T \times K]$, $[S \times K]$ and $[N \times K]$. This leads to a model with $K(T + S + N)$ parameters for a dataset with $T \cdot S \cdot N$ entries.
The latent variables dimensionality, K, regulates the complexity of the model. To evaluate the impact of K, different models with increasing complexity (increasing values of K)

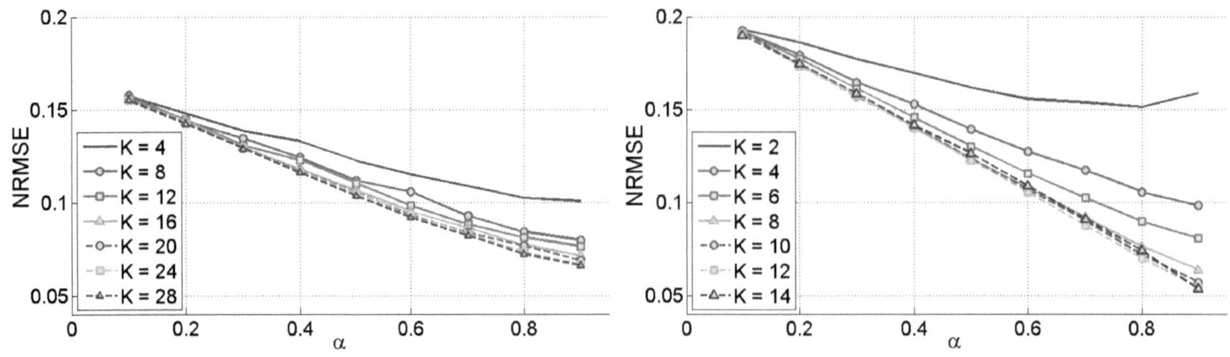

(a) (b)

Figure 2: Comparison of tensor factorization reconstruction of data for different values of K: (a) CIMIS dataset and (b) 3ENCULT

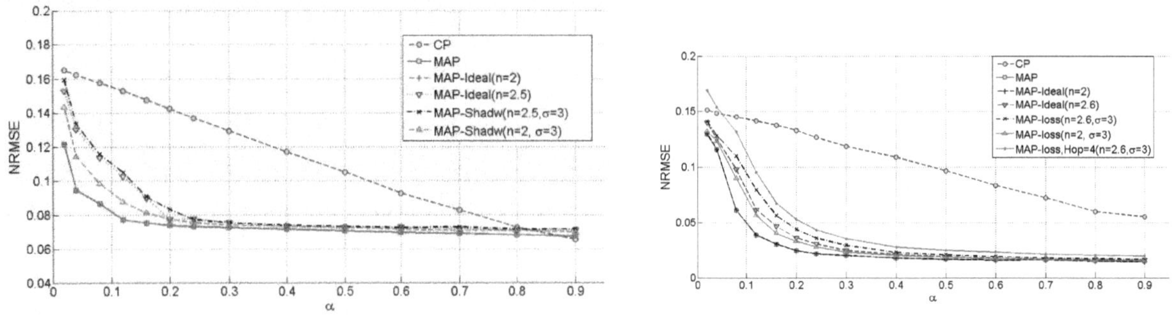

(a) (b)

Figure 3: Node duty cycling effects on the reconstruction error as computed from the standard tensor factorization approach (CP) and our technique (MAP): (a) CIMIS dataset and (b) 3ENCULT.

were learned from the data, using the standard CP tensor factorization technique. The whole dataset is reconstructed using the learned model and the $NRMSE$ between the real data and the reconstructed one is evaluated. This operation is repeated for different fractions of sampled data α used to learn the model. The $NRMSE$ shows how well the collected data can be summarized by a few latent variables, thus exploring the compression capabilities of our approach. The results for the two datasets are illustrated in Figure 2. In both cases we used blocks of 512 samples for the temporal duration, which were sub-sampled to test the algorithm. We can see a saturation effect on the quality of the reconstruction, with the increase of K. The exact choice of this parameter is application dependent and depends on the dimension of the network and the number of sensors. In our case K was set to 24 in the CIMIS and 12 in the 3ENCULT case.

5.3 Data recovery

In order to save energy, sensor nodes can apply aggressive duty cycling strategies, collecting just a portion of the original data. When applying a duty cycling policy, a node avoids sampling its sensors, resulting in an entire rows of missing entries in the data tensor. To analyze the ability of the proposed method to reconstruct the missing samples, we removed increasing percentages of rows from the collected data. The remaining data (*training data*) was used to learn our latent variable model, while the removed entries (*testing data*) were used to evaluate the recovering capabilities of the algorithm.

Figure 3 shows the reconstruction error of the missing data ($NRMSE$) as a function of the fraction of the sampled data (α) for the two analyzed datasets. We compare the two implementations of the tensor factorization algorithm: (1) the standard factorization technique (CP) that does not include correlations from the data, and (2) our approach that does incorporate the temporal, spatial, and inter-sensor correlation, where the variables are learned using the MAP estimation. In both cases we use a block of 512 samples from the whole network and set the dimension of the latent variables as indicated in the previous section. The correlations are learned directly from the data, using a block of 64 samples, taken just before the data blocks are considered for the reconstruction evaluation. The mean $NRMSE$ across all the variables is reported on the *testing data* for the two datasets.

In order to investigate the effect of the wireless transmission, we simulate the network conditions with different path loss exponents (n) and shadowing variances (σ) as described in Section 4.2 with the log-normal path loss model. Figure 3.(a) shows that in the CIMIS case our approach achieves a reconstruction error below 9%, with up to 80% of the missing samples under the worst wireless channel condition (i.e. n=2.5, σ=3). With the same sampling policy, Figure 3.(b) shows that for the 3ENCULT dataset we achieve a mean reconstruction error of 6.3%, when using a 4-hop network. The results show that the number of the network hops has a negligible effect on the reconstruction accuracy when the wireless channel conditions are stationary over the deployed area. Increasing the number of network hops by four de-

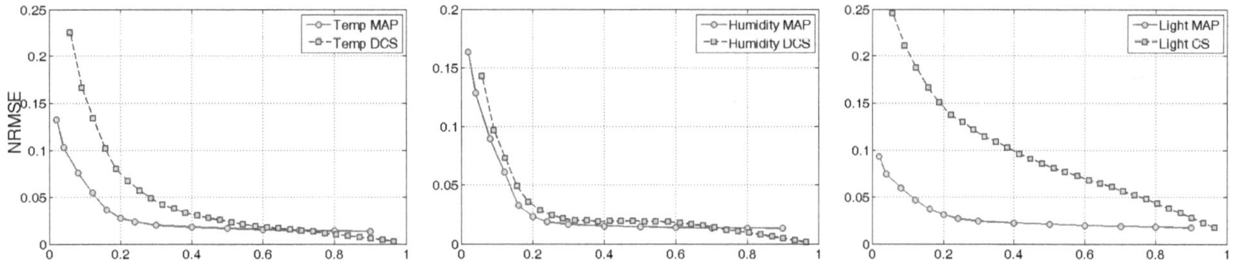

(a) (b) (c)

Figure 4: Comparison of our technique (MAP) with a distributed compressive sampling (DCS) technique for the different variables in the 3encult datast: (a) temperature, (b) humidity and (c) light.

creases the reconstruction accuracy by just 1%. Our technique consistently outperforms the standard tensor factorization approach with up to 90% of the missing samples. If there are more than 90% missing samples, our approaches still achieves less than 20% error.

The results outlined above are the average reconstruction errors among all sensors. If we look at the individual sensors, we see that the single variables exhibit different recovering proprieties. The ones characterized by strong correlation proprieties and smooth temporal transitions, such as temperature and solar radiation, are better reconstructed compared to the ones that have high variance or little periodicity, such as wind speed and direction.

5.4 Comparison with compressive sensing

To compare our approach with a state of the art technique, we used the same data with a compressive sampling reconstruction algorithm. To match our scenario, where just a portion of the desired data is collected due to duty cycling policies, we employed a sparse measurement matrix as in the Distributed Compressive Sampling (DCS) approach illustrated in [13]. A Discrete Cosine Transform (DCT) is used as the basis with a Basis Pursuit solver available in the SparseLab Matlab Toolbx to independently reconstruct the signals. The results of the comparison with the 3ENCULT data set are shown in Figure 4. Our technique, labeled MAP, performs better when a smaller portion of data is collected, thanks to the use of the inter-node correlations and the contribution from the whole network to reconstruct the data. For the reconstruction of the humidity signals we have comparable results for the two techniques. For the temperature our approach is better for smaller amounts of collected samples, gaining 6% of normalized reconstruction error at 20% of collected samples. In particular, the DCS algorithm has problems in the reconstruction of the light signal, which shows less temporal correlations and has higher variance. Indoor light patterns often present sharp changes due to artificial illumination, which is not well managed by the adopted compressed sensing approach. In this case we achieve more than 10% of gain in the NRMSE, when collecting 20% of the samples.

5.5 Energy savings

Using the energy characterizations of the nodes from Tables 3 and 4, we can estimate the average amount of energy savings associated with different sampling policies. Figure 5 shows energy savings for various combinations of sampling periods and duty cycling rates in the two case studies. Different sampling policies are compared to the case when all

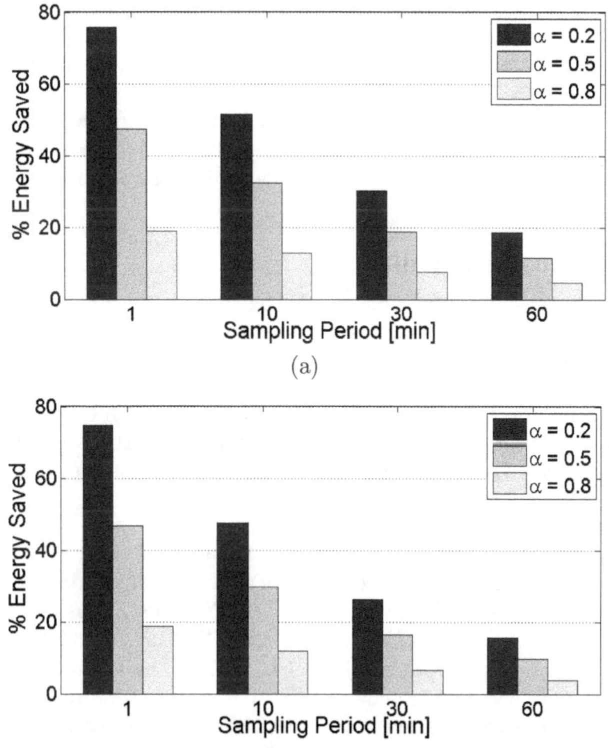

(a)

(b)

Figure 5: Energy saving (%) when applying a give sampling policy for different sampling periods: (a) CIMIS dataset and (b) 3ENCULT.

the data is sampled. Regardless of the type of hardware used in the two scenarios, we determine a similar result, showing that our algorithm can get large energy savings in a wide range of applications. Aggressively duty cycling on a dataset that samples the environment every minute yields significantly higher energy savings (76%) than the one which only samples every hour (20%). This is expected because with lower sampling frequencies, the sensor nodes spend most of the time in a low power sleep state. Thus, the energy consumption within the sleep state dominates and the overall power consumption is less influenced by the sampling policy.

6. CONCLUSION

This work presents a latent variable model for energy efficient data collection in wireless sensor networks. This approach takes advantage of the multivariate nature of the data collected by a heterogeneous sensor networks, and uses

tensor factorization methods combined with correlation.
Our model's performance allows us to employ aggressive duty cycling strategies on the sensor nodes for better energy conservation. Each node is able to save energy by sampling just a portion of the desired data. The available data is then used to learn a latent variable model and reconstruct the missing samples. The proposed technique does not require any kind of data processing on the sensor node, which only adopts the desired duty cycling policy and sends the collected samples.
Experiments with real-world sensor networks show that our algorithm can maintain a low mean reconstruction error, below 9%, with up to 80% of missing samples, even under harsh transmission channel conditions. This permits energy savings ranging from 20% to 80% depending on the sampling rates in the two cases dataset. When compared to an existing state of the art approach, such as the distributed compressed sensing, our approach shows 2 times better reconstruction performance with 80% of missing samples. Our approach takes advantage of inter-node correlations across the network, so has advantage when signals has low correlations.

Acknowledgments

This work has been funded by the NSF project Citisense (grant CNS-0932403), NSF OCI Award 1219504 and the European project 3ENCULT (Grant agreement 260162). Additionally it was supported in part by TerraSwarm, one of six centers of STARnet, a Semiconductor Research Corporation program sponsored by MARCO and DARPA. We also thank the Qualcomm Research center for their support.

7. REFERENCES

[1] 3ENCULT. www.3encult.eu/en/casestudies/.

[2] E. Acar and B. Yener. Unsupervised multiway data analysis: A literature survey. *IEEE Transactions on Knowledge and Data Engineering*, 21(1):6–20, 2009.

[3] C. Caione, D. Brunelli, and L. Benini. Distributed compressive sampling for lifetime optimization in dense wireless sensor networks. *IEEE Transactions on Industrial Informatics*, 8(1):30–40, 2012.

[4] B. Calhoun, D. Daly, N. Verma, D. Finchelstein, D. Wentzloff, A. Wang, S.-H. Cho, and A. Chandrakasan. Design considerations for ultra-low energy wireless microsensor nodes. *IEEE Transactions on Computers*, 54(6):727–40, 2005.

[5] D. Carli, D. Brunelli, L. Benini, and M. Ruggeri. An effective multi-source energy harvester for low power applications. In *Design, Automation Test in Europe Conference Exhibition*, pages 1–6, 2011.

[6] W. Chen, M. Rodrigues, and I. Wassell. Distributed compressive sensing reconstruction via common support discovery. In *IEEE International Conference on Communications*, pages 1–5, 2011.

[7] Y. Chen and A. Terzis. On the implications of the log-normal path loss model: an efficient method to deploy and move sensor motes. In *Conf. on Embedded Networked Sensor Systems*, pages 26–39, 2011.

[8] S. K. Chong, M. M. Gaber, S. Krishnaswamy, and S. W. Loke. Transactions on large-scale data and knowledge-centered systems. 2011.

[9] CIMIS dataset. www.cimis.water.ca.gov.

[10] J. Dauwels, K. Srinivasan, M. Ramasubba Reddy, and A. Cichocki. Multi-channel eeg compression based on 3d decompositions. In *Acoustics, Speech and Signal Processing (ICASSP)*, pages 637 –640, 2012.

[11] A. Deshpande, C. Guestrin, S. R. Madden, J. M. Hellerstein, and W. Hong. Model-driven data acquisition in sensor networks. In *Intl. Conf. on Very large data bases*, pages 588–599, 2004.

[12] Digi. Xbee pro zb. www.digi.com/xbee/.

[13] M. F. Duarte, M. B. Wakin, D. Baron, and R. G. Baraniuk. Universal distributed sensing via random projections. In *Information processing in sensor networks*, IPSN, pages 177–185, 2006.

[14] K. Herring, J. Holloway, D. Staelin, and D. Bliss. Path-loss characteristics of urban wireless channels. *IEEE Trans. on Antennas and Propagation*, 58(1):171–177, 2010.

[15] T. G. Kolda and B. W. Bader. Tensor decompositions and applications. *SIAM Review*, 51(3):455–500, 2009.

[16] L. Kong, M. Xia, X.-Y. Liu, M.-Y. Wu, and X. Liu. Environment reconstruction in sensor networks with massive data loss. In *Technical Report*, 2011.

[17] Y. Koren, R. Bell, and C. Volinsky. Matrix factorization techniques for recommender systems. *IEEE Transactions on Computers*, 42(8):30–37, 2009.

[18] J. C. Lim and C. Bleakley. Adaptive WSN scheduling for lifetime extension in environmental monitoring applications. *International Journal of Distributed Sensor Networks*, 2012(1958), 2012.

[19] G. Mao, B. D. Anderson, and B. Fidan. Path loss exponent estimation for wireless sensor network localization. *Computer Networks*, 51(10):2467 – 2483, 2007.

[20] OMNET. Simulator. http://omnetpp.org/.

[21] M. A. Prada, J. Toivola, J. Kullaa, and J. Hollmen. Three-way analysis of structural health monitoring data. *Neurocomputing*, 80(0):119 – 128, 2012.

[22] V. Raghunathan, S. Ganeriwal, and M. Srivastava. Emerging techniques for long lived wireless sensor networks. *IEEE Comm. Magazine*, 44(4):108–114, 2006.

[23] Vaisala. Wxt250. http://www.vaisala.com/en/products/multiweathersensors/Pages/WXT520.aspx.

[24] V. V. Veeravalli and P. K. Varshney. Distributed inference in wireless sensor networks. *Philosophical Transactions of the Royal Society*, 370(1958):100–117, 2012.

[25] N. Verma, P. Zappi, and T. Rosing. Latent variables based data estimation for sensing applications. In *IEEE Intl. Conf. on Intelligent Sensors, Sensor Networks and Information Processing, ISSNIP*, pages 335–340, 2011.

[26] World Meteorological Organization. Wind measurement and archival under the automated surface observing system (ASOS). www.aoml.noaa.gov/hrd/Powell/ArchiveASOS.pdf.

[27] P. Zappi, C. Lombriser, T. Stiefmeier, E. Farella, D. Roggen, L. Benini, and G. Troster. Activity recognition from on-body sensors: Accuracy-power trade-off by dynamic sensor selection. In *Eu. Conf. on Wireless Sensor Networks*, pages 17–33, 2008.

A Process Algebraic Framework for Estimating the Energy Consumption in Ad-hoc Wireless Sensor Networks*

Lucia Gallina, Andrea Marin, Sabina Rossi
Università Ca' Foscari Venezia, Italy
{lgallina,marin,srossi}@dais.unive.it

Tingting Han, Marta Kwiatkowska
University of Oxford, United Kingdom
{marta.kwiatkowska,tingting.han}@cs.ox.ac.uk

ABSTRACT

We present a framework for modelling ad-hoc Wireless Sensor Networks (WSNs) and studying both their connectivity properties and their performances in terms of energy consumption, throughput and other relevant indices. Our framework is based on a probabilistic process calculus where system executions are driven by Markovian probabilistic schedulers, allowing us to translate process terms into discrete time Markov chains (DTMCs) and use the probabilistic model checker PRISM to automatically evaluate/estimate the connectivity properties and the energy costs of the networks. To the best of our knowledge, this is the first work that proposes a unique framework for studying qualitative (e.g., by proving the equivalence of components or the correctness of a behaviour) and quantitative aspects of WSNs using a tool that allows both exact and approximate (via Monte Carlo simulation) analyses. We demonstrate our framework at work by considering different communication strategies based on gossip routing protocols, for a typical topology and a mobility scenario.

Categories and Subject Descriptors

C.4 [**Computer Systems Organization**]: Performance of systems—*modeling techniques*; C.2.1 [**Computer-Communication Networks**]: Network architecture and design—*Wireless Communication*

General Terms

Theory, reliability

Keywords

Process algebra, simulation, sensor networks

*Work partially supported by the MIUR Project CINA "Compositionality, Interaction, Negoziation, Autonomicity for the future ICT society".

MSWiM'13, November 3–8, 2013, Barcelona, Spain.
Copyright 2013 ACM 978-1-4503-2353-6/13/11
http://dx.doi.org/10.1145/2507924.2507958 ...$15.00.

1. INTRODUCTION

Wireless Sensor Networks (WSNs) [2] are collections of spatially distributed sensing devices equipped with limited computing and radio communication capabilities. They are employed in a variety of applications, ranging from military surveillance to health care or assisted living, and from smart cities to environmental monitoring. A typical sensor network is characterized by a large number of sensor nodes, which are densely deployed, and have frequent topology changes due to the mobility of its devices. Nodes communicate using wireless transmission in a specified range, with communication between nodes implemented in terms of routing protocols. A critical issue in wireless sensor networks is the limited availability of energy within the network devices. Therefore, judicious choice of routing protocols that can reduce the nodes' power consumption is crucial, not only for the performance of each single node, but also for the throughout of the network lifetime. In this paper we introduce a framework for the specification, modelling and automated analysis or simulation of connectivity properties and the evaluation or estimation of energy consumption in ad-hoc WSNs. The framework is based on a variant of the Probabilistic Energy-aware Broadcast Unicast and Multicast (PEBUM) calculus introduced in [5], and supports the automatic performance evaluation through (approximate) probabilistic model checking, e.g., using the PRISM model checker [9]. The advantages of using a process algebra rely on its compositional nature which allows us to decompose both the model construction and the qualitative analysis. Concerning the quantitative analysis we take advantage of the various kind of properties which can be specified in terms of a temporal logic and verified using the model checking technique. The proposed calculus is built around nodes, representing the sensor devices of the systems, and locations, identifying the position cells across which each device may move inside the network. Node mobility is governed by probability distributions. Instead, wireless synchronisations are controlled by sequential processes inside the nodes: each transmission broadcasts a message within a given transmission range. The semantics of our calculus is inspired by Segala's probabilistic automata [15] driven by schedulers to resolve the nondeterministic choice among the probability distributions over target states. Differently from [5], in this work we assume that nodes are not equipped with a unique identifier and they all share the same transmission frequency. These choices reflect the fact that transmissions in ad-hoc sensor networks are directed to a geographical location rather than to a specific node and, due to the low-cost hardware of sensors, only one frequency is used

Networks		**Processes**	
M,N ::= $\mathbf{0}$	Empty network	P,Q ::= $\mathbf{0}$	Inactive process
$\mid [P]_l^{\mathbf{J}}$	Sensor Node	$\mid (\tilde{x}).P$	Input
$\mid M_1 \mid M_2$	Parallel composition	$\mid \langle\tilde{w}\rangle_{L,r}.P$	Output
		$\mid [w_1 = w_2]P, Q$	Matching
		$\mid A\langle\tilde{w}\rangle$	Recursion

Table 1: Syntax

at a given time [17]. Moreover, in contrast to [6, 5], in this paper we employ *Makovian probabilistic schedulers*, mapping the non-deterministic choices among the different actions a system may enable into probability distributions. As a consequence, the labelled transition system underlying process terms is a discrete time Markov chain (DTMC), which can be used for automatically performing a range of qualitative and quantitative analyses by means of probabilistic model checking, e.g., using PRISM. We define a probabilistic observational congruence in the style of [13] to equate networks exhibiting the same connectivity behaviour. As in [5], and in contrast to [12], the notion of observability is associated with specific locations in the network reflecting the fact that in ad-hoc WSNs the transmissions are not addressed to specific nodes but to specific locations. We provide a coinductive characterization of the observational congruence based on a probabilistic labelled bisimilarity. Finally, we define an energy-aware preorder over networks, to contrast networks having the same behaviour, but different energy costs. We use our framework for a comparative study of gossip based routing protocols for wireless ad-hoc sensor networks. We address the problem of the state space explosion using the statistical model checking implemented in PRISM. The paper is organised as follows. Section 2 presents the calculus, its observational semantics expressed in terms of behavioural equivalences and a characterization of it based on a notion of probabilistic bisimilarity. In Section 3 an energy-aware preorder over networks is defined: it allows us to compare the average energy cost of different networks but exhibiting the same connectivity behaviour. Finally, in Section 4, gossip based routing protocols for different scenarios are considered and we show the framework at work studying the sensitivity of the performances of these protocols to some configuration parameters. Finally, Section 5 discusses the related bibliography and concludes the paper.

2. A CALCULUS FOR WSN

We present a variant of the PEBUM calculus presented in [5] which focuses on the main features of ad-hoc wireless sensor networks. Specifically, nodes are not equipped with a unique identifier and only one transmission frequency is used.

Syntax. We use letters l for *locations*, r for *transmission radii*, x and y for *variables*. *Closed values* contain locations, transmission radii and any basic value (booleans, integers, ...). *Values* include also variables. We use u and v for closed values and w for (open) values. We write $\tilde{v}$, $\tilde{w}$ for tuples of values. We write $\mathcal{N}$ for the set of all networks and **Loc** for the set of all locations. While movements may be assumed to be continuous, we identify locations as the countable set of cells that constitute the observing areas within the network. The syntax of our calculus is shown in Table 1. This is defined in a two-level structure: the lower one for processes, the upper one for networks. Networks are collections of sensor nodes running in parallel and communicating messages. As usual, $\mathbf{0}$ denotes the empty network and $M_1|M_2$ denotes the parallel composition of two networks. We denote by $\prod_{i\in I} M_i$ the parallel composition of the networks M_i, for $i \in I$. $[P]_l^{\mathbf{J}}$ denotes a sensor node located at the physical location l and executing the process P. $\mathbf{J}$ is the transition matrix of a discrete time Markov chain modelling node mobility: each entry $\mathbf{J}_{lk}$ is the probability that the sensor node located at l moves to the location k. Hence, $\sum_{k\in\mathbf{Loc}} \mathbf{J}_{lk} = 1$ for all locations $l \in \mathbf{Loc}$. Static nodes inside a network are associated with the identity Markov chain, i.e., the identity matrix $\mathbf{J}_{ll} = 1$ for all $l \in \mathbf{Loc}$ and $\mathbf{J}_{lk} = 0$ for all $l \neq k$. Processes are sequential and live within the nodes: $\mathbf{0}$ is the inactive process; $(\tilde{x}).P$ is ready to listen to a transmission, while $\langle\tilde{w}\rangle_{L,r}.P$ is ready to transmit. In $(\tilde{x}).P$, the variables in $\tilde{x}$ are bound with scope in P. As to the output form, the tag r represents the transmission radius of the sender, while the tag L is used to maintain the set of physical locations of the intended recipients: $L = \mathbf{Loc}$ represents a broadcast transmission, while a finite set of locations L denotes a multicast communication (unicast if L is a singleton). As stated in the introduction, communication protocols for ad-hoc sensor networks are usually intended to reach a certain location, rather than a specific device, due to the absence of global identifiers associated with the sensor devices. The remaining syntactic forms are standard: $[w_1 = w_2]P, Q$ behaves as P if $w_1 = w_2$, and as Q otherwise. $A\langle\tilde{w}\rangle$ is the process defined via a (possibly recursive) definition $A(\tilde{x}) \stackrel{\text{def}}{=} P$, with $|\tilde{x}| = |\tilde{w}|$ where $\tilde{x}$ contains all variables appearing free in P.

Probability distributions for networks. We denote by $\mu_l^{\mathbf{J}}$ the probability distribution associated with a node located at l with transition matrix $\mathbf{J}$, i.e., the function over **Loc** such that $\mu_l^{\mathbf{J}}(k) = \mathbf{J}_{lk}$ for all $k \in \mathbf{Loc}$. Let M be a network. We denote by $M\{[P]_k^{\mathbf{J}}/[P]_l^{\mathbf{J}}\}$ the network obtained by replacing l with k inside the sensor node $[P]_l^{\mathbf{J}}$. We also denote by $[\![M]\!]_{\mu_l^{\mathbf{J}}}$ the probability distribution over networks induced by $\mu_l^{\mathbf{J}}$ and defined by: for all networks M',

$$[\![M]\!]_{\mu_l^{\mathbf{J}}}(M') = \begin{cases} \mu_l^{\mathbf{J}}(k) & \text{if } M' = M\{[P]_k^{\mathbf{J}}/[P]_l^{\mathbf{J}}\} \\ 0 & \text{otherwise.} \end{cases}$$

Intuitively, $[\![M]\!]_{\mu_l^{\mathbf{J}}}(M')$ is the probability that the network M evolves to M' due to the movement of the sensor node $[P]_l^{\mathbf{J}}$. We say that M' is in the support of $[\![M]\!]_{\mu_l^{\mathbf{J}}}$ if $[\![M]\!]_{\mu_l^{\mathbf{J}}}(M') \neq 0$. We write $[\![M]\!]_\Delta$ for the Dirac distribution on the network M, i.e., the probability distribution defined as: $[\![M]\!]_\Delta(M) = 1$ and $[\![M]\!]_\Delta(M') = 0$ for all $M' \neq M$. Finally, we let θ range over $\{\mu_l^{\mathbf{J}} \mid \mathbf{J}$ is a transition matrix and $l \in \mathbf{Loc}\} \cup \{\Delta\}$.

$$\text{(R-Bcast)}\ \frac{}{[\langle\tilde{v}\rangle_{L,r}.P]_l^{\mathbf{J}} \mid \prod_{i\in I}[(\tilde{x}_i).P_i]_{l_i}^{\mathbf{J}^i} \rightarrow [\![[P]_l^{\mathbf{J}} \mid \prod_{i\in I}[P_i\{\tilde{v}/\tilde{x}_i\}]_{l_i}^{\mathbf{J}^i}]\!]_\Delta} \quad \text{where } \forall i \in I.d(l,l_i) \leq r \text{ and } |\tilde{x}_i| = |\tilde{v}|$$

$$\text{(R-Move)}\ \frac{}{[P]_l^{\mathbf{J}} \rightarrow [\![[P]_l^{\mathbf{J}}]\!]_{\mu_l^{\mathbf{J}}}} \qquad \text{(R-Par)}\ \frac{M \rightarrow [\![M']\!]_\theta}{M|N \rightarrow [\![M'|N]\!]_\theta} \qquad \text{(R-Struct)}\ \frac{N \equiv M \quad M \rightarrow [\![M']\!]_\theta \quad M' \equiv N'}{N \rightarrow [\![N']\!]_\theta}$$

Table 2: Reduction Semantics

Reduction semantics. The dynamics of the calculus is specified by the *probabilistic reduction relation* ($\rightarrow$) described in Table 2: it takes the form $M \rightarrow [\![M']\!]_\theta$ denoting a transition that leaves from M and leads to a probability distribution $[\![M']\!]_\theta$. As usual, reduction relies on structural congruence ($\equiv$), such that, e.g., $M|N \equiv N|M$, $(M|N)|M' \equiv M|(N|M')$ and $M|\mathbf{0} \equiv M$. Nodes cannot be created or destroyed, and move autonomously. Node connectivity is verified by looking at the physical location and the transmission radius of the sender: a message broadcast by a node is received only by the nodes that lie in the area delimited by the transmission radius of the sender. We presuppose a function $d(\cdot,\cdot)$ which returns the distance between two locations.

Rule (R-Bcast) models the transmission of a tuple of messages $\tilde{v}$ by a sensor node located at l and using a radius r. The index set I may be empty, i.e., the rule can be applied even if no nodes are ready to receive. The radius r associated with the output action denotes the transmission radius of that communication which may depend on the energy consumption strategy adopted by the surrounding protocol. All the nodes that lie in the range of the sender (i.e., such that $d(l,l_i) \leq r$) will receive the messages. Rule (R-Move) deals with node mobility: a node $[P]_l^{\mathbf{J}}$ executing a move action will reach a location with a probability described by the distribution $\mu_l^{\mathbf{J}}$ that depends on the Markov chain $\mathbf{J}$ statically associated with the node. The remaining rules are standard. Given a network M, we write $M \rightarrow_\theta N$ if $M \rightarrow [\![M']\!]_\theta$ and N is in the support of $[\![M']\!]_\theta$. Following [6], an execution for M is a (possibly infinite) sequence of steps $M \rightarrow_{\theta_1} M_1 \rightarrow_{\theta_2} M_2 \ldots$.

Observational Semantics. According to a standard practice, we formalise the observational semantics of our calculus in terms of a notion of *barb* that provides the basic unit of observation [13]. As in other calculi for wireless communication, the definition of barb is naturally expressed in terms of message transmission. We denote by $behave(M) = \{[\![M']\!]_\theta \mid M \rightarrow [\![M']\!]_\theta\}$ the set of the possible behaviours of M. In order to solve the nondeterminism in a network execution, we consider each possible probabilistic transition $M \rightarrow [\![M']\!]_\theta$ as arising from a *probabilistic scheduler* defined as follows.

DEFINITION 1 (SCHEDULER). *A* probabilistic scheduler *is a total function F assigning to a network M a distribution ϕ on the set behave(M).*

We denote by *Sched* the set of all probabilistic schedulers. Given a network M and a scheduler F, we define the set of all executions starting from M and driven by F as:

$$Exec_M^F = \{e = M_0 \rightarrow_{p_1\theta_1} M_1 \rightarrow_{p_2\theta_2} M_2 \ldots \mid M_0 \equiv M \text{ and } \forall j > 0:\ M_{j-1} \rightarrow [\![M_j']\!]_{\theta_j},\ p_j = F(M_{j-1})([\![M_j']\!]_{\theta_j}) \text{ and } M_j \text{ is in the support of } [\![M_j']\!]_{\theta_j}\}.$$

For a finite execution $e = M \rightarrow_{p_1\theta_1} M_1 \ldots \rightarrow_{p_k\theta_k} M_k \in Exec_M^F$ starting from M and driven by a scheduler F we define

$$P_M^F(e) = p_1 \cdot [\![M_1']\!]_{\theta_1}(M_1) \cdot \ldots \cdot p_k \cdot [\![M_k']\!]_{\theta_k}(M_k)$$

where $\forall j \leq k$, $p_j = F(M_{j-1})([\![M_j']\!]_{\theta_j})$. We denote by $last(e)$ the final state of a *finite* execution e, by e^j the prefix $M \rightarrow_{p_1\theta_1} M_1 \ldots \rightarrow_{p_j\theta_j} M_j$ of length j of the execution $e = M \rightarrow_{p_1\theta_1} M_1 \cdots \rightarrow_{p_j\theta_j} M_j \rightarrow_{p_{j+1}\theta_{j+1}} M_{j+1} \cdots$, and by $e\!\uparrow$ the set of $\bar{e}$ such that $e \leq_{prefix} \bar{e}$. We write $M \rightarrow_*^F M'$ if there exists a finite execution $e \in Exec_M^F$ with $last(e) = M'$.

We define the probability space on the executions starting from a given network M as follows. Given a scheduler F, $\sigma Field_M^F$ is the smallest sigma field on $Exec_M^F$ that contains the basic cylinders $e\!\uparrow$, where $e \in Exec_M^F$. The probability measure $Prob_M^F$ is the unique measure on $\sigma Field_M^F$ such that $Prob_M^F(e\!\uparrow) = P_M^F(e)$. Given a measurable set of networks H, we denote by $Exec_M^F(H)$ the set of executions starting from M and crossing a state in H. Formally $Exec_M^F(H) = \{e \in Exec_M^F \mid last(e^j) \in H \text{ for some } j\}$. We denote the probability for a network M to evolve into a network in H, according to the policy given by F, as $Prob_M^F(H) = Prob_M^F(Exec_M^F(H))$. Note that the use of probabilistic schedulers allows us to model networks as discrete time Markov chains (DTMCs). This is the result of the application of a *two level* probability distribution: the reduction semantics maps a network M into a probability distribution in the set *behave*(M) while, in turn, the probabilistic scheduler maps M into a probability distribution ϕ over the probability distributions in the set *behave*(M), giving rise to a fully probabilistic model.

The notion of barb introduced below denotes an observable transmission with a certain probability according to a fixed scheduler. We first introduce a notion of *strong barb*: for a network M, we write $M \downarrow_K$ when $M \equiv [\langle\tilde{v}\rangle_{L,r}.P]_l^{\mathbf{J}}|M'$ with $\emptyset \neq K \subseteq L$ and forall $k \in K$, $d(l,k) \leq r$. Roughly, a transmission is observable only if at least one location in the set of the intended recipients is able to receive the message. We say that a network M has a *barb* with probability p at the set K of locations, according to the scheduler F, written $M \Downarrow_p^F K$, if $Prob_M^F(\{M' | M \rightarrow_*^F M' \downarrow_K\}) = p$. Intuitively, for a given network M and scheduler F, if $M \Downarrow_p^F K$ then there is a positive probability that M, driven by F, performs a transmission and at least one of the intended recipients is able to correctly listen to it. In the following, we introduce a notion of probabilistic observational congruence relative to a specific set of schedulers $\mathcal{F} \in Sched$. Since our semantics is contextual, we need to ensure that the set of schedulers we consider allows the specific networks we analyse to interact with any possible context. Hence for a set $\mathcal{F}$ of schedulers we define the *contextual superset* $\mathcal{F}_\mathcal{C}$ of $\mathcal{F}$, as the largest set of schedulers allowing networks to interact with any pos-

$$\text{(Output)}\ \frac{-}{\langle\tilde v\rangle_{L,r}.P \xrightarrow{\tilde v_{L,r}} P} \qquad \text{(Input)}\ \frac{-}{(\tilde x).P \xrightarrow{\tilde v} P\{\tilde v/\tilde x\}}$$

$$\text{(Then)}\ \frac{P \xrightarrow{\eta} P'}{[\tilde v = \tilde v]P,Q \xrightarrow{\eta} P'} \qquad \text{(Else)}\ \frac{Q \xrightarrow{\eta} Q' \quad \tilde v_1 \neq \tilde v_2}{[\tilde v_1 = \tilde v_2]P,Q \xrightarrow{\eta} Q'} \qquad \text{(Rec)}\ \frac{P\{\tilde v/\tilde x\} \xrightarrow{\eta} P'}{A\langle\tilde v\rangle \xrightarrow{\eta} P'}\quad A(\tilde x) \stackrel{\text{def}}{=} P$$

Table 3: LTS rules for Processes

sible context even when driven by $\mathcal{F}$ (see [4] for a formal definition). It holds that $Sched_{\mathcal{C}} = Sched$. Hereafter, a context $C[\cdot]$ is a term with a hole defined by the grammar: $\mathcal{C}[\cdot] ::= [\cdot] \mid [\cdot]|M \mid M|[\cdot]$. Our probabilistic observational congruence relative to a specific set of schedulers is defined as follows.

Definition 2. *Given a set $\mathcal{F} \subseteq Sched$ and a relation $\mathcal{R}$ over networks:*
- $\mathcal{R}$ *is* barb preserving *relative to $\mathcal{F}$ if $M\mathcal{R}N$ and $M{\Downarrow}_p^F K$ for some $F \in \mathcal{F}_{\mathcal{C}}$ implies that $\exists\ F' \in \mathcal{F}_{\mathcal{C}}$ such that $N{\Downarrow}_p^{F'} K$.*
- $\mathcal{R}$ *is* reduction closed *relative to $\mathcal{F}$ if $M\mathcal{R}N$ implies that $\forall\ F \in \mathcal{F}_{\mathcal{C}}\ \exists\ F' \in \mathcal{F}_{\mathcal{C}}$ such that $\forall\ \mathcal{C} \in \mathcal{N}/\mathcal{R}$, $Prob_M^F(\mathcal{C}) = Prob_N^{F'}(\mathcal{C})$.*
- $\mathcal{R}$ *is* contextual *if $M\mathcal{R}N$ implies that $\mathcal{C}[M]\,\mathcal{R}\,\mathcal{C}[N]$ for every context $\mathcal{C}[\cdot]$.*
- Probabilistic observational congruence relative to $\mathcal{F}$, *written $\cong_p^{\mathcal{F}}$, is the largest symmetric relation over networks which is reduction closed, barb preserving and contextual.*

Two networks are related by $\cong_p^{\mathcal{F}}$ if they exhibit the same probabilistic (connectivity) behaviour relative to $\mathcal{F}$. In the next section a bisimulation-based proof technique for $\cong_p^{\mathcal{F}}$ is developed in order to provide an efficient method to check whether two networks are related by $\cong_p^{\mathcal{F}}$.

Deciding the Observational Congruence. We express the semantics of the calculus in terms of labelled transition systems (LTS) which are built upon two sets of rules: one for processes and one for networks. Table 3 presents the LTS rules for processes. Transitions are of the form $P \xrightarrow{\eta} P'$, where η ranges over input and output actions: $\eta ::= \tilde v \,|\, \tilde v_{L,r}$.

Table 4 presents the LTS rules for networks. Transitions are of the form $M \xrightarrow{\gamma} [\![M']\!]_\theta$, where M is a network and $[\![M']\!]_\theta$ is a distribution over networks. Probabilities are used to model the mobility of nodes. Tag γ ranges over the labels:

$$\gamma ::= L!\tilde v[l,r] \mid ?\tilde v@l \mid R!\tilde v@K \mid \tau.$$

Rule (Snd) models the sending of tuple $\tilde v$ to a specific set L of locations with transmission radius r, while rule (Rcv) models the reception of $\tilde v$ at l. Rule (Bcast) models the broadcast message propagation: all the nodes lying within the transmission cell of the sender may receive the message, regardless of the fact that they lie in one of the locations in L. Rule (Obs) models the observability of a transmission: every transmission may be detected (and hence *observed*) by any recipient lying in one of the observation locations within the transmission cell of the sender. The label $R!\tilde v@K$ represents the transmission of the tuple $\tilde v$ of messages: the set R is the set of all the locations receiving the message, while its subset K contains only the locations where the transmission is observed. Rule (Lose) models message loss. As usual, τ-transitions denote non-observable actions. Rule (Move) models node mobility according to the probability distribution $\mu_l^{\mathbf{J}}$. Finally, (Par) is standard.

Based on the LTS semantics, we define a probabilistic labelled bisimilarity that is a characterisation of our *probabilistic observational congruence.* It is built upon the actions:

$$\alpha ::= ?\tilde v@l \mid R!\tilde v@K \mid \tau.$$

We write *lbehave*(M) for the set of all possible behaviors of M, that is *lbehave*$(M) = \{(\alpha, [\![M']\!]_\theta) \mid M \xrightarrow{\alpha} [\![M']\!]_\theta\}$. A scheduler[1] for the labelled semantics is a function F assigning a probability to each pair $(\alpha, [\![M]\!]_\theta) \in$ *lbehave*(M) with a network M. We denote by *LSched* the set of schedulers for the LTS semantics. A labelled *execution* e of a network M driven by a scheduler F is a finite (or infinite) sequence of steps: $M \xrightarrow{\alpha_1}_{p_1\theta_1} M_1 \xrightarrow{\alpha_2}_{p_2\theta_2} M_2 ... \xrightarrow{\alpha_k}_{p_k\theta_k} M_k$. With abuse of notation, we define $Exec_M^F$, $last(e)$, e^j and $e\!\uparrow$ as for unlabeled executions.

Since we are interested in weak observational equivalences, that abstract over τ-actions, we introduce the notion of *weak action* as follows: $\Longrightarrow$ is the transitive and reflexive closure of $\xrightarrow{\tau}$; $\xRightarrow{\alpha}$ denotes $\Longrightarrow\xrightarrow{\alpha}\Longrightarrow$ $\forall \alpha \neq \tau$. We write $\xRightarrow{\hat\alpha}$ for the weak action $\xRightarrow{\alpha}$ if $\alpha \neq \tau$, and $\Longrightarrow$ otherwise. We denote by $Exec_M^F(\xRightarrow{\alpha}, H)$ the set of all executions that, starting from M, according to the scheduler F, lead to a network in the set H by performing $\xRightarrow{\alpha}$. We define the probability of reaching a network in H from M by performing $\xRightarrow{\alpha}$, according to a scheduler F as $Prob_M^F(\xRightarrow{\alpha}, H) = Prob_M^F(Exec_M^F(\xRightarrow{\alpha}, H))$. For $\mathcal{F} \subseteq Sched$, we denote by $\hat{\mathcal{F}}_{\mathcal{C}} \subseteq LSched$ its *contextual superset* for the LTS semantics (see [4]).

Definition 3. *Let M and N be two networks. An equivalence relation $\mathcal{R}$ over networks is a* probabilistic labelled bisimulation *relative to a set $\mathcal{F}$ of schedulers, if $M\mathcal{R}N$ implies: for all schedulers $F \in \hat{\mathcal{F}}_{\mathcal{C}}$ there exists a scheduler $F' \in \hat{\mathcal{F}}_{\mathcal{C}}$ such that for all α and for all classes $\mathcal{C} \in \mathcal{N}/\mathcal{R}$:*
- *if $\alpha \neq ?\tilde v@l$ then $Prob_M^F(\xrightarrow{\alpha}, \mathcal{C}) = Prob_N^{F'}(\xRightarrow{\hat\alpha} \mathcal{C})$;*
- *if $\alpha = ?\tilde v@l$ then either $Prob_M^F(\xrightarrow{\alpha}, \mathcal{C}) = Prob_N^{F'}(\xRightarrow{\alpha}, \mathcal{C})$ or $Prob_M^F(\xrightarrow{\alpha}, \mathcal{C}) = Prob_N^{F'}(\Longrightarrow, \mathcal{C})$.*

Probabilistic labelled bisimilarity *relative to $\mathcal{F}$, written $\approx_p^{\mathcal{F}}$, is the largest probabilistic labelled bisimulation relative to $\mathcal{F}$ over networks.*

Probabilistic labelled bisimilarity is a characterization of our probabilistic observational congruence [4].

Theorem 1. *$M \cong_p^{\mathcal{F}} N$ if and only if $M \approx_p^{\mathcal{F}} N$.*

[1] We abuse notation and still use F to denote a scheduler for the LTS semantics.

$$
\text{(Snd)}\ \frac{P \xrightarrow{\tilde{v}_{L,r}} P'}{[P]^{\mathbf{J}}_l \xrightarrow{L!\tilde{v}[l,r]} [\![[P']^{\mathbf{J}}_l]\!]_\Delta}
\qquad
\text{(Rcv)}\ \frac{P \xrightarrow{\tilde{v}} P'}{[P]^{\mathbf{J}}_l \xrightarrow{?\tilde{v}@l} [\![[P']^{\mathbf{J}}_l]\!]_\Delta}
$$

$$
\text{(Bcast)}\ \frac{M \xrightarrow{L!\tilde{v}[l,r]} [\![M']\!]_\Delta \quad N \xrightarrow{?\tilde{v}@l'} [\![N']\!]_\Delta}{M|N \xrightarrow{L!\tilde{v}[l,r]} [\![M'|N']\!]_\Delta}\quad d(l,l') \leq r
$$

$$
\text{(Obs)}\ \frac{M \xrightarrow{L!\tilde{v}[l,r]} [\![M']\!]_\Delta}{M \xrightarrow{R!\tilde{v}@K} [\![M']\!]_\Delta}\quad R \subseteq \{l' \in Loc:\ d(l,l') \leq r\} \quad K = R \cap L,\ K \neq \emptyset
$$

$$
\text{(Lose)}\ \frac{M \xrightarrow{L!\tilde{v}[l,r]} [\![M']\!]_\Delta}{M \xrightarrow{\tau} [\![M']\!]_\Delta}
\qquad
\text{(Move)}\ \frac{}{[P]^{\mathbf{J}}_l \xrightarrow{\tau} [\![[P]^{\mathbf{J}}_l]\!]_{\mu^{\mathbf{J}}_l}}
\qquad
\text{(Par)}\ \frac{M \xrightarrow{\gamma} [\![M']\!]_\theta}{M|N \xrightarrow{\gamma} [\![M'|N]\!]_\theta}
$$

Table 4: LTS rules for Networks

3. MEASURING ENERGY CONSUMPTION

In this section, based on the LTS semantics, we define a preorder over networks which allows us to study the performances, in terms of energy consumption, of different networks, but exhibiting the same connectivity behaviour. For this purpose we associate an energy cost with labelled transitions as follows. For a transmission with radius r, let

$$\mathtt{En}(r) = \mathtt{En}_{elec} \times \mathtt{packet\_len} + \mathtt{En}_{ampl} \times \mathtt{packet\_len} \times r^2$$

where $\mathtt{En}_{elec}$ (nJ/b) is the energy dissipated to run the transmitter circuit, while $\mathtt{En}_{ampl}$ $(pJ/b/m^2)$ is the radio amplifier energy (see [11]). We define

$$
\mathbf{Cost}(M, N) = \begin{cases} \mathtt{En}(r) & \text{if } M \xrightarrow{L!\tilde{v}[l,r]}_\Delta N \\ & \text{for some } L, \tilde{v}, l \text{ and } r \\ 0 & \text{otherwise} \end{cases}
$$

For an execution $e = M_0 \xrightarrow{\alpha_1}_{\theta_1} M_1 \xrightarrow{\alpha_2}_{\theta_2} M_2 \ldots \xrightarrow{\alpha_k}_{\theta_k} M_k$,

$$\mathbf{Cost}(e) = \sum\nolimits_{i=1}^{k} \mathbf{Cost}(M_{i-1}, M_i).$$

Let H be a set of networks; we denote by $Paths^F_M(H)$ the set of all executions from M ending in H and driven by F which are not prefix of any other execution ending in H. More formally, $Paths^F_M(H) = \{e \in Exec^F_M(H) \mid last(e) \in H$ and $\forall e'$ such that $e <_{prefix} e',\ e' \notin Paths^F_M(H)\}$.

DEFINITION 4. *The average cost of reaching a set of networks H from an initial network M according to the scheduler F is*

$$\mathbf{Cost}^F_M(H) = \frac{\sum_{e \in Paths^F_M(H)} \mathbf{Cost}(e) \times P^F_M(e)}{\sum_{e \in Paths^F_M(H)} P^F_M(e)}.$$

The average cost is computed by weighting the cost of each execution by its probability according to F and normalized by the overall probability of reaching H.

DEFINITION 5. *Let $\mathcal{H}$ be a countable set of sets of networks and let $\mathcal{F} \subseteq LSched$ a set of schedulers. We write*

$$N \sqsubseteq^{\mathcal{F}}_{\mathcal{H}} M,$$

if $N \approx^{\mathcal{F}}_p M$ and, $\forall$ schedulers $F \in LSched$ and $\forall\ H \in \mathcal{H}$, $\exists$ a scheduler $F' \in LSched$ such that $\mathbf{Cost}^{F'}_N(H) \leq \mathbf{Cost}^F_M(H)$.

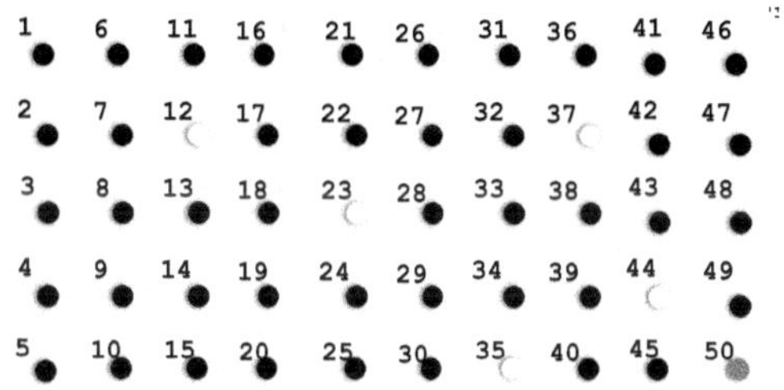

Figure 1: Topology of the Static Network (SN)

4. STUDYING GOSSIP PROTOCOLS

Gossip protocols are a family of communication protocols inspired by the way that gossiping disseminates information in social networks. A gossip protocol is a variant of the flooding algorithm, where each node forwards a message with some probability to reduce the overhead of the routing protocols. Gossiping based routing protocols are commonly used in large-scale networks (see, e.g., [3, 10, 7]) to reduce the number of retransmissions and the energy cost. In this section we show that our framework is suitable for providing an integrated automatic analysis of the gossip strategy in terms of both connectivity maintenance and energy consumption. In particular, we assume that, when a node receives a message, it forwards it with a fixed probability $\mathtt{psend}$ and discards it with probability $1 - \mathtt{psend}$. Common values for $\mathtt{psend}$ ranges from 0.6 to 0.8: it is shown that, in practical scenarios, these values provide a reduction of more than 30% of the forwarding transmissions without deteriorating the network connectivity [7]. Here we consider two different network configurations on a rectangular area of 50×100m. We assume omnidirectional antenna and a fixed transmission power for each sensor node, which covers circular areas with a radius of 10m. In the following, we denote by $[P_i]^{\mathbf{J}}_l$ the sensor node i located at l, executing the process P_i and moving according to the transition matrix $\mathbf{J}$. We study the behaviour of the networks by varying the value of the parameter $\mathtt{psend}$. The first network we consider consists of 50 static nodes, evenly distributed within the network area (see Figure 1). Node mobility is characterised by the identity matrix $\mathbf{I}$. In our tests, we consider a

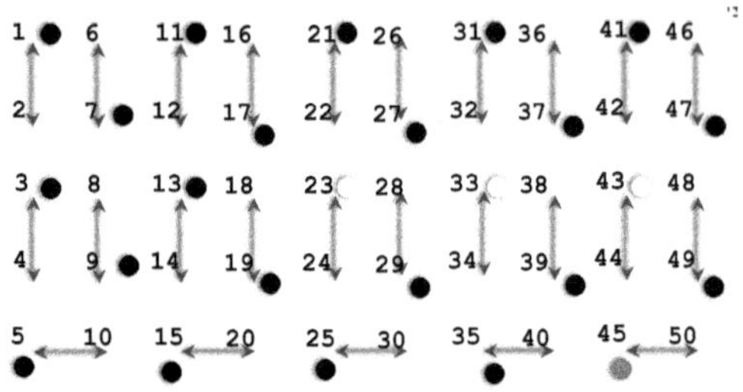

Figure 2: Topology of the Mobile Network (MN)

fixed receiver $[P_{50}]^{\mathbf{I}}_{50}$, while the sender node's location varies in the set $\{12, 23, 35, 37, 44\}$, in order to study how the connectivity behaviour of the network changes, depending on the distance between the sender node and the receiver. The network is expressed by the term:

$$M_j \stackrel{\text{def}}{=} \sum\nolimits_{i=1}^{50} [P_i]^{\mathbf{I}}_i,$$

with $j \in \{12, 23, 35, 37, 44\}$, and $P_i \stackrel{\text{def}}{=} (x_i).\langle x_i\rangle_{\{50\},10}.P_i$, $\forall i \notin \{j, 50\}$, $P_j \stackrel{\text{def}}{=} \langle x_j\rangle_{\{50\},10}.P_j$, $P_{50} \stackrel{\text{def}}{=} (x_{50}).P_{50}$, modelling the communication between $[P_j]^{\mathbf{I}}_j$ and $[P_{50}]^{\mathbf{I}}_{50}$.

The second configuration consists of 25 mobile sensor nodes again evenly distributed within the network area. Each sensor node can move between two adjacent locations, modelling the instability caused by, e.g., environmental conditions (see Figure 2). The probability distribution associated with node mobility can be captured by the transition matrix $\mathbf{J}$ such that: $\mathbf{J}_{l(l+5)} = \mathbf{J}_{(l+5)l} = \varepsilon\ \forall l \in \{5, 15, 25, 35, 45\}$, and $\mathbf{J}_{l(l+1)} = \mathbf{J}_{(l+1)l} = \varepsilon$ for all the other odd locations in the network area, and $\mathbf{J}_{ll} = 1 - \varepsilon$ for all the locations, with $0 < \varepsilon < 1$. Notice that the choice of ε and the definition of the scheduler allow us to model the relative speed between movements and transmissions. Henceforth we assume that $\varepsilon = 0.8$. This network is expressed by the term:

$$N_h \equiv \sum\nolimits_{i=1}^{25} [P_i]^{\mathbf{J}}_{(2i-1)},$$

with $h \in \{12, 17, 22\}$, where $P_i \equiv (x_i).\langle x_i\rangle_{\{45,50\},10}.P_i$, $\forall i \notin \{h, 25\}$, $P_h \equiv \langle x_h\rangle_{\{45,50\},10}.P_h$ and $P_{25} \equiv (x_{25}).P_{25}$, modelling the communication between $[P_h]^{\mathbf{J}}_{(2h-1)}$ and $[P_{25}]^{\mathbf{J}}_z$, with $z \in \{45, 50\}$ the set of locations where we expect to find P_{25}.

We model several different gossip strategies by varying the value of psend in the interval $[0.6 - 1.0]$. In particular, for each value of psend we assume a set $\mathcal{F}_{\mathsf{psend}}$ of schedulers such that, at each step, the probability for each node to perform a synchronisation or a movement is the same. Moreover, we do not consider message loss due to link failure or other environmental causes: a message can be lost only when a node discards it, consistently with the protocol. The analysis is performed using the PRISM model checker [8] (see the Appendix for details). The first step of our methodology consists in translating the process algebraic definition of our networks into the language supported by PRISM. This can be achieved in a purely algorithmic way. In general the exact analyses of real WSNs' models is unfeasible due to the explosion of the state space of the model. For this reason, we choose to perform an exact analysis to study problems of equivalences or performances in case of small components, e.g., to replace a network's node with a functionally equivalent one that has better performances in terms of throughput or energy consumption. Conversely, when studying the overall properties of wide WSNs we apply the *approximate model checking* (also known as *statistical model checking*), that relies on a Monte Carlo simulation of the underlying DTMC. As a consequence, PRISM will compute estimates of the desired indices rather then results, whose precision is controlled by means of confidence interval specifications (absolute width and confidence). When simulation is adopted, the estimates are obtained by sampling, i.e., generating a large number of random paths through the process underlying the model, hence avoiding the generation of whole DTMC. In our case studies we assume that the sender node keeps retransmitting the same packet until the destination node receives it. The outcomes of this study allow us to determine the expected number of retransmissions of the same packet that are needed to reach the intended recipient or, in more detail, which is the number of retransmissions needed in order to reach the destination with a probability higher than a given threshold. Our goal is the comparison between the different network configurations, according to the definition of energy aware preorder introduced in Section 3. Concerning the termination of the simulations, the next proposition states that, by varying the sender location, the packet eventually reaches the intended recipient.

PROPOSITION 1.

(i) $\forall\mathcal{F}_{\mathsf{psend}}$, $\mathsf{psend} \in [0.6{-}1.0]$ *and* $\forall j_1, j_2 \in \{12, 23, 35, 37, 44\}$

$$M_{j_1} \approx_p^{\mathcal{F}_{\mathsf{psend}}} M_{j_2}.$$

(ii) $\forall\mathcal{F}_{\mathsf{psend}}$, $\mathsf{psend} \in [0.6 - 1.0]$ *and* $\forall h_1, h_2 \in \{12, 17, 22\}$

$$N_{h_1} \approx_p^{\mathcal{F}_{\mathsf{psend}}} N_{h_2}.$$

Once we proved that the networks we are considering have the same connectivity, we are ready to compare their energy costs, by changing the value of **psend** and the distance among the sender and the receiver. Using the PRISM model checker, we exploit the possibility of defining reward measures to compute the energy cost function defined in Section 3. Assuming that the energy spent for each transmission is fixed and that all the nodes have the same physical characteristics, we simply count the number of transmissions rather than summing their energy cost. The cost function is expressed in terms of a Probabilistic Computation Tree Logic (PCTL) formula in the PRISM property specification language, augmented with *rewards* (or costs), which are real-valued quantities associated with states and/or transitions (see the Appendix for more details). Specifically, we verify the formula $\mathbf{R} = ?\ [\mathbf{F}\ \mathtt{goal}]$, which expresses the cumulative expected energy cost to complete the communication.

Validation of the simulator. We have validated our simulator by comparing our estimates with those obtained in [7] (see Figure 3 and 4).

Simulation of static Networks. The estimates for the static network are shown in Figure 5. The simulations have been performed with an average of 10000 experiments, a maximum confidence interval width of 1% of the estimated measure based on 95% of confidence. The plots show how the distance between sender and receiver critically influences the energy performance of the algorithm. For a distance larger then 30m we have a monotonic decreasing plot showing that, for large distances, the gossip protocol can cause energy waste. Using the standard flooding strategy (**psend** $= 1.0$)

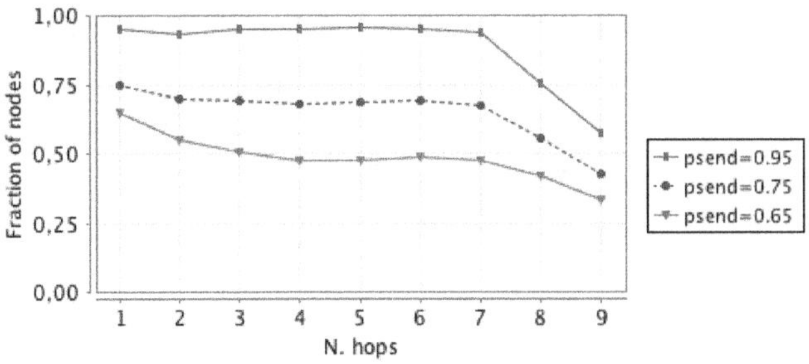

Figure 3: (SN) Fraction of nodes reached by a transmission

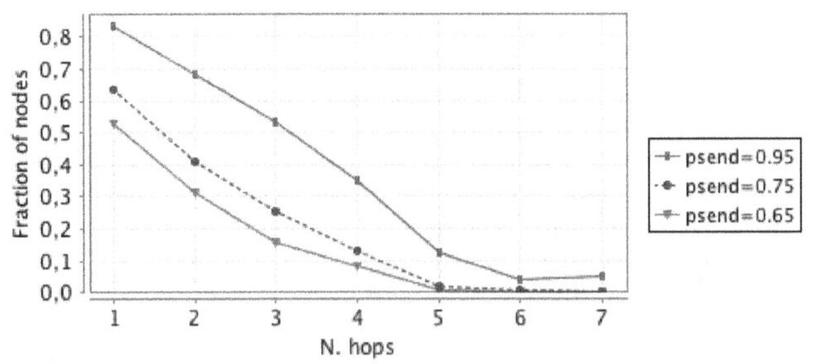

Figure 4: (MN) Fraction of nodes reached by a transmission

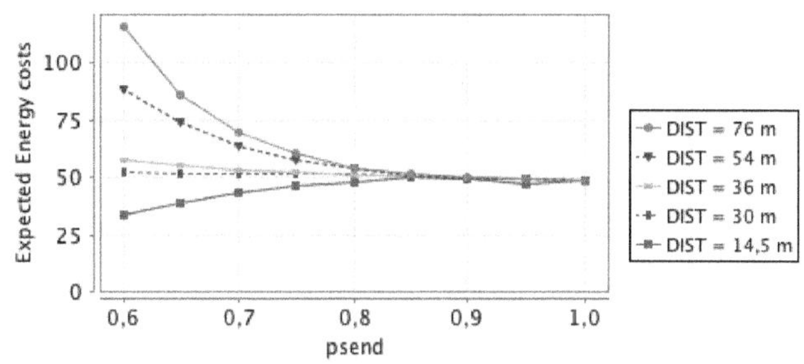

Figure 5: (SN) Expected energy cost

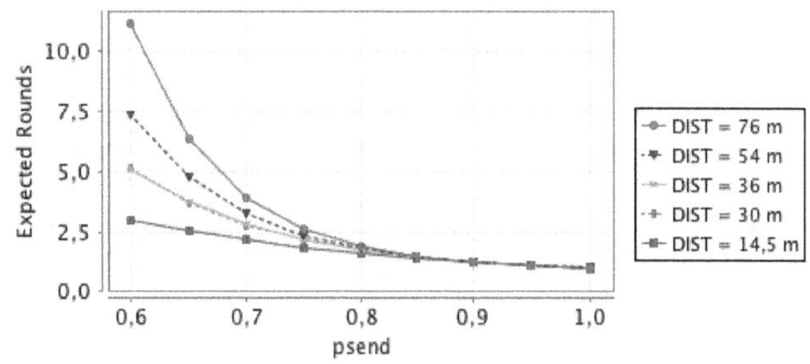

Figure 6: (SN) Expected number of transmissions for a successful communication

all the cases converge to 49, because each node will forward the message exactly one time. We can verify that there exists a preorder among different network configurations within the confidence of the simulation.

PROPOSITION 2. *For all* **psend** $\in \{0.6, 0.65, 0.7, 0.75, 0.8, 0.85, 0.9, 1.0\}$ *and for all* $j_1 < j_2 \in \{12, 23, 35, 37, 44\}$ *it holds that* $M_{j_1} \sqsubseteq_{\mathcal{H}}^{\mathcal{F}_{\mathbf{psend}}} M_{j_2}$*, where* $\mathcal{H}$ *is the set of network configurations where the communication has been successfully completed.*

Figure 6 shows the expected number of retransmissions that the sender node must perform before the communication is successfully completed. Notice that the smaller is the value of **psend**, the higher is the probability that the message is lost during the path, forcing a new transmission (for the sake of simplicity we don't model the acknowledges, but we assume that the sender node will wait for an acknowledge until a timeout occurs, then it will transmit again); hence, even if a small value of **psend** reduces the forwarding explosion, it may increase the number of replications.

Simulation of networks with mobility. Figure 7 shows the estimates of the expected energy cost for a successful transmission in the WSN with mobility.

The mobility of the nodes critically increases the size of the state space, hence the obtained results have wider confidence intervals than those of the static network simulation, based on 95% of confidence. However, the results are very similar to the previous case: for distances larger than 25m the gossip protocol causes a very high energy waste.

PROPOSITION 3. *For all* **psend** $\in \{0.6, 0.65, 0.7, 0.75, 0.8, 0.85, 0.9, 1.0\}$ *and for all* $h_1 < h_2 \in \{12, 17, 22\}$*, it holds that* $N_{h_1} \sqsubseteq_{\mathcal{H}}^{\mathcal{F}_{\mathbf{psend}}} N_{h_2}$ *where* $\mathcal{H}$ *is the set of network configurations where the communications has been successfully completed.*

Figure 8 shows the average number of retransmissions that the sender must perform before the communication has successfully completed.

5. RELATED WORK AND CONCLUSIONS

A large amount of research on sensor networks has been recently reported in the last decade. Several papers address the problem of studying the energy consumption for specific communication protocols. For instance, in [18] the authors define a Markov reward process (see, e.g., [14]) modelling some protocols for point to point reliable transmissions. A steady-state quantitative analysis is then obtained, and from this the average performance indices are computed. In [1], Bernardo et al. present a methodology to predict the impact of power management techniques on system functionality and performance. In [16], the authors define a set of metrics to analyse the energy consumption which are then estimated through simulation, and show how some modifications in the protocols can improve their efficiency. In [7], gossip protocols running on WSNs are studied but the authors develop an ad hoc simulator to estimate their performances. Conversely, in our setting, a general purpose tool, e.g., PRISM, can be used since the performance indices or properties to be evaluated (or estimated) can be formally specified according to a rigorous logic. Moreover, with respect to all the above mentioned contributions, the model we propose here aims at providing a common framework for automatically perform both qualitative and quantitative analyses. The energy preorder defined in Section 3 can be efficiently decided for small networks' components using model checking methods and hence one may decide to replace a node with

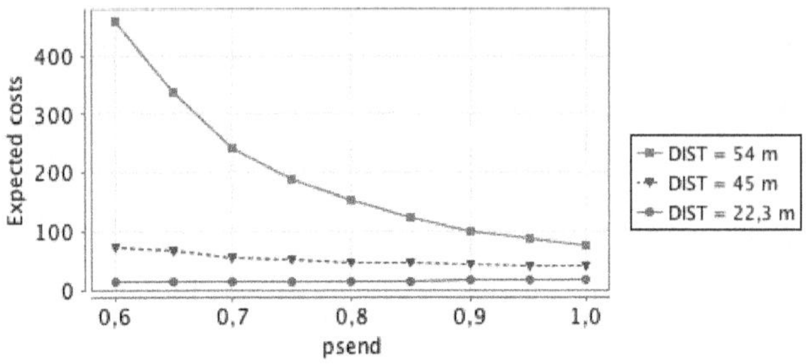

Figure 7: (MN) Expected energy cost

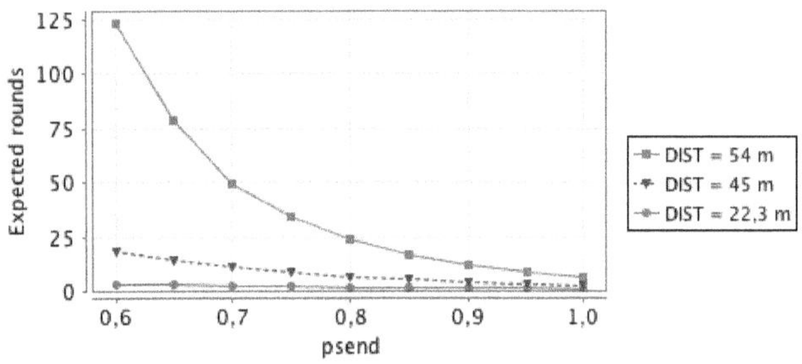

Figure 8: (MN) Expected number of transmissions for a successful communication

another which is behaviourally equivalent but less energy consuming; conversely, when the complexity of the process underlying the model makes exact analyses unfeasible, approximate (or statistical) model checking can be employed. This corresponds to the well-known Monte Carlo simulation; using the temporal logic implemented in the tool, one can verify a proposition within a certain level of confidence (e.g., the network equipped with a certain protocol is connected with a confidence of 99.9%). To the best of our knowledge such a qualitative and quantitative approach supported by the same tool represents a novelty in the study of WSNs.

6. REFERENCES

[1] A. Acquaviva, A. Aldini, M. Bernardo, A. Bogliolo, E. Bontà, and E. Lattanzi. A methodology based on formal methods for predicting the impact of dynamic power management. In *Formal Methods for Mobile Computing*, volume 3465 of *lncs*, pages 51–58. Springer Berlin / Heidelberg, 2005.

[2] I. Akyildiz, W. Su, Y. Sankarasubramaniam, and E. Cayirci. Wireless Sensor Networks: A Survey. *Computer Networks*, 38(4):393 – 422, 2002.

[3] A. Dimakis, A. Sarwate, , and M. Wainwright. Geographic Gossip: Efficient Aggregation for Sensor Networks. In *Proc. of the 5th international conference on Information processing in sensor networks*, pages 69–76. ACM, 2006.

[4] L. Gallina. *Formal Models for Qualitative and Quantitative Analysis of Mobile Ad Hoc and Sensor Networks*. PhD thesis, DAIS, University Ca' Foscari of Venice, 2013.

[5] L. Gallina, S. Hamadou, A. Marin, and S. Rossi. A probabilistic energy-aware model for mobile ad-hoc networks. In *Proc. of the 18th International Conference on Analytical and Stochastic Modelling Techniques and Applications (ASMTA'11)*, volume 6751 of *LNCS*, pages 316–330. Springer-Verlag, 2011.

[6] J. Goubault-Larrecq, C. Palamidessi, and A. Troina. A probabilistic applied pi-calculus. In *Proc. of the 5th Asian Symposium on Programming Languages and Systems (APLAS'07)*, volume 4807/2009 of *LNCS*, pages 175–190. Springer-Verlag, 2007.

[7] Z. Haas, J. Halpern, and L. Li. Gossip-based Ad Hoc Routing. *IEEE/ACM Trans. Netw.*, 14(3):479–491, 2006.

[8] A. Hinton, M. Kwiatkowska, G. Norman, and D. Parker. Prism: A tool for automatic verification of probabilistic systems. In *Proc. of the 12th International Conference on Tools and Algorithms for the Construction and Analysis of Systems (TACAS'06)*, volume 3920 of *LNCS*, pages 441–444. Springer-Verlag, 2006.

[9] M. Z. Kwiatkowska, G. Norman, and D. Parker. Prism 4.0: Verification of probabilistic real-time systems. In G. Gopalakrishnan and S. Qadeer, editors, *CAV*, volume 6806 of *Lecture Notes in Computer Science*, pages 585–591. Springer, 2011.

[10] P. Kyasanur, R. Choudhury, and I. Gupta. Smart Gossip: An Adaptive Gossip-based Broadcasting Service for Sensor Networks. In *Mobile Adhoc and Sensor Systems (MASS), 2006 IEEE International Conference on*, pages 91 –100, 2006.

[11] T. V. Madhav and N. Sarma. Maximizing Network Lifetime through Varying Transmission Radii with Energy Efficient Cluster Routing Algorithm in Wireless Sensor Networks. *International Journal of Information and Electronics Engineering*, 2(2):205–209, 2012.

[12] M. Merro. An observational theory for mobile ad hoc networks. *Information and Computation*, 207(2):194–208, 2009.

[13] R. Milner and D. Sangiorgi. Barbed bisimulation. In *Proc. of International Colloquium on Automata, Languages and Programming (ICALP'92)*, volume 623 of *LNCS*, pages 685–695. Springer-Verlag, 1992.

[14] S. M. Ross. *Stochastic Processes*. John Wiley & Sons, 2nd edition, 1996.

[15] R. Segala and N. Lynch. Probabilistic simulations for probabilistic processes. In *Proc. of the 5th International Conference on Concurrency Theory (CONCUR'94)*, volume 836 of *LNCS*, pages 481–496. Springer-Verlag, 1994.

[16] S. Singh, M. Woo, and C. Raghavendra. Power-aware routing in mobile ad hoc networks. In *Proc. of the 4th annual ACM/IEEE International Conference on Mobile Computing and Networking (MobiCom'98)*, pages 181–190. ACM, 1998.

[17] G. Zhou, C. Huang, T. Yan, T. He, J. A. Stankovic, and T. F. Abdelzaher. Mmsn: Multi-frequency media access control for wireless sensor networks. In *In IEEE INFOCOM*, page 7, 2006.

[18] M. Zorzi and R. Rao. Error control and energy consumption in wireless communications channels. In *Proc. of the 34th Annual Allerton Conference on Communication, Control and Computing*, pages 825 – 834, 1996.

Energy Management of Networked, Solar Cells Powered, Wireless Sensors

Soledad Escolar
Computer Science Dept.
University Carlos III of Madrid
Madrid, Spain
mdesdiaz@inf.uc3m.es

Stefano Chessa
Computer Science Dept.
University of Pisa Pisa, Italy
ISTI-CNR. Pisa, Italy
ste@di.unipi.it

Jesus Carretero
Computer Science Dept.
University Carlos III of Madrid
Madrid, Spain
jesus.carretero@uc3m.es

ABSTRACT

Solar cells combined with power management algorithms enable the dynamic scheduling of Wireless Sensor Networks applications in a reference period, where the objective of the scheduling is to maximize the application quality level while conserving an energy level sufficient to constantly maintain the sensor operation. In this paper we consider networked, solar cells powered wireless sensors and we propose an algorithm aims to find a global, (sub)optimal scheduling that maximizes the overall quality of service in the sensors and keeps the system energy neutral, thus ensuring that the system works uninterruptedly.

Categories and Subject Descriptors

C.2.m [**Computer-Communication Networks**]: Miscellaneous; I.6.4 [**Simulation and Modeling**]: Model Validation and Analysis—*Algorithms, Design, Simulation*

Keywords

Power Management; Solar Cells; Quality of Service; Wireless Sensor Networks.

1. INTRODUCTION

A Wireless Sensor Network (WSN) comprises a large number of low-power wireless embedded devices, called sensors, that can be easily deployed in a given area in order to collect environmental data. The sensors send any related sensed data to a special node (called sink) that act as a gateway between the WSN and external networks. Most of the commercial sensors available nowadays are powered by limited-capacity batteries that provide the energy required to sustain their operations. Consequently, the sensor lifetime is limited: when the battery drops below a minimum charge level, the sensor stops working. Such a limitation may be addressed by means of energy harvesting systems that use the energy obtained naturally from the environment to power on the sensors. However, since the energy production is generally not continuous, the sensors still use batteries that are recharged when there is an excess of energy production that guarantees their operation under an insufficient production. Therefore, an efficient energy management is necessary to guarantee an infinite sensor's lifetime while maintaining the activities of the sensors. In our work we model the sensors activities as tasks with a cost and a quality level, which expresses how much the task meets the user requirements. Based on this model, we devise a scheduling strategy that aims at maximizing the quality of service (QoS) while keeping the sensor energy neutral (i.e. within a time frame the energy production equals the energy consumption). Specifically, we consider a simple scenario that comprises two networked devices, one sensor and one sink, that communicate wirelessly and that employ an energy harvesting system based on solar cells combined with embedded batteries. We propose a low-complexity algorithm aimed at finding a (sub)optimal application scheduling that concerns to both the sensor and the sink, such that the overall quality of the scheduling is maximized, the energy is preserved to guarantee the applications execution even in conditions of darkness or low production, and the tasks selected at each time for the sensor and for the sink are compatible (i.e. they can work together).

MSWiM'13, November 3–8, 2013, Barcelona, Spain.
Copyright 2013 ACM 978-1-4503-2353-6/13/11 ...$15.00.
http://dx.doi.org/10.1145/2507924.2507991.

2. RELATED WORK

Adaptive sampling techniques adjust the sampling rate of a sensor based on the spatial/temporal correlation of the data [1] to save energy. These techniques are often used in sensors equipped with some energy harvesting system to estimate the energy that will be produced in a future time frame. Among the forms of energy harvested from the environment, the energy produced from the sun may be predicted with reasonable accuracy. In [4] the concept of *energy neutrality* is introduced to state that the energy consumed by a sensor in a period of time is always less or equal than the energy harvested from the environment in the same period. Based on this, they propose an algorithm that divides the sensor lifetime in time slots, and that assigns to each slot the maximum sampling rate that keeps the system energy neutral. Although QoS is not mentioned explicitly, we observe that increasing the sampling rate corresponds to rising the QoS of the application running on the sensor. QoS of the WSN applications is also related to other performance metrics such as throughput, service differentiation, coverage, exposure, reliability and, lately, energy consumption. We have addressed the QoS optimization while keeping the energy neutral condition in two previous works [2] [3]. Differently than the above works, in this paper we aim at optimizing the QoS in a context of networked sensors, where the optimization takes into account also the compatibility of the scheduling plans of different devices and the fact that energy production and consumption is, in general, not the same on all devices. To the best of our knowledge, this is the first work that consider the optimization of QoS in energy harvesting sensors under this perspective.

3. SYSTEM MODEL

We consider a scenario that comprises one sensor and one sink powered by solar cells. The efficiency of a solar cell (η) is a measure of the energy conversion efficiency of the incident light absorbed by a solar cell into electric power and is computed as $\eta = \frac{P_{max}}{D \times S}$, where P_{max} is the maximum output power provided (in Watts), D is the irradiance, defined as the density of incident power on a surface under standard assumptions (in W/m^2) and S is the surface area of the solar cell (in m^2). The output power is computed as $P_{out} = \eta \times D \times S$ and the average energy production E_p of the solar cell is P_{out}/V_{ld}. To obtain the instantaneous irradiance of the solar cell at time t, we apply a correction factor depending on the current day and solar time. Thus, at time t the instantaneous irradiance can be expressed as $D(t) = \frac{(t-h)^2}{4p} + D_{month}$, where t is any hour between 0:00 and 23:00, h is the hour of maximum solar light (12:00am), D_{month} is equal to the average irradiance in a month and $p = 9/D_{month}$, where 9 is the number of standard hours of solar light. The estimated energy production at time t is $E_p(t) = \frac{D(t) \times \eta \times S}{V_{ld}}$.

Our **task model** considers a sensor that executes a subset of the available tasks in $\Theta = \{T_0, \ldots, T_\alpha\}$ in a given period of time. A task T_i ($i > 0$) is represented by a triple $T_i = \langle t_i, p_i, w_i \rangle$, where t_i is the execution time of the task, p_i is the period of execution of the task (note that must be $p_i > t_i$), and w_i is the energy consumption of the sensor due to the execution of task T_i. A special task T_0 (also called Idle task) is executed when there is no other task to execute, which means that T_0 does not have a period and a predefined execution time. The sensor executes a scheduling plan P that is defined as a finite sequence of tasks in Θ. Note that since the tasks are periodic, P is also cyclic. The cost of execution of P per unit of time is given by $c = \sum_{T_i \in \Theta, T_i \neq T_0} \frac{w_i}{p_i} + w_0 \left(1 - \sum_{T_i \in \Theta, T_i \neq T_0} \frac{t_i}{p_i}\right)$. Let us assume n possible scheduling plans of the sensor $P_1^N, \ldots, P_n^N$ and m scheduling plans of the sink $P_1^S, \ldots, P_m^S$. We use notation P_i^X, with $X \in \{S, N\}$, to denote the scheduling plan i that is either of the sensor (if $X = N$) or of the sink (if $X = S$). For a given scheduling plan P_i^X are defined its energy cost per unit of time c_i^X and a defined quality level q_i^X. Let us also assume two scheduling plans P_i^N and P_j^S with $i \leq n, j \leq m$. To enable the communication between the sensor and the sink, it exists a sending task $T_x \in P_i^N$ and a receiving task $T_y \in P_j^S$. Then, P_i^N and P_j^S are compatible iff $(p_x) \geq (p_y)$ and $(p_x + t_x) \leq (p_y + t_y)$. To express the compatibility among any pair of scheduling plans of the sensor and of the sink, we use the matrix C, composed by n rows and m columns, that represent the compatibilities by using simple binary notation: if $C(i,j) = 1$ then P_i^N and P_j^S are compatible plans; otherwise $C(i,j) = 0$, which means that they are incompatible and cannot be run together.

In our **energy model** we define B_{max}^X and B_{min}^X to be the maximum and minimum battery capacity of the device, respectively. The energy available in the batteries may increase (or decrease) depending on the solar irradiance in a place and instant of time. As stated in [4] a sensor can operate uninterruptedly if its energy management is *energy neutral*. This means that, in a reference period of time $[t', t'']$, must be $B_{t'} = B_{t''}$. In our case, since the energy harvesting system is based on solar cells, we consider a time frame of 24 hours divided into σ slots of duration $\delta = \frac{3600 \times 24}{\sigma}$ seconds. Let $e_p^N(i)$ and $e_p^S(i)$ be the energy production at the end of slot i and $e_e^N(i)$ and $e_e^S(i)$ be the expected energy production (estimated by using the model discussed before) at the end of slot i, of the sensor and the sink, respectively. Similarly, let $c^N(i)$ and $c^S(i)$ be the energy cost due to the execution of a scheduling plan during the slot i, in the sensor and the sink, respectively. We denote with $B^X(i)$ the battery level at the end of slot i of the device X. Let also $\phi \in [0,1)$ be the charging efficiency of the battery and the rectifier function $[x^X]^+$ be defined as follows: if the charge x tends to overflow the battery above B_{max}^X, then the battery charge will be B_{max}^X also at the end of the slot. Similarly, if the charge tends to underflow the battery below 0, then the battery charge will be 0 also at the end of the slot. Under these assumptions, and disregarding the power leakage of the battery, we express the estimated battery level of the sensor and of the sink for each slot $i \in [1, \sigma]$ as $B^X(i) = \max\{B_{max}^X, B^X(i-1) + \phi[e_e^X(i) - c^X(i)]^+ - [c^X(i) - e_e^X(i)]^+\}$, where $B^X(0)$ is the initial battery level at the beginning of slot 1, the second term accounts for the energy which is produced and not consumed by X and the last term accounts for the energy that is drained from the battery in X.

4. POWER MANAGEMENT ALGORITHM

We assume that the scheduling plans and their quality levels for the sensor and the sink are known, and that they are energy neutral at least in some condition (e.g. the scheduling plans that keep in idle the sensor and the sink are always compatible). Different scheduling plans may implement completely different functionalities with different performance (e.g. different duty cycles). Our purpose is to find a (sub)optimal assignment of plans to slots such that the overall QoS in a time frame is maximized while maintaining the overall system energy neutral. The vectors S^N and S^S contain the allocation of the scheduling plans to each time slot for the sensor and for the sink, respectively, being its energy budget $B^X(\sigma) - B^X(0)$. We define the vector q of the quality level, the vector g of compatibility of the scheduling plans, and the vectors c^X the energy costs of X. Specifically, for a given S^N and S^S and a time slot $i \in [1, \sigma]$ let $S^N[i] = j$ and $S^S[i] = k$, we have that $q[i] = \min\{q_j^N, q_k^S\}$, where q_j^N and q_k^S are the quality of the plan j and k assigned for the sensor and the sink, respectively at slot i; $g[i] = C(j,k)$; $c^N[i] = c_j^N$, and $c^S[i] = c_k^S$. We formalize it as an optimization problem:

$$max \sum_{i=1}^{\sigma} q[i] \wedge \prod_{i=1}^{\sigma} g[i] = 1 \quad (1)$$

$$B^N(0) \leq B^N(\sigma) \wedge B^S(0) \leq B^S(\sigma)$$

$$B_{min}^N \leq B^N(i) \wedge B_{min}^S \leq B^S(i) \forall i \in [1, \sigma]$$

We propose an heuristic aimed at finding an admissible solution that approximates the optimal solution. Let Φ^X be a set of scheduling plans. We define $opt(\Phi^X)$ as the schedul-

Sensor Plan	T_1	T_2	T_3	T_4	T_0	c	$q(\%)$	Efficiency
$N1$	$\langle 2, 5, 10\rangle$	$\langle 1, 5, 15\rangle$	$\langle 1, 5, 8\rangle$	–	T_0^1	7.0	100	14.28
$N2$	$\langle 1, 10, 3\rangle$	$\langle 1, 10, 5\rangle$	$\langle 1, 10, 5\rangle$	$\langle 1, 10, 7\rangle$	T_0^6	3.2	90	28.12
$N3$	$\langle 5, 15, 10\rangle$	–	–	–	T_0^{10}	2.0	85	42.50
$N4$	$\langle 2, 20, 3\rangle$	$\langle 4, 20, 4\rangle$	–	–	T_0^{14}	1.75	80	45.71
$N5$	$\langle 20, 30, 10\rangle$	–	–	–	T_0^{10}	1.0	75	75
$N6$	$\langle 26, 30, 1\rangle$	–	–	–	T_0^4	0.3	70	233.3
Sink Plan	T_1	T_2	T_3	T_4	T_0	c	$q(\%)$	Efficiency
$S1$	$\langle 1, 3, 2\rangle$	$\langle 1, 3, 10\rangle$	$\langle 1, 3, 12\rangle$	–	T_0^0	8.0	100.0	12.5
$S2$	$\langle 1, 5, 10\rangle$	–	–	–	T_0^4	3.6	98.0	27.2
$S3$	$\langle 1, 6, 7\rangle$	$\langle 1, 6, 3\rangle$	$\langle 1, 6, 5\rangle$	$\langle 2, 6, 2\rangle$	T_0^1	3.16	95.0	30.0
$S4$	$\langle 2, 10, 3\rangle$	$\langle 6, 10, 10\rangle$	–	–	T_0^2	1.7	90.0	52.94
$S5$	$\langle 7, 10, 10\rangle$	–	–	–	T_0^3	1.6	85.0	53.13
$S6$	$\langle 1, 20, 2\rangle$	$\langle 1, 20, 1\rangle$	$\langle 1, 20, 3\rangle$	$\langle 10, 20, 1\rangle$	T_0^7	1.05	80.0	76.19
$S7$	$\langle 27, 30, 7\rangle$	$\langle 2, 30, 10\rangle$	–	–	T_0^1	0.63	60.0	94.73
$S8$	$\langle 32, 35, 1\rangle$	–	–	–	T_0^3	0.2	50.0	250.0

Table 1: Scheduling plans for the sensor and for the sink employed in the simulation.

ing plan $P_i^X \in \Phi^X$ such that $\forall P_j^X \in \Phi^X$ holds $\frac{q_i^X}{c_i^X} \geq \frac{q_j^X}{c_j^X}$ and $q_i^X > q_j^X$ if $\frac{q_i^X}{c_i^X} = \frac{q_j^X}{c_j^X}$ (i.e. P_i^X is the most efficient scheduling plan in Φ^X). Note that a plan P_j^X for which $q_j^X < q_i^X$ and $c_j^X \geq c_i^X$ for some i is inefficient and can be excluded. We define $\Phi_q^X = \{P_i^X \in \Phi^X : q_i^X > q\}$ as the set of scheduling plans in Φ^X that have a quality level above q, and $\Phi_c^X = \{P_i^X \in \Phi^X : c_i^X < c\}$ as the set of scheduling plans in Φ^X that have a cost below c. Given P_i^N and a set of plans of the sink Φ, the subset of scheduling plans in Φ compatible with P_i^N is $comp(\Phi, P_i^N) = \{P_j^S \in \Phi : C(i,j) = 1\}$. We make the following assumptions:

ASSUMPTION 1. *Given the scheduling plans P_i^N and P_j^N, let us consider two scheduling plans for the sink P_h^S, P_k^S such that P_h^S is the minimum cost scheduling plan for the sink in the set $comp(\Phi^S, P_i^N)$, and P_k^S is the minimum cost scheduling plan for the sink in the set $comp(\Phi^S, P_j^N)$. Then, $c_i^N \leq c_j^N$ iff $c_h^S \leq c_k^S$. Similarly, let P_h^S be the maximum quality level scheduling plan for the sink in the set $comp(\Phi^S, P_i^N)$, and P_k^S be the maximum quality level scheduling plan for the sink in the set $comp(\Phi^S, P_j^N)$. Then, $q_i^N \leq q_j^N$ iff $q_h^S \leq q_k^S$.*

Our algorithm progressively achieves a (sub)optimal solution in several iterations. It starts assigning to all the slots of the sensor the most efficient scheduling plan, and by finding, among the compatible schedules of the sink, the most efficient one. After this preliminary step, if the solution is admissible, then the algorithm enters a loop in which it tries to improve it. The improvement consists in increasing the overall QoS by considering only the scheduling plans of the sensor that have a better quality level than that of the scheduling plan used for the initial assignment. It selects among these the most efficient plan and tries to reassign slot by slot (starting from the slot at sunrise, in which the solar cells start producing energy again) the scheduling plan for the sensor and, for each reassignment, it also finds a (new) compatible scheduling plan for the sink that, according to Assumption 1, must have a better quality level, thus this reassignment improves the overall quality level of the solution. This loop ends only when there are no more better scheduling plans to try. Otherwise, if the solution is not admissible (it is not energy neutral or the battery level of the device drops below the minimum), the algorithm enters a loop in which it looks for solutions that cost less but that may have also a lower QoS. Only the scheduling plans of the sensor that have a smaller cost than that of the scheduling plan used for the initial assignment are considered. It selects among these the most efficient and tries to reassign slot by slot (starting from the slot at sunset, in which the solar cells stop producing energy) the scheduling plan for the sensor and, for each reassignment, it also finds a (new) compatible, scheduling plan for the sink that, according to Assumption 1, must have a lower cost, reducing thus the overall cost of the solution. This loops ends only when there are no more scheduling plans with a lower cost to try.

5. EVALUATION

We evaluated our approach by simulation. We select the plans for the sensor and for the sink that maximize the overall QoS according to our algorithm in a time frame of 24 hours divided in $\sigma = 300$ slots. To compute the energy production from the solar cell we take the average monthly solar irradiance in Madrid [5]. We compute the instantaneous energy production at any hour by using the model in Section 3 and then we distribute it equally among the slots in an hour ($\frac{\sigma}{24}$). B_{max}^X is 2500mAh, B_{min}^X is 1950mAh and B_0^X is 2000mAh. Table 1 shows the details for the scheduling plans of the sensor $N1, \ldots, N6$ and for the sink $S1, \ldots, S8$. The compatibility between these plans is presented in Table 2, which shows a compatibility of at most a 40 and 80 between plans. We proceed with the assignment algorithm for the 1st day of each month starting at 0:00am that corresponds to slot 0.

	S1		S2		S3		S4		S5		S6		S7		S8	
%	L	H	L	H	L	H	L	H	L	H	L	H	L	H	L	H
N1	0	1	0	1	1	1	0	1	0	0	1	1	0	1	1	0
N2	1	1	0	1	1	1	0	1	1	1	0	1	0	0	0	0
N3	0	1	1	1	1	0	0	1	1	1	0	0	0	1	0	1
N4	1	1	0	1	1	1	1	0	0	0	0	1	0	1	0	1
N5	0	0	0	1	1	1	1	1	0	1	1	1	0	1	0	0
N6	0	1	0	1	0	0	1	1	0	0	1	1	0	1	1	1

Table 2: Compatibility matrix. Legend: L: Low compatibility-40%; H: High compatibility-80%.

We obtain an overall energy neutral system for the compatibilities considered and for all months of the year, which means that the algorithm finds an assignment of scheduling plans to slots in the sensor and in the sink that verifies $B^X(300) > B^X(0)$. Figure 1 shows the battery level for the sensor for a compatibility of 40 . There is a clear relationship between the energy production and the battery level: the bigger is the production, the larger is the battery level achieved at the last light hour (close slot at the sunset r_2) and the lower is the battery level before the slot at the sunrise r_1, due to the fact that the most consuming plans can be

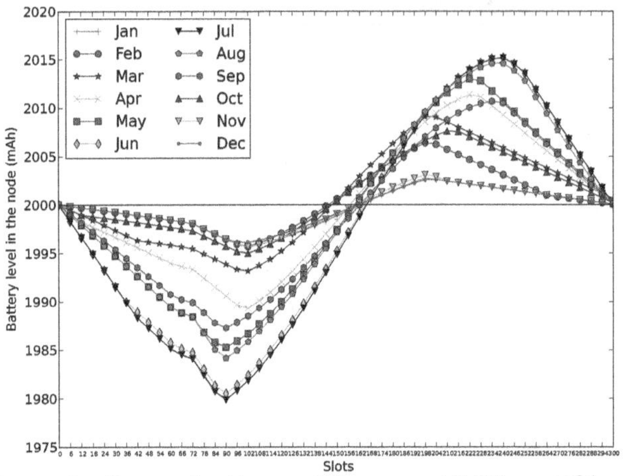

Figure 1: Sensor battery with compatibility=40%.

assigned when the production is larger. The largest battery level is achieved in uly at r_2. Correspondingly, the lowest battery level is achieved at r_1 in the same month in the sensor (the most consuming plans are assigned also in that month). The same experiment was done for the sink, and we observe that the battery level at slot 300 in the sink is rather larger than in the sensor, which means that a part of the energy production is accumulated in the battery (while it is lower than B_{max}) but it is not used to execute a plan with higher QoS.

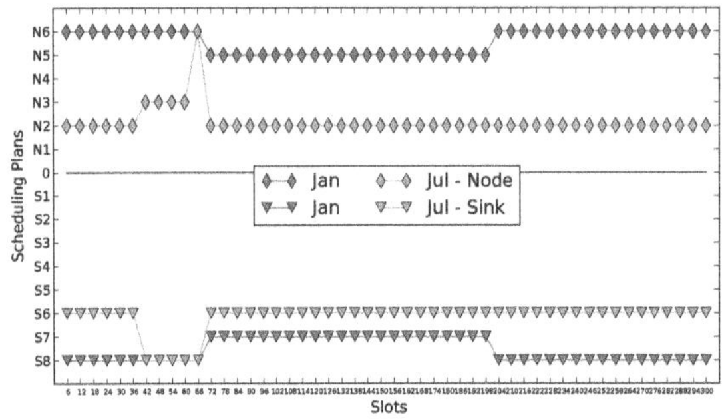

Figure 2: Assignment with compatibility of 80%.

Figure 2 shows the assignment for anuary and uly assuming at most 80 of compatibility. The axis y represents the plans in the sensor and in the sink and the axis x represents the slot where assigned. The order of the plans by efficiency is $N6, \ldots, N1$ and $S8, \ldots, S1$. In anuary, as observed, the algorithm starts assigning the most efficient plan in the sensor N6 and in the sink S8. When the first change occurs in the sensor at slot 72 and the plan N5 is selected, the sink looks for the first plan compatible with the new one. Since S8 is not compatible with N5, S7 is selected and starts to execute at the same slot. When the sensor selects again N6 at slot 204, the sink comes back to S8. We repeat the same experiments with a compatibility of at most 40 . A lower compatibility assigns plans that are farther from S8, which increase the overall QoS of the assignment. QoS is computed as the average quality level of the plans assigned and thus is higher in summer than in winter. As expected, the QoS in the sensor is larger than in the sink. Remind that the sink executes the first most efficient plan while compatible with the plan in the sensor, which leads to have a biggest production while the consumption is kept. If we reduce the compatibility we reduce, in turn, the probability of that a plan in the sensor be compatible with the most efficient plan in the sink. Note that the overall QoS with a 40 of compatible plans is higher than with a 80 and that in the months of bigger production the QoS achieved in the sensor is similar to the sink; this is because the sensor upgrades several times to achieve the plan with the highest quality able to execute and, at the same time, with a low compatibility we reduce the possibility of that such a plan be compatible with the plan of the sink, forcing to the sink to select another plan that is less efficient but has a higher consumption and a higher quality, which improves the QoS in the sink. However, with a higher compatibility, the QoS achieved in months of bigger production could be lower than in months of lower production; e.g. in April, May, and September the QoS in the sink is close to 50 , which indicates that S8 is compatible with most of the plans selected in the sensor.

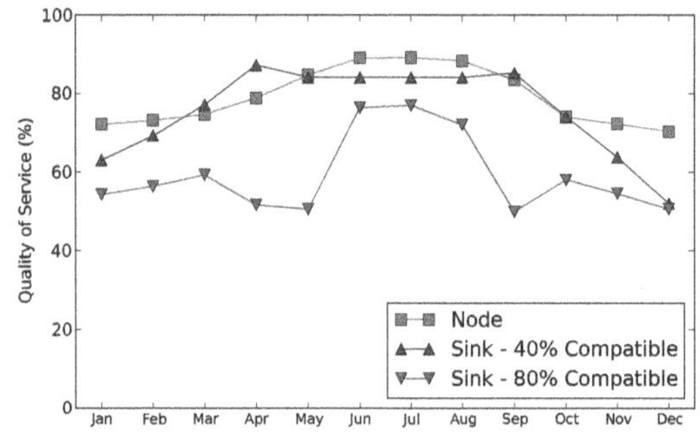

Figure 3: QoS for the sensor and for the sink.

6. FUTURE WORK

We address the problem of the energy management concerning to two networked devices, a sensor and a sink, equipped with solar cells, with the aim of achieving potentially infinite lifetimes. Our algorithm achieves a high QoS for the sensor and preserves a low cost in the sink, leading to accumulate the energy produced but not consumed into the battery, which could be further used to execute another tasks or attending a larger number of sensors. Our next step is to generalize our algorithm to consider N nodes.

7. REFERENCES

[1] C. Alippi, G. Anastasi, M. Di Francesco, and M. Roveri. Energy management in wireless sensor networks with energy-hungry sensors. *Instrumentation Measurement Magazine, IEEE*, 12(2):16–23, april 2009.

[2] S. Escolar, S. Chessa, and J. Carretero. Optimization of quality of service in WSN powered by solar cells. In *10th IEEE Int. Sym. on Parallel and Distributed Processing with Applications*, pages 1–8, Madrid, Spain, July 2012.

[3] S. Escolar, S. Chessa, and J. Carretero. Energy management in solar cells powered wireless sensor networks for quality of service optimization. *Personal and Ubiquitous Computing*, pages 1–16, 2013.

[4] A. Kansal, J. Hsu, S. Zahedi, and M. B. Srivastava. Power management in energy harvesting sensor networks. *ACM Trans. Embed. Comput. Syst.*, 6(4), Sept. 2007.

[5] N. S. meteorology and S. Energy. Retscreen. http://eosweb.larc.nasa.gov/sse/RETScreen/, 2011.

Analytical Revisit on the Use of Biased Random Walks for Data Forwarding in Wireless Sensor Networks

Issam Mabrouki
University of Manouba, Tunisia
issam.mabrouki@hanalab.org

Abdelfettah Belghith
University of Manouba, Tunisia
abdelfattah.belghith@ensi.rnu.tn

ABSTRACT

In recent years, the use of random walks (RW) for data forwarding in wireless sensor networks (WSN) has gained a lot of popularity. However, a negative effect is often caused by the fact that a completely uniform random choice of the next hop during the walk translates into a reduced progress towards the sink node, thereby yielding a long latency. Several strategies are proposed to attenuate this problem. Most of them are characterized by their dependence on state information stored in sensor nodes in order to bias the direction of the walk towards the target. Such information require additional capabilities and it is costly in terms of complexity and energy, which is inherently problematical in WSN. This leads to a tradeoff between mutually contradictory goals and raises the question as to what extent biasing RW can affect the performance of the data forwarding scheme. This question is our primary motivation in investigating the problem of biasing RW based data forwarding from a pure analytical perspective.

Categories and Subject Descriptors

C.2 [**Computer-Communication Networks**]: Distributed Systems

Keywords

Random Walk Theory; Wireless Sensor Network; Entropy

1. INTRODUCTION

To deal with the limited capabilities often encountered in WSN, one option consists in reducing the dependence of routing schemes on state information by constructing a data forwarding solution without recurring to topology-control mechanisms, thereby solving the routing problem strictly locally [1]. The idea of choosing forwarding nodes at random can be therefore applied. As it is most likely that a route will consist of multiple wireless hops, and by identifying data packets with particles and the network with the medium in which particles move, the resulting routing scheme induces a RW on the WSN graph.

Without any control, RW can lead to poor performance such as long latency. Indeed, the lack of such a control induces an *unbiased* RW that selects the next neighbor node to visit *uniformly* at random. Taking advantage of the broadcast nature of wireless communications, the unbiased RW does not rely on any state information. It only requires a connected node to keep data moving, which can be highly desirable in the context of WSN. However, with an unbiased RW, a negative effect is often caused by the fact that a completely uniform random choice of the next hop during the walk translates into a reduced progress towards the destination node, thereby yielding a long latency.

MSWiM'13, November 3–8, 2013, Barcelona, Spain.

http://dx.doi.org/10.1145/2507924.2507994

To attenuate the problem of latency, many strategies are proposed to *bias* the RW. Throughout the variety of works in this context, we realize that the common characteristic of existing strategies is their dependence on state information stored in the nodes in order to bias the direction of the walk. Since the RW is forced to visit new parts of the network, the latency is then expected to be reduced. However, this improvement would be achieved at the expense of a considerable amount of state information required at nodes, which increases the overhead and the complexity of the system. This results in a tradeoff between mutually contradictory goals and raises the question as to what extent biasing RW can affect the performance of the system. This question is our primary motivation in this paper. In particular, we approach this problem from an *analytical* perspective, and obtain some interesting answers for the influence of biasing mechanisms on the performance of RW through closed-form expressions. More precisely, we consider here a RW with bias running on a regular grid topology for the task of data gathering, where transition probabilities are instead altered in favor of a preferred direction. Moreover, our model does not involve any assumptions about the kind of state information driving the RW with bias. This makes our approach more intrinsic. To understand the influence of the biasing mechanism on the performance of the proposed data gathering scheme, we look closely at delay metrics. The main results obtained indicate that biased RW induce a significant improvement in delay properties.

The rest of this paper is organized as follows. In Section 2, we give backgrounds and theoretical elements of RW theory. In Section 3, we give a precise description of the network model. In Section 4, we study the performance of the proposed model through closed-form expressions. We conclude in Section 5 by pointing to some research directions.

2. ELEMENTS OF RW THEORY

2.1 Definitions and Assumptions

Let Ω be a countable subset contained in the d-dimensional real Euclidean space $\mathbb{R}^d$. Suppose a particle starts from a given site $\vec{\mathbf{r}}$ of Ω. It randomly selects a site as its next dwelling point, and moves to this site. Then the particle selects another site at random and move to it, *etc.* The random sequence of sites selected this way is a *RW*, Ω is called the *state space* of the walk, and the particle is called a *random walker*. Then the obtained random walk can be simply characterized by specifying for each $\vec{\mathbf{r}}$ and $\vec{\mathbf{s}}$ in Ω a real number $p(\vec{\mathbf{r}},\vec{\mathbf{s}})$, which is the probability to move from site $\vec{\mathbf{r}}$ to site $\vec{\mathbf{s}}$ in one step. Function $p(\vec{\mathbf{r}},\vec{\mathbf{s}})$ is called the *transition function* of the RW.

For all $n \geq 1$, we define $P_n(\vec{\mathbf{r}},\vec{\mathbf{s}})$ as the probability of a walker to be at site $\vec{\mathbf{s}}$ after n steps, given that the walk started at site $\vec{\mathbf{r}}$. We also denote by $F_n(\vec{\mathbf{r}},\vec{\mathbf{s}})$ the probability of arriving at site $\vec{\mathbf{s}}$ for the *first* time on the nth step, given that the walk started at site $\vec{\mathbf{r}}$. We shall refer to $P_n(\vec{\mathbf{r}},\vec{\mathbf{s}})$ and $F_n(\vec{\mathbf{r}},\vec{\mathbf{s}})$ as the *site occupation* and *first-passage probabilities* at time n respectively. We shall also adopt the only consistent and useful convention that $P_0(\vec{\mathbf{r}},\vec{\mathbf{s}}) = \delta_{\vec{\mathbf{r}},\vec{\mathbf{s}}}$, $F_0(\vec{\mathbf{r}},\vec{\mathbf{s}}) = 0$, and introduce

$$P(\vec{\mathbf{r}},\vec{\mathbf{s}}\,|\,z) = \sum_{n=0}^{\infty} P_n(\vec{\mathbf{r}},\vec{\mathbf{s}})\, z^n \text{ and } F(\vec{\mathbf{r}},\vec{\mathbf{s}}\,|\,z) = \sum_{n=0}^{\infty} F_n(\vec{\mathbf{r}},\vec{\mathbf{s}})\, z^n$$

as the generating functions associated with sequences $\{P_n(\vec{\mathbf{r}},\vec{\mathbf{s}})\}_{n\in\mathbb{N}}$ and $\{F_n(\vec{\mathbf{r}},\vec{\mathbf{s}})\}_{n\in\mathbb{N}}$ respectively.

LEMMA 1. *Generating functions $P(\vec{\mathbf{r}},\vec{\mathbf{s}}\,|\,z)$ and $F(\vec{\mathbf{r}},\vec{\mathbf{s}}\,|\,z)$ are related to each other according to the formula*

$$F(\vec{\mathbf{r}},\vec{\mathbf{s}}\,|\,z) = \frac{P(\vec{\mathbf{r}},\vec{\mathbf{s}}\,|\,z) - \delta_{\vec{\mathbf{r}},\vec{\mathbf{s}}}}{P(\vec{\mathbf{s}},\vec{\mathbf{s}}\,|\,z)} \tag{1}$$

for all $\vec{\mathbf{r}}$ and $\vec{\mathbf{s}}$ in Ω.

For a detailed proof, we refer the reader to [2].

In the general case, it is always possible to describe the random walk through a set of equations governing the walk evolution. Physically speaking, this set of equations represents the *evolution laws* of the walk.

LEMMA 2. *Generating function $P(\vec{\mathbf{r}},\vec{\mathbf{s}}\,|\,z)$ satisfies the evolution law*

$$P(\vec{\mathbf{r}},\vec{\mathbf{s}}\,|\,z) = \delta_{\vec{\mathbf{r}},\vec{\mathbf{s}}} + z \sum_{\vec{\mathbf{s}}'\in\Omega} P(\vec{\mathbf{r}},\vec{\mathbf{s}}'\,|\,z)\, p(\vec{\mathbf{s}}',\vec{\mathbf{s}}) \tag{2}$$

where Ω and $p(\vec{\mathbf{r}},\vec{\mathbf{s}})$ stand respectively for the state space and the transition function of the walk.

We refer the reader to [2] for a detailed proof.

2.2 Perfect Random Walks

In what follows, we explore a special class of random walks taking place on a *finite* square lattice $\mathfrak{T}$ of size $N \times N$, for which the components r_i of the position of site $\vec{\mathbf{r}}$ are integers satisfying the inequality $0 \leq r_i \leq N-1$ for $i = 1,2$. To cope with boundary effects, we assume that $\mathfrak{T}$ is equipped with *periodic boundary conditions* (PBC). Concretely, this means that finite square lattice $\mathfrak{T}$ is transformed into a torus lattice by connecting the opposite ends of $\mathfrak{T}$. This allows us to define on $\mathfrak{T}$ a transition function $p^{\dagger}(\vec{\mathbf{r}},\vec{\mathbf{s}})$ satisfying the translational invariance property, that is, $p^{\dagger}(\vec{\mathbf{r}},\vec{\mathbf{s}}) = p^{\dagger}(\mathbf{0},\vec{\mathbf{s}}-\vec{\mathbf{r}})$ where $\vec{\mathbf{s}}-\vec{\mathbf{r}}$ is interpreted modulo N, *i.e.*, periodically. Consequently, transition function $p^{\dagger}(\vec{\mathbf{r}},\vec{\mathbf{s}})$ is really determined by the single point function $p^{\dagger}(\mathbf{0},\vec{\mathbf{s}})$ where $\vec{\mathbf{s}}$ is interpreted modulo N. This random walk is therefore deemed *perfect* in the sense that all nodes behave similarly. We propose in the following to formally characterize this random walk. To this end, let us define $\lambda^{\dagger}(\vec{\mathbf{m}})$, the *structure function* of the walk, as the 2-dimensional discrete Fourier transform of $p^{\dagger}(\mathbf{0},\vec{\mathbf{s}})$, that is

$$\lambda^{\dagger}(\vec{\mathbf{m}}) = \sum_{\vec{\mathbf{s}}\in\mathfrak{T}} p^{\dagger}(\mathbf{0},\vec{\mathbf{s}})\, e^{i\frac{2\pi}{N}\vec{\mathbf{m}}\cdot\vec{\mathbf{s}}}, \qquad \vec{\mathbf{m}} \in \mathfrak{T}. \tag{3}$$

THEOREM 1. *If $P^{\dagger}(\vec{\mathbf{r}},\vec{\mathbf{s}}\,|\,z)$ denotes the site occupation probability generating function of the perfect random walk, then we have*

$$P^{\dagger}(\vec{\mathbf{r}},\vec{\mathbf{s}}\,|\,z) = \frac{1}{N^2} \sum_{\vec{\mathbf{m}}\in\mathfrak{T}} \frac{e^{-i\frac{2\pi}{N}\vec{\mathbf{m}}\cdot(\vec{\mathbf{s}}-\vec{\mathbf{r}})}}{1 - z\lambda^{\dagger}(\vec{\mathbf{m}})}. \tag{4}$$

For a detailed proof, we refer the reader to [2].

Even though (4) does not give us a simple form of generating function $P^{\dagger}(\vec{\mathbf{r}},\vec{\mathbf{s}}\,|\,z)$, it is of great importance and represents one basic relation upon which most of our contributions rely.

2.3 Imperfect Random Walks

We investigate now the effect of introducing perturbations into the perfect random walk defined in Subsection 2.2 at a *finite* number of sites denoted by $\vec{\mathbf{s}}_j$, $j = 1,2,\cdots,k$. We assume that at these sites a walker arriving there never leaves. In the literature, these sites are called *trapping* sites. Note in passing that such trapping sites can modelize real sink nodes used for data gathering. After introducing trapping sites, let $p^{\ddagger}(\vec{\mathbf{r}},\vec{\mathbf{s}})$ denote the transition function of the resulting random walk, called also *imperfect* random walk. Thus, we can formulate this walk by writing

$$p^{\ddagger}(\vec{\mathbf{r}},\vec{\mathbf{s}}) = \begin{cases} p^{\dagger}(\vec{\mathbf{r}},\vec{\mathbf{s}}) & \text{if} \quad \vec{\mathbf{r}} \neq \vec{\mathbf{s}}_j,\ j = 1,2,\cdots,k \\ \delta_{\vec{\mathbf{r}}\vec{\mathbf{s}}} & \text{else.} \end{cases}$$

Following Montroll [4], we give next a key relation to find a formal solution for the imperfect random walk once the perfect one is well-characterized.

THEOREM 2. *Let $P^{\ddagger}(\vec{\mathbf{r}},\vec{\mathbf{s}}\,|\,z)$ and $P^{\dagger}(\vec{\mathbf{r}},\vec{\mathbf{s}}\,|\,z)$ denote the site occupation probability generating functions associated with the imperfect/perfect random walks respectively. $P^{\ddagger}(\vec{\mathbf{r}},\vec{\mathbf{s}}\,|\,z)$ and $P^{\dagger}(\vec{\mathbf{r}},\vec{\mathbf{s}}\,|\,z)$ are related to each other according to*

$$\begin{aligned} P^{\ddagger}(\vec{\mathbf{r}},\vec{\mathbf{s}}\,|\,z) =& P^{\dagger}(\vec{\mathbf{r}},\vec{\mathbf{s}}\,|\,z) + \sum_{j=1}^{k} P^{\ddagger}(\vec{\mathbf{r}},\vec{\mathbf{s}}_j\,|\,z)\delta_{\vec{\mathbf{s}},\vec{\mathbf{s}}_j} \\ & - (1-z)\sum_{j=1}^{k} P^{\ddagger}(\vec{\mathbf{r}},\vec{\mathbf{s}}_j\,|\,z) P^{\dagger}(\vec{\mathbf{s}}_j,\vec{\mathbf{s}}\,|\,z). \end{aligned} \tag{5}$$

Proof. We refer the reader to [2] for a detailed proof.

Theorem 2 enables us to infer the value of $P^{\ddagger}(\vec{\mathbf{r}},\vec{\mathbf{s}}\,|\,z)$ as a function of $P^{\dagger}(\vec{\mathbf{r}},\vec{\mathbf{s}}\,|\,z)$, once we know $P^{\ddagger}(\vec{\mathbf{r}},\vec{\mathbf{s}}_j\,|\,z)$ for all trapping sites $\vec{\mathbf{s}}_j$. Indeed, it is easy to find $P^{\ddagger}(\vec{\mathbf{r}},\vec{\mathbf{s}}_j\,|\,z)$. To this end, we simply set $\vec{\mathbf{s}} = \vec{\mathbf{s}}_1,\vec{\mathbf{s}}_2,\cdots,\vec{\mathbf{s}}_k$ in (5) to obtain a set of k simultaneous linear equations for the trapping site occupation probability generating function $P^{\ddagger}(\vec{\mathbf{r}},\vec{\mathbf{s}}_j\,|\,z)$. As we shall see in what follows, Theorem 2 is of very great importance and represents one of the basic relations upon which relies some of our contributions in this work.

3. BORDER DATA GATHERING MODEL

3.1 Network Description and Assumptions

We look here at a common regular deployment topology where network nodes are spread over an area of interest with a square pattern. As illustrated in Figure 1, this pattern corresponds to a square unit cell, $\mathfrak{T}$, of size $N \times N$. Every node $\vec{\mathbf{r}} \in \mathfrak{T}$ is labeled with (r_1,r_2), where r_1 and r_2 are integers such that $0 \leq r_1,r_2 \leq N-1$. In this model, we assume that sink nodes are located at the border line corresponding to set $\mathcal{S}$ of nodes $\vec{\mathbf{s}}_j = (0,j)$ for $j = 0,\cdots,N-1$, whereas the other nodes of $\mathfrak{T}$ are sensor nodes.

To cope with boundary effects imposed by the finiteness of the network, we equip unit cell $\mathfrak{T}$ with periodic boundary conditions. The envisioned data gathering scheme is then defined as follows.

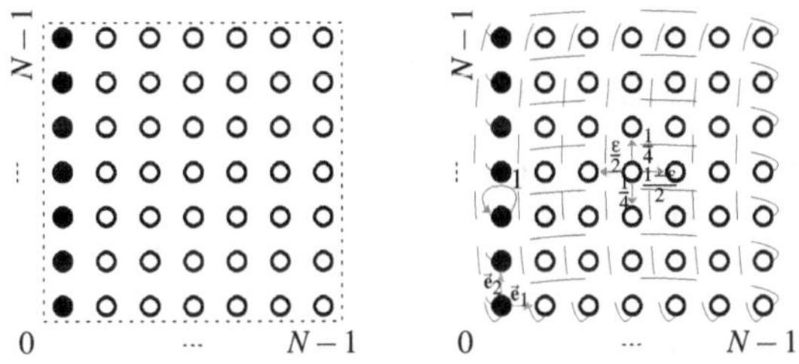

(a) $\mathfrak{T}$ (b) $\mathfrak{T}$ with PBC

Figure 1: Border data gathering model. The dark-filled circles are sink nodes while light-filled ones are sensor nodes.

At a given sensor node $\vec{\mathbf{r}}$, as indicated in Figure 1, we assume that the next hop occurs only to the 4-nearest neighbors with probability $\frac{1}{2}(1-\varepsilon)$ to the right neighbor $(0 \leq \varepsilon \leq 1)$, $\frac{1}{2}\varepsilon$ to the left neighbor, and $\frac{1}{4}$ to either top or bottom neighbor. However, for a given sink node a data packet arriving there never leaves. With this configuration, the induced RW is *biased* unless $\varepsilon = \frac{1}{2}$.

3.2 Problem Formulation

The data gathering scheme described above can be formulated as a problem of an imperfect RW taking place on torus lattice $\mathfrak{T}$. Indeed, since all nodes of $\mathfrak{T}$ have similar behaviors except sink nodes, where a data packet arriving there never leaves, one may view sink nodes as trapping sites whereas sensor nodes are deemed perfect ones. Thus, the proposed data gathering scheme induces an imperfect RW on torus lattice $\mathfrak{T}$ in the presence of a finite number of trapping sites corresponding to $\vec{\mathbf{s}}_j = (0, j)$ for $j = 0, \cdots, N-1$.

To characterize this scheme, we first introduce $P_n^{\ddagger}(\vec{\mathbf{r}},\vec{\mathbf{s}})$ and $F_n^{\ddagger}(\vec{\mathbf{r}},\vec{\mathbf{s}})$ as the node occupation and first-passage probabilities of the imperfect RW respectively. Let $P^{\ddagger}(\vec{\mathbf{r}},\vec{\mathbf{s}}\,|\,z)$ and $F^{\ddagger}(\vec{\mathbf{r}},\vec{\mathbf{s}}\,|\,z)$ be their associated generating functions. We also write $P_n^{\dagger}(\vec{\mathbf{r}},\vec{\mathbf{s}})$ and $F_n^{\dagger}(\vec{\mathbf{r}},\vec{\mathbf{s}})$ for the node occupation and first-passage probabilities of the induced perfect RW respectively. Let $P^{\dagger}(\vec{\mathbf{r}},\vec{\mathbf{s}}\,|\,z)$ and $F^{\dagger}(\vec{\mathbf{r}},\vec{\mathbf{s}}\,|\,z)$ denote their associated generating functions. We can therefore employ the perturbation techniques stated by Theorem 2, which enables us to find a formal solution to the imperfect RW once the induced perfect one is well-characterized.

PROPOSITION 1. *Generating functions $\{P^{\ddagger}(\vec{\mathbf{r}},\vec{\mathbf{s}}_j\,|\,z)\}$ satisfy the simultaneous linear equations*

$$P^{\dagger}(\vec{\mathbf{r}},\vec{\mathbf{s}}_k\,|\,z) = (1-z)\sum_{j=0}^{N-1} P^{\ddagger}(\vec{\mathbf{r}},\vec{\mathbf{s}}_j\,|\,z)P^{\dagger}(\vec{\mathbf{s}}_j,\vec{\mathbf{s}}_k\,|\,z), \qquad (6)$$

which involve coefficients only depending on $\{P^{\dagger}(\vec{\mathbf{s}}_j,\vec{\mathbf{s}}_k\,|\,z)\}$ for $0 \leq j,k \leq N-1$ and complex number z.

Proof. Applying Theorem 2, we can show that $P^{\ddagger}(\vec{\mathbf{r}},\vec{\mathbf{s}}\,|\,z)$ is related to $P^{\dagger}(\vec{\mathbf{r}},\vec{\mathbf{s}}\,|\,z)$ according to the formula

$$\begin{aligned} P^{\ddagger}(\vec{\mathbf{r}},\vec{\mathbf{s}}\,|\,z) =& P^{\dagger}(\vec{\mathbf{r}},\vec{\mathbf{s}}\,|\,z) + \sum_{j=0}^{N-1} P^{\ddagger}(\vec{\mathbf{r}},\vec{\mathbf{s}}_j\,|\,z)\delta_{\vec{\mathbf{s}},\vec{\mathbf{s}}_j} \\ &-(1-z)\sum_{j=0}^{N-1} P^{\ddagger}(\vec{\mathbf{r}},\vec{\mathbf{s}}_j\,|\,z)P^{\dagger}(\vec{\mathbf{s}}_j,\vec{\mathbf{s}}\,|\,z). \end{aligned} \qquad (7)$$

Setting $\vec{\mathbf{s}} = \vec{\mathbf{s}}_k$ into (7) and after some simplifications, we establish (6). ■

We can observe that the sum involved on the right-hand side of (6) can be interpreted as a cycle convolution of two N-periodic sequences, namely $\{P^{\ddagger}(\vec{\mathbf{r}},\vec{\mathbf{s}}_k\,|\,z)\}_{0\leq k\leq N-1}$ and $\{P^{\dagger}(\mathbf{0},\vec{\mathbf{s}}_k\,|\,z)\}_{0\leq k\leq N-1}$. This property stems from the periodic boundary conditions of $\mathfrak{T}$ and the translational invariance of the induced perfect RW, that is, $P^{\dagger}(\vec{\mathbf{r}},\vec{\mathbf{s}}\,|\,z) = P^{\dagger}(\mathbf{0},\vec{\mathbf{s}}-\vec{\mathbf{r}}\,|\,z)$, where $\vec{\mathbf{s}}-\vec{\mathbf{r}}$ is interpreted modulo N. Therefore, it is natural to make appeal to discrete Fourier transforms in order to get a more compact form of (6). For all $\vec{\mathbf{m}}_l = (0,l)$, $l = 0,\cdots,N-1$, we define $\widehat{P^{\ddagger}}(\vec{\mathbf{r}},\vec{\mathbf{m}}_l\,|\,z)$ and $\widehat{P^{\dagger}}(\mathbf{0},\vec{\mathbf{m}}_l\,|\,z)$ by

$$\widehat{P^{\ddagger}}(\vec{\mathbf{r}},\vec{\mathbf{m}}_l\,|\,z) = \sum_{k=0}^{N-1} P^{\ddagger}(\vec{\mathbf{r}},\vec{\mathbf{s}}_k\,|\,z)\, e^{i\frac{2\pi}{N}\vec{\mathbf{m}}_l\cdot\vec{\mathbf{s}}_k} \qquad (8a)$$

$$\widehat{P^{\dagger}}(\vec{\mathbf{r}},\vec{\mathbf{m}}_l\,|\,z) = \sum_{k=0}^{N-1} P^{\dagger}(\vec{\mathbf{r}},\vec{\mathbf{s}}_k\,|\,z)\, e^{i\frac{2\pi}{N}\vec{\mathbf{m}}_l\cdot\vec{\mathbf{s}}_k} \qquad (8b)$$

as the 1-dimensional discrete Fourier transforms of $\{P^{\ddagger}(\vec{\mathbf{r}},\vec{\mathbf{s}}_k\,|\,z)\}_{0\leq k\leq N-1}$ and $\{P^{\dagger}(\vec{\mathbf{r}},\vec{\mathbf{s}}_k\,|\,z)\}_{0\leq k\leq N-1}$ respectively.

PROPOSITION 2. *The discrete Fourier transform $\widehat{P^{\ddagger}}(\vec{\mathbf{r}},\vec{\mathbf{m}}_l\,|\,z)$ can be expressed in an explicit form as*

$$\widehat{P^{\ddagger}}(\vec{\mathbf{r}},\vec{\mathbf{m}}_l\,|\,z) = \frac{1}{1-z} \times \frac{\widehat{P^{\dagger}}(\vec{\mathbf{r}},\vec{\mathbf{m}}_l\,|\,z)}{\widehat{P^{\dagger}}(\mathbf{0},\vec{\mathbf{m}}_l\,|\,z)}, \qquad (9)$$

for all $\vec{\mathbf{m}}_l = (0,l)$, $l = 0,\cdots,N-1$ and $\vec{\mathbf{r}} = (r_1,r_2)$.

Proof. Multiplying both sides of (6) by $e^{i\frac{2\pi}{N}\vec{\mathbf{m}}_l\cdot\vec{\mathbf{s}}_k}$, summing over $0 \leq k \leq N-1$ and observing that convolution of sequences corresponds to multiplication of their discrete Fourier transforms, we obtain (9). ■

PROPOSITION 3. *Let $\lambda^{\dagger}(\vec{\mathbf{m}})$ denote the structure function of the induced perfect RW, where $\vec{\mathbf{m}} = (m_1,m_2)$: m_1 and m_2 are integers such that $0 \leq m_1,m_2 \leq N-1$. The discrete Fourier transform $\widehat{P^{\dagger}}(\vec{\mathbf{r}},\vec{\mathbf{m}}_l\,|\,z)$ can be then expressed in an explicit form as*

$$\widehat{P^{\dagger}}(\vec{\mathbf{r}},\vec{\mathbf{m}}_l\,|\,z) = \frac{1}{N}\sum_{k=0}^{N-1}\frac{e^{i\frac{2\pi}{N}(kr_1+lr_2)}}{1-z\lambda^{\dagger}(k,l)}, \qquad (10)$$

for all $\vec{\mathbf{m}}_l = (0,l)$, $l = 0,\cdots,N-1$ and $\vec{\mathbf{r}} = (r_1,r_2)$.

Proof. We derive this proposition by using Theorem 1, which provides the node occupation probability generating function of a perfect RW taking place on a finite lattice with periodic boundary conditions in terms of the structure function of the walk. Thus, we can write

$$\begin{aligned} P^{\dagger}(\vec{\mathbf{r}},\vec{\mathbf{s}}_j\,|\,z) &= \frac{1}{N^2}\sum_{\vec{\mathbf{m}}\in\mathfrak{T}}\frac{e^{-i\frac{2\pi}{N}\vec{\mathbf{m}}.(\vec{\mathbf{s}}_j-\vec{\mathbf{r}})}}{1-z\lambda^{\dagger}(\vec{\mathbf{m}})} \\ &= \frac{1}{N^2}\sum_{m_1=0}^{N-1}\sum_{m_2=0}^{N-1}\frac{e^{i\frac{2\pi}{N}(m_1r_1+m_2r_2)}\times e^{-i\frac{2\pi}{N}jm_2}}{1-z\lambda^{\dagger}(m_1,m_2)} \\ &= \frac{1}{N}\sum_{m_2=0}^{N-1}\left\{\frac{1}{N}\sum_{m_1=0}^{N-1}\frac{e^{i\frac{2\pi}{N}(m_1r_1+m_2r_2)}}{1-z\lambda^{\dagger}(m_1,m_2)}\right\}\times e^{-i\frac{2\pi}{N}jm_2}. \end{aligned} \qquad (11)$$

By the Fourier inversion theorem, the expression within braces can be recognized as the 1-dimensional discrete Fourier transform of sequence $\{P^{\dagger}(\vec{\mathbf{r}},\vec{\mathbf{s}}_j\,|\,z)\}_{0\leq j\leq N-1}$. After the change of variables $k = m_1$ and $l = m_2$, we finally obtain (10). ■

Finally, it turns out that by evaluating the structure function $\lambda^{\dagger}(\vec{\mathbf{m}})$ and plugging (10) into (9), it is possible to express the discrete Fourier transform $\widehat{P^{\ddagger}}(\vec{\mathbf{r}},\vec{\mathbf{m}}_l\,|\,z)$ in terms of analytically well-known functions. Then, by using the Fourier inversion theorem, we can recover the generating function $P^{\ddagger}(\vec{\mathbf{r}},\vec{\mathbf{s}}_j\,|\,z)$ from $\widehat{P^{\ddagger}}(\vec{\mathbf{r}},\vec{\mathbf{m}}_l\,|\,z)$, and hence the data gathering scheme becomes well-characterized. However, throughout what follows, it will be not needed to obtain an explicit evaluation of the generating function $P^{\ddagger}(\vec{\mathbf{r}},\vec{\mathbf{s}}_j\,|\,z)$, and rather only an explicit form for the discrete Fourier transform $\widehat{P}^{\ddagger}(\vec{\mathbf{r}},\vec{\mathbf{m}}_l\,|\,z)$ will be sufficient in order to derive many subtle and useful results regarding the properties of the proposed data gathering scheme. So, all the results of the present paper comes directly from an analysis of the consequences of Propositions 2 and 3.

4. PERFORMANCE EVALUATION

4.1 Bias and State Information

We introduce now the concept of *entropy* associated with a discrete random variable. In the context of RW, it can be defined as the opposite of the sum $\sum_{\vec{\mathbf{s}}\in\Omega} p(\vec{\mathbf{r}},\vec{\mathbf{s}})\,\log_2\big(p(\vec{\mathbf{r}},\vec{\mathbf{s}})\big)$. As regards our proposed biased RW, let $\mathcal{H}^{\ddagger}(\vec{\mathbf{r}},\varepsilon)$ be the associated entropy at sensor node $\vec{\mathbf{r}}$. Therefore, $\mathcal{H}^{\ddagger}(\vec{\mathbf{r}},\varepsilon)$ can be computed as

$$\mathcal{H}^{\ddagger}(\vec{\mathbf{r}},\varepsilon)=\frac{3}{2}-\frac{1}{2}\{\varepsilon\log_2(\varepsilon)+(1-\varepsilon)\log_2(1-\varepsilon)\}.$$

Suppose that at time $n=0$ a data packet is released from a given sensor node $\vec{\mathbf{r}}$. Let $\mathcal{R}_n(\vec{\mathbf{r}},\varepsilon)$ be the position of the data packet after n hops. We have then

$$\mathcal{R}_n(\vec{\mathbf{r}},\varepsilon)=\sum_{j=1}^{n}\mathcal{Y}_j(\vec{\mathbf{r}},\varepsilon), \tag{12}$$

where the random vector $\mathcal{Y}_j(\vec{\mathbf{r}},\varepsilon)$ represents the displacement of the data packet on the jth hop. We find by taking expectations of both sides of (12) that the mean position of the data packet after n hops can be given by

$$\mathbf{E}\big(\mathcal{R}_n(\vec{\mathbf{r}},\varepsilon)\big)=\sum_{j=1}^{n}\mathbf{E}\big(\mathcal{Y}_j(\vec{\mathbf{r}},\varepsilon)\big). \tag{13}$$

As long as the data packet survives for at least n hops without being trapped by sink nodes and since we have the same transition probability distribution over all sensor nodes, (13) reduces to

$$\mathbf{E}\big(\mathcal{R}_n(\vec{\mathbf{r}},\varepsilon)\big)=n\vec{\mu}(\varepsilon), \tag{14}$$

where $\vec{\mu}(\varepsilon)$ denotes the mean displacement on a single hop. A short calculation shows that $\vec{\mu}(\varepsilon)=\frac{1}{2}(1-2\varepsilon)\vec{\mathbf{e}}_1$. In RW theory, this vector is sometimes called the *bias* of the RW and represents the mean *velocity* of data packet propagation. When $\varepsilon=\frac{1}{2}$, this speed is zero and therefore the RW is unbiased. In this case, the data packet has a natural tendency to orbit around its source node. In contrast, when $\varepsilon\neq\frac{1}{2}$ so that the speed $\vec{\mu}(\varepsilon)$ is non-zero, the RW is biased and data packets drift in the direction of the bias. More precisely, if $0\leq\varepsilon<\frac{1}{2}$, data packets drift backwards the data gathering border, *i.e.*, to the right. The bias is called *repulsive*. On the other hand, when $\frac{1}{2}<\varepsilon\leq 1$, data packets drift towards the data gathering border, *i.e.*, to the left. The bias is called *attractive*.

4.2 Local Delay

We study in this subsection the time (in number of hops) it will take for a data packet released at a given sensor node to reach the data gathering border. We refer to this delay time as the *local delay*. Let $\mathcal{D}_N^{\ddagger}(\vec{\mathbf{r}},\varepsilon)$ be the local delay defined at a given sensor node $\vec{\mathbf{r}}$.

THEOREM 3. *Let $\mathcal{D}_N^{\ddagger}(\vec{\mathbf{r}},\varepsilon\,|\,z)$ be the generating function of random variable $\mathcal{D}_N^{\ddagger}(\vec{\mathbf{r}},\varepsilon)$. $\mathcal{D}_N^{\ddagger}(\vec{\mathbf{r}},\varepsilon\,|\,z)$ can be then expressed as*

$$\mathcal{D}_N^{\ddagger}(\vec{\mathbf{r}},\varepsilon\,|\,z)=\frac{\widehat{P}^{\dagger}(\vec{\mathbf{r}},\vec{\mathbf{m}}_0\,|\,z)}{\widehat{P}^{\dagger}(\mathbf{0},\vec{\mathbf{m}}_0\,|\,z)}, \tag{15}$$

where $\widehat{P}^{\dagger}(\vec{\mathbf{r}},\vec{\mathbf{m}}_0\,|\,z)$ is the discrete Fourier transform of sequence $\{P^{\dagger}(\vec{\mathbf{r}},\vec{\mathbf{s}}_k\,|\,z)\}_{0\leq k\leq N-1}$ at the origin.

Proof. Using the law of total probability, the event that a data packet generated at sensor node $\vec{\mathbf{r}}$ will be trapped by the data gathering border after n hops can be decomposed into the N mutually exclusive events that the data packet is gathered by sink node $\vec{\mathbf{s}}_j$ at the n-th hop, which has the probability $F_n^{\ddagger}(\vec{\mathbf{r}},\vec{\mathbf{s}}_j)$. So, we have

$$\mathbf{Pr}\{\mathcal{D}_N^{\ddagger}(\vec{\mathbf{r}},\varepsilon)=n\}=\sum_{j=0}^{N-1}F_n^{\ddagger}(\vec{\mathbf{r}},\vec{\mathbf{s}}_j),\qquad n\geq 0.$$

Multiplying both sides by z^n and summing over all n leads to

$$\mathcal{D}_N^{\ddagger}(\vec{\mathbf{r}},\varepsilon\,|\,z)=\sum_{j=0}^{N-1}F^{\ddagger}(\vec{\mathbf{r}},\vec{\mathbf{s}}_j\,|\,z). \tag{16}$$

Recalling Lemma 1, we find

$$F^{\ddagger}(\vec{\mathbf{r}},\vec{\mathbf{s}}_j\,|\,z)=\frac{P^{\ddagger}(\vec{\mathbf{r}},\vec{\mathbf{s}}_j\,|\,z)}{P^{\ddagger}(\vec{\mathbf{s}}_j,\vec{\mathbf{s}}_j\,|\,z)}. \tag{17}$$

However, since $\vec{\mathbf{s}}_j$ is a trapping site, $P_n^{\ddagger}(\vec{\mathbf{s}}_j,\vec{\mathbf{s}}_j)=1$ for all $n\geq 0$. It follows that $P_n^{\ddagger}(\vec{\mathbf{s}}_j,\vec{\mathbf{s}}_j\,|\,z)$ can be replaced by $1/(1-z)$. Hence, by plugging (17) into (16), we obtain

$$\mathcal{D}_N^{\ddagger}(\vec{\mathbf{r}},\varepsilon\,|\,z)=(1-z)\sum_{j=0}^{N-1}P^{\ddagger}(\vec{\mathbf{r}},\vec{\mathbf{s}}_j\,|\,z). \tag{18}$$

By remarking that the sum involved on the right-hand side of (18) is nothing but the discrete Fourier transform $\widehat{P}^{\ddagger}(\vec{\mathbf{r}},\vec{\mathbf{m}}_0\,|\,z)$ and then applying Proposition 2, we establish (15).■

From now on, we need to make $\widehat{P}^{\dagger}(\vec{\mathbf{r}},\vec{\mathbf{m}}_0\,|\,z)$ and $\widehat{P}^{\dagger}(\mathbf{0},\vec{\mathbf{m}}_0\,|\,z)$ explicit in order to derive useful statistics of the local delay $\mathcal{D}_N^{\ddagger}(\vec{\mathbf{r}},\varepsilon)$ in terms of analytically well-known functions. This is done in our previous work [3]. We obtain then the following theorem.

THEOREM 4. *At a given sensor node $\vec{\mathbf{r}}=(r_1,r_2)$, generating function $\mathcal{D}_N^{\ddagger}(\vec{\mathbf{r}},\varepsilon\,|\,z)$ can be rewritten as*

$$\mathcal{D}_N^{\ddagger}(\vec{\mathbf{r}},\varepsilon\,|\,z)=\frac{\rho_1(z)^{r_1}-\rho_2(z)^{r_1}}{\rho_1(z)^N-\rho_2(z)^N}+\big(\rho_1(z)\rho_2(z)\big)^{r_1}\frac{\rho_1(z)^{N-r_1}-\rho_2(z)^{N-r_1}}{\rho_1(z)^N-\rho_2(z)^N}, \tag{19}$$

where

$$\left\{\begin{array}{l}\rho_1(z)\\ \rho_2(z)\end{array}\right.=\frac{1\pm\sqrt{1-4A(z)B(z)}}{2A(z)}$$

and

$$\left\{\begin{array}{l}A(z)=z(1-\varepsilon)/(2-z)\\ B(z)=z\varepsilon/(2-z).\end{array}\right.$$

4.2.1 *Mean Local Delay*

Applying generating function techniques, the mean local delay, denoted by $\mathbf{E}\big(\mathcal{D}_N^{\ddagger}(\vec{\mathbf{r}},\varepsilon)\big)$, can be derived by taking the limit of the z-derivative of $\mathcal{D}_N^{\ddagger}(\vec{\mathbf{r}},\varepsilon\,|\,z)$ as $z\to 1^-$, so that

$$\mathbf{E}\big(\mathcal{D}_N^{\ddagger}(\vec{\mathbf{r}},\varepsilon)\big)=\lim_{z\to 1^-}\frac{\partial}{\partial z}\mathcal{D}_N^{\ddagger}(\vec{\mathbf{r}}\,|\,z). \tag{20}$$

Plugging (19) into (20) and after elementary calculus, we obtain the following result.

RESULT 1. *The mean local delay $\mathbf{E}(\mathcal{D}_N^{\ddagger}(\vec{\mathbf{r}},\varepsilon))$ can be written in an explicit closed-form expression as*

$$\mathbf{E}(\mathcal{D}_N^{\ddagger}(\vec{\mathbf{r}},\varepsilon)) = \frac{2(\eta+1)}{\eta-1} \times \left\{ r_1 - N\frac{1-\eta^{r_1}}{1-\eta^N} \right\}, \qquad (21)$$

where $\vec{\mathbf{r}} = (r_1, r_2)$ such that $0 \le r_1, r_2 \le N-1$ and $\eta = \dfrac{\varepsilon}{1-\varepsilon}$.

Discussion. Formula (21) seems to be valid only for $\varepsilon \neq \frac{1}{2}$ and $\varepsilon \neq 1$. However, expanding the right-hand side of (21) close to $\varepsilon = \frac{1}{2}$ and $\varepsilon = 1$ shows that $\mathbf{E}(\mathcal{D}_N^{\ddagger}(\vec{\mathbf{r}},\varepsilon))$ is continuous at all $0 \le \varepsilon \le 1$. Indeed, an easy computation shows that $\mathbf{E}(\mathcal{D}_N^{\ddagger}(\vec{\mathbf{r}},\varepsilon \to \frac{1}{2})) = 2r_1(N-r_1)$ $\mathbf{E}(\mathcal{D}_N^{\ddagger}(\vec{\mathbf{r}},\varepsilon \to 1)) = 2r_1$. Furthermore, it is possible to demonstrate that $\mathbf{E}(\mathcal{D}_N^{\ddagger}(\vec{\mathbf{r}},1-\varepsilon)) = \mathbf{E}(\mathcal{D}_N^{\ddagger}(N\vec{\mathbf{e}}_1-\vec{\mathbf{r}},\varepsilon))$, which means that the curves of $\mathbf{E}(\mathcal{D}_N^{\ddagger}(\vec{\mathbf{r}},\varepsilon))$ and $\mathbf{E}(\mathcal{D}_N^{\ddagger}(\vec{\mathbf{r}},1-\varepsilon))$ are symmetric about the axis $r_1 = \frac{N}{2}$. It is therefore sufficient to study the dependence of the mean local delay on parameter ε only over the range $\frac{1}{2} \le \varepsilon \le 1$.

Recalling from Section 4.1 that the bias of the RW can be interpreted as the mean velocity of data packet propagation, the first term of (21), proportional to r_1, represents the capture of data packets by the data gathering border when the bias is attractive ($\frac{1}{2} < \varepsilon \le 1$), while the term proportional to $N - r_1$ for large N represents the capture of data packets when the bias is repulsive ($0 \le \varepsilon < \frac{1}{2}$). Indeed, we have established in Section 4.1 that the bias, denoted by $\vec{\mu}(\varepsilon)$, is equal to $\frac{1}{2}(1-2\varepsilon)\vec{\mathbf{e}}_1$. Therefore, for $1/2 < \varepsilon \le 1$, the negative direction of the x-axis is favored by the walk. In other words, for $1/2 < \varepsilon \le 1$, data packets are attracted by the RW towards the data gathering border. A data packet issued from sensor node $\vec{\mathbf{r}}$ travels then the distance r_1 before being trapped by the data gathering border with a speed $|\vec{\mu}(\varepsilon)| = (\eta-1)/(2(\eta+1))$, hence the time required by the data packet before being trapped is simply the distance divided by the speed, that is, $2r_1(\eta+1)/(\eta-1)$. This is in good agreement with the first term of (21). On the other hand, when the bias is repulsive, a data packet issued from sensor node $\vec{\mathbf{r}}$ has to travel the distance $N - r_1$ before being trapped at the data gathering border. This observation follows from the the periodic boundary conditions. Thus, if we assume N to be large so that η^N can be neglected, formula (21) can be approximated by $2(N-r_1)(\eta+1)/(1-\eta)$, which implies the reasonable result that the time required for the data packet to be gathered is merely the distance $N - r_1$ divided by the speed $|\vec{\mu}(\varepsilon)| = (1-\eta)/(2(\eta+1))$.

The impact of the bias on the mean local delay is illustrated in Figure 2. In this figure, since the data gathering scheme is translationally invariant along the $\pm y$ directions (see Figure 1), the mean local delay is only depicted as a function of r_1 for different values of parameter ε. Furthermore, by symmetry considerations, we restrict our focus on the case of attractive bias, *i.e.*, $\frac{1}{2} < \varepsilon \le 1$. The plots of repulsive bias can be then readily deduced by a reflection transformation against the axis $r_1 = \frac{N}{2}$. The main result from this figure, as expected, is that an attractive bias towards the data gathering border accelerates the data delivery while a repulsive bias decelerates it. Interestingly enough, the case of $\varepsilon = \frac{1}{2}$ corresponds to an unbiased RW where no direction is favored. This represents the worst case for the efficiency of the data gathering scheme in terms of delay. Note also that for fixed ε such that $1/2 \le \varepsilon < 1$, the mean local delay increases with r_1. As we can see in Figure 2, though, there is a crossover in this behavior. Beyond a maximum value, the mean local delay decreases as r_1 increases. This observation can be explained by the fact that with the periodic boundary conditions, the data gathering border at $r_1 = 0$ is virtually replicated

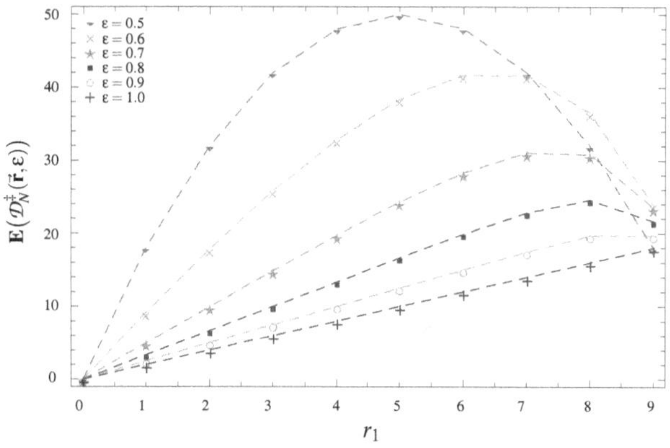

Figure 2: Impact of the bias on the mean local delay for different values of ε. $N = 10$.

to infinity by rigid translations among vectors $mN\vec{\mathbf{e}}_1$ where m is an integer. In particular, the axis $r_1 = N$ would correspond to a line of sink nodes. Hence, when r_1 increases, the attractive effect of the bias is countered by the farness from the data gathering border ($r_1 = 0$) until the proximity from the axis $r_1 = N$ takes hold, and therefore, the mean local delay goes down again.

Finally, we look closely at the full attractive RW ($\varepsilon = 1$) compared to the similar case obtained when the shortest path routing (SPR) is used. This implies that whenever a data packet is generated at a given sensor node $\vec{\mathbf{r}} = (r_1, r_2)$, it will be rather trapped by the closest sink node, namely the one located at $(0, r_2)$. Recalling that the mean local delay $\mathbf{E}(\mathcal{D}_N^{\ddagger}(\vec{\mathbf{r}},1)) = 2r_1$, it follows that the SPR scheme is only twice as efficient as the full attractive RW. This optimality, though, has the drawback that data packets are always delivered along the same path so that each sensor node becomes a critical point of failure. In contrast, the full attractive RW achieves relatively comparable delay while taking advantage of multiple routes to spread out the load evenly over a large number of nodes, thus, minimizing the impact of node failures.

5. CONCLUSION

We have examined analytically in this paper the influence of biasing mechanisms on the performance of RW. The main conclusion is therefore that the larger the applied bias is, the shorter is the data gathering task. However, this is indeed achieved at the cost of additional state information at sensor nodes, which is costly in terms of complexity and energy. There are many lines along which this work could proceed further. One consists of extending the basic model considered in this paper to more complex models, such as the random geometric graphs.

6. REFERENCES

[1] G. Froc, I. Mabrouki, and X. Lagrange. Design and performance of wireless data gathering networks based on unicast random walk routing. *Networking, IEEE/ACM Transactions On*, 17(4):1214–1227, Aug. 2009.

[2] B. D. Hughes. *Random Walks And Random Environments*, volume 1. Oxford University Press, New York, 1995.

[3] I. Mabrouki. *Random Walks in Wireless Sensor Networks*. PhD thesis, University of Rennes I, 2008.

[4] E. W. Montroll. Random walks on lattices. In *Proc. of Symposia on Applied Mathematics*, volume 16, pages 193–220, 1964.

Cactus: A Hybrid Digital-Analog Wireless Video Communication System

Hao Cui
University of Science and Technology of China
Hefei, 230027, P.R. China
hao.cui@live.com

Zhihai Song
Peking University
Beijing, 100871, P.R. China
zhhsng@gmail.com

Zhe Yang
Northeastern University
Shenyang, 110004, P.R. China
yangzhe.research@gmail.com

Chong Luo
Microsoft Research Asia
Beijing, 100080, P.R. China
chong.luo@microsoft.com

Ruiqin Xiong
Peking University
Beijing, 100871, P.R. China
rqxiong@gmail.com

Feng Wu
Microsoft Research Asia
Beijing, 100080, P.R. China
fengwu@microsoft.com

ABSTRACT

This paper challenges the conventional wisdom that video redundancy should be removed as much as possible for efficient communications. We discover that, by keeping spatial redundancy at the sender and properly utilizing it at the receiver, we can build a more robust and even more efficient wireless video communication system than existing ones.

In the proposed framework, inter-frame (temporal) redundancy in video is removed at the encoder, but intra-frame (spatial) redundancy is retained. In doing so, pixel values after a transform-domain scaling are directly transmitted with amplitude modulation. At the receiver, spatial redundancy is utilized by image denoising. Note that denoising in our decoder is not a post-processing, but have to be immediately performed on channel output. We implement the video communication system called *Cactus* on SORA platform, and make the denoising processing real-time through GPU implementation. Cactus is evaluated in 802.11a/g WLAN environment. On average, Cactus outperforms SoftCast by 4.7 dB in video PSNR and is robust to packet losses.

Categories and Subject Descriptors

C.2.0 [**Computer-communication networks**]: General—*Data Communications*

Keywords

Wireless video; hybrid digital-analog communication; joint source-channel coding

1. INTRODUCTION

In 2011, mobile video traffic exceeded 50 percent of mobile traffic for the first time, and it is predicted to increase 25-fold in the next five years, according to Cisco Visual Networking Index (VNI) [4]. Wireless video communications are facing a dilemma in achieving efficiency and robustness. On one hand, videos in their raw format are huge in size, and they need to be efficiently compressed for transmission. On the other, compressed video sequences have too little redundancy left, and therefore are susceptible to channel errors.

Direct application of Shannon's separation theorem [13] suggests that source redundancy should be completely removed and channel coding is responsible for adding redundancy against noise. However, joint source-channel coding (JSCC) suggests to keep certain amount of source redundancy and has been shown to achieve better performance at limited complexity and delay. This inspires us to consider the following questions: how much source redundancy should be retained in wireless video communications in order to achieve both efficiency and robustness? Is it possible to skip channel coding and completely rely on source redundancy for channel protection?

Interestingly, the answer to the second question is a resounding YES, and the answer to the first question becomes clear after we carefully examine the two types of redundancy in video and their respective characteristics. Our research finds that: 1) Inter-frame (temporal) redundancy should be removed as much as possible at the encoder for high efficiency while intra-frame (spatial) redundancy should be retained to protect videos against channel noise. 2) Residual frames should be transmitted in spatial domain (e.g. scaled pixel values) instead of transform domain (i.e. coefficients) through analog transmission to combat losses and noises. 3) The key to fully utilize the source redundancy is to perform image denoising at the decoder based on both source and channel characteristics.

Based on these findings, we propose a hybrid digital-analog video communication system called *Cactus*. At the sender, temporal redundancy is removed by motion-compensated temporal filtering [3]. The motion information is entropy coded into digital bits and protected by the strongest channel codes during transmission. Pixel values in residual frames are transmitted using amplitude modulation. In order to minimize the mean squared error (MSE) under the average power constraint, a transform-domain scaling is performed. However, we emphasize that the sender should transmit scaled pixel values instead of transform-domain co-

MSWiM'13, November 3–8, 2013, Barcelona, Spain.
Copyright 2013 ACM 978-1-4503-2353-6/13/11
http://dx.doi.org/10.1145/2507924.2507987 ...$15.00.

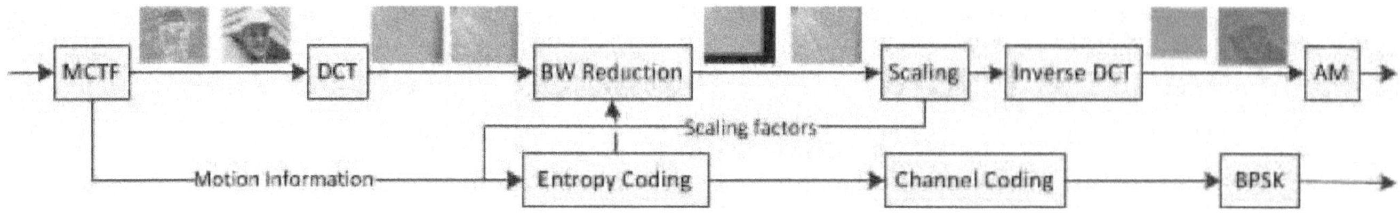

Figure 1: Cactus sender design

efficients. This allows the receiver to fully utilize the source redundancy through applying image denoising techniques. In particular, Cactus employs median filter [12] to deal with packet losses and BM3D [5] to deal with additive noises.

We have implemented Cactus on SORA [15] platform and have evaluated it in 802.11a/g-based wireless LAN environments. Evaluation results confirms that our design achieves high received video quality and is robust to channel variations. Besides, Cactus allows for graceful degradation in a wide range of receiver SNRs, and therefore can be readily used for multicasting. Trace-driven experiments show that Cactus outperforms a recent analog mobile video system SoftCast [8] by 4.7 dB in average video PSNR.

The rest of this paper is organized as follows. Section 2 briefly reviews related works on JSCC. Section 3 presents the Cactus system design. Section 4 describes the implementation of Cactus on SORA and the GPU implementation of BM3D algorithm. Section 5 evaluates the Cactus system and we finally summarize in Section 6.

2. RELATED WORK

The design of Cactus belongs to joint source-channel coding (JSCC), and in particular analog JSCC. This topic has been studied both from information theoretic perspective and for the specific application on video communications.

Theoretic work on analog JSCC mostly considers general source and channel. For instance, it is well-known that a Gaussian source achieves the capacity of an AWGN channel [7]. Gastpar et al. [6] observed that channel coding is not necessary in some cases for optimal communication, but the source and the channel have to be matched in a probabilistic sense. Compression techniques, like vector quantization (VQ) [14] and Wyner-Ziv coding [9, 17], have been adopted in hybrid digital-analog transmissions to match source and channel. Recently, Kochman and Zamir [10] showed that, by combining prediction and modulo-lattice arithmetic, one can match any stationary Gaussian source to any colored-noise Gaussian channel, hence achieve Shannon's capacity limit. They also pointed out that analog transmission scheme is more robust than its digital counterpart and is not sensitive to exact channel knowledge at the sender.

Recently, an analog mobile video system named SoftCast has been proposed [8]. In SoftCast, 3D-DCT is performed on a group of pictures, and the transform coefficients are transmitted through amplitude modulation (AM) after power scaling. SoftCast has shown that such pseudo-analog video transmission is robust to channel variations and is capable of achieving graceful degradation in a wide range of channel conditions. However, an important fact that has been neglected in SoftCast is that the retained source redundancy should be actively utilized at the receiver. Our work differs from Softcast in two main aspects. First, SoftCast is almost a pure analog scheme. All information (except scaling factors) are transmitted with AM. However, we discover that a hybrid digital-analog framework is more efficient and robust for video transmission. Second, Softcast keeps both temporal and spatial redundancy but does not utilize them at the receiver. In contrast, we remove temporal redundancy at the sender and adopt image denoising techniques at the receiver to utilize the spatial redundancy.

3. CACTUS DESIGN

3.1 Sender Design

Cactus is a hybrid digital-analog communication system. Fig.1 provides a block diagram of the sender design.

1) Reduction of temporal redundancy: At the sender, a video sequence is first divided into group of pictures (GOP). Temporal redundancy is removed via motion-compensated temporal filtering (MCTF) [3, 18]. MCTF is attractive to our system because it is based on an open-loop prediction model, i.e. the prediction is based on original pixel values not the reconstructed ones. Therefore, the drifting errors are much smaller than its closed-loop counterpart when the received signal contains errors. The motion information, including mode and motion vector, needs to be faithfully received by every receiver, so they are entropy coded and transmitted using a robust digital scheme.

2) Bandwidth allocation and reduction: The temporally filtered frames have exactly the same dimension as the original frames. Normally, the channel does not have enough bandwidth to transmit all the pixels, so part of them should be discarded. Directly discarding pixels in spatial domain will incur unrecoverable errors. Discarding small coefficients in frequency domain as conventional video encoder does is not a feasible solution too. This is because we will eventually transmit the frames in spatial domain, and the source bandwidth does not change after inverse-DCT no matter how many coefficients are discarded and set to zeros.

We propose L-shaped data reduction in frequency domain. As known, the truncation of image/video data should be performed in frequency domain in order to keep most of the energy. Considering the fact that the high-frequency and low-frequency MCTF frames differ greatly in energy, the data reduction is performed on GOP basis. For each MCTF frame, we first perform DCT and then compute the average energy for each inverse-L line on the bottom-right of a frame (corresponding to the highest horizontal and vertical frequency band). We gradually discard the inverse-L line which has the lowest energy in a GOP until the bandwidth requirement is satisfied. As the remaining coefficients possess a rectangular shape, we could later use the IDCT of smaller dimensions (equalling to the size of remaining coefficients) to generate spatial-domain frames of reduced size.

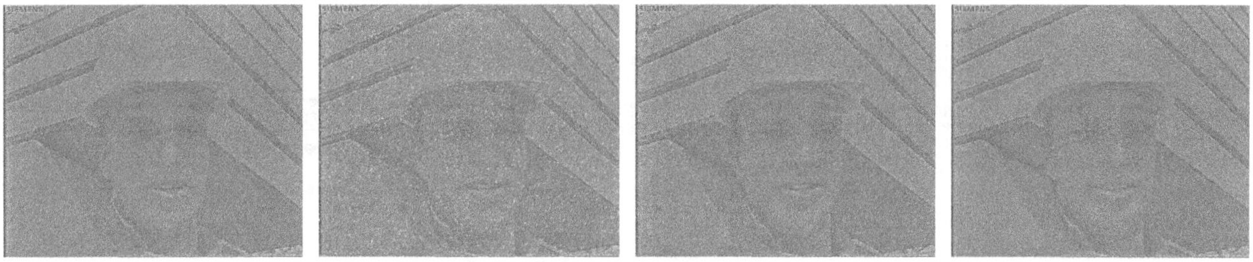

(a) Channel input (b) Channel output (c) After median filter (d) After BM3D

Figure 2: Transmitting a low-pass frame of Foreman over a 5dB AWGN channel and 1% loss rate

3) L-shaped chunk division and scaling: To optimally transmit a visual signal under MSE criterion in a power-constrained system, one should scale frequency-domain coefficients by a factor which is inversely proportional to the fourth root of its variance [11]. In order to reduce the overhead of transmitting the scaling factors, Jakubczak and Katabi [8] propose to group nearby coefficients into rectangular chunks and model the values in each chunk as random variables (RVs) from the same distribution. Then the sender only need to transmit one scaling factor per each chunk.

We observe that transform coefficients decay rapidly from low-frequency to high-frequency, and those belonging to similar frequency band are more likely to have similar values. Therefore, we propose a new adaptive (inverse) L-shaped chunk division method. Assuming we divides the coefficients into M L-shaped chunks, then the scaling factor for the ith chunk, denoted by g_i, is

$$g_i = \lambda_i^{-\frac{1}{4}} \sqrt{\frac{P}{\sum_i \sqrt{\lambda_i}}}, \tag{1}$$

where P is the total power budget and λ_i is the variance of the ith chunk.

An optimal chunk division should minimize $\sum_i \sqrt{\lambda_i}$. For L-shaped chunk division, the adjustable parameters are r_j ($j = 1, 2, ...M-1$), which are the positions of chunk boundaries. We adopt an iterative approach to search for the optimal set of $\{r_j\}$. The initial values of $r_j's$ are evenly spaced. Then the algorithm iteratively updates each r_j with other values fixed. The chunk boundaries and scaling factors are transmitted through digital method too.

4) Inverse DCT and transmission: Finally, inverse DCT is performed on each frame. This is a key step in our design in order to fully utilize the spatial redundancy, because the loss of pixels is more friendly to image denoising algorithms than the loss of frequency coefficients. Note that transmitting scaled pixel values does not change the overall power because IDCT is an orthonormal transform.

The scaled pixel values are interleaved and transmitted with AM. In particular, every two pixel values are transmitted as the I and Q components of a complex symbol. The AM we used is actually *pseudo-analog*, because we use a discrete modulation constellation, except that it is much denser than the commonly used 16-QAM or 64-QAM. This pseudo-analog implementation allows our design to be easily integrated into existing network stack.

3.2 Receiver Design

At the receiver, the digitally transmitted symbols are processed with a sequence of inverse operations including demodulation, channel decoding, and entropy decoding. Correct motion information and metadata can be obtained. Meanwhile, the receiver directly reads the scaled pixel values from the I/Q components of wireless symbols, and pieces together all the frames.

One key finding in our research is that source redundancy can provide channel protection under the premise that it is fully utilized at the receiver. We propose to perform image denoising at the receiver, and emphasize that denoising should be immediately applied on the scaled frames. Fig.2 uses an example to illustrate the denoising process in our decoder. We assume an AWGN channel with 5dB receiver SNR and additional 1% loss rate. Fig.2(b) shows the channel output where white dots indicate the lost pixels. They are randomly dispersed pixel "holes" in the frame under ideal interleaving. We first fill these holes with the median filter [12] and the resultant frame is shown in Fig.2(c). Then, the state-of-the-art denoising algorithm BM3D [5] is adopted to reduce the random noise. Fig.2(d) shows the result after BM3D denoising. It can be seen that this image is very close to channel input as shown in Fig.2(a).

After denoising, transform-domain de-scaling is performed on each frame. This is accomplished by DCT transform, scaling, and inverse DCT transform. If the frame size is smaller than the regular size, indicating a portion of the coefficients have been dropped, the decoder will pad zeros to form a frame of regular size, then perform inverse DCT. The de-scaled frames and decoded motion information will then be used to reconstruct the GOP by inverse MCTF.

4. IMPLEMENTATION

4.1 Cactus Implementation

In the Cactus encoder, we use a reference C code which implements the barbell lifting MCTF proposed by Xiong et al. [18], and perform 3-layer filtering for each 8-frame GOP. The other application-layer modules, including transform, bandwidth allocation and reduction, L-shaped chunk division and scaling, and entropy coding are implemented in Matlab. All the modules except MCTF could process CIF (352×288) videos in real-time. However, we believe that MCTF can be run in real-time, because it has very similar processing steps and complexity as hierarchical-B coding structure in H.264 [18]. The latter already has a real-time implementation x.264 [2], which can encode four 1080p streams in real-time on a single consumer-level computer.

Cactus PHY is implemented over OFDM as defined in IEEE 802.11a/g. Specifically, the channel is divided into 64 subcarriers and 48 of them are used to transmit modulation symbols. To reduce the overhead of PLCP header, we use

100 OFDM symbols in each PLCP frame for data transmission. Therefore, the total number of modulation symbols in each transmission is 4800. Metadata, including motion information and M chunk boundaries and scaling factors, are transmitted using BPSK and rate-1/2 channel coding to ensure successful transmission. In this implementation, M is set to 10. To resist packet loss, the adjacent symbols from a frame are pseudo-randomly shuffled across different PLCP frames. We limit the shuffling in a GOP of video frames to reduce the decoding delay. When a PLCP frame is lost, it creates randomly dispersed "holes" in the video frame, which can be easily processed by median filter.

In the Cactus decoder, we implement channel decoding, entropy decoding, and transform-domain de-scaling in Matlab. The inverse MCTF has a much lower computational complexity than MCTF encoder. Therefore, the decoder can also be implemented in real-time. We use the Matlab code published by the authors [1] to perform BM3D denoising for all the evaluations. The processing time for one CIF video frame is around 1.4 seconds using Intel Core Quad CPU (Q9550) 2.83GHz.

4.2 GPU Implementation of BM3D

We notice that the current implementation of BM3D has a high computational complexity. Fortunately, it is very suitable for parallel computing (e.g., a specially designed chip, a FPGA or a GPU). In order to validate that our system can run in real-time, we implement BM3D through GPU NVIDIA GTX680. It has 8 streaming multiprocessors (SMs). Each SM has 192 cores and 64KB shared memory in which 48KB can be used to store data. We implement BM3D in GPU following two optimization rules. The first rule is to fully utilize all 192 cores. Second, because accessing the display memory (size up to 2GB) is slow, the data processed by the 192 cores should not exceed the SM's memory size which is 48KB.

In addition to the parallel design, we make two simplifications to the original BM3D algorithm to reduce complexity. First, we only implement the basic estimate and skip the final estimate. Second, we replace the original bi-orthogonal transform with Haar wavelet transform for the matched blocks. We evaluate our GPU implementation over 16 CIF test video sequences under 5 dB AWGN channel. The anchor results is achieved by the official Matlab code [1]. On average, our implementation has 0.19 dB loss in video PSNR. On average, our GPU implementation can process CIF videos at the speed of 35 fps with only 0.19dB loss in video PSNR.

5. EVALUATION

5.1 Settings

Wireless environment: Evaluations are carried out with SORA (equipped with WARP radio board) over 802.11a/g-based WLAN. We perform 52 test runs. In each test run, we transmit data generated by Cactus encoder. The receiver records the received wireless symbols. These symbols are not only used for Cactus decoding, but are compared with the exact channel inputs to generate the traced channel noise. The traced data are labeled from 1 to 52 (according to the time they are obtained). Our comparisons with reference schemes are trace-driven to ensure fairness.

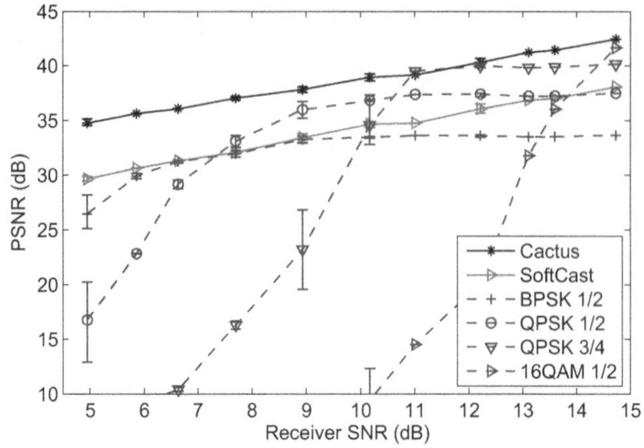

Figure 3: Compare Cactus against two reference schemes for CIF sequence in a multicast session when source bandwidth equals channel bandwidth.

Video Source: We create a monochrome CIF video sequence with resolution 352 × 288 for our evaluation. The frame rate is 30 fps (frame per second). This sequence is created by extracting the first 32 frames from 16 standard video test sequences including *akiyo, bus, coastguard, crew, ower, football, foreman, harbour, husky, ice, news, soccer, stefan, tempete, tennis, waterfall.* This test sequence is similar to the one used in SoftCast [8], with the only difference that the resolution used in SoftCast is 352 × 240.

Reference Schemes: Two reference schemes are considered. The first one is SoftCast [8]. Our implementation sets the GOP size to 8 in order for a fair comparison with Cactus. We actually evaluated both schemes for GOP size 16, and found that both schemes will have 0.3-0.5 dB performance gain in PSNR.

The other reference is based on H.264 or MPEG4 AVC digital video coding standard [16]. We adopt a publicly available encoder called x264 [2] to encode test sequences at different rates and obtain a R-D (rate-distortion) curve. Similarly, GOP size is set to 8 for fairness. The possible rates are those defined in 802.11a/g. We then calculate the Goodput rate for an entire test run, and find the corresponding distortion from the R-D curve, as if the encoder had known the channel conditions in advance. We do not compare with the Scalable Video Coding (SVC) extension of H.264/AVC because it has been shown in SoftCast that the performance is inferior to SoftCast.

Performance metric: We evaluate the video delivery quality with the standard peak signal-to-noise ratio (PSNR) in dB. We compute the PSNR for each video frame by $PSNR = 10log_{10}\frac{255^2}{MSE}$, where MSE is the mean squared error of all pixels. Then the PSNR is averaged across frames.

5.2 Performance

Fig.3 compares the performance of Cactus against two reference schemes, namely SoftCast and Omni-MPEG under multicast scenario. We run 52 traces over the CIF sequence to emulate a 52-receiver multicast session. For Cactus and SoftCast, in each test run, we compute the average receiver SNR across PHY packets and average video PSNR across sequences. To plot the video PSNR as a function of receiver SNR, we divide the receiver SNR range into 1 dB bins, and

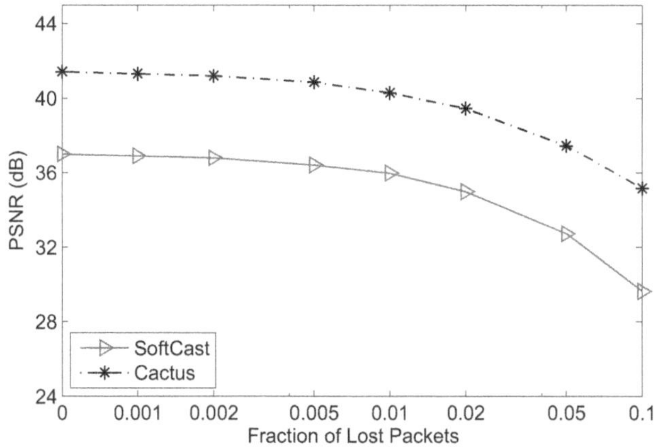

Figure 4: Error resilience capability of Cactus and SoftCast with trace #16 (receiver SNR = 13.59 dB)

average all the (receiver SNR, PSNR) pairs whose receiver SNR fall into the same bin. Results show that although both Cactus and SoftCast achieve graceful rate adaptation, Cactus consistently outperforms SoftCast in video PSNR, and the average gain is 4.7 dB.

For MPEG, the sender has to fix a transmission rate in each test run. We run four tests, using the lower half of the PHY rates defined in 802.11a/g. Once the transmission rate is fixed, the video PSNR can be found in the R-D curve. We run each trace for each PHY rate, if the instantaneous receiver SNR is higher than expected, transmission is successful. Otherwise, transmission fails. We average the PSNR along each trace, and also plot (receiver SNR, PSNR) in bins. Fig.3 clearly shows that Cactus outperform MPEG because the latter suffers from the threshold effect.

We next evaluate whether Cactus is robust to packet losses. The traces used in this experiment is #16 which has a receiver SNR of 13.59 dB. The packet loss is simulated by assuming an interferer who transmits packets at constant intervals. We evaluate both Cactus and SoftCast when the packet loss ratios are 0.001, 0.002, 0.005, 0.01, 0.02, 0.05, and 0.1. Fig.4 shows the average video PSNR achieved by Cactus and SoftCast as a function of loss rate. The x-axis is in logarithm. When the packet loss ratio is 0.1, the PSNR loss of Cactus with respect to no loss case is 6.3 dB. Under the same packet loss ratio, the PSNR loss of SoftCast with respect to its no loss case is 7.4 dB. This shows that Cactus has even higher robustness to packet loss than SoftCast.

6. SUMMARY

We have described in this paper an efficient and robust wireless video communication system - Cactus. Our design validates that it is possible in video communications to skip channel coding and solely rely on source redundancy for channel protection. Evaluations show that performing image denoising at receivers greatly improves the perceived video quality. The encouraging results suggest the great potential of such hybrid digital-analog framework.

7. REFERENCES

[1] Bm3d algorithm and its extensions. Technical report, http://www.cs.tut.fi/ foi/GCF-BM3D/.

[2] http://www.videolan.org/developers/x264.html.

[3] S.-J. Choi and J. Woods. Motion-compensated 3-d subband coding of video. *IEEE Trans. on Image Processing*, 8(2):155–167, Feb 1999.

[4] Cisco. Cisco visual networking index: Global mobile data traffic forecast update, 2011-2016. Technical report, http://www.cisco.com/en/US/ solutions/collateral/ns341/ns525/ns537/ns705/ ns827/white_paper_c11-520862.pdf, Feb 2012.

[5] K. Dabov, A. Foi, V. Katkovnik, and K. Egiazarian. Image denoising by sparse 3-d transform-domain collaborative filtering. *IEEE Trans. on Image Processing*, 16(8):2080 –2095, aug. 2007.

[6] M. Gastpar, B. Rimoldi, and M. Vetterli. To code, or not to code: lossy source-channel communication revisited. *IEEE Trans. on Information Theory*, 49(5):1147–1158, May 2003.

[7] T. Goblick. Theoretical limitations on the transmission of data from analog sources. *IEEE Trans. on Information Theory*, 11(4):558 – 567, Oct 1965.

[8] S. Jakubczak and D. Katabi. A cross-layer design for scalable mobile video. In *Proceedings of ACM Mobicom'11*, pages 289–300, 2011.

[9] Y. Kochman and R. Zamir. Joint wyner-ziv / dirty-paper coding by modulo-lattice modulation. *IEEE Trans. on Information Theory*, 55:4878–4899, Nov 2009.

[10] Y. Kochman and R. Zamir. Analog matching of colored sources to colored channels. *IEEE Trans. on Information Theory*, 57(6):3180–3195, June 2011.

[11] K.-H. Lee and D. Petersen. Optimal linear coding for vector channels. *IEEE Trans. on Communications*, 24(12):1283 – 1290, Dec. 1976.

[12] W. K. Pratt. Median filtering. Technical report, Image Processing Institute, University of Southern California, Sep. 1975.

[13] C. E. Shannon. A mathematical theory of communication. *Bell System Technology Journal*, 27:379–423, 623–656, 1948.

[14] M. Skoglund, N. Phamdo, and F. Alajaji. Design and performance of VQ-based hybrid digital-analog joint source-channel codes. *IEEE Trans. on Information Theory*, 48(3):708–720, Mar. 2002.

[15] K. Tan, H. Liu, J. Zhang, Y. Zhang, J. Fang, and G. M. Voelker. Sora: high-performance software radio using general-purpose multi-core processors. *Communications of the ACM*, 54(1):99–107, Jan. 2011.

[16] T. Wiegand, G. J. Sullivan, G. Bjontegaard, and A. Luthra. Overview of the H.264/AVC video coding standard. *IEEE Trans. on Circuits and Systems for Video Technology*, 13(7):560–576, Jul. 2003.

[17] M. P. Wilson, K. Narayanan, and G. Caire. Joint source channel coding with side information using hybrid digital analog codes. *IEEE Trans. on Information Theory*, 56:4922–4940, Jul 2010.

[18] R. Xiong, J. Xu, F. Wu, and S. Li. Barbell-lifting based 3-d wavelet coding scheme. *IEEE Trans. on Circuits and Systems for Video Technology*, 17(9):1256–1269, sept. 2007.

On the Compound Impact of Opportunistic Scheduling and D2D Communications in Cellular Networks

Arash Asadi
Institute IMDEA Networks
University Carlos III of Madrid
Leganes (Madrid), Spain
arash.asadi@imdea.org

Vincenzo Mancuso
Institute IMDEA Networks
University Carlos III of Madrid
Leganes (Madrid), Spain
vincenzo.mancuso@imdea.org

ABSTRACT

Opportunistic scheduling was initially proposed to exploit user channel diversity for network capacity enhancement. However, the achievable gain of opportunistic schedulers is generally restrained due to fairness considerations which impose a tradeoff between fairness and throughput. In this paper, we show via analysis and numerical simulations that opportunistic scheduling not only increases network throughput dramatically, but also increases energy efficiency and can be fair to the users when they cooperate, in particular by using D2D communications. We propose to leverage smartphone's dual-radio interface capabilities to form clusters among mobile users. We design simple, scalable and energy-efficient D2D-assisted opportunistic strategies, which would incentivize mobile users to form clusters. We use a coalitional game theory approach to analyze the cluster formation mechanism, and show that proportional fair-based intra-cluster payoff distribution brings significant incentive to all mobile users regardless of their channel quality.

Keywords

LTE; opportunistic scheduling; clustering; D2D.

Categories and Subject Descriptors

C.2.1 [**Computer-communication networks**]: Network Architecture and Design—*Wireless communication*

1. INTRODUCTION

Opportunistic schedulers have become a promising solution to cope with the mobile consumer traffic boom in cellular networks. This class of schedulers exploit multiuser diversity to reorder transmissions so that each user is served, with high probability, when it is in a relatively good channel state. However, the achievable opportunistic gain is restrained by user's fairness requirements, and by limited memory and computational resources at the base station. In fact, schedulers that achieve a good tradeoff between throughput and fairness, e.g., the renowned Proportional Fair scheduler (PF) [33], are too complex for the centralized architecture of cellular networks. In contrast, today's mobile devices are equipped with high processing power, large memory, and multiple radio interfaces. Therefore, mobile users may communicate with each other using 802.11 interfaces, e.g., using WiFi-Direct capabilities [31]. Particularly, multiple radios could be exploited for establishing cooperation via Device-to-Device (D2D) communications, e.g., to form clusters, as illustrated in Figure 1.

MSWiM'13, November 3–8, 2013, Barcelona, Spain.

http://dx.doi.org/10.1145/2507924.2507929.

Figure 1: Cellular network with clusters of dual-radio mobiles.

In this paper, we propose to use the multi-radio capabilities of newly designed mobile devices to form cooperative clusters. The presence of clusters simplifies the scheduling operation at the base station and enables efficient, opportunistic radio resource utilization. Specifically, we design a multi-layer cluster-based scheduling mechanism in which the base station *schedules clusters* instead of users, while intra-cluster resource distribution is left to cluster members using D2D communications.

Note that scheduling clusters instead of users means that each cluster connects to the base station via a *cluster head.* However, unlike existing clustering approaches, we propose to select the cluster head *opportunistically* in each frame. The resulting scheduling mechanism consists of two elements: an algorithm to schedule clusters, and an algorithm to select cluster heads opportunistically within each cluster. We primarily focus on the cluster scheduling part and show that cluster heads can be chosen in a pure opportunistic way.

The main contributions of this paper are as follows: (*i*) we design a novel network architecture based on cooperative D2D communications, combining clustering techniques and opportunistic scheduling; (*ii*) we design two novel cluster scheduling algorithms, and present a mathematical analysis of these schemes; (*iii*) we provide an analytic model for user power consumption in the proposed architecture; (*iv*) we provide a game theory-based description of the clustering formation and revenue distribution; (*v*) via extensive numerical simulations, we evaluate the compound impact of opportunistic scheduling and D2D techniques within the proposed architecture, and show that we achieve dramatic throughput gain, extremely fair throughput distributions among mobile users, and high energy efficiency.

The remainder of this paper is organized as follows. In Section 2 we discuss the related work. The system model is presented in Section 3. In Section 4 we model the scheduling algorithms used in this work. We provide a novel model for power consumption of clustered dual-radio mobile users in Section 5. In Section 6 we evaluate the clustering gain with static topologies. In Section 7 we propose a coalitional game theory approach to form clusters and evaluate our clustering proposal in realistic dynamic topologies. Section 8 concludes the paper.

2. RELATED WORK

Since our proposal defines opportunistic *cluster* scheduling using cooperative communications, here we review the literature related to opportunistic scheduling and cooperative communications.

Opportunistic scheduling. Proposals on opportunistic scheduling are very mature. Indeed, a simplified version of PF is already implemented in 3G systems [33]. However, there are other schedulers proposed in the literature, which promise better throughput performance than PF, at the expenses of either fairness or increased complexity. Knopp and Humblet proposed the so called MaxRate opportunistic scheduler in [14], which always schedules the user in the best channel condition. Since opportunistic gain of MaxRate relies on multiuser channel diversity, opportunistic beamforming was proposed in order to increase the user diversity [27,29]. MaxWeight [1] is another opportunistic scheduler that selects the user with the highest product of queue length and transmission rate. *Exp-rule* schedulers [26] are throughput-optimal schedulers that prioritize users based on an exponential formula using queue size and transmission rate of every user.

Our proposal leverages the MaxRate scheduler for communications between base station and cluster heads, thus achieving the maximum utilization of the airtime allotted to each cluster. Differently from existing (opportunistic) schedulers, we propose to schedule clusters as a whole, and show that *cluster* scheduling can be operated by means of simple and scalable schemes achieving high fairness, notwithstanding the use of MaxRate.

User cooperation. Research on cooperative communications in cellular networks has investigated different aspects of cooperation, such as base station-level cooperation [5] and user-level cooperation [13].

Relaying is an example of cooperation, in which mobile stations act as fixed base stations for long periods, hence increasing coverage without the need for setting up additional cells [15,32]. Specifically, Wu *et al.* [32] propose to use dual-radio relay stations (cellular and ad-hoc) to perform load balancing among different cells. Their approach does not consume cellular radio resources for relaying but it is not channel-opportunistic and introduces extra delay.

Another example of user cooperation is represented by clustering techniques. Clustering has been well studied in wireless sensor networks for energy saving, routing and coverage improvement purposes [4,10]. The work in [6,12,18,23, 30] studied clustering in WLANs and cellular networks. In particular, Lin *et al.* [18] proposed clustering to form robust multi-hop networks. In [6,23], mobile users are clustered to form a virtual antenna array which emulates a MIMO device via D2D communications. Furthermore, Dohler *et al.* [6] proposed to use a second wireless interface (e.g., bluetooth or WiFi) for intra-cluster communications. These proposals are either not suitable for cellular network protocols, or do not exploit opportunistic scheduling.

In general, D2D communications may be utilized for cooperative communications, e.g., packet forwarding, and relaying. In [7]and [17], the authors explore some applications of D2D communications in cellular networks such as P2P, multiplayer gaming, and multicast transmissions. Yu *et al.* [34] propose D2D communications in cellular networks for local traffic handling. In their view, D2D transmissions are meant to handle communications among two mobile devices, however users do not help each other to relay traffic to the base station. Also, all transmissions occur over the same interface as cellular communications, and D2D resources are allocated by the base station. Differently from our work, the existing proposals do not exploit opportunistic scheduling.

3. SYSTEM MODEL

We model downlink transmissions in a single LTE-like cell using a 20 *MHz* bandwidth in FDD mode [28]. There are N mobile users served either with legacy user-based schedulers or with our proposed cluster-based scheduling algorithms. Since we are interested in network capacity and fairness under heavy load conditions, we study the case of fully backlogged downlink flows. The total downlink capacity, in terms of transmission slots per frame, is indicated as S_{tot}, and the maximum achievable rate in the cell is 80.64 *Mbps*.[1]

Selection of Modulation and Coding Scheme (MCS). The downlink channel in between the base station and mobile node i is characterized by stationary Rayleigh fading. Therefore, the SNR can be described as a r.v. C_i with average SNR γ_i, so that pdf and CDF of the SNR have the following expressions, respectively:

$$f_i(z) = \frac{1}{\gamma_i} e^{-\frac{z}{\gamma_i}} u(z), \quad F_i(z) = \left[1 - e^{-\frac{z}{\gamma_i}}\right] u(z); \tag{1}$$

where $u(z)$ is the unit step function.We assume that user channels are independently distributed but not identically, and the channel state information is available at the base station. Transmissions occur at different rates according to M available MCSs. We assume that the MCS for user i is selected as a function of the instantaneous SNR, i.e.:

$$MCS_i = k \iff C_i \in [th_k; th_{k+1}[, \ k = 1 \dots M; \tag{2}$$

$$th_1 = 0; \quad th_p < th_q \iff p < q; \quad th_{M+1} = \infty.$$

Therefore, the probability that a scheduled user i receives a frame encoded according to the kth MCS is:

$$\pi_k^{(i)} = \int_{th_k}^{th_{k+1}} f_i(z)dz = e^{\frac{th_k}{\gamma_i}} - e^{\frac{th_{k+1}}{\gamma_i}}. \tag{3}$$

The number of data bits transferred in one OFDMA symbol using the kth MCS is denoted by b_k, see Table 1. The table shows the list of possible MCS's with their corresponding SNR thresholds for LTE-like networks [25]. The implementation margin (IM) in Table 1 is a value that represents the effects of non-ideal receiver. For the sake of tractability, in this paper we assume that mobile users belong to

[1]We neglect LTE protocol overhead, and consider that all available downlink resources can be used for data traffic.

Table 1: Modulation and coding schemes

Modulation	Coding Rate	SNR (dB)	IM (dB)	SNR+IM (dB)	b_k(Bits per symbol)
No transmission	-	$-\infty$	-	$-\infty$	0
QPSK	1/8	-5.1	2.5	-2.6	0.25
	1/5	-2.9		- 0.4	0.4
	1/4	-1.7		0.8	0.5
	1/3	-1		1.5	0.67
	1/2	2		4.5	1
	2/3	4.3		6.8	1.3
	3/4	5.5		8.0	1.5
	4/5	6.2		8.7	1.6
16QAM	1/2	7.9	3	10.9	2
	2/3	11.3		14.3	2.66
	3/4	12.2		15.2	3
	4/5	12.8		15.8	3.2
64QAM	2/3	15.3	4	19.3	4
	3/4	17.5		21.5	4.5
	4/5	18.6		22.6	4.8

one of three predefined SNR *classes*, which correspond to *poor*, *average*, and *good* mean SNR. The designated SNR for different classes are chosen in a manner that the mean achievable rates for *poor*, *average*, and *good* users are 20%, 50%, and 80% of the maximum transmission rate achievable in the system, respectively. With the thresholds and MCS values reported in Table 1, the designated SNR values are 7 dB, 16 dB and 23 dB, respectively for *poor*, *average*, and *good* users. Note also that using non-homogeneous channel qualities allows us to evaluate the long-term system fairness under different (opportunistic) scheduling mechanisms.

Clustering. We assume that mobiles can form clusters and receive downlink traffic through the *cluster head*, i.e., the node enabled to exchange data with the base station (see Figure 1). Note that each node is a potential candidate to act as cluster head, and cluster heads are selected on a per-frame basis. A cluster consists of several mobiles that form an ad-hoc wireless network and that are in radio range with each other, e.g., a WiFi clique. Hence, all intra-cluster communications take place over the ad-hoc wireless network. After cluster formation, the base station is aware of clustering decisions. Thus, whenever a packet is destined to a cluster member, the base station simply sends it to the cluster head, which maximizes the throughput at that epoch. Thereby, the base station schedules clusters as if they were regular users. From a modeling perspective, a cluster can be considered as a user whose SNR is the highest of the SNR values of cluster members. As for intra-cluster resource sharing, unless otherwise specified, we assume that the extra throughput gained from clustering is equally distributed among users.

Example of cluster impact. The incentive behind clustering can be easily observed by comparing the user's channel state probabilities, as defined in Eq. (3). Indeed, the primary effect of clustering is to increase the probability of transmitting with higher MCS's, due to the opportunistic selection of the cluster head. Figure 2 illustrates the impact of clustering on channel state probabilities π_k. Here, a cluster is considered as a user whose channel state is the highest of the channel states among cluster members. As shown in the figure, cluster formation highly boosts the transmission rate of *poor* and *average* users, while the impact on *good* users is less significant. Nonetheless, we will show that with our proposal the throughput of *good* users can improve as well by a non-negligible quantity. Therefore, *good users* can

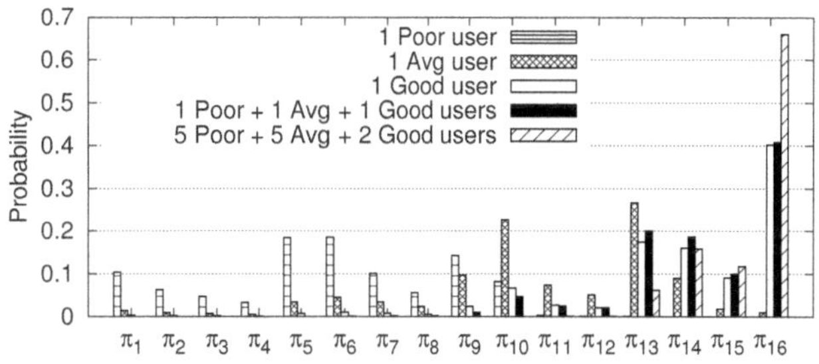

Figure 2: Impact of clustering on channel state probabilities.

be incentivized to help users with lower channel qualities. In practice, *good* users can be encouraged to participate in clustering by receiving an extra quota for the portion of traffic that they forward for others users. A more detailed discussion on clustering incentives and costs is provided later in Section 7.

4. CLUSTER-BASED SCHEDULING

In the following, we introduce a new class of schedulers, namely *cluster-based schedulers*. We consider the case in which the base station schedules N_c clusters instead of N normal users. This means that the base station decides which cluster has to be served, and then transmissions will be managed by the current cluster head.

Defining X_n as the SNR of cluster n, we have:

$$X_n = \max\{C_j, j : U_j \in CL_n\},\ n \in \{1 \dots N_c\}. \quad (4)$$

The CDF of X_n can be readily computed considering that the random variables C_j are all independent:

$$F_{X_n}(z) = \prod_{j:U_j \in CL_n} F_j(z) = u(z) \prod_{j:U_j \in CL_n} \left(1 - e^{-\frac{z}{\gamma_j}}\right); \quad (5)$$

the corresponding pdf, $f_{X_n}(z)$, can be obtained by derivation from $F_{X_n}(z)$. The adopted MCS, for each transmission, only depends on the instantaneous SNR of the best channel in the scheduled cluster, i.e., it only depends on X_n at the scheduling epoch:

$$\pi_k^{(CL_n)} = \int_{th_k}^{th_{k+1}} f_{X_n}(z)dz. \quad (6)$$

CL(WRR): **Cluster Weighted Round Robin.** Let us call N_n the number of members of cluster CL_n. With *CL(WRR)*, clusters are scheduled according to a WRR mechanism, with each cluster CL_n having weight w_n. For instance, using $w_n = N_n/N$ would correspond to assign each cluster an amount of airtime proportional to the number of members in the cluster.

In this system, the per-cluster scheduling probability is exactly w_n, $n \in \{1 \dots N_c\}$, while the average symbol rate depends only on the selected MCS, which, in turn, only depends on the selected cluster. Since resources are allocated in WRR, the average throughput of each cluster only depends on the cluster weight and the probability distribution of the cluster's MCS:

$$E[T_{CL_n}] = w_n \sum_{k=1}^{M} \pi_k^{(CL_n)} b_k S_{tot},\ n \in \{1 \dots N_c\}. \quad (7)$$

CL(MR): **MaxRate Between Clusters.** With this scheme, each frame is allotted to the cluster with the user experiencing the best SNR. The probability that cluster CL_n

is scheduled with the k-th MCS is:

$$P(CL_n|k) = Pr(X_n > Y_n|MCS_{CL_n} = k), \qquad (8)$$

where $Y_n = \max\{Cj\}, j \notin CL_n$, and X_n represents the SNR of cluster n (see Eq. (4)). The CDF of X_n, subject to $MCS_{CL_n} = k$, is:

$$F_{X_n}(z|MCS_{CL_n} = k) = \\ = u(z - th_k)\frac{F_{X_n}(\min(z, th_{k+1})) - F_{X_n}(th_k)}{\pi_k^{(CL_n)}}. \qquad (9)$$

Now we can rewrite (8) using the total probability formula, considering that X_n and Y_n are independent:

$$P(CL_n|k) = Pr(X_n > Y_n|MCS_{CL_n} = k) \\ = \int_0^\infty [1 - F_{X_n}(z|MCS_{CL_n} = k)]\, f_{Y_n}(z)dz. \qquad (10)$$

Finally, the average per-cluster throughput can be computed using the following formula:

$$E\left[T_{CL_n}\right] = \sum_{k=1}^{M} P(CL_n|k)\pi_k^{(CL_n)} b_k S_{tot}. \qquad (11)$$

5. POWER CONSUMPTION ANALYSIS

We derive the power consumption of mobiles from the empirical power models proposed for LTE and WiFi in [11] and [8]. The proposed models are desirable for two virtues: (i) they include the baseline power required to keep the interface up and running; (ii) they account for the variability of power consumption with transmission rate, and differentiate transmission from reception.

LTE consumption. Based on [11], the downlink power consumption of user i in the cellular network is:

$$W_{lte}^{(i)} = \beta_{lte} + \alpha_{rx} R_{rx}^{(i,lte)}, \qquad (12)$$

where β_{lte} is the baseline power, α_{rx} is the downlink power consumption per $Mbps$, and $R_{rx}^{(i,lte)}$ is the average data rate received by user i over the LTE interface:

$$R_{rx}^{(i,\,lte)} = \sum_{k=1}^{M} \pi_k^{(i)} b_k t_k^{(i)}, \qquad (13)$$

where $b_k t_k^{(i)}$ is the average data rate of user i when its MSC is k, b_k is the per-symbol throughput achieved with that MCS, and the value of $t_k^{(i)}$ represents resources allocated to user i, which depend on the scheduling policy adopted (see Section 4).

In particular, under cluster-based schedulers, only cluster heads receive packets from the base station, so that the power consumption of user i strongly depends on the probability of that user being the cluster head when it can use MCS k, namely $P_h^{(i|k)}$. Therefore, the fraction of resources allotted to user i when it is the cluster head and can use MCS k is:

$$t_k^{(i)} = S_{tot} P_h^{(i|k)} P(CL_n|k),\ i \in CL_n,\ n = 1 \dots N_c, \qquad (14)$$

where S_{tot} is the total number of symbols per frame transmitted by the base station, and $P(CL_n|k)$ is the probability that cluster CL_n is scheduled with the k-th MCS. Note that $P(CL_n|k)$ is equal to w_n for CL(WRR), while it is given by Eq. (8) for CL(MR).

Recalling that the mechanism for selecting *cluster heads* resembles a MaxRate scheduling policy, i.e., the cluster head is selected as the user i with the best channel within its cluster CL_n, we can compute $P_h^{(i|k)}$ with an expression similar to Eq. (10):

$$P_h^{(i|k)} = \int_0^\infty [1 - F_i(z|MCS_i{=}k)]\, f_{Y_i}(z)dz, \qquad (15) \\ Y_i = \max_{j\in CL_n\setminus\{i\}} \{C_j\}, \quad \forall i \in CL_n.$$

As a remark, the total cluster throughput $E[T_{CL_n}]$, which is defined as the sum of cluster members' throughputs $E[T_i]$, is also equal to the sum of the data rates received by all cluster members over the LTE interface:

$$\sum_{i\in CL_n} E[T_i] = E[T_{CL_n}] = \sum_{i\in CL_n} R_{rx}^{(i,\,lte)}. \qquad (16)$$

WiFi consumption. We use the accurate model proposed in [8], which accounts for the power required for packet processing as well as for transmission. The resulting power consumption of WiFi interfaces is:

$$W_{wifi}^{(i)} = \beta_{wifi} + \zeta_{tx}\tau_{tx} + \zeta_{rx}\tau_{rx} + \kappa_{tx}\lambda_{tx} + \kappa_{rx}\lambda_{rx}, \qquad (17)$$

where β_{wifi} is the baseline power of WiFi, ζ_{tx} and ζ_{rx} represent the power consumptions due to transmission and reception, respectively; τ_{tx} and τ_{rx} are the fractions of time spent in transmission and reception, respectively; κ_{tx} and κ_{rx} are the power consumptions due to packet processing in transmission and reception, respectively; eventually, λ_{tx} and λ_{rx} are the packet rates, respectively in transmission and reception.

The WiFi power related parameters introduced in Eq. (17) are computed as follows: τ_{tx} is the ratio between the transmission rate over the WiFi interface and the achievable rate of the WiFi connection, i.e., for user i, we have $\tau_{tx}^{(i)} = R_{tx}^{(i,wifi)}/R_{wifi}$. Similarly, user i transmits $\lambda_{tx}^{(i,wifi)}$ packets per second over WiFi.

In order to compute $R_{tx}^{(i,wifi)}$ and $\lambda_{tx}^{(i,wifi)}$, we need to estimate the fraction of traffic which is received by user i over the LTE interface and is then forwarded to other users over the WiFi interface. To this aim, let us define δ_i as the ratio between the user's throughout $E[T_i]$ and the total cluster throughput $E[T_{CL_n}]$, and assume that the traffic distribution over a scheduling interval is the same as the long term distribution of throughputs within the cluster CL_n. Therefore, we have the following expressions for δ_i and $R_{tx}^{(i,wifi)}$:

$$\delta_i = \frac{E[T_i]}{E[T_{CL_n}]} = \frac{E[T_i]}{\sum_{j\in CL_n} R_{rx}^{(j,\,lte)}}, \qquad (18)$$

$$R_{tx}^{(i,wifi)} = (1-\delta_i) R_{rx}^{(i,\,lte)} = (1-\delta_i)\cdot\sum_{k=0}^{M} \pi_k^{(i)} b_k t_k^{(i)}. \qquad (19)$$

Note that $E[T_i]$ can be expressed in terms of throughput without clustering plus clustering gain, as follows:

$$E[T_i] = E[T_i^{\text{no cluster}}] + E[T_i^{\text{cluster gain}}]. \qquad (20)$$

Therefore, both $E[T_i]$ and δ_i depend on the payoff allocation method adopted within the cluster, which will be further elaborated in Section 7.

As for $\lambda_{tx}^{(i,wifi)}$, we compute the average number of packets per second for the average packet size L_p:

$$\lambda_{tx}^{(i,wifi)} = \frac{R_{tx}^{(i,wifi)}}{L_p}. \qquad (21)$$

Similarly, to derive $\tau_{rx}^{(i)} = R_{rx}^{(i,wifi)}/R_{wifi}$, we need an expression for the traffic received over the WiFi interface by user i in cluster CL_n when it is not the cluster head. To this aim, consider that $R_{rx}^{(i,wifi)}$ is a fraction δ_i of all the traffic delivered by LTE to the other cluster members:

$$R_{rx}^{(i,wifi)} = \delta_i \cdot \sum_{j \in CL_n \setminus \{i\}} R_{rx}^{(j,lte)}. \quad (22)$$

The corresponding value of $\lambda_{rx}^{(i)}$ is as follows:

$$\lambda_{rx}^{(i,wifi)} = \frac{R_{rx}^{(i,wifi)}}{L_p}. \quad (23)$$

Eventually, assuming that the achievable WiFi rate in the ad-hoc network is $R_{wifi} > \sum_{i \in CL_n} R_{tx}^{(i,wifi)}$, the power consumed by user i to transmit over the WiFi interface is computed by plugging $R_{tx}^{(i,wifi)}$, $R_{rx}^{(i,wifi)}$, R_{wifi}, $\lambda_{tx}^{(i,wifi)}$, and $\lambda_{rx}^{(i,wifi)}$ in (17):

$$W_{wifi}^{(i)} = \beta_{wifi} + \left(\zeta_{tx} + \frac{\kappa_{tx}}{L_p}\right) \frac{1-\delta_i}{R_{wifi}} \sum_{k=1}^{M} \pi_k^{(i)} b_k t_k^{(i)} + \left(\zeta_{rx} + \frac{\kappa_{rx}}{L_p}\right) \frac{\delta_i}{R_{wifi}} \sum_{j \in CL_n \setminus \{i\}} \sum_{k=1}^{M} \pi_k^{(j)} b_k t_k^{(j)}. \quad (24)$$

Total power consumption. Putting together the results for LTE and WiFi consumptions, the resulting total power consumption of a clustered user is as follows:

$$W_{tot}^{(i)} = \beta_{lte} + \beta_{wifi} + \left[\alpha_{rx} + \frac{1-\delta_i}{R_{wifi}}\left(\zeta_{tx} + \frac{\kappa_{tx}}{L_p}\right)\right] \cdot \sum_{k=1}^{M} \pi_k^{(i)} b_k t_k^{(i)} + \left(\zeta_{rx} + \frac{\kappa_{rx}}{L_p}\right) \frac{\delta_i}{R_{wifi}} \sum_{j \in CL_n \setminus \{i\}} \sum_{k=1}^{M} \pi_k^{(j)} b_k t_k^{(j)}. \quad (25)$$

The first two terms in Eq. (25) represent the fixed power consumption due to activating the LTE and WiFi interfaces, respectively. The third term is the power spent to manage the overall cluster traffic when node i is the cluster head, and the last term is the power spent over the WiFi interface to receive packets from the cluster head when i is not the cluster head.

Energy efficiency. The overall power consumption with clusters increases due to the increased achievable throughput, which is fully utilized under the fully backlogged assumption we use. However, as we will show in Sections 6 and 7, clustering causes little increase in power consumption while enabling a much more efficient energy utilization. To evaluate the beneficial impact of clustering under fully backlogged traffic assumption, we use as metric the energy efficiency, i.e., the amount of data (bits) that can be transferred to the final user per energy unit (Joule), e.g., for user i, the energy efficiency is given by $E[T_i]/W_{tot}^{(i)}$.

6. PERFORMANCE OF STATIC CLUSTERS

The goal of this section is to provide a preliminary evaluation of throughput, fairness, and energy efficiency achievable with our clustering architecture and scheduling. For the sake of clarity, we consider a static scenario with a few clusters of different sizes, formed by users with heterogeneous average SNR.

We present results obtained via numerical simulation of the model presented in Sections 3 to 5. When we refer to the

Figure 3: Evaluation topology for static clusters.

CL(WRR) scheduler, for simplicity we fix the WRR weights as proportional to cluster sizes, i.e., $w_n = N_n/N$. For power computation we use an average packet size $L_p = 1000\ B$ and average WiFi net rate $R_{wifi} = 28\ Mbps$. The evaluation scenario includes three clusters with fixed sizes, as shown in Figure 3. In this scenario, clusters C1, C2, and C3 have 5, 10 and 15 users, respectively. In each experiment, the SNR class of each user is chosen as *poor*, *average*, or *good* with the same probability. We repeat each experiment 2000 times, and we plot the average and standard deviation of the achieved results. The values which are used for power related parameters are reported in Table 2 and are derived from [8, 11].

We benchmark our proposal against Round Robin (RR) and Proportional Fair (PF) schedulers. With RR, each user is scheduled for an equal amount of resources (e.g., *equal time* or *equal rate*) [9]. Here we consider equal time rather than equal rate, since the throughput of equal rate decreases drastically in the presence of *poor* users. With RR, the throughput of each user is simply computed as $E[T_i] = \frac{1}{N}\sum_{k=1}^{M} \pi_k^{(i)} b_k S_{tot}, \forall i \in \{1 \dots N\}$. Since PF is an opportunistic scheduler that is already implemented in 3G systems, it is a good benchmark to evaluate our proposal. PF is a priority scheduler that uses the ratio of feasible data rate to average throughput at time t (i.e., $R_i(t)/\mu_i(t)$, $\forall i \in \{1 \dots N\}$) as priority function. In every frame the users with top n_s priorities are scheduled. Since no accurate model is available, in this paper the performance results of PF are obtained from a home grown C++ simulator, in which the averaging window is 100 frames, and only one user is scheduled in each frame..

Figure 4 illustrates the average user performance under different schedulers, for the three SNR classes we adopted. In Figure 4(a), we observe the throughput of a user when it belongs to the *poor*, *average* or *good* SNR class. Users receive the lowest throughput under RR because they are scheduled irrespective to their channel quality. Instead, PF has remarkably better performance in terms of throughput, due to its opportunistic nature. Nevertheless, PF is still considerably outperformed by cluster schedulers for all SNR classes. Between cluster schedulers, CL(MR) provides *good* users with higher throughput in comparison to CL(WRR), because the former is a pure opportunistic scheduler. Figure 4(b) shows that throughput gained with clustering produces increased power consumption of users. Specifically, while this power increment is negligible for *poor* and *average* users, *good* users incur slightly higher power increment ($\sim 180mW$, i.e., +14% with respect to RR) because they will play the role of cluster head more often. However, this power increase is limited and is not proportional to the

Table 2: Parameters used in the power model

LTE		WiFi				
β_{lte}	α_{rx}	β_{wifi}	ζ_{tx}	ζ_{rx}	κ_{tx}	κ_{rx}
1.29 $[W]$	51.97 $[nW/bps]$	0.28 $[W]$	0.46 $[W]$	0.44 $[W]$	0.11 $[mJ]$	0.09 $[mJ]$

throughput increase. Indeed, Figure 4(c) shows that the energy efficiency of all classes of users sensibly increases with clustering. CL(WRR) achieves the best energy efficiency for *poor* users, CL(MR) favors *good* users.

To show the impact of cluster sizes, we report in Figure 5(a) the aggregate throughput of C1, C2, and C3. For comparison, we also report in the figure the aggregate throughput achieved by cluster members if they where scheduled according to RR or PF. Therefore, results with RR, PF scale linearly with the cluster size. Similarly, CL(WRR) shows linearity, while the high variability of results for CL(MR) does not allow us to confirm or reject the hypothesis that CL(MR) scales linearly. This behavior is due to the fact that CL(MR), differently from CL(WRR), does not guarantee any minimum airtime to any cluster, so that clusters not including *good* user will receive little throughput.

Figure 5(b) sheds light on the aggregate throughout performance achieved by the considered scheduling schemes. The figure reports results for two cases: (*i*) all users have the same probability of being *poor*, *average* or *good*, and (*ii*) the probability of being *poor* is much higher than one of being *average*, which in turn is higher than the probability to be *good*. The figure also reports the upper bound for the downlink throughput. The aggregate throughput of RR and PF is outperformed by cluster-based schedulers. CL(MR) practically hits the upper bound, while the worst case for CL(WRR), i.e., when the number of *poor* users is predominant, outperforms RR and PF under their best performance.

So far, CL(MR) outperforms all other schedulers. However, considering fairness, CL(MR) is always the most unfair, especially when more *poor* users are present, while CL(WRR) performs like PF or better, see Figure 5(c).

To summarize the results reported in this section, we have observed that the clustering proposal not only increases the throughput and the energy efficiency, but it can also increase the fairness level. In particular, CL(WRR) achieves similar throughput and energy efficiency results as CL(MR), but it is much fairer. Therefore, the advantage of using CL(WRR) is fourfold: (*i*) it offers the possibility to gain a high throughput with respect to legacy RR and PF schedulers; (*ii*) it allows each cluster to exploit the clustering gain proportionally to its size; (*iii*) it provides nearly perfect fairness among users; (*iv*) energy efficiency is increased with respect to RR and PF.

7. CLUSTER FORMATION: A GAME THEORY APPROACH

The goal of this section is to provide a simple model for the cluster formation process, and shed light on the impact of clustering when users experience non-stationary channel qualities, e.g., due to mobility. Here, we consider the realistic case of users that can choose to join or leave a cluster, depending on their revenue expressed in terms of energy efficiency. We only consider the case of CL(WRR) cluster scheduling, which is the method that yields the best trade-off between throughput, energy efficiency, and fairness (see Section 6). Since clustering yields increased throughput, we also discuss the impact of intra-cluster throughput distribution on fairness and energy efficiency.

The cluster formation in our proposed architecture can be modeled using *coalitional game theory* [21]. Coalitional games are a class of games studied in cooperative game theory and a coalition is simply a group of entities that agree on cooperating to increase their *social welfare*. In our case, a coalition is a group of users that agree on forming a cluster and acting as a single mobile user. Here, we use a simple dynamic coalition formation game that accounts for the basic cost to form a cluster—namely the power consumption—and for the basic clustering revenue—namely the increased throughput. Indeed, to determine which users should form a cluster and which users are better off alone, we use the energy efficiency as metric for the user's welfare.

7.1 Definition of the game

In the following, $U=\{u_1,\ldots,u_N\}$ denotes the set of users in the network and $S=\{S_1,\ldots,S_l\}$ is a partition of U, i.e., $\bigcup_{i=1}^{l} S_n=U$ and $S_n \cap S_j=\emptyset$ if $n \neq j$. The utility function $\nu(.)$ defines the value of a cluster S_n as:

$$\nu(S_n)=\begin{cases}\sum_{k=1}^{M} \pi_k^{(S_n)} b_k t_j^{(S_n)} & \text{if } d_{S_n}\leq d_{\mathrm{m}} \ \&\ \eta_i^{(S_n)}\geq \eta_i, \forall i\in S_n;\\ 0 & \text{otherwise;}\end{cases} \tag{26}$$

where $t_j^{(S_n)}$ is proportional to the resources allocated to the cluster S_n with the selected scheduler, see Eq. (14); d_{S_n} and d_{m} are the distances between the two farthest users in cluster S_n, and the maximum allowable distance among cluster members, respectively; $\eta_i^{(S_n)}$ and η_i are the energy efficiencies of user i when it joins cluster S_n and when it is not clustered, respectively. In particular, d_{m} accounts for the WiFi transmission range, and can be set to guarantee that any user inside a cluster can directly reach the rest of the cluster members. The constraint on the energy efficiency guarantees that users form a cluster only if energy efficiency increases.

7.2 Cluster formation algorithm

The problem of finding optimal coalitions is NP-complete because it requires evaluating all possible partitions of the set of users U in the network [19]. Obviously, the existing base stations with limited computational resources are not able to handle an NP-complete problem involving a few tens of users.

Hence, we adapt the simple *merge and split* algorithm to solve the coalition formation problem with low complexity [22]. Although merge and split is a trivial method for dynamic cluster formation, it was shown to be a good alternative when computational overhead is of concern [3,20]. The merge and split rules are defined as follows: merge any set $\{S_{a_1},..,S_{a_k}\}$ into a unique coalition (i.e., cluster), if the following inequality holds:

$$\sum_{i=1}^{k} \nu(S_{a_i}) < \nu\left(\cup_{i=1}^{k} S_{a_i}\right). \tag{27}$$

Similarly, if the previous inequality does not hold for a coalition that can be described as $\cup_{i=1}^{k} S_{a_i}$, then split it into its components (i.e., split the big cluster into smaller clusters). The authors of [2] have proven that the merge and split algorithm terminates and the result is D_{hp}-stable, i.e., the system reaches a state in which there are no cluster members willing to perform a merge or a split operation.

7.3 Payoff allocation

So far we have not investigated on how resources should be distributed among cluster members. We have generically

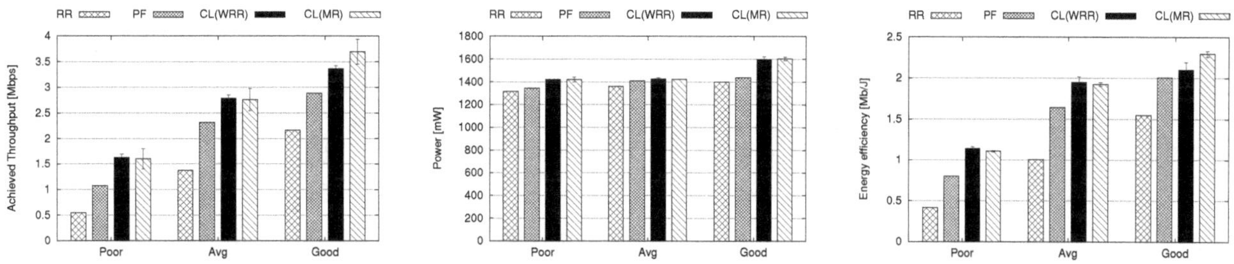

(a) Per-class per-user throughput (b) Per-class per-user power (c) Per-class per-user efficiency

Figure 4: Per-user per-class throughput and cost with equal user distribution (See Figure 3).

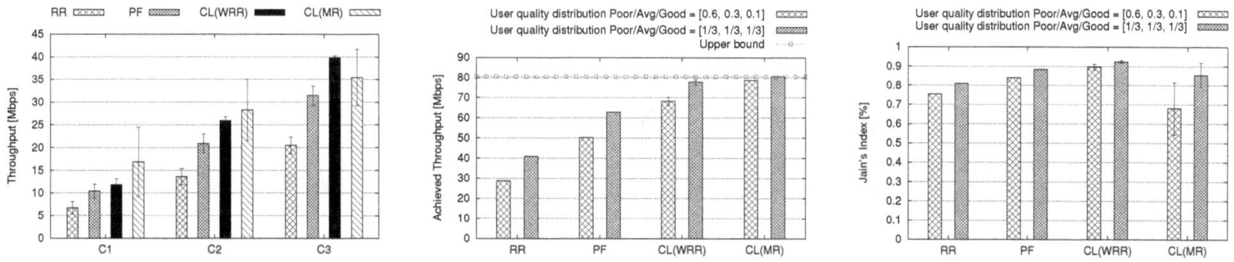

(a) Per-cluster throughput (b) Aggregate cell throughput (c) Jain's fairness indexes

Figure 5: Per-cluster and aggregate performance.

assumed that cluster revenue (i.e., the throughput gain) was equally shared by cluster members.

More in general, the *payoff* for a user is defined as the amount of throughput which is allotted to a member from the total cluster throughput. Formally, let $G \in S$ be a cluster of size $|G|$, and $\bar{x} = \{x_1, \ldots, x_{|G|}\}$ the payoff vector of members of G. A payoff vector is called *cost efficient* if $\sum_{i \in G} x_i = \nu(G)$ [20]. Of course, we are only interested in cost efficient payoff vectors.

As for the payoff distribution method, we chose to compare two mechanisms proposed in the literature, namely equal share and weighted share [20, 24]. These two mechanisms are simple and would allow us to easily illustrate how clustering can be made attractive for all classes of users.

Equal share. This is the simplest approach, in which the clustering gain is equally divided among members. The cost efficient payoff distribution used under equal share is formally expressed as follows:

$$x_i = \frac{\nu(G) - \sum_{j \in G} \nu(\{j\})}{|G|} + \nu(\{i\}), \quad i \in G. \tag{28}$$

Weighted share. Here, the cost efficient payoff distribution is computed based on the positive weights ω_i:

$$x_i = \frac{\omega_i}{\sum\limits_{j \in G} \omega_j} \cdot \left(\nu(G) - \sum_{j \in G} \nu(\{j\})\right) + \nu(\{i\}), \; i \in G. \tag{29}$$

As shown in Section 4, the clustering gain is mainly due to the presence of *good* users, whereas the channel state probability distribution of a cluster does not dramatically improve with the addition of a *poor* user (see Figure 2). Hence, equal share may not strongly motivate users with good channel quality to cluster with users with poor channel quality. In contrast, adjusting ω_i in Eq. (29), we can make sure that users with better channel quality receive enough incentive to cluster. Specifically, in our numerical simulation, we use values of ω_i which are proportional to the user non-cooperative throughput, so that the clustering gain share of each user is proportional to the user's throughput achieved without clustering.

7.4 Numerical evaluation

So far, we have shown that clustering gives substantial throughput increment. We also defined the rules to form clusters and distribute the resources within the cluster. Our proposal might not be attractive for *good* users when the channel quality diversity of cluster members is high and most of the cellular transmissions are carried on by *good* users. Hence, power consumption of these users would increase. Now the question is: *Is there always enough incentive for the good users to participate in clustering?*

To answer this question, we simulate a network with variable number of users (from 1 to 150) with varying channel quality, randomly placed in a circular-shaped cell with 500 m diameter. The SNR class of a user is selected at random with a probability distribution that changes according to the distance from the base station. In order to have a more realistic scenario, we assume that mobile users move with an average pedestrian speed between 0 and 5 km/h [16]. A cluster can have a maximum diameter $d_{\mathrm{m}} = 150$ m. Like in the static scenario, we use $L_p = 1000$ B and $R_{wifi} = 28$ $Mbps$.

Figure 6 illustrates the performance metrics for different user population sizes. In the figure, we report results achieved with RR, PF, CL(WRR) with equal share, namely CL(WRR)-ES, and CL(WRR) with weighted share, namely CL(WRR)-WS. Additionally, we report results for PF when $n \geq 1$ users are scheduled per frame (PF n in the figure). We report this comparison since user-based schedulers allocate multiple users per frame, and it is indeed common to schedule tens of users per frame, even when opportunistic schedulers are adopted. However, RR and CL(WRR) are not affected by the number of user scheduled per frame, due to the assumption that user's channels are independent and stationary (and so are the channels of cluster heads).

In Figure 6(a), we can observe that the clustering gain raises with the number of users in the system, and, as soon as about 30 users are present, CL(WRR) achieves the high-

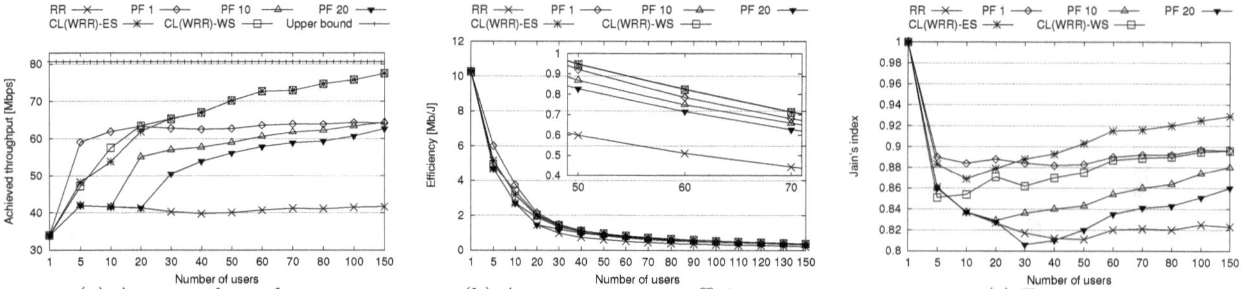

(a) Average throughput (b) Average per-user efficiency (c) Fairness

Figure 6: Throughput, efficiency and fairness under different scheduling mechanisms.

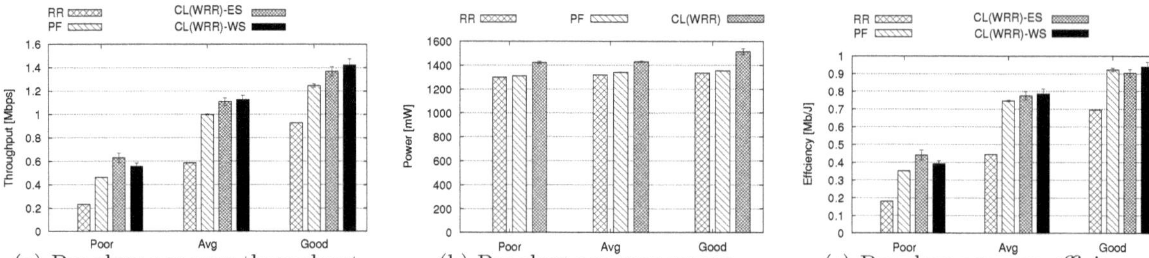

(a) Per-class per-user throughput (b) Per-class per-user power (c) Per-class per-user efficiency

Figure 7: Per-user per-class throughput, efficiency and power with 70 users.

est aggregate network throughput, which approaches the upper bound with a reasonable cell population size of 150 users. CL(WRR)-ES and CL(WRR)-WS do not sensibly differ over the aggregate network throughout. The throughput of PF reduces significantly as the number of scheduled users per frame increases. However, all PF curves converge, for high number of users, to a value well below the throughput of CL(WRR). In Figure 6(b), we can observe that the energy efficiency of CL(WRR)-WS is the best, and CL(WRR)-ES and PF 1 achieve similar efficiencies. Overall, the energy efficiency decreases with the number of users, due to the fact that each additional user incurs a minimum cost due to activating the network interfaces, while the cell capacity is upper bounded. However, e.g., with 70 users, the efficiency of CL(WRR) is higher than RR and PF 20 by $\sim 60\%$ and $\sim 15\%$, respectively. As regards fairness, Figure 6(c) shows that CL(WRR)-ES provides the highest fairness level, while CL(WRR)-WS achieves results comparable to the best results achieved by PF. The fairness improvement due to clustering with respect to RR and PF 10 or PF 20, which are realistic figures for PF performance, is remarkable.

We now zoom into the performance figures achieved by the three SNR classes. To this aim, in Figure 7 we fix the number of users to 70, which yields a reasonable cell size with reasonable opportunistic gain for PF and CL(WRR) schedulers. However, we verified that results for user populations larger than 30 are similar. In terms of throughput, Figure 7(a) shows that all users obtain the highest throughput under clustering schemes. In particular *good* users achieve more throughput with CL(WRR)-WS than CL(WRR)-ES, i.e., *good* users are more incentivized to form clusters with CL(WRR)-WS, at the expenses of *poor* users. In all cases, the incentive for clustering is high, especially if compared to RR throughputs. As for the power consumed by users, Figure 7(b) highlights that extra consumption due to clustering is quite limited, i.e., less than 15%, that is 200 mW in the worst case. However, Figure 7(c) confirms the superiority of cluster-based schemes also in terms of energy efficiency. In particular, *poor* users experience the best efficiency improvement, while *good* users experience similar performance as for the case of ideal PF scheduling with one user scheduled per frame.

8. CONCLUSIONS

In this paper, we proposed and modeled novel cluster-based scheduling schemes, which significantly improve the throughput of a cellular network (up to $\sim 50\%$), boost energy efficiency (+30% with realistic user-populations) and achieve fairness levels higher than PF. To show the impact of our proposal, we proposed a new model for the power consumption of dual-radio mobile devices using LTE and WiFi networking capabilities at the same time. Additionally, we used a game theory approach to model the cluster formation process in realistic network scenarios, in which throughput and fairness are boosted via user cooperation.

Our results show that CL(WRR)—which assigns resources to the clusters in weighted round robin and selects clusters heads opportunistically—achieves throughputs close to the maximum achievable. Furthermore, CL(WRR) outperform other opportunistic schedulers in terms of achieved fairness. Our numerical simulations confirmed that the compound impact of opportunistic scheduling and D2D techniques is beneficial for all users irrespective of their channel qualities, and dramatically improves energy-efficiency.

9. ACKNOWLEDGEMENTS

The research leading to these results was supported by the CROWD project, under the European Union's Seventh Framework Programme (grant agreement n° 318115).

This publication was supported in part by the Comunidad de Madrid MEDIANET Project, Ref.: S2009/TIC-1468.

10. REFERENCES

[1] M. Andrews, K. Kumaran, K. Ramanan, A. Stolyar, R. Vijayakumar, and P. Whiting. Scheduling in a queuing system with asynchronously varying service rates. *Probability in the Engineering and Informational Sciences*, 18:191–217, Apr. 2004.

[2] K. Apt and T. Radzik. Stable partitions in coalitional games. *Arxiv preprint cs/0605132*, 2006.

[3] K. Apt and S. Witzel. A generic approach to coalition formation. 2006.

[4] S. Bandyopadhyay and E. Coyle. An energy efficient hierarchical clustering algorithm for wireless sensor networks. In *Proceedings of IEEE INFOCOM*, volume 3, pages 1713–1723, 2003.

[5] W. Choi and J. Andrews. The capacity gain from base station cooperative scheduling in a MIMO DPC cellular system. In *IEEE International Symposium on Information Theory*, pages 1224–1228, July 2006.

[6] M. Dohler et al. *Virtual antenna arrays*. PhD thesis, University of London, 2004.

[7] F. H. Fitzek, M. Katz, and Q. Zhang. Cellular controlled short-range communication for cooperative P2P networking. *Wireless Personal Communications*, 48(1):141–155, 2009.

[8] A. Garcia-Saavedra, P. Serrano, A. Banchs, and G. Bianchi. Energy consumption anatomy of 802.11 devices and its implication on modeling and design. In *Proceedings of ACM CoNEXT*, pages 169–180, New York, NY, USA, Dec. 2012.

[9] E. Hahne. Round-robin scheduling for max-min fairness in data networks. *IEEE Journal on Selected Areas in Communications*, 9(7):1024–1039, 1991.

[10] W. Heinzelman, A. Chandrakasan, and H. Balakrishnan. Energy-efficient communication protocol for wireless microsensor networks. In *Proceedings of System Sciences*, pages 10–pp, 2000.

[11] J. Huang, F. Qian, A. Gerber, Z. Mao, S. Sen, and O. Spatscheck. A close examination of performance and power characteristics of 4G LTE networks. In *Proceedings of ACM MobiSys*, pages 225–238, June 2012.

[12] E. Jon Vergara and N. Nadjm-Tehrani. Watts2share: Energy-aware traffic consolidation. In *Proceedings of IEEE GreenCom*, 2013.

[13] K. Khalil, M. Karaca, O. Ercetin, and E. Ekici. Optimal scheduling in cooperate-to-join cognitive radio networks. In *Proceedings of IEEE INFOCOM*, pages 3002–3010, Apr. 2011.

[14] R. Knopp and P. Humblet. Information capacity and power control in single-cell multiuser communications. In *Proceedings of IEEE ICC*, volume 1, pages 331–335 vol.1, June 1995.

[15] L. Le and E. Hossain. Multihop cellular networks: Potential gains, research challenges, and a resource allocation framework. *IEEE Communications Magazine*, 45(9):66–73, 2007.

[16] S. Lee, K. Kim, K. Hong, D. Griffith, Y. Kim, and N. Golmie. A probabilistic call admission control algorithm for WLAN in heterogeneous wireless environment. *IEEE Transactions on Wireless Communications*, 8(4):1672–1676, 2009.

[17] L. Lei, Z. Zhong, C. Lin, and X. Shen. Operator controlled device-to-device communications in LTE-advanced networks. *IEEE Wireless Communications*, 19(3):96–104, 2012.

[18] C. Lin and M. Gerla. Adaptive clustering for mobile wireless networks. *IEEE Journal on Selected Areas in Communications*, 15(7):1265–1275, 1997.

[19] D. Ray. *A game-theoretic perspective on coalition formation*. OUP Oxford, 2007.

[20] W. Saad, Z. Han, M. Debbah, and A. Hjorungnes. A distributed merge and split algorithm for fair cooperation in wireless networks. In *Proceedings of IEEE ICC Workshops*, pages 311–315, 2008.

[21] W. Saad, Z. Han, M. Debbah, A. Hjorungnes, and T. Basar. Coalitional game theory for communication networks. *IEEE Signal Processing Magazine*, 26(5):77–97, 2009.

[22] W. Saad, Z. Han, M. Debbah, A. Hjorungnes, and T. Basar. Coalitional games for distributed collaborative spectrum sensing in cognitive radio networks. In *Proceedings of IEEE INFOCOM*, pages 2114–2122, 2009.

[23] A. Sendonaris, E. Erkip, and B. Aazhang. User cooperation diversity. Part I. System description. *IEEE Transactions on Communications*, 51(11):1927–1938, 2003.

[24] M. Sereno. Cooperative game theory framework for energy efficient policies in wireless networks. In *Proceedings of ACM e-Energy*, pages 1–9, May 2012.

[25] S. Sesia, I. Toufik, and M. Baker. *LTE–the UMTS long term evolution: from theory to practice*. Wiley, 2011.

[26] S. Shakkottai, R. Srikant, and A. L. Stolyar. Pathwise optimality of the exponential scheduling rule for wireless channels. *Advances in Applied Probability*, 36(4):1021–1045, 2004.

[27] N. Sharma and L. Ozarow. A study of opportunism for multiple-antenna systems. *IEEE Transactions on Information Theory*, 51(5):1804–1814, May 2005.

[28] Third Generation Partnership Project (3GPP). Physical layer procedures (Release 10) for Evolved Universal Terrestrial Radio Access (E-UTRA). 3GPP TR 36.213 v 10.5.0, Mar. 2012.

[29] P. Viswanath, D. Tse, and R. Laroia. Opportunistic beamforming using dumb antennas. In *IEEE Transactions on Information Theory*, page 449, June 2002.

[30] Q. Wang and B. Rengarajan. Recouping opportunistic gain in dense base station layouts through energy-aware user cooperation. In *Proceedings of IEEE WoWMoM*, pages 1–9, 2013.

[31] Wi-Fi Alliance Specification. Wi-Fi Peer-to-Peer (P2P) Specification v1.1, 2011.

[32] H. Wu, C. Qiao, S. De, and O. Tonguz. Integrated cellular and ad hoc relaying systems: iCAR. *IEEE Journal on Selected Areas in Communications*, 19(10):2105–2115, 2001.

[33] J. Yang, Z. Yifan, W. Ying, and Z. Ping. Average rate updating mechanism in proportional fair scheduler for hdr. In *Proceedings of IEEE GLOBECOM*, volume 6, pages 3464–3466, 2004.

[34] C.-H. Yu, K. Doppler, C. B. Ribeiro, and O. Tirkkonen. Resource sharing optimization for device-to-device communication underlaying cellular networks. *IEEE Transactions on Wireless Communications*, 10(8):2752–2763, 2011.

An Open Source Model for the Simulation of LTE Handover Scenarios and Algorithms in ns-3

Nicola Baldo
Centre Tecnològic de Telecomunicacions de Catalunya (CTTC)
Castelldefels, Spain
nbaldo@cttc.es

Manuel Requena-Esteso
Centre Tecnològic de Telecomunicacions de Catalunya (CTTC)
Castelldefels, Spain
mrequena@cttc.es

Marco Miozzo
Centre Tecnològic de Telecomunicacions de Catalunya (CTTC)
Castelldefels, Spain
mmiozzo@cttc.es

Raymond Kwan
Ubiquisys Ltd.
Swindon, UK
raymond.y.c.kwan@gmail.com

ABSTRACT

In this paper, we present an open source simulation model for the ns-3 simulator that allows the simulation of LTE handover scenarios, to support the design and evaluation of handover decision algorithms. In addition to the features supported by other publicly available open source LTE simulators, such as mobility, propagation, channel, PHY and MAC modeling, our model provides additional features such as the modeling of the RRC protocol, the MAC random access procedure, and the X2, S1 and S11 interfaces. On top of these features, the LTE handover procedure is modeled, following closely the 3GPP specifications. We present in detail the characteristics of each component of the simulation model, highlighting the modeling assumptions that were made in each case.

Categories and Subject Descriptors

I.6.5 [**Simulation and Modeling**]: Model Development—*Modeling methodologies*; I.6.7 [**Simulation and Modeling**]: Simulation Support System—*Environments*

Keywords

Simulator; ns-3; LTE; handover algorithm; RSRQ

1. INTRODUCTION

Long Term Evolution (LTE) is today's cutting edge mobile communication tecnology, improving significantly over previous technologies such as 3G and High Speed Packet Access (HSPA). One of the key factors that make LTE better performing and more appealing to Mobile Network Operators is its Self Organized Network (SON) capabilities, i.e., the ability of the LTE network to self-configure and self-optimize itself to automatically improve its performance and reliability, with minimal or no intervention by network engineers. In practice, SON capabilities are realized by designing and implementing a set of SON algorithms that intelligently take care of network management tasks (e.g., admission control, radio resource management, mobility management and load balancing) by leveraging on a wide pool of measurements and performance indicators provided by the various network elements. Such SON algorithms are in general quite complex, and their efficient design and implementation is often pursued by network equipment manufacturers as a key element for achieving product differentiation and being more competitive on the market.

MSWiM'13, November 3–8, 2013, Barcelona, Spain.

ACM 978-1-4503-2353-6/13/11 ...$15.00.
http://dx.doi.org/10.1145/2507924.2507940

Many prior publications already pointed out that LTE network simulation models are crucial in the process of designing LTE SON algorithms [1,2]. In simulation, there is a clear tradeoff between the complexity of the model and its usefulness, and there is no generally optimal tradeoff point, but rather each particular problem (e.g., a particular SON algorithm to be designed) will require a different modeling granularity.

In this paper, we focus in particular on the modeling associated with the design of LTE SON algorithms for mobility management, focusing in particular on handover algorithms. A description of the LTE handover procedure and the associated technical challenges goes beyond the scope of this paper; on this matter, the reader is referred to the 3GPP specifications [3] as well as to the abundant literature on the topic (see for instance [4] and [5]).

Several handover algorithms have been proposed in the recent literature, which consider different aspects of network performance optimization such as coverage maximization/outage minimization [6,7], handover signaling minimization [8–11], load balancing [12,13], interference management [14] and energy efficiency [15]. In order for an LTE network simulator to provide adequate support for the design and evaluation of these algorithms, several aspects have to be modeled:

1. Practically all LTE simulators used for the evaluation of handover algorithms include some mobility model and radio propagation models in order to evaluate the

most basic aspect of a handover scenario, i.e., whether a user is in coverage of a certain cell as a function of how he is moving.

2. In order to study aspects such as load balancing and interference coordination, it is also needed to model some PHY and MAC layer aspects, such as Adaptive Modulation and Coding, MAC scheduling, PHY error modeling and, possibly, HARQ.
3. A model of handover preparation (including UE measurements) and execution is needed in order to plug handover decision algorithms onto it;
4. An evaluation of the radio interface aspects that affect handover delay and failure probability would require the modeling of control signalling protocols, in particular the RRC protocol, the RLC AM protocol over which RRC handover-related messages are transmitted, and the MAC layer aspects related with the Random Access procedure.
5. An evaluation of the core network aspects that affect handover delay shall involve the modeling of core network interfaces such as the X2-C, S1-C and S11 interfaces. The aspects to be modeled could be different according to the handover scenario considered, e.g., S1-based vs X2-based handover, and whether the handover is intra/inter SGW/MME.
6. Characterizing the QoE degradation of a handover algorithm on data communications requires an LTE data protocol stack model, covering the RLC and PDCP radio link protocols as well as the S1-U and the X2-U protocols.

In this paper, we describe the open source LTE simulation model that we developed with the aim of covering all of the above aspects. The motivation behind our work was that, previous to it, no such publicly available open source simulation tool was available to the research community. Among pre-existing open source LTE simulators, the Vienna LTE system-level simulator [16] covered mostly the aspects 1-2, and did not cover 3-6; extending it to do so appeared overwhelmingly complex, due to its focus being on the PHY and MAC layer only. LTE–Sim [2] covers the aspects 1-3; it would need to be extended in order to cover the aspects 4-6. The LTE module of the popular ns-3 network simulator, which is the result our prior work carried out within the LENA project [1,17], covered the aspects 1-2 as well as some parts of 4 (the RLC AM protocol and its interaction with the MAC scheduler) and 6 (the S1-U interface). The simulation model that we are now presenting is thus an extension of our prior work aimed to include aspects 3 and 5 and the previously missing features of aspects 4 and 6. This paper describes in detail such extension.

2. THE PROPOSED MODEL EXTENSION

The proposed model extension consists of the addition of new features both to the LTE model, which is responsible for the radio access aspect of the system, and to the Evolved Packet Core (EPC) model, which describes the core network aspects of the system. These additions have been done over our previous work [1,17].

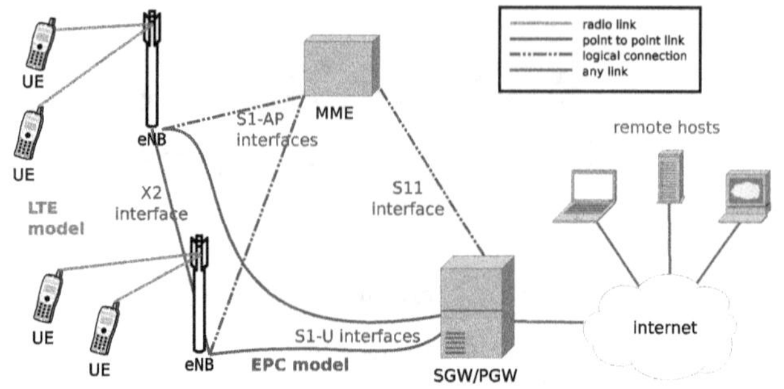

Figure 1: Network architecture of the proposed simulation model

In detail, the following new features have been added to the LTE model:

- A model for the MAC Random Access procedure
- A model for the RRC protocol.
- An implementation of the RRC management logic for both the UE and the eNB.
- A model for the NAS management logic.

The resulting relations among the different entities of the LTE Radio Protocol Stack are represented in figures 2 and 3 for the eNB and the UE nodes, respectively.

For the EPC model, the following new features have been added:

- A model of the X2 interface, including both the user plane and the control plane.
- A model for the MME entity.
- A model for the control plane part of the S1 interface and for the S11 interface.

These new features are shown on figure 1.

In the upcoming subsections, we will describe separately each new feature.

3. MAC RANDOM ACCESS

In our prior work [1,17], the MAC Random Access (RA) procedure was not modeled at all. We added model of the Random Access procedure based on some simplifying assumptions, which are detailed in the following for each of the messages and signals described in the specification [18].

- **Random Access (RA) preamble**: in real LTE systems this corresponds to a Zadoff-Chu (ZC) sequence using one of several formats available and sent in the PRACH slots, which could in principle overlap with PUSCH. The RA preamble is modeled using the *LteControlMessage* class, i.e., as an ideal message that does not consume any radio resources. The collisions of preamble transmissions by multiple UEs in the same cell are modeled using a protocol interference model, i.e., whenever two or more identical preambles are transmitted in the same cell at the same TTI, no one of these identical preambles will be received by the eNB. Other than this collision model, no error model is associated with the reception of a RA preamble.

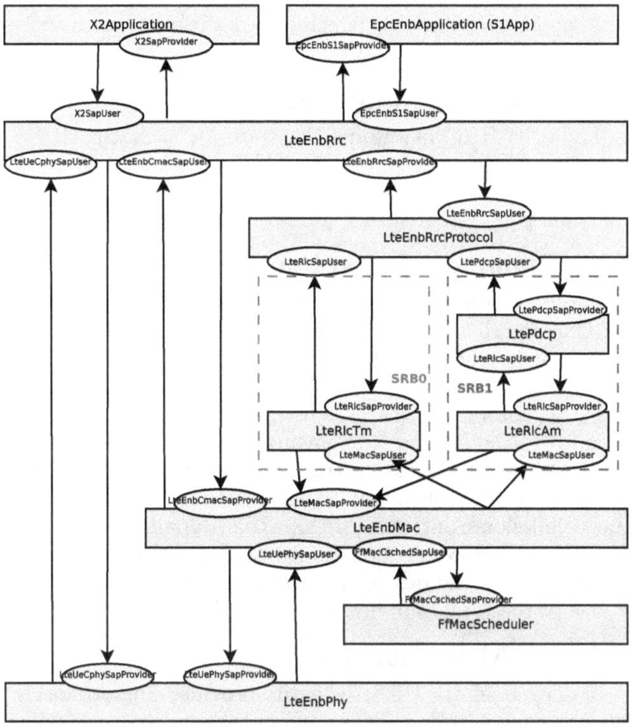

Figure 2: LTE radio protocol stack architecture for the eNB on the control plane

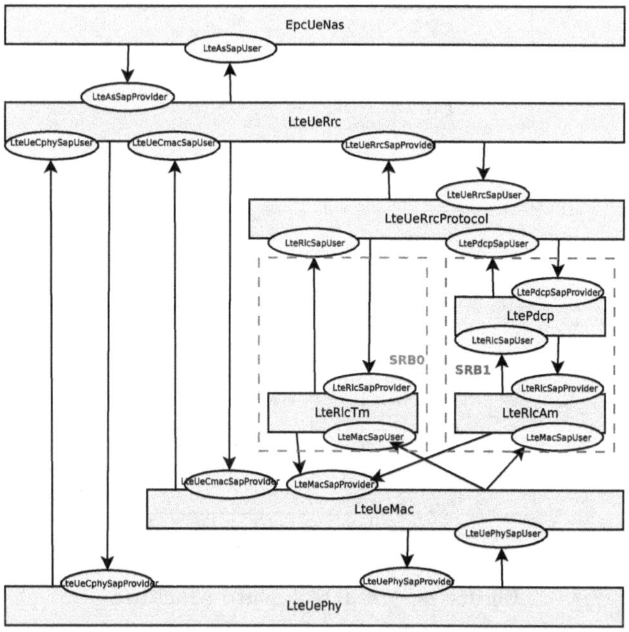

Figure 3: LTE radio protocol stack architecture for the UE on the control plane

- **Random Access Response (RAR)**: in real LTE systems, this is a special MAC PDU sent on the DL-SCH. Since MAC control elements are not accurately modeled in the simulator (only RLC and above PDUs are), the RAR is modeled as an *LteControlMessage* that does not consume any radio resources. Still, during the RA procedure, the *LteEnbMac* will make a request to the scheduler to allocate resources for the RAR using the FF MAC Scheduler primitive SCHED_DL_RACH_INFO_REQ. Hence, an enhanced scheduler implementation (not available at the moment) can then have the option to allocate radio resources when this primitive is called, and thereby modeling the consumption of Radio Resources for the transmission of the RAR.

- **Layer 3 Message**: in real LTE systems, this is an RLC TM SDU sent over resources specified in the UL Grant in the RAR. In the simulator, this is modeled as a real RLC TM PDU whose UL resources are allocated by the scheduler upon call to SCHED_DL_RACH_INFO_REQ.

- **Contention Resolution (CR)**: in real LTE system, the CR phase is needed to address the case where two or more UE sent the same RA preamble in the same TTI, and the eNB was able to detect this preamble in spite of the collision. Since this event does not occur in the simulator, due to the protocol interference model used for the reception of RA preambles, the CR phase is not modeled, i.e., the CR MAC CE that would be sent by the eNB is not simulated, and the UEs just consider the RA to be successful upon reception of the RAR. As a consequence, the radio resources consumed for the transmission of the CR MAC CE are not modeled.

4. RRC

In real LTE systems, the RRC protocol provides the functionality of system information transmission and acquisition, connection control, mobility and measurement configuration and reporting; for a more detailed description, the reader is referred to [19]. Our prior LTE model [1,17] did not model the RRC protocol at all. It assumed that the simulation started with all UEs already in the RRC CONNECTED state, without modeling the RRC connection establishment procedure. System Information transmission was not modeled, and neither mobility nor measurement configuration and reporting were supported.

To overcome these limitations, we designed and implemented an explicit RRC model that provides the following features:

- transmission (by the eNB) and acquisition (by the UE) of System Information
- RRC connection establishment procedure
- RRC reconfiguration procedure, supporting in particular the use cases of data radio bearer setup, reconfiguration of the PHY TX mode (for MIMO support) and the SRS configuration index, and handover
- UE measurement configuration and reporting.

4.1 RRC Model Architecture

The RRC model is divided into the following components:

- the RRC entities *LteUeRrc* and *LteEnbRrc*, which implement the state machines of the RRC entities respectively at the UE and the eNB;

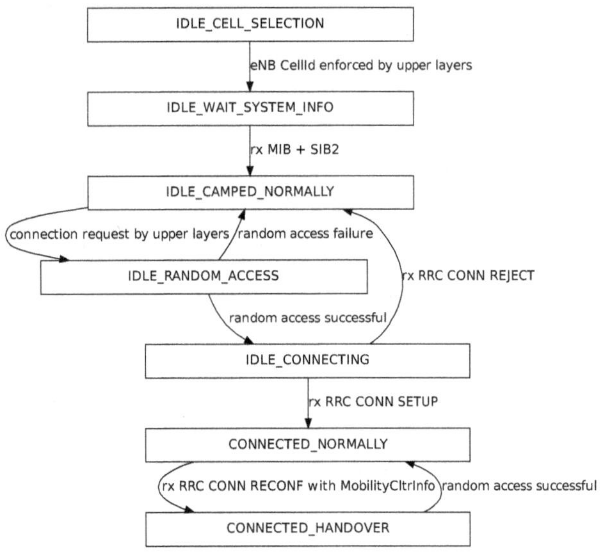

Figure 4: UE RRC State Machine

- the RRC SAPs *LteUeRrcSapProvider*, *LteUeRrcSapUser*, *LteEnbRrcSapProvider*, *LteEnbRrcSapUser*, which allow the RRC entities to send and receive RRC messages and information elmenents;
- the RRC protocol classes *LteUeRrcProtocolIdeal*, *LteEnbRrcProtocolIdeal*, *LteUeRrcProtocolReal*, *LteEnbRrcProtocolReal*, which implement two different models for the transmission of RRC messages. In the "Ideal" model, RRC messages do not consume any radio resources and are always correctly delivered with zero delay. Conversely, the "Real" model features an implementation of the ASN.1 encoding of Information Elements as specificed in [19], which allows to model the allocation and consumption of radio resources and to use the PHY error model for the transmission of RRC messages.

Additionally, the RRC components use various other SAPs in order to interact with the rest of the protocol stack. A representation of all the SAPs that are used is provided in the figures 2 and 3.

4.2 UE RRC State Machine

In Figure 4 we represent the state machine as implemented in the RRC UE entity. It is to be noted that most of the states are transient, i.e., once the UE goes into one of the CONNECTED states it will never switch back to any of the IDLE states. This choice is done due to the fact that the focus of the LTE-EPC simulation model is on CONNECTED mode. In particular, radio link failure is not currently modeled, so a UE cannot go IDLE because of radio link failure; furthermore, RRC connection release is currently never triggered neither by the EPC nor by the NAS. On the other hand, the IDLE state is modelled explicitly, because a realistic UE RRC configuration is needed for handover, which is a required feature, and in order to have a cleaner implementation it makes sense to use the same UE RRC configuration also for the initial connection establishment. Additionally, having an IDLE state facilitates the implementation of the idle mode cell selection, which is a desirable feature to be included in the future.

4.3 eNB RRC State Machine

The eNB RRC maintains the state for each UE that is attached to the cell. In our model, the state of each UE is contained in an instance of the *UeManager* class. The state machine is represented in Figure 5.

4.4 Radio Admission Control

Radio Admission Control is supported by having the eNB RRC reply to an RRC CONNECTION REQUEST message sent by the UE with either an RRC CONNECTION SETUP message or an RRC CONNECTION REJECT message, depending on whether the new UE is to be admitted or not. In the current implementation, the behavior is determined by the boolean attribute `ns3::LteEnbRrc::AdmitRrcConnectionRequest`. The development of smart Radio Admission Control algorithms that dynamically decides whether a new connection shall be admitted or not is left open. In fact, the design and evalution of such algorithms is one of the target application of our simulation model.

4.5 UE Measurements

In our model, the UE RRC entity provides support for UE measurements; in particular, it implements the procedures described in Section 5.5 of [19], with the following simplifying assumptions:

- only E-UTRA intra-frequency measurements are supported;
- measurement gaps are not modelled, as they are not needed for intra-frequency measurements;
- only event-driven measurements are supported; the other type of measurements are not supported;
- only the events A2 and A4 are supported;
- time-to-trigger is not supported, i.e., a time-to-trigger value equals to zero is always assumed;
- layer 3 filtering assumes that the periodicity of the measurements reported by the PHY is equal to 200ms;
- in measurement reports, the reportQuantity is always assumed to be "both", i.e., both RSRP and RSRQ are always reported, regardless of the trigger quantity.

The eNB RRC entity configures the UE measurements. The eNB RRC entity sends the configuration parameters to the UE RRC entity in the MeasConfig IE of the RRC Connection Reconfiguration message when the UE attaches to the eNB or the RRC Handover Request message when the target eNB initiates the handover procedure.

In our model, the eNB RRC entity implements the configuration parameters and procedures described in Section 5.5 of [19], with the following simplifying assumptions:

- only E-UTRA intra-frequency measurements are configured, so only the downlink carrier frequency of the serving cell is configured as measurement object;
- only the events A2 and A4 are configured;
- only the RSRQ threshold is configured for both events;

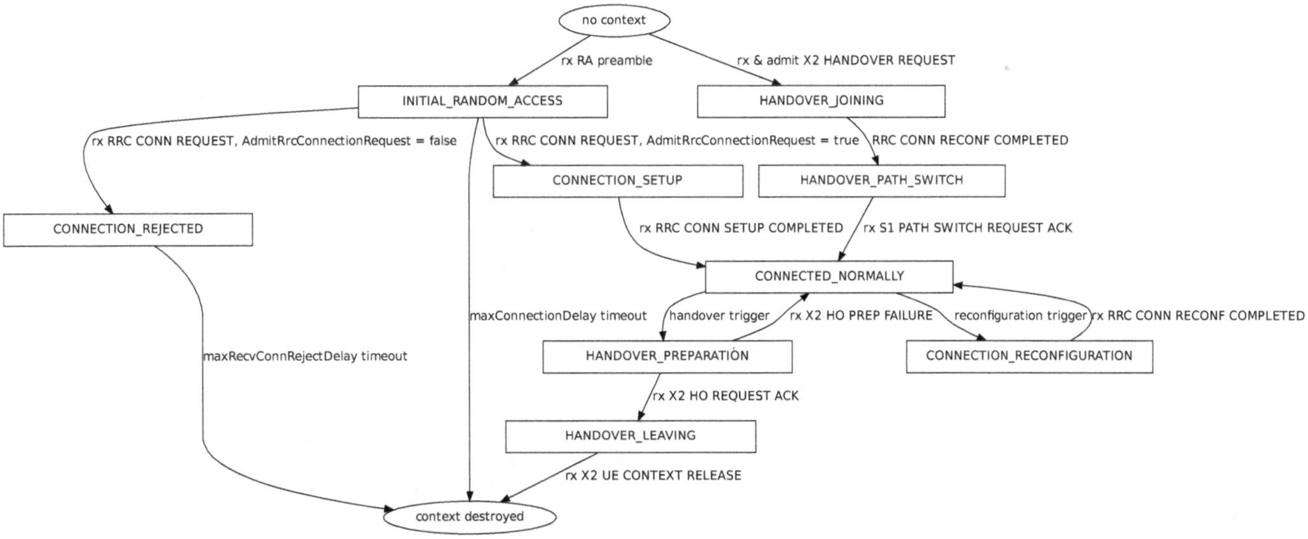

Figure 5: ENB RRC State Machine for each UE

- the *reportInterval* parameter is configured to 480 ms, so once the events are triggered, the UE will send the measurement reports with this periodicity;
- the filterCoefficientRSRQ parameter is configured to fc4, which is the default value specified in the protocol specification [19];
- the hysteresis and timeToTrigger parameters are configured with values equal to zero;
- a one-to-one mapping between the PCI and the E-UTRAN Global Cell Identifier (EGCI) is assumed.

4.6 Handover

The RRC model supports the execution of an X2-based handover procedure. The handover procedure can be triggered via either the simulation program by scheduling an execution of the method `LteEnbRrc::SendHandoverRequest()`, or the eNB RRC entity. In the latter case, the algorithm shown in Fig. 6 is executed upon reception of a UE measurement report by the eNB. The two parameters which affect the behavior of this algorithm are:

- *servingHandoverThreshold*: if the RSRQ value measured by the UE in its serving cell is less than or equal to this parameter, i.e., the channel quality of the UE in the serving cell is unsatisfactory, the eNB evaluates neighbor eNBs as potential handover targets for this UE;
- *neighbourHandoverOffset*: if the difference between the best neighbour RSRQ and the serving cell RSRQ is greater than or equal to this parameter, then the handover procedure is triggered with that neighbor eNB as the target.

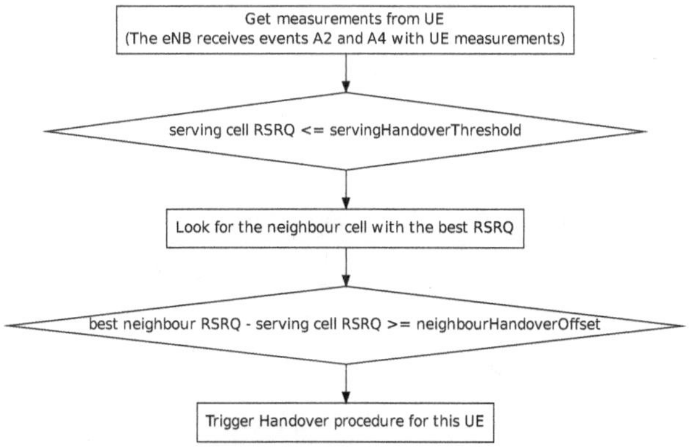

Figure 6: Algorithm to automatically trigger the Handover procedure

5. S1-AP

The S1-AP interface provides means for control plane interaction between the eNB and the MME. In the simulator, a logical model is used for this interface, which consists of modeling a subset of the primitives defined in [20], but, unlike what done for the X2-AP, X2-U and S1-U intefaces, without modeling the encoding of the corresponding messages and information elements specified in [20], and without simulating their transmission using existing ns-3 devices and link models.

The currently modeled S1-AP primitives are: INITIAL UE MESSAGE, INITIAL CONTEXT SETUP REQUEST, INITIAL CONTEXT SETUP RESPONSE, PATH SWITCH REQUEST, and PATH SWITCH REQUEST ACKNOWLEDGE.

6. X2

According to the 3GPP specifications, the X2 interface interconnects two eNBs [21]. From a logical point of view, the X2 interface is a point-to-point interface between the two eNBs. In a real E-UTRAN deployment, this logical interface could be realized over different network topology, e.g., it could be implemented over a dedicated physical point to point connection as well as over a multi-hop network local area network connection or even over the internet. In our

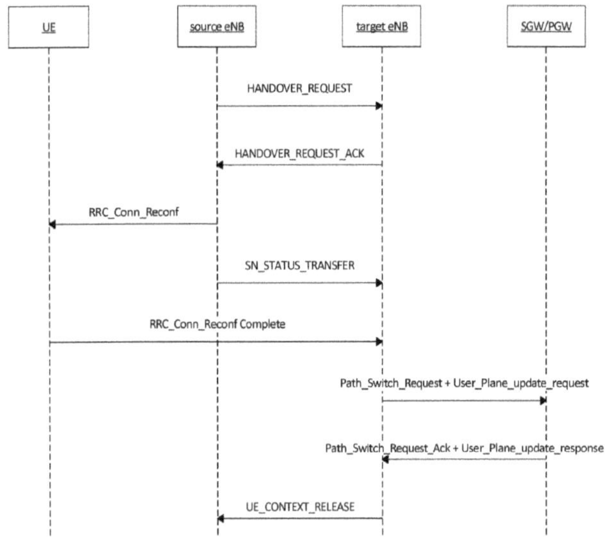

Figure 7: Sequence diagram of the X2-based handover

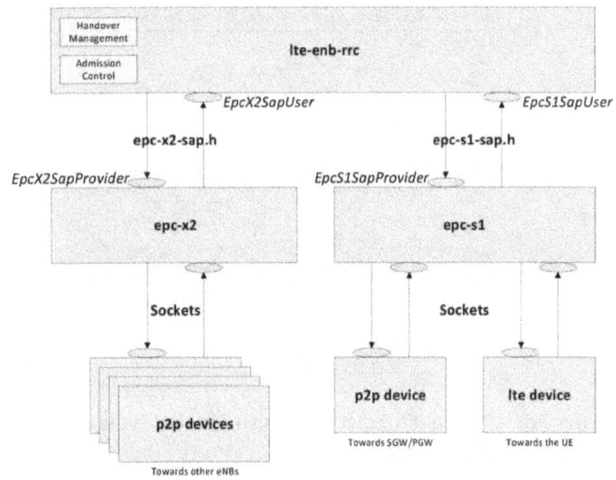

Figure 8: Implementation Model of X2 entity and SAPs

simulation model, the X2 interface is implemented over a point-to-point link (modeled using the existing ns-3 point-to-point module) which can be deployed between each eNB pair of choice, according to the specification of the simulation program. A point-to-point device is created in both eNBs and the two point-to-point devices are attached to the point-to-point link. Figure 1 shows a representation of how the X2 interface fits in the overall architecture of the LENA simulation model.

The X2 interface implemented in the simulator provides a detailed implementation of the following elementary procedures of the Mobility Management functionality [22]: (1) Handover Request procedure, (2) Handover Request Acknowledgement procedure, (3) SN Status Transfer procedure, and (4) UE Context Release procedure. These procedures are involved in the X2-based handover. The reader can find the detailed description of the handover in section 10.1.2.1 of [3]. We note that our model currently supports only the *seamless handover* as defined in Section 2.6.3.1 of [5]; in particular, *lossless handover* as described in Section 2.6.3.2 of [5] is not supported.

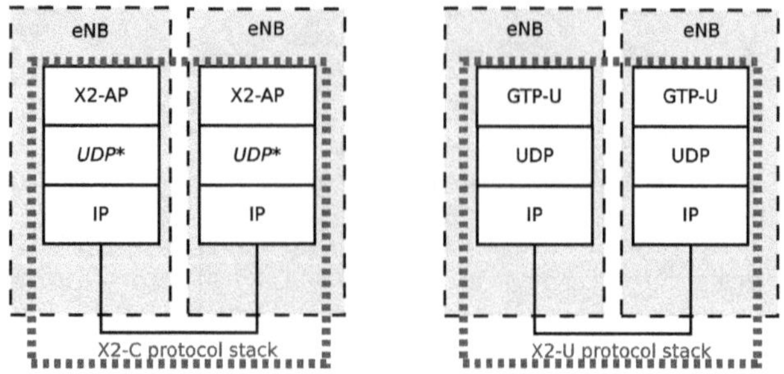

Figure 9: X2 interface protocol stacks

Figure 7 shows the interaction of the entities of the X2 model in the simulator. The X2 model is composed of an entity that sends/receives the X2 messages over the point-to-point devices to/from the peer X2 entity. The sender X2 entity builds the X2 message with the RRC message received from the sender RRC entity and the receiver X2 entity retrieves the RRC message from the X2 message and delivers it to the receiver RRC entity.

Figure 8 shows the implentation model of the X2 entity and its relationship with all the other entities and services in the protocol stack. We note that the RRC entity manages the initiation of the handover procedure. This is done in the Handover Management submodule of the eNB RRC entity. The target eNB may perform some Admission Control procedures. This is done in the Admission Control submodule.

6.1 X2 interfaces

The X2 model contains two interfaces:

- the X2-C interface. It is the control interface and it is used to send the X2-AP PDUs corresponding to the X2 elementary procedures.
- the X2-U interface. It is used to send the bearer data when there is *DL forwarding.*

Figure 9 shows the protocol stacks of the X2-U interface and X2-C interface modeled in the simulator. The X2-C interface is the control part of the X2 interface and it is used to send the X2-AP PDUs. In real 3GPP systems, the X2 control protocol uses SCTP [23] as the underlying transport protocol; unfortunately, no SCTP protocol model was available in the ns-3 simulator at the time our model was developed. Therefore, we used UDP instead of SCTP as the transport protocol for the X2 control protocol.

The X2-U interface is used to send the bearer data when there is *DL forwarding* during the execution of the X2-based handover procedure. Similarly to the S1-U interface, data packets are encapsulated over GTP/UDP/IP when being sent over this interface. Note that in our model the EPS Bearer QoS is not enforced on the X2-U links; rather, it is assumed that the overprovisioning of the link bandwidth is sufficient to meet the QoS requirements of all bearers.

6.2 X2 Service Interface

The X2 service interface is used by the RRC entity to send and receive messages of the X2 procedures. It is divided into two parts:

- the EpcX2SapProvider part is provided by the X2 entity and used by the RRC entity;
- the EpcX2SapUser part is provided by the RRC entity and used by the X2 entity.

The primitives that are supported in our X2-C model are described in the following subsections.

6.2.1 X2-C primitives for handover execution

The following primitives are used for the X2-based handover: HANDOVER REQUEST, HANDOVER REQUEST ACK, HANDOVER PREPARATION FAILURE, SN STATUS STRANSFER, and UE CONTEXT RELEASE. All these primitives are used by the currently implemented RRC model during the preparation and execution of the handover procedure. Their usage interacts with the RRC state machine; therefore, they are not meant to be used for code customization, unless it is desired to modify the RRC state machine.

6.2.2 X2-C SON primitives

The X2 model supports the primitives LOAD INFORMATION and RESOURCE STATUS UPDATE to implement Self-Organized Network (SON) functionalities. Note that the current RRC implementation does not actually use these primitives. They are included in the model within the RRC logic for future SON algorithm developments. The details regarding the variable associated with the above primitives are specific to the SON algorithms being implemented, and hence are beyond the scope of this paper.

7. S11

The S11 interface provides control plane interaction between the SGW and the MME using the GTPv2-C protocol specified in [24]. In the simulator, this interface is modeled in an ideal fashion, with direct interaction between the SGW and the MME objects, without actually implementing the encoding of the messages and without actually transmitting any PDU on any link.

The S11 primitives that are modeled are CREATE SESSION REQUEST, CREATE SESSION RESPONSE, MODIFY BEARER REQUEST and MODIFY BEARER RESPONSE. Of these primitives, the first two are used upon initial UE attachment for the establishment of the S1-U bearers; the other two are used during handover to switch the S1-U bearers from the source eNB to the target eNB as a consequence of the reception by the MME of a PATH SWITCH REQUEST S1-AP message.

8. TESTING AND VALIDATION

To test the correct functioning of the new features of our simulation model, as well as to validate the simulation output, some new test suites were developed and integrated with the ns-3 test framework. These test suites are described in the following subsections.

8.1 UE Measurements Tests

The test suite lte-ue-measurements provides system tests recreating an inter-cell interference scenario with two eNBs, each having a single UE attached to. The test evaluates the correctness of the RSRP and RSRQ measurements performed by the UE at two different points of the network architecture: the source, i.e., the PHY layer of the UE, and the destination, i.e., the RRC entity of the eNB. The test vectors for RSRP and RSRQ are obtained by means of a dedicated separate octave program which performs link budget calculations for the particular topology being considered.

8.2 RRC Tests

The test suite lte-rrc tests the correct functionality of the following aspects: i) MAC Random Access, ii) RRC System Information Acquisition, iii) RRC Connection Establishment and iv) RRC Reconfiguration. The test suite considers a type of scenario with a single eNB and multiple UEs that are instructed to connect to the eNB. Each test case implements an instance of this scenario with specific values of the following parameters:

- number of UEs
- number of active Data Radio Bearers to be activated for each UE
- time t_0^c at which the first UE is instructed to start connecting to the eNB
- time interval d^i between the start of connection of UE n and UE $n+1$; the time at which user n connects is thus determined as $t_n^c = t_0^c + nd^i$
- a boolean flag indicating whether the ideal or the real RRC protocol model is used

Each test cases passes if the condition "UE is connected to eNB" is positively evaluated for each UE after a delay d^e from the time it started connecting to the eNB. The delay d^e is determined as

$$d^e = d^{si} + d^{ra} + d^{ce} + d^{cr}$$

where:

- d^{si} is the max delay necessary for the acquisition of System Information. We set it to 90ms taking into account 10ms for the MIB acquisition and 80ms for the subsequent SIB2 acquisition;
- d^{ra} is the delay for the MAC Random Access (RA) procedure. This depends on preamble collisions as well as on the availability of resources for the UL grant allocation. The total amount of necessary RA attempts depends on preamble collisions and failures to allocate the UL grant because of lack of resources. The number of collisions depends on the number of UEs that try to access simultaneously; we estimated that for a 0.99 RA success probability, 5 attempts are sufficient for up to 20 UEs, and 10 attempts for up to 50 UEs. For the UL grant, considered the system bandwidth and the default MCS used for the UL grant (MCS 0), at most 4 UL grants can be assigned in a TTI; so for n UEs trying to do RA simultaneously the max number of attempts due to the UL grant issue is $\lceil n/4 \rceil$. The time for a RA attempt is determined by 3ms + the value of LteEnbMac::RaResponseWindowSize, which defaults to 3ms, plus 1ms for the scheduling of the new transmission;
- d^{ce} is the delay required for the transmission of RRC CONNECTION SETUP followed by RRC CONNECTION SETUP COMPLETED. We consider a round

trip delay of 10ms plus $\lceil 2n/4 \rceil$ considering that 2 RRC packets have to be transmitted and that at most 4 such packets can be transmitted per TTI;

- d^{cr} is the delay required for eventually needed RRC CONNECTION RECONFIGURATION transactions. The number of transactions needed is 1 for each bearer activation. Similarly to what done for d^{ce}, for each transaction we consider a round trip delay of 10ms plus $\lceil 2n/4 \rceil$. delay of 20ms.

The condition "UE is connected to eNB" evaluates to positive if all the following conditions are satisfied:

- the eNB has the context of the UE (identified by the RNTI value retrieved from the UE RRC)
- the RRC state of the UE at the eNB is CONNECTED_NORMALLY;
- the RRC state at the UE is CONNECTED_NORMALLY;
- the UE is configured with the CellId, DlBandwidth, UlBandwidth, DlEarfcn and UlEarfcn of the eNB;
- the IMSI of the UE stored at the eNB is correct;
- the number of active Data Radio Bearers is the expected one, both according to the context information at both the UE and the eNB;
- for each Data Radio Bearer, the identifiers EPS bearer id, DRB id and LCID are consistent between the UE and the eNB.

8.3 X2 handover execution tests

The test suite `lte-x2-handover` checks the correct functionality of the X2 handover procedure. The scenario being tested is a topology with two eNBs connected by an X2 interface. Each test case is a particular instance of this scenario defined by the following parameters:

- the number of UEs that are initially attached to the first eNB;
- the number of EPS bearers activated for each UE;
- a list of handover events to be triggered, where each event is defined by: 1) the start time of the handover trigger , 2) the index of the UE doing the handover, 3) the index of the source eNB, and 4) the index of the target eNB;
- a boolean flag indicating whether the target eNB admits the handover or not;
- a boolean flag indicating whether the ideal RRC protocol is to be used instead of the real RRC protocol;
- the type of scheduler to be used (Round Robin or Proportional Fair);

Each test case passes if the following conditions are true:

- at time 0.06s, each UE is connected to the first eNB;
- for each event in the handover list, at the indicated event start time, the indicated UE is connected to the indicated source eNB; at 0.1s after the start time, the indicated UE is connected to the indicated target eNB; at 0.6s after the start time, for each active EPS bearer, the uplink and downlink sink applications of the indicated UE have achieved a number of bytes which is at least half the number of bytes transmitted by the corresponding source applications.

The condition "UE is connected to eNB" is the same introduced previously in Section 8.2.

8.4 Automatic X2 handover

The test suite `lte-x2-handover-measures` checks the correct functionality of the handover algorithm. The scenario being tested is a topology with two, three or four eNBs connected by an X2 interface. The eNBs are located in a straight line in the X-axis. A UE moves along the X-axis going from the neighbourhood of one eNB to the next eNB. Each test case is a particular instance of this scenario defined by the following parameters:

- the number of eNBs in the X-axis
- the number of EPS bearers activated for the UE;
- a list of check point events to be triggered, where each event is defined by: 1) the time of the first and the last check point event, 2) the interval time between the two check point events, 3) the index of the UE doing the handover, and 4) the index of the eNB where the UE must be connected;
- a boolean flag indicating whether the ideal RRC protocol is to be used instead of the real RRC protocol;
- the type of LTE MAC scheduler to be used.

Each test case passes if the following conditions are true:

- at time 0.08s, each UE is connected to the first eNB
- for each event in the check point list, at the indicated check point time, the indicated UE is connected to the indicated eNB, and 0.5s after the check point, for each active EPS bearer, the uplink and downlink sink applications of the UE have achieved a number of bytes which is at least half the number of bytes transmitted by the corresponding source applications.

Again, the condition "UE is connected to eNB" is the one introduced previously in Section 8.2.

9. HANDOVER SCENARIO EXAMPLE

The example `lte-x2-handover-measures` provides a scenario where a UE performs a handover across several eNBs. The handover is triggered automatically according to the algorithm described in Section 4.6.

The scenario is configured with four eNBs located along the X-axis with a distance of 1000m between each eNB. Each eNB is configured with a different cellId, namely 1, 2, 3 and 4. The UE is initially attached to the eNB with cellId = 1, and moves along the X-axis at a constant speed of 20m/s. Figure 10 shows a simplified diagram of the scenario topology; the EPC elements (i.e. SGW/PGW and MME) are omitted from the figure for simplicity.

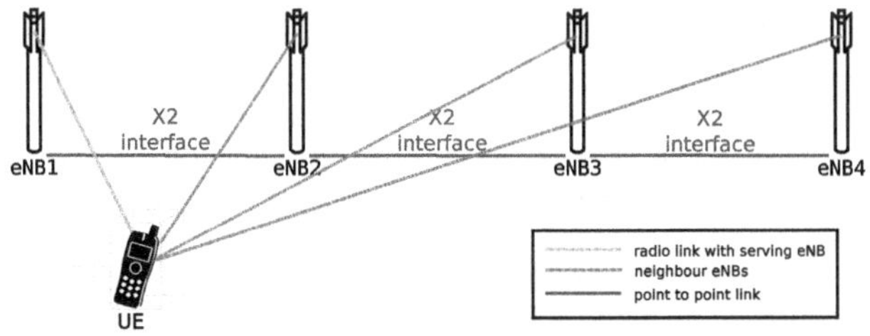

Figure 10: Physical topology of the automatic X2-based handover

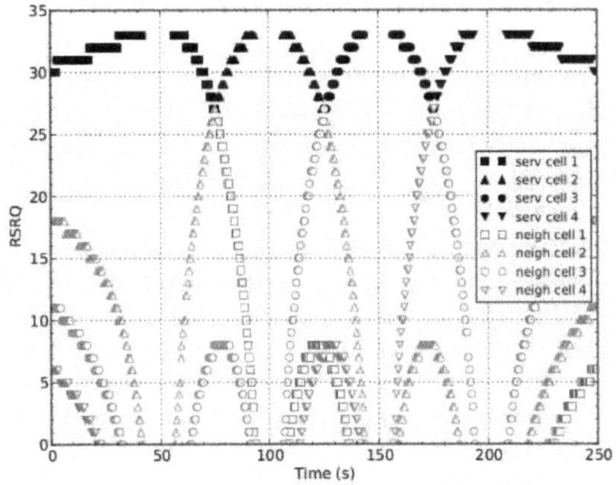

Figure 11: RSRQ measurements reported by the UE to its serving eNB

Figure 11 shows the RSRQ measurements provided by the UE RRC to the eNB RRC. The filled black markers show the RSRQ values of the serving cell, whereas the empty colored markers show the RSRQ values of the neighbour cells. The shape of the marker indicates the cellId. For example, at time = 10s, the UE is sending the measurement report of its serving cell equals to 1, and its neighbour cells 2, 3, and 4.

In this scenario, there are three handovers occurring at different times: (1) at around 75s, the UE performs a handover from eNB1 to eNB2; (2) at around 125s, from eNB2 to eNB3; (3) at around 175s, from eNB3 to eNB4.

10. SIMULATION FOOTPRINT

In order to assess the the CPU and memory consumption of the proposed simulation model, we ran some simulations with the `lena-dual-stripe` program, which models the Dual Stripe scenario definde in [25]. We used changeset 2c5b0d697717 of the simulation module which is available at [26]; the ns-3 build was configured with the parameters `-d optimized --enable-static`, which are the recommended ones for production use. The Dual Stripe scenario was configured with a single femtocell block having 10 apartments per row, no macro cell site, a unitary HeNB activation ratio, variable HeNB deployment ratio (which generated a variable number of eNBs in the scenario) and variable number of UEs per eNB. The duration of the simulation was set to 10 s, and the "Real RRC" model was chosen between the two model described in Section 4. We ran the simulations on a Intel Pentium IV 3.00 GHz machine with 1GB of RAM running Fedora Core 10 with a 2.6.27.41-170.2.117 kernel, enabling PHY, MAC, RLC and PDCP traces, which were output directly to the hard disk. The obtained results are shown in Figures 12 and 13.

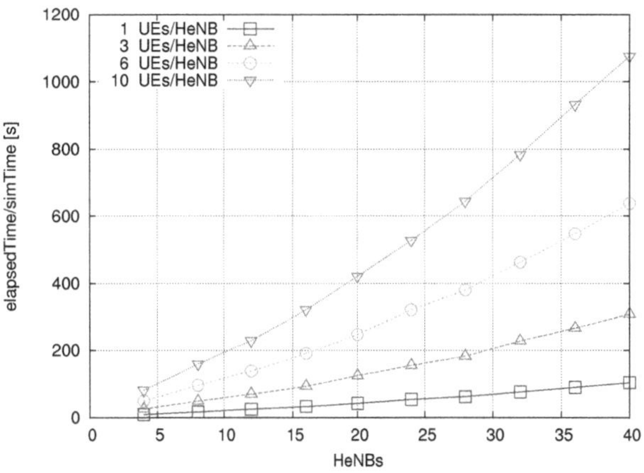

Figure 12: Execution time of the experiments normalized to the simulation time

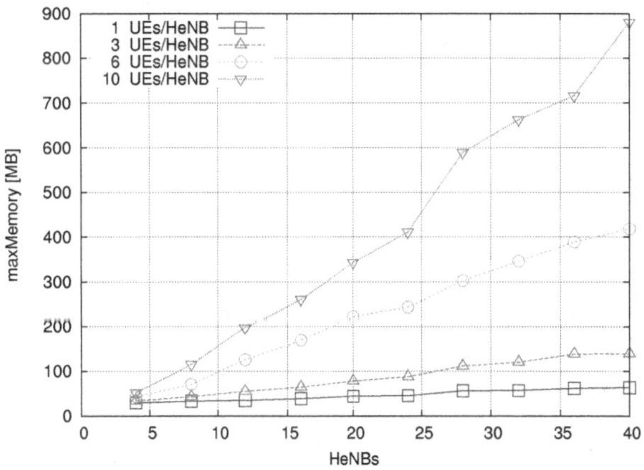

Figure 13: Peak memory consumption of the experiments

11. CONCLUSIONS

In this paper, we presented our ns-3 based model for the simulation of LTE handover scenarios. The model is licensed on the terms of the GNU General Public License v2, and is publicly available at [26]. Possible future development directions for this model include the support for inter-frequency UE measurement, and the implementation of new handover decision algorithms.

12. ACKNOWLEDGMENTS

The work at CTTC has been partially funded by the Spanish Ministry of Science and Innovation under grant number TEC2011-29700-C02-01 (project SYMBIOSIS), by the Catalan Regional Government under grant 2009SGR-940, and by Ubiquisys Ltd.

13. REFERENCES

[1] N. Baldo, M. Miozzo, M. Requena-Esteso, and J. Nin-Guerrero, "An open source product-oriented LTE network simulator based on ns-3," in *Proc. of ACM MSWiM*, Nov. 2011.

[2] G. Piro, L. A. Grieco, G. Boggia, F. Capozzi, and P. Camarda, "Simulating LTE cellular systems: an open-source framework," *IEEE Trans. Veh. Technol.*, vol. 60, no. 2, pp. 498–513, 2011.

[3] "E-UTRA and E-UTRAN overall description," TS 36.300, Mar. 2012.

[4] K. Dimou, M. Wang, Y. Yang, M. Kazmi, A. Larmo, J. Pettersson, W. Muller, and Y. Timner, "Handover within 3GPP LTE: design principles and performance," in *Proc. of IEEE VTC Fall*, Sep. 2009.

[5] S. Sesia, I. Toufik, and M. Baker, *LTE – The UMTS Long Term Evolution: From Theory to Practice.* Wiley Online Library, 2009.

[6] J.-M. Moon and D.-H. Cho, "Efficient handoff algorithm for inbound mobility in hierarchical macro/femto cell networks," *IEEE Commun. Lett.*, vol. 13, no. 10, pp. 755–757, 2009.

[7] D.-W. Lee, G.-T. Gil, and D.-H. Kim, "A cost-based adaptive handover hysteresis scheme to minimize the handover failure rate in 3GPP LTE system," *EURASIP Journal on Wireless Communications and Networking*, vol. 2010, p. 6, 2010.

[8] B. Jeong, S. Shin, I. Jang, N. W. Sung, and H. Yoon, "A smart handover decision algorithm using location prediction for hierarchical macro/femto-cell networks," in *Proc. of IEEE VTC Fall*, Sep. 2011.

[9] A. Ulvan, R. Bestak, and M. Ulvan, "Handover scenario and procedure in LTE-based femtocell networks," in *Proc. of UBICOMM*, Oct. 2010.

[10] H. Zhang, W. Ma, W. Li, W. Zheng, X. Wen, and C. Jiang, "Signalling cost evaluation of handover management schemes in LTE-advanced femtocell," in *Proc. of IEEE VTC Spring*, May 2011.

[11] H. Zhang, X. Wen, B. Wang, W. Zheng, and Y. Sun, "A novel handover mechanism between femtocell and macrocell for LTE based networks," in *Proc. of ICCSN*, Feb. 2010.

[12] A. Lobinger, S. Stefanski, T. Jansen, and I. Balan, "Coordinating handover parameter optimization and load balancing in LTE self-optimizing networks," in *In Proc. of IEEE VTC Spring*, May 2011.

[13] R. Kwan, R. Arnott, R. Paterson, R. Trivisonno, and M. Kubota, "On Mobility Load Balancing for LTE Systems," in *Proc. of IEEE VTC Fall*, Sep. 2010.

[14] D. López-Pérez, A. Ladányi, A. Juttner, and J. Zhang, "OFDMA femtocells: Intracell handover for interference and handover mitigation in two-tier networks," in *Proc. of IEEE WCNC*, Apr. 2010.

[15] D. Xenakis, N. Passas, and C. Verikoukis, "An energy-centric handover decision algorithm for the integrated LTE macrocell–femtocell network," *Elsevier Computer Communications*, vol. 35, no. 14, pp. 1684–1694, Aug. 2012.

[16] C. Mehlführer, J. C. C. Ikuno, M. Šimko, S. Schwarz, M. Wrulich, and M. Rupp, "The Vienna LTE simulators-Enabling reproducibility in wireless communications research," *EURASIP Journal on Advances in Signal Processing*, vol. 2011, no. 1, pp. 1–14, 2011.

[17] N. Baldo, M. Requena-Esteso, J. Nin-Guerrero, and M. Miozzo, "A new model for the simulation of the LTE-EPC data plane," in *Proc. of WSN3*, 2012.

[18] 3GPP, "E-UTRA Medium Access Control (MAC) protocol specification," TS 36.321, Jan. 2009.

[19] ——, "E-UTRA Radio Resource Control (RRC)," TS 36.331, Sept. 2010.

[20] ——, "E-UTRAN S1 Application Protocol (S1AP)," TS 36.413, Jan. 2011.

[21] ——, "E-UTRAN X2 general aspects and principles," TS 36.420, Jan. 2009.

[22] ——, "E-UTRAN X2 Application Protocol (X2AP)," TS 36.423, Oct. 2009.

[23] R. Stewart, "RFC4960," *Stream control transmission protocol*, 2007.

[24] 3GPP, "Tunnelling Protocol for Control plane (GTPv2-C)," TS 29.274, March 2013.

[25] ——, "Simulation assumptions and parameters for FDD HeNB RF requirements," TSG RAN WG4 R4-092042, May 2009.

[26] "LENA project web page," http://iptechwiki.cttc.es/LTE-EPC_Network_Simulator_(LENA).

ERCA: Efficient and Robust Cipher Algorithm for LTE Data Confidentiality

Soran Hussein, Hassan Noura, Steven Martin, Lila Boukhatem, Khaldoun Al Agha
Labaratoire de Recherche en Informatique
Université Paris-Sud, CNRS
Paris, France
soran.hussein@lri.fr, noura-h@lri.fr, steven.martin@lri.fr, lila@lri.fr, alagha@lri.fr

ABSTRACT

In this paper, a new ciphering algorithm is proposed for Long Term Evolution (LTE) data confidentiality. The proposed cipher scheme is based on a novel stream cipher framework which uses Substitution-Diffusion (SD) structure to provide key-streams that possess acceptable cryptographic performance (avalanche effect and key sensibility). Standards have been already adopted by 3GPP for LTE data confidentiality; EEA1, EEA2, and EEA3 which are based on Snow 3G, Advanced Encryption Standard (AES), and ZUC, respectively. Although the above mentioned algorithms have sufficient security strength against attacks, our solution is constructed to ensure less complexity with similar security strength. The proposed algorithm consists of an addition layer and a modified RC6 substitution layer which could require no memory and has stronger cryptographic properties compared to RC6. Furthermore, a new dynamic non invertible diffusion layer technique is introduced, which is constructed from the output of the substitution layer. Theoretical and simulation results show that our algorithm is immune against liner, differential, chosen/known-plain-text, brute force and statistical attacks. Equally important to note, our proposed cipher algorithm has a lower computational time compared to AES, and could be adapted for other kinds of wireless networks.

Categories and Subject Descriptors

[Security and privacy of mobile/wireless systems]

Keywords

LTE Data Confidentiality, Non Invertible matrix, Key dependent matrix, Diffusion layer, Efficient Stream cipher, Security Analysis

1. INTRODUCTION

The 4G LTE of mobile networks is designed to be an IP-based packet network. Hence it should provide a robust defense mechanism to protect users' data from diverse attacks and threats which its security architecture is about to face. Data Confidentiality (DC) is one of the most important features of any secure communication that requires prevention of an unauthorized disclosure of data between two communication nodes to the third party attackers or intruders, such as individuals, entities or processes. In the LTE system architecture as described in [4], User Equipment (UE) and eNode B (eNB) are connected through the Access Stratum (AS), where both security features of DC and data integrity are carried out in the Packet Data Convergence Protocol (PDCP) layer. The PDCP performs ciphering/deciphering of user and control plane data at both UE and eNB sides. The 3rd Generation Partnership Project (3GPP) had already standardized three algorithms for DC to ensure confidentiality of user and signaling data in LTE-Service Architecture Evolution (LTE-SAE). The first algorithm is a 128-bit key Evolved Packet System Encryption Algorithm (128-EEA1), which is a stream cipher algorithm, based on SNOW 3G that is already deployed in Universal Mobile Telecommunication System (UMTS). The second one is 128- EEA2 which is based on the AES block cipher algorithm used in its CounTeR mode (CTR mode) [8]. The next standard 128-EEA3 has been recently designed and it is now published for public evaluation, its core is based on ZUC stream cipher [4]. However, designing a less complex DC algorithm that has adequate security strength and consistency with the standards is preferred, since it would require lower computation power and consequently lower energy consumption at both eNB and UE sides during ciphering/deciphering procedure.

Shannon demonstrated in [14], that the conventional technique to obtain a powerful encryption of a block of bytes is achieved by using the confusion and diffusion layers for several rounds. In this paper we propose a novel stream cipher technique based on SD structure which its main advantage is its reduced complexity to one round, and possesses similar security strength compared to the standardized solutions. It consists of an addition, a substitution and a diffusion layer. The addition layer uses binary XOR operation with constant block value to ensure key uniformity. The Substitution layer is constructed from the nonlinear transformation of RC6 to add confusion. Finally, the diffusion layer is constructed from the output of the substitution one by forming a sub-matrix. The rest of this paper is organized as follows: a description of LTE-SAE architecture as well as the functionality of current DC standards is presented in Section 2. In Section 3, we introduce and describe our proposed algorithm and the functionality of each layer is explained in detail. Simulation tests of the cryptographic strength and performance are introduced in Section 4. Finally in Section 5, conclusion and future works are presented.

2. LTE SECURITY ARCHITECTURE AND CONFIDENTIALITY STANDARDS

The security architecture of mobile networks has been subjected to subsequent evolutions since the first analog system, which later

MSWiM'13, November 3–8, 2013, Barcelona, Spain.
Copyright 2013 ACM 978-1-4503-2353-6/13/11 ...$15.00.
http://dx.doi.org/10.1145/2507924.2507946 .

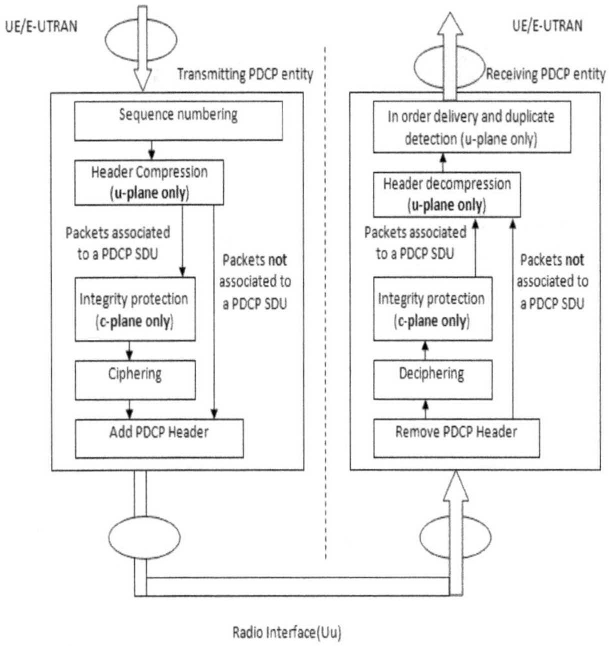

Figure 1: PDCP Layer.

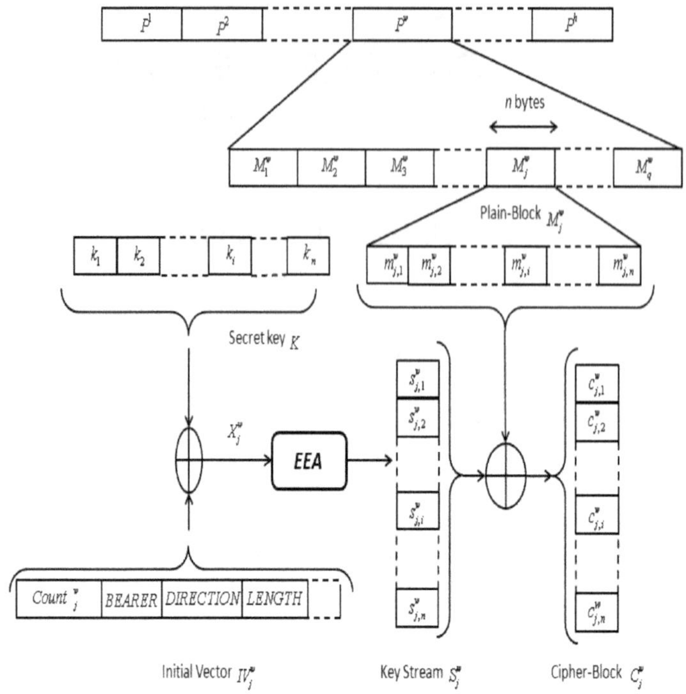

Figure 2: Ciphering a block of data.

evolved to Global System for Mobile communications (GSM) then 3GPP (UMTS) and now 3GPP LTE. GSM security has rather concentrated on the protection of the air interface. Substantial improvements had been adopted for UTMS security, such as adding security features for radio access networks and services. LTE is designed as an IP-based architecture to support heterogeneous radio access networks. As a consequence new and numerous threats exist that requires more powerful security mechanisms. The LTE-SAE, also denoted as Evolved Packet System (EPS), adds two security functions to the AS to ensure data security during transmission over air interface. An encryption algorithm has been employed to cipher both user and control plane data to achieve DC. The second feature is integrity protection of the control plane data which is called Data Integrity (DI) [2]. These two security features are applied at PDCP layer as shown in figure 1, which is located above the Radio Link Control (RLC).

The ciphering algorithm and the key to be used by PDCP are managed by upper layers, and the input parameters to the ciphering algorithm are; a 128-bit cipher key (K), and a 128-bit Initial Vector (IV), which is composed of a 32-bit counter, a 5-bit bearer identity, the 1-bit direction of transmission(shall be 0 for up-link and 1 for down-link) and the length of the required key-stream [5]. In general, the cipher algorithm considers a stream of packets in plain-text P exists at the source (UE or eNB) and requires to be transmitted safely. This stream is divided into many packets $\{P^1, \ldots, P^w, \ldots, P^h\}$, $w = 1, \ldots, h$ and each packet is divided into many blocks M_j^w, $j = 1, 2, \ldots, q$ of 128-bit length (16 bytes). The process of encryption/decryption in EEA is depicted in Figure 2 for the jth plain-block of the wth packet. More precisely, at the encryption side, the cipher-text $C_j^w = \{c^w_{j,1}, c^w_{j,2}, \ldots, c^w_{j,n}\}$ is obtained by XORing the bytes of the jth plain-data block (plain text) $\{m^w_{j,1}, m^w_{j,2}, \ldots, m^w_{j,n}\}$ with their corresponding output byte key-stream $S_j^w = \{s^w_{j,1}, s^w_{j,2}, \ldots, s^w_{j,n}\}$ obtained from the ciphering algorithm:

$$c^w_{j,i} = m^w_{j,i} \oplus s^w_{j,i} \qquad (1)$$

Likewise, at the decryption side, the ith byte of cipher block is XORed with the ith byte of key-stream $s^w_{j,i}$ to recover the ith byte of the plain block $m^w_{j,i}$:

$$m^w_{j,i} = c^w_{j,i} \oplus s^w_{j,i} \qquad (2)$$

However, 3GPP adopted till now three pairs of standards for DC and DI; (EEA1, EIA1), (EEA2, EIA2) and (EEA3, EIA3). In this paper, we are mainly focusing on DC and the related standards (EEA1, EEA2, and EEA3). In the next section the functionality and drawbacks of each of the three standard DC algorithms are explained.

2.1 EEA1-SNOW 3G

The core cipher of EEA1 is based on SNOW 3G which was originally used as the cryptographic kernel of the second set of UMTS confidentiality and integrity algorithms and has been kept as the first set of security algorithms for LTE. It is derived from the stream cipher SNOW 2.0, with improvements against algebraic cryptanalysis and distinguishing attacks. SNOW 3G is a word oriented stream cipher that generates a sequence of 32-bit words using a 128-bit key and a 128-bit initialization variable [15]. The structure of SNOW 3G is composed of a Linear Feedback Shift Register (LFSR) with 16 chained 32-bit stages and a Finite State Machine (FSM). SNOW 3G offers adequate protection against new forms of algebraic attacks, but computationally it is quite complicated especially in terms of hardware implementation.

2.2 EEA2-AES

The ciphering procedure of EEA2 is based on AES [10] (see Figure 3) using the mode CTR which is a block cipher that can

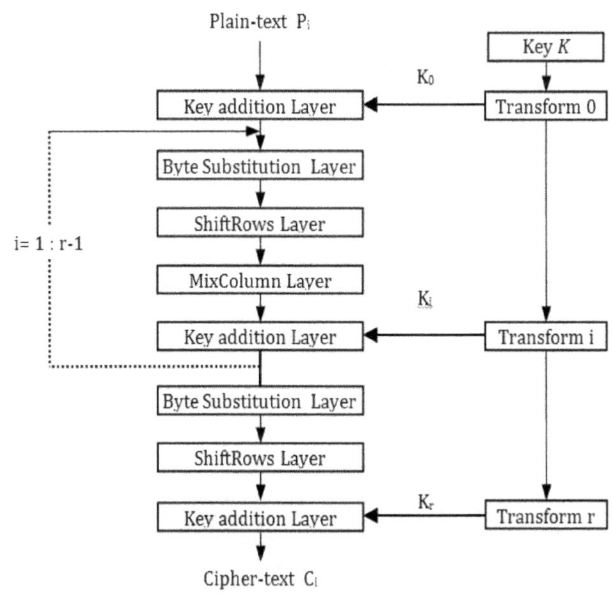

Figure 3: AES Algorithm

process data blocks of 128-bit (16 bytes block) using cipher keys of 128, 192 and 256-bit. Yet, 3GPP adopted 128-bit cipher key as a standard for EEA2. The design of AES depends on a principle called Substitution-Diffusion Network (SDN), as the encryption procedure for128-bit is composed of 10 rounds of processing. Each round except the last one includes four layers:*ByteSubstitution* layer (S-Box), *ShiftRow* layer, *KeyAddition* layer and *MixColumn* layer, which will be eliminated in the last round. First, a 128-bit round key XORed to the state is applied, then in the next layer a byte-by-byte substitution is performed using 16×16 look up table to provide the confusion property. Permutation is performed at the *ShiftRow* Layer at byte level. Finally, *MixColumn* Layer combines blocks of four bytes by using matrix operation. The *ShiftRow* and *MixColumn* layers provide the diffusion property. However, AES-CTR mode is similar to a stream cipher since, instead of encrypting the plain text directly, the counter is encrypted then Xored with the plain-text to produce the cipher-text for transmission. Apart from offering strong encryption via 128-bit keys, AES computational time is long since it uses 10 rounds of iterations.

2.3 EEA3-ZUC

The EEA3 algorithm core is based on a new stream cipher called ZUC [3], which is designed by Chinese Academy of Science to be permitted for use in China. ZUC is a word oriented cipher that takes as input 128-bit initial cipher key and 128-bit initial vector. The output is 32-bit word key-stream, also called key-word that would be used to encrypt/decrypt the plain text. The ZUC stream cipher has three main logical layers: LFSR, Bit-Reorganization (BR) and Non-Linear Function (NLF). The LSFR is composed of 16 registers, each one containing 31 bit and taking values from 1 to $2^{31}-1$. Additionally, it has two modes of operation: the initialization mode and the working mode. During initialization mode, LSFR takes a 31-bit input word computed by removing the rightmost bit from the XORing cipher key the initial vector. However, in the working mode, the LSFR does not receive any input. The BR makes four words by extracting 128 bits from LSFR states. The first three words are used by the NLF and the last one is used to construct a key-stream. Indeed, despite the fact that ZUC appears to have a sound design with large security spectrum, it requires more analysis to gain further confidence.

The standard ciphers are based on r multi-round function, where each one is composed of several simple iterated functions. The round function can be categorized into two classes: Feistel Networks (FN) and SDN. However, the security level depends on the number of rounds, which leads to a trade-off between high security level and required computational time (high complexity) and consequently high energy consumption.

3. THE PROPOSED ERCA ALGORITHM

In Section 2, the security architecture of the LTE and different standards adopted by 3GPP for DC were explained. This section features a new efficient secure stream cipher for practical LTE- DC. Usually, the term efficiency means having the fastest execution time while keeping security of the LTE network conditions. This permits to overcome the above-described disadvantages of related works. Our proposition is to add defense schemes into the LTE-DC concept. The main properties of our proposed solution are: high level of security, efficiency in computation complexity without any need for memory overhead. The effectiveness of secure stream cipher is a necessary condition for practical implementation. In this work, we design an efficient implementation, which is easy to function with mobile devices. The proposed stream cipher algorithm candidate has similar architecture to AES. Furthermore, our cipher is iterated for only one round, which leads to ensure less complexity.

The basic scheme of the proposed ciphering algorithm is presented in Figure 4. For each input block, the process of addition layer is applied first, then the process of substitution. After that, we reshape the output of substitution process (row) to form a sub-matrix, which is used to construct the diffusion matrix. Finally, the process of diffusion is applied using the obtained diffusion matrix on the output of substitution layer. The proposed cipher algorithm uses secret key $K = \{k_1, k_2, \ldots, k_{16}\}$ with 128-bit length. Indeed,the ciphering algorithm is performed on a set of bytes of input block $X_j^w = \{x_{j,1}^w, x_{j,2}^w, \ldots, x_{j,16}^w\}$, which is obtained from the XOR between the bytes of K and IV_j^w as below:

$$x_{j,i}^w = k_i \oplus IV_{j,i}^w, \quad i = 1, 2, \ldots, 16 \tag{3}$$

In the following, the functionalities of each layer are described in details.

3.1 Initial Key Addition Layer

The addition layer uses constant block value, that has been chosen with uniform bit distribution to provide the uniformity to the key-stream by mixing the input block with a constant block, which would be carried out on bytes (byte by byte) using logical XOR operation as follows:

$$y_{j,i}^w = x_{j,i}^w \oplus t_i \tag{4}$$

where $x_{j,i}^w$ is a byte of the input block and t_i a byte of the constant block. The use of logical operation XOR ensures the uniformity, which makes the differential cryptanalysis extremely difficult.

3.2 Substitution Layer

The substitution process is the most important operation in any cipher algorithm due to its non linearity which makes the algorithm immune against differential and linear cryptanalysis. The substitution layer could be in forms of S-box as in AES and ZUC, or could be a nonlinear transformation as employed here. Mathematically,

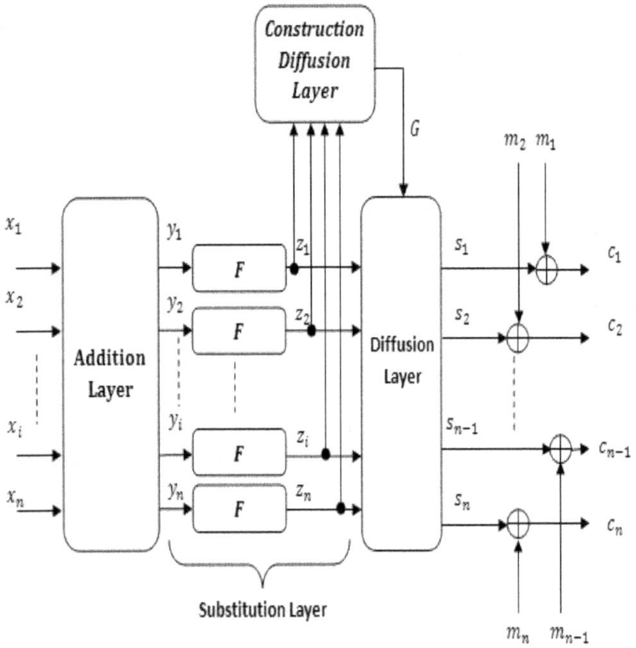

Figure 4: ERCA stream cipher

an $m \times m$ substitution layer is a nonlinear mapping $F : (0,1)^m \rightarrow (0,1)^m$, where $(0,1)^m$ represents the vector spaces of elements from binary Galois field. The proposed substitution layer uses the nonlinear transformation of RC6 [12], with an efficient modification, since RC6 has poor cryptographic properties, especially high differential probability approximation which makes it useless to be used as a substitution layer. The nonlinear transformation of RC6 is performed as below:

$$z = F(y) = mod(y \times (2 \times y + 1), 2^Q) >> log_2(Q) \quad (5)$$

where $>>$ is Bitwise right shift and Q is equal to 8, since the substitution layer is applied on byte level. This transformation is applied for multi-iteration $irs = 1, 2, \ldots, rs$. Hence, a substantial enhancement of its cryptographic properties is achieved. Starting with initial vector V, where $V_j = j$ and $j = 0, 1, \ldots, 255$. The output vector after each iteration becomes the input vector for the next one. The cryptographic performances of the proposed substitution layer are quantified for each iteration. The obtained results in Figure 7 and 8 show that the optimal number of iterations to attain a good performance (LP_F, SAC, BIC and DP_F) as described in Section 4.1 is $log_2(Q) = 3$. Therefore, in our implementation each byte is substituted by applying the RC6 nonlinear function for three iterations.

3.3 Diffusion Layer

The diffusion process includes two steps: secret matrix generation G; and Modular 256 vector matrix multiplication.

3.3.1 *Construction of the diffusion layer* G

The diffusion layers are linear transformation, which is represented as matrices. However, the proposed technique of key dependent diffusion layer is designed to be efficient and robust, which means that the avalanche effect has to be achieved in cooperation with the substitution layer. In addition, this method is based on a special rule of algebra, which can provide the properties of flexibility, effortless to be implemented in hardware, key dependent, and non invertible matrix as its determinant is equal to 0 (singular matrix). In the following, the proposed method to build a dynamic diffusion matrix is described. It is based on a particular matrix structure (non invertible 2D matrix), simple to realize and successful in terms of speed of calculation. The 2D matrix is presented below.

$$A = \begin{bmatrix} a & b \\ c & d \end{bmatrix}; det(A) = ad - bc \quad (6)$$

Hence, if $det(A) = 0$ then $a \times d = b \times c$. To obtain the proposed structure of non invertible key dependent diffusion layer, considering that d is equal to b, which leads to $a \times b = b \times c$. This gives us that a is equal to c. Then, the form of a secret matrix in 2D is defined as below:

$$A = \begin{bmatrix} a & b \\ a & b \end{bmatrix} \quad (7)$$

Assuming that b is equal to $a \times (2 \times a + 1) \bmod 2^{256}$, the non invertible matrix requires only one parameter a. In this formulation called back below, parameter a is replaced by the sub matrices A to form the diffusion matrix with n dimensions.

$$G = \begin{bmatrix} A & B \\ A & B \end{bmatrix} \quad (8)$$

A is a non-zero matrix of size $\frac{n}{2}$ $times\frac{n}{2}$. The elements of A can be freely chosen from any Galois field such that G is full rank. In our simulation, the elements of this sub-matrix varies between 0 and 255. Having a matrix G constructed from four sub-matrices (A, B, C, D), the non-invertibility of this matrix can be proven as follows.

Its determinant is given by:

$$\begin{aligned} det(G) &= det(A) \times det(D - CA^{-1}B) \quad (9) \\ &= det(A) \times det(B - ABA^{-1}) \\ &= det(A) \times det(B - B) \\ &= 0 \end{aligned}$$

where $D = B$, and $C = A$.

Therefore, the necessary condition to not have an inverse matrix is attained and the attackers cannot calculate the inverse secret matrix G^{-1} to get the original substituted data. An example to construct the secret matrix G is shown in figure 5 for $n = 16$. The output of the substitution layer is reshaped to form a sub-matrix parameter $temp$ with size $\frac{n}{4} \times \frac{n}{4}$. Later, this sub-matrix is replicated to form a sub-matrix A with size $\frac{n}{2}$ $times\frac{n}{2}$, which is required to form the final matrix (diffusion layer).

3.3.2 *The Proposed diffusion Process* G

The input of the diffusion layer is n bytes and diffusion is performed on a series of substituted bytes $\{F(y_1), F(y_2), \ldots, F(y_h)\}$, which the output from is the produced key-stream. The key-stream S is obtained by performing a modular multiplication matrix using the secret matrix G, which is obtained from the substituted data. The architecture of the diffusion process is shown in Figure 6. The coefficients vector $\{G_1, G_2, ..., G_n\}$ are described as the global diffusion matrix (G). Each global diffusion vector G_i is represented as a sequence of independent random numbers from a byte field. The relationship among input block data, G and S can be described as

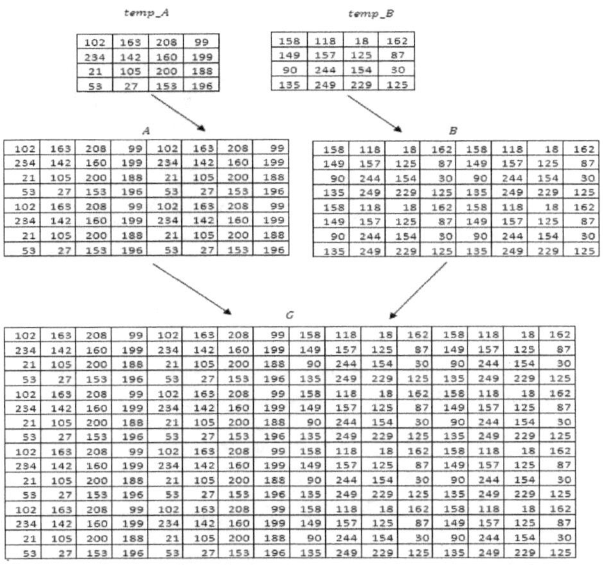

Figure 5: An example of creation of the diffusion Layer

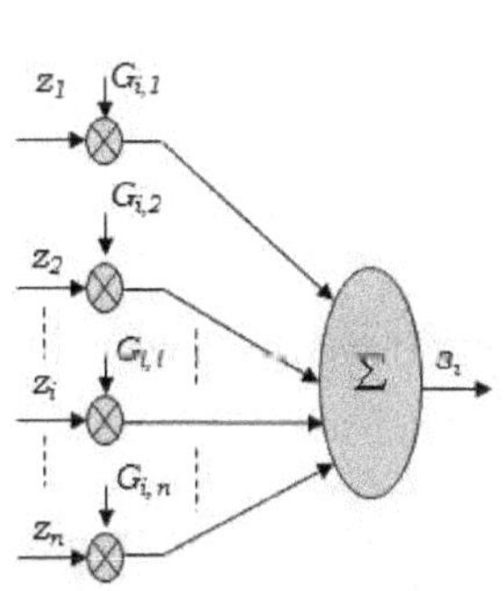

Figure 6: Proposed Diffusion Technique

follows:

$$S = G \times (F(Y)) = \begin{bmatrix} s_1 \\ s_2 \\ \vdots \\ s_n \end{bmatrix} = \begin{bmatrix} G_{1,1}G_{1,2}\cdots G_{1,n} \\ G_{2,1}G_{2,2}\cdots G_{2,n} \\ \vdots \quad \vdots \quad \ddots \quad \vdots \\ G_{n,1}G_{n,2}\cdots G_{n,n} \end{bmatrix} \cdot \begin{bmatrix} F(y_1) \\ F(y_2) \\ \vdots \\ F(y_n) \end{bmatrix} \quad (10)$$

Where $G_{i,j}$ is a diffusion coefficient that varies between 0 and 255 for the line i and column j and $i, j = 1,2,...,n$. $F(y_i)$ is a substituted byte, s_i is the resulting byte key-stream

Finally the output key-stream produced S is XORed with the plane text M to produce the cipher-text C.

4. CRYPTOGRAPHIC STRENGTH AND PERFORMANCE

In this section, the cryptographic properties of the proposed algorithm are presented. The algorithm is subjected to several tests such as uniformity, randomness, key sensitivity, etc. to assess its efficiency and to show how far it is consistent with security standards. In addition, the time complexity is quantified and compared to *AES* algorithm.

4.1 Cryptographic performance of the substitution layer

A strong $n \times n$ substitution layer must have some important properties, based on information theory analysis [9], [7], [16]. The main five properties are: bijectivity, non linearity, strict avalanche criterion (SAC), output bit independence criterion (BIC), and equiprobable input/output XOR distribution.

4.1.1 Linear Probability Approximation Boolean Function (LP_F)

One of the important properties of the substitution layer is non linearity to make it capable resisting linear cryptanalysis attacks. LP_F is used to measure the nonlinear degree of a given substitution layer, it is calculated according to [9]. In Figure 7-a, the variation of *LPF* against the number of iterations *rs* is shown .It attains the minimum after three iterations.

4.1.2 Differential Probability Approximation Function (DP_F)

Differential Uniformity is one of the important properties of any substitution layer for obtaining the nonlinear transformation and hence resisting differential cryptanalysis attacks [7]. DP_F is used to measure differential uniformity of our substitution layer as in [11]. Figure 7-b, shows the variation of DP_F against the number of iterations *rs*, which attains its minimum after 4 iterations.

4.1.3 Strict Avalanche Criterion (SAC)

Webster and Tavares were the first to present (SAC) when they generalized the avalanche effect [16]. A cipher system function is satisfying *SAC* whenever a single input bit is complemented, the output bit should be changed at least with a probability of half. Certainly, *SAC* is considered a desirable characteristic of any block ciphering algorithm and used to quantify the degree of security of the s-boxes of substitution-permutation networks. Therefore, any strong ciphering system should fulfill these criteria The average value SAC (mean of 8x8 values of the dependence matrix) versus the number of iteration *rs* is shown in Figure 8-a. We can observe that the SAC becomes very close to the ideal value 0.5 after three iterations.

4.1.4 Output Bit Iindependence Criterion (BIC)

BIC is another property which has also been also described by Webster and Tavares [16], which is considered a desirable characteristic of cipher algorithms. The *BIC* specifies that: two output bits j, k should change independently when a single input bit i is changed for all i, j and k. The average value of *BIC* (mean of 8x8 values of the *BIC* matrix without the diagonal) versus the number of iteration *rs* is shown in Figure 8-b. We can observe that the *BIC* becomes very close to the ideal value 0.5 after three iterations. This result is similar compared with *SAC*, so the number of iterations is set to be equal to 3 to attain an acceptable performance with as low complexity as possible.

However, when the number of iterations is 8, all properties become weak, this means that, increasing the number of iterations leads to eliminate totally the advantage of Bitwise right shift, since this function without >> is linear and cannot be used as substitution layer. The proposed function is periodic and its periods are 8 iterations. In conclusion, the proposed substitution layer possesses the most suitable properties for being used in the proposed stream cipher algorithm. To demonstrate the performances of the proposed substitution layer, its properties are compared with the substitution layer of AES and ZUC (S_0 and S_1) in Table 1. The results showed

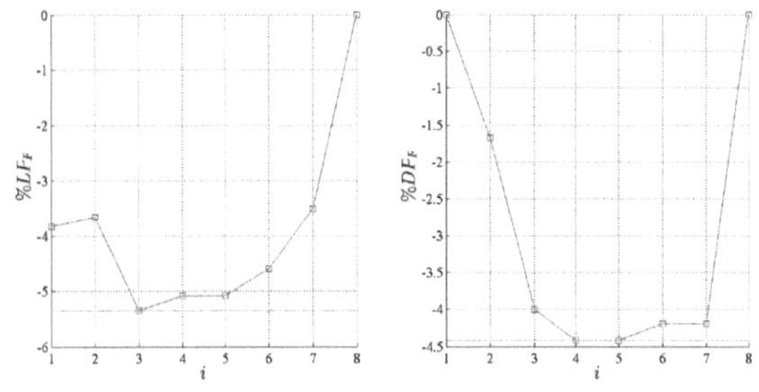

(a) (b)

Figure 7: Variation of the *LPF* (a) and *DPF* (b) against the number of iterations

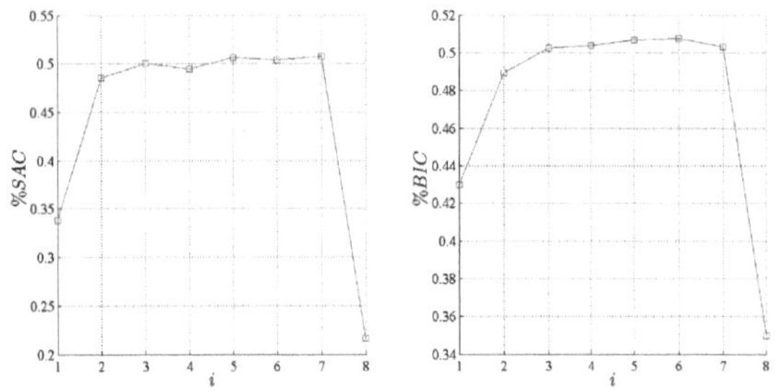

(a) (b)

Figure 8: Variation of the *SAC* (a) and *BIC* (b) against the number of iterations

that the proposed substitution layer is possessing sufficient cryptographic performances.

Table 1: Comparison Analysis of Substitution Layer

Test	Proposed	AES	S_0	S_1
LP_F	$2^{-5.3}$	2^{-6}	2^{-5}	2^{-6}
DP_F	2^{-4}	2^{-6}	2^{-4}	2^{-6}
SAC	0.5	0.4998	0.494	0.509
BIC	0.502	0.4998	0.4951	0.505

4.2 Randomness of the Produced Key-Stream

The security strength of the proposed stream cipher is depending on the produced key-stream, therefore the stream cipher should produce key-streams with high level of randomness. Some parameters of the LTE packet header are used in addition to the counter to form IV, which implies that the sub-matrix used in the construction of the diffusion layer is renewed for each block; consequently the produced key-stream is updated. In Figure 9, the recurrence (a) and distribution (b) for a random key-stream are shown. These results indicate clearly a good degree of randomness and uniformity. To prove these properties, the cipher key stream has been analyzed using the randomness test of NIST [13]. In order to get correct statistical results one needs to provide 100 secret keys and each key-stream sequence should be at least 1000000 bit long. The NIST test performs 15 tests on the data sample, and the total amount of executing NIST STS tests is 189. Results of testing the key-stream

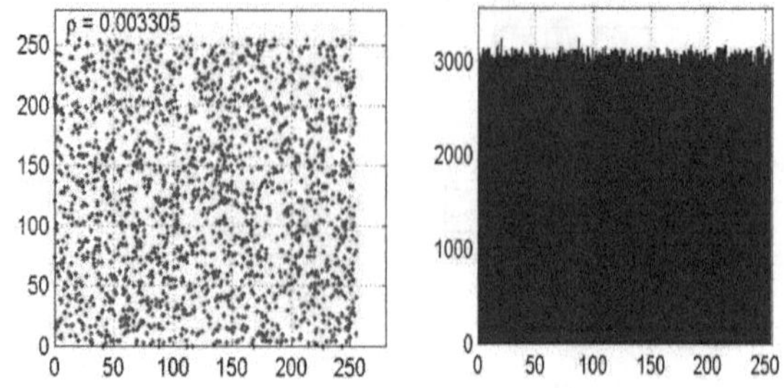

(a) (b)

Figure 9: Recurrence of producing key-stream (a) and its distribution (b) using a secret random key *K*

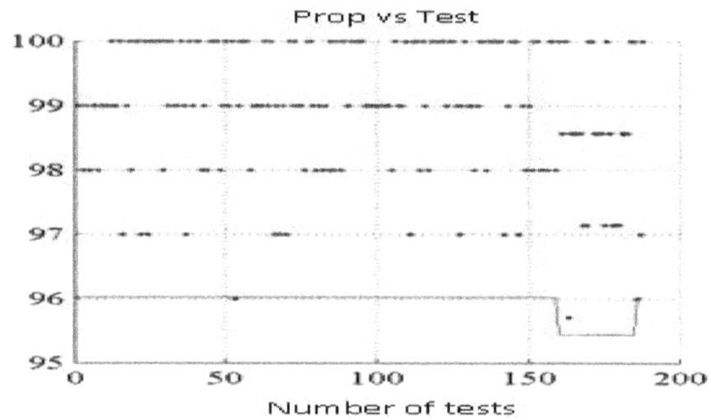

Figure 10: Proportion values of NIST tests

randomness are shown in Figure 10. The obtained proportion values (Success rate) show how many samples passed given tests. The red line marks minimum proportion values in order to consider the sequence to be random. Random Excursions and Random Excursions Variant tests represent 26 tests with different parameters, which have other minimum proportion values. The simulation results indicate clearly the randomness of the generated key-stream.

4.3 Key sensitivity

The sensitivity of the secret key is analyzed for 1000 random keys. All the elements of K'_i are equal to those of ith key K_i, except the Least Significant Bit (*LSB*) which was flipped . The percent of Hamming distance is calculated as follows:

$$PDH = \frac{\sum_{k=1}^{T} C_i \oplus C'_i}{T} \times 100\% \quad (11)$$

where T is the length in bit level of the encrypted packet, and C_i and C'_i are the corresponding cipher packets using K_i and K'_i respectively.

In Figure 11, the sensitivity of the secret key versus 1000 random keys is shown, while only the *LSB* of K^i is changed . This result indicates a high sensitivity, while the average Hamming distance percent is closer to the optimal values (50%) in bit level.

4.4 Statistical Properties

To demonstrate the safe use of our stream cipher, it is important to analyze its characteristics, in terms of random recurrence, mixing nature, and low coefficient correlation between original and encrypted data packets. In our simulation, the proposed stream cipher scheme is considered as a black box and randomly choosing a set of initial packets with a 125000 byte length, which are normally

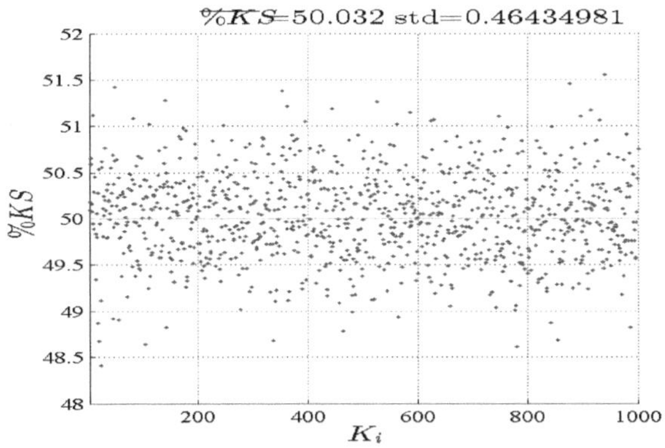

Figure 11: The key sensibility results for change random LSB of the secret key K versus 1000 random keys

distributed with a mean equal to 128 and a standard deviation equal to 8.

4.4.1 *Recurrence*

The recurrence plot serves to measure the evaluation of randomness and estimates the correlations among the data of a sequence as in [1]. Considering a packet sequence $x_i = x_{i,1}, x_{i,2}, \dots, x_{i,m}$, a vector with delay $t \geq 1$ can be constructed by:
$x_i(t) = x_i,\ x_{i+t},\ x_{i,2\times t}, \dots,\ x_{i,m\times t}$. In Figure 12 a-b, the variation between $x_i(t)$ and $x_i(t+1)$ from the original and the encrypted packets respectively are shown. We can observe that that no clear pattern is obtained after encryption.

4.4.2 *Mixing Nature*

The mixing nature serves as a measure of the uniformity and it can be quantified by a statistical approach. If the frequency counts of the encrypted generation are close to a uniform distribution, then it is possible to categorize that the concerned cipher under test have a good level of mixing. In Figure 13-a and b, the distribution of the original packets and its corresponding cipher packets respectively are shown. This result shows clearly that the contents of the encrypted packets are spread overall the space and have a uniform distribution. To validate this uniformity, the Chi-square test [6] is applied and works as follow:

$$\chi^2_{test} = \sum_{i=1}^{l} \frac{o_i - e_i}{e_i} \tag{12}$$

where l is the number of levels (here 256), o_i is the observed occurrence frequencies of each level of field size (0-255) in the histogram of ciphered generation contents, and e_i is the expected occurrence frequency of uniform distribution. For a significant level of 0.05, the null hypothesis is not rejected and the distribution of the histogram is uniform if $\chi^2_{test} \leq \chi^2_{theory}(255, 0.05) \approx 293$. The average results of the Chi-square test for 1000 different sets of generation for the whole ciphered packets against h is shown in Figure 14. The distribution of the tested histogram is uniform for $\approx 97\%$, that means a stronger mixing property is obtained.

4.4.3 *Low Coefficient Correlation*

Another important requirement for any encryption scheme must be attained is that the encrypted data should be greatly different from its original form. The encrypted packets should have redundancy and correlation as low as possible. First, the correlation coefficient between the original and encrypted packets is measured.

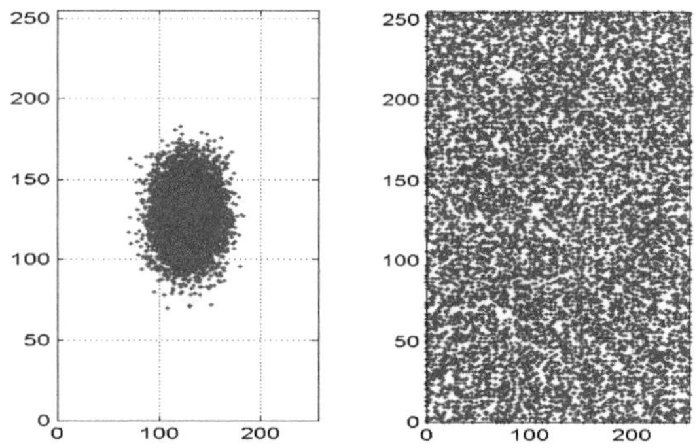

(a) (b)

Figure 12: Recurrence plot of the original packet (a) and its correspondent encrypted ones (b)

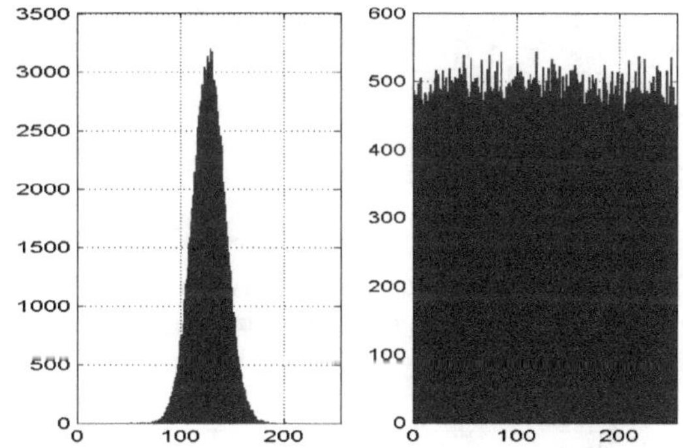

(a) (b)

Figure 13: The distribution of the contents original stream packet (a) and its correspondent encrypted one in (b)

The correlation coefficient is computed according to the following formulas:

$$\rho_{x,y} = \frac{cov(x,y)}{\sqrt{D(x) \times D(y)}} \tag{13}$$

$$where\ cov(x,y) = E[\{x - E(x)\}\{y - E(y)\}];$$

$$E(x) = \frac{1}{n} \times \sum_{k=1}^{n} x_i$$

$$and\ D(x) = \frac{1}{n} \times \sum_{k=1}^{n} \{x_i - E[x]\}$$

In Figure 15, the coefficient correlation between the original and encrypted packets versus 1000 different keys and data packets is shown. This result shows the correlation coefficient is always close to zero which indicates that no detectable correlation exists between the original and its corresponding cipher packets.

4.5 Execution Time

The execution speed is very important for any DC algorithms since it is directly related to the time and resources required for ciphering/deciphering.The excution time should be maintained very low, especially when a huge amount of data is to be transmitted such as in LTE systems. The average calculation times in *ms* (on

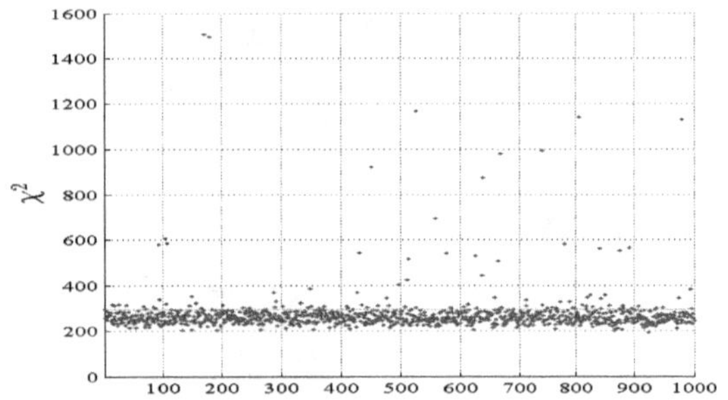

Figure 14: Variation of the χ^2_{test} of cipher packets for 12508 bytes length versus 1000 random keys

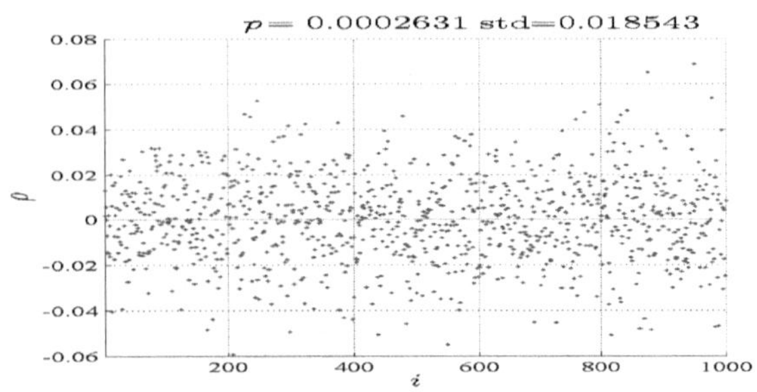

Figure 15: The coefficient correlation between the original and encrypted stream packets versus 1000 random keys

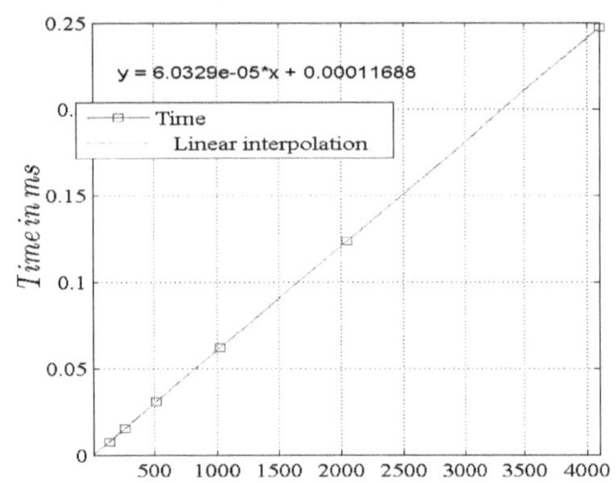

Figure 16: Variations of the average time for packets encryption in function to its length

10000 times) to encrypt a packet M against $Tb$is presented in Figure 16, where Tb represents the length of the block such as 128, 256, 512, 1024, etc. These calculations are performed under the following software and hardware environment 1: Matlab 2012 and micro-computer Intel Core 2 Duet 2.1 GHZ CPU with 2 GB RAM Intel, under Windows7. Clearly, the variation of average time is linear. The average time necessary against Tb is estimated (approximately) using the linear interpolation method. It shows that the proposed method is indeed sufficiently fast for LTE applications. Finally, we compared the mean encryption time (in ms), versus Tb, of the proposed cipher with AES. The proposed secure scheme is at least 5 times faster than the AES algorithm.

4.6 Discussion and Cryptanalysis

A cryptographic scheme is considered secure if it is strong enough to resist attacks. According to Shannon's theory, the confusion and diffusion process must be applied to provide resistance against the powerful attacks that is based on statistical analysis [14].These processes are repeated for several rounds to achieve the avalanche effect which leads to delay in terms of execution times (high computation complexity that lead to high delay and consumption of energy) especially for resource constrained devices. The proposed stream cipher is constructed in a new manner, where the diffusion process changes in a dynamic manner (pseudo-random) and doesn't possess the invertible property. In addition, the security is achieved with one round instead of 10 rounds as in *AES*, leading into a lower complexity and by consequence a lower energy consumption. The cryptographic security of our scheme relies on two properties:

- using a new efficient substitution layer
- using a dynamic diffusion layer with unpredictability and high sensitivity of the diffusion layer G

Moreover, the statistical properties of the proposed secure scheme (such as the uniformity of the cipher packets and the low coefficient correlation between the original and encrypted block of packets) are attained, which can provide immunity against the statistical attacks. Furthermore differential and linear attacks would become ineffective, since the avalanche effect is attained and the diffusion layer changes for each block. In fact, any change in any bit of secret key or public parameters causes a significant difference in the encrypted blocks as see in Figure 11. The key space of the secret key is 2^{128}, which is sufficiently large to make the brute-force attack infeasible. Additionally, the use of non invertible dynamic diffusion layer will limit the ability of the attackers who try to break out the cipher.

5. CONCLUSION

In this paper, a new stream cipher has been presented as an alternative candidate for the core of LTE-DC. Indeed the new proposed stream cipher is a round function consisting of an addition, a substitution and a diffusion layer. A new technique of key dependent stream cipher has been introduced, which achieves avalanche effect with an acceptable trade-off between security and complexity compared to ZUC and AES. Moreover, our algorithm has been subjected to all possible tests and attacks that are essential for any cipher system to be considered credible and robust. Simulation results show that computational time complexity of the proposed cipher is lower compared to AES cipher. This leads to less computational power and energy consumption during ciphering/deciphering processes. For the future work, we are working on developing a new data integrity and source authentication algorithm for LTE systems.

6. REFERENCES

[1] Thirteen Ways to Look at the Correlation Coefficient. *The American Statistician*, 42(1):59–66, 1988.

[2] Evolved Universal Terrestrial Radio Access (E UTRA); Packet Data Convergence Protocol (PDCP) Specification. Tech. Rep 3GPP TS 36.323. , March 2009.

[3] ETSI/SAG: Specification of the 3GPP confidentiality and integrity algorithms 128-EEA3 and 128-EIA3. document 1: 128-EEA3 and 128-EIA3 specification. Version 1.5. Tech. rep., ETSI , January 2011.

[4] 3GPP Technical Specification Group Services and Systems Aspects. System Architecture Evolution (SAE); Security Architecture (Release 11). Tech. Rep. 3G TS 33.401 v11.6.0,3 rd Generation Partnership Project., 2012.

[5] Digital cellular telecommunications system (phase 2+); Universal Mobile Telecommunications System (UMTS); mobile application part (MAP) specification (3GPP TS 29.002 version 11.5.0 Release 11) , February 2013.

[6] C. Bates and N. W. L. D. VA. *The Chi-square Test of Goodness of Fit for a Bivariate Normal Distribution*. Defense Technical Information Center, 1966.

[7] E. Biham and A. Shamir. Differential cryptanalysis of DES-like cryptosystems. In *Journal of Cryptology*, Vol. 4, No. 1 1991, pp. 3-72.

[8] C. M. Gutierrez. Recommendation for block cipher modes of operation:, 2007.

[9] M. Matsui. Linear cryptanalysis method for des cipher. In *Workshop on the theory and application of cryptographic techniques on Advances in cryptology*, EUROCRYPT '93, pages 386–397, Secaucus, NJ, USA, 1994. Springer-Verlag New York, Inc.

[10] F. P. Miller, A. F. Vandome, and J. McBrewster. *Advanced Encryption Standard*. Alpha Press, 2009.

[11] K. Nyberg. Differentially uniform mappings for cryptography. In *Workshop on the theory and application of cryptographic techniques on Advances in cryptology*, EUROCRYPT '93, pages 55–64, Secaucus, NJ, USA, 1994. Springer-Verlag New York, Inc.

[12] R. L. Rivest, M. J. B. Robshaw, R. Sidney, and Y. L. Yin. The RC6 TM Block Cipher. In *in First Advanced Encryption Standard (AES) Conference*, page 16, 1998.

[13] A. Rukhin, J. Soto, J. Nechvatal, E. Barker, S. Leigh, M. Levenson, D. Banks, A. Heckert, J. Dray, S. Vo, A. Rukhin, J. Soto, M. Smid, S. Leigh, M. Vangel, A. Heckert, J. Dray, and L. E. B. Iii. A statistical test suite for random and pseudorandom number generators for cryptographic applications, 2001.

[14] C. E. Shannon. Communication Theory of Secrecy Systems. *Bell Systems Technical Journal*, 28:656–715, 1949.

[15] S. Traboulsi, M. Sbeiti, F. Bruns, S. Hessel, and A. Bilgic. An optimized parallel and energy-efficient implementation of SNOW 3G for LTE mobile devices. In *in Proceedings of the IEEE 12th International Conference on Communication Technology (ICCT '10)*, pp. 535-538, Nanjing, China, November 2010.

[16] A. F. Webster and S. E. Tavares. On the design of s-boxes. In *Advances in Cryptology*, CRYPTO '85, pages 523–534, London,UK, 1986. Springer-Verlag.

A Representative and Accurate Characterization of Inter-contact Times in Mobile Opportunistic Networks

Enrique Hernández-Orallo, Juan-Carlos Cano,
Carlos T. Calafate, Pietro Manzoni
Departamento de Informática de Sistemas y Computadores.
Universidad Politécnica de Valencia. Valencia. Spain.
ehernandez@disca.upv.es, jucano@disca.upv.es, calafate@disca.upv.es,
pmanzoni@disca.upv.es

ABSTRACT

A representative characterisation of inter-contact times between nodes is essential for the performance evaluation of mobile networks. The most common characterization of inter-contact times is based on the study of the aggregate distribution of contacts between individual pairs of nodes. The problem with this aggregate distribution is that it is not always representative of the individual pair distributions, especially in the short term and when the number of nodes in the network is high. Thus, deriving results from this characterisation, can lead to inaccurate performance evaluations results.

In this paper, we propose and evaluate two new methods for characterising the inter-contact times distribution in mobile networks. We prove that these characterizations have a higher representativeness, thereby improving the accuracy of the derived performance results. For evaluating the precision of the different characterizations we use the epidemic routing protocol, which has an analytical performance expression that is based on a contact rate λ. We derive from each of the characterizations the corresponding λ values. Then, we compare the results obtained using the analytical expression with simulation results using both synthetic and real contact traces. It is shown that the new characterization methods are very accurate, even for reduced contact traces and high number of nodes.

Categories and Subject Descriptors

C.2.1 [**Network Architecture and Design**]: Wireless communication; I.6 [**Simulation and modelling**]: Model validation and Analysis

Keywords

Mobile Networking, Performance Evaluation, Inter-contact times

MSWiM'13, November 3–8, 2013, Barcelona, Spain.

http://dx.doi.org/10.1145/2507924.2507936.

1. INTRODUCTION

Mobile opportunistic networks collectively create dynamic networks that are built from short unpredictable contact times as nodes move in and out of connectivity. Applications of such networks include Mobile Ad-Hoc Networks (MANETs), Vehicular Ad-Hoc Networks (VANETs) and Mobile Social Networks.

Characterizing inter-contact times (or inter-meeting times) between nodes is essential for analyzing the performance of contact based protocols in cooperative or opportunistic networks. The established approach is to characterize the inter-contact times distribution between pairs of nodes using an *aggregate distribution* [2,7,9,13,15]. This distribution is obtained by *aggregating* the *individual pair distribution* of all combinations of pairs of nodes in the network. The *individual pair distribution* is defined as the distribution of the time elapsed between two consecutive contacts between the same pair of nodes [12].

Another form of characterizing the inter-contact times is to consider the time elapsed between contacts for any pairs of nodes in a group (known as *inter-any-contact times*). This characterization was briefly studied in [7] using human mobility traces. The conclusions were that inter-any-contact times are longer that individual pairs inter-contact times (as expected), but with a similar distribution shape. This paper also shows a time dependence in the contact distribution, with different pattern distributions for the diurnal and night periods.

The goal of a correct characterization of the inter-contact times distribution is to improve the precision of the performance evaluations derived from these characterizations. For example, there are many analytical performance models that assume that the inter-contact times distribution between pairs of nodes are exponentially distributed with a given rate λ. For example, using a contact rate λ we can obtain the transmission delay and cost of several mobile protocols, such as epidemic routing protocols [4,14], and the impact of node selfishness on mobile networks [5,6,10]. The precision of the previous models clearly depends on how accurate is the estimation of the contact rate λ, which depends directly on the representativeness of the characterized distribution.

Previous works have studied the distribution of the inter-contact times by collecting data from real mobile network environments [2–4,9,15]. Some works have shown that the aggregate inter-contact times distribution is exponential with rate λ for both human and vehicle mobility scenarios [4,11,15]. The work in [3] analyzed some popular mobility traces and found that over 85% of the individual pair distributions fit an exponential distribution. Nevertheless, there is some controversy about whether this exponential distribution relates to real mobility patterns. Some empirical results have shown that the aggregate inter-contact times distribution follows a power-law distribution and has a long tail [2], meaning that some pairs of nodes barely experience any contact. In [1], it is shown that in a bounded domain, the inter-contact distribution is exponential, but in an unbounded domain the distribution is power-law. The dichotomy of this distribution is described in [9], which shows a truncated power law with exponential decay appearing in its tail after some cutoff point. A recent paper [12], presents the dependence between the *individual pair distributions* and the *aggregate distribution*. It is stated that, starting from exponentially *individual pair distributions*, the *aggregate distribution* is distributed according to a Pareto law. It also verifies the dichotomy property of the aggregate distribution analytically.

Summing up, most of the literature is based on the aggregate distribution, assuming that it is representative of the individual pair distribution [12]. The practical reason of using the aggregate distribution is that is a more convenient approach, since obtaining enough samples for each individual pair of contacts is not feasible. The practical approach for obtaining the contact rate λ is to assume that all individual pair distributions are similar so the contact rate of the aggregate distribution is similar to the individual pair distributions contact rates. Nevertheless, as shown in [12], these contact rates are only similar when the length of the contact trace is large. Therefore, we need another method to estimate this individual pair distribution (and the contact rate), feasible to measure and more statistically representative.

In this paper, we evaluate better methods to characterize the inter-contact times distribution presenting higher representativeness and, thus, increasing the precision of the results obtained. Using different characterization methods, three inter-contact time distributions are considered: *Aggregate Pairs* distribution, that is the *established characterization*; the *Aggregate Nodes* distribution, that is obtained as the aggregate of inter-contact distributions between one node and the rest of nodes; and the *Any Contact* distribution, that is the inter-contact distribution between any nodes. First, we study its statistical representativeness showing that, for the same trace length, the Aggregate Pairs distribution has a very low representativeness, especially when the number of nodes is high, in contrast with the others that have a good representativeness. Second, we study the relation between these distributions. We prove that, if all individual pair distributions are exponentially distributed, the *Aggregate Nodes* distribution is simply a new exponential distribution. This is not true for the *Aggregate Pairs* distribution, that depends on the distribution of each individual λ [12]. This conclusion is very important, because it allows to obtain in a more precise way the value of λ used in the analytical models.

Finally, we evaluate the precision of the three distributions using both synthetic and real contact traces. The precision is evaluated using a well known analytical model, the epidemic routing, that is based on a given exponential contact rate λ obtained from the three previous characterization methods. Experimental results confirm that the established *Aggregate Pairs* distribution is under-representative

t	n_1,n_2	d	t	n_1,n_2	d	t	n_1,n_2	d
1	(1,2)	2	7	(2,3)	4	14	(2,3)	2
2	(2,3)	3	7	(1,2)	6	17	(1,2)	3
2	(3,4)	2	7	(1,5)	3	20	(1,3)	6
5	(1,3)	5	8	(3,4)	5	20	(2,5)	2
5	(1,2)	1	11	(1,4)	4	-	-	-

Table 1: Contact trace sample. Note that a contact (n_1,n_2) means that both nodes have visibility of each other.

and, consequently, the precision of the results obtained using the epidemic routing model are imprecise. This precision is very low when the number of nodes of the evaluated network is high. Instead, the results using the *Aggregate Nodes* and *Any-Contact* distributions are much more precise, requiring significantly smaller contact traces.

The rest of the paper is organized as follows. We introduce the three methods for characterizing inter-contact times distributions evaluating its representativeness in Section 2. Section 3 study the relation between these distributions. The evaluation of the representativeness and precision of the different characterizations is described in Section 4. Finally, Section 5 presents some concluding remarks.

2. CHARACTERIZING INTER-CONTACT TIMES DISTRIBUTIONS

In this section we describe three possible methods for characterizing the inter-contact times distribution from a contact trace. Then, we study their representativeness by introducing some metrics and evaluating these metrics through some real traces.

A contact trace is obtained measuring the times when contacts between pairs of nodes occur for a given interval time T. The result is a trace of length $C(T)$ (that is, the number of contacts), where each record is a 4-tuple (t_i, a_i, b_i, d_i), reflecting, that at time $t_i \leq T$, there is a contact between the pair of nodes (a_i,b_i) with a duration of d_i seconds. A *contact* is defined as an opportunity of transmission between a pair of nodes (that is, two nodes are able to communicate between them directly for a given time). Based on this definition, for practical issues, there is only one record for each contact between a pair of nodes (a_i,b_i), and this contact is reciprocal (in other words, there is no another record with the (b_i,a_i) contact).

Using a contact trace, we can characterize the inter-contact times distribution. This distribution is influenced by the trace's duration and resolution [2]. The resolution is defined as the smallest interval between two successive measurements. Inter-contact times that last more or are close to the duration of the experiment, and inter-contact times that last less than the time resolution, cannot be observed.

For clarity of exposition, we are going to use a simple contact trace as exemplified in Table 1. This trace corresponds to a network of five nodes ($N = 5$), which has a duration T of 20 seconds, resulting in 14 contacts ($C(T) = 14$).

From a contact trace we can characterize three possible inter-contact distributions:

- *Aggregate Pairs* (AP) distribution: the aggregate of inter-contact times distributions between the same pair of nodes. This is the established characterization, usually known as simply *inter-contact times* distribution [2–4, 9, 15]. This distribution is obtained by aggregating the *individual pair inter-contact times* of all node pair combinations in the network. We need at least 2 contacts between the same pair of nodes in order to obtain an inter-contact time. For example, using our contact trace, for the pair (1,2) we have the following contact times[1]: {1,5,7,17} and so the inter-contacts time are {4,2,10}. We can also obtain the inter-contact times for the following pair of nodes: (1,3), (2,3) and (3,4); however, for the rest of pairs, this is not possible. By aggregating all the inter-contact times calculated for the previous pairs, we can obtain the aggregate pairs distribution.

- *Aggregate Nodes* (AN) distribution: the aggregate of inter-contact distributions between one node and the rest of nodes. For example, using the sample trace, we can obtain the contacts of node 1 with the other nodes: (1,x)={1,5,5,7,7,11,17,20}, so the inter-contact times are {4,0,2,0,4,6,3}. For this trace all nodes have contacts with other nodes. By aggregating all the inter-contact times we can obtain the aggregate nodes distribution.

- *Any Contact* (AC) distribution: inter-contact distribution between all nodes. This is known as the *inter-any-contact times* in [7]. In this case there is only one distribution of inter-contact times, which corresponds to the difference between two consecutive contacts. For our sample trace we have 13 inter-contact time values: {1,0,3,0,2,0,0,1,3,3,3,3,0}.

A key factor of a contact trace characterization is its representativeness. This representativeness depends on the trace length $C(T)$, the number of nodes N in the network, and the method. Two metrics are defined to measure this representativeness: the contact ratio R_C and the *average* number of measures per individual distribution M_C. These metrics are detailed below for each distribution.

For the aggregate pairs (AP) distribution, in a network of N nodes, the number of possible combinations of pair of nodes is $V = N \cdot (N-1)/2$. If we denote with $\mathcal{P}(t)$ the set of pairs of nodes that has at least two contacts up to time t, the contact ratio is $R_C = |\mathcal{P}(T)|/V$ (where $|\mathcal{P}(t)|$ is the size of $\mathcal{P}(t)$). For our sample trace, this ratio is $R_C = 4/10 = 0.4$. The average number of measures M_C is computed as the sum of all inter-contact times divided by the number of node pair combinations, that is,

$$M_C = \frac{1}{V} \sum_{p \in \mathcal{P}(T)} (C_p(T) - 1) \tag{1}$$

where $C_p(T)$ is the number of contacts between pairs of nodes $p \in \mathcal{P}(T)$. So, in our example, we have M_C=$(3+2+1+1)/10$=0.7.

In the aggregate nodes (AN) distribution, the contact ratio is: $R_C = |\mathcal{N}(T)|/N$, where $\mathcal{N}(t)$ is the set of nodes that has at least two contacts up to time t. For our sample trace, this ratio is $R_C = 5/5 = 1$. The average number of measures

	Cambridge	*Shanghai*
Type	Human	Vehicle
Device	iMote	GPS+GPRS
Network Type	Bluetooth	WiFi
Duration (hours)	274	24
Resolution (seconds)	120	60
Nodes	36	2288
Contacts (C)	21200	1262498
Repr. AP distribution		
Contact ratio (R_C)	0.81	0.04
Aver. measures (M_C)	16	0.08
Repr. AN distribution		
Contact ratio (R_C)	1	0.99
Aver. measures (M_C)	459	474
Repr. AC distribution		
Contact ratio (R_C)	1	1
Aver. measures (M_C)	21199	1262497

Table 2: Description of contact traces and representativeness.

M_C is computed as:

$$M_C = \frac{1}{N} \sum_{n \in \mathcal{N}(T)} (C_n(T) - 1) \tag{2}$$

where $C_n(T)$ is the number of contacts for each node $n \in \mathcal{N}(T)$. So, in our example, we have M_C=$(7+6+6+2+1)/5$=4.2.

Finally, in the any contact distribution (AC) the ratio is 1 (if $C(T) > 1$) and the number of measures is $C(T) - 1$.

As expected, we can see that the representativeness of the AP distribution is very low: a contact ratio of only 0.4 and less than one measure per pair of nodes. In the AN distribution the representativeness is greater: full contact ratio and a mean of 4.2 measures for each node. The greatest representativeness corresponds to the AC distribution which has a full ratio and the highest number of measures.

In general, for the same trace time T, the lower representativeness is for the AP distribution, and this representativeness (the values of R_C and M_C) is inversely proportional to V, that exhibits quadratic growth with N. Therefore, when the number of nodes is high, the representativeness is very low. For the AN distribution it representativeness is inversely proportional to the number of nodes N. And finally the best representativeness is for the AC distribution.

We study the representativeness of the previous distributions using some well known real contact traces (see Table 2). The *Cambridge* mobility set trace [8] was gathered from a set of undergraduate students from the University of Cambridge carrying small devices (iMotes) in 2005. This trace has a duration of 274 hours and has 36 mobile nodes (students)[2]. The *Shanghai* Taxis GPS Trace [15] was collected from 2100 taxis in Shanghai city during February of 2007[3]. This trace does not contains the contacts (it contains GPS locations), so a pre-process for obtaining the contact trace is needed. Following the method used in [15] we assume that a contact occurs if both vehicles are in WiFi range (100 meters).

[1]In this paper, the inter-contact time is computed as the difference between the starting times of two consecutive contacts. Another way to compute this time (see [2]) is to obtain the difference between the end of a contact and the start of the next one. In this case, the duration of the contact is used to obtain the inter-contact times.

[2]Although this trace has also static nodes we only evaluate the mobile nodes.

[3]The trace used in [15] is for 4 weeks. In this paper we use only the trace for one day, that it is the only available online.

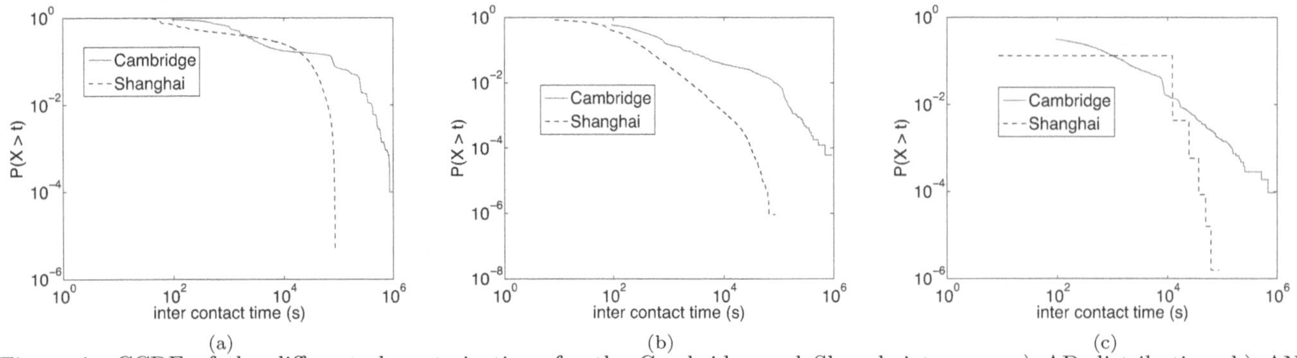

Figure 1: CCDF of the different characterizations for the Cambridge and Shanghai traces. a) AP distribution, b) AN distribution, c) AC distribution

Table 2 shows that in the Cambridge trace, which has only 36 nodes, the contact ratio for the AP distribution is high (although not 1) and the average number of measurements is relatively high. We can say that it has a moderate representativeness. Nevertheless, for the Shanghai trace, that has a high number of nodes, the AP distribution has a very low representativeness, so this characterization is not useful for obtaining information about the contact pattern on this network. For the AN distribution, both traces have a good representativeness (in terms of contact ratio and average measures). And finally, for the AC distribution, both traces have excellent representativeness (full ratio and the highest number of measures).

3. RELATION BETWEEN DISTRIBUTIONS

In this section we study the relation between the different distribution characterizations (AP, AN, AC). In order to study the inter-contact times distribution, the CCDF (Complementary Cumulative Distribution Function) is widely used [2, 9, 12]. The CCDF (also known as the *tail distribution*) is useful to study how often a random variable is above a particular level, that is, $\bar{F}(x) = P(X > x)$. So, first, we are going to introduce the relation between the different CCDFs. As we will show, if the individual pair distributions are not exponential we cannot obtain a simple relation between these distributions. Thus, we also study the relation between the average contact rates (λ) that are valid for any distribution.

3.1 Relation between CCDF

We can see in Figure 1 the CCDF of the different distributions for the Cambridge and Shanghai traces. In the CCDF for the AP characterization, we can clearly observe the dichotomy of the distribution: the inter-contact time follows a power-law decay up to a characteristic time (about $10^5 s \approx 12$ hours for the Cambridge set and $20000s \approx 6$ hours for the Shanghai set) and beyond this time, the decay is exponential. This confirms earlier studies [9, 15]. For the AN distribution, the previous dichotomy is not so evident, and it is clearer that it follows an exponential decay. Finally, for the AC distribution we can see an exponential decay. Note also the resolution issues in the Shanghai traces, where the inter-contact times are below the resolution time, and so its values are very discretized.

The relation between the CCDF of individual pair p ($\bar{F}_p(x)$) and the aggregate pairs CCDF ($\bar{F}_{AP}(x)$) for the AP distribution was established in [9] as:

$$\bar{F}_{AP}(x) = \sum_{p \in \mathcal{P}(T)} \frac{C_p(T) - 1}{C(T) - |\mathcal{P}(T)|} \bar{F}_p(x) \tag{3}$$

and when T tends to be large,

$$\bar{F}_{AP}(x) = \sum_{p \in \mathcal{P}} \frac{\lambda_p}{\Sigma \lambda_p} \bar{F}_p(x)) \tag{4}$$

where $1/\lambda_p$ is the average of inter-contact times for the pair p (in other words, λ_p is the average contact rate of the pair), and $\Sigma\lambda_p = \sum_{p \in \mathcal{P}} \lambda_p$. Expression 4 shows that the aggregate CCDF is equal to the weighted sum of individual CCDF with weight proportional to the rate of contacts λ_p. Furthermore, if all individual CCDF ($\bar{F}_p(x)$) are identical and the ratio of contacts (R_C) is assumed to be 1 (note that if $T \to \infty$ then $R_C \to 1$), then the aggregate CCDF and the individual CCDF are the same. Based on equation 4, when the individual distributions are different and exponentially distributed, we cannot obtain a simple relation between these distributions and the aggregate one. More information is needed about the distribution of the individual rates λ_p and, depending on this distribution, the aggregate distribution can follow an Exponential, Pareto, or Power Law with Exponential Decay distribution (see paper [12] for a detailed study about these relations).

In a similar way, we can establish a relation between the individual node n CCDF ($\bar{F}_n(x)$) and the aggregate nodes CCDF for the AN characterization:

$$\bar{F}_{AN}(x) = \sum_{n \in \mathcal{N}(T)} \frac{C_n(T) - 1}{C(T) - |\mathcal{N}(T)|} \bar{F}_n(x) = \sum_{n \in \mathcal{N}} \frac{\lambda_n}{\Sigma \lambda_n} \bar{F}_n(x) \tag{5}$$

where $1/\lambda_n$ is the mean value for the inter-contact times for node n, and $\Sigma\lambda_n = \sum_{n \in \mathcal{N}} \lambda_n$. If all individual CCDF ($\bar{F}_n(x)$) are identical and $R_C = 1$, then the aggregate CCDF is equal to the individual CCDF.

Now, we are going to study the relation between the three different distributions. Expressions 4 and 5 establish the relation between the aggregate distribution and the individual distributions. These expressions are derived on the basis that the aggregate distribution is obtained using the aggregation of the individual contact times.

First, we establish a relation between the AC distribution and the AP distribution, through the individual pair CCDF of the AP distribution ($\bar{F}_p(x)$). We can see that if a contact occurs at time t, the next contact time will be the minimum time of all possible contacts between pairs. That is, the minimum of the random variables associated with the individual distributions $F_p(x)$. So, we have:

$$\bar{F}_{AC}(x) = \min_{p \in \mathcal{P}(T)} \{F_p(x)\} \tag{6}$$

where min{} is the CCDF of the minimum of the random variables of the distributions. This minimum depends on the type of distribution. Fortunately, for exponential distributions, this expression is very simple. For n independent exponentially distributed random variables with rate parameters $\lambda_1, \ldots \lambda_n$, the minimum is also exponentially distributed with parameter $\lambda = \lambda_1 + \cdots + \lambda_n$. Then, if all distributions are exponentially distributed, the CCDF is also exponentially distributed:

$$\bar{F}_{AC}(x; \lambda_{AC}) = \bar{F}(x; \sum_{p \in \mathcal{P}(T)} \lambda_p) \tag{7}$$

were λ_{AC} is the contact rate of the AC distribution. We can see that this relation is more simple than expressions 4 and 5. Furthermore, it allows to obtain the average contact rate $\bar{\lambda}_p$ from λ_{AC}, when T tends to be large:

$$\lambda_{AC} = \sum_{p \in \mathcal{P}} \lambda_p \quad \rightarrow \quad \bar{\lambda}_p = \frac{\lambda_{AC}}{|\mathcal{P}|} = \frac{\lambda_{AC}}{\frac{1}{2}N(N-1)} \tag{8}$$

This relation is of special interest, as many analytical models based on Markov Chains use λ_p as the contact rate.

The relation between the AC distribution and the AN distribution is obtained in a similar way. If we use expression $\min_{n \in \mathcal{N}(T)} \{\bar{F}_n(x)\}$, we can see that for a given pair (a, b), $\bar{F}_n(x)$ is repeated twice, one for the first node on the pair $a \in p$, and another one for the second node of the pair $b \in p$. For the AC distribution the contacts are no longer repeated, and so we have:

$$\bar{F}_{AC}(x) = \frac{1}{2} \min_{n \in \mathcal{N}(T)} \{F_n(x)\} \tag{9}$$

Then, if all distributions are exponentially distributed, the CCDF is:

$$\bar{F}_{AC}(x; \lambda_{AC}) = \bar{F}(x; \frac{1}{2} \sum_{p \in \mathcal{N}(T)} \lambda_n) \tag{10}$$

Finally, we can obtain a similar relation between the individual distributions of the AP and AN distributions. For a node n, when a contact occurs at time t, the next contact time will be the minimum time of all contacts between pairs p that have node n. So, we have:

$$\bar{F}_n(x) = \min_{p \in \mathcal{P}(T) \wedge n \in p} \{F_p(x)\} \tag{11}$$

If all distributions are exponential distributed, the CCDF is:

$$\bar{F}_n(x; \lambda_n) = \bar{F}(x; \sum_{p \in \mathcal{P}(T) \wedge n \in p} \lambda_p) \tag{12}$$

In conclusion, we have shown that the AN and AC distributions have a simpler relation with the individual pair distribution than the previous AP distribution. Furthermore, if the individual pair distributions are exponentially distributed, the AN and AC distributions are also exponentially distributed. This fact confirms the exponential shapes shown in Figure 1.

3.2 Relation between Contact Rates

In this section we study the relation between the contact rates of the different characterizations, based on the individual contact rates. The following relations are valid for all types of distributions.

The relation between the average contact rate of the AC distribution (λ_{AC}) and the average contact rates of individual pair of nodes (λ_p) is obtained as follows[4]. For large values of T, the number of contacts generated up to time T in the AC distribution is $T \cdot \lambda_{AC}$. This number of contacts must be the same as the number of contacts for all pair of nodes p in the AP distribution. These contacts are obtained as the sum of the contacts of all pairs p. Thus, making equal both expressions and removing T on both parts, we have:

$$\lambda_{AC} = \sum_{p \in \mathcal{P}(T)} \lambda_p \tag{13}$$

The relation between λ_{AC} and the individual node contact rate λ_n is obtained in a similar way.

$$\lambda_{AC} = \frac{1}{2} \sum_{n \in \mathcal{N}(T)} \lambda_n \tag{14}$$

Note that in the previous expression we take into account repeated pair of nodes, as detailed for expression 9.

Now, we can obtain the relation between the average contact rate of the AP distribution λ_{AP} and λ_p. The number of contacts generated for each λ_p is $T \cdot \lambda_p$, so the total number of contacts is $T \cdot \sum_{p \in \mathcal{P}(T)} \lambda_p$. Note that this number of contacts must be equal to the number of contacts for the AP aggregate distribution, that depends on the number of pairs and its rate: $T|\mathcal{P}(T)|\lambda_{AP}$. Thus, making equal both expressions and simplifying, we have:

$$\lambda_{AP} = \frac{\sum_{p \in \mathcal{P}(T)} \lambda_p}{|\mathcal{P}(T)|} \tag{15}$$

Finally, the relation between the average contact rate for the AN distribution λ_{AN} and λ_n is obtained in a similar way:

$$\lambda_{AN} = \frac{\sum_{n \in \mathcal{N}(T)} \lambda_n}{|\mathcal{N}(T)|} \tag{16}$$

That is, the contact rate of the aggregate distribution is equal to the mean of the individual contact rates.

Combining expressions 13 and 15 we can obtain the relation between λ_{AP} and λ_{AC}, for T large enough, as:

$$\lambda_{AP} = \frac{\lambda_{AC}}{|\mathcal{P}(T)|} = \frac{\lambda_{AC}}{\frac{1}{2}N(N-1)} \tag{17}$$

and expressions 16 and 14:

$$\lambda_{AN} = \frac{2\lambda_{AC}}{|\mathcal{N}(T)|} = \frac{2\lambda_{AC}}{N} \tag{18}$$

and from expressions 17 and 18 we have:

$$\lambda_{AN} = (N-1)\lambda_{AP} \tag{19}$$

[4]Abusing notation, we denote the average contact rate using λ. This does not imply that the distributions must be exponential.

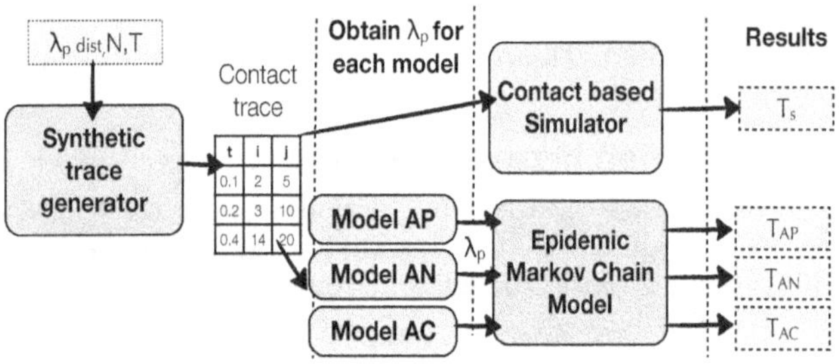

Figure 2: The evaluation process.

As a corollary, we can see, that if all λ_p values are equal, then $\lambda_{AP} = \lambda_p$, $\lambda_n = (N-1)\lambda_p$, and $\lambda_{AN} = \lambda_n$.

From the previous relations two important conclusions can be drawn. First, if the individual inter-contact times distribution between pairs of nodes is exponentially distributed, we can obtain the average λ in a simple way, using expressions 8 and 10. Since AN and AC distributions are more statistically representative than the AP distribution for the same contact trace time T, the value of λ obtained using these distributions will be more precise. Second, based on the relation between contact rates, we can also obtain the average contact rate between pairs of nodes, using the more representative AN and AC distributions.

4. EXPERIMENTAL EVALUATION

In previous sections we have studied the representativeness of the different distributions and the relation between them. We showed that the average node (AN) distribution, and especially the any contact (AC) distribution has better statistical representativeness that the widely established aggregate pairs (AP) distribution.

Now, we are going to evaluate the precision of these distributions. There are many analytical performance models that assume that the inter-contact times distribution between pairs of nodes is exponentially distributed [4, 10, 14, 15]. This fact allows using the contact rate λ in Markovian models. We use the model for the Epidemic Routing as a way to evaluate the precision of the different distributions. Specifically, the model we use, based on Markov chain models, was introduced in [4] for obtaining the average source-to-destination delivery delay ($T_d = E[T]$). This model assumes a unique contact rate λ between all pair of nodes and full probability of transmission when a contact occurs. So, all individual pair distributions must be equal and exponentially distributed with mean λ_p. As shown in section 3, when assuming the previous condition we have that:

$$\lambda_p = \lambda_{AP} = \frac{\lambda_{AN}}{N-1} = \frac{\lambda_{AC}}{\frac{1}{2}N(N-1)} \tag{20}$$

so λ_p can be estimated using any of the previous distributions.

The process for evaluating the distributions is the following (see Figure 2). We synthetically generate a contact trace for a given time T with inter-contact times between pairs of nodes that are exponentially distributed with a contact rate λ_p. This contact trace is used to estimate three different contact rates $\hat{\lambda}_p$ from the different contact rates of the distributions (λ_{AP},λ_{AN},λ_{AC}) using expression 20. Then, using the different $\hat{\lambda}_p$ generated for each distribution (AP,AN,AC) we can obtain the delivery time using the Markov model for epidemic routing. For validation purposes, we also implemented a custom simulator. This simulator reads the contact trace and simulates the transmission of a message between a randomly selected pair of nodes in the network. The simulation finishes when the message reaches the destination node. This evaluation is repeated 1000 times (that is, 1000 different traces are generated) in order to obtain a mean value. We also obtain the ratio of contacts on the simulator, that is similar to the ratio of contacts (R_C) obtained for evaluating the representativeness of the distributions. In case a simulation ends without the message being delivered to the destination node, we count this as a miss, and when the experiments end, we obtain the delivery ratio as $(1000 - misses)/1000$.

In the real trace experiments the process is very similar, except that in this case we used a real traffic trace as the input of the model and simulator. In order to evaluate the precision of the different distributions depending on the duration of the traffic trace, the original traffic trace is trimmed from T ranging from 0 to the maximum duration (that is, only the contacts with time $t \leq T$ are used). Finally, although the traffic trace is always the same, the simulation is repeated 1000 times, varying the pair of selected sender and destination nodes of the network.

4.1 Synthetic traces

The following experiments used synthetic traces as a way to validate the conclusions derived about representativeness and precision in sections 2 and 3. In Figure 3a we show the delivery delay time for the different distributions calculated using a synthetic trace with time T ranging from 1 to 200s that was generated assuming that all inter-contact times distributions between pairs are exponentially distributed with the same contact rate $\lambda_p = 0.1$ (that is, all distributions are homogeneous).

We can see that AN and AC distributions obtains the best results, converging very fast to the simulation results (for example, for $T = 200s$, the delay obtained through simulation is 0.918s and the delays obtained using the AN and AC distributions are the same: 0.905s, a relative error of 1.42%). Instead, the AP converges to the simulation results very slowly. As expected, these results clearly depend on the representativeness of the different distributions as shown in Figure 3b. The AP contact ratio is very low for a reduced trace time (T), reaching 1 for $T = 100$. Nevertheless, for this trace time the average number of measures is still very reduced ($M_C = 9.6$ is for $T = 100$ in the AP distribution compared to $M_C = 765.86$ in the AN distribution), so the precision is also low. Thus, as expected, the conclusions are clear, the most precise characterizations are the Aggregate Nodes (AN) and Any Contact (AC) distributions.

In the following experiment we study the case of heterogeneous exponential distributions. We generate a synthetic contact trace with the contact times between pair of nodes exponentially distributed, where the contact rate λ_p is also exponentially distributed with mean 0.1. The delay of a message using epidemic transmission is shown in Figure 3c. In this case we can see that the delay obtained using the AC and AN distribution is very precise (a relative error of 2.34% for $T = 200s$). Nevertheless, the delay obtained for the AP distribution converges to the solution very low. The reason is that, for an heterogeneous distribution the representative-

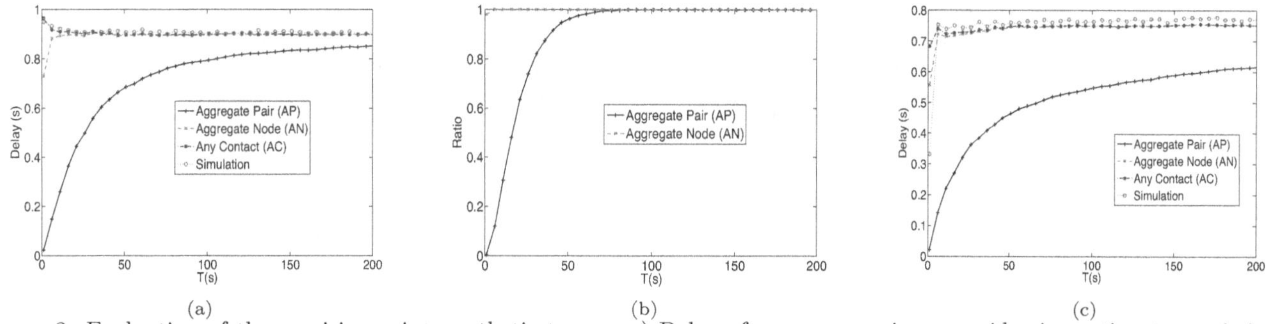

Figure 3: Evaluation of the precision using synthetic traces. a) Delay of a message using an epidemic routing transmission with an homogeneous trace, b) Contact ratio of the homogeneous trace (R_C), c) Delay with an heterogeneous trace

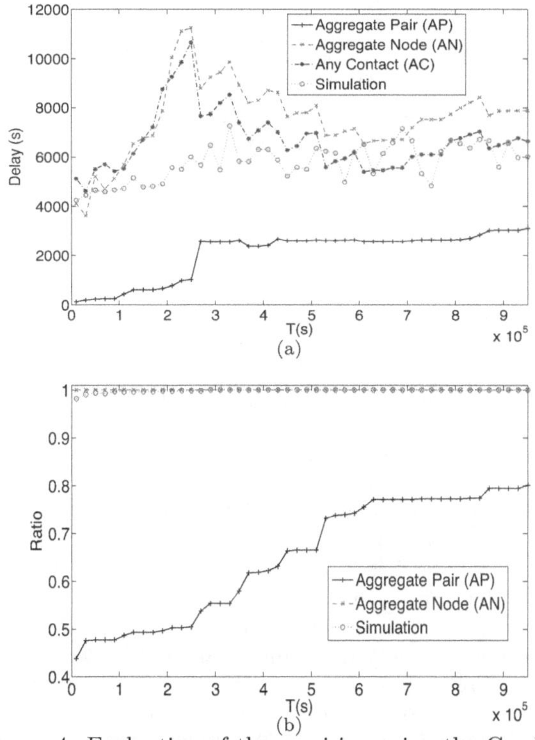

Figure 4: Evaluation of the precision using the Cambridge traces. a) Delay of a message using an epidemic transmission, b) Contact ratio (R_C).

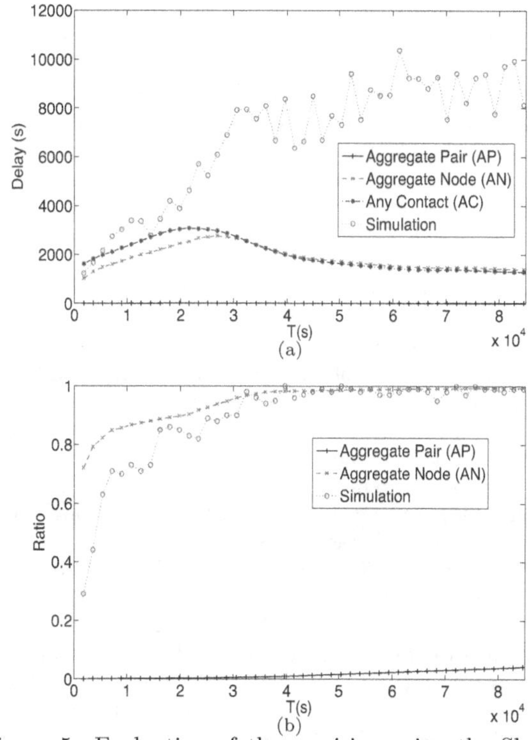

Figure 5: Evaluation of the precision using the Shanghai traces. a) Delay of a message using an epidemic transmission, b) Contact ratio (R_C).

ness of the AP distribution is lower than in the homogeneous case (for example, for $T = 200s$, $R_C = 0.92$ and $M_C = 23$). The rate of contact reaches 1 for approximately $T = 2000s$ with $M_C = 233$, and a relative error of 7.24%.

4.2 Real traces

We now, evaluate the precision of the different distributions using real traffic traces.

Figure 4 shows the results for the Cambridge trace depending on the duration T (that is, a trimmed traffic trace with duration T). Regarding the delay, the results obtained using the AC and AN distributions are close to the simulation results. There is a strong time dependence of this trace (the sawtooth shape), due to the high difference between contact rates in diurnal and night periods. Regarding the AP distribution, the precision increases as the contact ratio also increases (see Figure 4b), but it is very far of the results obtained using the other distributions.

Figure 5 shows the results for the Shanghai traffic traces. In this case, the delay obtained using the AN and AC distributions for traffic trace length T less than 20000 (about 5 hours) are close to the simulation ones, although the results for greater values of T show a higher error. The results using the AP distribution are quite poor, due to the low representativeness of this distribution (see Figure 5b). We can also observe how the contact ratio of the simulation is low for values less than 10000s, so the representativeness of the simulation is also low.

The conclusions drawn from the previous experiments for the AN and AC distributions are clear: the greater the contact trace duration, the lesser the precision. This is mainly due to the long-tail behaviour of the inter-contact times distribution between the same pair of nodes. If the duration of the trace is high (days in the case of Cambridge, or hours in the case of Shanghai), the probability of contact between some reduced number of pair of nodes is very low, so its inter-contact time is very high. In other words, the greater the duration of the trace, the greater the tail of the distribution[5].

We repeated the previous experiments using other performance models (such as the Two Hop multicopy protocol, and a more sophisticated model for evaluating the selfish detection introduced by the authors [6]), obtaining similar results in terms of precision.

5. CONCLUSIONS

In this paper we introduced new approaches to characterize the inter-contact times distribution in order to increase the representativeness, and thus the precision of the analytical performance models based on these distributions.

We have seen that the established characterization, the Aggregate Pairs (AP) distribution, has a very low representativeness especially when the number of nodes is high. This leads to poor results when applied to analytical models (such as the Epidemic routing). Therefore, we introduced and evaluated two alternative methods for characterizing the inter-contact times distribution: the Aggregate Nodes (AN) and Any-Contact (AC). The resulting distributions have an excellent representativeness for shorter trace durations. We also obtained a simple relation between the individual contact rate and the contact rate for the AP and AN distributions. Thus, we can use these distributions in order to obtain the individual pair contact rate used in analytical models.

The experiments confirm, that the representativeness and precision achieved using these new distributions is high. Using synthetic and real traces we showed that the Aggregate Nodes (AN) and Any-Contact (AC) distributions are more precise than the Aggregate Pairs (AP) distribution. Finally, regarding which distribution (AP or AC) choose, we found that the AC distribution is able to provide better results for very low trace sizes. However, when the number of contacts is moderately large, the results for both distributions are very similar.

Acknowledgments

This work was partially supported by the *Ministerio de Ciencia e Innovación*, Spain, under Grant TIN2011-27543-C03-01.

6. REFERENCES

[1] H. Cai and D. Y. Eun. Crossing over the bounded domain: From exponential to power-law intermeeting time in mobile ad hoc networks. *IEEE/ACM Trans. on Networking*, , 17(5):1578 –1591, oct. 2009.

[2] A. Chaintreau, P. Hui, J. Crowcroft, C. Diot, R. Gass, and J. Scott. Impact of human mobility on opportunistic forwarding algorithms. *IEEE Trans. on Mobile Computing*, 6:606–620, June 2007.

[3] W. Gao, Q. Li, B. Zhao, and G. Cao. Multicasting in delay tolerant networks: a social network perspective. In *Proceedings of the tenth ACM international symposium on Mobile ad hoc networking and computing*, MobiHoc '09, pages 299–308, 2009. ACM.

[4] R. Groenevelt, P. Nain, and G. Koole. The message delay in mobile ad hoc networks. *Performance Evaluation*, 62:210–228, October 2005.

[5] E. Hernández-Orallo, M. D. Serrat, J.-C. Cano, C. M. T. Calafate, and P. Manzoni. Improving selfish node detection in MANETs using a collaborative watchdog. *IEEE Communications Letters*, 16(5):642–645, 2012.

[6] E. Hernández-Orallo, M. D. Serrat Olmos, J.-C. Cano, C. T. Calafate, and P. Manzoni. Evaluation of collaborative selfish node detection in MANETS and DTNs. In *Proceedings of the 15th ACM international conference on Modeling, analysis and simulation of wireless and mobile systems*, MSWiM '12, pages 159–166, 2012. ACM.

[7] P. Hui, A. Chaintreau, J. Scott, R. Gass, J. Crowcroft, and C. Diot. Pocket switched networks and human mobility in conference environments. In *Proceedings of the 2005 ACM SIGCOMM workshop on Delay-tolerant networking*, WDTN '05, pages 244–251, 2005. ACM.

[8] P. Hui, J. Crowcroft, and E. Yoneki. Bubble rap: social-based forwarding in delay tolerant networks. In *Proceedings of the 9th ACM international symposium on Mobile ad hoc networking and computing*, MobiHoc '08, pages 241–250, 2008. ACM.

[9] T. Karagiannis, J.-Y. Le Boudec, and M. Vojnović. Power law and exponential decay of inter contact times between mobile devices. In *Proceedings of the 13th annual ACM international conference on Mobile computing and networking*, MobiCom '07, pages 183–194, 2007. ACM.

[10] M. Karaliopoulos. Assessing the vulnerability of dtn data relaying schemes to node selfishness. *IEEE Communications Letters*, 13(12):923–925, dec 2009.

[11] Y. Li, G. Su, D. Wu, D. Jin, L. Su, and L. Zeng. The impact of node selfishness on multicasting in delay tolerant networks. *IEEE Trans. on Vehicular Technology*, 60(5):2224 –2238, jun 2011.

[12] A. Passarella and M. Conti. Characterising aggregate inter-contact times in heterogeneous opportunistic networks. In *Proceedings of the 10th international IFIP TC 6 conference on Networking*, Networking'11, pages 301–313, 2011. Springer-Verlag.

[13] A. Passarella, M. Conti, C. Boldrini, and R. I. Dunbar. Modelling inter-contact times in social pervasive networks. In *Proceedings of the 14th ACM international conference on Modeling, analysis and simulation of wireless and mobile systems*, MSWiM '11, pages 333–340, 2011. ACM.

[14] X. Zhang, G. Neglia, J. Kurose, and D. Towsley. Performance modeling of epidemic routing. *Computer Networks*, 51(10):2867 – 2891, 2007.

[15] H. Zhu, L. Fu, G. Xue, Y. Zhu, M. Li, and L. M. Ni. Recognizing exponential inter-contact time in VANETs. In *Proceedings of the 29th conference on Information communications*, INFOCOM'10, pages 101–105, 2010. IEEE Press.

[5]Note that we are studying the average behaviour, thus, if we made a good estimate of the tail distribution, it can led to wrong average results

A Novel Scheduling Algorithm for Densely-Deployed Wireless Stations in Urban Areas

Hirozumi Yamaguchi
Graduate School of IST,
Osaka University
Suita, Osaka, Japan

Akihito Hiromori
Graduate School of IST,
Osaka University
Suita, Osaka, Japan

Teruo Higashino
Graduate School of IST,
Osaka University
Suita, Osaka, Japan

Shigeki Umehara
Sumitomo Electric Industries, LTD.
Osaka, Japan

Hirofumi Urayama
Sumitomo Electric Industries, LTD.
Osaka, Japan

Masaya Yamada
Sumitomo Electric Industries, LTD.
Osaka, Japan

Taka Maeno
Space-Time Engineering Japan, Inc.
Tokyo, Japan

Shigeru Kaneda
Space-Time Engineering, LLC.
Los Angeles, CA, USA

Mineo Takai
University of California, Los Angeles
Los Angeles, CA, USA

ABSTRACT

This paper presents a scheduling algorithm for a set of wireless stations such as road-side access points for vehicular networks and outdoor WiFi stations, which are deployed in wide urban areas and may compete with each other for limited wireless resources. Different from a number of conventional approaches most of which consider detailed information on individual stations and signal interference among them, we focus more on geography of the areas of interest, and provide a novel algorithm that pursues the best balance among (i) optimality of resource utilization, (ii) robustness to new station installation and traffic demand, and (iii) scalability to the population of stations and area size. We have confirmed the performance by experimental simulations with several scenarios, and the applicability of approach has been testified by a case study on a scheduling problem for roadside access points of vehicular networks in cooperation with a manufacturing corporation.

Categories and Subject Descriptors

C.2.1 [**Computer-Communication Networks**]: Network Architecture and Design—*Wireless communication*

Keywords

Resource allocation, wireless communication, scheduling

1. INTRODUCTION

Nowadays, a number of short range wireless stations are covering urban areas. For instance, outdoor public Wi-Fi access points (APs) have been deployed by AT&T, Time Warner Cable etc. to offload smartphone 3G or 4G traffic in large cities of US. In Japan, high-traffic volume in 3G cellular networks is the most critical issue, and KDDI has already launched Wi-Fi services for cellular subscribers. For Intelligent Transport Systems (ITS), installation of DSRC (Dedicated Short-Range Communication) road-side units at intersections and on highways and city streets has been started in Japan for vehicle collision warning, local traffic information broadcast and so on. Those APs or road-side units, which we call *stations* hereafter, are usually densely-deployed to accommodate more clients. However, dense deployment of stations may cause severe and undesired wireless interference among them.

A number of studies have been dedicated to resolve wireless interference problems in a variety of networks such as cellular networks, wireless mesh networks (WMNs) and wireless sensor networks (WSNs). In these approaches, scheduling algorithms have been proposed to reuse the wireless resources (either of time slots or wireless channels). That is, a channel or a time slot is concurrently used by two or more stations if they do not interfere with each other. In cellular networks, systematic resource allocation to hexagonal cells is a well-studied topic [17]. In WMNs or general wireless multi-hop networks, link scheduling is designed based on given network topology or interference graphs, and routing performance is often considered simultaneously [6].

However, most of these methods consider scheduling for individual stations and thus scalability and robustness issues may not be solved in urban scenarios. Firstly, it is quite expensive to gather interference information from a number of stations in city-wide areas. Therefore, some conventional link-based scheduling may not scale to the number of stations and size of the areas. Furthermore, some may not be robust to new station installation and traffic demand changes. Even for rapid growth of station population and traffic volume, we would like to maintain the current allocation since it is also expensive to reallocate resources to a number of stations.

MSWiM'13, November 3–8, 2013, Barcelona, Spain.

ACM 978-1-4503-2353-6/13/11$15.00.
http://dx.doi.org/10.1145/2507924.2507939.

In this paper, we deal with a scheduling problem of wireless stations in urban areas. We assume densely-deployed stations like outdoor Wi-Fi APs and road-side stations, which are subject to location changes, new station installation and so on. In order to allocate limited resources efficiently to a number of stations in a robust and scalable manner, we employ not a station-based but cell-based scheduling and provide a near-optimal algorithm. In the algorithm, we divide the area of interest by cells, and estimate "inter-cell interference", which is an abstract representation of multiple (and potential) interference relationships among stations in cells. It hides minor difference of signal propagation among individual stations and allows us to focus more on intrinsic features of interference that are often seen in urban environment, *e.g.*, signal propagation is tend to be directional along streets. Based on this feature, we propose a novel cell-based algorithm called *Vector-based Cell Cover (VCC)*. VCC first extracts a Common Interference Pattern (CIP) among cells and achieves near-optimal resource allocation. Then it considers irregular part and irregular traffic demand to finalize the allocation of resources to each station. Since the derived resource allocation rule is fully based on cell locations, resources can be allocated to stations without consulting the other allocations. This feature provides robustness to new station installation and traffic demand changes, as well as scalability to the population of stations and area size. We also pursue optimality of resource utilization by the CIP-based sub-algorithm, which is designed based on a vector space theory with correctness proof.

Experiments by simulations have been conducted to observe the performance. Compared with a heuristic approach that is tuned to achieve reasonable optimality using all the detailed inter-station interference information, the proposed VCC algorithm could achieve much better utilization of wireless resources while achieving robustness to new station installation. Furthermore, in cooperation with Sumitomo Electric Industries, the algorithm is applied to a real world scenario where TDMA scheduling of road-side units is required for I2V (Infrastructure-to-Vehicle) wireless communication. Our algorithm could achieve desired time slot scheduling satisfying constraints on bandwidth limitation in the designated frequency (*i.e.* 760MHz$\pm$5MHz band).

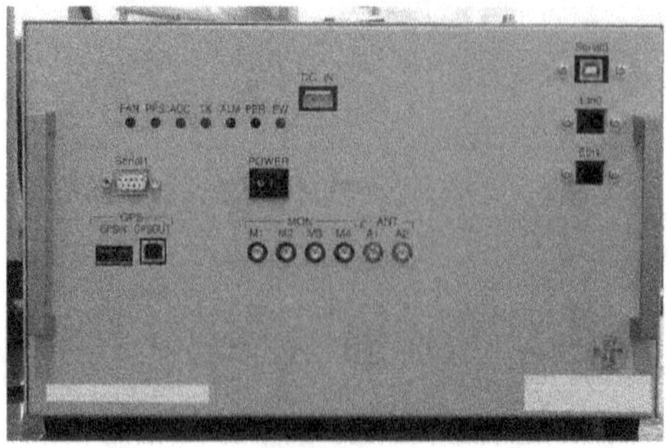

(a) Roadside Unit (Product by Sumitomo Electric Industries)

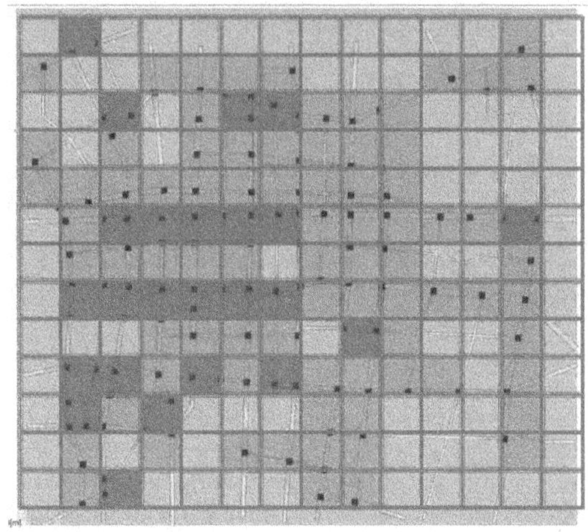

(b) Cells on Osaka Downtown Road-map

Figure 1: Roadside Unit (RSU) and Deployment Scenario in Osaka

2. RELATED WORK

A number of research contributions have been dedicated to manage and schedule radio frequencies in cellular networks. For example, Fractional Frequency Reuse (FFR), which allocates different frequencies to users around cell boundaries and the same frequency to those near base stations, has been developed so far. Ref. [7] has evaluated how the FFR increased the overall network capacity in rural environments. Our method has some similarity with those approaches in terms of cell-based resource scheduling, but most of them do not consider arbitrary, complex inter-cell interference in urban areas, and hence it is difficult to directly apply them to our case.

Network coordination is a well-known technique for spatial reuse of spectrum. For example, [10, 11] organize base stations into clusters to handle them as a single network antenna array. Interference is eliminated in the clusters since clients receive the same signal from all the base stations. However, such coordination requires a large amount of effort to collect information and to synchronize the stations, which is not applicable to densely-deployed large-scale networks. In uncoordinated environment, Jindal et al. [9] have formulated the problem of determining required slots to keep high spectrum efficiency and low interference, and have analyzed the network performance with different ratios of time-frequency resources and area resources. In addition, Ref. [15] has proposed a method to adjust slots and transmission power according to spatial channel characteristics of users in a distributed manner.

To avoid interference between communicating nodes, TDMA scheduling for wireless networks have been widely investigated so far [4, 12]. For example, Wang et al. [16] have proposed a TDMA scheduling method for wireless multihop networks. Ref. [8] has shown that complete knowledge of the interference environment can contribute to improvement of network capacity in Spatial reuse TDMA (STDMA) scheduling. Brar et al. [5] have proposed a polynomial algorithm for STDMA scheduling in wireless mesh networks. These STDMA scheduling techniques are similar to those for cellular networks in the context that they exploit geographical information. However, like the cellular network based allocation, only simple interference patterns (usually range-based interference) are allowed and therefore it is not suitable to our case.

In the technical aspect, the most relevant approach is the recent work in Ref. [2], where a slot scheduling problem for

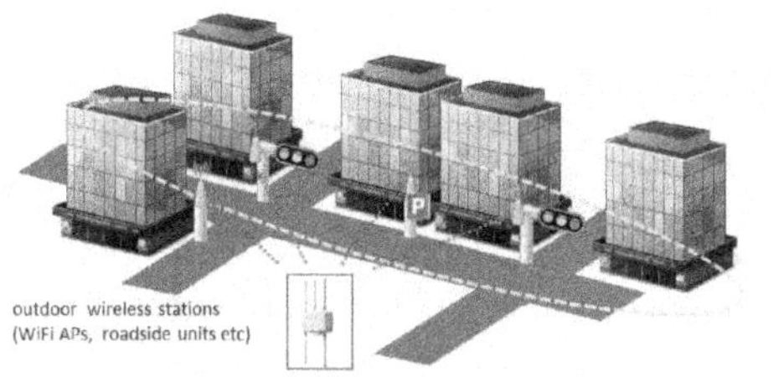

Figure 2: Typical Wireless Station Installation in Urban Scenario

wireless networks is formulated as a coloring problem. They employ the vector model to represent a periodic pattern, which we also use in this paper. However, it is quite different from our approach in the sense that we provide an algorithm that deals with arbitrary interference, stations, and geography, while only grid alignment of nodes is considered in [2]. We have also confirmed the effectiveness of our approach by a real world problem.

3. PROBLEM STATEMENT

3.1 Example Scenarios

An example scenario is channel management of public, outdoor WiFi stations in urban scenarios. Recently, the number of public WiFi APs is rapidly growing to accommodate more users in different areas, and those APs may compete for the limited number of 2.4GHz/5.2GHz channels. Therefore, efficient and global channel utilization policy depending on location is more preferable than relying only on channel adaptation mechanisms of local stations. A similar situation can be found in road-side station (or road-side unit (RSU)) management in Intelligent Transport Systems (ITS) [3]. Fig. 1(a) shows an RSU control unit, which is a wireless station to deliver/collect messages to/from vehicles. RSUs are usually installed at intersections, and the vehicles within 250m distance from the intersection are intended to communicate with RSU to notify the other vehicles' presence for collision warning or congestion information of nearby intersections for traffic-aware adaptive route selection. As seen in Section 5.2, each RSU may interfere with the others within around 1km range, and 10 or more intersections are included in the range in large cities of Japan. In order to provide the ITS services with severe bandwidth limitation, we need an efficient resource management scheme. For an Osaka downtown region, we show in Fig. 1(b) an RSU installation plan by Sumitomo Electric Industries [1], which is the top ITS system provider in Japan. In this figure, each red cell contains two or more RSUs (represented by small blue squares) and light-red and transparent cells have one and no RSUs, respectively.

The common feature of these scenarios is that stations are placed widely in urban area and they interfere with each other as illustrated in Fig. 2. Again, we consider the following two important requirements. (i) Allocations must be "robust" to environmental changes and "scalable" to the areas of interest. Such changes may be caused by installation/removal of new/existing stations and variance of traffic demand. Scalability is also a significant factor to deal with wide areas containing a number of stations. (ii) Resource allocation must be as optimal as possible.

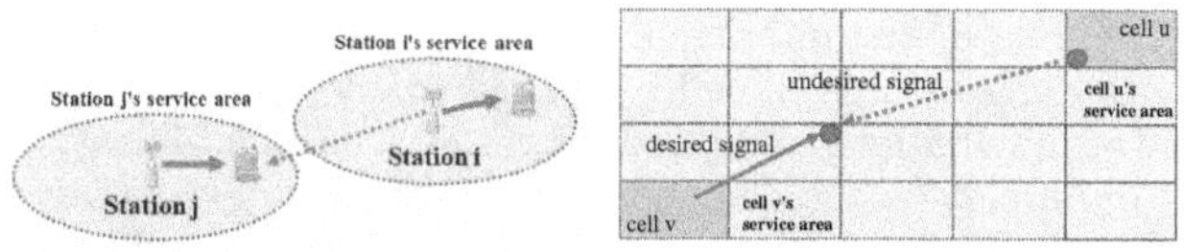

(a) Station Interference (b) Cell Interference

Figure 3: Interference Example

3.2 Problem Formulation

A wireless system consists of sets of stations and (mobile) clients, which are denoted as S and M, respectively. Each client may access to network services through a station and its back-haul. We assume that each station has its own service area, and clients in its service area are associated with the station. We would like to guarantee the clients' network performance by mitigating interference from the other stations. Fig. 3(a) illustrates this situation where solid and dotted lines represent propagation of desired radio signal and undesired (interference) radio signal, respectively. Station i interferes with a client of station j in the service area of station j. We let $\mathcal{I}_S : S \rightarrow 2^S$ denote *inter-station interference relation* where 2^S is the power-set of S. For stations i and j, $j \in \mathcal{I}_S(i)$ means that transmission of radio signal from i interferes with communication between station j and its clients if i and j use the same resource(s).

We let R denote a set of wireless resources (usually channels or time slots and simply called *resources*). Depending on traffic volume or for other reasons, each station s may require one or more resources for communication with their clients and the number of resources requested by station s is denoted as $reqs_S(s)$ ($\leq |R|$).

3.2.1 Conventional Resource Allocation Problem

A conventional resource allocation problem is often defined as a problem of minimizing the number of resources allocated to the stations. That is, for given sets of S and R with $\mathcal{I}_S(s)$ and $reqs_S(s)$ for each $s \in S$, the problem is to find such an allocation $\mathcal{A}_S : S \rightarrow 2^R$ that satisfies

$$\min |\bigcup_{i \in S} \mathcal{A}_S(i)| \quad (1)$$

subject to:

$$\forall i, j \in S;\ \mathcal{A}_S(i) \cap \mathcal{A}_S(j) \neq \emptyset \Rightarrow j \notin \mathcal{I}_S(i) \wedge i \notin \mathcal{I}_S(j) \quad (2)$$

$$\forall i \in S;\ reqs_S(i) \leq |\mathcal{A}_S(i)| \quad (3)$$

(2) guarantees that for any pair of stations that share the same resource there is no interference and (3) satisfies the resource request by each station.

3.2.2 Our Case

Our approach does not directly collect inter-station interference $\mathcal{I}_S$. Instead, we divide the area of interest into a set C of (rectangle) cells. Then we define the service area of stations in each cell as a set of cells, and examine *inter-cell interference relation* denoted as $\mathcal{I}_C : C \rightarrow 2^C$. We say that for a pair of cells u and v, $v \in \mathcal{I}_C(u)$ *iff* there is *at least* a pair of locations in cells u and v such that one station at the location of cell u may interfere with a client at the location in the service area of cell v. In Fig. 3(b), we may examine (or simulate) the interference at the closest point of cell u to the service area of cell v. We do not need to deal with individual stations and interference. We consider allocation of resources to each cell and later we further allocate these resources to the stations in the cell.

Then we formulate a cell-based resource allocation problem as follows. For given set C of cells and set R of resources with inter-cell interference $\mathcal{I}_C(u)$ and resource request $req_C(u)$ which is the number of resources requested by all the stations in a cell, the problem is to find such an allocation $\mathcal{A}_C : C \rightarrow 2^R$ that satisfies

$$\min |\bigcup_{u \in C} \mathcal{A}_C(u)| \quad (4)$$

subject to:

$$\forall u, v \in C; \ \ \mathcal{A}_C(u) \cap \mathcal{A}_C(v) \neq \emptyset \Rightarrow v \notin \mathcal{I}_C(c) \wedge u \notin \mathcal{I}_C(v) \quad (5)$$

$$\forall u \in C; \ \ req_C(u) \leq |\mathcal{A}_C(u)| \quad (6)$$

$$req_C(u) = \bigcup_{s \in u} req_S(s) \quad (7)$$

(5) and (6) correspond to (2) and (3), respectively. (7) is the definition of $req_C(u)$. Different from the conventional resource allocation in Section 3.2.1, our approach does not use information about stations or clients. We use $\mathcal{I}_C$ instead of $\mathcal{I}_S$ and consider resource allocation on the cells. Here the technical challenge is that by exploiting the merit from this cell-based abstraction, we have to pursue optimality, scalability and robustness as addressed earlier. We continue to discuss this issue in the following section.

3.3 Algorithm Overview and Example

For the problem in Section 3.2.2, we propose a centralized algorithm that obtains allocation $\mathcal{A}_C$. It has the following nice features.

1. [optimality] Although $\mathcal{A}_C$ may not be optimal in general, it approaches to the near optimal one as cells have more "similar interference patterns" with each other. If the patterns are identical among cells, then the solution is very close to the optimal one.
2. [scalability] It is scalable in terms of the number of stations and area size, since our algorithm derives a rule that uniquely determines resource allocation based on cell locations. This facilitates to manage resources allocated to a number of stations deployed over wide area.
3. [robustness] It is robust to increase/decrease of stations and traffic demand. Since a cell-location-based allocation rule is derived, adding additional resources to a cell does not affect the other stations in other cells.

To achieve these features, we first try to extract interference pattern that is common to "most" of the cells (this is called *common interference pattern* (or "CIP" in short). For instance, in conventional cellular networks, a distance-based interference model is often employed [7]. This may create CIP illustrated as orange cells in Fig. 4(a). Besides, we consider urban scenarios where stations are installed along streets or at intersections and they may have similar wireless propagation characteristics due to reflection on the surface of buildings and streets and diffraction by buildings. Assuming the propagation model in ITU-R P.1411-1 recommendation [13] in which radio signal from a source is likely to propagate along streets, each cell may have CIP as illustrated in Fig. 4(b) with some irregular part. In this figure, due to characteristics of propagation in urban area, most cells interfere with those in the orthogonal directions as well as its neighbors. We may extract these parts as CIP (red cells in Fig. 4(b)) and handle the rest of the cells as "irregular part" (blue cells).

Our algorithm can handle "any" patterns of interference as both CIP and irregular part. An allocation example is shown in Fig. 4(c) and Fig. 4(d) (both show the same allocation) where all the cells have CIP of Fig. 4(b) and the numbers in cells are the resource IDs. In Fig. 4(c), it can be seen that resource "2" is allocated to the red cell at location (4,3) and those cells in its common interference pattens (orange cells) do not use the same resource (they use IDs "0", "1", "3" and "4"). The same thing happens in Fig. 4(d) where we focus on the cell at location (5,3). Totally five resource are used in this allocation.

Secondly, the irregular part must be considered. In order to meet the condition of (5), such irregular part is handled as follows. Assume that cell (5,3) of Fig. 4(d) has blue cells in the right part of Fig. 4(b) as the irregular part. The allocation of Fig. 4(d) based only on CIP (without irregular part) allocates resource "3" to cells at (3,2) and (7,4), which are in the irregular part and therefore compete with cell (5,3) for the same resource "3". For those cells, an additional resource is allocated, and in this case, resource "8" (=3+5) is assigned as shown in Fig. 4(e). Since the CIP needs five resources, every new five resources, like "5"-"9" can be used as the secondly resources as the same rule as "0"-"4". In this case, the cells with resource "3" can use "$3+5*k$" ($k = 0, 1, 2, ..$) without conflicting with the other cells' resources. Therefore, six resources are used in this case.

Hereafter, k is called *level*, and this scheme can be applied to the general case where each cell needs more than one resource due to different traffic demand or different number of stations. Fig. 4(f) shows such a case that some cells request more than one resource (the number of resources requested is illustrated at the up-right corner in each cell; *e.g.* the cell at (6,3) requires three resources). Then for the cell at (6,3), the resources "4", "9" and "14" are allocated according to the rule above. As we have seen, we pursue the optimality (if there is no irregular part, the allocation is almost optimal for each level, which is shown later), with scalability and robustness to change of environment like increase of stations and variance of resource demand and station deployment.

In summary, we provide the two stage algorithm that consists of (i) determining the allocation rule that satisfies given CIP, and (ii) determining the final allocation considering the irregular part and the number of resources requested. They are explained in Sections 4.1 and 4.2, respectively.

4. RESOURCE ALLOCATION ALGORITHM

We call our algorithm *Vector-based Cell Cover* (VCC algorithm in short) and its correctness is validated by several theorems with proofs step by step.

4.1 CIP-based Allocation Algorithm

Here we present the algorithm to derive the allocation rule $\mathcal{A}_{CIP} : C \rightarrow R$ if CIP (common interference pattern) is

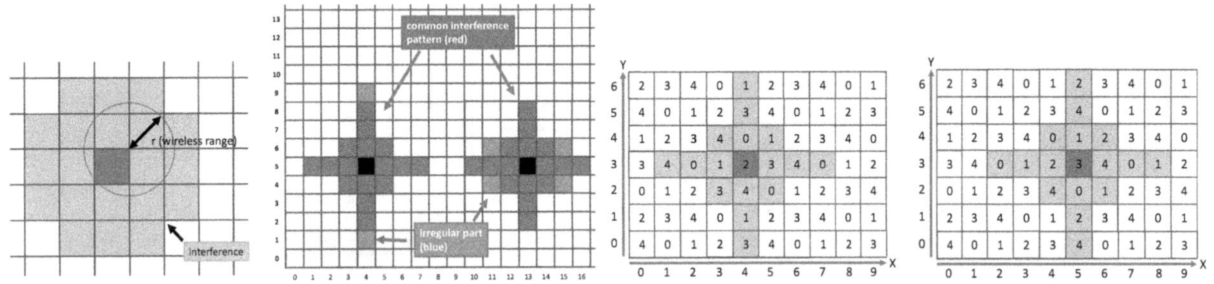

(a) interference pattern (distance-based) (b) common interference pattern typically seen in urban scenario (w/ irregular part) (c) resource allocation with common interference pattern of (b) (w/o irregular part) (d) resource allocation with common interference pattern of (b) (w/o irregular part)

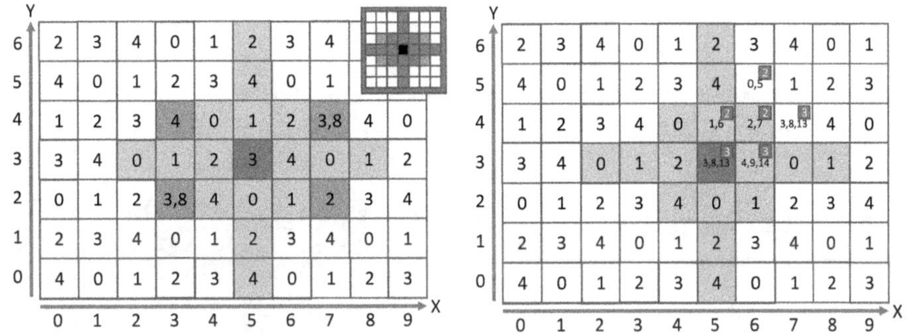

(e) resource allocation with common interference pattern of (b) (w/ irregular part) (f) resource allocation with different cell resource request

Figure 4: Two Examples of Interference Patterns and Corresponding Allocations

given[1]. The derived $\mathcal{A}_{CIP}$ is used in the second stage of the algorithm explained in Section 4.2. CIP can be extracted by investigating inter-cell interference $\mathcal{I}_C$. As stated earlier, inter-cell interference can be obtained by simulation or sample measurement, as it is easier to obtain than inter-station interference with a large number of stations.

CIP is a subset of original $\mathcal{I}_C$, where for any pair u and v of cells $\mathcal{I}_C(u)$ and $\mathcal{I}_C(u)$ have the same pattern. To distinguish CIP from $\mathcal{I}_C$, CIP is denoted as $\mathcal{I}_{CIP}$ hereafter. We let $\mathcal{F}$ denote a relation between two cells where they do not interfere with each other in $\mathcal{I}_{CIP}$. $\mathcal{F}$ is called *interference-free relation* in $\mathcal{I}_{CIP}$.

Hereafter, cells are identified by their coordinates on the integer field as illustrated in Fig. 5(a). Therefore, a cell is regarded as a vector on the coordinate system and we use the term "cell" and "vector" interchangeably. For non-zero vectors u and v, if there is no such an integer k that satisfies $u = kv$, they are said to be *independent.*

As a starting point, for an arbitrary vector (or cell) u, we define a set $V(u)$ of vectors as follows.

DEFINITION 1. *$V(u)$ is an non-empty set of vectors satisfying the following properties.*

1. $u \notin V(u)$
2. $u\mathcal{F}v \quad (\forall v \in V(u))$
3. $v \neq w \Rightarrow (v - w + u)\mathcal{F}u \wedge (w - v + u)\mathcal{F}u \quad (\forall v, w \in V(u) \cup \{u\})$
4. *p and q are linearly independent* $\quad (\forall p, q \in \overline{V}(u))$

Note that $\overline{V}(u)$ is the set of vectors obtained by shifting each vector in $V(u)$ by vector $-u$ (*i.e.* $\overline{V}(u) = \{w \mid w = v - u;\ \forall v \in V(u)\}$).

Due to property 2, vectors in $V(c)$ are interference-free with u and property 3 indicates that they are also interference-free with each other. Most significantly, they are linearly independent according to property 4. An example is shown in Fig. 5. CIP for $u = (7, 7)$ is shown in Fig. 5(a) and Fig. 5(b) illustrates $V(u) = \{(8, 9), (10, 8)\}$ and $\overline{V}(u) = \{(1, 2), (3, 1)\}$ where (1,2) and (3,1) are linearly independent. We note that $V(u)$ is not usually unique, and we add an index to $V(u)$ (*e.g.* $V_i(u)$) to distinguish multiple sets.

Secondly, we define the following property of $V(u)$.

DEFINITION 2. *We say that $V(u)$ is linearly interference-free with u iff $v\mathcal{F}u$ for any v which can be represented as $u + \sum_{p_j \in \overline{V}(u)} k_j p_j$ (k_j is an integer).*

This means that any linear combination of vectors in $\overline{V}(u)$ shifted by vector u does not interfere with u. Since $|\mathcal{I}_{CIP}(u)|$ is quite small in general, this can be checked easily by exhaustive search of possible integers k_j and comparison with $\mathcal{I}_{CIP}(u)$.

Then we let $W_i(u)$ denote a set of all the vectors with the form of $u + \sum_{p_j \in \overline{V}_i(u)} k_j p_j$ where k_j is an arbitrary integer. This is called a set of *cover vectors of u*. We prove the following theorem with respect to the isomorphism of cover vector set.

THEOREM 1. *For any u and v where $v \in W_i(u)$, $W_i(u) = W_i(v)$.*

[1]We would like to emphasize that only a single resource is allocated to a cell in this sub-algorithm ($\mathcal{A}_{CIP}$). The general case ($\mathcal{A}_C$) in considered in Section 4.2.

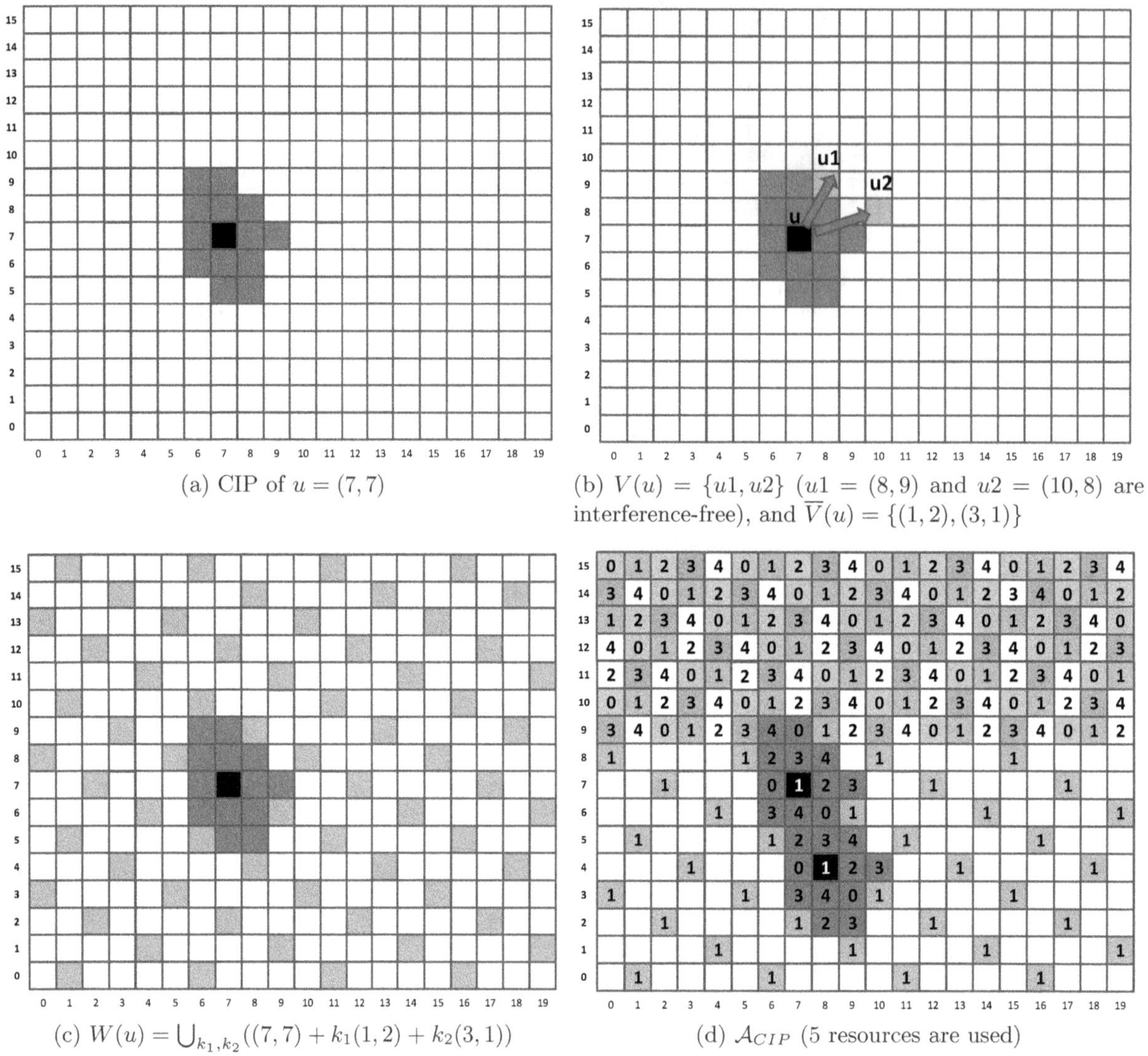

(a) CIP of $u = (7,7)$

(b) $V(u) = \{u1, u2\}$ ($u1 = (8,9)$ and $u2 = (10,8)$ are interference-free), and $\overline{V}(u) = \{(1,2),(3,1)\}$

(c) $W(u) = \bigcup_{k_1,k_2}((7,7) + k_1(1,2) + k_2(3,1))$

(d) $\mathcal{A}_{CIP}$ (5 resources are used)

Figure 5: Algorithm Description

proof: This is intuitively true but we formally show the correctness. Since (i) $\overline{V}_i(u)$ is a set of relative vectors with origin u and (ii) $\mathcal{I}_{CIP}(u)$ and $\mathcal{I}_{CIP}(w)$ are isomorphic for any w, $\overline{V}_i(u) = \overline{V}_i(w)$ for any w. Therefore, for any $v \in W_i(u)$, $v = w + \sum_{d_j \in \overline{V}_i(w)} h_j d_j = w + \sum_{d_j \in \overline{V}_i(u)} h_j d_j$. Since w is represented as $u + \sum_{d_j \in \overline{V}_i(u)} k_j d_j$ from definition, $v = u + \sum_{d_j \in \overline{V}_i(u)} (k_j + h_j) d_j$ meaning $W_i(v) = W_i(u)$. □

From the theorem above, we obtain the following.

THEOREM 2. *For any $W_i(u)$ that is linearly interference-free with u and for any $v, w \in W_i(u)$, $v\mathcal{F}w$.*
proof: From theorem 1, $\forall v, w \in W_i(u)$, $W_i(u) = W_i(v) = W_i(w)$. Because $W_i(v)$ is linearly interference-free with v, $u'\mathcal{F}v$ for any $u' \in W_i(v)$. Also because $u' \in W_i(u)$ for such u', $w\mathcal{F}v$ when $u' = w$. □

Finally, we obtain the following theorem. We let $u.x$ (or $u.y$) denote the x-coordinate (or y-coordinate) of u.

THEOREM 3. *For any $W_i(u)$ that is linearly interference-free with u and for any $v \in W_i(u)$, there exists w such that $w \in W_i(u)$, $v \neq w$ and $v.y = w.y$.*
proof: for any $v \in W_i(u)$, v can be represented as $u + \sum_j k_j \cdot d_j$. For this v, we pick w where $w = u + (d_2.y) \cdot d_1 - (d_1.y) \cdot d_2 + \sum_{j>2} 0 \cdot d_j$. Then such w is in $W_i(u)$ and has the same y-coordinate as v. □

Theorem 3 can be confirmed by Fig. 5(c) where cells (vectors) in $W(u)$ are aligned horizontally with equal spacing.

From theorem 2, $W(u)$ is regarded as such a set of cells where any cells in the set are interference-free with each other. This indicates that only one resource is used for these cells. Therefore, if the following sets of cell cover vectors that totally cover all the cells in the region are found, then the resource allocation, $\mathcal{A}_{CIP}$, is determined and the number of those sets is the number of resources used by $\mathcal{A}_{CIP}$. We let W^* and C_i denote a set of cover vector sets and a set of cells, respectively.

$$\text{minimize:} \quad \sum_{W_i \in W^*} |C_i| \tag{8}$$

$$\text{subject to:} \quad \bigcup_{W_i \in W^*} \bigcup_{u \in C_i} W_i(u) = C \tag{9}$$

From theorem 3, for a given W_i, $|C_i|$ can be obtained as follows;

$$|C_i| = \min_{v \in W_i(u)} \bar{d}_c(u, v) \qquad (10)$$

where $\bar{d}_c(u, v)$ denotes horizontal (or vertical) distance if u and v are aligned horizontally (or vertically), and ∞ otherwise. Therefore, in order to find such W^* in (9), we exhaustively search W_i, calculate $|C_i|$ for W_i correspondingly, and find the best combination of W's that minimizes (8) satisfying (9).

Fig. 5(d) shows an example where $W(u)$ of Fig. 5(c), $C_1 = ((7,7),(8,7),(9,7),(10,7),(11,7))$ and $|C_1| = 5$. In this figure, we can see that $\mathcal{A}_{CIP}(u)$= "1" for any $u \in W((7,7))$ (green and black cells) for instance.

4.2 Handling Irregular Part and Multiple Resource Request

$\mathcal{A}_{CIP}$ is an allocation of single resource to each cell. To complete the algorithm design and obtain $\mathcal{A}_C$ that resolves $\mathcal{I}_C$ satisfying req_C, we have to deal with (i) irregular part that has not been considered in $\mathcal{I}_{CIP}$ and (ii) req_C, which may request more than one resource for each cell.

For the first issue, there may still be interference among two or more cells under the allocation by $\mathcal{A}_{CIP}$. We let C_i denote a set of such cells that interfere with each other due to such irregular part, and r denote the number of resources used by $\mathcal{A}_{CIP}$. Without loss of generality, $R = \{"0", "1", "2", ...\}$ and we assume that $\mathcal{A}_{CIP}$ uses them in ascending order. Then for each cell in C_i to which resource ID s is allocated, we allow $\mathcal{A}_C$ to further assign the resources $s + r \cdot k$ using level "k" ($k \geq 1$) to the cell as exemplified earlier in Fig. 4(e) to resolve such interference. This does not violate the rule of $\mathcal{A}_{CIP}$, but extends the numbering in a hierarchical way. This can naturally be applied to solve the second issue. Back to the example in Fig. 4(f), we finally use {"0"-"4","5"-"9","13","14"} and totally 12 resources are used. For the level of k=2 ("10"-"14"), three resources still remain unused, and this can be used for future installation of new stations in those cells.

5. PERFORMANCE EVALUATION

5.1 Examination of CIP-based Allocation Performance by Simulation

In order to confirm the basic feature of CIP-based allocation (basically optimality and regularity of allocation), we conducted extensive simulation. The performance of whole algorithm has been evaluated with a real world scenario that contains a lot of irregular interference. This will be introduced in Section 5.2.

5.1.1 Simulation Settings

We have prepared scenarios with different station densities and different interference patterns, and have observed (i) optimality of resource utilization, and (ii) spatial regularity (*i.e.* scalability and robustness) of resource allocation. In order to quantify the spatial regularity, we define the *nearest cell vector* for each cell c. The nearest vector of cell c is the vector from cell c to cell c' which is interference-free with c with minimum distance among the others. Using the notion of nearest cell vectors, we introduce two metrics, *Average Neighbor Cosine* (ANC) and *Average Neighbor Distance* (AND). The ANC is the average cosine of the angles formed by every pair of two nearest cell vectors, and AND is the average norm of all the nearest cell vectors. For a pair of two nearest cell vectors, if their directions are similar, the cosine is close to one (is exactly one if they completely match). Therefore, intuitively, ANC represents directional similarity. Meanwhile, AND represents the degree of reuse of the same resource since a smaller value indicates more reuse of resources (meaning compact allocation). In summary, for spatial regularity, ANC should be closer to one and AND should be smaller.

In $1km \times 1km$ square region divided by $50m \times 50m$ cells (400 cells), we define the station density by the ratio of actual stations to 400 stations (400 is the number of stations when we put exactly one station in each cell). We have prepared different station density p ($p \in [0.1, 1]$ with step 0.1) by randomly choosing cells to which stations place, with probability p. We have used two types of interference. One is a popular model as introduced in Fig. 4(a) called *omni-directional model* assuming a conventional distance-based interference with 250m interference range. Hence if station density $p = 1$, each station interferes with about 80 stations. Another model assumes such situation where each station strongly interferes with others in some specific directions. This may happen with directional signal transmission or reception due to antennas or obstacles. This is called *directional model*. For the directional model we have used such CIP where for cell (0,0), $\mathcal{I}_{CIP}(0,0)$={(0,1), (0,2), (0,3), (0,4), (0,5), (1,0), (1,1), (1,2), (2,0), (2,1), (2,2), (3,0), (4,0)} as well as their (0,0) symmetries.

For comparison purpose, we have also implemented the following heuristic algorithm; Given inter-station (not inter-cell) interference $\mathcal{I}_S$, initially we pick a station randomly, and we repeatedly pick a new station that does not interfere with any already-chosen station and is nearest to one of the already-chosen stations, and make it as an already-chosen station. This is called *Nearest Neighbor Selection* algorithm (NNS in short) and does not work unless all information in $\mathcal{I}_S$ and station information (location) is collected and given. This does not use cell information to obtain the solution, and does not have spatial regularity due to its distance-based and station-based selection feature. Hence it is not realistic for real-world operations, but is a reasonable benchmark in terms of optimality of resource utilization. This is confirmed by the fact that AND of this algorithm is close to that of our algorithm, meaning similar efficacy of resource reuse in dense networks.

Since our algorithm (VCC algorithm) considers all the potential interference including those which may or may not appear in future, the number of resource utilization is always a constant independently of the station deployment. Therefore, with sparse deployment of stations the NNS algorithm may achieve better efficacy than our VCC algorithm. Meanwhile, ANC and AND are always one and constant value, respectively, that is, the perfect regularity is accomplished. Hence we carefully observe that in densely-deployed situations the optimality of the NNS algorithm drops down below the VCC algorithm, and also the NNS algorithm cannot achieve spatial regularity in any density situations.

5.1.2 Results

Fig. 6 shows the results. In each graph, the station density p is represented on x-axis where 1.0 means 400 stations. For each station density, we have prepared 10 different sta-

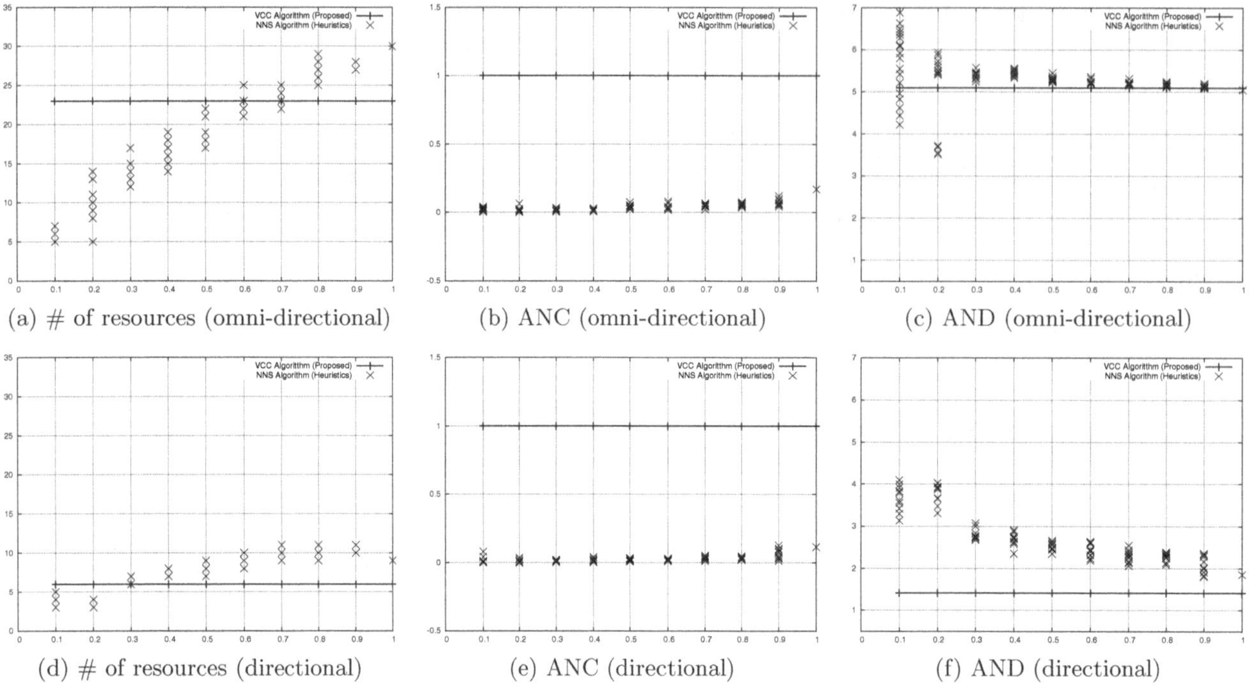

(a) # of resources (omni-directional) (b) ANC (omni-directional) (c) AND (omni-directional)

(d) # of resources (directional) (e) ANC (directional) (f) AND (directional)

Figure 6: Simulation Results

tion deployment scenarios and have plotted the corresponding number of resources used, ANC and AND. Fig. 6(a) and Fig. 6(d) show the number of resources used. As expected, the NNS algorithm (heuristics) needs less resources than our VCC algorithm with lower density, but with higher one it needs much more than VCC. In particular, in any settings with 0.7 or higher density, NNS needs more resources than VCC and with 1.0 density (which is the severest case where stations are very populated) in Fig. 6(a); NNS needs 30% or more resources than VCC. Also the ANC (average neighbor cosine that represents directional similarity of spatial resource assignment) values of NNS stay around zero values (in Fig. 6(b) and Fig. 6(e)). This means that there is almost no regularity in the NNS algorithm while it is always one in the VCC algorithm. On the other hand, in terms of resource reuse efficacy, AND of the NNS algorithm (in Fig. 6(c) and Fig. 6(f)) approaches to that of our VCC algorithm, and therefore the certain resource reuse has been accomplished also in NNS. Compared with the NNS algorithm which can achieve better optimality with no-crowded situation, our algorithm is beneficial in terms of optimality in densely-deployed scenarios and spatial regularity where resources can be uniquely determined by the cell location.

5.2 Case Study on Real World Problem

Although we have confirmed the basic performance and benefit of CIP-based allocation, we should examine the whole algorithm performance through real world scenarios. We conduct a case study in collaboration with Sumitomo Electric Industries [1] on a Road-Side wireless Unit (RSU) installation problem. They are now building I2V (Infrastructure-to-Vehicle) communication platform in metropolitan cities such as Tokyo and Osaka. The RSU module prototype by Sumitomo Electric Industries has been shown in Fig. 1(a).

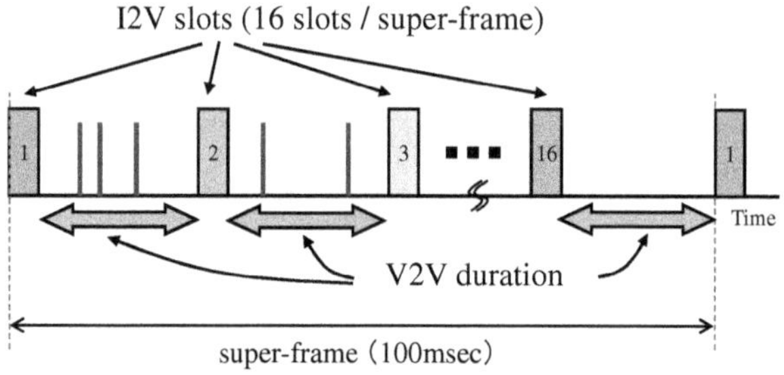

Figure 7: I2V slots and V2V duration in each 100ms super-frame [3]

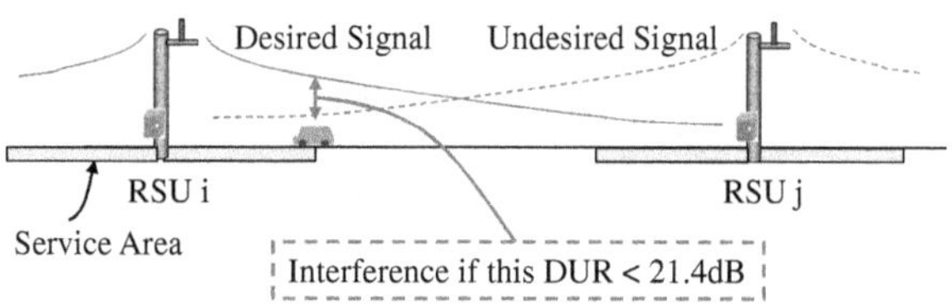

Figure 8: Desired to Undesired Signal Ratio (DUR)

5.2.1 *Background*

In Japan, the DSRC-based system called ETC (Electronic Toll Collection system) have been deployed nation-wide, and 5.8GHz band is reserved for the purpose. It is also discussed to use this frequency for V2V (vehicle-to-vehicle) communications. Meanwhile, as a new tread for ITS, reorganization of frequency reservation has been done lately, and 760MHz band with 10MHz bandwidth is reserved for ITS communications in December 2012. Since lower frequency's fea-

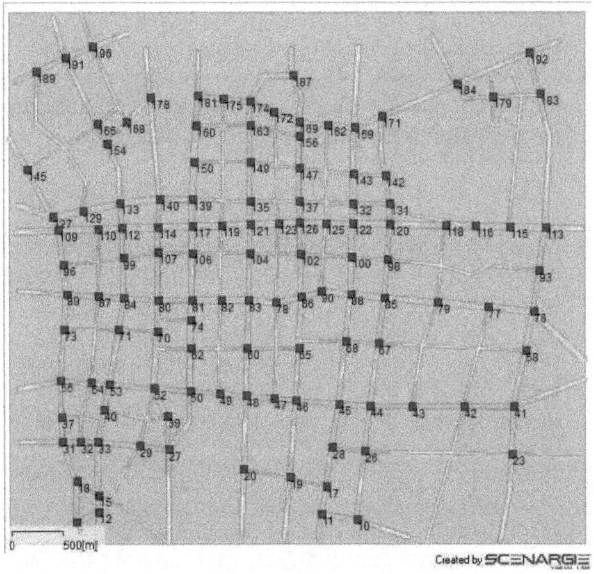

(a) 121 Road-side Unit Installation

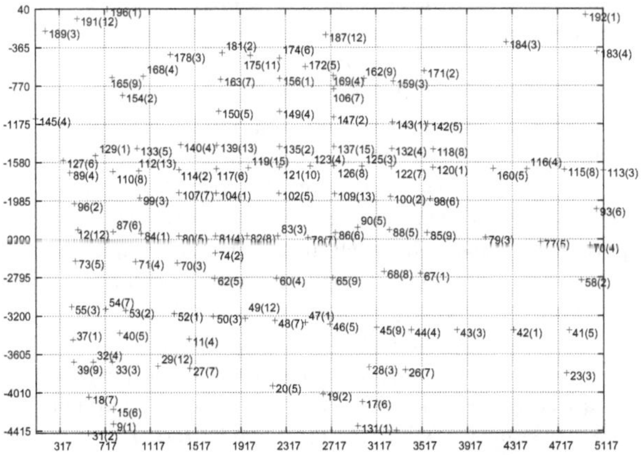

(b) Allocation of 13 Slots to 121 RSUs (13 slots are used)

Figure 9: 5km×5km Region in the Center of Osaka City, Japan

tures like diffraction beyond intersections in urban canyon are beneficial, this new frequency is critically premium. On the other hand, since only limited bandwidth (10MHz) is allowed to accommodate all I2V and V2V communications, efficacy of media access control is essential.

For efficient MAC control with existence of road-side equipment and vehicles, TDMA separating I2V and V2V has been designed and standardized by Japanese Association of Radio Industries and Businesses (ARIB) as documented in [3]. In this standard, duration of one frame transmission (this is called *super-frame*) is set to 100ms in which 16 subframes (called *slots*) are reserved for I2V communications in a TDMA fashion and the rest of duration is used for V2V communication by CSMA (see Fig. 7).

We have applied our VCC algorithm to determine the allocation of 16 slots (or less slots) to 121 road-side units (RSUs) in the 5km×5km central region of Osaka City, which is the second largest city in Japan. We have prepared the road map of Osaka downtown region with RSU installation as illustrated in Fig. 9(a).

Here, we have learned the following important experiences through the experiments.

Firstly, the size of cells significantly affects the number of required resources. Larger cells contain more RSUs per cell, and the form of inter-cell interference patterns may become simpler (due to course-grained classification of RSU locations) but inner-cell interference becomes severer. Therefore, more resources are needed inside each cell. For example, if each cell has 10 RSUs, 10 resources are needed at maximum in each cell as well as resources needed to avoid inter-cell interference. On the other hand, fine-grained cells may lead to more complex form of inter-cell interference, and resources are consumed more for avoiding inter-cell interference. Consequently, there may be few inner-cell interference. We have tried different cell sizes and have known that 400m×405m was the best size to optimize the number of resources where in each cell at most three cells exist (see Fig. 9(b)).

Secondly, inter-cell interference estimation is also significant. Our VCC algorithm may use some propagation model to estimate inter-cell interference. Overestimation of interference leads to waste of resources, and underestimation generates more irregular part for those RSUs that have oversized interference than the inter-cell interference estimation.

We have used an inter-cell interference model that is estimated considering the 760MHz propagation model of ITU-R. P.1411-4 [13] and DUR threshold (21.4dB) as shown in Fig. 8. This value is empirically determined considering fading margin, multipath attenuation effect and some other factors. For successful communication in service area around each RSU, achieving at least 21.4dB at the edge of the service area is required. The interference distance in LoS (lines of sight) cases is around 1km, and several hundred meters even in NLoS cases. Considering this fact, interference where each cell interferes with three cells in each horizontal or vertical directions (assuming LoS along streets), and two cells in any other directions (assuming NLoS by buildings). The inter-station interference by P.1411-4 was measured by the customized version of the Scenargie simulator [14] with the precise propagation model of P.1411-4 and detailed 3D maps of roads and buildings. Different from the cases in the previous section, each station's (or cell's) interference pattern is different, and is dependent on geography (*e.g.* building and street structures). Also the station density is not uniform.

5.2.2 Results

Given inter-cell interference $\mathcal{I}_C$ and determined cell size, we obtained that the number of resources needed for $\mathcal{A}_{CIP}$ was only five. Since each cell contains at most three RSUs, we allocated three resources for each cell, for example, if resource h ($1 \leq h \leq 5$) is allocated to a cell, it is also allowed to use $h+5$ and $h+10$. Therefore, we need fifteen at maximum at this moment. After that, we have verified that $\mathcal{I}_C$ (estimation) includes all the inter-station interference $\mathcal{I}_S$ (the ground truth) and have found that 22 pairs of RSUs (stations) did not satisfy the linear interference free property in Definition 2 (*i.e.* the irregular part) We have to prepare additional resources to resolve the irregular part of interference. On the contrary, overestimation of inter-node interference also happens and as a result some RSU pairs in two different cells which interference with each other may not actually interfere, *i.e.* they can use the same resources.

Since we would like to leverage these features, we have developed the following procedure to handle the irregular part where we seek all the possibility to allocate the three resources h, $h+5$ and $h+10$ to RSUs in the cell, which can resolve the irregular part. As a result of this procedure, we could finally determine the allocation of only 13 slots (*i.e.* $R = \{1, 2, ..., 15\} - \{11, 14\}$ where 11 and 14 were unused), and we could be successful to obtain the reasonable allocation under the limitation that 16 available slots. In order to confirm that this is reasonable enough, we run the NNS algorithm and an allocation using ten slots was obtained, *knowing all the ground truth data.* In this case study, we have also used the interference information but only limited information (22 pairs) was used to avoid the irregular par of interference. Also the station density in this case was around 0.6, and after the population of RSUs, it will grow quickly as confirmed in the simulations. Also the ANC value of NNS was 0.054, and therefore no spatial regularity was guaranteed (the value was 1 in our VCC algorithm). We illustrate the 13 slots allocation by the VCC algorithm in Fig. 9(b) to help visual confirmation of allocation regularity and efficacy.

6. CONCLUSION

We have dealt with a scheduling problem of wireless stations in urban areas like outdoor Wi-Fi APs and road-side stations, which are subject to location changes, new station installation and so on. Our goal is to pursue the best balance among (i) optimality of resource utilization, (ii) robustness to new station installation and traffic demand, and (iii) scalability to the population of stations and area size. The proposed VCC algorithm achieves a near-optimal resource allocation based on a Common Interference Pattern (CIP) extracted from inter-cell interference, and then handles irregular interference and traffic demand to finalize the allocation of resources to each station. The derived allocation is based fully on cell locations, and hence it provides robustness to new station installation and traffic demand as well as scalability to the population of stations and area size. We also pursue optimality of resource utilization by the CIP-based sub-algorithm, which is designed based on a vector space theory with correctness proof.

We conducted two types of experiments; one is exhaustive simulations to confirm the basic performance of CIP-based sub-algorithm, and another is based on a real world scenario where TDMA scheduling of road-side units is required for vehicular wireless communication. In particular, in the real scenario, we have worked together with Sumitomo Electric Industries and have shown that our algorithm could achieve desired time slot scheduling under bandwidth limitation in the designated frequency.

7. REFERENCES

[1] Sumitomo Electric Industries. `http://global-sei.com/`.

[2] I. Amdouni, P. Minet, and C. Adjih. Node coloring for dense wireless sensor networks. Technical report, Institut National de Recherche en Informatique et en Automatique, 2011.

[3] Association of Radio Industries and Businesses (ARIB). 700MHz band intteligent transport systesm. ARIB Standard ARIB STD-T109 version 1.0, April 2012. `http://www.arib.or.jp/tyosakenkyu/kikaku_tushin/tsushin_kikaku_number.html`.

[4] A. A. Bertossi and M. A. Bonuccelli. Code assignment for hidden terminal interference avoidance in multihop packet radio networks. *IEEE Transactions on Networking*, 3(4):441–449, August 1995.

[5] G. Brar, D. M. Blough, and P. Santi. Computationally efficient scheduling with the physical interference model for throughput improvement in wireless mesh networks. In *Proc. of MobiCom '06*, pages 2–13, 2006.

[6] R. L. Cruz and A. V. Santhanam. Optimal routing, link scheduling and power control in multi-hop wireless networks. *Proceedings of IEEE Infocom '03*, pages 702–711, 2003.

[7] R. Giuliano, C. Monti, and P. Loreti. WiMAX fractional frequency reuse for rural environments. *Wireless Communications, IEEE*, 15(3):60 –65, 2008.

[8] J. Grönkvist and A. Hansson. Comparison between graph-based and interference-based STDMA scheduling. In *Proc. of MobiHoc '01*, pages 255–258, 2001.

[9] N. Jindal, J. Andrews, and S. Weber. Bandwidth partitioning in decentralized wireless networks. *Wireless Communications, IEEE Transactions on*, 7(12):5408–5419, december 2008.

[10] S. Jing, D. N. C. Tse, J. B. Soriaga, J. Hou, J. E. Smee, and R. Padovani. Multicell downlink capacity with coordinated processing. *EURASIP J. Wirel. Commun. Netw.*, 2008:18:1–18:19, Jan. 2008.

[11] M. Karakayali, G. Foschini, and R. Valenzuela. Network coordination for spectrally efficient communications in cellular systems. *Wireless Communications, IEEE*, 13(4):56 –61, 2006.

[12] V. S. A. Kumar, M. V. Marathe, S. Parthasarathy, and A. Srinivasan. Algorithmic aspects of capacity in wireless networks. *Proc. of SIGMETRICS*, 33(1):133–144, June 2005.

[13] Recommendation ITU-R P.1411-5. Propagation data and prediction methods for the planning of short-range outdoor radiocommunication systems and radio local area networks in the frequency range 300MHz to 100GHz, October 2009.

[14] Space-Time Engineering, LLC. Scenargie. http://www.spacetime-eng.com/.

[15] R. Veronesi, V. Tralli, J. Zander, and M. Zorzi. Distributed dynamic resource allocation with power shaping for multicell sdma packet access networks. In *Proc. of IEEE WCNC 2004*, pages 2515 – 2520, 2004.

[16] W. Wang, Y. Wang, X.-Y. Li, W.-Z. Song, and O. Frieder. Efficient interference-aware TDMA link scheduling for static wireless networks. In *Proc. of MobiCom '06*, pages 262–273. ACM, 2006.

[17] J. Yang, Q. Jiang, D. Manivannan, and M. Singhal. A fault-tolerant distributed channel allocation scheme for cellular networks. *IEEE Trans. Comput.*, 54(5):616–629, May 2005.

RECAST: Telling Apart Social and Random Relationships in Dynamic Networks

Pedro Olmo Vaz de Melo
Universidade Federal de Minas Gerais, Brazil
olmo@dcc.ufmg.br

Aline C. Viana
INRIA, France
aline.viana@inria.fr

Marco Fiore
IEIIT - CNR, Italy
marco.fiore@ieiit.cnr.it

Katia Jaffrès-Runser
University of Toulouse, IRIT, France
kjr@enseeiht.fr

Frederic Le Mouël
INSA Lyon, France
frederic.le-mouel@insa-lyon.fr

Antonio A. F. Loureiro
Universidade Federal de Minas Gerais, Brazil
loureiro@dcc.ufmg.br

ABSTRACT

In this paper, we argue that the ability to accurately spot random and social relationships in dynamic networks is essential to network applications that rely on human routines, such as, e.g., opportunistic routing. We thus propose a strategy to analyze users' interactions in mobile networks where users act according to their interests and activity dynamics. Our strategy, named *Random rElationship ClASsifier sTrategy (RECAST)*, allows classifying users' wireless interactions, separating random interactions from different kinds of social ties. To that end, RECAST observes how the real system differs from an equivalent one where entities' decisions are completely random. We evaluate the effectiveness of the RECAST classification on real-world user contact datasets collected in diverse networking contexts. Our analysis unveils significant differences among the dynamics of users' wireless interactions in the datasets, which we leverage to unveil the impact of social ties on opportunistic routing.

Categories and Subject Descriptors

H.2.8 [**Database Management**]: Database Applications—*Data Mining*; I.6.4 [**Simulation and Modeling**]: Model Validation and Analysis

Keywords

dynamic social networks; edge classification

1. INTRODUCTION

Recent studies have analyzed data generated from mobile individuals in urban regions, such as cab drivers in San Francisco (USA) [1] or students in large campuses [2, 3]. Particular attention has been paid to the dynamics of user movement, whose real-world complexity cannot be fully captured through synthetic models. Indeed, understanding user mobility is of fundamental importance when designing new communication protocols that exploit opportunistic encounters among users. In this case, the problem mainly lies in correctly forecasting future contacts. To that end, the regularity of daily activities comes in handy, as it enforces periodic (and thus predictable) space-time patterns in human mobility [4]. Building on such a feature, protocols have been designed to estimate the potential of mobile users to act as data forwarders, mainly leveraging complex network analysis metrics such as centrality measures.

MSWiM'13, November 3–8, 2013, Barcelona, Spain.
Copyright 2013 ACM 978-1-4503-2353-6/13/11 ...$15.00.
http://dx.doi.org/10.1145/2507924.2507950.

Although human behavior is characterized by an elevated rate of regularity, random events are always possible in the routines of individuals. Those are hardly predictable situations that deviate from the regular pattern and are unlikely to repeat in the future; they originate from the fact that users are reasonable beings, whose connections represent decisions they take based on their personal motivations [5], which may also change over time. We refer to contact networks deriving from systems where users are reasonable beings as *Dynamic Complex Wireless Networks (DCWN)*. For instance, a contact network composed of wireless hand-held devices is a clear example of DCWN, since the user mobility creates neither purely regular nor purely random connections among the entities composing the network.

The random events in DCWNs veil the ordinary patterns by introducing a significant amount of noise, thus making the process of knowledge discovery in such datasets a complex task. Therefore, the ability to accurately identify random and social events in DCWNs is essential to social analysis and to applications that rely on a precise description of human routines, such as recommendation systems, forwarding strategies and opportunistic dissemination protocols.

In this paper, we propose a *Random rElationship ClASsifier sTrategy (RECAST)* to classify relationships among users so as to spot contacts due to random events in DCWNs. To that end, RECAST examines how the real system would evolve if users' decisions were random. More precisely, we use the temporal graph originated from the real network dataset and a random counterpart of the same to tell apart edges representing random events from those created by actual social relationships, such as friendship or professional interactions. RECAST has a single and intuitive parameter, which makes it preferable to conventional methods for filtering and cleaning social network data that require arbitrary thresholds, many parameters, and often a deep knowledge of the system.

In summary, the contribution of this paper is threefold:

- We introduce RECAST, a simple yet very effective way of classifying wireless contacts by leveraging metrics that reflect two major features of social networks: frequent user encounters and shared acquaintances.
- We unveil the large differences among contact datasets, and claim that conclusions drawn from evaluating a single dataset should not be generalized; rather, the validation of networking protocols or services has to consider different types of datasets.
- We show that the knowledge of the wireless relationship a pair of users share can be leveraged for the design of opportunistic routing schemes.

The paper is organized as follows. Section 2 discusses the related work. Section 3 details the design behind RECAST. Section 4 shows how we model real-world network traces into complex temporal networks. Section 5 details the RECAST implementation. Section 6 shows how RECAST can improve opportunistic routing solutions. Finally, conclusions are drawn in Section 7.

2. RELATED WORK

Social network analysis builds on the high predictability of human behaviors [6], which are mostly driven by regular, routine activities. As a consequence, connections among social network nodes can be modeled by mechanisms such as preferential attachment [7] and triangle formation [5], that leverages the existence of communities or highly connected hubs [8] in the network. This makes social networks different from random ones, such as the Erdős and Rényi network [9], where node connections are purely stochastic, being determined by a constant probability.

Given this predictability, social ties have been widely exploited in opportunistic mobile networks so as to favor network services. The considered problems range from multi-hop message forwarding [10] and multicasting [11], to network security [12]. To the best of our knowledge, the works of Miklas et al. [13] and Zyba et al. [14] are those most closely related to ours. These studies differ in that they classify either *users* or their *interactions* (i.e., vertices and edges in the social graph), respectively. Zyba et al. distinguish social and vagabond users according to their social mobility behavior. They analyze regularity of appearance and duration of visits in a given area of traces to sort out users. Hence, the resulting classification only works on a per-individual per-area basis. Miklas et al. classify links between friends and strangers. They assume that frequent pairwise node encounters represent friendship interactions, and empirically decide that pairs of users meeting 10 days or more out of 101 days are friends, whereas others are strangers.

Overall, our work extends the investigations in [13, 14] in the following ways. First, we propose a finer grained classifier, able not only to clearly characterize random interactions, but also to identify different kinds of social interactions: *Friends*, *Acquaintances* and *Bridges*. As such, we go a step further than [13] as we are able to identify edges corresponding to, e.g., *familiar strangers*, as defined by Milgram [15]: indeed, the users sharing a bridge interaction repeatedly encounter but may never experience an explicit social relationship. In addition, unlike the proposal by Zyba et al. [14], our strategy has no geographical dependency, i.e., it is of general validity.

3. RATIONALE

We consider social networks composed of individuals who are wirelessly connected over time. Such wireless encounters in these networks are driven by behaviors that tend: (i) to be regular and to repeat periodically; (ii) to build persistent communities of individuals or to generate commons acquaintances between them. The classification strategy we present in this paper leverages these two behaviors to efficiently distinguish social from random encounters in DCWNs. In the following, we detail our methodology and present the real world datasets considered in our analysis.

Social vs. random interactions: In DCWNs, interactions among the system entities are usually a consequence of semi-rational decisions. We say "usually" and "semi-rational" decisions because any system is subject to random events and irrational choices. Nevertheless, because most of the interactions still arise from conscious decisions made by their entities, the evolution of DCWNs is significantly different from the evolution of random networks, e.g., Erdős and Rényi networks [9]. Indeed, while in DCWNs the edges are created from semi-rational decisions, which tend to be regular and to repeat over time, in a *random network the edges are created independently of the attributes of the network entities, i.e., the probability of connecting any two entities is always the same.*

More formally, an individual may execute a *social decision*, or a *random decision*. Intuitively, if its probability of performing a social decision is greater than its probability of a random one, the network evolves to a well-structured social network. If the opposite it true, the network evolves as a random network, such as the Erdös and Rényi one.

Differentiating social from random network: The second major feature of DCWNs that we exploit in our study is the presence of communities, i.e., groups of individuals who are strongly connected to each other because they share the same interests or activity dynamics [5]. In contrast, communities can not be found in random networks where, as previously stated, edges are created stochastically and independently of the attributes of each node.

The network clustering coefficient has been widely used to discriminate random from social networks. Given an undirected graph $G(V, E)$ (where V represents the set of network graph nodes, e.g., individuals, and E is the set of links describing relationships among entities, e.g., contacts among individuals), the clustering coefficient cc_i measures the probability that two neighbors of a node i are also connected among them. Formally, it is calculated as $cc_i = 2|E_i|/|N_i|(|N_i| - 1)$, where N_i is the set of neighbors of i, E_i is the set of edges between nodes in N_i and $|\cdot|$ is the cardinality of the included set. The clustering coefficient $\overline{cc}$ of the whole network is the average of all node clustering coefficients $cc_i, \forall i \in V$.

By introducing the equivalent random network G^R as the random network constructed with the same number of nodes, edges and empirical degree distribution of its real world counterpart G, Watts and Strogatz [16] show that the clustering coefficient of a social network G is one order of magnitude higher than the clustering coefficient of G^R. Thus, when a given network G exhibits a clustering coefficient that is significantly (i.e., orders of magnitude) higher than that of its random equivalent G^R, then we can state that (part of) the decisions made by the entities that compose the network graph G are non-random.

Real-world DCWN datasets: Our evaluations are performed on three real-world datasets (also referred to as *traces* in the following) that describe movements of entities in campus and city scenarios. The Dartmouth dataset [3] is a mobility trace of more than $1,000$ individuals in the university campus, recorded over eight weeks using WiFi network access information. The USC dataset [2] is also a mobility trace in a campus scenario, comprising movement information of more than $4,000$ individuals over eight weeks, again collected through WiFi access. Finally, the San Francisco dataset [1] contains records of the mobility of 551 taxis in San Francisco, CA,

USA, over one month, gathered through GPS logging at each cab in the urban area. For both the Dartmouth and USC traces, two individuals are assumed to generate a contact if they are using the same WiFi access point to connect to the wireless network on campus. In the San Francisco trace, two taxis are in contact if their distance is lower than 250 meters. Extensive experimental analysis in [17] shows that a distance of $250m$ grants a 50% packet delivery ratio in urban environments, under common power levels (15-20 dBm) and with robust modulations (3-Mbps BPSK and 6-Mbps QPSK). In all cases, the contact events between two individuals are traced using start date of contact and its duration. Table 1 summarizes the features of the different datasets.

4. MODELING

This section introduces the basic operations performed on the dataset before RECAST is executed. Section 4.1 shows how we model the dynamic DCWN as a temporal aggregation graph. Section 4.2 details the algorithm we employ to obtain the equivalent random graph of a given temporal aggregation graph, and discusses how these two graphs compare in terms of clustering coefficient.

4.1 Temporal Aggregation Graph

As previously discussed, the datasets we employ list contacts among individuals or vehicles, and associate to each encounter a start time and a duration. In order to generate the temporal graph, we discretize time into steps of duration δ [1], and represent all the encounters occurring at time step k as a graph $\mathcal{G}_k(\mathcal{V}_k, \mathcal{E}_k)$. The set of vertices $\mathcal{V}_k$ is composed of all network nodes (i.e., individuals or vehicles) involved in a contact during the k-th time step, while the edges in the set $\mathcal{E}_k$ represent the pairwise contacts during the same time step. Therefore, an edge between two nodes i and j, with $i, j \in \mathcal{V}_k$, exists in $\mathcal{E}_k$ if i and j have met during time step k.

We can then define a time varying representation of the DCWN using a temporal accumulation graph $G_t = (V_t, E_t)$. Formally, $G_t = \{\mathcal{G}_1 \cup \mathcal{G}_2 \cup ... \cup \mathcal{G}_t\}$. As such, V_t (respectively E_t) is the set of all vertices (edges) that appeared in the dataset between time 0 and time step t included. Note that G_t evolves over time and aggregates all the contacts in the dataset, thus comprising both social encounters and random encounters between network entities.

4.2 Comparison with Random Graphs

The first step to analyze the mobility patterns of the temporal accumulation graph G_t is to build its random version G_t^R. The latter must feature similar topological characteristics as the original G_t graph, i.e., the same number of nodes, edges, and empirical degree distribution. That way, the only difference between G_t and G_t^R lies in the way nodes are connected to each other. While in G_t the nodes connect in a "semi-rational" way, in G_t^R the connections happen in a purely random fashion. As we will show later, this difference can be leveraged to accurately determine the extent of randomness in the mobility of individuals in DCWNs.

We use two algorithms to to generate G_t^R from G_t. The first algorithm, which we will call `RND`, is well known in the network science community [18]. The algorithm G^R=`RND` (G) receives a graph $G(V, E)$ as a parameter and returns a random graph $G^R(V, E^R)$ with the same topological characteristics as G, i.e., the same number of nodes, number of edges and degree distribution. In this way, we guarantee that the only difference between the real graph G and G^R is to whom each node connects, that is the focus of our analysis. Thus, given the degree distribution $D = (d_1, d_2, \ldots, d_n)$ of G with n nodes, this algorithm assigns an edge between nodes i and j with probability $p_{ij} = (d_i \times d_j)/\sum_{k=1}^{|V|} d_k$.

[1]In our study, we considered a duration of $\delta = 1$ day, since the data sets originate from human activities that feature daily routines.

The second algorithm, which we call `T-RND`, is an extension of `RND` and is able to generate random graphs from a temporal network G_t. As mentioned in Section 4.1, the temporal aggregation graph $G_t = \{\mathcal{G}_1 \cup \mathcal{G}_2 \cup \ldots \cup \mathcal{G}_t\}$ is the union of event graphs $\mathcal{G}_t$. Thus, the algorithm G_t^R =`T-RND` $(\mathcal{G}_1, \mathcal{G}_2, \ldots, \mathcal{G}_t)$ receives as parameters a set of consecutive event graphs $\mathcal{G}_t$ and returns a random temporal graph G_t^R. It constructs G_t^R by executing `RND` in each event graph $\mathcal{G}_t$ and then aggregating it in a way that $G_t^R = \{\text{RND}(\mathcal{G}_1) \cup \text{RND}(\mathcal{G}_2) \cup \ldots \cup \text{RND}(\mathcal{G}_t)\}$. In summary, both `RND` and `T-RND` randomly replicate the total number of contacts with distinct persons each individual had in a given time snapshot.

We first demonstrate the analytical power of random comparison in Figure 1, where we show the behavior of the clustering coefficient for graphs G_t and G_t^R over time for the three analyzed networks. As we have previously mentioned, the clustering coefficient is a good metric to differentiate social networks from random networks. As we observe in Figure 1-a, for the Dartmouth dataset, the clustering coefficient of G_t and G_t^R are different in orders of magnitude over the first days. However, as time goes by, their values get closer, as random encounters grow in number and tend to veil the social network structure. On the other hand, as we see in Figure 1-b, the clustering coefficients of G_t and G_t^R for the USC dataset are almost constant over time. However, the difference between them is not exceedingly high, since they have the same order of magnitude. We discuss these differences in detail later on.

Finally, as we observe in Figure 1-c, the clustering coefficients of the San Francisco networks are practically the same, being close to 1. In fact, after a few hours, the network becomes similar to a clique, indicating a global high mobility, allowing each individual taxi encountering most of the other taxis at some point of the day. Formally, this indicates that G_t and G_t^R are very similar for the San Francisco dataset, i.e., the probability of random encounters is much higher than the probability of social contacts, what makes the San Francisco network similar to a random mobile network. This makes sense since taxis' decisions depend on occasional customers' requests rather than on routine mobility patterns of the driver.

5. CLASSIFIER

In this section, we describe the *Random rElationship ClASsifier sTrategy (RECAST)* we propose to differentiate relationships among individuals in a social network. More precisely, the purpose of RECAST is to tell apart random interactions from social-driven ones. To that end, Section 5.1 presents the DCWN features used by RECAST. Then, Section 5.2 introduces the RECAST algorithm and, finally, Section 5.3 discusses the results obtained by applying RECAST to the previously introduced datasets.

5.1 Social Networks Features

In order to identify social relationships, we must point out which features distinguish a social relationship from a random one. Indeed, two characteristics are always present in social relationships [19]:

1. **Regularity**. It is well known that social relationships are regular, in that they repeat over time. If two individuals are, for example, friends, co-workers, or daily commuters, they see each other regularly.

2. **Similarity**. It is expected that two individuals who share a social relationship have common acquaintances between

Table 1: Datasets used in the presented investigations.

Dataset	Local	Number of entities	Duration	Entities type	Avg. # encounters/node/day
Dartmouth [3]	University campus	1156	2 months	Individuals	145.6
USC [2]	University campus	4558	2 months	Individuals	23.8
San Francisco [1]	City	551	1 month	Cabs	834.7

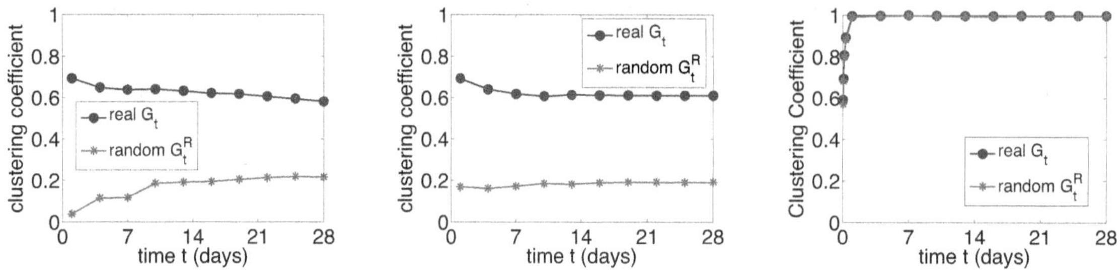

(a) Dartmouth (b) USC (c) San Francisco

Figure 1: Evolution of the clustering coefficient in the G_t of the three datasets, and in their random equivalents G_t^R.

them. As an example, two individuals who share a large number of friends will most probably know each other as well.

Regularity and **Similarity** can be mapped into DCWN features that, in turn, can be computed from a contact dataset so as to identify what kind of relationship two individuals share. In the following, we discuss such features.

5.1.1 *Edge Persistence*

A complex network metric mapping of the **Regularity** of a relationship is the edge persistence. Basically, considering the set of event graphs $\{\mathcal{G}_1, \ldots, \mathcal{G}_t\}$[2], the edge persistence $per_t(i,j)$ measures the percentage of times the edge (i,j) occurred over the past discrete time steps $1, 2, \ldots, t$. Formally, it is defined as $per_t(i,j) = \frac{1}{t}\sum_{k=1}^{t} \mathbb{1}_{[(i,j)\in\mathcal{E}_k]}$, where $\mathbb{1}_{[(i,j)\in\mathcal{E}_k]}$ is an indicator function that assumes value 1 if the edge (i,j) exists in $\mathcal{E}_k$ at time k, and 0 otherwise.

For instance, assuming that each day of the week is a time step, if Smith and Johnson met each other twice in a week, their edge persistence is the number of times they encountered, i.e., 2, divided by the total number of time steps, i.e., 7, or $per_{t=7}(\textit{Smith}, \textit{Johnson}) = 2/7$. The edge persistence allows spotting regular relationships between two entities.

We show in Figure 2 (first column) the edge persistence as measured in the three datasets. Considering the set of event graphs $\{\mathcal{G}_1, ..., \mathcal{G}_t\}$ of all three real networks and their RND-generated random counterparts[3] $\{\mathrm{RND}(\mathcal{G}_1), ..., \mathrm{RND}(\mathcal{G}_t)\}$, we portray the complementary cumulative distribution function (CCDF) $\overline{F}_{per(i,j)}(x) = P[per_t(i,j) > x]$. There, the time step is one day and each curve is obtained by analyzing four weeks of contacts, since $t = 28$ corresponds to the length of the shortest considered dataset, i.e., the San Francisco one. From Figures 2-a and 2-c, we observe that the Dartmouth and USC networks have edge persistence distributions that significantly differ from those computed in their random equivalents. More precisely, while the CCDFs of random networks show an exponential decay, the individuals in the real network tend to see each other regularly, i.e., for reasons beyond pure randomness, leading to a heavy-tailed distribution. Conversely, as from Figure 2-e, the encounters in the San Francisco dataset show an edge persistence similar to that obtained in the random equivalent graphs.

5.1.2 *Topological Overlap*

The **Similarity** of contacts can be mapped to the topological overlap feature of a complex network. This metric is extracted from the aggregated temporal graph G_t. The topological overlap $to_t(i,j)$ of a pair of nodes i and j is defined as the ratio of neighbors shared by two nodes, or, formally,

$$to_t(i,j) = \frac{|\{k \mid (i,k) \in E_t\} \cap \{k \mid (j,k) \in E_t\}|}{|\{k \mid (i,k) \in E_t\} \cup \{k \mid (j,k) \in E_t\}|}.$$

In Figure 2 (second column), we show the CCDF $\overline{F}_{to(i,j)}(x) = P[to_t(i,j) > x]$ of the topological overlap of the edges of the real networks G_t and their respective random networks G_t^R, generated by the T-RND mechanism[4]. Again, we pick one day as the time step and consider four weeks of contacts (i.e., $t = 28$ days). Similar to what occurred to the edge persistence, we note that the Dartmouth and USC network CCDFs significantly differ from their random counterparts, in Figures 2-b and 2-d. Indeed, pairs of individuals in these datasets share common neighbors in a way that could not happen randomly. Conversely, in Figure 2-f, the San Francisco network again behaves like a random contact network. Since all results indicate that the San Francisco network is random by nature, in the remainder of this work we will focus on the Dartmouth and the USC datasets.

5.2 The RECAST algorithm

We have seen that both the edge persistence and the topological overlap behave differently in contact graphs generated from real-world social networks and in their random equivalent graphs. We exploit such a diversity to identify which edges are consequences of random or social events. In particular, we propose a classification of relationships among network entities into four categories, depending on whether the edge corresponding to the relationship features random-like persistence and topological overlap. The four

[2]Note that edge persistence is computed over the set of graphs $\mathcal{G}_t$ and not over the temporal accumulation graph G_t.

[3]We generated five instances for every random graph and the cumulative distribution considers all of them.

[4]Again, we generated five instances for every random graph and the cumulative distribution considers all of them.

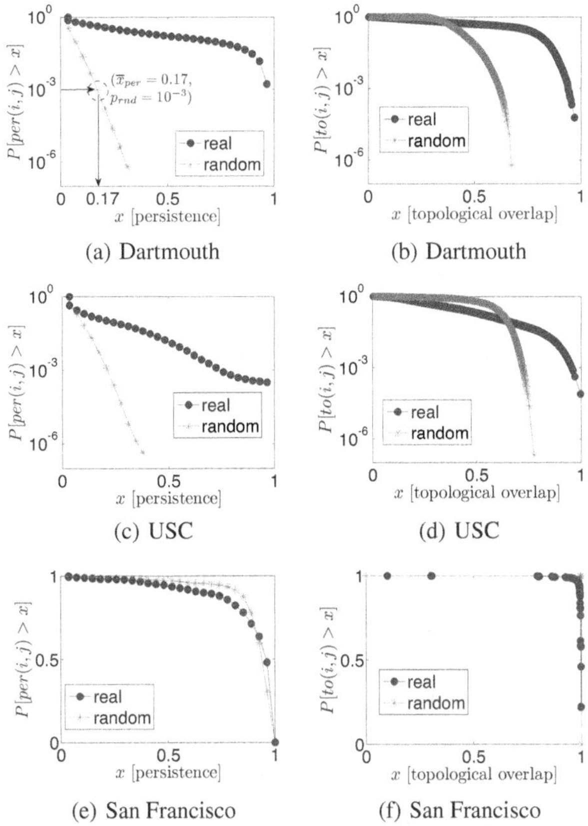

Figure 2: The complementary cumulative distribution function of the edge persistence (a)(c)(e) and topological overlap (b)(d)(f) for the G_t of the three datasets and for their random correspondents G_t^R after four weeks.

classes of relationships are described in Table 2. A feature value is called "social" if there is an almost zero probability of this value being generated randomly. On the other hand, a feature value is called "random" if there is a significant probability of this value be generated randomly. In fact, as we explain in the following paragraphs, the unique parameter p_{rnd} of RECAST defines if a given feature value is social or random.

Table 2: RECAST relationships classes.

Class	Edge persistence	Topological overlap
Friends	social	social
Acquaintance	random	social
Bridges	social	random
Random	random	random

Relationships classified as *Friends* characterize pairs of individuals whose connection shows social edge persistence and topological overlap, i.e., who meet each other regularly and also tend to know the same people[5]. The *Acquaintance* class includes relationships among individuals sharing many common encounters, but not meeting often. As an example, friends of friends who see each other once in a while, in occasions such as birthday parties, graduation ceremonies or weddings, would be classified as *Acquaintance*. The last social class is that of *Bridges*, characterizing pairs of individuals who see each other regularly, but do not share a large number of common acquaintances. E.g., the so-called familiar strangers, people who meet every day but do not really know each other (e.g., because they just commute between common home and work areas) are very likely to be classified as *Bridges*. Finally, when an edge is neither persistent nor characterized by topological overlap, it is considered the result of a random contact, and we classify it as *Random*.

In order to distinguish "social" from "random" values of the DCWN's features, we resort to the distributions we previously discussed. More precisely, we define a value p_{rnd}, the *only* parameter in RECAST, and we identify the feature value $\bar{x}$ for which $\overline{F}(\bar{x}) = p_{rnd}$ for the random network G_t^R. The value $\bar{x}$ represents then a threshold, such that feature values higher than $\bar{x}$ occur with a probability lower than p_{rnd} in a random network. If we set p_{rnd} to some small value, we can finally state that feature values higher than $\bar{x}$ are very unlikely to occur in a random network, i.e., they are most probably due to actual social relationships. The parameter p_{rnd} can also be seen as the expected classification error percentage. For instance, in Figure 2-a, consider $p_{rnd} = 10^{-3}$. This gives a threshold $\bar{x} = 0.17$, then all values higher than $\bar{x} = 0.17$ will be classified as social. However, there is a $p_{rnd} = 10^{-3}$ probability of randomly generating values that RECAST classified as social edges (i.e., false positives). In other words, we expect that $10^{-3} = 0.1\%$ of the edges classified as social to be, in fact, random. The full RECAST mechanism is described in Algorithm 1, where the criteria used in each classification are detailed. In this algorithm, index t is omitted for *per* and *to* metrics for clarity purposes.

Algorithm 1 RECAST: classify edges of G_t

Require: $p_{rnd} \geq 0$
 return class(i, j) $\forall (i, j) \in \cup_t E_t$
 Construct G_t^R and set $\{\texttt{RND}(\mathcal{G}_1), ..., \texttt{RND}(\mathcal{G}_t)\}$ using T-RND
 Get $\overline{F}_{to}(x)$ and $\overline{F}_{per}(x)$ from G_t^R
 Get $\bar{x}_{to} \mid \overline{F}_{to}(\bar{x}_{to}) = p_{rnd}$ and $\bar{x}_{per} \mid \overline{F}_{per}(\bar{x}_{per}) = p_{rnd}$
 for all edges $(i, j) \in E_t$ **do**
  if $per(i, j) > \bar{x}_{per}$ and $to(i, j) > \bar{x}_{to}$ **then**
   class$(i, j) \leftarrow$ *Friends*
  else if $per(i, j) > \bar{x}_{per}$ and $to(i, j) \leq \bar{x}_{to}$ **then**
   class$(i, j) \leftarrow$ *Bridges*
  else if $per(i, j) \leq \bar{x}_{per}$ and $to(i, j) > \bar{x}_{to}$ **then**
   class$(i, j) \leftarrow$ *Acquaintance*
  else
   class$(i, j) \leftarrow$ *Random*
  end if
 end for

The complexity of RECAST is upper bounded by the construction of G_t^R using T-RND, which is $O(t \times (|\mathcal{V}_t| + |\mathcal{E}_t^R|))$, i.e., the minimum complexity for the generation of a degree sequence-based random graph available to date [18]. After the construction of G_t^R, the complexity of the classification mechanism is $O(|E_t^R| \times |V_t|)$, where $O(|V_t|)$ is the cost of computing the topological overlap of an edge.

5.3 Classification results

We apply RECAST to the Dartmouth and the USC networks. We are omitting the results for the San Francisco dataset, since, as previously stated, the random-like nature of taxi routes makes the analysis uninteresting, with all edges classified as *Random*. In Figure 3, we show the number of edges per class as a function of

[5]It is worth mentioning that, although the *friend* terminology implies attachment among two individuals by affection or personal regard, we use it here to describe strong social ties in terms of regularity and similarity.

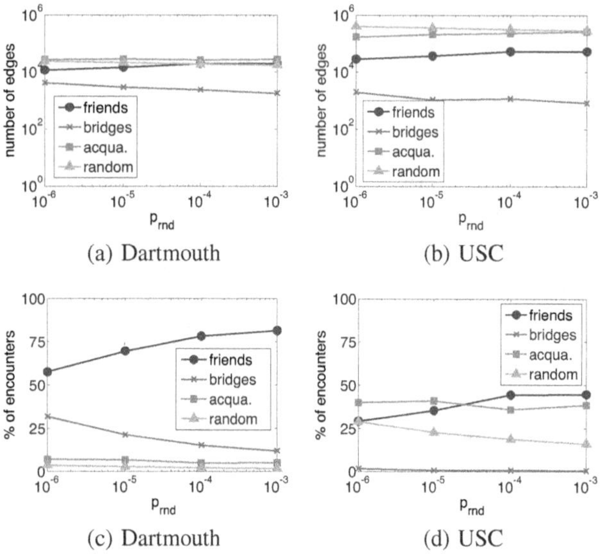

(a) Dartmouth (b) USC

(c) Dartmouth (d) USC

Figure 3: The number of edges (a)(b) and percentage of encounters (c)(d) of a given class that appears in the first four weeks of data versus p_{rnd}.

the p_{rnd} value. An initial and quite surprising observation is that, by varying p_{rnd} through four orders of magnitude, the number of edges per class stays in the same magnitude. This shows that RECAST is robust with respect to p_{rnd}, i.e., it does not need a fine calibration of the parameter to return a consistent edge classification.

Secondly, in both datasets, the number of *Bridges* is orders of magnitude lower than the other classes, a clear indication that in the analyzed social networks regular connections among different communities are rare. Also the number of *Friends* edges is similar in the two networks, implying similar dynamics in tight relationships among individuals in the two campuses. This also agrees with the biological constraint on a social interaction that limits human social networks' size, i.e., the number of *Friends* relationships [20]. However, the two datasets differ when looking at the number of edges classified as *Acquaintances* and *Random*, that are one order of magnitude larger in USC than in Dartmouth. This is the result of the actual size of the two campuses, USC accounting for a population around ten times larger than that of Dartmouth. This aspect is also reflected by the size of the traces in Table 1 that clearly leads, in the USC network, to (i) many more *Random* contacts among individuals who do not actually know each other, but just happen to cross each other while strolling on campus, and (ii) an increased presence of strangers who happen to know the same people, leading to more *Acquaintances* edges.

The observations above are even more evident when observing the percentage of individual encounters of each type in the Dartmouth and USC networks. In Figure 3, we show the percentage of encounters of a given class that appear in the first four weeks of data for a given value of p_{rnd}. The percentage of *Random* encounters in the Dartmouth network is close to zero, varying from 1.7% to 3.6% as p_{rnd} decreases. On the other hand, in the USC network, this percentage varies from 16% to 29%. In fact, the proportion of *Random* encounters provides a good estimate of the probability of random decisions mentioned in Section 4. Thus, the USC network has a significantly higher tendency to evolve to a random topology than the Dartmouth network.

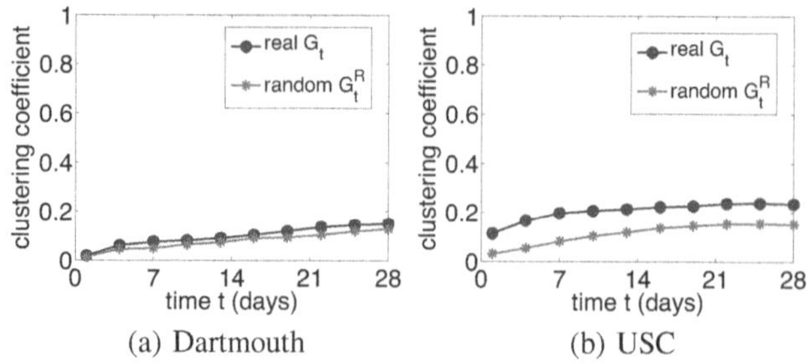

(a) Dartmouth (b) USC

Figure 5: Evolution of the clustering coefficient of G_t when only *Random* edges are present, compared to their random correspondents G_t^R.

The analysis is confirmed by Figure 4, portraying the snapshots of the Dartmouth and USC networks after two weeks of interactions, when considering only social edges (i.e., those classified as *Friends*, *Acquaintances* and *Bridges*) or only edges tagged as *Random*. Edges of the former networks in Figures 4-a and 4-c are distinguished by colors, according to the same code used in Figure 3 (*Friends* edges are in blue, *Bridges* in red, *Acquaintances* in gray, and *Random* in orange). The difference between the social-only networks and the random-only ones is striking. Social networks are characterized by a complex structure of *Friends* communities, linked to each other by *Bridges* and *Acquaintances*. More precisely, when comparing the Dartmouth and USC social networks, the former appears to be dominated by *Friends* interactions, while the sheer number of *Acquaintances* in the latter drives its graph structure.

Conversely, networks containing only *Random* edges do not show any structure and look like random graphs. A rigorous way to verify the randomness of such networks, and thus validate the efficiency of the RECAST classification, is to perform a clustering coefficient analysis. Figure 5 compares the clustering coefficients of the Dartmouth and USC networks G_t *when only Random edges are present* against the same metric computed in their random counterparts G_t^R. The clustering coefficient, commonly employed to determine the actual randomness of a network, has very similar evolutions in G_t and G_t^R: this proves that the network of contacts tagged as *Random* by RECAST is actually a random network. Therefore, RECAST is able to extract from a real-world contact dataset edges that correspond to random encounters.

6. RECAST APPLICATION

In this section, we use the Dartmouth and USC contact traces to simulate an epidemic dissemination. We consider that the users communicate with each other in an opportunistic fashion, i.e., without any infrastructure and exchanging messages only when they are within physical proximity. Thus, if user i wants to send a message to user j, he (she) has to deliver it personally to j or has to ask other users to relay it for him (her), through a multi-hop carry-and-forward path. Also, we consider the transfer to be epidemic, i.e., in order to reach j, user i sends a message to all other users he (she) is in contact with at a given time t. The latter forward it to all of the users they later meet and so on, until user j is reached. Such an epidemic approach allows us characterizing the lower bound on the delay required by the opportunistic transfer.

For both Dartmouth and USC contact traces, we use RECAST to classify the relationships between users over one month of contact data, which we refer to as the *classifying stage*. Then, we simulate the opportunistic transfer scenario above during the two following

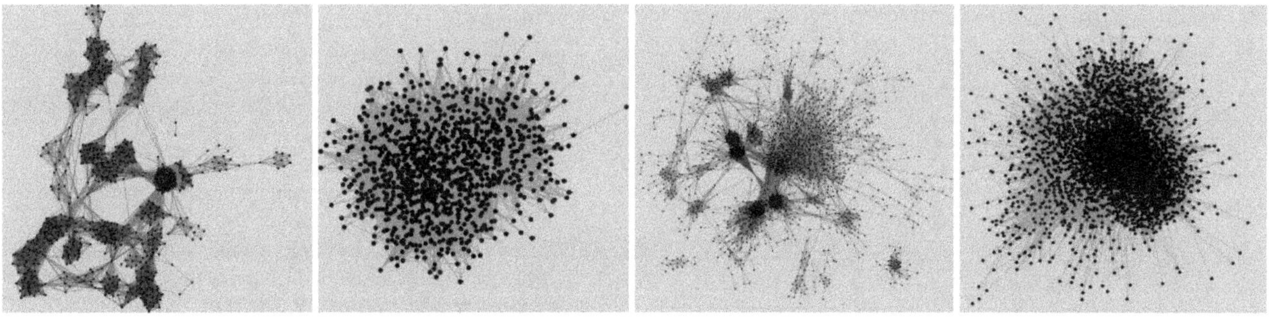

(a) Dartmouth, social edges (b) Dartmouth, random edges (c) USC, social edges (d) USC, random edges

Figure 4: Snapshots of the Dartmouth and USC networks after two weeks of interactions, considering only the social edges and only the random edges. *Friends* edges are painted in blue, *Bridges* in red, *Acquaintances* in gray and *Random* in orange. This figure is best viewed in colors.

weeks, termed the *routing stage*, containing only future encounters, not known previously by RECAST. For each user i, we randomly pick a time $t_{0,i}$ within the first week of the *routing stage* for him/her to start the epidemic transfer process, and a destination user j. We leave one week for the message to reach its destination: if the message is not delivered by then, the transfer is deemed failed and the data lost.

In Figure 6, we show the overall forwarding efficiency. Figures 6-a and 6-b show the percentage of messages that were successfully delivered to their destinations in the Dartmouth and in the USC scenarios, respectively. Each bar represents one relationship shared by the message source and destination, and within each bar we depict the fraction of edges of a given class of relationship that was used to deliver the message. First, we observe that all the messages reached their destinations in the Dartmouth scenario, a consequence of the limited network size. Moreover, the edges classified as *Friends* were the most used to deliver the messages and the *Random* ones the least used. In fact, considering all the paths directed to *Friends*, less than 2% of the hops in these paths were given by users who share a *Random* relationship.

Different from the Dartmouth scenario, not all messages are delivered in the USC scenario. The lower delivery ratio is partially due to the larger network that is harder to navigate. However, that is not the only reason, and the social relationship between the source and destination significantly affects the probability of success. Socially connected pairs (tagged as *Friends*, *Bridges* and *Acquaintances*) can actually exchange data: 90% of the messages were successfully delivered to *Friends*, 92% to *Bridges* and 77% *Acquaintances*. If one wants to send a message to a *Random* contact in the USC scenario, there is only 44% of chances that this message will arrive successfully. Moreover, although the majority of the classified edges in the USC scenario are *Random* (see Figure 3), the majority of the hops in the paths are between users who share a social relationship. Considering all the paths directed to *Friends*, less than 13% of the hops in these paths were given by users who share a *Random* relationship.

In Figure 7, we show how much time it was necessary for the messages to reach their destinations. We grouped together all the routings from source user i to destination user j by the class of relationship $c$that i and j share. Then, we cumulatively count how many destinations of the class c are reached per each hour, considering the total number of routings that were performed between sources and destinations of class c. Observe that the expected time to reach a *Random* contact is significantly higher than the time needed to reach a social contact. Moreover, observe that the majority of the messages sent to *Friends* arrive in the first hours for both scenarios.

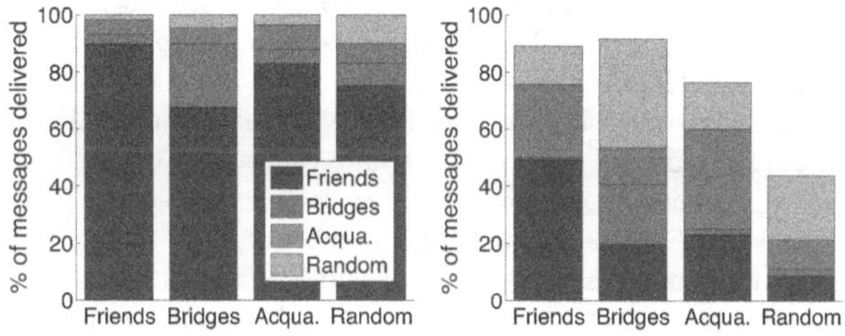

(a) Dartmouth (b) USC

Figure 6: The forwarding efficiency when user i sends a message to user j in the opportunistic network, and i and j share a specific RECAST relationship. Within each bar we also show the fraction of edges of a given class of relationship that was used to deliver the message.

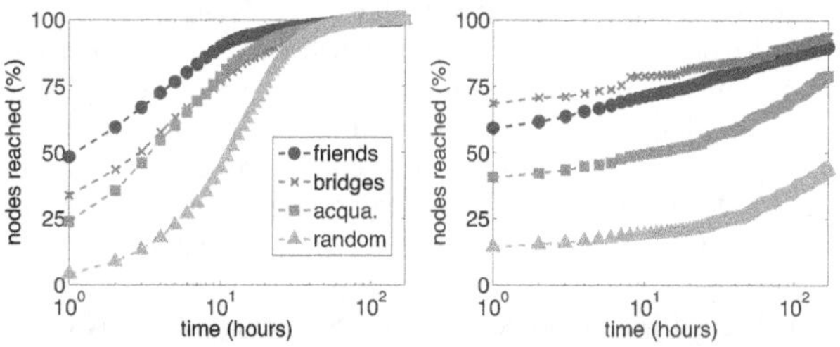

(a) Dartmouth (b) USC

Figure 7: The % of users who were reached over the time.

It is not only the time it takes for a message to arrive at its destination that is relevant to the design of forwarding solutions for opportunistic networks. Another fundamental aspect is the number of hops required to reach the destination. In Figure 7, we show the cumulative distribution function (CDF) of the path lengths of messages between users i and j who share a determined class of relationship. Observe that the expected number of hops for a message to arrive at a *Random* contact is significantly higher than to arrive at a social contact. For the USC scenario, 89%, 92% and 81% of the routes to *Friend*, *Bridge* and *Acquaintance* destinations, respectively, have path lengths lower or equal to 3. In the meanwhile, only 65% of the routes to *Random* destinations have path lengths

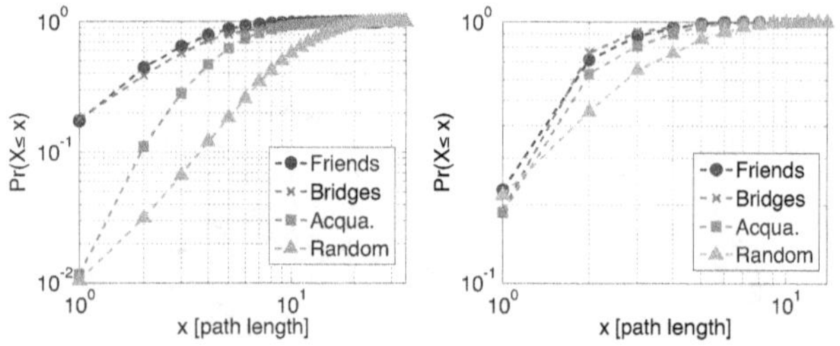

(a) Dartmouth (b) USC

Figure 8: The histogram of the path lengths of messages between users i and j who share a determined class of relationship.

lower or equal to 3. This difference is even more striking for the Dartmouth scenario, where 65%, 57% and 28% of the routes to *Friend*, *Bridge* and *Acquaintance* destinations, respectively, have path lengths lower or equal to 3, and only 6% to *Random* destinations have path lengths lower o equal to 3.

Overall, our results show how the RECAST classification allows identifying those who share social relationships with the sender, whose opportunistic paths are usually short and reliable. In fact, such paths usually pass through a few number of hops, mostly using social ties among users, and rarely leverage random encounters. As an intuitive corollary, reaching users that share some social relationship is significantly easier than attaining users one does not know, especially in large systems. These results may serve to leverage the performance of various routing solutions for opportunistic networks. If we previously know the class of relationship the destination share with the source, we also know the chances and the probable time the message will take to arrive.

7. CONCLUSIONS

The contribution of this paper is threefold. First, we modeled three real-world mobile user encounter datasets as temporal contact graphs and we proposed the use of random equivalent graphs to outline their hidden social structure. Our original approach shows that different mobility traces can yield completely different social structures, determined by diverse behaviors of the entities participating in the system. These results let us speculate that researchers should not generalize their results based on the analysis of a single dataset. Second, we proposed the RECAST strategy to lazily classify random and social relationships in temporal social networks, and demonstrate its simplicity and effectiveness. Third, we employed the RECAST classification to the case of epidemic opportunistic transfers, and showed its relevance towards the identification of faster, reliable paths leveraging social ties among users.

As future work, we plan to analyze other mobility scenarios, both real and synthetic. Moreover, it would be interesting to apply the RECAST to other social networks, such as communication networks from phone calls or SMSs.

8. REFERENCES

[1] A. Rojas, P. Branch, and G. Armitage, "Experimental validation of the random waypoint mobility model through a real world mobility trace for large geographical areas," in *Proceedings of the 8th ACM MSWiM*, MSWiM '05, (New York, NY, USA), pp. 174–177, ACM, 2005.

[2] W. jen Hsu and A. Helmy, "Impact: Investigation of mobile-user patterns across university campuses using wlan trace analysis," *CoRR*, vol. abs/cs/0508009, 2005.

[3] T. Henderson, D. Kotz, and I. Abyzov, "The changing usage of a mature campus-wide wireless network," in *Proceedings of the 10th annual international conference on Mobile computing and networking*, MobiCom '04, (New York, NY, USA), pp. 187–201, ACM, 2004.

[4] M. C. Gonzalez, C. A. Hidalgo, and A.-L. Barabasi, "Understanding individual human mobility patterns," *Nature*, vol. 453, pp. 779–782, 2008.

[5] J. Leskovec, L. Backstrom, R. Kumar, and A. Tomkins, "Microscopic evolution of social networks," in *KDD '08: Proceeding of the 14th ACM SIGKDD*, (New York, NY, USA), pp. 462–470, ACM, 2008.

[6] E. Cho, S. A. Myers, and J. Leskovec, "Friendship and mobility: user movement in location-based social networks," in *Proceedings of the 17th ACM SIGKDD*, KDD '11, (New York, NY, USA), pp. 1082–1090, ACM, 2011.

[7] A. Barabasi and R. Albert, "Emergence of Scaling in Random Networks," *Science*, vol. 286, no. 5439, p. 509, 1999.

[8] R. Albert, H. Jeong, and A.-L. Barabási, "Diameter of the World Wide Web," *Nature*, vol. 401, pp. 130–131, September 1999.

[9] P. Erdös and A. Rényi, "On the evolution of random graphs," *Publ. Math. Inst. Hung. Acad. Sci.*, vol. 7, p. 17, 1960.

[10] A. Mtibaa, M. May, C. Diot, and M. Ammar, "Peoplerank: Social opportunistic forwarding," in *IEEE Infocom*, 2010.

[11] W. Gao, Q. Li, B. Zhao, and G. Cao, "Multicasting in delay tolerant networks: a social network perspective," in *ACM MobiHoc*, 2009.

[12] M. Conti, R. Di Pietro, A. Gabrielli, L. V. Mancini, and A. Mei, "The Smallville Effect: Social Ties Make Mobile Networks More Secure Against the Node Capture Attack," in *ACM MobiWac*, 2010.

[13] A. G. Miklas, K. K. Gollu, K. K. W. Chan, S. Saroiu, K. P. Gummadi, and E. De Lara, "Exploiting social interactions in mobile systems," in *Proceedings of the UbiComp '07*, (Berlin, Heidelberg), pp. 409–428, Springer-Verlag, 2007.

[14] G. Zyba, G. M. Voelker, S. Ioannidis, and C. Diot, "Dissemination in opportunistic mobile ad-hoc networks: The power of the crowd," in *Proceedings of IEEE INFOCOM 2011*, pp. 1179–1187, IEEE, Apr. 2011.

[15] S. Milgram, *The individual in a social world*, ch. The Familiar Stranger: An Aspect of Urban Anonymity, pp. 51–53. Addison-Wesley, 1977.

[16] D. J. Watts and S. H. Strogatz, "Collective dynamics of "small-world" networks," *Nature*, vol. 393, pp. 440–442, 1998.

[17] F. Bai, D. Stancil, and H. Krishnan, "Toward understanding characteristics of dedicated short range communications (dsrc) from a perspective of vehicular network engineers.," in *ACM MobiCom*, 2010.

[18] F. Chung and L. Lu, "Connected Components in Random Graphs with Given Expected Degree Sequences," *Annals of Combinatorics*, vol. 6, pp. 125–145, Nov. 2002.

[19] C. A. Hidalgo and C. Rodriguez-Sickert, "The dynamics of a mobile phone network," *Physica A: Statistical Mechanics and its Applications*, vol. 387, no. 12, pp. 3017 – 3024, 2008.

[20] R. I. M. Dunbar, "The social brain hypothesis," *Evol. Anthropol.*, vol. 6, no. 5, pp. 178–190, 1998.

Epidemic Content Distribution: Empirical and Analytic Performance

Ljubica Pajevic, Gunnar Karlsson, Ólafur Helgason
KTH Royal Institute of Technology
Linnaeus ACCESS Center
Stockholm, Sweden
{ljubica, gk, olafurr}@kth.se

ABSTRACT

Epidemic content dissemination has been proposed as an approach to mitigate frequent link disruptions and support content-centric information dissemination in opportunistic networks. Stochastic modeling is a common method to evaluate performance of epidemic dissemination schemes. The models introduce assumptions which, on one hand make them analytically tractable, while on the other, ignore attested characteristics of human mobility. In this paper, we investigate the fitness and limitations of an analytical stochastic model for content dissemination by comparison with experimental results obtained from real mobility traces. Our finding is that a homogeneous analytic model is unable to capture the performance of content dissemination with respect to content delivery delays.

Categories and Subject Descriptors

C.2.1 [**Network Architecture and Design**]: Wireless comunication; C.4 [**Performance of Systems**]: Modeling techniques

Keywords

Epidemic modeling, opportunistic networks, ad hoc networks, content distribution

1. INTRODUCTION

Opportunistic networking is seen as a feasible way to provide communication between mobile devices in absence of infrastructure, or as a mean to off-load existing mobile networks. Both cases are seen as scalable solutions for content distribution that adopts a *store-carry-and-forward* paradigm: a node downloads and stores contents; it then carries the contents through its mobility and shares the contents with other nodes it encounters.

A variety of opportunistic routing schemes have been proposed and epidemic spreading is central to many. Epidemic content distribution schemes are able to achieve minimum delivery delay at the expense of increased use of resources, such as buffer space, transmission power, and bandwidth. In order to exploit trade-off between delivery delay and resource consumption, different schemes limit the number of hops for contents to be carried. Adopting the principles of epidemic modeling from the field of mathematical biology to study spreading of diseases, stochastic modeling has become a common approach.

In this paper, we empirically study the performance of epidemic content spreading by using real-world mobility traces. Then, we consider an analytic model proposed in [8], and examine if this homogeneous model can be utilized to evaluate the performance of opportunistic networks. We consider a basic epidemic scheme, where all nodes participate in content forwarding.

The rest of the paper is organized as follows. In Section 2 we describe the analytic model for epidemic content distribution. We present the empirical study and compare it with analytic evaluation in Section 3. Section 4 summarizes related work and in Section 5 we draw main conclusions of this study and give directions for our future work.

2. OPPORTUNISTIC CONTENT DISTRIBUTION MODEL

2.1 Application scenario

The application scenario we consider here is that of disseminating information by utilizing opportunistic contacts and based on user interest. Sharing local news, traffic and tourist information in public areas, public announcements at massive events, or mobile advertisements are common examples where this can be used. From the perspective of a publisher, questions of interest could be: "how many users will the information reach in a period of one hour?", or "what is the probability that the information will reach a certain number of users?". Such questions can be answered by analytic modeling of information spreading.

2.2 Homogeneous system model

We consider a network $\mathcal{N}$ with $|\mathcal{N}| = N$ mobile nodes, equipped with short-range radios and moving in a bounded area. The network is assumed to be relatively sparse, with node density insufficient to establish a connected network. The data is stored and carried by nodes, and transferred through intermittent contacts occurring owing to node mobility. Let us introduce the definitions and assumptions that we will use in this text. The *contact time* is the duration of time when two nodes are in transmission range of each other. The *inter-contact time* for a pair of nodes is defined as the time elapsed between two consecutive contacts.

MSWiM'13, November 3–8, 2013, Barcelona, Spain.

ACM 978-1-4503-2353-6/13/11
http://dx.doi.org/10.1145/2507924.2507998

We assume that the mobility of nodes is such that the inter-contact times between any pair of nodes can be modelled by independent identically distributed (i.i.d.) random variables that are exponentially distributed. Then, we assume that nodes in the network are *homogeneous*, that is, all the nodes have the same mobility and contact patterns that follows the same exponential inter-contact distribution with average rate λ.

The content spreading scheme works as follows. At time $t = 0$, there is a single node in the network that possesses the content item and all other nodes in the network are interested in obtaining it. Nodes that obtained the content are willing to forward the content to other nodes they meet. We study the performance by investigating the time it takes for the content to reach all the other $N - 1$ nodes. The transmissions are assumed to be instantaneous and every contact results in a successful transmission.

We are interested in two metrics which characterize the process of content distribution, namely *overall* and *individual delivery time*. Consider a network $\mathcal{N}$ and an arbitrarily chosen node i, $i \in \mathcal{N}$. Given that content is available at i at time $t = 0$, the *overall delivery time*, denoted by T_{odt}, is the time until the content has reached all the other $N - 1$ nodes. The time until a node j, $j \in \mathcal{N}$ has obtained the content is the *individual delivery time*, T_{idt}. From a performance perspective, T_{odt} measures the performance of the entire system, while T_{idt} is a measure of the system performance seen from an arbitrary node.

Borrowing the terms from epidemic modeling [3], we denote nodes that carry contents as *infected*, and nodes that are interested in obtaining contents as *susceptible* nodes. In our model, once a susceptible node is infected, it stays in that state for the remainder of the epidemic process.

2.3 Stochastic model

In the field of epidemic modeling, there are two main approaches to analyse spreading: stochastic and fluid-based modeling. Stochastic models are preferable when studying networks of small scale, as they allow some randomness in the final number of infected. The fluid models present a deterministic approximation of the stochastic spreading and can therefore only produce accurate results for networks of larger scale. From an engineering point of view, only stochastic models are able to predict the distribution of time until a certain percentage of network has been infected. Herein, we consider a stochastic model for content distribution, based on a continuous-time Markov chain. We present only the basic description referring interested readers to [8] for the complete analysis.

Let the random variable $X(t)$ be the number of infected nodes at time $t, t \geq 0$ with $X(0) = 1$. Since all the i infected nodes spread the content further, the process $\{X(t); t \geq 0\}$ is a pure-birth process with with rates $\lambda_i = i(N - i)\lambda$ for all the states $i = 1, ..., N - 1$.

T_{odt} is the time it takes the system to reach the absorbing state $X(T_{odt}) = N$. The time the system spends in each transient state i is exponentially distributed with the expected value $1/\lambda_i$, and the average absorption time is given by the sum:

$$E[T_{odt}] = \sum_{i=1}^{N-1} \frac{1}{\lambda_i} = \frac{1}{\lambda} \sum_{i=1}^{N-1} \frac{1}{i(N-i)} = \frac{2}{\lambda N} H_{N-1} \quad (1)$$

where $H_n = \sum_{i=1}^{n} 1/i$ is the n-th harmonic number.

To obtain $E[T_{idt}]$, denote by the random variable $T_{k,N-1}$ time until k out of the $N - 1$ susceptible nodes have become infected, and introduce the event K that a given node is the k-th to become infected. Since all nodes are identical and inter-contact times are i.i.d., the probability of this event is $Pr\{K\} = 1/(N - 1)$ and

$$E[T_{idt}] = \sum_{k=1}^{N-1} E[T_{k,N-1}] Pr\{K\} = \frac{1}{N-1} \sum_{k=1}^{N-1} E[T_{k,N-1}].$$

Omitting a few steps of derivation (complete proof in [8]), the expected individual delivery time is

$$E[T_{idt}] = \frac{1}{\lambda(N-1)} H_{N-1}. \quad (2)$$

Expressions (1) and (2) describe epidemic spreading with respect to contents delivery times. In the next section, we will empirically analyse the spreading in four scenarios, by means of simulation.

3. ANALYSIS WITH MOBILITY TRACES

3.1 Mobility Datasets

To cover various scenarios, we use four experimental datasets different in time granularity, number of participants and in duration. The datasets report pairwise contacts between users moving in relatively restricted areas: a conference venue, a university and office buildings. Note, however, that the areas are not strictly bounded, thus users may leave the areas and return after longer periods (even days). Below we describe the contexts where the traces were collected, the acquisition methodologies used, and our methodology of pre-processing the traces.

Infocom mobility traces [12] were obtained during four days at Infocom 2006. The dataset reports direct contacts between a group of 78 attendees of a workshop, who were carrying iMotes. The scanning interval was 120 seconds. Thus, it is likely that many shorter contacts were not recorded. Also, contacts between two users scanning simultaneously are missing. Therefore, we assume that two nodes were in contact if either of the nodes reported that event. As our model assumes a closed system (no nodes leaving), we consider only the time intervals when most of the nodes were active and seen by other users. The experiment lasted for four days; we extracted from the trace only the contacts during daytime: between 9:00 and 18:00 on the first and the third day, between 9:00 and 21:00 on the second, and between 9:00 and 16:00 on the fourth day.

Humanet trace [1] describes human mobility of participants in an office building. The data collection was carried out in a company building and contains traces of 52 participants, company employees, during one working day. The users were carrying Bluetooth devices, which were scanning

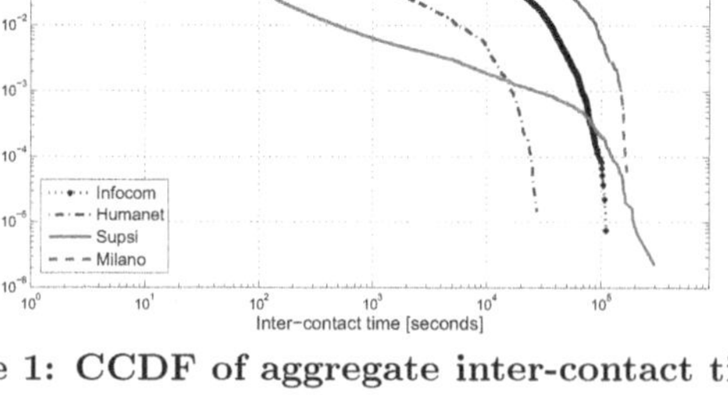

Figure 1: CCDF of aggregate inter-contact times.

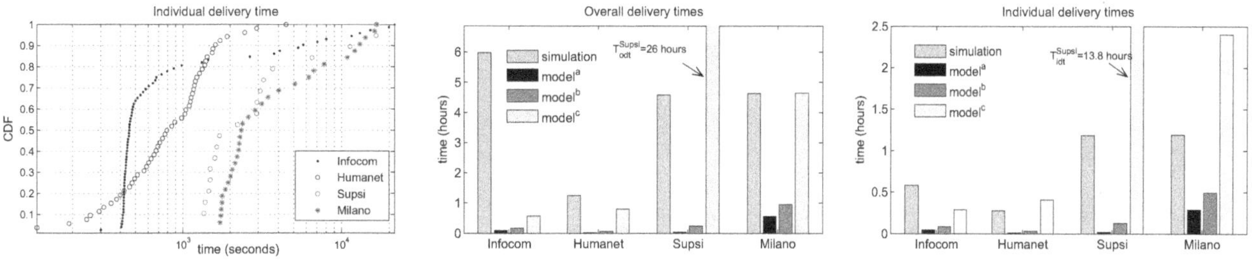

(a) (b) (c)

Figure 2: (a) CDFs of the delivery times. Comparison of the (b) overall and (c) individual delivery times.

every 5 seconds to capture direct contacts with other devices. For each user, contact entries contain the time when the contact started and when it ended. First, we processed the trace to account for all the contacts recorded by either of the two nodes, and when both nodes recorded the same event, we took the entry with longer contact duration. Some entries contained contacts of zero duration; if either of two nodes reported a contact with non-zero duration, we chose that entry. The next step was to merge multiple consecutive contacts of zero duration if their inter-contact time was shorter than one second into a single contact with the duration equal to the sum of their inter-contact times, and finally, omit contacts that occurred before 10:00 or after 19:00.

Supsi dataset [4] includes contacts between 39 participants from three institutes, located in two buildings. The experiment was carried out in December 2010 and lasted more than three weeks. We use records of eleven days when the largest number of contacts was recorded. Proximity information was collected by sensor nodes, carried by the users. The nodes were configured to have a transmission range of 5 meters and perform neighbour discovery every 10 milliseconds. Similarly as with the previous traces, we consider only contacts from 9:00 to 18:00. This comes from the assumption that the contacts took place in the area of interest, and that they represent real mobility of people, as some devices collected contact information during the night when left by the users in the offices. This leaves records of 34 users in total; the number of active users per day varied from 13 to 27.

Milano dataset [5] was collected at the University of Milano in November 2008 from 44 mobile devices carried by faculty members, graduate students, and technical staff. The experiment area comprised offices and laboratories located in a three-floor building, and nearby premises where participants took breaks during lunch times. Contacts were logged by devices operating with a transmission range of 10 meters and a configurable scanning interval of around one second. By using the same procedure of filtering out sparse contacts during the night or during the days when few participants were active, we extract only the contacts during work hours from 9:00 to 18:00 over twelve days.

Note that all traces capture direct contacts between the experiment participants, and, aside from the *Infocom* trace, with scanning intervals in the order of seconds. Due to the long scanning interval, the *Infocom* trace may be missing shorter contacts.

3.2 Aggregate inter-contact time distributions

We calculate the inter-contact times between any two nodes, and assume that all the samples come from one and the same distribution, the *aggregate* inter-contact time distribution. The distribution of samples of inter-contact times for a specific pair of nodes is denoted by *pair-wise* inter-contact time distribution. The aggregate distributions are plotted in Fig. 1. The average inter-contact times of these distributions are: 2347 (*Infocom*), 312 (*Humanet*), 323 (*Supsi*) and 7996 seconds (*Milano*) ($\bar{\tau}_{ag}$ in Tab. 1). Only the *Milano* trace seems to resemble exponential distribution, and only up to around 6 hours (found by looking carefully into a lin-log scale). All distributions exhibit fast decay after a certain value (usually order of hours), which however, could simply be an artefact of the finite duration of the traces.

In opportunistic networking, accurately characterising inter-contact times between nodes is crucial for evaluating system performance. In earlier works, the common approach has been to look at aggregate distributions. However, recent studies such as [2], [10] indicate the risk of treating aggregate distributions as representative of pair-wise distributions. The authors in [10] prove that aggregating various pair-wise distributions can lead to false conclusions on the characteristics of node interactions on a pair level. We confirm this in the following section.

3.3 Experimental evaluation

In this section, we assess the capability of the homogeneous epidemic model to capture the process of content spreading in real-life scenarios.

We simulated four scenarios by replaying the pre-processed traces in 3.1. For each of the traces, we choose a single day when the nodes were most active, seen as the number of contacts recorded during that day. The reason for this is twofold: first, to observe the spreading we needed enough interaction between users, and the second, some nodes were missing from the traces during multiple days. *Humanet* trace is only one day long; for *Infocom* and *Milano* we choose the first day and for *Supsi* the eleventh. The number of nodes during those days was 72, 52, 19 and 32, for *Infocom, Humanet, Supsi* and *Milano*, respectively. The spreading works as follows. We start by infecting a single node and evaluate the time until it infects all other nodes. The same process is repeated for all the nodes in the trace. To account for the daily variations, nodes spread new content every hour during the active part of the day. We consider only the simulation runs when all the nodes were eventually infected and find the average overall delivery times and individual delivery times. Cumulative distribution functions (CDFs) for individual delivery times are plotted in Fig. 2(a).

The analytic model is an efficient tool to estimate the system performance; its simplicity stems from the fact that it requires only two input parameters: the number of nodes in the network and the node inter-contact rate. In order to validate the analytic model, we compute the same metrics,

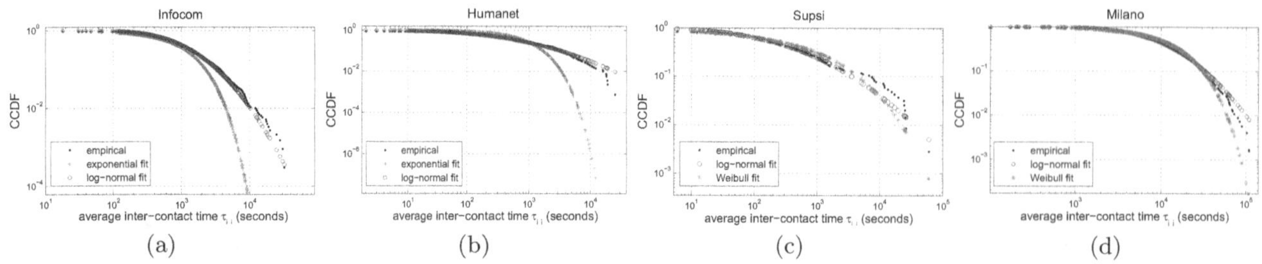

Figure 3: CCDF of average pair-wise inter-contact times: (a) Infocom, (b) Humanet, (c) Supsi, (d) Milano.

overall and individual delivery times given by formulas (1) and (2), and assume that node interactions can be described by the aggregate inter-contact time distributions. The inter-contact rates are reciprocal to average inter-contact times. Fig. 2 (b, c) depicts the simulation results and the computed delivery times (denoted by model^a).

We observe large discrepancies between simulation results and the delivery times predicted by the model. The average overall delivery times obtained from the simulations are: 359, 74, 275 and 278 minutes; while the model predicts delivery times: 316, 54, 118 and 2012 seconds. Clearly, the model does not match any of the scenarios, and it underestimates the overall delivery time for the *Supsi* trace by three orders of magnitude. With respect to the average individual delivery times, the situation is similar; the simulation yields: 2089, 993, 4264 and 4291 seconds, and the model gives: 160, 28, 62 and 1039 seconds.

The explanation for this lies in several factors:

1. The aggregate inter-contact time distribution is not representative of the pair-wise inter-contact distributions in any of the examined traces. This can be seen from the aggregate distributions for *Humanet* and *Supsi* in Fig. 1. Their average inter-contact times are relatively short (order of minutes), while the distributions are long tailed. This is due to finite duration of the traces: pairs that meet more frequently will contribute more samples of their inter-contact times.
2. Many node pairs never meet. In some scenarios, we see that even the most "social" nodes meet very few other nodes and hence, all of their inter-contact times are not observable.
3. To estimate spreading times, we calculated the delivery times by averaging only over those simulations in which all the nodes were infected. In theory, the average overall delivery times would be infinite, since some nodes never get infected.

We investigate the first two findings in further detail in the following sections.

3.4 Pair-wise inter-contact time distributions

In all four traces, we have seen that the aggregate inter-contact time distribution does not give a complete view of the contact patterns in the network. Thus, we look at inter-contact times on a node-pair level. However, fitting different distributions for each node pair would lead to an intractable

Table 1: Estimated average inter-contact times.

	Infocom	Humanet	Supsi	Milano
$\bar{\tau}_{ag}$	2347	312	323	7996
$\bar{\tau}_{i,j}$	4386	1473	2397	14841
$\bar{\tau}^C_{i,j}$	15187	16346	4495	66445

*all times are given in seconds

model. Hence, on a node-pair level some approximation is usually assumed. The important is that all distributions have exponential decay or at least exhibit exponential tails. For each pair of nodes in a trace, we find the average inter-contact time and plot the distributions of these average times in Fig. 3. For all the traces, log-normal distribution seems to be a good fit; we observe that tails of empirical data are bounded by log-normal and Weibull curves. We then applied curve fitting with log-normal and estimated the average inter-contact times. The average values are given in Tab. 1, denoted by $\bar{\tau}_{i,j}$. By plugging these values in the formulas, we find that the delivery times are still underestimated, although they yield better estimates than in the case of inter-contact rates calculated from the aggregate distributions. The overall delivery times are: 591, 256, 882 and 3736 seconds, and the average individual delivery times are: 300, 130, 465 and 1928 seconds (model^b in Fig. 2 (b, c)).

Clearly, node contacts are too heterogeneous: notice from Fig. 3 that average inter-contact times for different pairs differ by two orders of magnitude. Still, we want to examine if, by simply treating the traces in a different way, we can improve the estimation using the homogeneous model.

3.5 Compensating for the missing contacts

In a network of N nodes, there are $\binom{N}{2}$ node pairs, and each pair can generate different pair-wise inter-contact time distributions. Our idea is to model contact patterns with an average inter-contact time for each node pair. Then, contact patterns in the network can be described with the *contact matrix* $\mathbf{T}=[\bar{\tau}_{i,j}]$, where $\bar{\tau}_{i,j}$ is the average inter-contact time for a pair of nodes (i, j). $\mathbf{T}$ is a symmetric, zero-diagonal matrix since $\bar{\tau}_{i,j} = \bar{\tau}_{j,i}, \forall(i, j)$. Thus, to describe a network we need $n(n-1)/2$ matrix elements, but many node pairs are missing from the traces. For example, only 30% of all node pairs in the *Supsi* trace are observable. This raises the question how to model interaction between those node pairs and to fill in the missing elements of the contact matrix.

We use the following method: assume that all the nodes i and j, whose contact is not captured in the processed trace, meet with some average inter-contact time T_m. First, we set the value T_m to be equal to the duration of the entire trace: 36, 9, 103 and 62 hours. Then, we calculated the average inter-contact times for the traces by averaging over the elements of the contact matrix; these values are given in Tab. 1, denoted by $\bar{\tau}^C_{i,j}$. The results for delivery times are plotted in Figs. 2 (b, c) and 4 (model^c). Fig. 2 shows that the proposed method is unable to accurately estimate the delivery times in any of the scenarios. In case of the *Infocom* trace, the analytic model underestimates both overall and the individual delivery times, while for the *Supsi* trace, both times are overestimated. For the *Milano* trace, the model gives good estimation of the overall delivery time, while it

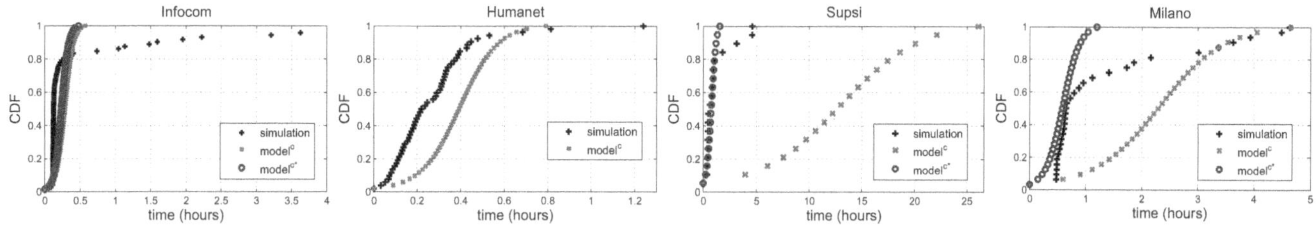

(a) (b) (c) (d)

Figure 4: CDF of infected population: (a) Infocom, (b) Humanet, (c) Supsi, and (d) Milano trace.

significantly overestimates the individual delivery time. The only scenario were we observe a fairly good approximation for both delivery times is the *Humanet* scenario. However, the inconsistency of the method makes it unsuitable for use on an arbitrary trace, when the properties of the trace are not known a priori. This implication is also evident from Fig. 4; the model does not capture the evolution of the epidemic process. We also tested if filling the contact matrix with a different value for T_m would give a better fit. Curves in Fig. 4 (a, b, d), denoted by model$^{c^*}$, correspond to the cases where inter-contact times T_m are equal to the length of a work day (around 9 hours). Although the curves in Fig. 4 (c, d) show asymptotic behaviour in the beginning, it cannot be estimated when the simulated spreading starts to deviate from the model. For example, an accurate estimation of the time until a certain fraction of the network is infected, e.g. 80% of nodes in the *Milano* scenario, would not be possible by using this model.

The usefulness of the homogeneous model is in its simplicity, as it requires only two input parameters. However, we conclude that the homogeneous model is not accurate enough to be used for studying epidemic spreading in general, and we show methodologically, what recent studies use as a starting point and assumption but without proving, that node heterogeneity cannot be neglected when evaluating the network performance.

4. RELATED WORK

This paper mainly relates to the performance evaluation of epidemic content spreading. Epidemic models, adopted from the field of mathematical biology, are widely used in networking to study spreading of messages. Our study focuses on a stochastic Markov model for epidemic content distribution in opportunistic networks, proposed in [8]. A Markov model was also used in [6] to model the message delay in ad hoc networks until a specific destination was reached. The other line of work in stochastic modeling uses transient analysis of random graphs, as in [14], where the hop-limited broadcasting of messages was analysed. Studies such as [7], [15] use ordinary differential equation models, and consider the epidemic spreading process as a fluid flow. Common for all these works is that they assume homogeneous system. Heterogeneity is introduced by separating network nodes into multiple mobility classes in [9], [13], or modeling completely heterogeneous networks, as in [11]. However, it is debatable whether using these analytic models gives enough insight over simulations to account for their complexity.

5. CONCLUSION

We empirically evaluated the content delivery times by using four mobility datasets, chosen to represent a small system of pedestrians, moving in a relatively bounded area, and compared the empirical results with analytic model. We proposed three methods of treating the statistical data obtained from the traces. Our main finding is that a homogeneous model is unable to accurately capture the epidemic process in real-life scenarios and our future work will aim at modeling epidemic spreading in heterogeneous systems by using stochastic models.

6. REFERENCES

[1] J. M. Cabero, V. Molina, I. Urteaga, F. Liberal, and J. L. Martin. CRAWDAD data set Tecnalia Humanet (v. 2012-06-12), June 2012.

[2] V. Conan, J. Leguay, and T. Friedman. Characterizing pairwise inter-contact patterns in delay tolerant networks. In *Proc. Autonomics '07*, pages 19:1–19:9, Brussels, Belgium, 2007.

[3] D. J. Daley and J. Gani. *Epidemic modelling: an introduction.* Cambridge United Kingdom: Cambridge University Press, 1999.

[4] A. Förster, K. Garg, H. A. Nguyen, and S. Giordano. On context awareness and social distance in human mobility traces. In *Proc. ACM*, MobiOpp '12, New York, NY, USA, 2012.

[5] S. Gaito, E. Pagani, and G. Rossi. Fine-grained tracking of human mobility in dense scenarios. In *Proc. SECON*, 2000.

[6] R. Groenevelt, P. Nain, and G. Koole. The message delay in mobile ad hoc networks. *Perform. Eval.*, 62(1-4):210–228, Oct. 2005.

[7] Z. J. Haas and T. Small. A new networking model for biological applications of ad hoc sensor networks. *IEEE/ACM Trans. Networking*, 14(1):27–40, Feb. 2006.

[8] O. R. Helgason, F. Legendre, V. Lenders, M. May, and G. Karlsson. Performance of opportunistic content distribution under different levels of cooperation. In *European Wireless Conference (EW)*, pages 903–910, 2010.

[9] C.-H. Lee and D. Y. Eunt. Heterogeneity in contact dynamics: helpful or harmful to forwarding algorithms in DTNs? In *WiOPT'09*, Piscataway, NJ, USA, 2009.

[10] A. Passerella and M. Conti. Characterising aggregate inter-contact times in heterogenous opportunistic networks. In *IFIP Networking*, pages 301–313, 2011.

[11] A. Picu, T. Spyropoulos, and T. Hossmann. An analysis of the information spreading delay in heterogeneous mobility DTNs. In *Proc. IEEE WoWMoM*, pages 1–10, 2012.

[12] J. Scott, R. Gass, J. Crowcroft, P. Hui, C. Diot, and A. Chaintreau. CRAWDAD trace cambridge/haggle/imote/infocom2006 (v. 2009-05-29), May 2009.

[13] T. Spyropoulos, T. Turletti, and K. Obraczka. Routing in delay-tolerant networks comprising heterogeneous node populations. *IEEE Trans. on Mobile Computing*, 8(8):1132–1147, 2009.

[14] M. Vojnovic and A. Proutiere. Hop limited flooding over dynamic networks. In *Proc. IEEE INFOCOM*, 2011.

[15] X. Zhang, G. Neglia, J. Kurose, and D. Towsley. Performance modeling of epidemic routing. *Elsevier Comput. Networks*, 51(10):2867–2891, 2007.

Gateway Relocation Avoidance-Aware Network Function Placement in Carrier Cloud

Tarik Taleb
NEC Europe
Heidelberg, Germany
talebtarik@ieee.org

Adlen Ksentini
IRISA - INRIA - University of Rennes 1
Campus Universitaire de Beaulieu
Rennes, France
adlen.ksentini@irisa.fr

ABSTRACT

Building mobile networks, on demand and in an elastic manner, represents a vital solution for mobile operators to cope with the modest Average Revenues per User (ARPU), on one hand, and the ever-increasing mobile data traffic, on the other hand. An important research problem towards this vision of carrier cloud pertains to the development of adequate technologies and methods for the on-demand and dynamic provision of a decentralized and elastic mobile network as a cloud service over a distributed network of cloud-computing data centers, forming a federated cloud. An efficient mobile cloud cannot be built without efficient algorithms for the placement of network functions over this federated cloud. In this vein, this paper argues the need for avoiding or minimizing the frequency of mobility gateway relocations and discusses how this gateway relocation avoidance can be reflected in an efficient network function placement algorithm for the realization of mobile cloud. The proposed scheme is evaluated through computer simulations and encouraging results are obtained.

Categories and Subject Descriptors

C.2.1 [**Network Architecture and Design**]: Distributed networks

Keywords

3GPP, mobile cloud, carrier cloud, network function virtualization, and network function placement

1. INTRODUCTION

There has been continuous need for higher data rates, shorter end-to-end communication delays and short latencies for connection setup. This has pushed for the development of diverse fast radio, backhaul, and mobile core network technologies. This, in return, has favored the launch of smart user equipment, even racing ahead of mobile networks, supporting diverse operating systems and offering both users and developers a wide plethora of tools to generate thousands, if not millions, of mobile applications [1][2]. This wide variety of mobile applications is not only changing the basic assumptions based on which mobile networks have been designed, but is also changing the users' behavior and having a strong impact on them. They further introduce important technological as well as economic challenges to mobile operators, particularly noting the modest average revenues per user (ARPU). Different protocol-level as well as architectural solutions have been proposed to cope with these challenges [3][4]. Most of these solutions present short-term "cosmetic" remedies to an ever-complicating problem. The concept of carrier cloud is perceived as an important long-term solution for mobile operators to cope with the tremendous increase in their mobile data traffic, the so-called mobile IP tsunami, and to get into the cloud computing area, seeking new business opportunities and defining new business models and strategies. Indeed, thanks to their interesting features such as pay-as-you-go, full elasticity support, and multiple tenancy support, cloud computing technologies will help mobile operators to decentralize their networks on demand, elastically, and in the most cost-efficient way, enabling operators to invest small in building virtualized mobile networks and growing on demand as per increase in the mobile data traffic.

As an important enabler of the carrier cloud concept, network function virtualization (NFV) is gaining great momentum among industries. NFV aims for decoupling the software part from the hardware part of a carrier network node, traditionally referring to a dedicated hardware, single service and single-tenant box, and that is using virtual hardware abstraction [5]. Network functions become thus a mere code, runnable on a particular, preferably any, operating system and on top of a dedicated hardware platform. The ultimate objective is to run network functions as software in standard virtual machines (VMs) on top of a virtualization platform in a general purpose multi-service multi-tenant node (e.g., Carrier Grade Blade Server). A suitable Software Defined Networking (SDN) technology can be used to interwork between the different virtualized network functions on the different VMs within the same data center or across multiple data centers, to ultimately realize a flexible, dynamic, rapidly deployable, and elastic mobile network on the cloud. To build an efficient mobile cloud that meets the general requirements of a mobile operator, the placement of network functions, namely the mobile Radio Access Network (RAN) functions, the mobile core network functions, and the caches or servers for the Packet Data Network, is of

MSWiM'13, November 3–8, 2013, Barcelona, Spain.

ACM 978-1-4503-2353-6/13/11 ...$15.00.
http://dx.doi.org/10.1145/2507924.2508000 .

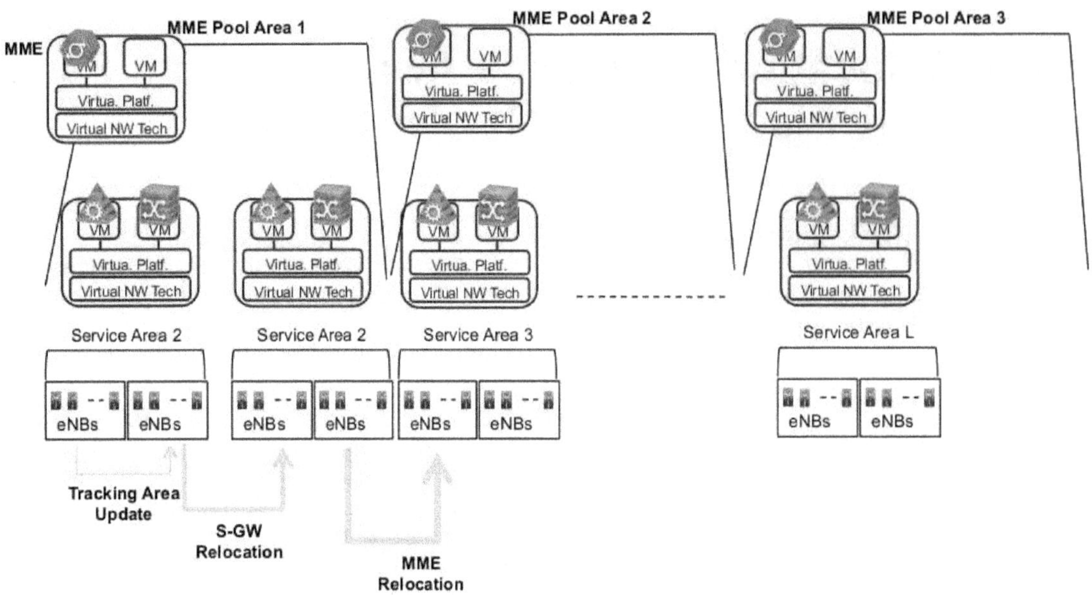

Figure 1: Need for avoiding mobility gateway relocation when placing network functions in carrier cloud.

utmost importance and shall be based on different metrics such as application type [6], data center location, data center load, end-to-end Quality of Service (QoS)/Quality of Experience (QoE), [3] that shall render the overall end-to-end communications optimal [7]. Another important metric for the network function placement consists in the avoidance of gateway relocation, due to the cost incurred with these processes and the impact they may have on the overall QoE [8]. Indeed, with the deployment of mobile network functions on multiple regional data centers, geographically distributed and interconnected, and forming a federated cloud network, the serving areas of mobility gateways (e.g., serving gateways in the context of the Evolved Packet System) and the pool areas of Mobility Management Entities (MMEs) are likely to get smaller and that is for the purpose of localizing mobility management. Frequents handovers with gateway and/or MME relocations may occur as shown in Fig. 1, resulting in additional delay to handoff, additional signaling overhead for bearer establishment and admission control [8][9]. Given these reasons and more, the specifications [9] indicate that gateway and MME relocation during handoff for user equipment in ECM (EPS Connection Management) connected mode (i.e., active mode) is to be avoided when possible. It is therefore the objective of this paper to reflect this recommendation in the planning of service areas and MME pool areas when deciding on where, when and at what scale to place virtualized network functions pertaining to these mobility gateways.

The remainder of this paper is organized in the following fashion. Section 2 presents some research work related to mobile network decentralization and gateway relocation avoidance. The proposed virtualized network function placement scheme, in terms of service areas planning and its modeling, is described in Section 3. Section 4 follows with an evaluation of the proposed scheme. The paper concludes in Section 5 with a summary recapping the main features discussed in this paper.

2. RELATED WORKS

With the introduction of the 3GPP Long Term Evolution (LTE), certain network decentralization features focusing, on both network architecture and network management were brought forward significantly improving the former UMTS (Universal Mobile Telecommunications System). Specifically, considering the network architecture, LTE merged the former Radio Network Controller (RNC) within NodeB introducing a new radio access element called eNB that flattens and simplifies the priori UMTS architecture [9].In terms of network management, LTE advances the prior UMTS-based configuration and optimization methods towards a distributed Self-Organized paradigm [11]. A further step towards an even more flatten UTMS architecture is in [12], where the GGSN (Gateway GPRS Support Node) and SGSN (Serving GPRS Support Node) are integrated in the NBs, while in [13] a similar approach is introduced in the context of EPS with the aim of bringing gateway functions to the edge of the network, merging in this way the radio access and core network split.

In principle, there is a fundamental technology and cost related trade-off behind the adoption of either centralized or distributed network architecture. Costly network equipment are usually shared, creating centralized architectures. This was the case in the initial phase of 3G deployment, wherein a centralized architecture was preferred to share core network utilities and processing resources, while keeping the base station cost low [12]. Nowadays the evolution of computer technology has significantly reduced equipment costs, advancing their deployment flexibility. However, the increased mobile-oriented data volumes still maintains the network utilization cost high, creating significant revenue problems for operators. For this reason operators are looking for data offloading solutions towards the network edge, introducing PDN-GW/S-GW (Packet Data Network Gateway and Serving Gateway) functionality close to eNBs (evolved Node B). Additionally, the provision of Content Distributed Networks (CDN) services towards the network edge may complement

data offloading, reducing further network costs as within the backhaul and via a more efficient resource usage.
A tutorial regarding the data offloading techniques including LIPA (Local IP Access), SIPTO (Selective IP Traffic Offload) and IFOM (IP Flow Mobility and Seamless Offload) focusing on 3GPP Rel-10 is available in [14], while further details on LIPA/SIPTO data offloading are provided in [4], which illustrates specific network architectures and service requirements that meet the current decentralized needs, enlightening also network management and deployment issues with emphasis on QoS and service continuity. A complementary analysis on the architecture and main benefits associated with the use of decentralized architectures from the IETF perspective is documented in [15], with the most important being route optimization and increased robustness. Currently the research efforts towards decentralized cellular networks focus on mobility and service continuity as well as on efficient resource management related to gateway selection and relocation. Ensuring service continuity and QoE for active user with reduced signaling, by avoiding the use of core network equipment, is the ultimate goal of decentralized mobile networks. Nevertheless, the means of achieving decentralization is distributed mobility management. A study that examines and compares centralized and distributed mobility in the context of 3GPP is presented in [16], elaborating also a dynamic and distributed mobility management solution, which merges the mobility anchor gateways and base stations. In particular, mobility is realized by the use of tunneling to forward traffic upon a handover, allowing also the user to establish flows via different mobility anchors for efficient resource usage. The fundamental concepts of gateway-based load balancing with respect to user performance are analyzed in [17], where an inter-GW load balancing protocol and policies are presented and evaluated considering a gateway pool in association with group of base stations. A more advanced solution to provide service continuity focusing on distributing the content of a centralized mobility anchor to a set of distributed mobility agents utilizing the concept of virtual routers and Distributed Hash Tables (DHT) is introduced in [18], with substantial benefits in load balancing and resiliency.
For highly mobile users, i.e. on board vehicles, decentralized mobile networks would also have a significant impact on the conventional Tracking Area Update (TAU) procedure and on the maintenance of PDN connections of UEs in idle mode. Although TAU approaches as in [10] aim to allocate to UEs a gateway that could potentially serve them for a large geographical area, considering the initially associated eNB position, this approach mostly holds for centralized architectures. In decentralized schemes, we envision smaller serving areas, thus additional mechanisms to compensate frequent serving area relocations are recommended. In [19], a self-organized method, which adopts the tracking areas according to the user mobility taking into account long term history data is introduced based on graph partitioning heuristics.

3. GATEWAY RELOCATION AVOIDANCE-AWARE NETWORK FUNCTION PLACEMENT SCHEME

3.1 Problem statement

As shown in Fig.1, each service area is managed by one virtual S-GW and consists of several Tracking Areas (TAs). Each TA consists, in turn, of several cells. In order to reduce the S-GW relocation it is important to ensure an optimal planning of the service areas considering the mobility patterns of users as well as their data traffic load. Furthermore, it is important to dimension the virtual function by defining the optimal number of virtual S-GWs to create. It shall be noted that throught the remainder of this paper, the focus is on service areas, but the same logic applies to pool areas of MMEs.
Let N denotes the number of Tracking Areas as planned by any underlying mobile network planning algorithm [21]. The set of TAs in the mobile network is denoted by $N_{TA} = \{1, \ldots, N\}$, and the set of SAs currently employed is $N_{SA} = \{1, \ldots, S\}$. The vector $SA = [s_1, \ldots, s_N]$ denotes the service area planning (i.e., mapping TA to SA), whereby s_i is the Service Area of TA i. This mapping can be represented by a binary symmetric matrix (NxN), denoted by $adj(SA)$. An element $adj(SA)$ represents the case whether or not two TAs are in the same SA, in other words

$$adj_{i,j}(SA) = \begin{cases} 1 & \text{if } s_i = s_j \\ 0 & \text{Otherwise} \end{cases}$$

Let $w(i)$ denotes the traffic load at a TA i, during a specific period of time. Intuitively, $w(i)$ equals to the aggregate load of traffic exchanged over cells belonging to TA i. Let $h_{i,j}$ denote the number of UEs moving from TA_i to TA_j during the same period of time. For the sake of simplicity, we assume that each time a UE moves from one TA into another TA, a S-GW relocation occurs incurring a cost denoted by $C_{relocation}$. Intuitively, in real life networks, a UE has to cross a number of TAs before a S-GW relocation takes place. Moreover, we assume that each S-GW has the capacity to handle SGW_{max} amount of traffic load generated by the covered service area.
At this point the problem of service area planning, i.e., placement of virtualized S-GW functions on a federated cloud or a distributed network of data centers, can be formulated as follows:

$$min \sum_{i\in N} \sum_{j\in N} Cost = C_{relocation} h_{i,j}(1 - adj_{i,j}(SA))$$

Subject to
$for\ i = 1\ to\ N,\ \sum_{j\in N} w(j) adj_{i,j}(SA) \leq SGW_{max}$
$adj_{i,j}(SA) \in \{0, 1\}$

In other words, the optimization problem consists in finding the optimal service area planning, and therefore the location of data centers where to place the virtualized S-GW functions, that minimizes the overall S-GW relocation cost, while ensuring that each SA traffic load does not exceed the capacity SGW_{max} of a SGW. Accordingly, the problem becomes an Integer Linear Program (ILP). This problem is similar to the TA planning algorithm, which is known as NP hard [21]. Solving optimality the service area planning problem may require excessive computational effort in view of its complexity. In the following section, we propose an effective solution based on a greedy algorithm, which finds an effective solution for this problem.

3.2 Greedy-based algorithm for virtualized SGW placement in carrier cloud

The proposed greedy algorithm (GA) successively builds up a solution for the service area planning. It selects step

Algorithm 1 Greedy algorithm for virtualized S-GW placement in carrier cloud

```
procedure CHECK_NEIGHBOR(k)
    Neighbor(k) ← ∃m ∈ SA : adj_{k,m}(SA) = 1;
    for all m ∈ SA : adj_{k,m}(SA) do
        if w(m) + load_s ≤ SGW_max then
            SA(m) ← S
            load_s ← w(m) + load_s;
        end if
    end for
end procedure
procedure MAIN
    SA ← {0, 0, 0, ..., 0}
    S ← 0
    while ∃i ∈ SA : adj_{i,j}(SA) do
        S ← S + 1
        Neighbor(j) ← ∃j ∈ SA : adj_{i,j}(SA) = 1;
        load_s ← w(i);
        Check_Neighbor(i);
        for all j ∈ Neighbor(i) do
            Check_Neighbor(j);
        end for
    end while
end procedure
```

by step the TAs assigned to a SA. This is repeated until the S-GW capacity is exceeded.

In the first run, the greedy algorithm selects a TA (i.e., starting TA noted TA_i) from the SA set. Then, it affects this TA to a SA. For each neighbor of TA_i (noted TA_j), it checks if it can be assigned to the same SA (S). A TA is assigned to S if the traffic load generated by this TA added to the current traffic load of (S) does not exceed the capacity SGW_{max}. If TA_j is assigned to the same SA, the GA continues to consider candidates TA from the neighbor set of TA_j. Since there is no more candidate in the neighbor of TA_j, the operation is repeated for another neighbor of the TA i. When there is no possibility to add a further TA to S, the greedy algorithm selects then another TA from the SA set (i.e., the selected TA is not yet assigned to any SA) and increments S. The algorithm ends when all TAs are assigned to a specific SA (S). Note that the proposed greedy algorithm is not efficient, as it does not take into consideration the cost. In order to address this issue, we propose another version of this algorithm, namely Repeated Greedy Algorithm (RGA), which improves the GA version by adding a loop on the initial TA for the GA. So, RGA respectively executes GA with different starting TA. The final Serving Area configuration or (SA_i) is the one that incurs the minimum cost, i.e. the minimum number of S-GW relocation.

It is worth noting that RGA gives a near optimal number of virtual S-GWs to be instantiated and deployed for a certain configuration of traffic load and mobility pattern, while reducing the number of S-GW relocations. The algorithm complexity is $O(N^3)$.

On the other hand, the RGA algorithm can be launched periodically, or if the mobile operator detects a noticeable change in the network traffic load or user mobility, so it can scale up or down the number of virtual S-GWs given some network load conditions.

Table 1: Simulation parameters.

	$w(i)/min$	$h_{i,j}/min$	SGW_{max}
Scenario1	Random [0, 25]	Random [0, 50]	200
Scenario 2	Random [0, 25]	Random [0, 25]	200
Scenario 3	Random [0, 50]	Random [0, 50]	200
Scenario 4	Random [0, 50]	Random [0, 25]	200

4. SIMULATION RESULTS

In this section, we present the results of our experiments conducted using MATLAB to evaluate the efficiency of RGA in gateway relocation avoidance. We compare the GRA results against those of GA (i.e., only one TA is used for initiating the greedy algorithm). We generated a random network topology, where each TA has an average of six neighbors. We considered four scenarios as described in Table 1. Scenario 1 represents the case of low traffic load and high mobility. Scenario 2 also shows the case of low traffic load, but considers users with low mobility features. Scenario 3 represents the case of high traffic load and high mobility features. Finally, scenario 4 illustrates the case of high traffic load and low mobility features. We varied the number of TAs for each scenario from 10, representing a small area, to 80, simulating a large area.

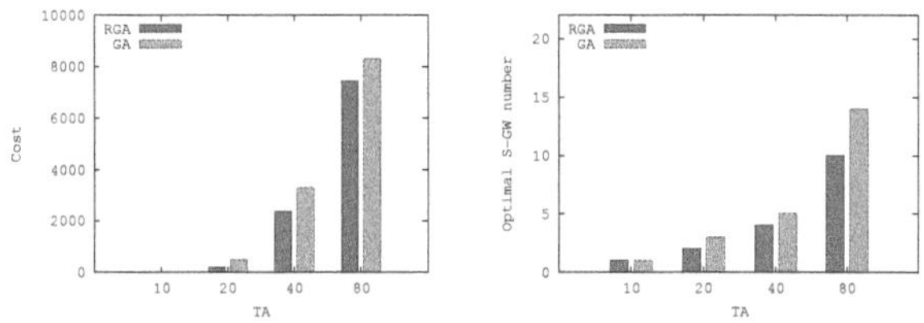

Figure 2: Scenario 1

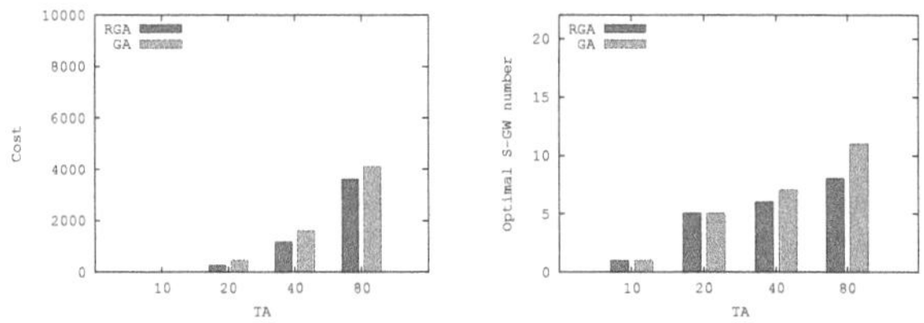

Figure 3: Scenario 2

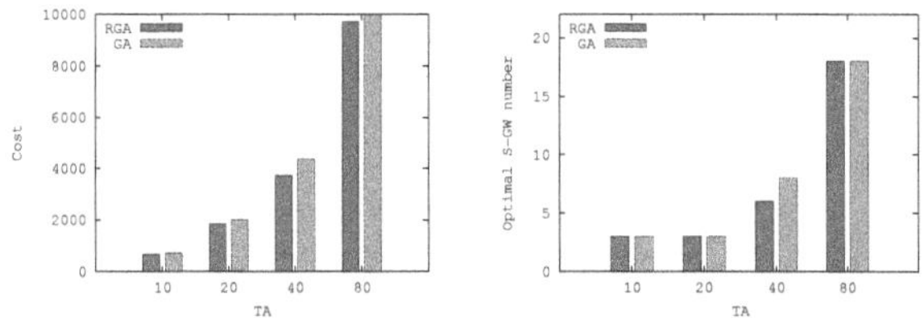

Figure 4: Scenario 3

Figs. 2 - 5 show the results obtained for the four simulated scenarios. The results are presented in terms of incurred cost and the required number of virtual S-GWs. From these results, we clearly observe that high traffic load implies the need for higher number of S-GWs, and when the mobility is high, the cost (S-GW relocation) incurred by both the GRA

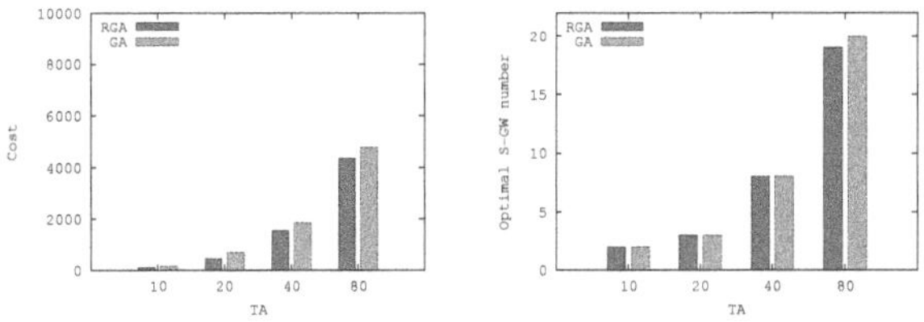

Figure 5: Scenario 4

and GA is high. For instance, in case of low traffic load (i.e., scenarios 1 and 2), the required number of S-GWs is one when TA=10, and this number exceeds 20 in case of scenario 4 (i.e., high traffic load) for TA=80. We also observe that the cost is highly skewed between scenarios 1 and 2, even they have the same traffic load. Scenario 1 incurs higher cost than scenario 2, which is intuitive as there are frequent handovers with TA change, which increases the probability of S-GW relocation. We notice the same behavior when comparing between scenarios 2 and 3. Finally, we remark that RGA always finds a better solution than GA, ensuring lower cost in terms of gateway relocations and involving less number of virtual S-GWs to instantiate.

Acknowledgment

The research work presented in this paper is conducted as part of the Mobile Cloud Networking project, funded from the European Union Seventh Framework Program under grant agreement number [318109].

5. CONCLUSION

In this paper, we presented a new algorithm for avoiding or minimizing the frequency of mobility gateway relocations in carrier cloud and that is via optimal placement of virtualized relevant network functions over federated clouds. We focused on the case of S-GW relocation in case of EPS, and formulated the network function placement as a service area planning optimization problem, where the aim is to reduce the cost of gateway relocation. This problem is NP-hard problem. We therefore introduced a heuristic based on a greedy algorithm. Simulation results indicate the efficiently of the proposed algorithm in reducing the gateway relocation cost.

6. REFERENCES

[1] T. Taleb and A. Ksentini, "Impact of Emerging Social Media Applications on Mobile Networks," in Proc. IEEE ICC 2013, Budapest, Hungary, Jun. 2013.

[2] T. Taleb and A. Kunz, "Machine Type Communications in 3GPP Networks: Potential, Challenges, and Solutions," in IEEE Commun. Mag., Vol. 50, No. 3, Mar. 2012.

[3] T. Taleb and A. Ksentini, "QoS/QoE Predictions-based Admission Control for Femto Communications," in Proc. IEEE ICC 2012, Ottawa, Canada, Jun. 2012.

[4] K. Samdanis, T. Taleb, and S. Schmid, "Traffic Offload Enhancements for eUTRAN", in IEEE Communications Surveys and Tutorials J., Vol. 11, No. 3, Aug. 2012, pp. 884-896.

[5] Authored by network operators, "Network Functions Virtualization: An Introduction, Benefits, Enablers, Challenges, & Call for Action," Oct. 2012

[6] T. Taleb and A. Ksentini, "On Efficient Data Anchor Point Selection in Distributed Mobile Networks," in Proc. IEEE ICC 2013, Budapest, Hungary, Jun. 2013.

[7] T. Taleb and A. Ksentini, "Follow Me Cloud: Interworking Federated Clouds & Distributed Mobile Networks," to appear in IEEE Network Magazine.

[8] T. Taleb, K. Samdanis, and F. Filali, "Towards Supporting Highly Mobile Nodes in Decentralized Mobile Operator Networks," in Proc. IEEE ICC 2012, Ottawa, Canada, Jun. 2012.

[9] 3GPP, "General Packet Radio Service (GPRS) enhancements for Evolved Universal Terrestrial Radio Access Network (E-UTRAN) access," TS 23.401, V10.2.1, Jan. 2011.

[10] A. Kunz, T. Taleb, and S. Schmid, "On Minimizing SGW/MME Relocations in LTE", in Proc. ACM IWCMC'10, Caen, Jun. 2010.

[11] 3GPP, "Technical Specification Group Radio Access Network, Evolved universal Terrestrial Radio Access Network (E-URAN), Self-configuring and self-optimizing network (SON) use cases and solutions", (Rel 9), TR 36.902, Apr. 2011.

[12] P. Bosch, L. Samuel, S. Mullender, P. Polakos, and G. Rittenhouse, "Flat Cellular (UMTS) Networks", IEEE WCNC Hong Kong, Mar 2007.

[13] Z. Yan, L. Lei, and M. Chen, "WIISE A Completely Flat and Distributed Architecture for Future Wireless Communication Systems", WWRF 21, Stockholm, Oct 2008.

[14] C.B. Sankaran, "Data Offloading Techniques in 3GPP Rel-10 Networks: A Tutorial", IEEE Communication Magazine, Vol.50, No.6, Jun 2012.

[15] R. Kuntz, D. Sudhakar, R. Wakikawa, and L. Zhang, "A Summary of Distributed Mobility Management", IETF Internet Draft, Feb 2011.

[16] P. Bertin, S. Bonjour, and J-M. Bonnin, "Distributed or Centralized Mobility?", IEEE GLOBECOM, Honolulu, Dec 2009.

[17] C. Xue, J. Luo, R. Halfmann, E. Schulz, and C. Hartmann, "Inter GW Load Balancing for Next Generation Mobile Networks with Flat Architecture", IEEE VTC-Spring, Barcelona, May 2009.

[18] M. Fischer, F-U. Andersen, A. Kopsel, G. Schafer, and M. Schlager, "A Distributed IP Mobility Approach for 3G SAE", IEEE 19th PIMRC, Cannes, Sep 2008.

[19] M. Toril, "Automatic Re-planning of Tracking Areas", SOCRATES Final Workshop on Self-Organisation in Mobile Networks, Karlsruhe, 22 Feb 2011.

[20] S. Pack, T. Kwon, and Y. Choi, "A Performance Comparison of Mobility Anchor Point Selection Schemes in Hierarchical Mobile IPv6 Networks", in Elsevier J. Computer Networks, Vol. 51, No. 6, Apr. 2007.

[21] Y. Bejerano, M-A. Smith, J. Naor, and N. Immorlica. "Efficient Location Area Planning for Personal Communication Systems", in IEEE/ACM Transactions on Networking, Vol. 14, No. 2, Apr. 2006.

How Does Interference Dynamics Influence Packet Delivery in Cooperative Relaying?

Udo Schilcher
University of Klagenfurt
Networked and Embedded Systems
Klagenfurt, Austria
udo.schilcher@aau.at

Stavros Toumpis
Athens University of Economics and Business
Department of Informatics
Athens, Greece
toumpis@aueb.gr

Alessandro Crismani
University of Klagenfurt
Networked and Embedded Systems
Klagenfurt, Austria
alessandro.crismani@aau.at

Günther Brandner
University of Klagenfurt
Networked and Embedded Systems
Klagenfurt, Austria
guenther.brandner@aau.at

Christian Bettstetter
University of Klagenfurt
Networked and Embedded Systems
Lakeside Labs GmbH
Klagenfurt, Austria

ABSTRACT

We show by means of stochastic geometry that interference dynamics has a strong impact on the performance of cooperative relaying. For both conventional and multi-hop-aware cooperative relaying we show that the packet delivery probability significantly changes with the dependence of interference among the links. Depending on the scenario under consideration, this change could be either an increase or decrease of the packet delivery probability. Especially for multi-hop-aware cooperative relaying, the performance gain is heavily reduced when interference possesses high temporal and spatial dependence.

Categories and Subject Descriptors

C.2.1 [**Computer-communication networks**]: Network architecture and design—*wireless communication, network communications*; G.3 [**Probability and statistics**]: Stochastic processes

General Terms

Performance, Theory

Keywords

Cooperative relaying; interference; diversity; multi-hop-aware relaying; fading.

MSWiM'13, November 3–8, 2013, Barcelona, Spain.
ACM 978-1-4503-2353-6/13/11
http://dx.doi.org/10.1145/2507924.2507926.

1. INTRODUCTION AND MOTIVATION

The behavior of interference in wireless networks has a huge impact on system design and performance [9, 14]. In simple terms, interference is caused if, for a given transmitter-receiver pair, at least one additional node is transmitting at the same time and at the same carrier frequency in the vicinity of the receiver. The signals of all such nodes interfere at the receiver with the intended signal from the transmitter due to the broadcast nature of the wireless medium. Such co-channel interference limits the overall network capacity in terms of bit/s/Hz/m^2 [10]. Besides the average interference level, the time-varying and space-varying properties of interference should be considered for the design of communication techniques and protocols, and notably for temporal and spatial diversity schemes [21]. If, e.g., a basic scheme retransmits lost packets, this might lead to problems for highly dependent interference. In such scenarios interference is unlikely to change significantly between two transmissions and hence the retransmission is likely to fail.

Along this line of argumentation, this paper applies methods from spatial stochastics to analyze the impact of interference dynamics on cooperative diversity [15] (also called cooperative relaying) with simple selection combining. Most of the research in the past analyzed cooperative relaying without considering such interference dynamics.

In particular, we present the following contributions:

- We extend previous results on the time-varying behavior of packet delivery under interference [3] to the spatio-temporal case.
- We derive the packet delivery probability of a cooperative relaying scenario with selection combining. Additionally, we compare the performance of such relaying under dependent and independent interference for several channel conditions.
- Finally, we analyze multi-hop-aware cooperative relaying [1] assuming that interference is spatially dependent, and compare our results with the case where interference is assumed to be independent.

The organization of the paper is as follows: Section 2 presents the models and assumptions used for the analysis. Based on these, in Section 3, we derive the spatio-temporal dependence of packet delivery at different locations and time slots by obtaining the joint probability that a number of transmissions is successful under dependent interference. Next, in Section 4, we use these results to calculate the packet delivery probability in a cooperative relaying scenario where the destination relies on selection combining. This analysis is done for both the single iteration and the multiple iterations cases. In Section 5 we calculate the packet delivery probability for multi-hop-aware cooperative relaying [1]. Here, the main focus of our analysis lies in comparing the protocol's performance gain for the dependent and independent interference scenarios. Finally, Section 6 presents an overview of the related work and Section 7 concludes.

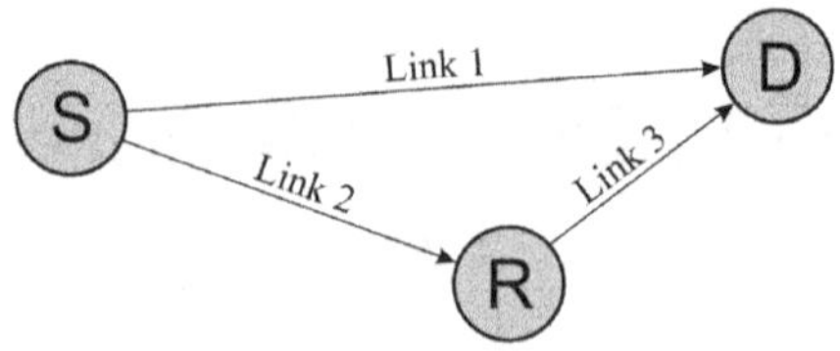

Figure 1: Relaying scenario.

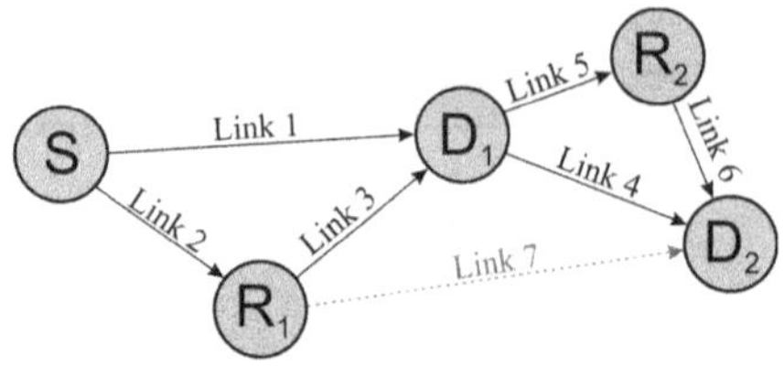

Figure 2: Multi-hop-aware relaying scenario.

2. MODELING ASSUMPTIONS

2.1 Node Setup and Channel Characteristics

Consider a wireless scenario where nodes are distributed according to a Poisson point process (PPP) Φ with density λ [19]. For simplicity, let Φ denote both the PPP and the nodes' locations. Time is divided into time slots, and each node transmits in each slot with probability p. This is similar to random access with slotted ALOHA.

For a given slot t, we denote the transmitter by $s(t)$ and the receiver by $d(t)$. In general, also other nodes besides $s(t)$ are transmitting at slot t, which causes interference at $d(t)$. The set of all nodes transmitting at slot t is denoted by $\Psi(t) \subseteq \Phi$; the density of the thinned process Ψ is λp. For simplicity of notation we often skip the index t. The symbols s and d indicate both the nodes and their coordinates.

The channel is modeled using a distance-dependent path loss, where transmissions are subject to Rayleigh fading. Hence, when the node s sends a packet to the node d, the signal power received at d is

$$S_d = h(s,d)\, g(\|s-d\|)\,. \tag{1}$$

The function $g(\|s-d\|)$ represents the path loss between the transmitter s and the receiver d. We apply the path loss function $g(\|s-d\|) = \|s-d\|^{-\alpha}$, where α is the path loss exponent. The random values $h(s,d)$ model Rayleigh fading caused by multipath propagation. These values are independent and exponentially distributed and have a mean of unity. We have

$$\mathrm{P}\left[h \geq \alpha\right] = \exp\left(-\alpha\right)\,. \tag{2}$$

The interference level at d in a given slot is the sum of all power values from all interfering signals arriving at d, i.e.,

$$I_d = \sum_{u \in \Psi \setminus \{s\}} h(u,d)\, g(\|u-d\|) \tag{3}$$

with u indicating both a particular interferer and its position.

The signal-to-interference ratio at the receiver d is

$$\mathrm{SIR}_d = \frac{S_d}{I_d} = \frac{h(s,d)\, g(\|s-d\|)}{\sum_{u \in \Psi \setminus \{s\}} h(u,d)\, g(\|u-d\|)}\,. \tag{4}$$

We assume interference to be much higher than noise and therefore omit the noise term.

Let A denote the event that a packet transmission over the link from a node s to a node d at time slot t is successful. We assume that the transmitter technology used is such that the event A occurs if and only if $\mathrm{SIR}_d \geq \theta$, where θ denotes the receiver threshold. During the operation of the network, in general, several such success events occur for different transmitters and different receivers. A set of N such events is denoted by $\{A_1, A_2, \ldots, A_i, \ldots, A_N\}$. To avoid misinterpretation, note that i is an identifier of the event, neither a time index nor an identifier of the receiver.

2.2 Cooperative Relaying Schemes

In this paper we study both conventional cooperative relaying with a single relay [18] and multi-hop-aware (MHA) cooperative relaying [1]. In the conventional relaying system (Figure 1), the relay is assumed to be selected in advance and used over several slots. The receiver decodes the signals received from the transmitter and the relay using selection combining. It works as follows: Node S transmits a data packet to D. The relay R overhears this transmission and tries to decode the packet. If the decoding is successful, the relay forwards the packet to D. The whole process is successful if D is able to decode at least one of the two transmissions. Note that in our model the relay always forwards the packet independent of whether the direct link succeeds or not. The relaying procedure is described in Algorithm 1.

Algorithm 1 Cooperative relaying

```
S transmits a data packet
if R can decode the packet then
    R forwards the packet
end if
if D can decode the packet from S or R then
    success
else
    failure
end if
```

In MHA relaying each relay along a multi-hop path is selected by considering its ability to serve the following two hops. In this paper we show results for a two-hop example, however the analysis is general and may be applied to scenarios consisting of many hops. The two-hop example depicted in Figure 2 works as follows. First, S sends its packet to D_1. The relay R_1 overhears the packet and retransmits it. This retransmission might be overheard by the receiver of the second hop (node D_2). Next, D_1 sends the packet to D_2. The relay R_2 tries to decode this transmission and, in the case of success, retransmits the packet. Finally, the scheme is successful if D_2 receives at least one of the packets from R_1, D_1, and R_2 correctly. Here, Link 7 in Figure 2 is the link that distinguishes MHA relaying from the conventional two-hop cooperative relaying. The MHA relaying procedure is detailed in Algorithm 2. The motivation for such a setup is that the path over S, D_1 to D_2 can be kept stable for a long time. It has to be altered only if a node fails. However, the relays can be reselected each time the channel changes significantly.

Algorithm 2 MHA cooperative relaying

```
S transmits a data packet
if R1 can decode the packet then
    R1 forwards the packet
end if
if D1 can decode the packet from S or R1 then
    D1 transmits the packet
    if R2 can decode the packet then
        R2 forwards the packet
    end if
end if
if D2 can decode the packet from D1 or R1 or R2 then
    success
else
    failure
end if
```

3. SPATIO-TEMPORAL DEPENDENCE OF TRANSMISSION SUCCESS

First, we calculate the joint probability $\mathrm{P}[A_1A_2\cdots A_N]$ that N arbitrary transmissions in the network are successful. To do so, we follow the approach of [3], where Ganti and Haenggi calculate the joint probability for packet delivery over a given link at two or more different time slots. We extend this result by deriving the joint probability for packet delivery over both different time slots *and* different links.

Observe that

$$\mathrm{P}[A_1\dots A_N] = \mathrm{P}\Bigg[\frac{h(s_1,d_1)\,g(\|s_1-d_1\|)}{\sum_{u\in\Phi} h(u,d_1)\,g(\|u-d_1\|)\,\mathbf{1}(u\in\Psi\backslash\{s_1\})} \geq \theta,\dots, \frac{h(s_N,d_N)\,g(\|s_N-d_N\|)}{\sum_{u\in\Phi} h(u,d_N)\,g(\|u-d_N\|)\,\mathbf{1}(u\in\Psi\backslash\{s_N\})} \geq \theta\Bigg], \quad (5)$$

where $\mathbf{1}$ is the indicator function.

By substituting $\theta_i := \frac{\theta}{g(\|s_i-d_i\|)}$ into (5), the ith term in the brackets yields

$$h(s_i,d_i) \geq \theta_i \sum_{u\in\Phi} h(u,d_i)\,g(\|u-d_i\|)\,\mathbf{1}(u\in\Psi\backslash\{s_i\})\,. \quad (6)$$

From the independence of the fading terms h and (2) we get

$$\mathrm{P}\big[h(s_1,d_1)\geq\alpha_1,\dots,h(s_N,d_N)\geq\alpha_N\big] = \prod_{i=1}^{N}\exp(-\alpha_i)\,. \quad (7)$$

Applying this expression in (5) yields

$$\begin{aligned}
\mathrm{P}[A_1\dots A_N] &= \\
&\overset{(a)}{=} \mathrm{E}_{\Phi,h}\Bigg[\prod_{i=1}^{N}\exp\Big(-\theta_i\sum_{u\in\Phi} h(u,d_i)\,g(\|u-d_i\|)\,\mathbf{1}(u\in\Psi\backslash\{s_i\})\Big)\Bigg]\\
&= \mathrm{E}_{\Phi,h}\Bigg[\prod_{u\in\Phi}\prod_{i=1}^{N}\exp\Big(-\theta_i\,h(u,d_i)\,g(\|u-d_i\|)\,\mathbf{1}(u\in\Psi\backslash\{s_i\})\Big)\Bigg]\\
&= \mathrm{E}_{\Phi}\Bigg[\prod_{u\in\Phi}\prod_{i=1}^{N}\mathrm{E}_h\Big[\exp\Big(-\theta_i\,h(u,d_i)\,g(\|u-d_i\|)\,\mathbf{1}(u\in\Psi\backslash\{s_i\})\Big)\,\Big|\,\Phi\Big]\Bigg]\\
&\overset{(b)}{=} \mathrm{E}_{\Phi}\Bigg[\prod_{u\in\Phi}\prod_{i=1}^{N}\Big(\frac{p}{1+\theta_i g(\|u-d_i\|)}+1-p\Big)\Bigg]\\
&\overset{(c)}{=} \exp\Bigg(-\lambda\int_{\mathbb{R}^2} 1-\prod_{i=1}^{N}\Big(\frac{p}{1+\theta_i g(\|x-d_i\|)}+1-p\Big)\,\mathrm{d}x\Bigg)\,.
\end{aligned} \quad (8)$$

In the above derivation (a) holds since the coefficients $h(s_i,d_i)$ are exponentially distributed and independent and we take the expected value over the PPP and the channel coefficients $h(u,d_i)$ of the interferers; in (b) we calculate the expectation over $h(u,d_i)$; (c) is due to the probability generating functional of Φ (cf. [8], (4.8)).

4. COOPERATIVE RELAYING

In the following we compute the packet delivery probability of cooperative relaying with selection combining. By considering the dependence of interference, we provide a deeper characterization than related work does (see Sections 6.2 and 6.3). The packet delivery probability is obtained by applying the tools developed in the previous section.

4.1 Packet Delivery Probability for a Single Iteration

We consider a three node relaying scenario as depicted in Figure 1. Let A_i denote the event that a packet is successfully transmitted via link i, with $i\in\{1,2,3\}$. Let B denote the event that the overall scheme is successful, i.e., that D is able to receive at least one of the packets from S or R. The overall packet delivery probability can in general be calculated as

$$\begin{aligned}
\mathrm{P}[B] &= \mathrm{P}[A_1\cup A_2A_3]\\
&= \mathrm{P}[A_1]+\mathrm{P}[A_2A_3]-\mathrm{P}[A_1A_2A_3]\,.
\end{aligned} \quad (9)$$

All terms in this equation can be calculated using (8). For the special case of independent interference, we have

$$\mathrm{P}[B] = \mathrm{P}[A_1]+\mathrm{P}[A_2]\,\mathrm{P}[A_3]-\mathrm{P}[A_1]\,\mathrm{P}[A_2]\,\mathrm{P}[A_3]\,. \quad (10)$$

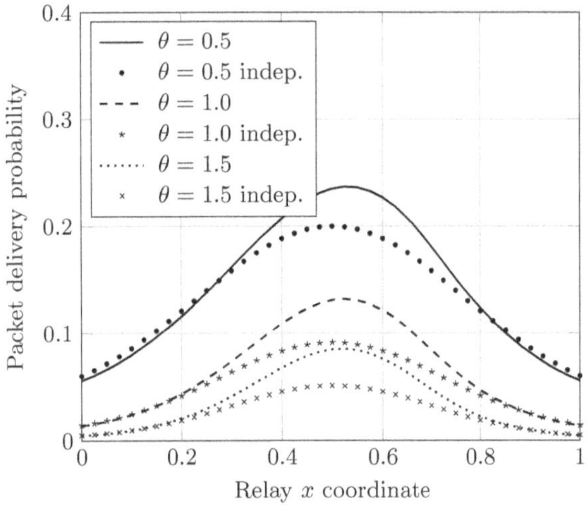

Figure 3: Packet delivery probabilities for cooperative relaying with dependent vs. independent interference over different positions of the relay for an overall transmitter-receiver distance of 1. Parameters are $\lambda = 1$, $p = 1$, and $\alpha = 4$.

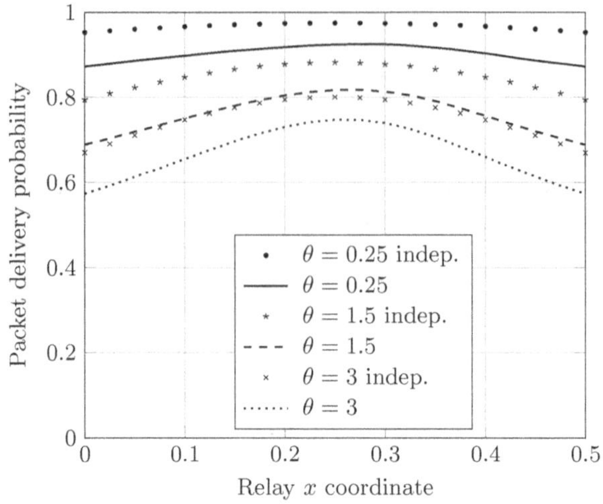

Figure 4: Packet delivery probabilities for cooperative relaying with dependent vs. independent interference for an overall transmitter-receiver distance of 0.5. Parameters are $\lambda = 0.4$, $p = 1$, and $\alpha = 4$.

Figure 3 shows a plot of the packet delivery probability $\mathrm{P}[B]$ for independent interference (marks) given in (10) and for dependent interference (lines) given in (9) when varying the relay's position. We consider a scenario where the transmitter is located at $(0, 0)$, the receiver at $(1, 0)$ and the relay is placed somewhere on the line between the transmitter and the receiver. Hence, the y coordinate of the relay is 0, while the x coordinate varies between 0 and 1.

This scenario leads to very harsh conditions and hence to very low packet delivery probabilities. It has been chosen on purpose to be able to make the following observations.

First, the optimal relay position for independent interference is exactly in the middle between S and D. For dependent interference, however, it is slightly closer to D.

Second, if R is roughly in the middle between S and D, having dependent interference *increases* the performance. This is because the delivery probability for the two-hop path from S via R to D increases for increasing dependency of interference. This can be best seen in two extreme cases. If interference is independent, we have $\mathrm{P}[A_2A_3] = \mathrm{P}[A_2]\mathrm{P}[A_3]$ since the two events are independent. In the opposite case, if interference is highly dependent, we have $\mathrm{P}[A_2A_3] = \mathrm{P}[A_2]\mathrm{P}[A_3 \mid A_2]$. Here, $\mathrm{P}[A_2A_3]$ is higher since in the highly dependent case the probability $\mathrm{P}[A_3 \mid A_2] \gg \mathrm{P}[A_3]$ (see [3]).

Third, if the relay is located close to either S or D, the direct $S - D$ link plays a dominant role on the overall performance. In this case, a dependency in interference will *decrease* performance — if the direct link fails also the two-hop path does so and vice versa.

Figure 4 shows results of the same network setup as Figure 3, except that the distance between S and D is halved to 0.5 and λ is changed to 0.4. This significantly improves the performance of the direct link with respect to the two-hop path. Therefore, having dependent interference *always decreases* the performance of the relaying scheme. Additionally, the position of the relay has much less influence on the overall performance compared to the case having an R-D distance equal to unity.

Figure 5 shows the packet delivery probability over the transmission probability p. In scenarios with weak interference (low λp), it is better to have independent interference. In scenarios with strong interference (high λp), dependence helps due to the highly dependent hops of the two-hop path. The explanation is as follows: the direct link between S and D is unlikely to be useful for strong interference while the two-hop path still works due to the multi-hop gain. Thus the increased dependence between direct and two-hop paths plays a less important role than for weak interference. This effect can also be seen in Figure 6, which shows a plot of the

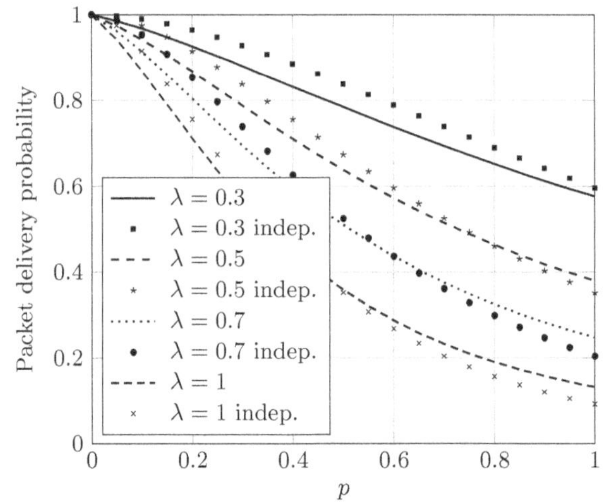

Figure 5: Dependence of packet delivery probabilities for cooperative relaying with dependent vs. independent interference for different sending probabilities p. Parameters are $\theta = 1$, $\alpha = 4$ and an overall transmitter-receiver distance of 1, where the relay node is located in the middle between transmitter and receiver.

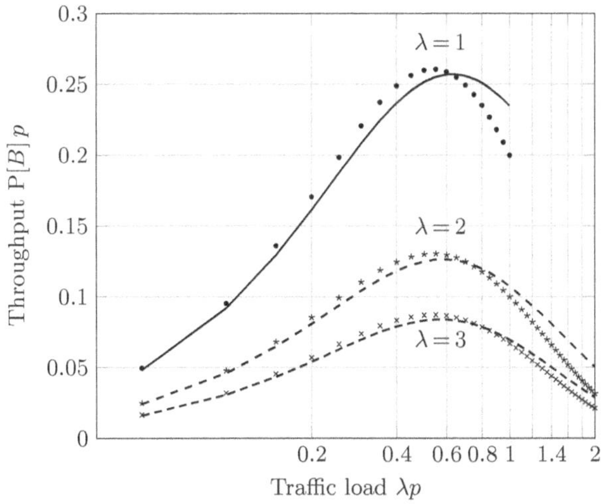

Figure 6: Normalized throughput (in 1 per slot) for cooperative relaying with dependent (lines) vs. independent (marks) interference for different normalized traffic loads λp (in 1 per slot and unit area). Parameters are $\theta = 0.5$ and an overall transmitter-receiver distance of 1, where the relay is located in the middle between transmitter and receiver.

normalized throughput. For higher traffic load the difference between dependent and independent interference cases in terms of throughput increases. Additionally it can be seen that for dependent interference the maximum throughput occurs at a slightly higher traffic load than for independent interference.

4.2 Packet Delivery Probability for Multiple Iterations

We now consider a scenario where cooperative relaying is repeated until D receives the packet. In every time slot with an odd number ($2 \nmid t$) the node S transmits; in every time slot having an even number ($2 \mid t$), the relay node R transmits assuming it received the transmission from S in the previous slot. Otherwise, the slot stays empty. This procedure is continued until D successfully receives the packet.

In the following, we compute the probability $\mathrm{P}[B^T]$ that the receiver correctly receives the packet at time slot T. The event B^T occurs if and only if all transmissions in slots $t = 1, \ldots, T-1$ are unsuccessful and the transmission in slot T is successful. Let $C(t)$ denote the event that the transmission in slot t is successfully received by D, i.e.

$$C(t) = \begin{cases} A_1(t), & \text{if } 2 \nmid t, \\ A_2(t-1) \cap A_3(t), & \text{if } 2 \mid t\,. \end{cases} \tag{11}$$

Here, $A_i(t)$ denotes the event that a packet is sent successfully using link i in the relaying scenario (Figure 1) in slot t.

$$\begin{aligned} \mathrm{P}\left[B^T\right] &= \mathrm{P}\left[C(T) \cap \bigcap_{t=1}^{T-1} \bar{C}(t)\right] \\ &= \sum_{\mathcal{T} \subseteq \{1,\ldots,T\}} (-1)^{|\mathcal{T}|}\, \mathrm{P}\left[C(T) \cap \bigcap_{t \in \mathcal{T}} C(t)\right], \end{aligned} \tag{12}$$

where $\bar{C}(t)$ denotes the complementary event of $C(t)$. The last equality holds due to the inclusion-exclusion principle. The joint probabilities can be computed using (8). For independent interference we can simplify this equation to

$$\mathrm{P}\left[B^T\right] = \mathrm{P}[C(T)] \sum_{\mathcal{T} \subseteq \{1,\ldots,T\}} (-1)^{|\mathcal{T}|} \prod_{t \in \mathcal{T}} \mathrm{P}[C(t)]\,. \tag{13}$$

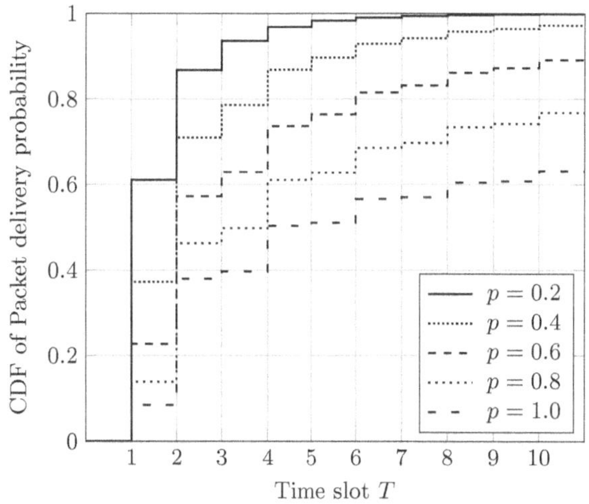

Figure 7: CDF of packet delivery probability $\mathrm{P}[B^T]$ in slot T for different transmit probabilities p. Parameters are $\lambda = 2$, $\theta = 1$, $\alpha = 4$, an overall transmitter-receiver distance (from R to D) of 0.5 and the relay placed in the middle between R and D.

In Figure 7 the cumulative distribution function (CDF) of the probability $\mathrm{P}[B^T]$ is plotted over T for different interference levels (i.e., for different sending probabilities p). As can be seen in the plot, the relay transmission significantly increases the packet delivery probability (i.e., the CDF also

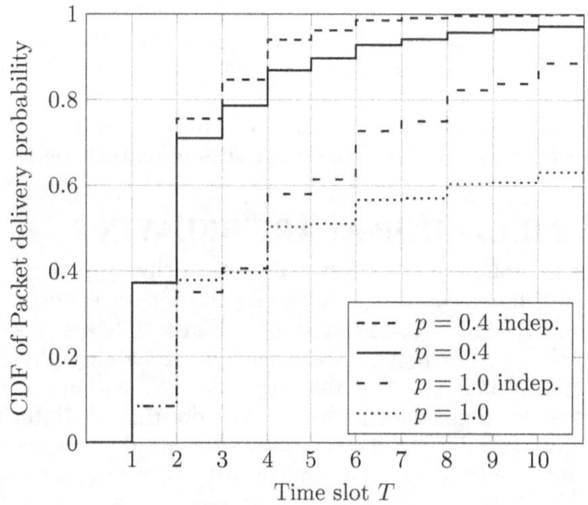

Figure 8: Comparison of the CDFs of the packet delivery probability $\mathrm{P}[B^T]$ in slot T for dependent and independent interference. Parameters are $\lambda = 2$, $\theta = 1$, $\alpha = 4$, an overall transmitter-receiver distance of 0.5 and the relay is placed in the middle between transmitter and receiver.

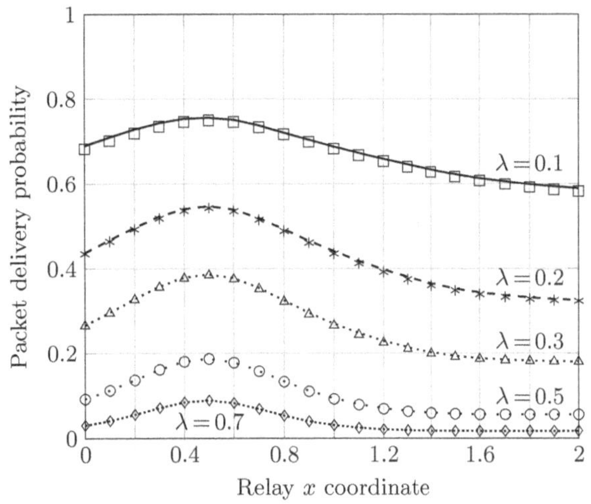

Figure 9: Packet delivery probability of MHA relaying (lines) and dependent two-hop relaying (marks) for different positions of the first relay R_1. The distance for each R-D hop is 1 and R_2 is located at 1.5. Parameters are $\theta = 1$, $p = 1$, and $\alpha = 4$.

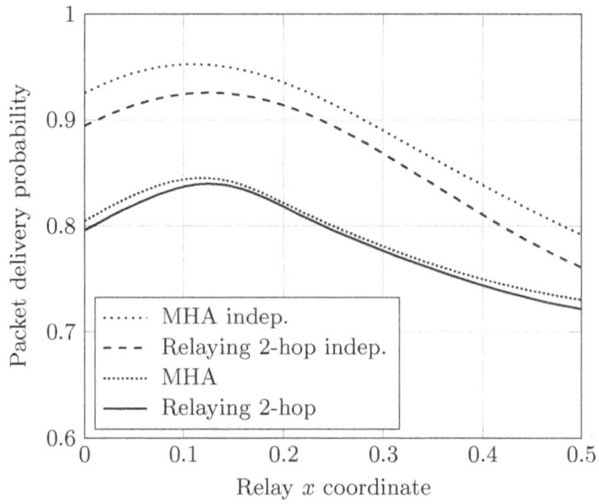

Figure 10: Packet delivery probability of MHA relaying with/without interference dependencies and two-hop relaying with/without dependencies. Parameters are $\lambda = 1$, $\theta = 1$, $p = 1$, $\alpha = 4$, and the distance of each R-D hop is 0.25.

increases in even slots). Furthermore, while the first few iterations of the scheme increase the overall packet delivery probability significantly, in later iterations this increase becomes smaller. This smaller increase can still contribute to the overall packet delivery probability, although the retransmission process has to stop at some point. The reduced increase is explained by noting that if the first iteration is unsuccessful, the probability of having success later is small due to dependent interference. If two or more iterations already failed, this effect is even stronger.

Figure 8 compares the packet delivery probabilities $\mathrm{P}[B^T]$ for dependent and independent interference. It can be seen that the CDF converges much faster toward 1 for independent interference than for dependent interference. This shows that the dependence of interference significantly reduces the benefits of retransmissions. This is an example which shows that considering interference dynamics may significantly change the performance of a protocol and therefore must be considered in order for results to be realistic.

5. MULTI-HOP-AWARE RELAYING

In the following we study the packet delivery probability of multi-hop-aware cooperative relaying with selection combining [1]. The topology appears in Figure 2.

First, we derive the packet delivery probability $\mathrm{P}[B]$ of a conventional two-hop relaying link, i.e., without using Link 7, for dependent interference. Note that the interference power values of the two hops are dependent, hence we cannot simply square the result in (9). Therefore, we have

$$\begin{aligned}\mathrm{P}[B] &= \mathrm{P}\big[(A_1 \cup A_2A_3)(A_4 \cup A_5A_6)\big]\\ &= \mathrm{P}[A_1A_4] + \mathrm{P}[A_1A_5A_6] - \mathrm{P}[A_1A_4A_5A_6]\\ &\quad + \mathrm{P}[A_2A_3A_4] + \mathrm{P}[A_2A_3A_5A_6]\\ &\quad - \mathrm{P}[A_2A_3A_4A_5A_6] - \mathrm{P}[A_1A_2A_3A_4]\\ &\quad - \mathrm{P}[A_1A_2A_3A_5A_6] + \mathrm{P}[A_1A_2A_3A_4A_5A_6]. \quad (14)\end{aligned}$$

In case of independent interference this simplifies to

$$\begin{aligned}\mathrm{P}[B] &= \mathrm{P}\big[(A_1 \cup A_2A_3)(A_4 \cup A_5A_6)\big]\\ &= \big(\mathrm{P}[A_1] + \mathrm{P}[A_2]\mathrm{P}[A_3] - \mathrm{P}[A_1]\mathrm{P}[A_2]\mathrm{P}[A_3]\big)\cdot\\ &\quad \big(\mathrm{P}[A_4] + \mathrm{P}[A_5]\mathrm{P}[A_6] - \mathrm{P}[A_4]\mathrm{P}[A_5]\mathrm{P}[A_6]\big). \quad (15)\end{aligned}$$

Second, we address the case where Link 7 is also used by node D_2, i.e., applying MHA cooperative relaying. The overall packet delivery probability for this scenario under dependent interference is given by

$$\begin{aligned}\mathrm{P}[B_{\mathrm{MHA}}] &= \mathrm{P}[B] + \mathrm{P}[A_2A_7] - \mathrm{P}[A_1A_2A_4A_7]\\ &\quad - \mathrm{P}[A_2A_3A_4A_7] + \mathrm{P}[A_1A_2A_3A_4A_7]\\ &\quad - \mathrm{P}[A_1A_2A_5A_6A_7] - \mathrm{P}[A_2A_3A_5A_6A_7]\\ &\quad + \mathrm{P}[A_1A_2A_3A_5A_6A_7] + \mathrm{P}[A_1A_2A_4A_5A_6A_7]\\ &\quad + \mathrm{P}[A_2A_3A_4A_5A_6A_7] - \mathrm{P}[A_1A_2A_3A_4A_5A_6A_7]. \quad (16)\end{aligned}$$

For independent interference we have

$$\begin{aligned}\mathrm{P}[B_{\mathrm{MHA}}] &= (1 - \mathrm{P}[A_2])\cdot\\ &\quad \Big(\mathrm{P}[A_1]\big(\mathrm{P}[A_4] + \mathrm{P}[A_5]\mathrm{P}[A_6] - \mathrm{P}[A_4]\mathrm{P}[A_5]\mathrm{P}[A_6]\big)\Big)\\ &\quad + \mathrm{P}[A_2]\Big(\mathrm{P}[A_7] + (1 - \mathrm{P}[A_7])\cdot\\ &\quad \big(\mathrm{P}[A_1] + \mathrm{P}[A_3] - \mathrm{P}[A_1]\mathrm{P}[A_3]\big)\cdot\\ &\quad \big(\mathrm{P}[A_4] + \mathrm{P}[A_5]\mathrm{P}[A_6] - \mathrm{P}[A_4]\mathrm{P}[A_5]\mathrm{P}[A_6]\big)\Big). \quad (17)\end{aligned}$$

The probabilities in the last equations can be again calculated by applying Equation (8).

Figure 9 compares the packet delivery probabilities of multi-hop-aware cooperative relaying and conventional cooperative relaying. The position of S is at the origin, while D_1 and D_2 have x-coordinates of 1 and 2, respectively. The location of the relay used in the first hop is altered while the position of the second relay is kept fixed at 1.5. As we can see, the optimal position of the first relay is at about 0.5, i.e., in the middle between S and D_1. Furthermore, the plot shows that the gain for the additional link (Link 7 in Figure 2) is very small for the considered scenario.

Next we want to see if the gain of MHA relaying improves when we consider independent interference. Figure 10 compares the performance of multi-hop-aware cooperative relaying and conventional two-hop relaying for the dependent and independent interference cases. The upper two curves show the performance of the two relaying schemes for independent interference. Here, the performance of MHA cooperative relaying is significantly better than the performance of two-hop relaying. Again, if we consider dependent interference, the performance improvement is much smaller. These results show that the performance gain of MHA cooperative relaying is significantly reduced if we consider a model of dependent interference.

6. RELATED WORK

6.1 Temporal and Spatial Properties of Interference

A number of recent papers aim to analyze the temporal and spatial characteristics of interference. In particular, Haenggi introduced the 'uncertainty cube', which models the stochastic aspects of the network under consideration [7]. The author also derives the correlation of interference for network scenarios represented by the vertices of this cube.

The authors of [17] extended the results of Haenggi by considering a wider set of sources of correlation, including the nodes' locations, the temporal correlation of the wireless channel and the particular traffic pattern adopted by communicating stations.

This work is also strongly related to the analysis in [3], where Ganti et al. derive the conditional probability of outage situations at different time slots for scenarios that exhibit correlated interference. In particular, our work adapts and extends some aspects of the above-cited work to the spatial domain by addressing cooperative communications.

6.2 Performance of Cooperative Communication Systems

The performance of cooperative techniques has been extensively investigated in recent years, and some of the contributions that are closer to the analysis contained in this work are briefly reviewed in the following.

Gupta and Kumar derive the capacity of the relay-aided wireless channel assuming point-to-point coding [6]. Their analysis is extended by Gastpar and Vetterli in [4], which accounts for more general channel access schemes and coding solutions, where the single relays are allowed to help each other in a 'network coding' fashion.

Laneman et al. address the design of cooperative protocols including outage probability as a performance metric [15]. The authors show that the proposed relaying schemes are capable of performing within 1.5 dB from the optimum and provide a significant resource gain compared to non-cooperative solutions.

Amplify-and-Forward schemes, where the relay does not decode the signal received from the transmitting station, are analyzed in [12], where Nakagami-m fading is assumed. The authors derive the outage probability characterizing the considered network scenario, and verify that the analysis closely matches the simulated performance.

The outage probability of coded cooperation schemes, where relays follow an incremental forwarding rule, instead of simply retransmitting the same information sent by the transmitter, is studied in [11]. The authors show that coded cooperation is fundamentally different from decode-and-forward schemes, and they further prove that such a forwarding technique is beneficial for the network performance compared to non-cooperative and repetitive solutions.

Incremental systems are also studied in [2], where the authors obtain the throughput, delay and outage performance of cooperative coded systems consisting of multiple transmissions. The analysis of [2] is not based on capacity considerations, but it relies on the sphere-packing bound and hence accounts for the effect of the number of symbols that are transmitted in each attempt, without loosing generality since the bound is not limited to using a particular encoding and decoding engine.

All the above-mentioned works characterize in detail the performance of the cooperative link, though they do not consider the influence of interference from external stations, which is the ultimate aim of this contribution. Hence, the presented paper may be seen as an effort for extending previous theoretic works to the interference limited scenario.

6.3 Influence of Interference on Cooperative Communications

Despite extensive research efforts on cooperative communications, few papers considered the influence of interference on the performance of a cooperative scenario. The most recent contributions are summarized in the following.

A look at cooperation between the base stations of different cells grouping users is presented in [5], though that work is quite distant from the single link point of view analyzed in this contribution. Particularly, the authors investigate the possibility of enabling cooperative decoding of signals received at different base stations, for the sake of obtaining an increased performance by exploiting interference in order to create a virtual multiple-input multiple-output channel.

A capacity bound for scenarios consisting of two transmitter-receiver pairs is studied in [16], assuming that stations from the different pairs may cooperate, though they cause interference to the other communicating pairs. The paper shows that a significant performance increase is achieved when the two transmitters are allowed to cooperate following the rule proposed by the authors, and further proves that the capacity bound is achieved when the cooperation channel gain is infinite.

Reference [20] studies the sum-rate and energy efficiency of a cooperative network and highlights a tradeoff between the throughput gain provided by cooperative communications and the amount of interference introduced by relay stations in an asynchronous multi-user scenario. The authors derive through numerical analysis and simulations the optimal size of a cooperative region for maximizing the network sum-rate and energy efficiency.

The performance of decode-and-forward relaying schemes is analyzed in [13] assuming that the cooperative link is affected by co-channel interference. Particularly, the authors derive the outage probability of the system and provide optimal energy allocation strategies under an adaptive relay selection assumption, where only stations that successfully decoded the transmission of the source node may cooperate.

The works summarized above are a step toward analyzing

the behavior of cooperation when the communication is affected by interfering nodes, though the results obtained do not consider the correlation properties of interference, which may significantly influence the network performance. This paper aims at extending the above-cited references by introducing spatial correlation of interference experienced by nodes at different locations, hence providing a more accurate analysis of cooperative techniques in interference limited networks.

7. CONCLUSIONS AND FURTHER WORK

In the paper at hand we derived the joint probabilities of successful packet delivery at multiple receivers under spatially and temporally dependent interference. This tool was then applied to selected cooperative relaying scenarios. We showed how the performance of cooperative relaying changes under dependent interference compared to the case of independent interference. For good communication conditions, dependence decreases the end-to-end performance, while for harsh communication conditions it increases the performance. We analyzed the probability of full packet delivery at a given slot for repeated cooperative relaying. The outcome was as follows: repetitions of the relaying process significantly improve packet delivery for independent interference; this gain can be smaller for dependent interference.

Next, a scheme called multi-hop-aware cooperative relaying was analyzed. We showed that the performance gain of this protocol is reduced when interference exhibits high temporal and spatial dependencies. Overall, results show that the spatial and temporal dependence exhibited by interference has a large impact on the performance of cooperative relaying. Many related works, however, derive performance metrics without considering the dependence of interference.

As a next step, we plan to generalize our work to the case of multiple relays. Here, some relay selection protocol can be assumed to choose the best relay with regard to some metric. Additionally, we will analyze the performance of maximum ratio combining using the same tools.

Acknowledgments

This work has been supported by the Austrian Science Fund (FWF) under grant P24480-N15 and by the ERDF, KWF, and the state of Austria under grants KWF-20214/15935/23108 (RELAY) and 20214/20777/31602 (Research Days). It has been performed in the research cluster Lakeside Labs. The work of S. Toumpis has been partly done during a research stay at Lakeside Labs GmbH.

8. REFERENCES

[1] H. Adam, C. Bettstetter, and S. M. Senouci. Multi-hop-aware cooperative relaying. In *Proc. IEEE Vehicular Technology Conf. (VTC)*, Barcelona, Spain, Apr. 2009.

[2] F. Babich and A. Crismani. Cooperative coding schemes: Design and performance evaluation. *IEEE Trans. Wireless Commun.*, 11(1):222–235, Jan. 2012.

[3] R. Ganti and M. Haenggi. Spatial and temporal correlation of the interference in ALOHA ad hoc networks. *IEEE Commun. Lett.*, 13(9):631–633, Sept. 2009.

[4] M. Gastpar and M. Vetterli. On the capacity of wireless networks: the relay case. In *Proc. IEEE Intern. Conf. on Communications (ICC)*, pages 1577–1586, June 2002.

[5] D. Gesbert, S. Hanly, H. Huang, S. Shamai Shitz, O. Simeone, and W. Yu. Multi-cell MIMO cooperative networks: a new look at interference. *IEEE J. Select. Areas Commun.*, 28(9):1380–1408, Dec. 2010.

[6] P. Gupta and P. R. Kumar. The capacity of wireless networks. *IEEE Trans. Inform. Theory*, 46:388–404, 2000.

[7] M. Haenggi. Outage, local throughput, and capacity of random wireless networks. *IEEE Trans. Commun.*, 8(8), Aug. 2009.

[8] M. Haenggi. *Stochastic Geometry for Wireless Networks.* Cambridge University Press, 2013.

[9] M. Haenggi and R. Ganti. *Interference in Large Wireless Networks.* now publishing, 2009.

[10] R. Hekmat and P. Van Mieghem. Interference in wireless multi-hop ad-hoc networks and its effect on network capacity. *Wirel. Netw.*, 10(4):389–399, July 2004.

[11] T. Hunter, S. Sanayei, and A. Nosratinia. Outage analysis of coded cooperation. *IEEE Trans. Inform. Theory*, 52(2):375–391, Feb. 2006.

[12] S. S. Ikki and M. Ahmed. Performance analysis of cooperative diversity wireless networks over Nakagami-m fading channel. *IEEE Commun. Lett.*, 11(4):334–336, Apr. 2007.

[13] S. S. Ikki, P. Ubaidulla, and S. Aissa. Regenerative cooperative diversity networks with co-channel interference: performance analysis and optimal energy allocation. *IEEE Trans. Veh. Technol.*, 62(2):896–902, Feb. 2013.

[14] A. Iyer, C. Rosenberg, and A. Karnik. What is the right model for wireless channel interference? *IEEE Trans. Wireless Commun.*, 8(5):2662–2671, 2009.

[15] J. N. Laneman, D. N. C. Tse, and G. W. Wornell. Cooperative diversity in wireless networks: efficient protocols and outage behavior. *IEEE Trans. Inform. Theory*, 50:3062–3080, 2004.

[16] Y. Peng and D. Rajan. Capacity bounds of half-duplex Gaussian cooperative interference channel. In *Proc. IEEE Intern. Symp. on Inform. Theory (ISIT)*, pages 2081–2085, July 2009.

[17] U. Schilcher, C. Bettstetter, and G. Brandner. Temporal correlation of interference in wireless networks with Rayleigh fading. *IEEE Trans. on Mobile Computing*, 11(12):2109–2120, Dec. 2012.

[18] A. Sendonaris, E. Erkip, and B. Aazhang. User cooperation diversity - Part I: system description. *IEEE Trans. Commun.*, 51:1927–1938, Nov. 2003.

[19] D. Stoyan, W. S. Kendall, and J. Mecke. *Stochastic Geometry and Its Applications*, chapter 2.4. John Wiley & Sons Ltd, 1995.

[20] S. Vakil and B. Liang. Cooperative diversity in interference limited wireless networks. *IEEE Trans. Wireless Commun.*, 7(8):3185–3195, Aug. 2008.

[21] Y. Zhong, W. Zhang, and M. Haenggi. Managing interference correlation through random medium access. 2013. Submitted. Available at `http://www.nd.edu/~mhaenggi/pubs/twc13c.pdf`, accessed on May 7th, 2013.

Efficient New Delayed ACK for TCP: old problem, new insight

Ming Li
Aalto University, Finland
ming.li@aalto.fi

Andrey Lukyanenko
Aalto University, Finland
andrey.lukyanenko@aalto.fi

Sasu Tarkoma
University of Helsinki, Finland
sasu.tarkoma@helsinki.fi

Antti Ylä-Jääski
Aalto University, Finland
antti.yla-jaaski@aalto.fi

ABSTRACT

When a TCP connection experiences a timeout, the sender must wait at least RTO_{min} (Minimum Retransmission Timeout) before doing the retransmission, during which the channel may be completely idle, undermining the throughput and channel efficiency. In this paper, we investigate the origin of RTO_{min} and find that it is needed to mitigate against spurious timeouts when the Delayed ACK (DA) scheme for TCP is implemented.

Motivated by this observation, we propose a deployable and TCP-compatible new Delayed ACK (NDA) to replace the legacy DA. Our solution differs with previous work is that instead of using complex algorithms or fine-grained timer to tune RTO_{min}, we modify the DA scheme with minor changes to allow the sender to remove the RTO_{min} constraint while reserving the delayed ACK function at the receiver. In order to eliminate the aggressiveness of RTO (Retransmission Timeout) after removing RTO_{min}, we use coding techniques to encode the timeout retransmitted packets to make the potential spurious retransmissions useful.

The simulation results demonstrate that in lossy wireless networks, NDA is efficient, because it achieves much higher TCP goodput and channel efficiency compared to DA. The gain we obtain by the use of NDA comes from two-order effects. One effect comes from removing the RTO_{min} constraint, because small RTO timer makes TCP react quickly to timeouts, resulting in small transmission idle. The other effect comes from eliminating consecutive RTO by allowing the receiver to acknowledge each timeout retransmission, which further reduces the RTO idle.

Categories and Subject Descriptors

C.2.2 [**Computer-Comms Nets**]: Network Protocols

MSWiM'13, November 3-8, 2013, Barcelona, Spain

http://dx.doi.org/10.1145/2507924.2507948

General Terms

Algorithms, Design, Performance

Keywords

TCP, Minimum RTO, Delayed ACK, Spurious RTO, NS-3

1. INTRODUCTION

A significant amount of today's Internet traffic is carried by TCP. In its 35 year history, TCP has evolved to function well in various environments, e.g., gigabit networks, long/fat networks, satellite and wireless environments. In this paper, we examine the area that still has space to optimize the performance of TCP: lossy wireless networks, especially in case of last mile wireless users connected to high-speed backbone links. The optimization space lies in the events of RTO (Retransmission Timeout) that cause non-trivial transmission idles when the Delayed ACK (DA) [5] is used. DA is an extension of TCP. With DA, every second segment is acknowledged in order to improve network performance and reduce host resources.

Although DA runs at the receive side, it affects the setting of the RTO timer at the send side. Specifically, the sender sets a Minimum RTO (RTO_{min}) as the lower bound of RTO timer to avoid spurious timeouts. Therefore, we say that RTO_{min} was bound to DA as default. In this paper, we study the impact of the TCP's DA scheme and RTO_{min} on TCP performance using the Network Simulator NS-3 [1]. Our study is based on the NewReno [10] flavor of TCP, as it is by far the most popular implementation in the Internet today. We show that during each RTO, DA causes non-trivial transmission idle (e.g., 200 ms), during which no data is delivered, undermining the TCP performance and channel utilization.

In order to mitigate the transmission idles during timeouts, some existing works proposed to use adaptive or fine-grained timeout timers. However, their proposals require either complicated tuning algorithms [17] or high resolution timer in OS kernel [20]. Some understood the problem in a different way. For example, they avoid the RTO events by tuning certain buffers during congestion [2, 8, 22] or add congestion control at receiver [21]. Although all the existing solutions claim to either be effective on mitigating the problem or solve it completely, we concern that they seem to unnecessarily complicate the problem. Can't we just remove the RTO_{min} constraint at the sender while reserve the DA

Table 1: Notations

Symbol	Semantics
DA	Legacy Delayed ACK scheme
NDA	New Delayed ACK scheme
RTO	Retransmission timeout
SRTO	Spurious RTO
RTO_{min}	Minimum RTO
TCP-RTO	RTO timer without the constraint of RTO_{min}
DACK	Delayed ACK timer
SRTT	Smoothed RTT
RTTVAR	RTT variation
AP	Access point
V^t	Random coefficient vector
CTF	Cross-traffic flow
p_i	Packet
c	Coded packet

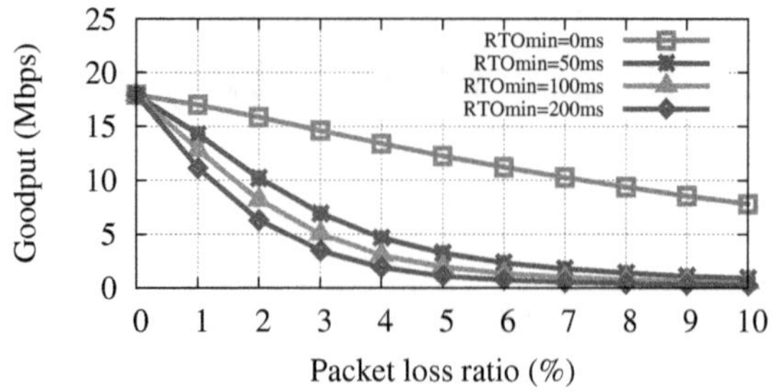

Figure 1: Goodput over packet losses. No CTF (cross-traffic flow) is injected.

function at the receiver? If this goal could be achieved with minor expense, it will not only have significant influence on TCP performance but also on TCP Incast problem in Datacenters [6]. In this paper, we investigate the possibility to achieve that goal.

In this paper, we propose a new Delayed ACK (NDA) as an extension to TCP to replace the legacy DA. An important feature of NDA is that it clears the bind between RTO_{min} and the delayed ACK function by allowing the sender to retransmit *coded packets* (instead of original packets) after a timeout. By removing the RTO_{min} constraint from the RTO timer, the TCP sender is able to react rapidly to RTO so that the transmission idle is greatly reduced to an affordable granularity.

Simulation results show that NDA is efficient, because it leads to large gains on goodput and channel utilization over lossy wireless networks. In addition to the effort provisioned by the coding techniques, the gains also come from the change of retransmission pattern. For example, the simulations show that removing RTO_{min} (or small RTO_{min}) makes the TCP flow more likely to recover missing packets by fast retransmission instead of resorting to timeout retransmission. Therefore, instead of incurring extra spurious RTO events, NDA reduce the number of them, obtaining further gains on goodput and channel utilization. The simulation also demonstrates that TCP using NDA can coexist with TCP using DA in the absence of losses, without affecting fairness.

The remainder of the paper is organized as follows. In Section 2, we first review the background of DA for TCP as well as the origin of RTO_{min}, and then present the impact of RTO_{min} on TCP performance. In Section 3, we introduce how we integrate coding techniques to NDA and discuss its deployment issues in practice. Section 4 includes our extensive performance evaluation. In Section 5, we discuss the related work. Section 6 concludes the paper.

2. BACKGROUND

The notations and definitions utilized in this paper are summarized in Table 1. In this section, we first investigate DA and the origin of RTO_{min}, and then present the impact of RTO_{min} on TCP performance in lossy wireless networks.

DA is a popular scheme for TCP among the vast majority of OSs. It is useful both in saving the network bandwidth and in reducing the protocol processing overhead. We summarize the rules of DA as follows.

1. The receiver generates one ACK for every other packet, unless the packet arrives out of order.
2. The receiver delays sending an ACK for the first in-order arriving packet, for as long as the DA timer suggests.

In order to avoid spurious timeouts when DA is enabled, the sender sets an explicit configuration parameter, RTO_{min}, as the lower bound of the RTO timer. In addition to DA, the other reason the conservative lower bound is used is the coarse grain clocks that were implemented in OSs a few decades ago [4]. Nowadays, the OS clock granularity is not a matter of concern for modern OSs any more [17]. Therefore, in this paper we only consider DA as the constraint on RTO timer.

The RTO timer now is modelled by RFC 6298 [16] as

$$\mathrm{RTO} = \max\left(\mathrm{SRTT} + 4 * \mathrm{RTTVAR}, \mathrm{RTO_{min}}\right), \quad (1)$$

where SRTT holds the smoothed RTT and RTTVAR the RTT variation. The same RFC also specifies that RTO_{min} should be 1 second, i.e., whenever RTO is computed, if it is less than 1 second, then the RTO should be rounded up to 1 second. Currently, there exists no explicit official instruction on the setting of RTO_{min}. The most common value for RTO_{min} and DA timer is 200 ms.

In order to differentiate SRTT+4*RTTVAR from RTO_{min}, we name the former TCP-RTO in the rest of the paper.

2.1 TCP Performance Degradation

Our interest is in the impact of RTO_{min} on the TCP performance. Therefore, we assume TCP-RTO is less than RTO_{min}. Otherwise, RTO_{min} will add no extra waiting time in case of timeouts.

We now investigate the impact of RTO_{min} on the TCP goodput. We simulate a pair of client and server connected through a wireless connection. Please refer to Section 4 for more information on the simulation settings and topology. In order to exclude interference by other factors, we add no cross-traffic flow (CTF) in the network. Fig. 1 shows the goodput of a TCP flow as we increase the packet loss ratio using different RTO_{min} values. We notice that the goodput reduces when the packet loss ratio grows, and the larger the RTO_{min} is, the more significantly the goodput degrades. We deduce that removing the lower bound of RTO would significantly improve the TCP performance.

To understand how RTO_{min} affects the performance of TCP, let us review a process of a timeout retransmission

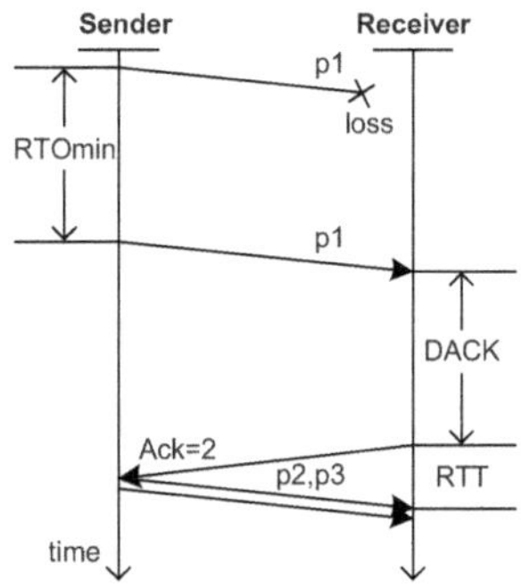

Figure 2: TCP timeout using DA

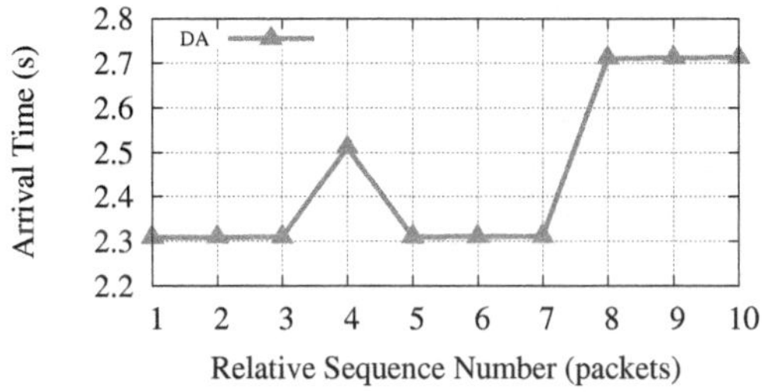

Figure 3: Packet Arrival Time. RTO_{min}=200 ms

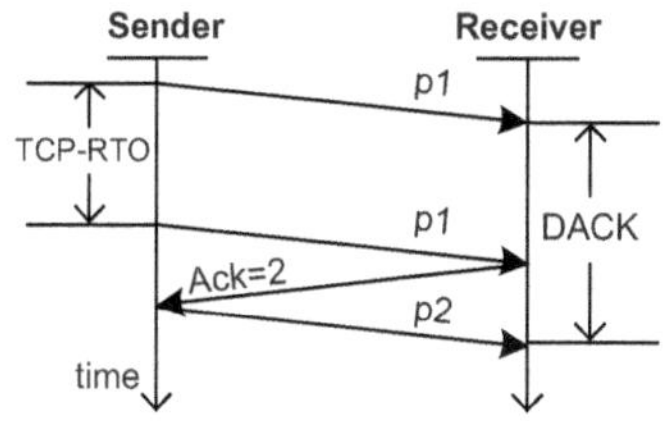

Figure 4: Removing RTO_{min} directly without modifying any rule of DA accordingly

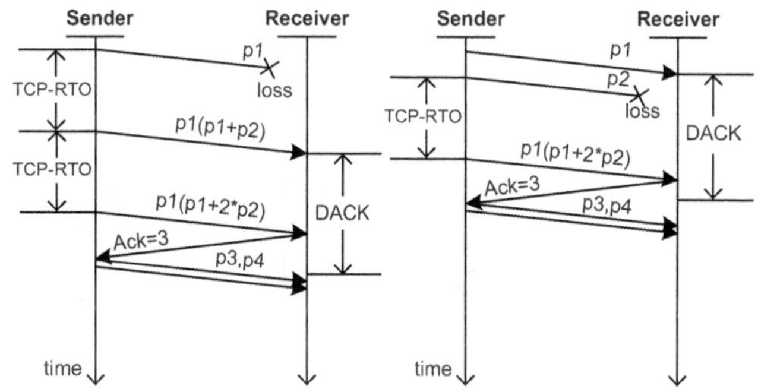

(a) Timeout caused by packet loss (b) Timeout caused by Delayed ACK

Figure 5: TCP timeout using NDA

using DA. As shown in Fig. 2, the packet p_1 is lost without subsequent packets coming. According to the rules of TCP RTO, p_1 will be retransmitted after RTO_{min}. According to the rules of DA, when p_1 reaches the receiver, the receiver will delay sending an ACK until the DA timer (DACK) expires so that the sending of p_2 and p_3 is also delayed for RTO_{min}.

To demonstrate the correctness of the RTO process discussed above, we still use the same simulation topology as above. We set the DA timer and RTO_{min} to 200 ms and set the loss ratio of the wireless connection to 0.5%. Fig. 3 presents the packet arrival time. We observe that the 4th packet (corresponding to p_1 in Fig. 2), expected to reach the destination at around 2.3s, is delayed to arrive at the receiver for 200 ms. We deduce that the packet is lost and is retransmitted after RTO_{min}. The 8th packet (corresponding to p_2 in Fig. 2) arrives at the receiver after $RTO_{min} + RTT$ of the arrival of the 4th packet.

In summary, RTO_{min} is usually smaller than RTT. If DA is enabled, RTO will result in non-trivial transmission idle compared to RTT. Therefore, large number of RTOs will impact the TCP performance and the channel utilization severely.

3. NEW DELAYED ACK FOR TCP

NDA aims to remove the RTO_{min} constraint at the sender while to reserve the delayed ACK function at the receiver. To achieve this goal, we need to study a number of issues. First, removing the RTO_{min} directly may cause extra spurious RTOs. To avoid them, instead of retransmitting an original packet, we want to retransmit a coded packet to make the potential spurious retransmissions useful. Second, the introduction of coding operations after timeout may incur computational overhead. Third, we need to modify the rules of DA. But the change is minor. In this section, we investigate these issues and evaluate potential solutions.

3.1 Spurious Timeout Retransmission

RTO_{min} was designed to avoid spurious timeout retransmission when DA is implemented. If we remove RTO_{min} directly without modifying any rule of DA, spurious retransmission will happen. The graph in Fig. 4 shows the process of a timeout retransmission where we remove the RTO_{min} directly without modifying any rule of DA accordingly. We notice that when the first retransmitted p_1 reaches the destination, the ACK is delayed for as long as the DA timer suggests (i.e., 200 ms) during which one more retransmission of p_1 will be introduced.

In order to avoid successive retransmissions of the same packet, we propose to retransmit a coded packet instead of an original one. For example, as shown in Fig. 5(a), when the TCP enters RTO, instead of waiting for RTO_{min}, the sender will do the retransmission after TCP-RTO and retransmit a coded packet ($p_1 + p_2$) by linearly combining p_1 and the next packet p_2. p_2 may be the next unsent packet or the next unacked packet. Please refer to the Section 3.3 for the coding design. According to the rules of DA, the receiver will delay sending the ACK when it receives $p_1(p_1 + p_2)$, causing the sender to do another retransmission of a new coded packet $p_1(p_1 + 2 * p_2)$ after TCP-RTO. Note that the two coded packets will carry the same sequence number as p_1. When the coded packets reach the destination, the receiver will decode both p_1 and p_2, and send an ACK immediately. After that, the data will start to follow the normal transmission until the next timeout appears.

The scenario above considers the timeout retransmission

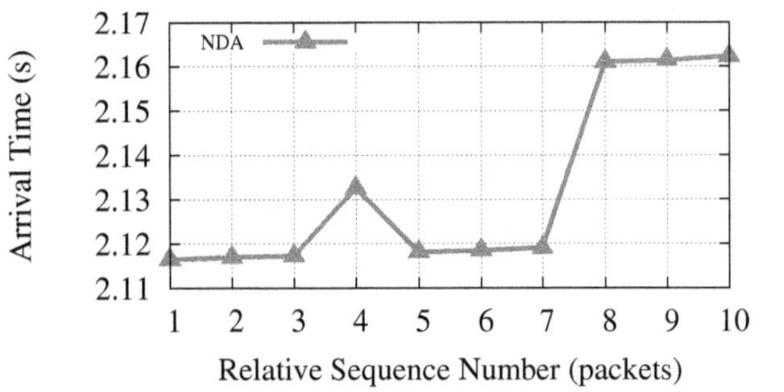

Figure 6: Arrival Sequence of TCP using no RTOmin. No ACK for coded RTO packets

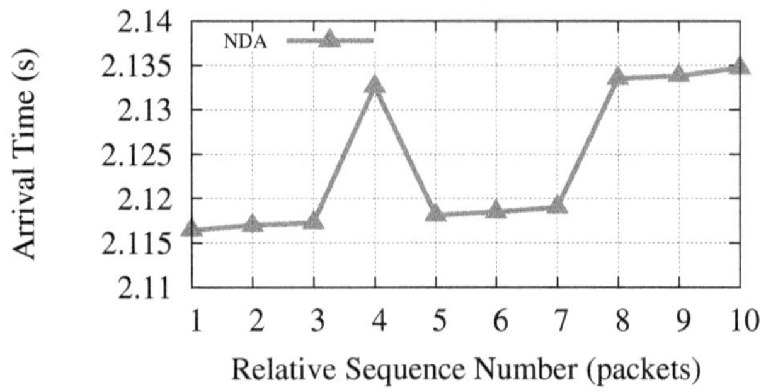

Figure 8: Arrival Sequence of TCP using RTOmin. Instant ACK for coded RTO packets

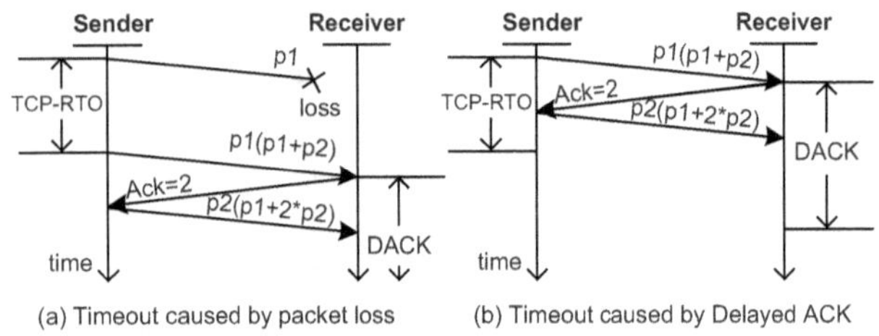

Figure 7: Optimized NDA

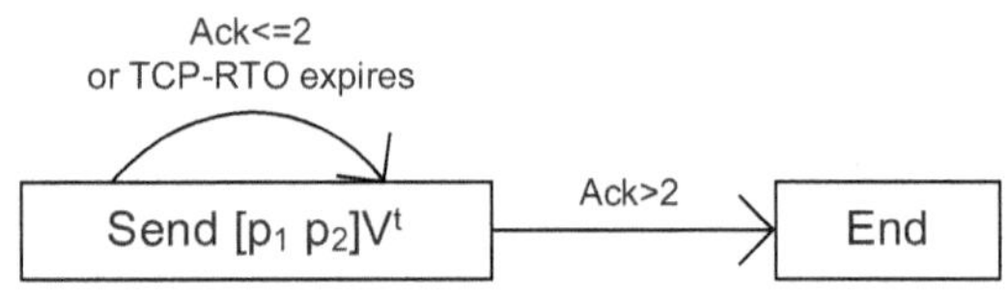

Figure 9: Processing flow of RTO using NDA

caused by the packet loss or congestion. We now discuss another scenario, where timeout is caused by delayed ACK. As shown in Fig. 5(b), the receiver receives p_1 and will delay sending an ACK. Because TCP-RTO is smaller than the DA timer, the sender will retransmit p_1 after TCP-RTO. When the coded packet reaches the destination, the receiver decodes p_2 (the receiver already has p_1) and immediately sends an ACK asking for p_3. After that, the data will start to follow the normal transmission until the next timeout appears.

Fig. 6 plots the simulation result of the packet arrival time of the same scenario shown in Fig. 5(a). We observe that the 4th packet is retransmitted after TCP-RTO so that the idle time period is greatly improved, e.g., reducing from 200 ms to a few milliseconds.

3.2 Eliminate Consecutive Timeout

We now focus on the 8th packet (see Fig. 6) that corresponds to $p_1(p_1 + 2 * p_2)$ in Fig. 5(a). When the 4th packet (corresponding to $p_1(p_1 + p_2)$ in Fig. 5(a)) arrives at the receiver, the receiver holds the ACK until the 8th packet arrives after another timeout. In order to further improve the transmission idle, we propose to allow the receiver to acknowledge every coded packet immediately so that the second coded packet, instead of being sent out as a retransmitted packet after a successive timeout, could be retrieved after one RTT. We draw the optimized process in Fig. 7. Fig. 8 plots the packet arrival time using the optimized NDA. We observe that, as we expect, the 8th packet could reach the destination one RTT after the arrival of the 4th packet.

In the optimized NDA, the ACK pattern changes because the receiver will send an ACK immediately if it receives a coded packet. In Section 4.4, we evaluate whether this acknowledgement pattern will result in the fairness issue.

Note that consecutive timeout is not introduced by NDA, but inherits from DA (see Fig 3). In the rest of the paper, without explicit specification, we use NDA to denote the optimized NDA.

3.3 Coding Design

In this section, we describe the coding design used in NDA. According to the discussion in the last two sections, in each RTO, the encoding/decoding process involves two original packets. We use p_1 and p_2 to denote them, where p_1 is the packet for retransmission and p_2 is the next unacked packet or the next unsent packet. In our coding design, we interpret each packet as a symbol over the field $GF(2^s)$, where s indicates the packet size. We assume each packet has the same size. If two packets have different sizes, the shorter one will be padded to the same size of the other one. The processing flow of the timeout retransmission is described in Fig. 9 where if the sender receives an $ACK \leq 2$ or does not receive any ACK at all before the RTO timer expires, a new coded packet will be sent out. Otherwise, the process will end.

$$c = [p_1 \quad p_2]V^t \tag{2}$$

As shown in Eq.(2), we use c to denote the new generated packet. Each time a coded packet c is generated by linearly combining the two packets, a random coefficient vector V will be used to guarantee all the coded packets are linear independent to each other. To simplify the coding operation without losing generality, we use predefined two-dimensional coefficient vectors to encode the packets. For example, V could choose from, but not limited to, $(1, 1), (1, 2), \cdots, (1, m)$. For each retransmission for the same packet pair, the sender will choose a unused coefficient vector.

The coding operations in NDA introduces negligible com-

Table 2: Deployment Difficulty

	Changes
1	RTO_{min}
2	Acknowledge
3	Encoding
4	Decoding

putational overhead, because they occur only in the presence of timeout and require few linear computation.

3.4 Deployment of New Delayed ACK for TCP

Based on the discussion above, we summarize the rules of NDA together with RTO timer as follows.

1. The receiver generates one ACK for every other packet, unless the packet is a coded packet or it arrives out of order.

2. The receiver delays sending an ACK for the first in-order arriving packet, for as long as the DA timer suggests.

3. The sender retransmits a packet after TCP-RTO.

4. If timeout happens, the sender will retransmit a coded packet.

By comparing the rules of DA (see Section 2) and NDA, we find that the changes from DA to NDA may cause some deployment issues that prevent NDA from being used in practice. We now discuss the difficulty of deployment for each change.

As shown in Table 2, NDA faces four deployment issues. The first two are minor. For example, to remove RTO_{min}, we just need to set RTO_{min} to zero as default, and in order to allow the receiver to acknowledge each coded packet, we need to add at least one-bit field in the TCP header to indicate whether the packet is encoded or not.

The other two issues are the main concern because they require to extend coding techniques to TCP stack at both the sender and the receiver. However, we are not the first to utilize packet coding into TCP. In last decade, various coding techniques have emerged as an important potential approach to optimize the network performance [11, 12, 14]. Sundararajan *et al.* [19] have already explained how network coding can be integrated into TCP-Reno by both theory and real implementation. Therefore, integrating coding techniques into NDA setting in a practical way is not a challenging task any more.

According to the discussion above, an important point to note is that NDA does not require any change in the basic features of TCP, such as sliding-window, congestion control, flow control, sequence number integrity and so on. The main change introduced by NDA to TCP is that the retransmitted segments after timeout are transformed by the encoder. This transformation is removed by the decoder, making it invisible to applications and the lower layer. Thus, NDA, as an extension of TCP, could be applied in a manner compatible with TCP.

In Section 4.4, we study the fairness of TCP using NDA to demonstrate that it could coexist with TCP using DA.

Table 3: Wifi Device Parameters

Node	WifiPhy	Mac	Rate control
AP	YansWifiPhy	Nqos	AARF
Clients	YansWifiPhy	Nqos	AARF

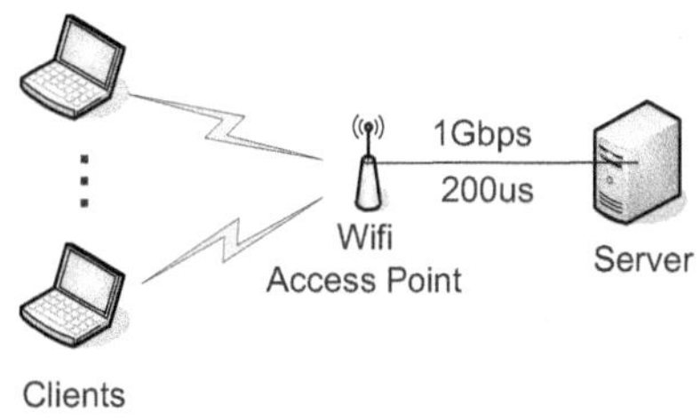

Figure 10: Topology

4. EVALUATION

In this section, we evaluate the performance of TCP using different delayed ACK strategies. We use four performance metrics:

- The number of RTOs and spurious RTOs,
- Goodput of single TCP flow,
- Bandwidth utilization (aggregate goodput of all flows),
- Protocol fairness.

The simulation platform is Network Simulator NS-3.11. We work with TCP-newReno, which is a widespread and practical variant of TCP. The segment size is 1000 bytes. Without explicit specification, the default RTO_{min} and the DA timer is set to 200 ms. For every set of parameters we consider, we repeat the simulation 10 times with different global random seeds.

Our focus is on the performance evaluation in the presence of RTO. In order to introduce RTO naturally, we choose a wireless access network connected to a backbone server as our simulation target. Fig. 10 shows the topology where the clients use Wi-Fi (complies with 802.11a) interfaces to send data to the server and the AP connects to the server using a wired connection. The bandwidth and transmission delay of the wired connection are set to 1 *Gbps* and 200 *us* respectively. The bottleneck queue of the wired connection is DropTail with the maximum queue length of 100 packets. The parameters set in the Wi-Fi devices (in the context of NS-3) are listed in Table 3. In theory, the maximum speed of the Wi-Fi connection is 54 $Mbps$, but in our simulation, the maximum speed is around 19 $Mbps$. Each client runs a FTP application transferring a file until the performance is stable. When we study the performance of an individual TCP flow, all the other flows are regarded as cross-traffic flows.

4.1 RTO and Spurious RTO

We define *RTO percentage* as the ratio between the number of RTO events and the number of sent out packets and define spurious RTO (SRTO) percentage as the ratio between the number of spurious RTO events and the number of sent out packets. Moreover, we define Transmission Idle as the sum of waiting time during all RTOs.

Fig. 11 presents the RTO/SRTO percentage and transmission idle over different RTO_{min} values. In the simulation,

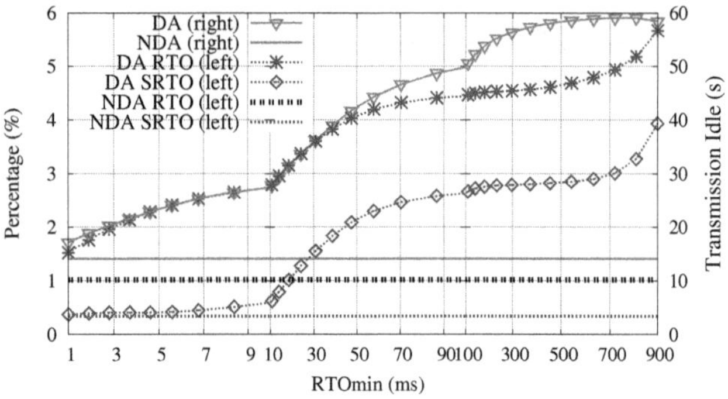

Figure 11: RTO/SRTO Percentage and Transmission idle VS. RTO_{min}

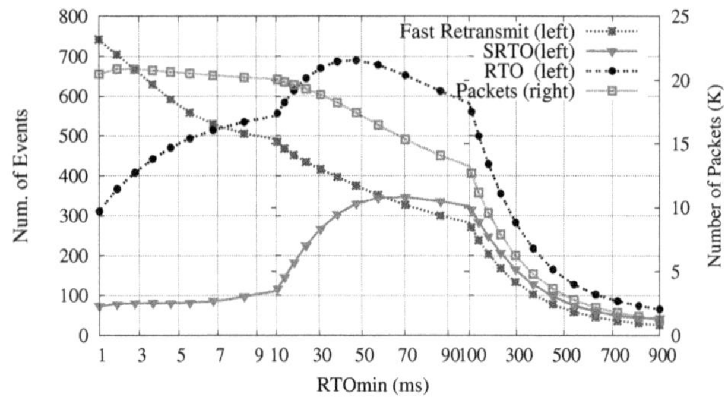

Figure 12: Retransmission events and packets sent out VS. RTO_{min}

we inject 5 CTFs, set the packet loss ratio to 5% and run the simulation for 60 s. In order not to introduce extra SRTO, we set the DA timer the same value as RTO_{min}. In the figure, the x-axis groups the RTO_{min} into three levels of granularity, i.e., 1-10ms, 10-100ms, 100-900ms. We notice that RTO/SRTO percentage and transmission idle of DA grow as we increase the value of RTO_{min} . In the extreme case where RTO_{min}=900 ms, the RTO percentage is around 6% and the transmission idle is almost 60 s that substantially exceeds the transmission time, resulting in very poor performance. The three horizontal lines indicate the RTO percentage, SRTO percentage and transmission idle of NDA (RTO_{min}=0) respectively. Compared with the corresponding curves of DA, the horizontal lines demonstrate the efficiency of NDA.

According to the intuition, there should be a trade-off between RTO_{min} and SRTO, which was also mentioned by Allman in [3]. For example, small RTO_{min} causes extra SRTO. But Fig. 11 shows the opposite result. We use the simulation result (using the same simulation settings as above) drawn in Fig. 12 to explain the reason. When we increase RTO_{min} from 1 ms to 60 ms, we expect to see the result that the number of SRTOs decreases, but in the simulation result, the number increases. Now note the curve of the fast retransmit events. We observe that it is a decreasing curve as the function of RTO_{min}. We deduce that when RTO_{min} is small plus the receiver acknowledges every coded packet, the congestion window grows quickly resulting in more packets on the fly. Therefore, when a packet is missing, it becomes more likely to trigger the fast retransmission. When RTO_{min} is above 60 ms, the SRTO events reduce dramatically, because the congestion window grows slowly after each timeout so that the TCP flow starts to be more likely to resort to RTO for recovery.

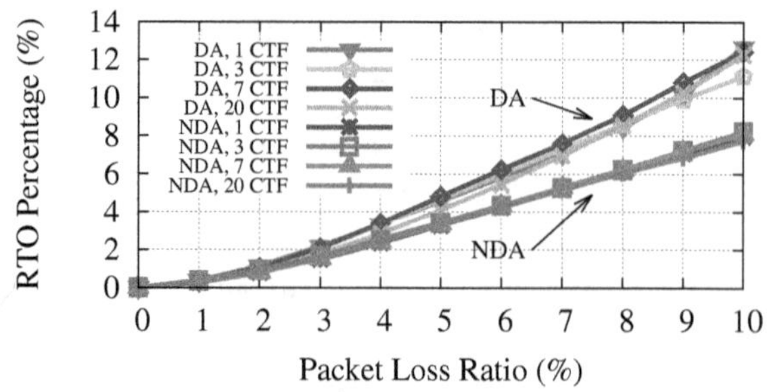

Figure 13: NDA reduces timeouts

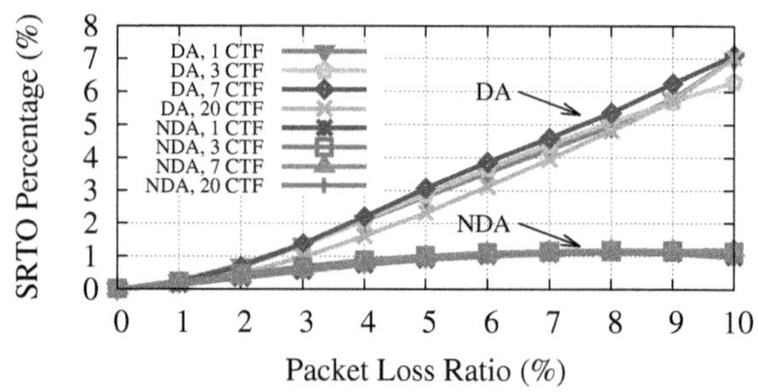

Figure 14: NDA reduces spurious timeouts

We now want to explain another phenomenon in Fig. 11, e.g., the SRTO percentage of DA increases as RTO_{min} grows even thought the events of SRTO decreases when RTO_{min} is above 60 ms. The reason is that when RTO_{min} is above 60 ms, the reducing speed of data packet sent out decreases faster than the reducing speed of SRTO events. The same explanation also works for RTO percentage.

In the following simulations, we set RTO_{min} and DA timer to 200 ms in DA and study the RTO and SRTO as the function of packet loss ratio. Fig. 13 presents the RTO percentage of a single TCP flow as we increase the loss ratio using different number of cross-traffic flows. We observe that the curves are divided roughly into two groups belonging to NDA and DA respectively. Each group has four curves. The RTO percentage in the NDA group is always less than the DA group. Another observation is that the curves in each group almost overlap with each other. This phenomenon implies packet loss is the main cause of timeouts in our simulation. In the worst case, e.g., loss ratio is 10%, the RTO percentage of NDA is reduced by up to 37% against DA.

Fig. 14 presents SRTO percentage as we increase the packet loss ratio using the same simulation settings as above. We have the similar observation as Fig. 13. For example, the curves of NDA and DA are also divided into two groups of NDA and DA respectively, and the four curves in the same group almost overlap with each other. By comparing the curves of DA and NDA, we see that in the worst case, NDA

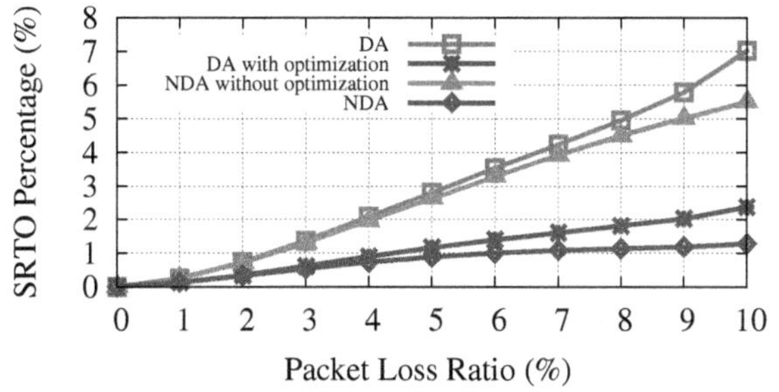

Figure 15: SRTO percentage using different Delayed ACK strategies. One CTF is injected.

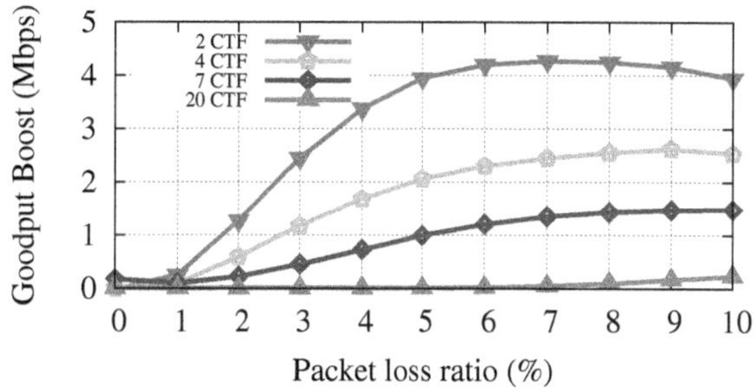

Figure 17: Goodput Boost VS. Packet loss

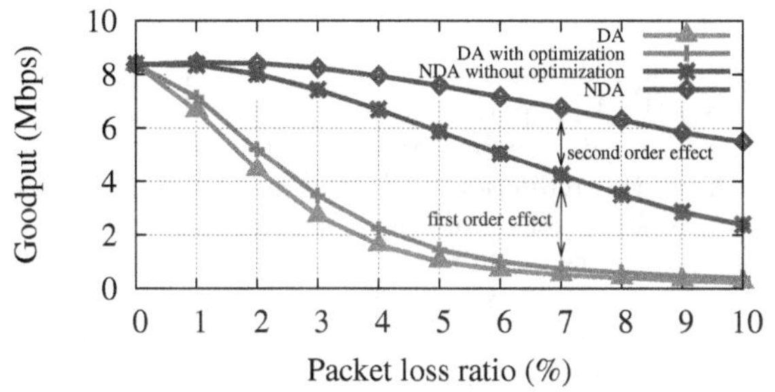

Figure 16: Goodput VS. Packet loss. One CTF is injected.

reduces the SRTO by 86% against DA in the worst case.

The discussion above demonstrates that NDA is efficient on reducing RTO and SRTO. We now investigate the impact of NDA/DA optimization and coding techniques on SRTO. Recall that in Section 3, in order to avoid consecutive timeout we propose to optimize NDA by allowing the receiver to acknowledge each coded packet. The curves in Fig. 15 present the SRTO percentage using four different Delayed ACK strategies: DA, DA with optimization, NDA without optimization and NDA (optimized as default). The strategy of DA with optimization means that in DA, we also allow the receiver to acknowledge each timeout retransmitted packet. In the figure, we only present the curves of one CTF because the curves of more CTFs have the similar shape as that of one CTF. By comparing the curves, we have two observations. First, allowing the receiver to acknowledge each timeout retransmission reduces SRTO percentage for both DA and NDA. Second, with and without optimization, NDA further reduces the SRTO percentage against DA, because of coding techniques integrated into NDA.

In summary, NDA is efficient on reducing the RTO and SRTO events. The reasons are: 1) coding techniques in timeout retransmission mitigate the spurious timeouts, 2) in TCP using DA, a timeout may further incur a consecutive RTO, whereas NDA removes it by allowing the receiver to acknowledge each coded packet, 3) the TCP sender using NDA responds more quickly to timeout so that more packets are on the fly to trigger the fast retransmission.

4.2 Single TCP Performance

In Fig. 1, we draw the goodput of a TCP flow as the function of loss ratio without any cross-traffic. We now introduce flow multiplexing to study the extent to which NDA is able to boost the goodput by suppressing transmission idles during timeouts. We first consider the scenario of one CTF and then extend to more CTFs.

Fig. 16 shows the goodput of a TCP flow as the function of loss ratio using four different Delayed ACK strategies respectively. According to the figure, TCP using DA has the worst performance. This is because it is not able to saturate the shared bandwidth due to transmission idles caused by timeouts. By comparing the two curves of DA, we find that optimized DA could also improve the goodput, but the improvement is limited. This phenomenon implies that the transmission idle during each RTO is the main reason of TCP performance degradation.

We now focus on the three Delayed ACK strategies of DA, NDA and NDA without optimization. Their curves show that the use of NDA without optimization results in large gains in goodput because it reduces the transmission idle during timeout. This gain could be considered as a "first order effect". The gain could further be obtained by optimizing NDA, i.e., allowing the receiver to acknowledge each coded packet so that the number of RTO/SRTO reduces. We consider this gain as a "second order effect".

Moreover, by comparing the curves of DA and NDA, we notice that the goodput boost offered by NDA does not increase monotonically as the function of packet loss ratio. We find that the goodput difference between NDA and DA is the largest, by up to 640%, when the loss ratio is around 5%. This is because as the loss ratio grows, the curve of DA decreases exponentially, whereas the curve of NDA decreases almost linearly. Thus, largest goodput boost will appear in the middle.

Next we study the goodput improvement the NDA offers to TCP in more scenarios. We define the goodput boost as the difference between the goodput provisioned by NDA and DA respectively. According to the simulation results shown in Fig. 17, we have a few observations. First, on a fixed packet loss ratio, the goodput boost becomes smaller when more flows share the channel. This is because when more flows share the same channel, each individual TCP flow shares less bandwidth and the shared bandwidth further decreases because of signal interference so that their difference becomes smaller. Second, in accordance with the observation in Fig. 1, the highest goodput boost appears in a middle position. Third, if the number of cross-traffic is large, the goodput boost by NDA becomes minor. This is

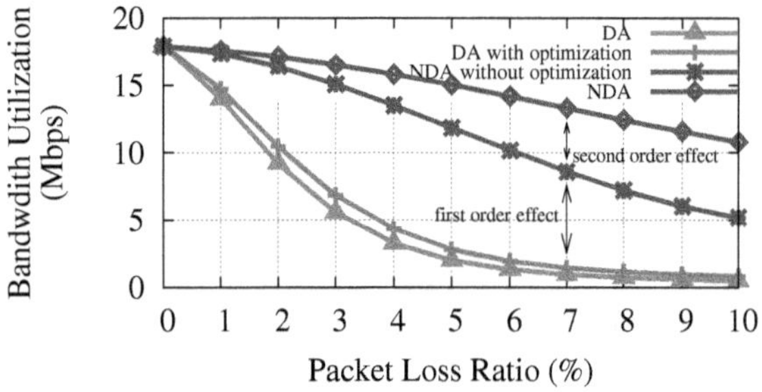

Figure 18: Bandwidth Utilization VS. Packet Losses. One CTF is injected.

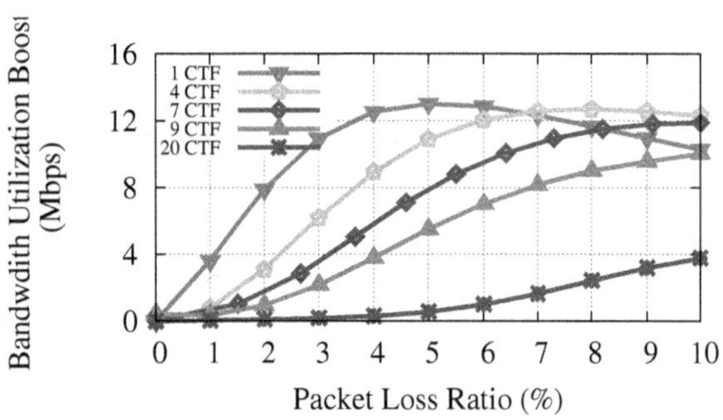

Figure 19: Bandwidth Utilization VS. Packet Losses

because in wireless networks, more competitive flows incur more frame collision and retransmission to counteract the goodput boost by TCP layer effort.

4.3 Bandwidth Utilization

We now study the impact of packet losses and bandwidth competition on the bandwidth utilization. We define the bandwidth utilization as the aggregate goodput of all TCP flows (including the cross-traffic flows). We first inject one cross-traffic flow to study the bandwidth utilization as the function of loss ratio. Fig. 18 draws the simulation result. We have a few similar observations as Fig. 16. For instance, DA has the worst performance and DA with optimization could only improve the performance a little bit. NDA without optimization improves the performance a lot because it reduces the transmission idle during each RTO from RTO_{min} to TCP-RTO, one- or two-order granularity reduction. NDA could further improves the performance because it eliminates a goodly number of RTO and SRTO. The highest goodput boost also appears at the loss ratio of around 5%. The boost is up to 680%, the same level of boost compared with the single TCP flow using NDA (see Fig. 16).

We now further study the bandwidth utilization boost in more scenarios by introducing more flow multiplexing. Fig. 19 shows the bandwidth utilization boost of NDA compared to DA as the function of packet loss ratio using different number of CTFs. We observe that each curve of the bandwidth utilization follows the same trend as the individual TCP flow with the same number of running flows (see Fig. 17). The reasons are the same as we have explained in the last section.

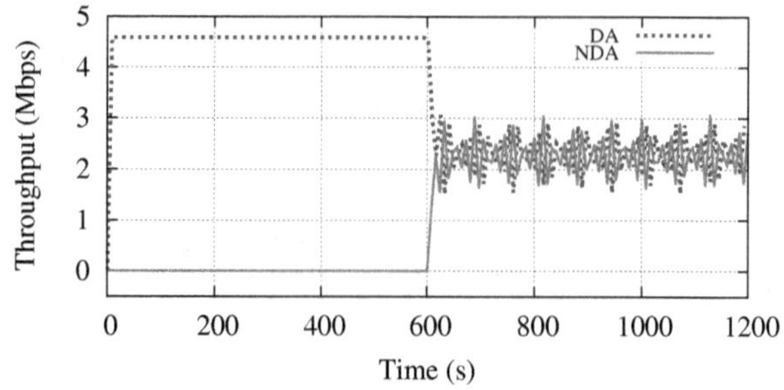

Figure 20: Protocol fairness - two TCP flows using DA and NDA respectively

In summary, we have demonstrated that NDA is efficient to improve the TCP performance as well as the channel utilization. The gains come from two-order effects. The first comes from the reduction of RTO transmission idle from RTO_{min} to TCP-RTO, in which process the coding techniques play a role of mitigating the SRTO events. The second effect comes from allowing the receiver to acknowledge each timeout retransmitted packet. The highest performance boost appears in the middle, i.e., the larger packet loss ratio may not result in higher goodput boost. More intense channel contention could counteract the effort of TCP layer on goodput boost.

4.4 Fairness of the Protocol

In the last few sections, we demonstrate that in the context of lossy wireless networks, NDA could improve the performance of TCP compared to DA. In this section, we study the fairness property of TCP using NDA in the absence of packet loss. TCP fairness means that if two similar flows compete for the same channel, they should have an approximately equal share of the channel bandwidth without dependence on the order in which the flows join the network.

We use the same topology shown in Fig. 10 where we use two clients. One of them uses DA and the other uses NDA. The loss ratio is set to 0%. In order to introduce enough contention, we set the bandwidth of the wired connection between AP and server to 5 $Mbps$. We set the simulation time to 1200 s. The TCP flow using DA starts first at the beginning and the TCP flow using NDA starts at 600 s. The throughput is calculated at intervals of 8 s. The evolution of the throughput over time is shown in Fig. 20. We notice that after the second flow starts, the bandwidth gets redistributed fairly.

Thus, TCP using NDA can coexist with TCP using DA in the absence of losses, without affecting fairness.

5. RELATED WORK

Delayed ACK is a two edged sword for TCP. For example, it reduces the number of ACKs so that the network bandwidth is saved and protocol processing overhead reduces, whereas it requires the sender to set a conservative lower bound for RTO timer, which may degrade the TCP performance significantly in the presence of timeout. To solve this problem, researchers propose several solutions in different ways.

Psaras *et al.* [17] demonstrated that the conservative RTO_{min} setting may cause severe TCP performance degradation. They propose a mechanism named Adaptive MINRTO to identify the packets whose ACKs are (possibly) going to be delayed and apply extended RTO_{min} to those packets only, in order to avoid spurious RTO. Vasudevan *et al.* [20] propose to reduce RTO_{min} to microseconds so that there would be a shorter idle time upon RTO. They demonstrate that their solution is effective, if we make use of a high resolution timer in OS kernel. However, the availability of such timer for each TCP connection is a stringent requirement to many OSs.

Several other solutions try to solve the problem to tune certain buffers to avoid severe drops. For example, the authors in both [8] and [22] suggest to modify the IEEE 802.1Qau switch to regulate flow rate, so that severe drop that causes RTO is less likely to happen. Shpiner *et al.* [18] propose to use two queues to prioritize flows with lower packet arrival rate, so that it can reduce throughput disparity and make TCP less likely to resort to RTO for recovery. Alizadeh *et al.* [2] propose DCTCP to allow senders to start reacting as soon as queue length on an interface exceeds a thresh value so that more buffer space is available to absorb transient micro-bursts, greatly mitigating costly packet losses that can lead to timeouts. Das *et al.* [7] tries to improve DCTCP by resetting the congestion indicator after every timeout to avoid successive timeout.

Some also tried to solve the problem in another direction. For example, Kulkarni *et al.* [13] propose to use spontaneous proactive retransmission. In order to avoid timeout, they make TCP senders to retransmit unacknowledged packets periodically without waiting for signals from the receiver. However, their solution does not scale well in dynamic networks and the proactive retransmission may cause spurious retransmission. Haitao *et al.* [21] propose a receiver side congestion control scheme to mitigate the effect of timeout. In their solution, the receive window size of the TCP connections are dynamically adjusted to alleviate the congestion. Gurtov *et al.* [9] present an enhanced version of the Eifel algorithm [15] to detect spurious RTO and recover the connection state saved before the timeout. Their simulations show that their algorithm can increase throughput by up to 250%. However, they only consider the spurious RTO but do not solve the transmission idle during each needed RTO.

6. CONCLUSION

RTO_{min} is the lower bound of RTO timer to avoid spurious timeout when DA is implemented at the receiver. In lossy wireless networks, the transfer is lengthened whenever a RTO occurs. If RTO happens regularly, the degraded performance is very noticeable.

To improve the TCP performance, we propose NDA with minor changes to DA. Extensive simulations show that NDA improves the TCP goodput as well as channel utilization significantly, especially in lossy wireless networks. For example, at the loss ratio of 5% and light channel contention, NDA improves both the goodput of a single TCP flow and channel utilization by more than 600% against DA.

Although lowering RTO_{min} reduces the time spent waiting on needed RTOs, intuitively we believe that it may lead to more spurious RTOs. However, in fact it works in an opposite way. Our simulation results show that smaller RTO_{min} does not cause extra spurious timeouts, because first quickly reacting to timeouts makes the TCP flows more likely to recover missing packets by fast retransmission, and second allowing the sender to send coded packets instead of original packets can make the potential spurious timeout retransmissions useful.

In addition, intense channel contention may counteract the effort of TCP layer on goodput boost. Thus, NDA is more suitable to be used in wireless access networks with light channel contention or wired lossy networks which have no signal interference. Although our simulation is based on 802.11a, the same idea works in any lossy networks.

7. ACKNOWLEDGEMENT

This work was supported in part by the Academy of Finland (grant number 253860) and Tekes within the ITEA2 project 10014 EASI-CLOUDS.

8. REFERENCES

[1] Network simulator (ns-3) [Online] Available: http://www.nsnam.org.

[2] M. Alizadeh, A. Greenberg, D. A. Maltz, J. Padhye, P. Patel, B. Prabhakar, S. Sengupta, and M. Sridharan. Data center TCP (DCTCP). *ACM SIGCOMM Computer Communication Review*, 40(4):63–74, 2010.

[3] M. Allman. Retransmission Timeout Considerations. *Internet draft*, May 2012.

[4] M. Allman and V. Paxson. On estimating end-to-end network path properties. In *ACM SIGCOMM Computer Communication Review*, volume 29, pages 263–274. ACM, 1999.

[5] R. Braden. Requirements for Internet hosts-communication layers. *IETF RFC 1122*, 1989.

[6] Y. Chen, R. Griffith, J. Liu, R. H. Katz, and A. D. Joseph. Understanding TCP incast throughput collapse in datacenter networks. In *Proceedings of the 1st ACM workshop on Research on enterprise networking*, pages 73–82. ACM, 2009.

[7] T. Das and K. M. Sivalingam. TCP improvements for data center networks. In *2013 Fifth International Conference on Communication Systems and Networks (COMSNETS)*, pages 1–10. IEEE, 2013.

[8] P. Devkota and A. N. Reddy. Performance of quantized congestion notification in TCP incast scenarios of data centers. In *2010 IEEE International Symposium on Modeling, Analysis & Simulation of Computer and Telecommunication Systems (MASCOTS)*, pages 235–243. IEEE, 2010.

[9] A. Gurtov and R. Ludwig. Responding to spurious timeouts in TCP. In *INFOCOM 2003. Twenty-Second Annual Joint Conference of the IEEE Computer and Communications. IEEE Societies*, volume 3, pages 2312–2322. IEEE, 2003.

[10] T. Henderson, S. Floyd, A. Gurtov, and Y. Nishida. The NewReno modification to TCP's fast recovery algorithm. *RFC6582*, 2012.

[11] T. Ho, M. Médard, R. Koetter, D. R. Karger, M. Effros, J. Shi, and B. Leong. A random linear network coding approach to multicast. *IEEE Transactions on Information Theory*, 52(10):4413–4430, 2006.

[12] S. Katti, H. Rahul, W. Hu, D. Katabi, M. Médard, and J. Crowcroft. XORs in the air: practical wireless

network coding. *IEEE/ACM Transactions on Networking (TON)*, 16(3):497–510, 2008.

[13] S. Kulkarni and P. Agrawal. A probabilistic approach to address TCP incast in data center networks. In *2011 31st International Conference on Distributed Computing Systems Workshops (ICDCSW)*, pages 26–33. IEEE, 2011.

[14] J. Kumar Sundararajan, D. Shah, and M. Médard. ARQ for network coding. In *IEEE International Symposium on Information Theory. ISIT 2008.*, pages 1651–1655. IEEE, 2008.

[15] R. Ludwig and R. H. Katz. The Eifel algorithm: making TCP robust against spurious retransmissions. *ACM SIGCOMM Computer Communication Review*, 30(1):30–36, 2000.

[16] V. Paxson, M. Allman, J. Chu, and M. Sargent. Computing TCP's retransmission timer. *IETF RFC 6298*, June 2011.

[17] I. Psaras and V. Tsaoussidis. On the properties of an adaptive TCP Minimum RTO. *Computer Communications*, 32(5):888–895, 2009.

[18] A. Shpiner, I. Keslassy, G. Bracha, E. Dagan, O. Iny, and E. Soha. A switch-based approach to throughput collapse and starvation in data centers. *Computer Networks*, 2012.

[19] J. K. Sundararajan, D. Shah, M. Médard, S. Jakubczak, M. Mitzenmacher, and J. Barros. Network coding meets TCP: Theory and implementation. *Proceedings of the IEEE*, 99(3):490–512, 2011.

[20] V. Vasudevan, A. Phanishayee, H. Shah, E. Krevat, D. G. Andersen, G. R. Ganger, G. A. Gibson, and B. Mueller. Safe and effective fine-grained TCP retransmissions for datacenter communication. In *ACM SIGCOMM Computer Communication Review*, volume 39, pages 303–314. ACM, 2009.

[21] H. Wu, Z. Feng, C. Guo, and Y. Zhang. ICTCP: Incast Congestion Control for TCP in data center networks. In *Proceedings of the 6th International COnference*, page 13. ACM, 2010.

[22] Y. Zhang and N. Ansari. On mitigating TCP incast in data center networks. In *Proceedings IEEE INFOCOM 2011*, pages 51–55. IEEE, 2011.

Congestion Control in Reliable CoAP Communication

August Betzler, Carles Gomez, Ilker Demirkol, Josep Paradells
Department of Telematics Engineering
Universitat Politecnica de Catalunya
i2CAT Foundation
Barcelona, Spain
{august.betzler, carlesgo, ilker.demirkol, josep.paradells}@entel.upc.edu

ABSTRACT

The development of IPv6 stacks for wireless constrained devices that have limited hardware resources has paved the way for many new areas of applications and protocols. The Constrained Application Protocol (CoAP) has been designed by the IETF to enable the manipulation of resources for constrained devices that are capable of connecting to the Internet. Due to the limited radio channel capacities and hardware resources, congestion is a common phenomenon in networks of constrained devices. CoAP implements a basic congestion control mechanism for the transmission of reliable messages. Alternative CoAP congestion control approaches are a recent topic of interest in the IETF CoRE Working Group. New Internet-Drafts discuss the limitations of the default congestion control mechanisms and propose alternative ones, yet, there have been no studies in the literature that compare the original approach to the alternative ones. In this paper, we target this crucial study and perform evaluations that show how the default and alternative congestion control mechanisms compare to each other. We use the Cooja simulation environment, which is part of the Contiki development toolset, to simulate CoAP within a complete protocol stack that uses IETF protocols for constrained networks. Through simulations of different network topologies and varying traffic loads, we demonstrate how the advanced mechanisms proposed in the drafts perform relative to the basic congestion control mechanism.

Categories and Subject Descriptors

C.2.1 [**Network Architecture and Design**]: Wireless Communication; C.2.2 [**Network Protocols**]: Applications, Protocol Architecture

General Terms

Algorithms, Performance, Experimentation, Verification

MSWiM'13, November 3–8, 2013, Barcelona, Spain.

ACM 978-1-4503-2353-6/13/11 ...$15.00
http://dx.doi.org/10.1145/2507924.2507954.

Keywords

CoAP; RPL; 6LoWPAN; IEEE 802.15.4; Cooja; Contiki; End-to-end Reliability; Congestion Control

1. INTRODUCTION

The challenge of designing protocols and standards for constrained devices has become greater, as the networks they form are no longer only of local character but also get connected to the Internet as part of the Internet of Things [12]. The Internet Engineering Task Force (IETF) has been focusing on finding solutions for different aspects of the communication protocol stack that are trimmed to the requirements of networks of constrained devices. The IPv6 Routing Protocol for Low-Power and Lossy Networks (RPL) [15], IPv6 over Low Power Wireless Personal Area Network (6LoWPAN) [8] and CoAP [13] are some of the protocols designed by the IETF working groups in this space.

The limited hardware capacities of sensor nodes and the limited link capacities of the radio channel may lead to congestion in constrained networks. Congestion may result in increased delays, because packets remain longer in node buffers before being successfully transmitted over wireless links or it may lead to packet losses, when internal message buffers overflow or the simultaneous transmission of packets in the radio channel leads to collisions that render packets useless.

Congestion control mechanisms are able to detect congestion and/or apply measures to avoid or dilute congestion, which can have an important effect on the network performance. Thus, the investigation of congestion control mechanisms in the ambit of constrained networks that run CoAP is also crucial. As an alternative to the basic mechanisms applied by CoAP, the CoAP Simple Congestion Control/Advanced (CoCoA) draft [1] proposes more complex but potentially improved congestion control mechanisms for CoAP. However, performance evaluations are needed to confirm if the proposed mechanisms result in a more efficient congestion control. In a novel approach, we use the Cooja simulation environment for Contiki, an operating system employed by many constrained devices, to carry out simulations that determine the performance of the alternative CoAP congestion control mechanisms for different network topologies and varying traffic loads. We evaluate these mechanisms over a stack of protocols which includes protocols specified by the IETF for networks of constrained devices. To the best of our knowledge, this is the first work to evaluate CoCoA performance and furthermore the first study that evaluates congestion control for CoAP.

The rest of the paper is organized as follows. In Section 2, the basic CoAP congestion control mechanism is explained along with the alternative CoCoA mechanisms. In Section 3, the communication protocol stack used for the evaluation of the CoAP congestion control performance is detailed. Also, the simulation parameters and network setups are explained. The results of the simulations are presented in Section 4. Section 5 concludes the paper, giving a resume of the obtained results and giving indications for further analysis on CoAP congestion control for constrained networks.

2. COAP CONGESTION CONTROL

CoAP is a Representational State Transfer style (RESTful) [5] protocol developed for constrained devices that allows interactions between clients and servers over the Internet. In the environment of constrained devices, CoAP can be used for the manipulation of resources, such as sensor measurements or actuator states.

For simplicity, CoAP uses UDP as the transport protocol by default. Since UDP does not implement end-to-end reliability but this may be required by the application, CoAP introduces optional application layer end-to-end Acknowledgements (ACKs). By setting the confirmable (CON) flag in an outgoing CoAP message, an end-to-end ACK is requested from the destination node. If no ACK is received within the retransmission timeout (RTO) interval, a retransmission is initiated for the outstanding transaction. The initial RTO for any CoAP transaction as specified by the base CoAP specification [13] is randomly chosen from the fixed interval [2s, 3s].

A relatively high initial value is chosen, because packets that travel through the Internet may suffer large delays and round-trip times (RTTs). Apart from that, a CoAP request may trigger an action at the destination device that requires intensive processing, which can increase the RTT due to processing delay.

If a message is not confirmed during the RTO interval, CoAP assumes that its transmission has failed. However, the cause for an unsuccessful confirmation is not explicit, since the CoAP message or its corresponding ACK may have been delayed beyond the duration of the RTO interval or they may have been lost, because of congestion or due to lossy wireless links. Because of this ambiguity it is difficult to determine an optimal RTO. On one hand, it should not be too short, to avoid spurious retransmissions in the case that confirmation of the request suffers from delay. On the other hand, it should not be too long, to avoid the originator of the CoAP request to idle unnecessarily before retransmitting the packet in the case that the request or confirmation packets were lost. In this context, the basic RTO calculation of CoAP (a fix interval of possible values) is quite trivial and inflexible. It may not provide an optimal performance for all types of scenarios.

Apart from retransmitting the message, once the RTO timer expires, CoAP applies a binary exponential backoff (BEB) as in the Transmission Control Protocol (TCP), effectively throttling the generation of more packets, as it assumes that the network is congested. CoCoA, amongst other things, proposes to run two RTO estimator algorithms for each destination of CoAP transactions, the so called strong and weak estimators. The strong estimator uses the RTT that is measured if an ACK was received for a transaction that did not require retransmissions. The weak estimator uses the RTT that is measured when an ACK is received after retransmitting the CoAP request at least once. Both RTO estimators use the RTO formulas introduced in RFC 6298 [11]. When the overall RTO is updated, a weighted average of the previous overall RTO and the last obtained RTO estimation, being a weak or strong one, is calculated. The overall RTO is initialized to 2 seconds in CoCoA.

The evaluation of the CoAP congestion control performance in this paper includes the evaluation of the default and two alternative RTO calculations. The first alternative is the RTO calculation as proposed in CoCoA, which requires additional state information and program logic. As a lightweight alternative we evaluate a second congestion control algorithm, CoCoA Strong (CoCoA-S), which only considers the strong estimator.

Another important CoAP parameter that is discussed in CoCoA is the NSTART parameter, which determines how many CoAP transactions may be created to one destination endpoint in parallel. The base CoAP document states that this value must be set to 1. Higher values can lead to congestion of the network, since it allows various CoAP transactions between two nodes simultaneously. How the performance of the default and advanced congestion control changes when using a NSTART value of 4 is also analyzed in the experiments presented in Section 4. For the case of non-confirmable messages, CoCoA proposes some restrictions, however in this paper we only focus on reliable communication.

3. SIMULATION SETUP

This section introduces the Cooja simulator and gives an overview of the Contiki communication protocol stack used in this study. Also, this section covers the configuration of the nodes and explains the tested network topologies, as well as the test run configuration used to do the performance evaluations.

3.1 Contiki OS and the Cooja Simulator

Contiki OS is an open source operating system designed for constrained devices and the Internet of Things and is the choice of many sensor motes. Fig. 1 shows the IETF protocols over IEEE 802.15.4 and how they are implemented in Contiki OS, along with other Contiki specific layers. It implements the uIPv6 stack that provides the functionality for IPv6 networking. uIPv6 includes Contiki-RPL, an implementation of the routing protocol for low-power lossy IPv6 networks, and SICSlowpan, an implementation of the 6LoWPAN adaptation layer. Contiki also comes with the Erbium CoAP implementation [7], which currently supports CoAP up to draft version 13, together with observe and blockwise transfers [6, 2]. In the layer based model of the communication protocol stack, CoAP is located at the application layer on top of uIPv6.

RPL, as part of the uIPv6 Stack, is responsible for the network formation, packet routing and the maintenance of the network topology. In RPL, one or more root nodes generate a network topology that trickles down to the leaf nodes, resulting in Directed Acyclic Graphs (DAGs). If the network contains a single root, it is called Destination Oriented DAG (DODAG). Contiki 2.6 only supports the storing mode for RPL, where each node stores routing entries that indicate the next hop(s) to the RPL-root and to its child nodes. The RPL objective function (OF) determines which links are

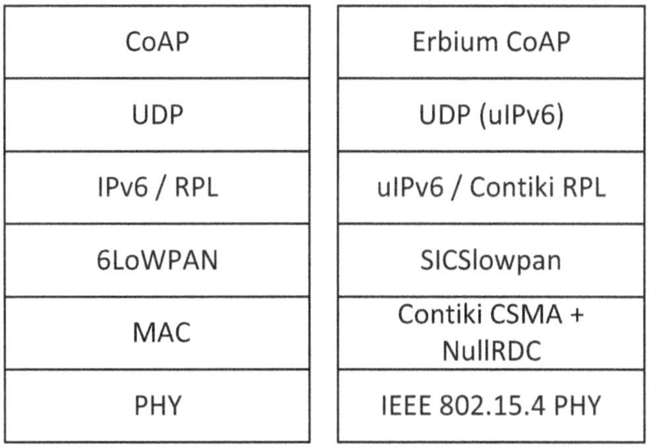

Figure 1: A comparison between the IETF communication protocol stack (left) and its implementation in Contiki (right).

chosen to be part of the RPL-DAG. Contiki comes with two predetermined OFs, the expected transmission count (ETX) OF [4] is the default OF and is used in the evaluation carried out in this paper.

The 6LoWPAN implementation of the uIPv6 stack, SICSlowpan, applies header compression of IPv6 packets at the sender site, and fragmentation if necessary to transport IPv6 packets on top of IEEE 802.15.4 MAC layer frames. At the receiver side, SICSlowpan takes care of decompressing the headers to reestablish their original content and performing reassembly if needed. Underneath the layers that are part of uIPv6, Contiki implements a MAC driver with Carrier Sense Multiple Access (CSMA) and link layer reliability. Contiki allows choosing from different radio duty cycling (RDC) drivers that determine when a mote turns off the radio to save energy.

Cooja is a network simulator that can execute Contiki OS-based code, designed to be a rapid development platform for Contiki. Cooja supports simulation of sensor networks at three levels: the application level, the operating system, and the machine code instruction set [10]. As an outstanding feature, the binary image of compiled Contiki code designed for real motes can be uploaded to be used for simulations. Cooja also is capable of emulating the real hardware for several types of nodes. All together a high degree of simulation realism is achieved, since memory restrictions, the real node periphery and internal processing of the motes are simulated as well.

Cooja allows three-dimensional deploying of nodes inside the simulated environment and offers several radio models. The radio models determine how radio signals propagate in the network. The radio channel model used is the unit disk graph radio model, which defines the link delivery ratio within the transmission range to be 100%. The interference range, set to be twice the transmission range, indicates up to which distance the radio signal is capable of interfering the radio of other nodes. If a node receives two packets at the same time (being in transmission or interference range), the simulator assumes a packet collision, rendering both packets useless for the receiving node. More complex models like a ray-tracing based model are under development or not yet fully implemented.

3.2 Sensor Mote Configuratio

Cooja provides the necessary software to emulate the hardware of a set of real sensor nodes. This means that real hardware limitations like memory and processing capacities are respected in the simulation environment. From the types of devices that are supported by Cooja, two IEEE 802.15.4 capable motes with the same type of radio transceiver (CC2420 [14]) are chosen for the simulations: the Z1 from Zolertia [16] and the Tmote Sky from Moteiv [9], latter being equivalent to TelosB motes [3] in terms of hardware. The most relevant features of the two motes are stated in Table 1. As seen in the table, the motes differ in ROM and RAM capabilities and the MCU. While Z1s offer more ROM for application code, the Sky Motes have higher RAM storage capacity.

Table 1: Hardware Specifications of the Zolertia Z1 and Moteiv Tmote Sky Wireless Sensor Nodes.

	Tmote Sky	Z1
RAM	10 KB	8 KB
ROM	48 KB	92 KB
MCU	MSP430F1611	MSP430F2617
Radio	CC2420	

The simulated network topologies used for CoAP performance evaluation include two types of nodes that differ in their resource requirements: CoAP nodes and RPL border routers. Each topology includes one RPL border router that implements the communication stack introduced in Section 3.1 up to UDP and that acts as RPL-root node. The simulated network topologies are local networks that do not require the border router to establish external connections.

According to the RPL specifications, when a node is missing a routing table entry for the destination node, it forwards the packet to the next node in direction of the RPL-root. This process is repeated, until a node has a valid routing entry to forward the packet in direction of the requested destination address. In the case that none of the nodes on the way to the RPL-root has valid routing information stored, the RPL-root eventually receives the packet. The RPL-root then in the optimal case looks up the entry with the destination address for the packet from the routing table and forwards it to the next hop in direction of the destination node. To achieve that, the RPL border router needs to be able to store routing table entries for all possible destinations in the network, which is why the RAM requirement of this node is relatively high. Because of that, the RPL border router runs on Tmote Sky nodes that have a higher RAM capacity compared to the Z1 motes. Since the analyzed network topologies are of limited size, it is possible to assign sufficient routing table sizes to the RPL-root beforehand for each topology.

The rest of the motes in the network topologies are nodes that run the full Contiki OS stack and the Erbium CoAP implementation based on CoAP version 13. In contrast to the RPL-root, the nodes with CoAP require more ROM to fit the additional application code that is part of the Erbium CoAP implementation and also for the user application that controls the high level behavior of the node. Z1 nodes are better suited for this type of tasks, since they have higher ROM capacities when compared to Tmote Sky nodes.

The two types of motes are part of all network topologies that are used for simulation experiments in this paper. In

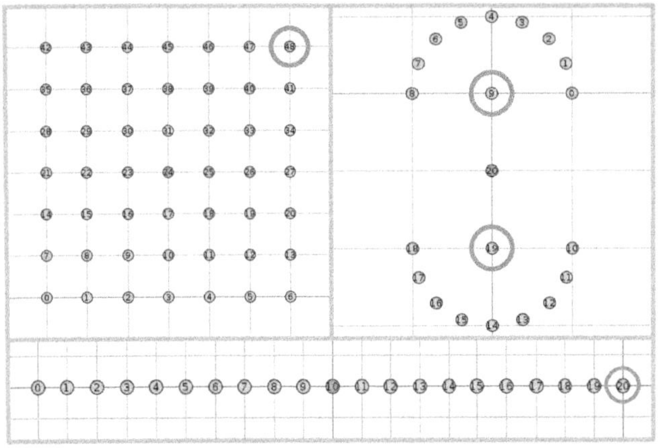

Figure 2: The three network topologies used for performance analysis (grid, dumbbell, and chain). The width of a square corresponds to 10 m. Nodes with a blue circle are sink nodes for CoAP messages. Green nodes are RPL border routers.

each of the network topologies, there is always a single RPL-root, while the rest are CoAP nodes, out of which one or two are set as the destination (sink) nodes as detailed in Section 3.3.

Another factor that influences the performance of the network essentially is the size of Contiki's MAC layer queue and the RDC mode. All packets that are generated or forwarded by a node need to traverse a queue located at Contiki's MAC layer. The queue is used to store packets that are pending to be sent and that need to wait the CSMA procedure before being transmitted by the radio. Since the amount of RAM for constrained devices is very restricted, the number of MAC layer queue entries is set to 4 for CoAP nodes and 6 for the RPL border router. Contiki disposes of different RDC mechanisms, such as NullRDC, B-MAC, X-MAC and ContikiMAC. For the evaluations carried out in this paper, the NullRDC is chosen. In NullRDC, nodes do not sleep and their radio is constantly turned on. For the performance analysis of CoAP, we discard to use any RDC alternative, thus avoiding the cross-layer interactions they require.

3.3 Network Topologies

To carry out the performance evaluation of CoAP congestion control mechanisms, three different network topologies are defined for the simulations. They differ in the number and positioning of the nodes, which amongst other things lead to differences in the number of direct neighbors of the nodes, the lengths of routes between source and destination of CoAP requests, and the number of nodes that may compete for the radio channel simultaneously. The evaluated topologies are i) a chain of nodes with 21 nodes, ii) a rectangular grid of 49 nodes (7x7), and iii) a dumbbell topology with 21 nodes.

Figure 2 depicts snapshots of the Cooja simulator GUI showing the two-dimensional positioning of the nodes for the three different topologies. The transmission range is set to 10 meters, whereas the interference range is set to be twice of the transmission range, i.e., 20 meters. The distance between nodes in the chain topology is chosen in such a way that only direct neighbors are in transmission range. Since the interference range is twice the transmission range, a packet transmission may interfere the radio of nodes up to two hops away. Each node may therefore have up to two neighbors. The same distance rule applies for the grid topology, where each node may have up to 4 direct neighbors. In the dumbbell topology, the nodes on the half circles are exactly 10 meters away from the node that is part of the dumbbell's axis.

To observe the performance of the CoAP congestion control algorithms, we want to avoid that RPL malfunctioning distorts the results. The network topology determines the configuration for some of the RPL parameters, that, when not configured adequately, may lead to performance drops. The routing table and neighbor table sizes are two important parameters that determine if packets can be routed correctly throughout the network. For the simulations carried out in this paper, the neighbor tables are able to store information about all direct neighbors. The RPL border route has a routing table large enough to store entries for all nodes of the network. Due to the strict RAM limitations of CoAP nodes, their routing tables need to be smaller. Adjusted to the introduced topologies, the storable amount of RPL neighbor and routing table entries is set to the values shown in Table 2.

Table 2: Configurations of the RPL Routing and Neighbor Table Sizes.

	Chain Topology	Dumbbell Topology	Grid Topology
Neighbor Table (all nodes)	2	10	4
Routing Table (CoAP node)	10	10	20
Routing Table (RPL bord. router)	20	20	48

Since the RPL border router acts as dispatcher for messages that need to be forwarded through the RPL root, it should be located in a central position of the network to make it equally accessible from all nodes in the network. In the chain topology, the RPL border router is located in the middle of the chain. In the grid it is located at the center of the topology, where the 4th line of nodes crosses with the 4th column. In the dumbbell topology the RPL border router is the center node that connects the two laterals of the dumbbell formation. In all the topologies, CoAP messages are created by the CoAP nodes and directed to one or two sink nodes. Except for the dumbbell topology, each network has a single sink, marked with a circle in the topology overviews. In the dumbbell topology there are two sink nodes. They are the destinations of traffic that is generated by nodes from the opposite side of the dumbbell topology. While in the chain and grid topologies the sink nodes do not generate any CoAP requests, in the dumbbell topology each of the sink nodes also creates CoAP requests for the sink node on the opposite side.

3.4 Test Run Configuratio

When a test run is started, the simulated nodes are initialized and the RPL-root creates the RPL-DODAG by spreading DAG Information Objects (DIOs) throughout the network. CoAP performance tests begin after the complete RPL-DAG is built. After this, the nodes start generating periodical CoAP requests. The generation of periodic traffic is implemented by running cyclic timers that upon their depletion create a new CoAP request. The CoAP request is a POST message that sets the color of a LED at the sink node and increases an internal counter of the sink node by one. Additionally an increasing message ID and the short address (node ID) of the originator node are included in the payload of the CoAP request. The sink node that receives this CoAP request carries out the requested actions and responds to the originator node with a confirmation message. A CoAP request message including all headers and the payload has a size of 95 bytes.

If a node generates a CoAP request, but the limitation of parallel transaction to the destination node dictated by NSTART does not permit to generate another request, the generated packet is dropped. Since all CoAP requests in the analyzed network topologies only have one possible destination, packets at the application layer are only dropped when a node is waiting for a confirmation of the previously sent CoAP request in the case of NSTART=1. If NSTART is larger, packets at the application layer are only dropped, if already NSTART transactions are active. In real life scenarios, where a single sink node is employed, NSTART can play an important role for possible congestion of the network. Thus, we also analyze the performance of congestion control mechanisms for CoAP with a higher NSTART value.

The duration of the simulation phase during which CoAP requests are generated is always 360 seconds. After this time, the test script generates a signal for all nodes in the network that tells them to stop spawning further CoAP requests. Subsequently the simulation terminates. All events that occur during the simulation and are of interest for the performance evaluation are collected from the nodes over their virtual serial interface. During the simulation, the nodes can send messages over their serial port hat can be intercepted by the simulation script and can then be stored into log-files for further evaluation. Such messages can contain the status of internal variables, such as buffer sizes or can be used to notify about an event, such as the reception of a confirmation message.

In the following section, the performance results of the investigated approaches are presented.

4. SIMULATION RESULTS

This section presents the results of the experimental evaluation of the congestion control mechanisms in reliable CoAP communication for the three previously introduced network topologies. As the performance metric, the relation of carried load against the offered load is chosen. The offered load refers to the total amount of data created by the nodes per second on average when CoAP requests are generated, and is given in kilobits per second (kbps). The carried load indicates the average amount of data that is successfully delivered to the sink node(s) per second, and also given in kbps.

For all analyzed configurations of the CoAP congestion control mechanisms, the test runs have been repeated three times with different random simulator seeds to obtain meaningful average results.

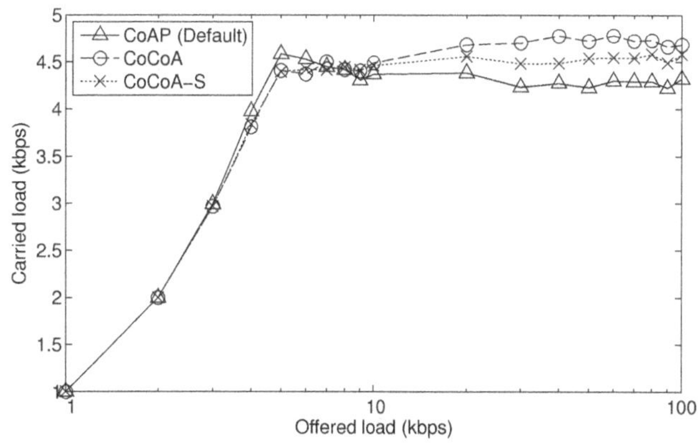

Figure 3: Throughput achieved for different offered loads in the dumbbell topology with NSTART=1.

4.1 Congestion Control Performance for Different Traffi Loads

When NSTART is set to 1, the main difference of the analyzed congestion control algorithms lies in the RTO calculation algorithm. The results show that this mechanism has a high impact on the network performance and that it influences the effectiveness of the CoAP congestion control.

Fig. 3 illustrates how the carried load evolves as the offered load increases when using the three RTO algorithms for the dumbbell topology evaluated. Since at low traffic rates, the network does not reach a state of congestion and nearly all packet transmissions across the network are successful, the carried load is identical to the offered load, independently of the RTO algorithm used. As the offered load increases, the ratio of successfully delivered CoAP requests decreases because of congestion. This is where differences in the performance of the different congestion control algorithms become visible.

The performance of the three congestion control algorithms is almost identical up to an offered load of 3 kbps. For offered traffic loads up to 7 kbps, CoCoA and CoCoA-S show a slightly worse performance in terms of throughput. Since the number of hops between source and destination routes is small and there is almost no congestion in form of packet collisions or packet drops, the CoCoA algorithms have small RTO estimations. As the estimated RTO gets smaller and reaches the real RTT, the probability for spurious retransmission increases and sometimes causes the nodes to unnecessarily retransmit a packet they assumed to have been lost. These spurious retransmissions can lead to drops in the throughput performance. The default CoAP RTO does not suffer from these effects, as the initial RTO for transactions always is 2 s or higher. As the offered traffic load increases beyond 7 kbps, the congestion control mechanisms of CoCoA and CoCoA-S take effect, outperforming default CoAP. CoCoA-S has a slightly lower performance than CoCoA. At high traffic rates that lead to increased packet drop rates across the network, CoCoA-S has a lower probability to obtain valid RTT measurements, thus it is not able to calculate improved RTO estimations.

The relevance of RTO estimations becomes clearer when looking at the amount of packets that are dropped during the simulation. Packet drops occur when i) the MAC layer buffer overflows, or ii) when CoAP refuses to send a packet, because the number of parallel transactions allowed for a

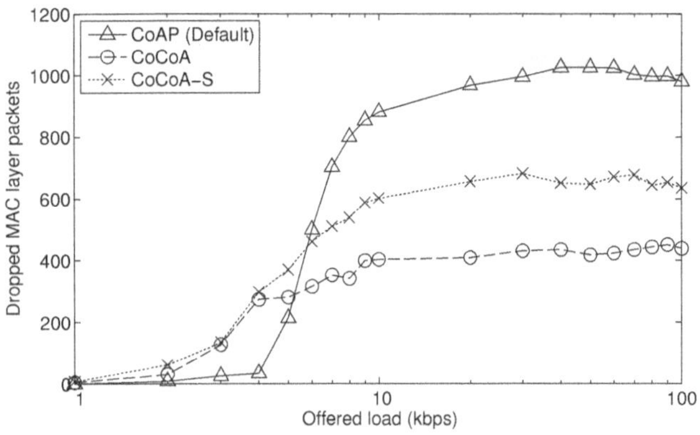

Figure 4: Dropped MAC layer packets for different offered loads in the dumbbell topology with NSTART=1.

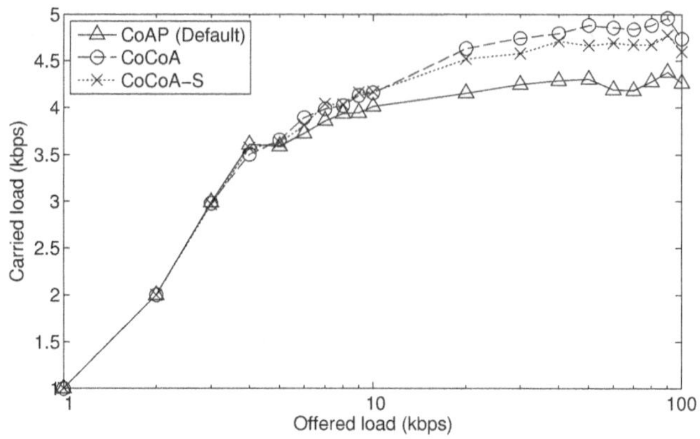

Figure 5: Throughput achieved for different offered loads in the chain topology with NSTART=1.

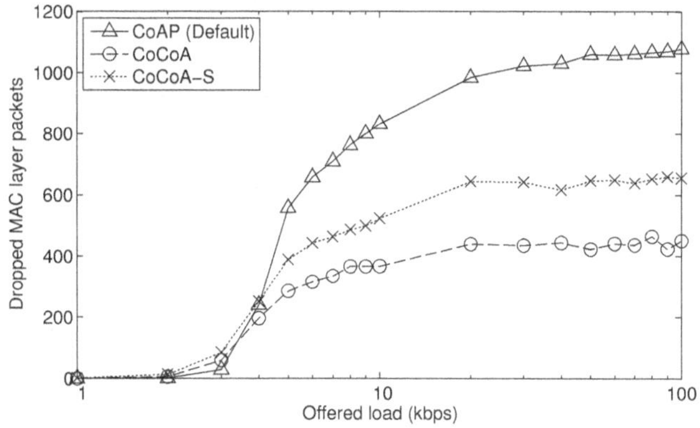

Figure 6: Dropped MAC layer packets for different offered loads in the chain topology with NSTART=1.

destination, i.e., NSTART parallel transactions, has been reached for the destination of the packet.

MAC layer buffer overflows are a clear sign of congestion, as they indicate that a high amount of packets are created and intended to be forwarded throughout the network, exceeding the capabilities of the network. The effect of the RTO algorithm on the amount of dropped packets is deducted for the dumbbell topology and Fig. 4 shows the overall amount of dropped MAC layer packets for this topology.

As seen in the figure, when applying the default RTO algorithm, the number of MAC layer packet drops grows quickly above 3 kbps of offered traffic load and reaches an asymptotic value at around 20 kbps. When using the alternative RTO algorithms for CoAP congestion control, a slower increment of the number of dropped packets and a much lower asymptotic value are observed. This means that the CoCoA algorithms are capable of effectively decreasing the congestion in the network. The clear difference in the number of dropped MAC layer packets between CoCoA and CoCoA-S is a result of the different RTO estimations they apply. In contrast to CoCoA-S, CoCoA additionally uses weak RTT measurements from retransmissions that may lead to large RTOs. This throttles the output of packets and leads to a further reduction of buffer overflows in the network.

An asymptotic behavior of the amount of dropped MAC layer packets is observable, because the actual amount of traffic transmitted over the radio channel does not increase significantly further with the offered load at high traffic rates. On the other hand, due to the limitation given by NSTART=1 and increasing packet generation frequencies at each node, the probability of dropping newly generated CoAP messages gets higher with the offered load. For offered load beyond the threshold where the amount of dropped MAC layer packets reaches its asymptotic value, the CoAP packet drop rate is observed to increase almost linearly with the amount of generated packets.

As mentioned before, the amount of hops between source and sink nodes in the dumbbell topology is low, resulting in small RTTs. How the congestion control algorithms perform when larger RTTs are observed can be demonstrated in the chain topology, where packets may have to travel along many hops before reaching their destination. The radio links along the chain are not utilized equally. The links closer to the sink will be required more frequently for transmissions, as all the packets from the other end of the chain need to traverse them. On the other hand, due to spatial reuse, it is possible for several nodes to transmit in parallel along the chain, without interfering each other.

For this particular setup, the difference between the default CoAP and the CoCoA mechanisms becomes larger, as can be seen in Fig. 5. This shows that the CoCoA mechanisms are able to adapt to different RTT values and to the traffic characteristics of the network. This observation can be backed up by observing the amount of dropped MAC layer packets (Fig. 6), showing a similar behavior as in the dumbbell topology, where the drop rates for the CoCoA mechanisms are much smaller than for default CoAP.

On the other hand, in the grid topology, the number of hops between source and destination nodes varies a lot, since many combinations of links for the connection of source and sink nodes are possible. Therefore, RTTs of different scales can be observed. Since within the transmission, and also the interference range of a node there will be more nodes, a congestion of the radio channel is more likely than in the other analyzed topologies.

The performance comparison for the grid topology reveals that CoCoA mechanisms are able to perform significantly better than default CoAP. Fig. 7 shows that CoCoA and CoCoA-S perform better than the default CoAP, even when the offered load is small (starting at 4 kbps). However, the performance achieved by the two advanced congestion control mechanisms is very similar for this topology. For the intermediate traffic rates, CoCoA gets many weak RTT measurements from retransmissions, increasing the es-

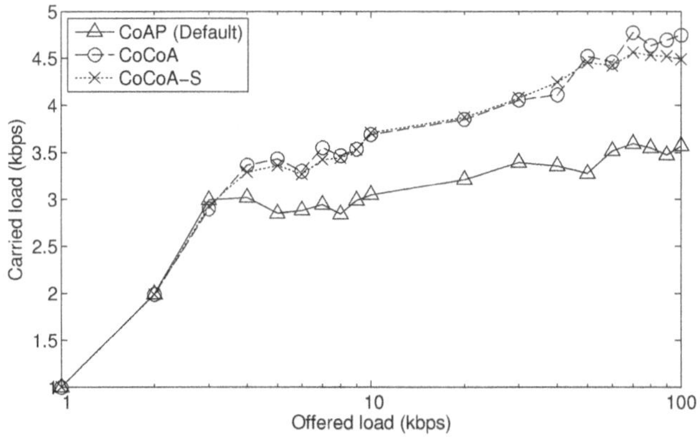

Figure 7: Throughput achieved for different offered loads in the grid topology with NSTART=1.

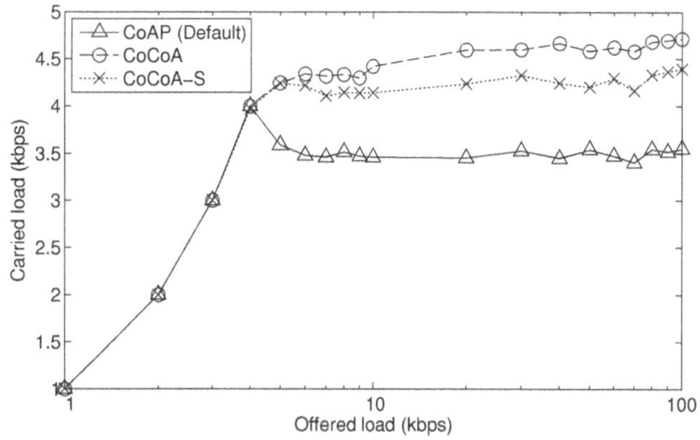

Figure 8: Throughput achieved for different offered loads in the dumbbell topology with NSTART=4.

timated RTO to large values. In case of a loss this results in a long idle period. CoCoA-S and default CoAP use shorter RTOs. The amount of valid RTT measurements gets lower with higher traffic for nodes that apply CoCoA-S and that are not very close to the sink. Thus the CoCoA-S RTO estimations do not grow as much as CoCoA RTO estimations, while default CoAP maintains the default initial interval. Due to these lower RTO estimations, CoCoA-S will use more retransmissions in a fixed time interval for nodes that have difficulties to successfully complete transactions on their first transmission, when compared to CoCoA. This can increase the PDR, until the traffic rates become higher and this behavior is the cause of more congestion. This is the case above 60 kbps, where the performance of CoCoA-S is lower than the performance of CoCoA. The results for the MAC layer packet drops are very similar to the results for the chain and dumbbell topology and will not be detailed further. As before, CoCoA and CoCoA-S lead to a much lower drop rate of MAC layer packets.

The applicability of the observations to several network topologies confirms that the improvements obtained by using CoCoA and CoCoA-S are crucial for reliable CoAP communication. In the following, this conclusion is strengthened by observing the performance of the congestion control mechanisms when allowing multiple parallel CoAP transactions to a destination node (NSTART=4).

4.2 Effect of NSTART on Congestion Control Performance

When NSTART is set to 4, the amount of maximum parallel transactions to one destination is increased from 1 to 4. Nodes that apply the basic CoAP congestion control initialize independent RTO timers for each transaction. Nodes that create transactions when using CoCoA and CoCoA-S can resort to already obtained RTO information for a destination node.

With a higher NSTART value, the potential degree of congestion in the network is higher, increasing the importance of an efficient congestion control mechanism.

Fig. 8 illustrates the carried load in the dumbbell topology. As seen in the figure, the default congestion control mechanism is not able to cope with NSTART=4. When using the default CoAP congestion control mechanism the performance drops noticeably compared to the performance achieved with NSTART=1. For default CoAP, offered load above 4 kbps leads to a relevant drop and the carried load starts fluctuating around a value of 3.5 kbps. Analogical to the NSTART=1 scenario, CoCoA and CoCoA-S are able to surpass the performance of the default CoAP congestion control. However, the differences in the performance are greater for NSTART=4. When analyzing the amount of dropped MAC layer packets (Fig. 9a), it becomes clear that the default CoAP is not able to control several parallel transactions efficiently. The number of MAC layer packet drops is 3 to 4 times higher, compared to the number of drops observed for CoCoA and CoCoA-S. This means that the advanced congestion control mechanisms are able to better detect congestion and reduce it.

Figs. 9b and 9c show the throughput results for the chain and grid topology, respectively. The observations for NSTART=1 also apply for NSTART=4, but with a greater difference between the three congestion control mechanisms in the dumbbell and chain topologies. Due to space limitations, the figures for the number of MAC layer drops are omitted.

5. CONCLUSIONS

In this paper, we have carried out a performance evaluation of different CoAP congestion control mechanisms proposed for reliable end-to-end communication. For that, we used the Cooja simulation environment to evaluate CoAP within the Contiki communication protocol stack that includes IETF protocols for constrained networks. Three different network topologies are simulated with different network traffic loads.

We showed that the recently proposed CoCoA congestion control mechanism for CoAP on average performs equal to or better than the default congestion control mechanism in terms of throughput. CoCoA is able to reduce the quantity of MAC layer buffer overflows for congested networks, an important aspect in constrained networks. The results obtained with NSTART set to 1 could be confirmed for the case where NSTART is set to 4, where an even greater difference between the performance of the default CoAP congestion control and CoCoA was observed.

We also evaluated a simplified version of CoCoA, namely CoCoA-S. The simplified CoCoA-S mechanism does not perform as well as the CoCoA mechanism, accentuating the need to use the weak RTO estimator, as opposed to using only the strong RTO estimator. However, CoCoA-S is able

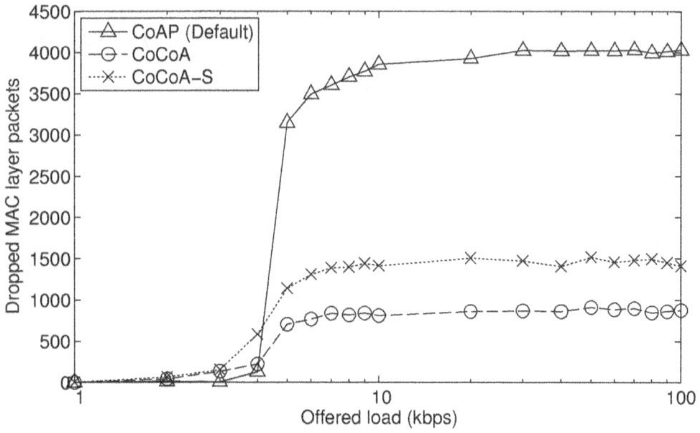

(a) Dropped MAC layer packets for different offered loads in the dumbbell topology with NSTART=4.

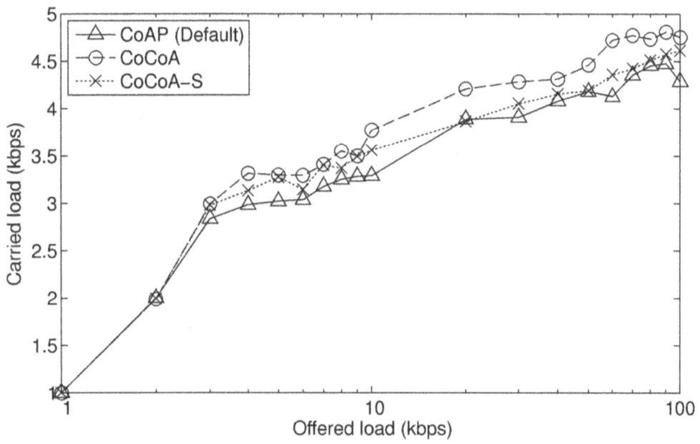

(b) Throughput achieved for different offered loads in the grid topology with NSTART=4.

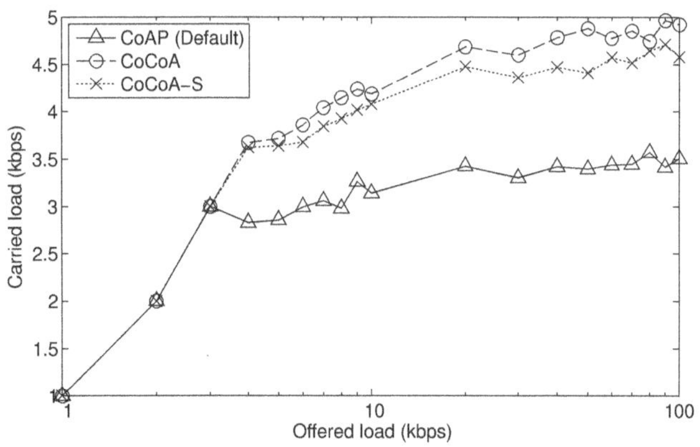

(c) Throughput achieved for different offered loads in the chain topology with NSTART=4.

Figure 9: Congestion control performances for NSTART=4.

to outperform the default CoAP congestion control mechanism, while not requiring as much state information as CoCoA. With the results obtained in this paper, we can confirm the relevance of advanced congestion control mechanisms and confirm that for this purpose CoCoA is an interesting candidate.

As future work, the advanced congestion control mechanisms will be tested in more network topologies, other performance metrics will be evaluated and different traffic generation patterns will be applied.

6. ACKNOWLEDGMENTS

This work has been supported by the Spanish Government's Ministerio de Economía y Competitividad through project TEC2012-32531 and by MICINN through project TEC2009-11453, as well as by the Comissionat per a Universitats i Recerca del DIUE from the Generalitat de Catalunya, the Social European Budget (Fons Social Europeu), and FEDER.

7. REFERENCES

[1] C. Bormann. CoAP Simple Congestion Control/Advanced (work in progress), August 2012.

[2] C. Bormann and Z. Shelby. Blockwise transfers in CoAP (work in progress), Feb. 2013.

[3] Crossbow Technology Inc. TelosB mote platform, 2009.

[4] D. S. J. De Couto, D. Aguayo, J. Bicket, and R. Morris. A high-throughput path metric for multi-hop wireless routing. In *Proceedings of the 9th annual international conference on Mobile computing and networking*, MobiCom '03, pages 134–146, New York, NY, USA, 2003. ACM.

[5] R. T. Fielding. *Architectural styles and the design of network-based software architectures.* PhD thesis, 2000. AAI9980887.

[6] K. Hartke. Observing Resources in CoAP (work in progress), Feb. 2013.

[7] M. Kovatsch, S. Duquennoy, and A. Dunkels. A low-power coap for contiki. In *Proceedings of the 8th IEEE International Conference on Mobile Ad-hoc and Sensor Systems (MASS 2011)*, Valencia, Spain, Oct. 2011.

[8] N. Kushalnagar, G. Montenegro, and C. Schumacher. IPv6 over Low-Power Wireless Personal Area Networks (6LoWPANs): Overview, Assumptions, Problem Statement, and Goals. RFC 4919 (Informational), August 2007.

[9] Moteiv Corporation. TMote Sky: Ultra low power IEEE 802.15.4 compliant wireless sensor module, June 2006.

[10] F. Osterlind, A. Dunkels, J. Eriksson, N. Finne, and T. Voigt. Cross-level sensor network simulation with cooja. In *Local Computer Networks, Proceedings 2006 31st IEEE Conference on*, pages 641–648, 2006.

[11] C. Paxson, M. Allman, J. Chu, and M. Sargent. Computing TCP's Retransmission Timer (RFC 6298), June 2011.

[12] Z. Shelby and C. Bormann. *6LoWPAN: The Wireless Embedded Internet.* Wiley Publishing, 2010.

[13] Z. Shelby, K. Hartke, and C. Bormann. Constrained application protocol (CoAP), May 2013.

[14] Texas Instruments. Chipcon products: CC2420 Datasheet: 2.4 GHz IEEE 802.15.4 / ZigBee-ready RF Transceiver, March 2013.

[15] T. Winter, P. Thubert, J. Hui, P. Kelsey, P. Levis, K. Pister, R. Struik, J. Vasseur, and R. Alexander. RPL: IPv6 Routing Protocol for Low-Power and Lossy Networks. Technical Report 6550, RFC Editor, Fremont, CA, USA, Mar. 2012.

[16] Zolertia. Z1 low-power wireless sensor network module, March 2010.

Analyzing the Effect of Client Queue Size on VoIP and TCP Traffic over an IEEE 802.11e WLAN

Sajib Datta
CReWMaN
Dept of Computer Science and Engineering
University of Texas at Arlington, TX, USA
sajib.datta@mavs.uta.edu

Sajal K. Das*
Dept of Computer Science
Missouri University of Science and Technology
Rolla, MO, USA
sdas@mst.edu

ABSTRACT

In this paper we introduce a mathematical model to analyze the performance of Wi-Fi networks carrying voice calls and TCP controlled file downloads. We derive the voice call capacity, the TCP throughput, and the bandwidth utilization using the proposed five-dimensional Markov model. We show that there exists a correlation among the queue size of client nodes and the capacity and throughput of the network. We also demonstrate how bandwidth utilization is affected by variable packet arrival rates. The analytical results match well with the simulation results generated by Qualnet simulator. Moreover, we conduct an experimental study of the Enhanced Distributed Channel Access (EDCA) mechanism of the IEEE 802.11e standard with a real-environment testbed consisting of 1 access point and 11 laptops to further validate the analytical and simulation results.

Categories and Subject Descriptors

C.2.1 [**Computer-Communication Networks**]: Wireless communication

Keywords

Markov model; EDCA; QoS; Simulation; Experimentation

1. INTRODUCTION

Wi-Fi networks have gained extensive acceptance with the preamble of the IEEE 802.11 standard. Because of the pervasive aspect of the wireless access networks, the need for real-time video-conferencing, video streaming, and voice calls over Wi-Fi networks have started to be recognized. As a result, associated issues have recently become dynamic research areas. A Wi-Fi network is comprised of one or more access points (APs) and a number of mobile stations/STAs. Performance analysis and capacity estimation of Wi-Fi networks have been vibrant research areas for a long time. It is quite difficult to model wireless local area networks (WLANs), where multiple traffic classes are present and functioning in real-time because of the intricate architecture of the medium access control (MAC) layer. Meeting the QoS objectives is a key challenge in WLANs due to the limited bandwidth availability. In order to guarantee the QoS support and to handle multimedia applications in WLANs, the IEEE 802.11e standards group has proposed Enhanced Distribution Channel Access (EDCA), which enhances the MAC protocol.

The 802.11e employs a hybrid coordination function (HCF) which essentially augments both the point coordination function (PCF) and the distributed coordination function (DCF). The HCF offers two modes for channel access, named HCCA (HCF controlled channel access) and EDCA (enhanced distributed channel access). The EDCA is comparable to DCF but has provision for four different traffic classes such as AC0, AC1, AC2 and AC3, where AC0 is the least privileged and AC3 is the most privileged class. For instance, voice call is considered AC3 and web browsing is considered AC1. We will use the terms 'access categories' and 'traffic classes' inter-changeably in the reminder of this paper. Through the differentiation of MAC parameters, the EDCA offers service differentiation among these traffic classes.

This paper proposes a mathematical model to analyze the performance of EDCA-based IEEE 802.11e WLAN when VoIP traffic and TCP controlled data traffic are present in the network. We use the number of nonempty AC3 queues (mobile STAs), the number of packets waiting in those AC3 queues, the number of nonempty AC1 queues, the number of packets waiting in those AC1 queues, and the variable to keep track of which ACs are allowed to attempt in a channel slot to form the Markov states. This model is accurate and computationally easier. Using the proposed model, we calculate VoIP capacity, TCP throughput, and bandwidth utilization in EDCA WLAN. We demonstrate that there exists a correlation among the queue size of mobile STAs and the capacity and throughput of the network. We analyze the effect of arbitrary queue size on voice capacity and TCP throughput. This work is useful in the capacity planning and bandwidth management of Wi-Fi networks.

2. RELATED WORK

In this section, we summarize the existing works on performance analysis of EDCA WLANS. In [1], a complex mathematical model for EDCA performance is proposed for generic non-saturated and saturated cases, and it estimates the av-

*The work presented in the paper was completed during 2012-13, when Dr. Das was affiliated to the University of Texas at Arlington.

MSWiM'13, November 3–8, 2013, Barcelona, Spain.
Copyright 2013 ACM 978-1-4503-2353-6/13/11 ...$15.00.

erage delay, standard deviation of the delay, and average throughput. In [2] and [3], the evaluation of 802.11e WLAN is based on Markov model; the authors assume that the number of active STAs changes only at certain periods. However, two unrealistic assumptions of these models are: (i) a new packet always arrives at empty queue, and (ii) each queue only contains at most one packet at any time, which means a queue always becomes empty after transmitting a packet. In contrast, some works consider infinite queue (e.g., [4], [5]). In [6], the authors propose a simplistic analytical model, which relaxes the assumptions of ([2], [3]) but the model is only applicable for one traffic class, namely VoIP. In [7], the authors demonstrate a technique for measuring one-way delay in an 802.11e real-environment testbed; they also study delay in the context of protecting a voice call competing against data traffic.

The analysis presented in [8] is based on the following assumptions: (i) a fixed number of mobile STAs and each of the STAs is saturated with only one traffic class, and (ii) the probability of collision for each traffic class is same in each channel slot. In our proposed model, we tackle few limitations in some of the existing works such as new packets arrive at empty queue all the time and a queue becomes empty immediately after a packet transmission [2], number of STAs in the network is fixed [8], and fixed packet arrival rate [3]. The proposed model is more generic compared to the other existing models in the literature; for example, some of the existing approaches ([3], [2]) indeed become special cases of our model when the queue size is 1.

3. MODELING AND ASSUMPTIONS

Let the WLAN comprises of one access point (AP) and a number of mobile clients; we also assume the AC3 and AC1 traffic as initiating from different mobile STAs. So, let M_{AC3} be the number of mobile STAs carrying two way AC3 (VoIP) traffic and let M_{AC1} be the number of mobile STAs downloading AC1 (TCP) traffic with one session each. We consider the basic access mechanism for the channel access of the access categories (ACs). In [2], it has been illustrated that if the number of mobile clients is too big, then the performance of each client with multiple queues matches with that of each client with one queue. Therefore, we assume that each client has one queue without loss of generality and this will reduce the complexity of our analysis. In the AP, there is one queue for AC3 traffic to serve all voice calls and another for AC1 traffic to provide all TCP data downloads and so AP can be viewed as 2 nodes. Therefore, we have a total of $(M_{AC3}+M_{AC1}+2)$ nodes and thus the equal number of queues. We denote the queue of an AC3 STA as $QSTA_{AC3}$, that of an AC1 STA as $QSTA_{AC1}$. Similarly, queue of an AP for AC3 traffic as QAP_{AC3}, and that of an AP for AC1 traffic as QAP_{AC1}.

4. MATHEMATICAL MODEL

We consider the presence of AC3 and AC1 traffic classes in the network. In our framework, a channel is a wireless medium in which 802.11e traffic is transmitted with no packet loss as a result of noise. Here, channel activity is stated as any sort of action carried out by a queue at any time. For instance, at any time, a queue may participate in a collision, stay idle or transmit a packet successfully.

Let Y_j^{AC3} be the number of nonempty $QSTA_{AC3}$s, N_j^{AC3} be the number of packets waiting in all the $QSTA_{AC3}$s, Y_j^{AC1} be the number of nonempty $QSTA_{AC1}$s, and N_j^{AC1} be the number of packets waiting in all the $QSTA_{AC1}$s at the end of jth channel slot. So, $0 \leq Y_j^{AC3} \leq M_{AC3}$, $0 \leq Y_j^{AC1} \leq M_{AC1}$, $0 \leq N_j^{AC3} \leq M_{AC3} \cdot V$ and $0 \leq N_j^{AC1} \leq M_{AC1}$.

We use the variable F_j^{AC} to keep track of which ACs are allowed to attempt in a channel slot. Let $F_j^{AC} = 0$ indicate that the prior channel slot was idle and therefore, any node (either AC3 or AC1) can attempt at j^{th} channel slot. Let $F_j^{AC} = 1$ represent that the prior channel slot had an activity and so, only AC3 nodes can attempt at j^{th} channel slot. Our Markov state is defined at j^{th} channel slot as $St_j = (Y_j^{AC3}, N_j^{AC3}, Y_j^{AC1}, N_j^{AC1}, F_j^{AC})$.

4.1 Packet Arrival and Departure

To derive the transition probability $P(St_j | St_{j1})$, we note that state changes because of the arrival and/or departure of packets. Let λ define the packet arrival rate in a single channel slot. Let $\{A_j^{AC3}, j \geq 0\}$ be the packet arrival process, in which A_j^{AC3} is the total number of new VoIP packets arrived in AC3 queues/mobile STAs in the jth channel slot. Let L_j be the length of the jth channel slot and $L_j = l$. Then M_{AC3} number of $QSTA_{AC3}$s, each of size V, can hold at most $M_{AC3} \cdot V$ packets. Applying Poisson formula,

$$P[A_j^{AC3} = a \mid l] = (M_{AC3}\lambda l)^a e^{(M_{AC3}\lambda l)}/a! \qquad (1)$$

where $M_{AC3}\lambda$ is the cumulative average of packet arrival in M_{AC3} mobile clients. Let D_j^{AC3} be the number of packets transmitted from $QSTA_{AC3}$s, D_j^{AC3AP} be the number of packets transmitted from QAP_{AC3}, D_j^{AC1} be the number of packets transmitted from $QSTA_{AC1}$s, and D_j^{AC1AP} be the number of packets transmitted from QAP_{AC1} in the jth channel slot. We know that at any channel slot at most one transmission/departure can occur. A variable *totalstate* is defined to denote the total number of valid Markov states. Here, $totalstate = 2 \cdot (M_{AC3}+1) \cdot V \cdot (M_{AC1}+1)$.

4.2 Deriving Markov Property

We use the attempt probabilities of [2] to determine D_{j+1}^{AC3}, D_{j+1}^{AC3AP}, D_{j+1}^{AC1}, and D_{j+1}^{AC1AP}. Let β_j^{AC3} be the attempt probability of any AC3 queues (including QAP_{AC3}) in the jth channel slot and β_j^{AC1} be the attempt probability of any AC1 queues (including QAP_{AC1}) in the jth channel slot. β_j^{AC3} and β_j^{AC1} can be derived, given that there are Y_j^{AC3} nonempty queues of AC3 and Y_j^{AC1} nonempty queues of AC1 in the jth channel slot applying the saturation fixed point analysis [2]. Let there be Y_j^{AC3} and Y_j^{AC1} nonempty queues of AC3 and AC1 respectively at the jth channel slot; Since by assumption, both QAP_{AC3} and QAP_{AC1} always contend for the channel, so including the AP of both ACs we have $Y_j^{AC3}+1$ and $Y_j^{AC1}+1$ nonempty queues of AC3 and AC1 in total correspondingly. From the equation (1) intended for VoIP packet arrivals and the attempt probabilities of AC3 and AC1 traffics, we can say that St_j creates a five-dimensional discrete-time Markov chain at j^{th} channel slot. We can determine the stationary probabilities $\{\Pi_j; \sum_{j=1}^{totalstate} \Pi_j = 1\}$ for all the Markov states by using available transition probabilities and solving a set of linear equations.

5. PERFORMANCE EVALUATION

5.1 VoIP Capacity

Our proposed Markov model is used to compute the voice call capacity for WLAN. Let $R(t)$ be the number of successfully transmitted packets by AP (QAP_{AC3}) in time t, then the AP service rate is calculated as

$$\Theta_{AP-AC3} = \lim_{t\to\infty} \frac{R(t)}{t} \quad (2)$$

We can obtain Θ_{AP-AC3} by taking expectation on the value of R_j at each Markov state and then divide the expected value of R_j by the expected length of a channel slot. The detail is deferred to the extended version because of page limitation. To ensure the QoS requirements, the service rate of AP must be greater than or equivalent to the cumulative traffic arrival rate. Therefore,

$$\Theta_{AP-AC3} \geq M_{AC3}\lambda \quad (3)$$

5.2 TCP Throughput

Let $U(t)$ be the number of successfully transmitted packets by AP (QAP_{AC1}) in time t, then the AP service rate is calculated as

$$\Theta_{AP-AC1} = \lim_{t\to\infty} \frac{U(t)}{t} \quad (4)$$

We can obtain Θ_{AP-AC1} by taking expectation on the value of U_j at each Markov state and then divide the expected value of U_j by the expected length of a channel slot. Again, the detail is deferred to the extended version.

5.3 Bandwidth Utilization

Let each of the AC3 STA in the WLAN requires bandwidth of τ_{AC3}, which means each STA requires to transmit at a rate of τ_{AC3} bits/sec so as to meet the QoS requirements. If there are M_{AC3} mobile STAs in the network, then the required bandwidth for VoIP (AC3) traffic is $\tau_{AC3}.M_{AC3}$. Moreover, the AP (QAP_{AC3}) transmits packets at a rate of Θ_{AP-AC3}. So, the total bandwidth utilized by the $QSTA_{AC3}$s and the QAP_{AC3} is $\Theta_{AP-AC3} + \tau_{AC3}.M_{AC3}$. Similarly, let each of the AC1 STA in the WLAN requires bandwidth of τ_{AC1}, which means each STA requires to transmit at a rate of τ_{AC1} bits/sec. If there are M_{AC1} mobile STAs in the network, then the required bandwidth for TCP (AC1) traffic is $\tau_{AC1}.M_{AC1}$. Moreover, the AP (QAP_{AC1}) transmits packets at a rate of Θ_{AP-AC1}. So, the total bandwidth utilized by the $QSTA_{AC1}$s and the QAP_{AC1} is $\Theta_{AP-AC1}+\tau_{AC1}.M_{AC1}$. Now, if the bandwidth of H bits/sec is supported by the wireless channel, then the bandwidth utilization is obtained by dividing the sum of the above expressions by H.

6. EXPERIMENTAL RESULTS

Now, we evaluate our proposed model for EDCA-based IEEE 802.11e WLAN. We believe our method is applicable to any IEEE 802.11 variant as the scheme is generic. Here, we validate our analytical model using simulation results produced by the Qualnet simulator [9] and experimental results produced from real-environment testbed. We have implemented the EDCA model according to the IEEE 802.11e specifications.

6.1 Testbed Setup

To perform our experiments we built a testbed composed of 11 laptops, each with wireless connectivity running under the infrastructure mode. All laptops ran on Windows operating system. One laptop acted as a server with the remaining ones acting as clients generating traffic. All laptops were equipped with Edimax EW-7811Un 150 Mbps Wireless IEEE 802.11b/g/n nano USB Adapters which fully implement the EDCA mechanism of the standard. All laptops ran Iperf [10], a real-time traffic generator software. Linksys WAP610N Wireless-N Access Point was used as access point. The laptops were connected to a wireless router with the 802.11e feature enabled which forwarded the packets from client nodes to server and vice versa. Iperf software enables a laptop to send four different types of traffic, each with different QoS priorities. The four different traffic classes are as follows: voice traffic (AC3), video traffic (AC2), best-effort traffic (AC1), and background traffic (AC0). All of the tests are performed using the 802.11b physical maximal transmission rate of 11Mbps with RTS/CTS disabled and the channel number explicitly set. As we are interested in the effect of client queue, we have varied the size of certain queues.

Table 1 shows the VoIP capacity obtained from both analysis, simulation, and real-life experiments with respect to the number of TCP sessions and when queue size is either 1, 10 or 20. We observe that when queue size is 1 and no TCP session is present in the network, 11 STAs are supported without QoS degradation. Simulation results illustrate that 11 mobile STAs are supported whereas experimental results show that 10 mobile STAs are supported. From the table we see that for queue size 10, when no TCP session is present in 802.11e WLANs, 8 voice calls can be supported analytically, 7 voice calls can be supported in terms of simulation results, and 6 voice calls can be supported in terms of real-time experimental results without compromising QoS objective. We also observe that 6 voice calls can be supported without service degradation in case of ten TCP sessions and when queue size is 10; which is same as when only one TCP session was present. The effect of one TCP session is similar to that of ten TCP sessions because the QAP_{AC1} is already saturated with one TCP. So, the number of VoIP calls will not change much with increasing TCP sessions. Simulation results also confirm our analytical results whereas experimental results show that 4 voice calls are supported.

Moreover, we notice that the VoIP capacity is same in terms of analysis and simulation results when queue size is equal to 20 and there is no TCP session. We observe from analysis that 7 voice calls can be supported without service degradation and from real experiment we observe that 6 voice calls can be supported. The effect of 10 queues is almost similar to that of 20 queues because the QAP_{AC3} is saturated. We also examine that 6 voice calls can be supported without service degradation in case of ten TCP sessions and when queue size is 20; which is same as when only one TCP session was present. The effect of one TCP session is similar to that of ten TCP sessions because as mentioned earlier the QAP_{AC1} is already saturated with one TCP. So, the number of VoIP calls will not change much with increasing TCP sessions. Simulation results almost match with our analytical results whereas experimental results show that 3 voice calls are supported. Table 1 shows the simulated VoIP capacity with 95% confidence intervals.

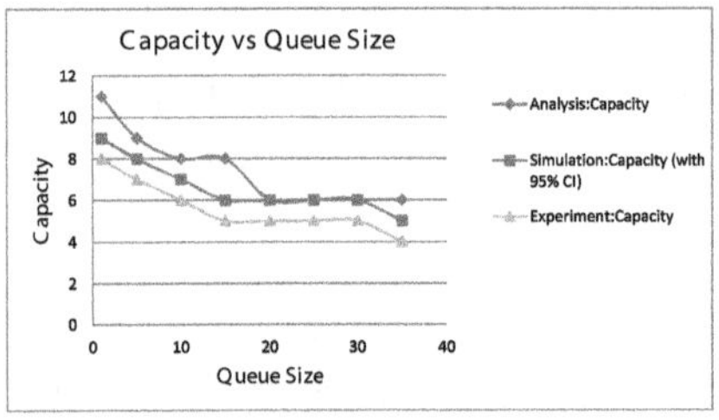

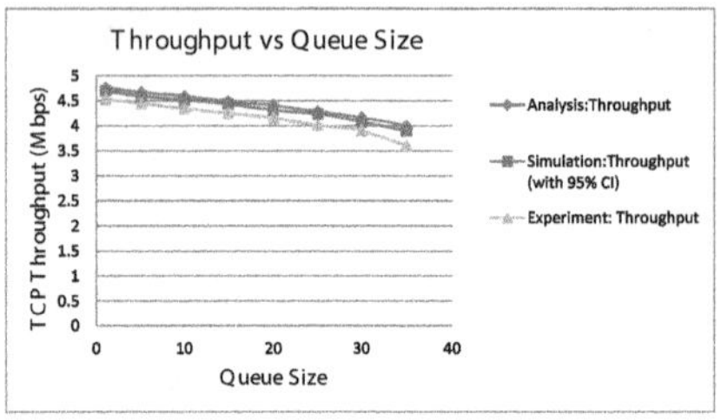

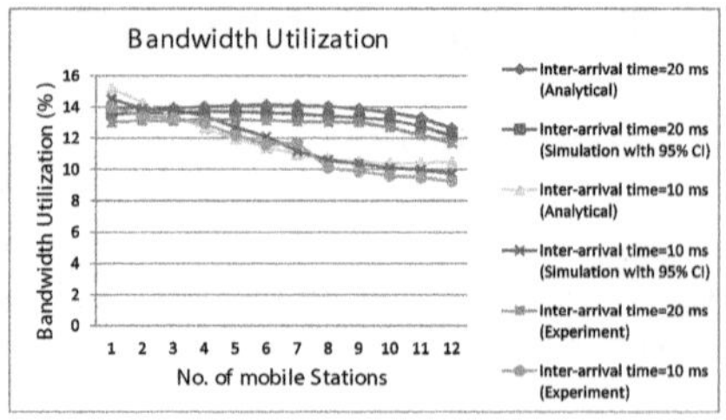

Figure 1: VoIP Capacity comparison for arbitrary queue sizes

Figure 2: TCP Throughput comparison for arbitrary queue sizes

Figure 3: Bandwidth Utilization in IEEE 802.11e WLAN

Table 1: VoIP Capacity Comparison

	Voice calls for Queue size=1	Voice calls for Queue size=10	Voice calls for Queue size=20
No TCP (Analytical)	11	8	7
No TCP (Simulation)	11	7	7
No TCP (Experiment)	10	6	6
One TCP (Analytical)	9	6	6
One TCP (Simulation)	9	6	5
One TCP (Experiment)	8	5	4
Ten TCP (Analytical)	9	6	6
Ten TCP (Simulation)	9	5	4
Ten TCP (Experiment)	8	4	3

Figure 1 shows the VoIP capacity for arbitrary queue sizes, diverse between 1 and 35. Since the QAP_{AC3} is saturated, the queue size of 40/50 packets or more will yield almost the same performance as an infinite queue. We examine that as we augment the queue size, initially the capacity changes instantly and afterward tends to become stable. From the plot, we note that initially the capacity decreases about 20%. Thus, the larger the size of the queue, the more the collision in the network and hence we observe substantial decrease in the capacity. The reason is as we increase the queue size, it introduces more packet delay in the queues and hence causes packet drop. Therefore, the service rate of AP and so the capacity of the network decreases. Similarly, Figure 2 shows the TCP throughput for arbitrary queue sizes in IEEE 802.11e WLANs. The plots show the simulated VoIP capacity and TCP throughput with 95% confidence intervals.

From Figure 3, we notice that as the number of STAs increases, the bandwidth utilization declines. The reason is more bandwidth is required for the packet transmission of larger number of STAs and thus there will be more collision in the network. Consequently, the service rate of AP and so the bandwidth utilization in the network declines. Note that, the bandwidth utilization is less for the packet inter-arrival time of 10ms compared to the packet inter-arrival time of 20ms. It elucidates the truth that if the STAs generate packets at a higher rate then more collisions occur in the network. Results are further validated by real-environment experimental results.

7. CONCLUSIONS

In this paper, we identify relationships among size of queues of STAs, VoIP capacity, and TCP throughput. From our analysis, we see that client nodes with larger queue introduces more collision and hence reduces throughput, even though application is generating packet at the same rate. In addition, reduced throughput accounts for reduced capacity in WLAN. Moreover, bandwidth utilization for variable packet arrival rate is analyzed. The proposed model does not depend on MAC parameters and so is generic for any access categories. Also, some of the existing approaches become special cases of our model for queue size of 1. Our model is validated by comparing analytical, simulation, and real-life experimental results.

8. REFERENCES

[1] P. Serrano, A. Banchs, P. Patras, and A. Azcorra, "Optimal configuration of 802.11e EDCA for real-time and data traffic," *IEEE Transactions on Vehicular Technology*, vol. 59, no. 5, Jun. 2010.

[2] V. Ramaiyan, A. Kumar, and E. Altman, "Fixed point analysis of single cell IEEE 802.11e WLANs: Uniqueness and Multistability," *IEEE/ACM Transactions on Networking*, vol. 16, no. 5, Oct. 2008.

[3] S. Harsha, S. V. R. Anand, A. Kumar, and V. Sharma, "An analytical model for capacity evaluation of VoIP on HCCA and TCP file transfers over EDCA in an IEEE 802.11e WLAN," *ICDCN*, Dec. 2006.

[4] S. Rashwand and M. J., "IEEE 802.11e EDCA under bursty traffic - how much TXOP can improve performance," *IEEE Transactions on Vehicular Technology*, vol. 60, no. 3, Mar. 2011.

[5] J. Hu, G. Min, M. Woodward, and W. Jia, "A comprehensive analytical model for IEEE 802.11e QoS differentiation schemes under unsaturated traffic loads," in *IEEE ICC*, May 2008, pp. 241–245.

[6] S. Imon, S. Datta, and S. K. Das, "A simplistic approach to model capacity estimation and bandwidth utilization of IEEE 802.11e WLAN," in *IWCMC*, Jul. 2011, pp. 1569–1574.

[7] I. Dangerfield, D. Malone, and D. Leith, "Experimental evaluation of 802.11e EDCA for enhanced voice over WLAN performance," *WiNMee*, pp. 1–7, 2006.

[8] Y. Lin and V. Wong, "Saturation throughput of IEEE 802.11e EDCA based on mean value analysis," in *WCNC*, Apr. 2006, pp. 475–480.

[9] Qualnet simulator, http://www.scalable-networks.com/boards/qualnet/.

[10] Iperf, http://iperf.sourceforge.net/.

CEDO: Content-Centric Dissemination Algorithm for Delay-Tolerant Networks*

Francisco Neves dos Santos
EPFL, Switzerland
fmnsantos@gmail.com

Benjamin Ertl
University of Nice, France
benjamin.ertl@asamnet.de

Chadi Barakat
INRIA, France
Chadi.Barakat@inria.fr

Thrasyvoulos Spyropoulos
Eurecom, France
spyropou@eurecom.fr

Thierry Turletti
INRIA, France
Thierry.Turletti@inria.fr

ABSTRACT

Emerging challenged networks require new protocols and strategies to cope with a high degree of mobility, high delays and unknown, possibly non-existing routes within the network. Researchers have proposed different *store-carry-and-forward* protocols for data delivery in challenged networks. These have been complemented with appropriate drop and scheduling policies that deal with the limitations of the nodes' buffers and the limited duration of opportunistic encounters in these networks. Nevertheless, the vast majority of these protocols and strategies are designed for end-to-end transmissions. Yet, a paradigm shift from the traditional way of addressing the endpoints in the network has been occurring towards content-centric networking. To this end, we present CEDO, a content-centric dissemination algorithm for challenged networks. CEDO aims at maximizing the total delivery-rate of distributed content in a setting where a range of contents of different popularity may be requested and stored, but nodes have limited resources. It achieves this by maintaining a delivery-rate utility per content that is proportional to the content miss rate and that is used by the nodes to make appropriate drop and scheduling decisions. This delivery-rate utility can be estimated locally by each node using unbiased estimators fed by sampled information on the mobile network obtained by gossiping. Both simulations and theory suggest that CEDO achieves its set goal, and outperforms a baseline LRU-based policy by 72%, even in relatively small scenarios. The framework followed by CEDO is general enough to be applied to other global performance objectives as well.

*This work is supported by the French national project ANR Connect and the European ICT Labs Activity on Information-Centric Networking (ITA 12191).

Categories and Subject Descriptors

C.2 [**Computer-Communication Networks**]: Network Architecture and Design

Keywords

Delay-Tolerant Networks; Content-Centric Networks; Storage management and content scheduling.

1. INTRODUCTION

Challenged networks like tactical networks, exotic media networks (e.g. underwater, interplanetary), sensor networks, and pocket-switched networks require new protocols and strategies to handle a high degree of mobility, high delays and unknown, possibly non-existing routes between nodes in these networks [4]. Many researchers have proposed different protocols to overcome these emerging challenges within the area of delay tolerant networking (DTN) [23]. Most of the propositions imply a paradigm shift from the traditional network architecture of addressing the endpoints in the network with the current TCP/IP model towards a *"bundle"* overlay or named content network architecture. However, these new architectures also pose new challenges for example in the field of routing, security or buffer management.

To deal with the high degree of mobility and possibly unknown or non-existing paths between the source node(s) and the target node(s) in these networks, researchers have proposed routing protocols based on the *store-carry-and-forward* routing principle [9][10][18][22]. Following this principle, nodes store messages or contents in their buffers and carry them until an opportunity to forward or replicate them arises. These routing protocols disseminate data in an epidemic, probabilistic, or utility-based manner, with recent protocols trying to exploit known and measured patterns in human mobility in a sophisticated manner [25].

Nevertheless, such long-term storage and heavy replication impose a heavy toll on the resources of the nodes involved. While the focus of existing routing protocols has been on the selection of the right next hop(s), the performance of these protocols is tightly coupled to the storage capacity of the nodes in the network as well as the amount of bandwidth available during a contact with another node. It is thus key to implement efficient buffer management policies for dropping data upon nodes' buffers saturation and scheduling it for transmission upon nodes' encounters [13]. To this end, researchers have studied the effect of simple policies such as *Drop Last*, *Drop Front*, *Drop Oldest*, etc. [24]. Furthermore, a theoretically optimal buffer management policy, along with an efficient distributed implementation for it have been proposed in [14].

However, in the majority of these works, the buffer management and scheduling problem is formulated and solved in the context of *end-to-end* traffic sent by one device to another well defined device. Yet, an increase in user demand for content has been observed, due to multimedia streaming and data sharing. This has led the Internet community to shift towards content-centric architectures that care less about addressing specific endpoints and more about the content and data themselves (e.g. CCN [9][23]). Wireless and opportunistic networks are no exception to this trend, with cellular traffic being dominated by content related to streaming and social applications [15]. It becomes of prime importance to be able to inject new content and rely on network architecture to forward it to all nodes that request it. Yet, given the increasing abundance and size of content available, and the limited, in comparison, resources of handheld nodes, interesting questions arise in this context, especially when the number of requesting nodes varies over time and from one content to another: *How can one optimize (or even define) the global performance of such a network? How can one serve content requests in a "fair" manner?* While such questions are not new, when it comes to content-centric approaches, answering them in the context of DTNs poses interesting new challenges. As a result, developing efficient drop and scheduling policies for content-centric delay-tolerant networks is an important research objective [7][8][20][21][25].

To this end, in this paper we formulate and propose efficient content-delivery strategies for Delay Tolerant Networks (DTN). We consider a setting where different contents of varying popularity exist in the network, and where nodes can store copies for only a small subset of them due to storage limitations. This turns the scheduling and drop problem into a storage allocation problem. Our main contribution in this paper is to study this problem in depth, in the context of DTN, proposing both optimal and practical (i.e. implementable) solutions. Specifically, our contributions can be summarized as follows:

- We formulate the centralized optimization version of the problem and derive the *theoretically* optimal allocation that maximizes network-wide content hit rate as a function of content popularity distribution, number of nodes, rate of mobility, and nodes' buffer capacity.
- We use the above formulation to derive appropriate utilities per content, that can be used *locally* by each node to make drop and scheduling decisions; this distributed implementation of the optimal policy, based on content utilties, can be shown to converge to the globally optimal one.
- In order to obtain global quantities (e.g. popularity, measured as request rate) needed to calculate a content's utility, we propose appropriate (*unbiased*) estimators. This leads to our practical policy for the problem in hand, where nodes: (*a*) estimate key quantities (per content), (*b*) use them to derive the utility of a content (i.e. marginal gain from keeping or replicating it), and (*c*) use the utilities to choose which content to drop or forward, when encountering other nodes. This sequence of actions, while not provably optimal at all times, is designed to closely resemble the optimal actions *in the average sense.*
- Finally, we have implemented our distributed solution, called CEDO, within the CCN architecture [9, 3] and evaluated its performance using different simulation scenarios in NS-3 [6]. CCN is a promising architecture for content-centric networking and provides a set of building blocks that allow a smooth support of CEDO. Our first results suggest that, even in small networks, CEDO outperforms baseline policies, as for example $60-72\%$ higher throughput than with LRU (Least Recently Used), in different mobility scenarios.

In the following section, we describe our solution CEDO and the storage allocation problem behind. Section 3 discusses the implementation of CEDO and explains the details of its integration with the CCNx architecture. Simulation results over synthetic mobility traces are presented in Section 4. Section 5 concludes the paper with some perspectives on our future research.

2. CONTENT-CENTRIC DISSEMINATION ALGORITHM (CEDO)

We cast the problem of scheduling and drop as a network-wide content allocation problem where the question is *how nodes should replicate contents so that the network throughput is maximized.* We formulate the problem as follows. Suppose there are L nodes in the network, each of which has a buffer of capacity B, which can be used to store contents. We assume that each node generates at random times requests for random contents, and that each such request has some "deadline" (denoted as TTL) after which it disappears from the requesting node and the network. Whenever a node E comes within transmission range of node F, and is interested in a content available in the buffer of F, E can retrieve the content. If E successfully retrieves the content before the deadline (i.e. less than TTL time units since it issued the request), we say that *the request is satisfied.* If not, then there is a *miss.*

It is clear from the above discussion that, the more nodes store a copy of a given content, the faster on average can this content be found by an interested node (with the actual statistics depending on the mobility model). However, if we assume that many different contents exist in the network, then each node can use its buffer space to store only a small subset of them. Hence, having more copies for content X in the network implies fewer copies for some other content Y, which creates a tradeoff behind the allocation problem we are interested in.

Furthermore, we assume that different contents might have different request rates, as some might be more popular than others. This is highly realistic as skewed popularity distributions have commonly been observed in a variety of contexts [2][5][19]. In this case, intuition suggests that more popular content should be allocated more buffer space. But how much? To what extent and under which network conditions can popular contents "kill" less popular ones?

Next, we first elaborate on our assumptions and formulate an optimization problem that aims at maximizing the long-term rate of satisfied requests (referred to as "delivery rate" hereafter), in the setting described above (Section 2.1). We then use this formulation to come up with a distributed solution for the problem: this solution is based on the notion of *utility per content* that each node can calculate locally and use to rank contents it stores. In this case, the drop strategy is simply to remove contents with minimum utilities and the scheduling strategy is to forward contents to encountered nodes by decreasing order of utilities (Section 2.2). Nevertheless, these utilities require the knowledge of content-related metrics (e.g. popularity), which are not available locally. Thus, as a final step, we show how each node can estimate these quantities locally so as to derive reliable estimates of the optimal utilities (Section 2.3).

2.1 Formulation of the Optimal Content Allocation Problem

For tractability reasons, we consider that nodes' inter-meeting times are IID, following an exponential distribution with a constant parameter λ; in other words, if node E meets node F, it expects to meet F again after $1/\lambda$ seconds. This assumption is commonly made in related work, and has also received some support (as a useful approximation) by recent trace analysis [11]. To further validate our policies, we will use in Section 4 a simulation scenario that greatly departs from this assumption. With the above assumption, the probability that a receiver obtains a replica of content i can be easily derived as (see e.g. [13]):

LEMMA 2.1. *Given the node meeting rate λ, the average lifetime for a content request TTL, and the number of replicas of content i, $n^{(i)}$, the probability that a node obtains a copy of content i is: $p^{(i)} = 1 - exp\{-\lambda TTL \cdot n^{(i)}\}$.*

Hence, by duplicating content i (i.e., increasing $n^{(i)}$), relaxing the request deadline TTL, or augmenting the meeting rate λ, we improve the likelihood $p^{(i)}$ that a device obtains a copy of content i.

The above probability refers to the success of a *single* request for content i. If we look at *all* requests for content i, we can define its delivery rate $DR^{(i)}$ that measures the number of replicas of this content successfully delivered to the intended destinations per unit of time:

DEFINITION 2.2. *Given the request rate for content i, $q^{(i)}$, and the probability of receiving a replica of content i, $p^{(i)}$, we define the delivery rate for content i as $DR^{(i)} = q^{(i)} \cdot p^{(i)}$.*

Our framework, CEDO, attempts to maximize the total delivery rate, which is the sum of the delivery rates of all contents, subject to the following constraints: (i) the total number of replicas of all content cannot exceed the amount of storage of all nodes, (ii) a node cannot store duplicate copies of a content i, and (iii) there must exist at least one replica of each content i in the network. This corresponds to the following optimization problem:

$$\begin{aligned} \underset{n^{(1)},\ldots,n^{(k)}}{\text{maximize}} \quad & f(n^{(1)},\ldots,n^{(k)}) = \textstyle\sum_{i=1}^{k} DR^{(i)} \\ \text{subject to} \quad & \textstyle\sum_{i=1}^{k} n^{(i)} - L.B \leq 0, \\ & n^{(i)} - L \leq 0 \quad \text{for all content } i, \\ & n^{(i)} \geq 1 \quad\quad\;\; \text{for all content } i. \end{aligned} \tag{1}$$

k is the number of contents, L is the number of mobile nodes and B is the buffer capacity of each node.

Given that the constraints in (1) are linear [13], that the objective function is concave, and assuming that $n^{(1)}, \ldots, n^{(k)}$ are real random variables, we get a convex optimization problem that is tractable and has a unique solution in terms of the number of replicas per content [13]. A key difference compared to the problem in [13] (end-to-end case) is that, in addition to the success probability of a request, the delivery rate per content is now also directly proportional to its popularity value. This will push the optimal algorithm towards an unbalanced allocation of resources ($n^{(i)}$) to contents, favoring popular contents (as expected). Yet, the concave nature of the delivery probability implies *diminishing returns* when further and further turning the balance in favor of more popular contents. The optimal allocation is thus the tradeoff between these two "forces".

2.2 Deriving per Content Utilities

While the above problem leads to the optimal allocation, in the context of DTNs, we cannot access all the buffers of all nodes in parallel and in one shot, choosing exactly $n^{(i)}$ nodes to store content i, $n^{(j)}$ nodes to store content j, etc. Instead, each node is faced with a *local* decision, whenever it encounters another node: it has to decide which contents to forward and which contents to drop, if its buffer is full and the encountered node has new contents to offer.

Since the above problem is convex, it can be generally solved with a *gradient ascent* strategy. CEDO allows for a distributed implementation inspired by [13]. When a given allocation exists in the network, taking the gradient of the objective function w.r.t the number of replicas, $n^{(i)}$, leads to a sum of the marginal gains in the total delivery rate with respect to increasing (or reducing) the number of replicas, $n^{(i)}$, for each content i. Hence, this marginal gain is the *utility of content* i with respect to the problem of maximizing the delivery rate. Each node can then use these utilities to *locally* compare different contents between which it must make a drop or transmission decision. This leads to a distributed implementation of the global algorithm that can be proven to converge to the optimal solution.

DEFINITION 2.3. *Given the delivery rates for all available contents, $DR^{(1)}, \ldots, DR^{(k)}$, the delivery-rate utility for a content i is defined as:*

$$U^{(i)} = \frac{\partial}{\partial n^{(i)}} \sum_{j=1}^{k} DR^{(j)}. \tag{2}$$

Using this definition of the utility and the expression of the delivery rate given above, we can express $U^{(i)}$ in a more convenient form, as explained next.

LEMMA 2.4. *The delivery-rate utility is proportional to the request-rate for content i, $q^{(i)}$, and decays exponentially with the number of replicas $n^{(i)}$:*

$$U^{(i)} = q^{(i)}(\lambda TTL) exp\{-\lambda TTL \cdot n^{(i)}\}. \tag{3}$$

The above result follows easily by taking the derivative of the expression for $DR^{(i)}$ given by Definition 2.2 and Lemma 2.1. In other words, as nodes replicate a particular content i, the marginal gain in the delivery rate of i is gradually smaller; as $n^{(i)}$ tends to infinity, $U^{(i)}$ tends to zero. This effect allows less popular contents to not "starve", provided there is some minimum buffer space available. We will return to the issue of starvation and fairness later.

With these utilities in hand, the *optimal policy* for each node is simply (a) to drop the contents with the minimum utility, when its buffer is full, and (b) when it encounters another node, to replicate the contents with the maximum utility (among the ones that the latter node does not already have). Consequently, the optimal policy essentially attempts to equalize the utilities of all contents: according to Eq. (3), action (a) reduces the number of replicas $n^{(i)}$ of content i thus increasing its utility; action (b) increases the number of replicas $n^{(i)}$ of content i thus decreasing its utility.

The following lemma converts the per-content utility into a different form that: (a) provides us with additional insight as to what the optimal allocation is really aiming at, and (b) will allow us to derive efficient estimators for these utilities (in the next section).

LEMMA 2.5. *The delivery-rate utility for content i, $U^{(i)}$, can alternatively be expressed as:*

$$U^{(i)} = \lambda TTL(q^{(i)} - DR^{(i)}). \tag{4}$$

Proof. We can rewrite (3) as follows:

$$\begin{aligned} U^{(i)} &= q^{(i)}(\lambda TTL)exp\{-\lambda TTL \cdot n^{(i)}\}, \\ &= q^{(i)}(\lambda TTL)(1 - (1 - exp\{-\lambda TTL \cdot n^{(i)}\})), \\ &= \lambda TTL(q^{(i)} - q^{(i)} \cdot p^{(i)}), \\ &= \lambda TTL(q^{(i)} - DR^{(i)}). \end{aligned}$$ □

Eq. (4) suggests that a content's utility is in fact proportional to the miss rate, defined as the number of unsatisfied requests for content i per second: $MR^{(i)} = q^{(i)} - DR^{(i)}$. Since the optimal policy, as we saw, attempts to equalize utilities in order to solve the optimal allocation problem, this is in fact equivalent to equalizing the miss rate of contents, irrespective of their request rate or popularity.

This latter interpretation allows to have a practical implementation of the optimal policy, that we call CEDO. CEDO essentially estimates miss rates of contents and manages buffer and scheduling accordingly. When a device's buffer is full, CEDO discards the content replica with the smallest rate of unsatisfied requests; by definition, this replica has the smallest impact on the total delivery rate. When a node meets another node, it sends first the content with the highest rate of unsatisfied requests; by replicating this item, the device will increase the probability that a receiver obtains a copy of this content. This gradient ascent strategy, illustrated in Figure 1, shall converge to the number of replicas per content that maximizes the objective function f in (1), provided the iteration step is such that CEDO reaches the efficient allocation before the network changes substantially [13]. Note that the iteration step is decided by the speed at which nodes move. For a proper functioning of CEDO, there should be enough node encounters before the traffic demand changes.

Although we now have a distributed implementation of the optimal policy, miss rates are *global* quantities (one needs to know every request made and whether this was successful), but need to be known locally by each node. Hence, miss rates must be estimated, in an efficient manner, by each node in order to calculate (or rather estimate) utilities and apply the above algorithm. This brings us to the final, and important, component of CEDO.

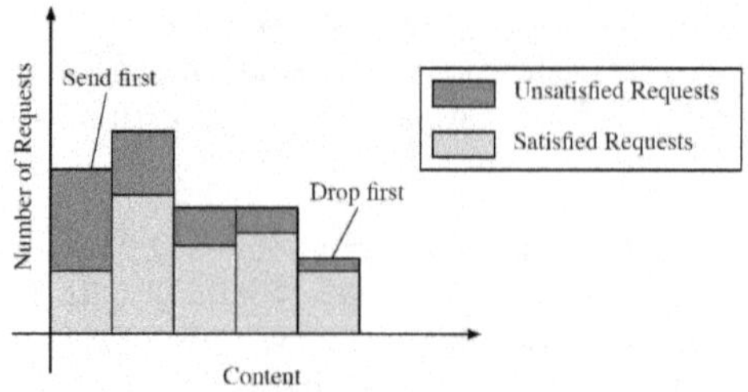

Figure 1: CEDO strategy for scheduling and drop as a function of content popularity and content miss rate.

2.3 Estimating the delivery-rate utility

To calculate the miss rate for a content i (as explained earlier the utility is proportional to the miss rate), a node must estimate the corresponding request and delivery rate. CEDO performs this estimate by requiring each node to record the time when the application running on it requests content i and when the corresponding request is fulfilled. This provides a first local estimation. To refine this local estimation, the node merges its own rate estimate with those received from other encountered nodes. Using the two approximate values for the request and delivery rate, the node computes the utility of content i by applying (4). Next, we define our unbiased estimators for $q^{(i)}$ and $p^{(i)}$. Without loss of generality, we consider in the sequel their normalized values with respect to the network size.

Definition 4 *Let $X_n^{(i)}$ be a random variable denoting the n-th measurement of the number of requests for content i per node, issued by the n-th encountered node in the past W seconds, such that $E[X_n^{(i)}] = q^{(i)}W$. Then our estimator for the request rate for content i per node, $q^{(i)}$, is given by*

$$\hat{q}_n^{(i)} = \alpha\hat{q}_{n-1}^{(i)} + (1 - \alpha)X_n^{(i)}/W, \tag{5}$$

where $\hat{q}_n^{(i)}$ is the value of the estimator $\hat{q}^{(i)}$ after considering the n-th node meeting and $\alpha \in (0, 1)$ is the weight given to the old estimate of the request-rate for content i, $\hat{q}_{n-1}^{(i)}$.

In other words, the estimator for the request rate of content i is computed as the exponentially weighted moving average (EWMA) of the observed samples $X_0^{(i)}, X_1^{(i)}, \ldots, X_n^{(i)}$, applying a weight of $(1 - \alpha)$ to the most recent sample, $X_n^{(i)}$. This allows on one hand to average over different measurements, and on the other hand to forget about the very past ones for reactivity reasons. One can easily show that this estimator is consistent and unbiased, i.e., $E[\hat{q}^{(i)}] = q^{(i)}$, meaning that its average over all nodes approaches the real popularity and it moves towards the real popularity as long as we add more samples.

In a similar way, we define the estimator for the delivery rate of content i per node, $DR^{(i)}$.

Definition 5 *Let $Y_n^{(i)}$ be a random variable denoting the n-th measurement of the number of satisfied requests for content i issued in the past t seconds, where $t \in [TTL, W + TTL]$, and such that $E[Y^{(i)}] = p^{(i)}q^{(i)}W$. Then our estimator for the delivery rate of content i, $\widehat{DR}^{(i)}$, is given by*

$$\widehat{DR}_n^{(i)} = \beta\widehat{DR}_{n-1}^{(i)} + (1 - \beta)Y_n^{(i)}/W, \tag{6}$$

where $\widehat{DR}_n^{(i)}$ *is the value of the estimator after considering the n-th node meeting and* $\beta \in (0, 1)$ *is the weight given to the previous estimate of* $DR^{(i)}$.

In other words, the estimator for the delivery rate of content i is computed as the exponentially weighted moving average of the observed samples $Y_0^{(i)}, Y_1^{(i)}, \ldots, Y_n^{(i)}$, applying a weight of $(1-\beta)$ to the most recent sample, $Y_n^{(i)}$. Here we shift back the time window by TTL seconds to allow the content requests issued in the last TTL seconds to receive an answer or, if none is received, to be classified as "unsatisfied". As the previous estimator for request rate, this one is also consistent and unbiased, i.e., $E[\widehat{DR}^{(i)}] = DR^{(i)}$.

In addition to refining the estimators for request and delivery rates using local measurements at other encountered nodes, a mobile node might also have the possibility to combine its estimators with those at other encountered nodes, if available. This allows local estimates to permeate the network. If two estimates for the same content i are available at two nodes that meet, CEDO combines them as a weighted sum with the weight of each estimator being inversely proportional to its variance [12][13].

3. ALGORITHM IMPLEMENTATION

We present hereafter details on the implementation of our algorithm and the main functions and building blocks required for its support. We start by a general description of the implementation, supported by pseudo code for the different modules (Modules 1-5), then move into a specification to the CCNx architecture [3][9]. CCNx is a promising solution for content-centric networking that provides a set of functions allowing a smooth support of CEDO.

3.1 Outlining the algorithm

Our content-centric dissemination algorithm resides between the application and the network layer: it receives interest messages from the application and attempts to find matching content cached in the mobile device's buffer or available from a neighbouring node. When CEDO fails to find matching content in the local buffer, it writes the query to the pending interest table of the underlying CCNx protocol [3] until it can satisfy the request. Periodically, each mobile device issues a hello message (HM) that signals its presence. When CEDO captures a hello message, it prepares a message with all its pending queries, known as the pending interests message (PIM). A mobile node within range attempts to satisfy the pending requests by searching its local storage and sending all matching content. CEDO relies on a node's ability to estimate the request and delivery rate, $\hat{q}^{(i)}$ and $\widehat{DR}^{(i)}$, for each content i, in order to compute the delivery-rate utility for this content, $U^{(i)}$, as stated in the previous sections. To reduce the load on nodes and avoid them storing and continuously updating estimators for different contents, we assume that each content i carries in its header the estimates for the two rates, which are initialized by the content origin server and updated by intermediate nodes thanks to gossiping. When a mobile device's buffer is full, CEDO uses the content utility to erase the least useful content from the memory. Similarly, when exchanging content with a neighbour, it prioritizes transmissions by decreasing utility. This ensures that the most useful content reaches the other node in case the connection stops before all requested content is transmitted. In the following, we will present the different steps performed by the algorithm.

Module 1 Processing interest messages received by the application at a device

```
Require: interest for content i from application
record time of request for i in statistics table
if buffer contains i then
    deliver content i to application
    record time when request for i satisfied in statistics
    table
else
    write interest to pending interest table
end if
```

Module 2 Processing hello messages

```
Require: hello message from network
if a hello message is waiting to be sent then
    delay transmission of hello message
end if
create new pending interests message
for each interest in the pending interest table do
    write interest to pending interests message
end for
schedule transmission of pending interests message
```

Module 3 Processing pending interests messages

```
Require: pending interests message from network
if a pending interests message is waiting to be sent then
    delay transmission of pending interests message
end if
for each interest in the pending interests message do
    if exists matching content i in buffer then
        write content i to list
    end if
end for
sort list in order of decreasing DR utility
for each content i in list do
    write request and delivery rate to content i
    schedule transmission of content i
end for
```

3.1.1 *Processing application queries*

When the application issues a content query, expressed as an interest message (IM), CEDO records the time at which it receives the interest in the statistics table and searches the mobile device's buffer for matching content. The statistics table is a data structure, independent of the content buffer, that stores the time when requests are issued and when they are satisfied, from which CEDO calculates the request and delivery rate of each content seen. If the buffer contains the desired content, CEDO delivers this data immediately to the application; otherwise, the device stores the query in the pending interest table. The pending interest table is a data structure that stores all the unsatisfied queries issued by the application. Note that the interest remains in the pending interest table until CEDO retrieves this data from an encountered node. Periodically, CEDO iterates through the statistics table to update the request and delivery rate of all content seen using Equations (5) and (6).

A mobile device cannot satisfy all content requests with its cache alone; in such a case, the device stores the query in the pending interest table while waiting for a response. Periodically, a device emits a hello message, which serves to alert other nodes of its presence; the delay for transmitting the next hello message, d_{hello}, is calculated as follows:

$$d_{\text{hello}} = d_{\text{hello}}^{\min}(b_{\text{hello}} + r), \quad (7)$$

where $d_{\text{hello}}^{\min}$ is the minimum delay between hello messages, $b_{\text{hello}} \in [0, b_{\text{hello}}^{\max}]$ is the hello backoff-counter, $b_{\text{hello}}^{\max}$ is the maximum hello backoff, and $r \in [0, 1]$ is a uniform random value. By randomizing the transmission delay of the hello message, CEDO reduces the probability of interfering with ongoing but yet undetected transmissions. When a mobile device receives a hello message, it delays the transmission of its own message by increasing the backoff counter, b_{hello}, as shown in lines 1-3 of Module 2; this avoids congesting the network with an excessive amount of hello messages. As a response to a hello message, CEDO prepares a pending interests message, comprising requests in its pending interest table, and schedules the transmission of the message to all devices within range; see lines 4-8 of Module 2.

Module 4 Processing incoming content

```
Require: datagram with content i from network
 1: if a pending interest exists for content i then
 2:     deliver content i to application
 3:     record time when request for i satisfied in statistics
        table
 4: end if
 5: average request-rate in statistics table and rate in data-
    gram
 6: average delivery-rate in statistics table and rate in
    datagram
 7: if buffer contains i then
 8:     discard content i
 9: else
10:     store-content(i)
11: end if
```

Module 5 Storing content in the buffer

```
 1: function store-content(i)
 2: if buffer not full then
 3:     write content i to buffer
 4:     return true
 5: end if
 6: let m ← content with lowest DR utility in buffer
 7: if i's utility > m's utility then
 8:     replace replica m with i in buffer
 9:     return true
10: end if
11: discard content i
12: return false
13: end function
```

CEDO computes the transmission delay of the pending interests message, d_{PIM}, as following:

$$d_{\text{PIM}} = d_{\text{PIM}}^{\min}(b_{\text{PIM}} + r), \quad (8)$$

where $d_{\text{PIM}}^{\min}$ is the minimum waiting time before transmitting the pending interests message (PIM), $b_{\text{PIM}} \in [0, b_{\text{PIM}}^{\max}]$ is the PIM backoff-counter, bounded by 0 and the maximum backoff $b_{\text{PIM}}^{\max}$, and $r \in [0, 1]$ is a random value. When a node receives a pending interests message, it defers the transmission of a possibly pending PIM by increasing the backoff-counter, b_{PIM}, see lines 1-3 of Module 3; this enables a mobile device to satisfy a part or all of its own pending interests by overhearing the upcoming data exchange, thus reducing the number of entries in its next PIM. To process an incoming PIM, a node retrieves from its buffer all the content items that satisfy the interests expressed in the message, see lines 4-8 of Module 3. It then orders the sought content by decreasing utility order and updates their estimated request and delivery rates, see lines 9-13 of Module 3.

3.1.2 Processing incoming content

Whenever a mobile device receives a content object, it checks the pending interests table for interests corresponding to this data; in case the content object matches an interest in the table, CEDO delivers the data to the application and records the time at which the interest was satisfied, see lines 1-4 of Module 4. As each mobile device may have its own estimate of the request and delivery rates, CEDO computes the arithmetic mean of the two estimates and updates the statistics table, as shown in lines 5-6 of Module 4. Finally, CEDO caches the replica of content i if no such copy exists in the device's buffer, see line 10 of Module 4.

The function **store-content()** implements CEDO's buffer management strategy, see Module 5. It accepts to store all unique content published by the user and replicas of other content received from the network as long as there is enough storage capacity, see lines 2-5 of Module 5. Whenever the buffer is full, the function selects the replica with the lowest delivery-rate utility from memory, say m, and compares it with the utility of replica i; it keeps only the replica with the highest utility from the pair $\{i, m\}$, see lines 6-12. By definition, the replica with the lowest utility has the lowest impact on the total content delivery-rate, if dropped.

3.2 Integration within CCNx

We implemented CEDO on the PARC CCNx implementation [3], version 0.6.0, which is based upon the Content-Centric Networking (CCN) architecture [9]. This open source software reference implementation is available under the GNU General Public License version 2. It is divided into two main components: (*i*) the client, which acts as a mediator between the server and the application and provides an interface for the application to issue interests and obtain content objects from the network, and (*ii*) the server, which propagates interests to the network and obtains content objects from other servers. The main changes required to deploy CEDO over CCNx consist in modifying the header of the content object to include the request and delivery rate estimates, disabling the propagation of interest messages to network peers, and introducing two control packets that implement the *hello* and *pending interests* messages.

A content object contains four units: `Signature`, `Name`, `SignedInfo` and `Content`, as illustrated in Figure 2. The `Signature` contains a digest of the `Name`, `SignedInfo` and `Content` components, computed using a signature algorithm [3]; the `Name` unit holds the hierarchical CCNx name of the content; the `SignedInfo` component specifies the signer of the message, the time when the object was signed, the type of content conveyed and the message's expiration time.

The original CCNx server stores each content object received from the network in a hash table. For each content replica received, the server divides the content object into two parts: (*i*) the first part comprises the **Signature** and **Name** units and (*ii*) the second consists of the remaining components of the content object. The server computes a hash value of the first part of the content object to index each replica stored in the buffer. We introduce the estimates of the request and delivery rates as two integer fields in the **SignedInfo** section of the message. Because the **SignedInfo** section belongs to the second half of the content object, recomputing the two rate estimates for each stared replica does not affect its hash value; hence, the server can still locate content in the buffer after updating the rate estimates of the stored replicas.

A message in the CCNx protocol is encoded using the CCNx binary (CCNB) format [3]. Each section of a message is labelled by a `DTAG`, which is an unique identifier drawn from an internal dictionary. The parser or decoder outputs the byte number at which each message element starts and ends. We encode each estimate as a four-byte `BLOB`, representing an integer value, enclose each estimate with a `DTAG` and modify the content-object parser so as to locate the boundaries of the two values. By using `BLOB`s of fixed length, we can recompute the estimates for the two rates, encode them using the CCNB format and replace the old values in the content object without generating a new message-header. Figure 2 illustrates the components of the content object, including the section where we encode the two estimated rates.

To compute the value of the two rates, we added a statistics table to the server that records the history of content requests; by storing content requests as a separate data structure, we ensure that its lifespan is independent of other server events, such as the removal of stale content from the buffer. Each table entry contains a list of all requests issued and satisfied in the preceding $W + TTL$ seconds for a specific content, where W denotes the measurement period and TTL is the maximum lifetime of an information request; each entry is indexed by the CCNx name of the content being tracked. To calculate the value of the request-rate estimator, $\hat{q}^{(i)}$, we apply (5) and measure $X_n^{(i)}$ by counting the number of requests sent in the preceding W seconds recorded in the content-requests table. We estimate the delivery rate, $\widehat{DR}^{(i)}$, using (6), and evaluate $Y_n^{(i)}$ by tallying all the satisfied requests transmitted in the preceding $[TTL, W + TTL]$ seconds. Knowing the two estimates, $\hat{q}^{(i)}$ and $\widehat{DR}^{(i)}$, we determine the utility of content i using (4) and record this value alongside each replica stored in the buffer. Whenever the buffer exceeds a storage threshold, which is controlled by the parameter `CCND_CAP` [3], we sort the buffer in order of increasing utility and discard the least-useful replicas until the buffer size is below the storage limit.

Finally, we implement CEDO's hello and pending interests messages as content objects. The hello message consists of a content object with **Name** set to **/CEDO/hello**, the **type** field set to **CCN_CONTENT_HELLO**, and having an empty **Content** section. A pending interests message has a CCNx name of **/CEDO/pit**, a **type** field set to **CCN_CONTENT_PIT** and the **Content** section of the message holds a list of the content-

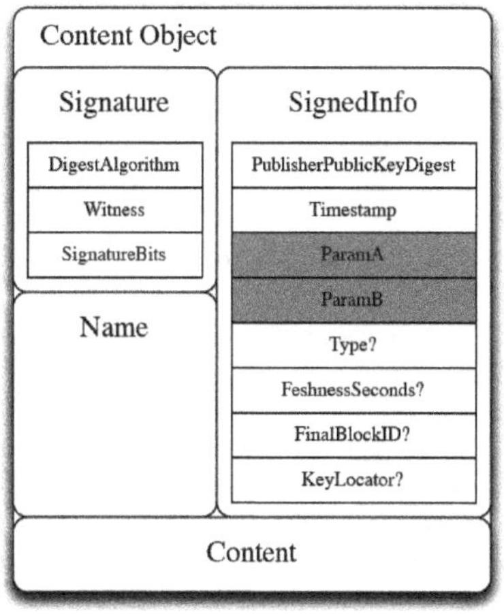

Figure 2: Structure of the CCNx content object [3][9]. Fields with "?" are optional. Red fields, param-A and param-B, carry the request and delivery rates.

names requested by the application and stored in the source node's pending interests table; this message is generated as a response to a hello message. Upon receiving a pending interests message, CEDO reads each name entry in the pending interests message's payload and locates matching content in the device's memory; the algorithm sorts all matching content by decreasing utility before scheduling each transmission. We use CCNx's built-in scheduler to implement the transmission delay equations (7) and (8) for the pending interests message and the hello message, respectively. Additionally, we rely on CCNx's procedure for sending data that introduces an additional random delay before each transmission; this helps reducing the likelihood of collision with ongoing communications.

The CCNx's forwarding-information base comprises a list of IP addresses for dispatching interest messages for which there is no matching content in the local content-store. Because we use the hello and pending interests messages for a similar purpose, we disabled the interest-forwarding procedure found in CCNx. However, we use the forwarding-information base table to store a default entry with CCNx name "/" that points to CEDO's multicast address; a device always uses this address to send data to other devices.

4. EVALUATION

In this section, we aim to verify if CEDO exhibits the behavior predicted in Section 2 for the optimal policy. The practical implementation of CEDO is based on estimated values of the content utilities (rather than actual ones), and also involves a number of additional implementation steps. It is thus important to examine the extent to which these factors affect the desired behavior. To this end, we first check whether CEDO succeeds in equalizing the delivery-rate utility of disseminated content, which, as explained in Section 2, is what an optimal policy should be doing. We then compare our policy to a baseline policy, to evaluate the potential performance benefits.

4.1 Simulation Setting

We simulate a mobile delay-tolerant scenario using the network simulator NS-3 [6] and use the direct-code execution (DCE) feature [16] to deploy the same version of CEDO conceived for real mobile-devices on the simulated nodes. Although this simulation method poses a significant performance penalty (in terms of simulation speed), we believe it increases the credibility of our results and facilitate a future deployment of CEDO on real devices.

We have based our simulations on two mobility models: (*i*) the simple *Random Direction model (RD)*, which has approximately exponentially-distributed inter-meeting times [13], consistent with our assumptions, and (*ii*) the *Self-Similar Least-Action Human Walk (SLAW)* synthetic mobility model, whose inter-contact times follow a truncated power-law [17]. This latter model thus departs from our assumption, but has been shown to better capture inter-contact times and contact durations observed in a large number of real mobility traces. The mobility trace file from each model was generated with the *BonnMotion* mobility scenario generation tool according to the simulation parameters in [1]. Finally, all mobile devices communicate using IEEE 802.11b radios with a PHY data rate of 1 Mbps and a transmission range of 50 to 100m.

We further assume that each node publishes one or more content items and requests one or more content items published by other nodes (the exact numbers are random) with a given randomized rate for requests, to avoid synchronous queries. We model the popularity of content according to a Zipf distribution with parameter $\alpha = 0.8$ (this is consistent with estimated values from measurements reported for web content popularity [2][5][19]). Hence, each new request issued by a node will be for a specific content i with a probability that is defined according to this distribution. We also assume that published content does not expire (only requests for it do), and that there always exists at least one replica for each content in the network (at the node publishing it). For each content, we collect the number of requests and the number of satisfied requests and average the data gathered over independent trials.

Table 1: Simulation parameters.

Parameter	Value
Simulation time	4,000s
Network size	50 nodes
Deployment field	500 m x 500 m
Mobility model	random-direction, SLAW
Node speed	2 m/s (constant)
Node travel direction	changes every 2s
Content published per node	1 content item
Content requested per node	15
Content request lifetime	30s
Radio	IEEE 802.11b, PHY rate = 1 Mbps
Transmission range	50 m, 100 m
Data collected	number of requests per content
Number of Trials	10 independent test runs

Finally, regarding the actual implementation, each node runs an instance of the CCNx server process which contains the implementation of CEDO. We model the behaviour of the user's application by generating events from within the simulation script. Initially, each application calls the CCNx client process to create a default entry in the forwarding-information base, named "/", that points to the CCNx multicast address `255.1.2.4` and multicast port `9695` through which all inter-device communication takes place. Because content does not expire, each application publishes content once, at the beginning of the simulation, and stores it permanently in the node's buffer. The application requests content by generating an interest message with the name of the desired content. All processes interchange data using Unix sockets and all nodes transmit data using the UDP transport protocol running over an IP network.

All simulation parameters are listed in Table 1. The source code of CEDO along with the simulation scripts are also available in the public domain[1] so as to be able to reproduce the figures presented in this paper.

4.2 Results

In our first scenario, captured in Figure 3, we consider a mobility generated by the Random Direction model and a wireless range of 100m. The figure shows the total number of requests (blue), the number of satisfied requests (green) and the number of unsatisfied requests or miss rate (red) for each content, listed in order of decreasing popularity. The first interesting observation is that there is no correlation between the number of unsatisfied requests per content, and the content popularity. This is the desired behaviour that maximizes the total delivery rate, as suggested by our previous analysis. The second observation is that more requests are satisfied for more popular contents, as also expected. While this is indeed the behavior consistent with optimizing the *total* delivery rate, this also implies that, when resources are quite limited in relation to the amount of different contents, low popularity contents might suffer significantly when it comes to the percentage of their satisfied requests. This is better captured in Figure 3b, where we plot the relative number of unsatisfied requests over the total number of requests for a given content, in other words the probability of satisfying a request for content i.

Digressing slightly, we could modify the objective function f in Equation (1), to achieve fairness in relative terms:

$$f(n^{(i)}, \ldots, n^{(k)}) = \sum_{i=1}^{k} \frac{DR^{(i)}}{q^{(i)}}, \tag{9}$$

and derive the utility function for each content i as

$$U^{(i)}(DR/q) = \frac{\partial}{\partial n^{(i)}} f(n^{(i)}, \ldots, n^{(k)}). \tag{10}$$

In this case, we would expect the plot in Figure 3b to exhibit a constant line, implying the same success probability for each content, regardless of its popularity. This is a completely different objective than our original one aiming to maximize the network throughput. Clearly, a number of intermediate policies in between these two extremes could be derived, by manipulating the objective function between Eq. (1) and (9). We defer this investigation to future work.

Table 2: Requests' statistics w/o CEDO.

Policy	Mobility	Range	Total Requests	Satisfied (%)	Unsatisfied (%)
LRU	RD	100m	26,493	14,322 (54%)	12,171 (46%)
CEDO	RD	100m	22,629	18,125 (80%)	4,504 (20%)
LRU	SLAW	100m	25,821	14,951 (58%)	10,870 (42%)
CEDO	SLAW	100m	22,261	18,499 (83%)	3,762 (17%)
LRU	SLAW	50m	28,367	12,315 (43%)	16,052 (57%)
CEDO	SLAW	50m	27,056	13,722 (51%)	13,334 (49%)

In Figure 4, we turn our attention to a network which is more "challenged", where we reduce the transmission range

[1]see URL http://planete.inria.fr/Software/CEDO/

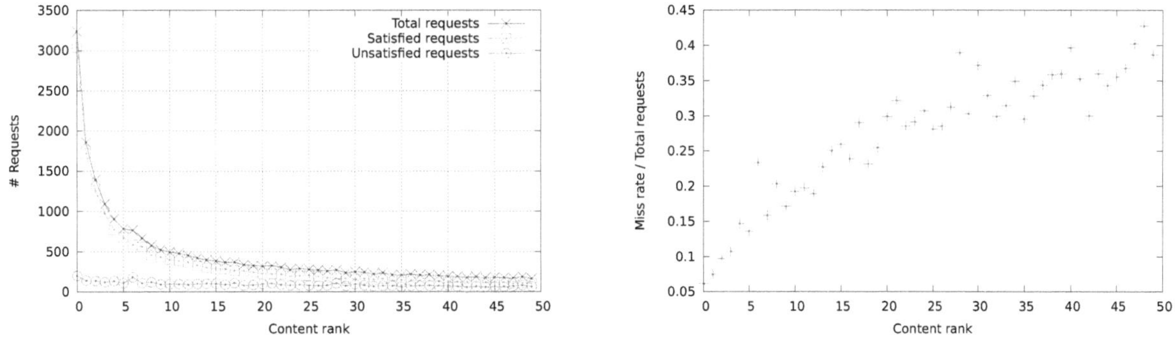

(a) Constant Miss Rate. (b) Increasing $\frac{MissRate}{TotalRequestsRate}$.

Figure 3: CEDO maximizes the total delivery-rate by equalizing the number of unsatisfied requests for all content. As expected, the plot in Figure 3a evidences a constant number of unsatisfied requests for all content, for ranked on the x-axis by decreasing popularity. CEDO does not attempt to equalize the MR/q value, hence the proportion of unsatisfied requests per number of requests increases as the popularity of content decreases; this phenomenon is illustrated in Figure 3b.

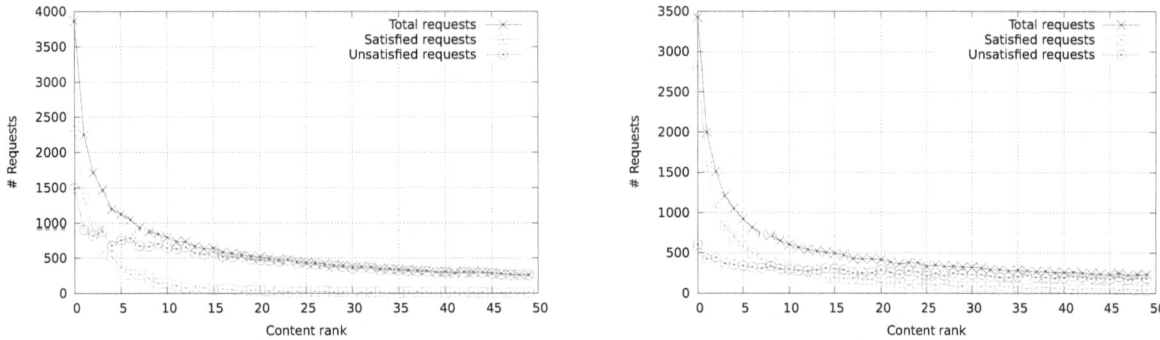

(a) Random direction. (b) Self-Similar Least-Action Human Walk (SLAW).

Figure 4: The number of total requests, satisfied and unsatisfied, for all content ranked on the x-axis by decreasing popularity. The figures correspond to a challenged scenario with a reduced transmission range of $50m$ and therefore less number of encounters within the transmission range. For both random mobility, Figure 4a, and SLAW mobility, Figure 4b, CEDO can still achieve an almost constant miss rate for all content.

to 50m. With a simulation time of $4,000s$, this results in nodes having fewer encounters and of shorter duration, which makes the need for good scheduling decisions (and thus CEDO) during these encounters more pressing. We also consider now two mobility scenarios, RD and SLAW. As is evident by this figure, CEDO achieves an almost constant miss rate for all content regardless of popularity, but higher than that of Figure 3, for both mobility scenarios. The effect of limited resources is even more evident for the random direction scenario, where the resources are so limited that requests are only satisfied for the 15-20 most popular contents. Consequently, as predicted by our analysis, when there are enough resources, the optimal policy will favor popular contents but will still allow requests for less popular contents to obtain a good chance of success (Figure 3). However, when resources become too limited, the optimal policy introduces a "cutoff" below which less popular contents are starved (i.e. they will only be served directly by their sources in this case).

In our final scenario, we compare CEDO to a reasonable baseline policy where nodes implement *Least Recently Used (LRU)* as drop policy in a non-collaborative way (this is often the default policy in CCN), and that schedule content upon encounters according to a simple First-In First-Out policy. Results for both mobility scenarios are shown in Table 2 and Figure 5. As can be seen there, CEDO achieves a 72% improvement in terms of satisfied requests for the random direction model and a 60% improvement for the SLAW mobility trace with a transmission range of $100m$. Even with a reduced transmission range of $50m$, CEDO still achieves a 19% improvement in terms of satisfied requests compared to LRU as indicated.

5. CONCLUSION

We designed CEDO, a content delivery algorithm for disseminating named data over a delay-tolerant network. We showed that the delivery rate is maximal when the delivery-rate utility of all contents equals a constant. We also showed that for this particular global objective function, the delivery rate utility for a content is no other than its miss rate. Hence, CEDO must strive to equalize the miss rates of all contents in order to optimize the network throughput. Compared to a *Least Recently Used* baseline drop policy, CEDO achieves up to 72% better performance on delivered content in the network as claimed by our simulation results. Although the initial results are promising, we must perform additional tests with larger networks, comprising hundreds of nodes that publish and subscribe a greater amount of content and measure the convergence time of the utility estimators. We also need to extend CEDO to account for other global performance objectives than network throughput.

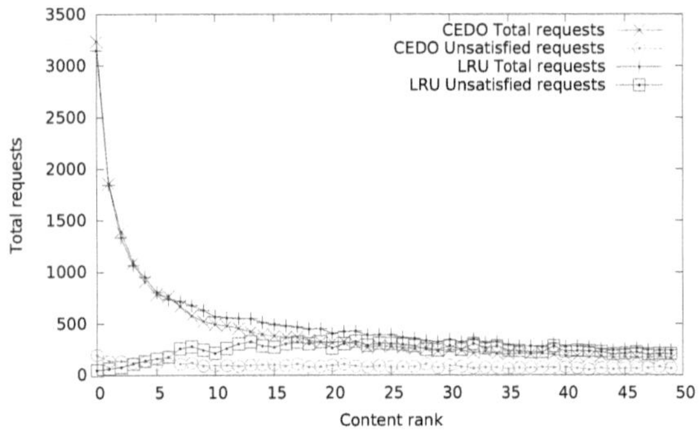

Figure 5: CEDO shows a constant number of unsatisfied requests, regardless of content popularity. LRU from its side shows a high satisfaction rate for very popular content, which means that unlike CEDO, it can not satisfy requests for unpopular content in favour of very popular content.

6. ACKNOWLEDGMENTS

Experiments presented in this paper were carried out using the Grid'5000 experimental testbed, being developed under the INRIA ALADDIN development action with support from CNRS, RENATER and several Universities as well as other funding bodies (see https://www.grid5000.fr).

7. REFERENCES

[1] BonnMotion, A mobility scenario generation and analysis tool. URL `http://net.cs.uni-bonn.de/wg/cs/applications/bonnmotion/`

[2] Lee Breslau, Pei Cue, Pei Cao, Li Fan, Graham Phillips, Scott Shenker. Web Caching and Zipf-like Distributions: Evidence and Implications.In *Infocom.* March 1999.

[3] *Project CCNx.* URL `http://ccnx.org/`.

[4] Kevin Fall. A Delay-Tolerant Network Architecture for Challenged Internets. In *ACM Sigcomm.* August 2003.

[5] Christine Fricker, Philippe Robert, James Roberts, Nada Sbihi. Impact of Traffic Mix on Caching Performance in a Content-Centric Network. *Technical report, 1202.0108v1 INRIA.* February 2012.

[6] Thomas R. Henderson, Mathieu Lacage, George F. Riley. Network Simulations with the ns-3 Simulator. In *ACM Sigcomm (demo session).* August 2008.

[7] Liang Hu, Jean-Yves Le Boudec, and Milan Vojnovic. Optimal channel choice for collaborative ad-hoc dissemination. In *IEEE Infocom.* 2010.

[8] Stratis Ioannidis, Laurent Massoulie, Augustin Chaintreau. Distributed caching over heterogeneous mobile networks. In *ACM Sigmetrics.* 2010.

[9] Van Jacobson, Diana K. Smetters, James D. Thornton, Michael F. Plass, Nicholas H. Briggs, Rebecca L. Braynard. Networking Named Content. In *ACM CoNEXT.* December 2009.

[10] Sushant Jain, Kevin Fall, Rabin Patra. Routing in Delay Tolerant Network. In *ACM Sigcomm.* August 2004.

[11] Thomas Karagiannis, Jean-Yves Le Boudec EPFL, Milan Vojnovic. Power law and exponential decay of inter contact times between mobile devices. In *ACM Mobicom.* New York 2007.

[12] Timothy Keller, Ingram Olkin. Combining Correlated Unbiased Estimators of the Mean of a Normal Distribution. *Technical report, Stanford.* 2002.

[13] Amir Krifa, Chadi Barakat, Thrasyvoulos Spyropoulos. Message Drop and Scheduling in DTNs: Theory and Practice. in *IEEE Transactions on Mobile Computing,* vol. 11, no. 9, 2012.

[14] Amir Krifa, Chadi Barakat, Thrasyvoulos Spyropoulos. Optimal Buffer Management Policies for Delay Tolerant Networks. In *IEEE SECON.* June 2008.

[15] Amir Krifa, Chadi Barakat, Thrasyvoulos Spyropoulos. MobiTrade: Trading Content in Disruption Tolerant Networks. In *ACM Chants.* September 2011.

[16] M. Lacage. Outils d'expérimentation pour la recherche en réseaux. *Ph.D. thesis, Université de Nice Sophia-Antipolis.* 2010.

[17] Kyunghan Lee, Seongik Hong, Seong Joon Kim, Injong Rhee, Song Chong. SLAW: Self-Similar Least-Action Human Walk. In *IEEE/ACM Transactions on Networking.* July 2011.

[18] Anders Lindgren, Avri Doria, Olov Schelén. Probabilistic routing in intermittently connected networks. In *ACM Sigmobile.* July 2003.

[19] Anirban Mahanti, Carey Williamson, Derek Eager. Traffic analysis of a web proxy caching hierarchy. In *IEEE Network,* Vol. 14, June 2000.

[20] Joshua Reich, Augustin Chaintreau. The age of impatience: optimal replication schemes for opportunistic networks. In *ACM Conext.* 2009.

[21] Giuseppe Sollazzo, Mirco Musolesi, Cecilia Mascolo. TACO-DTN: a time-aware content-based dissemination system for delay tolerant networks. In *MobiOpp Workshop.* 2007.

[22] Amin Vahdat, David Becker. Epidemic Routing for Partially-Connected Ad Hoc Networks. *Technical report, CS-200006.* April 2000.

[23] Athanasios V. Vasilakos, Yan Zhang, Thrasyvoulos Spyropoulos. Delay Tolerant Networks Protocols and Applications. *CRC Press.* 2012.

[24] Xiaolan Zhang, Giovanni Neglia, Jim Kurose, Don Towsley. Performance modelling of epidemic routing. In *IFIP Networking.* May 2006.

[25] Xuejun Zhuo, Qinghua Li, Guohong Cao, Yiqi Dai, Boleslaw Szymanski, Tom La Porta. Social-Based Cooperative Caching in DTNs: A Contact Duration Aware Approach. In *IEEE MASS.* 2011.

Efficient Relay Deployment for Controlling Connectivity in Delay Tolerant Mobile Networks

Zhiyu Wang, Mario A. Nascimento and Mike H. MacGregor
Department of Computing Sciences, University of Alberta
Edmonton, Alberta, Canada
zhiyu1@cs.ualberta.ca, mn@cs.ualberta.ca, macg@cs.ualberta.ca

ABSTRACT

In mobile networks, node movements may lead to a situation called network partition where an end-to-end path may never exist because the network is divided into several isolated subnetworks. Deploying stationary relays introduces new transmission opportunities leading to the improvement of network connectivity and performance. The majority of the proposed solutions concentrated on deploying the minimum number of relays in the network. However, relay deployment should also be resilient regarding relay node failures. In this paper, we show how the relay deployment problem can be modelled as a k-element connectivity problem in which multiple relay-disjoint paths are deployed to connect isolated subnetworks. To solve this problem, we present three heuristic algorithms targeting at finding the minimum number of relays to form k-element connected networks. Our experiments using synthetic and real data showed that the proposed greedy algorithm is 2 or 3 orders of magnitude faster and never worse than the other two algorithms.

Categories and Subject Descriptors

B.8 [**Performance and reliability**]: Reliability, Testing, and Fault-Tolerance

Keywords

mobile networks; relay deployment; connectivity

1. INTRODUCTION

In Delay Tolerant Mobile Networks (DTMNs), communications depend on finding a set of sequential opportunistic encounters between pairs of mobile nodes in a store-and-forward fashion. However, it is possible that the network is partitioned into isolated subnetworks, *i.e.*, there is no path between mobile nodes from unconnected subnetworks. Hence messages that must travel between disconnected subnetworks cannot be delivered.

To connect isolated subnetworks, additional encounter opportunities are required to deliver messages across different subnetworks. In general, there are two approaches to address the problem: (1) message ferrying and (2) deploying stationary relays. Message ferrying aims to provide extra encounter opportunities by having dedicated ferries or regular nodes acting as ferries to carry and forward messages between regular nodes in permanently partitioned environments. Deploying relays adds additional nodes into the network that serve as buffers for nodes that encounter the same relays at different times. Having dedicated ferries or using existing nodes as ferries by changing their original movements can be expensive and infeasible in some applications. For example, in military applications expensive unmanned aerial vehicles (UAVs) can be deployed as ferries. However, in civilian applications such as in vehicular ad hoc networks such a dedicated ferry deployment is infeasible. Even though taxis may change their trajectories to improve network connectivity, additional charges may apply causing high cost of using the ferries. Therefore, we focus on the relay deployment problem.

When the network is disconnected, there is no direct encounter between mobile nodes from different isolated subnetworks. However, it is possible that mobile nodes from different subnetworks visit the same locations but at different times. For example, in the university people from different departments rarely physically encounter each other, but they frequently meet people from the same department. Most of the time different groups of people are disconnected from each other. It would be very difficult to deliver a message through people from one department to the other. However, there are locations that both groups of people may visit, *e.g.*, cafeteria during lunch time and subway/bus stations during commute time. By setting up message boards at these locations, people from one department can write message on the boards, and people from another department can read the message when they visit the locations of the message boards. In this example people can be treated as mobile nodes whereas message boards serve as relays in the network. In disconnected environments, effectively deploying relays can help increase encounter opportunities leading to the improvement of network connectivity and performance.

In relay deployment, relay failure may pose significant degradation to the performance of the whole network. If a relay is critical to join disconnected subnetworks, its failure will disconnect the whole network. Therefore, instead of only deploying the minimum number of relays in the network simply to reduce delivery delay for example, the route diversity in the network is also very important to improve routing robustness so that the network is more resilient to relay node failures. In our study, *route diversity* is defined as the existence of multiple disjoint paths for routing between mobile nodes in the network.

Our study in this paper has the following contributions: (1) we show how to model the relay deployment problem as a k-element connectivity problem where the minimum number of relays is deployed to guarantee route diversity in the network where k relay-disjoint paths exist between mobile nodes, and (2) we present three heuristic algorithms, an iterative algorithm, a greedy algorithm and a shortest-path based algorithm, to solve the relay deployment problem. Our experiments using synthetic and real data showed that the proposed greedy algorithm is 2 or 3 orders of magnitude faster and never worse than the other two algorithms.

The remainder of this paper is organized as follows. An overview of relay deployment is discussed in Section 2. Section 3 presents the formal problem statement and approaches to solve the problem. To examine the performance of proposed algorithms and deployment solutions, experimental results that use synthetic data and real mobility traces are discussed in Section 4. Finally, conclusions and future work are given in Section 5.

2. RELATED WORK

There are mainly two approaches to join disconnected subnetworks: message ferrying and deploying relays. Message ferries act as mobile relays that travel between disconnected nodes whereas stationary relays buffer messages for mobile nodes who visit the same places at different times.

In DTMNs, previous studies have shown the impact of adding relays to the network with respect to increasing connectivity (delivery ratio) and decreasing average delivery delay [15, 6, 7, 2, 14]. A study also considered the use of different infrastructure deployment approaches [2]. In that study, the authors investigated the trade-offs of three different infrastructure deployment: relays, base stations and meshes. The authors showed that with the ease and cost of deployment, a mesh network or disconnected relays is a better choice compared to deploying base stations in many scenarios. However, to achieve similar performance in a network with base stations, it requires 2 times the number of mesh nodes or 5 times the number of relay nodes.

In [15], the authors proposed deploying throw-boxes (relays) to impose additional encounter opportunities to enhance message delivery ratio. In their analyses, different deployment approaches are considered based on the availability of contact histories and/or traffic demands of mobile nodes in the network. Pereira *et al.* presented different challenges in Vehicular Delay Tolerant Networks (VDTNs), a special network of DTMNs [13]. To address the routing problem in VDTNs, they focused on the optimal deployment of relay nodes. The authors argued that finding the smallest Connected Dominating Set is a feasible solution to their problem. Because the complexity of finding an optimal deployment in general is a NP-hard problem, two greedy-based heuristic algorithms were proposed to minimize (1) the average hop count and (2) the average message delivery time with the deployment of relays [6, 7].

The previous solutions mainly aimed to increase delivery ratio and reduce delivery delay without considering route diversity in the network. Because mobile networks can be very dynamic, if relays that are used to join disconnected subnetworks fail, the whole network would fall apart and become disconnected again. Therefore, increasing route diversity is also very important with respect to relay deployment, and that is the very focus of our work.

3. RELAY DEPLOYMENT PROBLEM

To connect partitioned subnetworks, our objective is to deploy the minimum number of relays in the network while maintaining route diversity, *i.e.*, disjoint paths in the network. We propose to use the k-connectivity problem paradigm to model the relay deployment problem.

3.1 k-connectivity problems

In the network, metrics such as throughput, reachability, reliable transportation, fault-tolerance and load balancing can be modelled as or related to k-connectivity problems. Targeting at relay failure, we concentrate on the k*-element connectivity problem.* In this problem, vertices in a graph are partitioned into two categories: terminals and non-terminals (or elements). A graph is said to be k-element connected if and only if there does not exist a set of k-1 *elements* whose removal disconnects the graph. In other words, there are k element-disjoint paths connecting every pair of terminals; and these paths are allowed to share terminals.

For a given k, finding an optimal sub-graph for the k-connectivity problem is NP-hard [9]. Although finding an optimal sub-graph with k-connectivity is NP-hard, finding the maximum k-connectivity in a graph or checking whether a graph is k-connected can be solved in polynomial time using max-flow algorithms based on Menger's theorem [12]. Max-flow algorithms such as Ford-Fulkerson algorithm [10] and Edmonds-Karp algorithm [5] can be used to find element-disjoint paths in the network. A max-flow algorithm actually computes the maximum number of element-disjoint paths for a given source and destination. As a result, the maximum k of the input graph equals the minimum max-flow over all node pairs.

3.2 The problem statement

Disconnected networks are composed of isolated subnetworks. In this study, we assume mobile nodes within subnetworks are strongly internally connected and do not fail. Thus, we can use a single vertex to represent each isolated subnetwork where each vertex captures the semantic of a strongly internally connected subnetwork with underlying mobile nodes. Because subnetworks are disconnected, their representative vertices are also disconnected. In other words, there is no path between any pair of representative vertices. The problem now is to deploy the minimum number of relays to connect those vertices such that the failure of relays does not disconnect the network. As we discussed before, this problem can be modelled as a k-element connectivity problem where vertices representing subnetworks are terminals, and vertices representing relays are elements in the graph.

An example of building an input graph to our problem is presented in Figure 1. As shown in Figure 1 (a), the network is composed of three isolated subnetworks represented by three terminals (T_1, T_2 and T_3). In order to connect those subnetworks, three candidate relays (R_1, R_2 and R_3)can be deployed as shown in Figure 1 (b). By treating each subnetwork as a single vertex, *i.e.*, a terminal in the graph, we obtain an input graph to the relay deployment problem in

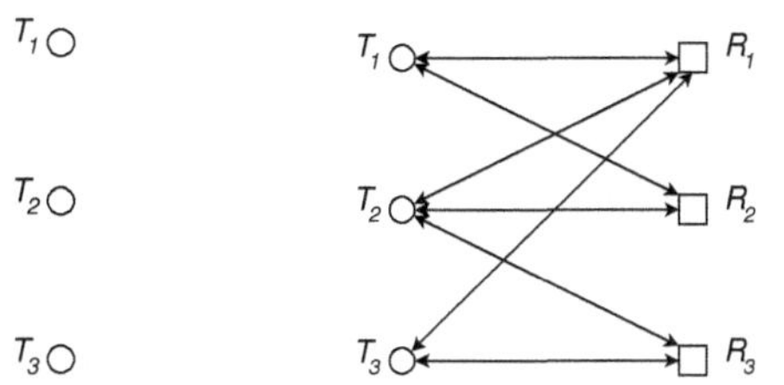

(a) A disconnected network with three isolated subnetworks

(b) A connected network with the presence of relays

Figure 1: A sample scenario to the k-element connectivity problem

Figure 1 (b). To create an unconnected infrastructure by deploying stationary relays, we assume there is no interaction between relays, *i.e.*, no edge connecting relays in the graph. As a result, the graph is a bipartite graph where terminals and relays are two disjoint sets, and no two vertices within the same set are connected. In this example, the minimum deployment to build a 1-element connected sub-graph connecting all terminals is using relay R_1. Similarly, the minimum deployment to build a 2-element connected sub-graph connecting all terminals is using all three relays because the failure of one relay will not disconnect the network.

Given an input bipartite graph whose vertices are divided into two disjoint sets terminals T and relays R such that every edge, in E, connect a vertex in T to one in R, we define the relay deployment problem as follows.

Definition 1. Given an integer k and a bipartite graph $G = (T, R, E)$, *the relay deployment problem* is to find the minimum k-element connected sub-graph of G. In other words, our objective is to find the minimum number of relays such that every pair of terminals in the sub-graph has k relay-disjoint paths.

It is clear that the relay deployment problem above is just the minimum-cost k-element connectivity problem in a special graph class. To solve this problem, approximation algorithms based on a linear programming relaxation of the problem have been proposed [8]. They can be solved by the ellipsoid algorithm [11]. However, the ellipsoid algorithm is relatively computationally expensive. In the section, we present heuristic algorithms to solve the relay deployment problem.

3.3 Heuristic algorithms

In this section, we introduce three heuristic algorithms, an iterative algorithm, a greedy algorithm and a shortest-path based algorithm.

3.3.1 Iterative Algorithm

As we described before, given an integer k, a max-flow algorithm can be used to check whether a graph is k-element connected in polynomial time. Taking advantage of this approach, we present an iterative algorithm that checks the k-element connectivity every time a relay node is inserted into the graph. Initially, the sub-graph only contains terminals. The algorithm iteratively adds relays into the sub-graph and checks its connectivity. There are two phases in this algorithm: (1) the algorithm sorts the relays according to the number of terminals they connect and then gradually expands the graph by iteratively inserting relays that connect to the most terminals first into the sub-graph in the decreasing order, (2) once the sub-graph is k-element connected, the algorithm prunes the relays that have been selected in the reverse order. The objective is to remove redundant relays in the sub-graph.

Because checking whether a graph is k-element connected can be solved using a max-flow algorithm *i.e.*, Edmonds-Karp algorithm, the complexity of this algorithm is dominated by the underlying max-flow algorithm and the number of relays being inserted.

3.3.2 Greedy algorithm

The input graph to our problem is bipartite graph. It is easy to see that an input bipartite graph can be viewed as an instance of the set cover problem. The objective is then to find a minimum subset of relays which cover all terminals. However, the relay deployment problem is not equivalent to the set cover problem. Let us look at an example presented in Figure 2. The universe includes four terminals where $U = \{T_1, T_2, T_3, T_4\}$, and there are three sets $S = \{R_1, R_2, R_3\}$. We assume that R_1 covers terminals $\{T_1, T_2\}$, R_2 covers terminals $\{T_2, T_3\}$, and R_3 covers terminals $\{T_3, T_4\}$. As shown in Figure 2 (a), it is clear that the set $\{R_1, R_3\}$ is the minimum subset that contains all terminals. However, simply adopting the solution from the set cover problem does not solve the relay deployment problem. For example, as shown in Figure 2 (b), deploying relays R_1 and R_3 does not connect the whole graph because sub-graphs $\{T_1, R_1, T_2\}$ and $\{T_3, R_2, T_4\}$ are still disconnected. To connect the whole graph, relay R_2 is also required.

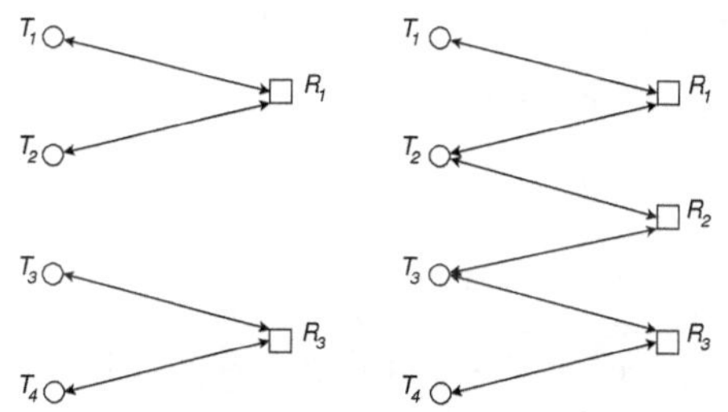

(a) A solution for the set covering problem

(b) A solution to build a 1-element connected sub-graph

Figure 2: The difference between the set covering problem and the relay deployment problem

In spite of the difference above, we develop a greedy algorithm inspired by the greedy algorithm for the set cover problem [3]. The pseudo-code of the algorithm is presented in Algorithm 1. The idea is simple, our greedy algorithm gradually builds a k-element connected sub-graph by always building a (k-1)-element connected graph first. To be specific, the algorithm constructs the k-element connected sub-graph by greedily connecting terminals with a degree of k-1 in the (k-1)-element connected sub-graph.

The idea is materialized in Algorithm 1. When i equals 1, set U contains all terminals because their degrees are less than i. To cover all terminals in U, the *greedy covering* function is called at line 14. The greedy covering function first chooses a relay containing the most uncovered terminals.

Algorithm 1 Greedy algorithm to find relays to build k-element connected graph($G = (T, R, E), k$)

1: **if** G is not k-element connected **then**
2:     **return null**
3: **end if**
4: $G' \leftarrow T$ //initialize a graph only with terminals
5: $U \leftarrow \emptyset$ //U contains terminals with a degree less than i
6: $C \leftarrow \emptyset$ //C contains a set of selected relays
7: $i \leftarrow 1$ //counter
8: **while** $i \leq k$ **do**
9:     **for** each terminal $t \in T$ **do**
10:         **if** degree(t)$< i$ **then**
11:             $U \leftarrow U \cup t$
12:         **end if**
13:     **end for**
14:     $C \leftarrow$ calling greedyCovering(U,G',G) function
15:     **if** $C \neq \emptyset$ **then**
16:         $G' \leftarrow G' \cup C$
17:         $U \leftarrow \emptyset$
18:     **else if** $C == \emptyset$ **then**
19:         //no solution is returned by greedy covering
20:         $C \leftarrow$ use the iterative algorithm to find the rest of relays to build k-element connected sub-graph
21:         $G' \leftarrow G' \cup C$
22:         **return** G'
23:     **end if**
24:     $i++$
25: **end while**
26: **return** G'
27:
28: **function** greedyCovering (U,G',G)
29:     $C \leftarrow U$ //initialize a graph only with terminals
30:     $S \leftarrow \emptyset$ //terminals that have been covered
31:     select a relay $r \in G$ and $r \notin G'$ that covers the most uncovered terminals in U
32:         $S \leftarrow S \cup S_r$ //S_r are the terminals covered by r
33:         $C \leftarrow C \cup r$
34:         $U \leftarrow U \setminus S_r$
35:     **while** $U \neq \emptyset$ **do**
36:         select a relay $r \in G$, $r \notin G'$ and $r \notin C$ such that it covers the most uncovered terminals in U and $S_r \cap S \neq \emptyset$
37:             $S \leftarrow S \cup S_r$
38:             $C \leftarrow C \cup r$
39:             $U \leftarrow U \setminus S_r$
40:     **end while**
41:     **return** C
42: **end function**

After selecting the first relay, the greedy covering function chooses the second relay that covers the most uncovered terminals left in U. Meanwhile, the second relay must cover at least one terminal that has already been covered because we want to build a connected network and avoid scenarios presented in Figure 2 (a). The process of selecting the second relay repeats until all terminals are covered. By doing this, the greedy covering function guarantees that terminals in U are connected. It is not hard to see that the greedy covering builds a 1-element connected sub-graph to connect all terminals in set U. As i increases, the sub-graph returned by our greedy algorithm always connects terminals whose degree is less than i. The greedy covering function is applied to connect those terminals until i equals k. When i is equal to k, the returned sub-graph is k-element connected.

Let us look at the if-statement at lines 18 to 24 in Algorithm 1 where the greedy covering function fails to return a feasible covering. Because greedy covering is used to find relays covering terminals with a degree less than the current connectivity i where $i \leq k$, if no relay can be used to connect those specific terminals, greedy covering fails to find a feasible solution, and thus the iterative algorithm in Section 3.3.1 is called to finish searching for relays.

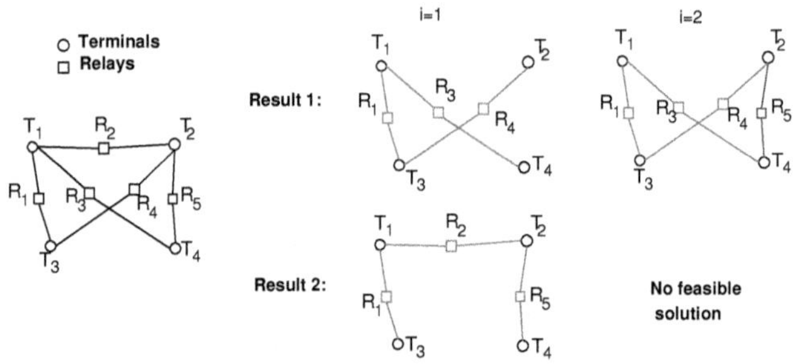

Figure 3: An example of failure of the set covering

An example to illustrate the failure is presented in Figure 3. In this example, it is trivial to see that the graph on the left side is 2-element connected. To find a 2-element connected sub-graph, the greedy algorithm first builds a 1-element connected sub-graph. When i equals 1, both results 1 and 2 are valid 1-element connected sub-graphs that can be returned by greedy covering. When i is increased to 2, in result 1 the greedy algorithm will select R_5 to connect terminals T_2 and T_4 because their degree is less than 2 when $i = 1$. As a result, the sub-graph is 2-element connected. However, in result 2 no such a relay can be found to connect terminals T_3 and T_4. Therefore, greedy covering fails to return a feasible solution. Thus, the greedy algorithm calls the iterative algorithm to find relays on top of the ones that have already been selected to build a 2-element connected sub-graph. In this example, all five relays will be selected. Both the sub-graphs returned in results 1 and 2 are valid, the greedy algorithm has equal probability of choosing either one. If the greedy algorithm returns result 2, it would be more computationally expensive to find a feasible solution. In addition, the sub-graph returned by calling the iterative algorithm will contain more relays compared to the number of returned relays in result 1.

We now prove the correctness of our greedy algorithm. In the cases where greedy covering fails to deliver a solution, the iterative algorithm is called to find a result. It is obvious that the iterative algorithm is correct. Therefore, the theorem focuses on the cases where the greedy algorithm does return a k-element connected sub-graph.

THEOREM 1. *Given an integer k and a bipartite graph $G = (T, R, E)$, the greedy algorithm returns a k-element connected sub-graph.*

PROOF. The greedy algorithm gradually builds a sub-graph towards k-element connectivity. We let the set of relays being added at state i be R^i in this proof where $1 \leq i \leq k$.

When i equals 1, it is clear that the greedy algorithm builds a 1-element connected sub-graph using a set of relays R^1.

When i equals 2, the greedy algorithm adds a set of relays, R^2, into the sub-graph to connect the terminals with a degree 1 in the 1-element connected sub-graph. As a result, the resulting sub-graph is still connected if a relay $r \in R^1$ is removed. This is because the sub-graph is connected by relays in R^2. Similarly, if a relay $r \in R^2$ is removed, the sub-graph is also connected by relays in R^1 because the sub-graph is 1-element connected when i equals 1. In the resulting sub-graph, because there are two independent sets of relays connecting the sub-graph, removing one relay from two independent sets does not disconnect the sub-graph. Therefore, the sub-graph generated is 2-element connected.

The same analyses apply as i increases. Therefore, we conclude that our greedy algorithm returns a k-element connected sub-graph. □

If greedy covering in the proposed greedy algorithm returns feasible solutions, the complexity of the algorithm is bounded by the complexity of the greedy algorithm from the set cover problem, otherwise it is dominated by the complexity of the iterative algorithm.

3.3.3 Shortest path Heuristic Algorithm

To deploy the minimum number of relays in a disconnected network, we can also find the relay-disjoint paths with the minimum total weight in the corresponding graph if a unit weight is assigned to vertices whereas edges have a zero weight. To find relay-disjoint paths with the minimum total weight, we use a shortest-path based heuristic algorithm to find a k-element connected sub-graph.

Initially, every vertex in the input graph has a unit weight, and edges have a zero weight. For each pair of terminals, the idea is to run a shortest path algorithm to find k relay-disjoint paths. The weight of relays that are selected by previous terminal pairs is set to zero in the graph. Changing their weights to zero is to mimic that the relays have been deployed for previous terminal pairs; therefore, it is free to reuse those deployed relays for the rest of terminal pairs to find their relay-disjoint paths since we want to minimize the number of relays being deployed towards a k-element connected sub-graph containing all terminal pairs.

The complexity of the shortest-path based algorithm is bounded by the running time of a shortest path algorithm and the total number of terminals in the graph.

4. EXPERIMENTS

In this section, we present experiments to evaluate the performance of the proposed heuristic algorithms. First, we conduct a set of experiments using real mobility traces. Because the instances derived from real mobility traces are relatively small, we also evaluate the three heuristic algorithms against synthetic data containing large instances.

4.1 Experiments using networks derived from real mobility traces

In trajectory-based traces, there exist a large number of candidate positions where relays can be set up. In order to reduce the search space, previous studies made different assumptions such as dividing the entire area into a grid of cells where relays are placed at the center of those cells [15]. However, making such assumptions may impact the results of the relay deployment problem. In this section, we concentrate on AP-based traces. In this type of mobility trace, we consider each AP as a candidate relay.

In the experiments, we focus on four real mobility traces: (1) the Dartmouth traces[1], (2) the MIT Reality traces [4], (3) the MIT corporate WLAN traces [1], (4) USC Summer and spring traces[2]. By examining those mobility traces over their entire durations, we found that the derived networks are connected as a single component. In order to have disconnected networks, we reduce the examined duration of each type of trace. Based on preliminary results, we found that a random period of consecutive 14 days is a reasonable duration where disconnected subnetworks can be connected by relays. In addition to reducing the duration of the examined traces, we propose a constraint, d, on the degree of the vertices in a graph. In a graph, some vertices may be loosely connected to the rest of the graph, *i.e.*, with a degree equal to one. If we set the constraint $d = 2$, the vertices with a unit degree will become disconnected from other vertices. As a result, the graph will become disconnected. Using the degree constraint, we are able to derive disconnected networks from real mobility traces. Because the results of all five traces are qualitatively similar to each other, we concentrate on the Dartmouth College traces in this section.

Table 1: Relay deployment in the Dartmouth college traces

(a) Dartmouth traces

	$d=2$	$d=3$	$d=4$
n	14	20	30
m	482	485	497
p	24.7%	18.2%	15.8%
k	3	2	2

(b) Relays for Dartmouth traces

Algorithm	# of returned relays		
	$d=2$	$d=3$	$d=4$
greedy	8	12	14
iterative	8	12	15
shortestPath	28	41	66

Table 1 presents the results regarding the Dartmouth College traces. By varying the degree constraint d from 2 to 4 in Table 1 (a) , four characteristics that control the complexity of the network have been measured in the generated networks:

1. n: the number of disconnected subnetworks, *i.e.*, the number of terminals in the graph.
2. m: the number of candidate relays that connect to at least two terminals.
3. p: the percentage of coverage. It measures the percentage of terminals in average that each candidate relay connects.
4. k: the maximum element connectivity in the graph.

For example, when d equals 2, the generated network contains 14 terminals, 482 candidate relays where each relay in the network connects to 24.7% of the terminals in average,

[1]Downloaded from crawdad.cs.dartmouth.edu/dartmouth/campus
[2]Downloaded from crawdad.cs.dartmouth.edu/usc/mobilib

and the maximum element connectivity in the network is equal to 3.

As the degree constraint d increases, both n and m increase. It is trivial that the number of disconnected subnetworks increases because more nodes are partitioned as d increases. In addition, the number of candidate relays increases because of more terminals in the network, and p decreases because the increasing number of terminals impacts the average coverage. Lastly, the element connectivity decreases because candidate relays may not cover all terminals as the number of terminals increases in order to be k-element connected.

Let us look at the results returned by our heuristic algorithms in Table 1 (b). Because the minimum element connectivity equals 2 among three different values of d in the last row of Table 1 (a), for a fair comparison, we set k to be 2, *i.e.*, building 2-element connected networks, to obtain the results in Table 1 (b). On one hand, the greedy and iterative algorithms return the same number of relays to connect disconnected subnetworks except when the degree constraint equals 4. One note here is that even though the number of returned relays from both algorithms are identical, the actual candidates may not be the same. On the other hand, the shortest-path based algorithm returns more relays compared to the ones returned by the other two algorithms.

There are three observations from the results:

1. The number of returned relays increases for all three algorithms as the number of terminals n increases. This is because as n increases, more relays need to be deployed in order to connect all terminals.
2. The greedy algorithm returns the smallest number of relays whereas the iterative algorithm returns identical or similar results. However, the shortest-path based algorithm returns the highest number of relays to form 2-element connected sub-graphs. This could be caused by the differences in our heuristic algorithms. In the greedy algorithm, the relays connecting the most uncovered terminals are always selected first whereas in the iterative algorithm, relays are selected in the descending order based on the number of terminals that they connect. Furthermore, the pruning process in the iterative algorithm eliminates the redundant relays to reduce the number of returned relays. The greedy covering and greedy selection in the greedy and iterative algorithms help to reduce the number of returned relays. However, in the shortest-path based algorithm, terminal pairs may have completely different sets of shortest relay-disjoint paths. As a result, relays being selected may not be reused by other terminal pairs leading to a large number of returned relays.
3. The difference between the numbers of relays returned by the shortest-path based algorithm and the number returned by the greedy/iterative algorithm increases as the degree constraint increases. For example, the difference between the number of relays returned by the shortest-path based algorithm and the iterative algorithm equals to 20 (28-8) when $d = 2$, 29 (41-12) when $d = 3$ and 51 (66-15) when $d = 4$. The cause could be the increase of n and/or the decrease of p. Because in the shortest-path based algorithm terminal pairs may have completely different sets of shortest relay-disjoint paths, the increase in n introduces more relays to form relay-disjoint paths between terminal pairs. In addition, as the coverage p decreases, relays in average connect to fewer terminals. It also reduces the probability of finding the relays that can be reused by multiple terminal pairs.

Because the network instances being examined in the real mobility traces are relatively small, we conduct experiments against synthetic data containing large network instances in the next section.

4.2 Experiments using synthetic networks

In this section we use synthetic networks to understand the performance of different heuristic algorithms. By constructing synthetic networks, we can control the characteristics of synthetic networks such as the number of candidate relays and the percentage of coverage.

We use three control variables to create synthetic networks:

1. n controls the number of terminals in a network.
2. m defines the number of relays in a network.
3. p is used to control the percentage of terminals covered by relays in average. For example, if p equals 5%, it means that each relay in the network randomly connects to 5% of the terminals in average. Given a fixed p, we assume that the percentage of coverage from candidate relays in the network follows a normal distribution. This variable mainly controls the overall connectivity in a network.

Two metrics are examined in our experiments: (1) the number of returned relays and (2) the running time. The number of returned relays indicates how good each heuristic algorithm is whereas the running time measures the efficiency of each algorithm.

In the following experiments, 100 random networks are generated for each combination of these three variables. We first set $k = 3$ by default in each combination of the three variables, and then vary k to examine heuristic algorithms in networks with different k connectivity.

4.2.1 *Varying* n

In Figure 4, we vary n while keeping the other three variables fixed. As the number of terminals increases, the number of relays required to connect those terminals increases as well. This explains the increases of the number of selected relays for all three heuristic algorithms. Among the three heuristic algorithms, the greedy and iterative algorithms return the smallest number of relays. This is because the greedy algorithm always selects the relays covering the most uncovered terminals first whereas the iterative algorithm always chooses the relays connecting to the most number of terminals first. The number of relays returned by the greedy algorithm at different n is slightly less than the one returned by the iterative algorithm; however, it may be difficult to recognize the difference in the figure. The shortest-path based algorithm returns the highest numbers of relays. In the shortest-path based algorithm, even though we set the weight of selected relays to be zero to reuse them, there could be so many relays that can be used to form the shortest relay-disjoint paths between terminal pairs that the ones can be reused by other terminal pairs may not be selected at all. This explains why the shortest-path based algorithm returns the largest number of relays.

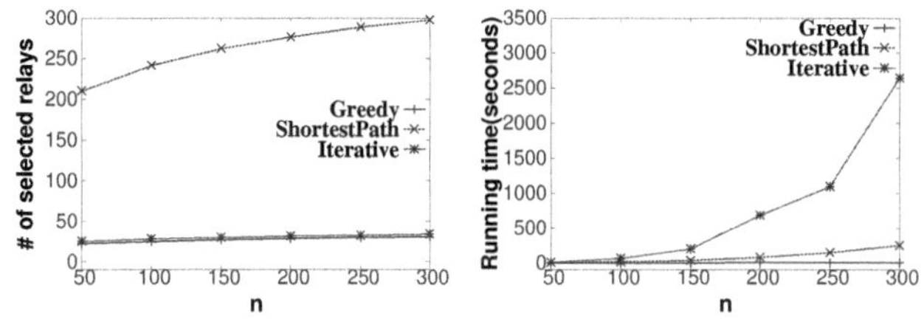

(a) The number of result relays (b) Running time

Figure 4: Varying n while $m = 400$, p =20% and $k = 3$

Regarding the running time, all three algorithms use more time to find the results as the number of terminals increases. The greedy algorithm takes the smallest amount of time because of adopting the greedy algorithm from the set cover problem. The iterative algorithm uses a significant amount of time to find a solution because it needs to check k-element connectivity at every insertion of a relay. The running time of the iterative algorithm increases as the number of terminals increases. This is because the iterative algorithm needs to include more relays as the network size increases. The running time of the shortest-path based algorithm increases because the number of times that the underlying shortest path algorithm needs to be run increases as the number of terminals n increases in the network.

4.2.2 *Varying* m

In Figure 5, we examine the three heuristic algorithms by varying m. Given a fixed p, we assumed the percentage of coverage from candidate relays follows a normal distribution. As the number of candidate relays increases in the network, even though p is fixed, the absolute number of relays with a high percentage of coverage increases. Because the absolute number of candidate relays with a high percentage of coverage increases, both the greedy and iterative algorithms demand fewer relays to connect a fixed number of terminals. As a result, there is a slight decrease in the results of both algorithms with respect to the number of selected relays. Similar to our discussion for Figure 4, as the number of candidate relays increases in the network, more relays can be used to form the shortest relay-disjoint paths between different pairs of terminals so that the ones can be reused by other terminal pairs may not be selected by the shortest-path based algorithm. This causes the increase in the number of selected relays, and it also explains the reason that the shortest-path based algorithm still returns the largest number of relays.

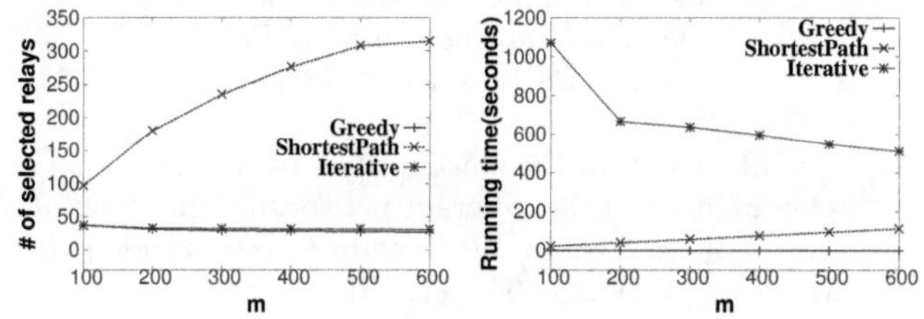

(a) The number of result relays (b) Running time

Figure 5: Varying m while $n = 200$, p =20% and $k = 3$

By selecting fewer relays, the running time of both the greedy and iterative algorithms decreases because their greedy approaches only need to examine fewer relays. However, the increase of the network size due to the increase of m leads to the increase in the running time of the shortest-path based algorithm. This is because the underlying shortest path algorithm takes longer time to find solutions in large networks.

4.2.3 *Varying* p

In Figure 6, we test the effect of varying the percentage of coverage p. As the average coverage increases, candidate relays now connect to more terminals. As a result, fewer relays are required to form a 3-element connected sub-graph. This explains that all three algorithm return fewer relays as p increases in Figure 6 (a). In the figure, the number of relays returned by the shortest-path algorithm decreases very quickly. This is because the number of feasible solutions to build an optimal/sub-optimal 3-element connected subgraph increases leading to a high probability of selecting reusable relays by the shortest-path based algorithm.

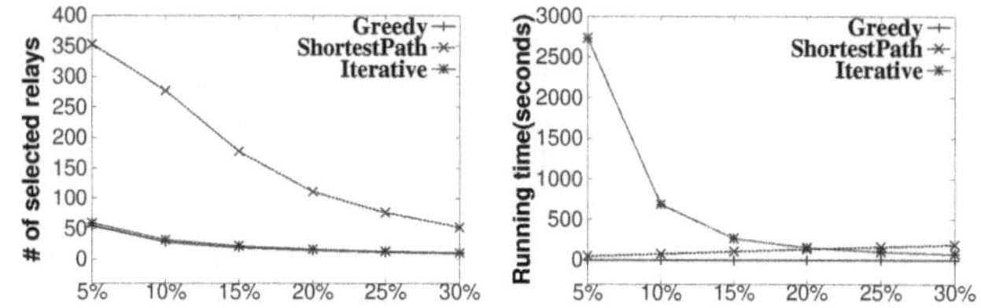

(a) The number of result relays (b) Running time

Figure 6: Varying p while $n = 200$, $m = 400$ and $k = 3$

As p increases, the resulting networks become dense. As a result, the shortest-path based algorithm takes longer time to find relay-disjoint paths. With respect to the greedy and iterative algorithm, both their running time decrease as the percentage of coverage increases because fewer relays are required to form 3-element connected sub-graphs. The running time of the iterative algorithm is lower than that of the shortest-path based algorithm once p is greater than 20%. As p increases, in Figure 6 (a), the iterative algorithm returns fewer relays. For example, only approximately 10 relays in average are returned by the iterative algorithm to form 3-element connected sub-graphs when p equals 30%. Therefore, the number of times to checking the k-connectivity of sub-graph decreases because fewer relays are required; however, the shortest-path based algorithm needs to find k relay-disjoint paths for every pair of terminals no matter what the value of p is. When p is large enough and the network is dense enough, the iterative algorithm takes less time than the shortest-path based algorithm.

4.2.4 *Varying* k

When we set $n = 200$, $m = 400$ and p =20%, the maximum connectivity of the generated synthetic networks can be equal to 7. Figure 7 presents the results regarding the performance of the three heuristic algorithms in networks with different connectivity. As k increases, more relays are required in order to form a k-element connected network. This explains the increase in the number of selected relays in Figure 7 (a) for all three heuristic algorithms. However, because the shortest-path based algorithm may not select the reusable relays, the number of returned relays is significantly higher than the numbers returned by the other two algorithms in the networks with different connectivity.

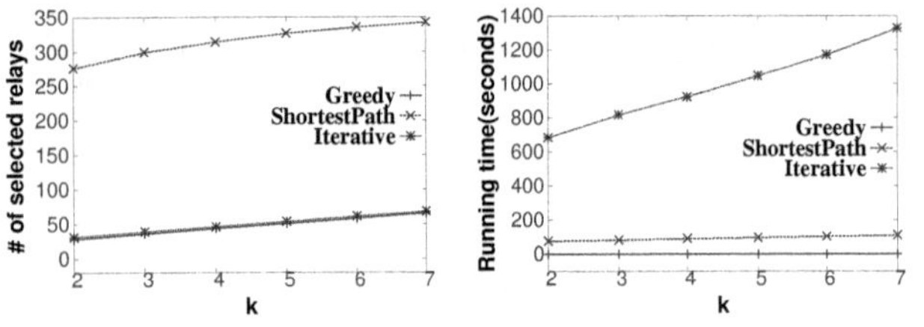

(a) The number of result relays (b) Running time

Figure 7: Varying k while n = 200, m = 400 and p =20%

In Figure 7 (b), the running time of all three algorithms increase as the value of k increases because they need to use more relays to build k-connected networks. The running time of the iterative algorithm is significantly higher than that of the other two algorithms because checking whether a sub-graph is k-element connected after each insertion of a relay is very expensive. Because more relays are required when k increases, the number of times that the iterative algorithm checks k-connectivity in the sub-graph increases.

In summary, our experimental results against synthetic networks have confirmed our observations from using the real mobility trace. We found that the greedy algorithm has the best performance in both synthetic and real data regarding both the running time and the number of selected relays. Without checking the k-connectivity of the subgraph, the greedy algorithm is very efficient and effective in terms of finding solutions for the relay deployment problem. The iterative algorithm has competitive results compared to the greedy algorithm. Greedily selecting the next relays which connect the most terminals and pruning redundant relays help to reduce the total number of returned relays. However, the iterative algorithm takes the longest time to find solutions among the three algorithms because iteratively checking k-connectivity at every insertion of a relay is time-consuming. With respect to the shortest-path based algorithm, even though running a shortest path algorithm to find relay-disjoint paths for terminal pairs is relatively fast, the shortest-path based algorithm fails to utilize the reusable relays because the returned shortest-paths may not always choose those reusable relays.

5. CONCLUSION AND FUTURE WORK

In DTMNs, mobile movements may lead to a situation called network partition where the network is divided into several isolated subnetworks. To connect isolated subnetworks, we proposed to deploy stationary relays to form k-element connected networks where there are k relay-disjoint paths between isolated subnetworks. The whole network is still connected if k-1 relays fail. To solve the relay deployment problem, we proposed three heuristic algorithms: a greedy algorithm, an iterative algorithm and a shortest-path based algorithm. The experimental results showed that the greedy algorithm returns the smallest number of relays to form k-element connected networks.

In DTMNs, mobile nodes failures and encounter failures are the norm rather than the exception. How to properly model those failures in the scope of the k-connectivity problem in general graphs requires further investigations.

6. ACKNOWLEDGMENTS

This research was partially supported by NSERC, Canada.

7. REFERENCES

[1] M. Balazinska and P. Castro. Characterizing mobility and network usage in a corporate wireless local-area network. In *Proc. of the Conf. on Mobile Systems, Applications and Services*, pages 303–316, 2003.

[2] N. Banerjee et al. Relays, base stations, and meshes: enhancing mobile networks with infrastructure. In *Proc. of the Conf. on Mobile computing and Networking*, pages 81–91, 2008.

[3] V. Chvatal. A greedy heuristic for the set-covering problem. *Mathematics of Operations Research*, 4(3):233–235, 1979.

[4] N. Eagle et al. Inferring social network structure using mobile phone data. In *Proc. of the National Academy of Sciences*, volume 36, pages 15274–15278, 2009.

[5] J. Edmonds and R. Karp. Theoretical improvements in algorithmic efficiency for network flow problems. *Journal of the ACM*, 19(2):248–264, 1974.

[6] F. Farahmand et al. Relay node placement in vehicular delay tolerant networks. In *IEEE GlobeCom*, pages 1–5, 2008.

[7] F. Farahmand et al. Performance of vehicular delay tolerant networks with relay nodes. *Wireless Communications and Mobile Computing*, 11(7):929–938, 2011.

[8] L. Fleischer et al. An iterative rounding 2-approximation algorithm for the element connectivity problem. In *IEEE Symp. on Foundations of Computer Science*, pages 339–347, 2001.

[9] M. Garey and D. Johnson. *Computers and Intractability: A Guide to the Theory of NP-Completeness.* W. H. Freeman, 1979.

[10] A. Goldberg and R. Tarjan. A new approach to the maximum-flow problem. *Journal of the ACM*, 35(4):921–940, 1988.

[11] M. Grotschel et al. *Geometric Algorithms and Combinatorial Optimization.* Springer-Verlag, 2nd edition, 1993.

[12] K. Menger. Zur allgemeinen kurventheorie. *Fundamenta Mathematicae*, 10(1):96–115, 1927.

[13] P. Pereira et al. From delay tolerant networks to vehicular delay tolerant networks. *IEEE Communications Surveys Tutorials*, 14(4):1166–1182, 2012.

[14] S. Shahbazi et al. On placement of passive stationary relay points in delay tolerant networking. In *Proc. of the Conf. on Advanced Information Networking and Applications*, pages 764–771, 2011.

[15] W. Zhao et al. Capacity enhancement using throwboxes in DTNs. In *Proc. of the IEEE Conf. on Mobile Adhoc and Sensor Systems*, pages 31–40, 2006.

Measurement-Based Simulation of WiFi Interference

Mustafa Al-Bado
University College Cork
Western Road, Cork, Ireland
m.albado@4c.ucc.ie

Cigdem Sengul
Oxford Brookes University
Wheatley, Oxford, UK
csengul@brookes.co.uk

ABSTRACT

A typical wireless network exhibits time-varying channel conditions and complex interference relationships, which are also influenced by different vendor implementations. Therefore, to improve the mapping between wireless simulation and real life, site and device specific models are needed. In this paper, we propose such interference models, called BOWLsim-advanced, based on measurements in two WiFi testbeds. We validate BOWLsim-advanced in complex interference scenarios comprising of hidden terminals, multi-hop flows, and inter-flow interference and show that it has better accuracy compared to both our earlier work and the default interference model of ns-3 (Network Simulator 3). However, the maximum improvement is observed for hidden terminals at the PHY layer, and for multi-hop flows and unicast communication, performance varies based on whether nodes are able to carrier-sense each other or have asymmetric interference. Essentially, our results show that PHY-layer models become insufficient for asymmetric interference, which requires better MAC layer models for higher accuracy.

Categories and Subject Descriptors

C.4 [**Performance of Systems**]: Modeling Techniques; I.6 [**Simulation and Modeling**]: Model Validation and Analysis

Keywords

WiFi; interference; measurements

1. INTRODUCTION

In [1], Partridge points at the "poisonous situation in wireless research" where results are not trusted due to limitations in both real-world experimentation and simulation. Therefore, the main goal of our research is to contribute to recovering the loss of confidence in wireless simulators [2, 3]. As interference-limited scenarios are typical in wireless networks, in this paper, we develop site-specific, measurement-based interference models for a WiFi network. Our models take into account that interference may be caused by multiple interferers. Also, the direct effects of interference e.g., packet drops and low channel utilization, result from several cross-layer interactions. For instance, interference may lead a transmitter to backoff based on IEEE 802.11 MAC. MAC effects, in turn, are expected to be amplified by a congestion-controlled transport layer (e.g., TCP). Therefore, in this work, we try to understand such effects by investigating simulation accuracy both at the PHY and transport layers.

Despite the complexity of interference scenarios, current simulators typically use simple models [2]. For instance, the ns-3 simulator [4] uses an additive Bit Error Rate (BER) based model, which evaluates pieces of a packet separately if they are affected by different interferers (see Figure 1). However, the accuracy of the model is low due to assuming a very steep and narrow transition between BER 0 and 1, which represents clear channel conditions [5]. In contrast, in this paper, we propose measurement-based interference models, BOWLsim-advanced, which are able to represent real link diversity. These models build on our earlier simulation work in, BOWLsim-basic [6, 7].

We validate the accuracy of BOWLsim-advanced against measurements in indoor and outdoor testbeds of the BOWL project [8] in ns-3. Comparing BOWLsim-advanced with the ns-3 BER-based model and BOWLsim-basic [6] shows that BOWLsim-advanced achieves the highest accuracy in hidden terminal scenarios, where we turn carrier-sensing off and use broadcast communication. This serves to bypass the MAC layer effects due to back-off and ACK transmissions and, the importance of site-specific PHY-layer models is better observed. On the other hand, with multi-hop and multi-flows, carrier sensing is on and, unicast communication is evaluated. Here, certain interference conditions e.g., nodes experiencing asymmetric interference, have significant effects on accuracy and require improved MAC layer models.

2. RELATED WORK

The simplicity of interference models in simulators has been frequent subject to criticism in the wireless networking community and led to loss of trust in simulation-based evaluations [2, 3]. To design better models, it is necessary to understand the factors that lead to interference-based losses. For instance, several works show that synchronization errors result in high losses [10, 11], but do not agree on a threshold signal to interference ratio (SIR) for correct reception since synchronization and detection is largely hardware-specific.

MSWiM'13, November 3–8, 2013, Barcelona, Spain.

ACM 978-1-4503-2353-6/13/11
http://dx.doi.org/10.1145/2507924.2507990 ...$15.00.

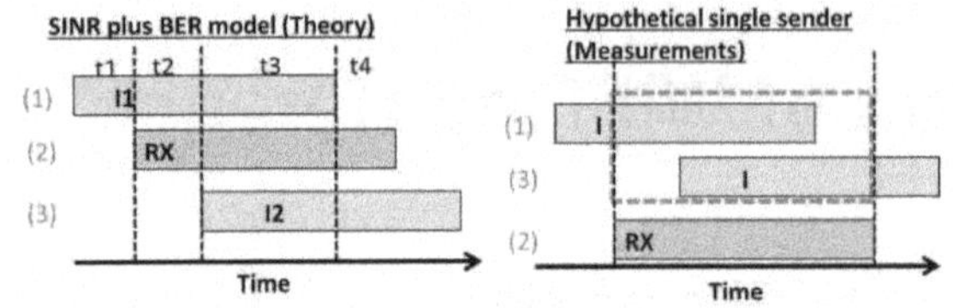

Figure 1: BER model in ns-3 considers overlapping packets in a piecewise manner. The hypothetical single sender model [9] bases on measurements but assumes all interferers affect the entire frame.

Equally, capture, the ability to receive the stronger signal even when the receiver is synchronized to another, affects correct reception [6]. Note that, capture is also device-specific. Ăś For instance, Atheros chipsets implement MIM (Message in Message), which captures frames even if they arrive after the preamble of the weaker frame [12].

These issues motivate site and device-specific, or simply, measurement-based models [7, 9]. In [9], the authors propose the *hypothetical single sender* model, where, using separate RSS (Receive Signal Strength) measurements, the probability that a receiver decodes a packet from its main transmitter is calculated assuming all interfering transmitters behave like a single sender that completely coincide with the sender's transmission (see Figure 1). This model is also used in our earlier work, BOWLsim-basic [6], and here, we extend this model and its evaluation to more complex scenarios.

In [13, 14] more powerful models are proposed for multiple interferers, unicast communication, and unsaturated senders. However, all these models [9, 13, 14], assume the interferer always start at the same time with the main transmission. Furthermore, these models may not be directly used in a simulator, that, for instance, relies on a standard MAC (e.g., IEEE 802.11) implementation. In our work, we follow the piece-wise model of ns-3. This also agrees with [5] that shows that SINR distribution in a frame period, which is determined by interference, decides whether a frame can be received or not. However, their measurements are based on Micaz motes while our validation is on WiFi radios, and our models are fully integrated into the ns-3 simulator.

3. BOWLSIM-ADVANCED MODELS

BOWLsim-advanced builds on the RSS, frame detection (FD) and frame error (FE) models of BOWLsim-basic [6]. The interference model of BOWLsim-basic is the *hypothetical single sender* model [9] described in Section 2. This model calculates the RSS in the presence of multiple interferers t_i, $i \geq 0$, from the sender s to the receiver r, $RX_{sr}^{t_i}$ as (Equation 9 in [9], with no transmission power changes, and hence $\alpha = \alpha_i = 1$):

$$RX_{sr}^{t_i} = \overline{R}_{sr} - \delta_r \sum_i (\overline{R_{t_i r}} - \overline{I}_r), \qquad (1)$$

where the mean RSS from sender s to r is $\overline{R}_{sr}$, the mean external interference at r is $\overline{I}_r$. The SINR threshold of r to successfully decode a packet is δ_r . Using $RX_{sr}^{t_i}$, and our FD and FE models, we decide whether a packet from s can be received in the presence of t_i. In addition, we implement the MIM capability of our Atheros radios.

BOWLsim-basic achieved good accuracy in the indoor testbed. However, it did not perform as well for the outdoor testbed, due to, we discovered, the varying link quality. Next, we detail how we tackle this issue by modifying the frame detection and interference models.

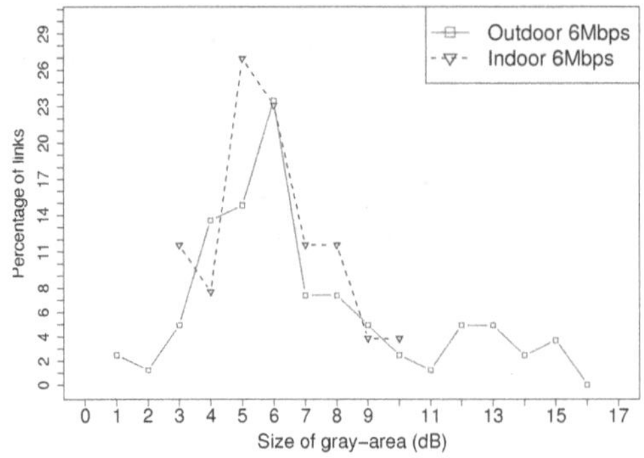

Figure 2: The % of links with increasing size of their gray area, where the FER is 5%-95% at 6Mbps.

3.1 Handling Varying Link Quality

Varying link quality dictates selecting δ_r carefully. In [9], δ_r is selected as the RSS at the knee of the delivery curve resulting from their attenuator-based measurements. Similarly, BOWLsim-basic selects δ_r based on FER measurements over all links, and sets it as the RSS value where the FER drops 50%. In indoor which has low link variability, indeed there is a point, where the FER decreases sharply. However, for the outdoor links, this transition is slower, and also changes per link. To show this we group links based on the RSS range that results in $5-95\%$ FER, which we define as the size of their gray area. Figure 2 that the gray area size varies significantly across the outdoor links. Therefore, for the outdoor network, we used a different δ_r for each link.

Also, BOWLsim-basic FD model uses the same per-rate FD threshold for all nodes. This works well in indoor, but not in outdoor due to a higher number of packets being detected and FE model, which built based on measurements without interference, decides falsely correct reception. To address this problem, we propose a new FD model, and calculate per-receiver FD thresholds. To do this, for each link i of a given receiver, we measure the mean RSS at 6 Mbps, denoted as $\overline{RSS}^i_{6Mbps}$. Next, we look up the FDR for the higher rates corresponding to $\overline{RSS}^i_{6Mbps}$. We combine the RSS and FDR values for each link of a receiver in its own table. In the simulator, to decide whether to detect a frame or not, the frame detection probability, $p_{detect}(r, RSS)$, for a given rate, r and RSS is compared to a uniformly sampled random variable q $(0 \leq q \leq 1)$. If $q < p_{detect}(r, RSS)$, the frame is detected, and otherwise, dropped.

3.2 Improving Interference Models

One of the main issues with the hypothetical sender model is that it considers all interferers fully overlap with an ongoing transmission. In contrast, ns-3 BER-based interference model correctly takes into account partial overlaps as the SINR distribution in a frame period determines FER [5]. However, ns-3 model uses theoretical BER models. To improve accuracy, we combined these models so that RSS of the piece with minimum $RX^{t_i}_{sr}$ in Equation 1 determines the final RSS of the packet. The RSS of the interferers are drawn from measurements. Figure 1 shows a scenario with multiple interferers. In BOWLsim-advanced, at time $t2$, the receiver *captures* the frame R, which has a stronger RSS. Note that, ns-3 drops this frame. At the end of reception, RSS of each piece is calculated, e.g., at $t3$, the interference from both $I1$ and $I2$ is taken into account. Finally, R's RSS is calculated as the minimum RSS of the three pieces and is used to decide whether a frame can be detected or not based on the FD model in Section 3.1. If the frame is detected, we calculate FER as:

$$p_{FE} = 1 - \prod_k 1 - FER(RX^{t^k_i}_{sr}), \qquad (2)$$

where $RX^{t^k_i}_{sr}$ is the RSS of the piece k, where t^k_i is its set of interferers, $FER(x)$ is looked up from measurements.

4. MEASUREMENT-BASED EVALUATION

In this section, we compare the accuracy of BOWLsim-advanced and BOWLsim-basic with measurements in different scenarios. As the base case, we also evaluate the default ns-3 BER-based interference model (*Default*), which also uses our measurement-based RSS model instead of a stochastic propagation model.

4.1 Measurement and Simulation Set-up

We run two type of measurements: (1) To build a link profile database for our simulation models and (2) to compare the simulation models in different interference scenarios. For all our measurements, we used the BOWL indoor and outdoor testbeds [6]. In outdoor, we created several different interference scenarios using 10 of these nodes, which carrier-sense 3-9 nodes (average 4.5). There are 4 asymmetric links. In indoor, we used nine nodes spanning two floors. We do not consider the carrier sensing relationships among these nodes, as they were only used in scenarios when carrier-sensing is disabled.

Our *link profiling measurements* use a well-known method, where one randomly selected node broadcasts, while all the other nodes record statistics during its transmission. Since the traffic is *broadcast*, no RTS, CTS or ACK frames are transmitted. We also configured the senders in *ahdemo mode*, which disables management frames such as beacons. Hence, our experiments are free of control overhead. Also, the receivers were setup in *monitor mode* we collected information about RSS, frame detection success and frame errors with different power levels, transmission rates, and packet sizes. Note that we cannot measure the RSS of the frames that were dropped by the radio signal detection unit. However, we know exactly how many frames were transmitted and, for each lost frame, we represent its RSS as the noise floor plus a *data-rate specific* correction factor [7].

We first evaluate the simulation models in *hidden-terminal scenarios*, where one sender broadcasts to a receiver in the presence of up to two and three interferers in indoor and outdoor, respectively. To ensure senders do not carrier sense each other, we set the CCA (Clear Channel Assessment) threshold to a very high value. Also, the Atheros-specific weak signal detection and ANI (Adaptive Noise Immunity)[1], which enhance robustness against interference, were disabled at the senders but enabled at the receiver. In *unicast experiments*, we used ns-3 as a traffic generator to have the same transport protocol implementation for both measurements and simulations. For all senders and receivers, both weak signal detection and ANI were on. For simulations, we used ns-3 version 3.13. We configured the same IEEE 802.11a PHY settings as in the measurements.

[1] US Patents 7349503 and 7522669

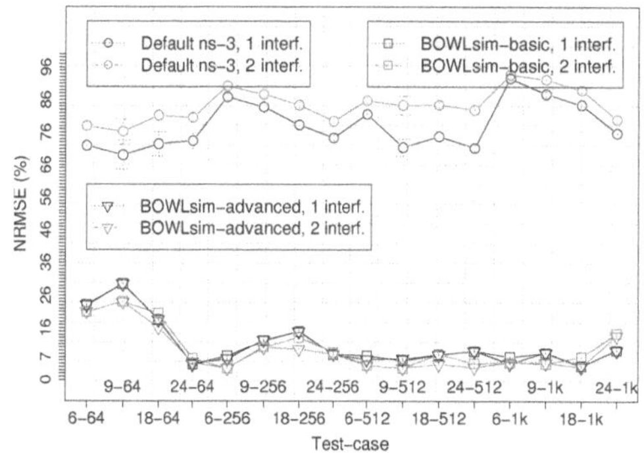

Figure 3: NRMSE of FRR vs. different (rate, packet size) combinations for indoor.

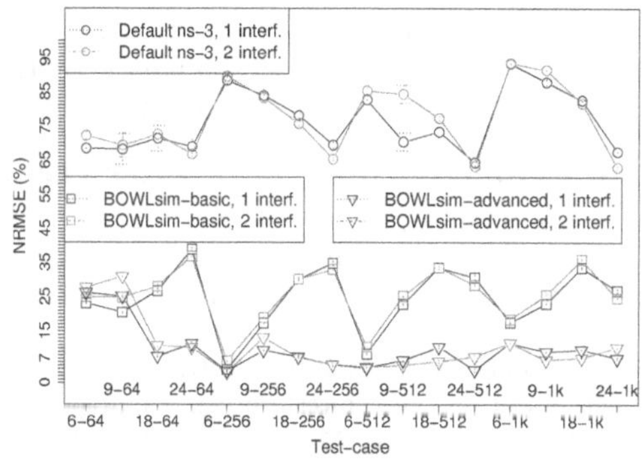

Figure 4: Outdoor: BOWLsim-advanced achieves significantly low error (9 times better in some cases).

4.2 Hidden-Terminal Scenarios

In these scenarios, we evaluate single-hop flows with 1-3 interferers, which send at the base rate of 6 Mbps, and packets of size 2000 B. Hence, this serves as a worst case scenario, where the interferer is always saturating the channel. The main sender sends with different packet sizes ranging from 64 to 1024B and rates 6-24 Mbps (higher rates were not possible). To vary interference, we first changed the transmit power of the sender in steps, while keeping the interferer power levels constant. Second, we kept the sender power level constant, and changed the power level one of the interferers in steps.

Figures 3 and 4 depict the NRMSE of FRR for different rate and packet size combinations. Each case was run for ten times and all simulation results are presented with their 95% confidence intervals. For all cases, BOWLsim-basic and BOWLsim-advanced perform 2-10 times better than *Default.* Also, for the indoor scenario, BOWLsim-basic

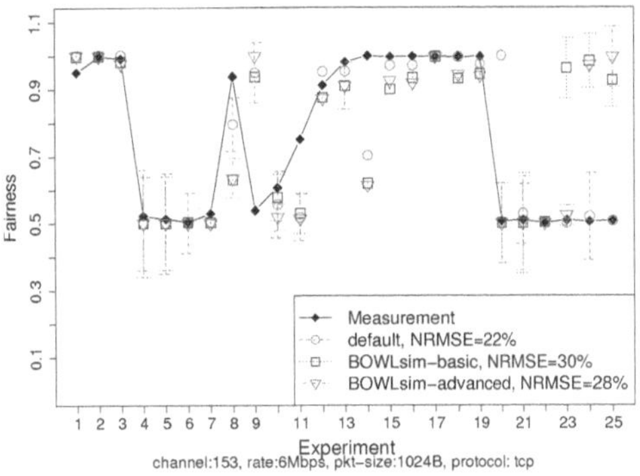

Figure 5: TCP fairness in multi-hop flows scenarios.

performs as well as BOWLsim-advanced, as these set-ups do not show high link variability (see Figure 2). However, for the outdoor scenarios, BOWLsim-advanced achieves higher accuracy. Especially, in the case of one interferer, the improvement reaches upto 9 times for *Outdoor*.

4.3 Multi-Hop and Inter-Flow Interference

We ran these experiments only in outdoor, as in the indoor network, the number of multi-hop and multi-flow configurations is limited. The measurements comprise 25 sets of experiments. Each set includes two flows that run over two hops. Each node is involved in exactly one flow to avoid any interactions other than interference. Finally, we operate with 6Mbps, 1024B and 17dBm. Based on the results in Section 4.2, in this setting, we do not expect much difference between BOWLsim-basic and BOWLsim-advanced. We evaluated both UDP and TCP flows but present only TCP results due to space limitations.

In terms of goodput, all models agreed with the measurements and achieved ≈2Mbps except one scenario in *Default*. However, Figure 5 shows that, in terms of fairness, results vary. For instance, shows that while our models are able to mimic some to some extent, they are more pessimistic or optimistic in others. *Default* also either shows very good agreement with the measurements or is completely off.

Closer inspection reveals two classes of scenarios:

Both flows are able to share the medium equally: In this case, nodes are able to carrier sense each other and all models represent this case well, with the exception of scenario 8 (see Figure 5).

One flow dominates or starves the other: These scenarios contain hidden terminals and asymmetric interference, which affect both data and ACK reception for TCP flows. The simulation models do not represent these scenarios well. If the issue is due to hidden terminals, our models work (scenarios 20 and 21). Otherwise, PHY layer models become limited and the interaction between PHY, MAC and transport layers need to be better modeled. Still, in some scenarios, our models are able to mimic TCP performance due to TCP amplifying PHY and MAC problems. For UDP, not shown due to space limitations, we see more problems as some senders are able to take advantage of asymmetric interference. Here, as our models implement capture, the timing of the frames become very important in determining the fate of a frame. Therefore, the advantage of our models compared with *Default* diminishes. To model interference in these scenarios, the MAC layer timings need to be modeled very precisely in the simulator. This constitutes our future work.

5. CONCLUSION

In this paper, we investigate the simulation of complex interference scenarios considering hidden terminals, multi-hop flows and various transmit rate and powers. We show that our site-specific model, BOWLsim-advanced significantly outperforms the current default model of ns-3 and improves over our previous simple model, BOWLsim-basic. For our future work, we will focus on addressing the challenges in modeling asymmetric interference, which require a deeper understanding of PHY, MAC and transport layer interactions.

6. REFERENCES

[1] C. Partridge, "Forty data communications research questions," *SIGCOMM Comput. Commun. Rev.*, vol. 41, no. 5, Oct. 2011.

[2] A. Iyer, C. Rosenberg, and A. Karnik, "What is the right model for wireless channel interference," *IEEE WC*, vol. 8, no. 5, May 2009.

[3] J. Liu, Y. Yuan, D. M. Nicol, R. S. Gray, C. C. Newport, D. Kotz, and L. F. Perrone, "Empirical validation of wireless models in simulations of ad hoc routing protocols," *Simulation*, vol. 81, Apr. 2005.

[4] "ns-3," http://www.nsnam.org/.

[5] S. Woo and H. Kim, "An empirical interference modeling for link reliability assessment in wireless networks," *IEEE/ACM NET.*, vol. 21, no. 1, 2013.

[6] M. Al-Bado, C. Sengul, and R. Merz, "What details are needed for wireless simulations? – a study of a site-specific indoor wireless model," in *INFOCOM*, Mar. 2012.

[7] M. Al-Bado, R. Merz, C. Sengul, and A. Feldmann, "A site-specific indoor link model for realistic wireless network simulations," in *SimuTools*, Mar. 2011.

[8] R. Merz, H. Schiöberg, and C. Sengul, "Design of a configurable wireless network testbed with live traffic," in *TridentCom '10*, May 2010.

[9] C. Reis, R. Mahajan, M. Rodrig, D. Wetherall, and J. Zahorjan, "Measurement-based models of delivery and interference in static wireless networks," in *ACM SIGCOMM*, 2006.

[10] V. Sridhara, H. Shin, and S. Bohacek, "Performance of 802.11b/g in the interference limited regime," in *ICCCN*, 2007.

[11] A. Kochut, A. Vasan, A. U. Shankar, and A. Agrawala, "Sniffing out the correct physical layer capture model in 802.11b," in *ICNP*, Oct. 2004.

[12] J. Ryu, J. Lee, S. Lee, and T. Kwon, "Revamping the IEEE 802.11a PHY simulation models," in *MSWIM*, 2008, pp. 28–36.

[13] A. Kashyap, S. Ganguly, and S. R. Das, "A measurement-based approach to modeling link capacity in 802.11-based wireless networks," in *MobiCom*, 2007, pp. 242–253.

[14] L. Qiu, Y. Zhang, F. Wang, M. K. Han, and R. Mahajan, "A general model of wireless interference," in *MobiCom*, 2007.

Energy Saving Strategies in WiFi Indoor Localization

Azin Neishaboori
School of Computer Science
Carnegie Mellon University Qatar
azin.neishaboori@gmail.com

Khaled A. Harras
School of Computer Science
Carnegie Mellon University Qatar
kharras@cs.cmu.edu

ABSTRACT

Despite extensive research on WiFi indoor localization, very few solutions are widely deployed, largely due to their high energy consumption. In this paper, we propose several energy saving strategies with varying localization accuracy and energy consumption tradeoffs in WiFi indoor localization. Instead of localizing every single device, these strategies exploit short range low-power communication technologies, to localize clusters of mobile devices, via a representative cluster head. We propose various cluster head selection algorithms that offer different trade offs between localization accuracy and power consumption. The outcome of this work provides insights into the effectiveness and cost of a particular strategy depending on the needs of the application requiring varying localization service levels.

Categories and Subject Descriptors

C.2.4 [**Computer Systems Organization**]: Computer Communication Networks—*Distributed Systems*

Keywords

Localization; Energy efficiency; Clustering; Accuracy

1. INTRODUCTION

With the exponential growth in location-based services and applications, WiFi indoor localization has become a mature area of research after more than a decade of extensive studies. It has evolved from RSSI signature based techniques such as RADAR [2] and HORUS [3] to more unsupervised methods with higher accuracy such as CompAcc[6], EZ [8], and UNLOC [5]. The achievable accuracy has also moved from room level resolution ($3-5$ meters) to finer resolutions of less than 1 meter. Despite the advances made in this area, to date, WiFi indoor localization solutions are not commonly deployed on our mobile devices largely due to their high energy consumption.

We observe that mobile users tend to move in groups in indoor public environments such as shopping malls, universities, or airports. Exploiting this fact, we convert the task of localizing individual mobile devices to a more hierarchical task of localizing *clusters* of them via one or more cluster representative(s), i.e. cluster head(s) [12]. Such collaborative scheme reduces the frequency of localization updates per device. While device collaboration leading to improved accuracy was proposed [4, 9, 10] without requiring higher energy consumption, it has not been utilized to reduce energy consumption with minimal loss in accuracy. Also, while clustering nodes to lower energy consumption is known in Wireless Sensor Networks (WSNs) [15], unlike homogenous WSNs, cooperation amongst members cannot be presumed when localizing typically selfish users. In addition, in WSNs, clusters are decided upon before cluster heads while the opposite occurs in localization.

In this paper, we propose energy saving localization strategies that exploit group mobility patterns, and the availability of low-energy network interfaces on mobile devices. By offering different methods for selecting cluster head(s), we make informed trade offs between the localization system's energy consumption, and its accuracy and energy variance across cluster members. We propose techniques for effectively selecting these cluster head(s) and estimating cluster members' locations. We do this with the following potentially conflicting objectives in mind: (*i*) maximizing localization accuracy, (*ii*) minimizing energy consumption, and (*iii*) preserving fairness in energy consumption across members.

We particularly study and evaluate the following algorithms. (1) Constant cluster head selection: this is the basic method proposed in [12], and formalized here, where one device which initially has the most nodes in proximity becomes the cluster head. (2) Round-Robin cluster head selection: members take turn to act as a cluster head, leading to a more even distribution of energy consumption among cluster members. (3) Multi-cluster head selection: more than one member serves as cluster head at any point in time, improving accuracy at the cost of higher energy consumption. (4) Hybrid round-robin multi-cluster head selection: more than one cluster head is present at a time, and sets of devices take turn to serve as cluster head. As in the round robin scheme, energy consumption is evenly distributed among members.

We study the trade-offs of the proposed algorithms via analysis and simulation using Qualnet 5.0 [1]. We evaluate our algorithms in terms of the objectives stated earlier under various environmental conditions reflected by many parameters. These parameters include the neighborhood range, cluster size, and cluster velocity since they have the most impact in identifying clusters and in the resulting localization accuracy. We observe from our results that multi-cluster

MSWiM'13, November 3–8, 2013, Barcelona, Spain.

head selection algorithms are more desirable as the cluster size increases; they mitigate the accuracy loss incurred by clustering without much increase in average power consumption. We also conclude that both round-robin and multi-cluster head round-robin methods offer fair power consumption profiles without loss in localization accuracy.

2. ENERGY SAVING STRATEGIES

In this section, we introduce several energy saving Cluster Head (CH) selection strategies, and discuss their localization accuracy versus energy cost. These methods are designed to be built on top of existing localization systems. The CH selection mechanisms introduced in this paper are built using the **GreenLock** system architecture introduced in [12].

2.1 Constant Selection of Cluster-Head (CSC)

In CSC, initially all nodes are CHs and send their own localization updates. Each CH frequently uses a Short-Ranged (SR) wireless technology, such as BlueTooth (BT) or Bluetooth Low Enrtgy (BLE) [11] to run a Neighbor Discovery Protocol (NDP) in background. At every update, a CH sends the server, via WiFi, a list of nodes in SR-proximity along with the WiFi Received Signal Strength Indication (RSSI) perceived from Access Points (APs) in its range. This update (or lack thereof) allows the server to merge (or split) clusters. The *follower* members have their WiFi radio turned off (if not used for other applications) and only use their SR radio to communicate with the CH. This communication is mainly in the context of NDP and scanning the wireless channel to sense a periodical Short-Ranged beacon (SR-beacon) broadcasted by the CH.

The server compares the list of neighbors sent by each CH to its previous state. If for a CH, A, this list contains another CH, B, for several consecutive updates (*joining confidence interval*), and if the neighbor list of B is a subset of the neighbor list of A, the server merges both clusters. The bigger group's CH, A, then becomes the CH for the merged group. Once selected as CH, a node remains in this state until it either leaves the cluster or the cluster it belongs to is merged with another cluster. If a CH leaves the cluster, followers detect it by not receiving the periodical SR-beacons broadcast by the CH for a certain duration (*splitting confidence interval*). Each follower then turns its WiFi radio back on and resumes transmitting RSSI updates to the server. More details on this method can be found in [12]. The main objective of that paper was to illustrate the advantage of localizing clusters to individual nodes, and CH selection methods were not discussed.

- CSC Localization Accuracy: The accuracy of CH selection method is, loosely speaking, inversely proportional to the size of its *Feasible Solution Region*(FSR). If all points in the FSR are equally probable, this relationship becomes strict. In the CSC, the FSR includes all points within the circle with radius $r_{prox} + \delta_p$ around the CH. r_{prox} is the proximity range, and $\delta_p = \mu_p + \sigma_p$ is the average error of the localization mechanism plus one standard deviation. We use μ_p and σ_p to denote the mean and variance of localization error respectively.

- CSC Energy Consumption and Fairness: We use the following notations: w_{LRI} and w_{LRS} denote the energy spent by a Long-Ranged (LR) interface (WiFi assumed herein) when idle, and scanning followed by transmitting, respectively. w_{SRI} and w_{SRS} denote the energy spent by the SR interface, when idle and active respectively.

In a cluster of size N, the average power spent by each cluster member in CSC is:

$$p_{avg} = \frac{1}{TN}\{ \sum_{T-N_U \times T_{ST}} (w_{LRI} + w_{SRI}) + \sum_{N_U \times T_{ST}} (w_{LRS} + w_{SRS})\} + \frac{N-1}{TN}\{\sum_{T}(w_{LRI} + w_{SRI})\} \quad (1)$$

where N_U is the number of WiFi updates sent during interval T, and T_{ST} is the duration it takes for a WiFi interface to perform one scan and transmission. In the above display, it is assumed that the number of WiFi RSSI updates and low-ranged neighbor list updates are the same. We assume this since one WiFi transmission to the server can convey both pieces of information, and hence, save energy.

In CSC, the CH carries the burden of transmitting localization updates as well as performing NDP. This requires the CH to spend more energy than if it did not participate in the cluster. Remaining members participate in the NDP using a SR wireless technology.

2.2 Round Robin Cluster Head Selection (RR)

Assume that all nodes are in each other's proximity range and therefore could serve as CH. In Round Robin (RR) CH selection, the server assigns each member a priority which indicates its turn in becoming CH. The period with which CH changes does not have to be the same as the localization update interval. However, herein we assume that to simplify power consumption equations.

To realize the Round-Robin CH selection, members of a cluster listen to the SR-beacon, broadcasted by the current CH. This beacon contains the ID of the current CH and an ordered list of members specifying their turns in acting as CH. This list is communicated by the server to the current CH after the CH sends a WiFi RSSI update to the server. If the node with priority succeeding that of the current CH does not hear the beacon for a period longer than $T_{SR-Beacon}$, it will become a CH.

The rest of the RR operation is as follows. If the scheduled CH departs the cluster, followers will not sense its SR-beacon. If this absence takes longer than $T_{no-Beacon} = m \times T_{SR-Beacon}$ (with m being an integer greater than one), the next member in line prepares to become the CH. The server notes the departure of the scheduled CH by either not receiving a WiFi RSSI and neighbor list update, or receiving a different set of neighbors. Subsequently, the server receives a request from a follower member to change status to CH. The server then eliminates the departed CH from the ordered priority list. When the next in line CH communicates with the server to request its status to become CH, it also receives the new priority list from the server. When two clusters merge (under the same conditions as in CSC), the server sends a command to the CH of the smaller cluster to change status to follower along with the new ordered priority list. Before settling as a follower, this former CH broadcasts one last SR-beacon announcing the new priority list to its former followers.

To assure a cluster is fully connected, every member device performs a periodic scan operation. This is accomplished in RR as every node obtains a chance to be CH and sends its updated neighbor list to the server. The server monitors the connectivity of the cluster and enforces full connectivity through the ordered priority list it sends to its CH.

- RR Localization Accuracy: In the absence of additional information, localization accuracy of each node in RR is $\frac{(N-1)}{N} \times Error_F + \frac{1}{N} \times Error_{CH}$ where N is the cluster size. RR's accuracy may be enhanced if the following information is available: (i) the distance between the CH and each follower, (ii) the velocity of each follower, (iii) a reference for the previous location of all members. Below we explain how such information can be acquired:

(1) The distance between the CH and each follower can be inferred using the short-ranged RSSI received from each follower at the CH.

(2) Approximating the velocity is more difficult. Using the last two location updates obtained from a certain member can give a crude estimate of speed due to infrequent updates from each member. We therefore resort to using accelerometers, present in most new mobile devices. Even if the velocity is obtained accurately for the CH, it is only used at a later point. During this time lapse, the velocity of this node may change in both magnitude and direction. We may be able to improve this estimate by adjusting it using the velocity of the current CH, e.g. using $\vec{v}_F[n] \simeq \alpha_k \vec{v}_F[n-k] + (1-\alpha_k)\vec{v}_{CH}[n]$ where N is cluster size, $0 \leq \alpha_k \leq 1, \forall k$ is a design parameter, n is the discrete time index, $0 < k < N-1$ is the discrete delay between the current time n and the time the velocity of the node in question was sent to the server, and $\vec{v}_{CH}$ and $\vec{v}_F$ are the speed vectors of the CH and follower F respectively.

(3) Every node is a CH at some point and is localized by the server, hence there is a reference location of it.

Given the above additional information, the server can calculate each follower's location as illustrated in Figure (1(a)) for a cluster of size 2. This figure also includes the error sources for this scheme: error of the localization mechanism (δ_p), error in calculating the inter-node distances (δ_d), and the velocity estimation error. The intersections of the two circular rings defines the FSRs like in [10].

- RR Energy Consumption and Fairness: In RR, each cluster member is a CH for $1/N$ of the time and a follower for $N - 1/N$ of the time. Therefore, the average power consumption of all cluster members is the same and equal to that of the CSC scheme (in 1) except for additional energy required for the CH to receive priority lists from the server. We denote the time required for this action by T_{RX} and use $T_X = T_{ST} + T_{RX}$ in the display to simplify the notations. Therefore, the average power consumption is:

$$p_{avg} = \frac{1}{TN}\{ \sum_{T-N_U \times (T_X)} (w_{LRI} + w_{SRI}) + \sum_{N_U \times (T_X)} (w_{LRS} + w_{SRS} + w_{LRI})\} + \frac{N-1}{TN}\{\sum_T (w_{LRI} + w_{SRI})\} \quad (2)$$

2.3 Multi-Cluster Head Selection (MC)

Depending on the size of the cluster, more than one CH may be selected. We refer to this method as Multi-Cluster head selection (MC). The operation of MC is similar to that of CSC except for the possible concurrent presence of more than one CH. Members listen to SR-beacons broadcast by all CHs, and only if they do not hear any SR-beacon, the next members in line will turn on their WiFi radio and contact the server to request changing status to CH.

- MC Localization Accuracy: The FSR for a follower in MC can be reduced if its distance with all the CHs are known (via SR communication). This is shown for the case of two CHs in Figure (1(b)).

- MC Energy Consumption and Fairness: In MC, the CHs carry the burden of sending localization updates on behalf of the whole cluster. Assuming M simultaneous CHs in a cluster of size N, the average power consumption per cluster member is:

$$p_{avg} = \frac{M}{TN}\{ \sum_{T-N_U \times T_{ST}} (w_{LRI} + w_{SRI}) + \sum_{N_U \times T_{ST}} (w_{LRS} + w_{SRS}))\} + \frac{N-M}{TN}\{\sum_T (w_{LRI} + w_{SRI})\} \quad (3)$$

2.4 Multi-Cluster Head Round Robin (MCRR)

Hybrid Multi-Cluster head selection Round-Robin (MCRR) scheme follows a Round-Robin CH selection order, but at every turn a **set** of CHs is selected. For fair energy consumption across members, all of them should appear the same number of times in one complete transmission cycle. Priorities are assigned to sets of members instead of individual members. Like in RR, the frequency of change of CHs may or may not be the same as that of localization updates. But herein we assume it is. The operation of MCRR is a straightforward extension of that of RR except that it is in the multi-CH context similar to that of MC. Details of MCRR's operation are omitted to save space.

- MCRR Localization Accuracy: When there are M concurrent CHs in MCRR, the feasible solution shrinks to the intersection of M circular rings. If, like in RR, the nodes' velocity information is also used, an additional circular ring can shrink the FSR even further. This is depicted in Figure (1(c)) for $M = 2$.

- MCRR Energy Consumption and Fairness: In MCRR, the average energy consumption for all nodes is the same, and equal to that of the MC except for the additional energy required for the CH to receive the ordered priority list from the server. This is similar to the adjustment made from (1) to (2) and is omitted due to space limits.

3. SIMULATION STUDY

3.1 Simulation Set up

We evaluate the localization accuracy of the above four clustering algorithms via simulation using Qualnet 5.0 [1]. The average and variance of energy consumption for these algorithms are also calculated from the formulas derived in the previous sections for the simulated scenarios and presented in this section for easier references.

A generic indoor localization system, PLoc, very similar to RADAR [2], is implemented and used to localize nodes based on the RSSI values observed from different APs. 36 APs are uniformly placed in a $200m \times 200m$ area spaced $40m$ apart, and using $1m \times 1m$ grids. More details on PLoc may be found in [12]. For MC and MCRR, 2 CHs are assigned concurrently to a cluster only if the cluster includes more than 2 nodes; otherwise just one CH is selected. For both methods, when possible, we chose the two most distant nodes as the two CHs. When implementing RR, MC and MCRR, to localize nodes we apply a search algorithm and declare as solution the first point found in the FSR. Since there are two intersection regions in case of RR and MC with two CHs, this method selects a point in one of the regions. If no point is found after the search, we use the location of the single CH and the average of two CHs for RR and MC or MCRR respectively.

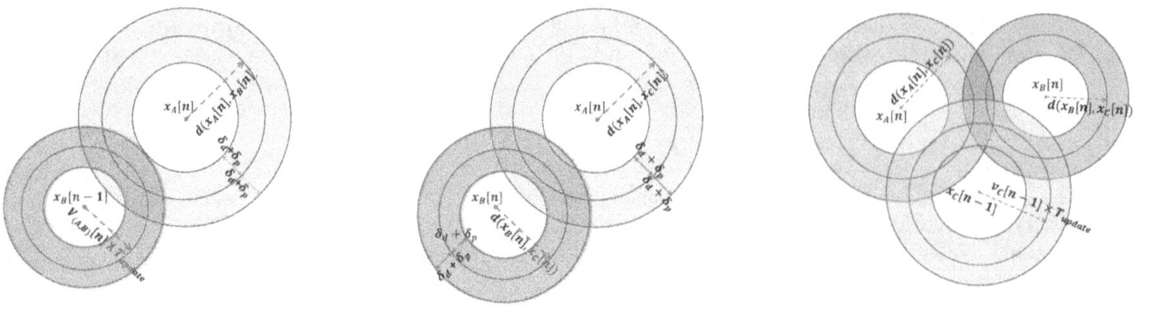

(a) FSR in cluster of size 2 in RR (b) FSR of C with CHs A and B in MC (c) FSR of C with CHs A and B in MCRR

Figure 1: Different Solution regions in RR, MC and MCRR

The simulation set up uses a single group of nodes with a constant constellation that moved from one corner of a $200m \times 200m$ square to the diagonally opposite corner with a constant speed. Nodes were placed uniformly on the perimeter of a circle with a diameter slightly less than the specified neighborhood range ($0.2m$). The mobility traces were generated separately and then fed to Qualnet.

We note that, in the case of RR and MCRR in constant cluster constellations, the server can collect the inter-node distances using SR wireless RSSIs. It can therefore eventually find the constellation of the cluster using trilateration. However, inaccuracies induced by the localization error itself, exacerbated by lower localization frequencies, and error in measuring the inter-node distances, all introduce uncertainty in the solution.

3.2 Simulation Parameters

We single out a few parameters expected to have more significant impact on identifying clusters and affecting the performance of each method: (i) group velocity, (ii) cluster size (cardinality), and (iii)neighborhood range. These parameters are varied only in an expected reasonable range of 1m/sec to 4m/sec (1.5 m/sec nominally) for velocity, 3-8 nodes (4 nodes nominally) for cluster size, and 1m-5m (5m nominally) for neighborhood range. The rest of the parameter values are fixed. We set the BT confidence, i.e. the percentage of times two nodes in each other's BT range perceive each other, at 100% to reflect full visibility. Also since we tested the performance of different CH selection methods on one group with fixed constellation, we set the joining and splitting confidence to 1. $\delta_{d0} = \mu_{d0} + \sigma_{d0}$ (average plus one standard deviation of inter-distance measurement error between two nodes per unit distance) was set to 0.3 akin to the corresponding values in [14]). α_k is chosen as 0.2, its empirically optimal value in terms of localization accuracy. σ_v is selected at 0.3, close to the value inferred from [9].

We borrow the power consumption values for WiFi and BT from [13]: P_{LRS}, P_{LRI}, P_{SRS} and P_{SRI} at 1290, 770, 120 and 10 mW respectively. We set the time required for one WiFi scan followed by transmission at 0.75 seconds, one WiFi scan and data reception at 0.25 seconds, and one BT scan at 4 seconds. The required power to turn WiFi radio on and off is not reflected in the simulation results. We would like to point out that the period with which CH changes does not have to be the same as the localization update interval. Increasing the ratio of the former to the latter can decrease the average power consumed due to WiFi radio being turned on and off. We do not address this issue herein.

3.3 Results

Figure (2) shows the localization error for: (1) PLoc with localization period of 1 sec (PLoc1), (2) PLoc with localization period of 5 sec (PLoc5), (3) CSC, (4) RR, (5) MC with 2 CHs, and (6) MCRR with 2 CHs (the same period used for methods $2-6$). In each figure, the unvaried parameters are set at their nominal values. We note that in all of these figures, error may exceed the neighborhood range due to the localization error of PLoc itself and the error introduced due to the localization update period of 5 seconds used in the simulation. Therefore, the accuracy of each CH selection algorithm must be compared with that of PLoc5 in all figures. We now briefly discuss the effect of the CH selection algorithms shown in Figure (2).

- Cluster Head Selection Method: We observe that the localization error of RR is close to that of CSC. The use of velocity seems to not have made any significant improvement in localization error. This is due to the inaccuracy introduced in the location estimate of the CH when the localization update period is 5 seconds. However RR's power consumption fairness still makes it more appealing than CSC. Comparing the performance of MC with two CHs with that of RR shows an accuracy improvement albeit at the cost of slightly higher power consumption. MCRR offers fairness in power consumption compared to MC, with little to no compromise in localization accuracy.

- Group Speed Effect: It seems that even when speed is constant and unidirectional, and there is no intra-group mobility, localization error is still exacerbated at higher speeds. This is expected as the localization update frequency remains constant. In presence of varying speed and directions or within-group mobility, estimating a mobile node's disposition from its previous value may be very difficult. Therefore, the location of the CH is less representative of the its followers' location in times between consecutive updates, rendering clustering less effective.

- Cluster Size Effect: Two factors influence the performance of clustering when cluster size is increased in a given area: (1) members are located on average closer to each other, rendering CHs better representatives of their followers. This is reflected by slight improvements in the error performance of CSC as group size is increased. (2) For RR and MCRR, there is longer time elapse between two consecutive updates by the same member. This seems to cancel the effect of the previous factor yielding no significant difference in the performance of RR and MCRR when the group size is increased.

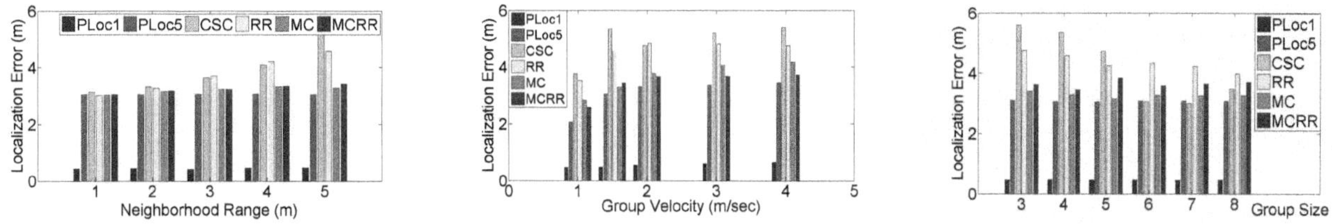

(a) Loc Error Vs. Range (b) Loc Error Vs. Group Velocity (c) Loc Error Vs. Group Size

Figure 2: Localization error vs. different parameters

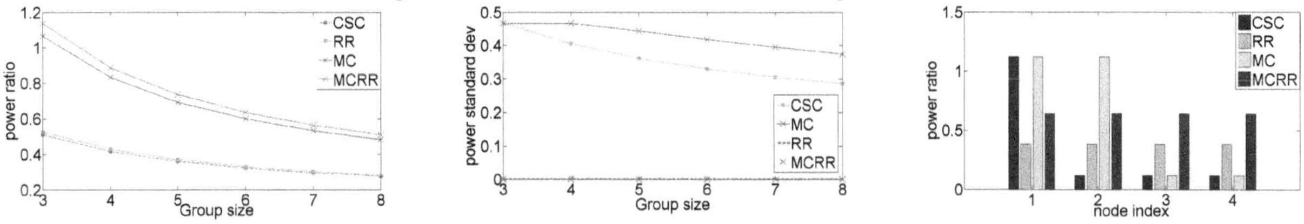

(a) avg power ratio of CH methods to no CH (b) SD of nodes's power in CH methods (c) power ratio of CH methods to no CH

Figure 3: Average and standard deviation of power consumption

- Neighborhood Range: As the neighborhood range increases, so does the localization error for all four CH selection methods. In smaller ranges, there is little accuracy performance difference between these methods, as the location of the CH is a relatively accurate estimate of those of other nodes. Both multi-clustering methods, MC and MCRR, offer meaningful improvement in their localization accuracy compared to the other methods.

- Notes on Power Consumption and Fairness: For different cluster sizes, Figure (3(a)) shows the ratio of power consumption per node with different CH selection methods to the same quantity in the case of no clustering. The ratio gets smaller as cluster size grows suggesting more energy saving. We also notice that the difference in average power consumption ratio between single and multi-CH selection schemes decreases with cluster size. This, together with their accuracy improvements, makes multi-CH algorithms compelling solutions for larger clusters.

Figure (3(b)) shows the standard deviation of power consumption across cluster members for clusters of different sizes. We can see that the standard deviation of power consumption is zero for both RR and MCRR. For both CSC and MC, this quantity decreases in larger cluster sizes as there are more followers.

Finally, in Figure (3(c)), we depict the ratio of power consumption by each node to the same quantity in case of no clustering in a cluster of size 4 for the four CH selection methods. It is assumed that node 1 is the CH for CSC, and nodes 1 and 2 are both CHs in MC. As reflected in this figure, in case of CSC and MC, this ratio is higher than 1 for the CH. This is due to the use of low-range NDP *in addition* to WiFi scanning and transmissions. However, the power consumption ratio is much lower for the follower nodes, which only have to participate in the NDP. This difference between power consumption across nodes does not exist in RR and MCRR making them more fair.

4. CONCLUSION AND FUTURE WORK

We have studied several methods for selecting CH(s) in clusters of mobile nodes. These CHs send the localization server RSSI updates on behalf of the whole cluster. The server uses these updates to localize the CHs and extrapolate the location of other members. Four CH selection algorithms were studied: constant, round-robin, multi-CH and multi-CH round robin. We have evaluated these algorithms in terms of the trade offs they offer in accuracy, total energy consumed, and energy consumption fairness across members. Consideration for maximum or residual energy in CH selection, multi-level hierarchical clustering based on the requirements of different localization applications, and deployment of the proposed methods, are left for future work.

5. REFERENCES

[1] Qualnet 5.0. http://www.scalable-networks.com.

[2] P. Bahl and V. Padmanabhan. RADAR: An In-Building RF-based User Location and Tracking System. In InfoCom2000.

[3] M. Youssef, A. Agrawala. The Horus location determination system, In Wireless Networks journal, 2008.

[4] L. Chan, J. Chiang, Y. Chen, C. Ke, J. Hsu, and H. Chu, Collaborative Localization: Enhancing WiFi-Based Position Estimation with Neighborhood Links in Clusters. In PerCom2006.

[5] H. Wang, S. Sen, A. Elgohary, M. Farid, M. Youssef, R. Choudhury. Unsupervised Indoor Localization. In Mobisys2012.

[6] I. Constandache, R.R. Choudhury, and I. Rhee. Towards mobile phone localization without war-driving. In InfoCom2010.

[7] K. Lin, A. Kansal, D. Lymberopoulos, F. Zhao, Energy-Accuracy Trade-off for Continuous Mobile Device Location. In MobiSys2010.

[8] K. Chintalapudi, A. Lyer, V. Padmanabhan. Indoor Localization Without the Pain. In MobiCom2010.

[9] T. Higuchiy, H. Yamaguchiy, and T. Higashino, Clearing a Crowd: Context-Supported Neighbor Positioning for People-Centric Navigation. In PerCom2012.

[10] H. Yamaguchiy, T. Higuchi and T. Higashino, Collaborative Indoor Localization of Mobile Nodes, In ICMU2012.

[11] J. Liu, Canfeng Chen Radio Systems Lab, Nokia Research Center, Energy Analysis of Neighbor Discovery in Bluetooth Low Energy Networks, Technical Report.

[12] M. Abdellatif, A. Mtibaa, K. Harras, M. Youssefy, GreenLoc: Energy Efficient WiFi Localization on Mobile Phones, in IEEE ICC2013.

[13] G. Ananthanarayanan and I. Stoica. Blue-fi: enhancing wi-fi performance using bluetooth signals. In MobiSys2009.

[14] N. Banerjee, S. Agarwal, P. Bahl.Virtual Compass: relative positioning to sense mobile social interactions, Technical Report MSR-TR-2010 – 5, Microsoft Research.

[15] D. P. Dahnil, Y. P. Singh, C. Kuan Ho. Energy-efficient cluster formation in heterogeneous Wireless Sensor Networks: A comparative study, in ICACT2011.

[16] B. Nazir and H. Hasbullah. Energy Efficient Multi Hierarchy Clustering Protocol for Wireless Sensor Network, in ICIIT2010.

Solution of Detecting Jamming Attacks in Vehicle Ad Hoc NETworks

Anh Tuan Nguyen
Laboratoire LACL
University of Paris-Est
tuan.ant117@gmail.com

Lynda Mokdad
Laboratoire LACL
University of Paris-Est
lynda.mokdad@univ-paris12.fr

Jalel Ben-Othman
Laboratoire L2TI
University of Paris 13
jalel.ben-othman@univ-paris13.fr

ABSTRACT

Today, vehicular ad hoc network (VANET) is currently researched and achieved by several organizers to develop the intelligent transportation system (ITS). Research on Vehicular Ad hoc Network (VANET) has been conducting for long time. Nowadays, several organizers has obtained remarkable achievements contributing to the development of the Intelligent transportation system, ITS. The communication protocol in VANET named 802.11p protocol, has been improved to adapt to the high-speed environment. However, the communication among vehicles can be interfered even by Denial of Service (DoS) attacks such as jamming attacks. The vehicles communicate with each other in the high-speed environment. The time of data exchange between them must be extremely short. Solutions for detection of jamming attacks must occur quickly to detect more precisely. In order to detect jamming attacks more precisely, solutions therefore must occur very fast. In this paper, we propose one solution to detect jamming attacks. The following solution is based on the combination of the packet delivery ratio and its diminution.

Categories and Subject Descriptors

C.2.0 [**Computer-Communication Networks**]: General - Security and protection; D.4.6 [**Operations Systems**]: Security and Protection; I.6.2 [**Simulation and Modeling**]: Simulation Languages

General Terms

Theory; Performance; Reliability; Security;

Keywords

ACM proceedings, Jamming attacks, Detect; Vehicular Ad hoc Network (VANET); security; availability; security attack; Denial of Service (DOS).

MSWiM'13, November 3–8, 2013, Barcelona, Spain.

1. INTRODUCTION

Vehicular ad hoc network (VANET) is a specific case of mobile ad hoc network (MANET) in which the participants nodes are vehicles [17]. A major objective of VANET is to enable to communicate between vehicles (V2V) or vehicle and infrastructure (V2I) in the high-speed environment on the frequency of approximately 5.9GHz. Its most particular feature is that vehicles can directly communicate with each other without any infrastructure. In VANET, 802.11p protocol is used for this communication. It is an approved amendment to the 802.11 standard to add wireless access in vehicular environments (WAVE)[1]. WAVE consist of the standard of IEEE 1609 which is the upper layer standard and the 802.11p protocol which contains the Physical layer (PHY) and the Medium Access Control layer (MAC). The 802.11p protocol was published on July 2010 [3].

The goal of the construction of a VANET network is to make sure its safety and reliability. We must develop methods against DoS attacks, such as jamming. Attackers can execute several types of interference at different moments. Since VANET is a dynamic network, its vehicles move quickly and can join or leave the network at any time, and traffic jam can always occur. Consequently, we need to differentiate between jammed scenarios and others conditions such as traffic congestion during the jam, interruption of communication due to failures of the transmitter when it is opposite the natural barrier. Jamming attack is like a more serious threat to the security in the domain of wireless networks. It continuously sends repeated signals to interfere with the communication between the stations for denial of the use of the transmission. The victim feels that the state of the channel is still busy. Therefore, it cannot send or receive the legal signal in the jammed area.

When jamming is effective, it will interfere with the legitimate communication. The sender does not detect an idle channel for sending packets. Even it successfully sends packets; the receiver cannot receive all the packets sent by the sender, because the attacker does not respect the communication protocol to intervene over the canal. Hence, its packet delivery ratio (PDR) is low. On the MAC layer of the receiver, all the received packets cannot be decoded correctly. Only packets sent by the sender can pass the Cyclic Redundancy Check (CRC). CRC is an error-detecting code. PDR is measured by using the ratio of the number of packets passing the CRC check with respect to the number of packets (or preambles) received. The packets received are packets sent by the sender or by the attacker. Hence, we will be able to detect the presence of jamming attack by verifying PDR and its changes.

The remaining parts of this paper is structured as follows: Section 2 describes the amendments of 802.11p protocol. Section 3 exposes the overview of the related work in the domain of Jamming, In Section 4, we describe the proposed solution for detecting a jamming attack in VANET. Section 5 presents some numerical results to verify feasibility of the proposed solution. Finally, we summarize the main contribution of this study and its perspectives in Section 6.

2. AMENDMENT OF 802.11P IN VANET

802.11p protocol combines two parts. The first part, on the PHY layer, is a particular variant of 802.11a. The second part, on the MAC layer, is an amendment of 802.11e MAC protocol to provide quality of service (QoS) in wireless network [19, 11], and it also uses the method Carrier Sense Multiple Access with Collision Avoidance (CSMA/CA) to minimize the collisions and to guarantee fair access to the channel.

2.1 PHY amendment

The PHY layer of 802.11p is modified from 802.11a to adapt to a high speed vehicular environment. It is also based on Orthogonal Frequency Division Multiplexing (OFDM). It is able to offer a flow rate between 3, 4.5, 6, 9, 12, 18, 24 and 27 Mbps (for distances up to 1000 meters) with a modulation of OFDM type [17].

802.11p protocol uses the mode of 10 MHz bandwidth while 802.11a uses a bandwidth of 20MHz [16]. This reduction is to increase the power of the signal against fading in the high-speed environment. Due to this change, the transmission rate of the 802.11p protocol is half that of 802.11a, 27Mbps compared to 54Mbps. However, because of the narrow channel bandwidth, it will increase the ability to reduce inter-symbol interference (ISI).

The frequency band of 802.11p is used to 5.85GHz - 5.925GHz, regulated in Europe by ETSI (European Telecommunications Standards Institute) and by FCC (Federal Communication Commission) in the United States. It segments into 7 channels of 10 MHz each. In all channels, the channel 178 is the control channel (CCH); four channels 174, 175, 180 and 182 are service channels (SCH); two channels 172 and 184 is reserved for special uses [6].

2.2 MAC amendment

- WAVE BSS[14, 10]: MAC layer 802.11p protocol has been upgraded to adapt to the communication in the high-speed environment. Firstly, it modifies the algorithm of communication. It changes the concept of basic services set on mode WAVE (WBSS) instead of the normal basic services set (BSS) which is a group of stations and an access point. In the VANET, all vehicles are similar. There is no difference between vehicles nor between vehicle and infrastructure. The 802.11p MAC algorithm has been improved to reduce the time of communication. There are no authentication nor association in the MAC layer. if a vehicle want to join the network directly. It must receive a WAVE advertisement and configures itself according to the advertisement to join the WBSS. With this improved algorithm before joining the network, we can increase the transmission capacity and the reception of packets.

- CSMA/CA: MAC layer 802.11p protocol is based on the CSMA/CA to reduce collisions and ensure access to the channel[11]. A vehicle sends the control frame RTS/CTS before sending data frames. After joining the network, each vehicle will initiate a transmission by listening to the channel, then detect an idle channel in the DIFS time interval (Distributed Inter Frame Space). During DIFS, if the channel is free and the backoff time reaches 0, it will start to send packets. Firstly, it sends a RTS packet containing information and duration of the transmission to avoid collisions during transmission. The receiver vehicle receives the RTS packet, waits for a SIFS time interval (Short Inter Frame Space) and then sends a CTS packet. The sender vehicle receives the packet CTS and then begins transmitting data after waiting for a SIFS time interval. Lastly, the receiver vehicle sends an ACK packet to the sender after successfully receiving the data frames and waiting for a SIFS time interval.

If the channel is busy during the DIFS time interval, the vehicle must execute a procedure BACK_OFF.
The BACK_OFF algorithm is executed as follows: (1) it initiates backoff time with CWmin where CW is Content Window size, (2) it doubles its size up to CWmax if the transmission failes, (3) its size decreases step by step when the channel is idle, (4) when backoff time reaches 0, it sends immediately. If other transmissions occur while the backoff time decreases, it will block its backoff time. The backoff time will continue decreasing after other transmissions end and waiting for a DIFS. Values CWmin and CWmax are dependent access class (ACs). In 802.11e MAC protocol, there are four categories of data traffic available with different priorities: the background traffic (BK or AC0), best effort traffic (BE or AC1), video traffic (VI or AC2) and voice traffic (VO or AC3) [2].

When CSMA/CA is executed, the attacker can jam control frames RTS/CTS, data frames or ACK message. When the RTS frame is jammed, the channel will be unavailable for the demand of transmission. The transmission fails. It then retransmits. If transmission repeats continuously, the collision will occur. Even if the frames RTS, CTS had successfully been transmitted, the collision would still occur on the data frames if the attacker had not followed the rules and emited bad packets to the receiver. Furthermore, the attacker can jam the ACK message. Data packets will be dropped, if the sender reaches the limit of retransmission.

In the next section, we provide the previous work on the domain of jamming attacks.

3. RELATED WORKS

In [9], attackers and possible attacks have been explained. Authors proposed five different classes of attacks and solution for classify, identify their attacks in VANET. Thus, the communication security in VANET has been discussed by [12], [15]. Maxim Raya and al. analyze potential security threats and design robust security architecture.

- *Denial of Service (DOS) Attack and Its Possible Solutions in VANET[8]*: Authors described many kind of the possible attacks in VANET that include DOS attack. They explain that DoS attacks are executed by three levels with three ways. In this DOS basic level attack, the attacker denies a communication of nodes by keeping their state become busy every time.

In this high level of DOS attack, the attacker jams the channel, thus other users in the jammed area can not access the network. The third level of DOS attack is Distributed Denial of Services (DDOS), the attackers launch attack from different locations. After explain DOS attacks, they propose a solution for avoidance them using Channel Switching, Technology Switching, Frequency Hopping Spread Spectrum (FHSS), Multiple Radio Transceivers.

- *Detection of radio interference in VANET[4]*: Authors proposed a new model based on the measure of correlation between errors and correct reception time to detect the presence of interference in vehicular ad hoc networks. The correlation coefficient (CC) used is a statistical measure of relation between two random variables. A node calculates and compares two values: the probability of error (PE) and the correlation coefficient (CC). If the CC is greater than the EP, the network is considered like jammed.

- *Improving Reliability of Jamming Attack Detection in Ad hoc Networks [7]*: Authors presented physical jamming, virtual jamming and collision probability in wireless ad hoc network. They use collision calculating to detect jamming attack. They claim that collisions due to jamming attack are not different from other collisions such as collision due to hidden terminal or network congestion.

- *Jamming Attack Detection and Countermeasures In Wireless Sensor Network Using Ant System [13]*: Authors presented types of physical jamming. This technique is based on the distributed intelligence using multiple performance parameters such as power, distance, packet loss, SNR, BER to build an algorithm for detecting physical jamming. This system bases on their parameters and the nodes' behavior to determine jamming attacks. The decline of energy and the rate of fault decision are important, they decide the system capacity. If they are lower, the detection capability would be higher.

- *JAM [5]* is software to detect a jammed area in the sensor network, It permit continue routing in the rest of the network by a warning around this area. A node uses this software to calculate the JAM algorithm and distribute a message to its neighbors in which it informs that it is jammed or none jammed.

- *The Feasibility of Launching and Detecting Jamming Attacks in Wireless Networks [18]*: Authors presented four types of virtual jamming that can be used against the WSN. Then they explore techniques for detecting a jamming such as the signal strength, the carrier sensing time, or the packet delivery ratio (PDR). They proposed two detection algorithms using the PDR and the signal strength information or the position like consistency checks.

In the methods of jamming attacks detection that has been proposed, they consider the low value of PDR and other parameters to detect the presence of jamming attack. No solution considers the PDR decrease when it is high. Hence, their methods cannot be in accord with the VANET which is the dynamic network. For this reason, we have proposed a one solution for detecting jamming attacks in vehicle ad hoc networks that can detect more precisely. Our method is described in the next section.

4. PROPOSED SOLUTION

This solution is based on the change of PDR value consisting of the PDR value and the rate of PDR reduction. In normal environment, all packets sent by the sender must be received at the receiver. There is no obstacle for communication. When a vehicle moves on the road, it is considered as jammed as soon as the change of PDR surpasses a threshold. It will broadcast the warning messages which have high priority.

At the receiver, PDR value is calculated at the MAC layer; by ratio of packets number passing the CRC check to the packets number received. Packets passing the CRC check are sent by the sender. Received packets are packets sent by the attacker or the sender.

The rate of PDR decrease is calculated by:

$$Down\_PDR = \frac{previous\_PDR - current\_PDR}{current\_time - previous\_time}$$

Current_PDR: the new PDR value at present
Previous_PDR: the old PDR value at previous
Current_time: the present moment
Previous_time: the previous time

INPUT : Current_PDR= procedure_of_calcul_PDR,
Down_PDR = calcul of down_PDR,
State_jam = false
OUTPUT: annonce_jam (position, State_jam, current_time, Vector_V)

```
if Down_PDR ≥ threshold_of_Down_speed then
  | State_jam = true;
end
if (0 < current_PDR ≤ threshold_of_PDR) then
  | if Down_PDR > 0 then
  |   | State_jam = true;
  | else
  |   | State_jam = false;
  | end
end
if current_PDR = 0 then
  | State_jam = true;
end
Position = (x, y) ;
Get Current_time;
Lock Vector_V;
Reture;
```

Algorithm 1: Jamming attacks detection algorithm

When a vehicle travels on the road, it is considered as jammed if at least one of the two following cases happens:

- The rate of PDR decrease is greater or equal to a decrease rate threshold.

- The PDR value is less than or equal to a PDR threshold and the rate of PDR decrease is strictly positive until the PDR value equals 0.

The decrease rate threshold and the PDR threshold can be defined. When it is considered as jammed, State_jam will be *"true"*, it will broadcast a warning message containing information of its state, direction, jammed time and jammed position. The State_jam *"true"* always happens when it is in the jammed area until it gets out.

In the case a vehicle enters the jammed area, the parameter Down_PDR is considered first to detect that it is jammed. At the beginning of the jammed period, its PDR is still high but the rate of PDR decrease is great. During the jammed period, this vehicle cannot receive packets sent by the sender; it only receives packets sent by the attacker. Hence, its PDR still decreases. For this reason the rate of PDR decrease is strictly positive until the PDR value equals 0. Finally, using the parameter Down_PDR, it is possible to detect jamming attacks at the earliest when the jamming attack is effective.

In case a vehicle participates in WBSS at the jammed area, the PDR value is considered to detect that it is jammed. Normally, before participating in WBSS, it must set the WBSS advertisement to join. But if it is jammed, it cannot receive their packets. Hence, its PDR is null. The State_jam will be *"true"* without interest the parameter Down_PDR until it got out of this area.

This vehicle considers that it leaves the jammed area if the PDR value is less than a PDR threshold and the rate of PDR decrease is less than or equal to 0, or the previous PDR value was equal to 0 and the rate of PDR decrease must be strictly negative. In this case, this vehicle can receive packets sent by the sender.

As soon as this vehicle exits the jammed area, the State_jam is *"false"*. It broadcasts a warning message if its State_jam changes from *"true"* to *"false"* to inform that it got out of this area. This message also contains information of the position, direction and time. The parameter vector_V informs the vehicle direction to forecast the jammed area.

With this solution, each vehicle can detect the presence of jamming attacks when it considers as jammed and when it got out of this area. After summarizing the information in the warning messages, we can specify a jammed area at each moment.

5. NUMERICAL RESULTS

We use the NS-3 simulator to design, implement and validate the proposed solution. With the NS-3 simulator, we can compare performance of the communication between vehicles in the case where there is no jamming attacks and where there is jamming attacks.

The simulation was restricted in place of 600m x 30m where the vehicle placements happen in two lanes. Parameters in Table 1 are used in the simulations.

Simulation parameters	
Transmission rate	OfdmRate3MbpsBW10MHz
Protocol	802.11p
Simulation time (s)	80
Packets size (bytes)	1000
Access class	AC_VO

Table 1: Parameters of the simulation network

Nodes send packets with the constant transmission rate using mode OfdmRate3MbpsBW10MHz. Nodes communicate with 802.11p protocol. Simulations occur during 80s. Packet size is 1000 bytes. We use the access class AC_VO with CWmin value of 3 and CWmax value of 15. Simulations were produced by two models: without mobility and with mobility of constant speed.

In the simulations below, the performance metric which was discussed is the packets delivery ratio (PDR) according to the communication between the nodes.

5.1 Simulation in the mobility model with constant speed

100 vehicles which are receivers move on the two lane road with the speed of 10m/s. We made three simulation cases to verify these changes of PDR. In these cases, the sender and the attacker does not move.

In the first case, simulation of one sender and one receiver going into the jammed area:

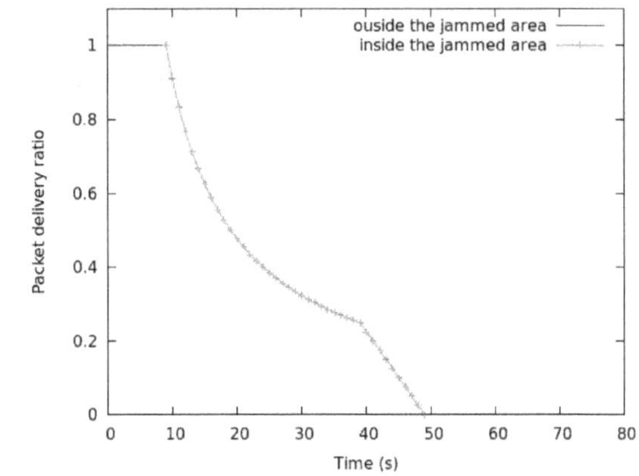

Figure 1: The PDR change in the first case

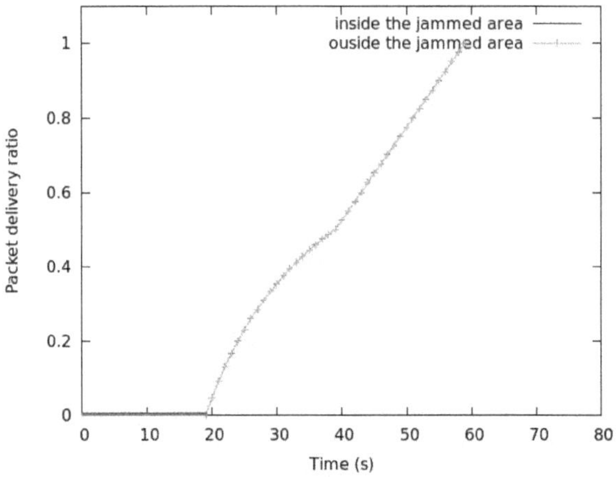

Figure 2: The PDR change in the second case

We observe a random vehicle on the road, the result in the first case denotes that the PDR of vehicle is 100% when it has not yet jammed. Its PDR begins to decrease as soon as entering the jammed area. After doing certain simulations with others vehicles, we find out that the rate of PDR decrease depends on the moment when the vehicle enters this area. If a vehicle enters this area earlier, the rate of PDR decrease is faster. Otherwise, there is a small area where the PDR begins to decrease.

In the second case, simulation of the receiver goes out of the jammed area and approaches the sender:

The attacker executes the reactive jamming before the examined vehicles take part in the network. They are in the jammed area, after they went to the sender. In the jammed area, these PDR are null. These PDR increase as soon as they go out of this area. Thus, a signal marking the state when a vehicle has been out of the jammed area is that the rate of PDR decrease (Down_PDR) is less than or equal to 0. It is denoted in the figure 2.

In the third case, simulation of the receiver goes into the jammed area; it then passes this area and goes to another sender:

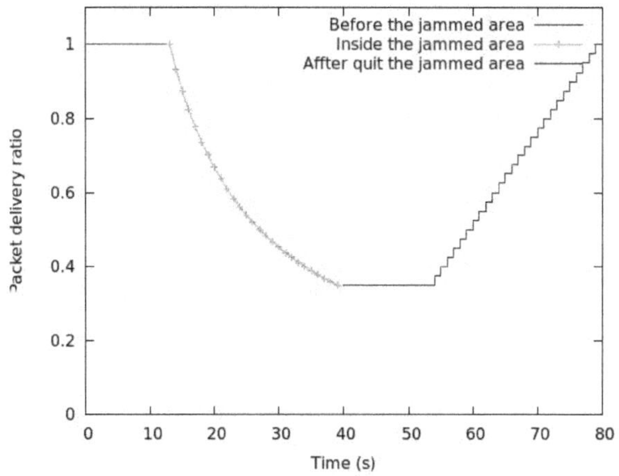

Figure 3: The PDR change in the third case

At the beginning, a vehicle is near the first sender. It passes the jammed area and goes to the second sender. The result in the third case shows that vehicle's PDR was decreased when it passed the jammed area, because it could not receive any packets. This PDR decrease occurs until it comes out of this area. After going out to this area, its PDR does not decrease, because it can receive from the second sender. Therefore, the rate of PDR decrease is less or equal to 0. For this reason, in the proposed solution, if Down_PDR is less than or equal to 0, it is considered as moved out the jammed area.

5.2 Simulation in the model without mobility

Attacker runs a jamming attack after the communication between 2 vehicles. We observe certain vehicles that are in the small area where these PDR begin decrease. We change the position of vehicle of δx (δx = 5 m). If the distance between the examined vehicle and attacker is the distances between other vehicles and the attacker are (d - x) (x + d), (d + 2x). We calculate these PDR values.

These results in the figure 4 show:

In this area, there are large differences of their PDR decrease. It gets smaller if the distance is longer. Hence, a

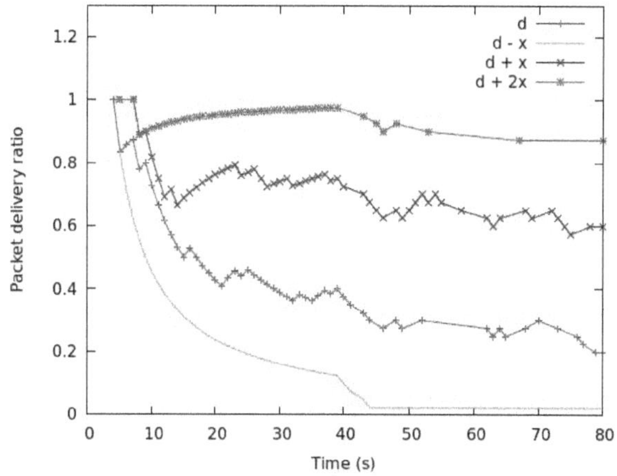

Figure 4: The PDR change in the simulation in the model without mobility

vehicle which is in this area is not completely jammed. It can still receive or send packets. In this proposed solution, a vehicle will broadcast warning messages while passing this area.

Summary of results:

With these separated simulations, we can verify feasibility of this solution. At the receiver, it will be considered like jammed if the rate of PDR decrease exceeds a threshold or PDR value is lowered and the rate of PDR decrease is strictly positive. The rate of PDR decrease will be firstly considered,if a vehicle runs into the jammed area. PDR value will be considered, if it departs this area. It sends warning messages as soon as it goes into the jammed area, and until it gets out of this area with a message informing the exit this area.

6. CONCLUSION

Vehicular ad hoc networks are dynamic networks. Vehicles move all the time and communications between them are very short.Hence, they are vulnerable to DOS attacks, such as the jamming attack and models of jamming attacks detection have to be produced very rapidly for preciser detection.

In this study, we proposed one solution based on the change of packets delivery ratio which consists of PDR value and rate of PDR decrease. It can detect the presence of jamming attacks as soon as their attacks are effective.

In the future, we will ameliorate this solution with more parameters for approach the real mode of VANETs

7. REFERENCES

[1] http://en.wikipedia.org/wiki/ieee _802.11p.

[2] http://en.wikipedia.org/wiki/ieee_802.11e-2005.

[3] Part 11: Wireless lan medium access control (mac) and physical layer (phy) specifications amendment 6: Wireless access in vehicular environments. Technical report, IEEE, 2010.

[4] Lynda Mokdad Ali Hamieh, Jalel Ben-Othman. Detection of radio interference attacks in vanet. *IEEE "GLOBECOM" 2009 proceedings*, 2009.

[5] Charalampos Konstantopoulos Aristides Mpitziopoulos, Damianos Gavalas and Grammati Pantziou. A survey on jamming attacks and countermeasures in wsns. *IEEE COMMUNICATIONS SURVEYS - TUTORIALS*, 2009.

[6] Christoph Sommery David Eckhoff and Falko Dressler. On the necessity of accurate ieee 802.11p models for ivc protocol simulation. 2011.

[7] Sumita Mishra Geethapriya Thamilarasu and Ramalingam Sridhar. Improving reliability of jamming attack detection in ad hoc networks. *International Journal of Communication Networks and Information Security (IJCNIS)*, 3, 2011.

[8] Jamalul-lail Ab Manan Halabi Hasbullah, Irshad Ahmed Soomro. Denial of service (dos) attack and its possible solutions in vanet. *World Academy of Science, Engineering and Technology 65*, 2010.

[9] Jamalul-lail Masood-ur-Rehman Irshad Ahmed Sumra, Halabi Hasbullah. Trust and trusted computing in vanet. *Computer Science Journal*, 2011.

[10] Daniel Jiang and Luca Delgrossi. Ieee 802.11p: Towards an international standard for wireless access in vehicular environments. In *VTC Spring'08*, pages 2036–2040, 2008.

[11] Barend J. van Wyk Lusheng Miao, Karim Djouani and Yskandar Hamam. A survey of ieee 802.11p mac protocol. *Multidisciplinary Journals in Science and Technology, Journal of Selected Areas in Telecommunications (JSAT)*, 2011.

[12] Jean-Pierre Hubaux Maxim Raya, Panos Papadimitratos. Securing vehicular communications. 13:8–15, 2006.

[13] Rajani Muraleedharan and Lisa Ann Osadciw. Jamming attack detection and countermeasures in wireless sensor network using ant system. *Proceedings of SPIE, the International Society for Optical Engineering*, 6248, 2006.

[14] Yongho Seokt Taekyoung Kwon Nakjung Choi, Sungjoon Choi and Yanghee Choi. A solicitation-based ieee 802.11p mac protocol for roadside to vehicular networks. 2007.

[15] Maxim Raya and JeanPierre Hubaux. The security of vehicular ad hoc networks. 2004.

[16] Rohde and Schwarz. Wlan 802.11p measurements for vehicle to vehicle (v2v) dsrc.

[17] Yuh-Shyan Chen Angela Irwin-Aamir Hassan Sherali Zeadally, Ray Hunt. Vehicular ad hoc networks (vanets): status, results, and challenges. 2010.

[18] Y. Zhang W. Xu, W. Trappe and T. Wood. The feasibility of launching and detecting jamming attacks in wireless networks. 2005.

[19] Bhaskar Krishnamachari Yi Wang, Akram Ahmed and Konstantinos Psounis. Ieee 802.11p performance evaluation and protocol enhancement. *Proceedings of the 2008 IEEE International Conference on Vehicular Electronics and Safety Columbus*, 2008.

On the Selection of Optimal Broadcast Schemes in VANETs

Julio A. Sanguesa, Manuel Fogue, Piedad Garrido, Francisco J. Martinez
University of Zaragoza, Spain
{jsanguesa, mfogue, piedad, f.martinez}@unizar.es

Juan-Carlos Cano, Carlos T. Calafate, Pietro Manzoni
Universitat Politècnica de València, Spain
{jucano, calafate, pmanzoni}@disca.upv.es

ABSTRACT

In Vehicular ad hoc Networks (VANETs), efficient dissemination of messages is a key factor to speed up the development of useful services and applications. In this paper, we propose a novel algorithm that automatically chooses the best dissemination scheme trying to fit the warning message delivery policy to the current characteristics of each specific vehicular scenario. Our mechanism uses as input parameters the vehicular density and the topological characteristics of the environment where the vehicles are located, in order to decide which dissemination scheme to use. Simulation results demonstrate the feasibility of our approach, which is able to support more efficient warning message dissemination in vehicular environments.

Categories and Subject Descriptors

C.2.1 [**Computer-Communication Networks**]: Network Architecture and Design—*Wireless communication*

General Terms

Experimentation, Performance

Keywords

Vehicular ad hoc networks, warning message dissemination, adaptive systems, vehicular density estimation, VANETs

1. INTRODUCTION

Vehicular ad hoc Networks (VANETs) are wireless communication networks supporting cooperative driving among vehicles on the road. Vehicles act as communication nodes and relays, forming dynamic vehicular networks together with other nearby vehicles [1].

The specific characteristics of VANETs favor the development of attractive and challenging services and applications, including road safety, traffic flow management, road status monitoring, environmental protection, and mobile infotainment [8, 16]. In this work we focus on traffic safety and efficient warning message dissemination, where the main goal is to reduce the latency and to increase the accuracy of the information received by nearby vehicles when a dangerous situation occurs.

In a VANET, any vehicle detecting an abnormal situation (i.e. accident, slippery road, etc.) rapidly starts notifying the anomaly to nearby vehicles to spread the alert information in a short period of time. Hence, broadcasting warning messages can be useful to alert nearby vehicles. However, this dissemination is strongly affected by: (i) the signal attenuation due to the distance between the sender and receiver (especially in low vehicular density areas), (ii) the effect of obstacles in signal transmission (very usual in urban areas, e.g., due to buildings), and (iii) a reduced message delivery effectiveness due to serious redundancy, contention, and massive packet collisions provoked by simultaneous forwarding, usually known as broadcast storm (prone to occur in highly congested areas) [14].

We consider that adapting the dissemination policy to the specific environment, accounting for the current vehicular density as well as for the scenario where the vehicles are located, can be beneficial in order to reduce broadcast storm related problems, and also to increase the efficiency of the warning message dissemination process.

In this paper, we propose an adaptive algorithm that automatically chooses the best dissemination scheme to adapt the warning message delivery policy to each specific scenario. Our mechanism uses as input parameters the vehicular density and the topological characteristics of the environment where the vehicles are located, using them to decide which dissemination scheme to use. The main goal is to maximize the message delivery effectiveness while generating a reduced number of messages and, thus, avoiding or mitigating broadcast storms. In addition, we also propose the Nearest Junction Located (NJL), our novel warning message dissemination scheme specially designed for being used in highly congested urban areas.

The paper is organized as follows: in Section 2 we review previous works closely related to our proposal, highlighting the main similarities and differences. In Section 3 we introduce our novel NJL scheme, and the optimal broadcast selection algorithm. Section 4 shows the simulation environment used to validate our proposal. Section 5 presents and discusses the obtained results. Finally, Section 6 concludes this paper.

MSWiM'13, November 3–8, 2013, Barcelona, Spain.

http://dx.doi.org/10.1145/2507924.2507935.

2. RELATED WORK

In the networking literature we can find several works that present adaptive mechanisms specially designed to enhance message dissemination in vehicular communications. In this section we present some of the most representative works.

Xue-wen et al. [15] proposed the Transmission Range Adaptive Broadcast (TRAB), a broadcast algorithm for VANETs. Considering the transmission ranges of vehicles together with the inter-vehicle distances, TRAB calculates the waiting time to select the relay vehicles in accordance with the additional coverage area of adjacent vehicles to ensure that fewer relay vehicles will be used to forward the emergency packets. In addition, TRAB guarantees the dissemination reliability by adopting two types of answering mechanisms called implicit ACK and explicit ACK. However, this scheme is designed to obtain efficient propagation of warning messages in highway scenarios alone, making it unsuitable for scenarios with complex topologies where we would want to disseminate warning messages in all directions surrounding the critical area.

Slavik et al. [12] proposed the Rate-Adaptive Broadcast (RAB) protocol for information dissemination in VANETs. RAB adapts to the network conditions, although it does not require any knowledge of network topology. By assuming a VANET dissemination application with fixed periodic updates, RAB is able to use a decision threshold control algorithm based on the rate of both messages. It tracks both the rate of received new messages and duplicate messages received. If the new message rate dips below its long-run average, the decision threshold is adjusted to improve message propagation. Otherwise, RAB adjusts the decision threshold to keep the duplicate message rate within an efficient range. Thus, RAB jointly optimizes the broadcast message delivery rate and the bandwidth consumption. Unlike the TRAB scheme, the use of RAB is not restricted to highways; nevertheless, the roadmap layout is not used to select the vehicles to forward the messages. Instead, the scenario is treated like a free space environment where vehicles only try to send messages as far away as possible, without accounting for the different blind areas that buildings may produce during the dissemination process.

Sommer et al. [13] proposed the Adaptive Traffic Beacon (ATB), a fully distributed message dissemination protocol which uses adaptive beaconing based on two key metrics: message utility and channel quality. Authors show that adaptive beaconing leads to a much broader dissemination of messages (in terms of penetration rate) than flooding-based approaches, although at a slower rate. The main objective of ATB is to exchange information in knowledge bases by sending beacons as frequently as possible, while maintaining a congestion-free wireless channel. However authors only tested their proposal in a roadmap portion of Ingolstadt, Germany.

Schwartz et al. [11] proposed a data dissemination protocol for VANETs that distributes data utility fairly over vehicles while adaptively controlling the network load. The protocol relies only on local knowledge to achieve fairness with concepts of Nash Bargaining from game theory. Simulation results show that their algorithm presents a higher fairness index, and it maintains a high level of bandwidth utilization efficiency compared to other approaches. In addition, the rate of transmissions is adaptively controlled as new information about the environment is collected. However, the vehicular density of the scenarios where their proposal was tested was very low (i.e., only 20 $vehicles/km^2$). Additionally, it is not clearly explained if their simulations accounted for the effect of obstacles in wireless signal propagation, and the benefits of their proposal in terms of vehicles informed.

As shown, existing adaptive dissemination techniques for VANETs usually consider features related to vehicles in the scenario, such as their density, speed, and location, to adapt the performance of the dissemination process. However, most of the works in the literature are designed for highway scenarios where messages are only propagated in one direction, or focused on end-to-end routing. Additionally, most of them do not account for the effect of buildings and other obstacles during the dissemination of messages, which may lead to wrong conclusions. Hence, these approaches are not useful when attempting to warn the highest possible number of vehicles about dangerous situations in realistic vehicular environments. We consider that new adaptive proposals for warning message dissemination in urban environments are needed, offering efficient broadcasting techniques around the affected area, taking into account both the number of nearby vehicles, as well as the topology of the scenario.

3. SELECTING THE OPTIMAL BROADCAST SCHEME IN VANETS

Over the years, several schemes have been proposed to address the broadcast storm problem in vehicular networks. Some of the most representative ones are presented below.

3.1 Broadcast Schemes

- The *Counter-based scheme* [14]. Initially proposed for Mobile Ad Hoc Networks (MANETs), this scheme aims at mitigating broadcast storms by using a threshold C and a counter c to keep track of the number of times a broadcast message is received. Whenever $c \geq C$, rebroadcast is inhibited.

- The *Distance-based scheme* [14]. This scheme accounts for the relative distance d between vehicles to decide whether to rebroadcast or not. When the distance d between two vehicles is short, the additional coverage (AC) area of the new rebroadcast is lower, and so rebroadcasting the warning message is not recommended. Forwarding is only beneficial when the additional coverage is nearly maximum.

- The *enhanced Street Broadcast Reduction* (eSBR) [6]. This scheme is specially designed to be used in VANETs, taking advantage of the information provided by maps and built-in positioning systems, such as the GPS. Vehicles are only allowed to rebroadcast messages if they are located far from their source ($> d_{min}$), or if the vehicles are located in different streets, giving access to new areas of the scenario. The eMDR scheme uses information about the roadmap to avoid blind areas due the presence of urban structures blocking the radio signal.

- The *enhanced Message Dissemination for Roadmaps* (eMDR) [4]. As an improvement to the eSBR scheme, eMDR increases the efficiency of the system by avoiding multiple forwardings of the same message if nearby

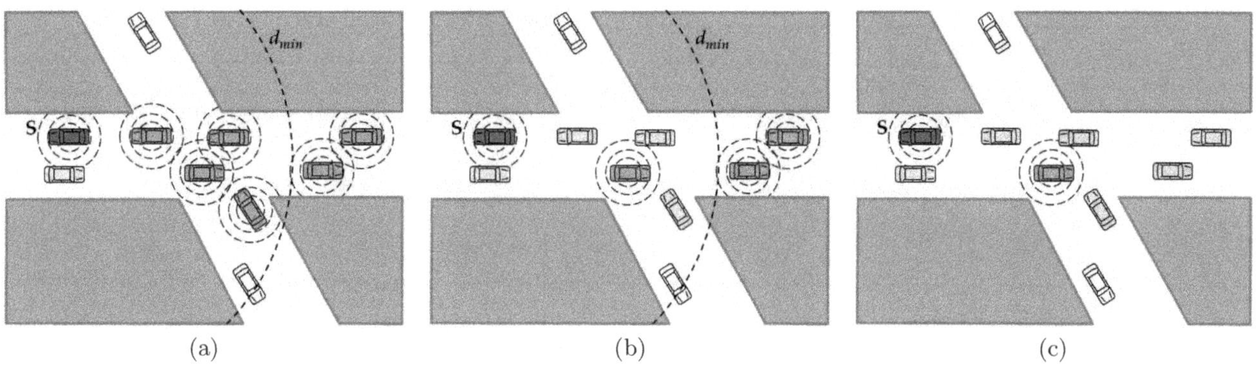

Figure 1: Comparison of different dissemination schemes for VANETs: (a) eSBR, (b) eMDR, and (c) NJL.

vehicles are located in different streets. Specifically, vehicles use the information about the junctions of the roadmap, and only the vehicle closest to the geographic center of the junction, according to the geopositioning system, is allowed to forward the messages received. This strategy aims at reducing the number of broadcasted messages while maintaining a high percentage of vehicles informed.

3.2 Nearest Junction Located: our Novel Broadcast Scheme

The eMDR and eSBR schemes proved to be specially effective in sparse urban environments. However, the number of messages produced may become excessive in scenarios with a high vehicle density. To cope with this deficiency, in this paper we proposed a novel dissemination scheme called *Nearest Junction Located* (NJL) that is completely based on the topology of the roadmap, allowing vehicles to rebroadcast a message only if they are the nearest vehicle to the geographical coordinates of any junction obtained from the integrated maps. This scheme follows a procedure similar to the eMDR algorithm, although ignoring the distance between sender and receiver; thus, it only focus on the location of the receiving vehicle. Although the performance of this algorithm is not optimal in sparse environments, it performs quite well in high-density scenarios where the dominant factor to improve the dissemination process is the position of the vehicles, achieving results similar to those obtained by the eMDR and eSBR schemes, while requiring only a fraction of the messages.

Figure 1 shows the differences between the eSBR, eMDR and NJL schemes in a specific VANET scenario, where vehicle S broadcasts a warning message. The line labeled as d_{min} represents the minimum rebroadcast distance used by eSBR and eMDR. Darker vehicles will be allowed to forward the messages received from S, and it is noticeable how the eSBR is the less restrictive scheme, whereas the NJL is the most restrictive one, and thus more suitable for scenarios with a high vehicle density.

3.3 Optimal Broadcast Selection Algorithm

To select the optimal broadcast scheme for a specific scenario, we must account for different performance metrics, which will allow us to determine which scheme is the most efficient. These metrics should be quantitative to be easily adapted to different scenarios and environments, i.e., highways and urban maps.

During a warning message dissemination process, the most important objective to accomplish consists on informing the highest possible number of vehicles in the shortest time. Hence, a critical metric to be used is the percentage of informed vehicles at different time instants (Inf_T). We propose to measure the percentage of vehicles receiving warning messages after 10, 30, and 120 seconds since the time when the dangerous situation started being notified, providing information about both the speed and completeness of the dissemination process. The first 10 seconds provide a good reference of the dissemination speed, the second period (30 seconds) offers a balance between dissemination speed and the completeness, and the state of the scenario after 120 seconds shows the stationary value when no evolution is observed.

These three values were combined using a weighted average, thereby obtaining a single value representing the efficiency of the dissemination process (P_{inf}). In our results, the weights applied to the values collected during the different time intervals are 0.5 (10 seconds), 0.3 (30 seconds), and 0.2 (120 seconds), respectively, since the stationary values of the different broadcast schemes do not tend to vary significantly, and the most noticeable differences occur during the first seconds of the process.

Another important metric for the dissemination schemes is the number of messages produced (M_{recv}). If the wireless channel is saturated with packets, the high contention and the occurrence of collisions will reduce the performance of the process, producing broadcast storms. Hence, the number of messages must remain as low as possible without compromising the efficiency of the dissemination.

Our Optimal Broadcast Selection Algorithm makes use of these two metrics (P_{inf} and M_{recv}) to select the scheme to be used on each particular situation. It works following a three step process, as shown in Algorithm 1:

- *Step 1*: For each considered broadcast scheme, the first metric (P_{inf}) is computed, and the scheme with the highest percentage of informed vehicles in the shortest time is selected. Due to the importance of this metric, only the dissemination schemes with a deviation lower than 10% with respect to the best one are considered for the second step of the algorithm, and they are stored in set $\mathbb{C}$.

Algorithm 1: Optimal Broadcast Selection

input : $\mathbb{B}$: set of broadcast schemes
input : $Inf_{10}(b), Inf_{30}(b), Inf_{120}(b)$: percentage of informed nodes after 10, 30, and 120 seconds
input : $M_{recv}(b)$: number of messages received per vehicle
output : $Optimal_{bcast}$: optimal scheme in terms of informed vehicles and messages received

/* Step 1: Maximize percentage of informed vehicles */
forall $b \in \mathbb{B}$ **do**
  $P_{inf}(b) = Inf_{10}(b) \cdot 0.5 + Inf_{30}(b) \cdot 0.3 + Inf_{120}(b) \cdot 0.2$;
$max_{inf} = max(P_{inf}(b)) \ \forall \ b \ \in \mathbb{B}$
$\mathbb{C} = \{\}$
forall $b \in \mathbb{B}$ **do**
  if $(max_{inf} - P_{inf}(b)) < 10\%$ **then** $\mathbb{C} = \mathbb{C} \cup \{b\}$

/* Step 2: Minimize received messages */
$min_{recv} = min(M_{recv}(b)) \ \forall \ b \ \in \mathbb{C}$
forall $b \in \mathbb{C}$ **do**
  $dev_{inf}(b) = max_{inf} - P_{inf}(b)$
  $dev_{recv}(b) = \dfrac{M_{recv}(b) - min_{recv}}{min_{recv}}$

/* Step 3: Selection of the optimal broadcast scheme */
$Optimal_{bcast} = \arg\min_{b \in \mathbb{C}} \ (dev_{inf}(b) \cdot K + dev_{recv}(b)) \ \forall \ b \ \in \mathbb{B}$

- *Step 2*: Considering only the broadcast schemes in $\mathbb{C}$, the scheme producing the lowest number of messages per vehicle (M_{recv}) is obtained, in order to reduce the probability of broadcast storms, and the percentage variation with respect to this value is computed for each scheme.

- *Step 3*: The optimal scheme will be selected as the one minimizing the deviation with respect to both the maximal P_{inf} and the minimal M_{recv}. Depending on the vehicle density, it may become more important to minimize the number of messages for high densities, and in that case our algorithm varies the degree of importance of the two metrics by using the K value, calculated as follows:

$$K = \frac{100}{density \ of \ vehicles} \qquad (1)$$

In particular, we used the value of reference 100 to compute K, since our experiments showed that the differences in terms of informed vehicles decrease noticeably for densities above 100 vehicles/km^2 (see Figure 2), and, hence, a higher weight is assigned to the number of messages received when this density is exceeded.

4. SIMULATION ENVIRONMENT

Our optimal broadcast selection algorithm was tested using the ns-2 simulator [2], modified to consider the IEEE 802.11p standard[1]. In terms of the physical layer, the data rate used for packet broadcasting is 6 Mbit/s, as this is the maximum rate for broadcasting in 802.11p. The MAC layer was also extended to include four different channel access priorities. Therefore, application messages are categorized into four different Access Categories (ACs), where AC0 has the lowest and AC3 the highest priority.

[1]All these improvements and modifications are available in http://www.grc.upv.es/software/

Table 1: Parameter settings in the simulations.

Parameter	Value
roadmaps	Rome, Valencia, Sydney, Amsterdam, Los Angeles, San Francisco, Madrid
number of vehicles per km^2	$[25, 50, 100, 150, 200, and\ 250]$
number of collided vehicles	3
roadmap size	$2000m \times 2000m$
warning message size	$256B$
beacon message size	$512B$
warning messages priority	$AC3$
beacon priority	$AC1$
interval between messages	1 second
MAC/PHY	802.11p
radio propagation model	RAV [7]
mobility model	$Krauss$ [5]
channel bandwidth	$6Mbps$
max. transmission range	$400m$
d_{min} (used in distance-based, eSBR, and eMDR schemes)	$200m$

The simulator was also modified to make use of our *Real Attenuation and Visibility* (RAV) scheme [7], which proved to increase the level of realism in VANET simulations using real urban roadmaps in the presence of obstacles. As for vehicular mobility, it has been obtained with CityMob for Roadmaps (C4R) [3], a mobility generator able to import maps directly from OpenStreetMap [9], and make them available for being used by the ns-2 simulator.

With regard to data traffic, vehicles operate in two modes: (a) warning mode, and (b) normal mode. Warning mode vehicles inform other vehicles about their status by sending warning messages periodically with the highest priority at the MAC layer; each vehicle is only allowed to propagate them once for each sequence number. Normal mode vehicles enable the diffusion of these warning packets and, periodically, they also send *beacons* with information such as their positions, speed, etc. These periodic messages have lower priority than warning messages, and so they are not propagated by other vehicles. All the results represent an average of over 50 repetitions with different random scenarios, obtaining for all of them a degree of confidence of 90%; each simulation run lasted for 120 seconds. Table 1 shows the parameters used for the simulations.

The roadmaps used in the simulations were selected in order to have different profile scenarios (i.e., with different topology characteristics). Table 2 shows the main features of the cities simulated. Note that we added a column labeled as *SJ Ratio*, which represents the result of dividing the number of streets between the number of junctions. As shown, the first 4 cities (Rome, Valencia, Sydney, and Amsterdam) present an SJ ratio greater than 1, which indicates that they have a complex topology, while the rest of the cities (Los Angeles, San Francisco, and Madrid) present a lower SJ value, which indicates that they have a simple topology.

We are interested in the following performance metrics: (i) percentage of informed vehicles, and (ii) number of messages received per vehicle. The percentage of informed vehicles is the percentage of vehicles that do receive the warning messages sent by warning mode vehicles. The number of messages received per vehicle (including beacons and warning messages) gives an estimation of channel contention and the overhead of the selected approach.

Table 2: Map features.

Map	Streets	Junctions	SJ Ratio
Rome	1655	1193	1.387
Valencia	2829	2233	1.267
Sydney	872	814	1.071
Amsterdam	1494	1449	1.031
Los Angeles	287	306	0.938
San Francisco	725	818	0.886
Madrid	628	715	0.878

Table 3: Simulation Results in San Francisco after 120 seconds.

	25 veh./km^2		250 veh./km^2	
	% informed	mess./veh.	% informed	mess./veh.
eSBR	89.9%	345	99.9%	4661
eMDR	89.5%	301	99.9%	4275
NJL	83.9%	174	99.9%	2184

5. SIMULATION RESULTS

In this work we performed a total of 10,500 experiments, since we made 50 repetitions while also varying the city roadmaps, the density of vehicles, and the broadcast scheme used. Due to space restrictions, it is not possible to present the results of all of the cities simulated, so in some cases we only included the results obtained for San Francisco and Valencia since, according to our previous work [10], the simulation results obtained in these roadmaps are closer to the average ones.

In this section, we present: (i) the performance results of our proposed NJL broadcast scheme, (ii) a comparison between the studied broadcast schemes in terms of informed vehicles, (iii) a comparison in terms of messages received per vehicle, and finally, (iv) the performance of our Optimal Broadcast Selection algorithm.

5.1 Performance of the Nearest Junction Located Scheme

Tables 3 and 4 compare the simulation results after 120 seconds in two different maps (San Francisco and Valencia). The values of the *percentage of informed vehicles* and the *number of messages received per vehicle* are shown. As can be seen, the NJL scheme allows informing about 3-6% less vehicles under low densities (25 veh./km^2) in both maps, but the percentage of informed vehicles when the vehicle density is high is the same. However, the number of messages received per vehicle is reduced by half in all the scenarios tested using the NJL scheme. This makes the NJL scheme specially suitable for scenarios with a high density of vehicles where broadcast storms are prone to occur. It would be beneficial to use less restrictive schemes under low vehicle density conditions, such as the eSBR and the eMDR, to reach as many vehicles as possible since the number of messages produced is too low to produce broadcast storms.

5.2 Comparison in Terms of Percentage of Informed Vehicles

As mentioned earlier, the most important metric to be considered when designing a warning message dissemination scheme for VANETs is the percentage of notified vehicles. We performed several experiments using roadmaps with different features and varying the density of vehicles. Figure 2 presents the evolution of the dissemination process in terms of notified vehicles for the maps of San Francisco and Valencia under four different vehicle densities: 25, 100, 150, and 250 vehicles/km^2.

Table 4: Simulation Results in Valencia after 120 seconds.

	25 veh./km^2		250 veh./km^2	
	% informed	mess./veh.	% informed	mess./veh.
eSBR	40.6%	55	99.7%	3360
eMDR	38.8%	48	99.7%	2451
NJL	37.4%	41	99.7%	1521

It is noticeable how the topology of the area and the number of vehicles are determinant factors affecting the performance of the broadcast scheme. The dissemination process develops faster in every situation when the vehicle density increases. For sparse networks, the counter-based scheme provides the best results in terms of informed vehicles, whereas for densities above 150 vehicles/km^2, the process presents a very similar behavior for all the selected schemes. The exception is the distance-based scheme in the map of Valencia, which proved to be very inefficient due to the high amount of obstacles interfering with the radio signal.

In addition, we corroborated that simple and regular city profiles like San Francisco allow an easier propagation of the radio signal, increasing the number of informed vehicles at a given time. The most restrictive schemes, such as the NJL, require a very high density of vehicles to achieve an efficiency similar to other dissemination schemes.

These results indicate that basing the selection only on the percentage of vehicles informed could lead to wrong decisions that could affect the efficiency of the system, justifying the need for additional metrics to perform the broadcast scheme selection.

5.3 Comparison in Terms of Messages Received per Vehicle

The number of messages produced by a given dissemination scheme may become very important in VANETs due to the high number messages sent and received by the vehicles involved. This could increase channel contention and the frequency of collisions. Therefore, a reduction of the number of messages sent under this situation would improve the warning message dissemination process, allowing other applications sharing the channel to operate adequately. To this end, it is necessary to evaluate the different dissemination schemes, taking into account the number of messages received by each vehicle in order to select the optimal scheme for each specific situation.

Figure 3 shows the number of messages received per vehicle in two of the maps under study. As shown, the selected dissemination scheme presents a determinant influence over the amount of messages produced; some of them produce only a fraction of the messages required by other schemes. In general, the counter-based scheme produces the highest number of messages, whereas the distance-based is the most restrictive one. As we might suppose, the NJL scheme produces the smallest amount of messages of all the schemes which used the information topology of the map to select the forwarding nodes.

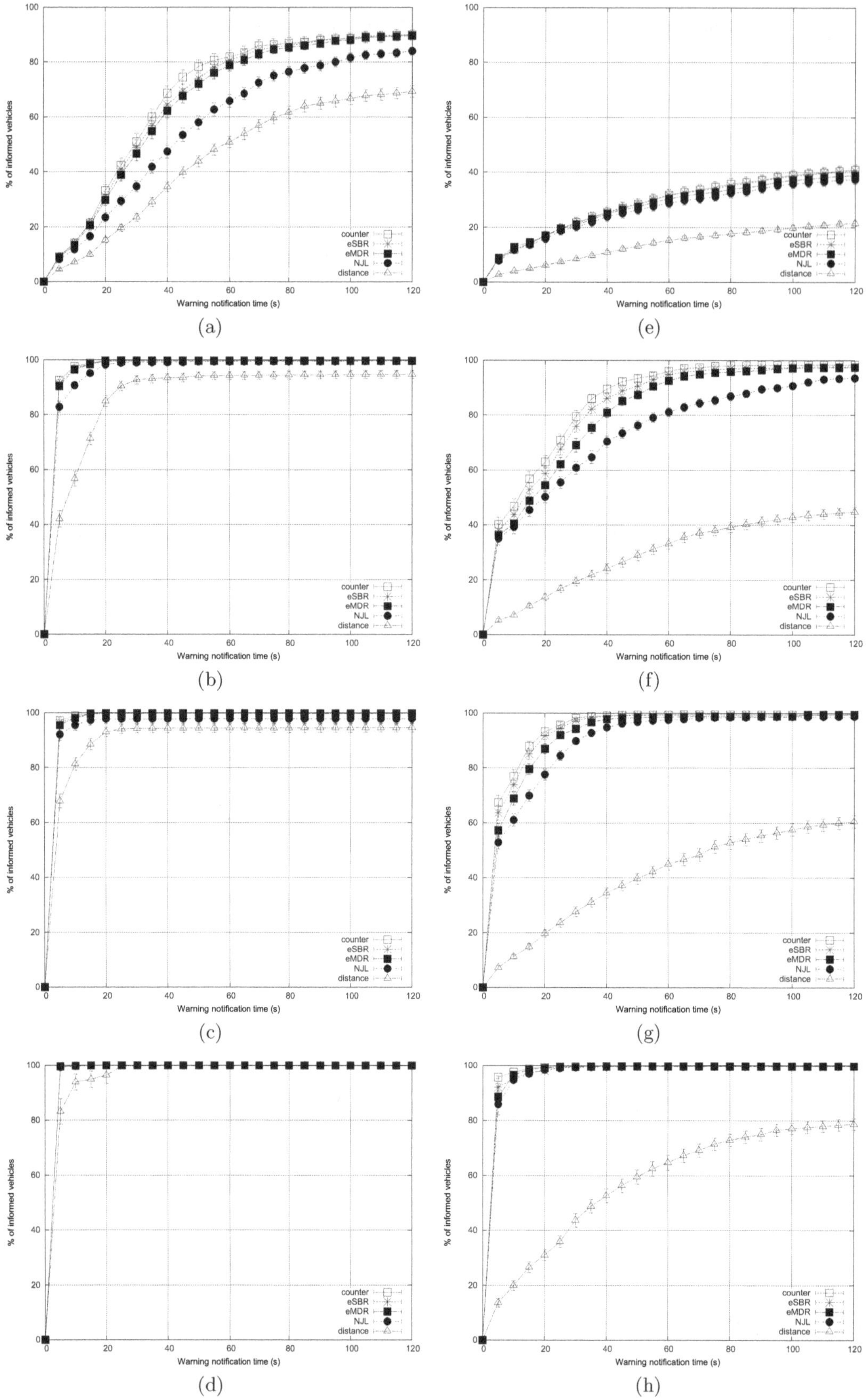

Figure 2: Percentage of informed vehicles in San Francisco for: (a) 25, (b) 100, (c) 150, and (d) 250 vehicles/km^2, as well as in Valencia for: (e) 25, (f) 100, (g) 150, and (h) 250 vehicles/km^2.

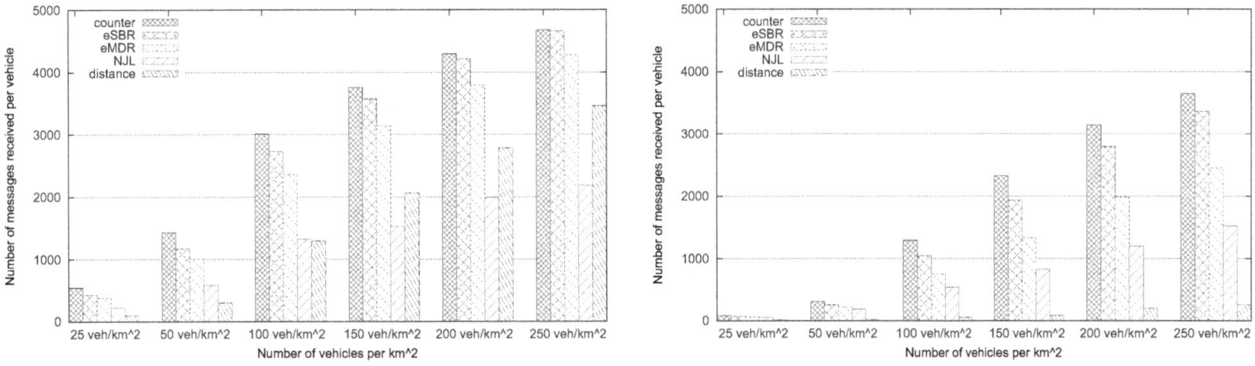

(a) (b)

Figure 3: Number of messages received per vehicle when varying the broadcast scheme and the vehicular density in: (a) San Francisco and (b) Valencia.

Again, the features of the map are determinant for the performance of the system. Simple maps allow a faster dissemination at the cost of noticeably increasing the number of messages received per vehicle, thereby increasing the probability of broadcast storms. Thus, more restrictive schemes are recommended for this kind of roadmaps.

5.4 Optimal Broadcast Scheme Selection

Table 5 contains an example of the performance of our broadcast scheme selection algorithm presented in Section 3. Specifically, it shows the results obtained for Valencia when simulating 100 vehicles/km^2. All the values are obtained as the average of 50 repetitions for each configuration. It is noticeable how only three of the selected schemes are considered after the first step of the algorithm: i.e., the counter-based, the eSBR, and the eMDR broadcast schemes. Since the eMDR produces the lowest number of messages while maintaining a high percentage of informed vehicles in a small time period, our algorithm considers it as the optimal broadcast scheme for this specific situation.

Table 6 shows the selected broadcast scheme for each of the simulated scenarios according to our proposed Optimal Broadcast Selection Algorithm. Notice that the proposed NJL scheme is selected as the optimal one in most cases, especially under high vehicle densities or simple maps with a small SJ ratio, where the radio signal can reach long distances and broadcast storms are prone to occur. On the contrary, eMDR and eSBR schemes offer better results in scenarios where broadcast storms are not a problem, and the main objective is informing as many vehicles as soon as possible.

It is remarkable that almost all the schemes selected by our proposed algorithm rely on topology information to select the most appropriate forwarding vehicle, highlighting the importance of this factor in the warning dissemination process. In fact, broadcast schemes that only make use of the distance between the sender and the receiver, or which only focus on avoiding repeated messages, present a worse trade-off between performance and the amount of messages required. We also observed an anomaly in the results obtained in Table 6 corresponding to the map of Madrid. The selected scheme when simulating 25 vehicles/km^2 is the counter-based one, while the overall trend indicates that the chosen one should be the eMDR scheme. This is due to the thresholds selected for Step 1 of the algorithm, where only those schemes with less than 10% variation with respect to the maximum value are considered. The eSBR and eMDR schemes achieve a value of 10.2% and 10.51% variation, respectively, which causes them to be ignored after the first step of the selection algorithm. This indicates that the use of fixed thresholds may lead to inaccurate decisions in some specific cases. We consider that a possible improvement of the broadcast selection algorithm could be using fuzzy logic to decide upon protocol adequacy, thereby avoiding those cases where values close to the threshold are completely ignored.

6. CONCLUSIONS

In this paper we proposed a quantitative algorithm that allows selecting the optimal broadcast scheme in a VANET scenario depending on two different metrics: (i) the percentage of informed vehicles, a particularly determinant factor in warning message dissemination, and (ii) the number of messages received by each vehicle, an important factor which indicates the channel contention and the possibility of broadcast storms during the dissemination of alert messages. In addition, we presented a new broadcast scheme called Nearest Junction Located (NJL), which was specially designed for scenarios presenting high vehicular densities or simple topologies, where broadcast storms are prone to occur. The NJL scheme is designed to reduce the number of messages received per vehicle without noticeably affecting the percentage of informed vehicles. We showed how our broadcast selection algorithm is able to select the optimal scheme in almost all the scenarios tested.

7. ACKNOWLEDGMENTS

This work was partially supported by the *Ministerio de Ciencia e Innovación*, Spain, under Grant TIN2011-27543-C03-01, by the Fundación Universitaria Antonio Gargallo and the Obra Social de Ibercaja, under Grant 2013/B010, as well as the Government of Aragón and the European Social Fund (T91 Research Group).

Table 5: Simulation results for 100 vehicles/km^2 in Valencia.

Broadcast	Inf_{10}	Inf_{30}	Inf_{120}	P_{inf}	dev_{inf}	$\mathbb{C}$ (Step 1)	M_{recv}	dev_{recv} (Step 2)	dev_{Tot}	Optimal (Step 3)
Counter	46.6%	79.5%	98.3%	66.81	**0%**	✔	1196	**77.9%**	**75.55**	✖
Distance	7.10%	19.4%	44.7%	18.31	**72.59%**	✖	-	-	-	-
eSBR	43.7%	75.8%	97.7%	64.13	**4.01%**	✔	940	**39.87%**	**43.89**	✖
eMDR	40.4%	69%	97.4%	60.38	**9.62%**	✔	672	0%	**9.62**	✔
NJL	39.2%	60.8%	93.4%	56.52	**15.40%**	✖	-	-	-	-

Table 6: Broadcast Scheme Selected According to our Optimal Broadcast Selection Algorithm.

City	SJ Ratio	Vehicle Density (veh./km^2)					
		25	50	100	150	200	250
Rome	1.387	eSBR	eSBR	eSBR	eSBR	NJL	NJL
Valencia	1.267	eMDR	eMDR	eMDR	eMDR	NJL	NJL
Sydney	1.071	eMDR	eMDR	eMDR	NJL	NJL	NJL
Amsterdam	1.031	eMDR	eMDR	NJL	NJL	NJL	NJL
Los Angeles	0.938	eMDR	eMDR	NJL	NJL	NJL	NJL
San Francisco	0.886	eMDR	eMDR	NJL	NJL	NJL	NJL
Madrid	0.878	Counter	eMDR	NJL	NJL	NJL	NJL

8. REFERENCES

[1] F. Ahammed, J. Taheri, A. Zomaya, and M. Ott. VLOCI2: improving 2D location coordinates using distance measurements in GPS-equipped VANETs. In *Proceedings of the 14th ACM international conference on Modeling, analysis and simulation of wireless and mobile systems*, MSWiM '11, pages 317–322, New York, NY, USA, 2011. ACM.

[2] K. Fall and K. Varadhan. ns notes and documents. The VINT Project. UC Berkeley, LBL, USC/ISI, and Xerox PARC, February 2000.

[3] M. Fogue, P. Garrido, F. J. Martinez, J.-C. Cano, C. T. Calafate, and P. Manzoni. A Realistic Simulation Framework for Vehicular Networks. In *5th International ICST Conference on Simulation Tools and Techniques (SIMUTools 2012), Desenzano, Italy*, pages 37–46, March 2012.

[4] M. Fogue, P. Garrido, F. J. Martinez, J.-C. Cano, C. T. Calafate, and P. Manzoni. Evaluating the impact of a novel message dissemination scheme for vehicular networks using real maps. *Transportation Research Part C: Emerging Technologies*, 25:61–80, December 2012.

[5] S. Krauss, P. Wagner, and C. Gawron. Metastable states in a microscopic model of traffic flow. *Physical Review E*, 55(5):5597–5602, 1997.

[6] F. J. Martinez, M. Fogue, M. Coll, J.-C. Cano, C. Calafate, and P. Manzoni. Evaluating the impact of a novel warning message dissemination scheme for VANETs using real city maps. In M. Crovella, L. Feeney, D. Rubenstein, and S. Raghavan, editors, *NETWORKING 2010*, volume 6091 of *Lecture Notes in Computer Science*, pages 265–276. Springer Berlin / Heidelberg, 2010.

[7] F. J. Martinez, M. Fogue, C. K. Toh, J.-C. Cano, C. T. Calafate, and P. Manzoni. Computer simulations of VANETs using realistic city topologies. *Wireless Personal Communications*, 69(2):639–663, 2013.

[8] F. J. Martinez, C. K. Toh, J.-C. Cano, C. T. Calafate, and P. Manzoni. Determining the representative factors affecting warning message dissemination in VANETs. *Wireless Personal Communications*, 67(2):295–314, November 2012.

[9] OpenStreetMap. Collaborative project to create a free editable map of the world, 2012. Available at http://www.openstreetmap.org.

[10] J. A. Sanguesa, M. Fogue, P. Garrido, F. J. Martinez, J.-C. Cano, C. T. Calafate, and P. Manzoni. An infrastructureless approach to estimate vehicular density in urban environments. *Sensors*, 13(2):2399–2418, 2013.

[11] R. Schwartz, A. Ohazulike, C. Sommer, H. Scholten, F. Dressler, and P. Havinga. Fair and adaptive data dissemination for traffic information systems. In *IEEE Vehicular Networking Conference*, pages 1–8, 2012.

[12] M. Slavik, I. Mahgoub, and M. Alwakeel. Adapting statistical multi-hop wireless broadcast protocol decision thresholds using rate control. In *9th International Conference on High Capacity Optical Networks and Enabling Technologies (HONET)*, pages 32–36, 2012.

[13] C. Sommer, O. Tonguz, and F. Dressler. Traffic information systems: efficient message dissemination via adaptive beaconing. *IEEE Communications Magazine*, 49(5):173–179, 2011.

[14] Y.-C. Tseng, S.-Y. Ni, Y.-S. Chen, and J.-P. Sheu. The broadcast storm problem in a mobile ad hoc network. *Wireless Networks*, 8:153–167, 2002.

[15] W. Xue-wen, Y. Wei, S. Shi-ming, and W. Hui-bin. A transmission range adaptive broadcast algorithm for vehicular ad hoc networks. In *Proceedings of the 2010 Second International Conference on Networks Security, Wireless Communications and Trusted Computing - Volume 01*, NSWCTC '10, pages 28–32, Washington, DC, USA, 2010. IEEE Computer Society.

[16] X. Zhuo, J. Hao, D. Liu, and Y. Dai. Removal of misbehaving insiders in anonymous VANETs. In N. B. Abu-Ghazaleh, L. Bononi, B. Bensaou, and V. R. Syrotiuk, editors, *Proceedings of the 12th ACM international conference on Modeling, analysis and simulation of wireless and mobile systems*, MSWiM '09, pages 106–115, New York, NY, USA, 2009. ACM.

Traffic Aware Video Dissemination Over Vehicular Ad hoc Networks

Guilherme Maia[1,2], Cristiano Rezende[2], Leandro A. Villas[3], Azzedine Boukerche[2]
Aline C. Viana[4], Andre L. L. Aquino[5], Antonio A. F. Loureiro[1]

[1] Federal University of Minas Gerais, Belo Horizonte, MG, Brazil
{jgmm, loureiro}@dcc.ufmg.br

[2] University of Ottawa, Ottawa, ON, Canada
{creze019, boukerch}@site.uottawa.ca

[3] University of Campinas, Campinas, SP, Brazil
leandro@ic.unicamp.br

[4] INRIA, Saclay, Orsay, France
aline.viana@inria.fr

[5] Federal University of Alagoas, Maceió, AL, Brazil
alla@ic.ufal.br

ABSTRACT

Video dissemination to a group of vehicles is one of the many fundamental services envisioned for Vehicular Ad hoc Networks. For this purpose, in this paper we describe VoV, a video dissemination protocol that operates under extreme traffic conditions. Contrary to most existing approaches that focus exclusively on always-connected networks and tackle the broadcast storm problem inherent to them, VoV is designed to operate under any kind of traffic condition. We propose a new geographic-based broadcast suppression mechanism that gives higher priority to broadcast to vehicles inside especial forwarding zones. Furthermore, vehicles store and carry received messages in a local buffer in order to forward them to vehicles that were not covered by the first dissemination process, probably as a result of collisions or intermittent disconnections. Finally, VoV employs a rate control mechanism that sets the pace at which messages must be transmitted in an attempt to avoid channel overloading and to overcome the synchronization effects introduced by the channel hopping mechanism employed by IEEE 802.11p. When compared to two well-known solutions – UV-CAST and AID – we show that our proposal is more efficient in terms of message delivery, delay and overhead.

MSWiM'13, November 3–8, 2013, Barcelona, Spain.

http://dx.doi.org/10.1145/2507924.2507962.

Categories and Subject Descriptors

C.2 [**COMPUTER-COMMUNICATION NETWORKS**]: Network Protocols—*Routing protocols*; H.4 [**Information Systems Applications**]: Miscellaneous

Keywords

VANETs, Video Dissemination, Broadcast Suppression, Intermittent Connected

1. INTRODUCTION

The scientific and auto maker communities envision video dissemination in Vehicular Ad hoc Networks (VANETs) as a fundamental service for traffic management and entertainment applications [6, 9]. For instance, it is unquestionable that disseminating a video showing lines of cars stuck in traffic conveys a much compelling message to a driver deciding which route to take than a text message stating heavy traffic conditions at a region of a city.

Toward this task, many solutions have been proposed in the literature [2, 8, 17, 18, 19]. Surprisingly, most of them were designed for always-connected networks, in which a path from the source vehicle to intended recipients is always guaranteed. Furthermore, relying on fixed infrastructures, such as roadside units and repeaters at intersections, is common practice. However, it is common knowledge that VANETs are inherently intermittently connected networks, independently of the traffic density, due to non-uniform demographic distribution of vehicles, congestion or simply traffic lights [6, 9, 15]. Besides, during the first years of VANETs deployments, the number of vehicles equipped with DSRC technology [7] and the availability of fixed infrastructure may not be enough for the proper functioning of existing video dissemination solutions.

With these issues in mind, in this paper we propose VoV, a video dissemination protocol for VANETs that works under the most diverse traffic conditions inherent to these networks. For high traffic densities, we propose a new geographic-based broadcast suppression mechanism that chooses vehicles inside high priority regions to rebroadcast. Furthermore, after receiving a message, vehicles store it in a local buffer to be later forwarded to uninformed neighbors that failed to receive them in the primary dissemination process. We show that this increases the message delivery capability for our protocol not just for sparse traffic scenarios, but also for heavy traffic conditions, since it works as a recovery mechanism for message losses caused by collisions. Due to the demanding nature of video dissemination, such as high bandwidth usage and strict time delivery requirements, we also propose a rate control mechanism to avoid channel overload and to overcome the synchronization effects introduced by the channel hopping scheme used by the IEEE 802.11p MAC layer [5]. Finally, by means of simulations, we compare our proposal to two existing solutions – UV-CAST [16] and AID [2] – and we show that, overall, our protocol delivers more messages in the least amount of time by consuming less network resources.

The remainder of this paper is organized as follows. In Section 2 we outline the related work and describe the two protocols used in our performance analysis. In Section 3, we describe in detail our proposed solution. Then, in Section 4, we compare our proposed protocol to two existing solutions in the literature under different traffic scenarios. Finally, in Section 5, we present our final remarks and discuss some future work.

2. RELATED WORK

Video dissemination, and data dissemination in general, is a well-studied topic in VANETs. However, despite the fact that VANETs are intermittently connected by nature [15], most solutions focus exclusively on always-connected scenarios. Moreover, the solutions that do focus on both connected and intermittently connected scenarios either employ some kind of infrastructure, such as roadside units or repeaters at intersections, or a combination of GPS and street mapping information. Among the solutions that focus on both scenarios are DV-CAST [14] and SRD [10]. These protocols rely exclusively on local one-hop neighbor information and do not employ any kind of fixed infrastructure. However, both were designed to perform directional data dissemination and they are used solely for highway environments. Data dissemination protocols proposed for highways do not perform well when deployed in urban environments [13].

Korkmaz et al. [8] propose the Urban Multi-hop Broadcast protocol (UMB), a medium access control (MAC) solution designed to avoid the hidden terminal and broadcast storm problems. UMB employs a Request to Broadcast/Clear to Broadcast handshaking procedure in which the farthest vehicle from the sender is selected to acknowledge the reception of the message and also to forward it to further vehicles. Furthermore, UMB employs repeaters at intersections to propagate the messages to all road directions. However, it assumes the network is always connected. Yi et al. [18] propose the StreetCast protocol, which, similarly to UMB, is a MAC solution. Under this scheme, roadside units deployed at intersections select the best relaying vehicles to forward the messages. Furthermore, the protocol employs a beacon suppression mechanism to avoid excessive periodic beacons at crowded intersections. Nevertheless, StreetCast works only under connected networks.

Zhao et al. [19] propose the Data Pouring protocol for data dissemination under urban environments. Despite working under both connected and intermittently connected networks, the protocol employs repeaters at intersections for buffering and forwarding messages along the intersecting roads. Wisitpongphan et al. [17] propose three broadcast suppression techniques – weighted-p-persistence, slotted-1-persistence and slotted-p-persistence – that do not require any neighbor information or special infrastructure. For instance, in the slotted-1-persistence technique, vehicles decide based on the distance to the sender when to rebroadcast a message. However, these techniques assume a connected network setup. Bakhouya et al. [2] propose the Adaptive Information Dissemination (AID), a distributed statistical-based broadcast suppression protocol for VANETs. Based on the inter-arrival time between message receptions, a vehicle decides whether to rebroadcast or not. For instance, in a high density traffic scenario, after receiving some redundant retransmissions for a given message, a vehicle may decide to not rebroadcast it by assuming it was already transmitted by many other vehicles. The protocol does not use any neighbor information or any kind of infrastructure. However, it assumes an always-connected scenario.

Viriyasitavat et al. [16] propose the Urban Vehicular Broadcast (UV-CAST) protocol for connected and intermittently connected networks. In UV-CAST, when a vehicle receives a message, it uses its local one-hop neighbor information to determine whether it should operate under a broadcast suppression or store-carry-forward regime. If it decides for the broadcast suppression regime, then it uses street mapping information to verify whether it is at an intersection or not to properly calculate its waiting time to rebroadcast. On the other hand, if the vehicle decides for the store-carry-forward regime, then it verifies whether it is a boundary vehicle or not. UV-CAST assumes boundary vehicles have a higher probability of encountering new neighbors. Therefore, these vehicles store and carry the message around until they encounter uninformed neighbors. UV-CAST uses implicit acknowledgements piggybacked in periodic beacons to identify these uninformed neighbors. Notice that, only boundary vehicles store, carry and forward messages to other vehicles. An interesting fact is that when a vehicle receives a beacon from an uninformed neighbor, it immediately rebroadcasts the message without any kind of explicit or implicit coordination with its neighbors. Such lack of coordination leads to an increase in the number of redundant retransmissions, especially under dense network scenarios, as shown in our performance analysis (c.f. Section 4).

3. PROPOSED SOLUTION

Video dissemination is a demanding task for any kind of network because of high bandwidth utilization and strict delay requirements. In VANETs, due to their intrinsically characteristics, such as the wireless medium and high dynamicity, this task becomes even harder. Therefore, the main goals of our proposed approach is to perform video dissemination in a reliable and efficient way without incurring a high load into the network. Toward these goals, VoV selects a minimum set of vehicles to broadcast and also determines when the broadcast should take place and at what pace. This way, the protocol tries to reduce the load sent to the link layer by decreasing the amount of redundant retransmissions. Moreover, given that network partitioning is very common in these networks, independently of the traffic density, received messages are kept in a local buffer to be later forwarded to uninformed vehicles. We assume every vehicle is equipped with a GPS and periodically broadcasts its $<$ *latitude*, *longitude*, *heading* $>$ information in beacons known as Cooperative Awareness Messages [6], which are used by many other applications in VANETs, especially for traffic safety. Figure 1 shows the general architecture of our proposed protocol. As can be observed, our solution operates immediately above the IEEE 802.11p MAC layer [7] and has three main components: the broadcast suppression, store-carry-forward and rate control mechanisms. The main steps of the protocol are depicted in Algorithm 1.

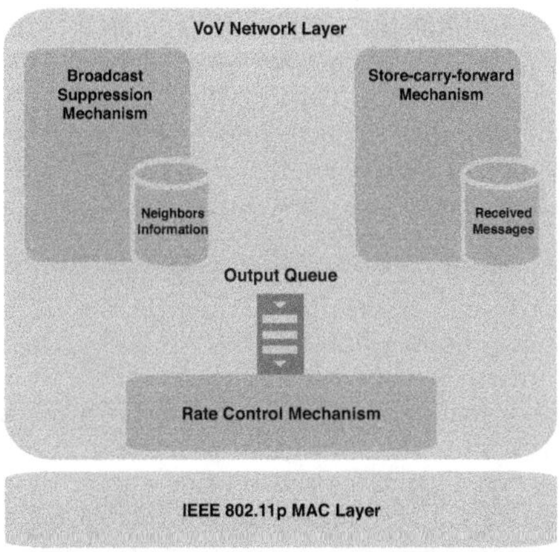

Figure 1: General architecture of VoV

In summary, the broadcast suppression mechanism determines whether a vehicle is inside high priority broadcast regions or not, and use such information to decide when the vehicle should rebroadcast. In principle, vehicles inside these high priority regions suppress the rebroadcast of vehicles outside them. The store-carry-forward mechanism keeps already disseminated messages in a local buffer and forwards them whenever it identifies a neighbor that has not received them. Finally, the rate control mechanism determines the pace at which messages are sent to the MAC layer in an attempt to avoid channel overloading. Moreover, it also tries to break synchronization effects introduced by the channel hopping mechanism proposed in the IEEE 802.11p MAC standard [5]. Hereafter, we provide a detailed description to each of these components.

3.1 Broadcast Suppression Mechanism

The goal of any broadcast suppression mechanism is to avoid the well-known broadcast storm problem, which is caused by uncoordinated and redundant retransmissions, and is characterized by severe packet losses, high delay and ultimately, service disruption. To avoid these issues, we propose a new broadcast suppression mechanism that combines geographical and timer-based approaches. At first, when a vehicle receives a broadcast with a new message (Line 7), it decides whether a rebroadcast is required or all vehicles in its neighborhood have already been covered by the broadcast. For that, the vehicle verifies whether there are any neighbor with a distance to the sender of the message greater than

Algorithm 1: The VoV algorithm

```
1  Initialize
2  N ← set of one-hop neighbors for this vehicle;
3  R ← communication radius;
4  θ ← size of the forwarding zone;
5  T ← base delay;
6  datarate ← base data transmission rate;
7  Event data message m received from neighbor s
8  if m is not a duplicate then
9      add message to the list of received messages;
10     insert m ID in subsequent beacons;
11     everybodyCovered ← true;
12     foreach n ∈ N do
13         if distance(n, s) > R then
14             everybodyCovered ← false;
15     if everybodyCovered = false then
16         D ← distance to s;
17         D ← minimum between D and R;
18         percentageDistance ← D/R;
19         if vehicle is inside forwarding zone of s then
20             delay ← T × (1 − percentageDistance);
21         else
22             delay ← T × (2 − percentageDistance);
23         schedule rebroadcast_timer for m to fire up at
           currentTime + delay;
24 else
25     if rebroadcast_timer for m is scheduled then
26         cancel rebroadcast_timer for m;
27 Event beacon b received from neighbor s
28 update neighborhood information;
29 foreach message m in the list of received messages do
30     if m is not acknowledged in b then
31         D ← distance to s;
32         D ← minimum between D and R;
33         percentageDistance ← D/R;
34         if vehicle is inside forwarding zone of s then
35             delay ← T × percentageDistance;
36         else
37             delay ← T × (1 + percentageDistance);
38         schedule rebroadcast_timer for m to fire up at
           currentTime + delay;
39 Event scheduled rebroadcast_timer for m expires
40 Insert message into output queue;
41 Event rate_control_timer expires
42 m ← dequeue from output queue;
43 send m down to MAC layer;
44 delay ← size(m)/datarate;
45 if in currentTime + delay the Control Channel will be
   active then
46     schedule rate_control_timer to fire up at the
       beginning of next Service Channel period;
47 else
48     schedule rate_control_timer to fire up at
       currentTime + delay;
```

the communication radius (lines 11-14). If there are no such neighbor, the vehicle will not attempt to rebroadcast, thus avoiding a redundant retransmission. Otherwise, the vehicle determines whether it is inside a forwarding zone or not to calculate its waiting time to rebroadcast (lines 15-23).

The **forwarding zone** is defined according to the direction of the sender, as outlined in Figure 2. Let the direction of a vehicle be a value in the interval $[0, 2\pi]$. Moreover, let the size of the forwarding zone be controlled by an input parameter θ that lies in the interval $[0, \frac{\pi}{2}]$. When θ is 0, there is no forwarding zone, and when it is $\frac{\pi}{2}$, all neighbors of the sender are inside the forwarding zone. Therefore, using the position and direction of the sender and its own position, a vehicle is said to be inside the forwarding zone of the sender if it lies in any of the four intervals $[0-\theta,\ 0+\theta]$, $[\frac{\pi}{2}-\theta,\ \frac{\pi}{2}+\theta]$, $[\pi-\theta,\ \pi+\theta]$ or $[\frac{3\pi}{2}-\theta,\ \frac{3\pi}{2}+\theta]$. The rationale is that vehicles inside these regions have a higher priority over vehicles outside it, i.e., vehicles inside the forwarding zone have a lower waiting time to rebroadcast. Notice that, the information required for a vehicle to determine whether it is inside the forwarding zone of the sender or not is embedded in received data messages. For instance, in Figure 2, vehicle E is inside the forwarding zone of the *Sender*, since it lies in the interval $[0-\theta,\ 0+\theta]$. Vehicles A and B also are inside it, since they lie in the interval $[\frac{\pi}{2}-\theta,\ \frac{\pi}{2}+\theta]$. However, vehicle C is outside it, since C does not lie in any of the four previously defined intervals.

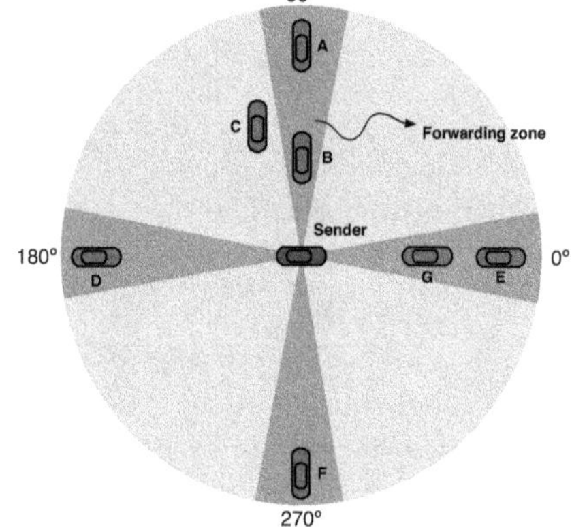

Figure 2: Forwarding zone

In hand of the above information, the vehicle proceeds to calculate its actual waiting time to rebroadcast (lines 20 and 22). The waiting time is inversely proportional to the distance between the vehicle and the sender, i.e., the father from the sender the vehicle is, the lower the waiting time to rebroadcast. Moreover, vehicles inside the forwarding zone always have a lower waiting time than vehicles outside it. Therefore, when the farthest vehicle inside the forwarding zone rebroadcasts, it suppresses the rebroadcast of vehicles closer to the sender, both the ones inside and outside the forwarding zone (lines 24-26). For instance, in Figure 2, vehicles A, D, E and F have the lowest waiting times to rebroadcast, since they are the farthest vehicles from the *Sender* that are also inside its forwarding zone. Therefore, when they broadcast, they will suppress the rebroadcast of vehicles B, C and G, thus avoiding 3 redundant retransmissions. Finally, it is worth noticing that when the waiting time to rebroadcast fires up, the vehicle does not broadcast immediately. Instead, it places the message in an output buffer (lines 39-40), which is used by the rate control mechanism (c.f., Section 3.3).

3.2 Store-carry-forward Mechanism

Despite the fact that the aforementioned mechanism is intended to guarantee high data delivery to intended recipients by avoiding channel overloading, some message losses may still happen due to the demanding nature of video dissemination. Furthermore, as shown elsewhere [1, 9, 15], VANETs are naturally intermittently connected networks. This means that even if the channel is not overloaded and there are no message collisions, 100% data delivery cannot be guaranteed due to the lack of a lasting end-to-end path from source to intended recipients. Therefore, with this in mind, we propose a store-carry-forward mechanism to increase the data delivery capability of VoV by serving vehicles that have lost some messages due to collisions and those that have failed to receive messages from the initial dissemination process.

When a vehicle receives a message for the first time, it stores it in a local buffer of received messages until the message's time-to-live expires or the vehicle leaves the region of interest for the message (Line 9). Notice that, both parameters are specified by the application that generated the message. For instance, the time-to-live for a message may be 2 minutes long and the region of interest may comprise all vehicles in a 1 km^2 area around the source. Besides storing the message, the vehicle needs to notify its neighbors about all the messages it has received so far that are still in its local buffer. This way, if a neighbor finds out that the vehicle has not received some already disseminate messages, it will forward them to the vehicle. To accomplish that, the IDs of all stored messages are piggybacked in the periodic beacons exchanged among vehicles (Line 10). For instance, if a vehicle A has received messages with IDs 1 and 2, then for every beacon it transmits, it will insert these IDs in the beacons to act as a list of received messages. Therefore, if a neighbor of A, say B, has received messages with IDs 1, 2 and 3, when it receives the beacon from A and notices the missing ID 3, it will forward this message to A. It is worth noticing that, the IDs piggybacked in periodic beacons act as a acknowledgement mechanism for the messages received so far and that are still relevant.

Assuming that the store-carry-forward mechanism is used not just for sparse traffic scenarios, but also for high traffic conditions, e.g., to recover from message collisions, some coordination must be employed when a vehicle decides to forward a message to an uninformed neighbor. For instance, imagine that in the scenario depicted in Figure 2, the *Sender* is the only vehicle that has not received a given message. Therefore, when it transmits a beacon that does not acknowledge the receipt of this message, all its neighbors will attempt to forward the message, probably leading to message collisions, contention and waste of network bandwidth. To overcome such issue, VoV also relies on a broadcast suppression mechanism similar to the one used for the normal dissemination process (lines 27-38). When a vehicle receives a beacon from an uninformed neighbor, it first verifies whether it is inside the forwarding zone of the neighbor. The rationale is the same as explained in Section 3.1. Then, it calculates its actual waiting time to forward the message to the uninformed neighbor. Here, however, vehicles closer to the uninformed neighbor receives a lower waiting time than vehicles farther away (lines 35 and 37). When the vehicle finally forwards the message, it suppresses the transmissions of other vehicles waiting to forward. For instance, going back to the example depicted in Figure 2, when all vehicles receive the beacon from the *Sender*, they verify whether they are inside the forwarding zone of the *Sender* and then calculate their waiting time to broadcast. Since vehicle B is the closest one to the *Sender*, it broadcasts first, thus cancelling the transmissions from all other vehicles, avoiding 6 redundant retransmissions. Notice that, if there is any other neighbor of B that also has not received the same message as the *Sender*, when B transmits it, such neighbor will also receive the broadcast.

3.3 Rate Control Mechanism

The two above mechanisms are sufficient for video dissemination under conventional mobile ad hoc networks based on the IEEE 802.11 technology. However, under vehicular environments, due to the use of the new WAVE standard [7], a third mechanism must be employed. WAVE was proposed to enable the reliable operation of safety applications. For that, WAVE relies on the use of multiple channels. The U.S Federal Communications Commission, for instance, reserved seven non-overlapping channels in the 5.85 GHz frequency range just for vehicular communication. One of these channels is designated as the Control Channel (CCH) and the remaining six as the Service Channel (SCH). Since the standard does not mandate the use of several antennas, a channel hopping scheme is proposed. Under such scheme, every 50 ms the transceiver is allowed to go from the CCH to the SCH, and then, after additional 50 ms, go from the SCH back to the CCH, as shown in Figure 3. At the beginning of each channel operation, there is a guard interval period in which the channel is treated as busy. It is assumed that beacon messages, mostly used by safety applications, will use the CCH, while general applications will use one the SCH.

The channel hopping scheme introduces an undesirable synchronization effect. As shown in Figure 3, when the MAC layer of a vehicle receives many data messages from the above layer to be transmitted, and the MAC is currently under the CCH, then it buffers the messages until the SCH becomes active. When the SCH finally becomes active, then the MAC attempts to transmit all buffered messages at the beginning of the SCH with maximum throughput. However, this also happen at other vehicles, which leads to a synchronization at the beginning of the SCH. This causes severe packet losses, especially for burst transmissions like video dissemination [5]. Notice that, such synchronization effect also happens at the beginning of the CCH for beacon dissemination, since beacons are also buffered at the MAC layer when the SCH is currently active.

To overcome the aforementioned issue, we propose a rate control mechanism that determines when VoV must send messages down to the MAC layer and at what pace (lines 39-48). For that, we assume that VoV can inquire the MAC layer about its current active channel and how long it will remain active. At first, when the rate control timer fires up (Line 41), VoV gets the next message from the output queue (Line 42) and sends it down to the MAC layer (Line 43). Then, it calculates how long it should wait to send the next message waiting on the queue down to the MAC (Line 44).

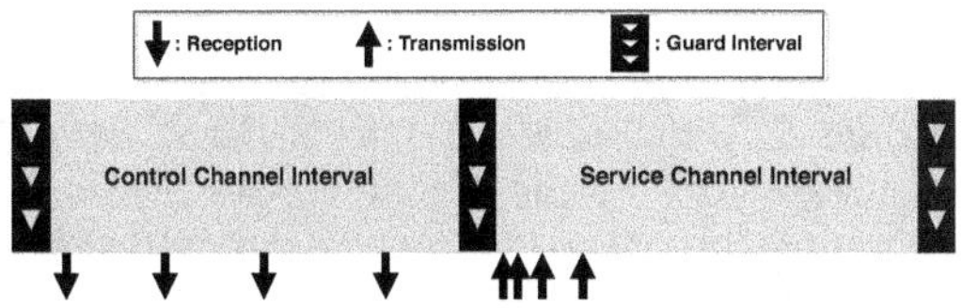

Figure 3: Synchronization at the beginning of the Service Channel leads to severe packet collisions

Such calculation takes into account the size of the previous message sent to the MAC, an input data rate parameter and which channel is currently active and for how long it will remain active (lines 45-48). This way, VoV guarantees that data messages are sent down to the MAC layer only when the SCH is active. This avoids the concentration of messages at the beginning of every SCH cycle, thus overcoming the previously described synchronization effect.

4. PERFORMANCE ANALYSIS

To evaluate the performance of our proposed solution, we conducted a series of simulations using the well-established OMNet++ 4.2.2 network simulator[1] and compared it to two protocols – UV-CAST [16] and AID [2]. Recall from our discussions on Section 2 that UV-CAST, like our solution, was designed to work under varying traffic conditions, since it implements both broadcast suppression and store-carry-forward mechanisms. On the other hand, AID was designed for always-connected networks. We use this protocol in our evaluation to show that even under dense networks, store-carry-forward still is a useful artefact to recover from message losses caused by collisions.

4.1 Simulation setup

Aiming to show that VoV is a proper solution for video dissemination under varying traffic conditions, we evaluated all protocols under low, normal and high traffic densities in a Manhattan grid. The streets layout comprises ten evenly-spaced vertical and horizontal double-lane roads in an area of 1 km^2. We also consider signal attenuation effects caused by buildings. For that, we assume that each block in the grid contains a 80 m x 80 m obstacle, representing a high-rise building. Moreover, we use the SUMO 0.17.0 mobility simulator [3] to build the street layouts and to generate realistic vehicle movements.

We also use the Veins 2.1[2] framework [11], since it implements both an obstacle model for signal attenuation effects and the WAVE standard for vehicle communications. As parameters to our simulations, we set the bit rate at the MAC layer to 18 Mbit/s and the transmission power to 0.98 mW. This results in a transmission range (R) of about 200 m under the two-ray ground propagation model. In VoV, we set θ to $\frac{\pi}{6}$ and the base delay (T) to 250 ms. Beacon messages are generated every 1 s and are transmitted only on the Control Channel. A vehicle approximately at the center of the network act as the source for video dissemination. We use the well-known and widely used *akiyou_cif*, a MPEG video with a resolution of 360x486 and composed of 300 frames. These frames are packed up into 560 messages of at most

[1]`http://www.omnetpp.org`
[2]`http://veins.car2x.org`

1024 bytes to be disseminated to all vehicles in the network. Moreover, the video messages are inserted into the network at three different data rates, 100 kbps, 500 kbps and 1 Mbps. These messages are transmitted only on the Service Channel. All results represent the mean of 30 executions for each evaluated scenario with a confidence interval of 95%. Finally, the metrics used to assess the reliability, efficiency and scalability of all protocols are the frame loss, frame delay, total number of messages transmitted and the Peak Signal-to-Noise Ratio (PSNR) [4].

4.2 Results

Figure 4 shows the average frame loss for different traffic densities and for different transmission rates. At 100 kbps (Figure 4(a)) both VoV and UV-CAST have similar frame losses. Notice that, the high losses for this result are not due to channel overloading, but the low transmission rate, especially under sparse densities (< 200 vehicles/km^2). When the network is intermittently connected, the connections among vehicles are short-lived, and at lower transmission rates it takes too much time to transfer the entire video from one vehicle to another, resulting in high losses. AID has a comparable performance to both VoV and UV-CAST only at high densities (≥ 300 vehicles/km^2). At lower densities, since it does not rely on store-carry-forward, the dissemination process stops at the first disconnection, resulting in a poor delivery.

At 500 kbps (Figure 4(b)), the channel starts to become overloaded and the benefits of the mechanisms used in VoV become more apparent. For instance, when compared to the previous result, the frame loss for VoV decreases to almost 0% at densities greater than 100 vehicles/km^2, while for UV-CAST and AID it increases. Observe that at 500 kbps, the video can be transferred from one vehicle to another much faster than at 100 kbps, which increases the chances for more frame deliveries. However, it also increases the channel load. Therefore, it is possible to notice the first effects of synchronization caused by channel hopping (see Section 3.3). For instance, at 100 kbps and 200 vehicles/km^2, AID lost about 20% of the frames, but at 500 kbps, the loss goes up to more than 40%. Another interesting fact in this results is that for very low traffic densities, where, theoretically, the channel is not overloaded, VoV still can deliver more frames than UV-CAST, regardless of both protocols perform store-carry-forward. Recall that, UV-CAST employs only a subset of the vehicles to perform such task, while VoV uses all vehicles inside the region of interest.

Increasing the transmission rate to 1 Mbps (Figure 4(c)), the channel becomes highly overloaded. The frame loss increases for all protocols at higher densities when compared to the previous results. For instance, the frame loss for AID at 200 vehicles/km^2 is now 60%. Notice, however, that the frame loss for VoV and UV-CAST does not increase at the same pace as it does for AID at higher densities. The explanation for such fact, as discussed in Section 3.2, is that the store-carry-forward schemes employed by these two protocols are acting as a recovery mechanism for message losses caused by collisions. This way, even if a vehicle does not receive the original dissemination, other vehicles doing store-carry-forward still can deliver it.

Figure 5 shows the total number of data messages transmitted. We can observe that, at 100 kbps, VoV and UV-CAST transmits the same amount of messages. However, when the transmission rate increases to 500 kbps, UV-CAST transmits more messages than VoV at higher densities, despite the fact that VoV can deliver more frames, as shown in Figure 4(b). This is an indication that the channel is overloaded, synchronization effects are happening, messages are colliding and it is the store-carry-forward who is keeping up the message delivery. At a transmission rate of 1 Mbps, this fact becomes even more clear. For instance, at a density of 400 vehicles/km^2, UV-CAST transmits about 57% more messages than VoV. However, as shown in Figure 4(c), the difference in delivery is just about 5%. This indicates that UV-CAST is transmitting a lot of extra messages to recover from losses. It also shows that our proposed broadcast suppression mechanism avoids unnecessary retransmissions, thus freeing the channel from more load, and our rate control mechanism is controlling when to send messages down to the MAC layer to avoid the synchronization effects.

Figure 6 shows the average delay to deliver frames to intended recipients. Notice the inverted-v shape for the VoV and UV-CAST curves at lower densities. This is due to the fact that, as the density increases, connection times start to last longer. This way, more messages can be delivered, most of them using store-carry-forward, explaining the increase in delay. As the density keeps increasing, the number of messages transmitted using the store-carry-forward decreases, resulting in a decrease of the delay. The higher delay for VoV and UV-CAST when compared to AID at high densities, such as 400 vehicles/km^2, is another indication that these protocols are using store-carry-forward to recover from message collisions, as already discussed in previous results. Therefore, we observe a trade-off between frame delay and delivery.

Finally, Figure 7 shows the average Peak Signal-to-Noise Ration when reconstructing the disseminated video at intended recipients. A PSNR between 30 and 40 indicates that the video can be reconstructed with a good quality at receivers. We can see that, at 100 kbps, only for densities greater than 60 vehicles/km^2, the video is reconstructed with an acceptable quality when using VoV. This value decreases to 20 vehicles/km^2 at a transmission rate of 500 kbps, a direct consequence of a better delivery ratio (see Figure 4(b)). However, at 1 Mbps, none of the evaluated protocols guarantee a good video reproduction at receivers. From the results presented in this section, we can argue that for traffic densities greater than 200 vehicles/km^2 and a transmission rate between 100 kbps and 500 kbps, VoV is a viable solution for video streaming applications over VANETs, since these applications require a delay and frame loss no higher than 5 s and 5%, respectively, according to the CISCO Quality Service requirements [12].

5. FINAL REMARKS

In this paper, we proposed VoV, a video dissemination protocol for VANETs with diverse traffic conditions. For high traffic density scenarios, VoV selects vehicles in high priority regions to rebroadcast. This increases the delivery ratio of the protocol by avoiding redundant retransmissions and diminishing the load in the channel. Moreover, vehicles store received messages in a local buffer and immediately forward them whenever they encounter an uninformed neighbor. This increases the delivery capabilities for VoV under both low and high traffic density scenarios. A rate control mechanism is proposed in order to set the pace at

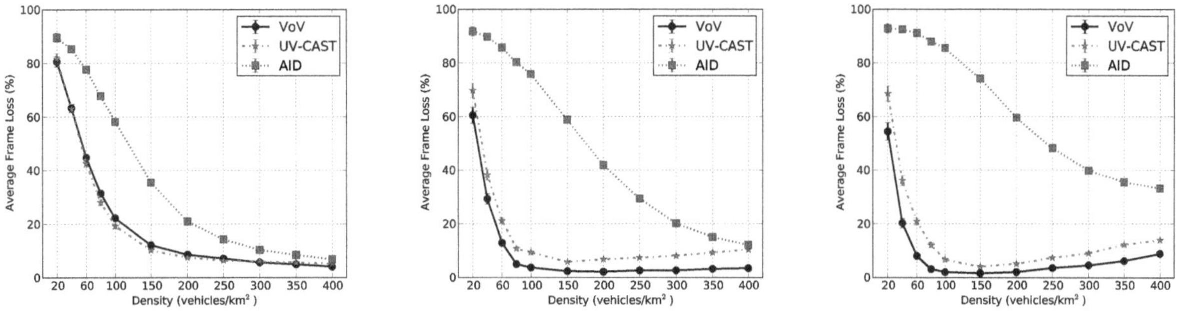

(a) 100kbps (b) 500kbps (c) 1Mbps

Figure 4: Average frame loss

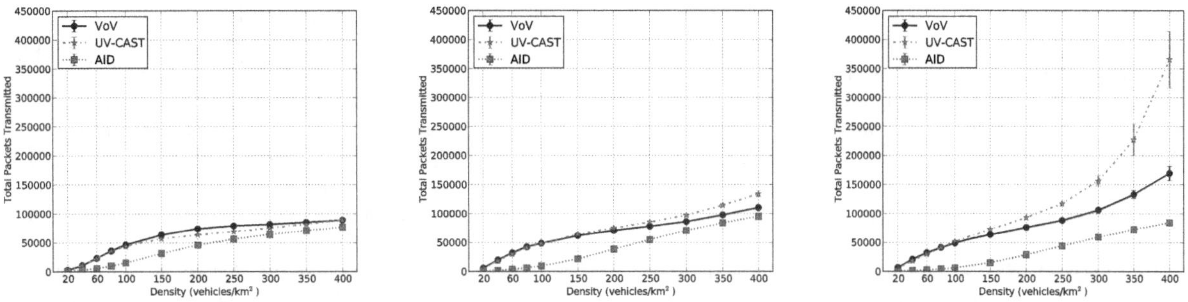

(a) 100kbps (b) 500kbps (c) 1Mbps

Figure 5: Total number of data messages transmitted

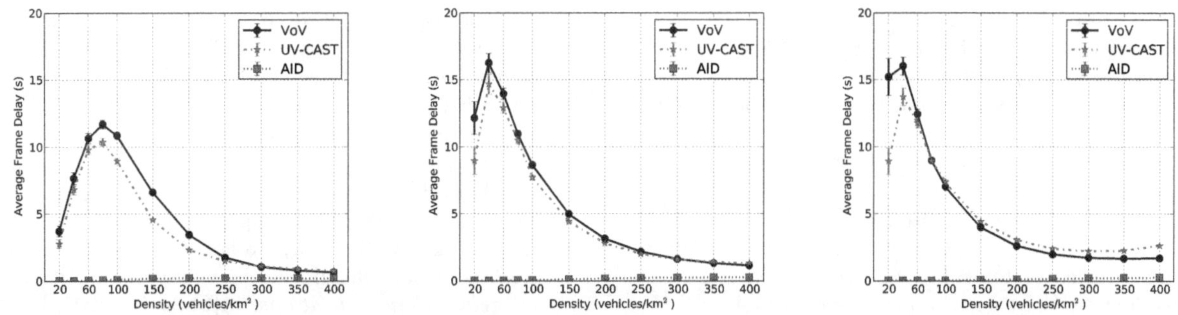

(a) 100kbps (b) 500kbps (c) 1Mbps

Figure 6: Average frame delay

which vehicles should transmit data messages and also to avoid the synchronization effects introduced by the channel hopping scheme employed by IEEE 802.11p. When compared to two related protocols, we show that VoV delivers more messages in the least amount of time by conserving the available network resources. Finally, we outlined some scenarios in which VoV is a perfect solution for some video dissemination applications with strict quality of service requirements, such as video streaming. As future work, we intend to investigate network coding techniques as a possible means for decreasing even more the current average frame loss of our solution.

Acknowledgments

This work was partially supported by CNPq, FAPEAL, FAPEMIG, NSERC DIVA Strategic Network, Canada Research Chairs Program and MRI/ORF Funds.

6. REFERENCES

[1] F. Bai and B. Krishnamachari. Exploiting the Wisdom of the Crowd: Localized, Distributed Information-Centric VANETs. *IEEE Communications Magazine*, 48(5):138–146, 2010.

[2] M. Bakhouya, J. Gaber, and P. Lorenz. An adaptive approach for information dissemination in vehicular ad

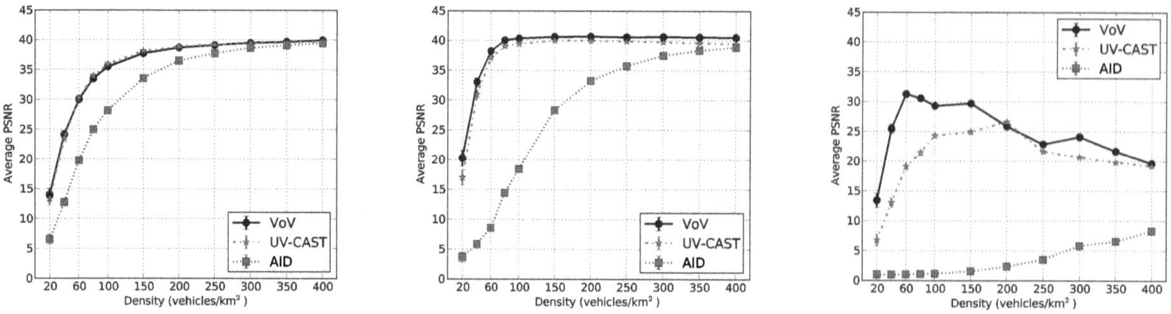

(a) 100kbps (b) 500kbps (c) 1Mbps

Figure 7: Peak Signal-to-Noise Ratio

hoc networks. *Journal of Network and Computer Applications*, 34(6):1971–1978, 2011.

[3] M. Behrisch, L. Bieker, J. Erdmann, and D. Krajzewicz. SUMO - Simulation of Urban MObility: An Overview. In *International Conference on Advances in System Simulation (SIMUL '11)*, pages 63–68, 2011.

[4] A. Chan, K. Zeng, P. Mohapatra, S.-J. Lee, and S. Banerjee. Metrics for evaluating video streaming quality in lossy IEEE 802.11 wireless networks. In *IEEE Conference on Information communications (INFOCOM '10)*, pages 1613–1621, 2010.

[5] D. Eckhoff, C. Sommer, and F. Dressler. On the Necessity of Accurate IEEE 802.11p Models for IVC Protocol Simulation. In *IEEE Vehicular Technology Conference (VTC '12)*, pages 1–5, 2012.

[6] H. Hartenstein and K. P. Laberteaux. A tutorial survey on vehicular ad hoc networks. *IEEE Communications Magazine*, 46(6):164–171, 2008.

[7] IEEE. Wireless LAN Medium Access Control (MAC) and Physical Layer (PHY) Specifications Amendment 6: Wireless Access in Vehicular Environments. IEEE Standards, 2010.

[8] G. Korkmaz, E. Ekici, F. Ozguner, and U. Ozguner. Urban multi-hop broadcast protocol for inter-vehicle communication systems. In *ACM International Workshop on Vehicular Ad hoc Networks (VANET '04)*, pages 76–85, 2004.

[9] U. Lee and M. Gerla. A survey of urban vehicular sensing platforms. *Computer Networks*, 54(4):527–544, 2010.

[10] R. S. Schwartz, R. R. R. Barbosa, N. Meratnia, G. Heijenk, and H. Scholten. A directional data dissemination protocol for vehicular environments. *Computer Communications*, 34(17):2057–2071, 2011.

[11] C. Sommer, R. German, and F. Dressler. Bidirectionally Coupled Network and Road Traffic Simulation for Improved IVC Analysis. *IEEE Transactions on Mobile Computing*, 10(1):3–15, 2011.

[12] T. Szigeti and C. Hattingh. *End-to-End QoS Network Design: Quality of Service in LANs, WANs, and VPNs (Networking Technology)*. Cisco Press, 2004.

[13] O. K. Tonguz, W. Viriyasitavat, and F. Bai. Modeling urban traffic: a cellular automata approach. *Communications Magazine*, 47(5):142–150, 2009.

[14] O. K. Tonguz, N. Wisitpongphan, and F. Bai. DV-CAST: a distributed vehicular broadcast protocol for vehicular ad hoc networks. *IEEE Wireless Communications*, 17(2):47–56, 2010.

[15] S. Uppoor and M. Fiore. Insights on metropolitan-scale vehicular mobility from a networking perspective. In *ACM International Workshop on Hot Topics in Planet-Scale Measurement (HotPlanet '12)*, pages 39–44, 2012.

[16] W. Viriyasitavat, F. Bai, and O. Tonguz. UV-CAST: An urban vehicular broadcast protocol. In *IEEE Vehicular Networking Conference (VNC '10)*, pages 25–32, 2010.

[17] N. Wisitpongphan, O. Tonguz, J. Parikh, P. Mudalige, F. Bai, and V. Sadekar. Broadcast storm mitigation techniques in vehicular ad hoc networks. *IEEE Wireless Communications*, 14(6):84–94, 2007.

[18] C.-W. Yi, Y.-T. Chuang, H.-H. Yeh, Y.-C. Tseng, and P.-C. Liu. Streetcast: An Urban Broadcast Protocol for Vehicular Ad-Hoc Networks. In *IEEE Vehicular Technology Conference (VTC '10)*, pages 1–5, 2010.

[19] J. Zhao, Y. Zhang, and G. Cao. Data Pouring and Buffering on The Road: A New Data Dissemination Paradigm for Vehicular Ad Hoc Networks. *IEEE Transactions on Vehicular Technology*, 56(6):3266–3277, 2007.

Distributed Base Station Activation for Energy-Efficient Operation of Cellular Networks*

Ali Abbasi
Department of Computer Science
University of Calgary
aabbasi@ucalgary.ca

Majid Ghaderi
Department of Computer Science
University of Calgary
mghaderi@ucalgary.ca

ABSTRACT

Dynamic base station activation (DBA) has recently emerged as a viable solution for reducing energy consumption in cellular networks. While most of the works on this topic focused on centralized decision making algorithms, in this paper we investigate distributive solutions. These solutions are particularly desirable due to importance of self-organization and self-optimization in future cellular networks. The goal of DBA is to achieve an optimal trade-off between network operator's revenue and operational cost while guaranteeing coverage for network users. The problem is posed as a network utility maximization aiming to find the optimal activation schedule of each base station. Using Lagrangian duality, the problem is decomposed into smaller subproblems, where each subproblem is solved locally at its associated base station. Controlled message passing among base stations ensures convergence to the global optimal solution. Moreover, this general solution is further extended to capture the combinatorial nature of DBA. Finally, numerical results are provided to demonstrate the behavior of our solution in terms of utility and cost trade-off and convergence in some example network scenarios.

Categories and Subject Descriptors

C.2.3 [**Network Operations**]: Network management

General Terms

Algorithms, Performance

Keywords

Energy Efficiency, Cellular Networks, Network Utility Maximization

*This work was supported in part by the NSERC Smart Applications on Virtual Infrastructure (SAVI) Strategic Network grant.

MSWiM'13, November 3–8, 2013, Barcelona, Spain.

ACM 978-1-4503-2353-6/13/11
10.1145/2507924.2507961 ...$15.00.

1. INTRODUCTION

With the proliferation of smartphones, cellular service providers have witnessed massive increase of data traffic in their networks. For example, one cellular operator in the US reported 8000% growth in data traffic from 2007 to 2010 [3]. It is expected that the cellular data traffic will continue to grow and will increase 13-fold over the next 5 years [4]. The increase in data traffic has put high pressure over cellular operators to enhance their network capacity by adopting new solutions and technologies [2]. Most notably, operators are moving towards denser deployment of base stations (BSs). In dense deployments, each base station covers a small geographical area and serves a small number of users which allows it to provide them with higher data rates.

While with the dense deployment of base stations, better data service is provided to users, more energy is also consumed to activate different parts of the radio access network. As a result, in addition to initial investment to expand the network capacity, higher operational expenditure, *e.g.*, electricity bill, is also a challenge that need to be considered by network operators. The issue is more highlighted to note that among various elements of a cellular network, base stations account for 60-80% of the total network energy consumption. With current base stations, 80-90% of peak energy[1] is consumed even in idle or low traffic state [18]. This energy is spent in cooling system and idle-mode signaling and processing as soon as the base station is powered on. In other words, current base stations are not *energy-proportional*[2]. However as we discuss later, by taking the characteristics of cellular traffic into consideration, energy-proportional base station operation can be emulated in the network, albeit at a coarser granularity.

Measurement studies have shown that cellular traffic exhibits periodic fluctuations both in time and space [21]. This behavior can be attributed to different usage patterns during days and nights, weekdays and weekends, and across residential and business areas. Nevertheless, cellular operators often deploy as many base stations as necessary to satisfy the peak traffic demand, while keeping them active (*i.e.*, in the On state) all the time. While it might seem that energy consumption issue could be addressed via dynamic transmission power control in base stations, the benefits of such mechanisms are marginal due to the mentioned sources of energy consumption in BS equipment (*e.g.*, cooling system).

[1]Energy consumed during the peak traffic load.
[2]Base stations in which energy consumption is proportional to the amount of traffic passing through.

Recent analysis of cellular traffic [20,23] has demonstrated that by dynamically activating base stations in a network, significant energy savings can be achieved. The idea is to completely power off underutilized base stations when their traffic load could be handled by nearby base stations. In turn, when the load in some parts of the network exceeds the capacity of the current active base stations, power on some inactive base stations so as to satisfy the demand. In this paper, we consider distributed base station activation problem in the context of a densely-deployed network. Specifically, we develop distributed mechanisms that explore the high coverage overlap in the network [12] to select an active set of base stations that results in the optimal matching between the provisioned network capacity and traffic load.

To this end, a measure is needed for evaluating the quality of a particular active set of base stations with respect to network users' satisfaction. A common approach to achieve such a measure, is to model user's satisfaction via the well-established notion of *utilities*. In this framework, a utility function is associated to each user, where the user utility is an increasing function of the amount of resources allocated to the user. Then, base station activation problem is modeled following the framework of *Network Utility Maximization* (NUM) [22]. There are however some subtle differences between our problem and classic NUM problems as follows. First, traffic requirements of cellular users are different from typical Internet users. Consequently the types of utility functions considered in our work are different from those considered in classic NUM problems. Second, due to the On/Off operation of base stations, this problem has a combinatorial nature, which adds to the complexity of the problem.

There are only a few recent works on this subject. In [21] a location-dependent traffic profiling study is conducted on real 3G network traces showing that 23-53% energy saving is possible via dynamic base station activation. Operators cooperation is investigated in [17], where optimal switch-off frequencies of base stations are computed in order to achieve balanced energy savings and roaming costs. Assuming a sinusoidal traffic profile, and following a threshold-based activation rule by each base station, an analysis of achievable energy savings is provided in [20]. The closest works to ours are presented in [26] and [23]. In [26], centralized and heuristic methods are presented for finding and deactivating the base station with the lowest load. The joint problem of base station activation and user association is studied in [23], where the objective is to minimize a joint energy and delay cost function. What distinguishes our work from the aforementioned works is that unlike them, we develop *distributed algorithms* that do not rely on a centralized controller.

Having a centralized decision maker, each base station is required to report its local state including load distribution in its coverage area and average channel gains to the central controller. These local states, collectively, define the state of the network. As network state changes over time, regular feedback is required to keep the controller informed about it. Thus, exchanging the state information between base stations and the controller imposes a high communication and computation overhead on the backhaul links, which is highly undesired in cellular networks [7]. A simpler scheme (in terms of the communication overhead) can be designed by delegating the role of the centralized controller to the base stations, as described in this paper. The distributed algorithm lets each base station decide on its activation/deactivation schedule by communicating only with its neighboring base stations without the need to communicate with a single centralized controller.

Our contributions in this paper can be summarized as follows:

- The DBA problem is formulated as a NUM problem with the objective of finding an optimal trade-off between operator revenue and network operational cost. Characteristics of cellular data traffic are considered in the formulation.
- The formulated problem features many local optima thus does not adhere to a distributed solution easily. Accordingly, an appropriate transformation is introduced in the objective function to make it strictly concave.
- A distributed algorithm is devised based on the Lagrangian dual decomposition, in which each base station computes its optimal activation probability through message exchange with its neighbors. In addition, each base station independently decides to activate or deactivate itself based on a locally computed activation probability.
- The DBA problem formulation is extended to more appropriately reflect the On/Off feature of the problem by considering general BS activation cost functions. The solution to the extended problem is obtained via difference of convex functions programming [25].

The rest of the paper is organized as follows. Section 2 describes the system model considered in the paper. The problem is formulated in section 3. Our distributed algorithm is presented in section 4. Sample numerical results are provided in section 6. Finally, section 7 concludes this paper.

2. SYSTEM MODEL AND ASSUMPTIONS

2.1 Network Model

The system considered in this paper includes the radio access part of a cellular network which consists of a number of base stations that collectively provide coverage for the network. The area under the coverage of the base stations is discretized to a set of locations. Let $\mathcal{B} = \{b_1, \dots, b_n\}$ and $\mathcal{L} = \{l_1, \dots, l_m\}$ denote the set of base stations and the set of locations respectively. Activating each base station b_i incurs a cost of c_i ($c_i \geq 0$) which is determined based on the total energy consumed at the base station while it is powered on. It is assumed that c_i is constant as the total power consumed at a base station is relatively constant (recall that base stations are not energy-proportional). Let $\mathcal{L}_i$ denote the subset of locations that can be covered by base station b_i (The notion of coverage will be clarified in the next section). Let $\mathcal{B}_j$ denote the set of all base stations that cover location l_j. Furthermore, let $\mathcal{S}_i$ denote the set of locations that are associated to b_i. By association of l_j to b_i, we mean that b_i is responsible for determining the amount of resources allocated to l_j from every BS in $\mathcal{B}_j$. We assume that a location might receive service from multiple BSs but it is associated to only one of them based on *e.g.*, proximity. The set of neighbors of base station b_i, denoted by $\mathcal{N}_i$, is defined as the set of all base stations that cover at least one common location with b_i, *i.e.*, $\mathcal{N}_i = \{b_j | \mathcal{L}_i \cap \mathcal{L}_j \neq \emptyset\}$.

Time is divided into scheduling epochs. At the end of each epoch, a subset $\mathcal{A}$ of base stations is selected for activation in the next scheduling epoch. Decisions are made only based on downlink traffic which is readily available to BSs[3]. Expectedly, $\mathcal{A}$ should match the traffic load of $\mathcal{L}$, while incurring the minimal total cost. The cost of activating the base station set $\mathcal{A}$ is given by $C(\mathcal{A}) = \sum_{b_i \in \mathcal{A}} c_i$.

Frequently switching base stations between On and Off states consumes energy, takes time, and generates huge amount of signalling traffic to re-associate users. To avoid unnecessary overhead due to transient network states, user association and resource allocation are carried out on a *different timescale* than the base station activation. The former is done at a *fast* timescale (*e.g.*, every few milli-seconds) based on current users' channel states, while the latter is done at a much *slower* timescale (*e.g.*, every few minutes) based on average network information, *i.e.*, capacity and demand, in the next scheduling epoch.

2.2 Resource Allocation

As implemented in the current 3GPP LTE systems [1], the radio access interface is assumed to be based on OFDMA. In OFDMA systems, available frequency bandwidth is partitioned into orthogonal subchannels which are the allocable resources to users. The total base station power P is divided between these subchannels. In our model, instead of dealing with individual users, we consider *locations*, where multiple users can be present in a single location. We further assume that channel variations across the channels allocated to a location are negligible as our model only considers *long-term* average rates that can be achieved over subchannels, as opposed to instantaneous rates that depend on short-term channel fluctuations.

Assume that base station b_i uses a subchannel to communicate with a user at location l_j. Let p_{ij} and g_{ij} denote the transmission power and long-term average power gain of the subchannel. Then, the average [4] received signal power at location l_j is given by $g_{ij} \cdot p_{ij}$. A location is considered covered by a base station if the received power of the pilot signal at that location is higher than a prespecified threshold. Let r_{ij} denote the received rate at location l_j. Using the Shannon capacity formula, we have $r_{ij} = \log(1 + \beta \frac{g_{ij} p_{ij}}{n_j + I_j})$, where β is the SINR gap due to limited modulation. Also, n_j and I_j denote background noise power and interference power at location l_j respectively. Similar to [19], to make the formulation tractable, we use an upper bound I on the interference power instead of using the exact I_j. I is the maximum multi-cell interference temperature or (maximum tolerable interference level) as mentioned in [10]. Doing so, we achieve a conservative rate function that does not need substantial amount of signaling to compute the actual value of interference at each location. We further borrow some simplifying assumptions from the literature [14,16] given as follows:

- We assume that each subchannel can be fractionally shared among users [14]. This is indeed the case in OFDMA systems such as WiMax and LTE as each subchannel is shared among multiple users using TDMA, *i.e.*, resources are shared in frequency and time. The assumption is particularly true for our model as we consider the long-term system averages.
- We assume the total transmission power P is divided equally among all subchannels. Therefore, if there exists R subchannels then the allocated subchannel power is $p = P/R$. As shown in [14], this scheme is nearly-optimal.
- As provisioned in LTE networks [16], we assume that neighboring cells are able to coordinate allocation of resources to users in overlapping regions such that orthogonal resources are allocated from neighboring BSs to locations in overlapping regions.

In the rest of the paper, we use the term *resource* to refer to the subchannels at a base station. Let γ_{ij} denote the fraction of resources allocated to location l_j from base station b_i. Following the third assumption, the total received rate at location l_j is given by:

$$r_j = \sum_{b_i \in \mathcal{B}_j} \gamma_{ij} \cdot R_{ij}, \tag{1}$$

where, R_{ij} is the rate received from base station b_i if all of its resources were to be allocated to location l_j, *i.e.*,

$$R_{ij} = R \cdot \log(1 + \beta \frac{p g_{ij}}{n_j + I}). \tag{2}$$

Consider a set $\mathcal{A}$ of active base stations. Let $\boldsymbol{r} = [r_j]_{l_j \in \mathcal{L}}$ denote a vector of rates achievable at location set $\mathcal{L}$. Define the set of all rate vectors achievable at location set $\mathcal{L}$ by the active base station set $\mathcal{A}$ as the *rate region* of $\mathcal{A}$, which is denoted by $\mathcal{R}_{\mathcal{A}}$. We then have

$$\mathcal{R}_{\mathcal{A}} = \Big\{\boldsymbol{r} = [r_j] : \sum_{b_i \in \mathcal{A}} \gamma_{ij} R_{ij} = r_j, \sum_{l_j \in \mathcal{L}_i : b_i \in \mathcal{A}} \gamma_{ij} \leq 1\Big\}. \tag{3}$$

2.3 User Traffic and Utility

Cellular data traffic is a mix of elastic and inelastic traffic. Cellular networks support real-time audio and video streaming applications that require certain minimum rate guarantees to function properly. There are also applications such as file transfer that do not have this constraint. This mix of elastic and inelastic applications can be modeled as *rate-adaptive* applications with a minimum rate requirement. In this work, we consider *α-critical* functions to model utility of this type of applications. In α-critical functions [9], the function value is 0 before a certain threshold. Once the threshold is met, the increase of the utility value is based on a concave function. Moreover, we combine user utilities at each location and represent the aggregate utility as a single function. Specifically, at each location l_j, the utility function $U_j(\cdot)$ is defined as follows:

$$U_j(x_j) = u_j([x_j - d_j]^+), \tag{4}$$

where $u_j(\cdot)$ is an increasing concave function, x_j is the rate received at location l_j, d_j is the base demand at l_j, and $[x]^+ = \max(0, x)$. For an active base station set $\mathcal{A}$, the *system utility* of $\mathcal{A}$ is defined as follows:

$$U(\mathcal{A}) = \max_{\boldsymbol{x} \in \mathcal{R}_{\mathcal{A}}} \sum_{l_j \in \mathcal{L}} U_j(x_j). \tag{5}$$

[3]The model can be extended to take into consideration the uplink traffic as well.

[4]The term 'average' is omitted hereafter without ambiguity.

For an active set $\mathcal{A}$, the *net utility* $N(\mathcal{A})$ is defined as the difference between its system utility and cost, *i.e.*,

$$N(\mathcal{A}) = U(\mathcal{A}) - C(\mathcal{A}). \tag{6}$$

3. PROBLEM FORMULATION

To be able to make optimal activation decisions, each base station needs to know the state of its neighbors a priori. Due to inter-dependence of all BS decisions, this information cannot be made available to all BSs at the same time. Therefore, in our formulation, the next likely configuration of each base station is computed and propagated to its neighbors. To this end, an activation probability is assigned to each base station. The probabilities are assigned so that the expected net utility is maximized. To find the optimal activation probabilities without the need for a centralized controller, we design a distributed iterative message passing algorithm among base stations. Overall, the base station activation works as follows:

1. In each scheduling epoch, every base station iteratively solves a local problem to find its activation probability and exchanges its results with its neighbors until a stable solution is found.
2. At the end of a scheduling epoch, each base station decides to become active or inactive based on the optimal activation probabilities computed via the iterative algorithm of step (1).

Let α_i denote the activation probability associated with base station b_i. Accordingly, the net utility (6) maximization problem is given by

$$\max_{\alpha} \sum_{b_i} U_i(\alpha_i, \{\alpha_{i'}\}_{i' \in \mathcal{N}_i}) - \alpha_i c_i, \tag{7}$$

where $U_i(\cdot,\cdot)$ is the utility of base station b_i, which depends on its activation probability as well as the activation probabilities of its neighbors, *i.e.*, $\{\alpha_{i'}\}_{i' \in \mathcal{N}_i}$. In (7), both system utility and system cost are expressed as functions of activation probabilities. We intend to express both system utility and cost as functions of allocated resources. Let y_{ij} denote the fraction of b_i resources allocated to l_j conditioned on the activation of b_i. Then, the expected fraction of resources allocated to l_j from b_i is given by $x_{ij} = \alpha_i y_{ij}$. It follows that

$$\sum_{l_j \in \mathcal{L}_i} \alpha_i y_{ij} = \sum_{l_j \in \mathcal{L}_i} x_{ij}. \tag{8}$$

When a base station is activated, all its available resources are allocated to users, *i.e.*, $\sum_j y_{ij} = 1$. Thus, the relation between α_i and x_{ij}'s is given by

$$\alpha_i = \sum_j x_{ij}. \tag{9}$$

Utility of base station b_i is defined as the sum of location utilities for all locations under its coverage assuming fixed rate contribution from its neighbors to each location. In other words, $U_i(.,.)$ is defined as follows

$$\begin{aligned} U_i(\alpha_i, \{\alpha_{i'}\}_{i' \in \mathcal{N}_i}) &= \sum_{l_j \in \mathcal{L}_i} u_j(x_{ij}, \{x_{i'j}\}_{b_{i'} \in \mathcal{B}_j \setminus b_i}) \\ &= \sum_{l_j \in \mathcal{L}_i} u_j(x_{ij} r_{ij} + \sum_{b_{i'} \in \mathcal{B}_j \setminus b_i} x_{i'j} r_{i'j}) \end{aligned} \tag{10}$$

Accordingly, we can express (7) as follows

$$\max_{\boldsymbol{x}} \sum_{l_j \in \mathcal{L}} u_j(\sum_{b_i \in \mathcal{B}_j} x_{ij} r_{ij} - d_j) - \sum_{b_i \in \mathcal{B}} (\sum_{l_j \in \mathcal{L}_i} x_{ij}) c_i. \tag{11}$$

In addition to maximizing the net utility, the minimum rate demand should be satisfied at each location as well. Thus, the optimization problem (11) has the following set of constraints

$$\sum_{b_i \in \mathcal{B}_j} x_{ij} r_{ij} \geq d_j, \ \forall l_j \in \mathcal{L}. \tag{12}$$

There is also another set of constraints on the resources available to BSs as

$$\sum_{l_j \in \mathcal{L}_i} x_{ij} \leq 1, \ \forall b_i \in \mathcal{B}. \tag{13}$$

Problem (11) is a convex optimization problem that can be solved efficiently using interior-point methods, however, applying duality techniques on (11) is not straightforward since these methods need the objective to be strictly concave. Although the objective function of (11) is strictly concave w.r.t resources allocated from a specific BS, *e.g.*, b_i to l_j, when the total received, *i.e.*, $\sum_{b_i \in \mathcal{B}_j} x_{ij} r_{ij}$ is fixed, the objective value is constant. This may result in indifferentiability of the dual of (11) at some points. Similar problem arises in utility maximization problem for communication networks with multipath routing [15] and a similar solution method can be applied to circumvent the issue. Specifically, the *proximal point* [6] method is employed according which a quadratic term is added to the objective function for every variable x_{ij}. Doing so, the objective function is modified as follows

$$\begin{aligned} &\sum_{l_j \in \mathcal{L}} u_j(\sum_{b_i \in \mathcal{B}_j} x_{ij} r_{ij} - d_j) - \sum_{l_j \in \mathcal{L}} \sum_{b_i \in \mathcal{B}} \frac{e_j}{2}(x_{ij} - y_{ij})^2 \\ &+ \sum_{b_i \in \mathcal{B}} c_i(\sum_{l_j \in \mathcal{L}_i} x_{ij}) \end{aligned} \tag{14}$$

where $e_j > 0$. The optimal value of (14) coincides with the one from (11); that is if $\mathbf{x}^*$ is an optimal solution of (11), then $\mathbf{x} = \mathbf{x}^*, \mathbf{y} = \mathbf{x}^*$ is the optimal solution of (14). Problem (14) can be solved by Gauss-Seidel method in which the following steps are performed alternately. First, while keeping $\mathbf{y}$ fixed and considering constraints (12) and (13), $\boldsymbol{x}$ is found as follows

$$\begin{aligned} \mathbf{x(t+1)} = \max_{\boldsymbol{x}} &\sum_{l_j \in \mathcal{L}} u_j(\sum_{b_i \in \mathcal{B}_j} x_{ij} r_{ij} - d_j) \\ &- \sum_{l_j \in \mathcal{L}} \sum_{b_i \in \mathcal{B}} \frac{e_j}{2}(x_{ij} - y_{ij})^2 + \sum_{b_i \in \mathcal{B}} c_i(\sum_{l_j \in \mathcal{L}_i} x_{ij}). \end{aligned} \tag{15}$$

Then $\boldsymbol{y}$ is updated according to

$$\mathbf{y(t+1)} = \mathbf{x(t+1)}.$$

It is easy to show that $\mathbf{x(t)} = \mathbf{x}^*$ as $t \to \infty$. Also, (15) can be solved using dual methods. Lagrangian of (15) is given by

$$L(\boldsymbol{x},\boldsymbol{\lambda},\boldsymbol{\nu}) = \sum_{b_i\in\mathcal{B}} \Big(\sum_{l_j\in\mathcal{S}_i} \big(u_j(\sum_{b_k\in\mathcal{B}_j} x_{kj}r_{kj} - d_j) - \frac{e_j}{2}(x_{ij}-y_{ij})^2\big) - c_i(\sum_{l_j\in\mathcal{L}_i} x_{ij})\Big) + \sum_{l_j\in\mathcal{L}} \lambda_j(\sum_{b_i\in\mathcal{B}_j} x_{ij}r_{ij} - d_j) + \sum_{b_i\in\mathcal{B}} \nu_i(1-\sum_{l_j\in\mathcal{L}_i} x_{ij}) \tag{16}$$

where $\boldsymbol{\lambda} = [\lambda]_{|\mathcal{L}|}$ and $\boldsymbol{\nu} = [\nu]_{|\mathcal{B}|}$ are Lagrange multipliers for the sets of constraints (12) and (13) respectively. The associated Lagrange dual function for Lagrangian (16) is then expressed as

$$\max_{\boldsymbol{x}} L(\boldsymbol{x},\boldsymbol{\lambda},\boldsymbol{\nu}) = \sum_{b_i\in\mathcal{B}} \max_{\boldsymbol{x}} D_i(\boldsymbol{x},\boldsymbol{\lambda},\nu_i) - \sum_{l_j\in\mathcal{L}} \lambda_j d_j + \sum_{b_i\in\mathcal{B}} \nu_i \tag{17}$$

where D_i is given as follows

$$D_i(\boldsymbol{x},\boldsymbol{\lambda},\nu_i) = \sum_{l_j\in\mathcal{S}_i} \Big(u_j(\sum_{b_k\in\mathcal{B}_j} x_{kj}r_{kj} - d_j) - \sum_{b_k\in\mathcal{B}_j} \frac{e_j}{2}(x_{kj}-y_{kj})^2 \sum_{b_k\in\mathcal{B}_j} \lambda_j x_{kj} r_{kj} - \sum_{b_k\in\mathcal{B}_j} x_{kj}(c_k+\nu_k)\Big) \tag{18}$$

and represents the local subproblem that is solved at BS b_i. Then the dual of (15) is represented as

$$\min_{\boldsymbol{\lambda}\geq 0,\boldsymbol{\nu}} g(\boldsymbol{\lambda},\boldsymbol{\nu})\,. \tag{19}$$

Since the objective function of (19) is differentiable at all locations based on Danskin's theorem [5], we have

$$\frac{\partial g}{\partial \lambda_j} = \sum_{b_i\in\mathcal{B}_j} x_{ij}r_{ij} - d_j, \qquad \frac{\partial g}{\partial \nu_i} = 1 - \sum_{l_j\in\mathcal{L}_i} x_{ij}\,. \tag{20}$$

Therefore, problem (15) can be solved by a gradient projection algorithm in which the dual variables are updated as follows

$$\lambda_j(t+1) = \Big[\lambda_j(t) - \xi(\sum_{b_i\in\mathcal{B}_j} x_{ij}r_{ij} - d_j)\Big]^+, \qquad \nu_i(t+1) = \nu_i(t) - \xi(1-\sum_{l_j\in\mathcal{L}_i} x_{ij}) \tag{21}$$

where ξ is a sufficiently small step-size. In the next subsection, the message passing algorithm among base stations to implement the above solution is presented.

4. ALGORITHM DESIGN

The solution method presented in the previous section consists of an outer Gauss-Seidel loop and an inner gradient projection loop. In each iteration of the outer loop, before updating $\boldsymbol{y}$, it is assumed that the gradient projection algorithm has converged to its optimal solution. However, ensuring convergence of the inner loop in a distributed manner is cumbersome, so another algorithm is presented here in which the number of iterations of the inner loop is constant (in our case, it is limited to 1). The new algorithm is as follows

I. Fix $\boldsymbol{y} = \boldsymbol{y}(t)$. Assume $\boldsymbol{x}(t)$ is the primal variable that maximizes (17) given $\boldsymbol{y}$, $\boldsymbol{\lambda}(t)$, and $\boldsymbol{\nu}(t)$. Update dual variables $\boldsymbol{\lambda}(t+1)$ and $\boldsymbol{\nu}(t+1)$ according to (21).

II. Let $\boldsymbol{z}(t)$ be the point that maximizes (17) given the new dual variables $\boldsymbol{\lambda}(t+1)$ and $\boldsymbol{\nu}(t+1)$. Update $\boldsymbol{y}$ as follows

$$\boldsymbol{y}(t+1) = \boldsymbol{y}(t) + \tau(\boldsymbol{z}(t) - \boldsymbol{y}(t)) \tag{22}$$

where $\tau \in (0,1]$. The algorithm is guaranteed to converge to the optimal solution. For details of the convergence, see [15]. Following the algorithm, each BS b_i operates as follows. Knowing r_{kj} for each neighboring BS b_k to all the locations $l_j \in \mathcal{S}_i$, it solves (18) and then sends the obtained primal variable x^*_{kj} to the corresponding BS b_k. Each BS b_k, updates ν_k according to (21) based on the received and locally-computed x^*_{kj}'s. Then it updates all its neighbors with the new ν_k. This allows b_i to compute $\boldsymbol{z}(t)$ and update $\boldsymbol{y}$. Following this procedure, the algorithm can be implemented in a completely distributed manner by message passing between neighboring base stations.

Now we would like to show how to find the optimal value of local optimization problem from the current set of Lagrange multipliers $\boldsymbol{\lambda},\boldsymbol{\nu}$. According to Karush-Kuhn-Tucker (KKT) theorem, the stationary point of the Lagrangian, *i.e.*, the solution to $\nabla_{\boldsymbol{x}} L(\boldsymbol{x},\boldsymbol{\lambda},\boldsymbol{\nu}) = \mathbf{0}$, gives the unique solution to problem (17). Based on (18), we have

$$\frac{\partial D_i}{\partial x_{kj}} = r_{kj}u'(\sum_{b_k\in\mathcal{B}_j} x_{kj}r_{kj} - d_j) - e_j(x_{kj}-y_{kj}) + \lambda_j r_{kj} - (c_k+\nu_k) \tag{23}$$

then by setting $\frac{\partial D_i}{\partial x_{kj}} = 0$, for every x_{kj}, we obtain x^*_{kj}. Motivated by the definition of *weighted proportional fairness*, let us assume that the utility of each l_j is defined as

$$u_j(\sum_{b_k\in\mathcal{B}_j} x_{kj}r_{kj} - d_j) = w_j \ln(\sum_{b_k\in\mathcal{B}_j} x_{kj}r_{kj} - d_j)\,.$$

Then we have

$$\frac{\partial D_i}{\partial x_{kj}} = \frac{w_j r_{kj}}{\sum_{b_k\in\mathcal{B}_j} x_{kj}r_{kj} - d_j} - e_j(x_{kj}-y_{kj}) + \lambda_j r_{kj} - (c_k+\nu_k) = 0 \,. \tag{24}$$

Note that all the BSs that could provide service to l_j are related according to (24). Therefore, to compute the corresponding x^*_{kj}'s, both sides of (24) are multiplied by r_{kj} then summed over all $b_k \in \mathcal{B}_j$. This gives the following relation

$$\frac{w_j \sum_{b_k\in\mathcal{B}_j} r^2_{kj}}{\sum_{b_k\in\mathcal{B}_j} x_{kj}r_{kj} - d_j} - e_j \sum_{b_k\in\mathcal{B}_j} x_{kj}r_{kj} + \sum_{b_k\in\mathcal{B}_j} \big(e_j y_{kj} r_{kj} + \lambda_j r^2_{kj} - (c_k+\nu_k) r_{kj}\big) = 0\,. \tag{25}$$

Define s_j, θ_j and μ_j as follows:

$$s_j = \sum_{b_k \in \mathcal{B}_j} x_{kj} r_{kj}$$

$$\theta_j = \sum_{b_k \in \mathcal{B}_j} \left(e_j y_{kj} r_{kj} + \lambda_j r_{kj}^2 - (c_k + \nu_k) r_{kj} \right)$$

$$\mu_j = w_j \sum_{b_k \in \mathcal{B}_j} r_{kj}^2$$

Then, (25) is simplified as follows

$$\frac{\mu_j}{s_j - d_j} - e_j s_j + \theta_j = 0$$

which results in the following quadratic equation

$$-e_j s_j^2 + (e_j d_j + \theta_j) s_j + (\mu_j - \theta_j d_j) = 0$$

Solving the above equation, s_j is given by

$$s_j = \frac{(e_j d_j + \theta_j) + \sqrt{(e_j d_j + \theta_j)^2 + 4 e_j (\mu_j - \theta_j d_j)}}{2 e_j}. \quad (26)$$

After finding s_j, every x_{kj}^* can be computed by replacing the corresponding value of s_j in (25) as follows

$$x_{kj}^* = \left[\frac{1}{e_j} \left(\frac{w_j r_{kj}}{s_j} + e_j y_{kj} + \lambda_j r_{kj} - (c_k + \nu_k) \right) \right]_{[0,1]},$$

where $[x]_{\mathcal{S}}$ is the projection of x onto the set $\mathcal{S}$.

5. GENERAL CONCAVE COST

In previous section, activation probability of a base station is shown to be equal to the fraction of resources allocated to users from that base station. Also, cost of activating a BS was considered linearly dependent on its probability of activation (fraction of allocated resources). However, this model may not appropriately reflect the energy consumption at base stations which is highly dependent on energy consumed for cooling, *etc.* and not the transmission power. This base energy cost can be included in the model by considering concave cost functions instead of linear ones. Such functions feature steep slope at lower values and become less steep as they move toward higher values. This behavior approximately resembles the zero-one nature of the cost function. Specifically, *sigmoidal cost functions*[5] are considered which are defined as follows

$$C(\alpha) = \frac{c}{1 + e^{-d(\alpha - \alpha_0)}}. \quad (27)$$

These functions are concave where $c, d > 0$ and $\alpha > \alpha_0$. A sigmoidal function along with a linear one are illustrated in Figure 1. Employing a concave cost function changes the problem (7) as follows

$$\max_{\alpha} \sum_{b_i} U_i(\alpha_i, \{\alpha_{i'}\}_{i' \in \mathcal{N}_i}) - C_i(\alpha_i), \quad (28)$$

where each $C_i(.)$ is an increasing, concave and continuously differentiable function in $[0, 1]$. Problem (28) is in fact the difference of two concave functions, so it is not a convex optimization problem. However, it can be tackled using convex-concave procedure (CCCP) [25]. In CCCP, instead of dealing with (28) directly, a sequence of convex programs is formulated. At each step the following problem is solved

$$\alpha_i^{l+1} \in \arg\max U_i(\alpha_i, \{\alpha_{i'}\}_{i' \in \mathcal{N}_i}) - \alpha_i \nabla C_i(\alpha_i^l), \quad (29)$$

The premise behind (29) is to replace the convex part of the objective, *i.e.*, $-C_i(\alpha_i)$, with an affine approximation to make the problem locally convex. To do so, first-order Taylor approximation of the cost function around the current solution, *i.e.*, α^l, is utilized. Then, the new one, *i.e.*, α^{l+1}, is obtained by solving (29). Since $C_i(.)$ is concave, we have

$$C_i(y) \leq C_i(x) + (y - x) \nabla C_i(x),$$

for all $x, y \in [0, 1]$. Therefore, we have

$$U_i(\alpha_i^{l+1}) - C_i(\alpha_i^{l+1}) \geq U_i(\alpha_i^{l+1}) - C_i(\alpha_i^l) - (\alpha_i^{l+1} - \alpha_i^l) \nabla C_i(\alpha_i^l) \quad (30)$$

Since $\alpha_i^{l+1} \in \arg\max U_i(\alpha_i) - \alpha_i \nabla C_i(\alpha_i^l)$, we also have

$$U_i(\alpha_i^{l+1}) - \alpha_i^{l+1} \nabla C_i(\alpha_i^l) \geq U_i(\alpha_i^l) - \alpha_i^l \nabla C_i(\alpha_i^l). \quad (31)$$

Combining (30) and (31) we have

$$\begin{aligned} U_i(\alpha_i^{l+1}) - C_i(\alpha_i^{l+1}) &\geq U_i(\alpha_i^l) - C_i(\alpha_i^l) - (\alpha_i^l - \alpha_i^l) \nabla C_i(\alpha_i^l) \\ &\geq U_i(\alpha_i^l) - C_i(\alpha_i^l). \end{aligned} \quad (32)$$

The above argument shows that the sequence of α's is ascent, therefore, (29) converges to a local maximum. See [24] for detailed discussion of the convergence of CCCP.

Adapting our previous solution to the new sigmoidal cost function is straightforward. The only change that is needed to be made is the value of c_k. In this case, c_k is not constant anymore but varies in each iteration. Specifically, the value of $c_k(t)$ depends on the fraction of resources allocated in the previous iteration as follows

$$c_k(t) = \nabla_x C(x(t)).$$

Assuming sigmoidal cost function (27) with inflection point of 0, c_k is given by

$$c_k(t) = \frac{c d e^{d x(t)}}{(e^{d x(t)} + 1)^2} \quad (33)$$

in problem (18). In this case, each base station b_i, in addition to updating its neighbors with the current value of ν_i, needs to update them with the current value of $c_i(t)$ in each iteration.

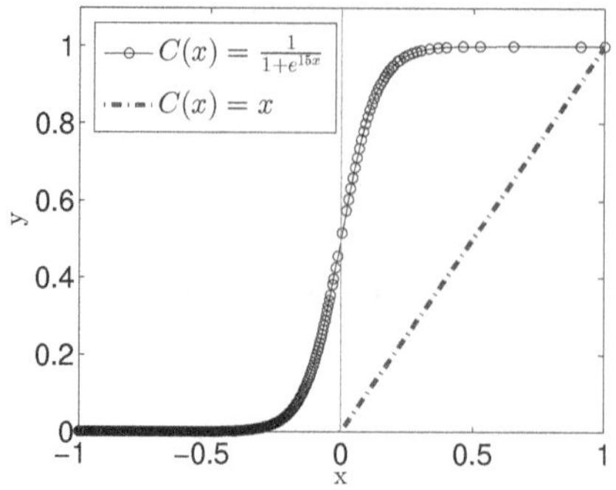

Figure 1: Comparison of different cost functions.

[5] An increasing function $f(x)$ is called a sigmoidal function, if it has one inflection point x_0, and $f''(x) > 0$ for all $x < x_0$ and $f''(x) < 0$, for all $x > x_0$.

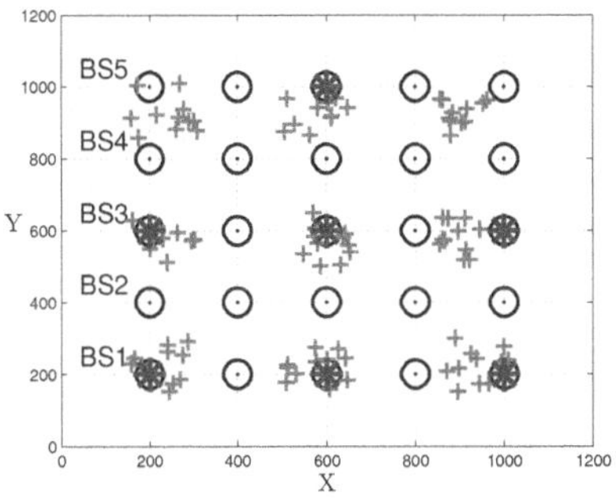

Figure 2: Snapshot of activated base stations ('*') in a network with non-uniform user distribution .

6. NUMERICAL RESULTS

We consider a network of size $1200m \times 1200m$. Base stations are placed on a regular grid. Distance between each two neighboring BSs is $200m$. There are a total of 25 base stations in the network. A base station is able to cover users which are up to $150m$ away from it.

The propagation parameter values are adopted from [8] as the assumptions regarding channel gains are consistent with the standard 3GPP propagation models. Power gain between a sender and a receiver is obtained as $g = f(d)$ where d is the distance between the sender and the receiver in (km). $f(d) = 10^{h_0} d^{-\kappa}$ with path loss exponent $\kappa = 3.5$ and $h_0 = -14.4$. Background noise is $N_0 = -174$ dbm (Hz^{-1}). Bandwidth is 1 MHz and maximum power P varies from $P = 4W$, to $P = 16W$.

Our goal is to study the behavior of the distributed algorithm. Two scenarios for distribution of users in the network are considered: *uniform* and *non-uniform*. In the uniform case, location of a user is chosen uniformly at random in the network. To distribute users non-uniformly, nine crowded regions are considered in the network. Each crowded region is a circle of radius $160m$. Users are divided equally among these crowded regions and distributed uniformly within each region.

6.1 Convergence of Distributed Algorithm

In the first set of results, we would like to demonstrate convergence of the algorithm to the optimal solution. Users are distributed non-uniformly in the network. In Figure 2, a snapshot of base station locations, user distribution and activated base stations is demonstrated. As it is apparent from the figure, base stations are activated mainly in more populated areas (higher utilities). Maximum transmission power for all BSs is set to $4W$. Cost of BS activation is assumed to be the 250. Demand at all locations is 0, so some users might not be covered.

In 3, variation of activation probabilities of five nearby base stations (BSs in the left vertical line of the network snapshot) are shown throughout the execution of the algorithm. Two of the aforementioned base stations are located in crowded regions, one of them is in a lightly-loaded region, and the other two in regions with no users. Activation probabilities of the BSs in crowded regions converge to 1, the base station in the lightly loaded region to almost 0, and the other two to 0. As demonstrated, the algorithm converges in about 350 iterations with step-size $\xi = 0.02$. To demonstrate the sensitivity of the algorithm to step-size selection, convergence of the probabilities are also shown for another step-size $\xi = 0.01$ in figure 4. In this case, convergence happens in about iteration 700. This shows that the algorithm can be slow for lower values of ξ.

6.2 Effect of Utility and Activation Cost

To see the behavior of the distributed algorithm, both activation cost and utilities have been varied. To increase the utilities, BSs maximum transmission power have been increased from $P = 4W$ to $P = 16W$. Figure 5 and 6 shows the number of activated base stations for different values of P and activation costs. As can be seen in the figure, increasing the utilities allows more base stations to be activated while increasing the activation cost reduces the number of active base stations. In addition, uniform user distribution associates approximately the same number of users to base stations which results in similar utilities for them. In comparison to the non-uniform user distribution, this allows activating more base stations when the activation cost is low. The opposite is true when the cost is high.

What is interesting in these results is the matching between the activated base stations and the crowded regions which is demonstrated in Figure 7. The figure depicts snapshots of the network and the corresponding activated base stations as activation cost is increased. The snapshots are taken from the above results where $P = 16W$. As the snapshots highlight, although the algorithm is randomized, it results in a good match between populated areas and activated base stations.

7. CONCLUSION AND FUTURE WORK

Distributed algorithms to the base station activation problem are investigated in this paper. The presented algorithm is designed to find the optimal operating point of the network in terms of utility and cost while guaranteeing network coverage. In the algorithm, finding appropriate step-size to ensure fast convergence of the distributed algorithm is difficult. As a future work, we plan to investigate distributed algorithms based on resorting KKT conditions [13], which do not use step-size and seem to result in faster convergence. Also, in this work, a randomized rounding procedure is used to activate base stations after finding the optimal activation probabilities. Other rounding methods [11] might be considered to guarantee coverage of inelastic demands.

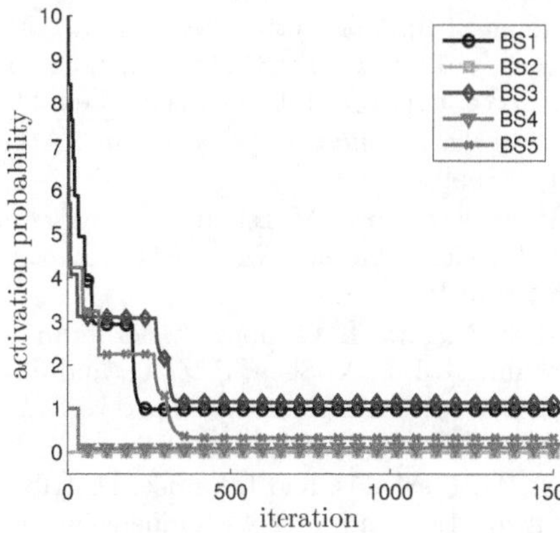

Figure 3: Convergence of BS activation probabilities with step-size $\xi = 0.02$.

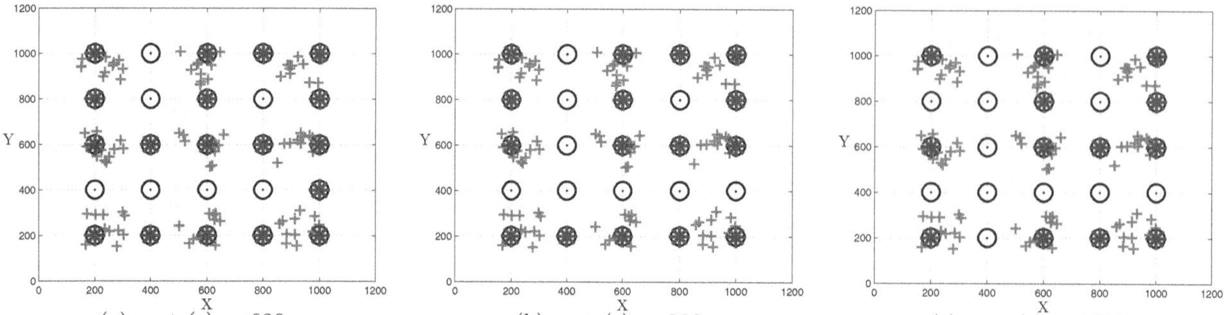

(a) cost (c) = 600. (b) cost (c) = 800. (c) cost (c) = 1000.

Figure 7: Snapshots of network and activated base stations ('$*$').

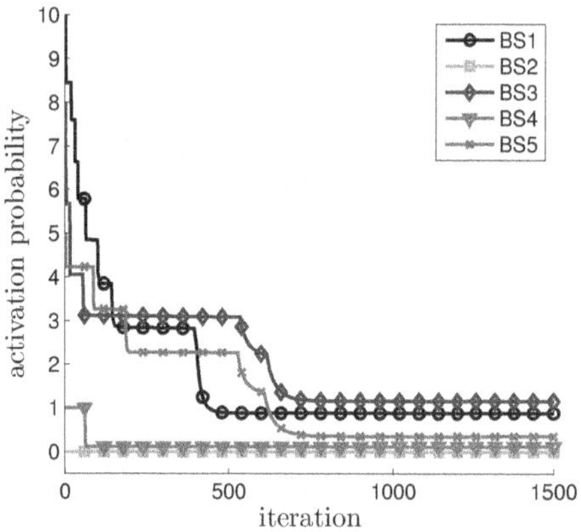

Figure 4: Convergence of BS activation probabilities with step-size $\xi = 0.01$.

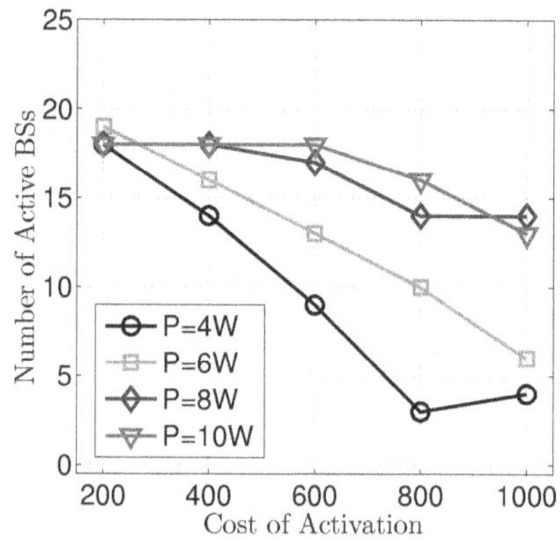

Figure 5: Number of active BSs versus transmission power and activation cost in a network with uniform user distribution.

8. REFERENCES

[1] Long term evolution of the 3gpp radio technology. `http://www.3gpp.org/LTE/`.

[2] LTE-Advanced. `http://www.3gpp.org/article/lte-advanced`.

[3] AT&T SXSW Press Release. `http://www.att.com/Common/docs/SXSW_Network%20Fact_Sheet.doc`, Mar. 2011.

[4] Cisco visual networking index: Global mobile data traffic forecast update. `http://www.cisco.com/en/US/solutions/collateral/ns341/ns525/ns537/ns705/ns827/white_paper_c11-520862.pdf`, Feb. 2013.

[5] D. P. Bertsekas. *Nonlinear Programming.* Athena Scientific, 1999.

[6] D. P. Bertsekas and J. N. Tsitsiklis. *Parallel and Distributed Computation: Numerical Methods.* Prentice Hall Inc., 1989.

[7] P. Bhat, S. Nagata, L. Campoy, I. Berberana, T. Derham, G. Liu, X. Shen, P. Zong, and J. Yang. LTE-Advanced: An Operator Perspective. *IEEE Commun. Mag.*, 50(2):104–114, 2012.

[8] S. Borst, M. Markakis, and I. Saniee. Distributed Power Allocation and User Assignment in OFDMA Cellular Networks. In *In Proc. Allerton Conference on Communication, Control, and Computing*, pages 1055–1063, Urbana, USA, Sep 2011.

[9] M. H. Cheung, A. H. Mohsenian-Rad, V. W. Wong, and R. Schober. Utility-Optimal Random Access for Wireless Multimedia Sensor Networks. *IEEE Commun. Lett.*, 1(4):340–343, 2012.

[10] FCC Spectrum Policy Task Force. Report of the Spectrum Ffficiency Working. `http://www.fcc.gov/sptf/reports.html`, Nov. 2002.

[11] R. Gandhi, S. Kuller, S. Parthasarathy, and A. Srinivisan. Dependent Rounding and its Applications to Approximation Algorithms. *Journal of the ACM*, 53(3):324–360, 2006.

[12] J. Gong, S. Zhou, Z. Niu, and P. Yang. Traffic-Aware Base Station Sleeping in Dense Cellular Networks. In *Proc. IEEE IWQoS*, pages 1–2, Beijing, China, Jun 2010.

[13] J. Huang, R. A. Berry, and M. L. Honig. Distributed Interference Compensation for Wireless Networks. *IEEE J. Sel. Areas Commun.*, 24(5):1074–1084, 2006.

[14] J. Huang, V. G. Subramanian, R. Agrawal, and R. A. Berry. Downlink Scheduling and Resource Allocation for OFDM Systems. *IEEE Trans. Wireless Commun.*, 8(1):288–296, 2009.

[15] X. Lin and N. B. Shroff. Utility Maximization for Communication Networks with Multipath Routing. *IEEE Trans. Automat. Contr.*, 51(5):766–781, 2006.

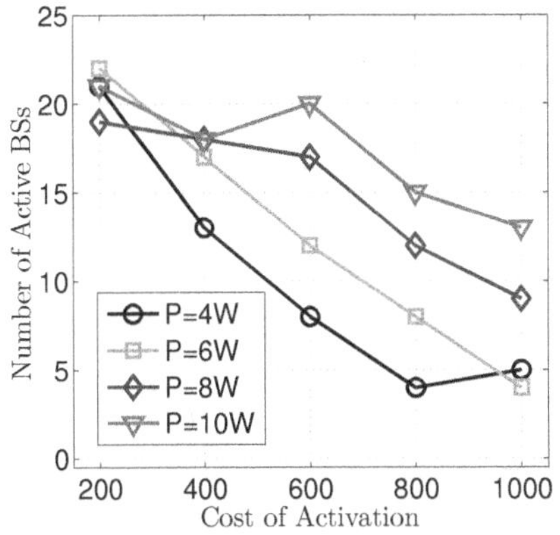

Figure 6: Number of active BSs versus transmission power and activation cost in a network with uniform user distribution.

[16] D. Lopez-Perez, I. Guvenc, G. D. L. Roche, M. Kountouris, T. Q. S. Quek, and J. Zhang. ENHANCED INTERCELL INTERFERENCE COORDINATION CHALLENGES IN HETEROGENEOUS NETWORKS. *IEEE Wireless Commun. Mag.*, 18(3):22–30, 2011.

[17] M. A. Marsan and M. Meo. Energy Efficient Management of two Cellular Access Networks. *ACM SIGMETRICS Performance Evaluation Review*, 37(4):69–73, 2010.

[18] M. A. Marsan and M. Meo. Green Wireless Networking: Three Questions. In *Proc. IFIP Med-Hoc-Net*, pages 41–44, Sicily, Italy, Jun 2011.

[19] D. W. K. Ng and R. Schober. Resource Allocation and Scheduling in Multi-Cell OFDMA Systems with Decode-and-Forward relaying. *IEEE Trans. Wireless Commun.*, 10(7):2246–2258, 2011.

[20] E. Oh and B. Krishnamachari. Energy Savings Through Dynamic Base Station Switching in Cellular Wireless Access Networks. In *Proc. IEEE GlobeCom*, pages 1–5, Miami, USA, Dec 2010.

[21] C. Peng, S.-B. Lee, S. Lu, H. Luo, and H. Li. Traffic-Driven Power Saving in Operational 3G Cellular Networks. In *Proc. ACM MobiCom*, pages 121–132, Las Vegas, USA, Sep 2011.

[22] S. Shakkottai and R. Srikant. Network Optimization and Control. *Foundations and Trends® in Networking*, 2(3), 2007.

[23] K. Son, H. Kim, Y. Yi, , and B. Krishnamachari. Base Station Operation and User Association mechanisms for Energy-Delay Tradeoffs in Green Cellular Networks. *IEEE J. Sel. Areas Commun.*, 29(8):1525–1536, 2011.

[24] B. Sriperumbudur and G. Lanckriet. On the convergence of the concave-convex procedure. In *Proc. NIPS*, pages 1759–1767, Vancouver, Canada, Dec 2009.

[25] A. Yuille and A. Rangarajan. The Concave-Convex Procedure (CCCP). In *Proc. NIPS*, volume 2, pages 1033–1040, Vancouver, Canada, 2002.

[26] S. Zhouy, J. Gongy, Z. Yangy, Z. Niuy, and P. Yang. Green Mobile Access Network with Dynamic Base Station Energy Saving. In *ACM MobiCom posters*, Beijing, China, Sep 2009.

Modelling and Analysis of Link Adaptation for LTE-Advanced

Parth Amin
Department of Computer Science and Engineering
Aalto University,
PO Box 15400, Aalto 00076, Finland
parth.amin@aalto.fi

Sassan Iraji
Department of Communications and Networking
Aalto University,
P.O.Box 13000, Aalto 00076, Finland
sassan.iraji@aalto.fi

Jukka K. Nurminen
Department of Computer Science and Engineering
Aalto University,
PO Box 15400, Aalto 00076, Finland
jukka.k.nurminen@aalto.fi

ABSTRACT

We present the detailed system model for adaptive modulation and coding (AMC) in the physical layer, and hybrid automatic repeat request (HARQ) in the data link layer, which play key roles in link layer of future wireless technologies as for e.g. LTE-Advanced. The packet combining schemes hard combining and weighted hard combining are compared in an attempt to reduce packet error rate (PER) and increase spectral efficiency. Simulation results show that both combining schemes will always keep the required quality of service (QoS) and increase spectral efficiency significantly over the system without AMC/HARQ. Moreover, with severe interference, hard combining will improve the system spectral efficiency more than weighted hard combining.

Categories and Subject Descriptors

C.2.1 [**Network Architecture and Design**]: Wireless communication; I.6.5 [**Simulation and Modeling**]: Model Development—*Modeling methodologies*

Keywords

link adaptation; hybrid automatic repeat request; adaptive modulation and coding; hard combining; weighted hard combining; Long Term Evolution; quality of service

1. INTRODUCTION

The principle of link adaptation is fundamental to the design of a radio interface which is efficient for packet-switched data traffic. We present a detailed system model to design link adaptation for packet network, for e.g. Long Term Evolution (LTE). Adaptive modulation and coding (AMC) and hybrid automatic repeat request (HARQ) are the key LTE link layer techniques to achieve high spectral efficiency for a interference limited cellular network. AMC resides in the physical layer and HARQ in the link layer of LTE. The core idea of AMC is to dynamically choose a mode, called Modulation and Coding Scheme (MCS), depending on the Channel Quality Indicator (CQI). The objective is to maximize spectral efficiency while maintaining quality of service (QOS) requirements[1]. HARQ combines the use of forward error correction (FEC) and retransmissions to significantly decrease packet error rate (PER). For each received copy of a packet, the receiver can combine the information to achieve time diversity[2].

Review of AMC and HARQ implementation in IEEE 802.16 and 3GPP LTE is given in [3]. In [4], HARQ and AMC is optimized for the delay constrained networks, based on the feedback from HARQ. [5] analyzes the impact of AMC and HARQ with chase combining to MIMO systems performance in LTE downlink at low, medium and high user mobile speed. [6] presents the iterative packet combining method based on both soft and hard information, that corrects both the even and odd errors in an erroneous packet by combining the current erroneous copy with the previous one. Work has been done also to find good thresholds for when to choose a specific MCS. A simplified approach with plain ARQ was investigated in [7]. This doesn't use any forward error correction in the link layer, and also no packet combining. They consider the modulation orders and coding rates of HIPERLAN/2 plus BPSK over a Nakagami-m fading channel. In [8] HARQ and an Incremental Redundancy (IR) scheme is used to combine retransmitted packets to improve the work of [7], in the special case of a Rayleigh fading channel. This is just one way of combining packets.

In this paper we present a detailed system model to design HARQ and AMC for LTE and future mobile networks, which maximizes spectral efficiency while keeping a certain QoS. Our work focuses on adding HARQ to the work previously done in [7]. As opposed to [8], which uses IR scheme, we compare hard combining and weighted hard combining. Both of the investigated techniques namely hard combining and weighted hard combining improve the system spectral efficiency. One important task is to choose MCS using our two packet combining schemes and implement the combining schemes in Link Layer Simulation Environment (LiLaS)[9].

The rest of this paper is organized as follows. The system model and assumptions are presented in Section 2. Section 3 presents the system design. In Section 4 we give the simula-

MSWiM'13, November 3–8, 2013, Barcelona, Spain.

ACM 978-1-4503-2353-6/13/11...$15.00.
http://dx.doi.org/10.1145/2507924.2507986.

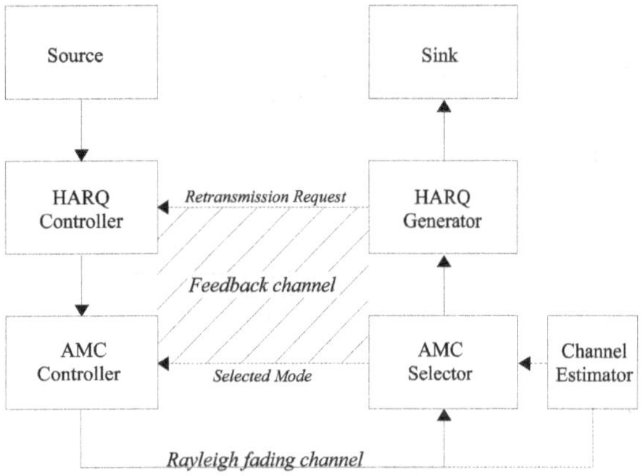

Figure 1: System Structure

tion model and present numerical results. Finally, in Section 5, conclusions are drawn.

2. SYSTEM MODEL

Consider the system structure in Fig. 1. The higher layers can be seen as the source generating information bits. In the receiver the bits are delivered to the corresponding sink. The processing unit in the link layer is *packet*, consisting of bits, while in the physical layer it is *frame*, consisting of symbols.

The responsibility of the HARQ Controller in transmitter is to add a Cyclic Redundancy Check (CRC) for residual error detecting purposes, then to add FEC by encoding the resulting packet using a fixed rate convolutional encoder with rate R_{HARQ}. It must also hold a buffer for the last transmitted packet in case of retransmission. The HARQ Generator in receiver uses the CRC after decoding to determine whether to send an acknowledgment (ACK) or negative acknowledgment (NAK) to the HARQ Controller. Upon reception of a NAK, the HARQ Controller will retransmit the same packet again. The approach is to wait for ACK/NAK before sending again. This is commonly referred to as a Stop-n-wait protocol. The HARQ Generator stores the packets received in subsequent retransmissions to combine them before decoding.

It performs variable convolutional coding with rates $R_{AMC,1}, ..., R_{AMC,N_r}$ using Rate Compatible Punctured Convolutional (RCPC) codes, where N_r is the number of code rates available. The bits are modulated using M_k-ary QAM, where $M_k = 2^k$, and the demodulation is coherent. One modulation scheme and associated coding rate results in an AMC mode or MCS. Based on CQI, a mode selection is made. CQI means in our case instantaneous signal to noise ratio (SNR). Each MCS comes with a threshold value for the SNR. The lower the thresholds, the higher is the MCS selected for a given SNR.

The information packet size from upper layers is assumed to be constant, containing N_i bits. Denote by N_{CRC} the number of bits added as CRC redundancy. Since the HARQ encoder has a memory of $N_{tail,HARQ}$ bits, one needs to add the same number of zeros in order to reset the memories. The number of bits after the HARQ encoder is then $N_{HARQ} = (N_i + N_{CRC} + N_{tail,HARQ})/R_{HARQ}$. Those bits are encoded by the AMC code using rate $R_{AMC,n}$ for mode n and $N_{tail,AMC}$ tail bits. The resulting number of bits are $N_{AMC} = (N_{HARQ}+N_{tail,AMC})/R_{AMC,n}$. The final number of symbols transmitted over the channel for mode n using modulation order k_n (bits/symbol) is

$$\begin{aligned} N_s &= \frac{N_{AMC}}{k_n} \\ &= \frac{(N_i + N_{CRC} + N_{tail,HARQ})}{k_n \cdot R_{HARQ} \cdot R_{AMC,n}} + \\ &+ \frac{N_{tail,AMC}}{k_n \cdot R_{AMC,n}} \end{aligned} \tag{1}$$

For comparison purposes, the assumptions and simplifications adopted in this paper are the same as in [8] and [7].

A1) For each transmitted frame, the channel is frequency flat and constant. The channel varies from frame to frame according to the Rayleigh distribution. As a consequence, AMC mode is selected on a frame-to-frame basis. For a Rayleigh fading channel, the instantaneous SNR is exponentially distributed[10] with mean γ_0 according to

$$f_\Gamma(\gamma) = \frac{1}{\gamma_0} \cdot e^{-\frac{\gamma}{\gamma_0}} \tag{2}$$

A2) The receiver has perfect knowledge of the channel. If the channel is denoted by H and the receiver estimate by $\hat{H}$, then $H = \hat{H}$.

A3) Mode selection messaging and ACK/NAK are fed back without error or delay, using the feedback channel.

A4) Error detection by CRC is perfect, detecting all errors. This is reasonable since we will use CRC polynomial from [11] with 24 redundancy bits, which has an undetected error rate $< 2^{-24}$ [12].

Further perfections of our assumptions are left for future research.

3. SYSTEM DESIGN

AMC at the physical layer is to be combined with HARQ at the link layer. General formulas are derived to determine threshold values given QoS constraints. In sections 3.1–3.2 we present a relationship between the packet error rate (PER) delivered to the user and the bit error rate (BER) in the physical layer. In section 3.3 we present the relationship between the BER in the physical layer and the received SNR.

A system with delay requirements can only allow a finite number of retransmissions. Hence error-free delivery cannot be guaranteed. We construct the first constraint as in [7]:

Constraint 1) The maximum number of re-transmissions allowed in the system is N_t.

The upper layers will also have requirements on the packet loss probability. This number can be given with the application at hand. It imposes the following constraint 2,

Constraint 2) The probability of packet loss after N_t transmissions must be less than P_{loss}.

Now that we have specifications for the HARQ at the data link layer, we can *design the AMC to maximize spectral efficiency while fulfilling constraints 1 and 2*, which is the objective of the cross-layer design.

3.1 Performance Requirement at the HARQ Decoder

From now on, we differ between packet error probabilities and bit error probabilities by denoting them by P and P_b, respectively. Denote simply by P the average PER delivered to upper layers from the HARQ. From constraints 1–2 we get [8]

$$P^{N_t} \leq P_{loss} \tag{3}$$

and from that we get the maximum PER we can have in one transmission [8]:

$$P \leq P_{loss}^{1/N_t} = P_{target} \tag{4}$$

For a convolutional code with hard-decision Viterbi decoding and independent errors at the channel input, the PER upper bound[13] can also be written as

$$P \leq 1 - (1 - P_u)^L = P_{target} \tag{5}$$

where L is the packet length delivered to the HARQ Decoder, and P_u is the union bound of the first-event error probability for the given code, given by

$$P_u = \sum_{d=d_f}^{\infty} a_d \cdot P_d \tag{6}$$

where d_f is the free distance of the code, and a_d is the total number of error events of weight d. P_d is the probability of an incorrect path at distance d from the correct path being chosen by the Viterbi decoder. It can be approximated as [14]

$$P_d \approx (4 \cdot P_{b,HARQ} \cdot (1 - P_{b,HARQ}))^{d/2} \tag{7}$$

where $P_{b,HARQ}$ is the bit error rate delivered to the decoder in HARQ. Since $P_{b,HARQ}$ is usually very small [8], P_u in Eq. (6) is dominated by its first term. Inserting (7) into (6) and simplifying yields

$$\begin{aligned} P_u &\approx a_{d_f} \cdot P_{d_f} && (8) \\ &\approx a_{d_f} (4 \cdot P_{b,HARQ} \cdot (1 - P_{b,HARQ}))^{d_f/2} && (9) \\ &\approx a_{d_f} \cdot 2^{d_f} \cdot P_{b,HARQ}^{d_f/2} && (10) \end{aligned}$$

Solving for $P_{b,HARQ}$ in (10), inserting equations (4) and (5) gives

$$\begin{aligned} P_{b,HARQ} &= \left[\frac{1 - (1 - P_{target})^{1/L}}{a_{d_f} \cdot 2^{d_f}}\right]^{2/d_f} && (11) \\ &= \left[\frac{1 - (1 - P_{loss}^{1/N_t})^{1/L}}{a_{d_f} \cdot 2^{d_f}}\right]^{2/d_f} && (12) \end{aligned}$$

$P_{b,HARQ}$, which is the bit error into the HARQ decoder, is related to the bit error probability delivered from the physical layer, $P_{b,phy}$. To satisfy (4), P_{target} exerts a requirement on $P_{b,phy}$, namely $P_{b,phy} \leq P_{b,target}$. Without packet combining we have $P_{b,HARQ} = P_{b,target}$, that is, the BER delivered to the HARQ decoder originates directly from the physical layer. By using packet combining in between, $P_{b,HARQ}$ will decrease with each retransmission.

3.2 Packet Combining

Two ways of packet combining are compared in this paper – hard combining and weighted hard combining. The retransmitted packets are buffered in the receiver. Before the packet is fed to the HARQ decoder, all stored packets are combined. The idea is to increase the probability of error correction in the decoder, by getting time diversity. We next explain the two combining schemes.

3.2.1 *Hard Combining*

In hard combining, the bit that is in majority will be chosen. If there are equal number of ones and zeros, we will make a guess. That can only happen after an even number of transmissions.

3.2.2 *Weighted Hard Combining*

In weighted hard combining, each bit is weighted by its corresponding SNR – as an attempt to improve the hard combining scheme in even transmissions. First, all zeros of each packet are converted into minus ones (-1). The packets are then multiplied by its respective SNR. When they are added together, looking at the sign of the sum gives the combined bits. Lastly, the minus ones are converted back to zeros and the packet is fed to the decoder. The procedure after i transmissions is shown below.

$$\begin{array}{cccccc} & [b_0^{(1)} & b_1^{(1)} & \dots & b_{L-1}^{(1)}] & \cdot\gamma^{(1)} \\ & [b_0^{(2)} & b_1^{(2)} & \dots & b_{L-1}^{(2)}] & \cdot\gamma^{(2)} \\ & \dots & \dots & \dots & \dots & \dots \\ + & [b_0^{(i)} & b_1^{(i)} & & b_{L-1}^{(i)}] & \cdot\gamma^{(i)} \\ \hline \text{sign}(& . & . & . & . &) \end{array}$$

The BER calculations will be similar to hard combining, but taking into account the SNR of each transmission. A correct decision can be made even if only one bit is correct, if its SNR is high enough. Mind that a wrong decision also can be made on the same basis.

3.3 AMC Mode Selection

We need to achieve a certain BER from the physical layer, as mentioned earlier. $P_{b,target}$ will approximately follow the expression used in [7]:

$$P_{b,target}(\gamma) \approx a_n exp(-b_n \gamma) \tag{13}$$

where n is the mode and γ is the received SNR. Parameters a_n and b_n are found by fitting (13) to the exact numerically found BER.

We decide that mode n is chosen when $\gamma \in [\gamma_n, \gamma_{n+1})$. γ_n is set to be the minimum SNR required to achieve $P_{b,target}$. Solving for γ in (13) gives us

$$\gamma_n^{(i)} = \frac{1}{b_n} ln\left(\frac{a_n}{P_{b,target}^{(i)}}\right) \tag{14}$$

where i is the number of transmissions performed.

Using (14) together with $P_{b,target}^{(i)}$, one can find the threshold for mode n in transmission i. This analysis will give separate thresholds for both hard combining and weighted hard combining, as depicted in Tables 3 and 4.

Mode	Modulation	Code Rate	a_n	b_n
Mode1	QPSK	1/2	10.5205	3.2358
Mode2	QPSK	3/4	3.1265	1.4730
Mode3	16-QAM	9/16	0.4545	0.3984
Mode4	16-QAM	3/4	0.4448	0.2138
Mode5	64-QAM	3/4	2.9770	0.0987

Table 1: Fitting parameters a_n and b_n

	Mode1	Mode2	Mode3
γ_n (dB)	7.3288	14.3186	20.5509

Table 2: Thresholds for original LiLaS, $P_{loss} = 10^{-1}$

4. SIMULATOR MODEL AND RESULTS

We use LiLaS simulator[9], which is already using a system with adaptive modulation. Fixed information packet length, $N_i = 735$ bits, will lead to that the number of bits delivered to the physical layer is $N_{HARQ} = 1020$ bits. We use 24-bit CRC, as used in [11] and HARQ convolutional encoder/decoder with rate 3/4 for error correction purposes. Variable coding rate in the physical layer are 1/2, 9/16 and 3/4. Parameters a_n and b_n for Eq. (14) are found by fitting the exact BER to equation (13) the same way as done in [8] and [7]. For each mode, a_n and b_n are summarized in Table 1.

To see a difference between the two combining schemes, we need to simulate a high error situation – which will lead to many retransmissions and thus combining. We therefore set $P_{loss} = 10^{-1}$. For a packet loss of P_{loss} one needs to send P_{loss}^{-1} packets just to have *one* packet in error (in average). But in order to have more accurate statistics, at least 100 lost packets is be needed. Hence $P_{loss}^{-1} \cdot 100$ transmitted packets are needed. In our simulations, we will run 1000 channel realizations for each SNR. For each realization one packet is transmitted (and possibly retransmitted up to $N_t - 1$ times). $N_t = 4$ is chosen, and the simulations will be carried out for every third SNR from 0 to 21 [dB]. Simulation parameters and calculated thresholds for all cases are summarized in Tables 1, 3 and 4. The following cases are simulated:

- Spectral efficiency vs. SNR – comparing the performance of hard combining and weighted hard combining with Original LiLaS simulator, which does not have the added HARQ and AMC functionality. All designed for $P_{loss} = 10^{-1}$. In the original LiLaS where only adaptive modulation is present, the thresholds are calculated from equations (6) and (7) in [15]. We will also add LiLaS using only AMC, which is a special case having $N_t = 1$.

	Mode1	Mode2	Mode3	Mode4	Mode5
$\gamma_n^{(1)}$ (dB)	-0.0471	2.6359	6.4231	8.8452	14.8239
$\gamma_n^{(2)}$ (dB)	-0.0471	2.6359	6.4231	8.8452	14.8239
$\gamma_n^{(3)}$ (dB)	-3.1136	-1.1613	2.5041	4.7506	10.6629
$\gamma_n^{(4)}$ (dB)	-3.1136	-1.1613	2.5041	4.7506	10.6629

Table 3: Thresholds for Hard combining, $P_{loss} = 10^{-1}$

	Mode1	Mode2	Mode3	Mode4	Mode5
$\gamma_n^{(1)}$ (dB)	-0.0471	2.6359	6.4231	8.8452	14.8239
$\gamma_n^{(2)}$ (dB)	-0.0471	2.6359	6.4231	8.8452	14.8239
$\gamma_n^{(3)}$ (dB)	-0.4238	2.1943	5.9722	8.3814	14.3554
$\gamma_n^{(4)}$ (dB)	-0.9797	1.5434	5.3059	7.6935	13.6594

Table 4: Thresholds for Weighted hard combining, $P_{loss} = 10^{-1}$

- Average number of retransmissions per transmitted packet vs. SNR – comparing hard combining and weighted hard combining.

The objective was to maximize spectral efficiency for a given QoS constraint. We designed our system for a maximum of four transmissions and packet loss of 10^{-1} to the upper layers. The thresholds used in the simulations will therefore always make sure these constraints are fulfilled. We next present what the spectral efficiencies are for this QoS. The spectral efficiency is affected by the modulation order, coding rate and number of retransmissions.

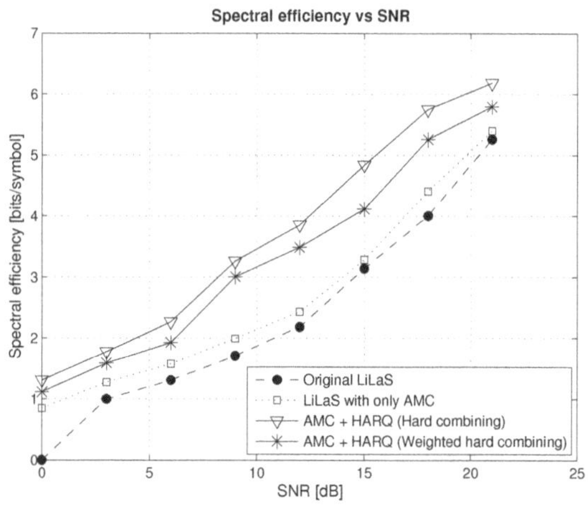

Figure 2: Spectral efficiency vs. SNR

The performance of link adaptation in terms of spectral efficiency is depicted in Figure 2. The figure shows that hard combining improves the spectral efficiency higher than weighted hard combining, as hard combining has lower thresholds for third and fourth transmissions compared to weighted hard combining, as shown in Tables 3 and 4. Lower thresholds leads to higher AMC modes and thus better spectral efficiency. A more fine-grained SNR scale would show a bigger difference between hard and weighted hard combining in the lower parts of each threshold interval – and consequently a smaller difference in the higher parts of the interval. This is because the AMC mode is constant in the interval, but the SNR changes.

Figure 2 also depicts that the system with only AMC does slightly better than the original LiLaS, because of the addition of adaptive coding. Finally we note that both of our complete systems, using either hard or weighted hard combining, outperform the original LiLaS where only adaptive modulation was used.

Figure 3 shows the average number of retransmissions per packet. This gives what delay the user will experience in average. For each SNR, the number of retransmissions will be different for the two combining schemes - not only because the combining methods are different, but also because they have different thresholds and may use different AMC modes for each SNR. Figure depicts the limitation of weighted hard combining resulting to slightly higher retransmissions compared to hard combining at lower SNR.

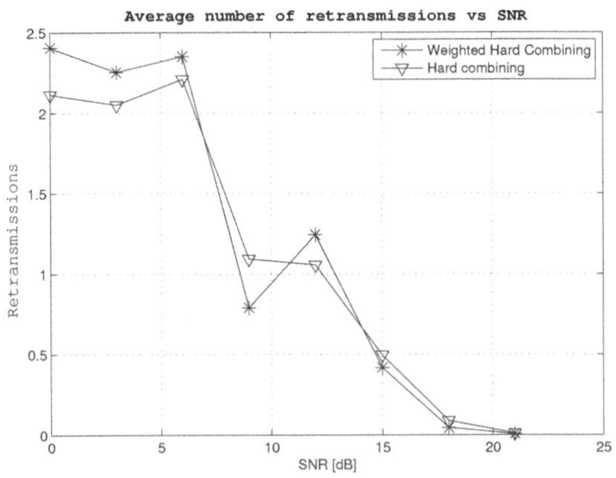

Figure 3: Average number of retransmissions per transmitted packet vs. SNR

5. CONCLUSIONS

In this paper, we have presented a detailed system design for link adaptation incorporating adaptive modulation and coding (AMC) and hybrid automatic repeat request (HARQ) in the LTE-Advanced system. The AMC was designed to maximize spectral efficiency while keeping constraints on the quality of service (QoS). Two packet combining schemes namely hard combining and weighted hard combining have been compared in an attempt to reduce packet error rate (PER) and increase spectral efficiency. The simulation results show that our link adaptation design significantly improves spectral efficiency. For a high bit error rate, as in a deep fading scenario or with severe interference, hard combining will improve the system spectral efficiency more than weighted hard combining. Weighted hard combining is only possible to implement if the combining unit has access to the received signal to noise ratio (SNR) for each packet.

6. ACKNOWLEDGMENTS

Authors wish to thank Daniel Göker, Tania Villa, Bilal Zafar, Jinliang Huang, Ben Slimane and Svante Signell for profound discussions.

7. REFERENCES

[1] 3GPP. Physical channels and modulation (release 11). Technical Report TS 36.211 V11.2.0, 2013.

[2] 3GPP. Medium access control (mac) protocol specification (release 11). Technical Report TS 36.321 V11.2.0, 2013.

[3] A.M. Cipriano, P. Gagneur, G. Vivier, and S. Sezginer. Overview of arq and harq in beyond 3g systems. In *Personal, Indoor and Mobile Radio Communications Workshops (PIMRC Workshops), 2010 IEEE 21st International Symposium on*, pages 424–429, 2010.

[4] Tania Villa, Ruben Merz, Raymond Knopp, and Uday Takyar. Adaptive modulation and coding with hybrid-arq for latency-constrained networks. In *European Wireless, 2012. EW. 18th European Wireless Conference*, pages 1–8, 2012.

[5] Alexandra Oborina, Martti Moisio, and V. Koivunen. Ergodic system capacity of mobile mimo systems using adaptive modulation. In *Personal Indoor and Mobile Radio Communications (PIMRC), 2010 IEEE 21st International Symposium on*, pages 2375–2380, 2010.

[6] O. Ur-Rehman, N. Zivic, S.A. Hossein, and A. E. Tabatabaei. Iterative enhanced packet combining over hybrid-arq. In *Wireless Communication Systems (ISWCS), 2011 8th International Symposium on*, pages 21–25, 2011.

[7] Qingwen Liu, Shengli Zhou, and G.B. Giannakis. Cross-layer combining of adaptive modulation and coding with truncated arq over wireless links. *Wireless Communications, IEEE Transactions on*, 3(5):1746–1755, 2004.

[8] Dalei Wu and Song Ci. Cross-layer combination of hybrid arq and adaptive modulation and coding for qos provisioning in wireless data networks. In *Proceedings of the 3rd international conference on Quality of service in heterogeneous wired/wireless networks*, QShine '06, New York, NY, USA, 2006. ACM.

[9] Svante R. Signell and Jinliang Huang. Lilas: a link layer simulator in matlab/octave. In *Proceedings of the 12th ACM international conference on Modeling, analysis and simulation of wireless and mobile systems*, MSWiM '09, pages 143–146, New York, NY, USA, 2009. ACM.

[10] Zander J. Slimane B. Ahlin, L. *Principles of Wireless Communications*. Studentlitteratur AB.

[11] 3GPP. Multiplexing and channel coding (release 11). Technical Report TS 36.312 V11.2.0, 2013.

[12] D. Chase. Code combining–a maximum-likelihood decoding approach for combining an arbitrary number of noisy packets. *Communications, IEEE Transactions on*, 33(5):385–393, 1985.

[13] M.B. Pursley and D.J. Taipale. Error probabilities for spread-spectrum packet radio with convolutional codes and viterbi decoding. *Communications, IEEE Transactions on*, 35(1):1–12, 1987.

[14] J. Proakis. *Digital Communications*. McGraw-Hill, New York, 1995.

[15] Jinliang Huang and S. Signell. Adaptive mimo systems in 2 x 2 uncorrelated rayleigh fading channel. In *Wireless Communications and Networking Conference, 2007.WCNC 2007. IEEE*, pages 1114–1118, 2007.

Channel Fading Impact on Multi-hop DSRC Safety Communication

Xiaoyan Yin
Duke University
Durham, USA
xy15@duke.edu

Xiaomin Ma
Oral Roberts University
Tulsa, USA
xma@oru.edu

Kishor S. Trivedi
Duke University
Durham, USA
ktrivedi@duke.edu

ABSTRACT

In this paper, we propose an accurate and efficient analytic model to evaluate the impact of channel fading on multi-hop safety message disseminations in vehicular ad hoc networks (VANET). A multi-hop relay strategy is also proposed by setting distance-based timers (the longer the distance, the shorter the timer) so that the farther receiver has the higher priority for it to rebroadcast the message. Important performance and reliability metrics are derived and analyzed for a thorough understanding of the safety message transmission behavior. Extensive simulations are conducted in Matlab to verify the correctness of our proposed model under realistic network parameter settings.

Categories and Subject Descriptors

C.4 [**Performance of Systems**]: *Modeling techniques, Performance, Reliability, availability, and serviceability.*

Keywords

analytic model; channel fading; multi-hop; safety; simulation

1. INTRODUCTION

In the U.S., Dedicated Short Range Communication (DSRC) [1] spectrum consists of seven channels to support both safety and non-safety applications in vehicular ad hoc networks (VANET). Channel 172 at one edge is preserved for event-driven safety message, which is broadcast in case of an emergency situation (*e.g.*, accidents, hard-braking, road hazard). Since some event-driven safety applications may be required to cover longer distances than the communication range (usually less than 1 *km* in DSRC), multi-hop message dissemination is necessary in such scenarios. For multi-hop broadcast scheme, the protocols proposed in the literature [2] focus on minimizing the number of retransmissions while attempting to ensure that a broadcast packet is delivered to every vehicle within the intended coverage area. In this paper, we adopt a robust relay selection strategy proposed in our previous work [3] for multi-hop propagation of event-driven safety message utilizing distance-based timers to choose the farthest node as the relay. An accurate and efficient analytic model is proposed to evaluate the performance and reliability of multi-hop safety message dissemination. Since event-driven safety message is occasionally generated (only when an emergency event is detected), we can reasonably assume that during the lifetime of an event-driven safety message, no other event-driven safety message is generated. Therefore, concurrent transmissions and hidden terminal problem do not exist in such a system. The main focus of this paper is the impact of channel fading on the system performance and reliability.

MSWiM'13, November 3–8, 2013, Barcelona, Spain.

2. SYSTEM DESCRIPTION AND ASSUMPTIONS

Once an emergency message is generated, its header contains the information about the originating source node, the type of message and the message propagation direction. Based on this information, we propose and evaluate an efficient multi-hop broadcast scheme for the emergency notification services. We adopt a multi-hop relay scheme similar to the one proposed in [3], which provides a reliable way to select a routing node to rebroadcast the emergency message. A vehicle will be selected to rebroadcast the message under the following conditions:

- the vehicle has successfully received the message;
- the vehicle's distance to the sender is the farthest among all one-hop vehicles that have received the message successfully.

The second condition is guaranteed by setting a deterministic timer in each vehicle that received the message [3]. The timer is a function of the distance from the sender x and is defined as:

$$t_{AD}(x) = \begin{cases} T_{\max}\left(1-\dfrac{x}{R}\right) & \text{if } x \le R \\ 0 & \text{if } x > R \end{cases} \tag{1}$$

where T_{max} is chosen as the one-hop lifetime of the emergency message and R is the average transmission range of a node.

All vehicles received the message will trigger the AD timer according to Eq. (1). The one whose AD timer expires first is chosen to rebroadcast the emergency message. If such rebroadcast message is received by some vehicles in the hop, they will cancel their AD timers and stop attempts to relay the message. In case that the rebroadcast message from the selected node fails to reach some nodes in the hop due to fading channel condition, those candidate nodes keep counting down their AD timer until one of the candidates is selected as a new relaying node. This process continues until at least one rebroadcast is successful in the hop.

The following assumptions are made in this paper to produce a simplified yet high fidelity analytic model. The network is considered one-dimensional (1D). The number of vehicles in a line is Poisson distributed with parameter λ (vehicle density), *i.e.*, the probability of finding i vehicles in a lane of length l is:

$$P\left(N(l)=i\right) = \frac{(\lambda l)^i}{i!}e^{-\lambda l} \tag{2}$$

In addition, all vehicles are assumed to have the same transmission range, receiving range, and carrier sensing range R. Vehicle mobility is not taken into account in this paper. The 1D

VANET model is a good approximation of ad hoc networks on highway when the distances between lanes on the highway are negligible compared with the length of the highway. Furthermore, recent statistical analysis of empirical data collected from real-world scenarios [7][8] show that Poisson model is a good fit for sparse highway vehicle traffic in terms of inter vehicle distance.

3. ANALYTIC MODEL

3.1 Channel Fading Model

In this paper, we concentrate on the impact of channel fading on multi-hop safety message transmission. DSRC channel modeling involves two important aspects: large scale path loss and small scale fading. The former is used to determine the average received signal strength at a particular distance from the transmitter, whereas small scale fading generally involves the detailed modeling of multi-path fading statistics, power delay profile, and Doppler spectrum. The *Nakagami* distribution has been shown to fit the amplitude envelope of empirical data for DSRC channel well [9]. Hence, incorporating the *Nakagami* channel fading model in [10], we obtain the probability of successfully receiving a message at a distance x:

$$P_s(x) = 1 - \frac{m^m}{\Gamma(m)} \int_0^{(x/R)^\gamma} z^{m-1} e^{-mz}\, dz \quad (3)$$

where m is the fading parameter, and γ is the path loss exponent.

3.2 Rebroadcast Probability

Due to the unfavorable characteristics of channel fading, various performance metrics for multi-hop message delivery are impacted. One important metric is the rebroadcast probability. We evaluate the rebroadcast probability from two perspectives: one from a broadcast message's perspective, and the other from a receiver's perspective:

- Message-centric rebroadcast probability P_{rb} is defined as the probability that a message can be rebroadcast by a receiver within this hop given the message is broadcast within a hop.
- Receiver-centric rebroadcast probability $P_{rbA}(x)$ is defined as given a receiver located with distance x from the sender, the probability that this receiver can rebroadcast the message.

3.2.1 Message-centric rebroadcast probability

In Figure 1, sender O broadcasts a safety message to all one-hop receivers. This message can be rebroadcast if at least one one-hop receiver in the rebroadcast direction receives the message successfully.

Suppose that there are n vehicles located on the rebroadcast direction within O's transmission range R. According to Theorem 6.2 in [5], the conditional *pdf* of the n nodes' un-ordered locations $T_1, T_2, \ldots, T_n$ respectively is given by:

$$f_{T_i}\left[t_i \mid N(R)=n\right] = \frac{1}{R}, \quad x \le t_i \le R, \ i = 1,2,\ldots,n \quad (4)$$

Therefore, we obtain the probability that at least one vehicle receives the broadcast message successfully, which is equivalent to the message-centric rebroadcast probability:

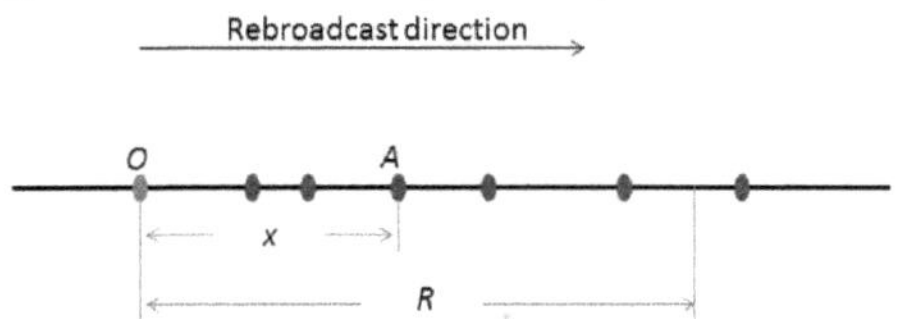

Figure 1. Message rebroadcast in a hop

$$\begin{aligned} P_{rb} &= 1 - \sum_{n=0}^{\infty} \left\{ \prod_{i=1}^{n} \left[\int_{t_i=0}^{t_i=R} (1 - P_s(t_i)) \cdot f_{T_i}\left[t_i \mid N(R)=n\right] dt_i \right] \right\} \cdot P\left(N(R)=n\right) \\ &= 1 - e^{-\lambda R + \lambda I(0)} \end{aligned} \quad (5)$$

where

$$\begin{aligned} I(x) &= \int_{t=x}^{t=R} (1 - P_s(t))\, dt = \int_{t=x}^{t=R} \left(\frac{m^m}{\Gamma(m)} \int_0^{(t/R)^\gamma} z^{m-1} e^{-mz} dz \right) dt \\ &= \int_{t=x}^{t=R} \frac{m^m}{\Gamma(m)} \cdot \left(\int_0^{(t/R)^\gamma} z^{m-1} e^{-mz} dz \right) dt = f(x,m) \end{aligned} \quad (6)$$

Normally, the fading parameter m is a piecewise constant function of communication distance in most MANET channels:

$$m = m_i \ \text{ for } x_i \le d < x_{i+1}, i = 1,2,\ldots; \qquad x_1 = 0 \quad (7)$$

where x_i are jump points and m_i are constant fading parameter values. By changing the order of integration in the double integral, $f(x,m)$ in Eq. (6) can be significantly simplified to reduce the computational complexity as:

$$\begin{aligned} f(x,m) &= \left\{ \sum_{i=N_2+1}^{N_1} \left[g(x_i, m_{i-1}) - g(x_i, m_i) \right] \right\} + g\left(R, m_{N_1}\right) - g\left(x, m_{N_2}\right) \\ N_1 &= \max\{i : x_i \le R\} \qquad N_2 = \max\{i : x_i \le x\} \end{aligned} \quad (8)$$

where

$$\begin{aligned} g(d,m) &= \frac{d}{\Gamma(m)} Y\left[m, m\left(\frac{d}{R}\right)^\gamma \right] - \frac{R}{\Gamma(m) m^{1/\gamma}} \cdot Y\left[\frac{1}{\gamma} + m, m\left(\frac{d}{R}\right)^\gamma \right] \\ Y(a,b) &= \int_{u=0}^{u=b} u^{a-1} e^{-u} du \end{aligned} \quad (9)$$

3.2.2 Receiver-centric rebroadcast probability

Besides the message-centric rebroadcast probability, we are also interested in: given a receiver located at a distance x from the sender, what is the probability that this receiver will rebroadcast the message? Based on the two conditions for selecting a relay node in Section 2, we know that a vehicle will rebroadcast a message if it successfully receives the broadcast message from the sender, and all one-hop nodes farther than this vehicle have not received this message.

Denote a random receiver in the rebroadcast direction to be A, located at a distance x from the sender O as shown in Figure 2. In addition, assume that there are n nodes located farther than node A from the sender O but within O's transmission range R. According to Theorem 6.2 in [5], the conditional *pdf* of the n nodes' un-ordered locations $T_1, T_2, \ldots, T_n$ respectively is given by:

$$f_{T_i}\left[t_i \mid N(R-x)=n\right] = \frac{1}{R-x}, \quad x \le t_i \le R, \ i = 1,2,\ldots,n \quad (10)$$

Therefore, the rebroadcast probability of node A, conditioned on there being n one-hop nodes farther than A, can be computed as:

- If n=0

$$P_{rb1}\left(x \mid N(R-x)=0\right) = P_s(x) \quad (11)$$

- If n>0

$$\begin{aligned} &P_{rb2}\left(x \mid N(R-x)=n\right) \\ &= P_s(x) \cdot \left\{ \prod_{i=1}^{n} \left[\int_{t_i=x}^{t_i=R} (1 - P_s(t_i)) \cdot f_{T_i}\left[t_i \mid N(R-x)=n\right] dt_i \right] \right\} \\ &= P_s(x) \cdot I(x)^n \cdot \left(\frac{1}{R-x} \right)^n \end{aligned} \quad (12)$$

Therefore, the un-conditioned rebroadcast probability for A (*i.e.*, the rebroadcast probability for a receiver located at a distance x from the sender) is given by:

$$P_{rbA}(x) = P_{rb1}(x)\cdot e^{-\alpha(R-x)} + \sum_{n=1}^{\infty}\left[P_{rb2}(x)\cdot\frac{(\alpha(R-x))^n e^{-\alpha(R-x)}}{n!}\right] = P_s(x)\cdot e^{-\alpha(R-x)+\alpha I(x)} \quad (13)$$

3.3 Average Rebroadcast Distance

For multi-hop message dissemination, the number of hops to reach a specific distance is one of the most important metrics to evaluate how fast a message can be transmitted. Hence, one-hop rebroadcast distance needs to be analyzed first, based on which the number of hops to reach a distance can be easily computed.

In Section 3.2, the un-ordered statistics for vehicles are considered for both message-centric and receiver-centric rebroadcast probability calculation, since the output measures do not depend on the order of vehicles within an area. However, to assess the rebroadcast distance for a message, we need to pay attention to the ordered statistics of the receivers because their locations impact the rebroadcast distance.

Suppose there are n vehicles located in the rebroadcast direction of the sender O within its transmission range R. According to the Theorem 6.1 in [5], the conditional joint *pdf* of the n vehicles' ordered locations $Y_1, Y_2, \ldots, Y_n$ is given by:

$$f\left[y_1, y_2, \cdots, y_n \mid N(R)=n\right] = \frac{n!}{R^n},\ 0 \le y_1 \le y_2 \le \cdots \le y_n \le R \quad (14)$$

Any vehicle among these n vehicles has the potential to rebroadcast the message originally broadcast from the sender. Suppose the ith vehicle with distance y_i rebroadcasts the message, the average rebroadcast distance is:

$$J_1(n,i) = \int_{y_n=0}^{y_n=R}\cdots\int_{y_2=0}^{y_2=y_3}\int_{y_1=0}^{y_1=y_2}\left[P_s(y_i)\prod_{j=i+1}^{n}\left(1-P_s(y_j)\right)\right]\cdot y_i\cdot\frac{n!}{R^n}\cdot dy_1 dy_2\cdots dy_n = \frac{n!}{R^n}K_1(n,i) \quad (15)$$

where

$$K_1(n,i) = \frac{1}{(i-1)!}\int_{y_n=0}^{y_n=R}\cdots\int_{y_i=0}^{y_i=y_{i+1}}\left[P_s(y_i)\prod_{j=i+1}^{n}\left(1-P_s(y_j)\right)\right]\cdot y_i^i dy_i\cdots dy_n \quad (16)$$

Due to the computational complexity of Eq. (16), we use polynomial to approximate the integrand for $P_s(y_i)$, and then do the multiple integrals symbolically to obtain $K_1(n,i)$. Next, considering all receivers' behavior and unconditioning on the number of receivers, the average rebroadcast distance is:

$$D_{rb} = \sum_{n=0}^{\infty}\left[\sum_{i=1}^{n}J_1(n,i)\right]\cdot P(N(R)=n) = \sum_{n=0}^{\infty}\left[\sum_{i=1}^{n}K_1(n,i)\right]\cdot\alpha^n e^{-\alpha R} \quad (17)$$

3.4 Average Number of Hops to Reach a Distance

Based on the average rebroadcast distance for a message derived in the previous section, we can compute the average number of hops to reach a specific distance l for a broadcast safety message:

$$E_h(l) = \left\lceil\frac{l}{D_{rb}}\right\rceil \quad (18)$$

3.5 Average Rebroadcast Delay

As mentioned in Section 1, one-hop receivers that successfully receive the broadcast message from the sender will trigger their respective distance-based AD timers before the winner whose timer expires first rebroadcasts the message. Such AD timer leads to delay in the message rebroadcast process. Following an approach similar to the one in Section 3.3 for rebroadcast distance computation, we utilize the ordered statistics for receivers and obtain the average delay if the ith vehicle with distance y_i rebroadcasts the message given that there are n one-hop receivers:

$$J_2(n,i) = \int_{y_n=0}^{y_n=R}\cdots\int_{y_2=0}^{y_2=y_3}\int_{y_1=0}^{y_1=y_2}\left[P_s(y_i)\prod_{j=i+1}^{n}\left(1-P_s(y_j)\right)\right]\cdot t_{AD}(y_i)\cdot\frac{n!}{R^n}dy_1 dy_2\cdots dy_n = \frac{n!}{R^n}K_2(n,i) \quad (19)$$

where

$$K_2(n,i) = \frac{1}{(i-1)!}\int_{y_n=0}^{y_n=R}\cdots\int_{y_i=0}^{y_i=y_{i+1}}\left[P_s(y_i)\prod_{j=i+1}^{n}\left(1-P_s(y_j)\right)\right]\cdot y_i^{i-1}\cdot T_{\max}\left(1-\frac{y_i}{R}\right)\cdot dy_i\cdots dy_n \quad (20)$$

Considering all receivers rebroadcast behavior and unconditioning on the number of receivers, the average rebroadcast delay induced by AD timer for a message is:

$$E_{AD} = \sum_{n=0}^{\infty}\left[\sum_{i=1}^{n}J_2(n,i)\right]\cdot P(N(R)=n) = \sum_{n=0}^{\infty}\left[\sum_{i=1}^{n}K_2(n,i)\right]\cdot\alpha^n e^{-\alpha R} \quad (21)$$

4. NUMERICAL RESULTS

To evaluate the accuracy and efficiency of our proposed analytic model, we compare the analytic-numeric results with the discrete event simulation results conducted in Matlab. The network parameters in Table 1 are chosen reasonably and most of them are from real testbeds [4][6]. The assumptions made in Section 2 are all applied to the simulative solution as well. We conducted 300 simulation runs. The mean for an output measure is computed for every 10 runs and hence the number of means obtained for each output measure is 30. Due to the Central Limit Theorem, normal distribution is assumed for these 30 sample means to compute 99% confidence intervals for the population mean.

Figure 2 shows the NRP incorporating channel fading impact and receiver-centric rebroadcast probability (P_{rbA}) with respect to distance from the sender. The lines represent the analytic-numeric results, whereas the symbols represent the simulation results for 99% confidence interval. In Figure 2, NRP decreases as distance increases due to channel fading's effect. In addition, the receiver-centric rebroadcast probability for a receiver $P_{rbA}(x)$ is nearly zero when the distance is less than 150m, and it generally increases when the distance approaches the transmission range R=300m. This is because the rebroadcast vehicle is most likely to be the farthest one from the sender, which is close to the transmission range. In addition, at the transmission range point R=300m, we notice that NRP almost equals P_{rbA}. This observation results from the fact that P_{rbA} is the probability that the vehicle located at R receives the message (given by NRP) and no farther receivers receive the message. Since there is no receiver farther than the one located with distance R, the P_{rbA} is equivalent to NRP for such a vehicle. The good match between the simulation and analytic results validates the accuracy of our model.

Figure 3 shows that as the distance becomes larger, the average number of hops generally increases. For better comparison, the

Table 1. Network parameter setting

Parameters	Values	Parameters	Values
Transmission range R	300 m	Packet length PL	300 *bytes*
$DIFS$	64 *us*	T_{max}	1 *second*
PHY preamble T_{H1}	40 μs	path loss exponent γ	2
MAC header T_{H2}	272 *bits*	Fading Parameter m	3 for d<50m
PLCP header T_{H3}	4 μs		1.5 for 50m≤d<150m
Data rate R_d	6 *Mbps*		1 for d≥150m

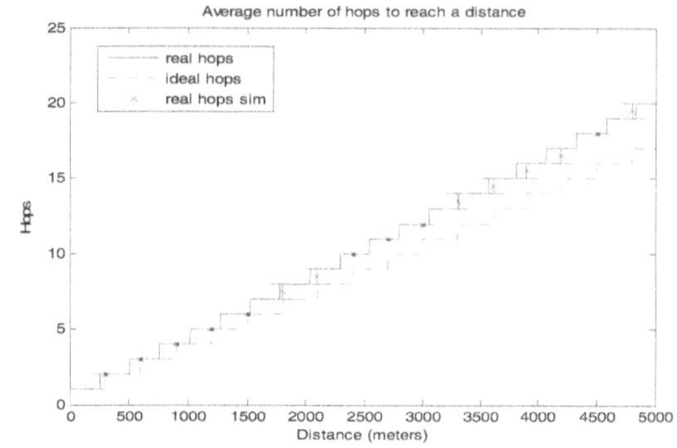

Figure 3. Number of hops to reach a distance

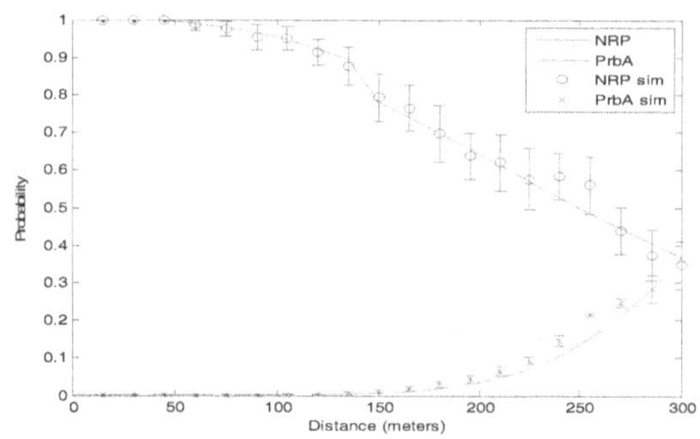

Figure 2. NRP and receiver-centric rebroadcast probability

ideal hop to reach a distance l is also plotted, which is defined as:

$$E_{h\_ideal} = \left\lceil \frac{l}{R} \right\rceil \tag{22}$$

The figure shows that the real number of hops for a message to reach a specific distance is larger than the ideal hop number. Such difference is more obvious when the distance is larger. This phenomenon results from the fact that the rebroadcast vehicle is at a distance less than the transmission range. The simulation results match very well with our analytic results, which again verifies the correctness of our approach.

The other output measures, which are not distance-based metrics, are listed in Table 2. The average rebroadcast distance is around 254*m*, which is less than the transmission range 300*m*. The average rebroadcast delay is about 0.139*s*, which accounts for the AD timer delay in the rebroadcast process. Compared to the simulation results, the analytic results fall within 99% confidence interval of the simulation results. Hence, this verifies the accuracy of our proposed analytic models. In addition, the analytic model takes about 1 minute to obtain the numerical results, whereas the simulation takes 28 minutes. The simulation time will be longer if we need to obtain tighter confidence intervals. Therefore, our analytic model is much more efficient than simulations.

5. CONCLUSIONS

This paper presents an accurate and efficient analytic model to evaluate the impact of channel fading on multi-hop safety message disseminations in VANET. We utilize a distance-based timer to ensure the farthest node from the sender has highest priority to be chosen to relay the safety message. Various important performance and reliability metrics are derived and analyzed for thorough understanding of the safety message transmission behavior. Simulations conducted in Matlab cross validate the accuracy of our proposed model. In addition, our model is much more efficient in terms of evaluation time than simulations. The analytic model can also be used to analyze essential metrics that are difficult to capture in simulations as shown in Table 2.

Table 2. Non distance-based metrics

Definitions	Symbols	Analytic Results	Simulation Results 99% CI	
			Low bound	High bound
Average rebroadcast distance (m)	D_{rb}	2.544e+02	2.501e+02	2.631e+02
Average rebroadcast delay (s)	E_{tAD}	0.138577	0.122911	0.166271
Message-centric rebroadcast probability	P_{rb}	0.999993	-	

6. ACKNOWLEDGMENTS

The authors would like to thank NSF grants (CNS-1018605 and CNS-1017722) to support this research.

7. REFERENCES

[1] J. B. Kenney, "Dedicated short range communications (DSRC) standards in the United States", *Proc. of the IEEE*, 2011.

[2] B. Williams, and T. Camp, "Comparison of broadcasting techniques for mobile ad hoc networks." *Proceedings of the 3rd ACM international symposium on Mobile Ad Hoc Networking & Computing*, 2002.

[3] X. Ma, et al. "Design and analysis of a robust broadcast scheme for vanet safety-related services." *IEEE Transactions on Vehicular Technology*, 61(1): 46-61, 2012.

[4] G. Marfia, M. Roccetti, A. Amoroso, and G. Pau, "Safe Driving in LA: Report from the Greatest Intervehicular Accident Detection Test Ever," *IEEE Transactions on Vehicular Technology*, 62(2), February 2013.

[5] K. S. Trivedi, *Probability and Statistics with Reliability, Queuing and Computer Science Applications*, Second Edition, John Wiley & Sons, INC., 2002.

[6] F. Bai, D. D. Stancil, and H. Krishnan, "Toward understanding characteristics of Dedicated Short Range Communications (DSRC) from a perspective of vehicular network engineers," in *Proc. 16th Annu. Int. Con. MobiCom*, 2010, pp. 329–340.

[7] N. Wisitpongphan, B. Fan, P. Mudalige, V. Sadekar, and O. Tonguz, "Routing in Sparse Vehicular Ad Hoc Wireless Networks," *IEEE J. Selected Areas in Comm.*, 25(8), pp. 1538-1556, Oct. 2007.

[8] H. Zhu, L. Fu, G. Xue, Y. Zhu, M. Li, and L. Ni, "Impact on traffiC Influxes: Understanding Exponential Inter-Contact Time in VANETs," *Proc. IEEE INFOCOM'10*, 2010.

[9] C. Patel, G. Stuber and T. Pratt. "Simulation of Rayleigh-Faded Mobile-to-Mobile Communication Channels", *IEEE Transactions on Vehicular Technology*. 53(11): 1876-1884, Nov 2005.

[10] X. Yin, X. Ma, K. S. Trivedi, "Performance of BSM Dissemination in Multi-channel DSRC", *IEEE 77th Vehicular Technology Conference*, June, 2013.

SA and PSO Assisted Joint Scheme of Channel Estimation and PPIC for MIMO-SDMA/OFDM System

Islam E. Shaalan
Fac. of Engineering, Port Said University,
Port Said, Egypt
is_shaalan@eng.psu.edu.eg

Khairy A. Elbarbary
Fac. of Engineering, Suez Canal University,
Ismailia, Egypt
khbar2000@yahoo.com

Ahmed A. S. Dessouki
Fac. of Engineering, Port Said University,
Port Said, Egypt
dessouki2000@yahoo.com

Mohamed S. Abo El-Soud
Fac. of Engineering Science, Sinai University,
Al Arish, Egypt
msamysoud@gmail.com

ABSTRACT

In this paper, a new scheme of Joint Channel Estimation and Partial Parallel Interference Cancellation using Simulating Annealing (SA) or Particle Swarm Optimization (PSO) algorithms is proposed. This scheme is proposed for multiuser Multiple-Input Multiple-Output /Space Division Multiple Access (MIMO-SDMA) Orthogonal Frequency Division Multiplexing (OFDM) systems. The proposed scheme tries to reduce the cancellation error in Conventional Parallel Interference Cancellation (CPIC) detection schemes used in MIMO SDMA-OFDM system. The SA and PSO algorithms are employed in searching the optimal weights of the PPIC for multiple access interference cancellation. The proposed scheme is shown to provide a performance improvement as compared to MMSE and CPIC detectors especially in an overloaded scenario where number of users is high as compared to the Base Station (BS) antennas. In this scenario, channel estimation becomes more challenging, owing to the increased number of independent transmitter-receiver links to be estimated and the constraint imposed by the rank of the MIMO channel matrix. The proposed scheme provides a reasonable solution to the multiuser MIMO channel estimation problem and multiuser detection in the above-mentioned overloaded scenario.

Categories and Subject Descriptors

G.4 [**MATLAB**]

General Terms

Algorithms, Performance, Design.

Keywords

Partial Parallel Interference Cancellation (PPIC), Multiple Input Multiple Output (MIMO); Space Division Multiple Access (SDMA); orthogonal frequency division multiplexing (OFDM); Simulating Annealing (SA); Particle Swarm Optimization (PSO).

MSWiM'13, November 3–8, 2013, Barcelona, Spain.

1. INTRODUCTION

With the growth of broadband internet access and the development of multimedia services in cellular mobile wireless communications, an ever-increasing demand for high capacity and high speed transmission with good Quality-of-Service (QOS) has been created. The capacity of wireless communication systems can be increased by exploiting the spatial dimensions by using multiple antennas at both the transmitter as the receiver. A system using this technique will further be referred to as Multiple-Input Multiple-Output (MIMO) system. The use of MIMO system basically provides many benefits such as array gain, diversity gain and/or Multiplexing gain.

Spatial Division Multiple Access (SDMA) is a MIMO arrangement which aims to maximize the number of supported users [6]. In MIMO-SDMA system, each Mobile Station (MS) utilizing a single transmitter antenna simultaneously communicates with the Base Station (BS) exploiting an array of receiver antennas. In practice, it is desirable to combine MIMO with OFDM technique to combat the effect of frequency selective fading. Currently, MIMO-OFDM is being adopted in WLAN standard (IEEE 802.11n) and is recognized as a strong candidate for the future 4th generation (4G) mobile system [9].

Numerous multiuser detection (MUD) schemes have been presented for MIMO SDMA-OFDM systems during these years; such as the Maximum-Likelihood (ML) MUD, the Zero-Forcing (ZF) and Minimum Mean Squared Error (MMSE) [6], [7]. In the literature, various suboptimal nonlinear MUDs have also been presented, such as "Successive Interference Canceller (SIC) [7]" or "Parallel Interference Canceller (PIC) [9], [1]". In contrast to ZF and MMSE MUDs that detect the users' signals in a separate manner, in SIC and PIC MUDs, all detected signals generated during the previous detection iteration are demodulated and fed back to the input of the MUD in successive or parallel manner for the next iteration. Since the philosophy of both the PIC and SIC MUDs is based on the principle of removing the effects of the interfering users during each detection stage, they are subjected to error propagation occurring during the consecutive detection stages due to the erroneously detected signals of the previous stages [6]. So, the interference cancellation does not necessarily reduce interference. To alleviate this problem, partial PIC (PPIC) was then developed in which the interference is partially cancelled with the aid of Partial cancellation factors (PCFs). PCFs ranging from zero to unity were introduced to control the signal cancellation level. As far as we are concerned, however, most of the above-mentioned MUD schemes in uplink are invoked for detecting the different users' transmitted signals with the aid of their unique, user-specific spatial signature constituted by their Frequency-Domain CHannel Transfer Functions (FD-CHTFs). However, in these schemes accurate channel estimation is required at the receiver for the sake of invoking both coherent demodulation and interference cancellation [5]. Compared to Single-Input-Single-Output (SISO) systems, channel estimation in the MIMO scenario becomes more challenging, since a significantly increased number of independent transmitter-receiver channel links have to be estimated simultaneously for each subcarrier. Moreover, the interfering signals of the other transmit antennas have to be suppressed. Furthermore, the poor performance associated with the overload scenarios, were investigated under the assumption of under-loaded [6], [5], will certainly lead to a rough propagation of error in decision-directed channel estimation schemes [3].

Against this background, in this paper, we propose a new iterative Joint Channel Estimation and partial interference cancellation detector assisted by one of two uniquely different optimization algorithms (Simulating Annealing (SA) and Particle Swarm Optimization (PSO))for MIMO SDMA-OFDM systems, which provides an effective solution to the multi-user MIMO signal detection and channel estimation problems in the above-mentioned overloaded scenario. Our ambitious goal of supporting an excess number of users is possible, because the proposed technique dispenses with any constraints concerning the rank of the channel matrix.

2. SYSTEM OVERVIEW

A block diagram of uplink MIMO SDMA-OFDM system is shown in the Figure 1, where each of the L simultaneous mobile users employs a single transmit antenna, while the BS's receiver exploits P antennas.

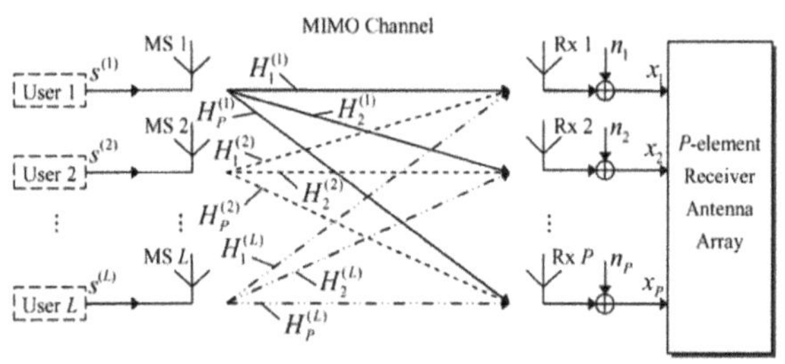

Figure 1. Block diagram of the uplink MIMO SDMA-OFDM model

At the kth subcarrier of the nth OFDM symbol received by the P-element receiver antenna array, we have the received complex signal vector x, which is constituted by the superposition of the independently faded signals associated with the L mobile users and contaminated by the AWGN, expressed as

$$x = Hs + n \qquad (1)$$

where the $(P \times 1)$-dimensional vector $\boldsymbol{x} = [x_1, x_2, \ldots x_P]^T$, the $(L \times 1)$ dimensional vector $\boldsymbol{s} = [s^{(1)}, s^{(2)}, \ldots, s^{(L)}]^T$ and the $(P \times 1)$ dimensional vector $\boldsymbol{n} = [n_1, n_2, \ldots n_P]^T$ are the received, transmitted and noise signals, respectively. The $(P \times L)$-dimensional matrix $\boldsymbol{H}$, which contains the frequency-domain channel transfer functions (FD-CHTFs) of the L users, are given by

$$\boldsymbol{H} = [H^{(1)}, H^{(2)}, \ldots, H^{(L)}]^T \qquad (2)$$

where $H^{(l)}$ is the vector of the FD-CHTFs associated with the transmission paths from the lth user's transmit antenna to each element of the P-element receiver antenna array, which is expressed by

$$H^{(l)} = [H_1^{(l)}, H_2^{(l)}, \ldots, H_P^{(l)}]^T, \quad l = 1,2,\ldots,L \qquad (3)$$

In (1)–(3), it is assumed that the complex signal $\boldsymbol{s}$ transmitted by the lth user has zero-mean and a variance of σ_l^2. The AWGN signal $n_p$also exhibits a zero-mean and a variance of σ_n^2. The FD-CHTFs $H_p^{(l)}$of the different receivers or users are independent, stationary, complex Gaussian distributed processes with zero-mean and unit variance [6].

Let us first briefly review MMSE algorithm, for MIMO SDMA-OFDM detection. This algorithm can be described by

$$\tilde{s} = W^H \boldsymbol{x} \qquad (4)$$

where $\tilde{s}$ denotes the decision statistics of the transmitted symbol vector $\boldsymbol{s}$ and W^H denotes the weight matrix. The transmitted data symbols can be recovered by passing the elements of $\tilde{s}$ through a decision device. For MMSE algorithm, W is generated according to the MMSE criterion and is given by [6]

$$W = (\boldsymbol{H}\boldsymbol{H}^H + \sigma_n^2 I)^{-1} \boldsymbol{H} \qquad (5)$$

where σ_n^2 is AWGN noise variance, superscript H stands for the complex conjugate transpose, and I denotes the identity matrix. As expected, the detector's performance improves upon increasing the number of array elements P and it degrades, when increasing number of users L.

3. ITERATIVE JOINT CHANNEL ESTIMATION AND PARTIAL PARALLEL INTERFERENCE CANCELLATION

The proposed iterative scheme is shown in Figure 2. It is assumed that each OFDM symbol composed of K subcarriers. A predefined pilot Binary Phase Shift Keying (BPSK) sequence is transmitted in the first OFDM symbol in each frame j of all the L users. Within the first OFDM symbol duration ($n = 0$), the pilot controller seen in Figure 2 feeds the pilots to the Initial Channel Estimator in order to obtain an initial estimate of the FD-CHTFs. Each user's pilot OFDM symbol is multiplied by a user-specific spreading code before it is transmitted. In the proposed system, orthogonal Walsh-Hadamard-Transform (WHT) [1], [8] based spreading codes of length L are used. Note that no spreading is applied to the data OFDM symbols. With the aid of the spread pilot OFDM symbols, an initial FD-CHTF estimate $\widetilde{H}_p^{(l)[j]}(l = 1,\cdots,L;\ k = 1,\cdots,K;\ j = 1,\cdots,J)$ can be generated. Depending on the specific performance-versus-throughput design tradeoff targeted, this process of generating initial channel estimates can be invoked at pre-defined time intervals. Here we denote the pilot overhead as ϵ, which is defined by the ratio of the number of pilot OFDM symbols to the total number of transmitted OFDM symbols. If the 2nd OFDM symbol duration carries a data symbol rather than a pilot symbol, the initial FD-CHTFs estimates $\widetilde{H}_p^{(l)[j]}$will be fed to the joint PPIC-Channel Estimator and the L-dimension MMSE detector to be used in next symbol estimation. The pilot controller will enable the L-dimension MMSE detector with decision circuits to generate an initial guess of the L users' transmitted symbols $\tilde{s}^{(l)}(l = 1,\cdots,L)$ with aid of the pilot-assisted initial estimates of the FD-CHTFs $\widetilde{H}_p^{(l)[j]}$ associated with the 1st OFDM symbol. The resultant symbol estimates after decision $\hat{s}^{(l)}$, the FD-CHTF estimates $\widetilde{H}_p^{(l)[j]}$ as well as the corresponding received signals $x_p[n = 1, k](p = 1,\cdots,P;\ k = 1,\cdots,K)$ are then fed to the joint PPIC-Channel Estimator, where the FD-CHTFs and PCFs of the L users associated with the 2nd OFDM symbol are jointly optimized by SA or PSO algorithm to be used in partial cancellation process. At each partial cancellation stage i, the optimized PCFs are used to generate an interference free signal $\hat{x}_{PIC,p}^{l[i]}(p = 1,\cdots,P;\ l = 1,\cdots,L$which is forwarded

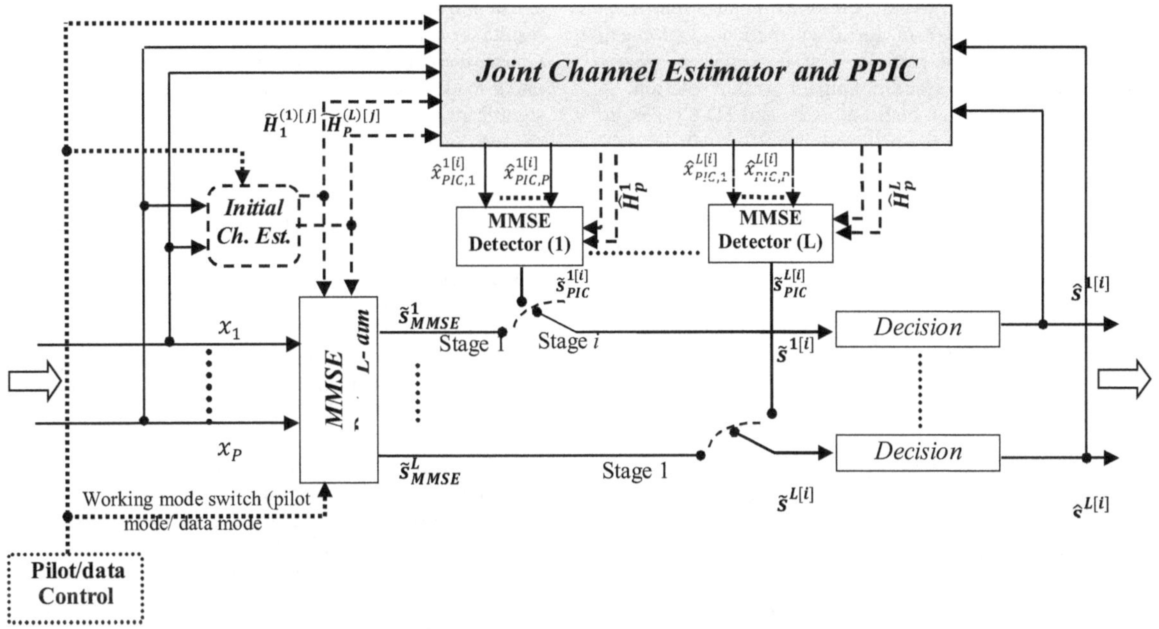

Figure. 2. The schematic diagram of the proposed iterative joint channel estimator and Partial Parallel Interference Canceller.

together with the FD-CHTF estimates $\hat{H}_1^{(1)[sym\,2]}$ to (L) MMSE detectors. Based on the optimized channel estimates and the interference free signals, the MMSE MUD is now capable of providing a better initial estimate of the transmitted symbols. This decision-directed process can be invoked for a number of stages for further performance enhancement [4].After the final stage, the lth user detected soft symbol $\tilde{s}_{PIC}^{(l)}$ corresponding to the 2nd OFDM symbol is directed to the decision circuit to get the output symbol $\hat{s}_{PIC}^{(l)}$. However, for the 1st stage of next nth OFDM symbol detection in ith frame, the MMSE detector generates an initial estimate of the L users' transmitted symbols with aid of the estimates of the FD-CHTFs $\hat{H}_1^{(1)[symn-1]}$ associated with the previous$(n-1)^{th}$OFDM symbol.

3.1 Generating Initial Symbol Estimates

As previously mentioned, the initial symbol estimate of lth user $\tilde{s}_{MMSE}^{l}$ is generated firstly with the MMSE detector assist at the first-stage [6], which invokes the initial FD-CHTF estimate obtained within the previous OFDM symbol duration. More clarity, the lth user symbol vector estimate is

$$\tilde{s}_{MMSE}^{(l)} = w^{(l)H}\boldsymbol{x} = w^{(l)H}(\boldsymbol{Hs}+\boldsymbol{n}) \\ = w^{(l)H}H^{(l)}s^{(l)} + w^{(l)H}\sum_{\substack{i=1\\ i\neq l}}^{L} H^{(i)}s^{(i)} + w^{(l)H}\boldsymbol{n} \qquad (6)$$

where $w^{(l)}$is the lth column of matrix W described in equation (8). To improve the system performance, a PPIC MUD is proposed. During the first stage each user is detected by means of the MMSE detector as shown in Figure 2. The MMSE detector's output vector is demodulated resulting in the vector of symbols that are most likely to have been transmitted by the L different users. During the ith detector stage a potentially improved estimate of the complex symbol $\hat{x}_{PIC,p}^{(l)[i]}$ transmitted by the lth user and received by p^{th} receiver antenna is obtained upon partial subtracting in a first step the $L-1$ interfering users' estimated signal contributions, from the original vector x_p of signals received by the different antenna elements, this partial subtraction depends on the specified PCFs for each interfering user. An estimated signal $\tilde{s}_{PIC}^{(l)[i]}$is extracted from the lth user's PPIC-related array output vector $\hat{x}_{PIC,p}^{(l)[i]}(p=1,\cdots,P)$, and then the symbol $\hat{s}^{l[i]}$, that is most likely to have been transmitted by the lth user, is delivered to the output. The lth interference signal at ith stage is

$$x_{MAI}^{(l)[i]} = \hat{H}^{(l)[i]}\boldsymbol{\alpha}^{[i]}\hat{s}_{free}^{(l)[i-1]} \qquad (7)$$

where $\hat{s}_{free}^{(l)[i]} = \hat{s}^{[i]}|_{lthrow=0}$ is the decisions at i^{th} stage with l^{th} row =0 and $\boldsymbol{\alpha}^{[i]} = [\alpha_1^{[i]}, \alpha_2^{[i]}, \dots, \alpha_L^{[i]}]$ is the PCFs at ith stage.

The lth estimated interference-free received signal is

$$\hat{x}_{PIC}^{(l)[i]} = \boldsymbol{x} - x_{MAI}^{(l)[i]} \qquad (8)$$

In the proposed scheme, the FD-CHTFs $\hat{H}^{(l)[i]}$ and the PCFs in PPIC was jointly optimized by SA or PSO search algorithm. The PCF $\alpha_l^{[i]}$of the PPIC ranging from -1 to +1 reflects the reliability of tentative decision and gives the ability of inverting the incorrect previously estimated symbol which makes the proposed scheme outperforms the conventional detection.

During the initialization stage, the (SA/PSO) constitutes directed (single agent / population of particles) based on the initially estimated symbols and FD-CHTFs from the previous stage. More expressly, at the ith stage in the kth subcarrier at the $(n+1)^{th}$OFDM symbol duration, the initial FD-CHTF estimates are:

$$\begin{cases} \hat{H}_p^{(l)} \quad iff\, i=1, \quad (n=0) \\ \hat{H}_p^{(l)[n][laststage]} \quad iff\, i=1, \quad (n\geq 1) \\ \hat{H}_p^{(l)[n+1][i-1]} iff\, i>1 \end{cases} \qquad (9)$$

The initial symbol estimates are

$$\begin{cases} \hat{s}_{MMSE}^{L} iff\, i=1 \\ \hat{s}_{PIC}^{L} iff\, i>1 \end{cases} \qquad (10)$$

3.2 PSO-assisted Joint FD-CHTF and Data Optimization

The joint optimization of the channel estimation and symbol detection requires a simultaneous search of the best values of the FD-CHTFs coefficients along with the PCFs. PSO, as a swarm intelligence algorithm, is distinguished from other evolutionary computation algorithms in that it stores the best solutions in memory and these best solutions are exploited by all of particles [1]. PSO applies the concept of social interaction to problem solving using a number of particles that constitute a swarm moving around in the search space looking for the best solution. The PSO search is applied on both the PCFs and FD-CHTFs in decision-directed manner to find the optimum$\alpha_l^{[i]}$ and $\hat{H}_p^{(l)[i]}$ that minimize the "fitness" objective mean squared error (MSE) function.

$$\min_{\alpha_j^{[i]}} E\left[\left|x - x_{MAI}^{(l)[i]}\right|^2\right] \qquad (11)$$

The detection algorithm can be outlined as follows [1]

i) Set the initial particles for both PCFs and FD-CHTFs.
ii) Initialize the PSO parameters; velocity v_i is initialized to zero, *pbest* is initialized for each particle position and *gbest* is initialized for the global best position.
iii) Evaluate the (MSE) of each particle searching for minimum

$$f = \left[\left|x - x_{MAI}^{(l)[i]}\right|^2\right], \qquad (12)$$

searching for best PCFs estimate, while the FD-CHTFs are set at their initial values.
iv) Find the new *pbest* and *gbest* and update its values.
v) Update particles velocity and positions on the basis of :

$$v_q^{m+1} = \varphi v_q^m + \alpha_1 rand\left(pbest - x_q^m\right) + \alpha_2 rand\left(gbest - x_q^m\right) \qquad (13)$$

$$x_q^{m+1} = x_q^m + v_q^{m+1} \qquad (14)$$

vi) If the minimum fitness isn't met, go to (iii), otherwise go to (iii) to find best FD-CHTFs values, while PCFs are set to their best values. Otherwise
vii) STOP if minimum fitness is met; otherwise go to (iii).

3.3 SA-assisted Joint FD-CHTF and Data Optimization

SA is a numerical optimization technique based on the principles of thermodynamics. SA is motivated by an analogy to annealing in solids. In contrast of PSO algorithm, SA is a trajectory-based algorithm typically uses a single agent or one solution at a time, which will trace out a path as the iterations continue [2]. The joint channel estimation and symbol detection can be optimized by SA search algorithm to estimate the best values of the FD-CHTFs coefficients along with the PCFs in decision-directed manner by minimizing the fitness MSE function.

The detection algorithm can be outlined as follows [2]:

i) Set the initial particles for both PCFs and FD-CHTFs.
ii) Initialize the SA parameters; initial solution, initial best solution, initial temperature, maximum time, cooling rate and constant β.
iii) Evaluate the fitness MSE function.
iv) Randomly select a position from set of all possible neighbors of the initial solution and calculate Δ=selected position fitness – initial fitness
v) If Δ< 0, (set the selected position to be the initial solution and if selected position fitness < Best fitness, update the best solution) otherwise, if $r < e^{-\Delta/temperature}$, where r is uniformly distributed number in the interval [0,1]; then this selected position is worse and no change in current solution remains unchanged.
vi) Update temperature according to cooling rate.
vii) STOP if the temperature is less than stopping temperature, otherwise go to (iv).

4. SIMULATION RESULTS

This section presents the MIMO SDMA-OFDM system performance using the adopted joint channel estimation and partial parallel interference cancellation multiuser detector assisted by SA or PSO algorithms. Basically, the simulation results show that the adopted detector outperforms the MMSE and Conventional Parallel Interference Cancellation (CPIC) MUDs in under-loaded, fully loaded and overloaded scenarios, but it has a significant performance improvement in overloaded scenario. The channel model was employed as flat Rayleigh fading channel having a normalized Doppler frequency of$FD = f_d T_s$, where $f_d$and $T_s$are the maximum Doppler frequency and the OFDM symbol duration, respectively [5]. The channel was assumed to be a symbol-invariant channel, but the transmitted symbol was faded at the beginning time of its duration. Also, it was assumed that each user has unity transmitted power.

Figure 3 shows a performance comparison in the Bit Error Ratio (BER) versus Signal-to-Noise Ratio (SNR) of a single stage SA-aided PPIC, PSO-aided PPIC, CPIC and MMSE detectors in under-loaded (4x6), fully-loaded (4x4) and overloaded (4x2) MIMO SDMA-OFDM systems under assumptions of normalized Doppler frequency FD = 0.0005 and a pilot overhead of ϵ=2.5%. This figure shows that the proposed PSO-aided PPIC outperforms the linear MMSE, the CPIC and the SM-aided PPIC especially in fully loaded and overloaded scenarios.

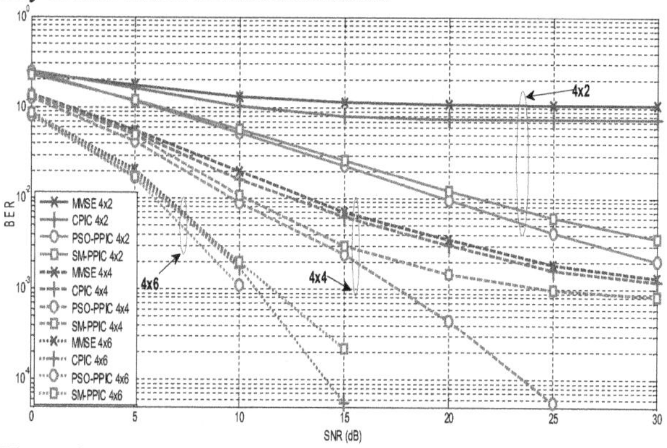

Figure 3. BER performances of SA and PSO assisted-, CPIC and MMSE detectors in 4x2, 4x4 and 4x6 MIMO SDMA-OFDM systems (ϵ = 2.5%.FD=0.0005)

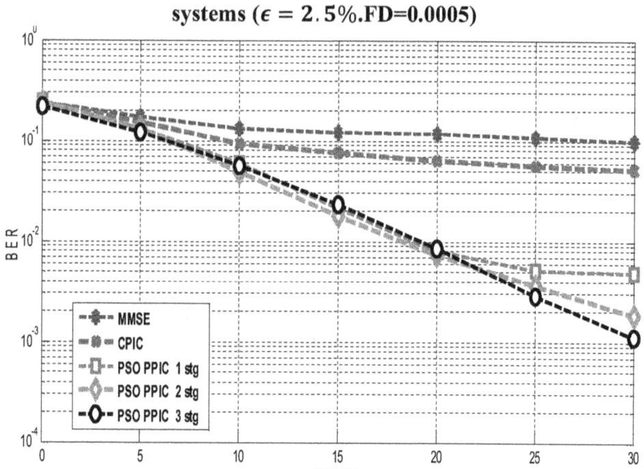

Figure 4. BER performances of (1, 2 and 3 stages) PSO-JCEMUD, CPIC and MMSE detectors in 4x2 MIMO SDMA-OFDM systems (ϵ = 1%. FD=0.0005)

Figure 4 represents a BER performance comparison of 1, 2 and 3 stages PSO-aided PPIC in overloaded 4x2 MIMO SDMA-OFDM system in conjunction with normalized Doppler frequency FD =0.0005. The proposed PSO-JCEPPIC scheme for different stages outperforms the linear MMSE and the CPIC, but with slightly

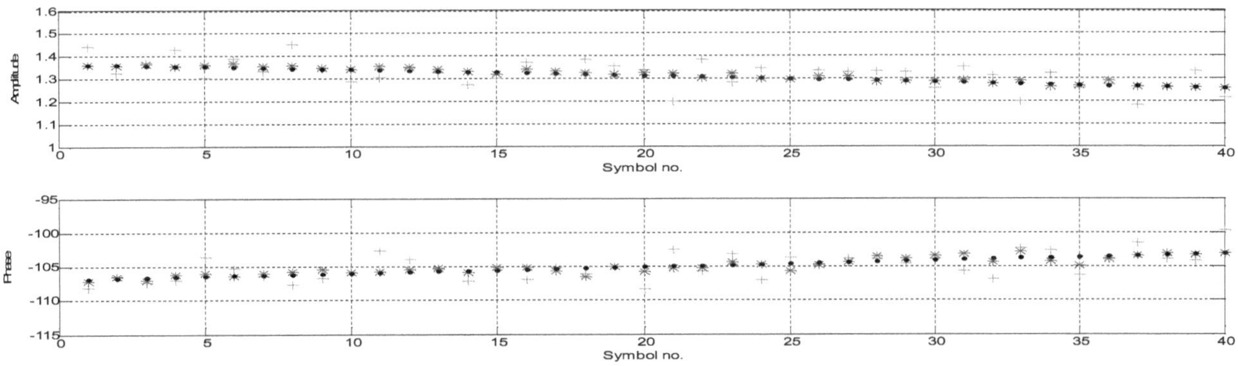

Figure 5. Channel estimation of the SA and PSO-assisted in 4x2 SDMA-OFDM system. A comparison between the estimated FD-CHTF $\hat{H}_1^{(2)}$ and true FD-CHTF $H_1^{(2)}$ amplitude and phase respectively, at a SNR =20dB over 40 consecutive OFDM symbols with FD=0.001.

performance difference between different stages, all assuming with a pilot overhead of $\epsilon = 1\%$.

Figure 5 shows a comparison between the true and estimated FD-CHTF ($H_1^{(2)}$ and $\hat{H}_1^{(2)}$) of a frame of 40 successive OFDM symbols at a SNR equal to 20dB. The decision-directed channel estimation is optimized by both SA and PSO algorithms. As shown in subfigures, the true-channel amplitude and phase are marked as dots and the SA-aided and PSO-aided estimated-channel amplitude and phase are marked as + and * respectively. From this figure, it is shown that the PSO-aided channel estimator outperforms the SA-aided one; as expected the population-based algorithms (as PSO) are less-likely to be trapped in local minima than single-agent based algorithms.

Figure 6 shows the metric evaluations required for both SM and PSO algorithms; SA algorithm requires about 540 metric evaluations to converge while PSO algorithm requires about 120 and 200 metric evaluations for 20 and 100 particles swarm-size respectively. It can be concluded that PSO-aided PPIC converges faster than SA algorithm and attains less cost value with less number of evaluations.

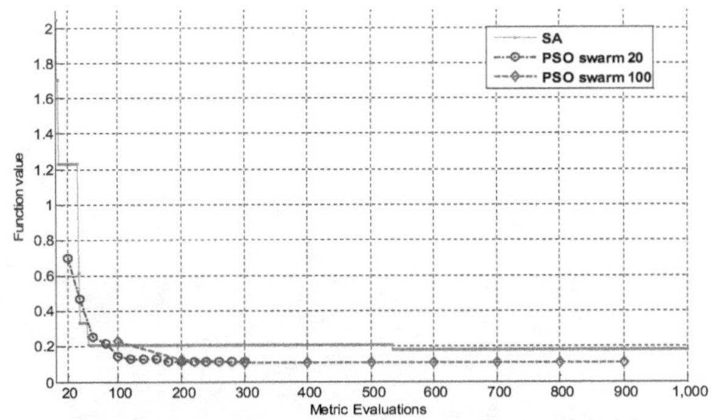

Figure6. Convergence of SA and PSO algorithms

5. CONCLUSIONS

From the simulation results and discussions, we conclude that the adopted PSO-assisted joint channel estimation and PPIC detector outperforms the SA-assisted one in both error performance and channel estimation. In addition to, it attains less complexity in terms of metric evaluations. Also, both suggest a reasonable solution to the channel estimation/data detection issue in MIMO SDMA-OFDM systems. Moreover, the PSO-assisted PPIC exhibits an acceptable performance that outperforms MMSE and conventional PIC especially in overloaded scenarios. With these featured properties, the SDMA-OFDM system is capable of potentially supporting an extra number of users in comparison to that supported by conventional MUDs.

6. REFERENCES

[1] C. Cheng, H. Hsu, Y. Huang, J. Wen and H. Hsu. 2010. Performance of an adaptive PSO partial Parallel Interference Cancellation for CDMA Communication Systems. *Wireless Internet Conference (WICON). The 5th Annual ICST*. pp.1– 7, March 2010.

[2] I. Zelinka and L. Skanderova. 2012. *Simulated Annealing - Single and Multiple Objective Problems*. Dr. M. S. Tsuzuki (Ed.).InTech, DOI: http://www.intechopen.com/books/simulated-annealing-single-and-multiple-objective-problems

[3] M. Chen and A. Burr. 2012. Low-Complexity Iterative Detection for Overloaded Uplink Multiuser MIMO OFDM System. *Smart Antennas (WSA). International ITG Workshop* on, pp.338– 342, March. 2012.

[4] M. Choudhry, M. Zubair and I. Qureshi. 2010. MUD for WCDMA using Modified PSO Algorithm. *Wireless Comm. and Signal Processing (WCSP). International Conference*. pp.1– 4, Oct. 2010.

[5] M. Jiang, J. Akhtman and L. Hanzo. 2007. Iterative Joint Channel Estimation and Multi-User Detection for Multiple-Antenna Aided OFDM Systems. *IEEE Transactions on Wireless comm*. Vol. 6, No. 8, pp.2904–2913, August 2007.

[6] M. Jiang and L. Hanzo. 2007. Multiuser MIMO-OFDM for Next-Generation Wireless Systems.*IEEE Proceedings*. vol.95, no.7, pp. 1430–1469, July 2007.

[7] P. Hammarberg, F. Rusek and O. Edfors.2012. Iterative receivers with channel estimation for multi-user MIMO-OFDM: complexity and performance.*EURASIP Journal on Wireless Communications and Networking*, vol. 75, no. 1, pp.1–17, 2012.

[8] R. Zhang and L. Hanzo. 2010. Harmony Search Aided Iterative Channel Estimation, Multiuser Detection and Channel Decoding for DS-CDMA. *72nd Vehicular Technology Conference. IEEE*. pp.1– 5, Sept. 2010.

[9] Y. Hsieh and W. Wu. 2008. Performance analysis of an adaptive two-stage PIC CDMA receiver in AWGN channels.*Signal Processing Journal*. vol. 88, Issue 6, pp.1413– 1427, Dec. 2008.

Author Index

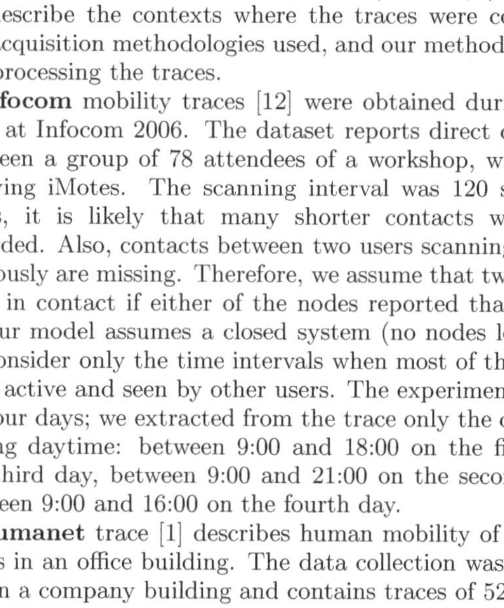

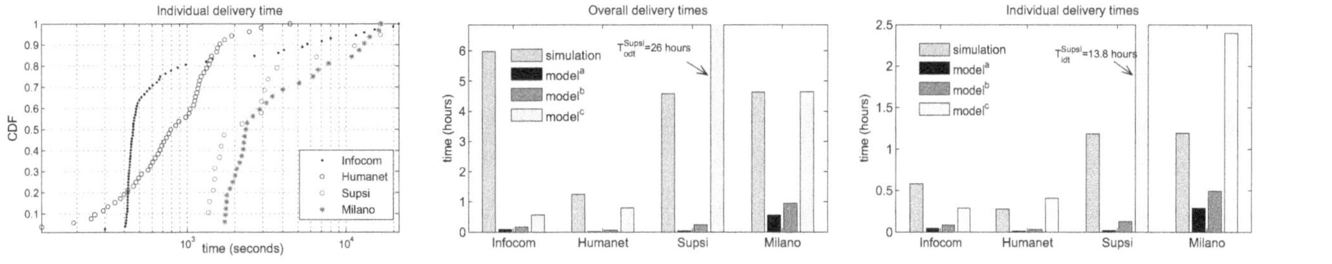

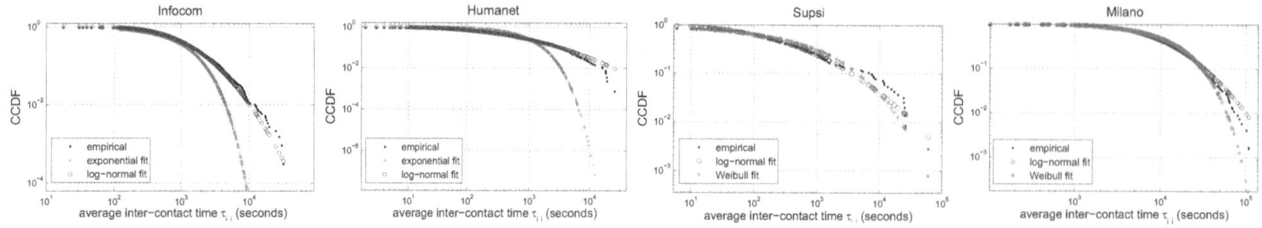

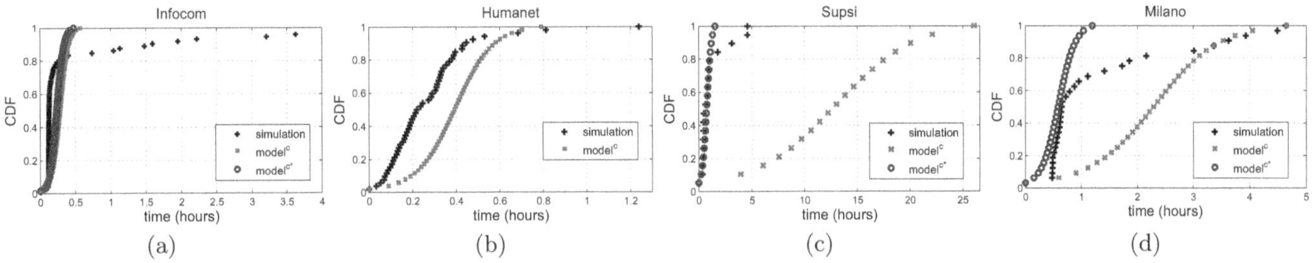

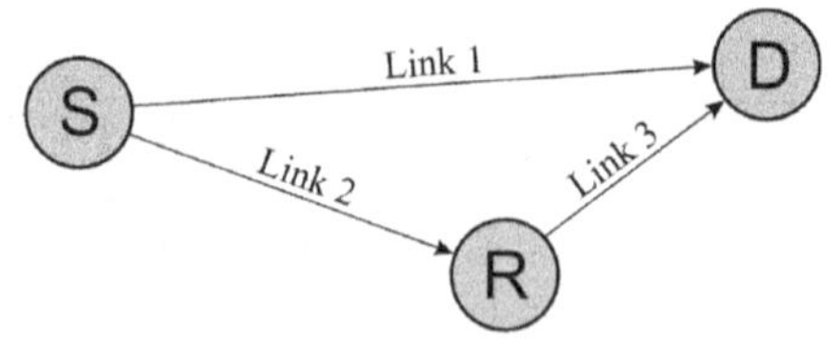

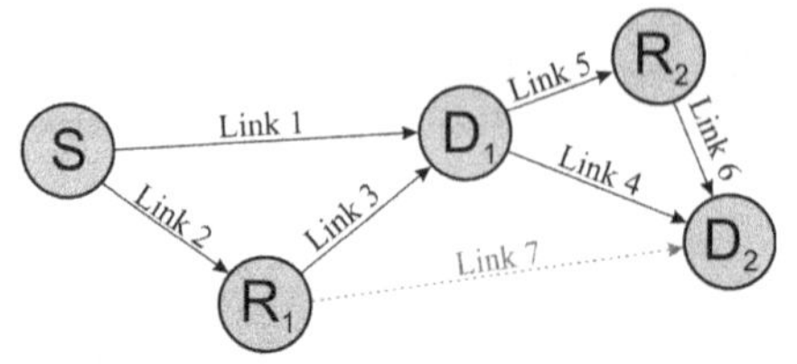

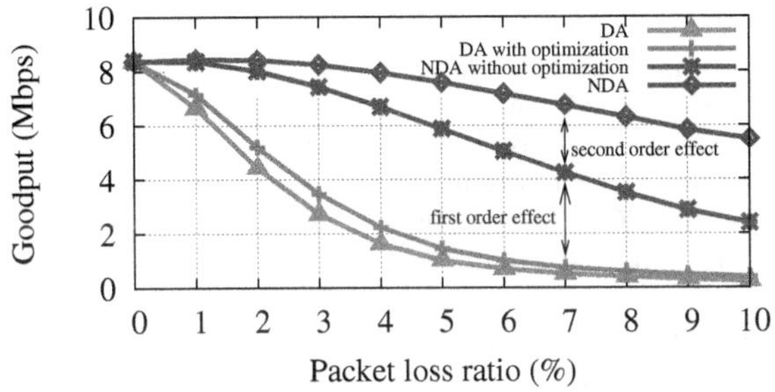

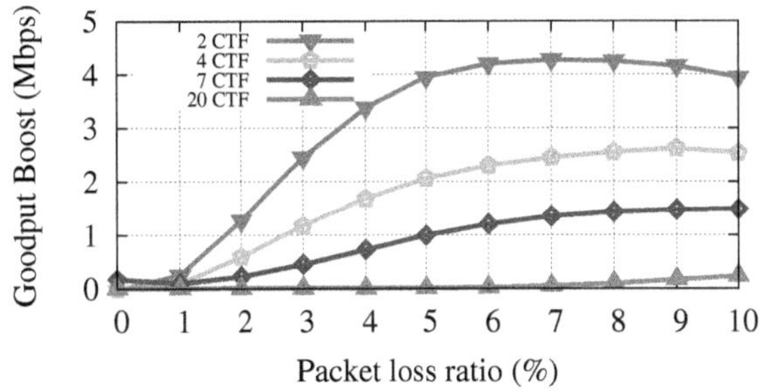

MSWiM'13, November 3–8, 2013, Barcelona, Spain.

$$d_{\text{PIM}} = d_{\text{PIM}}^{\text{min}}(b_{\text{PIM}} + r), \tag{8}$$

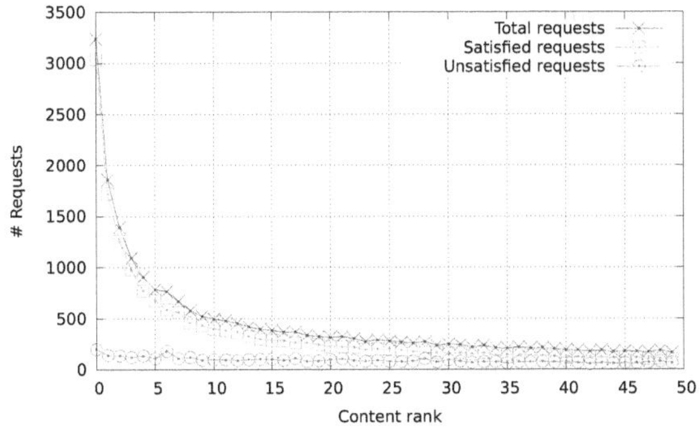

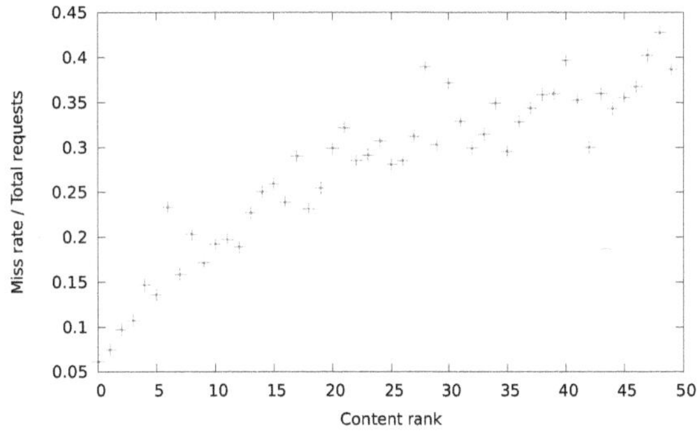

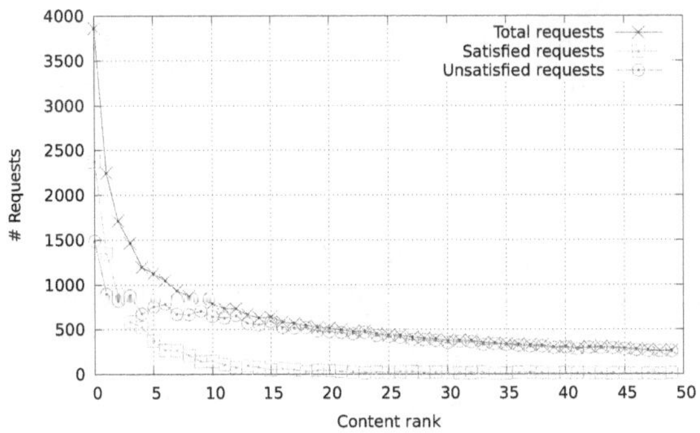

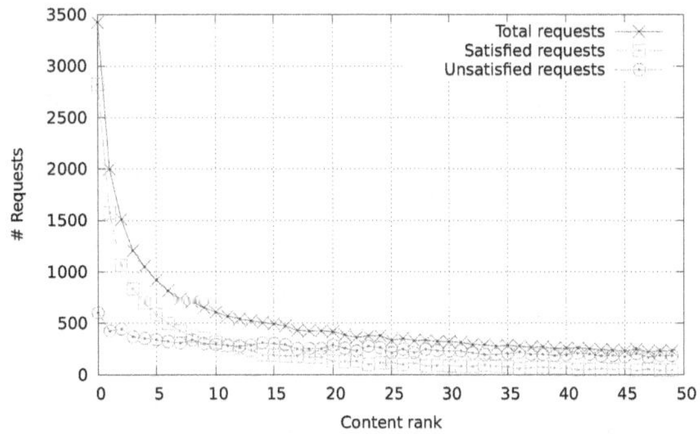

MSWiM'13, November 3–8, 2013, Barcelona, Spain.

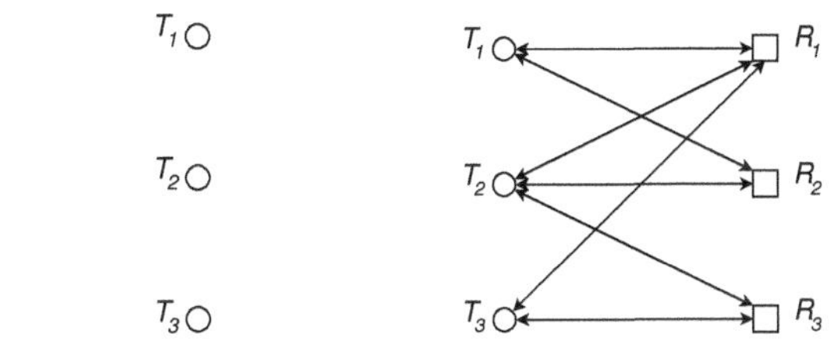

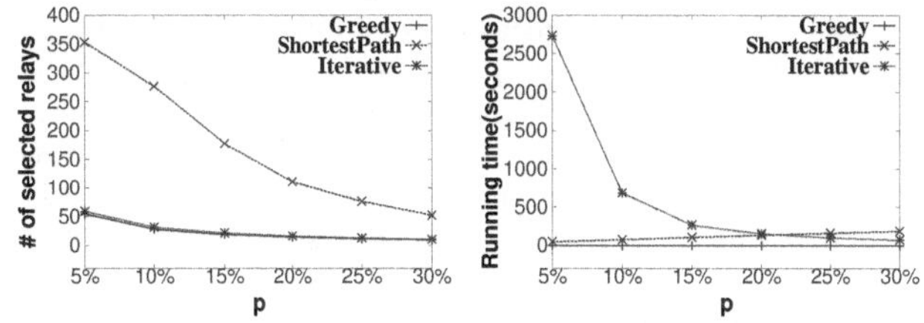

Equally, capture, the ability to receive the stronger signal even when the receiver is synchronized to another, affects correct reception [6]. Note that, capture is also device-specific. Äś For instance, Atheros chipsets implement MIM (Message in Message), which captures frames even if they arrive after the preamble of the weaker frame [12].

These issues motivate site and device-specific, or simply, measurement-based models [7, 9]. In [9], the authors propose the *hypothetical single sender* model, where, using separate RSS (Receive Signal Strength) measurements, the probability that a receiver decodes a packet from its main transmitter is calculated assuming all interfering transmitters behave like a single sender that completely coincide with the sender's transmission (see Figure 1). This model is also used in our earlier work, BOWLsim-basic [6], and here, we extend this model and its evaluation to more complex scenarios.

In [13, 14] more powerful models are proposed for multiple interferers, unicast communication, and unsaturated senders. However, all these models [9, 13, 14], assume the interferer always start at the same time with the main transmission. Furthermore, these models may not be directly used in a simulator, that, for instance, relies on a standard MAC (e.g., IEEE 802.11) implementation. In our work, we follow the piece-wise model of ns-3. This also agrees with [5] that shows that SINR distribution in a frame period, which is determined by interference, decides whether a frame can be received or not. However, their measurements are based on Micaz motes while our validation is on WiFi radios, and our models are fully integrated into the ns-3 simulator.

3. BOWLSIM-ADVANCED MODELS

BOWLsim-advanced builds on the RSS, frame detection (FD) and frame error (FE) models of BOWLsim-basic [6]. The interference model of BOWLsim-basic is the *hypothetical single sender* model [9] described in Section 2. This model calculates the RSS in the presence of multiple interferers t_i, $i \geq 0$, from the sender s to the receiver r, $RX_{sr}^{t_i}$ as (Equation 9 in [9], with no transmission power changes, and hence $\alpha = \alpha_i = 1$):

$$RX_{sr}^{t_i} = \overline{R}_{sr} - \delta_r \sum_i (\overline{R_{t_i r}} - \overline{I}_r), \qquad (1)$$

where the mean RSS from sender s to r is $\overline{R}_{sr}$, the mean external interference at r is $\overline{I}_r$. The SINR threshold of r to successfully decode a packet is δ_r . Using $RX_{sr}^{t_i}$, and our FD and FE models, we decide whether a packet from s can be received in the presence of t_i. In addition, we implement the MIM capability of our Atheros radios.

BOWLsim-basic achieved good accuracy in the indoor testbed. However, it did not perform as well for the outdoor testbed, due to, we discovered, the varying link quality. Next, we detail how we tackle this issue by modifying the frame detection and interference models.

$$p_{FE} = 1 - \prod_k 1 - FER(RX_{sr}^{t_i^k}), \quad (2)$$

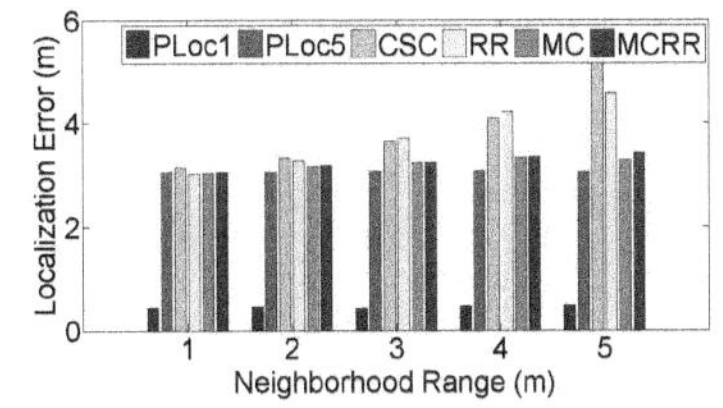

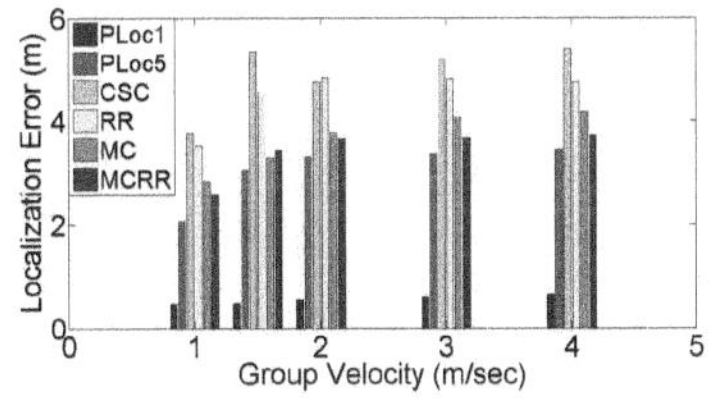

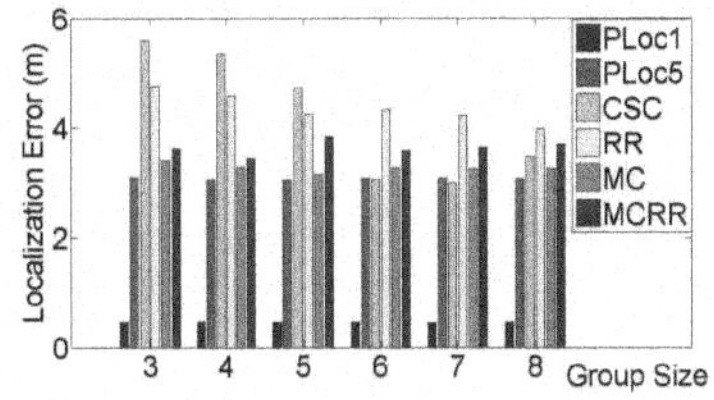

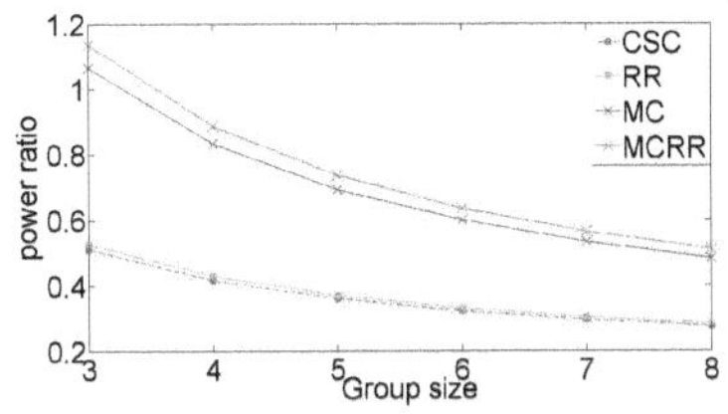

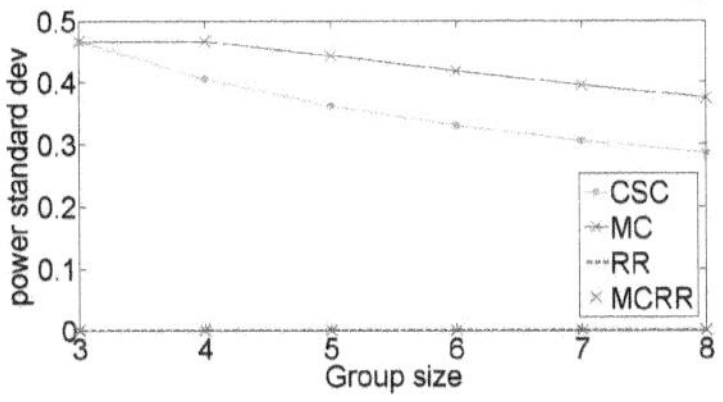

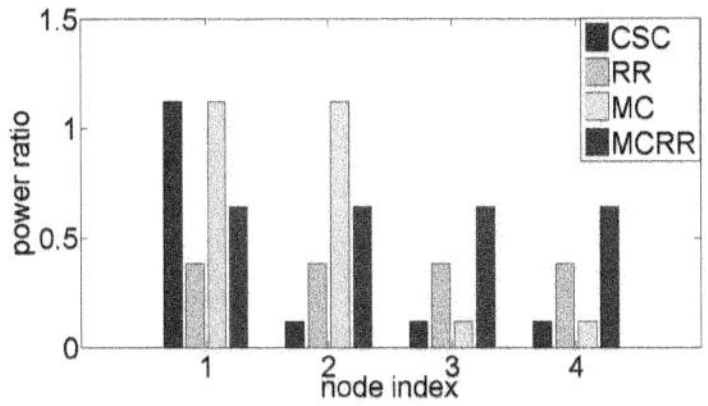

MSWiM'13, November 3–8, 2013, Barcelona, Spain.
Copyright 2013 ACM 978-1-4503-2353-6/13/11 ...$15.00
http://dx.doi.org/10.1145/2507924.2507935.

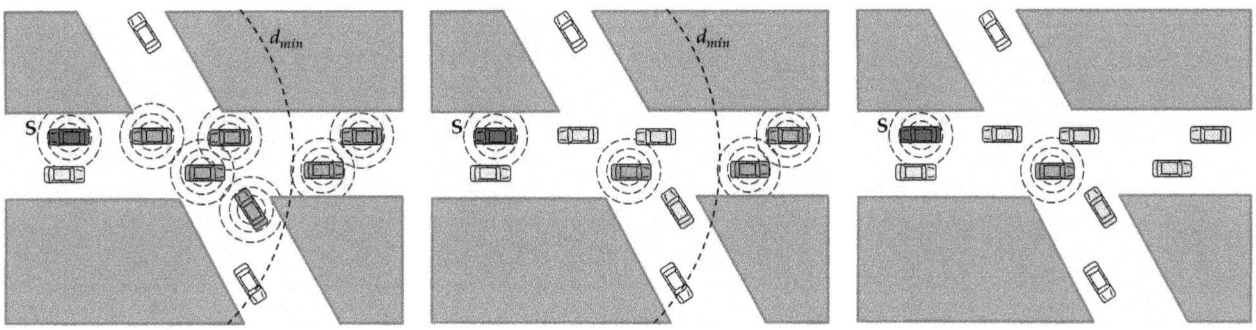

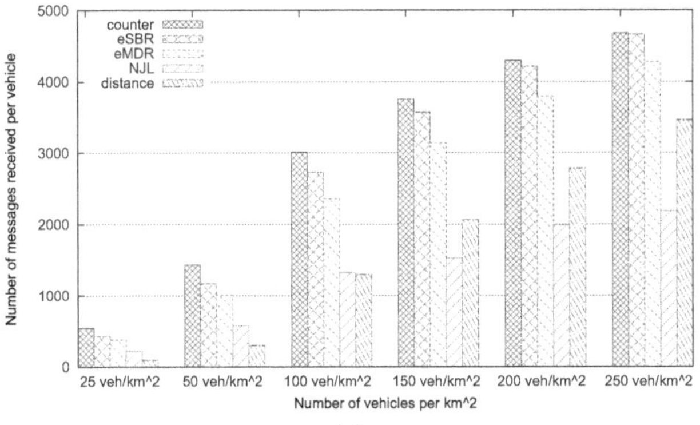

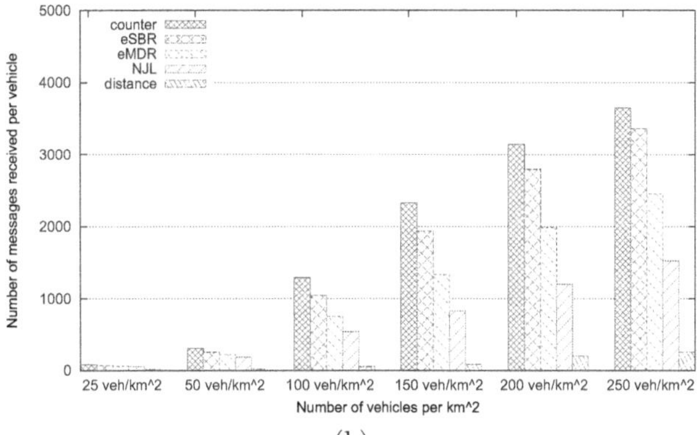

MSWiM'13, November 3–8, 2013, Barcelona, Spain.
Copyright 2013 ACM 978-1-4503-2353-6/13/11 ...$15.00.
http://dx.doi.org/10.1145/2507924.2507962.

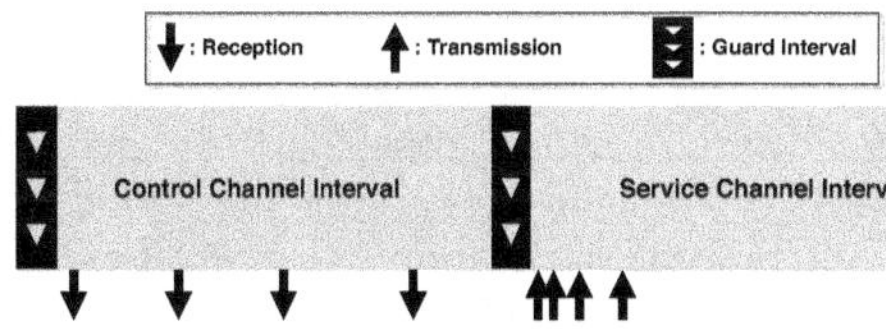

Figure 1: Comparison of different cost functions.

of dealing with (28) directly, a sequence of convex programs is formulated. At each step the following problem is solved

$$\alpha_i^{l+1} \in \arg\max U_i(\alpha_i, \{\alpha_{i'}\}_{i' \in \mathcal{N}_i}) - \alpha_i \nabla C_i(\alpha_i^l), \quad (29)$$

The premise behind (29) is to replace the convex part of the objective, *i.e.*, $-C_i(\alpha_i)$, with an affine approximation to make the problem locally convex. To do so, first-order Taylor approximation of the cost function around the current solution, *i.e.*, α^l, is utilized. Then, the new one, *i.e.*, α^{l+1}, is obtained by solving (29). Since $C_i(.)$ is concave, we have

for all $x, y \in [0, 1]$. Therefore, we have

$$U_i(\alpha_i^{l+1}) - C_i(\alpha_i^{l+1}) \ge U_i(\alpha_i^{l+1}) - C_i(\alpha_i^l) - (\alpha_i^{l+1} - \alpha_i^l) \nabla C_i(\alpha_i^l) \quad (30)$$

Since $\alpha_i^{l+1} \in \arg\max U_i(\alpha_i) - \alpha_i \nabla C_i(\alpha_i^l)$, we also have

$$U_i(\alpha_i^{l+1}) - \alpha_i^{l+1} \nabla C_i(\alpha_i^l) \ge U_i(\alpha_i^l) - \alpha_i^l \nabla C_i(\alpha_i^l). \quad (31)$$

Combining (30) and (31) we have

$$\begin{aligned} U_i(\alpha_i^{l+1}) - C_i(\alpha_i^{l+1}) &\ge U_i(\alpha_i^l) - C_i(\alpha_i^l) - (\alpha_i^l - \alpha_i^l) \nabla C_i(\alpha_i^l) \\ &\ge U_i(\alpha_i^l) - C_i(\alpha_i^l). \end{aligned} \quad (32)$$

The above argument shows that the sequence of α's is ascent, therefore, (29) converges to a local maximum. See [24] for detailed discussion of the convergence of CCCP.

Adapting our previous solution to the new sigmoidal cost function is straightforward. The only change that is needed to be made is the value of c_k. In this case, c_k is not constant anymore but varies in each iteration. Specifically, the value of $c_k(t)$ depends on the fraction of resources allocated in the previous iteration as follows

Assuming sigmoidal cost function (27) with inflection point of 0, c_k is given by

$$c_k(t) = \frac{c d e^{d x(t)}}{(e^{d x(t)} + 1)^2} \quad (33)$$

in problem (18). In this case, each base station b_i, in addition to updating its neighbors with the current value of ν_i, needs to update them with the current value of $c_i(t)$ in each iteration.

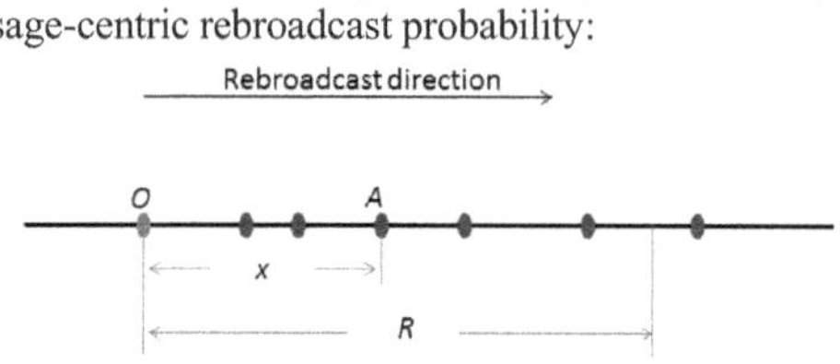

$$f(x,m) = \left\{\sum_{i=N_2+1}^{N_1}\left[g(x_i,m_{i-1})-g(x_i,m_i)\right]\right\}+g(R,m_{N_1})-g(x,m_{N_2})$$
$$N_1 = \max\{i : x_i \le R\} \qquad N_2 = \max\{i : x_i \le x\} \qquad (8)$$

$$\boldsymbol{x} = \boldsymbol{Hs} + \boldsymbol{n} \tag{1}$$

$$\boldsymbol{H} = [H^{(1)}, H^{(2)}, \dots, H^{(L)}]^T \tag{2}$$

www.ingramcontent.com/pod-product-compliance
Lightning Source LLC
LaVergne TN
LVHW082014200926
848481LV00010B/2856